Critical Concerns in the Field of DRUG ABUSE

OTHER ISSUES

Critical Concerns in the Field of DRUG ABUSE

Proceedings of the Third National Drug Abuse Conference, Inc., New York, 1976

NATIONAL DRUG ABUSE CONFERENCE, INC.

Conference Chairperson	Joyce H. Lowinson
Conference Co-Chairpersons	Beny J. Primm Shirley D. Coletti
Conference Coordinator	Ira J. Marion
Editorial Compilers	Arnold Schecter Harold Alksne Edward Kaufman

MARCEL DEKKER, INC.   NEW YORK · BASEL

ADAPTED

Library of Congress Cataloging in Publication Data

Proceedings of the National Drug Abuse Conference, Inc.
New York, 1976.
    Critical concerns in the field of drug abuse.

    Includes index.
    1. Narcotic habit--Congresses. 2. Drug abuse--
Congresses. I. National Drug Abuse Conference, Inc.
II. Title
[DNLM: 1. Drug abuse--Congresses. W3 NA561 3d
1976c / WM270 N283 1976c]
RC566.N376 1976   616.8'63   78-12871
ISBN 0-8247-6483-8

MARCEL DEKKER, INC.
270 Madison Avenue, New York, New York 10016

Current printing (last digit):
10 9 8 7 6 5 4 3 2 1

PRINTED IN THE UNITED STATES OF AMERICA

CONFERENCE CHAIRPERSON

JOYCE H. LOWINSON
Associate Clinical Professor of Psychiatry
Albert Einstein College of Medicine
Bronx, New York

CONFERENCE CO-CHAIRPERSONS

BENY J. PRIMM
Executive Director
Addiction Research and Treatment Corporation
Brooklyn, New York

SHIRLEY D. COLETTI
Executive Director
Operation P.A.R.
Comprehensive Drug Abuse Program
St. Petersburg, Florida

CONFERENCE COORDINATOR

IRA J. MARION
Drug Abuse Service
Albert Einstein College of Medicine
Bronx, New York

EDITORIAL COMPILERS

ARNOLD SCHECTER
Department of Preventive Medicine and Community Health
    and Office of Primary Health Care Education,
    Office of the Dean
New Jersey Medical School - College of Medicine and Dentistry
    of New Jersey

HAROLD ALKSNE
Department of Sociology
C.W. Post College of Long Island University
Greenvale, New York

EDWARD KAUFMAN
Associate Clinical Professor of Psychiatry
Department of Psychiatry and Human Behavior
University of California, Irvine Medical Center
Orange, California

SPONSORING ORGANIZATIONS

Albert Einstein College of Medicine of Yeshiva University
Alcohol and Drug Problems Association of North America
Bronx Psychiatric Center
Christopher D. Smithers Foundation
Do It Now Foundation
Drug Abuse Council
Greater New York Coalition on Drug Abuse
International Council on Alcohol and the Addictions
National Association of Drug Abuse Problems
National Association of Puerto Rican Drug Programs
National Association of State Drug Abuse Program Coordinators
National Coordinating Council on Drug Education
National Council on Alcoholism
National Federation of Concerned Drug Abuse Workers
National Free Clinic Council
National Institute on Alcohol Abuse and Alcoholism
National Institute on Drug Abuse
North American Association of Therapeutic Communities
Therapeutic Communities of America

ADVISORY COMMITTEE

Harold Alksne
Paul Blachly
Irving Blumberg
Peter Bourne
Thomas E. Bryant
Joseph Corcoran
Virginia Davidson
Elizabeth Dubois
Robert L. DuPont
Frances Rowe Gearing
Avram Goldstein
Samuel Grafton
William H. Harvey
Rayburn Hesse
Jerome H. Jaffe
Milan Korcok
John Langrod

Conrad Maugé
Robert B. Millman
Lonnie E. Mitchell
Helen H. Nowlis
Msgr. William O'Brien
Arnold Schecter
Frank Seixas
Edward C. Senay
Vernon J. Shorty
Jane Silver
David E. Smith
R. Brinkley Smithers
Barry Stimmel
Harold Trigg
Ray Trussell
Norman E. Zinberg

CONFERENCE STAFF

Catherine D. Latronica

Suzanne M. Mondo

Susan L. Rosenberg

PLANNING COMMITTEE

Ramon Adame
Larry Alan Bear
Carol Moody Becker
Bernard Bihari
Virginia Borrok
Leon Brill
Edward Brown
Laurence K. Brown
Sherry Calloway
Tommy Chung
Ron Clark
Paul Cushman
Charles Devlin
Sara Dowdy-Glenn
Roy Evans
Mathea Falco
Leona Ferguson
Ross Fishman
Melissa Freeman
Barbara Gibson
Matthew Gissen
Ralph Glatfelter
Harvey Gollance
Seymour Halpern
Pleasant Harris
Herman Joseph
Eric Josephson
Edward Kaufman

Elizabeth Khuri
Benjamin Kissin
Lee Koenigsberg
Anita Kurman-Gulkin
Susan Lachter
Frank Lima
Harriet Manley
Julio Martinez
Clifton Mitchell
Robert Moore
James Murphy
George Nash
Frank Nelson
John Orraca
Vernon D. Patch
John Phillips
Bianca Podesta
Mitchell S. Rosenthal
Michael Sack
Leon Salzman
Lawrence Santora
N. T. Schramm
Jacob Schut
Robert L. Shevin
Shirley Stone
William Vasquez
Don Wesson
Charles Winick

SPECIAL ACKNOWLEDGMENTS

The Conference and these Proceedings would not be possible without the tireless efforts of the following people:

Virginia Borrok

Laurence K. Brown

Barbara Gibson

Catherine Latronica

Suzanne Mondo

Susan Rosenberg

Lawrence Santora

Jane Silver

CONTENTS

PUBLIC POLICY

TREATMENT

MEDICAL COMPLICATIONS

ISSUES

LEGAL

CRIMINAL JUSTICE

ALCOHOL ABUSE

DRUGS AND ALCOHOL

POLYDRUG ABUSE

FAMILY THERAPY

ADMINISTRATION AND MANAGEMENT

GENERAL

FUNDING

ISSUES AND PROBLEMS OF STAFF DEVELOPMENT

RESEARCH

BASIC PHARMACOLOGY

PREFACE

The Third National Drug Abuse Conference, held in New York City in March, 1976, was attended by 3500 individuals, including social scientists, epidemiologists, researchers, physicians, program administrators, criminal justice representatives, lawyers, government officials, paraprofessionals, and consumers. Previous conferences in this series had focused on treatment. This Conference had as its theme "primary prevention" of substance abuse, and attempts were made to seek and understand etiological factors leading to substance abuse.

The Conference served a didactic purpose by offering numerous presentations meeting the requirements of Category I Credits for the Physicians Recognition Award of the American Medical Association; these included a number of panels and a one-day course on "The Medical Management of Drug and Alcohol Abuse," with lectures on opiate receptors and endorphins as well as other recent developments in basic science and clinical research. In addition, a Certificate Program was offered by the Conference in conjunction with the Manpower and Training Branch of the National Institute on Drug Abuse. This was accomplished with the cooperation of Dr. Lonnie E. Mitchell.

The papers presented in this Conference bear witness to the great strides that have been made in our understanding of substance abuse. Areas of controversy have been clarified, if not resolved, and our view of the nature of the problem rests on a broader base. There has been a continuing effort to transcend the differences that once characterized this field.

These conferences have been a primary force in defining significant areas for research. Moreover, they have helped workers in the field to keep abreast of recent developments.

The purpose of these Proceedings is to disseminate to as wide an audience as possible the papers presented at the Conference. This publication is intended to stimulate further research that will lead to more effective courses of action. Especially valuable are the papers of Drs. Robert DuPont and Ernest Noble in terms of their presentation of federal strategies in the area of substance abuse. Dr. Peter Bourne gives a global perspective to the heroin problem that is spreading across national borders and focuses on the international nature of substance abuse.

In the broadest sense, this Conference was a coalition. Professionals and paraprofessionals discussed ways of cooperating more closely to avert fragmentation of treatment. Many papers and panels focused on polydrug abuse and the fundamental changes in the demography and increasing complexity of today's substance abuser. Broadly discussed were practical problems affecting health services in general and the field of substance abuse in particular, especially the need to become increasingly effective in the face of fiscal stringencies which will be with us for some years to come. With this as a stimulus, participants discussed better deployment of existing resources.

Those responsible for the success of this Conference are too numerous to list. But we want especially to thank Dr. Robert DuPont of the National Institute on Drug Abuse and Dr. Thomas Bryant of the Drug Abuse Council for their moral and financial support. Their faith and confidence sustained us throughout the difficult months of planning for this Conference. The members of the Planning and Program Committees gave selflessly to the organization and development of the Conference. Their efforts, talent, and devotion are responsible for the final product. However, one individual must be singled out. Ira Marion, who served as Conference Coordinator, was the unifying element. He bridged gaps in communication, he furthered understanding between disparate groups, he gave full attention to major and minor details. He never lost sight of our main purpose and enabled the rest of us to focus on what really mattered.

These Proceedings reflect the efforts of all of the above and many more. We hope they will further our understanding of the nature of substance abuse.

Joyce H. Lowinson
Beny J. Primm
Shirley D. Coletti

Critical Concerns in the Field of DRUG ABUSE

INTRODUCTION

Harold Alksne

C.W. Post College of Long Island University
Greenvale, New York

The Development of the National Drug Abuse Conference

The importance of the National Drug Abuse Conference can best
be assessed by viewing some of the events that preceded it. The
year 1960 was a significant beginning. At that time it became
evident to an increasing number of those who had devoted their lives
to the treatment and rehabilitation of drug addicts that their best
efforts had failed. It was acknowledged for the first time that
both hospital-based and psychoanalytically-oriented treatment had
proven to be of little or no value to the addict in controlling his
dependence on drugs. In New York City, the Riverside Hospital for
the Treatment of Adolescents, which had delivered comprehensive and
quality service, was closed down when the recidivism rate was discovered to be close to 100%. (In its place a detoxification service accommodating less than 100 adolescents and adults was established at Metropolitan Hospital in Manhattan, obviously inadequate
to meet the needs of the tens of thousands of addicts in the City.)
Similar findings of failure were published for the Public Health
Hospital at Lexington, Kentucky, at about the same time. Some of
those who had been involved in traditional methods of treatment
continued to defend the value of these methods despite all evidence
to the contrary, but analysis of the poor results led to innova-
tional approaches and this proved advantageous to the field.

During the early 1960's, a number of events of great significance
occurred. Charles Diedrich, a recovered alcoholic, took an extraordinary step in organizing a program using the techniques of
Alcoholics Anonymous to help a small group of narcotic addicts.
His impressive results were widely recognized. Synanon, in Santa
Monica, California, was developed as a model for treatment of narcotic addicts through a process of resocialization and modification

1

of their values and life styles. This system has had a profound effect not only on the treatment of drug abusers but also on the treatment of ex-offenders, the mentally ill, and other dysfunctional individuals. Synanon was the precursor of Daytop Village, established on the East Coast in New York City under the leadership of Monsignor William O'Brien in association with Dr. Daniel Casriel and the charismatic David Deitch, one of the early participants at Synanon. Synanon, since then, has proliferated from the one therapeutic community in Santa Monica to scores of therapeutic communities throughout the United States, and it has developed various techniques for the treatment of patients in and outside of therapeutic communities such as the encounter and marathon.

At about the same time, beginning in 1964, Drs. Dole and Nyswander began to explore alternate ways of treating drug addicts and developed the methadone maintenance treatment method. Dr. Marie Nyswander, a psychoanalyst, had for 20 years prior to that time attempted to provide treatment to drug addicts through traditional psychotherapeutic approaches. Her recognition of the inadequacy of these approaches led to joint research with Dr. Vincent Dole at the Rockefeller Institute and to their pursuit of a method that would take into consideration the powerful craving for narcotics which drove addicts to continue their drug use. They explored the effects of morphine but found this to leave patients sedated, apathetic, unmotivated and drug-oriented. However, when patients were placed on stable doses of methadone they began to take on positive characteristics, talking about the future, their special interests and demonstrating an ability to become involved in productive activities. This suggested that maintenance on methadone had considerable potential for permitting patients to become accessible to rehabilitation, if freedom from drug use was not demanded as a prerequisite.

Dole and Nyswander, with the help of Dr. Mary Jeanne Kreek, then devoted their time and resources at Rockefeller Institute to explore in great detail the pharmacological, physiological and psychological effects of methadone maintenance treatment. A preliminary report of their findings was first published in 1965. In February of 1965, they were invited by Mayor Robert Wagner to begin at Manhattan General Hospital a pilot program which provided treatment to 100 patients.

The promise of methadone maintenance treatment was that it could reach large numbers of addicts, was acceptable to many addicts who could not be helped by other methods, and was inexpensive. After a one year period of exploration it was decided that methadone maintenance treatment could be attempted on an ambulatory care basis and numbers of clinics were established to provide this. By March of 1968, the Morris Bernstein Institute had 375 patients in treatment; an additional 496 patients were in treatment at other facilities in New York City.

At this point others were beginning to explore methadone maintenance as a treatment for heroin addiction. It was felt that it
would be important to gather together some who had experience in
this area to compare notes. In June of 1968, Drs. Dole and Nyswander
invited 75 researchers and administrators to Rockefeller University
to convene the First National Conference on Methadone Maintenance
Treatment in the effort to exchange observations and ideas concerning
the new modality. The Conference resulted in a set of proceedings
which was widely read in the field.

As a result of this experience it became apparent that interest
in methadone maintenance extended beyond those who were present at
the Conference, and it was decided that a new conference would be
held the following year and each successive year as long as it
served a purpose.

The ground rules for the organization of the conference were
something as follows: It was felt that the conference would be
oriented toward the sharing of new developments or problems in the
field of methadone maintenance treatment. The orientation of the
conference planning committee was that this conference was to be
specifically geared to service the needs of people who worked in the
area of methadone maintenance treatment; should those needs be fulfilled, making the conferences unnecessary, the conferences should
self-destruct.

The conference organization was geared to selecting a chairperson who would be responsible for selecting a planning committee
to organize the program. A co-chairperson would be selected who
would then become the chairperson for the successive year.

As we indicated, in the first year, 75 scholars and researchers
were in attendance. In the second year 280 were fitted into the
"Dome" auditorium of Rockefeller University。 The Third National
Conference, under the chairmanship of Dr. Marvin Perkins, involved
the participation of 1800 researchers, physicians, nurses, and a
variety of para-professionals who had developed an interest and
skills in methadone maintenance treatment. The Fourth Conference,
held in San Francisco (the first outside of New York City) began to
develop a character of monumental proportions, with 2800 individuals
in attendance. It was chaired by Dr. Avram Goldstein. Finally,
the Fifth National Methadone Treatment Conference, the Chairman of
which was Dr. Robert Dupont, included almost 3,000 individuals drawn
from the United States, Canada, and other parts of the world.

With each successive conference, new participants broadened the
base of interest to include the roles and contributions of those who
were to provide support services to patients who were successfully
stabilized on methadone. The growth of methadone maintenance treatment from experimentation with six patients at Rockefeller Institute

in 1964 to a treatment system that now serves 80,000 individuals
throughout the United States is a remarkable feat.

Beginning with the 100 patients on the original pilot program
at Morris J. Bernstein Institute, their performance was carefully
monitored by a committee of independent scientists, not involved in
methadone treatment, who evaluated this modality through the facilities of an independent system at the Columbia University School of
Public Health. Dr. Frances R. Gearing developed and has maintained
this evaluation to the present time when there are 36,000 methadone
maintenance patients in New York City.

The early experience with this modality demonstrated that between 80 and 85% of the clients who were enrolled in the program did
well by a series of criteria. These criteria, used in the evaluation,
involved cessation of criminal activities, maintenance of normal
family living, and employment in the community. Although this success rate has dropped over the years with the rapid expansion of
patients receiving this treatment, its effect on returning the majority
who attempt it to normal life styles ramains impressive.

The Value of the Methadone Maintenance Treatment Conferences

The holding of the National Conferences on Methadone Treatment
was important for the purpose of sharing information concerning the
problems, issues and new developments in this treatment modality.
But beyond that they were important in providing the basis for the
dissemination of information to the general public concerning the
effectiveness of this approach. The later conferences were significantly responsible for breaking down many of the resistances of
federal agencies to the use of a maintenance system in treating drug
abuse. Although maintenance treatment has been present in dealing
with such illnesses as diabetes and mental illness, the fundamental
prejudice of the public and major public agencies has inhibited free
exploration and rendering such treatment approaches to drug abusers.

By 1973 the specialized methadone maintenance treatment conferences had fulfilled their original goals. Originally it was believed that those rendering methadone maintenance treatment required
a communication system in order for them to share experiences and
encourage each other's development. By 1973 methadone maintenance
was accepted as a legitimate treatment in the United States and the
conference organizers felt that there was no longer a need to hold
such specialized conferences. A forum for communication and cross-
fertilization of ideas remained a prominent need in the general area
of drug abuse, and it was therefore decided by those who organized
the five methadone conferences that the base of future conferences
be broadened to include all treatment modalities and all new approaches
to the field of drug abuse treatment.

It was as a consequence of this that the first National Drug
Abuse Conference was held in Chicago in 1974, under the chairmanship

of Edward Senay and the co-charimanship of Vernon Shorty. Dr. Senay's organization of the Conference stressed representation of all elements of the drug abuse field, especially those that had previously not been represented in national forums of this kind. Senay was especially careful in developing minority and regional representation so that the Conference participants could share in the experiences of all categories and areas of the work in drug abuse. The success of this Conference was demonstrated in the publication of the proceedings under the title, Developments in the Field of Drug Abuse where close to 200 articles dealing with all areas in drug abuse interest appeared.

The Second National Drug Abuse Conference, held in New Orleans in the spring of 1975, was chaired by Vernon Shorty, who continued Dr. Senay's orientation toward a broad representation of workers and issues.

The Third National Drug Abuse Conference, under the chairmanship of Dr. Joyce Lowinson and the co-chairmanship of Dr. Beny Primm and Shirley Coletti, has moved from a professionally controlled conference to one that now is guided by representatives from both professional and non-professional areas in the field of drug abuse. The papers presented in this volume represent a final product of a process that began in 1968 and evolved to the execution of eight major conferences which we believe have significantly altered and advanced the cause of drug abuse research, prevention, treatment and rehabilitation in the United States.

Public Image of the Drug Abuser

One of the great problems in the field of drug abuse today involves the image that the public has of those people who suffer from this difficulty. The consequence of this is that drug abusers are excluded from treatment in many medical facilities and they are segregated when they are treated, almost as if they were pariahs. They are viewed as different from other troubled people despite the fact that their feelings and problems cut across all of those experienced by others, and finally when they are rehabilitated they encounter difficulty in finding work because of their identification as ex-drug abusers. It appears that one of the priorities of all of the participants in the National Drug Abuse Conference must be "normalization" of the problem of drug abuse in the United States.

We must recognize that success is measured not only by functioning within our treatment facilities but also in the communities, families and work settings to which rehabilitated addicts return. Clearly, the re-entry of the recovered addict to an acceptable and satisfying life is being blocked by continuing prejudices in the community. If we are to complete our job of rehabilitating our clients, we must go one step further to use our skills in changing some of these systems into which our clients must re-enter.

Alien as it may be to many of us, it may become necessary that
we become protagonists for the recovered drug abuser. Without this
final exertion of our efforts to re-orienting the community to accept
the return of our clients, what we have done may be doomed to failure.

The Development of a Constituency for Drug Abusers

There is insufficient awareness in the United States that drug
abuse is a monumental problem affecting tens of millions of individuals and their families. Drug abuse may no longer be seen as
characterized by heroin addiction; it now involves polydrug abuse,
alcoholism, and the misuse of such prescribed substances as tranquilizers, sedatives and amphetamines. Despite the fact that
staggeringly large numbers of the American people are touched directly and indirectly by drug abuse, very few of them are mobilized to
support treatment or rehabilitation centers by lobbying in behalf
of greater funding for treatment and research.

Yet we find in many groups -including Blacks, Hispanics,
Asian-Americans, gays, women, Native Americans- that people are
beginning to develop an awareness of their common problems. Each
was represented in this Third National Drug Abuse Conference. There
may be a great deal of value in attempting to develop a similar
consciousness among all those people who have suffered the problem
of drug abuse in the past and in the present.

Prevention as an Approach to Drug Abuse

We must turn our attention more and more to prevention in order
to identify and intervene with those factors that support the development of drug abuse. The media might be encouraged, for example, to
examine their responsibility in perpetuating such dangerous values
as "No discomfort should be tolerated" or "There is a pill for everything." Textbooks should be examined for their stress of immediate
gratification as a goal in life. It is our responsibility to change,
where we can, values and conditions that appear to make drug abuse
a reasonable alternative to confronting and overcoming problems which
originate in unhealthy social milieux.

We recognize that a great variety of mind-altering drugs are
becoming available to Americans. They are sought out and used extensively by all age groups, ethnic groups and regions. We know too
little about the cognitive functions that are affected by these drugs
and the needs they fulfill for those who take them. We seriously lack
scientific approaches which willhelp us identify the uses, functions
and potentially destructive elements of these drugs. The National
Drug Abuse Conference should address itself to these problems in
the future if it is going to be responsive to what is really happening in the streets and in the homes of America.

Political Power and Drug Abuse

We recognize more and more that our efforts to intervene with the drug abuse problem are inhibited because we have not addressed one of the critical problems involved with it. The drug abuse field is highly political and we must approach the power groups which affect the political quality of this field. Recognizing that politics are involved we must become increasingly sensitive to the use of power in the field.

This is especially relevant to the support systems that are developed for drug abuse programs. Funds are made available not necessarily on the basis of the value of treatment approaches but on the basis of public opinion and public manipulation of community awareness. Although this is not a customary orientation of treatment personnel they must develop approaches to "intervening" with these power groups.

Resistances to Medical Innovation in the Field of Drug Abuse

As with methadone maintenance treatment a great deal of resistance exists among public figures concerning any approach that is new to the drug abuse field, such as narcotic antagonists and l-alpha-acetylmethadol (LAAM). We must recognize that this resistance occurs and continues to inhibit the growth and development of efforts to deal with drug abuse. Just as we must become aware of the political forces so we must also be conscious of the fact that whatever innovations we present must be considered in the framework of resistances. It may be necessary for us to develop a media approach which will help the public understand and accept the new techniques that must be developed in drug abuse prevention and treatment.

Awareness of the Need for Multi-Modality Approaches

It has become sharply evident over the last several years that a need for a multi-modality approach to the treatment of drug abuse has become a critical issue. Drug addicts are heterogeneous, as are patients who are emotionally ill or those who suffer from different kinds of physical ailments. Each individual requires a careful diagnosis, and an assignment to a treatment approach which is more appropriate for him/her, and this requires the development of and agreement on more precise diagnostic criteria, and less concern with our "own" modality as the "only" approach. This special kind of modality egocentrism has to be modified if we are to provide our clients the quality treatment they deserve.

Our clients can only benefit from cooperation among representatives of different modalities. Deepening our theoretical insights and sharpening our technical tools can result from freeing ourselves from identification with one modality or another. Our purpose –

to control drug abuse - requires that we do not lose sight of the drug abuser while focussing on his treatment. "What does he/she need?" should be our main concern, and putting this concern foremost will produce better treatment approaches.

Other Unmet Needs

No treatment method is acceptable to all drug dependent people. For those who cannot be helped by methadone maintenance, experimentation with other forms of chemotherapy may become critical for the future of this field. Cyclazocine, naloxone and other drugs must be explored with greater intensity to determine which kinds of heroin addicts respond to these approaches. In recent years we have found that heroin maintenance is being entertained as a possibility for patients who cannot be touched by other approaches.

Therapeutic communities must always be considered in our evaluation of different and relevant approaches. Some have developed extensions of their work through such innovations as collectives to support those who have graduated their programs. We expect to see new developments reported in their work in forthcoming conferences.

Consensus becomes critical in defining the future approaches we will have to make toward the development of the field of drug abuse prevention and treatment. We have seen the beginnings of this in the first three National Drug Abuse Conferences.

PUBLIC POLICY

THE FUTURE OF PUBLIC SUPPORT FOR DRUG ABUSE PROGRAMS

Robert L. DuPont, M.D.

Director, National Institute on Drug Abuse
Rockville, Maryland

Rayburn has given us each 10 minutes to talk about the issue
of community support for drug abuse services. Today, we are seeing
across the country a weakening or at least a questioning of that
support. In order to understand this process, it is necessary to
go back and trace how we got where we are. We may be able to learn
from how we got here, how we can build a stronger future.

The first Federal commitment to deal with the drug abuse problem came abruptly in 1970 and 1971. Prior to that, there was only
a tiny Federal investment in this field. The Federal response
produced a tenfold rise in funding for both law enforcement and
treatment over a five-year period.

Why did the Federal Government get involved in the drug abuse
issue? There were three main reasons but to find them we have to
look back to 1970. The first reason for Federal intervention in
drug abuse was the concern about the crime problem. This was very
much in the public agenda in the late 1960's. It was a highly
publicized issue of great concern to the public and therefore to
politicians. Much of the crime increase in the 1960's was thought
to be related to heroin use. In fact, at that time, drug use in
general was associated with an unspecific fear that was linked to
the fear of crime.

Secondly, there was in the late 1960's a fear of the widespread use of drugs to middle-class communities. The dramatic
spread of marihuana use, and to a much lesser extent the spread of
the use of other illicit drugs, was quickly translated into public
support for drug abuse programs.

The third important issue was much more explosive than either
the crime issue or the marihuana issue. It grew out of the terror
and revulsion that tens of thousands of American soldiers in
Viet Nam were addicted to heroin. It seems like ancient history
now--its hard to even imagine it--but this proved to be the
triggering event that involved the Federal Government with the
drug abuse issue.

Today, all three of these concerns are either gone or
seriously eroded. There is nothing like the Viet Nam issue now.
The crime problem, to a substantial extent, has been discredited as
a political issue. It was tied to Richard Nixon and John Mitchell,
therefore it is not a subject that many politicians want to take
up. The middle class now has a much better understanding of the
distinction between casual marihuana use and heroin addiction than
it did in the 1960's. It is much less likely to react violently to
that issue. The fear of crime may make a comeback, but even if it
does, I doubt that it will hit as hard as it did in 1970. Where
does that leave the drug abuse field? It leaves us in a compromised position in terms of public support, along with the many
other social and health programs in the United States that were
funded during the boom decade of the 1960's. All of them are in
serious trouble in terms of community support right now for two
reasons: First, the current funding environment is dismal. Government is out of money. Second, these programs have had a very
difficult time proving that they work. This skepticism is running high just when budgets are running low. In no way is this
crisis unique to drug abuse.

Where do we go from here? These are two broad bases of support which can be tapped. First of all, we have the clear and
growing evidence of dramatic increases in the rates of drug use
and drug problems in the United States in the last decade. This
is literally without precedent. In other words, beyond any issue
of misunderstanding either of middle class marihuana use or Viet
Nam heroin addiction, there is clear fundamental evidence of a
change in social behavior taking place in the United States. Drug
use, both licit and illicit, is up. These trends are continuing
and they merit major public attention.

The second base of public support is contained in our drug
abuse treatment programs themselves. From their origins in the
early 1960's, these programs have been preoccupied with specifying their objectives. Basically, there are just three: reduced
illicit drug use, reduced crime, and increased productivity
(mostly that means working). The evidence which is available on
these points suggests that drug abuse treatment programs generally meet these objectives. The Federal Government's initial
evaluation of 44,000 drug abuse clients entering treatment
between 1969 and 1973 shows that $1 of investment in treatment
returned an average of $13 in reduced crime and increased employ-
ment while the clients were in treatment. Now the clients who
entered treatment between 1969 and 1971 have been followed up for
an average of 5 years after entering treatment, and it has been
shown that substantial decreases in crime and drug use and
increases in employment have held up over that long period of time.

The commitment of our field to evaluation distinguishes it
from most other social service and health programs. While it is

painful to subject our cherished programs to this kind of evalua-
tion--in candor, we must admit that not all evaluations of drug
abuse treatment programs have produced such positive results--it
is one of the strongest bases for building public support.

In conclusion, it is possible that the concern about crime
will return and will again be translated into support for drug
abuse treatment and prevention programs. Whether or not that
occurs, we can build a new and far more secure base of support on
the growing concern for the progressive rises in the use of both
licit and illicit drugs on the record of achievement of drug
abuse prevention and treatment program themselves.

REMARKS TO NATIONAL DRUG ABUSE CONFERENCE

Ernest P. Noble, M.D., Ph.D.

Director
National Institute on Alcohol Abuse and Alcoholism

With this distinguished group of scientists and physicians I feel that I am among friends. And in this ambience I would like to share some of the impressions collected in the first months away from my familiar clinical and academic stomping grounds...

In the next months, I will be giving much attention to increasing communication between Federal and private workers in our field of interest...between scientist and non-scientist. A major thrust will be efforts to stimulate cordial dialogues and increased cooperation among the diversified groups seeking answers to alcohol-related problems.

In the meantime, it is a refreshing experience to sit down to exchange views with fellow researchers and physicians. As a beginning for our conversations, it is appropriate for me to introduce myself. As you may already know, I began my scientific adventure with biochemistry. And I held a doctorate in that field before the decision was made to study medicine. In the medical school classroom and on the hospital wards, psychiatry became a compelling interest. I believe the combination is important enough to highlight because it has produced in me a particular--perhaps somewhat unique --approach to alcoholism. The biologist, the pharmacologist, the neurochemist in me demands examination of this disorder from one direction. The clinical psychiatrist in me demands examination from another.

I do not believe that the single great key to the complex riddle with which we are presented is to be found in our laboratory test tubes and experimental processes. At the same time, I must recognize the massive failure of clinical medicine--psychiatry in particular--to make real strides in managing one of the nation's most serious public health problems.

Alcohol has played a role in the functioning of civilized society as far back as memory goes. And--as with arthritis and certain other ancient diseases--the disorder we call alcoholism has afflicted some individuals throughout the whole of that history. How surprising it is that only today are we beginning to label alcohol a drug and that--even in this era of scientific enlightenment--we encounter some raised eyebrows and expressions of tolerance when we do so. In spite of all we have seen and read, some still consider the "drug" reference to be a bit of an exaggeration -- a kind of scare-tactic most appropriate to groups such as the Women's Christian Temperance Union. It may be safe to say that other elements of our overall prevention effort are received in the same manner.

Clearly, the public is responding in two ways to those who work in the field. On the one hand, it spares us the great indignant hue and cry which a health problem of this magnitude could be expected to generate. On the other (and in exchange) it shrugs at our warnings and ignores our labels. If there is any doubt that this is taking place, it is easily removed by a quick glance at the statistics showing accelerated alcohol abuse among women, the disadvantaged, and young people in particular. It appears that we have neither frightened nor deterred anyone. I sometimes wonder if we have even succeeded in informing many.

But before I'm accused of bearing only bad news, let me tell you about some good news! At NIAAA, we point with pride to accomplishments made over the past 12 months. For example--with an appropriation of $146 million in FY 1975, areas of progress include: 1) Results of the first large-scale follow-up study of clients treated by NIAAA-funded Alcoholism Treatment Centers indicated a 70 percent improvement rate 18 months after intake; 2) the first 42 alcoholism programs were accredited by the Joint Commission on Accreditation of Hospitals under newly adopted national standards; 3) the Institute carried out high priority programs for Spanish-Americans, Blacks, the aged, youth, women and Indians; 4) occupational alcoholism programs were greatly expanded. More than 100 Institute-trained occupational program consultants are presently employed at the State level, promoting and assisting in the development of State and local programs. More than 275 new occupational programs now have been established and currently serve a work force of nearly 2,750,000 people. Significant partnerships also have been developed with the Civil Service Commission and the Department of Defense to foster Congressionally-mandated occupational programs for Federal employees and servicemen with alcohol-related problems...

Our pamphlets and speeches tell our audiences that alcohol is a drug, that it must be used with discretion. We warn the young to consider what they do before they elect to use alcohol. We speak of the need to make responsible choices. All sound advice. But the alcoholism statistics continue to increase. Somewhere we have been falling down.

I suspect we will continue to do so until we come up with answers to some basic questions and learn to put those answers to effective use. It is at this point that we must involve our researchers more fully. We must avoid locking ourselves into an exclusively treatment-oriented approach. The door must be opened to our laboratories to give us clearer understandings of the etiology and mechanisms of alcoholism. To do this we will require cooperation of the best our scientific community has to offer. At present NIAAA

directly supports two Nobel Prize winners and several members of the
National Academy of Sciences. But we must go further. During my
tenure as Director we will be working to encourage the nation's best
minds to join our team. Hopefully, we will be able to supply adequate funding for this purpose. As you know, the recent Senate bill
allots $22 million for research and $6 million for treatment centers
--permitting us to expand our intramural program.

In urging participation of research scientists, I lay down a series of challenges. As the studies they undertake move along, our
researchers will expand the list. But for a beginning, I see us
examining basic biochemical processes involved in alcohol use--whe-
ther that be moderate or heavy. We cannot deal intelligently with
biological response to any substance until we can at least begin to
explain what takes place in the brain, the liver, and the G.I. and
endocrine systems.

We cannot approach the "why" of alcoholism--or work to identify
those at risk--until we understand more about metabolic, genetic,
environmental and other factors which appear to have a role in problems related to alcohol abuse.

This leads me to a series of questions having to do with the offspring of alcoholics. Are they indeed a high risk group? Certainly
we have thought so for a good many years. But now that theory may
be open to question--perhaps the greater problem lies with the next
generation, the grandchildren.

Who can describe for us the effect of maternal alcohol consumption on the unborn child? Does anyone know what level of consumption over what period leads to what level of fetal involvement?

What of the psychosocial area? We have a comprehensive study of
alcohol use among adolescents. In nudging away some of our notions
about the dynamics of drinking in this group, the investigation may
have raised more questions than it answered. Contrary to earlier
thinking, the effect of peer pressure, for example, seems to be
much less than that of implied or direct parental sanction. And so
we go around and around.

The temptation may be to throw up one's hands. Our task is too
complex, frustrating--and the answers will be too long in coming.
We lack adequate resources. Perhaps we should simply focus on
treatment for the visibly ill and leave the hard work to someone
else.

I think not.

It is my conviction that if we can encourage increased activity
on the part of our scientific community, if we can forge new alli-
ances--real progress is entirely within reach.

In this age of ecological awareness, investigators cannot proceed without deep concern for the quality of life around us. Our
skills are too greatly needed. But, after 25 years of research
involvement, I know well the tendency to "tend to our knitting", to
involve ourselves more and more deeply with our individual investigations. To meet the requirements of today's complex world, our
thinking must change. We cannot proceed singlemindedly only along
those paths of individual research interest. We must come forward

to give at least a portion of our attention to matters of concern to society as a whole. We can do so with complete assurance that the effort will enhance--rather than impinge upon--our various personal programs.

The studies required for clearer understandings in the alcoholism field may be long or short range. They may cover a wide variety of investigative categories. They can proceed in complete compatibility with other programs in which we are involved. In fact, they demand only two things which may be a little unfamiliar to some of us: First, it is necessary to expend more intellectual energy outside the laboratory than may be customary for us. We must get out into the community and acquaint ourselves with both scientific and non-scientific efforts which are underway. To identify areas where our contribution will be most meaningful, we must learn more about programming at our own state and local levels. This process of increasing awareness may be somewhat tedious, but I can promise that it opens up highly challenging research vistas. Second, we must insure that--after becoming involved--we find ways to share our findings in ways which are meaningful to the community as a whole. It is not enough for us to sit about talking to ourselves. We need to insure that our language is understood by--and our contacts include --those who may have difficulty understanding the nature of our contribution...

I would like to examine the prevention issue in terms of NIAAA emphasis during the next twelve months.

Some would have us focus on primary prevention. That is, total elimination of risk, abstinence, increased control in the form of labelling, age limits, and the like. My personal view is that, while some vigorous efforts in these directions are appropriate, too much concentration on primary prevention leaves us open to charges that we are out of touch with reality. Most people will consume alcohol in some social or religious setting. Drinking is so deeply enmeshed in the fabric of our society that to tamper with it requires that we subject ourselves to a kind of cultural shock. And this, quite obviously, must be managed with great care.

To date, workers in our field have been successful in alerting the public to incidence and prevalence of alcohol-related problems. We have gone a step further in encouraging self-examination and stimulating early identification. The next hurdle--the development of effective techniques of intervention--lies before us. A large piece of that action will take place in the laboratory. But the balance will be undertaken as part of the overall process of social enlightenment which can follow development of new insights into the means of producing cultural change.

It is useful for us to conceptualize prevention in ways which will strengthen restraining elements already present in each segment of society. If, at every level, we can help the individual to say to himself, "This far and no further", we can motivate him to apply a brake far more effective than any we have utilized so far. As part of this process, it is important for society as a whole to stop excusing itself for frequent or occasional alcohol-related "embarrassments." In teaching the concept of responsible alcohol use, we must help people to focus more fully on those parameters which enhance well-being within the culture or the community in which they function.

Thus it seems to me that a promising avenue for prevention investigation involves determining ways in which social and cultural constraints can be employed to insure that elements within our structure bolster--rather than weaken--efforts to achieve responsibility in drinking behavior. Just exactly what these means are--and the identification of appropriate programming to implement them--is now the subject of considerable thought within NIAAA and on the outside.

Another high priority issue for me relates to the quality of services we render to those who have not responded to prevention efforts. Sophisticated quality assurance techniques are in place in the physical health field. Effective evaluation processes exist to a lesser degree in the mental health area. In social health there are, for all practical purposes, none at all.

Quality care has, of course, three elements: The derivation of standards; appropriate licensing or certification of treatment staff; and development of post treatment audit review. We have made some progress with the first two. The task before us now is the identification of meaningful criteria for measuring treatment results. We know, for example, that we have good follow-up data for 18 months, but we must ask if that period is long enough. Is the criteria by which we have measured improvement or "cure" valid? And, with national health insurance on the horizon, a sense of urgency must attend our search for answers...

We intend to build upon what has gone before. In doing so we will discard that which has failed to realize its promise. Our emphasis will be on developing cooperative relationships with all who are prepared to engage in the battle against alcohol abuse. Where divisions have developed, we will seek to conciliate. Under my direction, NIAAA will hold its door open to every point of view--acknowledging no special interests or questions of "turf." We are all in this together and without the cordial participation of every interested group at every level--Federal, state and local--we cannot hope to handle the massive job of eliminating one of the nation's most serious public health problems.

To those of you who have not become deeply involved, to those who have felt concern about the significance of research in alcoholism programming, I hold out the hand of welcome. As a colleague I urge you to "come on in--the water's fine."

THE INTERNATIONAL HEROIN PROBLEM - A GLOBAL PERSPECTIVE

Peter G. Bourne, M.D.

Drug Abuse Council
Washington, D.C.

Ten years ago heroin addiction was still considered to be primarily an American problem with a rather minor spillover in Britain. Elsewhere in the world heroin addiction was almost non-existent and even though opium was smoked widely and eaten for medicinal purposes in parts of Asia and the Middle East, its use was effectively controlled by social mores that restricted it largely to older men and maintained a certain stability in its consumption.

In the last five years and particularly in the last two years, what was once the "American Disease" has become a world-wide affliction. Heroin addiction has become a major problem in a dozen new countries, with the numbers of addicts continuing to increase by several thousand every month. Not only are those becoming addicted for the most part the children of the social and intellectual elite of these countries and hence their future leaders, but the massive amounts of money now involved in traf-ficking have corrupted many high level officials and undermined already limited and unstable economies. Many factors are in-volved, but our own international efforts to interdict the flow of heroin to the United States have contributed substantially to what can only be described as a worldwide heroin epidemic.

In 1972 we persuaded the Turkish government to discontinue the cultivation of opium and at the same time we convinced the French to clamp down aggressively on the laboratory operators in Marseilles. The result was a significant temporary drying up of heroin supplies, particularly along the East Coast of the United States. Within a year, however, the vacuum left by the curtail-ment of Turkish heroin was filled by a massive influx of the drug from a new source - Mexico. In 1972 the heroin coming from Mexico represented only 20 percent of all heroin consumed in the United States, by 1975 it amounted to more than 90 percent of that coming in. Perhaps even more important, it is estimated that in the last twelve months, seven tons of heroin produced in Mexico have come into the United States. This heroin sells for $45,000 a kilo at the border for a total that is conservatively estimated at $315,000,000. The entire legitimate annual exports from Mexico amount to only 2.5 billion dollars. The heroin trade amounts to six percent of the gross national product, and is the number two foreign currency earner behind tourism. In the six northern states in the country opium cultivation is now the key element in the economy. In the three states of Sinaloa, Durango, and Chihuahua, American officials estimate from aerial surveys that 27,875 acres of opium were grown in 1975.

To date the number of Mexicans who have become addicts remains small, but it is increasing. Should there be any success in interdicting the flow of heroin to the United States, which at present seems unlikely, then it is probable that the traffickers accustomed to a lucrative income would turn to the Mexican population and the rest of Latin America as a market for their heroin.

Despite our initial success in cutting off the flow of heroin from Turkey by paying the Turks $35 million a year to stop cultivating opium, a change in government has resulted in a reversal of that policy and Turkish farmers are again growing this lucrative crop.

While there is little evidence yet that the new crop is being diverted, there has been a significant increase in heroin use in Europe, particularly in Germany, Italy, Denmark and the Netherlands. It appears that should Turkish opium start being diverted again there will be a convenient, accessible and affluent market for it without any longer having to worry about the risks of bringing it all the way to the United States.

In Southeast Asia over a ten year period of time a multi-million dollar business developed supplying heroin to United States troops. Some was consumed in Asia, but a significant amount was shipped back here to be sold on the streets of our cities. This opium was cultivated in the "Golden Triangle" where Laos, Burma and Thailand came together in a region where little or no government control exists. The tribespeople in this area had long been growing opium for domestic use, but the American market provided an entirely new level of economic opportunity.

Even before we began to pull our troops out of VietNam heroin had begun to catch on among young Asians. In Hong Kong, with a labile social situation and a history of traditional opium use, the incidence of heroin addiction rose during the early seventies to one of the highest levels in the world.

As the lucrative market evaporated as we pulled our troops out of Southeast Asia, the traffickers turned even more to the

indigenous populations, particularly the young urban males, many
of whom had problems of alienation in a rapidly changing society
that did not differ much from what existed in this country. In
Thailand it is now estimated that there are as many as 600,000
heroin addicts, up from 300,000 only three or four years ago. In
Burma a similar problem exists. A limited economy with few jobs
even for the most highly educated, an oppressive political system,
and a policy that prohibits emigration has created a sense of frustration and hopelessness. Young college students and graduates who
can find no work are turning to heroin in enormous numbers. One
physician in Mandalay estimated that three percent of the college
students in that town were heroin addicts. The profits for traffickers may not be as great as selling to Americans, but the risk
is minimal and the income is steady and growing. In Malaysia and
Indonesia, the use of heroin has climbed dramatically in the last
three years, and while it does not approach the magnitude that it
has in Burma and Thailand, the rapidity with which new people are
becoming addicted and the inability of the governments in those
countries to control the problem effectively is causing considerable alarm.

There is a belief held by some authorities that our intensive
efforts to get countries such as Thailand and Laos to pass laws
outlawing the traditional use of opium has encouraged the shift to
the odorless and more easily concealed heroin, triggering the widespread use of this drug not among the older male population who
previously had been the only ones using narcotics, but among the
youth of these countries who had no preexisting or controlled patterns of use. In these countries, the areas where opium is grown
are often outside the control of the central government, the immense profits have dramatically compounded preexisting problems of
police corruption and made control of supply almost impossible and
the capacity to provide treatment is almost nonexistent. One is
forced to the conclusion that the problem can only continue to get
steadily worse in the future.

One region of particular interest is Afghanistan and Pakistan
which appears to be the area of the world that will be of the
greatest significance in international narcotics trafficking in
the immediate future. This area has long produced large quantities of opium which for the most part have been consumed locally
or in neighboring Iran. The mountainous terrain where the opium
is grown is largely out of control of the central governments of
these two countries. While there has been no evidence in the past
that opium here was ending up in the international traffic elsewhere in the world, this is now suddenly changing. For the first
time last year a heroin processing laboratory was found in
Pakistan. The international traffickers are clearly increasingly
aware of Afghanistan and Pakistan as an easy source of narcotics,
and nationals of those two countries are showing a sudden reali-

zation of this immense potential wealth in their otherwise poverty
stricken countries.

The development of a major heroin trade out of these two
countries poses a threat not only as a new source for the markets
in the United States and Europe, but also for the largely unex-
ploited potential in Africa and certain parts of the Middle East.

Although Iran has long been an opium consuming country, it is
only in the last few years that significant quantities of heroin
have begun to appear. As a result, there has been an increasing
shift of heroin use to younger people and particularly those living
in the urban rather than rural areas. The increase in use seems
to be continuing and there is little evidence that any steps by
the Iranian government are containing it. There are at present
300,000 heroin and opium addicts in the country.

Conclusions

Based on this information that has become available recently
concerning the international trafficking patterns and the spreading use of heroin in many new locations the following conclusions
can be drawn.

(1) Once opium is being grown in a country, it is almost impossible to eliminate it. Despite international agreements such
as we had with Turkey, crop substitution programs as in Thailand,
or direct diplomatic pressure, as we have applied in Mexico, there
has not been any significant reduction in the amount of heroin
being grown. And the longer opium cultivation has existed, the
harder it is to eliminate because those profiteering from it become unwilling to relinquish their new affluence. Similarly
in many instances the money from opium creates a new level
of corruption among government officials that undermines any desire to move against the growers.

(2) When a heroin market dries up or trafficking routes are
successfully interdicted, the growers do not stop growing opium,
they look aggressively for new markets. Perhaps the best example
of this is the switch to local indigenous populations by traffickers in Southeast Asia after United States troops were pulled
out.

(3) Although we think in terms of opium cultivation occurring
only in certain countries namely where it currently grows there
are many other locations in the world where it could be grown, but
where it has not been grown to date. This means that even if
opium cultivation could be eliminated in those places where it
presently grows traffickers would have inumerable other potential
growing sites available to them.

(4)   While heroin addiction has spread in recent years to involve the youth of many previously unaffected nations there remain
large areas of the world which are highly vulnerable to its further
spread. Particularly in Africa and South America, social change,
urbanization and the increasing alienation of youth as in industrialized nations have created an ideal situation for the spread
of this problem. Increasing affluence will only increase the vulnerability of these regions and their desirability as profitable
markets.

(5)   The immense financial profits which heroin trafficking
offers makes people willing to take considerable risks. It also
not only corrupts but builds into national institutions a vested
interest in not interfering effectively with the cultivation or
trafficking. In poor countries it leads to a serious undermining
of the national economy.

(6)   All of our efforts to deal with this problem had had
little, or no impact. Most countries do not have effective law
enforcement agencies to deal with this problem and treatment for
the addict is limited or nonexistent. All of the steps that we
have taken in this country to retard the spread of addiction few
other countries are capable of applying.

The problem of heroin addiction is getting steadily worse
worldwide with all the evidence suggesting that we are heading into
a catastrophic situation with serious implications for the stability of the economies of several small nations and for the youth
and future leadership of much of the world.

Our efforts by the United States as well as those of the
United Nations organizations seem to have failed to come to grips
with the problem. We need in the United States to begin to see
the problem as one which must be dealt with on a worldwide basis
and not merely as an effort to keep heroin out of this country.
We must help other nations to develop the expertise to deal with
their own addiction problems with a far greater level of commitment
than we are making at present. It is not merely a question of
sending narcotics agents all over the world which seems to have
had minimal effectiveness and to have generated a great deal of
hostility. What is needed is a well funded program to offer assistance in the prevention and treatment of drug abuse so that we
can reduce the spread of the problem and the casualties it causes.
Any such program must be linked to economic development in those
countries so that heroin is no longer seen as a major source of
national income.

Above all we must recognize that narcotic addiction is now
a global problem not merely an American problem, and we must have
a unified coordinated effort to deal with the problem on that
basis. We can no longer afford to blame other nations for the

23

drug problems that have developed in the United States. The prospects for dealing with the problem are not good under the best of circumstances, but unless we change our attitude and recognize the magnitude of heroin addiction and the threat it poses now to the entire world, we may as well abandon our efforts before we even begin.

PROPOSAL FOR A NATIONAL BEHAVIORAL AND SOCIAL HEALTH COMMISSION

Rayburn F. Hesse

Executive Director
National Association of
State Drug Abuse Program Coordinators

M. Chairman:

I propose that the Congress create, for a period of three
years, a National Behavioral and Social Health Commission whose
principal function will be to recommend new policies to Federal,
State and local governments, and the health and social services
fields, for a behavioral health approach to the problems of drug
abuse, alcoholism, mental health, dysfunctional behavior and related social problems.

At minimum, the expectation is that this Commission's work
would result in the establishment, identification, recognition
and acceptance of a behavioral health science, distinct and apart
from the biomedical or physical health sciences.

That a behavioral health problem exists is an inalienable
fact. That a social health problem exists is an inalienable
fact. That we have amalgamated a behavioral-social health field
from key components of biomedical health is an inalienable fact.

That this behavioral health field is subject and vulnerable
to the rules, regulations, program standards -- and professional
biases and prejudices--of the biomedical, physical health
sciences is an inalienable fact.

That we must constitute this behavioral health field as a
behavioral-social health science is an undeniable certainty.

The resolution of critical problems in service delivery; long-
term funding; program accreditation and licensing; personnel
certification and credentialling; third-party payments under Title
19 and 20, as well as from national health insurance and non-public
resources; health planning, such as mandated by P.L. 93-641; and,
very importantly, the establishing of a truly comprehensive primary

prevention system as an integral component of a network of support
for all of our social casualties, can be significantly facilitated
by this change of approach -- and may in fact be directly dependent
upon this systems change.

At minimum, the expectation is that the new policies and
programmatic initiatives to be recommended by this Commission will
result in the adoption of comprehensive behavioral-social health ·
approaches to the problems of alcoholism, drug abuse, mental health
and dysfunctional behavior -- approaches that address cause as well
as effect -- approaches that interface the totality of our societal
resource in the human process of behavioral rehabilitation and
social re-integration.

Maximally, this Commission's recommendations could result in
the elimination of ADAMHA, NIDA, MIAAA, and NIMH -- to be replaced
by a Behavior and Social Health Administration.

In the coming weeks, I will submit a formal proposal to key
Congressional leaders. I offer this proposal as one individual --
not as Executive Director of the National Association nor in behalf
of the National Association.

It is my ardent hope that this proposal will be supported by
the Congress -- by the States who are the National Association --
and by program practitioners throughout the alcoholism, drug abuse,
mental health and social health fields.

I offer, not a final solution, but a challenge -- a forum on
which we can debate strategies for resolving or at least containing the multiple behavioral problems that confront this country. I
encourage and anticipate the constructive inputs of fellow professionals throughout the nation.

Let me share the highlights of the proposal with you.

Specifically, this Commission, modeled in part on the
Marihuana Commission, would be mandated to:

1. Assess the relative effectiveness and eficiency of current
policies, approaches, and programs related to alcoholism, drug
abuse, mental illness and dysfunctional behavior.

As a major function of such analysis, the Commission would evaluate
the continuum of services directed to target populations, factoring
for the host of client needs in different circumstances and
situations, and making determinations as to unmet client needs,
with attention focused on the needs for ancillary services. The
Commission would -- as a first step in fostering a total behavioral-
social health approach -- make recommendations relative to changes
in the service missions of system components, i.e., broadening the

service mission, obtaining the needed services through other care providers or services agents, etc. In this first category, a very top priority must be assigned to an analysis of resource systems for the purpose of identifying and recommending long-term funding strategies that ensure a continuum of effort in response to the problem dynamic critically important, this Commission would identify deterrents to effective programming -- deterrents which may be functions of short-sighted or impractical policies, deficient funding strategies, public apathy, professional jealousies, and inefficient management -- and recommend decisive actions to eliminate these deterrents.

2. Examine, as a major component of problem analysis, both the epidemiological and etiological characteristics of alcoholism, drug abuse, mental illness and other dysfunctional behavior, with specific emphasis upon the identification and analysis of societal and human conditions which contribute to or manifest themselves in dysfunctional behavior.

3. Determine and recommend, after appropriate study of existing roles and relationships, the appropriate roles, relationships, and responsibilities of Federal, State and local governments and services programs in behavioral and social service funding, planning, service delivery, program management, evaluation, research, program development, and manpower development. Such recommendations on structural and component relationships and inter-relationships would be based and be dependent upon the results of analyzing the current and future problem dynamic and companion recommendations for the most efficient and effective systems for problem resolution.

4. Determine and recommend the extent to which administrative management and services delivery systems should be integrated at the Federal, State and local levels.

5. Examine and evaluate the interfaces --theoretical, real and desired -- between the physical or biomedical health sciences and the behavioral sciences, with the objective of identifying separate spheres of influence, problem orientation, programmatic constructs, operating characteristics, performance standards, etc., so as to recommend ultimately a separate series of policies, regulations, standards and operating procedures for behavioral and social health programs.

This Commission should, in my opinion, specifically analyze the need for and implications of creating a new Behavioral and Social Health Administration, within the Department of Health, Education and Welfare, such Administration to assume and discharge the current functions of the Alcohol, Drug Abuse and Mental Health Administration, and its three constituent institutes -- the National Institute on Drug Abuse, the National Institute on Alcohol

Abuse and Alcoholism, and the National Institute of Mental Health --as well as those functions of the Health Resources Administration, Health Services Administration, the Social and Rehabilitative Services Administration, the Office for Human Development, and other HEW components which impact upon behavioral and social health problems.

Realistically, it is possible that the Commission could recommend a Behavioral Health Administration, as a counterpart to and coordinating authority with a Social Services Administration.

Admittedly, the Commission could recommend the continuation of ADAMHA, the three Institutes, and the existing system of interface relationships. Such a status quo recommendation regarding structure would have to be accompanied, in my opinion, by major changes in mission, policies, operating procedures, inter-relationships with the States, etc. It would be short-sighted, in my opinion, to merge NIDA and NIAAA as a singular act.

It is not a condition of the proposal that all existing service units must be merged -- or that the Single State Agencies must merge, although many now combine alcoholism and drug abuse management and most are actually units within Health and Mental Health Departments -- or that the three Institutes must merge, although at least one U.S. Senator is developing legislation to combine NIDA and NIAAA.

I believe further study is needed and I do not think I or anyone else should pre-empt the Commission. So, I do not stipulate such conditions.

Administrative and management approaches, like service systems, must relate to and be a function of strategies and policies that are, in the first instance, a product of careful analysis of the most effective methods of responding to the problem dynamic.

It is obvious from the outset that a multi-modality response system is mandatory. For example, there must be intensive care units for the mentally ill. We may continue to have therapeutic centers for heroin addicts, especially units that relate effectively to minority and cultural differences. But, the role relationships will be defined and undoubtedly different. Those treatment centers that continue will not only be evaluated, there will also be mechanisms to provide services other than counselling and treatment per se; there would be intake mechanisms to ensure that programs receive those clients with whom they have the highest potential of success; we would eliminate the need for every program to replicate the total range of social and health services.

But, those decisions are the product of analysis and should not be pre-judged.

Again, as a matter of highest priority, this Commission should be charged specifically with the obligatory task of recommending, not later than one year after its creation, program policies, regulations, standards and new programmatic concepts for a true behavioral health approach to the problems of alcoholism, drug abuse, mental health and dysfunctional behavior.

An orientation to and adaptation to behavioral health approaches is considered an absolute prerequisite to any reorganization within fields or merger of fields. Indeed, it is my opinion that these fields should adopt true behavioral health approaches regardless of any future realignments of service systems.

This condition is in keeping with a belief that the three major fields of alcoholism, drug abuse and mental health -- a problem grouping which should be expanded to include dysfunctional behavior -- have unfinished business -- major tasks that must be completed even as new system approaches are devised and implemented.

Thus, the prospect envisioned is that any major merger or realignment, if such if recommended, is a minimum of two and as many as four years away.

The rationale for the Commission is rooted in a perception of the changing problem dynamic, and in an analysis of why we do not cope effectively with dysfunctional behavior.

There is compelling evidence that we must alter strategy and modify systems -- but -- there is no convincing indication that the leadership or even the stimulus for change will be supplied by the Domestic Council, HEW, ADAMHA, or the three Institutions. Congress must exert the leadership through legislative mandate. We have an obligation to advise the Congress on need and policy -- but an even more imperative mandate upon us is to provide the energy, resources, wisdom and experience that can ensure a beneficial product. The cooperation of every professional and paraprofessionals in our fields is essential. I am quite sure our Federal colleagues will participate readily when the issue is joined.

FEDERAL PERSPECTIVES ON DRUG ABUSE

Lee I. Dogoloff

Federal Drug Management
Office of Management and Budget
Washington, D.C.

Today, I want to talk about where the Federal Government is
in relation to the drug abuse program. I obviously don't need to
go into long explanations about the seriousness of the problem and
why it should be a national priority. As workers in the field,
you know that better than any one. However, I do want to take a
few minutes for a brief historical review and then move into a
more detailed discussion of happenings over the past year and a
brief look into the immediate future.

Drug abuse is a phenomenon that can be traced back for
literally thousands of years. In 1729, 47 years prior to the
founding of our nation, the Chinese Emperor, Yung Cheng, issued
the first imperial ban on opium, prescribing severe penalties,
including death for opium shop proprietors in an attempt to stamp-
out the problem. There are many reports of a severe opium problem
in the United States during the latter half of the 17th century.
In China, in 1900, an estimated 27% of the adult male population
was addicted to opium to some degree. In 1909, the United States
officially recognized the international implications of the drug
problem by convening the Changhai Conference, the first in a long
history of international initiatives which continue today as part
of our program to deal with the problem.

Drug abuse was more recently rediscovered as an American
problem when, in the late 1960's and early 70's, it was both
linked to a growing crime rate in our large urban centers and
began to spread to our middle class and suburban communities.
During that time narcotic addiction among Vietnam forces approached 20%. There is no escaping from the conclusion, later verified
by key indicators, that the United States was, in fact, in the
grips of a heroin epidemic.

In response to the problem, a great deal of money was made
available to create a capacity to treat large numbers of drug

abusers and to increase our law enforcement efforts. And for a time there was the sweet smell of success. We interrupted the major drug trafficking route of Turkish grown opium, and created a nation-wide system that can now treat nearly a half million persons per year. Heroin indicators, on the major East coast cities of Washington and New York, began to turn down, and to some of us it certainly appeared that the worst was over.

Luckily, however, one of the results of the national priority for the drug program was the ability to monitor the problem. And as we continued our monitoring efforts we discovered in the summer of 1974 what many of you probably began to see a good six months earlier -- that things were getting worse. Retail heroin purity and drug related deaths were up -- Our treatment system was rapidly filling to capacity -- We had not solved the problem as many of us had hoped. We had merely experienced some temporary and largely regional successes.

As we began to try and understand what was happening, we became all to familiar with "Mexican brown" -- a new source of heroin supply that began to engulf our country. Today, the Drug Enforcement Administration estimates that Mexican heroin accounts for nearly 80-90% of all heroin coming into our country. We also began to appreciate the fact that heroin and other dangerous drug use was spreading -- first to other major cities like Miami and Los Angeles, and then to even smaller places like Jackson, Mississippi and Cheyenne, Wyoming. No longer could we think of New York City as having half of the nation's addicts. In addition, we began to recognize that the drug problem involved more than just heroin -- more and more people were getting into trouble with the use of barbiturates and amphetamines. They began appearing in emergency rooms with increasing frequency and a survey estimated that the current active non-medical use of these drugs among the adult population to be 5%, or 7 to 8 million Americans.

In response to these alarming statistics, President Ford directed the Domestic Council, under the leadership of the Vice President, to undertake a priority review of the overall Federal effort in the treatment and prevention of drug abuse, to give him a frank assessment of our effectiveness and to make recommendations concerning ways to improve the program.

I was fortunate to be able to participate as one of the key staff for that review and in the preparation of the resulting White Paper on Drug Abuse. This experience not only gave me a chance to directly impact on the treatment portion of the review, but also helped to broaden my perspective regarding the law enforcement and international aspects of the problem.

The White Paper experience helped me to understand the critical importance of a Federal program which balances the effort

to control and ultimately reduce the supply of drugs using law
enforcement efforts with an effort to control and ultimately reduce
the demand for drugs by providing effective treatment and
prevention services. I would like to share some interesting
apsects of our supply reduction program.

The objectives of the law enforcement program are to make
drugs expensive, inaccessible, inconvenient and dangerous to obtain
in order to discourage potential users, keep experimenters from
advancing to chronic use, and to encourage committed users to
abandon drugs.

There are a number of points at which we could impact drug
supply beginning with the growing of the raw materials and extending to the lowest street-level dealer. And just as our demand
program is much more than methadone, so the supply program is much
more than just kicking in doors. In fact, one of the major
recommendations of the White Paper was for Federal drug enforcement efforts to cease involvement in street-level busts and
instead to concentrate on developing conspiracy cases on high-
level traffickers. This recognizes that the further back in the
distribution chain we go, the more fruitful our efforts are likely
to be -- so, if we can use diplomatic initiatives to get opium
producing countries to better control their crops or, as in the
case of Mexico, work together or destroy illegal poppy fields
before the opium is harvested, this is much better than having to
interrupt street-level trafficking as the distribution system fans
out.

However, since we do not grow opium, this requires the
commitment of foreign countries where it is grown. Work at the
diplomatic levels includes such things as President Ford's direct
discussions of the drug situation with the Presidents of Mexico
and Colombia and the Prime Minister of Turkey. At the same time
we are offering law enforcement training and equipment to increase
the ability of foreign governments to deal with this problem.
However, the situation is much more complex that I have described
-- many of the growing areas are quite remote -- in rugged
mountainous terrain -- and in some areas of the world the national
government's power cannot be forcibly exercised over quasi-
independent tribal peoples or insurgent groups.

On the demand side there is also an international role. To
the extent that producing countries can see opium not only as a
U.S. problem, but also a problem affecting their people, these
countries will be more likely to afford high priority to enforcement efforts. Technical assistance in establishing treatment and
prevention programs helps to both focus attention on the problem
and to identify the numbers of people who are involved in drug
abuse in a given country. An interesting side note to this aspect
of the problem comes from my experience in representing the United

States in providing such technical assistance; I come away with the impression that although we are, generally speaking, much more economically able to provide services, the problems invovled are strikingly similar. For example, I participated in the Venezuelan discussion as they tried to determine what it is they wanted to prevent as part of defining drug abuse prevention. The Iranians are into issues like central intake units, in-patient versus out-patient services, and, of course, data management systems. The Thai's are struggling with issues like coordination of community resources and follow-up services after discharge from in-patient care -- so I conclude that all the cultural differences aside, drug abuse is truly an international phenomenon.

Returning to the White Paper, one of its major themes is that we must make distinctions between different drugs and different patterns of drug use -- that all drug use is not equally destructive. With limited resources on both the law enforcement and treatment sides we must give priority to those drugs which are most likely to cause the greatest problems to society and to individuals -- heroin, amphetamines and barbiturates are listed as the top priority group. However, we should also provide treatment to compulsive users of any drug, and continue law enforcement aimed at major traffickers of any drug.

The White Paper also called attention to the need for increased focus on rehabilitation efforts -- specifically vocational training and job placement activities and called for better interagency coordination at the Federal level to make certain that persons in or completing treatment get their fair share of such services.

In the area of prevention, where I suggest the White Paper is weakest, there was a recognition of the importance of local community involvement in non-drug specific prevention programs which, it suggests, is a local rather than Federal responsibility.

Lastly, the White Paper made three specific recommendations regarding program management: the revitalization of the Strategy Council on Drug Abuse to provide overall policy guidance; the creation of a Cabinet Committee for Drug Abuse Prevention with an active subcommittee structure (under the leadership of NIDA) to continue the coordination of prevention and treatment activities formerly provided by SAODAP; and the continuation of a small staff in the Office of Management and Budget to provide assistance to the Strategy Council and the Executive Office.

Now for the important discussion of what has happened since the White Paper was presented to and later endorsed by the President.

For one thing, drug abuse has been clearly established as a priority domestic program by the President. One of the best expressions of this priority is in the FY77 budget that is now before the Congress. The budget requests sufficient funds to implement all of the White Paper's major recommendations. For example, additional resources are provided for treatment demonstrations for abusers of amphetamines and barbiturates and 20 new positions are requested for the Drug Enforcement Administration to increase our ability to control the availability of these drugs. Seven thousand new community treatment slots are slated for NIDA — the first such increase in three years. In addition, funds are provided for a joint HEW/Labor program to investigate ways to provide employment opportunities for persons in and completing treatment and positions to improve the intelligence and research capability of our law enforcement program.

The Office of Federal Drug Management has been expanded from one to three persons and we have been working to establish government-wide programmatic leadership in the National Institute on Drug Abuse and in the Drug Enforcement Administration. Several interagency work groups have been formed under FDM and/or NIDA leadership to provide Federal coordination of demand programs in the areas of evaluation, criminal justice, prevention, employment and international programs. In each instance, NIDA either has or is scheduled to assume leadership of these committees in anticipation of the creation of the Cabinet Committee for Drug Abuse Prevention, the working group of which will be chaired by Bob DuPont.

The Domestic Council Drug Abuse Task Force which prepared the White Paper has been directed to conduct a thorough review of the problem of heroin flowing acorss the Southwest border and make specific recommendations to the President for improving law enforcement efforts. That report should be completed within the next few weeks.

I am now moving from a discussion of what was and what is to the more risky and dangerous realm of predicting what will be. These comments represent both a statement of goals as well as how things are likely to unfold in the months ahead. But, if the past few years have taught us anything, it is that one should be terribly cautious about such statements because things are subject to rapid and abrupt change.

Given these introductory disclaimers it does seem that the interagency committees can, in the next several months, develop some products -- for example, I anticipate that the evaluation group will develop a chapter in the National Strategy to be issued this summer. This will be a clear statement of what is known about treatment outcome. The statement will hopefully reveal what has happened to clients in terms of drug use, employment, and criminality during their treatment experience. Obviously, this is an over-simplification of a difficult and complex issue. But, there is a real commitment to not only developing a state of the art statement, but also planning for updating such evaluation as a regular part of our program.

The criminal justice group will move toward increased cooperation between the various Federal agencies -- with better linkages for drug involved persons who become known to the Federal criminal justice system and who needs specialized drug treatment in the community. In addition, I envision the development of detoxification standards for all persons coming into Federal detention centers who are addicted to either heroin or methadone to be certain that they get good care.

The prevention group will obviously have its work cut out for them. I am encouraged by the prospect of bringing in some outside thinking to help us to define what it is we want to prevent and to offer some guidance on how this can best be done. This would mean bringing together what we know about the problem of drug abuse, how it spreads, and what years of research concludes about influencing such human behavior. Then we will be in a better position to consider appropriate policy recommendations as to roles that different government agencies and that various levels of government might play in a prevention program.

The employment group should make specific recommendations regarding what, if anything, needs to be done to make certain that persons in and completing treatment have access to available programs for vocational rehabilitation, training, and job place-ment. These recommendations will be presented to the appropriate body for approval and implementation. In addition, it should develop the specifics of a joint HEW/Labor initiative to improve employment opportunities as requested in the FY77 budget.

Within the next several weeks the President will be sending a special message on drug abuse to the Congress. I anticipate the reactivation of the Strategy Council and the formal creation of the Cabinet Committee on Drug Abuse Prevention in the near future. A legislative package, affecting both the supply and demand programs, is in its developmental stages and I would suggest that this will be presented to the Congress along with the message.

Later this week I am scheduled to participate in a briefing on the drug abuse program for the President. His commitment to this program is clear. The level of activity is increasing tremendously. However, there are some striking differences in what is happening today as compared to when we rediscovered drug abuse a few years ago. Two essential differences deserve special mention -- first, that there is a commitment to and respect for the Cabinet departments and agencies dedication and ability to get the job done. NIDA and DEA are the leaders and they are going to

be the agencies that both the Executive offices and the field will
look to.

The second difference is terribly important -- it relates back
to the point I made in the beginning -- that drug abuse has been
with us for a long time -- and what follows is that it is not
likely to go away. We recognize this: we are not likely to be
able to stop all illegal drug traffic no more than we are going to
be able to cure all drug abusers or prevent all new drug abuse.
But, even if the problem will not be solved, there are things that
can and must be done to improve our current efforts to contain the
problem. History seems to indicate that the alternative to such
action is to face the prospect of a large portion of Americans who
are in serious trouble with drug abuse. Let's not fall into the
trap of over-promising -- instead, let's be realistic in our
expectations of what can be achieved. Let's not promise cures,
-- nor talk of wars. But, at the same time, let's be honest with
ourselves and most importantly be honest with clients. Let's give
them the full measure of our ability and concern so that we can
all achieve the realistic expectations of doing the best we can
given the difficulty of the problem and the limitations of both
our internal and external resources.

A VIEW OF THE FUTURE ADMINISTRATION
OF DRUG ABUSE AND ALCOHOLISM PROGRAMS
IN NEW YORK STATE

Lawrence C. Kolb, M.D.

Commissioner
State of New York
Department of Mental Hygiene

On behalf of our Governor, Governor Hugh Carey, I have the
honor and pleasure today to express for him his good wishes to all
those participating in this Third National Drug Abuse Conference.

Earlier this year Governor Carey delivered the first formal
State of the Health Message in the history of our State. In it
he outlined a series of proposals to both improve the accessibility
and increase the affordability of our system of health care.

One of the areas which the Governor stressed was improvement
in the specialized care involved in the treatment of those who
abuse drugs or are addicted to their use. Over the past decade the
State of New York has supported and operated separate alcohol and
drug abuse treatment programs. On the basis of the reports of a
study made by his Mental Health Task Force, there has been a disproportionate allocation of suggested state resources between the
separately administered services for drug abuse and alcoholism.

The increasing evidence of overlap of usage among the groups
served by these programs and the need to reduce duplication in
services wherever possible argued strongly in favor of the merger.
It has become clear that a totally new approach, encompassing new
treatment philosophies, a modification of traditional state responsibilities, and development of a more realistic understanding of
the goals and expectation of services provided in these areas is
essential.

I am certain that everyone in this knowledgeable audience
accepts the fact that drug use, abuse, and addiction derives from
multifactorial causes. These rest in biological, sociological,
cultural, and societal factors complexly intertwined and difficult
to tease apart when one is confronted with the consequences of that

37

abuse in any individual. If all or any of the above statements
could achieve a consensus in this audience, the need for coordination of efforts between the agencies concerned in the correction of
personality disturbances for any one of the forms of drug abuse,
would be a matter of agreement among all those present here today.

In New York State, the Department which I represent administers
the programs for the mentally ill, the retarded, and the alcoholic.
It has a remote relationship to the Drug Abuse Commission. There
is no question that in the past, as with other areas of the field
of medicine, the alcoholic and the drug abusers were accepted with
reluctance into the treatment services of the Department of Mental
Hygiene. Major efforts to effectively bring about those actions in
the preventive and therapeutic fields for those entrapped into
seeking help received short shrift. The recognition of the alcoholic and drug abuser as individuals to be cared for by our traditional mental health and welfare systems has only been addressed
clearly during the last decade. This is in contrast to the long-
term responsibility of the government and voluntary agencies in
regard to the problems of mental illness and mental retardation.
Further, as the newcomers to the field of health care and welfare
problems, there exists an evident disparity in the allocation of resources.

Beyond the difficulty of assessing the proper distribution of
funding that the Federal government and each of the states should
provide for those suffering disabilities as a result of psychopathology, retardation or one of the forms of drug abuse, there has
occurred an even greater maldistribution of resources as a consequence of the countercultural movements of the late 1960's and early
1970's which induced so many of our young people to experiment with
narcotics, hallucineogenics and hypnotics. Even at the height of
that period, the numbers abusing alcohol as the socially approved
drug always exceeded the numbers in trouble as a consequence of
their usage of the other agents.

As is so common in our country, major programs were initiated
to bring about control of and provide treatment for the young in
the non-alcoholic drug abuse craze. In New York State this movement was massive. The results perhaps are known to all of you but,
if not, allow me to report to you in terms of the allocation of resources.

Through the studies made by the Governor's Task Force on
Mental Health undertaken during the winter and fall of 1974, it became clear that this state was expending 150 million dollars on
drug abuse and 10 million on alcohol. The Governor's Task Force
emphasized the disparity in the funding. It recommended a fusion
of the several agencies to effectively balance the distribution of
resources in relation to the currently existing problem areas.
This proposal was partially based on findings that there were many

polydrug users whose appropriate placement was quite unclear in the separate agencies.

It is predictable that legislation mandating such a fusion of effort would produce much debate. Those active in the alcohol field and those active in the drug abuse field have both achieved a degree of identity and take pride in the development of programs they have established. Some quarters suggest that any massive attempt to meld the programs for the primary alcoholic or primary drug addict is unlikely to be seen as therapeutically wise. The pressure of the professional and non-professional workers in the several separate agencies or the establishment of credentials identifying them as such is a clear indication that several groups have achieved a degree of self-esteem and pride in their work, as well as material rewards, which will mitigate against other than a reluctant bondage under a single agency.

The "turf" problems, many believe, are contrary to the opinions of scientists who hold that the basic etiologic factors, (biological, psychological, cultural and societal), for all forms of drug abuse, will be found to have certain general properties and that the ultimate approach to their understanding should be unitary.

As a matter of fact, some of the leading research institutes in this country already have established sections on the "consumptive disorders". They include not only the several drug abuse problems of interest here today, but also those related to other socially condoned, if sometimes medically deplored, activities including the use and abuse of tobacco, caffeine-containing delights and food stuffing or food denial.

It is the conviction of this state government that it is desirable to proceed through a coordinated, comprehensive planning process which must bring together state, local and voluntary agencies to develop a working consensus expressive of the views both from providers and consumers to a greater degree than presently exists.

The planning process must recognize the reality of the scarcity of fiscal resources. This will require from the planners the painful decision-making of establishing priorities in the distribution of funding. That planning process too must relate itself to the new health service agencies and the functions they will assume in decision-making throughout the country.

It would be my hope that through a coordinated approach we would be able to convince the health insurance carriers to provide more adequately in coverage for the treatment of alcoholism and drug abuse and to develop more effective working relationships and increased fiscal sharing between those agencies of government concerned with the subject matter which shall come under discussion here today and the social service systems as well as the general health system. Only through the development of such relationships will we be able to bring about the social rehabilitative efforts that are so imminently required for the seriously impaired who entered services identified as either mentally ill, drug abusers or alcohol abusers.

On the preventive side, a coordinated educational effort in which resources are shared to pre-test the educational process on higher risk populations is much more likely to succeed than the piece-meal, shotgun-like and poorly-evaluated methodology that now typifies the various health fields. So too, the coordinated effort encouraging business, industry, organized labor and governmental agencies to develop programs of early identification of workers suffering the consequences of drug abuse and alcohol will be stronger than the confusing separate efforts of various agencies. Today, the narrow-focus approaches allow too many to suffer the consequences of failure of the initial study which leads them to the most appropriate therapeutic support.

One final word in regard to our efforts in the several fields. It would appear inevitable that any approach today must come under evaluative scrutiny as to its effectiveness if it is to receive public support. There are many serious issues confronting us in regard to evaluative processes.

Few undertaking service specify the expectation of change in behavior that they assume will occur as a result of the intervention provided. Even fewer indicate the length of time that must ensue before observable modifications and socially adaptive modification of behavior is likely to take place following one or another type of intervention as regards any services provided in these fields.

And, finally, there is a tendency to deny the ever-prevailing existence of long-continuing, irreversible or deteriorating illness as well as drug dependency. The evaluative process must recognize and give due credit to therapeutic support from those so suffering and for those administering to the chronically debilitated.

I close with an appeal for a broad and comprehensive approach, the sharing of knowledge and resources and the eschewing of narrow and limited territorial rights. By so moving, we will come together to dedicate ourselves to those suffering from the consequences of drug abuse and the underlying pathologies which force men and women into those kinds of behavioral servitudes.

THE ROLE OF THE REGULATORY AGENCIES:
THE NATIONAL INSTITUTE ON DRUG ABUSE

Stuart L. Nightingale, M.D.

Assistant Director for Medical & Professional Affairs
National Institute on Drug Abuse
Rockville, Maryland

The National Institute on Drug Abuse (NIDA) is not a regulatory
agency in the traditional sense, but it does participate in a
variety of "regulatory" activities with other Federal agencies,
Single State Agencies and treatment programs. The Special Action
Office for Drug Abuse Prevention, the Division of Narcotic Addiction and Drug Abuse of the National Institute of Mental Health
(the predecessor of NIDA) and the Bureau of Narcotics and Dangerous
Drugs [the predecessor of the Drug Enforcement Administration (DEA)]
all worked with the Food and Drug Administration (FDA) on developing the present methadone regulations authorized by and monitored
by FDA. If one uses methadone as an example of the regulatory
model, then NIDA can be characterized as working closely with FDA
and DEA on implementation of the regulations, reviewing the problems which arise, and participating in the development of suggested
revisions of the regulations. This is done through a working-level
group known as the Interagency Methadone Treatment Policy Review
Board which represents the directors of the above agencies, as well
as the Veterans Administration (VA). Compliance activities, a
primary concern of regulatory agencies, are not carried out by NIDA.
NIDA has no inspectors who go into the field to ascertain adherence to the methadone regulations, although NIDA does have personnel who monitor multiple aspects of NIDA-funded methadone programs.
NIDA is concerned both with its own methadone programs (which are
inspected by DEA, FDA and, in some cases, by state agency personnel) and with all programs whether private, state, local or pri-
vately funded through its cooperative efforts with the Federal
regulatory agencies. NIDA programs must operate under the same
regulations that non-NIDA funded programs do. Thus, we are very
concerned that the FDA methadone regulations are fair, reasonable,
and cost-efficient. We are concerned both about the substance of
the regulations and how they are enforced. Obviously, inappropriate regulations are very poor even if they are enforced with great
precision. Similarly, well-developed and written regulations

inappropriately enforced can be harmful. NIDA joins the other Federal agencies in these concerns but, like the VA, it is a major service provider and is impacted, perforce, more comprehensively by these regulations. Both DEA and FDA appreciate these concerns.

NIDA AND METHADONE TREATMENT: CURRENT ACTIVITIES

A. Methadone Regulations

NIDA will soon be jointly publishing revisions to the current methadone regulations with FDA, based on the recent legislation transferring licensing authority to DEA (Narcotic Addict Treatment Act of 1974). NIDA's role in the development of treatment standards is increasing. The Interagency Methadone Treatment Policy Review Board continues to be a forum for both regulation development and monitoring. The methadone regulations will continue to represent the minimal criteria necessary to grant Federal licensure to operate methadone programs. Meanwhile, NIDA continues to support state licensure of programs which may be the same or more detailed than Federal standards, depending on state and local needs and concerns.

B. Federal Funding Criteria

NIDA has published "Federal Funding Criteria" (FFC) for all treatment modalities as regulations. Those applicable to methadone are somewhat more detailed in certain areas than the current methadone regulations. The publishing of the FFC, although not supported by current legislation, is the closest that NIDA has come, to date, to approximating a regulatory agency approach in terms of its own funded programs. Though withdrawal of funds from a service delivery program can lead to program closure, it is not in itself, of course, a regulatory act.

C. Drug Abuse Treatment Standards of the Joint Commission on Accreditation of Hospitals

NIDA has sponsored the development of standards by the Joint Commission on Accreditation of Hospitals (JCAH) for drug abuse programs. Currently, these standards are being pilot tested in 88 programs across the country. These were developed as "optimal achievable standards" rather than minimal criteria (e.g., FDA methadone regulations) or minimal for purposes of funding (FFC). They were developed by professionals and paraprofessionals in the field, not the Federal Government per se. How they are "weighted" (prioritized), if they are found reasonable, will be critical to any implementation. The level of compliance which will be needed

42

to "pass" an inspection is just as important as what the standards are in any implementation as discussed above.

NIDA is currently analyzing and comparing the current FDA methadone regulations, those portions of FFC relevant to methadone detoxification and maintenance, and the JCAH standards and will then detail the minimal requirements necessary and publish them in concert with other relevant Federal agencies in regulatory form. NIDA will concomitantly disseminate and make available as appropriate the less essential (non-mandatory) elements in a training or technical assistance mode.

The process of arriving at final regulations and standards will be quite complex due to the following issues and problem areas:

1. The state of our evaluation knowledge related to methadone programs is fairly unsophisticated. There are some very well-performed studies, but few that detail specifics related to defining the most effective staffing pattern or medication "pick-up" schedule. Ideally, regulations should be reasonable and lead to improved efficiency, improved outcome, and minimize risks to public health. Fiscal problems might complicate our efforts because of a tendency to try to minimize the most expensive program elements (staff, urine surveillance, etc.) when such elements might not be the most appropriate to de-emphasize. On the other hand, such elements in the current regulations might very well be most appropriately dealt with in this way.

2. The scope of regulations are somewhat ill-defined in certain areas. The portions of the current regulations which are related to the quality of patient care vs. drug control/security vs. "approved use" of the drug are not always as clear-cut as one might think or hope.

3. How detailed should the final regulations be, based on certain unique issues which relate specifically to methadone treatment?

A. Methadone diversion.

B. Appropriate procedures for involuntary termination of patients: What is reasonable? Federal licensing allows program operations, but the program may have a monopoly on methadone treatment in a particular community.

In summary, NIDA has a diverse and comprehensive role in the methadone treatment area. NIDA's influence will be felt in the area of regulation, development, monitoring, and enforcement, even though NIDA is not a regulatory agency. NIDA will also assist in the area of training and technical assistance to programs in a variety of ways, as well as its more traditional approach to funding methadone treatment programs as part of its overall multi-modality approach.

GENERAL REFERENCES

1. Methadone Regulations, 39 Federal Register 11680, March 29, 1974.

2. S.L. Nightingale, Methadone Treatment Programs, Quarterly Bulletin of the Association of Food and Drug Officials of the United States, 38(2):99-101, 1974.

3. Federal Funding Criteria, 40 Federal Register 23062, May 27, 1975.

4. Standards for Drug Abuse Treatment and Rehabilitation Programs, Accreditation Council for Psychiatric Facilities, Joint Commission on Accreditation of Hospitals, Chicago, Illinois, 1975.

5. A Prescriptive Package: Methadone Treatment Manual, Law Enforcement Assistance Administration, U.S. Department of Justice, Washington, D.C. 20402, 1973.

44

OPENING REMARKS

Eva J. Tongue, LL.D.
Assistant Director, ICAA

It is my pleasure and privilege to bring to this conference, the
warmest greetings of the world community represented by the International Council on Alcohol and Addictions and its President, the
Honorable Harold E. Hughes, former United States Senator.

Headquartered in Lausanne, Switzerland, ICAA has had over 70 years
of experience in attempting to coordinate the international efforts
that were and are being made to combat the varied addictions which
have become a global problem in this century.

Addiction is truly an international problem. It rears its ugly
head in places diverse as Bangkok, Chicago and Marrakech. It is
an area in which many approaches have evolved and the variety of
philosophies, treatment, techniques and research represent fertile
ground for truly international cooperative action. This action
involves treatment, rehabilitation and indeed, the exerting of
pressure on the demand for drug substances through varied educational, informational and even political mechanisms.

Recent history has shown that for too many years the international
community has been overly preoccupied with control measures and
that this area, until recently, has been the salient feature of
international drug cooperation. It is time that this saturation
of effort in the control area be changed. It is fitting that in
1976, which marks the Bi-Centennial celebration of the United
States of America's Declaration of Independence that the international community re-dedicate itself to the task of freeing mankind from the mounting epidemic of addictions. The leadership
that the Western World has given in the field of substance abuse
must be supplemented by the insights and advances garnered in
Asia and Africa.

We at ICAA are especially concerned with a major area of drug
dependence - alcohol - and I am glad to see that alcohol related
problems are within the purview of this Conference. It is unfortunate that in the United Nations, alcohol dependence receives
very little attention from the drug organizations and only the
World Health Organization includes some activity concerning

45

alcohol in its mental health programs. It is depressing that
there is hardly a country that has been able to reduce its
alcohol problem significantly and alcohol consumption has spread
to cultures such as the Moslem and Buddhist worlds where religious
sanctions against its use have existed for centuries.

It is clear that in spite of many substance competitors, alcohol
more than holds its own and seems to have a very bright future in
our society. For this reason, there is an international trend
discernible to highlight alcohol dependence as the major national
and international drug problem and to place it and dependence on
other substances in the right perspective. This can obviously
have important implications in many areas of concern to us.

The thrust towards moving into true international cooperation is
about to be actualized with a major world conference of therapeutic communities in Norrkoping, Sweden, on September 27th, 1976.
The Conference will be dealing with therapeutic techniques,
patient problems, research and indeed, cover the gamut of the many
complex parts that together constitute the whole that is the
therapeutic community.

In conclusion, I am certain that we are all aware of the urgency
of the problems that we face together and I wish this Conference
every success in its deliberations. I would also like to reaffirm
ICAA's desire to stimulate the closest international contact between the group assembled here and their colleagues around the
world.

ON HEROIN MAINTENANCE

Alfred R. Lindesmith

Department of Sociology
Indiana University
Bloomington, Indiana

The irony and unreality of the argument on heroin maintenance is best indicated by calling attention to various relevant aspects of the traditional prohibition system which are usually ignored. When this is done, as I shall try to show in this paper, the heroin maintenance debate seems to resolve itself into a kind of Alice-in-Wonderland argument in a world of myth, fiction and pretense.

I. DO-IT-YOURSELF HEROIN MAINTENANCE

In practical terms, we presently have an extensive national heroin maintenance program which supplies this drug to most of our addicts. It is true, of course, that this is called "prohibition," that its goals are to cut off the supply of the drug and promote total abstinence. During more than a half-century these goals have not been achieved often enough or to a degree sufficient to make any difference and the program has probably promoted rather than prevented the spread of heroin addiction. Officials and citizens alike know that addicts are not cured by punishment and expect them to resume their habits when released from prison. Everyone also knows that the flow of illicit heroin has never been cut off effectively and never can be. Even if the poppy were to become an extinct plant, the illicit traffic would undoubtedly turn to synthetic opiate equivalents and continue to function. In short, disregarding meaningless rhetoric, what we have in fact, is a do-it-yourself heroin maintenance program operated for monetary gain by gangsters. The goals of maximizing profits and minimizing risks that are basic to the illicit heroin industry, automatically maximize the degradation and exploitation of the ordinary heroin addict who is furnished with garbage quality drugs at exorbitant prices and allowed to use it as he wishes. All of

47

this is generally known and taken for granted. The choices we have is thus, not between addiction and abstinence, but between a maintenance program operated by criminals and a legal one operated and supervised by medical personnel.

II.   PRICE SUPPORT FOR HEROIN INDUSTRY

It is ironic that, while the do-it-yourself system is passionately denounced by virtually everyone, many of the measures employed by the Government to combat it, actually function as price support program or as subsidies of the illicit heroin industry. Examples are the purchase and destruction of twenty-six tons of opium in northern Thailand and the paying of Turkish farmers not to grow opium poppies. Similar measures by the Department of Agriculture at home are known as price support programs for the benefit of farmers. The "buy-and-bust" tactic used by the narcotics police in apprehending drug peddlers and smuggles channels millions of dollars of public funds into the illicit trade and little of it is ever recovered. Even the routine arrest of heroin dealers and the confiscation of illicit heroin tends to keep prices high by increasing risks and reducing supply at the lowest level of the trade.

While the police commonly cite the high cost of illicit heroin as an indication of efficient law enforcement, they sometimes depart from the indicated patterns by themselves engaging in the illicit distribution of heroin. As will be indicated later, the police also commonly operate what amounts to a heroin maintenance system of limited scope for their stool pigeons.

III.   HEROIN VS. METHADONE

It is commonly argued that methadone is superior to heroin as a maintenance drug. There is, however, debate and disagreement on this issue. If one concedes that the ultimate tests of an effective program in the long run will be what it does, (1) to undermine the economic basis of the black market by reducing demand, and (2) to reduce the rate of recruitment of new addicts, a process that is associated with the illicit traffic,--if one concedes this, one must be seriously concerned with the fact that addicts generally prefer heroin over methadone. If addicts are not attracted to methadone programs in sufficiently large numbers then these programs alone will not be effective in achieving the above two purposes.

In Britain, heroin is not outlawed as it is here and is presently being used to some small extent as a maintenance drug in some of the clinics. British doctors involved in the drug program disagree on the relative merits and demerits of heroin and methadone. It is reported that a long range comparative study is being made there of these two drugs and their effectiveness in maintenance. There is, however, no reason to expect British experience, or any foreign experience for that matter, to resolve this issue in the United States.

While there are many ways in which present methadone and other treatment programs could be improved and their coverage extended, the status of heroin as a maintenance drug is not yet sufficiently clear to warrant excluding it as a possible resource, either in general medical practice or as a maintenance drug. An issue of this sort, one would think, could only be settled by research and experiment, not by lowest-common-denominators decisions of inter-bureau conferences of Washington officials or by politicians.

IV.   OTHER MAINTENANCE PROGRAMS IN THE U.S.

In addition to the methadone and the heroin do-it-yourself maintenance programs there are three other maintenance programs that may be worthy of mention. They are the following: (1) legal maintenance on opiate type drugs of patients with terminal diseases such as cancer or elderly patients with serious ailments that might make drug withdrawal dangerous to life; (2) police maintenance systems for addicted informers who are assisting in the enforcement of narcotic laws; (3) the illegal provision of opiate type drugs, usually morphine, by physicians to a limited number of especially privileged addicts. This is sometimes done with the explicit or tactic consent of narcotics agents. All three of these practices are at least as old as the prohibition system itself and are virtually part of it.

Concerning the first of these, differences sometimes arise between narcotic agents and doctors as to whether a specific patient ought to be provided with drugs (e.g., morphine) regularly, or, if the patient is already addicted, whether he can be safely withdrawn. If the police in this situation wish to threaten the physician with criminal prosecution in such cases, they invariably win the argument. Heroin, of course, is an outlawed drug in this country, not by medical decision but by that of bureaucrats. It actually seems well established that in some cases heroin has therapeutic advantages over morphine. Thus, an English physician once told me that when morphine was administered to his father when he was dying of heart disease, it caused him to retch and vomit. When heroin was substituted for morphine this did not occur. My informant thanked God that heroin was not outlawed in Britain!

A. Heroin Maintenance for Stool Pigeons

Heroin maintenance for addicted informers again illustrates the fact that the police presently seem to enjoy greater discretion with respect to heroin maintenance than physicians do. The use of addicts as stool pigeons is no doubt necessary in the law enforcement process and addicted informers are useful in other enforcement areas than that of narcotics. To motivate them to perform this often dangerous function it is a common practice to provide them in one way or another with confiscated illicit heroin. The Knapp Commission has amply demonstrated how this system operated in New York City. Reduction of charges and penalties may also be used for the same ends.

In view of the flexibility that the police have granted themselves in this matter, it seems fair to ask why similar privileges are denied physicians.

B. Privileged Junkies

The third of these systems is the most significant. It may be dramatically illustrated by the story of how the former United States Commissioner of Narcotics and head of the old Federal Bureau of Narcotics personally arranged for a life long maintenance program for an addicted member of Congress. Commissioner Anslinger himself has told the story. [1] Mr. Anslinger did not even require that the congressman go to Lexington for a cure but only demanded a promise that he would not buy illicit drugs. The congressman agreed readily. Anslinger then authorized a physician to write prescriptions for this man and arranged to have these prescriptions filled at a specific pharmacy somewhere on the outskirts of Washington. He told the junkie legislator that what he was doing for him was legal because of his age--a false statement.

The practice of exempting certain addicts from the sanctions of the criminal law in this manner has been commented on only now and then in the literature. The most informative study concerning it may be found in a study by John A. O'Donnell. In this study, O'Donnell made a painstaking study of the sources of narcotics that had been utilized by a sample of 190 addicted male residents of Kentucky who had been discharged from the Lexington hospital. He found that 45 of the 190 had, throughout their addiction, obtained their narcotics only from one doctor at a time. Ninety-one percent of these had never been sentenced by a court. [2]

Obviously it is grossly unjust that this sort of privileged status be granted to some addicts. The practice ought either to be eliminated or recognized and legalized with the criteria for admission to the program openly stated. Presumably such criteria would not include wealth, being a member of Congress, or personal friendship with a narcotic official. The possible advantages in legalizing and extending this practice are that it would involve more of the medical profession in the addiction problem and would not necessitate the creation of vast new bureaucracies since the medical bureaucracy is already there and since doctors are scattered throughout the country.

V. DISMANTLING THE FEDERAL NARCOTIC BUREAUCRACY

On its record, the federal drug law enforcement agency has earned oblivion. Had it been something other than an enforcement agency it would no doubt have been dismantled or had its funds impounded long ago. In the case of another drug prohibition fiasco, that of alcohol, when the 18th amendment was repealed the problem of dealing with alcohol abuse was turned over to the states and the federal enforcement agency was greatly reduced in size, powers and functions. The same procedure is, I think, now indicated for the narcotic enforcement bureaucracy. The Drug Enforcement Administration is the natural bureaucratic enemy of reform of any kind that would threaten its powers and its lush budget.

REFERENCES

1. Harry J. Anslinger and Will Oursler, The Murderers: The Story of the Narcotic Gangs. Farrar, Straus and Cudahy, New York, 1961, pp. 181-2.

2. John A. O'Donnell, Narcotic Addicts in Kentucky, Public Health Service Publication No. 1881, Chevy Chase, Md., 1969, p. 115.

THE NEW YORK EXPERIENCE UNDER
THE 1973 DRUG LAW

Mark C. Morril
Attorney

Legal Action Center
New York City

Over two and one half years have now passed since the implementation of New York's harsh 1973 drug legislation. Experience
with the law to date supports the conclusion that it has not only
failed to curb drug use or to reduce violent or other crime; it
has also deterred addicts from seeking desperately needed treatment
and has increased the burden on already over-taxed defense, prosecutorial, and court resources.

Worse of all from the point of view of those of us interested
in the treatment and rehabilitation of drug abusers, it is clear
that the law has had a disparately harsh impact on addicts in the
early stages of treatment who quite typically continue to experiment with small amounts of illicit drugs. No discretion exists
under the law for the sentencing judge to take into account an addict's treatment status, willingness to enter treatment, or prognosis for treatment. As a result, many persons who would otherwise
have an excellent prognosis for rehabilitation face lengthy mandatory minimum prison sentences, mandatory life maximum sentences,
and lifetime parole if they are ever released from prison. There
is little doubt that any progress which has been made towards rehabilitation is effectively destroyed by such a sentence. Moreover, under this law, vast numbers of addicts who sould not be
dealth with at all by the criminal justice system are stigmatized
with serious criminal records which will make them subject to the
various employment and other disabilities suffered by all ex-
offenders.

Because of these concerns, in December, 1975, the Legal Action
Center filed a federal court challenge to the law. That case, Car-
mona v. Ward, is currently pending in the United States District
Court for the Southern District of New York before Judge Constance
Baker Motley. We hope to demonstrate to the Court that the law

52

constitutes cruel and unusual punishment and violates the equal
protection and due process clauses of the United States Constitution.

What follows are short synopses of those specific aspects of
the law we believe to be most objectionable from a treatment and
rehabilitation viewpoint and which we will challenge in our court
action.

1. THE CLASSIFICATION SCHEME IN GENERAL

Under the New York Penal Law the weight of the illicit drug
sold or possessed is the principal determinant of the degree of the
crime charged. The 1973 drug law dramatically decreased the amount
of illicit substance possession or sale of which leads to the most
severe penalties. Thus, the sale of one aggregate ounce of narcotic-plus-diluent or the possession of two or more aggregate
ounces of narcotic-plus-diluent is an A-1 felony, punishable by a
mandatory minimum of 15-25 years and a mandatory maximum of life.
The sale of one-eighth aggregate ounce of narcotic-plus-diluent
is an A-II felony punishable by a mandatory minimum of 6 to 8 1/3
years and a mandatory maximum of life. Finally, the sale or possession with intent to sell of any amount of narcotic is an A-III
felony, punishable by a mandatory maximum of life.

The severity and fundamental injustice of this scheme is compounded by the drug law's use of the aggregate weight standard for
narcotic and certain other drug crimes. This standard classifies
degrees of drug offenses in terms of the aggregate weight of the
active drug plus whatever inactive substance it is mixed with,
rather than by the pure weight of the prohibited substance. Thus
the sale or possession of the same amount of illicit substance may
be punished as an A-I, A-II, or A-III felony depending solely upon
the weight of the inert material with which it is combined.

Because drugs such as heroin are generally distributed in increasingly dilute forms the lower the level of the drug offenders
involved, this scheme tends to result in the classification of
relatively minor drug offenders together with the most serious.
Thus under this scheme the street addict, who sells primarily to
keep his own habit going, is likely to be classified together with
the whoesaling profiteer, and accordingly treated with the same
severity. And since the law enforcement system is dependent upon
undercover "buys" for arrests, the street addict is far more likely
to be arrested than the entrepreneur. All this is contrary to the
popular conception that the new drug law operates primarily as an
instrument for reaching the higher-ups in the drug-trafficking
industry.

This analysis of the predictable effect of the laws has been
confirmed by experience of the last few years under the law. Very

few high-level drug offenders have been arrested or incarcerated. Instead the law has resulted in subjecting in an indiscriminate manner large numbers of small-time drug sellers and users, including addicts-in-treatment, to its extraordinarily severe sanctions.

2. THE SENTENCING STRUCTURE IN GENERAL

The New York drug law, as presently written, takes away from individual judges the power to fit the punishment to the particular offense and offender. Judges have no discretion to grant probation or a suspended sentence to marginal offenders based on an assessment of relevant individual factors such as the circumstances of the offense and the nature of the offender. Thus people are being sentenced to long prison terms who should never be sent to prison as all.

However, the assumption behind mandatory sentences -- that prison terms of a certain length will be assured -- is simply misguided. What happens, in fact, is that discretion is simply shifted from judges to the police and prosecutors who set arrest policies, frame the charges and work out the plea, and to the Parole Board which sets the release date. Thus a great deal of discretion remains in the system, but, unlike judicial discretion, it is not subject to public scrutiny and evaluation or to any form of review.

The result is that many persons for whom jail is totally inappropriate are being sent to prison under this law. Not only has the proportion of jail sentences for first offenders risen sharply -- from about 20% to 90% -- but also many of the defendants are truly marginal offenders. Significant numbers of college student experimenters, addicts in treatment who quite typically dabble in drugs during the early stages of treatment, and Viet Nam veterans who have acquired drug habits overseas but become resocialized rapidly upon their return, have been charged with offenses which merit a greater degree of reasonableness and discretion than is permitted under the present law.

3. PLEA BARGAINING RESTRICTIONS

The 1973 drug law prohibits a plea of guilty to a charge of less than an A-III felony to all persons indicted for any A drug felony (which includes approximately 80% of all drug indictments). The effect of this provision is to subject all those charged with even the marginal type of offenses encompassed within the A drug category to the drug law's extraordinarily severe sanctions. Further, the fact that one charged with an A-I or A-II drug felony is permitted to plead down to an A-III felony, while the person

charged in the first instance with an A-III felony cannot reduce
the charges against him, irrationally provides flexibility in
sentencing only to the more serious A felony offenders.

Data presently available reflect that plea bargaining took
place in some 80% of new law dispositions where an A-I or A-II was
charged, and that about half of the dispositions were pleas to
A-III felonies. Yet in New York City, A-I and A-II defendants who
pleaded down to an A-III charge uniformly received the same one
year minimum sentence as persons originally indicted for A-III
felonies. Thus, as predicted, those accused of offenses classified
by the law as the most serious drug offenses are generally receiving the same treatment as those accused of more minor drug offenses.

4. LIFETIME PAROLE

Under the 1973 drug law everyone who is convicted of an A drug
felony is subject to parole supervision for the rest of his life
if he is paroled after serving his mandatory minimum prison term.

Lifetime parole rejects the proposition that the convicted individual can make progress towards eventual resocialization. Thus
the law recognizes the drug offender as someone who may be sufficiently rehabilitated to be released from prison. But after release from prison the drug offender's reintegration into society
ceases, because for him parole supervision never ends.

Parold supervision creates substantial hardships for the parolee. His legal rights are abridged, including, e.g., his right to
travel, his Fourth Amendment right to be free of unwarranted
searches and seizures and his Fifth Amendment right to remain silent when confronted with charges. In addition, he is not entitled
to bail or release pending parole revocation hearings, and he is
subject to revocation and return to prison on grounds that would
not support a criminal conviction. No presumption of innocence at-
taches to him during revocation proceedings. Unlike other citizens
he cannot vote or hold public office, serve on juries, hold elective or appointive office in a union or participate in strikes or
picketing.

In addition to these legal disabilities, the parolee faces substantial practical burdens. His supervising parole officer can in-
trude into the most private areas of the parolee's life, including
the choice of living companion or his choice of marriage partner.
The fact that a person is a parolee significantly limits his employment opportunities.

5. THE PROBATION EXCEPTION

The only exception to the mandatory prison term faced by all drug felons is a provision that permits the court to sentence the offender to probation if the District Attorney recommends such a sentence because the offender has cooperated or is providing assistance in law enforcements efforts. The restricted nature of this single exception to the mandatory prison sentences of the drug law highlights the harsh and inequitable way the law deals with offenders who fall into its broad sweep. The informer exception is very narrow. It is designed simply to reward those who possess information useful to the State and are willing to divulge it. One cannot be an informer if one does not possess information useful to the State and are willing to divulge it. One cannot be an informer if one does not possess information which the District Attorney deems significantly useful to the State. Many marginal offenders do not possess the criminal contacts necessary to buy their freedom under this section of the law. Indeed it is only the most serious offenders who are ordinarily eligible for this exception, just as it is only the most serious offenders -- those charged with A-I and A-II felonies -- who are provided with the benefits of plea bargaining.

EPIDEMIOLOGY

THE IMPORTANCE OF EPIDEMIOLOGY

Robert L. DuPont, M.D.

Director, National Institute on Drug Abuse
Rockville, Maryland

The epidemiology field is one of the most interesting areas in the whole drug abuse area with a fantastic, yet largely untapped potential. For those of you who are not physicians and who are not trained in public health, let me urge you not to be put off by the word "epidemiology," thinking that this concept is tied in a negative way to what's called the "medical model." What I'm calling epidemiology is simply a matter of observing, counting, and establishing trends in drug use over time in various populations and the process of searching for the reasons for changes which are observed. This approach encompasses a broad range of investigative techniques and is in no way limited to the traditional medical approach to understanding "a disease."

One of the great questions that hangs over the drug abuse field is the question of what happened in the last decade to change so dramatically the levels of drug use in our society. There can be no doubt that there has been a historic change and yet our explanatory hypothesis are inadequate to describe what has happened. Let me just give you two pieces of data to show what I'm talking about. In terms of marihuana use by college students in 1967, not very long ago, a Gallup poll showed that 5 percent of American college students had used marihuana at least once. Last year the number was 55 percent. This is a dramatic change in a national group in a short period of time. Similarly, the national indicators of intravenous drug use, as reflected in the serum hepatitis rate, show a tenfold increase in the last decade. During that decade, there was no similar increase in the infectious hepatitis rate, so the change was not just a reporting artifact.

A major change in behavior has gone on in the United States in the last decade and there are exciting possibilities of trying to understand that change. I encourage all of you in your programs not to be discouraged by the sense that you must make sweeping observations describing the whole country. As I look over the epidemiology field, the really exciting contributions have come from local programs, from people who have worked with relatively small groups on a day-to-day basis. There are potentials to under-

stand various aspects of what's going on, not only what happened in
the last decade, but where we are going now--where are these trends
taking us. These opportunities exist primarily on the local level.
That is my main message this morning.

Now to tick off some of the major conceptual breakthroughs in
the epidemiology of drug abuse, I start with the Hughes hypothesis.
This epidemiological concept came out of Chicago and was contributed to by Ed Senay, Jerry Jaffe, and most especially by Gail
Crawford. The hypothesis states that the introduction of a treatment program in a relatively small community, in this case as a
housing project, significantly reduces the heroin use rate in that
community. I consider this to be one of the most exciting concepts
in our field. The work of Mark Greene and a number of others in
Washington, including Richard Katon, who I am pleased to see in the
audience, described the application of that concept to a whole community. The Washington group produced clear evidence, on a community-wide basis, of unmistakable reductions in heroin use which appeared to be related to a broad range of intervention activities, including both heroin supply reduction and the provision of specific treatment for heroin addicts on a large scale. The Washington work was
an application of the Hughes hypothesis to an entire city.

Secondly, I call your attention to the Hunt hypothesis or the
defusion hypothesis of heroin use developed by Leon Hunt. He
showed that drug-using behavior has spread in the United States
from larger cities to smaller cities. Hunt's findings confirm the
concept John Newmeyer talked about earlier this morning that
San Francisco and other large cities are in the vanguard of
national drug use trends. The spread of heroin use from larger
cities to smaller cities is predictable, and it has major implications in terms of treatment and prevention. Leon has shown that
this is similar to the diffusion of other innovations. (I guess
I'd almost have to put that in quotation marks because normally we
think of innovations as good!) Leon showed, for example, that the
spread of television stations in the United States followed
essentially the same pattern as the spread of heroin epidemics,
although the peak of heroin use incidence spread much more quickly
than television did. That speeded-up process may have to do with
the relatively simpler technology of heroin-using behavior and
distribution.

Another landmark epidemiological study that I commend to you
is the Lee Robins study of returning American veterans of the Viet
Nam war. Robins has now followed up this group for three years
after they left Viet Nam and returned to the United States.
She has produced such a rich data source that it defies brief
summary. That study raised questions about the permanence of
heroin addiction which must now be considered by all of us. Much
of our understanding of heroin-using behavior has been based on an
understanding that is clearly not wrong, but may be much more

limited than many of us thought. There are now a whole series of
other studies which support Robins' basic idea that heroin use,
like alcoholism and other drug problems, shows a turnover rate more
often than most of us thought. Rather than being either an
"alcoholic" or a "heroin addict," Robins has shown that most
people with drug problems go in and out of periods of problems with
these drugs over the course of their lives even without treatment
intervention. In other words, the natural history of the problem
involves a turnover that goes on with substantial periods of non-
use or use of the substance without significant problems. That is
an important and a new concept.

The fourth and last new epidemiological concept that I will
present is the concept of progression from one drug to another.
Most of us, conditioned by the experience of the late 1960's when
there was so much irrational concern that marihuana use led automatically to heroin addiction, jumped to the hasty conclusion that
there was nothing at all to this concept. It is, surprisingly, now
being looked at again. Three important data sources--Denise
Kandel's work in New York State, which was reported in Science
magazine a few months ago, as well as a number of other sources,
including the work of Lloyd Johnston and Jack O'Donnell, all
suggest that the idea of progression is more than the raving of the
neanderthals. These new studies show that as a birth cohort ages
there are clear stages of drug use in contemporary American
populations. The first drug that is consumed is alcohol in the
form of beer and wine. Beer and wine appear to be the initiating
substances in terms of drug-using behavior. Following this, there
is a divergence into two paths as described by Kandel. One route
is to cigarettes and the other is to hard liquor or distilled
spirits. People don't necessarily go to both, although there is
some crossover. Then the first movement into illicit drugs is to
marihuana--and that is nearly universal for those who go on to the
use of illicit drugs.

Marihuana is the gateway into illicit drug use. Jack
O'Donnell's study, for example, showed that if a person did not
drink alcohol, he certainly did not use other drugs. But there
was such a small percentage of the population of 20-to 30-year-old
American men who did not drink alcohol, that this finding wasn't
very helpful in terms of explaining behavior. On the other hand,
there was a substantial percentage of the population he studied
which did not use marihuana, and these people also did not use
other illicit substances. Those who used other illicit substances
almost all first used marihuana. I don't mean this to raise that
old negative specter that somehow the marihuana problem is causing
our heroin problem. Truly, that is not the case, and I hope we've
learned something since the days when people thought that, but the
issue of progression needs to be looked at again. To carry the
idea just one step further, after marihuana the steps in the
progression in non-medical drug use include tranquilizers,

amphetamines, and barbiturates, next the hallucinogens, and finally heroin and cocaine. Each of these ascending steps is associated with relatively smaller percentages. The bigger percentages stay on the lower steps. Interestingly, there is some data that when people are giving up drugs they come down the same steps in the reverse order. My experience with my friends who are "giving up drugs," shows this tendency to come down these same steps. People generally back down in the same way rather than leap over the steps, although of course there is some of that too.

The National Institute on Drug Abuse (NIDA) is developing a national data base in drug abuse epidemiology which has integrity. I notice that Fred Shick, for example, put his Chicago study into perspective a few minutes ago by using the National Marihuana Commission national survey data. It is important for local people to be able to use this growing national data base to compare to their local data. This building process is a high priority with us at NIDA.

John Newmeyer mentioned the Heroin Trends Report which we released at a national press conference two weeks ago. It describes, for the first time, a series of national indicators of heroin use trends in the United States. The experience we had in talking about "turning the corner" on heroin use in the Nation two years ago was not a happy one, and I hope we have learned the importance of specifying our data sources.

Let me summarize the current status of this national data base. First, it involves surveys. The survey work is central. NIDA is now sponsoring annual national surveys of the American population over the age of 12, and we will continue to do that on an annual basis until we feel the use rates stabilize. An example of the important data which came from the most recent survey relates to marihuana use, the leading edge of illicit drug use. There was no increase between 1972 and 1974 in marihuana use by people over the age of 25 as the marihuana-using population aged. There was a surprising stability in rates of marihuana use between those two years in the over 25-age group. But what did occur between 1972 and 1974 was nearly a doubling of the rates of marihuana use in the 12- to 17-year-old group. That also surprised many of us. This younger group clearly is where the volatile activity is in terms of marihuana use.

The second national data source is the Drug Abuse Warning Network (DAWN) system, which was jointly funded by the Drug Enforcement Administration and NIDA. DAWN surveys emergency rooms and medical examiners in 24 major metropolitan areas in the United States, plus a national sample of emergency rooms. DAWN reports, on a monthly basis, rates of problems with a variety of drugs. We hope to have a press conference and a DAWN Report similar to the Heroin Trends Report in the next couple of months.

The third major national data source is the Client Oriented Data Acquisition Process (CODAP) that reports on NIDA-funded treatment. There are now over 160,000 admissions a year on a nationwide basis in CODAP.

Finally, the national hepatitis data from the Center for Disease Control has been turned into a useful drug abuse indicator. There are other data sources which I won't describe now.

I will end by saying that one of the most important questions in the drug abuse field is this: Is there anything a community or a nation can do to change the rates of drug problems with or without influencing drug use? Are there practical steps that can be taken or is our drug abuse response simply putting up money to deal with our consciences? Such efforts in prevention and treatment help people who have problems in a variety of ways, and God knows that's worth doing too, but let's be clear as to whether that is all we are doing. In addition, is there something we can do to influence the overall trends of drug problems? I think the jury is clearly out on this fundamental question. I encourage all of you to think about that and to do what you can to answer it.

PRECURSORS TO HEROIN: A COMPARISON OF
HEROIN ADDICTS AND THEIR NONADDICTED FRIENDS

Gail A. Crawford, Ph.D.

The University of Chicago
Department of Psychiatry
Chicago, Illinois

At one time it was thought that virtually everyone who tries
heroin eventually becomes an addict. Recently a number of studies
have shown that addiction is not an inevitable consequence and that
a large, though unknown, proportion of users continue to "chip"
heroin over extended periods without becoming addicts. With this
realization, increasing attention has been directed to the questions of why some people become addicted whereas others who experiment with heroin do not become addicted and still others, though
presented with ample opportunities, refuse to try heroin even once.

To begin to answer these questions, I interviewed a sample of
young heroin addicts and their nonaddicted friends to determine
whether there might have been differences in their life styles,
patterns of identification, or involvement in illegal activities
that preceded first use of heroin and help to account for their
differential career outcomes.

METHODS

During the winter of 1971 and the spring of 1973, tape recorded personal interviews were administered to three samples of
young people: 15 heroin addicts who were patients in the Illinois
Drug Abuse Program, 15 current or former experimenters who tried
heroin at least once but did not become addicts, and 15 nonusers
who never tried heroin. Addict subjects tried heroin for the first
time between 1967 and 1970; experimenters first tried heroin between 1966 and 1973.

Experimenters and nonusers were chosen from the addict's self-
defined friendship group according to the following procedures. I
asked each addict to list the people he "hung with" prior to his
initiation to heroin and to assign them to one of the three categories of heroin use. Where present, an experimenter and a non-
user were selected from the friendship group and the addict's help

enlisted in arranging interviews with them. Each nonaddict was paid $10 for his participation immediately following the interview; each addict was paid $30 upon completion of interviews with his triad.

The total sample (N = 45) consisted of 18 whites (six addicts, six experimenters, six nonusers), 21 blacks (seven addicts, seven experimenters, seven nonusers), and 6 Puerto Ricans (two addicts, two experimenters, two nonusers). Thirty-six subjects were males, nine were females. Subjects ranged in age from 18 to 29 years, with a mean age of 22.0 years (sd = 2.6). Although addicts were slightly older than their nonaddicted peers ($\bar{x}$ = 22.8 years, sd = 2.5 for addicts; $\bar{x}$ = 21.5 years, sd = 2.4 for experimenters; $\bar{x}$ = 21.8 years, sd = 2.9 for nonusers), the differences were not statistically significant.

RESULTS

Patterns of Identification

One indicator of identification with conventional versus deviant (though not necessarily criminal) life styles might be the kinds of role models young people select. I asked addicts and experimenters to think back to the year or so before they first tried heroin and to describe the kinds of people they "wanted to be like;" nonusers were asked to think back to the year before their addict friends began to use heroin.

Table I shows that among addict and experimenter subjects there was considerable diversity in the choice of role models. Two-thirds (n = 10) of each subgroup, however, identified with "deviant" as opposed to conventional role models, in other words, with other drug users or "hippies," with people who were "getting over" through either legal or illegal means, or with successful hustlers or drug dealers. In contrast, 10 of the 15 nonusers selected as role models working people who strive for success through the legitimate opportunity system.

Although only a few of the heroin using subjects may have aspired to criminal "careers," most of them were involved in some kind of illegal activity during the year prior to first heroin use. Table II shows that within the addict subgroup only three subjects (two of them females) reported no illegal activities. The greatest proportion (n = 7) engaged in at least periodic drug dealing, usually of marijuana or other non-narcotics. Within the experimenter subgroup, six subjects reported no involvement in illegal activities prior to first heroin use. The remainder had occasionally dealt drugs and/or committed other kinds of offenses.

Eight of the nonusers reported no illegal activities during the year before their addict friends first tried heroin. Furthermore, unlike addicts and experimenters, only two nonusers reported any involvement in drug dealing.

Drug Use Histories

Studies (1,2) suggest that heavy multiple drug users are more likely than others to try heroin when given the opportunity. To

65

clarify the relationship between frequency and variety of drug use and subsequent patterns of heroin use, I obtained detailed drug history data from all subjects in the present study.

For the total sample (N = 45) the mean age at first drug use (other than heroin) was 16.1 years (sd = 2.4). As a group, non-heroin users were more than a year older than addicts or experimenters when they began to use drugs: $\bar{x}$ = 17.0 years, sd = 2.4; $\bar{x}$ = 15.8 years, sd = 2.2; $\bar{x}$ = 15.4 years, sd = 2.5 respectively).

Addicts and experimenters were asked to list the drugs they had tried prior to heroin. They were then asked to think back to the period of heaviest use of each drug and to describe their frequency of use during that period. Non-heroin users were asked simply to recall the period of heaviest use of any given drug and their frequency of use during that period. Subgroups were compared on their frequency of use of the following classes of drugs: cannabis, stimulants, sedatives, codeine cough syrup, and hallucinogens.

"Light" use of cannabis, stimulants, sedatives, or codeine cough syrup was defined as use of any of these drugs one or two days per week for three or more months; "moderate" use was defined as three to six days of use per week; and "heavy" use as daily use of any of these drugs for three or more months. "Light" use of hallucinogens was defined as use of any of these drugs one or two days per month for three or more months, "moderate" use as three to nine days per month, and "heavy" use as ten or more days per month.

Table III shows that all of the subjects reported at least light use of cannabis, but the greatest proportion of heavy users are found in the addict subgroup. Thus, 11 addict subjects reported daily use of cannabis prior to heroin. With respect to hallucinogens, however, most addicts (n = 11) either had had no experience with this class of drugs or had used them less than four times. In contrast, over half of the experimenter subgroup (n = 8) had used hallucinogens with some regularity (i.e., at least once or twice a month).

Drug use patterns of addicts and experimenters are roughly similar with respect to use of stimulants, sedatives, and codeine cough syrup. At least half of each subgroup reported no use of stimulants or cough syrup prior to heroin, or had used these drugs less than four times. On the other hand, a majority reported at least light use of sedatives prior to heroin. The moderate and heavy sedative users, however, are found primarily in the experimenter subgroup where eight subjects reported using these drugs three or more days per week.

The lack of moderate or heavy drug use among non-heroin users is in marked contrast to the drug use patterns of their addict and experimenter friends. No more than three subjects reported even moderate use of any class of drug other than cannabis.

Attitudes Toward Heroin

I asked addict and experimenter subjects what kinds of fears they had about heroin before they first tried it, and nonusers what kinds of fears they had before their addict friends first tried heroin. Only six subjects (two addicts, three experimenters, one nonuser) reported they had no fears about trying heroin. Among experimenters the most commonly expressed fears were fear of a "habit" (n = 7) and fear of needles (n = 4); among addicts the most commonly expressed fears were fear of an overdose (n = 7) and fear of needles (n = 7). Interestingly, only two addict subjects recalled that before they ever tried heroin they had some fears about becoming addicted. In marked contrast, ten of the 15 nonusers reported fear of a habit as their only fear about trying heroin, while two others reported multiple fears, including fear of addiction.

To obtain more definitive data regarding their fears about a habit, subjects were asked specifically whether they thought they would become addicted if they should try heroin. Thirteen addicts and 13 experimenters assumed they would not become addicted. Many of these subjects reported that they had only wanted to check out the high and never thought they would use heroin on a daily basis. Others thought they had enough "will power" to control their use of heroin. Although most of these subjects had known other people who started out with an "I can handle it" attitude and yet became addicted, they rationalized that they were stronger or smarter than those who had become addicted.

SUMMARY AND CONCLUSIONS

To summarize, the findings suggest that nonusers may have differed from addicts and experimenters in several important respects prior to exposure to heroin. Nonusers were more than a year older at the time they began to use drugs and they were considerably less involved in drug usage, drug dealing, and other so-called deviant activities than their heroin using friends. At the same time, they were more likely to report that they thought they would become addicted if they should try heroin.

Differences between addicts and experimenters, though generally in the expected direction, were not dramatic. Both subgroups tended to have been heavy multiple drug users, to have been involved in other illegal activities, and to have identified with "deviant" rather than conventional role models. Many of them assumed they had enough "will power" to be able to use heroin but avoid becoming addicted.

There are several limitations to this study. Although I am confident that subjects attempted to give truthful responses to the questions, in some cases their memories may have been faulty or their answers colored by subsequent events. Furthermore, the sample is small and the nonaddicts were obtained by asking addicts to identify their experimenter and nonuser friends. Therefore, it is perhaps not surprising that most of the subjects, including the non-heroin users, had histories of multiple drug use. Despite these limitations, the findings are consistent with those of other studies (3,4) and suggest that willingness to try heroin can be better understood within the context of a broader commitment to a deviant way of life.

TABLE I. SUBGROUPS COMPARED BY TYPES OF ROLE MODELS

Role Models	Add.			Exp.			Non.			
	B	W	L	B	W	L	B	W	L	Total
"Hippies"	–	3	–	–	4	–	–	3	–	10
Other drug users	–	1	–	–	1	–	–	–	–	2
Working people	4	1	–	5	–	–	5	3	2	20
People "getting over"	1	1	1	2	–	1	2	–	–	8
Dealers/hustlers	2	–	1	–	1	1	–	–	–	5
Total	7	6	2	7	6	2	7	6	2	45

TABLE II. SUBGROUPS COMPARED BY ILLEGAL ACTIVITIES

Illegal Activities	Category of Heroin Use			
	Add.	Exp.	Non.	Total
No illegal activities	3	6	8	17
Dealing non-narcotic drugs	6	4	–	10
Dealing heroin	1	1	–	2
Other illegal activities	3	1	5	9
Dealing & other ill. act.	2	3	2	7
Total	15	15	15	45

TABLE III. SUBGROUPS COMPARED BY FREQUENCY OF DRUG USE

Frequency of Use	Cannabis			Hallucinogens			Stimulants			Sedatives			Cough Syrup		
	Add.	Exp.	Non.	Add.	Exp.	Non.	Add.	Exp.	Non.	Add.	Exp.	Non.	Add.	Exp.	Non.
Never tried	–	–	–	8	6	5	7	6	3	2	4	4	6	8	9
1-3 experiences	–	–	–	3	1	6	4	2	4	2	1	3	2	3	5
Light use	1	5	5	1	3	2	3	4	5	7	2	6	3	1	1
Moderate use	3	3	4	–	1	1	1	1	3	–	3	2	1	2	–
Heavy use	11	7	6	3	4	1	–	2	–	4	5	–	3	1	–
Total Users	15	15	15	7	9	10	8	9	12	13	11	11	9	7	6

ACKNOWLEDGMENT

Portions of this paper are based on a doctoral thesis in sociology at the University of Illinois, 1973.

REFERENCES

1. L.N. Robins, J.E. Helzer, and D.H. Davis, <u>Arch</u>. <u>Gen</u>. <u>Psychiat</u>., <u>32</u>: 955 (1975).
2. P.H. Hughes and G.A. Crawford, <u>Arch</u>. <u>Gen</u>. <u>Psychiat</u>., <u>24</u>: 149 (1972).
3. D. Glaser, B. Lander, and W. Abbott, <u>Soc</u>. <u>Prob</u>., <u>18</u>: 510 (1971).
4. J.E. Helzer, L.N. Robins, and D.H. Davis, <u>Drug</u> <u>Alc</u>. <u>Depend</u>., <u>1</u>: 183 (1975/76).

A COMPARISON OF RURAL DRUG USE PATTERNS, RURAL BASED TREATMENT
PROGRAM SERVICE DELIVERY AND PROGRAM UTILIZATION IN THE STATE OF
IOWA

Richard R. Swanson

Training and Technical Assistance Manager
Iowa Drug Abuse Authority
Des Moines, Iowa

I. INTRODUCTION

This paper was designed to investigate two primary and interrelated problems in the delivery of chemical dependency services
to rural populations. First, the researchers wanted to look at the
incidence of drug abuse in rural areas within the State of Iowa to
determine if there was a significant use pattern differential
between rural populations and urban populations within the state.
Second, the researchers wanted to examine the treatment modes
being offered in rural areas to determine if they were primarily
extentions of the urban model or if they were attempting to meet
the specific needs of the rural drug abuser should a difference be
established. Finally, a combination of these factors should show
that those treatment programs which had altered their treatment
modes in rural areas to meet rural needs should show a greater
degree of success than should those programs which had established
rural programs which were primarily designed to meet urban needs.

II. METHODOLOGY

During an eight month period of time in 1975, the researchers
audited a random sample of CODAP admission report forms submitted
by treatment programs to the Iowa Drug Abuse Authority. Each
individual clinic, though part of a larger program, is identified
on those admission report forms by a separate clinic identifier
number. Those clinic identifier numbers of clinics located in
towns with populations between 1000 and 15,000 were defined as
rural. Among the 125 rural report forms reviewed, card 2, block
19-a indicates the primary drug problem diagnosed. These data
were then compared with 125 admission report forms, card 2, block

19-a data obtained of urban Iowa treatment programs. Those programs classified as being urban are located in cities ranging from 60,000 to 200,000 population. These data were analyzed to indicate differences in the frequency of use of different drugs or drug classes leading to the client's entrance into the treatment program.

During the period of program study, both urban programs studied began operation of "rural component" clinics under differing philosophies. Program #1 operated under the philosophy that local planning and continued input regarding the types of problems exhibited in the rural community were important factors to be taken into account in the establishment of the clinic and the design of its program. Program #2 offered a rural delivery system that was comprised of its urban treatment regimen placed in a rural setting. The philosophy of program #2 was that they were familiar with performing well in one arena and did not want to cast themselves in the role of being all things to all people.

A statistical projection was completed on the percent of capacity at which each program would have operated had they not opened their rural treatment components. This projection was then compared to the actual percent of capacity at which the program was operating. A comparison of these statistics will show which program's rural satellite components are more utilized.

If we consider that clients tend to select those programs that they believe most adequately meet their needs, then the program believed to be more adequately meeting client needs should show a greater increase in the percent of capacity utilized than should a program less adequately meeting those needs.

III. FINDINGS

A comparison of the urban/rural drug differential noted by drug or drug category with reference to the primary drug of abuse upon admittance to treatment, displays several important and significant differences. First, individuals presenting themselves for treatment with heroin as the primary drug of use comprised 30% of all clients entering the urban programs studied while in rural programs, the heroin user comprised 6% of the total client population. This represents an 80% difference between heroin primary drug diagnosis rates. Second, individuals presenting themselves for treatment with marijuana as the primary drug of use comprised 28% of all clients entering the urban program while in the rural program, the marijuana user comprised 48% of the client population. This represents a 41% difference between marijuana primary drug diagnosis rates. The remainder of the differences were not significant.

As may be seen in reference to program number I (fig. 1), beginning with the first month of tracking, the program was operating at 100% of capacity. This percent of capacity moves to 96%, 97% and 95% during the second, third and fourth months. During the fifth month, program number one opened its rural outreach component. Using the previous monthly percentage of capacity statistics the researchers have statistically projected where the programs percent of capacity statistics should have been. These were then compared to the actual monthly percent of capacity statistics from the fifth month, the point at which the rural outreach component operation began. The mean reported percent of capacity from the 5th through the 9th month studied was 138% while the projected mean during the same period was 85%. By operating an outreach component, program number 1 was able to increase its percent of capacity by 51% over that projected.

As may be seen in reference to program number 2 (fig. 2) the program began operation in month number 3 with .9% of capacity. This moved to 35% during the fourth month and 44% during the fifth month. During the sixth month, the program opened a rural outreach component. Using the three previous monthly percent of capacity statistics, the researchers statistically projected where the programs percent of capacity statistics should have been. These were compared with the actual monthly percent of capacity statistics from the fourth month, the point at which the rural outreach component operation began. The mean reported percent of capacity from the sixth through the ninth month studied was 95% while the projected mean during the same period was 101%. By operating an outreach component, program number 2 has shown a mean decrease of 6% from the percent of capacity projected over the period studied.

IV. ANALYSIS

The researchers believe that the primary difference between the two programs studied is that program number 1 included in its program planning phase, the formation of a rural board of advisors whose job it was to oversee the operation of the rural outreach component, setting the focus of treatment. Program number 2 did not have such planning behind its rural component.

The differences between rural and urban clients examined in phase I of this paper indicates that a program of an urban ilk must reorient its treatment objectives and methods in order to adequately meet the needs of a rural population. The evidence presented by programs number 1 and 2 indicate that this is the case by the numbers of clients who believe that their needs will be met by entering treatment.

V. AREAS FOR FURTHER RESEARCH

First, program number 2 (fig. 2) shows some increase over the projected percent of capacity statistics during months five and six with decreases during months number eight and nine with a mean decrease from the percent of capacity projected. The situation may exist that rural areas are so starved for programs of any sort, that some success is guaranteed though only partially meeting client needs. This, however, is subject for further research.

Second, program number 2 (fig. 2) shows an abnormal regression in percent of capacity statistics during month number eight. It occurs to the researchers that as new programs approach the "100% of capacity" mark, there may be other variables than program acceptability which account for a leveling off period. This, however, is also subject for further research.

Third, program number 1 (fig. 1) begins to show a drop in the percent of capacity from the sixth month to the end of the period of study. Whether this indicates a regression to the mean phenomena is topic for further research.

Fourth, the researchers intend to follow these two programs for an additional twelve months to note any additional trends in the percent of capacity at which the programs operate.

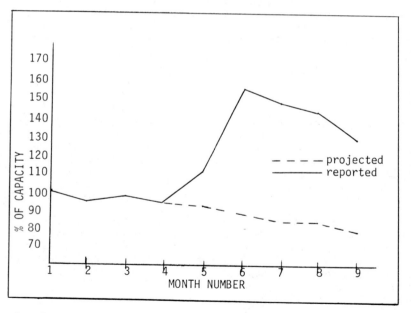

Fig. 1. Program # 1 Monthly Comparison of Projected % of Capacity to Reported % of Capacity.

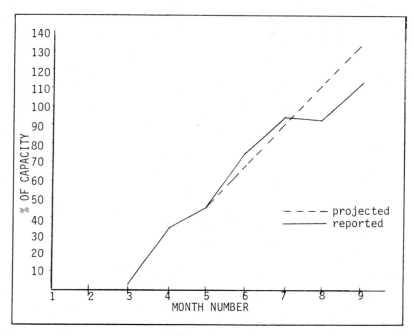

Fig. 2.   Program # 2 Monthly Comparison of Projected % of Capacity
to Reported % of Capacity.

VI. BIBLIOGRAPHY

1. Bourne, Peter G., M.D. in Journal of Psychedelic Drugs, 6:2
   (1974).
2. Geisler, Suzanne and Siverson, John in Minnesota Medicine, 56:
   3 (1973).
3. Glaser, Frederick B. in Southern Medical Journal, 67:5 (1974).
4. Horrisberger, Paul and Raabe, Jean in Proceedings of the Third
   Annual Iowa Conference on Chemical Misuse (Iowa Drug Abuse
   Authority, ed.), 1975.
5. James, George, M.D. in East Central Journal of Public Health,
   52:7 (1962).
6. Motto, Jerome in Standards for Suicide Prevention and Crisis
   Centers, 1970.
7. Schecter, Arnold, M.D. in Journal of Psychedelic Drugs 6:2
   (1974).
8. Smith, Roger C. in Drug Abuse: Proceedings of the International
   Conference,(Zarafonetis, Chris J., ed.), 1972.

THE "GERMAN CONNECTION"
A Survey of the Antecedents and Patterns of Drug Abuse Veterans
Returning from European Service

John R. Stafford, M.D.*
Jose A. Chorens, M.D.
George Dempsey, Ph.D. **
Vastine Hightower, MSW

Staff on Drug Dependence Treatment Unit, Veterans Administration
Hospital. Also on staff at Baylor College of Medicine* and the
University of Houston**, Houston, Texas

I. BACKGROUND

Prior to June 1971 active duty servicemen were discovered to be
users of drugs principally through evident intoxication or other
drug-related offenses committed against the Uniform Code of Military Justice. In 1967 4.8% of the cases received by the Army Criminal Investigation Repository were drug abuse cases. By 1969 that
percentage had increased eight-fold to 37.4%.[1] In 1962 only 1% of
admissions to a large Army general hospital on the East Coast had
drug-related causes. By 1969 this percentage had increased twenty-
five fold to 25%.[2]

The discovered drug-user was typically subjected to local disciplinary action and if refractory to change of behavior, eventually
evaluated at a military psychiatric facility. If "major mental disorders" were excluded the typical conclusion was that the subject
manifested a "character disorder" antedating entry into the military service. Recommendations were then made for administrative
separation for reasons of unsuitability or in extreme cases, bad
conduct.

Recognition of the "rising tide" of drug use among American forces
in Southeast Asia coincided with the "epidemic of drug abuse" in
the United States.[3] This led during 1969 to 1970 to the establishment of "amnesty" programs which minimized punitive action and
offered treatment and rehabilitation. In June 1971 the armed forces received a presidential mandate prohibiting the discharge of
drug dependent servicemen without signal efforts at rehabilitation.

This was accompanied by the establishment of random urine screening procedures for drug detection among active duty personnel at key re-embarkation centers, and eventually, at all military facilities. Simultaneously, certain military and Veterans Administration Hospitals were designated drug abuse treatment and rehabilitation centers.

II. CURRENT SITUATION

For the past 4½ years the Veterans Administration Hospital, Houston, Texas has operated two drug dependency treatment programs: a 35-bed hospital unit and an outpatient clinic, providing services to 260 veterans, predominantly those receiving methadone maintenance. The majority of admissions to both programs are voluntary. A small proportion of the hospital admissions are active duty military personnel undergoing final-phase processing for discharge under "Chapter 13" relating to the Armed Services Medical .Regulating Office (ASMRO). Prior to arriving at this facility they have undergone detoxification" and "rehabilitation" at one or more military facilities. In a previous study reported from this unit[5], the active duty military group constituted 13 of 100 consecutive hospital admissions. They were noted to rate themselves as healthier and to "appear healthier" on most psychologic and vocational rating scales, than 87 volunteer veterans. Fifty-four percent insisted they intended to further treatment and the remainder were at best highly ambivalent regarding their needs for rehabilitation. A similar ASMRO population has been noted by Van Stone in his description of a San Francisco VA Program.[6]

That their optimism may not be unrealistic has been documented in a series of papers by Robins et. al. describing a 10-month follow-up of servicemen leaving Vietnam in September, 1971.[7,8,9] Inasmuch as this population comprises that portion of soon-to-be veterans returning to the Southwestern United States from all possible duty stations we had anticipated a substantial decline in their number once American involvement in Southeast Asia had terminated.

The conditions peculiar to Vietnam, (1) low cost and high-grade heroin, capable of producing addiction by inhalation, (2) combat stresses, (3) maximal geographic and cultural separation from families, have been described by Baker.[2,4] Robins and associates have speculated that the thus far favorable outcome among ex-Viet Nam addicts was attributable to these atypical conditions, compared to U.S. "street" addicts or physician addicts.[10]

We have observed no decline in the number or percentage of active duty personnel among our program population. During 1975, 44 of 515 total program admissions (200 consecutive first admissions) were active duty personnel undergoing separation because of "treatment failure". Of this number over half (24/40) were noted to have undergone their "terminal" tour of duty in Germany.

We began the study of this group with the construction of a questionnaire containing twenty-eight (28) measures modeled after those employed by Gosolow and Childs in the first description of Vietnam era addicts.[11]

III. REVIEW OF FINDINGS

Questionnaire responses were obtained from 20 servicemen returning from German service enroute to their homes to receive discharge as having failed rehabilitation efforts for drug dependence. All were male, between the ages of 18 and 28 (mean age = 21.5 years), and belonged to the lower enlisted ranks (E_1 - E_4). Nineteen of the twenty respondents had enlisted. Length of service ranged from less than one year to five years.

A. Personal Background

Ethnic composition of our sample was -- 7/20 (35%) Black, 11/20 (55%) Caucasian and 2/20 (10%) Mexican-American, percentages which resemble those found in the Houston Independent School District (45% - 45% - 10%) and a 20-county surrounding region. Seven of our subjects were from a large metropolitan setting, ten from middle-sized cities, and only three from towns of under 5,000 population.

Twelve of the 20 were high-school dropouts, although four of these had subsequently achieved General Educational Development (G.E.D.) equivalency certificates, and two had entered college thereafter. A total of 6 of the 20 subjects had completed from one to three years of college but none had graduated. Six of twenty acknowledged a history of juvenile delinquency (all of these were from among the dropout group and were evenly divided between subsequent GED and non-GED achievers. Seven reported conflicts with military authority; interestingly, only two of those were previously "overtly delinquent").

Only three of twenty were married, two of the spouses had been present in Germany, and one of those two marriages was characterized by current separation.

B. Drug History

Seventeen of our 20 subjects had used one or more illicit drugs prior to service but in only five of these were drugs other than marijuana used (2 amphetamines, 2 LSD, 1 cocaine). Pre-service alcohol use was characterized as light or moderate by 11 subjects.

Seventeen of the twenty had been found by their commands to have urinalysis positive for opiates and three for amphetamines. Eleven of the twenty subjects described intravenous drug administration; most had experimented with smoking heroin in combination with marijuana.

Nine acknowledged addiction by self-report and description of abstinence syndrome. In at least two of these, abstinence symptoms were of relatively brief (24-48 hours duration). All of the subjects had undergone initial hospitalization in Europe and most had promptly (within 1 month) again been discovered to have opiate-positive urine specimens, resulting in their designation as treatment failures. This initiated a series of transfers from one hospital to another progressing to a "stateside" base and finally Veterans Administration Hospital near the "home of record".

In all but one case the subjects were "satisfied" with current status, i.e., not considering themselves in need of treatment, denying current drug problems and "relieved" at the prospect of immediate discharge from military service. The one who had longest military service (5 years) was embittered, claiming that a post-treatment positive urine was a laboratory error which was unjustly depriving him of a desired career.

An orientation to the hospital-outpatient clinic drug abuse treatment programs was given and each subject introduced to the "outreach" social worker who serves as contact for follow-up studies or desired treatment service.

IV. DISCUSSION OF "MOTIVATING FACTORS"

Eleven of our subjects responded to questionnaire and interview regarding factors influencing personal decisions to use heroin. Only three of eleven considered European service to resemble their expectations. Boredom, loneliness, and absence of freedom were prominent complaints. Few of the subjects had even considered availing themselves of optional language courses and none had learned a foreign language. They perceived themselves as isolated in a strange land with only fellow soldiers as companions. Friends and family were missed as were many artifacts of American culture. The European tour came to be perceived as an alternation of muddy maneuvers and the escape of getting high, rather than an opportunity for sightseeing or personal enrichment.

Peer pressure was a powerful determinant in patterning choice of euphoriant agent. Discrete groups of alcohol-only, marijuana and alcohol only, and polydrug users were described, with senior enlisted and officer personnel favoring alcohol. The implications for identification with or rebellion against "parental" drug choice seen clear.

Drug cost, while greater than described for Vietnam, was initially moderate and supportable in an environment in which all basic needs were provided and salary was viewed as largely recreational. Three of our subjects claimed that they had used drugs "only enough to get caught", insuring that they would be "treated", "fail treatment", and be discharged. These alleged that they had found military service so intolerable that they considered the "drug discharge" a pleasant alternative, and had exaggerated reports of their drug use. Other subjects reported less drug use to our interviewers than at Army hospitals overseas and in transit.

Prior to the 1971 revision of military policy such discontent would have likely led to unauthorized absences, successive disciplinary actions, and eventual "unsuitable" discharge. The "Chapter 13 Discharge", carrying no substantive stigma or loss of benefits, may be acquiring a status not originally considered or intended.

REFERENCES

1. Ruben, HL. A review of the first year's experience in the U.S. Army alcohol and drug abuse program. Am J Public Health 64(10): 99-1001, 1974.

2. Baker, SL. Drug abuse in the United States Army. Bull NY Acad Med 46(4):540-549, 1971.

3. Siegel, AJ. The heroin crisis among US forces in Southeast Asia: An overview. J Am Med Assoc 223(11):1258-1261, 1973.

4. Baker, SL. Present status of the drug abuse counteroffensive in the armed forces. Bull NY Acad Med 48(5):718-733, 1972.

5. Wallace, D; Hiner, D. Some descriptive measures on 100 consecutive VA Hospital drug abuse admissions. Int J Addict 9(3):465-473, 1974.

6. Van Stone, WW. Treating the drug dependent veteran - Perspective from a VA Hospital. Int J Addict 9(4):593-604.

7. Robins, LN; Davis, DH; Goodwin, DW. Drug use by US Army enlisted men in Viet Nam: A follow-up on their return home. Am J Epidemiol 99(4):935-941, 1974.

8. Robins, LN; Davis, DH; Nurco, DN. How permanent was Viet Nam drug addiction? Am J Public Health (Supplement)64:38-43, 1974.

9. Robins, LN; Helzer, JE; Davis, DH. Narcotic use in Southeast Asia and afterward. Arch Gen Psychiatry 32:955-961, 1975.

10. Modlin, HC; Montes A. Narcotics addiction in physicians. Am J Psychiatry 121:358, 1964.

11. Golosow, N; Childs, A. The soldier addict: A new battlefield casualty. Int J Addict 8(1):1-12, 1973.

GEOGRAPHY AND SPREAD OF HEROIN ADDICTION

Alex Richman, M.D.

Beth Israel Medical Center, 307 Second Avenue, New York, N.Y. and
the Mount Sinai School of Medicine of the City University of N.Y.

This paper considers the factors to which the geographic
concentration and diffusion of heroin addiction have been attributed. Although biological and psychological factors are important,
social factors are critical with respect to spread. For prevention and effective intervention, we need better understanding of
the dynamics and role of social factors in spread.

BACKGROUND

Research on the spread of narcotic addiction is hampered by
scanty data on distributions by time, place and person; lack of
demographic standardization of rates, transiency of the denominator and relative mobility of the numerator; difficulties in
definition of the disorder, its onset and clinical characterization of type and severity; and social area differentials in
identification of the disorder, and in the duration of the disorder among those ascertained. (1)

Although maps of the distributions of "narcotics" arrests may
show increased numbers of arrests from year to year and spatial
extension,data on arrests do not indicate prevalence,and changes
in the number of individuals arrested do not reflect incidence. (2)

It is not yet clear whether certain geographic areas "produce"
addicts; whether ascertainment factors differ; or whether addicts
seek particular cultural environments.

SOCIAL FACTORS IN SPREAD

It is generally reported that the vast majority of heroin
addicts are introduced to heroin in the setting of previously
established peer group activity. (3, 4)

Hughes and Crawford found that there were multiple channels for obtaining heroin in endemic areas. (5,6) Rather than one person being responsible for "infecting" the others, different group members simultaneously obtained heroin through different contacts. (7)

Evang recognized that communication from person to person was "the most important element", but emphasized that the concept of person-to-person spread deflected interest from the more important social and individual factors involved in the causation of drug dependence. (8)

Intervention efforts must be directed at high-risk groups and high-risk places. We need better understanding of the spread of heroin use in high-risk populations in high-risk neighborhoods. Adverse social circumstances, by themselves, do not explain why these areas (where heroin is available and addicts have lived for many years) provide the majority of addicts in the country.

APPLICATION OF GEOGRAPHERS CONCEPTS

It is not overly simplistic to consider the spread of narcotic addiction as diffusion of innovation. High risk groups have a peer network which promotes diffusion; diffusion is enhanced in high-risk neighborhoods. It is necessary to determine what is diffused. To what extent is there diffusion of information on heroin availability, instructions and techniques for the behavior; or acceptance of or compliance with the idea of heroin usership?

The geographer conceptualizes diffusion in terms of goods, people or ideas. These concepts also apply to spread of heroin addiction.

1) Flow of goods. Much attention has been directed to the source, transportation and availability of heroin. Pushers are alleged to market the drug and create a demand. Although a significant target for law enforcement efforts, distribution mechanisms do not account for the rapid, massive changes in incidence which occur in endemic areas.

2) Transmission of behavior patterns or migration. Network analysis often attributes spread of heroin addiction to a visitor from out of town or the return of a migrant. Quarantine is not effective when there are multiple sources of introduction. (5,6,7)

3) Spread of ideas or innovation. Innovations are rapidly spread in a social network which is spatially concentrated, internally cohesive, resistant to external values or forces, and interaction is intense and frequent. Spread in such settings is rapid and highly resistant to intervention.

MECHANISMS FOR DIFFUSION OF IDEAS

Diffusion research contends that information about an innovation is spread almost entirely by oral communication - by person-to-person transmission within small groups whose members live close together. A two-step flow is postulated, first, to the opinion leader of the group, and if the innovation is accepted, then other members of the group tend to follow. (10)

Since frequency of contact between individuals has a strong inverse relationship with geographic distance, first followers should be located closer to the group innovation leader and the laggard adopters further away. Maps showing the spatial growth pattern overtime would help assess whether this neighborhood level clustering occurs. (9) The appropriate units of observation for assessing the diffusion of heroin use in the inner-city would be at the level of blocks, which have the close, intense social networks within which heroin use is spread. Such maps are now being prepared by the author.

ROLE OF THE SOCIAL ENVIRONMENT

A geogen is defined as an environmental factor known or believed to be correlated with a disease or its pathogens. (11) A whole set of unfavorable life circumstances, low social status, unemployment, spatial mobility, minority group status, family disruption and single person households collectively assume their greatest intensity in the inner areas of the city. Addiction occurs in places which have many adverse social circumstances for the individual but which also contain the essential mechanism for spread - a strong social network. Places are geogenic because of their population's interpersonal relationships which foster diffusion of heroin addiction.

IMPLICATIONS FOR INTERVENTION

Traditionally intervention efforts consider the natural history of the disorder and the role of agent, host and environment. Intervention strategies for heroin addiction have been based on early identification and extension of treatment. "If all new cases were then rapidly treated, they would no longer be contagious and further spread might be prevented." (5)

Spread has been studied in areas which were selected because of a marked increase of new cases. (3, 4, 5, 6, 12) Studies of areas with a marked increase of new cases are bound to show that the later cases were, of course, of recent onset and in close temporal relation to the time of first use. (13) The apparent contagiousness of new cases in such studies is an artefact of the

ascertainment process and does not necessarily represent the usual
or frequent pattern of transmission.

Early identification of new cases in endemic areas is difficult since new users do not readily enter treatment. If anything,
there is evidence that early entry into treatment is mediated more
by law-enforcement efforts, which in itself, is counterproductive
since such efforts do not favor persistent therapeutic involvement. (14)

Secondly, we have not yet developed treatment approaches that
are attractive alternatives to heroin for new users. Many heroin
addicts, like other substance users, can persist in treatment only
after a number of unsuccessful, voluntary attempts to abstain. (15)

Provision of immediate treatment in an endemic area can result
in rapid admission of street addicts. However, the Chicago studies
showed a return of prevalence to pre-intervention levels within
six months and concluded short-term outreach efforts produced only
transitory reduction. (7, 12)

It is possible to define the targets for intervention in terms
of person or place but current approaches at intervention are not
yet effective in endemic areas.

CONCLUSION

This paper considers spread of heroin addiction in terms of
diffusion of ideas rather than as the flow of heroin or as migration of proselytizers. The communicable disease model of agent/
host/environment must be modified to stress those factors which
result in the host seeking out the agent quite consciously and
actively. (16) This perspective stresses the role of belief-
systems; social network; and the interactions between adverse
social environment and the individual.

Intervention must be directed towards the values, and leadership of social networks in order to achieve any durable change in
the spread of heroin addiction.

The assistance of Ms. T. Dubrow and the support of Research
Grant Number DA-00666-03 from the National Institute on Drug
Abuse is acknowledged.

REFERENCES

1. A. Richman in Proceedings of the System Sciences Conference on the Current Issues on the Epidemiology of Drug Abuse, Miami, 1974

2. L.B. de Fleur, Am. Soc. Rev., 40: 88 (1975)

3. R. de Alarcon, U.N. Bull. Narc., 21: 17 (1969)

4. R. Levengood, P. Lowinger and K. Schoof, Am. Jl. Pub. Hlth., 63: 209 (1973)

5. P.R. Hughes, and G. A. Crawford, Arch. Gen. Psych 27: 149 (1972)

6. P.R. Hughes, G. A. Crawford and W. Dorus in Developments in the Field of Drug Abuse (E. Senay, V. Shorty and H. Alksne eds.) Schenkman Publishing Company, Cambridge, 1975.

7. E. C. Senay and R. Parker, in Proc. Second National Drug Abuse Conference, New Orleans, 1975

8. K. Evang, Am. Jl. Pub. Hlth., 63: 927 (1973)

9. A. D. Cliff, Trans. Inst. Brit. Geog., 44: 75 (1968)

10. E. M. Rogers and F. F. Shoemaker, Communication of Innovation The Free Press, New York, 1971

11. J. M. May in American Geography: Inventory and Prospect, Syracuse, 1954

12. P. R. Hughes, Prev. Med., 2: 554 (1973)

13. M. Greene and R. L. Dupont in Report of the Thirty-Sixth Annual Meeting of the Committee on Problems of Drug Dependence, Mexico City, 1974, National Academy of Sciences, Washington, D.C., 1974

14. E. L. Richman and A. Richman in Proceedings Fourth National Conference on Methadone Treatment, San Francisco, 1972, National Association for the Prevention of Addiction to Narcotics, (New York), 1972

15. A. Richman and H.L. Trigg in Proceedings Fourth National Conference on Methadone Treatment, San Francisco, 1972 National Association for the Prevention of Addiction to Narcotics, (New York), 1972

16. E. Drucker and V. W. Sidel, The communicable disease model of heroin addiction: A critique, Annual Meeting American Public Health Association, San Francisco, 1973

RECENT STATUS OF NEW YORK CITY NARCOTIC ADDICTS
DETOXIFIED 1961-1963

A. Richman and E.V. Bowles

Beth Israel Medical Center, 307 Second Avenue, New York
City and the Mount Sinai School of Medicine of the City
University of New York

This paper describes the recent status of New York City heroin
addicts who were detoxified in 1961-1963.

BACKGROUND - THE PATIENT SETTING

Heroin users were first admitted for detoxification to the
Morris J. Bernstein Institute (formerly the Manhattan General Hospital) of the Beth Israel Medical Center in early 1961. Admission
was based on the patient's willingness to appear and medical criteria; there was no screening on the basis of subjective estimates
of motivation or "suitability". Hospitalization was voluntary and
patients could leave against medical advice. The patient was provided with a program of supervised medical withdrawal under the
clinical direction of a psychiatrist, as well as, general health
care. Parallel with reducing the heroin users' habit, attempts
were made to alter attitudes and to have the patient enter long-
term rehabilitation programs in the community. (1)

BACKGROUND - CASE REGISTER FOLLOW-UP

A sample (N=500) of individual narcotic addicts first admitted
during 1961-1963 was followed, in collaboration with the Narcotics
Register of the New York City Department of Health, on the basis
of reports received from a wide variety of health, social, law
enforcement and addiction agencies.

There was evidence of contact with these agencies more than
five calendar years after their index admission for over one-half
of the patients. For one-fifth there were no reports received
by the Narcotics Register following their index hospitalization.

This study of reported contacts shows where some patients have been, but not necessarily "where they're at". (2, 3)

Additional evidence is necessary to supplement this perspective of outcome based on reported contact with agencies. In order to determine outcome for patients without recent Register reports, we must learn whether they are alive and assess their "addiction status" through more direct forms of follow-up. (4, 5, 6)

RESULTS

We have now located 96% of our sample of 100 former patients. Four of the patients have not yet been located and, in fact, show no trace of further contact with any agency after their hospitalization.

One-sixth of these patients (17%) were found outside New York City after considerable effort had been expended. It is noteworthy that the proportion found outside New York City was similar for those considered to be no longer "using" narcotics (9/25 = 36%) and those still "using" narcotics (3/8 = 37.5%).

One-fourth of the former patients have now died. There is an increasing number of deaths in recent years. Since the number-at-risk is decreasing, the death rate is increasing even faster than the absolute number would indicate. How does this mortality compare with the general population? Some reports have compared mortality with that for the general population on the basis of age-sex specific mortality rates and concluded that mortality was relatively higher in the addicted group. (7) However, people living in poverty areas have far higher crude death rates than those living in areas with more adequate incomes. Death rates for persons living in poverty areas are generally 50 to 100% higher for most cities. Violent deaths are 91% higher for whites in poverty areas than non-poverty areas, and 55% higher for non-whites. (8)

Whether the increasing mortality is due to an aging factor; the cumulated effects of earlier life-hazards and complications of narcotic addiction; or a correlate, for some, of alcohol use can not yet be differentiated.

One-fourth (N=25) of the original group were alive and reported as not using narcotics by some informant other than themselves. Previous treatment experience varied widely in this group - some had been extensively involved in treatment programs while others have abstained since the time of their first detoxification.

The treatment needs of this group are generally being met in the sense that there are 36 patients in contact with narcotic treatment agencies in comparison to eight persons using narcotics and not in contact. Most of the current treatment is within methadone maintenance treatment programs but some of these patients have now had their methadone dosage reduced to zero.

SUMMARY

The course of heroin addiction in this sample is highly variable. Some patients have long histories of abstinence while others have required continuous treatment. The treatment needs of this group are largely being met. Mortality is increasing for this group and is considered a major problem.

The assistance of Ms. T. Dubrow and Ms. P. Zappel and the support of the Research Grant Number DA-00666-03 from the National Institute on Drug Abuse is acknowledged.

FOLLOW UP OF

100

NARCOTIC ADDICTS

DETOXIFIED 1961-1963

NOT FOUND	4	December, 1975
DEAD	25	
USERS	8	
IN TREATMENT	36	
JAIL	2	
OFF NARCOTICS	25	

REFERENCES

1. A. Richman, M.A. Feinstein and H.L. Trigg, in Drug Abuse –
    Current Concepts and Research, (W. Keup, ed.) Charles C. Thomas
    Thomas, Springfield, Ill. 1971.

2. A. Richman, J.E. Clark, L. Bergner and S.W. Patrick in Report
    of the Thirty-third Annual Meeting of the Committee on Problems
    of Drug Dependence, Canada, 1971, Washington, D.C.: National
    Academy of Sciences, 1971.

3. A Richman, J.J. Fishman, L. Bergner and S.W. Patrick, Social
    Psychiatry, 6: 179, (1971)

4. A. Richman and R. Sarnoff, presented at the Annual Meeting of
    the American Psychiatric Association, Dallas, 1972

5. A. Richman, M.E. Perkins, B. Bihari and J.J. Fishman, Am. J.
    Public Health, 62: 1002, (1972)

6. A. Richman in Proceedings of the Fifth National Conference on
    Methadone Treatment, Washington, D.C., March 17-19, II, 1494,
    1973.

7. O. Watterson, D.D. Simpson and S.B. Sells, American J. Drug &
    Alcohol Abuse, 2: 99(19750

8. Ventura, S.J. Taffel, S.M. and Spratley, E., Selected Vital and
    Health Statistics in Poverty and Non-Poverty Areas of 19 Large
    Cities, United States, 1969-71. Vital and Health Statistics:
    Series 21, Data from the National Vital Statistics System, No.
    26 DHEW publication No. (HRA) 76-1904.

THE UTILITY AND AVAILABILITY OF ARREST DATA
IN EVALUATING DRUG ABUSE TREATMENT

George Nash, Ph.D.

Deputy Director of Evaluation and Research
Westchester County Community Mental Health Services
White Plains, New York

and

Kay Foster, M.A.

Research Associate
Westchester County Community Mental Health Services
White Plains, New York

I.   INTRODUCTION

The purpose of this paper is to describe the advantages of using
arrest data in evaluating the impact of drug abuse treatment. In
recent years there has been rapid growth in centralized criminal
identification units on the state level. At present one exists
in almost every state.

Our study of the impact of 42 drug abuse treatment programs on
criminality conducted in New Jersey between 1972 and 1975 used
state wide arrest data as supplied at relatively low cost by the
Records and Identification Section of the New Jersey State Police.

In this paper we will first discuss the disadvantages of other
types of post-treatment outcome data. We will then describe the
disadvantages and advantages of arrest data.

II.   THE DISADVANTAGES OF OTHER TYPES OF POST-TREATMENT
      OUTCOME DATA

At Abt Associates the senior author participated in a study for
the National Institute on Drug Abuse which considered and compared
the wide variety of indicators of successful treatment outcome
that are potentially available. We concluded that there were

relatively few useful indicators and most of the measures had
disadvantages. The biggest problems are:
1.   It is hard to locate and personally interview
     previous recipients of treatment.
2.   Most of the more interesting measures can't be
     obtained for the pre-treatment period.
3.   Useful control or comparison groups are almost
     unobtainable.

We will now briefly describe the disadvantages of the most commonly used measures of drug abuse treatment outcome.

A.   Retention - Retention in treatment is seemingly easy to
     measure and has become one of the most widely cited
     statistics proporting to describe treatment program
     effectiveness. Unfortunately, it has many shortcomings.

     Is a person who has left a methadone treatment program
     and been incarcerated or gone into the hospital still
     considered in treatment? The answer depends on the
     policy of the program. Some programs continue to supply
     methadone to those in hospitals or jails, while others
     do not. This brings up the whole question of the dis-
     charge policy of the program.

     Studying retention is more difficult than it appears on
     the surface. It is difficult to determine when a person
     enters treatment and it is difficult to determine when
     a person leaves treatment or is still in treatment
     during the final stages. Once all this is determined,
     it is still difficult to say what retention itself means.

B.   Employment and Social Functioning - As assessment of a
     client's work history prior to entry into treatment or
     after leaving is complicated. Our New Jersey study
     showed that many clients in treatment actually have
     fairly positive job histories, having earned respectable
     sums of money by the week, and having worked on one type
     of job for a reasonable length of time. However, they've
     had interruptions due to incarceration, and so their
     histories are more complex than those of middle-class
     folk. Most drug-users will have had periods in which
     they functioned well, as well as times when they didn't.

     Most of the same cautions that apply to the study of
     work histories apply to an understanding of social
     functioning and family relationships. All of these
     problems make pre- and post-treatment comparisons
     difficult.

C. Drug Use and Abuse - It is difficult to measure and
describe drug use. Drug users, and especially those
who are not primarily heroin users, are much more
heterogeneous than is commonly imagined. Drug use may
vary by type of drug, intensity or quantity of usage
and availability.

It is extremely difficult to estimate the cost of drugs
used for most consumers because so many users are involved in distribution networks and they obtain drugs
at wholesale price or less.

The basic problem with using either employment, social functioning
or drug use data is that it is essentially non-linear data. Prior
to treatment (and especially immediately prior to treatment) most
clients had periods of unemployment or low employment, periods of
heavy drug use and they did not get along with their families.
These same problems may occur, at least periodically, subsequent
to treatment. Depending on the specific point at which post-
treatment information is gathered, a person may be doing either
well or poorly. Because the data is essentially ordinal rather
than linear it is hard to compare pre- and post-treatment
functioning and very difficult to determine how to deal with
behavior which has fluctuated. Although a large proportion of
former treatment clients have used drugs at one point in time
subsequent to beginning treatment, the proportion using at any
given specific time is much smaller. The results obtained asking
whether the person is currently using drugs will be quite different. Furthermore because the person certainly used drugs prior
to beginning treatment, meaningful pre- and post-treatment
comparisons are difficult.

III. THE DISADVANTAGES OF ARREST DATA

Simply knowing whether a person is or isn't arrested subsequent to
beginning treatment doesn't describe the full range of intended
treatment outcomes. This is especially true for younger non-
opiate users who may not have been arrested before beginning
treatment. Employment, the cessation of drug use, social functioning and retention in treatment are all valid goals of
treatment.

Arrests don't correspond perfectly to criminal behavior. Not all
crimes result in arrests and not all arrests are justified. Many
arrests don't result in convictions.

The likelihood of arrest varies substantially from one geographical area to another. The level of police activity is a factor
and younger minority group males, and especially those with
records, are more likely to be arrested for most types of
criminality.

92

Self reported arrest data is not necessarily valid. There is both
under reporting and over reporting. Similarly attempting to use
a counselor's report of arrests is likely to result in under reporting. Lukoff has estimated that using counselors' records
compared to actual police data will result in an under reporting
of approximately 40%[1]. Our experience shows that the greatest
discrepancy arises with those who have a large number of arrests.

Comprehensive state wide data of the type on which we depended in
our New Jersey study is not generally available for those under 18.

IV. THE ADVANTAGES OF PRE- AND POST-TREATMENT ARREST DATA OBTAINED FROM A CENTRALIZED STATE IDENTIFICATION BUREAU

The data is available at reasonable cost on all those who have
entered a treatment program, not just those who had stayed in
treatment or are known to the program or can be reached for
personal interviews.

Arrest data presents a comprehensive record in linear form over a
period of time which allows pre- and post-treatment comparisons.
Data obtained for just a short period of time prior to entering
treatment and a short period of time subsequent to entering treatment is biased in the direction of a favorable outcome on the
principle of regression toward the mean.

Because of the potential variety of charges, arrests can be
broken down into various types such as whether or not they were
drug related and whether or not violence had been involved.

The use of centralized arrest data increases the possibility of
including comparison groups in a study. We were able to include
three different comparison groups in New Jersey that would not
have been possible in the absence of centralized arrest data.

V. THE NEW JERSEY'S FINDINGS AND HOW THEY RELATE TO THE DISADVANTAGES DESCRIBED ABOVE

In New Jersey we first collected data on approximately 30 clients
each in nine methadone treatment programs and in six residential
and two non-residential drug free treatment programs. At these
17 programs, 30 consecutive entrants into treatment in the Fall
of 1971 were followed up for approximately 17 months. For both
types of treatment programs we computed the number of arrests per
year subsequent to age 18 before entry into treatment and after
entry into treatment. In each case the post-treatment rate was
lower and we were able to say that there was an abatement in
arrests. We then related the abatement rate to a number of other
factors about individuals and treatment programs.[2]

Although our study answered many questions about the impact of
drug abuse treatment upon criminality it did not deal with most of
the disadvantages of arrest data referred to above.

In our attempt to resolve some of these issues we correlated data
from three different sources on a sub-sample of 141 males who
entered methadone treatment in the Fall of 1971 and who were
followed up for 18 months.

For these men we have: pre-treatment arrest data from personal
interviews; post-treatment behavior as reported by them in the
same interviews done between 12 and 16 months after beginning
treatment; and assessments of their post-treatment behavior at
the same time from their counselors in methadone treatment. In
addition we have arrest data. Attempts to generalize from this
sub-sample should be limited because all of these clients stayed
in treatment for some time and they were alll in methadone
treatment.

This analysis reveals a number of significant correlations between other forms of post-treatment behavior and post-treatment
arrests. These correlations allow us to place more confidence in
post-treatment arrest data as an indicator of post-treatment
success.

There were four types of post-treatment behavior that were
strongly correlated with not being arrested after beginning
treatment. All described behavior at the time of the interview.
All of these correlations were in the expected direction. All
of the relationships reported are statistically significant. The
four items that were positively related with not being arrested
after beginning treatment were (in order of the strength of the
correlation):   Correlation
                                                      Coefficient

1. The client reporting that he had a regular job
    or was enrolled in school.   .60
2. The client reporting that he was not using drugs.   .57
3. The client reporting that he was happy.   .41
4. The client reporting that he was contributing to
    the support of someone else.   .39

As mentioned above we also had reports of these 141 male methadone
treatment clients behavior from their counselors. Each of the
clients was rated on the basis of illegal activities, drug abuse,
alcohol abuse, and employment. Two of the four items were
positively related with no post-treatment arrests. These related
to behavior in the last three months.   Correlation
                                                      Coefficient

1. Not being involved in illegal activities, insofar
    as the counselor knew about them.   .68
2. Not having a problem of drug abuse as known to
    the counselor.   .39

94

All of this shows that there is a strong relationship between the arrest data we obtained from the New Jersey State Identification Bureau and other forms of functioning.

Bearing in mind that these findings apply to male heroin addicts in methadone treatment, we can say that there is a relationship between the record obtained on an existing arrest, the staff at the treatment program's awareness of criminal involvement and both the client's and the staff members' reports on drug abuse and the clients' reports on employment. There is also a strong correlation between the staff members' perceptions of clients' behavior and the clients' anonymous self reports.

This strong set of relationships is probably due to the nature of heroin abuse itself. Once a person in treatment starts using heroin again, he is likely to lose his job and get into trouble with the criminal justice system. The staff at the program knows this and knowing that the facts are known to others, the client is truthful in his self report.

For the reasons cited above, arrest data would be useful even if it weren't strongly related to other outcome measures. The fact that it is related to drug use and employment gives us more confidence in arrest data as an overall measure of treatment program effectiveness.

More information on the availability of arrest data from state identification bureaus is available through Project Search of the California Crime Technological Research Foundation in Sacramento, California which has issued a number of publications on the functioning and capability of state identification bureaus.[3]

                                REFERENCES

1. Lukoff, Irving F. "Issues in the Evaluation of Heroin
    Treatment" in Josephson, Eric and Carroll, Eleanor E.
    (editors), Drug Use: Epidemiological and Sociological
    Approaches. Washington, D.C. Hemisphere Publishing, 1974.

2. Nash, George, The Impact of Drug Abuse Treatment Upon
    Criminality: A Look at 19 Programs. Upper Montclair, New
    Jersey, Montclair State College Drug Abuse Treatment Infor-
    mation Project, 1973.

3. Project Search State Identification Bureau, Design of a
    Model State Identification Bureau. Sacramento, California,
    California Crime Technological Research Foundation for
    Project Search, 1973.

DRUG ARREST DATA:
AN EPIDEMIOLOGICAL MONITORING SYSTEM INDICATOR

Blanche Frank, Richard Brawn, and Joy Dawson

Bureau of Research
New York State Office of Drug Abuse Services
New York City, New York

I. INTRODUCTION

The Bureau of Research of the New York State Office of Drug
Abuse Services has embarked on a pilot investigation under the
title, The Epidemiological Monitoring Stations Project. The purpose of the project is to determine the feasibility of establishing an information system to monitor the use of drugs in the State
of New York by means of unobtrusive techniques rather than by direct survey techniques. Four counties--varying from urban to
rural--make up the major locus of the project. These counties include Westchester, Rensselaer, Tompkins, and Columbia. In each of
the counties, certain "behavioral residuals," traditionally considered indicators of drug use, are being monitored as they are recorded in the criminal justice system, the health delivery services
system, and the treatment and rehabilitation system. In this paper we report on the monitoring and information value of arrest
data as they relate to drug use in the four counties.

II. LIMITATIONS OF THE DATA

For several reasons an analysis of arrest data must be approached with caution. The literature is replete with the caveats
associated with such an analysis, generally stating that arrest
data are more suggestive of police activity and its own pressures
than any other behavioral phenomenon (1).
Still there are certain characteristics that make arrest data
particularly suitable for our purposes. Arrest data are one of
the few possible indicators of drug use which are readily available and readily available in an almost on-going fashion. In addition, the ways in which an indicator can be analyzed may enhance
its information-producing capability. In our case drug arrests
will be studied alongside non-drug arrests. Regularities found in
drug arrests and persistent differences from non-drug arrests may
enable us to make some statements about drug acitvity. Ultimately,

findings with regard to the arrest data will be related to findings with regard to indicators from the health delivery services
system and the treatment and rehabilitation system for corroba-
tion.

However, in dealing specifically with the data at hand, it was
soon apparent that there were many shortcomings. New York State's
Division of Criminal Justice Services in Albany provided the investigation with data concerning fingerprintable arrests made in
the four counties under study. In order to get the broadest view
of drug activity, a drug arrest was defined as an arrest including at least one drug charge, irrespective of the severity of the
charge. Consequently, a non-drug arrest was an arrest including
no drug charges. Originally it was anticipated that the data
could be studied from 1970 through 1975. However, it was learned
that for the earlier years the data were not complete and not comparable due to new computerization of the system, a change in the
fingerprint law, and the fact that in some cases fingerprints are
returnable. As a result, only the years from 1973 through 1975
were studied because of their completeness and comparability. An
additional limitation resulted from the lack of identifying numbers for arrestees, inhibiting the ability to discuss incidence or
recidivism. Finally, the data included only arrests made within
the counties. We had no information about county residents arrested in other places.

It was necessary to also deal with population data for the counties in order to put a comparison of prevalence into proper perspective. Here again there were limitations. Population estimates and not enumerations were available for the years 1973
through 1975, with significant differences among the estimates made
by the several governmental agencies responsible for them. Wherever possible the Bureau of the Census estimates were used.

Given the limitations of the data, we now look at the information they yielded with respect to drug activity in the counties.
We start at the large focus of total arrests made in the counties,
and we eventually come to arrests as they relate only to the residents of the county and the local places in which the arrestees
reside.

III. THE FINDINGS

Examining, first, total arrest activity in the counties, we try
to identify trends and specific characteristics about the arrestees. With respect to trends over the three years, 1973 through
1975, it is apparent that drug arrests have universally declined
and non-drug arrests have universally risen. However, the arrest
rates for our two urban counties--Westchester and Rensselaer--are
lower than the arrest rates for our two rural counties--Tompkins
and Columbia. In 1975, the drug arrest rates range from 175 per
100,000 population for Westchester and Rensselaer to more than 215
per 100,000 population for Tompkins and Columbia; the non-drug arrest rates range more widely from 614 per 100,000 population for

Rensselaer to 937 per 100,000 population for Westchester to somewhat more than 1400 per 100,000 population for Tompkins and
Columbia.

With respect to the demographic characteristics of arrestees,
the greatest number of arrests altogether occur universally in the
ages between 16 and 24, with the median age of drug arrestees approximately three years younger than the median age of non-drug
arrestees. Although males universally represent the substantial
portion of arrests, a larger representation of the males is found
in drug arrests and a larger representation of the females is
found in non-drug arrests. Although white arrestees universally
represent the substantial portion of arrests, a larger representation of the whites is found in drug arrests and a larger representation of the blacks is found in non-drug arrests.

When we inquire into the place of residence of those arrested in
the four counties, the role of physical mobility becomes apparent,
especially among drug arrestees. It appears that those arrested
on drug charges are more likely to live outside of the county and
locality of residence than do those arrested on non-drug charges.
These findings are particularly apparent in the smaller counties
of Rensselaer, Tompkins, and Columbia, where almost 40% of those
arrested on drug charges live outside of the county compared to
25% of those arrested on non-drug charges. The extent of the
factor of physical mobility among known drug arrestees within
the county brings to question the number of county residents arrested for drug crimes outside the county, a population we know
nothing about. In the absence of this information we turn to the
county residents we do know about--those arrested within the county
--in an attempt to assess drug abuse among county residents.

Examining, secondly, arrest activity among county resident arrested within their counties, we try to identify trends and specific characteristics about the arrestees. With respect to trends
over the three years, again it is apparent that drug arrests have
universally declined and non-drug arrests have universally increased. However, the decline in drug arrests among county residents is not as dramatic as the total arrest picture indicated.
Furthermore, 1973 was generally the year of greatest drug arrests
when the total arrest picture is considered; 1974 was generally
the year of the greatest number of drug arrests when only county
residents are considered.

With respect to the age of arrestees who are county residents,
again we see the median age of drug arrestees as being approximately three years younger than the median age of non-drug arrestees,
with a median age of 21 for drug arrestees and a median age of 24
for non-drug arrestees.

When we examine the arrest rates for the minor civil divisions
or towns within the counties where the arrestees reside, two
interesting characteristics become apparent. First of all, more
than half of the minor civil divisions have drug arrest rates that
are 25% higher or lower than the county average. With respect to
25% higher or lower than the county average. With respect to the
non-drug arrest rate, the rates for the minor civil divisions

tended more to the average for their respective counties. Secondly, when we examine the arrest rates among the minor civil divisions, we see a strong correlation between drug and no-drug arrest rates in the same quartiles. However, in several deviant
cases these correlations do not exist. For instance, the minor
civil division of Mamaroneck in Westchester has a high drug arrest
rate but a low non-drug arrest rate. Such a minor civil division
may become especially interesting in the attempt to determine significant factors accounting for the presence or absence of drug
activity.

IV. DRUG ARREST DATA AS AN EPIDEMIOLOGICAL MONITORING SYSTEM INDICATOR

In assessing the value of drug arrest data for our purposes and
in the way we described, two important drawbacks emerge. First
of all, we have no knowledge of county residents arrested outside
the county. Considering the mobility of drug arrestees, this unknown population can be significantly large, and our knowledge will
always be incomplete.

Secondly, findings as a result of the analysis of drug arrest
data alone lend themselves to two polar models of interpretation:
as an indicator of drug activity or as an indicator of police activity. For instance, the fact that drug arrests have declined
lends itself to two extreme explanations. For instance, to the
extent that drug arrests are an accurate indicator of drug activity in our counties, it might be said that illicit drug activity
has diminished. On the other hand, to the extent that drug arrests are simply an indicator of police activity, the decline in
drug arrests may reflect less police concern with tracking down
illicit drug activity. This may have resulted from relaxed pressure on the police, the public's growing reaction to the harsh
New York State Drug Law of 1973, or more concern with non-drug
crime. The truth may be somewhere in between the two models of
interpretation. What we will be looking at eventually are data
gathered from the health delivery system and the treatment and
rehabilitation system which will support or refute our findings
with respect to arrest data.

Thus our experience with data from official sources has generally indicated that a procedure in interaction with the system that
generated the data is required in order to properly know the
limits of the data. Secondly, arrest data as an indicator of drug
activity cannot stand alone. For it to be meaningful, it appears
that triangulation with other indicators is required.

REFERENCES

1. For example, D. Seidman and M. Couzens, in Law and Society
   Review, 8: 457-493(1974); A. Riess, Jr., The Police and the
   Public, Yale University Press, New Haven, 1971; L. DeFleur,
   American Sociological Review, 40: 88-103(1975)

GERIATRIC DRUG ABUSE:
A Report of 23 Cases

Milton E. Burglass, M.D., M.P.H., M.S., M.Div.

Instructor in Psychiatry, Harvard Medical School at
The Cambridge Hospital; Director, Thresholds Unit,
Polydrug Treatment Program; Cambridge, Mass.

I. INTRODUCTION

This report describes selected aspects of the case histories
of 23 elderly individuals, 60 to 93 years of age, whose inappropriate use of psychoactive and/or somatic ethical drugs resulted
in clinical conditions necessitating medical and/or psychiatric
intervention.

II. SOURCES OF CASES

The cases reported here derive from the author's direct clinical experience over a two year period with a total of 283 geriatric
patients for whom he was medically and/or psychiatrically responsible. Of this total, 130 were seen upon admission to a chronic
care hospital; 91 as out-patients in a municipal geriatric clinic;
and 62 in office or general hospital psychiatric consultations. In
some cases the facts were gathered retrospectively through histories from the patient, a relative, or friend thereof; conversations
with the physicinas involved; and review of medical records. In
others, the author was involved as consultatnt. Cases involving
abuse of alcohol, caffeine, nicotine, illicit, or over-the-counter
drugs were excluded from the present report in order to focus on
the abuse of prescription of drugs and problems in the diagnosis
thereof.

III. SCHEDULE OF CASES

Table I presents the cases in tabular form and indicates the
major variables of age and sex of patient, substance of abuse,
circumstances of diagnosis, source of original supply, source of
ongoing supply, and presence of life precipitant. Narrative ex-
position of so many lengthy cases is precluded in this brief
report.

IV. DISCUSSION

In this report it is possible to discuss only a limited number of the more salient variables and factors. Future reports will explore the intrapsychic, pharmacodynamic, and developmental aspects of the 23 cases.

A. Pharmacological Class of Substance

Given the frequency with which minor tranquilizers and sedative-hypnotics are prescribed for the elderly, it is, perhaps, not surprising that drugs in these two classes were involved in 10 of 23 cases. The low frequency of abuse of major tranquilizers (2 of 23 cases) is interesting in that 5 of the 23 patients were using inappropriate drugs to suppress clearly psychotic symptoms. One is led to wonder if there is something in the sociology of knowledge about drugs that makes anti-psychotics less likely to be selected for self-medication. Given their generally lower frequency of use in the general population, perhaps factors of availability or opportunity are operative.

The low frequency of analgesic abuse (3 cases) in this series is striking given the high prevalence in the geriatric age group of diseases and conditions associated with chronic pain, e.g., degenerative joint disease and impaired peripheral circulation.

That only one case involved abuse of an antidepressant is of interest given the prevalence of depression in this age group, and the frequency with which the diagnosis is missed by both primary care physicians and psychiatrists. The one case involved imipramine given to an 86 year old widower by an elderly friend when the former became depressed after the death of his dog. Shortly thereafter, the patient obtained a prescription from the receptionist of his family physician (without being seen by the physician) and over a two week period increased the dose. Five days later, he presented to an emergency room with complaints of chest pain, palpitations, flushing, and diaphoresis. Apparently, no drug history was taken. The patient was treated symptomatically and sent home. Only after returning two days later with a myocardial infarction was the drug history taken and entered in the chart.

B. Duration of Use

Sedatives and minor tranquilizers were used longest before the appearance of toxic symptoms or side effects. The stimulants were least well tolerated, even when used in low doses. A 93 year old man developed a cardiac arrhythmia and subsequently suffered a myocardial infarction after taking 20 mg. of d-amphetamine daily for three months. His eighteen year old greatgrandaughter, who had been using the drug for weight control, gave it to him to "make

101

him feel better" after he became depressed shortly after fracturing his forearm in a fall.

C. Initial Source of Supply or Suggestion to Use Drug

In 9 cases, the patient had been initially given a supply of the drug or informed of its "value" by a friend or relative. Clearly, drug-sharing is a common practice among the elderly. This "grey market" in which drugs are freely exchanged is commonly seen by the elderly as a natural part of their social life. There is little awareness of the risk inherent in the activity and a considerable reluctance to modify or curtail it. Daily conversation with friends or fellow residents in nursing homes, elderly centers, and hospitals often centers around illness, encounters with doctors, and previous hospital experiences. Misinformation abounds and is disseminated with alarming rapidity.

In twelve cases, the patient's physician was the initial source. In some instances, choice of drug, dosage, and monitoring of use by the physician were appropriate. In others, an inappropriate drug was prescribed, or there were errors in dosage and/or inadequate follow-up provided. In two cases, a pharmacist had initially recommended and supplied the drug.

D. Source of Continuing Supply

In 5 cases the patient managed to obtain a steady supply of drug through the "grey market" or from family members. In 8 cases, pharmacies were supplying patients either without prescriptions or by refilling long-expired ones. In 10 cases, the physician was supplying the patient, most commonly after a "telephone visit" and a telephoned renewal order to a pharmacy.

E. Life Precipitant

In 14 of 23 cases there was a clearly identifiable life stress precipitant preceding the onset of drug abuse. In 9 cases, the relationship between life events and drug abuse was unclear. Most significantly, in 21 of 23 cases there was clear evidence of pre-existing depressive symptoms. In 8 cases, object loss was the immediate precipitant. In 7 cases, a significant decrease in self-esteem antedated and seemingly provided the impetus to seek a pharmacological solution. In 8 cases, drugs were being used to treat physical symptoms: e.g., chronic pain and hypertension.

F. Circumstance of Diagnosis

In 9 cases the diagnosis was made when the patient presented with signs of withdrawal. Significantly, for several patients, the diagnosis was missed on one or more occasions, and was not made until the withdrawal symptoms became more obvious or extreme. It would seem that a drug withdrawal syndrome is not often enough considered by the physician formulating a differential diagnosis in an elderly patient.

In 8 cases, the diagnosis was made when the patient presented with toxic signs and symptoms. Even then the diagnosis was occasionally missed initially. In 5 cases, the diagnosis was made when a drug history was taken after the patient presented with a drug side effect. In one case, the diagnosis was apparently made serendipitously during a health screening exam.

V. CONCLUSIONS

The most salient facts of these cases strongly suggest the need for an assessment of physician attitudes toward the elderly, particularly those stereotypes and assumptions which compromise clinical judgement and result in erroneous or missed diagnoses. The importance of taking a careful drug history on each elderly patient is, I think, clearly indicated.

The high prevalence of depression in this group of patients bespeaks, I think, the need for a more careful appraisal of the elderly's psychiatric status by both primary care physicians and psychiatrists. When psychiatric illness is diagnosed, careful consideration must be given to dosage and possible drug interaction. Close supervision and follow-up of elderly patients receiving psychoactive medications is mandatory.

Lastly, these cases reveal the critical need for improved education of geriatric patients and health care professionals in matters pertaining to drug use and abuse.

TABLE I

Case Characteristics

Patient/ Sex/Age(yrs)	Substance	How Diagnosis Made[a]	Initial Supply Source[b]	Ongoing Supply Source	Life Precipitant Present
1/F/62	d-amphetamine	T	F	F	+
2/M/86	imipramine	T	MD	MD	+
3/M/60	diazepam	W	MD	P	+
4/F/64	diazepam	C	MD	MD	o
5/F/71	bisacodyl	S	P	P	o
6/F/65	d-amphetamine	W	F	MD	o
7/F/62	pentobarbital	W	MD	P	+
8/F/63	thioridazine	S	F	P	+
9/M/77	reserpine/diazepam	W	MD	P	+
10/F/61	diphenylhydantoin	T	F	P	+
11/F/80	propoxyphene	W	MD	MD	o
12/M/93	d-amphetamine	T	F	F	+
13/F/79	oxycodone	S	MD	MD	o
14/M/60	chlordiazepoxide	W	F	F	+
15/F/78	diazepam	W	MD	MD	+
16/F/66	diazepam	T	MD	MD	+
17/M/69	nitroglycerine	T	F	F	+
18/F/75	diazepam	T	F	MD	+
19/M/62	pentobarbital	W	MD	F	+
20/M/66	bisacodyl	S	P	P	o
21/M/72	chlorpromazine	S	MD	P	+
22/F/74	diazepam	T	F	MD	o
23/F/61	pentazocine	W	MD	MD	o

[a]T = toxic symptoms; W = withdrawal; C = chance; S = side effects

[b,c]F = family or friend; MD = physician; P = pharmacy

DRUG HISTORIES OF PRISONERS
Survey of Inmates of State Correctional Facilities

William I. Barton

5509 Yorktown Blvd.
Arlington, Virginia 22207

METHODOLOGY

The purpose of this survey was to gather detailed information on the characteristics of inmates of State Correctional Facilities. The survey was restricted to State Correctional Facilities retaining adult and youthful offenders; State operated juvenile facilities were excluded. Out of 710 facilities defined to be within scope of the survey, 190 facilities were selected using scientific sampling methods. Some 10,359 inmates of these facilities were selected for interview, again using scientific sampling methods. This represents about 1 out of every 18 inmates under jurisdiction of State Correctional Facilities.

There were two pretests for the questionnaire. The questionnaire gathered data on: (1) demographic characteristics, (2) incarceration history, (3) present conviction, and circumstances surrounding it, (4) labor force participation, and income (prior to arrest), and (5) drug and alcohol use.

Data were gathered using female Bureau of the Census interviewers. The interviews were conducted in the institutions in a one-to-one situation, in sight of guards, but not within hearing.

Data from this survey are intended to represent an estimated 191,400 inmates of State Correctional Facilities - or the entire population which falls within scope of the survey.

SURVEY POPULATION

Of an estimated 191,400 inmates of State Correctional Facilities, 98% were sentenced inmates. Inmates who had not received sentences were awaiting trial or release on bail, being held for other authorities, etc. Males were 97% of the population. Around one-half of the inmates were white, with close to one-half being black (47%). Median age was around 27, with around three-fourths of all inmates being between 18-34 years of age. Educational attainment of inmate population was lower (median of 10 years of schooling completed) than that for the noninstitutional population of males in the U.S. in 1972 (median of 12 years of schooling completed). Some 68% of the inmates stated they were employed most of the month prior to the arrest for their present offense(s). Close to one-half of the inmates who stated they were unemployed were not only looking for work, but did not want work (this is 14% of the total inmate population).

About two-thirds (69%) of the inmates who had held jobs at any time after December 1968 had worked most recently as nonfarm laborers, operatorives, or craftsmen. In constrast, such occupational categories accounted in 1972 for 47% of employed males age 16 and over in the general civilian population.

Among sentenced inmates, three criminal offenses predominated: homicide, burglary, and robbery. These offenses accounted for about three-fifths of the convictions that led to imprisonment. Inmates sentenced for robbery were the most numerous - making up some 23% of all sentenced inmates.

SURVEY RESULTS

Findings are that 61% of the 191,400 inmates stated they had used drugs such as heroin, methadone, cocaine, marijuana, amphetamines, or barbiturates at some point in their lives, without a doctor's prescription and outside of a treatment program. The percentage of inmates who had ever used these drugs were: heroin (30%), methadone (9%), cocaine (28%), marijuana (56%), amphetamines (29%), barbiturates (28%), and other drugs/illicitly used (16%).

Table I shows that heroin had been used on a daily, or almost daily, basis by one-fifth of the inmates, while marijuana had been used with the same frequency by one-quarter of the inmates. A subpopulation of all inmates is the population of inmates who have ever used any of these drugs. Among inmates who have ever used any of these drugs, marijuana had been used by nine out of 10 inmates (Table II). One-half of the inmates who had ever used any of these drugs had at least tried heroin, with one-third having used it daily. Among inmates who have ever used heroin, seven out of ten inmates have used it daily, or almost daily, during some portion of their lives. This is in contrast to marijuana for which roughly the same proportion had used it infrequently as had used it daily. (Table III).

The data showed that close to three out of four inmates (73%) who stated they had ever used drugs daily were using drugs with

this frequency at the time of any of the present offense(s) resulting in imprisonment. This means that around one in four of all
inmates of State Correctional Facilities were using drugs daily,
or almost daily, at the time of any of the present offense(s) resulting in imprisonment. Heroin was being used by 14%, and marijuana, by 15%, of all inmates of State Correctional Facilities on
a daily, or almost daily, basis at the time of any of the present
offense(s) resulting in imprisonment.

Around one in four of all inmates of State Correctional
Facilities responded that they were under the influence of drugs
at the time of any of the offense(s) causing their present imprison
ment. By drug, 13% of all inmates stated they were under the
influence of heroin, and 8%, under the influence of marijuana
(Table IV).

Four out of ten inmates stated they had been drinking at the
time of any of the offense(s) which resulted in present imprisonment (Table V). Regardless of type of alcohol, one-fifth of all
inmates stated they had been drinking heavily.

Only 4% of all inmates of State Correctional Facilities stated
they were in drug abuse treatment programs at the time of present
offense(s). Thus, only about 7% of inmates who had ever used
drugs were enrolled in drug treatment programs at the time of
present offense(s), and no more than 11% of inmates who had ever
used drugs daily, or almost daily, were enrolled in drug treatment.

Only 9% of all inmates of State Correctional Facilities stated
they had been enrolled in a drug treatment program prior to the
time of their present offense(s).

* * *

Table I. Extent of use, by drug: all inmates of State
Correctional Facilities

Drug use	Total Percent	Never Used	Ever Used	Extent of use Infrequent	Regular	Daily
Heroin	100%	70	30	7	3	21
Methadone ..	100%	91	9	5	*	3
Cocaine	100%	72	28	17	5	6
Marijuana ..	100%	44	56	22	11	24
Amphetamines	100%	71	29	14	4	11
Barbiturates	100%	72	28	16	4	8
Other drugs/ illicit use	100%	84	16	10	3	4

* means that number is too small to be statistically significant.

Table II. Extent of use, by drug: only inmates of State
Correctional Facilities who had ever used drugs.

Drug use	Total Percent	Never Used	Ever Used	Extent of use		
				Infrequent	Regular	Daily
Heroin	100%	50	50	11	4	35
Methadone ..	100%	85	15	9	2	5
Cocaine	100%	55	45	27	8	10
Marijuana ..	100%	8	92	35	18	39
Amphetamines	100%	52	48	23	7	18
Barbiturates	100%	54	46	26	6	13
Other drugs/ illicit use	100%	73	27	16	5	7

[a]Drug categories are not mutually exclusive.
[b]Percentages may not precisely total due to rounding.

Table III. Extent of use, by drug: Inmates of State Correctional
Facilities who had ever used a particular drug.

Drug use	Percent	Used	Subtotal Percent	Extent of use		
				Infrequent	Regular	Daily
Heroin	100%	30	100%	22	8	71
Methadone ..	100%	9	100%	58	12	31
Cocaine	100%	28	100%	60	18	22
Marijuana ..	100%	56	100%	38	20	42
Amphetamines	100%	29	100%	48	15	37
Barbiturates	100%	28	100%	57	14	29
Other drugs/ illicit use	100%	16	100%	58	18	24

[a]Drug categories are not mutually exclusive. Thus inmates who
have used more than one drug appear in more than one drug
category.
[b]Percentages may not precisely total due to rounding.

Table IV. Number and percentage of inmates stating they were
         under the influence of a particular drug at the time
         of any of the offense(s) resulting in present imprison-
         ment: all inmates of State Correctional Facilities.

Drug use	Number	Percent
Heroin	25,300	13
Methadone	2,200	*
Cocaine	4,900	3
Marijuana	15,000	8
Amphetamines ...	7,600	4
Barbiturates ...	8,100	4
Other drugs/ illicit use ..	5,500	3

* means that number is too small to be statistically significant.

Table V. Number and percentage of inmates who stated they had
         been drinking at the time of any of the offense(s) which
         resulted in present imprisonment: all inmates of State
         Correctional Facilities.

	Number	Percent
Total ...	191,400	100%
Not drinking.	107,600	56
Drinking	81,700	43
Not reported.	2,100	*

			Degree of use		
			Light	Moderately	Heavy
Beer	19,400	10%	5	2	3
Wine	7,900	4	*	*	2
Liquor ...	32,400	17	4	4	9
Combination	22,000	12	*	2	8
Total			12	9	22

UTILIZATION OF CENSUS TRACTS TO PROVIDE
EFFECTIVE OUTREACH MANPOWER SERVICES

Donald R. Bennett

Rubicon, Inc.
1208 West Franklin Street
Richmond, Virginia 23220

INTRODUCTION: THE OUTREACH CENTER

Outreach, a vital function in substance abuse (drug, alcohol) treatment programs, provides the supportive background necessary to reach the heart of the substance abusing population. The staff identifies, locates and recruits individuals within a community whose lifestyles may include a dependency or an addiction upon a particular or combination of chemical substances. Functionally, outreach activity can encompass planned operations for prevention, community education, crisis intervention, information and referral, and generally represents the apex of awareness in a community concerning the program it represents. Depending on both the size and mobility of outreach staff these multi-faceted activities can limit the overall program effectiveness and reach into the community.

This paper is concerned with the utilization of factual information that usually is not readily available to the outreach counselor. The premise is based on an observation that there is a veritable storehouse of information (arrest data) which is collected routinely in many moderate sized communities with standard metropolitan statistical areas of 200,000 persons or more. Additionally, there is potential for use of both program intake and population data when viewed via census tracts.

The development of the data system requires three sets of data (arrest, intake and population).

STAGE ONE - DEVELOPMENT OF THE ARREST DATA FILE

The arrest data is plotted against census tracts as provided by the United States Department of Commerce.

The first stage of system development is data collection. After the appropriate arrest codes have been isolated, manual search and transcription is necessary. Once the data is isolated from the collective body of arrest data by a code book, specific drug arrest data is ready for processing. If data is to be compiled manually, it is necessary to create a common format for transcription on a month to month/year to year basis.

STAGE TWO - DEVELOPMENT OF THE ARREST DATA FILE

Drug arrest data is sorted per census tract for each month of the year undergoing analysis. A profile of drug arrests per census tract is generated. Within each census tract a profile of drug arrests is enumerated per each indice: age, sex, race, type of arrest, location of arrest, and census tract of the arrestee. The next step is to compile this monthly data on a quarterly basis isolating the above mentioned categories.

Arrest data compiled by census tracts over time begins to generate insight about the arrestee population within the city. Inspection of arrest data will indicate patterns along age, sex and race lines along with the type of drugs seized (i.e., marijuana, heroin, controlled drugs, etc.)

Analysis of cumulative arrest data (monthly, quarterly, annually) will indicate a frequency of arrest within and between demographic lines and also within and between census tracts. This set of data can be used to interpret the nature and extent of the arrestee population and monitor changes of the demographic makeup of the population both within and between census tracts over time. Arrest data provides some empirical evidence designating, on the surface, known drug using/abusing populations.

DEVELOPMENT OF THE INTAKE DATA FILE

The second set of data, treatment intake data, can be used to focus on a portion of the drug/alcohol using/abusing population seeking treatment services. Intake data which describes the date of program entry, demographic lines and residence can be plotted against census tracts to define within a given area potential treatment seekers. Intake into drug programs tends to have seasonal vacillations. By plotting intake data by census trace over time a seasonal correlation can be established. Identifying peak intake periods and subsequent decreases over time within census tracts or groups of census tracts can give outreach workers clues as to when and where recruitment efforts can best be mobilized. The use of the treatment intake data to identify seasonal intake periods which also yields demographic line descriptions can assist the outreach counselor in preparing his/her recruitment tactic by anticipating the typology of the population to be recruited.

DEVELOPMENT OF THE POPULATION DATA FILE

The third set of data, population data, as compiled by the Bureau of the Census of the U.S. Department of Commerce can be used to describe, generally, aspects of the population within a given census tract. Once the drug program understands the typology of its treatment seekers then the census data will assist in defining both who and where the known drug using/abusing populations exist.

APPLICATION

The seasoned counselor through a tedious learning process can best assess and make quality decisions about the realities of the complex set of variables to be entertained in efforts to identify the location of potential treatment seekers. Yet, when this seasoned counselor loses contact with these sources of information either by change in a job or extended sickness a valuable asset may be lost by the substance abuse program. The loss may not directly affect the quality of the outreach effort in the long run, but the manpower used to train new counselors attempting to catch up and develop a storehouse of information about the drug/alcohol population is more or less at a disadvantage until the counselor fully experiences that population. The use of arrest data combined with intake and population data is intended to fill the gap of information created due to staff turnover. Also, this data can be used in planning the direction of manpower resources.

CONCLUSIONS

The data files described above collectively yield to an outreach staff an increased understanding of the drug/alcohol using/ abusing population within a given community. Independently, each set of data has certain limitations of interpretation; collectively the interpretive value is substantially increased viewed in light of effective planning of outreach manpower resources. Generally, most well seasoned outreach counselors are aware through their experience of the general characteristics of their potential service populations. However, the acquisition of such knowledge takes time and is usually present-oriented. The use of census tracts as described involves the use of empirical data to yield both past and present understanding of the community drug/alcohol use/abuse problem, and also assists the outreach counselor(s) in future planning of outreach activity. The less tangible, intuitive data used by counselors is still an important factor in interpreting arrest, intake and population data via census tracts.

The overall effect of these data files is on the utilization of outreach manpower resources which can be efficiently planned relative to specific sub-populations, timed in view of peak intake periods and generally place manpower when and where necessary to optimize outreach capability.

Moreover, this data provides needed documentation for the drug/alcohol program as it reflects program reach in a community, and also assists the program in mobilizing on organized, action-oriented planning process for its outreach effort. Finally, information derived for these three sets of data rely on already existing systems of data collection. The collection of data does not require a high level of sophistication in data analysis and interpretation. State and regional drug abuse monitoring agencies could act as resources for necessary technical assistance, at start up, and could distribute to drug programs monthly arrest data from local police departments. The planning functions of state and local monitoring agencies could use this data in their interpretation of program reach and effectiveness. In essence, the census tract concept provides more documented feedback to concerned parties about the success/failure of a drug/alcohol program. The field of substance abuse treatment and rehabilitation, a highly complex system, must learn as much as possible about its service population in order to deliver effective service. The census tract concept is intended to provide measurable insight about the nature and extent of the substance abusing population so that knowledge can be translated into effective service delivery, especially by outreach centers.

A DETAILED REPORT OF THE INCIDENCE OF NARCOTICS DEATHS
IN WESTCHESTER COUNTY OVER A FIVE YEAR PERIOD

Marvin E. Perkins, M.D., Director-CMHS; Samuel L. Rogers, MA,
Director of Research-MMTP; James P. O'Hanlon, Program
Administrator-MMTP

Westchester County Community Mental Health Services

In this paper, we will investigate the relationship between
the operation of the Westchester County-sponsored methadone
treatment program and deaths which occurred in the County-at-large
between 1970 and 1975 due to narcotics poisoning or its complications.

Westchester is an urban-suburban County which lies northeast
of New York City and immediately north of the Bronx. Its population is about 900,000 and currently nearly 1,000 individuals are
in drug free programs and 1,200 in the 8 methadone treatment
programs geographically dispersed throughout the County.

Most of the variables which affect the number of deaths due
to narcotics in the County are believed to have remained stable
during the period under study. An exception is the Methadone
Maintenance Treatment Program which, notably in its initial phase
(1970-72), grew very rapidly.

I. METHODOLOGY

Data for this report was obtained from 3 main sources. The
first and most important were reports issued quarterly by the
Medical Examiner's Office in which the number and category of
narcotics deaths are enumerated. These reports were supplemented
by meetings with the Medical Examiner in which numerous questions
concerning the attribution of cause of death were clarified.

It should be understood that in cases of death due to suspected drug overdose, a complete investigation is carried out by
the Medical Examiner's Office. This consists of 1) an investigation of the site 2) an autopsy which includes toxicology, biochemistry, histology, and microbiology in addition to gross examination 3) determination of cause and manner of death 4) verification of identity and, finally, 5) notification of proper agencies
for follow up.

The names of those dying from narcotics overdose or related causes were checked against a roster of all individuals with a current or past record of methadone treatment. Any names from the Medical Examiner's Office found on our current roster were then checked against clinic reports of patient deaths in our central office files and if necessary, the clinic was contacted to confirm and supplement information surrounding individual cases.

In determining if an individual was enrolled as a patient, the following criteria have been observed:

1. an individual is considered to be intreatment upon receiving his first dose of methadone,
2. an individual is considered terminated from treatment when a "Report of Termination from Treatment" is submitted to the State Authority. When a patient is lost to contact, this notification takes place within two weeks of his last missed appointment.

Monthly census data was obtained directly from clinic reports to the State Authority and was confirmed by reference to the number of "Admission to Treatment" and "Termination from Treatment" forms submitted each month.

II. DEATHS DUE TO NARCOTICS OF PATIENTS IN TREATMENT

At the outset, it should be emphasized that the death of a patient in methadone treatment either from an overdose of methadone or from heroin or other narcotic or narcotic-related cause is a rare event. In the history of the County Program, from 1970 through 1975, only two such deaths have occurred and these will be now briefly reviewed.

The first patient died in 1973 of methadone overdose and chronic intravenous narcotism. This individual, a 23-year-old black female had been in treatment for 22 days, and kept all her clinic appointments, was being maintained on 80 mgs. of methadone per day on a 7-day per week clinic visit schedule and had been observed ingesting her daily dose of methadone at the clinic on the day prior to her death. On the morning of her death, the deceased was up and around the apartment where she lived with her mother and she and her mother conversed. These circumstances make it almost certain that methadone administered at the clinic was not the cause of death. However, methadone was the only drug found at autopsy.

The second patient, a 28-year-old white male who had been in treatment for 18 months, died in 1974 of mixed drug poisoning involving methadone and chloryl hydrate.

This small number of program fatalities due to narcotics -- 2 over a period of 6 years, is even more impressive when compared to the 148 deaths from narcotics over the same period among County residents not in methadone treatment.

Those findings are corroborated by Gearing's work which shows a dramatic reduction in mortality for addicts entering methadone treatment.[1]

III. COUNTY-WIDE DEATHS DUE TO HEROIN

Table I deals exclusively with deaths occurring between 1970 and 1975 inclusively caused by methadone and heroin either acting alone or in combination with other drugs. The table shows a sharp decline in deaths due to heroin since 1971. In that year, which other indicators[2] show was probably the peak period for incidence of narcotics first-use in the County, 20 individuals died from heroin poisoning. If this rate had continued unabated, 100 people would have died from this cause between 1971 and 1975. Actually, about half this number of deaths occurred. In every year except 1972, there have been fewer heroin deaths than in the preceeding year and in 1975, there were 4, a reduction of 80% from the 1971 figure.

No such clear-cut trend can be discerned, however, in this category reflecting the total number of deaths in which heroin was involved. The range here was 9 deaths (1974) to 25 (1971) with a total of 91 deaths during the 6-year period. In the face of both prevention and treatment efforts, this category has shown remarkable intransigence.

It is noteworthy, however, that the early establishment of a County-wide network of treatment facilities almost certainly blunted the impact of a major narcotics epidemic.

However, coincident with the decreasing number of deaths from heroin alone, there has been a disturbing increase in deaths caused by methadone. This was first seen in 1971 when there were 10 deaths in this category compared to 0 in the previous year. With the advent of the stricter regulations, to be discussed shortly, this figure dropped to 7 deaths in 1972 and 4 deaths in 1973 before rising to 7 and 10 deaths in 1974 and 1975 respectively.

The category Methadone and Other Drugs has remained very stable between 3 and 4 since 1971, the first year the category was reported. Included are any drug in combination with methadone except heroin which appears in the category Methadone & Heroin.

The total number of deaths in which methadone was found either alone or in combination with other drugs increased from 0 in 1970 to 17 and 15 in 1971 and 1972 respectively. In 1973, the category reached a minimum of 7 deaths before increasing to 11 in 1974 and 16 in 1975. Over the 6-year period, there have been 66 deaths in this category. As might be expected, its pattern of ebb and flow closely resembles that of the Methadone category.

In responding to the problem of deaths caused by methadone, the program sponsors were aware that, due to its location, abutting New York City with its enormous supply of illicit drugs on its southern border, it was almost certain that some and possible a substantial amount of the illicit methadone on the streets of the County came from sources other than the County programs. Nevertheless, it was decided that a determined effort should be made to reduce the opportunity for methadone diversion from Westchester County clinics as much as possible within the guidelines of sound patient rehabilitation. To this end, 3 major steps were taken:

1. Of the 9 facilities then comprising the County's total methadone treatment network, the 7 which were not already open 7 days a week were directed to begin 7-day operation and where necessary, extra staff were hired to make extended hours of operation possible.

2. Clinics were directed to place all new patients on mandatory 7 days per week pick-up for the first 3 months of clinic attendance and to reduce pick-up schedules thereafter only on clear objective evidence of clinical improvement.

3. Wherever possible, maintenance levels were to be reduced to 80 mgs. per day.

These rather far-reaching changes in clinic operation required many adjustments on the part of both patients and staff. There were a considerable number of patients who, when first informed of the stricter policies, requested detoxification as a preliminary to leaving treatment and it is a tribute to both those patients and their counselors that very few actually left during this difficult period. Ultimately, the new regulations were accepted as being painful but necessary.

IV. RESULTS

The effectiveness of these steps in reducing the potential for methadone diversion is clear; following theri implementation:

1. The number of methadone take-home doses decreased from 40% of the total dispensed to 20% -- a reduction of 50% in take home.

2. The modal maintenance level was reduced from 100 to 80 mgs. per day.

Thus, both the absolute number of doses available for potential diversion as well as their potency was sharply cut. Furthermore, these limitations have continued to be effective. In December of

1975, 76% of the total methadone dispensed was ingested in the clinics.

Under this regime, deaths due to methadone poisoning in the County dropped from 10 in 1971 to 7 in 1972 and to 4 in 1973. (See Table I). In 1974 and 1975, however, this downward trend was reversed and in those years there were 7 and 10 deaths from methadone. Thus, in the 1975 figure for methadone deaths, there is a match with that of 1971. However, it must be borne in mind that in 1971 there was a monthly average of only 769 patients in treatment while in 1975 the average was 1,197 or over 1½ times as many patients.

It becomes clear, therefore, that a rational evaluation of the effectiveness of a methadone program in containing diversion from its facilities depends not only on a consideration of the number of deaths occurring due to methadone during a given time period, and the amount of methadone available to area residents from adjacent areas: e.g., New York City, but also the number of individuals in methadone treatment.

To clarify the latter relationship a simple ratio has been drawn, between the number of deaths where methadone alone or in combination was implicated and the average monthly program census. This is shown in Table II.

The dimunition of the ratio concurrent with more stringent program regulations, first local and later Federal is apparent; a reduction of 0.0221 in 1971 to 0.0063 in 1973.

The increase in 1974 and 1975 (0.0092 to 0.0134) is more difficult to explain. It is unlikely that the small (4%) percentage increase in methadone take-home between 1972 and 1975 would account for enough diversion to cause the observed increase in deaths even when coupled with a 5% increase in program census.

A more likely explanation is that drug users in the County, when they found that stricter rules within the County Clinic had sharply curtailed their supplies of methadone proceeded to develop alternate supplies in 1974 and 1975, probably from sources outside the County. However, since the recovery of labeled methadone medication bottles which can be traced back to individual programs is estremely rare, the source of "street" methadone remains purely conjectural.

ACKNOWLEDGMENT

This is to express the sincere appreciation of the authors to Dr. Henry Siegel, the Westchester County Medical Examiner, for making available much of the data upon which this paper is based.

This publication relates to a program funded by the New York State Office of Drug Abuse Services.

TABLE I

SELECTED CATEGORIES OF NARCOTICS DEATHS IN WESTCHESTER COUNTY

Category	1970	1971	1972	1973	1974	1975	Tot.
Heroin	13	20	10	12	5	4	64
Methadone	0	10	7	4	7	10	38
Combined Methadone & Heroin	0	3	4	0	0	2	9
Heroin & other drugs	-	2	3	0	4	9	18
Methadone & other drugs	-	4	4	3	4	4	19
Heroin involved	13	25	17	12	9	15	91
Methadone involved	0	17	15	7	11	16	66

TABLE II

WESTCHESTER COUNTY MMTP 1971 - 1975
METHADONE IMPLICATED DEATHS/AVERAGE MONTHLY CENSUS

	1971	1972	1973	1974	1975
Average monthly census-MMTP	769	1106	1107	1202	1197
Deaths - Methadone involved	17	15	7	11	16
Deaths/av. mo. census	0.0221	0.0136	0.0063	0.0092	0.0134

REFERENCES

1. Deaths Before, During, and After Methadone Maintenance Treat-
    ment in New York City; Francis Rowe Gearing, M.D., MPH,
    (Division of Epidemiology, Columbia University School of Public
    Health & Administrative Medicine, 21 Audobon Ave., N.Y.), 1972.

2. Westchester Community Mental Health Services, Methadone Main-
    tenance Treatment Program Annual Report 1974; (An Overview
    1970-74); Samuel L. Rogers; James P. O'Hanlon; Alice Epps;
    (Westchester County Community Mental Health Services, #1 County
    Office Building, Room 234, White Plains, N.Y.), 1975.

CHANGING PATTERNS OF STREET METHADONE USE

Joyce H. Lowinson, M.D., Lois S. Alksne, M.A.
and John Langrod, M.A.

Methadone maintenance Treatment Program
Albert Einstein College of Medicine-Bronx Psychiatric Center
Bronx, New York

Methadone maintenance programs have been under fire recently as a source of yet another drug which can be used illegally on the street. Diversion of program methadone cannot be defended, and rigorous steps are being taken to prevent it. It is essential to keep an eye on the illegal use of methadone and to determine the nature and intensity of the problem over time.

This paper describes the changing patterns of street methadone use examined through comparing the experiences of two cohorts of patients entering methadone maintenance treatment at two time periods. The patterns of each group are derived from responses to a questionnaire that was administered at the time of application. The first group consisting of 64 patients, was interviewed between late January and mid-March, 1975, and the second group, also consisting of 64 individuals, was interviewed between late March and mid-May, 1975. Additional data were obtained from two sets of urine reports - one for 37 applicants for the month of December, 1974, and a larger group of 84 applicants between mid-July and mid-September 1975. Patients transferring from another program were eliminated since they would have positive urines legally.

The samples, then, consist of patients who were very recently using drugs on the street and should, therefore, represent current conditions and changes with regard to illicit methadone use.

An important trend which cannot be attributed to differences in demographic characteristics is that significantly more (Chi Square = 3.977; Confidence level = .05)of the Time I group used street methadone, and those who did used it more frequently (Tables 1 and 2). A supportive finding is that more people (5%) in Time II preferred heroin to methadone. The urine reports substantiate these findings. Of the 37 applicant to the program in December, 1974, 86 percent tested positive for methadone as opposed to 56.4 percent of the later group of 84 applicants.

The indication of less involvement with street methadone in the more recent groups of applicants may reflect tighter controls to prevent diversion of program methadone and/or the presence of more and better quality heroin on the street. Concerning the quality of heroin, none of the Time II group complained that it was poor, although several in Time I did. This finding agrees with articles in the press stating that the heroin now coming from Mexico is relatively pure and abundant (1).

The illicit use of methadone remains a serious problem, however. The percentage of users is still considerably higher than that cited by Stephens and Weppner in their 1973 study of Lexington patients (2). Fifty-two percent of their respondents stated that they had used methadone illegally. This, in turn, is more than 43 percent claiming illegal use in their study of similar respondents the previous year.

Heroin continues to be used in combination with other drugs, only one of which is methadone. Exactly the same percentage of each of our two groups used heroin and methadone in combination with some other drugs (61%). The urine results support this picture. The fact that a larger percentage of Time II (14% vs. 0%) used no other drug in addition to heroin may indicate a tendency away from polydrug use for heroin addicts.

An important finding based on both sets of data is that a large majority of those who ever used street methadone began methadone use on the street rather than in a program. We have already noted the decreasing frequency of street methadone use among those who use it. No applicant in the Time II group had used street methadone without first using heroin, as opposed to all but one in the Time I group. This is evidence that methadone addicts are not created primarily via the programs, which is sometimes a criticism of methadone maintenance.

Ninety-six percent of Time I claimed to be "certain" about how much street methadone they obtained for the money they paid, contrasted with only 79 percent of those admitted somewhat later in Time II. There were complaints in both groups about the possibility of the liquid methadone being watered down. This decrease in certainty about the quantity of the methadone may be explained by the fact that Time II tended to buy liquid methadone rather than diskets. It is possible that the zeal to prevent diversion of program methadone by dispensing it in liquid rather than disket form may, ironically, result in a greater number of overdoses and larger profits for illegal salesmen.

Responses to the question, "Did the methadone you bought always come from a program?" must be regarded with caution. The question asks for an opinion or conjecture. The question and the responses are somewhat unstructured for two reasons: most methadone users on the street probably do not know the ultimate source of the drug, and direct questions concerning the person they bought it from would be threatening and probably responded to untruthfully as methadone users have a stake in protecting their sources. Over 80 percent of Time I stated a belief that their methadone did ultimately come from a program. The percentage decreased with Time II to just over 60 percent. In both groups, more frequent users claim that their methadone came from a program than do infrequent users.

Although the majority state that their methadone derives from a program, it does not follow that it was purchased from methadone patients who were selling part of their dosage. It may be, as Representative Charles Rangel has stated, basing his observations on an 18 month federal study (3), that break-ins and armed robberies account for a major part of the program methadone that appears on the street.

Responses to questions concerning circumstances under which methadone is used and reasons for preferring methadone or heroin are more enlightening. Here there is a very wide range, but some suggestive patterns can be detected. In general, we can say that 1) methadone is not as often seen as superior to heroin in Time II as it was in Time I (28% vs. 13%), and 2) a slightly larger percentage of individuals prefer heroin to methadone in Time II than in the first group (65% vs. 60%). Again, the picture is one of a move away from methadone. There seems to be in both groups a tendency to see methadone as safer, cleaner, more medicinal than heroin, but there is a slightly larger number in the second group who feel that methadone is another drug to use to get high. One individual pointed out that a high is especially possible with methadone if one combines it with alcohol. There were some individuals, however, who reserved it for kicking heroin or for use when the demands of heroin addiction became too great.

In Time I, only 25 percent who used methadone ever used it while drinking or using cocaine or another substance simultaneously, although many more did use additional substances. This also suggests that these methadone users may see their drug-taking as therapeutic and are cautious about the possibility of overdose and other consequences of extreme misuse.

A much wider variety of drugs - used in combination of up to five - was reported in the second group. Two individuals used heroin together with methadone; none in the first group did this.

Summary

    Tentatively we have concluded that street methadone is used to
lesser extent at the present time than it was just a few months
earlier, and that it is being used less as a medicine for withdrawing from heroin and more as a drug with merits of its won, just
as it had been years ago under the name of dolophine. A broader
statement, in fact, can be made with more certainty, and that is
that the drug scene is constantly changing. A great deal can happen in terms of what drugs are used and how they are used in a period as short as eight months. Some of these changes are attributable to availability of various drugs on the illicit market,
which may be due to action in drug control. Another source of
change may be the development of new fads and interests within
subpopulations of drug users. We need to raise questions about
the part variations in needs and interests of different groups
play in these swiftly changing patterns. In any event, methods
that agencies use in attempting to cope with the problem of drug
addiction and abuse must, it is clear, be flexible, and frequent
soundings of conditions on the street must be taken and acknowledged.

Table 1

PREVALENCE OF STREET METHADONE USE

	First Group (N=64)	Second Group (N=64)
Used street methadone only................	57 (89%)	48 (75%)
Used methadone only on program...........	5 (8%)	14 (22%)
Never used any methadone.................	2 (3%)	2 (3%)

Table 2

FREQUENCY OF STREET METHADONE USE*

	First Group (N=64)	Second Group (N=64)
Used street methadone frequently........	45 (79%)	31 (65%)
Used street methadone infrequently.......	12 (12%)	17 (35%)
DNA......................................	(7)	(16)

    *"Frequent" means "daily" to "Two or three times a week."
    "Infrequent" is "only once or twice" or "once in awhile."

123

REFERENCES

1. The Narcotics Scene: There's all you want, The New York Post, December 8, 1975.

2. Stephens, R. and Weppner, R. Legal and Illegal Use of Methadone: One Year Later, American Journal of Psychiatry: 130 (12) 1391-1394, December 1973.

3. Government Accounting Office. Security Controls for Methadone Distribution Need Improving, January 30, 1975.

PATTERNS AND EFFECTS OF COCAINE USE

Elaine Schuyten-Resnick, M.S.W.
Suzanna Pribyl, B.A.
Richard B. Resnick, M.D.

Department of Psychiatry
Division of Drug Abuse Research and Treatment
New York Medical College
5 East 102nd Street
New York, New York

INTRODUCTION

This study was undertaken to assess the incidence and effects of cocaine use in a population of opiate dependent individuals applying for treatment in a multi-modality program for narcotics abusers. Interest in the use of cocaine in this population became intensified when the clinical staff began to hear increasing reports of large amounts of cocaine being used by our clinic population. In addition, the recent increase in popular press reports of cocaine use in the general population and the medical awareness of a great deal of conflicting information about the effects of cocaine added to our decision to survey our drug abusing population.

METHODS

As part of our routine intake process all individuals applying for treatment of opiate abuse were asked about their use of cocaine. Interviews were conducted by professional staff, using open-ended questions and recording the information on a standardized form. The Cocaine Use Questionnaires were designed to get detailed histories of past and present cocaine use and to elucidate information on why this group uses cocaine, how it makes them feel and in what way they believe it affects their behavior and their lives. A study sample of two hundred twelve questionnaires were used for data analysis.

RESULTS

The population was predominately male, ranging in age from eighteen to fifty-six, with a mean age of twenty-seven. Subjects came from various socio-economic backgrounds with an ethnic distribution of 38% black, 38% Puerto Rican and 24% white. One hundred ninety-nine of the two hundred twelve individuals interviewed (94 percent of the sample) acknowledged having used cocaine at least one time. Sixty-eight percent of those who had tried it reported having used cocaine during the six months preceeding their intake interview. Twenty-eight percent said they had used it during the week of interview. Average cocaine use during the week and six months prior to being interviewed are shown on Tables 1 and 2.

The age at which cocaine was first tried ranged from twelve years to forty years, with the mean age of first use being twenty. Thirty-four percent said they had used it for the first time at twelve to seventeen years of age. Route of administration for first use was reported as 38 percent intravenous and 62 percent intranasal. Opiate users are the only major group of cocaine users who regularly self-inject the drug, and most who do so mix the cocaine with heroin, a combination referrred to as a "speedball."

All subjects were asked whether they considered themselves to have ever been a "regular user" of cocaine. Forty-four percent of the sample defined themselves as having been a "regular user" of the drug at some time. For three-fourths of this group, regular use was defined as being $10 to $50 of cocaine during each day of use and using three to seven days a week for periods ranging from weeks to months.

Following the first exposure to cocaine, 23 percent of the sample had used it again by the next day and another 23 percent used it by the end of the same month. By the end of the year in which they first tried cocaine, a total of 75.4 percent had used it at least one more time. Only 2 percent stated that they never used the drug again. The group of self-defined "regular users" tried cocaine a second time much sooner than the "not regular users." For example, 73 percent of the "regular users" used cocaine again within a week, but by the end of six months, only 69 percent of the other group had used cocaine a second time.

Since we were interested in finding out about peoples' subjective experience when they took cocaine, all subjects were asked to report the effects they got from the drug and to rate these effects as "good" or "bad." They were instructed to report all effects spontaneously and were not given categories within which to fit their perceptions. Those "good effects" most frequently reported were related to the stimulant properties of cocaine, as shown in Table 3. More than half the sample (51 percent) reported that they never had "bad effects" from cocaine. Those individuals who did experience "bad effects" reported a range of effects but most frequently noted feeling nervous and shaky, fear or paranoia, irritable or depressed, nausea and rapid heartbeat (Table 4).

Forty-eight percent of users reported a biphasic effect from cocaine that consisted of primarily euphoric acute effects, followed by dysphoric effects as the acute effects subsided. This dysphoria is referred to as "post-coke blues" or "crashing" and is characterized by feelings of fear and paranoia, depression, tiredness, wanting more cocaine and being nervous (Table 5). Interestingly many of the "crash" effects are similar to those reported as "bad effects" of cocaine; apparently many individuals do not distinguish between the effects of the drug and the effects of the drug wearing off.

Cocaine is most frequently used in social situations rather than being taken by individuals when they are alone. Asked in what setting they first took cocaine, 61 percent reported using it in a private setting (i.e. their apartment, a friend's home, motel room); 33 percent said they had used it in a public place such as school, a park, the street or in a bar.

Ten percent of the sample believed that they had a "problem" with cocaine. Three-fourths of whom stated they would elect to seek treatment for the problem, if such treatment were available. For the remainder of the group, cocaine was only seen as a problem in terms of its expense. As many of them put it: "It keeps me broke."

TABLE 1

AVERAGE COCAINE USE DURING THE WEEK PRIOR TO INTERVIEW (N=56)

FREQUENCY (DAYS PER WEEK):

1-2 DAYS	71%
3-4 DAYS	16%
5-7 DAYS	12%

AMOUNT (DOLLARS PER DAY):

LESS THAN $10	25%
$11-$49	54%
$50-100	16%
$100 OR MORE	5%

TABLE 2

AVERAGE COCAINE USE IN THE SIX MONTHS PRIOR TO INTERVIEW (N-130)

FREQUENCY (DAYS PER WEEK):

LESS THAN 1 DAY	56%
1-2 DAYS	23%
3 DAYS OR MORE	21%

AMOUNT DOLLARS PER DAY):

LESS THAN $10	25%
$10-$50	54%
$50 OR MORE	21%

TABLE 3

WHAT "GOOD EFFECTS" DO YOU GET FROM COCAINE"

NUMBER OF SUBJECTS REPORTING:

ALERT/ENERGETIC	61
UP	48
HIGH	36
TALKATIVE/SOCIABLE	36
SEXUALLY STIMULATED	30
RUSH	29
PLEASURABLE	21
CONFIDENT	9
FORGET MY TROUBLES	5
MORE RELAXES	5

TABLE 4

WHAT "BAD EFFECTS" DO YOU GET FROM COCAINE?

NUMBER OF SUBJECTS REPORTING:

NERVOUS/SHAKY	30
FEAR/PARANOIA	23
IRRITABLE/DEPRESSED	20
NAUSEA/VOMITING	18
RAPID HEARTBEAT	16
VIOLENT	3

TABLE 5

WHAT EFFECTS DO YOU GET WHEN YOU CRASH?

NUMBER OF SUBJECTS REPORTING:

FEAR/PARANOIA	29
DEPRESSION	28
TIRED	27
WANT MORE	26
NERVOUS	24
SWEATING/CHILLS	13
INSOMNIA	8
NAUSEA/VOMITING	8

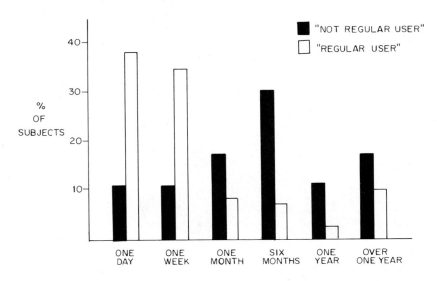

FIGURE 1. INTERVAL BETWEEN FIRST AND SECOND USE OF COCAINE

129

PREVENTION

PEOPLE ARE DRUG ABUSE PREVENTION

Robert L. DuPont, M.D.

Director, National Institute on Drug Abuse
Rockville, Maryland

Let me restrict my remarks this morning to just two points. Lee Dogoloff just mentioned that the integrated Federal drug abuse prevention strategy includes a broad range of supply reduction activities in addition to the more familiar demand reduction or treatment activities. Very few people in the treatment field are aware of this "other" aspect of the Federal approach. The most striking single change in the last 3 years in the entire drug abuse field has occurred on the supply side of the drug abuse equation. The emergence of Mexican heroin in large quantities throughout the United States has literally changed our lives. Many of the predictions made in 1972 and 1973 have changed because of the emergence of Mexican heroin. Last year 90 percent of the heroin seized or purchased by Federal agents in the United States had its origin in Mexico. This heroin comes from poppies grown in Mexico, processed in Mexican laboratories, and transported over our 2,000-mile border into the United States. I have, in the last 2 years, met with Mexican leaders on numerous occasions, including a long meeting with the Mexican President and the Mexican cabinet just 2 months ago to talk about this problem. I am convinced that the Mexican officials are sincerely concerned about this problem and that they are trying to do something constructive about it. The Mexican Attorney General has repeatedly said that he does not want Mexico to be made a scapegoat for inabilities of the United States to solve our drug abuse problems domestically. He has a point that is worth thinking about. The fact is that the distribution of heroin in the United States to heroin users is an American activity, carried on by American criminals some of whom are in the league with Mexican criminals. This heroin traffic is not something that is being done to us by an unfriendly country, but it represents a problem with deep roots in both of our countries, the solution to which will test the abilities of both of our governments. So that while we notice that the vast majority of heroin in the United States now comes from Mexico, we must avoid casting Mexico in the role of a scapegoat. The Mexicans are our neighbors and our friends.

I have had the experience of flying over and landing in a helicopter in the poppy fields in Mexico. They are not hard to find. There are thousands of small fields scattered throughout the Sierra Madre Mountains in western Mexico. All Mexican poppy cultivation is illegal. Poppies are not grown on legitimate farms at all, but on publically owned mountainous area. And, of course, this illicit crop is tremendously lucrative. The amount of money that's involved creates great difficulties for us and for the Mexicans. Whole sections of the Mexican economy are now dependent upon the income generated from illicit drug traffic with grave consequences for that country.

On the United States side, I can assure you that Secretary of State Kissinger and President Ford are personally aware of the seriousness of this problem and that both of them have made this a priority in dealing with Mexico. Today there is no doubt, either on the American side or the Mexican side, of the seriousness of the problem. The Mexican Government has taken what I consider to be a courageous step in using helicopter-borne defoliants to destroy the illicit poppy fields. That process started last fall, but it only got into high gear during the last 2 or 3 months. We don't yet know how successful this new Mexican eradication campaign will be, but at least there is the potential for some important progress, progress perhaps as great as that which followed the disruption of the Turkish-French Connection.

Whatever progress is made in our field can be traced to personal initiatives and personal hopes that have a collective spirit. Too often in the drug abuse field, we talk about budgets, plans, dollars, and slots. We've even called ourselves an "industry." But we haven't focused adequately on the people who are the drug abuse field -- the people who are the "industry." I'd like to take this opportunity to make a personal assessment of some of the people who have made a difference in all of our lives.

There are two new Federal officials in our field whom I want to commend to you. The first is Peter Bensinger, the new Administrator of the Drug Enforcement Administration in the U.S. Department of Justice. Peter is an energetic administrator who was the Director of the Corrections Department for the State of Illinois for 3 years before heading the Chicago Crime Commission; he ran for sheriff in Cook County and very nearly won in the 1974 election. I have met him on many occasions in the last 2 months and found him to be an outstanding, intelligent, and dedicated professional. He is uniquely open to collaboration with the drug abuse treatment field, at least in part, because of his experience with the "people-oriented" programs in the criminal justice field. One example of these characteristics was that Peter Bensinger, before he came to Washington, sat down and had a long talk with Ed Senay, Director of the Illinois Drug Abuse Program in Chicago, about how law enforcement could be more helpful to treatment. He has been open to the treatment people in Washington as well, and I look forward to real progress with DEA under Peter Bensinger's leadership.

The other new person that I want to bring to your attention is Ernie Noble, the Director of the National Institute on Alcohol Abuse and Alcoholism, who addressed you earlier in this Conference. Ernie is a scientist of great distinction himself; he's also a humanist and a dedicated public servant. He's not devoted to old bureaucratic lines - the old bureaucratic defensiveness - but he is open to collaborative activity with those of us in the drug abuse field. Ernie combines an extraordinary grasp of, and support for, research with a deep human concern for the sufferers from alcohol-related problems. Both Ernie Noble and Peter Bensinger are colleagues who are going to be helpful to us.

Now, I want to single out a few of the people directly in our drug abuse prevention field. I do this with some trepidation because there are many people who deserve recognition whom I won't have an opportunity to mention today. Those I have chosen will, I hope, represent the thousands of people who have literally created the drug abuse field over the last decade.

There were some dark days before the progress of the last decade -- before we evolved our modern drug abuse prevention strategy which balanced supply reduction with demand reduction approaches -- when law enforcement was seen by most Americans as the only way to approach the drug abuse problem. Unhappily, most of the Nation's doctors, social workers, psychologists and other "treaters" agreed with this narrow approach. But one man stood out as the champion of the treatment approach - Indiana Sociologist Alfred Lindesmith. He kept the idea alive despite harassment and ridicule. It is to him that we owe a special debt for his vision.

Two people, more than any others, who brought that dream of drug abuse treatment into reality were the great New York physicians, Vincent Dole and Marie Nyswander. This couple, through their brilliant pioneering work, literally made possible the widespread use of treatment for drug abusers in the United States. They too have suffered much misunderstanding. But their historic contributions will be respected as long as there is drug abuse prevention. Their approach, focusing on the development of methadone maintenance treatment, extends far beyond any "modality." They were committed to two ideas: First, drug abusers -- and they primarily dealt with heroin addicts -- were people who could be helped through voluntary medical treatment. Second, the results of any treatment must be subject to careful, dispassionate, objective study and the results -- good and bad -- made available to everyone. These concepts are the foundation of all our current treatment approaches.

Coming from quite a different background, Msgr. William O'Brien, formed the Daytop therapeutic community program in New York City in the early 1960's after working with Chuck Dederich, the creator of Synanon. This was the same time that Vince and Marie were beginning their experiments with methadone. Bill created an institution that not only flourished during the incredible years of the last decade, but his steady, open leadership has supported a cadre of degreed and non-degreed professionals who have taken all over the globe the "concept" that drug abusers working in a unique, structured environment, can help each other to solve their problems and to grow as people.

Frances Rowe Gearing was recruited in the mid-1960's by the Columbia University School of Public Health to conduct an independent evaluation of the original Dole-Nyswander methadone program. Her evaluations focused primarily on four easily measured variables: program retention, arrest, drug use, and employment. Fran's historic work laid the foundation for all subsequent evaluation studies in the area of drug abuse prevention. Her studies are models of clarity and objectivity and make all public health experts proud of their disciple.

I must reach a bit outside of our field to get to Edward Brecher, the distinguished journalist, whose book Licit and Illicit Drugs, published by the editors of Consumers Union in 1972, brought to the public the issues of drug abuse and its treatment in a form that was both interesting and reliable. Although written over 4 years ago, this book remains the single best general reference for those who would like to know more about drug abuse problems.

When the Nation first caught on to the major social changes caused by the epidemic of drug use in the late 1960's, Congress created a National Commission to study the subject. Although many distinguished people contributed to the historic work of the Commission, no other contribution was as important as that made by Richard Bonnie, the young lawyer who became the Associate Director of the Commission staff and who put together the two Reports and the many volumes of supporting material that were published by the Commission in 1971 and 1973. These publications not only put the drug abuse issue into perspective, they also gave it a firm intellectual foundation for the first time. While controversy still rages on almost every issue in our field, the Reports of the National Commission helped keep these controversies on track so that real policy and intellectual progress could be made. This was nowhere more evident than in the marihuana area where the Commission's work can be directly credited with moving that issue from one of pointless emotionalism into the relatively productive focus that we now have.

Closer to my own experience, I could not make even a short list of distinguished contributors to this field without noting the contribution of Jerome Jaffe, the first Director of the White House Special Action Office for Drug Abuse Prevention and the inventor of the concept of multimodality treatment. It may be hard for some of you in this room this morning to imagine that only 8 years ago there was no thought of a multimodality program in the country. In that era the various modalities -- which were in any event tiny by today's standards -- were fighting with each other; each claiming to be the "one true way." Jerry Jaffe created the Illinois Drug Abuse Program in 1968, bringing together the various modalities and offering to patients a choice of treatment approaches. In 1971 Jerry also bore the brunt of the political heat as the drug abuse field hit -- briefly -- as the Nation's number one domestic priority. He handled that impossible job with distinction.

Avram Goldstein, a distinguished academic pharmacologist, went to a lecture given by Vincent Dole at Stanford in the mid-1960's and discovered that his lab work had direct applicability to one of the major health and social problems in the Nation. Since that time, he has become the guru of our field, pioneering the use of lower doses of methadone for maintenance treatment, the use of antagonists and long-acting maintenance drugs, and, in general, bringing his sophisticated understanding of pharmacological research to our field. More recently, he has played a key role in the discovery of the morphine-like substance in the normal brain. This discovery is potentially of historic importance. There is a real possibility that we will discover new, perhaps natural, opiate-like substances with great therapeutic potential for the treatment of pain, other dysphoric states, and even for the treatment of addiction. Additionally, this work opens up new, fundamental areas of understanding of the nervous system.

In quite another area, Bill Harvey from St. Louis, has emerged as a leader in the drug abuse field. He has called our attention to the importance -- in a positive, constructive sense -- of the multicultural aspects of drug use and drug abuse prevention. Bill has done more than anyone else to get the problems of drugs and crime into the black political agenda. He has the deep roots in his own culture, as well as the firm academic training, needed to make a lasting contribution to our field.

Ramone Adame prefers to be called "Monchie." He tells you with his look and his words that he rejects pretentions and that he means business. The business he's about involves not only the tremendous unmet needs of the Chicano, (he created and heads the National Alliance) but the needs of all drug abusers and former drug dependent persons. As a graduate of 22 years of heroin addiction, Monchie has seen it and he interprets that experience for all of us.

137

I'm proud to say that Avram Goldstein, Richard Bonnie, Bill Harvey, and Monchie Adame are four of the 10 members of the new National Advisory Council on Drug Abuse formed by the Secretary of Health, Education, and Welfare. In this role these people have a direct voice in our Federal drug abuse prevention policy.

I promised you a short list. But I must add two more names before I close. Lee Dogoloff preceded me to the platform this morning. Lee was the key person working with me in creating the Narcotics Treatment Administration in Washington, D.C., in 1970. He left his job as Deputy Administrator of NTA to join Jerry Jaffe at the Special Action Office in 1972. He then, in 1973, set up the community assistance program in the new National Institute on Drug Abuse. Just a few months ago, he left NIDA to go back downtown to the White House and join the Office of Federal Drug Management in the Office of Management and Budget. Lee was in charge of the entire demand-side area of the White Paper on Drug Abuse, and I credit him with the fact that the President's budget for fiscal year 1977 has an increase in drug abuse treatment funds for the first time in 3 years.

In closing, I'd like to mention the name of Jim Fair. The other people I've mentioned could, each in his or her own way, be thought of as "big shots." Jim was never that. He was a former heroin addict who worked closely with Lee Dogoloff and me in the Narcotics Treatment Administration. Jim selflessly worked long hours taking on many responsibilities in the creation of NTA. His major contribution, however, was to communicate to the public -- most particularly the thousands of people who visited NTA between 1970 and 1974 -- the nature of heroin addiction and the experience of heroin addiction treatment. He was soft-spoken, sincere, and intelligent. He communicated with everyone from kids in high school classes, to then Governor Jimmy Carter of Georgia, to leaders of the House and Senate. He spoke for the drug abusers as well as for those who sought to help them. His was a unique, and unfortunately, not sufficiently recognized contribution. I hope that by singling Jim out this morning, I can in some small way express my personal indebtedness to him.

Well, that's it. A representative list of 14 people who have made a difference. These few people will have to stand for thousands of others. These are the kinds of people who bring budgets, plans, programs, and slots to life. They have helped create and sustain this field. Whatever the future fashion in funding may be, these contributions, and I mean the thousands of human contributions that have been made in the last decade, will live on and will grow.

I salute these people, and I salute each of you, for making a difference in the life of our Nation.

CRITICAL ISSUES IN DRUG ABUSE PREVENTION

Allan Y. Cohen, Ph.D.

Pacific Institute for Research and Evaluation,
Walnut Creek, California, and
John F. Kennedy University, Orinda, California
This article has been made possible in part
by a contract from the National Institute on
Drug Abuse, Division of Resource Development,
Prevention Branch

The emerging enthusiasm for drug abuse primary prevention engenders some special problems for programs and field practitioners. Some of the very strengths in the new philosophy of primary prevention have created confusion in definition and accountability. "Prevention people" and prevention strategies tend to be flexible, generic and humanistic, the very qualities associated with "soft-headed" thinking and programming.

Based on my previous confrontation with such issues, and the growing experience of Pacific Institute's PYRAMID Project, let me suggest a perspective potentially helpful in clarifying problems of definition and accountability.

I. DEFINITION

Let us recognize that any definition of prevention is arbitrary. Indeed, many program people dislike the word, since it connotes an overemphasis on the negative.

However, at the least, a definition allows communication among colleagues and between programmers and the community.

Literally, "prevention" means to "come before." In the drug abuse field, primary prevention is often used to describe strategies oriented to intervene before drug problems surface.

Prevention has historically emphasized either the prevention of supply and/or demand. The domain of supply prevention has devolved to law enforcement. To the extent (and it has not proven to be decisive) that potential users choose not to use drugs because of the risk of prosecution, the criminal justice approach also reduces demand.

The new breed of prevention theorists, however, are not impressed by the promise of fear-oriented approaches and are more inclined toward the enhancement of those personal qualities and societal conditions which reduce the attractiveness and necessity of drug use.

The special facet of primary prevention, [versus "early intervention" (secondary prevention) and "treatment" (tertiary prevention)] lies in its concern with future behavior. In this sense, the preventor is interested in the following objectives: (1) To reduce the future intensity and prevalence of drug use, among the populations who use drugs; (2) To reduce the future incidence of regular use among the population of experimenters; and (3) To reduce the future incidence of experimentation among the population of non-users. In contrast, strategies associated with early identification or treatment tend to be most concerned with a population's present or past behavior.

Previously, primary drug abuse prevention (of demand) featured drug information. Scare-oriented information broadened out into drug "education" designed more to produce rational decision-making than irrational conditioning against drugs. Recently, prevention strategies have emphasized skill and resource development through such foci as alternative involvements, self-esteem, personal values, interpersonal belonging, vocational relevance, and opportunity for meaningful responsibility and service to others. A basic assumption of many of these strategies is that drug-using behavior is essentially a matter of choice and that the probability of maladaptive drug use is inversely related to the individual's relative satisfaction with the non-intoxicated state of consciousness.

II. ACCOUNTABILITY

Most primary prevention strategists see drug abuse as only one symptom of underlying obstacles to the fulfillment of human potential. Effective prevention approaches should have impact also on alcohol abuse, mental illness, and criminal behavior. Ironically, most funding from the public sector is categorical, and prevention efforts often receive lower priority because of their more generic nature.

Whatever the logic of the situation, prevention programmers may be able to solve the accountability problem without compromising their principles.

I am suggesting that prevention efforts remain or become drug-specific when applying for support from drug abuse categorical funding. This requires the measurement of drug-relevant outcome variables. In many cases, drug incidence, prevalence or attitudes can be surveyed. Unless the situation changes, it is preferable to attempt to evaluate drug-use related measures than to rely merely on researching the "intermediary variables" (for example, self-esteem or value clarity). In fact, prevention programs may wish to collect data on a wide variety of outcome variables, depending upon their philosophies and funding sources. It is doubtful that funding agencies will criticize programs for preventing other social ills as long as drug-specific variables are being measured.

Ideally, a wide-ranging prevention program could collect data on most of the symptom categories of interest to funding agencies. The essence of the program need not be changed. For the foreseeable future, primary prevention will get its appropriate share of re-sources of drug money to the extent that it can demonstrate its direct relevance to the actual or potential use of drugs.

Needless to say, there are unique research and evaluation problems associated with measuring "something that doesn't happen." On the other hand, even with the inherent cost-efficiency in the preventive approach, an attempt at outcome evaluation, no matter how "soft" the data, is usually well worth the effort.

Even though the prevention community needs to maintain its essential position that there are causal variables producing the symptom of unnecessary drug use, it need not ignore the kind of symptom which may lead to even more damage to the individual and society. Furthermore, a specific focus on a measurable variable may help preventors better understand the real dynamics of human growth and adaptation. What causes a person to be "healthy" is perhaps too broad a question. The dynamics of drug abuse preven-tion may be more easily interpreted and ultimately generalizable to other developmental problems.

The critical issues in primary prevention are often frustrating and difficult, yet they can help sharpen thinking and move preven-tion toward a true science as well as an ongoing art.

PRIMARY PREVENTION

AN AVENUE WE MUST PURSUE

Andrew M. Mecca   MPH

Director, Substance Abuse
Community Mental Health
Marin County, California

"Public Health will never rise higher than the level of health established for the individual. The health of the many is but a summation of personal health. A nation can never be healthier than its citizens, and it is upon the welfare of the latter that our efforts must be concentrated.--" Vaughan

Sitting in the East Room of the White House in 1973, this author heard President Nixon proclaim to a National TASC (Treatment Alternatives to Street Crime) Conference delegation-that, "We have turned the corner on drug abuse." However, two years later, the S.F. Chronicle reported with authority, "A confidential White House white paper says the nation's war against drugs - once considered on the road to victory - is on the way to defeat..." Also, Florida's Attorney General Robert Shiven was quoted in the Florida Times Union, "America's taxpayers are losing a $50-billion dollar-a-year battle against drug abuse."

It was my belief in 1973, one even stronger today, that to continue relegating drug abuse solely to the treatment and prohibition strategy, dictates a perpetual need to expand ineffective treatment and prohibition activities. This belief emanates from seven years of running drug abuse treatment and diversion programs. For the thousands of clients seen, few have been rehabilitated. Drug abuse has traditionally been dealt with via the prohibition and/or treatment model. Both have demonstrated little impact.

In reviewing the abundant literature available, it is difficult to find any substantial data documenting positive outcomes. This sad fact has not precluded the federal, state and local governments pouring millions of dollars into these treatment programs that have demonstrated little impact on drug abuse. Additionally, hundreds of millions of dollars continue to go to drug enforcement activities that perpetuate their existence by, among other things, amassing impressive arrest records of "light weight" drug users.

This author will be the first to admit to the need for treating those in need, but the experience gained in developing and running drug treatment intervention programs, has sensitized me to the lack of success in treating most drug abusers and the need for energetically pursuing a primary prevention strategy. A new policy is required to begin balancing the disproportionate funding of treatment and prevention now taking place. In a one year period, 75 billion was spent on health care -- 93% was spent on treatment, 5% on research, 2% on prevention and one half of 1% on health education. (2) These figures emphasize our crisis-oriented approach to health care. The need for prevention is further supported by the ever-increasing incidence of drug and alcohol abuse, particularly among the youth of America. (3)

After my involvement in developing and running the drug US Army detoxification and treatment program in Vietnam, I returned to the US and established the Marin County TASC Program. In almost 3 years of operation the TASC program has referred over 1000 clients to treatment. One common denominator among this clientele is an almost total absence of self-esteem. This factor was empirically determined after hundreds of diagnostic workups. It was during these interviews that the consistent thread of low self image became evident. It was portrayed by a verbal description of how the individual felt about themselves. Statements like, "I don't have anything going for myself," or "I don't really care what happens to me", were common. The comments were almost always self-derogatory.

Now, behaviorists are in agreement that self-esteem is the single most effective coping tool one has in dealing with stress. Those lacking self-esteem, they say, are more inclined to act out adversely in a situation they are unable to cope with. This acting out may manifest itself in many forms, some as overt as drug abuse, alcohol abuse, criminality, and obesity; others as covert as cardiovascular, pulmonary, and gastrointestinal diseases.

A recent Behavior Today article stated that, "Researchers have found that medical utilization is closely associated with psychosocial stress." (4) Consistent with this is a comment by Dr. Carl Simonton in the August issue of Human Behavior, "Over and over again, we have seen that the cancer patient has certain recurrent character traits --- one of them is a low self-image." (5) Dr. M. Harvey Brenner of the John Hopkins School of Hygiene and Public Health was quoted recently in the San Francisco Examiner "...despite medical advances in the last half century, and the conquest of our physical environment and infectious disease, we are still plagued by high infant death rates, epidemics of suicide, violence, cancer and chronic disorders such as coronary heart disease, ulcers and depression. All these are conditions closely associated with stress." (6)

This then begins to expand the rationale for pursuing primary prevention. Enhancing self-esteem, particularly the youth, will enable them to better cope with stress and thus be less vulnerable to many health problems. It is, therefore, this author's contention that numerous health problems, including drug and alcohol abuse, can be prevented if people have an enhanced arsenal of personal resources that enable them to live successfully in today's complex, changing society. As stated in Prevention in Perspective, "...establishing a sense of identity and purpose, believing in one's personal worth and ability to meet the challenges of modern life, and gaining a clear idea of what successful living might mean --- are all conditions that help young people resist the temptation of drug abuse... (7) This led them to conclude that, "Children who have positive views of themselves tend to act in ways that bring further success: they are able to persevere, to remain committed in the face of stress and adversity. Children who do not regard themselves highly react in the opposite way." (8)

Affective education modes incorporated into school curriculums may be one method of enhancing our children's self esteem. Affective education has the common intent of aiding the individual in building a greater sense of self worth. This increases their ability to have meaningful relationships by enhancing their skills in communication, conflict-resolution, empathy, and group problem solving.

Our existing system of health care appears, on the contrary, to be reinforcing many of our problems. Taking drug abuse as an example, an individual manifesting an inability to cope with stress and lack of emotional support, ends up abusing drugs. This person then becomes involved in burglaries to support his drug use and winds up in jail. Immediately a legion of concerned persons arrives on the scene to help; a diversion screener, OR (Own Recognizance) interviewer, a probation officer, public defender, social worker, local drug program representative, just to name a few. All of a sudden this person has discovered a wealth of concerned, caring persons who's job it is to help. It seems possible that this abundance of attention may subconsciously reinforce this person's deviant behavior. A classic example of this reinforcing syndrome is captured in a statement by one of the TASC program's first clients. After being referred to treatment three times, and returning to jail on his third rearrest, this client candidly stated, "Well this is one warm home I can always count on."

The preceding scenario is one I have seen repeated hundreds of times. It represents a perpetuation of the disjointed-incremental problem solving approach that costs so much and does so little.

There is a dire need for more humane and innovative measures for dealing with drug abuse, alcoholism, and the criminality that surrounds their use. But by persisting in relying solely on treating and locking up these offenders, we will continue to see the nearly 100% recidivism rates currently being experienced; this, as a result of returning these individuals to the same endemic area they came from, one marked by a lack of self-esteem, little education, no viable job skills, poor family relationship, and sexual problems.

The funding of primary prevention cannot be left to any one particular area of concern (e.g. drug abuse). The responsibility

to support primary prevention needs to be shouldered by a comprehensive group of disciplines including education, criminal justice
and health care delivery (including drug and alcohol). This shared
responsibility is consistent with the potential impact of reducing
juvenile delinquency, adult arrest, drug abuse and alcoholism, not
to mention cardiovascular, gastrointestinal, pulmonary, and carsa-
nomic diseases.

This plan is by no means intended as a panacea for the ills
now decaying the marrow of our culture. Rather it is intended as a
seed to be sown that would provide an increasingly rich harvest
generation after generation as it increasingly prevails in the home
and society at large. The 104 year old American Public Health
Association strongly supported this position when they advocated in
their publication, "The Nation's Health" that, "...This crisis
oriented system of rewards for the treatment of sickness must be
changed to a system offering incentives for promoting health. It
further declared, "For these reasons it is time to redirect the
focus of health care to an emphasis on prevention and health promotion." (9)

I am the first to admit the long road ahead to realizing the
necessary support for a comprehensive primary prevention strategy.
The essential prerequisites to this program are: creation of a
political atmosphere that will provide the necessary financial commitment; creation of an effective developmental training program
for teachers (if the teachers don't feel good about themselves - it
is unlikely that they can assist the children in feeling better)
and development of a meaningful evaluation design.

The dissonance for the ineffectiveness of the existing models
is increasing rapidly. People are beginning to deman change - and
it is time we began attacking the real precursors to our problems.
Where is the age old wisdom of Hippocrates, Plato and Ben Franklin,
who expounded "an ounce of prevention is worth a pound of cure"?
Why can't we promote health rather than continually relegating ourselves to the game of just trying to stay even?

My friends continue to label me a lost optimist - but I share
very strongly a belief Rene Dubos articulately presented, "Optimism
is essential for action and constitutes the only attitude compatible with sanity. Optimism is a creative philosophical attitude,
because it encourages taking advantage of personal and social
crises for the development of novel and more sensible ways of life."
(10)

BIBLIOGRAPHY

(1) "Drug War - Losing Battle", Robert Greenberg,
     Chicago Daily News, San Francisco Chronicle,
     October 5, 1975.

(2) News Service: Legislative Alerts Monthly
     Report, NASDAPC, March, 1975

(3)   <u>White Paper on Drug Abuse</u>, September, 1975,
A Report to the President from the Domestic
Council Drug Abuse Task Force.

(4)   <u>Behavior Today</u>, June 30, 1975, Volume 6,
Number 26.

(5)   <u>Human Behavior</u>, "The Image of Cancer, C.C.
Elevell II, August, 1975.

(6)   "Feeling poorly? Blame Economy", Joann Rogers,
San Francisco Examiner and Chronicle, November,
1975.

(7)   <u>Prevention in Perspective Book I</u>, Pacific
Institute for Research and Evaluation, March,
1975.

(8)   Ibid.

(9)   "Prevention", The Nations Health - APHA Newspaper,
October, 1975.

(10)   "Optimism - The Creative Attitude", <u>Readers Digest</u>,
April, 1974.

STATE AUTHORITY
AND HER PATHETIC PREVENTION PHILOSOPHY

Bruce Bomier, M.P.H.

Executive Director
Minnesota Behavioral Institute
431½ East Main Street
Anoka, Minnesota 55303

Once there were two ghetto urchins who had a brief, but pleasant,
romance. One was a nice, simple, disorganized girl named State
Authority, and the other was a slimy, clever, manipulative kid
named Philip Morris Pfizer Phillips. State wanted to help people,
and Philip wanted to get rich quick, so State got a master's degree
in social work and Philip took a Dale Carnegie course.

Philip knew that the tobacco companies pay higher than any other
industry, so he started marketing cigarettes; he knew that alcohol
is one of the biggest industries on earth (one out of every 50 employed North Americans works in the alcohol industry), so he started writing alcohol advertisements; he knew that prescription drugs
are the most profitable products, ounce for ounce, in the nation,
so he wrote medical drug advertisements.

State, on the other hand, knew that tobacco kills, alcohol kills
and maims, and that prescription drugs kill, maim and addict, so
she decided to build a prevention program.

Philip had colorful, sexy pictures of healthy, strong people smoking cigarettes plastered up on billboards and in magazines. He had
sweet fruit juices added to cheap wine and dumped into cute little
bottles, with cute little names, and built ad campaigns aimed at
getting kids to start being cute and drinking young. He showed
young, sexy kids on TV drinking wine and beer while they played and
sang. For the older people, he showed proud Teutonic foresters
controlling wild bears; big, strapping men unleashing wild bulls,
inferring that their power came from beer. He showed how a "good
old boy" will walk out on family, job and civic responsibilities
when it comes to "thirst things first." Then he filled medical
magazines with patronizing articles showing how good doctors give

anxious patients, and any patients who might someday become anxious, lots of prescription happiness drugs.

Subtly, but certainly, people began to really believe that cigarettes denoted women as sophisticated and generally "having come a long way;" that alcohol made all people fun, healthy, sexy and powerful; and that unless everyone used lots of prescription drugs, something would go wrong with them.

Philip Morris Pfizer Phillips got pathetically rich. Although he developed a cigarette hack, had a few lost week ends, and started growing breasts from too much phenothiazine, he was overjoyed at his hard-won success.

Meanwhile, State Authority was trying to prevent the abusive use of recreational chemicals by publishing technical papers on metabolism rates of tetrahydrocannabinol, and the history of prehistoric fermentation processes. But people were using more and more recreational chemicals and getting more and more morbid at younger and younger ages. Twenty years of lecturing to professionals had failed, and State finally gave up and decided on a different course of action. She hired and married Ambrose Aardvark, whose qualifications included once having been a town drunk. She had Mr. Aardvark go to schools and churches and dynamically interact with small groups (everyone knows small groups learn more than big groups) about how he had wined, wenched and wallowed all over the country, until he died in the gutter one night outside Billy Graham's corporate headquarters, and was promptly resurrected. There were over 226 million people in North America, and although Mr. Aardvark talked to at least 226 of them, there still was more and more abuse, and the people became sicker and sicker.

State was desparate, so she decided to visit her dying flame, Philip, and ask him where the prevention program had gone wrong. State lived in a core city apartment with Mr. Aardvark, and Philip lived in a plush suburb, so State had to take an inter-city bus.

While she was waiting to transfer buses, State stopped in front of a TV store and saw five TV screens all going at once. One showed some teenage-ish, lusty people dancing around a beach fire, each holding a cute little jug of cheap wine; another showed a man who had just conquered a mountain, whereupon a blond on a motorcycle buzzed up and offered him a beer; the third showed a man's head with a little hammer pounding away inside until he took a drug; the fourth showed Sammy Davis, Jr. playing a "drinking game" with a bottle of Manischewitz wine; and the fifth showed a solid-looking cowboy puffing on a brown cigarette as he piloted a Viking ship into New York Harbor to the tune of a Wagnerian triumphal march.

When State walked onto the bus, she saw some posters that showed
clear streams, proud elk, blue skies and grazing buffalo with
superimposed "Drink Beer" signs. She saw billboards showing suggestive women offering whiskey; physically powerful men thirstily
quaffing beer and laughing; and a picture of eight dunderheads and
one reasonable person at a circus, with a superimposed question:
"Which one smokes Camels?"

"How come Mr. Aardvark and I couldn't stop alcohol and drug abuse?"
she wistfully kept asking herself.

As she walked up to the Phillips' mansion, she paused and admiring-
ly surveyed the massive, rococo architecture when all at once, she
saw something quite out of place. The Phillips' youngest son was
lying, passed out, on the driveway, surrounded by a case of empty
3.2 beer cans. She later learned that the boy was fortifying himself because of a recent tragedy. The Phillips' daughter, Annie
Greenspring, had been high on prescription amphetamines and had
driven her burnt-orange Opel into Mr. Phillips' wine cellar and
smashed everything in sight. This shock was too much for the ail-
ing Phillips, and he had died of complications from cirrhosis of
the liver, emphysema and gynocomestia. State tried to offer her
condolences to Mrs. Phillips, but the doctor had given her "something" for her sorrow and she was busy talking to the chandelier.

Suddenly, State had an inspiration. "Mr. Aardvark and I must be
talking about the wrong stuff; we won't think about drugs or alcohol at all--we'll just start sitting around in small, small groups,
talking about love, and touching and feeling, and doing real heavy
stuff; a whole 'bran' new language!' Boy, would Philip ever be
proud and happy about my idea," she thought, as she washed some
florinal down with a slug of Ripple in a toast to Philip's memory.

***

Prevention was born 200 years ago when a British physician deduced
that the government could change the water source of London and
substantially reduce the prevalence of an elusive fever. Environmental change meant improved public health through prevention.

Prevention, not therapy, is the most singular response any government can direct toward addressing a public health epidemic. It is
reassuring that eventually responsible public servants perceived
that prevention is a reasonable way to address the increase in the
prevalence of the misuse of recreational intoxication. Naturally,
the industry of responding to chemical dependency first fell back
on what it knew best: therapy, under the label of prevention.
Chemical misuse prevention programs are often staffed with, and
certainly always impacted by, those who have provided therapy.
Mini-therapy is marshalled against small, at-risk, but healthy

populations in an ill-thought-out attempt to "prevent." It is possible, even probable, that some individuals achieve prophylactic insulation from misuse, but the public health, as a whole, is untouched.

While grasping for programmatic sophistication in prevention in 1973, the American government correctly identified anti-drug, fear-oriented messages as a decade out of sync with reality. The messages had been unwise, but the new movement jettisoned even discussion relating to intoxication, along with the old messages. In the programmatic void, a last-minute communications effort directed toward abstractly extolling the general human virtues most often associated with treatment was plugged into "prevention." The only real variations in theme separating many of the "Bran New Language" messages from therapy, were depth, and the fact that intoxication was rarely mentioned.

The thinking seemed to be that if a lot of therapy was good for a sick population, a little therapy would be good for a healthy population. The analogy of giving a little shock therapy to people who are at risk of a severe mental disorder comes to mind.

To improve the public health through prevention, the environment must be impacted, and these days, that task is realistically obtainable. If the Pepsi Generation can be persuaded to drink pop wine, they can be persuaded not to drink it while driving; if women can be persuaded to inhale carcinogenic leaves to denote themselves as liberated, everyone can be persuaded not to inhale intoxicating weeds at times when it obviously interferes with employment.

The preferred role of government in "preventing" is not ambiguous, but relatively obvious:

1. Identify intoxication-related conduct that ought not be pursued;
2. Gain prime access to mass communication institutions and systems;
3. Employ artists (not scientists, social workers or counselors) to professionally manipulate images, beliefs, stereotypes, attitudes and sentiments into high-impact media messages designed to persuade macro-audiences not to misuse recreational intoxication.

The process of prevention is intricate, but the direction toward which a sound preventive response should move is clear. We must employ those persuasive public communications systems that have worked in the past for others, not provide scaled-down therapy on a random basis to small gatherings.

ARISE: AN ALTERNATIVE TO DRUG USE

Harvey B. Milkman, Ph.D.

Drug/Alcohol Institute
Metropolitan State College
Denver, Colorado

Although most drug users have experienced a variety of psychotropic agents, many experience a prolonged and distinct preference for a particular drug. Using Bellack and Hurvich's[1] Interview and Rating Scale for Ego Functioning, "preferential" users of heroin (N=10) or amphetamines (N=10) were interviewed under conditions of abstinence and intoxication with their respectively chosen drug. Normals (N=10) were interviewed twice while abstinent. Data were analyzed, qualitatively and quantitatively to answer: a) How do preferential users differ from normals and each other under abstinent conditions, b) How do they differ under conditions of intoxication, c) How does the drug user differ within himself under conditions of abstinence and intoxication?

In a sample of more than 30 drug admissions to Bellevue Psychiatric Hospital, more than 75 percent stated a specific preference for either heroin or amphetamine. All subjects had experienced both drugs, but the majority stated a strong preference and prolonged involvement with either heroin or amphetamine. The criteria for drug dependence were intravenous administration and minimal levels of use in the past month (amphetamines more than 9 times; heroin, more than 5 times). Subjects were white, male, middle class, 20-30 years of age and non-psychotic. Each heroin user was interviewed while abstinent and under the influence of 15 mg. morphine, given intramuscularly, in a clinical setting. Amphetamine users were interviewed while abstinent and intoxicated with 30 mg. (oral) dextroamphetamine sufate, also in a clinical setting. Normals were used as a control and interviewed twice while abstinent. Abstinence was determined by self-report and urine analysis. Interviews were spaced 1-2 weeks apart, taped, and the interviewer was blind to subject types and conditions of intoxication. The results pertain to a specific type of drug using population (white, middle class) but may also be applicable to minority groups.

Each subject participated in two semistructured interviews and was rated in accord with Bellak and Hurvich's[1] Interview and Rating

Scale for Ego Functioning. Scoring yields a composite quantitative index of "general adaptive strength", as well as specific scores for degree of impairment in each of 11 specified ego functions: 1) Autonomous Functioning, 2) Synthetic-Integrative Functioning, 3) Sence of Competence, 4) Reality Testing, 5) Judgment, 6) Sense of Reality, 7) Regulation and Control of Drives, Affects and Impulses, 8) Object Relations, 9) Thought Processes, 10) Defensive Functioning, and 11) Stimulus Barrier.(2)The scale also provides measures for Libindinal and Aggressive Drive strengths. The test data were submitted to analyses of variances for comparison of heroin and amphetamine users, under abstinent and intoxicated conditions, with a control group of unintoxicated normals. With the exception of Reality Testing, amphetamine users exhibited significantly higher ego strength than heroin users, whether or not they were intoxicated. Heroin users manifested significantly greater Aggressive Drive strength than amphetamine users and normals under the abstinent condition. Stimulus thresholds were markedly lower in heroin users while abstinent. Ego functioning, in both experimental groups, generally decreased in the intoxicated condition.

Clinical observations, in the abstinent condition, revealed marked differences between heroin and amphetamine users in the management of self esteem and styles of relating. The amphetamine user is characterized by active confrontation with his environment. While the heroin user feels overwhelmed by low self esteem, the amphetamine user utilizes a variety of compensatory maneuvers. He reassures and arms himself against a world perceived as hostile and threatening via physical exhibition of alienated symbols of power and strength. Identification with radical political groups further serves the need for active expression of hostility. Promiscuity and prolonged sexual activity may be the behavioral expression of needs to demonstrate adequacy and potency. High level artistic and creative aspirations are usually unrealized self-expectations, bordering on delusional grandiosity. Such beliefs often lead to compulsive and unproductive behavior. Active participation in hand crafts, music, drawing, or physical labor is striking in nearly all of the amphetamine users interviewed. To maintain his tenuous sense of self as a potentially productive individual, the amphetamine user deploys many defenses. Denial, projection, rationalization, and intellectualization are characteristically observed. Equilibrium is maintained at the cost of great expenditures of psychic and physical energy.

In contrast, conscious of his self-contempt and chronically depressed, the heroin user seeks to avoid confrontation with his surroundings. His major preoccupation is survival. Rarely identifying with people or causes, he believes that satisfaction is achieved through self-indulgence. Like the amphetamine user, he perceives the environment as hostile and threatening, but maintains equilibrium via withdrawal and passive expression of hostility. His parasitic relationship to the community is rationalized by perceiving himself as victim. For the heroin user, interpersonal communication is characterized by an initial front of honesty and openness in the service of opportunism. When the facade is relinquished, the user appears introverted, distrustful, and lacking in conviction. In contrast to the amphetamine user, thinking is more concrete and personalized, and defensive structures are more primitive and fragile. Under stress, repression is easily disrupted, permitting the emergence of self-derogation, hostile fantasy, and impulsive acting out.

As in the case of heroin, the alterations induced by amphetamine intoxication are syntonic with the user's characteristic modes of adaptation. The pharmacologic effect of heroin facilitates the user's ability to reduce anxiety via fantasy, repression and withdrawal. Amphetamine enables the user to more actively confront his environment while relying on intellectualization, projection and denial as primary coping mechanisms. In both cases, an underlying sense of low self esteem is defended against by the introduction of a chemically-induced altered state of consciousness. The drug state helps to ward off feelings of helplessness in the face of a threatening environment. Pharmacologic effect reinforces characteristic defenses which are massively deployed to reduce anxiety.

Differences in personality structure and function, such as those described in preferential users of heroin and amphetamine, provide clues which would permit careful delineation of a variety of treatment programs designed to meet the needs of a particular group of drug users. Prediction of the appropriateness of a particular user to a specific treatment program would increase the likelihood of the user remaining in treatment and increase the likelihood of successful outcome. Choosing the right drug in treating infection or psychosis is recognized as important, often crucial; a likely parallel is suggested in the treatment of drug use. A successful treatment program must provide the user with alternative modes of satisfying those inner needs and wishes previously resolved through drug use. Such alternative modes may include new patterns of discharge, gratification, or defense. Atmospheres may be engineered, whereby adaptive, drug-like regression in the service of ego (ARISE), is facilitated by non-chemical tools. This would allow for the crucial reversal from a pharmacologic to reality based orientation. In the case of heroin, for example, the approach provides a needed alternative to the contemporary and sometimes inhumane treatment of substituting a long acting pharmacologic defense mechanism, methadone. A drug-free residential treatment environment can be structured such that the user indulges his needs for withdrawal and fantasy with freedom to progress to more adaptive developmental levels.

The experimental program (ARISE) will recruit users who have expressed desire to attempt abstinence and cognitive reorganization.

The milieu will seek a balance of male and female residents so that dynamic issues are readily emergent and easily explored. While ethnic and social backgrounds are randomly controlled, there will be an effort to recruit young users (20-30 years of age) who are perceived as having greater potential for self-discovery and growth. Individuals in whom treatment motives may be contaminated by attempts to avoid incarceration are excluded prior to admission. The fundamental wish for productive change is bolstered by a written contract between the Program and client. ARISE participants agree to remain non-violent, abstinent, and within the confines of the center until they decide to discontinue treatment, with a maximum stay of two years. The Program provides room and board and a variety of therapeutic options, and may only initiate termination in case of breach of contract. Although support systems are available for terminated clientele, residential re-entry is not permitted.

Living quarters will include facilities for individual and group participation in activities designed to accommodate the user's underlying need structure. Rooms created as mini-atmospheres are developed to facilitate primary drug related motifs: anger, fantasy, withdrawal and stimulus numbing. These provisions aid in the user's transition to a non-drug orientation by reducing stress through structural reinforcement of characteristic defenses, formerly bolstered pharmacologically. The physical milieu is designed to accommodate self-paced developmental growth. While pictorial and written material with sexual and aggressive contents are readily obtained, a library is designed to provide more sublimated literature and art. Musical instruments, particularly such percussion toys as congas and bongos are available. Construction materials (wood, clay, paint, leathercraft, etc.) and moderately active sport areas (ping-pong, pool) are provided. Sleeping quarters are private and occupied at the user's discretion. A self-paced physical fitness program is included to transmute self-directed anger into life supporting energy.

In contrast to the supra-directive concept of forced therapy used in many residential drug centers, the user will have access to a variety of treatment modalities, on a choice basis. This model promotes internalization of growth inducing constructs while stimulating an increasingly higher sense of competence and self-regard. The perception of self, as victim, in a hostile and threatening environment, gradually dissipates in a climate of acceptance and warmth. The therapy program does include confrontation-encounter-attach groups geared at the productive displacement of aggressive energies. Although Attack Therapy is the core of treatment activities in many drug settings, ARISE offers it as one of a variety of treatment modalities. Biofeedback systems will assist the user in controlling his level of anxiety with the prospect of achieving an altered state of consciousness similar to the opiate experience. After relatively short exposure to the feedback program, control over the specific physiologic "involuntary" function (anxiety) generalizes to a control over more complex behavioral syndromes. The ease of mastering this technique heightens the user's sense of self-worth. Individual and group insight therapies will be offered to those who gravitate toward awareness of their developmental processes. The concepts of Transactional Analysis are readily grasped by academically unsophisticated individuals who are introspectively inclined. For those with a "don't look back" attitude, the more contemporary "now" therapies such as Gestalt, Rational Emotive or Reality are offered. Each has demonstrated utility in the treatment of disturbances in self-regard. Video-feedback in conjunction with psychodrama and other role playing techniques, are additional vehicles for self-exploration. Less crucial treatment modalities are dependent upon the particular predilections and biases of residents and staff.

Residential treatment is terminated upon the user's decision to re-enter the community. He is advised to give ample notice of his departure in order to work through intense attachments formed during his stay. Vocational rehabilitation counseling is available throughout residency, and the user may avail himself of state vocational rehabilitation services after graduation from the milieu. Re-entry into the community is facilitated by community based housing from which the user may participate in a job-related internship, resultant from vocational training. Out-patient psychotherapy is available to all residents, regardless of when they terminate. As "graduations" begin to accumulate, selected staff members will provide continuity of care by follow-up treatment in a community based setting.

Though not explicated in this work, a humanistic and developmental approach is equally applicable in the case of amphetamine use. The basic ARISE format can be used with primary differences in kinds of environmental tools and minimal changes in available therapeutic modalities. Other areas of emotional disorder could be approached in a similar fashion. Schizophrenia and geriatrics, for example, might better be handled through the careful engineering of an environment more suitable to specific client needs.

REFERENCES

1. L. Bellak and M. Hurvich, J. Nerv. Ment. Dis., 148, 569-585 (1969).

2. The scale for Adaptive Regression in the Service of the Ego and the scale for Superego were dropped from our study because of insufficient reliability in our population.

ALTERNATIVES AS A PROCESS -
DEVELOPMENT FOR ITS OWN SAKE

By William O. Zaslow, Deputy Director
Sanford Schwartz, Evaluation Specialist

St. Louis County Office of
Drug Abuse Prevention

The Office of Drug Abuse Prevention (ODAP) has been
operational in St. Louis County, Missouri since June
1975 with a staff of forty-two (42). The County encompasses some 500 square miles and consists of roughly
one million residents. St. Louis County is composed
of ninety-four (94) municipalities and numerous unin-
corporated areas accessed only by County Government
services.
    The formation of ODAP represented a marked change
in local government service provision. County
Government, by underwriting the Alternatives approach,
redefined the nature of the drug problem and Government's
role for intervention in that problem. Traditionally,
government's stance had been one of providing direct
services based on its own perceptions of both need and
appropriate response to that need. ODAP's belief was
that every community had the potential for identifying
and marshalling indigenous resources to deal with the
issue of drug abuse in a viable, constructive fashion.
Not only must an alternatives program deal with the root
causes of people abusing themselves through chemicals,
it must begin at the grassroots level.
    How one defines a problem largely determines
what (if anything) is done about it, the foci and
techniques of intervention and, consequently, excludes
certain other methods of problem solving. For example,
an ever-present criminal menace is markedly different
from a chronic medical or social problem in the public
reactions, funding priorities and operational programs
that may emerge. In the case of drug abuse, the type
of action (or inaction) taken will depend on whether

156

causes are seen as residing within individuals or within the environment. For at least the past 100 years, American society's perceptions of and attitudes toward drug dependent persons were explained in terms of the personal characteristics of the addict. This view fostered responses oriented toward micro-system interventions (e.g. law-enforcement and rehabilitation). Not until recently has the drug problem been framed in an ecological context wherein the environment is seen as playing an important causative role in the illicit misuse of chemical substances.

This approach views the addict as a victim beset upon by a mob of forces, and addiction as a symptom of other, more basic "problems" - alienation, boredom, frustration, and so on. What has emerged is the current trend toward primary prevention; community-based efforts with the dual focus of educating the entire community in ways of coping with and responding to a rapidly changing society as well as convincing important local decision-makers that a responsibility exists for the community to fulfill the broad range of legitimate human needs experienced by its residents. When the community accepts the environmental definition that societal forces contribute to abusive behavior, it simultaneously must accept some responsibility for rectifying the situation. The community, not just the "problem individual", must change.

The scope of the problem as represented by this definition is often seen as unmanageable by the community. The prevention programmer must engage the group in a process of sharing and clarifying their underlying assumptions. Once clarified, policy implications can be discussed from a common vantage point.

When a problem appears to be unmanageable, two basic options for resolution exist. Either the magnitude of the problem can be reduced to a "workable" level, or, the resources to deal with the seemingly unmanageable problem can be enhanced. Historically, attempts to limit the perception of the problem have yielded stop-gap, panacea-like interventions (e.g. State and Federal laws and uni-dimensional treatment modalities). The prevention approach, however, based on the scope of the problem as defined, precludes minimizing the situation and demands a multi-faceted approach. However, merely surfacing the complexity of the issue is not enough. Without the resources to provide alternatives at the grassroots level, a governmental dependency can result.

Traditionally, communities have tended to look elsewhere for a means of coping with substance abuse problems. As an agency of Saint Louis County Government, the Office of Drug Abuse Prevention's

community approach is geared to helping communities
marshall their own resources and develop their own
alternatives; movement away from mega-government. On
the belief that each community has, within itself, many
of the resources to deal with those abusing themselves
through chemicals, the program's field efforts focus
on brokering and facilitating alternative processes
within existing systems. Resources may range from an
initial willingness to acknowledge a problem, through
a core of volunteers mobilized to deal with a problem
to a well-developed service network designed to assist
clients-at-risk.

The community developer, when operating out of the
central assumption that he alone possesses the skills,
knowledge and ability to implement short-term projects
beyond the reach of the community at a particular
place in time, can provoke a natural rivalry between
the provider (himself) and the recipient of service
(the community). Community development is, in this
instance, perceived by the citizens as an enforced
process initiated through confrontation and metered-out
with considerable power. In these instances, development
becomes single-issue oriented, situational and often
unrepresentative of the community's actual needs.

What appears to offer a more long-term solution
to community-defined social problems is an engaging
process encompassing many of the basic tenets of community development. Attention must be paid to the
development and maintenance of this process or alternative projects may well fall short of their goals. The
following steps are part of a continuing sequence
utilized by the St. Louis County Office of Drug Abuse
Prevention. These individual areas of emphasis facilitate the prevention programmer's entrance into and
working with local communities in efforts to deal
with drug-abuse issues.

The sequence consists of six steps:

1. ASSESSMENT: the process through which the needs and
   values of the community are surfaced. Information
   is gathered in this phase from such sources as
   small group discussions among community residents,
   surveys, interviews with significant policy makers,
   census and other demographic data, arrest statistics, etc. The information generated from the
   above sources helps crystalize the formulation of
   the problem statement focusing through community
   value structures. It sets the direction of
   thinking about and acting on the problem. Values
   will strongly affect the community's interpretation of the data and therefore must be fully
   explored.

2. INVOLVEMENT: encompassing the contact with and motivation of significant community resources surrounding the issues raised in the assessment phase. The prevention network begins to form as contacts are made and new resources identified. It becomes a sounding board for many of the central assumptions generated by the assessment and forms the nucleus of those committed to take action around the perceived need.

3. EDUCATION: a mutual process wherein the theoretical knowledge of the prevention practioner is of equal value with the community's understanding of its own machinations. It is at this stage, in particular, where the problem to be tackled may appear to be insurmountable. The inconsistent blending of the theoretical and the situational, serves to upgrade citizen resources to manage the problem in all its complexities. As the skills and confidence of the group increase, they find themselves more willing to enter the developmental stage.

4. DEVELOPMENT: the process of generating action strategies, goals, and time frames. At this point the involved, educated participants solidify personal committments and assign individual and group tasks parameters around previously assessed needs.

5. IMPLEMENTATION: the process of mobilizing those involved to do what is needed. Tenets of program design, learned in earlier phases, are now actualized around specific goals. The program/project is operational.

6. EVALUATION: the re-examination of both the product and the process wherein the group reassesses where they have gone and how they got there. Feedback from the participants is encouraged and dealt with so as to apply current lessons to future projects.

These six phases, although sequenced, are highly interactional. The headings of each phase serve to function more as area of emphasis rather than as discrete activities. Each step is a mini-process consisting of the six phases described. Within each phase, all the others occur.

For example, the need to fully undertake an Assessment process varies depending upon the amount of readily accessible existing data. Therefore, one must assess the need for assessment, the manner in which it will be accomplished, and the scope of such activities. The Assessment phase offers easy access for the programmer into the community and initiates the potential for a non-partisan willingness to fully examine the community's needs. It becomes a focal point of involvement, wherein community members

develop ownership of and input to the product. The
community begins a mutual educational process with the
programmer, as to the identification of resources,
methodological concerns and the responsibilities inherent in acting on the acquired data. Development of
assessment instruments and strategies occurs, tasks are
assigned and commitments generated. The assessment
process is then implemented along the prescribed course
with all parties involved in and responsible for the
product. The results of the assessment are then
evaluated as to the process of development and the
outcome of the instruments used. Data is compiled and
conclusions are drawn.

The evaluation phase of the model likewise relies
upon each step of A-I-E-D-I-E process. The initial
need for an evaluation component must be fully assessed
by community participants. A preliminary idea is developed concerning how and what kinds of information
should be collected and monitored. Involvement
in and education about the methods and problems of
program evaluation follow wherein the prevention
programmer can encourage the community group to
explicate their expected measurable outcomes. An
appreciation for systematic evaluation of one's
efforts as a feedback mechanism is engendered. An
evaluation strategy can then be developed after the
above input is received. Accompanying this will be
the delineation and assignment of specific tasks in the
evaluation design. The agreed-upon procedure is then
implemented and the data collected. At this point the
community group will be able to examine the fruits of
its labor, discuss the strengths and shortcomings
(i.e. evaluate) of their evaluation, and make appropriate suggestions for future alterations.

The entire evaluative process represents the culmination of the alternative process for any particular
activity. The evaluation not only monitors the degree
to which the designed activity accomplished its goals,
but also paves the way for the assessment of new
community directions - towards the solution of a
broader scope of selected problems. The assessment
and evaluation phases as described above are illustrative of the way in which the other phases (Involve,
Educate, Develop, and Implement) of the process model
are likewise conducted.

A SUCCESSFUL COMMUNITY PRIMARY PREVENTION AND
EARLY INTERVENTION PROGRAM

Ronald J. Gaetano

Broome County Drug Awareness Center
Johnson City, New York

I. PURPOSE

The Broome County Drug Awareness Center, as it exists today, is
the result of almost five years of evolution and it would require
a major undertaking to set down on paper all of this agency's
"learning experience" and the various methods one might utilize
to create a similar program. Rather, it is our hope that this
paper will serve as a description of exactly what the "Center"
is, what it does and why it has been so successful. If, after
understanding the essence of the "Center," you are interested in
learning more about it an/or how you might establish a similar
program, just contact us; we are more than willing to share.

II. HISTORICAL PERSPECTIVE

Drug Abuse has been a topic of concern in this country for many
years, however, it was not until the mid 1960's that the street
crime in Washington D.C., heroin addiction among GI's in South
Vietnam, and evidence that heroin use was spreading to middle-
class suburbs created concern. Consequently, President Nixon conceived what has been described as "a limited heroin war, nothing
else." In New York State, Governor Rockefeller initiated a similar war in 1968 with the creation of the Narcotic Addiction Control Commission. The emphasis was on narcotics, addiction, and
rehabilitation. Governor Rockefeller announced in 1973 that the
New York State effort "achieved very little permanent rehabilitation, and we have found no cure." In late 1973, federal officials
optimistically declared that they had "turned the corner" on her-
ion use, only to have to retract that proclamation shortly after
when it was found that use was again increasing.

Why weren't these federal and state efforts successful? There
was no money shortage; the federal efforts have cost the taxpayer
more than $1 billion since 1971 and the New York State effort more
than $826 million since 1966. We feel these efforts were doomed

to very limited success because they concerned themselves almost entirely with the treatment and rehabilitation of the addict. Common sense dictates that earlier involvement such as primary prevention and early intervention offer greater hopes of success. Early intervention programs would prove the obvious, that almost all narcotic users were involved in polydrug, non-opiate abuse long before their involvement with narcotics.

In Broome County, which has an urban/suburban population of 200,000 and a rural population of 50,000, and a heterogenous mix of economic and ethnic and racial factors, the full-spectrum of drug and drug related problems can be found. In 1971, under the state given title, <u>Narcotics</u> Guidance Council, the Broome County Drug Awareness Center was established.

III. THE CENTER – WHAT IS IT?

The Center is a humanistic program based on the premise that the community is responsible for the solution of their own problems and that involvement is the key to any community problem. It's goal then was to mobilize the community and coordinate all of its resources, both human and material, to provide for effective prevention and control of drug abuse. Our strategies? Primary prevention and early intervention. Our tools? Education programs, a 24-hour hotline, and an ongoing counseling program.

<u>Educational Programs</u> – the education of the community regarding drugs is one of the brightest hopes for reducing drug abuse. The Center's education programs include such wide-ranging topics as pharmacology, law, self-awareness, role playing, drug problems (where to go), and a general drug overview. In 1975, the Center provided 159 programs for schools, colleges, businesses, civic and church groups. Nearly 10,000 individuals were present.

<u>Twenty-four Hour Hotline</u> – this is an information, referral, and crisis intervention service. The Center's buildings are open 9 AM to midnight but our hotline is in operation around the clock. In 1975 there were 967 requests for assistance received on our hotline. The immediate objective of the hotline is to take care of the crisis or provide information; the long range objective is to establish follow-up contact and, if needed, provide ongoing counseling.

<u>Ongoing Counseling Program</u> – this program is operated on an outpatient, drug-free basis and last year 448 individuals participated in this, and since the average client remained in the program for just over five months, our static capacity was 192 clients. Approximately 45% of our clients are referred by an agency, i.e., criminal justice system, school, hospital, social services, while the remainder are self-referrals or referred by their parents or friends.

The program makes no pretense of a clinical type of service; counseling is kept on a very practical basis and in most cases is a combination of education and problem solving. The technique most closely resembling what we do is Reality Therapy. Counseling takes place in coordination with ancillary services supplied by the Center itself, i.e., medical care, legal representation, welfare, psychiatric care, emergency food, clothing and housing. The primary service methodology for referring clients for services is the walk-through process whereby the client is accompanied to the various service agencies and their services are considered as an adjunct to our program, not as a substitute for it.

As the client fulfills his specific goals and demonstrates progressive behavior, he becomes more responsible and there is a gradual reduction of program requirements levied on him. Clients are not released immediately after a reduction in drug use and achievement of goals are met for it is felt that a re-integration process is essential to prevent backsliding. Thus, as the client is initially walked-through his individual treatment plan with the assistance of his counselor, he gradually works his way out of the treatment plan to function independently.

The average client is seen once a week. Our cost per slot is less than one quarter that recommended by the New York State Office of Drug Abuse Services for an outpatient, drug free program. The clients as well as the recipients of the education and hotline services are by no means limited to the young; drug abuse is not a problem of youth alone, for instance, we have found that the elderly take a lot of different drugs; they self-medicate. Yet most persons over 50 have never had a proper health education.

IV. THE VOLUNTEER CONCEPT

Involvement is the key to any cmmunity problem. Our volunteers offer the program a vast reservoir of knowledge and skills as well as the acting as the hands and legs, as well as the heart of the Center.

Our volunteers are divided into two groups. First, are the regulars, those who actually come to the Center to perform such tasks as counseling, phone rappers, typists, tutors, and clerical assistants. Secondly, are the special-help volunteers who act in such roles as medical, legal, and pharmaceutical consultants, trainers, and general manpower for specialized tasks. Our volunteers range in age from 15 to 60. Of our regular volunteers, 29% are currently high school or college students, 73% have had at least some college. Of our special-help volunteers, 75% have a four year or graduate degree from college.

Our recruitment of volunteers is a combination of publicity provided by local press, radio, and television coverage and our own outreach efforts. Most notable in our recruitment efforts is the self-propagating nature of our volunteer program. Almost 90% of our volunteers were recruited by people already involved at the Center (volunteer and paid staff members, clients) as opposed to referrals by other agencies or through the media. In addition 21% of all our volunteers either were clients, were parents of clients or were recruited by a client. A survey of the volunteer effort last year concluded that an estimated $120,000 worth of volunteers' hours were spent at our Center in 1974.

A basic eight-hour training course, which covers such topics as basic pharmacology, communications and phone rapping, the law, self-awareness and Center orientation, is required of all volunteers. Written materials accompany lectures and discussions. Advanced training sessions are held once a week on various topics of interest.

A newsletter, the "Center Bulletin" is distributed every other month to all volunteers. The Bulletin relates information regarding the Center's work and upcoming events and training as well as reporting on events on the state and national drug abuse prevention efforts.

V. DEMONSTRATED SUCCESS

The Center conducted a very successful research and demonstration project involving referrals from the criminal justice system in 1974-1975. The project is being considered by the National Institute on Drug Abuse and the National Association of Counties as a prototype. It was also presented as the topic of a workshop at the Annual Convention of the North America Association of Drug and Alcohol Problems. Currently we are conducting an education/training project for the National Free Clinic Council.

We have found that working with the drug abuser in the early stages of abuse does offer a great deal of hope for success. Our client's polydrug use - primarily marijuana and alcohol with some use of inhalants, hallucinogens, amphetamines, and barbiturates, is reduced in 90% of our cases.

It is our opinion that drug programs are faced with a very important decision. They can continue to demand higher degrees and pay more for professionals available on a 9-5 basis or they can develop economically reasonable programs such as ours. Such a program must be based in the community and the staff must be willing to respond immediately to those in need of their services.

Senator Jacob Javits has stated that "logic, common sense and honesty have had very little to do with the evolution of the national drug policy in the last 40 years." The 1975 Federal Strategies claimed to, at long last, have recognized that primary prevention and early intervention are essential yet they still almost totally ignore those strategies. At the proceedings of the 7th Annual Eagleville Conference, the following was said of the young polydrug user. "Although the population should be studied and researched to provide an understanding of what is truly happening at all levels of America's drug scene, it is uncertain whether massive funding and specialized treatment efforts to stop these individuals from using psychoactive drugs would be either successful or cost efficient." Drug abuse officials should be cognizant of the fact that tertiary prevention, the treatment and rehabilitation of seriously dysfunctional and addicted drug users has already been proven almost totally unsuccessful and _very_ expensive. The Eagleville Conference did note that "the capacity for early intervention does not exist at the present time. In most cases where substance abuse treatment capabilities exist, treatment is confined to heroin or alcohol delivery systems."

If it is at all true that, as the 1975 Federal Strategy states, "since the expansion of the federal efforts in the early 1970's, the Federal Government better understands the nature of the drug abuse problem in America," one should look forward to those officials leadership in the areas of primary prevention and early intervention, where there lies great potential for real success in containing and eventually reducing this country's drug abuse problem.

AN EARLY INTERVENTION DRUG PROGRAM

Edward Gottheil, M.D., Ph.D.

J. Anthony Rieger, M.Ed.

Bruce Farwell, M.S.

Daniel Lieberman, M.D.

Department of Psychiatry and Human Behavior
Thomas Jefferson University
Philadelphia, Pennsylvania

Although most patients admitted to Jefferson's drug-free, day treatment "Transition" program are seriously addicted adults, a small number have been polydrug using or abusing adolescents. As some of these youngsters responded to treatment, returned to school and continued to attend the program on an outpatient basis after school hours, a closer liaison developed between Transition and the personnel of these schools who then wished to refer additional patients to the program. During the summer school break, 25 drug using junior high school students in alternative programs were accepted for full day treatment services. Only six of these patients did not attend regularly throughout the summer and anecdotal reports from staff, students and parents were positive.

In view of these encouraging trends, the cooperation of Junior High Schools A and B was enlisted and a pilot project was planned for the fall school term which included data gathering for purposes of evaluation. The rationale for making Transition's services available to this population of less severely impaired individuals was that these youngsters, confused and often frightened, were felt to be at a stage in the development of their pattern of drug use where a series of positive experiences in a non threatening, non drug rewarding environment could possibly provide alternatives to drug abuse and the impetus to begin trying to function more effectively in a socially approved manner.

The referring schools A and B were located in South Philadelphia: A was approximately half white and half black while B was predominantly black in population. The 19 students from A were all in the alternative program: 12 were white and 7 black; 15 were male and

4 female. There were 23 students from B and all were black: 14 were in the alternative program and 9 were in regular classes; 17 were male and 4 were female. The group ranged from 12 to 16 years in age. They had been recognized by their teachers or school counselors as having problems with drugs and alcohol and were also found to have emotional, behavioral and family problems. They were not functioning well in school and were often truant. Approximately 75% were from families receiving public assistance. Control groups were selected at random from the remaining students in the same classes as the individuals in the treatment groups.

The students in the treatment groups were rostered at Transition by their schools for either a full morning or afternoon session once a week. They attended in groups of 8 to 12 and met with 3 or 4 staff members. The Transition staff viewed drug dependence as a symptom of dysfunction in personal, family and social adjustment. Drug dependent patients were seen as having difficulty in talking about or recognizing these dysfunctions, controlling behavior, expressing feelings, maintaining self-esteem and communicating with others. Treatment techniques were required, therefore, which would give them a chance to express themselves and to learn to deal more effectively with these attitudes, feelings and interpersonal behaviors. Group methods were used to provide opportunities for attempting less destructive alternative styles of coping with anxieties aroused by daily frustrations and interactions with others. Treatment plans and goals stressed positive growth experiences aimed toward self-acceptance and behavioral change. A considerable portion of the daily schedule was devoted to expressive forms of treatment in group settings. Music, art, relaxation, role-playing and recreational therapies were used extensively with particular emphasis placed on videotaping these activities for later feedback. Discussions during playback sessions focused on specific behaviors, expressions of feeling and relationship patterns (1,2,3).

Our evaluation following completion of the fall term was based on anecdotal reports and an examination of attendance records and grades in academics, behavior and work habits for the fall term and for the preceding spring term prior to the pilot project. It was observed during the course of the fall project that many of the patients became more free in discussing their personal problems and feelings in groups, formed relationships with staff members and requested individual counseling sessions. In several cases, family members visited Transition and became involved in treatment. Relationships among the youngsters became closer and acting out incidents decreased. Only 2 of the 42 patients did not complete the full program.

The staff maintained a high level of enthusiasm for the program and their work with these adolescent patients. There were frequent descriptions at staff conferences of how a patient who was hostile or another who was retiring had been made aware of their behaviors during ping pong, role-playing or videotaping and were making progress in developing alternative behaviors. School counselors and teachers also reported improved attention, behavior and relationships with others and decreased observable indications of drug use. We learned that some teachers and parents even used attendance at Transition as a reward for positive behavior in school and at home.

The attendance records of the treatment groups improved from spring to fall at both schools A and B to a greater degree than did the attendance of their respective control groups. Analysis of variance indicated that these differences were statistically significant (p.<05). Five of the remaining 6 comparisons for academics, behavior and work habits favored the treatment groups but these differences did not reach significance. The change in average attendance for the treatment groups was not due to only a few patients who improved markedly: 17 of the 19 patients from A (89%) and 15 of the 23 from B (65%) were absent from school less frequently in the fall than they had been in the previous spring. This compares to 56% at A and 29% at B for the control groups. Furthermore, improved attendance was not restricted to days on which the students were scheduled to come to Transition but extended to school attendance in general.

Rosenstock and Hansen (4) found that a small group of young adolescents with behavior problems improved in behavior and adaptability when given group therapy during school hours. Similarly, we found that group treatment for adolescents with drug problems in which students were rostered at the program facility during school hours was beneficial. Furthermore, we found that these generally nonverbal patients responded particularly well to treatment modalities designed to elicit expressiveness and communication such as art, music, recreation and role-playing therapies with videotape playback.

While the treatment groups tended to do somewhat better than the control groups in course grades, behavior and work habits, the differences were not significant. The major finding was in significantly better school attendance. Anecdotal reports were similarly favorable. Since more time in school allows less opportunity for drug taking and less time on the streets, it would appear that a major objective of the pilot project had been achieved. The usual trend toward increasingly poor school adjustment with more and more time on the streets was halted and even reversed for a period of time for these students.

As federal funds have become short, there is more and more emphasis on high priority drugs such as heroin, amphetamine and barbiturates and less emphasis on "less serious" polydrug use and abuse. The recent White Paper on Drug Abuse (5) suggests that "The use of outpatient drug-free slots for low priority drug users should be curtailed, and such funds used to provide effective treatment services for high priority drug users (p.72)." Nevertheless, we believe that opportunities for secondary prevention should not be overlooked. Drug taking adolescents are a clearly demarcated group of high-risk patients for whom primary preventive efforts obviously had not been effective. Early intervention, at this point, if successful, would clearly be a cost-effective approach as well as one which would reduce the personal and social consequences of later chronic addiction. The results of the Transition early intervention pilot project, while preliminary, appear promising. One must be cautious in generalizing from one pilot project, based on small samples from only two schools and a short term follow-up. We believe, however, that further studies of this type are warranted using larger samples, different populations and longer term follow-up periods.

References

1. M. E. Bernal, J. Nerv. Ment. Dis., 148: 375 (1969).
2. E. Gottheil, C. E. Backup, and F. S. Cornelison, J. Nerv. Ment. Dis., 148: 238 (1969).
3. F. H. Stoller, J. Res. Develop. Educ., 1: 30 (1968).
4. H. A. Rosenstock and D. B. Hansen, Am. J. Psychiat., 131: 1397 (1974).
5. White Paper on Drug Abuse. U.S. Govt. Printing Office, Washington, 1975.

SCHOOL-BASED COMMUNITY DRUG PREVENTION SERVICES - A TOTAL APPROACH

Mrs. Alice M. Riddell

Director, Project 25
Community School District 25
Flushing, New York

In September 1971, Project 25, Community School District 25's Drug Prevention Education and Intervention Program, was born after a gestation period of about 3 years.

To refresh the memory, it is important to state here that, at the end of the sixties and the onset of the seventies, New York City was experiencing a drug abuse epidemic. Drug free treatment programs and proponents of methadone recognized, along with legislative, law enforcement, civic and religious leaders, that as quickly as addicted clients were being serviced and returned to society as functioning individuals, hundreds of newly addicted individuals were roaming the streets or crowding the jails.

In addition, statistics revealed that the median age of the active addict was rapidly dropping to the mid and late teens and that drug experimentation had progressed downward from the junior high school to the elementary school.

In desperation, New York State allocated funds for Youthful Drug Abuse Programs (prevention programs) which were made available to school districts throughout the state. The sky was the limit - districts were encouraged to try anything that might work. What a wonderful opportunity to create, develop and implement a comprehensive meaningful program! Many districts decided to develop pilot programs.

Community School District 25 decided to make the full effort. As stated above, for 3 years prior to the inception of Project 25, the community had begun to address itself to its drug problem. Concerned teachers attended the first Narcotics Institute for teachers sponsored by the District Attorney of Queens, Queens College, and the newly formed New York City Addiction Services Agency. Concerned local groups formed organizations focusing explicitly on drug addiction. These included: The Concerned Citizens of Whitestone and Flushing, The Flushing Drug Alert Committee, The Greater

Flushing Drug Abuse Council, REACH, The College Point RARE Association, and Ministers Against Narcotics (MAN).

An Institute, Living Without Drugs, was held in 1970. Each of the
schools in the district was represented at the Institute by a principal, guidance counselor, teachers, and a parent. In addition, 4
or 5 students from each junior high school participated.

By the time money was made available for prevention programs, several basic facts had been clearly identified by various segments of
the district including school personnel, parents' associations,
community groups, business, religious, legal and medical groups,
fraternal and civic organizations, law enforcement agencies, and
the total criminal justice system.

1. The drug abuse problem is a total community problem and the
   school is part of that community.
2. In order to begin to scratch the surface, it would be neces-
   ssary to develop a network service system coordinating all related groups and agencies. Competition within or among
   groups would be counter-productive and counter-therapeutic.
   Individual professional interests would have to be submerged
   for the needs of individuals, families, and communities.
3. It was critical to reach out to students, parents and communities to build communication, to develop awareness and responsibility. Hopefully, action would follow.
4. Services had to be offered by a wide variety of individuals -
   whoever could best meet the needs of an individual. Services had to be available beyond the legal school day.

Thus, an exciting, challenging, new enterprise emerged, - Project
25, - a team approach to the drug problem for the total community.
District 25 is located in Northeast Queens and comprises several
small towns and communities - each unique and distinctive. One
community houses a low-rent city housing project, welfare hotels,
pocket poverty areas, multiple dwellings, and the main business
area. A second community houses a middle-income city housing project, a union cooperative, garden apartments, and some scattered
one and two family homes. A third community consists essentially
of one family affluent homes. A fourth is an old, staid community
separated geographically from the others and having only 2 main
roads in and out. Another consists of a combination of affluent
homes, expensive rental multiple dwellings, and a cooperative.

The population is a microcosm of New York City. Each area is in-
habited by people with different racial, ethnic and cultural backgrounds and different economic status. These include Blacks, Orientals, Spanish speaking from South and Central America, Haitians
and Caucasians; Catholics, Protestants, Jews and others; conservatives and liberals. Segments of each group can be found in the
low to middle income groups.

171

For effective saturation in all of the geographic areas, the district was divided into 6 action clusters. Each cluster consisted of a junior high school and its total community (including elementary and non-public schools and special agencies, i.e. religious, fraternal, civic, business, labor and civil service groups). Each cluster was the same in that the staff positions were identical; however, each cluster was different because of neighborhood areas, various sub-cultures, various religious groups and various economic levels. The cluster team included: 1 Cluster Coordinator; 1 Counselor; 1 Group Worker; 2 Streetworkers; 1 Family Worker; 1 Part-time Secretary. Teams were neighborhood based in order to establish neighborhood identity and be readily available to the community.

Weekly cluster team meetings and weekly job function meetings established ongoing communication, sharing of information, self-evaluation, case consultation, professional development and scheduled assignments for the following week based on team needs and appropriate staff who could best provide the service to the client. The team included professional and para-professional staff with a variety of skills. Some were licensed teachers, some were non-licensed degreed professionals, some rehabilitated drug abusers, some parents of rehabilitated children, some community organizers. All offered a unique quality and contributions of expertise to the program. Most had either lived or worked in the area. The Cluster Coordinator provided direct services in addition to coordinating activities of team members, distributing personnel and services in accordance with the needs of the local area.

Services are categorized in 2 general areas: 1) Prevention services including Magic Circle, Humanistic Education, workshops for parents, teachers and community groups, rap sessions (light groups), peer group training, curriculum development, community liaison, and providing resource material to cluster area; 2) Intervention services including Self-Awareness Groups, individual assistance, family assistance, home visits, parent groups (intensive), 3-5 Program (intensive after-school program), and referrals to Alternate School and other agencies.

Project 25's most intensive service is its Alternate School. Here again, the basic philosophy is a team approach involving therapeutic, psychological and educational services. Students who are identified by the field staff or who are referred by principals, assistant principals, deans, counselors, peers, self or parents for exhibiting negative acting-out behavior might display the following behavioral characteristics: experimentation with or abuse of alcohol and/or drugs; continued fighting in school; truancy; involvement with the criminal justice system; running away from home. The intake and screening process usually takes approximately 3 weeks after the case has been developed by the field staff. Part of the development includes individual assistance for students, parent conferences and consultation with school authorities. Separate informal orientation sessions are scheduled for the parents and the child. Subsequently, an intake interview for both parents and child is scheduled with the program School Psychologist and the Director of the Therapeutic Program. The interview requires 2 to 3 hours. At a weekly clinical meeting, the case is discussed by and with the entire staff of the Alternate School, the Outreach Coordinator (responsible for Alternate School parent program), and the field staff person. The following week the case is discussed by the District Consultative Team which includes the District Guidance Coordinator, the Supervisor of Attendance, a school representative, Project 25 Director, Psychologist and Director of Therapeutic Program. If the client is involved in private therapy or another agency, a representative is invited to the Consultative Team meeting. In other words, all personnel involved in the case participate in the review and decision.

Students who are accepted in the Alternate School attend for an average of 1 year. The student must complete 5 phases with specific behavioral objectives in each phase. The psychologist conducts weekly static groups for identified students, provides individual assistance to specific students, participates in family conferences in addition to his intake and screening responsibilities. He also acts as liaison to mental health agencies, therapists, hospitals and related agencies. The teachers provide individualized instruction on a contract system according to grade and ability levels. Standardized tests, report cards, parent conferences, and high school applications are handled in the same manner as a regular school. Students remain on the home school register and there is no indication on the records that they have been in an Alternate School setting. Teachers meet briefly daily with therapeutic staff before and after class.

The therapeutic program includes morning meetings, seminars, encounter groups, individual assistance and family contact and follow up. Confrontation, commitment and development of individual responsibility are stressed. Peer group pressure is one of the primary tools employed under direction of staff.

Parents of students in the Alternate School are required to attend weekly parent groups. Tuesday groups are for orientation, information, feedback and light groups. Usually, parents of students attending less than 3 months attend Tuesday groups. Thursday groups are regular encounter groups and focus on the parents themselves and their problems as individuals and couples. In order to ascertain progress of clients (students and parents) or lack of it, the Director of Project 25, the School Psychologist and the entire therapeutic staff meet weekly for case review and consultation. Clients are divided into 3 groups which are rotated. This system guarantees that each case is discussed at least once every 3 weeks. A second clinical meeting is held weekly which includes the Alternate School teachers, and related Project 25 field staff. At this meeting crisis situations would be handled in addition to in-depth reviews, new cases, referrals of Alternate School students to other agencies or programs.

This blend of therapeutic, psychological and educational philosophies, approaches, techniques and methodology results in a comprehensive service to each client. Even though the consultation process in itself is difficult and time-consuming, the team approach does work. It forces all staff who are involved in a client's case to jointly discuss the case, design an individual treatment program and continually follow up, evaluate, redesign and re-evaluate. By using the team approach subjectivity is avoided, personal identification and likes or dislikes of individual clients are checked, and the total group ultimately agrees on the prognosis. Consequently, students and parents cannot manipulate staff and staff do not undermine each other. School administrators are always amazed that students who have been chronic "troublemakers", truants, and cutters attend the Alternate School daily and on time. The team approach provides a concentrated focus and effort immediately on any problem.

Since its inception Project 25 has maintained the team approach concept even though the number of staff has decreased over the years due to funding cuts and increased costs. Because of the team approach and the concept of community problem and a total effort, the program has viewed the local universities as part of the community. As a result, an internship program for Criminal Justice students from St. John's University has been operating for 3 years. In addition, health majors in their junior and senior year at Queens College are assigned to Project 25 for field experience.

Project 25's team approach in the field as a cluster team and in the Alternate School can be utilized in any community - inner city, suburban or urban. Internal organization is a key factor in effective implementation. It is and has been a unique experience to have designed a program and have brought together a wide variety of individuals who would not normally ever have come into contact, and experience them functioning as a cohesive, coordinated, dynamic team providing a multiplicity of services to a broad population. We've proven it works. Try it - you will be amazed at the results.

174

PRIMARY PREVENTION AT THE ALPHA CENTER

G. Hale Pringle

Director of Research
Thee Door of Orange County, Inc.
Orlando, Florida

Judi Gregory

Director
The Alpha Center
Orlando, Florida

Rosemary DuRocher

Teacher
The Alpha Center
Orlando, Florida

Drug abuse among adolescents is accepted as a symptom of more real problems such as poor home environment, low academic achievement, insufficient self-control and motivation, and low self-concept. Since, however, these situations are operative and developing into problems long before puberty, there is a real need to intervene at an early age.

The Alpha Center, a prevention and education program cooperatively operated by Thee Door of Orange County, Florida, (a comprehensive drug rehabilitation agency) and The Orange County School System, was developed to work with children, ages 8 to 12 years old, who display maladaptive behaviors both at home and at school. As indicated above, such behaviors are judged to precipitate drug abuse. The purpose of the program is prevention and its philosophy is summarized appropriately by a statement in the 1975 White Paper on Drug Abuse:

> One conclusion well supported by experience is that drug abuse does not occur in isolation, so programs which address the broad developmental needs of children and youth are the most effective in preventing and reducing drug abuse and other forms of self-destructive behavior such as truancy, alcoholism, and juvenile delinquency.

Synopsis of Program Operation

One elementary school is targeted for eleven weeks and teachers, grades three through six, are asked to identify children who are displaying disruptive behavior in the classroom, failing to perform adequately in academic areas, and experiencing some family difficulties. Usually one, two, or three children per classroom qualify. This is not surprising in light of the declaration by the American Psychiatric Association (1964), which estimated between seven and twelve percent of all elementary school children are "emotionally disturbed." Based upon the recommendations of the classroom teacher, guidance counselor, school psychologist, and principal, Alpha Center

175

staff members contact the parents of each child and elicit permission for their child to participate in the program as well as their agreement to participate in weekly parent education classes and/or individual family counseling sessions. Once permission is obtained, for twenty students, pre-testing of academic skills and social behavior is carried out.

When screening is completed, the twenty students are transported to the Alpha Center three days a week where they are involved in an individualized math and reading program, arts and crafts, physical education, individual and group counseling, and other affective group activities.

The center is operated on basic behavior management techniques. Children are encouraged with positive reinforcement and disciplined by involving them in deciding consequences for their inappropriate behaviors. The children return to their regular classroom two days a week.

On the fourth day of each week, substitute teachers replace the regular teachers at the target school leaving the regular teachers free to attend inservice at the Alpha Center. (Each teacher attends a total of three inservice days.)

On the fifth day, the Alpha Center staff is in the targeted school working with the teachers and students. Staff encourage teachers to experiment with suggestions made in inservice and then discuss the experience with the teacher afterwards.

At the end of eleven weeks, the children are returned to their classrooms on a full-time basis and another elementary school is targeted.

Teacher Inservice Training Program

The goal of the inservice program is to expose teachers to several different classroom management techniques and interpersonal communication skills. The teachers are not shown "the way to teach", but rather are encouraged to take parts of each technique and integrate these parts into their own teaching styles in order to promote a more positive classroom environment.

Topics which are covered during the eleven week inservice program are Transactional Analysis, Reality Therapy, Behavior Management, positive reinforcement, and communication skills.

Transactional Analysis is presented in an effort to help teachers understand the development of disruption in the child and to present alternative ways of responding to different children.

Reality Therapy is presented as an alternative means of positive discipline within the classroom. Class meetings are discussed as a preventive measure to disruptive behavior.

Behavior management, contracting, positive reinforcement, and contingency management are also presented as ways of maintaining a positive classroom environment which lends itself to more infrequent displays of disruptive behavior.

Some basic communication skills which allow the teacher an opportunity to express his or her feelings in the classroom are discussed and teachers are encouraged to allow their students to know the teacher as a human being instead of a "role".

All inservice presentations involve teacher participation and discussion. Skills presented are modeled as much as possible by the facilitators. Also, most of the skills are used in the daily operation of the center with the same children with whom the teachers work on a daily basis. Positive classroom management and positive discipline are the goals of each technique presented. It should be noted that since the techniques presented are being used by the inservice presenters on the same children that the inservice recipients must deal with, the presentations have tremendous credibility.

Parents Activities

Parents attend meetings on a weekly basis. The meetings are held in the evenings with four meetings scheduled and the option to have further sessions if the parents so desire. The purpose of the parent meetings is to facilitate discussion among the parents about various means of handling situations with their children. Communication skills, positive reinforcement and problem solving techniques are presented, discussed and experienced during these sessions with direction as to their applicability back in the home. Because some parents are not able to attend these sessions, individual contact is made with them as often as possible.

Funding

Funding is a joint endeavor. Three teachers and a CETA aide, transportation, substitute teachers, a building, utilities, and building maintenance is supplied by the Orange County School Board. A Director, a counselor, a secretary, and all other operating expenses are provided by a grant from the State of Florida Office of Drug Abuse Prevention. (In 1975-76, the Edyth Bush Charitable Foundation will fund Thee Door's portion of the program and there will be a family counselor added to the staff.)

Research Results

The program in Orange County is a research and demonstration grant and as such, data is being collected on the operation and effectiveness of the program. Presentations based on these results have been made at the Florida Educational Research Convention and the National Drug Abuse Convention (where the Alpha Center was one of the four prevention programs in the United States to present).

Data is being collected on children's behavior before and after the program. On one instrument the children were rated by their teachers as significantly better in 17 out of 20 categories. On another, they were better in 4 out of 4 categories.

For the first two schools worked with during the 1975-76 school year, the average gain in math was 2.1 months per child per month in the center (which is 200% of expected gain for "average" children, much less disruptive children). The children were in the center for approximately three months and 86% of the children showed a three month or more gain. The test used was the Wide Range Achievement Test - Arithmetic.

In reading, 60% of the children gained three months or more while in the center. The average gain was four months. The test used was the Woodcock Reading Mastery Test.

Evaluations of the parent groups and the teacher inservice program have been excellent. The teacher comments indicate that several feel that the inservice provided by the Alpha program is the best they have ever attended.

Summary

In conclusion, the goal of the Alpha Center is to promote the prevention of drug abuse by intervening in a child's life at an early age and by involving those significant people in his life, i.e., teachers and parents in a supportive effort to redirect the child so that he will have a greater opportunity to succeed at home, at school, and in society.

More information about the program's operation or evaluation results is available upon request.

Bibliography

[1] American Psychiatric Association. Planning psychiatric services for children in the community mental health program. Washington, D.C.: American Psychiatric Association, 1964.

[2] White Paper on Drug Abuse - A report to the President from the Domestic Council Drug Abuse Task Force, September, 1975.

LOCAL FUNDING OF PRIMARY PREVENTION:
THE SAINT LOUIS COUNTY EXPERIENCE

Edward A. Bodanske, M.A.

Director, St. Louis County Office of Drug
Abuse Prevention (ODAP)

Perspective on the Environment

St. Louis County, Missouri has a 1970 census population of
952,000 making it the single largest jurisdiction in the state of
Missouri. As part of the nation's tenth largest metropolitan
area, the 500 square miles of St. Louis County contain 19 of the
fifty largest cities in the state. During the decade of the sixties, St. Louis County's population increased by 35.2%. St. Louis
County includes 92 cities, towns, and villages, second nationally
in this regard only to Cook County, Illinois. The 1973 assessed
valuation of property in the County was well over $3 billion and
median family income in 1970 was rated at $12,400.

In January of 1975, Gene McNary (R), former Prosecuting Attorney for St. Louis County, took office as County Supervisor. He
brought to that post an interest in and a commitment to drug abuse
prevention and alternatives. On January 15, McNary announced his
intent to establish a "people-to-people approach" to the problem
of substance abuse. He said: "It is my hope that by offering our
young people alternatives to the drug scene, they can be encouraged
to turn away from self-destructive behavior and enhance their own
growth and development as effective citizens." He also called for
establishing a community prevention network throughout the County
with local government providing the funds.

A program concept was developed, based on tenets of Cohen,
Dohner, Delphi II, the U.S.O.E. "Help Communities Help Themselves"
Program, and the National Drug Abuse Training Center youth program
model. Some 42 staff were hired and trained, whose backgrounds
ranged from drug counselors to teachers and from probation officers
to social workers. The new staff began needs assessment, followed
by action planning with civic and citizens' groups, agencies,
schools, churches, and youth themselves. Initiating, brokering,
and facilitating programs for schools, community centers, service
groups, and families started in the late summer of 1975.

As of March 1, 1976, ODAP had developed programs affecting 16,500 people. Examples of the variety of ODAP programs include: DRACON informational services; police training in youth intervention; teacher training; school counselor training; K-8 self-concept development programs; youth needs survey and action planning; outdoors adventure education; emergency department drug abuse training program; League of Women Voters parenting skills; Body-Mind-Spirit Health Fair; shoplifter discretionary diversion program; cab drivers' referral training; summer jobs coordination and solicitation; aid to victims of crime program development; wolf sanctuary and endangered species organizing; parent-child communication labs; opening of 22 field sites in 20 communities; local recreation directors' training; resource network design and coordination; mini-grant team development and technical assistance; and others.

Funding Structure and Issues

The Office of Drug Abuse Prevention receives its half-million dollar funding from two separate federal sources brokered through local government: revenue sharing and the Comprehensive Employment and Training Act (Title I). The $333,400 in revenue sharing comprises all overhead costs, direct programming expenses, and a portion of the salaries. The $215,000 in manpower funds is used only to pay the salaries of field specialists, referral unit specialists, and clerk typists.

Issues to be considered in local government funding are categorized by typology of policy. Promoting economic growth, providing or securing amenities, maintaining traditional services and arbitrating conflicting interests are widely held as broad types of primary prevention; ODAP's function is seen as a blending of amenities and services.

Translating the role of local government in primary prevention to issues of funding programs highlights four basic, political questions. The question of available revenue is clearly foremost. Federal funds amounting to some $21 million annually come to the County from revenue sharing and manpower sources. A trend toward earmarking a portion of those funds for human services is evident in Washington, D.C. and in Clayton, the St. Louis County Seat. The instability of these funds and the difficulty in predicting their quantity from year to year, in many ways is offset by the present drain on general fund or "hard" local tax revenues. It is in that latter category that most of the problems of local government can be found: costs rising at a pace greater than the increase in local taxing authority and receipts. It should be obvious, then, that the definition of "local funding" must be adjusted. For these purposes, the concept of local funding must include all forms of revenue and focus on the ways those funds are spent, be that for roads and bridges, hospitals, or primary drug abuse prevention.

Need is another issue confronting local government policy makers. Incidence and prevalence data, school surveys, client admissions, police reports, etc., all indicate a substantial drug/alcohol problem in the County. Far more significant than those mixed reports is the media interpretation and promulgation of their results. ODAP is expected to justify its existence as a function of need.

Evaluation of the program is a paramount issue to all approving levels of government. The primary prevention approach is slow-going, intangible, and therefore, open to questions. Distinctions between treatment and prevention, while eliminating duplication issues, raise new issues of how to measure and document the use of tax dollars. ODAP is expected to carry on evaluation activities to document progress and show results.

Oversight or monitoring by the County Council and Supervisor is the last of the funding issues. As an agency within the Executive branch, ODAP receives the same oversight as any other department. In addition, requirements for quarterly progress reports, regular budget control, and approval of citizen advisory board appointments were levied by Council.

Strategies for Replication

ODAP's funding structure and way of handling funding issues may be replicable in other local governments. Considering the oversight issue, ODAP's reporting system seems a viable strategy. Based on numbers of contacts, programs sponsored and participants in each, the system attempts to quantify the outreach and intervention function. The County Council performs evaluation/funding review on ODAP, much like a single state agency does on a 409 grant. Therefore, traditional skills of presenting data, documenting need, demonstrating community support, etc., are viable. Clearly, in-house research/evaluation activities are more useful for program development and improvement, but oversight can also be good feedback, particularly as relates to political issues that could be addressed.

A "common sense" approach to drug abuse prevention is an asset to the strategist in local government. Primary prevention is supported by conventional wisdom and has broad appeal if presented properly. Media also provides an on-going monitoring function for the public. Once funded, the program must use media to demonstrate progress, justify expenditures, and to gain community support.

The chief strategy is sharing resources. Although the Office of Drug Abuse Prevention is not a funding agency, ODAP's plan includes facilitating community prevention programs, owned and supported by the communities themselves. ODAP takes an active role in

helping community prevention programs meet financial requirements
by special program funding, resource identification, grants assistance and fund-raising support. All of the strategies relate to
the concept, and education, of the funding source around the concept of primary prevention is the key issue. The support of the
locally elected chief executive is critical for the program's initiation. However, the executive and the legislature must be included fully for program survival.

Conclusion

The ODAP experience includes relying on revenue sharing and
other federal funding programs which plow-back dollars to local
government. Trends indicate more, not less, of these programs in
the future. The wise strategist will understand the potential of
these funds for human services and will begin now to plan access
to and appropriate utilization of such monies.

Demands on local government to take over direct service responsibilities previously owned by the federal government are
rapidly increasing. A sense of the future indicates an accelera-
tion of demands for indirect and health maintenance services, as
well.

Primary prevention inherently includes a movement away from
mega-government. ODAP's role as broker or facilitator places
responsibility on the various communities for real systemic change.
Helping localities develop their own resources also reinforces a
shared responsibility notion. Local government as catalyst or
change agent, as broker or facilitator of preventive interventions
has been called for repeatedly. Shared responsibility is a community programming goal and idea which can be made real through
effective primary prevention initiatives by local government.

The most salient potentiality is concept-peddling. Primary
prevention is politically sound, supportable and cost-effective if
it is tempered with institutional realism. It can be a tool for
a politician, as well as for a disadvantaged group of young people.
It can be a government department as well as a private operation
in an old store front. The point is, it needs to be a part of
local government. Primary prevention needs the structure and accountability of local political processes. An idea whose time has
come, primary prevention has to grow up now. St. Louis County's
experience may serve as a marker for other pioneers.

EVALUATION

A NATIONAL FOLLOWUP STUDY TO EVALUATE THE
EFFECTIVENESS OF DRUG ABUSE TREATMENT. A REPORT
ON COHORT 1 OF THE DARP FIVE YEARS LATER

S. B. Sells, D. Dwayne Simpson, George W. Joe,
Robert G. Demaree, L. James Savage, and Michael R. Lloyd

Institute of Behavioral Research
Texas Christian University
Fort Worth, Texas

Introduction

This is the first report on the post-treatment status of
Cohort 1 of the nationally oriented, NIDA-TCU Drug Abuse Reporting Program (DARP) research on the effectiveness of treatment for
drug abuse. It is a preliminary report since the field work was
completed only within the past month. Nevertheless some gross
results available from firstrun tabulations are believed to be of
general interest.

The overall DARP program involves a file of approximately
44,000 admissions from 52 NIDA-supported agencies between June,
1969 and April, 1973 divided into three cohorts, as follows:

Cohort 1	11,383 patients	23 agencies	admissions between 6-1-69 and 5-31-71
Cohort 2	15,831 patients	36 agencies	admissions between 6-1-71 and 5-31-72
Cohort 3	16,729 patients	50 agencies	admissions between 6-1-72 and 3-31-73

The Cohort 1 population was restricted to daily heroin and other
opioid users, as a result of the legislation under which treatment was funded at that time. The admission criteria were later
broadened and the trends in the subsequent cohorts reflected
increasing percentages of youth, whites, females, and polydrug
users, as well as a shift away from methadone maintenance as the
most frequent treatment modality to outpatient drug-free treatment. Although these cohort samples were large and widely
dispersed throughout the United States the participating agencies
were selected mainly by administrative criteria and the DARP data

185

are not randomly representative of the federally supported drug abuse treatment population.

A treatment episode is only a small interval in the life of each patient and his outcomes at any point in time are influenced by many factors in each individual's total life space in addition to whatever the treatment experience per se may contribute. The task of evaluation research is therefore to identify and measure the relevant developmental and contextual factors and to isolate their effects from that of the treatment experience. In order to achieve results that can be generalized, for guidance of clinical and administrative decisions, it is also necessary to specify the treatment received by each patient and the criteria used to evaluate treatment effectivenes. Since patients vary in their involvement in and patterns of drug use and in their involvement in and prognosis for treatment, patient characteristics must also be specified and included in the data matrix.

Of the 11,383 admissions in Cohort 1, 9574 were eligible for inclusion in the followup study. The net cohort population of 9574 includes two distinct types of methadone maintenance (MM) treatment, three types of therapeutic community (TC), two types of outpatient drug-free (DF) treatment, and inpatient (DT-IP) and outpatient (DT-OP) detoxification, as well as a no-treatment (NT) group who went through admission but did not return for treatment. This is the nearest approximation to a control group available.

The sampling strategy, dictated by the plan to evaluate patient types across and within treatment types, time in treatment, during-treatment criterion performance, and type of termination, favored the restriction of the sample to subgroups for which adequate numbers of cases were available. As a result, only the MM, TC, and DT-OP treatments were sampled, along with an NT group. The sample included mainly Black and White males; Puerto Rican and Mexican-American males and Black and White females were retained only in the MM types in which they had substantial numbers.

The major portion of the field work was carried out by the National Opinion Research Center (NORC) of the University of Chicago under subcontract, beginning about March 1, 1975 and continuing through February, 1976. Interviewing for the agency in New Haven was carried out under a separate subcontract with the APT foundation. The overall response rate of 87% located and interviewed or otherwise accounted for is a reflection of the excellent performance of the outstanding professional organization at NORC and also at APT and a strong argument in favor of using professionals for this critical phase of the research. It is of interest that the response rate was highest for the two structured treatment modalities and lowest (but still exceptionally high) for the NT group, which had the longest interval between termination and followup.

186

Initial Gross Results

For this report we have been able to compare subgroups of the followup sample on three time-period measures for a number of outcome criteria. The three time period measures are: pretreatment level, the baseline representing the 2 months preceding admission; since termination, performance over the entire time from DARP termination to interview, which ranged from 1 year, at one extreme, to up to 6 years, at the other; and at interview, representing the 2-month period ending with the date of interview.

The outcome criteria involve a number of behavioral measures of opioid and nonopioid drug use, alcohol use and problems, criminality, gainful employment, and also return to treatment. The comparisons reported are mainly for a subsample of 1078 Black and White males, who comprise over three-fourths (77%) of the sample interviewed. Four treatment categories are compared: (1) MM, combining the two MM treatment types, (2) TC, combining the three TC treatment types, (3) DT-OP, and (4) NT.

From the data available it is possible to report some overall impressions gained from this followup study.

1. The at-interview levels shown in Table I compare favorably with the end-of treatment levels reported in earlier studies of Cohort 1. Table I shows percentages for 3 time periods for ten criterion measures for the 1078 Black and White males combined. Although some drug use persists, heavy drug use at the time of the followup interview is quite low, criminal indicators and somewhat reduced, and employment is up appreciably. Although the data shown are for any employment, the conclusion implied is supported by other available measures. It appears that alcohol problems may have increased in prevalence since termination from DARP treatment, but the baseline and followup report periods are not fully comparable.

The facts that 61% of this subsample returned to treatment after termination and that 28% were in treatment at interview are of major interest, but present problems. It will be necessary to analyze the other measures further comparing those who returned to treatment and those who did not. Most of those who returned to treatment--regardless of their DARP treatment modality-- returned to methadone maintenance.

From the data presented, subject to analysis of post-DARP treatment effects it appears that genuine post-treatment effects were found and that some degree of therapeutic change did indeed occur. The two major modalities, MM and TC, had clearly superior outcomes to the DT-OP and NT groups on most comparisons, but the DT and NT patients had higher rates of return to treatment and also showed impressive changes. However, because of the extent of post-DARP treatment reported, the NT group may lose some of its value as a comparison group, which is not unexpected.

2. Despite the differences in program duration, the gross post-treatment results for TC patients compare very favorably with those for MM and in some cases look superior. within

187

modalities, increased time in treatment appeared to produce favorable increments in outcomes.

3. Most of the gross comparisons available tend to confirm the clinical judgment of program personnel in that the post-treatment outcomes of individuals reported as having completed treatment are superior to those of all others. However, patients reported as having completed treatment also remained in most treatments longer than others.

4. One of the questions in the followup interview was-- "(No matter how you felt about your own experience there) was the program good enough to recommend it to others at that time?" The answers were overwhelmingly favorable: 83% of the MM patients, 83% of the TC, 72% of the DT-OP, and even 63% of the NT answered yes.

Conclusions

The initial gross results present a favorable picture of the status in 1975-1976 of a sample of patients admitted for treatment at 19 DARP agencies in 1969-1971, mostly between 4 and 6 years prior to the followup interview. There are nevertheless some sobering aspects of the data that will require further careful assessment. These include the large number (61%) of former DARP patients who returned to treatment, and the substantial number (over 25%) who reported living with other regular drug users after leaving treatment. Despite reduction of their drug habits and some success in finding jobs, many of these individuals continue to have close ties with the drug culture and feel a need for the kind of support that they received from their treatment program.

Acknowledgment

The work upon which this publication is based was performed under Contract H81 DA 01598-02S1 by the National Institute on Drug Abuse, Department of Health, Education and Welfare. This project is part of a nationally oriented research program pursued jointly by NIDA and IBR staff members since 1968. The continuing interest and support of Dr. Robert DuPont and the NIDA staff have contributed significantly to the effective completion of the research. The interpretations and conclusions presented in this report do not necessarily reflect the position of the National Institute on Drug Abuse or the Department of Health, Education and Welfare.

Table I

Percentages of Followup Subsample of 1078 Black and White
Males Described by Ten Criteria at Three Periods:
Pretreatment, Since Termination, and At Interview

| | Percentage of Subsample | | |
	Pretreatment	Since Termination	At Interview
Any Illicit Drug Use[a]	100	73	34
Any Nonopioid Use	62	54	23
Any Opioid Use	87	64	23
Daily or Weekly Nonopioid Use[a]	34	34	9
Daily Opioid Use	73	46	6
Any Time in Jail	75[b]	47	12[c]
Any Illegal Support	51	not avail.	18
Any Part-Time or Full-Time Employment	40	90	52
Any Major Problem with Alcohol	8[b]	24	7
Enrollment in any Other Treatment	52	61	28

[a] Does not include marijuana use.
[b] Unlike other variables, this is a life-time figure.
[c] An additional 11% were booked on criminal charges during the
2-month period preceding the interview.

PARAMETERS DEFINING THE ABILITY TO REMAIN ABSTINENT
AFTER DETOXIFICATION FROM METHADONE: A SIX-YEAR STUDY

Barry Stimmel, M.D., Edith Rotkopf,
Murry J. Cohen, M.D.

Departments of Medicine and Psychiatry
Mount Sinai School of Medicine of
The City University of New York
New York, New York

Three hundred and thirty-five persons successfully detoxified from
methadone maintenance were followed for six years to determine
their ability to remain free from narcotic use once abstinent. A
follow-up was able to be obtained on 269 (80%) of the 335 detoxifications. This represents a total of 6,965 person-months' exposure, with a mean person-month exposure of 20.8.

At the conclusion of this study, only 93 (28%) were found to remain
abstinent subsequent to detoxification. Narcotic use had occurred
in 155 (46%), with 6% of persons either dead or imprisoned and 20%
unknown. A demographic comparison with respect to ethnicity, sex,
family composition, employment, education and age on admission,
and years of private drug use revealed no significant difference
in any of these parameters with the exception of family composition. Of those individuals living alone, only 13 (24%) were found
to be narcotic free, with 33 (60%) having relapsed to narcotic use
(p=0.01).

A study of the relation of outcome to length of time on methadone
maintenance revealed that only 17% of those persons on methadone
maintenance for less than 12 months were able to maintain a drug-
free state (p < 0.01). In addition, with increasing duration of
methadone therapy, the percentage of individuals able to maintain
a narcotic-free state slowly increased from 46% of persons in
therapy from 12 to 23 months to 71% of persons in therapy from 48
months or longer. A significant relationship could not be demonstrated between outcome and length of time in follow-up.

This study relates to a program funded by the New York State
  Office of Drug Abuse Services.

190

The reason for detoxification in the 335 patients was reviewed. All patients were classified according to the following reasons for detoxification: 1) voluntarily discontinued; 2) violated rules; 3) arrested, and 4) treatment completed. Only 58 (17%) of the entire group of patients were considered to have completed treatment. Approximately 60% represented patients who were voluntarily discontinued or violated program rules. Arrests counted for 24% of detoxifications. Those individuals who were considered to have completed treatment had a considerably greater ability to remain narcotic free, with 42 (92%) of the entire group remaining abstinent through the period of follow-up ($p < 0.001$). Only 28% of those who voluntarily discontinued, 18% of those who violated rules, and 16% of those who were arrested were able to remain abstinent. No deaths were recorded in the treatment completed group and no persons were found to be in jail in this group at the conclusion of the study.

Demographic analysis of the treatment completed group compared to other groups revealed a significant difference only with respect to family composition and duration of methadone maintenance. Those individuals in the treatment completed group had a significantly greater duration of methadone maintenance, 29.8 v. 11.2 months, respectively ($p < 0.01$). With respect to family composition, only 5% of individuals in the treatment completed group lived alone as compared to 28% of persons in the other categories ($p = 0.001$).

In an attempt to define the characteristics of a group with a high probability of remaining narcotic free subsequent to detoxification from methadone, a multivariate analysis was performed. This analysis was able to correctly classify 68 of 93 (73%) narcotic-free persons and 142 of 175 (81%) persons in the other categories ($p < 0.01$).

The few most important variables in this analysis were found to be: reason for detoxification, length of follow-up, and duration of methadone maintenance, with reason for detoxification alone able to give significant discrimination ($p < 0.01$), being the single most important variable in distinguishing between narcotic-free groups and others.

Results of the study indicate that it is possible to achieve abstinence subsequent to detoxification from methadone; however, abstinence does not appear to be a realistic goal for all, and, if premature, detoxification from methadone with subsequent relapse to illicit heroin use is quite prevalent. It should be emphasized that this study only defines the ability of an individual to remain abstinent after initial detoxification from methadone maintenance. It is completely possible that individuals relapsing to narcotic use were subsequently able to achieve and maintain the abstinent state. It is also recognized that

abstinence from narcotic use does not in itself necessarily signi-
fy optimal functioning. Nonetheless, the current study indicates
that it is possible for some to progress from methadone maintenance
to abstinence and remain so for prolonged periods.

This study did indicate, however, that the single most important
factor in predicting the ability of a person to remain abstinent
was found to be a consensus among trained professionals that the
full benefits of methadone maintenance have been realized. The
presence of qualified staff in treatment programs is thus essential. This point is especially pertinent since the trend with respect to funding appears to be in the direction of minimizing both
the number and quality of treatment personnel. The data in this
study suggest that such a direction is not warranted.

A TWO-YEAR FOLLOW-UP ON PATIENTS
THERAPEUTICALLY DETOXIFIED FROM METHADONE MAINTENANCE

William Panepinto, M.S.W.
Frances Silver, M.S.
Gennaro Ottomanelli, Ph.D.
Benjamin Kissin, M.D.

Division of Alcoholism and Drug Dependence
Department of Psychiatry
Downstate Medical Center - State University of New York
Kings County Hospital
Brooklyn, New York

The methadone maintenance treatment approach to heroin addiction has succeeded in socially rehabilitating large numbers of addicts, as shown in early studies by Gearing (1). These studies were conducted on an addict population which was predominantly male, about 35 years of age, with at least a ten-year addiction history, and a record of numerous arrests and incarcerations. Since the early 1970's, a significant number of addicts entering methadone treatment have been in their early to mid-twenties with two-to-five-year addiction histories, lower rates of arrests and incarcerations, and more stable family and community ties (2).

Reported attempts at detoxification of patients in methadone maintenance programs have been quite discouraging. Chappel, Skolnick and Senay (3) have reported that one year after the start of detoxification, just 18.7% (14/75) of patients in the methadone maintenance clinic remained abstinent. Rabin and Stimmel (4) noted that of 168 patients who attempted detoxification, only 17% (34 patients) remained abstinent.

I. STUDY METHOD

A. Sample

The Family Maternity Clinic of the Kings County Addictive Disease Hospital has been treating a population of younger addicts since its inception in November 1971. The sample consisted of the 62 patients who completed detoxification from July 1972 to January 1974.

Women constituted 71% (44/62) of the sample. The average age of the women was 22.4 years, that of the men, 26.0 years. The sample was 77.4% black (48 patients), 11.3% white (7 patients), and 11.3% Puerto Rican (7 patients). This study sample appeared to be representative of the total clinic population. Since detoxification during pregnancy has many special considerations, all women who began their detoxification during pregnancy were excluded from the study.

B. Follow-up Procedures

Approximately one year after the group had detoxified, a clinic follow-up was made which examined patient contact in treatment after detoxification. Community follow-up, approximately two years after detoxification, evaluated outcome status by utilizing two data sources. A request was made to the Community Treatment Foundation, Methadone Information Center, to conduct a data search of the 62 patients in the study as to current registration in a methadone maintenance program, and history of methadone registration at any time after discharge from the Family Maternity Clinic. The follow-up team of the Drug Division conducted clinical interviews with study subjects and obtained patient self-report information and urinalysis results.

II. RESULTS

A. Results of the One-Year Clinic Follow-Up

1. OUTCOME OF DETOXIFICATION

Of the 62 patients completing detoxification, 44 (71.0%) remained drug free and in contact with the program an average of 11.5 months, and a range of 6-25 months.

Nine patients (14.5%) completed detoxification, but relatively soon thereafter requested a return to methadone treatment in the Family Maternity Clinic. These patients remained abstinent for an average of 4.0 months, with none drug free for more than six months. Nine patients (14.5%) were detoxified and soon dropped out of treatment. This last group was drug free an average of 2.7 months before losing contact with the program and none remained in contact more than six months.

2. AVERAGE METHADONE DOSAGE BEFORE DETOXIFICATION

The patients who remained drug free had been stabilized on an average methadone dose of 53.6 mg per day. The patients who returned to methadone received an average of 63.3 mg. However, those patients who dropped out of treatment had been stabilized on an average of 26.7 mg prior to detoxifying.

3. TIME IN TREATMENT BEFORE DETOXIFICATION

The patients who remained drug free were in treatment an average of 9.7 months before detoxification began. Those who returned to methadone were in treatment an average of 12.4 months. The patients who dropped out after detoxifying were in treatment only 4.1 months before beginning the procedure.

B. Results of the Two-Year Community Follow-Up

1. FOLLOW-UP PROCEDURES

Follow-up personal interviews, including urine examinations, were completed on 27 of the 44 patients who were reported as drug free in the first evaluation. These clinical interviews by a member of the follow-up team or by the clinic counselors indicated that 20 of the 27 patients had remained drug free according to patient self-report and urinalysis result.

2. DATA BANK SEARCH

The data bank search revealed that in every case the 20 patients who reported themselves as drug free in the interview had no current methadone registration or history of registration as reported by the data bank search. The 7 patients who reported themselves as having returned to methadone maintenance or illicit drug abuse, had either a history of methadone registration or current registration.

3. SUCCESS RATE

Therefore, of the 44 patients considered drug free at the first evaluation, 20 of the 44 patients (45.4%) have remained drug free. It is important to note that the 20 successful patients have been so for an average of 28.9 months, with a range of 19-37 months.

4. TIME IN TREATMENT

The 20 patients who were successful, were in treatment an average of 15.3 months after completing detoxification, with a range of 6-30 months.

5. ADDITIONAL DATA

The data bank search indicated that of the 17 patients who could not be located for a follow-up interview, 14 had no current methadone registration or history of registration. A chart review also revealed no objective data to indicate drug abuse by any of these 14 patients. However, since none of these 14 patients could be located for a follow-up interview, they have not been considered as having remained drug free. It is possible that some of these patients indeed are still drug free, so that the true two-year success rate may fall somewhere between the documented lower level of 32.3% (20/62 patients) and the possible upper level of 54.8% (34/62).

III. DISCUSSION

The principal finding of this paper is that 20 of 62 patients (32.3%) who completed detoxification, have remained drug free for an average of 28.9 months since detoxification and none for less than 19 months. This is the lowest valid success rate and the true level may be as high as 54.8%. This is a more encouraging result than the findings of previous studies with even less than two-year follow-ups.

The younger age and shorter addiction history of this study group suggests greater flexibility and potential for giving up methadone dependence as compared to the majority of older, more long-term addicts involved in earlier detoxification studies. The sample in this paper is not only 71.0% female (44/62 patients) but 77.3% (33/44) of these women entered the treatment program while they were pregnant, although none began their detoxification while pregnant. In addition, 12 of the 18 men also entered treatment while their wives were pregnant. This aspect of recent parenthood may be a powerful motivator for willingness to change.

The detoxification procedures were designed to consider the individuality of each patient and to allow maximum appropriate patient participation in the timing of dosage reductions and in the amount of such reductions. Patients who were successful had been maintained on a methadone dosage averaging 53.6 mg (with a range from 10 mg to 60 mg), much lower than methadone maintenance levels in most programs at that time. Furthermore, these patients had been in treatment an average of only 9.7 months before beginning detoxification, again a considerably shorter period of time than experience of most programs. Perhaps the lower stabilizing dosage helped the patient in taking the risk of requesting detoxification. The relatively short period of stabilization of 9.7 months likewise may result in less psychological and social dependence on the methadone program.

Patients are confronted that becoming drug free is not the end of the treatment process, but rather a new phase in their continuing growth. Staff encouraged patients to return to the program whenever they wished, even after formal discharge from treatment. The 20 patients who have remained drug free were in treatment an average of 15.3 months after completing detoxification, which underscores the real importance for long term supportive counseling of patients who have detoxified from methadone maintenance. Patients continue to need help with problems of family, employment, and socialization after detoxification.

IV. SUMMARY

Low dose methadone treatment leading to abstinence is a viable therapeutic approach, especially for patients in their early to mid-twenties who have less than a five-year addiction history and some stable family ties. Of 62 patients who completed detoxification, 44 were reported drug free at the first evaluation. The two-year follow-up on these 44 patients used clinical interviews and urinalysis tests, and a data search by the Methadone Information Center as to current methadone registration or history of registration. At the two-year evaluation, only 27 of the 44 drug free patients could be followed up and of these, 20 were still drug free for an average of 28.9 months. Of the remaining 17 patients not followed up, there was no positive evidence from the data bank search of return to methadone treatment or drug abuse in 14 patients. Consequently, the documented two-year success rate for this group was 32.3% (20/62) with the possibility of the true figure reaching as high as 54.8% (34/62).

REFERENCES

1. F. Gearing, Proc. Third Natl. Conf. Methadone Maintenance, 1: 2-16 (1970).
2. S. Ross and S. Smock, Proc. Fifth Natl Conf. Methadone Treatment, 1: 133-141 (1973).
3. J. Chappel, V. Skolnick, and E. Senay, Proc. Fifth Natl. Conf. Methadone Treatment, 1: 482-489 (1973).
4. J. Rabin and B. Stimmel, in Developments in the Field of Drug Abuse (E. Senay, V. Shorty, and H. Alksne, eds.), Cambridge, Mass. (1975).

THE ABILITY TO REMAIN NARCOTIC FREE FOLLOWING
DETOXIFICATION FROM METHADONE MAINTENANCE:
A FIVE-YEAR STUDY

Edith Rotkopf, Barry Stimmel, M.D.

Department of Medicine
Mount Sinai School of Medicine of
  The City University of New York
New York, New York

Methadone maintenance is now an accepted modality of therapy in the
treatment of heroin addiction. From 1968 when 1,230 persons were
admitted to methadone maintenance (MM) in New York City to the
present, increasing numbers of former heroin users have received
this therapy with approximately 35,000 individuals currently enrolled in MM in the metropolitan New York area. Although much
information has appeared in the literature with respect to difficulties encountered with MM as well as the statistical success of
this modality in "social rehabilitation" of the heroin addict, relatively little work has been published concerning the prognosis of
persons detoxified from MM with respect to the ability to remain
abstinent over a period of time.

The relevance of the knowledge of an individual's ability to remain
narcotic free after discharge from MM has been emphasized by recent
guidelines issued by both state and federal monitoring agencies.
Such guidelines imply the desirability of detoxifying individuals
in maintenance therapy once a greater than two-year period of time
has elapsed. In an attempt to provide information concerning long-
term follow-up of persons no longer on MM, the following study was
undertaken.

I. DESCRIPTION OF STUDY

The Mount Sinai Methadone Maintenance and Aftercare Treatment
Program (MMATP) was established in February, 1969, being one of the
first programs in New York City to initiate MM on an ambulatory

---

This study relates to a program funded by the New York State
  Office of Drug Abuse Services.

basis only. The program is community based, with most of its members residing in the East Harlem area. The staff is multidisciplinary and consists of both professionals and paraprofessionals working in a team approach to help the heroin addict better realize the full potential he/she is capable of achieving. From 1969 to the present, approximately 800 persons have been admitted to therapy, with 85% remaining on maintenance for at least a one-year period of time. Overall retention of persons in the program since its inception is approximately 60%. During any one period approximately 10% of persons are abstinent and participate in the aftercare component. An additional 10% of patients are usually in some phase of detoxification from methadone.

The present study focuses on those persons admitted to the MMATP for the first time between March 1969 and December 1973 and successfully detoxified from MM at any time from March 1969 through October 1974. All detoxifications were classified according to the following reasons: 1) voluntarily discontinued (VD); 2) violated rules (VR); 3) arrested (A), and 4) treatment completed (TC).

The term treatment completed (TC) applies to persons who the staff felt had spent sufficient time in MM to have achieved a degree of rehabilitation that would enable them to maintain a narcotic-free state. Following detoxification, these patients had the choice of either remaining in the program's aftercare component or being discharged.

The category voluntarily discontinued (VD) was applied to persons who either 1) felt that they had achieved the ability to remain abstinent but with whom the staff disagreed or 2) did not wish to remain on MM. Arrests (A) refer to individuals who were arrested while on the program and subsequently detoxified due to the likelihood of impending incarceration.

In this study detoxification is not considered synonomous with discharge. Discharges from the program included not only individuals who detoxified but also those who abruptly stopped coming to treatment, as well as those transferred to other programs.

All persons detoxified were then followed to determine those individuals who were able to remain free from opiate use. Inability to maintain a drug-free state was established by: 1) evidence of reapplication to the MMATP at The Mount Sinai Hospital; 2) evidence of admission to another program as determined by the data bank at the Rockefeller University; 3) personal admission of drug use to staff members or 4) presence of a positive urinalysis for illicit narcotics. An individual was considered to be abstinent only if he/she had been seen at periodic intervals by treatment staff with neither history, positive signs of opiate abuse, or positive urinalysis for narcotics being found. For the purpose of this study, any single documented evidence of narcotic use after discharge is considered as a "failure" regardless of whether the person subsequently became drug free.

II. RESULTS

The general characteristics of the population enrolled in MM during the study period revealed no difference between the Admission, Detoxification, and Discharge Groups. During this time there were 634 first admissions to MM, 134 discharges without detoxification, and 230 detoxifications.

Of all first admissions, 75% were men, 25% women. Ethnic breakdown revealed 63% hispanic, 26% black, and 11% white, closely reflecting the racial composition of East Harlem.

The remainder of the paper will deal with those 230 persons detoxified from MM. The reasons for detoxification can be seen in Table I.

The ability to adjust to the program regulations was quite good, with only 16% of detoxifications resulting from a violation of program rules. The largest number of detoxifications were performed at the patients' requests (VD) against staff advice (38%), with only 22% of all detoxifications being performed in persons who the staff felt would be able to maintain the abstinence state (TC). Arrests with subsequent sentencing were responsible for the remaining 24%. The relationship between length of time on MM and reason for detoxification revealed the following: Of all A resulting in detoxification, 85% took place within the first eleven months of therapy (p=0.001) and usually was related to old warrants. Similarly, within an eleven-month period, detoxification due to VR and VD occurred in 67% and 53%, respectively. In contrast, only 12% of persons in the TC group were detoxified within a short period (p=0.001), with 63% of TC detoxifications occurring in persons on MM for greater than a two-year period. In contrast, detoxifications due to VD, VR, and A occurred predominantly within the first two years of therapy (67%, 81%, and 91%, respectively).

The mean time on MM prior to detoxification for all patients was 16 months. However, those in the TC group had a mean duration of MM of 30.2 months (p=0.005), with a mean of 8.9 in the A group. The duration of follow-up ranged from 3 to 61 months, with a mean of 21 months. When classified as to reason for detoxification, the duration of follow-up was comparable in all groups, with the exception of TC which had a mean of 11.8 months (p<0.01).

The outcome with respect to recurrent narcotic use is illustrated in Table II. The ability to remain abstinent was seen in 31%,

200

return to narcotic dependency in 47%, with 18% of persons not able
to be located. Of the 106 persons returning to narcotic use, 54
(51%) were enrolled in MM programs, with the remainder having reverted to heroin injection.

A correlation was found between prior time on methadone maintenance
and prognosis. Only 11% of those on MM for less than 12 months
were able to maintain a drug-free state (p=0.001). This can be
compared with abstinence being maintained in 51% of those on therapy for one to two years, 67% of those on MM for two to three years,
48% for three to four years, and 67% for four to six years.

The effect that length of follow-up period might have on prognosis
with respect to recidivism to narcotic use revealed no difference
with follow-up periods of two years. Longer periods of time were
associated with a greater return to narcotic use. However, since
the percentage of persons not located in these groups correspondingly increases, the relevance of these figures must be questioned.

The relationship between reason for detoxification and prognosis
can be seen in Table III. Narcotic use resumed in 49% to 81% of
persons in all categories, with the exception of the TC group. In
this category 84% of persons detoxified who the staff felt were
ready to attempt abstinence were able to remain drug free
(p=0.001).

III. SUMMARY

The results of this continuing study suggest that although the
actual process of detoxification from methadone is not technically
difficult and, providing appropriate time is allowed, can be accomplished with a minimum of stress, recidivism to narcotic use is
high, with only one-third of persons detoxified being able to remain abstinent. Failure to maintain the abstinent state does not
necessarily imply reversion to illicit activities as approximately
50% of individuals will enter MM programs rather than resume injection of street heroin.

Factors can be identified which may have a predictive value with
respect to the ability to remain drug free. Characteristics of a
population at a low risk of recurrent narcotic use once detoxified
from methadone include 1) a period of MM of two years or greater
and 2) the ability of the patient to have reached sufficient goals
and realistic objectives so as to be considered by the staff to
have completed the phase of MM.

TABLE I: REASON FOR DETOXIFICATION FROM METHADONE

	Number	Percent
Treatment Completed (TC)	51	(22.2)
Violated Rules (VR)	36	(15.7)
Voluntarily Discontinued (VD)	87	(37.8)
Arrested (A)	56	(24.3)
TOTAL	230	(100)

TABLE II: GENERAL OUTCOME OF DETOXIFICATIONS

Outcome	Number	Percent
Narcotic Free (NF)	73	(31)
Narcotic Dependent (ND)	106	(47)
Jail (J)	4	(2)
Unknown (UK)	43	(18)
Dead (D)	4	(2)
TOTAL	230	(100)

TABLE III: REASON FOR DETOXIFICATION AND PROGNOSIS

	NF No. (%)	ND No. (%)	J No. (%)	D No. (%)	UK No. (%)	TOTAL No. (%)
TC	43 (84)*	4 (8)	- -	- -	4 (8)	51 (100)
VR	1 (3)	29 (81)**	- -	- -	6 (16)	36 (100)
VD	20 (23)	43 (49)	- -	3 (4)	21 (24)	87 (100)
A	9 (16)	30 (54)	4 (7)	1 (2)	12 (21)	56 (100)
TOTAL	73 (31)	106 (47)	4 (2)	4 (2)	43 (18)	230 (100)

  * p=0.001
 ** p=0.05

202

DISCHARGED PATIENTS AND DROP-OUTS FROM A
METHADONE MAINTENANCE TREATMENT PROGRAM: A FOLLOW-UP STUDY

Iradj Siassi, M.D.
Burleigh P. Angle, M.A.
Dominick C. Alston, B.A.

Comprehensive Drug Abuse Treatment Program
Western Psychiatric Institute and Clinic
University of Pittsburgh
Pittsburgh, Pennsylvania

For several years the need for research on methadone
maintenance treatment programs has been readily recognized. In
the early years, research was directed toward examining those
results of treatment which were readily quantifiable. Many
studies were conducted on arrest rates, employment rates, and
continued drug abuse as criteria for evaluation of success. (1-4)

As treatment programs and treatment personnel gained
experience and sophistication, research methodology was also
improved. However, one of the major difficulties in outcome
research in methadone maintenance is the failure in following up
patients who are discharged and/or the patients who drop out.
Most claims about the success or failure of methadone maintenance
as a treatment modality are vulnerable to this criticism. (5)
The problems of tracing and evaluating the patients who are no
longer in treatment are formidable. These problems are well
documented in the literature. (6-9) This paper discusses a) the
steps found necessary to carry out a one-year follow-up of 125
patients in a methadone maintenance program, and b) the treatment
outcome for these patients at the end of this one-year period.

The main purpose of this study was to assess the psychosocial
problems of the patient population of a methadone maintenance
clinic and then to evaluate any changes over time by a reassessment after 12 months. During the months of November and December,
1974, the entire patient population of a typical urban methadone
clinic was evaluated by a gattery of four tests. Briefly, the
four instruments used for testing can be described as follows:

MacMillan Health Opinion Survey (10) -- The MacMillan used
in this study is the abbreviated 13-item MacMillan Index used

203

in other studies. The items consist of questions about specific physical manifestations of mental disorder. A four point frequency scale is marked to respond from "Most of the Time" to "Never."

The Symptoms Checklist 90 (11) -- The SCL 90 is a development of the Hopkins Symptoms Checklist and consists of 90 items responded to on a four-point frequency scale. It is a personality inventory which produces nine factors titled: somatization, obsessive-compulsive, interpersonal sensitivity, depression, anxiety, anger-hostility, phobic-anxiety, paranoid ideation, and psychoticism. Estimates of reliability and validity have been established as well as norms on several different general and psychiatric populations.

The Michigan Alcoholism Screening Test (12) -- The MAST is a 25-item, true/false response questionnaire for detection of alcoholism. It has been used on different populations. Its validity as well as an estimate of its reliability have been established.

The Global Assessment Rating Forms (13) -- The Global consists of 8 items marked on a seven-point scale of severity where the patient indicates his perception of his present and past status. The Global has not been used enough to have established norms.

At the end of 12 months, 93 (74%) of the original 125 patients were still in treatment; and 32 patients had been discharged or had dropped out. During November and December, 1975, the 93 patients of the original group who had remained in the clinic were retested, while one researcher devoted his time exclusively to the efforts to locate and retest the other 32 members of the original group.

SETTING

The Methadone Maintenance Clinic of the Western Psychiatric Institute and Clinic (WPIC), Pittsburgh, Pennsylvania, has been in operation since July, 1969. The Clinic treats unselected heroin addicts who are at least 18 years of age, whose addiction histories extend back at least two years, and who are currently addicted. All who meet these criteria are accepted. It is a typical outpatient methadone maintenance program with emphasis on social rehabilitation of the patients.

THE SEARCH

To re-test the 32 ex-patients, it was necessary first to find them; and then to persuade them to consent to the re-test. Each a formidable task. With daily search for two months, all 32 ex-

patients were located and their status accounted for. However,
only 16 (50%) could be re-tested.

Among the sources of information used to locate the ex-
patients were the hospital records for their addresses and telephone numbers, and those of their relatives. Also available in
medical records were records of previous treatment histories and
documents of addiction, which were provided by friends, relatives,
and acquaintances who were contacted to find the ex-patient's
present location. The most current sources of information about
an ex-patient were patients still in the program. A non-threatening relationship between the patients and the researcher made the
patients a valuable source of information.

For most of the ex-patients who were either incarcerated or
in state mental hospitals, lack of cooperation by these agencies
became an unsurmountable obstacle to re-testing.

The task of persuading the ex-patients to participate in the
research posed a different problem. For some, no persuasion was
necessary. They were willing to help because they had been asked.
Others helped because they wanted to re-enter the program. Some
in jail wanted to get messages to counselors, lawyers, friends.
Whatever could be legally and responsibly done to obtain their
cooperation was done.

There were four elements that played a vital part in facilitating the location of all the ex-patients. The first was the
program's policy of thorough history-taking and record-keeping on
every patient upon admission and throughout their treatment.
Second, was a cooperative relationship between patients in the
program and the research staff of the program. Third, was the
immediate follow-up on a lead about any ex-patient. Fourth, was
the personal responsibility of the researcher to find the ex-
patient and collect the information needed himself. In contrast,
the failure to obtain greater than 50% re-test is striking. An
important step involves raising the consciousness of the
responsible institutions as to the importance of follow-up
studies. Under such condition, it would be expected that the rate
of information retrieval would be greatly increased.

RESULTS

For the sake of brevity, only the results is presented here.
The details are presented in a separate paper. A comparison
between the treatment and drop-out groups on a standard demographic data, using chi square tests showed no significant
differences. The drop-out group of 32 ex-patients consisted of
the total number of patients who, for whatever reasons, were unable to continue in treatment. An active search to locate all 32
of these drop-outs succeeded. Of these, six were in prison;

three were hospitalized; four had died, three were in other programs, and refused to be re-tested. The 16 others reached agreed
to be re-tested and interviewed. The majority of those clients
discharged were those breaking programmatic rules. Twenty were
discharged for this reason. Six were incarcerated. Four transferred to other programs. Two had psychiatric problems.

An analysis of variance was conducted on all instruments
between the treatment and drop-out groups. For the drop-out
group alone, test-retest comparisons showed a significant decrease
on the SCL 90 variable of psychoticism and on the MacMillan Inces
at the .05 and .01 levels, respectively. Test-retest comparisons
on the treatment group showed a significant decrease in scores on
the MacMillan Index at the .01 level. Test-retest comparisons
between the treatment and drop-out groups showed no significant
differences between the two groups.

In summary, the results shows that both the Treatment Group
and the Drop-Out Group have improved over the study period.
Scores on the SCL 90 have tended to decrease, indicating fewer
symptoms of psychoticism, obsessive compulsiveness, etc. Scores
on the MacMillan have also decreased indicating greater feelings
of satisfaction and self-esteem, which is also seen in the change
of scores on the Patient Global Assessment Form. It is important,
however, to see that the Michigan Alcoholism Screening Test scores
have increased for the Treatment Group. It seems that methadone
treatment is closely related to increased alcohol abuse.

DISCUSSION

Due to the short length of time (a year) over which this
study was conducted, we cannot make any major generalization.
Such generalizations will depend on following the study population
over a much longer period of time. Nevertheless, certain tentative conclusions may be drawn from the collected data.

Those who stay in treatment are significantly better off
(at least over the short run) than drop-outs. By following up
the 32 drop-outs; in essence, they go back on drugs, are incarcerated, institutionalized, or die.

But for 50% of the drop-outs, we found that they had gotten
better in many psychological areas. They were, in fact, slightly
better off psychologically than those who remained in treatment.
Furthermore, the patients who remain on methadone shows a
significantly greater problem with alcohol than the re-tested
drop-outs. Considering the known deleterious effects of alcohol
on this population, the long-term clinical picture may in fact
favor the latter group.

206

ACKNOWLEDGEMENT

Funded in part by NIDA Grant #5-H80DA01356.
Special thanks to Mrs. Jackie Moye for her kind assistance.
Requests for table data and reprints should be directed to either
Burleigh P. Angle or Dominick C. Alston.

REFERENCES

1. W.F. Wieland and C.D. Chambers, Methadone Maintenance,
    Einstein, Ed., New York, Marcel Dekker, 1971. pp. 85-92.

2. F.R. Gearing, Int J of Addict, 5:517-543, (1970)

3. J.H. Jaffe, M.S. Washington, E.N. Washington, Int J of
    Addict 4:481-490 (1969).

4. W.A. Bloom, E.W. Sudderth, Methadone Maintenance,
    S. Einstein, Ed., New York, Marcel Dekker, (1971) pp. 119-141.

5. J.F. Maddux, C.L. Bowden, Am J Psychiatry, 129 4:440-446
    (1972).

6. M.E. Perkins, and H.I. Bloch, Am J Psychiatry, 128:47-51
    (1971).

7. D.G. Levine, Am J Psychiatry, 129:4:456-460, (1972).

8. W. Morton, J. Sall, U. Petros, Pro. 5th Natl. Conf. Methadone
    Treatment, National Association for the Prevention of
    Addiction to Narcotics, New York, 1973, pp. 151-157.

9. G.E. Vaillant, Am J Drug Alcohol Abuse, 1 (1) 25-36, (1974)

10. A.M. MacMillan, Psychol. Rep., 1:325-329 (1957).

11. L.R. Derogatis, R.S. Lipman, K. Rickels, E.H. Uhlenhuth,
    and L. Covi, Mod. Probl. Pharmacopsychiatry, Vol. 7, pp. 79-
    110, (P. Pichot) Paris 1974.

12. R.A. Moore, Am J Psychiatry, 128:12:1565-1569, (1972).

13. H.H. Strupp, M.S. Wallach, M. Wozan, Psychol Monograph:
    General and Applied. 78:11, pp. 1-45, (1964).

A TEN YEAR STUDY OF ADDICTION TREATMENT

SUCCESSES AND FAILURES

Alfred V. Miliman

Maryland Drug Abuse Research and Treatment
Foundation, Inc.
222 E. Redwood Street, Baltimore, Maryland

This study began at a private psychiatric hospital in 1965.
During a 4 1/2 year period, ending in September 1969, there were
21 admissions of opiate addicts. The inpatient chemotherapy detoxification regimen of the hospital was excellent, with detox in
1 to 3 weeks. Complete stabilization, drug free, with comfort,
homeostasis, an equilibrium of mind and body, did not take place
until at least one to two months had passed. The minimum recommended inpatient treatment period was 15 weeks, though only 4 of
the addicts remained that long.

Follow-up showed that only one of 25 patients remained drug
free for one year or more following discharge. The most striking
phenomenon encountered was the resumption of physical symptons of
"withdrawal" following weeks and months of hospitalization and
forced drug abstinence, beginning from hours to days following release. This phenomenon also appeared during our study at a women's
prison where weekly sessions for 10 months served to provide valid
data on 30 inmates (1969-1970). Other subjects were included from
a correctional training center (minimum security jail) and the
USPHS Hospital at Lexington, Kentucky. Using drug abstinence for
a 12 month period as a goal, success rate of the private psychiatric hospital was 5%, the public hospital 1% and jail, from 7% to
17%. Only opiate addicts deemed by us to have a "habit" of 40 mg.
or more of morphine or equivalent, those who had been "strung out"
and by whom marked physical withdrawal symptoms had been experienced in the past were included.

A study of 53 addicts on a very large methadone program (900
patients) during a 1 year period (1970) illustrated the worth of
regular counselling-therapy. There were two groups; one "active",
totalling 33 patients, and one "inactive" with 20 patients. The
active group was seen on a regular basis for one to two hour sessions of what could be described as educative, supportive, directive reality therapy. All meetings were structured with most of the

time being spent on subjects and issues not directly related to
the participants. What the counselor deemed to be pathologic subjectivity was discouraged; during much of the session, the topic
of one's own self was prohibited. No effort was made to counsel
any of the second group other than in the initial interview(s) and
periodic brief follow-up sessions. Three husband-wife pairs were
in group 1; none in the inactive group; seven drop outs who remained less than 6 months are excluded. Therapy was discontinued as
program policy in November of 1970. The 3 abstinent patients subsequently relapsed. Maintenance dosage during this period ranged
from 20 to 300 mg. daily. Using responsible behavior as the criterion, the active group was 50% more successful.

A private outpatient program (1970-1971) used chemotherapy
other than methadone such as dilantin, phenobarbitol, prolixin,
mellaril, and serax. 22 of 27 patients required methadone only.
The major treatment effort was in "Reality Counselling-Therapy"
primarily in groups of 8 to 14, meeting twice weekly for 1 to 3
hours. Throughout this and the entire major study, the most striking factor was our realization that 80% to 90% of opiate addicts
did not have significant prior-existing psychopathology, that is,
prior to the first chemical of regular "abuse" (meaning to get
"high"), which was cannabis in over 80% of cases.

What we call the major study from 1967 to date, involved 411
addicts on 16 outpatient methadone programs. Methadone use appeared to benefit most patients for a period of several months up to
about one or two years after admission. The patient was always
blamed for the failure of treatment.

What was so rare up until the sixties, the combination of narcotics with alcohol, has now become most prevalent. Because of
poor detoxification techniques (160 cases), mandatory or punitive
detox (42 cases), or failure to elevate mental and environmental
status during maintenance (114 cases), the addict sought relief
from alcohol and other drugs.

M-DART divides drugs of abuse into three groups, depending upon
the affect on the brain: "ups","downs" and distorters. We consider only the "downs" (opiates, barbiturates, and alcohol) to have
the requisite addictive properties, physical and mental dependence,
and tolerance. We consider all reference to the abuse of caffeine,
nicotine, aspirin, etc. to be no part of our drug problem. Our
drug abuse problem relates to one's functioning in the area of
mental health. Cigars, coffee, and Pepsi Cola do not so relate.

Valium is a good minor tranquilizer, properly prescribed and
used, but for the drug dependent great caution should be exercised.
It produces marked feelings of pleasure or well-being and is addictive, with a significant tolerance factor. One addict, several
days after sudden cessation of 150 mg. daily, had a seizure and
"nearly bit his tongue off". This took place on the porch of the
drug program.

Effective treatment resulted from intensive therapy involving
the intellect, not the feelings or emotion. Over 90% of addicts
appeared to have the mentality to absorb and comprehend the steps

necessary to achieve a drug-free state with homeostasis. Treatment had 3 components: psychotherapy, chemotherapy and sociotherapy; and 3 goals, re-motivation, re-socialization and rehabilitation, if required.

Patient evaluation, both initial and periodic, was generally poor. This, combined with take-home medication privileges on the basis of time alone, was conducive to much traffic in illicit methadone and other drugs. Addiction was often created (12 cases), intensified (405 cases) or was so inadequately treated that addicts turned to other drugs for relief. This was tragic, for outpatient treatment requires methadone. Program ineffectiveness and lack of staff competence was generally concealed from public view, yet neighbors could see the obvious condition of many patients and at least sense the drug traffic going on. Any desired chemical contraband could be obtained within a block or two of all but 2 programs.

Outmoded, dogmatic, or verbal humanistic etiologic theory hampered effective education, training and treatment. The cycle of curiosity, pleasure, then dependence (or syndrome or addiction) was found in 582 of 650 cases. About 10% of addicts were believed to be particularly vulnerable to emotional or related disorder prior to their chemical abuse. M-DART found cause and effective treatment to be unrelated to race, religion, sex, materialism, Viet Nam, parents, the ghetto, pollution, the military-industrial complex, consumerism, etc., ad nauseum in the great majority of cases. In fact, reinforcement of these attitudes of criticism, pessimism and depression, though ego-protective, was most untherapeutic. Many group meetings consisted of little more than the ravings of ideologic fanatics or a rehash of revolutionary rhetoric or autobiographical stories by the great "dope fiends" present.

The prevalence of iatrogenic or physician induced addiction was found to be highly exaggerated. At most, 3 of 650 addicts were so addicted, and 2 of these were not verified.

M-DART found the greatest obstacle to successful treatment to be the Cannabis Syndrome, those patterns of thinking and behavior caused by regular marihuana use. We found well over 60% of patients (and 1/3 of staff) to have this condition and to be unaware of the usually subtle changes in their attitude, thinking and ability to achieve. Pot smoking in group sessions was found.

A study of existing addiction and methadone literature, found little reference to marijuana. Any competent behaviorist will concede the probable danger to the drug or alcohol dependent of using chemicals for pleasure. Pro-marihuana bias is most significant, and exists throughout the drug abuse field. A prime example might be the initial rejection by this Conference of the other study submitted by M-DART entitled "The Thought Disorder of the Cannabis Syndrome". We consider cannabis a most dangerous drug, with only about 3% of users graduating to other drugs.

Seven patients exposed to ardent behavior modification techniques on two methadone programs all failed in treatment. The main reason appeared to be gross lack of knowledge of methadone organicity by the therapist.

During the years 1969 - 1975 inclusive, 65 admissions to
Therapeutic Communities or psychiatric hospitals were noted where
15 mg. or no methadone or equivalent was given for detox to addicts
with daily doses of 60 mg. or higher. Average length of stay was
2 to 3 days. Some TC's do not distinguish a pothead from a methadone addict.

Criminal activity by addicts receiving methadone was reduced
by well over 40%, as an average, but crime by outpatients currently receiving methadone was noted in over 1/3 of cases. One addict
during 6 years of methadone treatment, had over 1,000 successful
shoplifts; one drug dealer grossed well over $50,000 from illicit
drug sales, and one addict was arrested and convicted for only one
of over 50 breaking and enterings.

Use of antagonists was and will not be successful, no more
than disulfuram (Antabuse) is with alcoholics. Effective treatment is a one to three year process, generally, during which time
a major change in thinking and attitude must take place. Methadone, properly used, permits these changes to occur, for the
patient can remain relatively comfortable. Most effective therapy
techniques noted were suggestion and persuasion.

The lack of competent and effective counselor-therapist was
disastrous. Counselor training to date, still so full of fancy
theory, was deemed equally disastrous.

Static dose "lifetime" methadone programs will not work either
because changes in mental status affect the need for or effect of
the methadone, generally in an inverse proportion. Improved mental and environmental status requires lowered doses to maintain
stability, while the opposite mandates use of additional methadone
or other drugs to maintain comfort. Heroin should not be used for
outpatient treatment because of its: high tolerance, short action,
difficulty of oral administration and extremely high pleasure
factor.

Use of hospitals in Maryland for addiction treatment was most
inadequate, one major exception being a case admitted to Montgomery General Hospital in 1972. Within one month, stabilization was
gained at 50 mg. methadone for a severe poly-drug dependent. The
inpatient chemotherapy regimen involved six types of medication
to treat 3 drug dependencies, guard against seizure and permit
sleep. This was an excellent use of neuroleptic and other drugs
by a skilled psychiatrist who obtained and used recommendations
of the referrer. At the time of admission, 200 mg. was not
"holding" this man.

Because of the cyclic, recurrent nature of addiction, and mood
and other swings, M-DART found it particularly effective to reintroduce very low analgesic level doses following detox of motivated patients. 5 to 10 mg. daily, maximum, will give the required comfort for several days or weeks. This should be done for
periods as long as one to three months following successful detox
in some cases, certainly if other drug or alcohol abuse is to be
prevented. This is a most effective way to suppress symptoms of
recurrent discomfort which can become catastrophic to recovery.

A principal conclusion by M-DART is that the concept of addiction as simply a sympton of some deeper, underlying disorder has been self-defeating and wrong. Addiction should be considered a specific illness entity to which anyone is susceptible. Further, when the behavior of the addict in doing everything necessary to obtain and inject drugs is viewed as normal under the circumstances, then, and only then, will our efforts pay off. Is it not logical that anyone who would undergo severe withdrawal without doing something about it, must be crazy? Keep in mind that the term "addict" does not include the teenybopper who gets high on a 5 mg. dolophine pill.

Another critical problem, probably an insurmountable one, is the fact that many of our experts, authorities and bureaucrats now in the field have been changed by their personal drug abuse without their awareness. The pronouncements and findings of those who have the thought disorder of the psychedelic drug syndrome have been ruinous. The expert who states withdrawal from cigarettes is worse than that from heroin, or recommends use of psychedelic drugs if guided by a witch doctor - is he an authority? We found too many instances where the drug abuse educator and healer was sicker than the patient. Has the pot smoker done valid research? M-DART beleives not.

Though field and clinical research and meaningful longitudinal studies such as this one do not fulfill exacting scientific requisites, the strong probability exists that this type of data must be considered before real progress can be made. References, bibliography and detailed study data will be furnished upon request.

THERAPEUTIC COMMUNITIES VS. METHADONE TREATMENT
FURTHER PRELIMINARY RESULTS FROM A RANDOMIZED COMPARISON

Richard N. Bale, Ph.D., William W. Van Stone, M.D.,
John M. Kuldau, M.D., Thomas M. Engelsing, M.D., L. Susan Cabrera, M.A.,
and Vincent P. Zarcone, M.D.

Stanford University School of Medicine and
the Veterans Administration Hospital
3801 Miranda Avenue
Palo Alto, California 94304

We present here the fourth in a series of progress reports of an ongoing follow-up study of some 613 male heroin addicts who were in
treatment at the VA Hospital in Palo Alto. In earlier reports at
this conference, we have described the study and early results of the
assignment procedure (Bale, et al., 1973), the characteristics of
patients accepting or rejecting treatment (Bale et al., 1974), and
the preliminary one-year follow-up results (Bale et al., 1975). Today we will review a few of our basic study questions and present
further results of some preliminary analyses.

In early 1972 we felt that the multi-modality drug abuse treatment
unit at the Palo Alto VA afforded us a unique opportunity to answer
some critical questions about treatment effects while maintaining
some experimental control over the assignment of patients to different modalities. We knew, for example, that major national reviews
by the Ford Foundation (1972) and the Consumer Union (Brecher, 1972)
had characterized the therapeutic communities as almost totally ineffective. Because there were so very few studies of therapeutic
community patients on which to base these conclusions, we were curious if careful, systematic follow-up assessment would show the same
result. We also knew that therapeutic communities were widely reported to attract primarily young, white addicts (Glasscote, 1972),
in some distinction to methadone treatment, which seemed more acceptable to older blacks and other minority groups. We were curious if
this was an artifact of the modality locations or the way different
addict groups learned about various treatment options. Would the
same pattern of age and race distribution obtain in retention patterns from a controlled situation where patients were initially randomly assigned to various treatments? What type of patient would
actually enter a treatment program? Would patients in the

This work was supported by research grant DA-00384 from the National
Institute of Drug Abuse.

therapeutic communities show comparable outcomes to those treated in the outpatient methadone clinic? Would time in treatment be a critical factor for TC patients? In order to answer these and other critical questions, a research group including clinicians and administrators (Drs. Zarcone, Van Stone, Kuldau and Engelsing) was formed to oversee the study and its execution. A research director (the principal author) not connected with any of the programs being studied was appointed to design and execute the study. NIMH funding was obtained which enabled the intake, treatment, and follow-up assessments to be conducted by outside Stanford University research personnel unaffiliated with the treatment programs. The treatment staff themselves were involved substantially in the determination of the assessment variables. The advantages of this multi-leveled approach have been discussed elsewhere (Bale, 1973). Before presenting further preliminary results of the study, let us first review the treatment modalities involved and the basic research protocol.

The drug abuse treatment program at the Palo Alto Veterans Administration Hospital is composed of three therapeutic communities treating 20-30 patients for an average stay of two to six months, and a methadone therapy program treating between about 60-100 patients at Palo Alto and 125 patients at its satellite in San Francisco. The multi-modal program as a whole has recently been described by William Van Stone, M.D., in the August 1974 issue of the International Journal of the Addictions (Van Stone, 1974). The 3 TC programs have been described elsewhere and include a peer confrontation ward (Van Stone and Gilbert, 1972), a second peer-run community treating only drug abusers (Hogan, 1975) and a psychodynamically-based program (Zarcone, 1975).

Most of the drug abuse patients entering these communities first complete a 5-day detoxification on a central admitting and detoxification ward. During an 18-month period in 1972 and 1973, 613 patients entered our detoxification ward (plus an additional number who were not included in the study because they were transferred to psychiatric wards or were not veterans eligible for treatment). Each patient was asked if he was interested in a treatment program following detoxification. Each of the 486 who answered "yes" to this question was randomly assigned to one of the four treatment programs. A patient who desired a different program than the one to which he was assigned could do so only by waiting 30 days and re-entering the hospital. Patients not eligible for methadone by federal guidelines were assigned only to one of the therapeutic communities. For this presentation, these 2 samples are combined. The remaining 217 patients who expressed no interest in further treatment are also included in our study as the "Detox Only" group. Of the 486 patients who were randomly assigned 230 actually entered a treatment program during the first year. This included 109 patients who waited the 30 days and entered a treatment program to which they had not been originally assigned. To this extent, the randomization design is compromised, which will be discussed in future reports.

214

Extensive background information on 335 variables, including drug use, employment, education, arrests and convictions, illegal activity and interpersonal relations was gathered on each patient during his initial period on the detoxification ward. Each patient was contacted by phone or mail at two points, six and twelve months following his date of admission to the detoxification ward. He was asked to return a short standard questionnaire by mail. This 3-4 page questionnaire assessed a few basic data such as current drug use, employment, legal status. Preliminary results from this follow-up data were presented at last year's conference (Bale et al, 1975). For this presentation we will review three actual questions:

1. *Do the therapeutic communities (in this controlled situation) attract primarily young, white addicts, while outpatient methadone treatment attracts older, black addicts?* In our experience, no. Patients randomized to the various programs who actually entered treatment did not show this pattern. Neither age nor ethnic background predicted entry significantly to either a TC or methadone treatment. This is not to say that there are no dramatic differences between the white and black subjects, which there are. Ethnic background is the single most powerful predictor of differences in many of the intake variables, which will be discussed in later reports.

2. *What does predict treatment entry?* For this preliminary analysis we have looked at entry to <u>any</u> program and entry to a TC. A linear discriminant function was computed to identify the relative contribution of different variables in predicting entry to treatment. Perhaps the most striking result is that while we can predict entry into a program with some 72-78% accuracy for white patients, we can predict only slightly better than chance for black patients. Generally, the white patient entering a treatment program has used more drugs including alcohol but not cocaine or illicit methadone which he has used less. While he may have had an alcohol problem he does not seem to now (suggesting that heavy heroin and alcohol use may be interchangeable but not concomitant). The white patient entering a therapeutic community shows a similar pattern with greater indications of dependent relationships. He is more likely to be living with relatives or parents and has received help for overdoses more frequently. He disagrees that heroin would be OK for his own use if it were legal (suggesting less interest in chemical solutions).

3. *What is the effect of time in treatment on outcome for the TC patients?* Our first follow-up results are consistent with other studies showing time in treatment to be positively correlated with good outcome.

Although methodologically limited, two studies of the Daytop Program in New York have found greater functioning with increased time in treatment, in terms of drug use and employment (Romond, 1975) as well as arrest rates and a wide variety of other social functioning (Collier and Hijazi, 1974). A number of investigations of the Phoenix House program in New York have shown time in treatment to be strongly positively related to outcome (Chambers, 1974; De Leon, 1972). Aron and Daily (1974) report large and significant differences in conviction records between short and long stay patients at the Camarillo State Hospital TC.

A major study from the Eagleville Hospital therapeutic communities for drug abusers and alcoholics (Barr 1973 a,b) reports time in treatment as the major predictor of outcome: 22% of patients in less than two months report a six month or more period of voluntary abstinence during a two year follow-up, compared with 55% of the full stay (six months) group. Similar patterns are reported with employment.

We examined mean days in treatment across several outcomes for all patients who had stayed one or more days in a TC. Patients who spent time in methadone treatment were included if their total TC days were greater. This table presents results of these analyses.

RELATIONSHIP OF TIME IN TREATMENT TO OUTCOME FOR TC'S

Variable	Mean Treatment Days		T-Test Significance (p<x)
heroin use during year:	Yes	30	
	No	80	.001
heroin use during past month:	Yes	55	
	No	96	.005
working at one year:	Yes	83	
	No	63	.005
convicted during year:	Yes	40	
	No	87	.001

The results indicate that time in treatment is strongly related to outcome. We are cautious in ascribing causal inferences to the data. Patients are not randomly assigned to different treatment durations and it may be that those patients with greater personal and social resources "predisposed to good outcome" are precisely those patients who choose to stay in treatment longer. Further analyses, including covariance procedures and results of our recently completed two-year follow-up may shed some light on this question.

REFERENCES

Bale, R.N., Van Stone, W.W., Kuldau, J.M., Engelsing, T.M. & Zarcone, V.P., Methadone treatment versus therapeutic communities: Preliminary results of a randomized study in progress. Paper presented at the Fifth National Conference on Methadone Treatment, Washington, D.C., April 1973.

Bale, R.N., Van Stone, W.W., Kuldau, J.N., Engelsing, T.M. & Zarcone, V.P. Therapeutic communities versus methadone treatment: Characteristics of patients accepting or rejecting treatment in a randomized study. In E. Senay & Shorty (Eds.), Developments in the field of drug abuse, Cambridge, Mass.: Schenkman Publishing Co. Inc., 1974.

Bale, R.N., Van Stone, W.W., Kuldau, J.M., Engelsing, T.M. & Zarcone, V.P. Preliminary one-year follow-up results from a comparative study of therapeutic communities versus methadone treatment. Paper presented at the Second National Drug Abuse Conference, New Orleans, April 1975.

Dealing with drug abuse: A report to the Ford Foundation. New York: Praeger Publishers, Inc., 1972.

Brecher, E.M & The Editors of Consumer Reports. Licit and illicit drugs. Little, Brown and Company, 1972.

Glasscote, R., Sussex, J.N., Jaffee, J.H., Ball, J., & Brill, L. The treatment of drug abuse: Programs, problems, prospects. Washington, D.C.: The Joint Information Service, 1972.

Bale, R.N. Program Evaluation: Who should do it? Paper presented at the meeting of the American Psychological Association, Montreal, August 1973.

Van Stone, W.W. Treating the drug-dependent veteran--perspective from a Veterans Administration Hospital. International Journal of the Addictions, August 1974, 9(4), 593-604.

Van Stone, W.W. & Gilbert, R. Peer confrontation groups: what, why, and whether? American Journal of Psychiatry, 1972, 129:5.

Hogan, D. Converting a confrontation ward to a therapy/vocational dual program. Paper presented at the Second National Drug Abuse Conference, New Orleans, April 1975.

Zarcone, V.P. Drug addicts in a therapeutic community: The Satori Approach. Baltimore, York Press, 1975.

Romond, A.M., Forrest, C.K., & Kleber, H.D. Follow-up of participants in a drug dependence therapeutic community. Archives of General Psychiatry, 1975, 32, 369-374.

Collier, W.R. & Hijazi, M.A. A follow-up study of former residents of a therapeutic community. International Journal of the Addictions, 1974, 9, 805-826.

Chambers, C.D. & Inciardi, J.A. Three years after the split. In E. Senay & V. Shorty (Eds.), Developments in the field of drug abuse. Cambridge, Mass.: Schenkman Publishing Co., Inc., 1974.

De Leon, G., Holland, S., & Rosenthal, M. Phoenix House: criminal activity dropouts. The Journal of the American Medical Association, 1972, 222(6), 686-689.

Aron, W.S. & Daily, D. Camarillo--short and long term TC'S: A follow-up and cost effectiveness comparison. International Journal of the Addictions, 1974, 9(5), 619-636.

(a) Barr, H.L., Ottenberg, D.J., & Rosen, A. Two year follow-up study of 724 drug addicts and alcoholics treated together in an abstinence therapeutic community. Paper presented at the Fifth National Conference on Methadone Treatment, Washington, D.C., April 1973.

(b) Barr, H.L., Rosen, A., Antes, D.E., & Ottenberg, D.J. Two year follow-up study of 724 drug and alcohol addicts treated together in an abstinence therapeutic community. Eagleville Hospital Monograph, 1973.

217

DATA NETWORKS: A PLANNING TOOL TO MONITOR
DRUG USING POPULATIONS

Donald R. Bennett

Rubicon, Inc.
1208 West Franklin Street
Richmond, Virginia 23220

INTRODUCTION

Generally, drug abuse planning on local, regional and state
levels is based on little empirical data about the population
being served by treatment agencies operating within these planning
entities. Usually, the potential service population has been defined by population statistics and in some rare cases quantifiable
arrest data. Most planning agencies utilize treatment program data
such as total clients served, those completing treatment, rates of
recidivism, urinalysis (methadone programs), and some demographic
description of the clients seen by the drug treatment programs.

The full picture of drug use/abuse activity is often scant and
devoid of detail. Treatment data is used for decision making
processes which ultimately affect, directly, populations both real
and potential who are or could be service recipients.

Within each community there are human service providers who
may or may not receive funds to deliver services to the drug
using/abusing population. This group of human service providers
may either attempt to give services within their own resources or
make referrals to known drug programs or simply exit the individ-
ual(s) for whom no resource is adequate to meet individual needs.
RAP houses, community living rooms and telephone crisis lines
represent such organizations. Hospital emergency rooms, police
vice units, county sheriffs' offices represent another group of
service providers who may serve this drug using/abusing population
in one way or another, yet receive no direct funds for their services unless they can document the need.

This paper is not an attempt to substantiate a process for
acquisition of monies for such groups, but rather the approach to
be discussed is the viewing of such agencies and organizations as
potential data sources for input into drug abuse planning. Available resources can be better and more efficiently planned, thus

reducing the potential for intuitive decision making processess on
all levels of local/regional/state monitoring agencies.

THE DATA NETWORK CONCEPT*

Richmond, Virginia, and its surrounding counties have a ple-
thora of human service agencies. There is generally very little
communication between agencies and organizations about specific
service populations with which they are concerned.

The nature of the agencies and organizations often prohibits
communications between respective facilities. Exceptions can occur
when an issue surfaces that would stimulate collaboration or policy
making. For example, it is rare that hospital emergency rooms and
drug treatment programs would ever collaborate unless a crisis involving a mutual client evolved or some general conflict coalesced.
Detail is about the internal operations of dissimilar agencies serving similar populations is usually peripherally known among some
personnel working within agencies. Often the notions of one agency about another as to its function, who it serves, its quality of
service and its acceptance in a community is derived from rumor and
incremental contacts with a few staff or their clients. Positive-
to-negative impressions build upon one another to a point where an
individual agency is viewed by other agencies as anything from mys-
terious to successful to unsuccessful. Over time, collaboration
between agencies can range from positive to neutral to negative.
Usually, human service agencies compile information on their service populations independently of one another and rarely if ever
share their experiences.

In Richmond, specifically, this situation has been apparent
among agencies serving the drug using/abusing population. The
Richmond regional drug abuse monitoring agency perceived this condition, and began to entertain ideas on the ways and means to provide for a catalyst for cooperation between agencies. Every agency
known to provide some service either directly or indirectly to the
drug abusing population was surveyed. The survey found that within each agency data was compiled on their service populations including drug abusers for distribution within the organization.
Some agencies had considered maintaining statistics on drug abusers realizing that a part of their effort involved service to the
drug using/abusing population. No credit was being given for this
service. In addition agencies were not sure who they should report
to or how to go about compiling the statistics. The monitoring
agency compiled its findings, and reported back to the survey participants suggestions on how the situation could be corrected. The
proposal encompassed the creation of a low cost/high yield regional
data network that was to be tailored to the reporting capability of
each agency, each of whom on a monthly basis would submit a report
of pertinent data relative to the drug using/abusing population
served within each agency. This information was to be compiled by

the monitoring agency, analyzed and grouped per agency monthly, quarterly and yearly for uniform statistical comparison.

METHOD

As commitments were received among agencies, plans were drawn for uniform reporting procedures. Agencies were grouped according to category (i.e., emergency rooms, police bureaus, sheriffs' offices, treatment programs, community action programs, laboratories (city and state), guidance counselors in high schools and other agencies such as rap houses, crisis telephone lines, and community living rooms. Within each category a data collection system was developed that reflected similar data from each agency within each category. This data included contact frequency, age, sex, race, durg(s) of abuse, type of service provided and referrals to other agencies. With permission from the Executive Director of each agency a staff person was assigned responsibility for statistical compilation and submission and reception of reports to and from the regional data network. The monitoring agency provided the necessary technical assistance to ensure uniform reporting among all network participants.

Each month a region-wide report was compiled comparing the data submitted by each agency within each category. Narrative comments by the monitoring agency accompanied the statistics and were returned to each participant. Comments were invited from participating agencies which were also included in the feed back reports. Every three months a quarterly report was compiled to indicate trends, fluctuations and significant changes occuring in the data.

RESULTS

Sharing of information among agencies created the catalyst for communication between agencies, and generated request for detailed descriptions of participating agencies. The united effort helped to stimulate volunteers for any number of activities from agencies who were not participants, but who requested reports and were generally interested in the field of drug abuse programming. Many agencies, for the first time, were able to give input into the state plan for drug abuse control. Rapport and support for the monitoring agency were developed in areas previously non-existent, prior to the establishment of the network. A comprehensive composite profile of the drug using/abusing population in the region and agencies both directly and indirectly involved in providing services to this population was finally available.

The counties surrounding Richmond which were often overlooked or poorly represented in the overall state plan for drug abuse control finally had a voice through which their concerns could be expressed. In some of the larger rural counties, for instance, a substantial rise in drug using/abusing activity and drug arrests was documented. The regional monitoring agency now enjoys closer, positive affiliations with the county areas, and has begun to provide more qualitative technical assistance in numerous areas, including referrals, inter-agency collaboration and techniques in documentation/statistical recording.

CONCLUSIONS

The regional data network has been in operation for almost two years in the regional planning district of Richmond, Virginia. The regional monitoring agency has a more efficient tool with which to plan the direction of its efforts. Constructive and viable cooperation among numerous dissimilar collective agencies is better than every before. Documentation of the drug using/abusing population as seen by numerous agencies, who usually have no voice in planning efforts, is a reality. A planning agency, especially one involved in the elusive area of drug abuse control, must have feedback from the community for which they plan. Often monitoring agencies are engaged in extensive data collection and impose substantial burden on those organizations rarely know what is done with the data they submit. Such situations can only serve to create less than harmonious affiliations. Public hearings are generally used to give an opportunity for feedback from consumers and agency representatives. However, such opportunities are often self-limiting in view of agency resources and agency initiative.

The Regional Data network is a process which helps to resolve these problems. An on-going, reciprocal arrangement that is constantly in touch with the community over time is and should always be the focus of such networks. Regional representatives of state agencies through this mechanism can be more responsive to their communities. The communities in turn are represented in the planning process. The network provides a natural link between localities to the highest levels of state government wherein such links are often disjointed and concentrated too much in major metropolitan areas. If government is to be truly responsive to the needs of its people especially in the area of drug abuse control then it must require comprehensive, on-going planning tools which act as gauges of the populations served and to be served. Moreover, planning must use tools which highlight community needs so the available resources can be properly and effectively allocated. Through the Regional Data Network for drug abuse control the channels of communication are open to a degree where no bureaucrat can in good conscience ignore the cries of community representatives attempting to serve their population. Moreover, the Network as a planning tool, presents a more comprehensive profile of drug abuse throughout a community beyond that population seen by treatment programs. The increased level of inter-agency communication provides more thorough coverage in cases where uncertainty about a referral to a drug program is indicated.

LATTER DAY RELIGION AS TREATMENT FOR DRUG ABUSE:
STATISTICAL ANALYSIS OF SURVEY DATA

Marc Galanter, M.D.
Peter Buckley, M.B., Ch. B.

Department of Psychiatry
Albert Einstein College of Medicine
Bronx, New York

In this paper we report on the role played by a charismatic
religious sect in the apparent marked decline in drug use among
its youthful members. Our data reveal that specific aspects of
the sect's activities contribute to the decrease in drug use. The
Divine Light Mission (DLM), the sect studied, had its origin in
the United States in 1971, when its leader the Guru Maharaj Ji
visited this country from India at the age of thirteen. He acquired a large following of American youths, many of whom had
grown disenchanted with their involvement in the counter-culture.
The Mission has chapters throughout the United States, and is now
also represented in Western Europe. In 1974 it sponsored a large
conclave in the Houston Astrodome which gave the group a broad
national exposure.

Initiation in the DLM occurs when agreement is reached with
a Mahatma, one of the apostolic figures of the Mission, that the
potential member is ready to receive Knowledge. After this spiritual ceremony, the initiate is designated as a premie, and is expected to fulfill the tenets of the DLM, which include Service,
Santsang, Meditation and Darshan. Service refers to all activities
which are dedicated to the DLM, ranging from formal religious tasks
to a variety of good deeds benefiting either premies or non-premies. Satsang is a polemical sermon or verbal exchange in which
issues related to the Knowledge are presented or discussed.
Darshan is the experiencing of the personal presence of Maharaj Ji;
this is usually done at national festivals which are held at regular intervals. The Meditation generally consists of a one hour
period both in the morning and in the evening, during which the
meditator sits in a lotus position with eyes closed and experiences various spiritual and sensate aspects of the Knowledge. It
is also observed by experiencing the holy "Word" throughout the
day by rooting one's consciousness in that experience, no matter
what the activity. Many of the premies live in religious resi-

dences called Ashrams in which they practice celibacy, vegetarianism and full obedience to the DLM. A larger portion live in communal residences, but, unlike those in Ashrams, may marry, maintain individual ownership of property, and work outside of the DLM.

Method

In October, 1975 the anniversary of the birth of Maharaj Ji's father was celebrated in Orlando, Florida. Agreement was secured from the DLM national organization to have a sample of those present at the festival fill out a computer-codeable questionnaire on various aspects of their psychological experiences and membership in the movement. It consisted of multiple choice items in the following areas:

(a) Aspects of membership: Relating to friends and relatives who were members; the amount of time spent working for the movement and living with members of the group in and out of Ashrams.

(b) Group cohesiveness: Ratings on how much the respondent cared for the ten premies he knew best, all premies, and the ten non-premies he knew best; how much they cared for him or were suspicious of him.

(c) Experiences with drugs: Drug use was examined for the following time periods: at any time prior to membership, in the few months immediately prior to first contact with the movement, in the few months immediately after receiving knowledge, and in the most recent two months.

(d) Psychiatric symptoms: Various psychiatric symptoms were examined for the same time periods outlined above, as well as adaptative difficulties due to psychiatric problems, and history of contact with mental health professionals.

(e) "Spiritual" experiences: Questions were asked regarding the aforementioned periods in relation to perceptual, visual, auditory, somatosensory, temporal, and sexual sensations, with particular relation to meditation.

The questionnaires were administered in a group setting by the authors, with the assistance of premies attached to the medical service unit for the Festival. These premies were trained and supervised by the authors in clarifying the various questions which were raised by respondents. An accord with the DLM was reached so that the responding to the questionnaire was designated as Service. Because of this designation, all those approached agreed to respond and diligently reviewed each question to assure that its intent was clear to them. Registrants were systematically approached at points during the registration process so as to assure a random selection. 119 questionnaires were filled out by fully-initiated members, and these were chosen for full data analysis.

Results

The premies studied were predominately single young adults who lived in communal residence with other premies (72% were single, and 53% were between the ages of 21 and 25), and typically had been members for between one and two years. 76% had at least some college.

Respondents rated their drug use level along a five point scale. Table I indicates the consistent decline in level of moderate to heavy drug use, in accordance with frequency levels indicated for each drug. T-tests of proportions were done to ascertain the statistical significance of changes in the relative incidence of drug use from the period immediately prior to joining to the most recent two-month period. Typical decreases in moderate and severe drug use for this interval were: 46 to 7% for marijuana ($t=6.79$, $p<.001$); 13 to 0% for alcohol ($t-4.11$, $p<.001$) and 7 to 0% for heroin ($t=2.86$, $p<.01$). A step-wise multiple regression analysis was performed to ascertain correlates of changes in marijuana and alcohol use in relation to the predictor variables related to meditation, cohesion and activity. The multiple correlation coefficient for marijuana was .41 ($p<.01$) and for alcohol .40 ($p<.01$). Significant predictor variables were drawn from all three categories.

Discussion

On the basis of our findings it can be concluded that sustained membership in The Divine Light Mission led to a considerable decline in the level of drug use among the respondents. In addition, as indicated by the examples of marijuana and alcohol use, different aspects of group membership played differential roles in the decline in use. The data revealed, however, that all three of the membership factors examined, namely, group cohesiveness, meditation, and group activity were contributory factors in influencing the members for change.

The remarkable capacity of a cohesive peer group to "deprogram" the young adult from his pattern of drug use should be noted. Kandel (1) has already pointed to the central role of the peer group in initiating drug use. The prominent role of meditation in generating psychological and behavioral change among their members is also of interest. This latter issue has been discussed by Benson and Wallace (2) and by Shafii (3), and with regard to the DLM, by Horton and Lerner (4). The plasticity of the intoxication state and the potential substitution of other altered states of consciousness has been discussed by Galanter in relation to marijuana (5). This latter point is further supported by historical references to the use of cannabis in the 19th century in which its numerous uses gave no clear indication of any potential or use as a social intoxicant (6).

In conclusion, one might operationally define the DLM as a "multi-modality drug abuse treatment program" which has achieved a striking degree of effectiveness for those "patients" who chose to become full members and stay with the movement. In applying this paradigm further we would be obliged to examine the "dropout" population to develop a clearer picture of those drug abusers for whom the treatment is most suitable. Nonetheless, it behooves us to reflect on current professional treatment activities with some humility, given the potential for such outcome outside the limits of traditional therapeutic modalities.

REFERENCES

1. D. Kandel, Science, 181: 1067 (1973).

2. H. Benson, and R.K. Wallace, in (C.J.D. Zarafonetis, ed.), Drug Abuse, Proc. Internatl. Conf., Lea and Febiger, Philadelphia, Pa., 369 (1972).

3. M. Shafii, R. Lavely, and R. Jaffe, Amer. J. Psychiat., 131: 60 (1974).

4. J. Horton, and M. Lerner, in (E. Senay, S. Shorty, and H. Alksne, eds.), Developments in the Field of Drug Abuse, Natl. Drug Abuse Conf., Schenkman Publishing Company, Inc., Cambridge, Mass., 738 (1975).

5. M. Galanter, Am. J. Psychiat., June, 1976, in press.

6. S.H. Snyder, Uses of Marijuana, Oxford University Press, New York, 1971, p. 13.

TABLE I

INCIDENCE OF MODERATE TO HEAVY DRUG USE IN FOUR TWO-MONTH PERIODS

Drug	Questionnaire Scale*	any time before DLM Contact	right before DLM Contact	right after receiving Knowledge	last 2 months
Marijuana	3,4	65%	45	10	7
Alcohol	3,4	17	13	1	0
Depressants	2,3,4	15	5	1	1
Stimulants	2,3,4	18	7	0	1
Hallucinogens	2,3,4	29	12	1	0
Heroin	1-4	14	7	1	0

*Scale choices: (0) never. (1) 1-3 times. (2) 1-2x/week.
(3) about daily. (4) 1x/day, most days.

INTEGRITY OF OUTCOME EVALUATION

George De Leon, Ph.D.

Director of Research
Phoenix House Foundation, Inc.
New York, New York

Some non-research elements cloud a perspective of drug-treatment effectiveness. Several of these are historical, or characteristic of human services work. Others stem from an adversary relationship between funder and treatment program.

"Nuts and Bolts" Accountability

Drug programs can benefit from monitoring their daily internal ("nuts and bolts") operations, e.g. number of staff, kinds of services rendered, furniture, space, and particularly, record keeping.

Maintaining an orderly house is desirable in its own right, but discrepancy between proposed and actual operations also weakens confident interpretation of treatment effects. In a therapeutic community (TC), 2 clinical directors trying to do the work of 5, lessens the overall impact and ultimately reduces the number of program successes.

More subtle, negative influences can arise. Well intentioned, but overburdened staff, have particularly raw sensitivity to administrative pressures. Sensing danger from outside evaluators and board members, program directors feel compelled to hide or distort on matters of record keeping, understaffing, census, treatment and management failures. Though rationalized in terms of program survival, or commitment to the disadvantaged, these non-disclosures are nevertheless deceptions, which **are** potentially erosive.

In the TC, for example, absolute honesty and total respect for role models, more than ideals, are essentials in the treatment process. Cumulating increments of deception insidiously affect staff morale, and reinforce the resident's mistrust of the "system" or earlier parental disappointments. Although these effects are not obvious or directly expressed, their covert contribution to staff turnover and split rates should not be ignored.

Thus, accountability of internal operations is an external reflection of the integrity of the program's personnel, who after all, are the significant mediators of positive therapeutic change.

Comparative Outcome and the "Numbers Game"

Does methadone reduce criminal activity more effectively than drug-free treatment? Or, more currently, is out-patient, drug-free service more cost effective than the "expensive" residential approach.

In no other area of health care have the questions of comparative treatment been as relentlessly asked or so flagrantly politicized. The methodological obstacles inherent in large scale effectiveness research are respectfully acknowledged (by funding sources) in the criminal corrections and mental health systems. In drug abuse treatment, however, these seem to be impatiently ignored.

Comparative treatment studies in breast cancer, for example, have only appeared some three decades after initial claims of success. In mental health, firm conclusions have yet to emerge on the effectiveness or cost effectiveness of drugs, shock, psychotherapy, in or out patient services; and, in criminal corrections, the price of the incarceration - recidivism cycle has simply eluded precise cost benefit analysis. (1)

Beginning in the mid-1960's, however, before approaches to mass-urban drug abuse were 10 years old, heightened public pressure polarized drug treatment modalities to vie, like "hungry siblings", for attention and money - forcing distortions, exaggerations, or unreliable claims of success numbers. (2)

The early reports of crime reduction with methadone, in synergistic combination with citizen anxiety, head-started this modality in the comparative numbers game, "proving" its superiority over other approaches.

A special casualty has been the therapeutic community. For, in retrospect, the divisive race between the chemical and TC modalities was a mismatch from the start.

Clearly, their treatment goals and modus operandi were entirely different. Cultivating individual life-style change in the TC was seen as a low-impact, slow process for the social urgency, while the chemical approach seemed to fit a public health model of rapid, mass innoculation.

Less obvious, was an historical-genealogical difference between these two modalities; one which profoundly biased their capability of entering the comparative contest.

Chemical approaches to drug abuse treatment descend from the medico-physical tradition with science oriented staff and training. Reared in the deterministic view of physical cause, course and cure, doctors and researchers could administer a chemical treatment and sensibly document it.

Understandably, these professionals competently designed studies, assembled conferences and presented their data - a sophistication which facilitated publication of a considerable volume of research papers.

In contrast, the TC evolved from quasi-religious roots, community consciousness, self-help and a guiding sense that the convert, or ex-sick, lead the sick. As sparse, nomadic undertakings, therapeutic communities could hardly identify themselves as fraternity, much less a treatment modality. The former addict, alcoholic and ex-criminal offender "para-professional", neither spoke, nor cared for, the language and logical rules of science. Quantified reports could not have surfaced while credible, descriptive narratives were only scattered appearances.

These legitimate differences in the language and consciousness of 2 treatment worlds soon became misunderstood imparities in the public arena. Too busy to formulate questions of outcome, and untrained in answering them, drug-free workers often experienced a puzzling self-doubt in their efficacy to compete in the numbers contest.

One serious consequence of this historical handicap is that policy makers are <u>still</u> remarkably naive
about the inner workings or effectiveness of the TC (as
are the health services, corrections and the public).
Funders have pursued information, but usually by re-
course to the "outside evaluation". This approach has
been costly and relatively unproductive, however,
chiefly because of psychological reasons.

Program people have perceived (often correctly)
the "outside evaluation" as a disguised, fiscal audit,
not an honest research effort to understand or improve
their treatment. In this climate of suspicion, only
scanty, superficial data could emerge, sketching
pictures as distant from the actuality as the evaluators themselves.

Today, the TC possesses a readiness and capability
for self assessment; and, in small chapters, has been
telling its <u>own</u> story. (3, 4, 5) Now, however, it must
be given the opportunity to tell that story more fully,
for the public still reacts reflexively to its social
pains.

Earlier, the drug epidemic galvanized indiscriminate
spending. The promise was immediate relief from crime
in the streets. Currently, crime, still unabated, and
the squeeze of tight money, provide an equally strong
counter-reaction for relief - underfunding. Then and
now, there is not enough valid information on treatment
process and outcome. Then and now, uninformed fiscal
decisions are the most expensive. These illusions of
solution are palliative. As temporary sedatives, they
dull the motivation needed to achieve permanent resolutions. Once impressive sums of money are given, or
taken away, we are lulled and distracted, until the
next crisis.

Perhaps the cold wind of economic austerity is
neutralizing the struggle among treatment modalities.
There is yet another encouragement. Various treatments
have matured, discovering the fallibility of imposing
any single therapeutic approach upon the diversity of
human behavior. Not all drug abusers are the same, nor
are the paths for individual change.

References

1. De Leon, George, The Issues of Effectiveness and
    Cost Effectiveness of Drug-Abuse Treatment, in
    preparation.

2. De Leon, George, Behavioral Science in the
    Therapeutic Community: Some Old Issues Revisited,
    Journal of Drug Issues, 435-442, 1974.

3. De Leon, George, Phoenix House: Studies in a
    Therapeutic Community, (1968-1973), New York:
    MSS Information Corporation, 1974.

4. De Leon, George, Phoenix House Therapeutic Com-
    munity: The Influence of Time in Program on Change
    in Resident Drug Addicts, Proceedings, 81st Annual
    Convention, APA, 1973.

5. De Leon, George, Psychologic and Socio-Demographic
    Profiles of Addicts in the Therapeutic Community,
    Final Report of Project Activities Under NIDA
    Grant #DA-00831-01, 1976.

EVALUATING DRUG CONTROL EFFECTIVENESS

Bernard A. Gropper, Ph.D.*
Office of Evaluation
National Institute of Law Enforcement
and Criminal Justice
Law Enforcement Assistance Administration

INTRODUCTION

Exploratory analyses of the effects of federal drug control on
abuse patterns and related indicators were made on data through
late 1974. Nine representative drugs were evaluated: (a) a
group of five anorectic stimulants orginally controlled in mid-1973
(Benzphetamine, Chlorphentermine, Diethylpropion, Phendimetrazine
and Phentermine) and (b) a group of four depressants scheduled
in late-1973, a non-barbiturate sedative (Methaqualone) and three
barbiturates (Amobarbital, Pentobarbital and Secobarbital).

These provided a representative set of drugs which, to the extent
possible within the constraints of the available cases, sampled
the control schedule levels and pharmacological categories,
offered reasonably large base periods of data both before and after
the change of control status, and had been newly scheduled or
rescheduled from lower to more stringent levels of control.

The primary data bases used were the Drug Abuse Warning Network
(DAWN) for abuse levels and the National Prescription Audit (NPA)
for licit availability through prescriptions. Additional exploratory investigations were also made, using other DEA information
resources, of effects on the availability of the controlled
drugs to the medically needy and on related drug arrests, in
order to supplement the interpretive picture available within the
primary data bases. However, information on these related topics
was very sparse, and much more data and study is needed to
satisfactorily identify and evaluate their interrelations.

---

* Formerly with the Office of Science and Technology, Drug
Enforcement Administration

The NPA statistics used in this paper are based on data
copyright by IMS America Limited, 1973 and 1974.
The full report is DEA # STS-TR-16, June 1975 (NTIS #PB246720)

A significant overall pattern of reductions in drug abuse rates was found for each of these drugs. Moreover, reviews of federal records and prescription data indicated these desired benefits did not tend to be associated with any appreciable levels of undesired side-effects--medical prescribing practices were not inhibited, ready availability of these drugs for legitimate medical needs was maintained, and no large arrest and criminalization of otherwise innocent users was found.

METHODS

Although the DAWN represents the best existing data base for continual nationwide and regional monitoring of incidents involving all types of drugs and user populations, and the NPA monitors nationwide prescription patterns at the consumer level, they provide data from operational systems which were not set up primarily to support these specific analyses and absolute long-term stability within these systems is not attainable. The DAWN system expanded from its initial pilot phase in July 1973, shortly before the change in these drugs' official control status. For comparisons across the pre-and post-control status periods that would extend back into the initial DAWN period we employed a normalized measure of abuse per reporting facility. In making this normalization, incidents from all facilities of a given type were weighted equally, as a reasonable first approximation. Comparisons were made against abuse levels observed for all other drugs within the data base which did not undergo a control status change at that same time.

For analysis of abuse rates with each drug, let:

$$FR = \text{Total Facility Rate} = \sum_i \frac{d_f}{n_f}$$

Where: f = facility type: ER = Emergency Rooms
                                  ME = Medical Examiners
                                  IP = Inpatient Units
                                  CC = Crisis Centers

           n = number of facilities of type f in interval i

           i = intervals for available data (i.e., monthly)

           d = data (i.e., frequency of DAWN mentions)

RESULTS

For the DAWN abuse data, as summarized in Figure 1, the effects of new control status or increased control level appear to be:

a) Near-term decreases in abuse incidents for every drug in these
    sample groups. Comparisons of the normalized pre-control to
    post-control rates for the test drugs showed a general pattern
    of decrease for the entire set below the relatively stable
    levels for the unchanged overall population of drugs (signifi-
    cant at the 0.998 level of confidence, using the binomial test
    for direction of change relative to the DAWN base levels).

b) Suggestions of possible differential effects within a
    therapeutic class which appear related to: 1) level of
    schedule (III > IV), and 2) the original relative abuse
    rates--with more effect found for the more stringent schedules
    and the more heavily abused drugs.

c) Newly controlled drugs appear to show a greater proportional
    decrease than those cases in which already-controlled drugs
    are shifted to a more stringent schedule, although decreases
    are obatined for both types of control increase. There is
    a suggestion of diminishing returns.

d) The tentative pattern of greater decrease being generally
    associated within a therapeutic group with larger prior
    abuse rates does not appear to hold for those drugs that
    are shifted from a lower to a higher control level, and other
    additional factors appear to be more significant within that
    sub-group.

e) When groups of related drugs are scheduled at approximately
    the same time, such class-action scheduling seems to leave the
    original relative positions intact, so that decreases in one
    drug are not accompanied by increases in other drugs within
    the controlled set.

A more detailed view of the month-by-month pattern of abuse
decreases is given in Figure 2, which shows the numbers of reported
incidents following control for each of the three barbiturate-
sedatives from the first quarter of FY 74 through the first quarter
of FY 75.

Overall, our analyses of NPA prescription trends show:

a) Long-term decreases in the amphetamine stimulants and
    barbiturate sedatives tending to be accompanied by increases
    in the non-amphetamines and non-barbiturates, which appear to
    reflect changes both in prescribing preferences and control
    status over the 6 year interval from 1969 through 1974.(Fig. 3)

b) General post-control decreases for both the licit prescription
    rates and overall abuse rates, with positive but widely
    varying correlations with time obtained for each of the drugs
    in the sample groups.

c) Within the sedatives, a much stronger correlation between pre criptions and abuse rates for the previously uncontrolled Methaqualone than for the three previously-controlled barbiturates. Figure 4 indicates the strong pattern of synchronous variations between its month-by-month abuse levels and NPA prescription levels (r = 0.953) over this period.

Possible side-effects attributable to drug control were also explored. Federal files involving purchases, seizures or arrests for these drugs were checked, and discussions held with the medical staffs of DEA and the National Institute on Drug Abuse.

Of the 294 federal cases involving these drugs in FY 74, the large majority (98%) were not classifiable as criminalizations of otherwise innocent citizens due to their possession of small quantities of these drugs for personal use since they involved wholesale quantities, Similarly, no significant evidence was found that drug controls inhibited physician prescribing practices to the degree that the drugs were not readily available to those with legitimate medical needs.

These near-term effects, of course, will not necessarily persist as a stable permanent picture. Further monitoring and evaluation of long-term trends are being made, to permit maintenance of these improved abuse patterns and develop additional insights into the complex relations affecting the balances between necessary drug availability and undesired drug abuse.

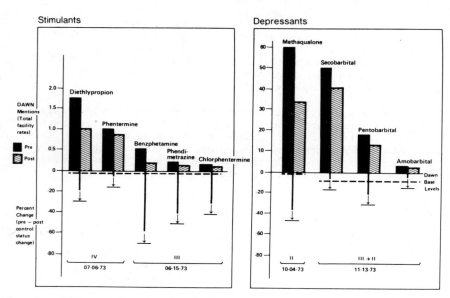

Fig. 1.   Effects of control schedule changes on abuse incident rates.

Fig. 2. Trends in drug abuse incidents: barbiturates.

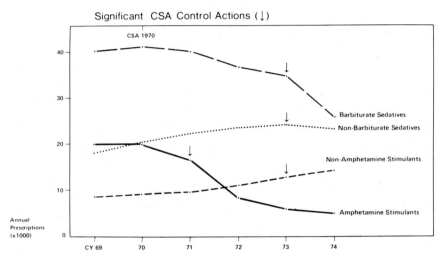

Fig. 3. Prescription trends: stimulants and depressants--1969-74.

238

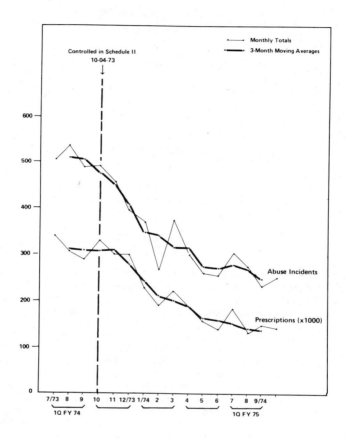

Fig. 4. Abuse incidents and prescription trends. Non-barbiturate
sedative: Methaqualone.

A MULTIDIMENSIONAL PROBLEM-ORIENTED
REVIEW AND EVALUATION SYSTEM

Allan J. Galonsky
Sherman Patrick

Addiction Research and Treatment Corporation
22 Chapel Street
Brooklyn, New York   11212

INTRODUCTION

With the advent of increasing pressures for more frequent and complete audits of drug abuse treatment agencies, the importance of building a method of internal assessment into treatment delivery systems is becoming clear.

BACKGROUND

A number of sophisticated and rather costly systems previously were developed by the Addiction Research and Treatment Corporation, as it was founded provided that the program both foster and submit to evaluation and research. These efforts could have functioned as a direct aid to the treatment programs and as useful tools in improvement of administrative procedures. Thus it would serve as a data resource for inquiry into various aspects of the narcotics abuse problem. Evaluative studies were carried out by Yale Medical School (monitoring of Medical Care Delivery System and the study of the efficacy of various dosage levels), Columbia University School of Social Work (assessment of overall impact of the program on the socio-economic behavior of drug abusers), and Harvard University Center for Criminal Justice, (examination of relationships between the Criminal Justice System and the impact by Addiction Research and Treatment Corporation treatment delivery). Federal grants independently obtained for these purposes were liberally supplemented by Addiction Research and Treatment Corporation, these studies ended in 1975 after five years. These efforts were the forerunners of the present effort. The present system is expected to function as a primary data collection and self-evaluation tool for Addiction Research and Treatment Corporation. It seeks to take note of the data and knowledge gaps already experienced, and thereby provide instructive feedback of data interpretation that can improve patient care and administrative procedures relevant to compliance with the Federal, State and/or local regulations. It will, of course, lack the objectivity of an independent approach based upon needs assessment. Yet it strives to explore and expose what the program does (output), what happens to its clients (outcome), and what kinds of patient needs were known to the program and were dealt with. It does not address post-discharge results due to cost factors.

DEVELOPMENT OF THE SYSTEM

When the system was conceived eight months ago, it was decided that from the outset it would be established in a manner that would allow for evaluation of service functions and treatment outcome as well as for reporting and program compliance recording. The treatment staff is interdisciplinary in function and professional composition; social workers, vocational specialists, educators, lawyers, psychologists, medical doctors and nurse-clinicians, all act in a generalistic role as well as in the specialist roles of their training and background. Each individual acts as the primary treatment service worker for a variety of patients. Patients are assigned to the staff on a rotating basis unless the initial referring information indicates an immediate specific need for a given modality treatment. When necessary, the special expertise of another professional is requested in consultation or referral. It is sometimes necessary to transfer the primary responsibility for a patient to another professional. This diversity served as an added stimulus to our desire to be able to evaluate the effectiveness of modalities approaching similar patient problems from different points of view.

The tasks in developing our new record-keeping system suited to both regulatory compliance and internal evaluation were multiple. Our system required: (1) a cost-conscious method of development and implementation with respect to man and materials; (2) a tool to be used for evaluation of a multi-modality delivery in meeting patient needs; (3) a tool for managing program ongoing operations with respect to, internal data needs, regulatory agency required reporting, and regulatory agency compliance. Inherent in the above tasks are untold checks and balances necessary to satisfy the many reporting agencies and ongoing audits of Addiction Research and Treatment Corporation. Data by modality of service and delivery, congruence of internal and external data bases including third party reimbursement data are all needed.

SYSTEM INPUT

One of our most difficult problems was to develop a way of briefly describing a patient at a time of his initial case review at admission, so as to be able later to measure the treatment outcome. Diagnostic data alone was felt to be insufficient, since it did not adequately describe the patient's basic needs, reason for his seek-help, his source of discomfort, or the plan for remedying these problem areas. Many things unrelated to drug taking could cause narcotics abusers to seek help. However, upon completion of treatment, the narcotics abuser diagnosis might still be appropriate, even though the patient's situation might have improved considerably. Intake evaluation on patients therefore was coupled with specifically listed identifiable problems, in lieu of the more preferable needs assessment surveys, since the latter would have meant an expense of staff time that we could not afford.

Instead, over a period of several months we met with treatment staff to review and list the presenting problems of patients as recorded by staff. At the end of this period, the problems generated from all modalities a categorical listing. Each staff supervisor was asked about special interest areas which could be included. Also, during this same period, a review was made of all applicable funding and regulatory agency policies and guidelines which applied. Data enabling conformity with the recording and reporting aspects of these regulations was incorporated into a one page form along with the areas already noted. Five versions, one designed specific to each treatment modality were formatted.

The worker uses his modality's form at each patient contact. He fills out the front page containing all data needed for compliance records. Process data relevant to what is happening, how and why, etc. is recorded in space provided on the back of the form. A form with both front and back completed, serves the patient's chart needs.

All of the information described here, is stored manually. One copy of the form is placed in the patient's record which is kept at the local clinic. The other is stored in the records department. Records at both locations are cross-referenced by our agency name and identification number. A new file is activated for each new case and the new intake record is immediately available to the treatment staff and, to the records department responsible for preparation and dissemination of external and internal reports.

SYSTEM OUTPUT

Actual data retrieved for various internal uses on a weekly basis include census, patient's medicaid status, medicaid visits made per week, methadone pick-ups and methadone dosage levels. Monthly data is generated on such items as patient visits, readmissions, terminations, transfers, number and types of services rendered, number of clients receiving chemotherapies and number drug free, as well as a clinic by clinic roster listing name, identification number, admission date and current status. Quarterly data includes cumulative totals for all the above plus additional demographic data breakdowns into sex, ethnicity and so forth. Also a "patient profile" is to be compiled bi-annually. The first of these included: Sex, Race, Age, Time in Program, Prior Treatment, Last Treatment, Medication and Admission Type.

Because this system is now a manual one, data retrieval includes the use of computerized "report data" obtained from various external regulatory agencies where available. Although this external feedback of data is not always current because of time lapses regarding reporting and input, it has proven to be surprisingly reliable when checked against in-house census data. This is because periodic record checks are made with all these data sources to insure that the recording validity and accuracy necessary for internal and external congruence is being maintained. (Note that when discrepancies are found, immediate steps are taken to correct them as a top priority).

1   Other output is also possible and highly desirable. This includes such things as production of patient problem index, average number service hours spent per patient seen, total patients seen, number and type of patient problems referred, and to whom, etc. These items can be retrieved for an individual staff member or patient, for individual clinics, and for modalities. However, manual handling makes routinized production of such tables impractical.

DISCUSSION AND CONCLUSION

As noted, several different types of output can be routinely available. For example, monthly outputs for modalities can be generated, giving each a summary of its data for the month and for the year to date. Although such reports represent simply a numerical summary of the items entered into the system, such reports allow for comparisons among modalities regarding their utilization by patients, and their results. Such reports will supply data useful in planning program expansion or modification, deployment of personnel and efforts expended. It also yields a monthly description of the population that allows examination of such areas as seasonal intake and discharge patterns, turnover, etc.

Finally, it should prove useful to have such a data base upon which to develop specific studies of qualitative concern because of the wide range of identifiable patient groups. The patients'' clinic records are available for data extraction of course. Thus areas such as required narrative data analysis and even direct interview technique, for data gathering becomes feasible. For example, we are now taking a look at case histories of patients who have had a drinking problem. The contact sheet exposes the problem area and gives us entre into the sample.

These and other comparisons necessary for evaluation and comparisons for relative effectiveness of modalities, staff, clinics, etc., are best generated by electronic data processing. To this event, the agency has applied to the National Institute on Drug Abuse for a small research grant that will underwrite the cost of computerization of data and the employment of a researcher to do the actual evaluations.

FOLLOW-UP RESEARCH FOR TREATMENT FACILITIES
WITH LOW RESEARCH PRIORITIES

William R. Schmelter M.S., Joseph C. Kern Ph.D.

Nassau County Department of Drug and Alcohol Addiction
and Hofstra University (Dept. of Psychology)

INTRODUCTION

Follow-up studies can provide very useful and practical information for any therapeutic or treatment program. Evaluation of
almost any aspect of a treatment program ultimately requires examination of the effect of that aspect on "treatment success".

The uses to which follow-up data can be put can be divided into two broad categories. First the data can be used to evaluate
how well a program - as it exists - performs the function it was
designed to perform. Under this category are included studies
which are intended to demonstrate that a program is worthy of its
existence (with implications for continued or additional funding,
public relations, etc.) and studies attempting to demonstrate that
one type of program is better than others [1]. A second way that
follow-up data can be utilized is to examine the relationship between client characteristics, program components or various combinations of the two and the behavior of clients subsequent to
treatment ("treatment success"). Here the results of the research
could be used for the development of prognostic indicators and
more importantly for general program modification and improvement
[2,3]. For lack of a better terminology these two potential uses
of follow-up information will be referred to as "external" use and
"internal" use respectively.

Follow-up research is typically an expensive and time consuming activity. Also, it is not difficult to find able criticism of
much of the work done to date [4,2]. This criticism generally revolves around one or more of the following points.
1) Lack of adequate control groups formed by random assignment of subjects to treatment and non-treatment groups.
2) Poor contact rates, resulting in a biased follow-up sample.
3) Poor reliability (accuracy) of obtained data.

A more complete version of this paper is available from the
authors.

Such criticism, and the prescriptions for how proper follow-up should be carried out have undoubtedly discouraged many programs from attempting organized follow-up studies due to the lack of staff, time and basically money.

The position taken here is that most of us are, and should be, interested in the "internal" use of follow-up information. That is follow-up information is considered useful if it can help us to discover ways to increase the "success" of "our" clients.

If this premise is accepted then the criticisms presented above (especially the first one) should not be viewed as prohibitive. The concern for generalizablity, representativeness and accuracy (in terms of "absolute" levels of success) are crucial if the data is to be used for "external" purposes (as defined above). However, when we are concerned with the "internal" use of the data we can be satisfied, at present, to 1) discover relations concerning the clients that seek "our" programs, 2) discover relations concerning "contacted" clients. (If our findings do not generalize to our "non-contacted" groups it is still infinitely better to learn about some of our clients than none at all). 3) Place our clients on at least an "ordinal scale" in terms of treatment success (5).

A follow-up tracking system is presented below which can be used by programs which do not or cannot place a high priority on research and which are primarily interested in the "internal" use of the obtained data. Before presenting the system it should be pointed out that the intention here is not to provide excuses for sloppy research. The point being made is that as concerned workers in an applied field, where money is scarce, we can obtain useful, practical information without carrying out perfectly designed studies.

A FOLLOW-UP TRACKING SYSTEM

Overview

The system presented here is not offered as a major innovation in follow-up research but as a system which: 1) spreads the work involved in a follow-up study over a number of staff members; 2) provides acceptable contact levels; 3) provides a means of obtaining fairly accurate information; 4) can be used (and is most appropriately used) on an ongoing basis; 5) provides some direct as well as derived therapeutic benefits and 6) seems to work in general. At any step in the procedure modifications can be made which either better suit a given program or seem more appropriate to those doing the research for whatever reason. Therefore, the system will be presented in its basic form and the possibility of modification at any step will be assumed.

Counselors (professional or para-professional) and a person assigned as part time "data coordinator" (secretary, research aide) perform the actual collection of the data and keep the system running. A person with some research skills would be required to determine the variables to be studied and to analyze data.

Specific Procedures

Step 1 - The first step is to obtain pertinent information from
the clients at intake or at appropriate points in time during treatment. This information is what we want to "relate" to some measure
of treatment success and it can take a variety of forms: demographic information, personality variables, behavior while in treatment,
etc.

Step 2 - At some point during treatment the client is told about
the follow-up study and its purpose and is asked to provide information which will facilitate subsequent contact with him. For
example, names, addresses and phone numbers of friends and relatives of the client can be obtained with the understanding that they
may be contacted to provide information on the whereabouts and/or
behavior of the client. This information along with the client's
name, address and phone number and his counselor's name are written
on an index card. This step can be completed by the data coordinator or counselor.

Step 3 - A starting point for the follow-up period must be determined. For inpatient facilities the client's discharge date is
most appropriate and for outpatient programs either the intake date,
discharge date, or perhaps the date that a client completes a
certain phase of treatment can be used. At the starting date for a
given client the index card completed in Step 2 is given to the
counselor who will actually be contacting the client in the following months. In addition a "Follow-up Face Sheet" containing the
clients name, the counselor's name and the starting date is entered
into a "Follow-up File". This file contains 31 sections each representing a day of the month and labeled 1st of month, 2nd of
month........31st of month. The face sheet is entered into the
section corresponding to the client's starting date. This step is
carried out by the data coordinator.

Step 4 - Once the system has started every Monday the data coordinator looks through the follow-up file under those "days of the
month" which correspond to the week beginning on that day. For example, if it is Monday, January 3rd, the data coordinator looks
through the 9th of the month. For each client whose face sheet is
found under these days of the month a "Follow-up Information Sheet"
with the client's name entered on it is given to the counselor responsible for that person. Each counselor then has a week to contact the people assigned to him and fill out the Follow-up Information Sheets. These contacts can be made by phone or in person.
Also other resources (hospitals, friends and relatives of the
client, police departments, etc.) can be used to obtain or verify
information. In order to increase the reliability of the data when
contacts are made by phone or in person, it is advisable to require that specific questions asking specific information be used
in their exact form by the counselors when conducting their interviews. On the following Monday the data coordinator gives each
counselor a new batch of Follow-up Information Sheets and picks up
those from the week before which are then attached to each client's
face sheet. This process continues until a client has 6 Follow-

up Information Sheets (for a 6 month study) attached to his face
sheet at which time it is removed from the file.
Step 5 - Once a client's follow-up period is completed his follow-
up information plus all other pertinent information are coded for
computer processing. This coding can be done by virtually anyone.
Although "computer processing" sounds forbidding to many people,
there are statistical packages (6) which can easily be used by some
one familiar with statistical procedures. In addition, computer
time and service can be obtained at reasonable rates from many
university computer centers.

Characteristics of the System

1) The principal advantage of the system is that no one person
is burdened with more than a reasonable amount of additional work.
We have run a pilot of the system in a 10 bed, 7 day detoxification
program and the system did not interfere with the daily activity of
the program. For a six month follow-up the average number of contacts per counselor (4 counselors) in this program was approximately 10 per week. Since this is the case the system can be carried
out on a continuing basis rather than as a one-shot study. An
important reason for making the system a permanent part of a program is that in most cases counselors would like to keep in touch
with their clients, but fail to because there is no systematic reminder. In our pilot study the counselors expressed that they felt
the system was beneficial both from the client's point of view and
their own since they now received constant feedback regarding their
work.

2) One criticism which could be leveled against the system is
that the counselors might provide biased follow-up reports. If the
counselors are trained and understand that the system is not to
evaluate them personally but rather to provide information for
program inprovement, this problem can be eliminated. Also, we feel
that the clients provide more accurate information to a counselor
whom they trust than to a researcher whom they don't know at all.

3) Contacting clients on a number of occasions rather than
just once has a number of advantages. First, it increases the
accuracy of the follow-up information. Since the clients are being
asked about their behavior during a short period of time they can
be more specific in their description. Also, receiving six reports
at equal intervals provides more resolution than could be achieved
if only one contact was made after six months. In addition, it is
more difficult for a client to fool a counselor six times than once

A second benefit of calling clients monthly is that a relative
-ly high contact rate can be maintained. Since we are dealing with
a population that "moves around" alot, calling the client or a
friend or relative of the client monthly makes it easier to keep
up with him than if we had waited 6 months before our first attempt
In the pilot study mentioned above, we attempted to follow-up 189
consecutive clients. We obtained complete information (i.e. all 6
months) on 132 of the clients (a contact rate of 70%).

As mentioned earlier this system is not offered as a major innovation in follow-up research nor is it offered as a final system. We, however, have found it to work well on a practical level and hopefully it will provide us with some useful information

REFERENCES

(1)   Emrick, C.D. A review of psychologically oriented treatment of alcoholism, II; the relative effectiveness of different treatment approaches and the effectiveness of treatment versus no treatment. Journal of Studies on Alcohol, 36, No. 1,88-108 (1975)

(2)   Trice, H.M., Roman, P.M. and Belasco, J.A. Selection for treatment; a predictive evaluation of an alcoholism treatment regimen. International Journal of Addiction, 4, 303-317 (1969).

(3)   Bateman, N.I. and Peterson, D.M. Variables related to outcome of treatment for hospitalized alcoholics. International Journal of Addiction, 6, 215-224 (1971).

(4)   Hill, M.J. and Blane, H.T. Evaluation of psychotherapy with alcoholics; a critical review. Quarterly Journal of Studies on Alcohol. 28, 76-104, (1967).

(5)   Nunnally, J.C. Psychometric Theory, New York: McGraw-Hill Book Co., (1970).

(6)   Nie, N.H., Bent, D.H. and Hull, C.H. SPSS: Statistical Package for the Social Sciences, New York, McGraw-Hill Book Co., (1970).

DRUG TREATMENT OUTCOMES: IS SEX A FACTOR?

Barry J. Rosenthal, M.S.
Bradford T. Greene, Ph.D.

Richard Katon and Associates, Inc.
11300 Rockville Pike
Rockville, Maryland 20852

William H. Spillane, Ph.D.

Director, Division of Scientific and
    Program Information
National Institute on Drug Abuse
11400 Rockville Pike
Rockville, Maryland 20852

I. INTRODUCTION

The latent belief that traditional approaches to drug treatment have been unable to meet the unqiue needs of women has been raised to the conscious level by various feminist groups, the media, and other social commentators. The few studies conducted suggest that the female addict has been differentially treated due to ingrained societal attitudes that relegate her to a more deviant position and cast her as much "sicker" than her male counterpart.[1,2] Others argue that the treatment afforded female abusers is often inadequate at best: it does not satisfy their unique needs which are shaped by different social/psychological reasons for using drugs and are manifested in different patterns of drug abuse.[3,4]

The purpose of this paper is to examine the impact of sex on treatment outcome and to identify variables which interact with sex to affect treatment outcome.

If differences in outcome and other treatment variables exist between males and females and if these differences can be explained by identifiable treatment factors, we may be able to structure our present service delivery system to more fully meet the needs of specific population groups and thereby improve the rate of successful treatment outcomes.

II. METHODOLOGY[5]

Factors used in this analysis are treatment outcomes, demographic characteristics, treatment history, and drug abuse pattern. Treatment outcome refers to "Reason for Discharge" on the CODAP discharge form where the program reports why the client was terminated. Demographic characteristics include the variables, sex, age, race, and the socioeconomic characteristics, employment and educational status. Treatment history is measured by the client's status at admission (first admission, readmission, transfer), number of prior treatment experiences, length of time in treatment; and drug abuse pattern, by primary drug and frequency of use of primary drug. (A more detailed description of the variables collected by the CODAP system can be found in the CODAP National Management Handbook, 1974.)

The source of data is a computer-generated random sample of 13,268 clients drawn from 146,681 clients in a Historical Client File of the Client Oriented Data Acquisition Process (CODAP) covering the period November 1974 to September 1975.

The purpose of this paper is to examine two categorical relationships. They are: (1) the relationship between treatment outcome and sex, and (2) the differential effects of demographic characteristics, treatment history, and patterns of drug abuse on treatment outcomes for males and females.

Because most of the data is either nominal (categorical) or ordinal, the analysis is based on data arrayed in contingency tables. Percentage differences in the independent variable determine the magnitude of the studied relationships. Differences of 0-4% are negligible (i.e., they could be due to measurement error alone); differences of 5-9% are small, 10-19%, moderate; and over 20%, large.

III. FINDINGS

The first relationship examined in this study is that between drug treatment outcomes and sex. When the five categories of treatment outcome are contrasted for males versus females, the differences are negligible. (The outcome categories include completed treatment, left treatment, transferred, non-compliance, and other.)

Although a difference does not exist between females and males regarding treatment outcome, the data are important: the finding of no association between outcomes and sex is contrary to previous research and inconsistent with the belief of many individuals in the field. For example, Levy and Doyle (1974) found that the split rate for females was 10-15% higher than for males. These data also are important in terms of noting the actual success rate (completed treatment outcome) among clients. Less than one in four clients discharged from federally-funded treatment is a "successful" treatment completion.

The finding of no association between sex and treatment outcome does not preclude the possibility that categorical sex differences may exist when control variables are introduced. The second part of this analysis examines whether the variables describing demographic characteristics, treatment history, and drug abuse patterns differentially affect treatment outcomes for males and females. This issue is both theoretically and practically important to understanding females' treatment outcomes and their role in drug programs: it can help to clarify the way in which sex differences may reflect important aspects of the treatment process.

When the impact of each demographic variable is considered, the percentage differences for male versus female treatment outcomes are small or negligible. However, one of the most pronounced sex differences occurs among the two youngest age groups who leave treatment before completion. In the under 18 age cohort, 48% of the females leave treatment compared to 42% of the males; in the 18-20 group, 49% of the females, but 43% of the males, leave before completing treatment.

Negligible differences in treatment outcome are present for men and women within racial categories. While sex is not a factor in explaining differences in treatment outcome, race is. White clients have the greatest occurrence of treatment completion and black clients have the greatest occurrence of non-compliance.

Differences between males and females at the various levels of educational attainment are negligible. Less than 23% of the females who did not finish high school complete treatment compared to 32% who have completed twelfth grade; a similar difference occurs among male clients.

Differences in treatment outcome for men versus women, when controlling for employment status at admission and participation in vocational improvement, are negligible. The outcome differences are not related to clients' sex but treatment completions are associated with whether a client of either sex is employed full-time or participating in vocational improvement.

The final part of this analysis focuses upon sex differences in treatment outcome for the variables describing treatment history and drug abuse patterns. The variable, number of prior treatment experiences, accounts for percentage differences between males and females that are negligible, with differences less than 3 percentage points in all instances except one: 33% of the females with three or more treatment experiences are either transferred or referred compared to 26% of the males in this same category.

Only negligible sex differences appear when examining length of time in treatment. As is true for clients with no prior treatment experience, there is also a relationship between clients' remaining in treatment for 3 or more months and the "completed treatment" outcomes. The relationships, however, are similar for males and females.

Another treatment history variable, admission status, yields negligible sex differences when examined on measures of treatment outcome. Overall, the highest percentage of admissions to treatment were first admissions, with 76% of the females and 72% of the males being first admissions to treatment. Though there is no outcome difference by sex for admission status, first admissions are more likely to complete treatment than readmissions or clients who have transferred from another clinic.

Most of the variables discussed above exhibit only negligible sex differences (of less than 4 percentage points) with males and females always consistent regarding their patterns of treatment outcome within categories of a third (control) variable.

One variable that shows somewhat larger differences is primary drug of abuse at admission. Overall, a higher percent of males use opiates (57%) than females (49%), but females are more often abusers of barbiturates and sedatives (11%) than their male counterparts (5%). Both groups use marihuana at about an equal rate.

In terms of actual differences in treatment outcomes for males and females who abuse different drugs, females with a primary problem of alcohol have the highest rate of treatment success (33%). The highest rate of treatment success among the male population occurs among primary abusers of marihuana (35%). Comparatively, the rate of treatment success for males with a primary problem of alcohol is 30% and for females with a primary marihuana problem, 32%.

The three most frequently occurring primary drugs of abuse for males are heroin (57%), marihuana (15%), and alcohol (7%) respectively. For females, the top three drugs are heroin (49%), marihuana (17%), and barbiturates-sedatives (11%). No matter which of these drugs is considered, female abusers exhibit the same treatment outcome patterns as male abusers.

An examination of sex differences within categories of frequency of use of primary drug reveals negligible differences and similar trends for females and males within the completed treatment category. However, among clients who are "infrequent" users females are more likely to leave treatment than males; 38% of the males and 45% of the females in this category leave treatment prior to completion.

253

VI.   CONCLUSIONS

This paper analyzes a large quantity of data to examine differences in treatment outcomes for males and females. The various relationships examined indicate there are only negligible or small percentage differences between males and females with respect to treatment outcomes. The introduction of a number of categorical control variables does not amplify the percentage differences.

The differences in treatment outcome that were seen in the analyzed data occur between the categories of certain demographic, treatment history or drug abuse pattern variables rather than between males and females. In fact, those differences that were noted in the other categorical variables tend to be similar for females and males.

The lack of a meaningful relationship between treatment outcome and sex does not mean that the female abuser does not have special treatment needs. Sex differences may not be reflected in the treatment outcome categories of the CODAP data. Further analysis of all clients admitted to treatment conducted at other levels of interest may amplify findings of this study.[7]

NOTES

[1] J. Chwast, "Special Problems in Treating Female Offenders: Social Psychological Aspects," International Journal of Offender Therapy, V (1971), pp. 24-27.

[2] Levy, Stephen J., and Doyle, Kathleen M., "Attitudes Toward Women in a Drug Treatment Program." Journal of Drug Issues, 4(4): 428-434, Fall, 1974.

[3] P. Chesler, Women and Madness (New York: Doubleday, 1972).

[4] G. Mellenger, et. al., "Patterns of Psychotherapeutic Drug Use Among Adults in San Francisco," Archives of General Psychiatry, 25:   383-394.

[5] Derived in part from "A Comparative Study of Treatment Outcomes of Male and Female Drug Abuse Clients," (Draft), for NIDA Statistical Series: A Quarterly Report, July-September, 1975.

[6] Norman H. Nie, et. al., SPSS: Statistical Package for the Social Sciences, Second Edition (New York: McGraw-Hill Book Company, 1974).

[7] Unabridged text and data tables available from the authors.

A DISCUSSION OF THE ROLE OF ONGOING EVALUATION
IN A DRUG PREVENTION PROGRAM

Louise Murray, CSW

The Children's Aid Society
New York, New York

Since 1970, the Children's Aid Society has sponsored a
Drug Prevention Program out of four community based centers
operated by the Society. Each of the four centers serves
approximately 55 youngsters between the ages of 8 and 15. All
participants in the program meet as groups for weekly discussion and at another time each week for a planned activity.
In addition to the group work services, youngsters receive
individual counselling, tutoring, and a complete physical
examination each year. On the three days when youngsters
are not involved in an activity with their group, they can
join in the general activities sponsored by the host center.

The Children's Aid Society originally applied for funds
to operate a specialized drug prevention program out of a
deep concern for drug abusing youngsters who were known to
the centers. Concomitantly, there was a keen interest in
examining both the extent to which the youngsters were
"vulnerable" to drugs and the impact of the program on youngsters served. In order to conduct systematic studies of the
Drug Prevention Program, the Children's Aid Society's proposal
has always included a request fo research monies.

This paper will describe the operating principles and
activities of the Research Unit from 1970 to 1976.

It has always been understood that the reports prepared
by the Research Unit will not identify a particular center or
division within any center, however desirous this information
may be for administrative staff. Although this method of data
collection has limited statistical and other kinds of analyses,
the Research Unit prefers to collect data anonymously, in
order to demonstrate to staff that they will never be identified by their responses or by study findings about their clients.

To date, the Research Unit has surveyed youngsters twice by means of pre-coded questionnaires which probed their attitude about drugs and their use of illicit drugs. Before either questionnaire was administered to the youngsters, the Research Unit has met with all levels of staff to explain the purpose of the questionnaire and the procedures for administering it. Because the group leaders have an ongoing relationship with the youngsters, they have always administered the questionnaire during a scheduled group meeting. Group leaders were asked to read the questionnaire in order to minimize individual differences in reading skills and to postpone administering the questionnaire if less than half of the group was present. It was strongly emphasized that youngsters should not sign their name and that after completing the questionnaire, they should place it in a box which a staff member of the Research Unit would pick up after the meeting. By reading the questionnaire, the group leader would not hover over any youngsters who had difficulty reading; and since the questionnaire was administered on only one occasion and youngsters would place their completed questionnaire in a sealed box, it was most unlikely that anyone could ascertain how a particular client responded.

In addition to measuring youngsters' attitudes and use of drugs, the Research Unit has also collected data directly from staff. In 1971 and 1972, staff were asked to describe social characteristics of youngsters and to assess the extent of their drug involvement and the prevalence of school and other difficulties. Neither of these reports presented data in terms of individual groups or particular centers. In 1971, data were obtained from 74% of those registered in the program; and a full year later the response rate increased over 20% and data were obtained on 96% of those registered in the drug prevention program.

The first report (1) describ ed 170 of 229 members of the Drug Prevention Program as of March 1971, and the second report (2) described 231 of the 239 youngsters in the prevention program as of March 1972. For each report, data were collected from questionnaires completed by the youngsters group worker. The six page pre-coded questionnaire asked about key characteristics of the population and for information about the frequency of services youngsters received.

In both 1971 and 1972, the modal age of the study population was twelve and the ethnic composition of the prevention population corresponded to that of the host center's population. Eighty percent of the study population had both natural parents alive, but only half lived with both parents. One surprising finding from the 1971 report was that group leaders reported a lack of school problems. However, in the 1972 report, academic difficulties were identified in over half of the cases; 57% were judged

to be disruptive in school; and 78% of the youngsters were estimated to be truant.

In both years, nineteen groups were organized at the four
centers. In 1971 a total of 1,100 group meetings were held
with a mean average of 58 group meetings for each group. An
80% attendance rate was computed for participation in group
meetings. In the following year, the mean average number of
group meetings declined to 42, but the majority of youngsters
attended more than 85% of the group meetings.

The third study (3), analyzed the drug vulnerability of
youngsters in the prevention program and other center youngsters with similar social characteristics. The latter con-
sittuted a "contrast group." A seven page questionnaire containing 48 multiple choice items was administered to drug
groups and center groups in May 1973. The questionnaire
probed youngsters' perception about the prevalence of drugs
in the community and at the center as well as to ask specific
questions about their own use of illicit drugs and what they
thought of drug abusers.

Usable data were obtained from 136 prevention youngsters
and 48 in regular programs. The overall rate of consistency
of responses was .82 on 2,994 pairs of responses for the 184
youngsters in the study population. A further check on the
accuracy of youngsters' responses included items asking about
the use of a fictitious drug named "Eljoz". Only five of the
184 study respondents reported ever using "Eljoz", a much
lower percentage than other national studies. The fact that
less than 3% reported ever using a fictitious drug provides
reasonable assurance that youngsters were accurate in reporting drug use. Somewhat less reassuring was the finding that
21 or 11% of the study group reported that they themselves
or persons in their neighborhood or center were either using
or had tried "Eljoz." Overall, however, the rates of invalid
responses by the procedures of fictitious drug listing are not
of sufficient magnitude as to challenge the confidence in the
data reported by the children in the study.

Comparison of patterns of drug use and attitudes about
drug abusers between prevention youngsters and others revealed
that youngsters in the Drug Prevention Program were significantly
less inclined towards drug use. Specifically:

> ...Older youth in the prevention program had a far lower
> rate of experience with illegal drugs and accounted for
> most of the difference between the two cohorts of drug
> prevention and regular program youngsters. (p. < .05)

...Both younger and older youth in the prevention
program had lower rates of current use than their
corresponding age group in other CAS programs.

...Thirty-nine percent of those in the prevention
program reported having stopped using illicit
drugs; whereas only 17% of the youngsters in
the contrast groups reported having stopped using
drugs.

...The difference between usage for males, who until
recently tended to be more drug abusing than females, from prevention groups and others was
significant ($p < .001$).

The 1974 report also included documentation illustrating
that all study respondents thought that illicit drugs were
readily available throughout their neighborhoods and in the
schools they attended. Yet despite these myriad influences,
youngsters in the Drug Prevention Program were less inclined
to use drugs than youngsters who had not been part of this
specialized program. The 1974 report gave evidence of the
efficacy of "primary prevention."

In the third report, the Research Unit could make the
assumption that the experimental and contrast groups were
equivalent at the beginning of program year since the program
admitted any youngster between the designated ages, the only
limitation being the number of youngsters the program could
accommodate. In July 1975, this open admissions policy was
altered at the stipulation of the funding agency. As of the
beginning of the fall 1975, youngsters admitted to the Drug
Prevention Program had to show some clear indication that they
were "vulnerable to drugs." Before a youngster could be
admitted to program, staff had to document that he was known
to be experimenting with illicit drugs, living with an addicted person or encountering serious family or academic difficulties.

The stipulation that youngsters meet specific criteria
for admission to the Drug Prevention Program raised several
questions. Some staff contended that virtually all youngsters
known to the centers met the criteria, while others maintained
that a careful intake process was necessary in order to comply
with the funding agency's requirements. The uncertainty about
how the selection criteria would affect the program prompted
the Research Unit to plan a Time One measure at the beginning
of program year in order to provide an independent measure of
the equivalence of Drug Prevention youngsters and those in
other services provided by the Children's Aid Society.

In November 1975 and again in April 1976, this instrument
was administered to youngsters in the Drug Prevention Program
and approximately 70 youth with similar social characteristics.
Analysis of these data will indicate the equivalance of the
two cohorts at the beginning of the program year and the
extent to which they manifest desirable changes.

In concluding, I would like to comment on the role of
"in-house" research. While it would be foolhardy to deny
that staff has questioned both the usefulness of research and
the manner in which data will be used, I think we have been
able to work through many of the inherent strains between
practice and research during the past six years. It seems
reasonable to assume that our policy of presenting results
in such a way that no one is identified has demonstrated that
we are interested in conducting systematic studies rather
than to assist administration in making evaluations for the
Children's Aid Society. Secondly, I think that by working
closely with all levels of staff to explain the purpose of
our research efforts and to work out the arrangements for
data collection, we have developed a sound basis for conducting research that is both legitimate and potentially beneficial to the Drug Prevention Program and The Children's Aid
Society.

REFERENCES

1. Goldie Sherman, <u>An Analysis of Basic Characteristics of
    Children Served and Assessment of their Drug Involvement</u>:
    The Children's Aid Society. 1971

2. Popie Martin, <u>Analysis of the Children's Aid Society Drug
    Prevention Program and Its Participants.</u> New York: The
    Children's Aid Society, 1972.

3. Herman Piven, Abraham Alcabes and Popie Martin, <u>Drugs and
    Urban Youth: A Study of The Children's Aid Society Drug
    Prevention Program</u>. New York: The Children's Aid
    Society, 1974.

A COMPARISON OF VOLUNTARY AND INVOLUNTARY ADMISSIONS TO TREATMENT FOR NARCOTIC ADDICTION

Carl G. Leukefeld, D.S.W.

Division of Resource Development
National Institute on Drug Abuse
Rockville, Maryland

Statements by various individuals indicate that the number of narcotic abusers have increased. Programs are providing treatment for voluntarily admitted narcotic abusers and authoritative court referred narcotic abusers. Yet there is a paucity of systemized knowledge or information about these two ways of entering treatment.

The purpose of this study is to add to that knowledge base by examining the extent to which differences in outcomes among voluntarily admitted narcotic abusers and authoritative court referred narcotic abusers varied separately in relation to the method of treatment.

Narcotic abusers were defined as individuals who were dependent upon: opium, heroin, and their compounds and derivatives. Coupled with this definition, two methods of treatment entry are core concepts. (1) Authoritative court referred narcotic abusers were defined as abusers in treatment who were on probation or parole; (2) Voluntarily admitted narcotic abusers were defined as abusers who were not on probation or parole. Three treatment methods were included (methadone maintenance treatment, drug-free outpatient treatment and therapeutic community treatment).

Brill and Leiberman[1] have reported that the use of authority from the judicial system was the single most important factor in the treatment of narcotic abusers. Levine and Monroe[2] also identified court pressure as the most important variable in retaining narcotic addicts in treatment. The findings of several follow-up studies[3], of abusers admitted to the Lexington and Fort Worth facilities, have shown that voluntary admissions function poorly in their community after discharge. The subjects of this study were narcotic abusers chosen from the Drug Abuse Reporting Program data which was a contract funded by the National Institute on Drug Abuse to Texas

The writer would like to thank the National Institute on Drug Abuse and the Institute of Behavioral Research, Texas Christian University for making this study possible.

Christian University. The February to May 1972 reporting periods were included. The number of new admissions from 30 agencies was reduced to meet the study's sample specifications.

Six outcome scales used to measure specific behaviors manifested by narcotic abusers in treatment were: opiate use, non-opiate use, alcohol use, arrests, employment, and time in jail. Demaree's[4] research report provides a detailed explanation of the statistical development and construction for the outcome scales used in this study. In order to capsulate an overall assessment of treatment outcome, the writer developed a composite outcome score.

The study's limitations are: (1) The subjects are only those who met the criteria for admission to and continuation in each of the treatment agencies; (2) Generalizability of the findings to specific agencies participating in the Drug Abuse Reporting Program data system or other treatment agencies cannot be suggested; (3) Only behavioral outcomes have been used in this study as measures of outcome; (4) Outcomes are influenced by intervening variables which could not be totally controlled.

The demographic characteristics for the 2027 subjects in the study are: About three-fourths (74.5%) were males, over one-third (38.9%) were twenty-one to twenty-five years of age, and Blacks made up almost one-half (48.6%) of the sample. 647 or 31.9% of the abusers were court referred and 1380 or 61.8% were voluntary. Males accounted for 81.3% of the court referrals as compared with 71.5% of the voluntarily admitted. The percentage of females was larger among voluntarily admitted (28.5% contrasted with 8.7%). 1,033 (74.9%) of the voluntary abusers and 262 (40.5%) of the court referrals received methadone maintenance treatment. Drug-free outpatient treatment was received by 402 (19.8%); 160 of the outpatients in drug-free treatment were voluntary and 242 were court referred. 330 abusers were provided therapeutic community treatment; 187 of these were voluntary and 143 were court referred.

Court referrals manifested more deviant behavior. Almost 1/3 of the voluntarily admitted had never been arrested before admission. This was substantially different for court referred with only about 1% who had never been arrested. Approximately 50% of the voluntarily admitted had never been incarcerated, while about 10% of the voluntary admissions had never been convicted. Over 3/4 of the sample used opiates daily for two months prior to commencing treatment. Voluntarily admitted retained jobs for a longer period of time than authoritative court referred.

The Hypotheses Tested

The first hypothesis, that there is a significant difference between the treatment outcomes of authoritative court referred and voluntarily admitted narcotic abusers, was tested using Hotelling's

T-Squared test and t-tests. The number of subjects in this analysis was 1,546. 481 users were excluded for this analysis. The percentage spread for the demographic characteristics is not substantially different from the study sample. Hotelling's T-Squared test result was non-significant (T = .525). In addition, the individual t-tests for the composite outcome score and the six specific outcome scores were not significant. The t-test for the composite outcome score was: t = .612. The hypothesis was not statistically supported.

Hypothesis 2 stated that there is a significant difference between the outcomes of authoritative court referred and voluntarily admitted narcotic abusers receiving methadone maintenance treatment, drug-free outpatient treatment and therapeutic community treatment. The analytic method used to test this hypothesis was two-way analysis of variance and analysis of covariance. Three covariates (sex, age and race-ethnic group) were significant (F = 3.97; P = .001). Six outcome measurements were utilized in addition to the composite outcome score. The number of subjects was 1,546. This analysis confirms findings of other research that sex, age and race-ethnic group should be taken into account in studies of narcotic users in treatment. It also reveals that there is no significant difference between the two levels of treatment entry (F = .46). Treatment method was significant beyond the .001 level (F = 11.53); however, this may be the result of the behavioral indices. The interaction of treatment entry and treatment method was also significant at the .05 level (F = 2.97). The analysis of variance findings for each of the six outcome scores separately revealed similar findings. The covariates were significant for five of the six outcome scores. Arrests (F = .90) was not significant. Treatment entry was not significant for five of the six outcome scores. The employment outcome score was significant (F = 5.94; P = .01). Treatment method was significant for the five outcome scores. It was not significant for time in jail (F = 1.21). The interaction of treatment entry and treatment method was significant for one of the six outcome scores - Non-opiate use (F = 4.57; P = .01). The hypothesis was not statistically supported.

Hypothesis 3 stated that there is a significant difference between the length of time narcotic abusers remain in treatment according to whether they are authoritative court referred or voluntarily admitted. For this hypothesis, the length of time in treatment was operationally defined as the number of bi-monthly Status Evaluation Records received for one year. 2027 narcotic abusers were included in this analysis. 34.8% of the subjects remained in treatment for one year. Specifically, 30.9% of the court referrals remained in treatment for one year and 36.7% of the voluntary abusers remained in treatment for one year. The Z-test, to determine if there was a difference, was significant (Z = 116; P = .001). The test revealed that voluntarily admitted remained in treatment significantly longer than court referred. The hypothesis was supported.

Findings and Conclusions

The most substantial finding from the analyses of the data may be concerning the non-significant difference between the types of treatment entry (court referred and voluntarily admitted). Regardless of the variables examined (treatment method or time in treatment), the results were not significant when the composite outcome score was used. The data from this study did reveal that before entering treatment narcotic abusers on probation or parole did manifest greater deviant behavior. In this respect, recognizing that there were no significant difference between the two group's outcomes, it seems that treatment did reduce deviant behaviors for court referrals because their behavioral outcomes were not significantly different from voluntary admissions.

Possibly the most interesting results were obtained when retention in treatment was examined. The finding from Hypothesis 3 revealed that voluntary admissions remained in treatment longer. However, this difference, when examined for court referrals and voluntary admissions by the three treatment methods separately, reveals that court referrals remained in treatment longer for methadone mainte-nance treatment (49.2% compared with 44.5%), drug-free outpatient treatment (21.9% compared with 16.9%), and therapeutic community treatment (12.6% compared with 10.2%). Thus, court referrals remained in each of the three treatment methods longer than volun-tarily admitted abusers.

As an addition to the findings of previous studies, the results of this study indicate that abusers on probation/parole not only re-mained in treatment longer for drug-free treatment but also for methadone maintenance treatment and therapeutic community treatment. The high retention rate for patients in methadone maintenance treat-ment on probation/parole is probably more an indication of methadone treatment since 44.5% (compared with 49.2%) of the voluntary admis-sions remained in methadone maintenance treatment. The following recommendations are presented:

1. Treatment agencies with low retention rates should seek to in-crease that rate by developing linkages with courts, probation departments and parole departments for referrals.

2. Methadone maintenance treatment programs should pay specific attention to the development of viable counseling/therapeutic ser-vices. This recommendation is presented in relation to the study's finding that methadone maintenance treatment had the highest reten-tion rate and by implication could be identified as having the greatest potential for achieving treatment objectives.

3. Treatment programs and policy makers should allocate sufficient resources for follow-up studies and further study of drug-free outpatient treatment. The recommendation for follow-up studies is based on the need to find out what changes are accomplished by treatment.

NOTES

1. L. Brill and L. Lieberman, Authority and Addiction, Little Brown and Company, Boston, 1969.

2. J. Levine and J. Monroe, "Discharge of Narcotic Drug Addicts Against Medical Advice," Public Health Reports 79, 1964: 13-18.

3. See: Z. Amsel et al, "Narcotics Register for Follow-up of a Cohort of Adolescent Addicts," International Journal of the Addictions 6 (June 1971): 225-39; H. Duvall et al, "Follow-up Study of Narcotic Addicts Five Years After Hospitalization," Public Health Reports 73 (March 1963): 185-94; J. O'Donnell, Narcotic Addicts in Kentucky; G. M. Pescor, "Follow-up Study of Treated Narcotic Addicts"; G. Vallient, "A Twelve Year Follow-up of New York City Addicts: In Relation to Treatment Outcome"; J. O'Donnell, "The Relapse Rate in Narcotic Addiction: A Critique of Follow-up Studies," in Narcotics, 1965, pp. 226-46.

4. R. G. Demaree and J. F. Newman, "Criterion Measures and Scales for Year Three," Texas Christian University, 1974 (typewritten); R. G. Demaree, J. F. Newman, L. Long and B. L. Grant, "Patterns of Behavioral Outcomes Over Time in Methadone Maintenance Treatment," Texas Christian University, 1974 (typewritten).

PREDICTING PRE-TREATMENT ATTRITION IN DRUG ABUSE PROGRAMS

Bruce Kleinhans,[1] Robert J. Harford,[2] James C. Ungerer,[2] Donald Wright,[1] and Joel Kleinberg[2]

[1] Addiction-Prevention, Treatment Foundation
100 Park Street
New Haven, Connecticut 06511

[2] Department of Psychiatry
Yale University School of Medicine
New Haven, Connecticut 06511

A chronic problem confronting drug treatment programs has been the failure of many applicants to enter treatment (1,2). This paper describes results of a procedure for predicting an applicant's likelihood of entering treatment.

Knowledge of how likely an applicant is to enter treatment can assist staff in several ways. Applicants identified as high-risk can be given special priority and attention during the intake process. In multi-modality programs, knowing an applicant's likelihood of entry can facilitate his assignment to the most appropriate treatment modality. Our understanding of the dynamics of failure to enter treatment also can be improved by the development of accurate predictive instruments. A systematic analysis of pre-treatment attrition could provide a basis for evaluating the entire intake process and may suggest ways to diminish the applicant's anxiety and ambivalence concerning treatment and to increase his identification with program goals.

METHOD AND RESULTS

Our total sample consisted of 162 applicants to the Connecticut Mental Health Center's Drug Dependence Unit (DDU). At the DDU a centralized screening unit evaluates applicants and assigns them to appropriate treatment modalities. Our data were collected at the screening unit during the intake process.

Beginning with an extensive set of variables, we used discriminant analysis to determine optimum weighted sets of predictors. The resulting discriminant functions were then applied on a case-by-case basis to predict the entry status of each applicant, allowing a comparison of predicted vs. actual entry status. We first identified four general categories of variables likely to affect entry: (a) demographic status and drug use history, (b) personality, (c)

This research was supported in part by grants from the National Institute of Drug Abuse: DA 01097 and H80 DA 16356.

legal pressure, and (d) treatment facility characteristics at time
of application. Demographic status and drug use history were represented by sex, age, race, principal drug of abuse, whether the applicant had applied to the DDU previously, and whether he had previously applied but failed to enter treatment. Personality measures
included the Rotter Locus of Control Scale, the Mosher Sex-Guilt
Inventory, the Extraversion, Neuroticism, and Lie scales of the
Eysenck Personality Inventory, the Taylor Manifest Anxiety Scale,
and the Rotter Interpersonal Trust Scale. In addition we constructed two different composite measures of psychological maladjustment.
The first measure consisted of the sum of an applicant's standardized scores for neuroticism, anxiety, and mistrust; the second was
the applicant's highest single standardized score of these three
measures. The legal pressure experienced by the applicant at his
time of application was measured by four separate variables, namely
probation, parole, pending court action, and referral by the criminal justice system, as well as by a composite of these four variables. In addition, for each applicant we counted the number of
persons applying for treatment, waiting for treatment, and in treatment at the DDU on his day of application. Finally, for applicants
using heroin, we noted whether methadone maintenance treatment was
offered.

We performed a separate analysis for each of four subsamples:
(a) nonheroin-using first applicants, (b) heroin-using first applicants, (c) White heroin-using applicants, and (d) Black heroin-using
applicants. Each analysis included both (a) a set of univariate t-
tests to compare applicants who entered with those who did not enter on each of the 24 initial variables and (b) a stepwise discriminant function procedure yielding the best weighted linear combination of predictors.

For the 45 nonheroin users without prior DDU contact, the univariate t-tests indicated that an applicant was more likely to enter if he had been referred by legal authorities, was on probation,
or applied when few others were applying. The discriminant function
for the first-application nonheroin users included three predictors:
Referral, Locus of Control, and Sex. Controlling for the other
variables in the function, having an internal locus of control and
being female were associated with entry. Using the function to predict entry, 82% of the applicants in the sample were correctly
classified.

For the 58 first-application heroin users, the univariate t-
tests revealed that clients who entered tended to apply when clinic
populations and the number awaiting treatment were small. The discriminant function for this group of applicants consisted of four
variables: Number of Clients Awaiting Treatment, Number of Clients
in Treatment, Locus of Control, and Parole Status. Controlling for
the other variables in the discriminant function, program entry was
associated with an internal locus of control and with being on parole. On a case-by-case basis, the function correctly predicted
the entry status of 72% of the applicants.

White heroin users were more likely to enter if they had applied when few applicants were awaiting treatment, if they had been
recommended for a methadone program, or if they were not on probation. In the discriminant analysis for the 53 White heroin users,
Number of Clients in Treatment was added to Number Awaiting Treatment, Methadone Recommendation, and Probation Status. Controlling
for the other three variables, entry was more likely when the clinic
population was small. The function correctly classified 76% of the
sample.

Relative to Black heroin users who did not enter, Black heroin
users who entered were more likely to have applied previously and
to have been referred by legal authorities. The discriminant analysis for Black heroin users yielded a 4-variable function consisting
of Prior Application, Legal Referral, Methadone Recommendation, and
Extraversion. Controlling for the other factors in the discriminant
function, entry was associated with an offer of methadone maintenance and with extraversion. Correct classification was obtained for
80% of the sample.

DISCUSSION

Our results demonstrate that entry into drug treatment programs
can be predicted with some degree of accuracy by combining a small
number of variables into a multivariate prediction equation. Furthermore, the results show the importance of sampling different
types of variables for use as predictors. The variables entering
into our optimum prediction equations included client demographic
and psychological characteristics, legal pressure, and treatment
facility characteristics. Failure to include any one of these four
classes of variables would have reduced our predictive power.

In addition to maximizing predictability, the multivariate procedures took account of the intercorrelations among variables, revealing a number of misleading univariate relationships. For example, first application nonheroin users who entered treatment had
higher maladjustment scores than those who failed to enter. However, the patterns of intercorrelations indicated that this difference was attributable to differences in Locus of Control and/or Referral.

The discriminant analyses also revealed several suppressor variables (3) which had no significant univariate relationship to the
criterion, but which significantly improved the multivariate prediction. For example, for first-application nonheroin users, sex
was related to entry only after we controlled for Legal Referral.

Some of the substantive results bear further comment. For example, referral from the criminal justice system was an important
determinant of entry for both non-heroin users and Black heroin
users. Fear of legal consequences may act as a powerful motivating
factor encouraging treatment entry. However, this finding should
be interpreted with caution. The other, more specific forms of
legal pressure, namely probation, parole, and pending litigation,

showed inconsistent and generally nonsignificant relationships with entry. In fact, for White heroin users, being on probation decreased, rather than increased, an applicant's likelihood of entry.

Furthermore, our results provide no evidence regarding the effects of legal pressure on treatment effectiveness, as opposed to treatment entry. In a separate investigation (4) we have found various forms of legal pressure to be either unrelated or negatively related to retention and successful completion of treatment. Legal pressure thus should not be considered as generally enhancing the efficacy of treatment for drug dependence.

The psychological measure most predictive of entry was Rotter's Locus of Control Scale. Regardless of drug abused, first-time applicants who entered treatment scored more internal on this measure than those who did not enter. This finding indicates that entry is facilitated by feeling in control of one's outcomes in life. However, locus of control was not predictive of entry when former applicants were included in the sample. This finding agrees with Rotter's (5) proposition that generalized expectancies such as locus of control will accurately predict behavior only in novel situations. According to Rotter, accurate prediction of behavior in a familiar situation requires an instrument specifically tailored to that situation. Thus, to predict entry for applicants familiar with the application process, a measure of expectancies for treatment success may be more appropriate than the general locus of control instrument. We are currently administering an instrument designed specifically to assess the applicant's treatment expectancies.

In studying pre-treatment attrition, it is a strong temptation to focus exclusively on characteristics of the applicant and to neglect characteristics of the treatment facility. We found that when clinical programs were operating near capacity, applicants were less likely to enter. Screening personnel are probably sensitive to the treatment programs' varying demand for new clients. When many empty treatment slots exist, the screening staff may facilitate entry by providing ample attention and encouragement to every applicant. When few spaces are available, however, intake personnel may lower entry rates by being more selective and concentrating their energies on those applicants who seem the best risks.

We should emphasize that our findings are tentative until they can be cross-validated on other samples. The extent to which our results generalize to other treatment facilities is unknown. Differences in client population as well as the size and organization of the particular facilities may result in different sets of optimum predictors of entry. Also, the additive models represented by our discriminant functions probably oversimplify the complex web of relationships involved in treatment entry. The contrasting sets of significant predictors emerging in different analyses demonstrated that race and drug of abuse interact with other variables to determine likelihood of entry. For example, although Blacks and Whites were equally likely to enter, previous application was a good predictor of entry for Blacks, but not for Whites.

The identification of those applicants least likely to enter treatment permits a more efficient allocation of program resources. Various remedial measures could be instituted to facilitate entry for applicants identified as high-risk. For example, the length of the pre-treatment waiting period would be reduced by assigning these applicants a special high-priority status and permitting them to complete all intake procedures in the shortest possible time. Also, some treatment functions such as counseling and/or dispensing of medication could be instituted for these applicants during the intake process itself.

We are beginning to understand the underlying dynamics determining entry into treatment for drug dependence. Entry appears to involve interrelated characteristics of both the applicant and the treatment facility. Future research should further clarify how drug abusers seeking help can be successfully engaged in treatment.

REFERENCES

1. A. E. Raynes and V. D. Patch, Int. J. Addict., 8: 839 (1973).
2. C. M. Rosenberg, N. McKain, and V. Patch, Drug Forum, 1: 145 (1972).
3. R. B. Darlington, Psychol. Bull., 69: 161 (1968).
4. R. J. Harford, J. C. Ungerer, and J. K. Kinsella, Proceedings, Second National Drug Abuse Conference, (in press).
5. J. B. Rotter, J. Consult. Clin. Psychol., 43: 56 (1975).

A SEVEN-YEAR FOLLOW-UP STUDY OF 186 MALES IN A RELIGIOUS
THERAPEUTIC COMMUNITY INDICATES BY PERSONAL INTERVIEW AND
URINALYSIS THAT 70% ARE DRUG FREE. 57% NEVER USED AN IL-
LEGAL DRUG FOLLOWING GRADUATION FROM THE PROGRAM.

Catherine B. Hess, M.D., M.P.H., F.A.C.O.G.

Research Director
Teen Challenge Training Center

I. HISTORY OF TEEN CHALLENGE

Teen Challenge, a therapeutic-type totally religious rehabilitation program for drug and alcohol abusers and addicts, was developed in New York City in 1958 by Rev. David Wilkerson from Phillips-
burg, Pa., author of The Cross and the Switchblade as well as doz-
ens of other books and brochures. In the early years it was exclusively a male program but it now includes females. The program has
the usual three phases: the induction center, the rehabilitation
center and re-entry into society. This report includes all admissions in 1968 to the Brooklyn Induction Center plus all admissions
to the rehabilitation center called the Teen Challenge Training
Center or the Farm. In 1968 there were eight induction centers in
the U.S. and Puerto Rico. In 1975 there were 50 induction centers
in 24 states, Puerto Rico, the District of Columbia, and 76 centers
throughout the world. No longer is it a small localized program
but international in scope, giving service to 14,000 youths each
week. 2,793 people were inducted into 49 residential programs; 36
for males, 16 for females. Although Teen Challenge appears to be
an exclusive drug and alcohol program, one must note that it is a
more far-reaching program in its ministry to troubled youth. The
impact of its Evangelistic outreach touches all corners of the
world. The Charismatic movement is being adopted by many denomin-
ations. This is a self-supported international program, growing by
leaps and bounds, which will not become extinct because some federal or state funding terminates. I see nothing but growth potential over the next decade for this successful program.

A. The Religious Component of Teen Challenge

From the first day of admission into the Induction Center the individual is instructed in Bible reading and how these teachings of the Old and New Testaments can affect their mental, physical and spiritual lives. The life and teaching of Jesus Christ is used to help the individual solve his problems. As they get to know Him, a time comes for many when a physical or spiritual change takes place with such emotional force that it is referred to as a conversion experience. This coming to the Lord in repentance and total submission is referred to as being "born again" or "saved", "converted" or "regenerated". This is an experience of salvation: growth sets in and the individual's life begins to change. The Baptism of the Holy Ghost is a spiritual experience subsequent to the "conversion" and becoming a born-again Christian. As a result of this acceptance there are some who develop the ability to "speak in tongues". This may be an actual language understood by those who also speak it or it may be an unrecognizable language not spoken on earth. The concept of being born again is identified as being Pentecostal. The Assembly of God church is one of the older Pentecostal groups but born-again Christians are identified today among Catholics, Lutherans, Episcopalians, Presbyterians, and many others.

Drugs are the symptom of a problem. The major problem is sin for which acceptance of Jesus Christ is the cure. Through faith in Jesus Christ you can be forgiven and cleansed from the power of sin. With this forgiveness you no longer have to be controlled by sin and you are free to change your life style. It is replacement therapy: take sin out, put Christ in. When sin is removed, so are the symptoms removed: drug use, hate, jealousy, anger, rebellion, selfishness and retaliation.

B. Program At Teen Challenge

1. INDUCTION CENTER - TRAINING CENTER (THE FARM) - RE-ENTRY

Anyone was admitted who desired to have his sins forgiven and to work with the Lord. Only homosexuals and severe emotional problems were referred elsewhere. This phase might last a week to several months, depending mostly on the availability of beds at the Training Center (the Farm) at Rehrersburg, Pa. The majority in this study, 335 out of 369, entered the Brooklyn Center. All Puerto Ricans came through Brooklyn, so this group of 37 had two induction periods. 23 came from 6 other induction centers across the U.S. 222 of 335 dropped out, leaving 113 to go to the Farm. During this phase one, each person stopped: using drugs (cold turkey), smoking, swearing, drinking, and seeing family or friends. Scripture reading was begun and verses memorized. Love, concern, and support were shared.

The Training Center (the Farm) is located on 220 acres in Eastern Pa. The average stay was 7.5 months. At the end, one quietly graduated and returned home. Features of the program included: physical work, upkeep of the property, Bible classes, all morning church, choir, vocational training in areas of printing, automotive mechanics, farming, milking, food management, bookstore, etc. In this phase there was an amazing lack of organized group therapy sessions or the handling and identification of their people problems. Living together (4 in a room) created much talking and general sharing. No trained counselors, therapists or psychologists were on the staff. There was little medical care because most physicians gave out too many pills. Reinforcement by going out into public speaking was excellent therapy and a continual high seemed to exist with praising the Lord. There was 42 staff for 100 males.

Little preparation was made for re-entry back into society with practically no follow-up. At the graduation point assistance was given upon request to get a job or to locate in some induction center as a staff person.

II. METHODOLOGY OF THE STUDY

The class of 1968 (369 males) was chosen so that a minimum of 5 years would have gone by. The main study is to determine the outcome of 144 young men who entered the farm that year. In addition a 20% random sample was selected out of the 222 Brooklyn Induction Center drop-outs. The goal: to locate, administer a 78-item questionaire, and to secure a urine specimen. The following populations were identified: P1 - 44 (20%) sample of 222 drop-outs from Brooklyn Induction Center, P2 - 77 drop-outs from the Training Center, and P3 - 67 graduates from the Training Center.

The actual location rate done in a 6-month period by the National Opinion Research Center of Chicago netted the following results: P1 - 70% (31), P2 - 78% (60), and P3 - 97% (65). The total number located was 199, 13 were dead (4 in P1, 8 in P2, 1 in P3), and 9 persons refused to give a urine. The National Medical Laboratory in Philadelphia, Pa. did the urine testing. Total confidentiality was maintained by establishing a code system so that the Teen Challenge Research Team did not know the identity of any respondent.

III. EPIDEMIOLOGIC FACTS FROM THE STUDY - INCLUDING AGE, RACE, RELIGION, EDUCATION, ARRESTS, FAMILY & DRUG USE

The youngest was 14, the oldest, 47. The mean age of P1 - 23, P2 - 25 and P3 - 24 years. 70% were under 25 years. 119 were Hispanic, 38 Black and 29 White. 335 came through Brooklyn (37 from Puerto Rico) and 34 from across the nation. 44% were Catholic,

30% Protestant, 23% said no religion, 5% other. The majority of entrants identified themselves as not religious, including 73% of the graduate P3 group. The school drop-out rate was highest at the 16th and 17th years. The P1 group had 21% drop-out, P2 - 30% and P3 - 19%. Not one family member was identified as being a drug user. Those who were married prior to Teen Challenge were: P1 - 41%, P2 - 32% and P3 - 23%. Only 22.5% were in trouble with the law at time of admission. The youngest arrest was at 7 years. Only 39 of the 186 had never been arrested. 147 had been arrested 1,020 times prior to Teen Challenge. For drug related arrests, 41 persons had 191 arrests.

Drug use: 39 individuals first used drugs between 11 and 13 years, 108 first used 14-17 years. 5 claimed first drug use under 10 years. The age of first heroin addiction showed 6 occurred at ages 11-13, 89 at 14-17 years and 45 at 18-20 years. The age of first marihuana use showed 3 used regularly before 10 years, 21 at 11-13, 81 at 14-17 years. The sequence of drug use showed cigarettes first, alcohol next, marihuana, then heroin. The other drugs usually came after heroin drug use. All, except 8 people, smoked cigarettes. 13 were alcohol abusers. 70 (36%) smoked marihuana, 45 smoked marihuana regularly. The degree of heroin addiction (more than once a day) was: P1 - 44 (70%) heavily addicted, P2 - 26 (63%) heavily addicted and P3 - 44 (73%) heavily addicted. Before Teen Challenge other treatment programs had been used: P1 - 28 (40%), P2 - 20 (38%) and P3 - 35 (55%).

IV. RESULTS OF THE STUDY

The mean length of stay at the induction centers for the 3 populations was: P1 - 13 days, P2 - 69 days and P3 - 87 days. The mean length of stay at the Training Center is: P2 - 90 days and P3 - 227 days. Adjustment to society is measured by: drug use, mental and physical health, conformity to law, employment, educational attainment and religious participation. 36 (57%) of the graduates never used any kind of cigarettes, alcohol, heroin, or illegal drugs since Teen Challenge. 70% of all three populations were not using drugs at the time of the interview (March through August, 1975). This is confirmed by the urinalysis report. 59 were hospitalized after Teen Challenge. 28 claim they still have nervous or emotional problems. 69 class themselves as having excellent health, 70 good health, 32 fair health and 15 poor health. In the P1 group 55 had 269 arrests since Teen Challenge. P2 group, 29 had 62 arrests and P3 group, 19 had 54 arrests. At the time of interview the employment shows: P1 - 37 working (50%), P2 - 29 working (56%) and P3 - 48 working (75%). In P1, 28 worked less than 1 year while in P3, 14 worked less than 1 year (significant difference in the employment category). 56 went back to school. 8 in P1, 5 in P2 and 6 in P3 got their High School Graduate Equivalence Diploma. 29 in the P3 group went on to Bible School - 14

became ministers. 11 in the P2 group went on to Bible School - 3
became ministers. 1 in P2 received his college degree. Church
attendance of two or more times a month showed there were: 13 in
P1, 21 in P2, and 38 in P3. Out of the total population of 168, 58
claim to be very religious, 99 somewhat religious and 29 not religious at all (8 in the graduate group, 13 in Farm drop-outs).

V. CONCLUSION

The high success rate of the Teen Challenge approach to drug addiction is based on several unusual facts not utilized in any other
program in the United States. All other treatment programs have
ignored the spiritual side of man. Other programs try to identify
and treat basic problems, few help the individual to handle his
anxieties or to recognize the existential vacuum in many people's
lives. The Teen Challenge approach produces faith so that nothing
appears in vain, no act remains unaccounted for, and nothing is
meaningless. Three basic elements are found: ideology, commitment
and forgiveness. The future is no longer dependent on the past and
one is free to clothe himself in a new identity. Previously he may
have had reason to act out in rebellion and hostility to self and
others where man-made rules were concerned but there is a different
focus in the arena of God-made rules.

Four basic needs are met in the Teen Challenge Program: 1) Security and self confidence. He learns to do some skills well and
is complemented for it. He finds a security through a trust and
faith in Christ and finds meaningful recognition in the sight of
God. 2) Love and affection. The atmosphere within Teen Challenge
is one of love and acceptance for the person as a human being. No
longer does he face rejection and criticism at every turn. No
longer does he need to fight back to win his point and preserve his
self image. 3) New experiences are found. If drugs are to be over
come and forgotten, emotional and satisfying highs must replace the
old feeling. Singing, giving your life to the Lord, receiving the
Baptism of the Holy Spirit, plus the whole array of charismatic
gifts which you pass on to others gives reinforcement and fulfills
the need of response. 4) Removal from the source of drugs, peer
pressure and a life style which enfolds him and captures him. In
a rural atmosphere one becomes aware of beauty, the warmth of soli-
tude, and develops strengths to find pleasure in things other than
drugs. Above all, he learns how to live within structure and like
it. He learns to enjoy work and to share feelings instead of acting out feelings.

Teen Challenge is based on a sateriological model (salvation or
conversion). The offender is alienated from God and man by "sin".
One must undergo a resocialization to conform to Biblical standards.
From this acceptance of new standards he can be reintegrated into
society. Change comes about by confession to Christ of his trans-
gressions and acceptance of Christ as his spiritual mentor.

SUCCESS RATES: VALIDITY AND RELIABILITY
OF TREATMENT FOLLOW-UP STUDIES

Joy A. Held

Project R.E.T.U.R.N. Foundation, Inc.
New York, New York

I. LITERATURE REVIEW

Numerous commentators have discussed and analysed the problems endemic to drug evaluation research. On the theoretical side, O'Donnell has discussed the problem of defining addiction, Bates has analysed problems involving conceptual clarity in this field and Glaser has lamented the paucity of theory and argued for more sophisticated and fruitful research questions. Petersen suggests that we study the interaction of client and milieu rather than examining them in isolation from one another. Hunt, Barret and Branch have suggested that the different addiction fields can profit from more interaction.
Considerable attention has been paid to problems of measurement, as well. Norris observes that attempts to evaluate TC's are confounded by the absence of standardized program criteria. O'Donnell has urged that we look at patterns of post-institutional drug use rather than using all or nothing measures of abstinence which bias the findings toward relapse, and DeLeon argues for measures of relapse by degree. O'Donnell further suggests that we rely upon "hard" rather than "soft" criteria of addiction wherever possible, and that measurement be done independently by at least two people. Glaser asks that we examine what we can learn from negative findings. Chambers and Inciardi note the necessity to follow up program splittees as well as graduates.
Finally, attention has focused upon the political context of evaluation research. Leinhardt has reflected upon the problem of credibility -- if research done by an insider is favorable, outsiders will doubt it; if it is negative, insiders will doubt it. And Bogdan has cautioned evaluators on the nature of pressures toward im-

morality that emanate from the political context of evaluation research.

The problems in drug evaluation research enumerated above reflect the problems of the field of evaluation research as a whole. These issues are analysed with care by Edward Suchman in his book Evaluative Research. Here Suchman provides a critique of Guides of Evaluative Research which he says encapsulates the problems extant in the field of evaluation research as a whole.

Suchman divides these problems into 3 general subject areas -- those of subject matter, methods of procedure, and administration, and has an additional section on recent problems in evaluation research. We have already seen in our review of the literature that drug program evaluation research suffers from shortcomings in each of these crucial subject areas. The remainder of this paper evaluates selected drug program follow-up studies according to Suchman's paradigm of problems common to evaluation research.

II. METHODOLOGY

This paper examines the reliability and validity of twenty-four drug treatment program follow-up studies. A purposive sample of follow-up studies was drawn to include programs from the major modalities of treatment, representing the various populations served, including both short range and long term follow-up, for the time period 1943 to 1975. Studies were drawn from major journals, books and conference proceedings.
The studies sampled varied in the following ways:
1. Characteristics examined -- criteria of program success: drug abstinence, absence of arrests, employment, or some combination of the above, with the occasional addition of other characteristics such as psychological or social adjustment or alcohol abstinence.
2. Population studied: adult, youth, and mixed; of both sexes and sex segregated.
3. Program type: hospital, therapeutic community, methadone maintenance, religious community, prison program, and community clinic.
4. Time elapsed between treatment and follow-up study: from zero (in the case of methadone maintenance) to 12 years, with most studies falling in the 6 months to 2 year range.
5. Year of study: with the exception of a few early works, studies ranged from 1961 to 1975, with most falling into the time period 1968 - 1975.

III. FINDINGS

Suchman's criticisms of Evaluation Research Guides are appropriate to drug treatment follow-up studies on almost every point. First let us consider the area of subject matter. All five of Suchman's points here are sustained by the studies examined. First, none of the studies attempt to distinguish elements within the treatment regimen. Second, follow-up studies of drug programs emphasize resources and facilities at the expense of measures of program effectiveness. Third, these studies tend to neglect program objectives except for the global objectives of drug abstinence and social adjustment. Furthermore, the studies examined employ different definitions of program success making comparisons extremely difficult. Fourth, these studies focus upon ultimate objectives, with little or no attention to intermediate objectives or the relationship between various functional levels of organization. Finally, these studies stress ideal standards rather than realistic goals. Hence, criteria of measurement for success tend to emphasize all or none results at the expense of degrees of success or the developmental sequence of behavior after treatment.

Substantial problems are also found with regard to the methodology of the studies in question. First, many of these studies did collect their own data, so Suchman's criticism concerning the utilization of existing records does not hold up. Second, there is a general failure to employ a control group, making inferences about causality extremely problemmatic. Third, these studies provide no evidence of the control of bias in measurement reliability and validity. We are being asked to take these measurements on faith. Fourth, most studies rely entirely upon self-reporting rather than upon objective criteria of measurement. Several researchers discussed the inability to get supportive data from other agencies due to limitations of confidentiality. Fifth, there is an inherent difficulty in comparing studies done at different communities due to the different properties of those communities. While the studies examined do not attempt such comparisons, the reader may, at considerable peril. Sixth, none of the studies examined go beyond descriptive analysis -- none do causal analysis, none examine intervening variables.

The area of administration also poses problems. Suchman's first point here is not wholly sustained, as many of these studies were done by qualified research personnel rather than service workers. As for the bias

inherent in evaluating one's own program, none of the
studies examined discussed this problem or ways of minimizing it. None of the studies followed Suchman's suggestion that program evaluation be done by a team of
outside and inside evaluators. Third is the strain
towards low quality evaluation research induced by scarce
time, personnel and facilities available for such studies.
One can assume that many of the problems observed in these
studies can be attributed to this source. Thus it is
easier to rely upon self-reporting and one-shot studies
than to cross-check data or do longitudinal analysis.

Suchman's fourth category for analysis is current
problems in evaluation research. Suchman comments upon
the relative lack of evaluation studies. While evaluation
studies of drug programs do exist there is little evidence
in the research literature on the success rates of therapeutic communities or community clinics and there is a
lack of comparative studies. Second, Suchman finds that
the evaluation studies that do exist are often of poor
quality and that point is confirmed by my survey. A third
point concerns the political pressures exerted upon researchers by administrators and/or funding sources. While
none of the studies surveyed here discuss this problem
directly, that should not be construed as evidence that
they did not experience it. Similarly strain between research and service workers was not discussed. Fifth is
the lack of guidelines for evaluation research. As already indicated, these evaluation studies fail to address
the question of standards or to propose any.

Thus we find Suchman's major criticisms of evaluation
research appropriate to drug treatment follow-up studies
on almost every point. These studies have been found
weak in the conceptualization of program goals, they have
by-in-large lacked experimental design, the control of
measurement bias and attention to causal analysis. Why
is this the case? Suchman's explanations suffice. He
asserts that evaluative research difficulties exceed those
of basic research due to problems involved in value
assessment, political pressures on the evaluation process,
and scarce resources for this kind of analysis. All the
problems he enumerates for evaluative research apply to
the drug abuse treatment setting. Research funds are
short; service pressures upon researchers are great.
Administrators do have vested interests in program evaluation. Evaluative research is not generally a high program priority. Misunderstandings do abound between
service and research workers. There is an absence of research standards. Research is sometimes conducted by
personnel without requisite training. Furthermore, the
fact that drug abuse is illegal may encourage an even
greater halo effect than is true of research on other
kinds of social programs.

IV. CONCLUSION

Drug treatment follow-up studies suffer from significant problems in validity and reliability, throwing both individual study findings and comparisons of programs into question. Thus, we are hard pressed to determine whether perceived differences in program success rates reflect actual differences in program effectiveness, bias in study design, artifacts of measurement, confounding factors or differences in clients served. However, even more formidable in my view are the constraints emanating from a sphere outside the jurisdiction and control of the researcher -- namely the political process.

The problem of scarce resources can be traced directly to the political arena. Evaluation studies would not be so rare, so poorly conceived and executed, and program researchers would not be so harried were programs or outside agencies adequately funded for this kind of work.

Furthermore, we see today not only the routinely low priority put on evaluation research but retrenchment in the area of drug treatment funding as well. In New York State today, state drug programs are being dismantled; ODAS, the state drug agency is contracting; New York City Addiction Services Agency is under threat of extinction; local programs are being extinguished or cut -- the very provision of drug abuse treatment is being called into question. It is indeed naive to expect that evaluation research, relatively ignored in times of plenty, will be enhanced in times of famine. In such a climate of program retrenchment, evaluation research becomes more than a luxury, it becomes a threat, since it is far more likely to result in eliminating than in enhancing programs.

Thus evaluation research has to battle not only the serious problems inherent in research design and practice but political neglect or assault as well. This paper has identified these serious obstacles to quality evaluative research. We do not yet know the answers to basic questions about the effectiveness of drug treatment programs, and in the existing political climate we are unlikely to learn them.

REFERENCES

1. E. Suchman, Evaluative Research, Russell Sage Foundation, New York, 1967.

DOES METHADONE MAINTENANCE LEAD TO INCREASED
ALCOHOL AND POLYDRUG USE?

Frances Rowe Gearing, M.D.
Dina A. D'Amico, B.A.
Sam Toussie, B.A.

Division of Epidemiology
Columbia University School of Public Health
Methadone Maintenance Evaluation Unit
New York, New York

I. INTRODUCTION

Among the many criticisms aimed at Methadone Maintenance Treatment is that "patients who continue in treatment tend to turn to alcohol or multiple drug use in order to obtain their high." This is a frequently repeated statement, but adequate quantification is hard to find. For instance, there have been no adequate answers to such questions as:

1. What proportion of patients are involved in these problems?
2. Which patients? The young? The old? The men? The women? Which ethnic group?
3. Are these problems transient, and remediable?
4. Did the patients who manifest these problems while in treatment have multiple drug abuse problems at the time of admission which were unrecognized?
5. Are the problems of alcohol abuse and polydrug abuse greater among patients in Methadone Maintenance Treatment than in the communities from which these patients are drawn?

We have reported previously that excessive alcohol has been a problem at some time during treatment for approximately 20% of the patients and was responsible for 16% of the discharges. Problems with alcohol involved a larger proportion of the Black patients and the older patients. We have also reported that continued multiple drug use has been a problem for approximately 5% of the patients and was responsible for 20% of the discharges. Polydrug use involved a larger portion of the White population, and was more prevalent among the younger patients. For both of these problems the proportion of Hispanic patients was in between the White and Black. We have further expressed the opinion that alcohol and polydrug problems were more prevalent in the patients admitted to the later cohorts (1970-1972), as compared with the earlier cohorts (1965-1969). These results were based on some initial very crude and unsophisticated methods of analysis.

We are presenting the same data, but our current analysis is a bit more refined and sophisticated and attempts to provide some possible answers to some of the questions posed earlier.

II. METHODOLOGY

One method of determining the alcohol and polydrug experience of patients in Methadone Maintenance Treatment is by analysis of involuntary discharge rates primarily due to continued alcohol or polydrug problems. The method used for this analysis is the modified life-table. This method determines the probability of survival for a group followed over time based upon those individuals under observation during each particular period. It allows for the examination of any particular cause of discharge by controlling for all other reasons for discharges. The probabilities for any given time period can then be used to calculate cumulative probabilities of continuing in treatment, which are based upon the experiences of the same cohort in preceding years.

Analysis by cumulative probabilities has the advantage of controlling for lag in reporting of discharges in successive years, and yields an indication of the cohort experience for the entire period of observation. This analysis is performed by the Mantel Haenszel method. The data are divided into two cohorts, those entering treatment from 1964-1969, and those entering treatment in 1970-1971. The divisions were made based upon differences in criteria for admission to treatment. Entry into treatment from 1964-1969 required the absence of detectable alcohol or polydrug problems. This cohort can be contrasted to the 1970-1971 entering cohort, where admission criteria were substantially relaxed.

Initially these data were analysed by age, and ethnic group within each cohort.* Cohort comparisons for the 1964-1969 and 1970-1971 groups are based upon seven and five years of follow-up, respectively. Statistical analysis between cohorts is based upon five years of follow-up. Comparisons of cohort, and ethnic group experiences are graphically presented in Figures 1 and 2.

*Due to lack of space, the data are reported only by cohort and ethnic group. All conclusions, however, were drawn based upon age within ethnic group within cohort analyses. Graphical representation and results of statistical tests are available for all groups upon request.

III. RESULTS - COHORT EXPERIENCES - MEN

Contrary to expectations, the 1970+ cohort had proportionately
fewer discharges for drug and alcohol problems. (Figure 1)   These
differences were significant (p < .001) for both drug and alcohol
problems.   While Figure 1 shows the total cohort experience, the
same patterns were observed for age and ethnic-specific rates within each cohort.   The greatest differences between discharge rates
related to drug abuse were seen among Black and Hispanic men entering at age 30, and among White men entering at age 20.

For discharges related to alcohol problems the same age-within-
ethnic group differences were noted between the early and later admission cohorts, with the greatest differences in the 30 year old
entry groups.   It is also seen that alcohol problems are more prevalent than drug problems within each cohort.

One may be tempted to conclude that methadone maintenance
treatment has led to increased drug and alcohol abuse, since those
entering treatment in the 1964-1969 cohort had fewer problems at
onset of treatment.   Analysis of total discharge rates, however,
casts doubt upon this conclusion.   Comparison of total discharge
rates shows approximately the same magnitude of differences as seen
for drug and alcohol associated discharges (p < .001).   These differences are consistent by age and ethnic group within cohort.
While the magnitude is the same, however, the direction is reversed.
Namely, the 1964-1969 cohort had significantly lower total discharge rates than the 1970-1971 cohort.   This would suggest that
the greater alcohol and drug problems of the early cohort are not a
function of time in treatment, but rather arise because a significantly greater proportion of patients in the early cohort have remained in treatment.

In Figures 1-2, the cumulative probabilities of survival are
plotted against years in treatment.   After the fourth year in
treatment, discharges due to severe alcohol and drug problems tend
to disappear.   While it can be argued that this is merely a reflection of those with problems being discharged for other causes or
voluntarily leaving treatment, total discharge rates (Figure 2) do
not show the same discharge patterns.   This suggests that severe
alcohol and drug problems do not increase during treatment, although the selectivity factor cannot be ignored.   Furthermore, the
fact that after the fourth or fifth year of treatment, the severe
alcohol and drug problems virtually disappear has implications for
restructuring counseling priorities during treatment.

Another interesting finding is the similarity between the discharge rates for drug, alcohol and total discharges in all cohorts
and ethnic groups.   While magnitudes vary, it seems that the greatest risk of discharge for any cause, is between the second and
fourth year of treatment.   This indicates that perhaps the emphasis

282

on encouraging patients to begin detoxification from Methadone
Maintenance after only two years of treatment may be premature.

IV. ETHNIC GROUP ANALYSIS

Figure 2 suggests that Blacks fare better than Whites in terms
of discharges for drug abuse. Hispanic men had essentially the
same drug discharge rates as Black men, and lower rates than White
men. These rates are consistent for age within ethnic group and
cohort with 20 year old at entry Whites in the 1970-1971 cohorts
having the highest discharge rate. Alcohol discharges are greatest
among Blacks, and are generally more prevalent for all groups.
Among the Blacks, men age 30 of the 1964-1969 cohorts had the highest discharge rate.

It would seem, therefore, that White men have significantly
greater drug problems in the early years of treatment, and Black
men have the most significant alcohol problems. Support for this
notion of true ethnic differences is supported since ethnic differences between cohorts for discharge rates for drug and alcohol abuse
are essentially the same. Furthermore, ethnic comparisons of total
discharge rates show Black men to have overall higher discharge
rates than White men, who have lower rates than Hispanic men. If
ethnic differences were an artifact of total discharge rates, one
would expect the same ethnic group relationships for problem discharges as for total discharges. This is not the case, however,
since Whites have fewest total discharges and most drug related discharges, Hispanics and Blacks have fewest drug related discharges,
Hispanics have fewest alcohol related discharges, and Blacks have
most total discharges. These relationships are consistent within
age and cohort.

V. REPORTED PROBLEMS

Rates of reported alcohol and drug problems differ from discharge rates in two important ways. First, they probably represent
less severe problems, and second, they are prevalence rates rather
than incidence rates. Since yearly rates are not mutually exclusive, except for the first year of treatment, life table methods for
statistical analysis cannot be used. Ongoing analysis however, has
yielded some interesting preliminary results. Contrary to belief,
reported alcohol and drug problems among patients who remain in
Methadone Maintenance Treatment seem to be transient in nature,
with an average duration of between 1.5-3 years of seven years of
follow-up. Furthermore, the problems seem to cluster around the
second-fourth years of treatment, and disappear by the sixth or
seventh. The fact that the reported problems of those in treatment
seems to parallel discharge patterns adds to the validity of discharge rates as representative of group experiences.

We must emphasize that these data are preliminary, and are presented here as much for provocation as for elucidation. We must further emphasize again that this prevalence data is based on patients remaining under observation.

VI. WOMEN

Evaluation of data on women in treatment is complex, both from an interpretative and a methodological point of view. Sample sizes are small, and as with the men, it is dangerous to combine cohort, ethnic, or age data, since the experiences of each sub-group are significantly different. We are currently evaluating the women's data more thoroughly, so we will mention only some preliminary findings.

The women appear to have a greater proportion of severe alcohol problems than the men and the early cohorts have fewer discharges. Like the men, however, Black women have a greater proportion of problems than either the Whites or Hispanic women.

Like the men, the White women have higher discharge rates for drug abuse than either the Black or Hispanic women, but again the rates are much higher than for the men. Cohort differences do not seem to be significant. Total discharge rates for women are greater than for men, and no definite cohort differences have been found. Ethnic differences of total rates disagree with those for the men. Unlike the men, Hispanic, as well as Black women had the highest discharge rates.

VII. SUMMARY AND CONCLUSIONS

The data we have presented leads us to answer some of the questions initially posed, as follows:

1. Alcohol problems are more prevalent among both Black men and Black women and tend to increase with age at onset of treatment, whereas polydrug problems are more prevalent among White men and women, and among the younger patients. It must be noted, however, that it cannot be concluded that alcohol and drug problems increase solely as a function of age. Ages represent the age at onset of treatment, and by the end of the study period, most patients starting in one age group were in the next older group.

2. Among the patients who have remained under observation and treatment with methadone for four years or longer, previously reported alcohol and drug abuse problems tend to disappear, supporting the hypothesis that in this group these problems are transient and remediable if necessary ancillary services are put into operation, and patients are not discharged too soon.

3. Unrecognized problems with alcohol and polydrug use in the early cohort (1964-1969) appear to have been somewhat more prevalent than expected.

4. In answer to the question of comparative figures for the communities from which these patients come, we have to admit complete defeat with reference to multiple drug use.

With reference to alcohol problems, we can only cite a study done for the Health Services Administration under Gordon Chase in 1972, which reviewed adult admissions to several Municipal and Voluntary Hospitals. The results were that 40% of these admissions to the Voluntary, and 50% of the admissions to the Municipal Hospitals were *alcohol* associated. If this is used as a crude index of the size of the alcohol problem in New York City, the proportion of patients in Methadone Maintenance Treatment who present major alcohol problems is certainly no greater than might be expected.

Supported under Grant No. DA 5PG004 from Special Action Office for Drug Abuse Prevention; Grant No. 8H81 DA 01777-01 and Contract No. 271-76-1107 National Institute on Drug Abuse.

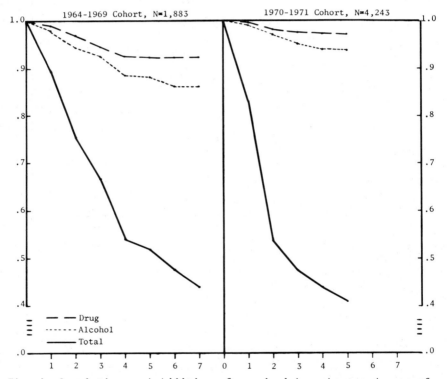

Fig. 1 Cumulative probabilities of survival by cohort and year of follow-up.
Men - Drug, Alcohol and Total Discharges.

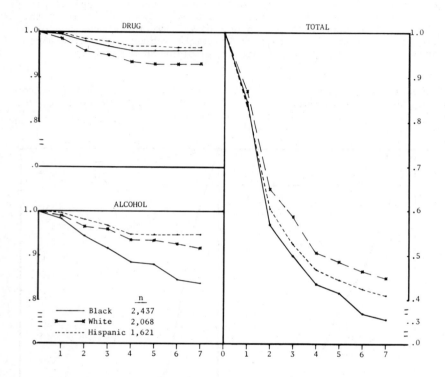

Fig. 2   Cumulative probabilities of survival by type of discharge
         and year of follow-up.
              Men - Black, White, and Hispanic.

A STUDY OF METHADONE TREATMENT EVALUATION

Gerald H. Dubin, M.D.

National Institute on Drug Abuse
Rockville, Maryland

Arnold I. Tannen

Creative Socio-Medics, Corporation
New York, New York

"In every house where I come I will enter only for the good of my patients ..."

Hippocratic Oath - Ethical code
of the medical profession

Whose Agent Is The Methadone Program?

Since methadone treatment is often considered a medical activity, we might expect that methadone programs primarily serve their clients. However, an analysis of the literature reveals that these programs are predominantly geared to represent the interests of society.

Methadone programs are largely funded by society, and not by clients; and since programs are dependent upon funding for their survival they are most sensitive to the demands of the funding agencies. The criteria for success in methadone programs are consistent with this reality, and largely reflect societal concerns. These criteria include reduction in criminal behavior, reduction in drug use, reduction in antisocial behavior and increase in social productivity.

In addition, large numbers of persons come to methadone programs through varying degrees of coercion; and the criminal justice system appears at this time inextricably involved in this process.

Finally, the semantics and phenomenology of methadone programs bear examination. Activities such as observed ingestion of metha-

done, urine surveillance, mandatory group therapy can hardly be
seen as consistent with a client advocacy approach to treatment.
Methadone programs often espouse "reintegration into the mainstream", and "shaping up" clients into "socially normal" individuals.

Role Conflict

Yet, there are many persons involved with methadone programs who
see themselves primarily as client advocates. These include some
physicians and counselors working within these programs.

Such persons may constantly be subjected to pressures over their
conflict in roles. On the one hand, they see themselves primarily
as serving the needs of the client. However, they are working
within a system which emphasizes principally the impact of programs
upon society (e.g., impact of methadone treatment on crime). How
does the methadone program employee cope with serving primarily
clients while being paid solely by the funding agency?

Implication for Evaluation

Conflicting philosophies and goals such as indicated above can
cause chaos and confusion within methadone programs. Within the
area of evaluation, one often notes a fundamental inconsistency
between treatment philosophy and evaluation methodology. This
occurs when a methadone treatment program, often headed by a
physician, cites as its principal mission to serve its clients.
However, possibly because of the pressures of funding realities,
the outcome criteria (criteria for success) reflect societal
concerns rather than client oriented factors.

In reality, we recognize a situation far more complex than the
dichotomy cited above of client advocacy vs. societal advocacy.
There are a host of often competing vested interests including
counselors, physicians, clients, community leaders, states,
federal government, politicians, pharmaceutical industries, etc.
The diagram on the following page, although perhaps an oversimplification, should serve to illustrate the problem.

Evaluation methodology cannot be constructed in the absence of
philosophies and goals, and a clear knowledge for whom the treatment services are intended. Therefore, the evaluation specialist
must enter into this arena of vested interests and assess the
philosophies and goals of the treatment program or agency. A Drug
Enforcement Agency (DEA) program needs a different evaluation
methodology from a client oriented program. A program that seeks
to impress Congress and the news media with how it has "shaped up"
the addict would have a far different evaluation methodology than

one that seeks to catalyze the growth and development of the individual addict. A program that sees addiction as a disease would have different criteria for success from one that sees it as moral decay or another that views addiction as simply the addict's free choice.

Most drug treatment programs and agencies have failed to adequately grapple with the issue of treatment philosophy. Until they have done that, a discussion of evaluation methodology is premature. An individual cannot evaluate his own life in the absence of underlying philosophies and purposes. Similarly, drug programs and agencies which attempt to establish evaluation methodologies in the absence of treatment philosophies will be wasting all of our time and money. Waiting for the results of these evaluation studies will be truly "waiting for Godot".

The absence of a clearly defined treatment philosophy is not accidental. It is a political tool useful in defending an agency or program from an assault from outside. Although the agency cannot show that it is effectively serving anyone, it can argue that it tries to effectively serve everyone. A succinct treatment philosophy might alienate those who do not share the viewpoint!

On the other hand, the lack of a treatment philosophy has enormous implications for those working in drug funding and drug treatment agencies. These funding agencies traditionally have had problems with employee morale, which may stem to a large degree from the failure to clarify a treatment philosophy. In the treatment programs, the treatment staff is caught in a clash of vested interests. The drug counselor may initially set his/her goals toward helping other human beings in trouble. However, he/she becomes pressured to a varying extent to be a tool of those political forces more interested in "social sanitation". The administrators may play the role of buffer between counselor and funding agency. If the counselor agrees to be an enforcer of program policy (e.g., observed urines, mandatory group therapy, etc.), then he will be permitted to remain in the program and try to assist the client in almost any way he can. This arrangement ultimately proves unsatisfactory to many individuals. The embracing of a treatment philosophy does involve the risk that the philosophy will not be supported financially. This underlines again the political expediency of avoiding a treatment philosophy. However, the absence of a treatment philosophy virtually assures the continuation of chaos, the stagnation of learning and the gradual withdrawal of finances.

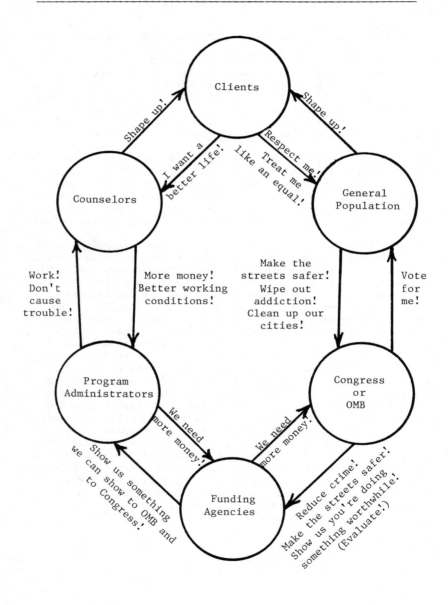

A FACTOR ANALYSIS OF ONE HUNDRED ADMISSIONS TO REALITY HOUSE, INC.

Melvyn Ellner, Ph.D.

Reality House, Inc.
New York, New York

Retention of clients and treatment success of drug abusers has been the major concern of rehabilitation centers. The results of studies of the federal facility at Lexington, Kentucky showed that immediately upon discharge one half of released patients used drugs (1), and that more than 80% returned to drug use within six months of discharge (2). Vaillant (3) found that 95% of discharged patients from the Lexington facility eventually returned to drug abuse. Daytop Village (4) reports that only slightly more than 50% of "their select addict population" (5) who "started" their program remained to completion. The Central Referral Unit of New York City reports that less than 20% of their referred drug abusers to treatment programs remained in treatment as long as several weeks (6). And a recent survey of all admissions during a five month span to the drug free program Reality House with an N of 416 found one month retention rate to be 34%, two month retention 27%, three month 18%, four month 14%, five month 13%, six month 9%, seven month 7%, eight month 7%, and nine month 6%.

To complicate matters relating to evaluation, most treatment programs do not release statistics of their retention rates in an adequate fashion. It is often the case that a client is not considered to be in a program until several weeks have elapsed since admission, or until several interviews are held which are separated by time. These criteria spuriously bolster retention rates, are misleading, and create confusion with regard to program evaluation.

During a four month period, the Intake Unit of Reality House administered to 100 consecutive clients who were black, male, heroin abusers who were to be admitted to our ambulatory program, questionaires which tapped his socio-psychological situation (see Results section for description of items). At a one month follow-up, it was determined that of these 100 clients, 39 did not return to the program after the interview, 32 did return and attended several sessions before dropping out, and 29 were successful in advancing to the therapy level, and remained in the program at least four weeks.

In an effort to resolve questions about subject variables and their relationship to short term retention in the program, a factor analysis of the data was performed.

METHOD

Subjects: One hundred consecutive admissions to the ambulatory program of Reality House who are black, male, heroin abusers.

Materials: Drug Abuse Reporting Program of NIMH (1971), Multiple Affect Adjective Check List (7), and the Opinions About Heroin Scale (8).

Procedure: The data were collected by the Intake staff, and prepared for factor analysis.

RESULTS

The results indicate that the sample group of 100 black, male, heroin abusers was on the average 30 years old, had completed about 11 years of education, and that 83% were unmarried. Less than half of the group was a product of a broken home, and with few exceptions the group had spent no time in orphanages. The group varied widely in work experience, and the average client had held a job for two years.

The average client began using heroin at 20 years of age and became addicted to it within 5 months of this experience. He had been using heroin for 10 years. The average client had been in one drug rehabilitation program before coming to Reality House, had stopped using drugs on his own on two occasions, and the average longest run of drug free experience was five and a half months. Currently he was not using heroin. As a youth, the average client was not declared a juvenile delinquent, and on an average, he was not arrested until he was twenty years of age. He has been convicted of a crime four times, and he had spent three and a half years in prison.

Emotionally, the client showed elevated anxiety, depression, and hostility. He reported an attitude against heroin, and he was generally honest in his report to the staff (based upon a lie scale of the Opinions about HEROIN scale). The average client had never been hospitalized for mental disorder and had not abused alcohol to the point of serious consequence.

292

It was concluded from the correlation matrix that there was not a single variable which significantly correlated with short term retention in the program. The variables which attained the highest correlation with retention, though not statistically significant, were: knowledge of father's occupation (-.20), alcoholism (-.16), parent's marital status (-.15), longest drug free run (.14), age of first heroin use (.14), number of times stopped using drugs (.13), longest time held job (.13), and age (.13). It is interesting to note that the correlation between legal status, e.g., probation, awaiting trial, welfare, and self referral, was not significantly related to short term retention in the program (r=-.05).

The nine factors obtained via the rotated factor analysis accounted for 63% of the variance. The results tend to indicate that at least nine separate types of clients enter our doors. These are The Long Time User, The Neurotic, The Later Drug User, The Manipulator, The Neighborhood Referral, Broken Home Syndrome, The Susceptible User, The Normal, and The Perpetual Client. These descriptive terms are interpretations of the data, and future research might assess their validity. Associated with each factor was a "success" score which represents a statistical approximation of a client's tenure at Reality House. It was deduced from the data that the individuals scoring highest in the "Broken Home" and "Late Drug User" categories were the most successful of the Intake population to progress to the "therapy" level (P<.05) and to remain in the program on a drug free basis for at least four weeks.

DISCUSSION

The results tend to indicate that at least nine types of clients were entering the Reality House program. This makes it difficult to find common denominators by which clients can be grouped for therapeutic purposes. Therefore approaches to an intake population and throughout a program need to include special attention to the unique needs of each client and might not be a fixed program.

While it would be correct to characterize one third of the sample population as having what is conventionally referred to as a character disorder, it would be a mistake to group most of the sample population into this catchall category. Although this term fits the drug abuser on the surface, the data of this research would not justify such a label for a majority of the clients. The range of factors indicates that the client population draws from the normal, the criminal, the impulsive, the labor force, the neurotic, the product of the broken home, and the community. Conservative approaches to diagnosis and treatment are thereby merited.

The data indicate that at Reality House we were most successful with the client who is the product of the "Broken Home". These individuals tended to come from families in which the parents were divorced, deceased, and particularly where the nuclear family con-

293

sisted of only a mother. These clients tended to delinquency in
their youth, and were underachievers at school. They tended to
drink alcohol to a lesser degree and had a longer drug free run
than other clients in the sample group. Perhaps Reality House re-
created the nuclear family for these clients.

The results also tend to indicate that the Reality House program
was somewhat more successful with the "Late Drug User" than the
other factorial groups. These individuals tend to be more closely
associated with the straight world than the other clients. They
regained direction to rejoin the drug free world, possibly as a result of their experiences with the paraprofessional staff, whom
they easily identified with.

When proper diagnosis is made of a client his treatment can be en-
riched. This will result in greater retention rates and enhanced
success rates. The "neurotic" user can be detected by his elevated tension, depression, and hostility. Early treatment by a trained mental health worker may be indicated in many of these cases.
The "susceptible" user can be detected by the shortness of time it
took him to become addicted to drugs (often he felt addicted after
only several shots). With this client, rapid induction, speedy
gratification, and the avoidance of difficult obstacles to program
entrance are required. The "manipulator" usually enters Intake
with a current drug habit, yet he says that he is down on drugs.
He must be outmanipulated in his game if he is to be helped. Encountering him would be most effective in the initial stages of
treatment.

The "neighborhood referral" user is usually a married man whose
life circumstances have led him to heroin use. In treatment, family therapy might be most effective. The "normal" user is psychologically and sociologically unextraordinary. His treatment might
concern itself more with counseling techniques than intense psychotherapy. Vocational guidance and opportunity might be concentrated
upon.

Every type of program system has its "perpetual client", and he is
detectable in our sphere by the many programs he's been in, the
many times he has stopped using drugs on his own, and the fact that
he is not using drugs now. He is a difficult client, but he can be
effectively treated either by making ultimatums of him, placing him
on long term detoxification, or by going along with his game until
he is genuinely involved in the program.

On the strength of the findings of the current research, it can be
concluded that the client population at the Intake level is diverse. The clients vary greatly, particularly with respect to age,
employment record, prison experience, drug free experiences, and
rehabilitation experience. Treatment methods of these clients
should be equally diverse.

It is quite possible that more questions and problems are posed by the results of this research than are answers provided herein. It is hoped that this work might present directions for future endeavors.

REFERENCES

1. M. Pescor, Pub. Health Rep., (1943, Supp. No. 170).

2. G. Hunt and M. Odoroff, Pub. Health Rep., 77: 41 (1962).

3. G. A. Vaillant, Am. J. Psychiat., 122: 727, (1966).

4. D. Casriel and G. Amen, Daytop: Three Addicts and Their Cure, Hill and Wang, New York, 1971.

5. F. Leavitt, Drugs and Behavior, W. B. Saunders Co., 1974, p. 139.

6. D. Glaser, Routinizing Evaluation: Getting Feedback on Effectiveness of Crime and Delinquency Programs, N.I.M.H., Center for Studies of Crime and Delinquency, Rockville, Md., 1973.

7. M. Zukerman and B. Lubin, Manual for The Multiple Affect Adjective Check List, Education and Industrial Testing Service, San Diego, 1965.

8. M. Ellner, Opinions About Heroin Scale, Reality House, Inc., New York, 1973.

PROCESS EVALUATION: EXPLAINING THE
IMPACT OF DRUG TREATMENT PROGRAMS

Kathleen M. Doyle, B.A.
Mark A. Quinones, Ph.D., M.P.H.
Darleen Young, B.A.
Jacqueline Hughes

Division of Drug Abuse
Department of Preventive Medicine & Community Health
New Jersey Medical School
Newark, New Jersey   07103

The most common method of evaluating the effectiveness of
drug treatment programs is the follow up or outcome study which
measures clients' post-treatment success in regard to criteria
such as employment, anti-social activity, or use of illicit drugs.
Although such evaluations can help in analyzing program success
or failure, they do not provide reasons for the results. Process
analysis is the study of activities by which a program produces
its results and is essential to an explanation of the descriptive
findings of the outcome evaluation (1). Unfortunately, a review
of the literature indicates that little of this type of research
has been done in the area of drug abuse.

Since September 1969, the New Jersey Medical School's
Department of Preventive Medicine and Community Health and its
Division of Drug Abuse have coordinated six drug treatment programs in Newark, N.J. During that time, the Division has collected data on patients moving through the system, including
detailed pre admission and post treatment psychosocial information; these data are being used for purposes of evaluating the
programs. We realized, however, that a process analysis of the
programs was necessary both to strengthen and to interpret the
outcome findings.

Methodology

The process evaluation was designed to determine the types,
intensity and quality of treatment regimens offered in the
various drug treatment programs and the ways in which these
treatments affected different types of clients. As a result, a
large number of interactional variables including staff and

client attitudes and behavioral changes, as well as general philosophy (as opposed to observed actions) were considered.

Data were collected from January 1 through November 30, 1975, from program directors, staff and clients of Integrity House, and Odyssey House (to 6/30, when it closed, only), both therapeutic communities, and Dana Clinic, a methadone maintenance program. Although DARE, another therapeutic community, closed in December, 1974, an extensive on-site evaluation had been performed there by the Evaluation staff and the results were incorporated in interpreting DARE outcome data. In addition, partial data (questionnaires but no on-site observation) were obtained from the two outpatient programs, New Well and Mt. Carmel Guild; because of their poor retention rate and our small staff, evaluation of these programs was limited.

The following methods and instruments were used:

1. Each program director completed a questionnaire in which he stated specific program goals of therapies offered to clients. These statements provided a base from which to compare actual treatment being given.

2. All staff (including the directors) completed a two-part questionnaire. Part I elicited demographic data and Part II measured their attitudes in terms of self-esteem, rigidity, dependency and feelings toward drug abuse, drug abusers and rehabilitation (hopefulness of "cure"). Instruments used were: Rosenberg's Self-Esteem Scale (2), Jones' Pensacola Scale (3) and Hart's Drug Abuse Questionnaire (4).

3. In January or upon admission, all clients at Integrity and Odyssey and a random sample of 187 at Dana completed a questionnaire which included the same attitudinal scales given to staff. These scales were re-administered in November to all still remaining in treatment. Ns on these were as follows:

	1st Q.	2nd Q.
Dana Clinic	187	156
Integrity House	239	57
Odyssey House	81	--

The Psychosocial Questionnaire (an instrument containing 150 items) was also routinely administered, for the purpose of correlating "success" with demographic and psychosocial variables.

4. In addition, data were gathered on interactional variables and behavioral changes through ongoing observations of staff meetings, group sessions, individual counseling, encounters, and intake interviews. Initially, interactions involving clients were videotaped by program staff and viewed later by the

297

evaluation team; after a few months, however, the observers had become "part of the scenery" and were allowed access to all activities.

All interactions were both written up and coded on an Interaction Reporting Form for statistical analysis. ID numbers of both staff and clients were included in the reports, providing data on the dynamics and outcome of specific individual interactions.

5. In measuring behavioral adjustment and change, different criteria were required for the methadone program and the therapeutic communities. For all clients, the baseline for such change was the "Social Functioning Score", drawn from drug abuse, employment, criminal, and psychiatric histories at the time of admission.

For the methadone program clients, behavioral changes within treatment were assessed by computing changes in employment, arrests, infractions against program rules (including drug and alcohol abuse) and take home privileges.

For therapeutic community clients, behavior in treatment was measured by computing job assignment records and contract (punishment) and privilege records.

Measures for both client types were obtained from patient files, thus providing a complete record on the whole sample, including those who were in treatment before the evaluation began.

Results and Discussion

The amount of data this effort has generated is massive. The purpose here is to demonstrate some ways of using such data and to illustrate them with some preliminary results.

Following the outline in Suchman's Evaluative Research, three basic areas may be covered.

1. Attributes of the program itself which contribute to program success or failure.

Examples of this would be such procedures as the intake process, services offered the patient in the early weeks of treatment, staffing patterns, etc. For example, one therapeutic community was found to have a higher proportion of graduates than other therapeutic communities. But in observing procedures, it was noted that this program used the "hard concept" type of encounter (in which the patient is required to "scream for help") as the main intake procedure, thus screening out and never admitting large numbers of potential clients who might not have remained long in the program. It was further noted that many patients were promoted quickly and attained graduate status in 7 to 8 months while in the other therapeutic communities the average time was 14-15 months.

This is admittedly an extreme example but it illustrates how differently outcome findings may be interpreted when process is considered.

In the area of staffing patterns and staff effectiveness, both sociometric data, in which each staff member indicates to whom he defers on certain matters, and also actual observation of staff interrelationships, should be considered. Thus, although the sociometric matrices at another therapeutic community showed almost the same strict hierarchy of relationships as did the program staffing chart, it became clear through observation that all power and authority in the program rested with three people. This explains the high level of frustration towards work exhibited by most middle management (house directors, etc.) at this program, and may partially explain the program's low retention rate.

2. The second area of consideration is program recipients - who the program does and does not reach.

Here basic demographic profiles of the programs were considered. In addition, clients' perceptions of self, attitudes towards drug abuse and feelings of dependency were tested; preliminary findings indicate self-esteem as the most significant of the variables. Data indicates for example that the self-esteem of methadone maintenance clients is significantly higher than that of therapeutic community patients ($t=3.31$, $p < .008$), despite the fact that the maintenance clients are not doing particularly well in terms of social functioning. This raw datum could be interpreted as meaning that methadone clients have less self perception than do therapeutic community clients, or as indicating that of themselves because they are on their own rather than in a residential program. However, when a comparison is made between behavioral functioning of both client groups before treatment with their functioning in treatment, this difference in attitudes and particulars of change can be clarified. Parenthetically, it might be noted that the differences in self-esteem cannot be explained by differences in demographic variables such as age, sex, ethnicity, mental status or educational attainment.

3. The final factor for consideration is the type (cognitive, attitudinal or behavioral) of effects produced by the program, including side effects and duration of effects. These will be determined by comparisons of functioning before and during treatment, and by comparisons of Time 1 vs. Time 2 attitude scales.

In addition, analysis of differences between "stays" and "splits" can indicate side effects as well as intended effects.

The field of drug abuse research has much to gain from applying combined process/outcome methodologies to evaluation of treatment program impact. Incorporation of such an approach gives us a more meaningful picture of our programs, distinguishing clearly between the ideal (that which is proposed or intended) and the real (that which actually occurs). Process evaluation not only enriches outcome evaluation but also offers the substantial possibility of altering outcome in beneficial fashion by modifying process.

REFERENCES

1. E. Suchman, Evaluative Research, Russell Sage Foundation, New York, 1967.
2. E. Rosenberg, in Measures of Social and Psychological Attitudes (J. Robinson and P. Shaver, eds.), Survey Research Center, Institute for Social Research, Ann Arbor, Mich. 1973.
3. L. Jones, in Measures of Social and Psychological Attitudes op. cit.
4. L. Hart, Intern. J. Addictions, 8:809 (1973).

FIELD EVALUATION AT THE CLINIC LEVEL:
A PRAGMATIC APPROACH - THE GREAT T.V. LOTTERY[1]

John Bradshaw, Ph. D.
Eric S. Blumberg, M. A.
Aldona Mikaila

Henry Ford Hospital
Detroit, Michigan 48202

ABSTRACT

The ideal method of discovering a clinic's effectiveness is generally said to be a field follow-up study of clients some time after discharge. The level of resources required for such studies conducted in the traditional manner has usually put them out of reach of most clinics and into the purview of the occasional independently funded researcher. The dearth of this sort of information must be remedied if a program is to be humanistic and ready to change as feedback suggests, rather than mechanistic in its processing of bodies. The current study reports on a follow-up effort made in a somewhat different fashion than the traditional. The basic element of this study can be replicated by any clinic at relatively little cost in either dollars or manhours. Both the method and a limited analysis of the study findings are reported.

THEORETICAL CONSIDERATIONS

Methods

In his paper on the Monitoring of Outcome Data, presented at the American Psychological Association in 1973, James Ciarlo[2] presented a plea for the study of program outcome measures, rather than the study of process objectives or quality objectives. In that paper and in a subsequent one [3] some important discussions on the topic outcome measures and their preparation and use are presented, including such methodological issues as scale development, inter-rater reliability in item coding, and validity of responses. They and other authors stress the importance of developing careful measures of how clients of human service programs change over time in various carefully established measurable objectives.

301

We certainly do not quarrel with the importance of the development of methodologically proper evaluative technology. At the same time we are extremely sensitive to the problem of the practical difficulties of adopting the approach and techniques of the purists. We question, for example, the denigration of "process objectives" by authors and wonder whether another perspective might not have greater utility. Are process objectives only summaries of what is "done to" clients, such as number of visits, number of training sessions or number of months in program contact? Or does the term also include in its users' minds what happens to the client while in treatment (and presumably at least in part as a consequence of)? If the latter, then some definite areas of disagreement appear between Ciarlo's position and ours. We would term certain kinds of observable changes as outcome measures, even if only small and perhaps reversible. Thus we are concerned with recording <u>changes</u> in employment, <u>changes</u> in educational attainment, <u>changes</u> in regularity of appointment keeping, and so on. The question which must then of course be raised is whether the changes remarked and recorded as a short-term outcome measure while the client is in the program have any correspondence to longer-term outcomes, and, if so, of what degree and of what kind is the correlation. This latter question was addressed in part by this current research and will be discussed further below.

The more rigid writers on the topic of program evaluation insist almost invariably on standards of design and sophistication which are impossible to meet except, if then, as part of a very special, highly controlled "social experiment."[4,5] Our concern is rather with the question of what kinds of evaluation can be done at the clinic level at a relatively low cost. This clearly takes from us the opportunity to influence important decisions   about the success and cost of basic national policy decisions. If one follows Carol Wiess' typology of levels of decisions which can be made[6] or Thomas Glennan's[7] since they are basically the same, then there are three general levels of decision-making related to programs which occur. These are policy decisions, emphasizing whether basic policy objectives on a broad national level are being met; strategic decisions; emphasizing the study of alternate strategies of intervention within a given policy framework; and tactical decisions in which the emphasis is on the evaluation of managerial efficiency.

It is our assertion that the clinic level evaluation must start first with a very firm grasp of the lowest level of evaluation sophistication, the tactical. When a strong system of internal measurement and record-keeping is in place, and program directors can discuss with confidence the nature of achievements reached by clients while in the program, then it is time to begin seeking farther afield in time, distance and money for the answers to questions which are at a strategic decision level. Reaching the point of beginning to work toward a limited long-term study of client outcomes is very important philosophically and programmatically to a clinic, because only with some answers to questions of that sort can certain basic questions about individual clinic operations be answered.

Very few drug treatment clinics actually attempt long-term outcome studies, even though many of them disdain to claim that they are working with their clients for anything other than 100% success on a difficult long-term goal-complete abstinence from all drugs. One reason why so few attempt studies is surely that the clinics secretly fear the results which may be found. Another is that field follow-up studies have commonly been lengthy and expensive processes, with questionable results from a statistical vantage point, because frequently only a relatively small number of the sample is located. The field study of client outcomes, when even simple descriptions are given, may also seem both generally difficult and more complicated with drug abuse treatment as the area being studied. A useful example of this latter problem can be presented using statements from a recent book on evaluation sponsored by NIMH, Daniel Glaser's "Routinizing Evaluation",[8] as a starting point.

As Glaser usefully summarizes, there are a number of methods which have been used by researchers to trace cohorts of persons to discover what has happened to them subsequent to some event such as receiving or not receiving treatment. The studies have commonly used school, juvenile court, and police records extensively, and in addition have variously employed such other sources of information as Welfare Departments, Mental Health and Medical Records, Selective Service records and Credit Bureau files.

Glaser suggests that records can be used to: (a) locate people in the study cohort for personal interviews; (b) discover what information has become a matter of public record; and (c) learn information which is not public under circumstances in which responsible researchers can provide adequate assurances that confidentiality will be maintained.[9]

In the case of research on ex-clients of drug abuse treatment programs, however, the ethics of confidentiality restrict information in a way opposite from that which concerns Glaser. Unless the identity of the researcher is concealed in some way, the very fact of making it known that a certain individual appears in one's study cohort is in itself a serious breach of the right of privacy of the individual being sought. To approach a Police Department with a list of names and ask for records on their arrest and incarceration, if one is Director of Evaluation for a number of treatment clinics, is to announce to a law enforcement world of undeterminable size (given the interlocking file systems which seem to exist) that those persons are all ex-clients and hence, at best, ex-addicts. Thus the problem becomes one of somehow locating and interacting directly with those persons being sought, without, if possible, stigmatizing them with the label of "drug addict" or "ex-drug addict."

303

Cost

In a time of decreasing funding of treatment programs, program directors are under pressure to justify their existence to legislators and administrators. At once they are, therefore, caught in a difficult bind. Long-term outcome studies are notorious for difficulty and expense, if field contact with clients is sought. Outcome studies using secondary data sources, if a humanistic concern for clients' rights to privacy are protected, seem difficult to accomplish. The expense for conducting studies of individual clinics' terminated populations generally seems too high. For example, Ciarlo[10] reported a cost of around $45.00 per client for a study with a response rate of around 70% and a cost of around $30.00 per client for a response rate of around 50%. The authors[11] of a superlative short manual on the techniques of follow-up evaluation report an average of three staff hours per successfully located client with an amazing 90% response rate, which is considerably less expensive than Ciarlo per located client, but still costing thousands of dollars for a program of any size.

There is at this point in time no solution that we know to the problem outlined above. If programs wish to locate terminated clients in sufficient numbers to be able to make reasonably appropriate generalizations about the long-term success of all clients, they will find it necessary to devote a good deal of money to the effort.

There is, however, a limited beginning solution to the problem. We were able to achieve a 25% response rate with a cost of under $1.00 per client. The inappropriateness of making broad generalizations on the basis of such a limited and presumably biased sample is known to everyone who has ever studied statistics and methodology. The possible utility may not be quite so obvious and we will further discuss the subject below with reference to data from our effort.

Pallister-Lodge Lottery

The method we used combined two techniques, with the intention of taking a "quick and dirty" pass at the problem of discovering what could be said about clients' drug use after leaving the clinic. The design of the study questions was oriented to seeking a very limited amount of information in order to get as high a response rate to a mailed questionnaire as possible. The "kicker" was the promise in bold letters that a returned questionnaire (a single addressed and stamped card) would enter the client into a raffle which would be held on a specified date (quite soon after the mailing went out) at which time a new television set would be given away. At the same time, an effort was undertaken to locate and interview by telephone all past terminations as well. Clinic

304

counselors were used for the telephone effort, and they were not encouraged to spend any more than a minimum of effort on any one client, in order to ensure coverage of all 469 follow-up eligible clients in a short period of time.

As we said above, the response rate we achieved can be considered good only in relation to cost or to having no information at all. We received 63 mailed responses (13% response) and located and interviewed 73 ex-clients by telephone (16% response). However, there were only 20 clients who appeared in both groups. Thus, by combining two very low-effort methods we were able to get information on 116 clients, or a 25% response rate overall. The total cost of the data collection was around $225.00 plus the cost of the limited amount of staff time spent telephoning.

One might ask, as we said above, whether information on such a limited percentage of the study group is useful. It is certainly not appropriate to generalize from any correlations found in the sample to the entire group. We found, for example, that of the 116 clients, 54, or 47%, reported being drug free. Between the likelihood of some "yea-saying" response bias and the probability that many of the most successful clients will be the easiest to locate, to name just the most obvious problems, we can certainly not conclude that 47% of all of our former clients are living drug free lives. (Since there are possible biases in the other direction, we cannot necessarily assume that the figure is worse, either).

Use of Data

There are several things which can be done with this kind of data. One is to analyze various associations within the response data to see what correlations may exist. The probability is that a significant positive or negative association might be moved by data from a greater number of responses to the point of zero order correlation, but it is unlikely to totally reverse direction.

An example of this general logic can be given by considering the following finding. The Final Termination Status item is coded by means of a fairly elaborate set of criteria which are all based on something mentioned previously that we feel is important-- analysis of short-term changes (outcomes) in the client while in treatment. The categories used are: urinalysis results; counseling attendance; methadone pick-up; detoxification status; social relations; psychological adjustment; educational status; and vocational status.(12) We feel that a clinic concerned about what is happening to its clients must maintain a constant awareness of factors such as these.

Final Termination Status (Prognosis)	Drug Use at Follow-Up			
	Drug Free	Not Drug Free	In Another Program	Total
Recovered	2	0	0	2
Improved	31	12	6	49
No Improvement	18	24	15	57
No Evaluation	3	5	0	8
Total	54	41	21	116

Chi Square = 14.23, df of 6, $p < .05$

There is a clear relationship between the rating of future prognosis at the point of terminating service and the reporting of no drug use at follow-up. Were the number of responses greatly increased, it is perfectly possible that there might be no association between the two. It is much harder to imagine, however, given that an association was found in this limited case, that it would be found that a rating of improved at time of leaving is related to being non-drug free at a later date. We will thus continue to use this coding process. Had there been a finding of a negative correlation we would not.

Another way data compiled in the manner which we used may be analyzed is through considering it to provide a certain minimal guidance about things which are not working and could be improved. If it is discovered that the number of persons reporting drug free status at follow-up is quite low, then one may begin to change program elements to attempt to change this result when the next group of clients are followed. This sort of data use requires that one assume that the same or similar biases are affecting the characteristics of the responding sample each time. Thus perhaps only the 25% most stable clients would be being located each time, and the clinic would be attempting to maximize the number of goals achieved in that population.

Another example of a similar nature can be given from our findings. We discovered that when analyzing the association

between drug free status and counselor when in the clinic certain
patterns emerged. Two counselors' were much less successful, on
the average, than those of all the others. We are using this
information as an indication that further attention should be
given to what is being done or not done by these persons.

We have discussed some of the reasons why undertaking a
follow-up study of treatment populations is both important and
difficult. There are problems of cost and confidentiality, if a
sophisticated study is undertaken, and problems of generalizability, if a simple study is done. In our opinion, the benefits
to programs and their clients more than compensate for the problems
at whichever level of sophistication is adopted. We strongly
recommend to programs which have never done any field follow-up to
begin to at least plan to do a project such as ours. As limited as
it was, it has given all members of the clinic a much greater sense
of being in touch with the reality around which treatment is
supposed to be oriented.

References

(1)   This study was in part supported by NIDA Grant #1 H80
      DA00955-03. A special note of thanks is owed to Ms. Lynda
      Amerine and Ms. Paula O'Neill for their work on this project,
      and to Ms. Sally Clark for her editorial aid.

(2)   Ciarlo, J.A. Monitoring of outcome data: steps toward a
      system for improving mental health program outcomes. Paper
      presented at American Psychological Association Convention,
      Montreal, Canada, 1973.

(3)   Ciarlo, J. and J. Reihman, The Denver community mental health
      questionnaire: development of a multi-dimensional program
      evaluation instrument. Mental Health Systems Evaluation
      Project. Northwest Denver Mental Health Center (unpublished
      paper).

(4)   Houston, T.R. The behavioral sciences impact effectiveness
      model, in Evaluating Social Programs (P.H. Rossi and
      W. Williams, eds.), Seminar Press, New York, 1972, pp. 51-65.

(5)   Stanley, J.C. Controlled field experiments as a model for
      evaluation, in Evaluating Social Programs (P.H. Rossi and
      W. Williams, eds.), Seminar Press, New York,1972, pp. 67-71.

(6)   Weiss, C. H. Alternative models of program evaluation,
      Social Work, 19:675-681 (1974).

(7)   Glennan, T.K. Jr. Evaluating Federal manpower programs: notes
      and observations, in Evaluating Social Programs (P.H. Rossi
      and W. Williams, eds.), Seminar Press, New York, 1972,
      pp. 187–220.

(8)   Glaser, D. Routinizing evaluation: getting feedback on
      effectiveness of crime and delinquency programs, Center for
      Studies of Crime and Delinquency, NIMH, 1973.

(9)   Glaser, D., op. cit., pg. 95.

(10) Ciarlo, J. and J. Reihman, op. cit.

(11) Bale, R.N.; Cabrera, S.L. and J.D. Brown, An Introduction to
      Follow-up Evaluation, Stanford University School of Medicine,
      1975.

(12) Coding guidelines for this item were developed by Eric
      Blumberg, with the assistance of Aldona Mikaila, and are
      available from one of them upon request.

FOLLOW-UP SURVEYS: TECHNIQUES AND EXPERIENCE

Lisa J. Anderson, Catherine K. Forrest, and Michael Spier

Addiction-Prevention, Treatment Foundation, Inc.
New Haven, Connecticut

Follow-up research in the field of drug abuse has received
much clinical and Federal emphasis. The manner in which this
research is conducted and the techniques employed to collect
follow-up data raise complex ethical and practical issues. Once
an individual leaves a treatment program, an inevitable conflict
arises between his or her right to privacy and the investigators'
desire for knowledge (1). Unlike research conducted on an inpatient population, the success of a follow-up project depends
entirely upon locating the client -- a process that often requires
the services of community agencies and the respondent's relatives.
The general trend towards mobility makes it difficult to maintain
contact with any group over an extended period of time (2).
Former drug patients seem to be particularly difficult to find.
Many move erratically without leaving forwarding addresses or
notifying relatives. Another complication of follow-up surveys is
that agencies allow research personnel less access to records than
previously. Within a two-year period, our local police department
moved from allowing total access to their records to complete
refusal to make police records available (3). This trend is encouraging for civil libertarians but frustrating for the researcher.

The primary responsibility of the follow-up research team
must be to balance the needs of research with the need to respect
individuals' rights to privacy. This paper outlines effective
methods of collecting follow-up data that do not violate the
client's right to confidentiality. This will be discussed drawing
from our experience in two follow-up studies of New Haven drug
abusers. In both, a follow-up interview was conducted with the
former client.

Research personnel need an explicit set of procedures which
make clear the ethical standards they are to maintain. From this
base, the details of research methodology, relationships with
other agencies, locating subjects and confidentiality can be decided. It is hoped that such standards will modify the current
trend to closing access to important research data.

The beginning step in this process comes from the Human Investigation Committees in our universities. The major charge of such groups is to ensure that the informed consent of subjects is obtained. To this end, the committee carefully examines the procedures and techniques of the research with particular attention to the adequacy of explanation of a study's potential benefit and risk to the prospective subject. Usually, a signed consent is required of those who agree to participate in the study. This requirement is more difficult to meet in follow-up studies of drug dependent people. Assuring a person of anonymity and confidentiality of his interview can seem contradictory to requiring his signature at the time of the interview. A respondent in one of the New Haven follow-up studies felt this incongruity. When asked to sign a consent form, he simply refused. He had been told that his name would not be associated with the data provided, and he felt that a request for a signature was an abridgment of that promise. A partial solution of this type of problem is to anticipate it at admission. Patients should be told that evaluation of treatment is part of the program and that they may be contacted at a later date. Accurate names, addresses, and phone numbers of persons who know the respondent well should be collected (4). The intent of such a procedure is to sensitize the respondent to the idea of follow-up research and to provide the researcher with contacts that the respondent has selected.

Associated with the issue of informed consent is the important ethical issue of confidentiality -- how it is explained to research personnel, communicated to subjects, understood by participating agencies and maintained throughout the research effort. From the beginning the nature of the study should not be revealed to anyone but the respondent. The subject may be living with individuals who do not know that he was a drug user. Although the person may give his parents' address on admission forms, they may not know that he was in a drug program.

Locating an individual who has left a program some time ago is a difficult process. Each case is different and must be treated as such. An outline of useful locating techniques will follow here. The best starting place is the addresses and phone numbers the person provides at intake. In the initial contact letter we sent out to these addresses, the research was described as a health study. The return address was equally non-revealing (5). In the majority of cases the respondent was not at that address; most of these letters were returned to us marked "Addressee or Address Unknown". Other letters did not come back. There was no way of knowing whether the letters were opened and read by people other than the person in our sample. Letters were sent out to new addresses as they were collected. Since all the envelopes were marked "Address Correction Requested", the Post Office notified us of any address change on file. In one New Haven follow-up study, only 27% of those interviewed were residing at their intake addresses.

A more efficient method to locate respondents is the telephone. We checked telephone directories for listings under the respondent's and his/her parent's name. Every effort was made to locate the respondent through these contacts. In many cases, the parent or family members refused to disclose the whereabouts of the respondents, although they were willing to pass on messages. It is interesting to note that family members often give cues that suggest that the respondent is incarcerated. They make evasive comments such as "he is out of town" or "he is not around".

After phoning or writing respondents, visiting their addresses is an effective means of locating them. If the respondent no longer resides at a particular address, his whereabouts may be known by neighbors, local bartenders or other neighborhood people. If individuals contacted at the initial address are unable or unwilling to help locate the respondents, additional addresses and names of family members can be obtained from social agencies.

In worrying about an agency's cooperation, a researcher may divulge more information than is necessary, unconsciously thinking that this will help get needed addresses. Agencies are usually responsive to direct and explicit requests and accept the demands of confidentiality readily. (We found the same was true of families. Parents appreciated our not disclosing the nature of the study even though they knew of their child's drug treatment.) Some agencies are more strict than others about confidentiality. We found that some State correctional institutions and State hospitals required that we submit requests for information to their Human Investigation Committees. The Motor Vehicles Departments and Probation Departments were less formal. Many would answer our request about updated addresses, etc. over the phone without question. Although it may be necessary to describe the nature of the study to a project director, this information should not be shared with the other staff members of the agency.

The best agency from which to seek information is the drug treatment facility. Periodically a member of the follow-up staff should check to see if the respondent has returned to treatment. 15% of our sample had returned and were currently in treatment when our study began. These respondents were interviewed first. In addition, the records maintained on patients during treatment provide useful locating information and admission forms often included names of family members.

Respondents in drug follow-up studies can be expected to have criminal records. Throughout our study, we checked regularly to see if any of the respondents were incarcerated in State facilities or Federal prisons. Probation Departments can often provide updated address information on respondents. Another agency which proved to be extremely useful was the Department of Motor Vehicles, since most adults have licenses. Address information is routinely updated by this agency, and often readily accessible via computer terminals. We were given permission to use these terminals ourselves and were therefore able to look up other leads such as parents' names and addresses. Because the information is organized by last name and date of birth, we often picked up respondents who had moved to other parts of the state.

These are only a few of the many agencies which can be used to gather updated address information on respondents. Others include the Welfare Department, schools or universities the respondents attended, reverse directories, and commercial records. The usefulness of a particular agency depends upon how accurate and accessible its records are and what demands of confidentiality they make upon the researcher. The important thing is to be resourceful when trying to locate an individual. We live in a society in which enormous amounts of information are collected on each of its members. Given adequate funding, the researcher can expect to locate at least 80% of his sample.

Locating respondents who have left a drug program some years ago is often very difficult and time-consuming. The need to maintain confidentiality only complicates the task. For this reason, it is extremely important that interviewers as well as the entire research staff understand the demands of confidentiality. This is especially crucial because follow-up studies frequently employ former clinical staff or ex-addicts as interviewers. People who have been in a clinical setting where information is freely communicated need detailed explanation of the importance of confidentiality, stressing the common, unintended slips of confidential information. An example of this is telling a counselor how well a subject is doing, thereby running the risk of this getting back to the subject who proceeds to question how much of what he said when interviewed was reported back to his former counselor.

An interviewer can expect to find respondents who are extremely suspicious and who may require extensive explanations (6). The ease with which he talks about confidentiality may directly effect whether or not he secures an interview with a particular respondent. It is essential that senior research personnel encourage interviewers to discuss the stresses they experience and dilemmas they face especially where confidentiality is concerned. The issue can be openly addressed, the interviewer reassured of the staff's acceptance of error or confusion, and the research effort maintained.

Lastly, for a successful follow-up study, interviewers should be involved in all phases of the research effort. The term "research" has many negative connotations, mostly as a result of misunderstanding. As a part of interviewer training the rationale for the study can be explained. Interviewers can understand how the interview method is preferable to the questionnaire. They can learn that precision and rigor are essential ingredients of research and how bias affects data. More generally, they can appreciate what questions the study hopes to answer -- and their crucial role in making that possible.

NOTES

1. S. Nelson and H. Grunebraum, *Amer. J. Psychiat.*, <u>128</u>: 11 (1972).

2. P. May, H. Tuma, and W. Kraude, *Amer. J. Orthopsychiat.*, <u>35</u> (1965).

3. A detailed report of validation procedures used in the NARA Study (1971) showed that many states did not allow access to police or institution records, even with patient consent in a few instances.

4. G. Valliant, *Amer. J. Drug & Alcohol Abuse*, <u>1</u>: 1 (1974).

5. In follow-up studies where the questionnaire instrument is used, it is important that researchers send out questionnaires to verified addresses only. The letter should be sent by registered mail.

6. We only accepted refusals given by the respondent himself. In one of our New Haven Drug Dependence Unit follow-up studies, the refusal rate was 5.6%. A follow-up study of psychiatric patients (Myers and Bean, 1968), sent three different interviewers to obtain an interview before accepting a refusal.

TREATMENT

PSYCHOSOCIAL PREDICTORS OF PREMATURE DISCHARGE FROM AN INPATIENT DETOXIFICATION UNIT FOR HEROIN ADDICTS

Jacob Schut, M.D.

and

Robert A. Steer, Ed.D.

West Philadelphia Community Mental Health Consortium, Inc.

A pernicious difficulty confronting any voluntary, inpatient detoxification service is the relatively high incident of patients failing to complete treatment. The premature discharge rates for inpatient detoxification have been reported by Baekeland and Lundwall[1] as ranging from 23 to 39 percent. Although the long-term efficacy and costs of inpatient detoxification have been challenged by Raynes et al.[2] because they found that only 13.5 percent of a sample of 100 narcotic addicts were drug free one year after leaving the hospital, these same researchers discovered that the addicts who had completed treatment were 3.7 times more likely to be drug free one year later than those who had not completed detoxification in the hospital.

The literature about prematurely leaving inpatient detoxification is sparse and equivocal. For example, Fortunato et al.[3] found that subcultural membership, the interaction between subcultural membership and age, and referral source were able to partially discriminate between completers and noncompleters in a New York City hospital, but Raynes et al.[2] reported that none of the addicts' background characteristics in their study differentiated between those who remained in and those who left a Boston hospital. Types of discharge were also studies by Lin[4] in an inpatient detoxification program that treated both alcoholics and drug abusers; the alcoholics were more likely than the drug abusers to leave prematurely, and men were more likely than women to be discharged against medical advice. Persons with psychopathic tendencies as measured by the MMPI were prone to leave without asking for any permission at all.

The present paper describes research which was conducted at the Inpatient Detoxification Unit of the West Philadelphia Community Mental Health Consortium, Inc., located at Philadelphia

General Hospital. The study tried to provide further data for deciding whether or not the psychosocial characteristics of heroin addicts can predict who will and will not complete inpatient detoxification. The unit has 20 beds - pregnant addicts and poly-drug abuse addicts are detoxified here also.

Method

The study proceeded in two stages. The first stage involved a post hoc search for any psychosocial variables that differentiated between persons finishing and not finishing detoxification in a sample of 115 consecutive admissions to the unit. During the second stage, a lapse of three months was allowed to occur, and the discriminating variables identified in the first stage were then used a priori to predict who would and who would not complete treatment in a sample of 30 subsequent admissions.

Samples

The first sample consisted of 77 men and 38 women of whom 37 were white and 78 were black. The mean age was 24.84 years (SD = 5.47), and the mean number of years spent seeking an education was 11.08 (SD = 1.49). Only 6 people were currently employed, whereas 52 were married. Nineteen persons were on probation, and the sample's mean number of arrests was 4.59 (SD = 6.23).

The patients' drug histories showed that 63 had been in treatment before, whereas 52 had not; eleven of the 63 had been referred from methadone programs. Heroin was being used daily by 94 patients, with the exception of 11 methadone referrals who reported that they were only using it two or three times per week. Interestingly, 26 persons were using other opiates, besides heroin and methadone, and the bimodal other opiates were morphine and dilaudid which were used weekly. Illicit methadone was also being taken infrequently by 14 patients, and approximately 10 percent were irregularly using barbiturates.

Within the first sample, there were 32 persons who left before completing detoxification and 83 who remained throughout. The average length of stay for the 29% who left prematurely was 6.63 (SD = 2.37) days, whereas the 72% who stayed lasted for a mean of 10.90 (SD = 4.34) days.

The second sample was comprised of 20 men and 10 women who entered the Unit three months after the first sample of consecutive admissions had been drawn. There were 5 whites and 25 blacks. The mean age of 26.83 (SD = 5.64) years, the mean educational attainment of 10.50 (SD = 1.57) years, and mean number of arrests at 4.67 (SD = 5.48) were comparable to those of the first sample's. The overall drug histories were also similar to the first sample's.

Twenty patients left prematurely, whereas 10 stayed on.

Data Analysis

Twenty-six psychosocial characteristics were selected from the information gathered during the first day upon entering the Unit. The variables represented a wide range of background data including personal information, such as age, race, and sex, drug and alcohol histories, previous treatments for drug, alcohol, and mental health problems, etc. The patients scores on the Lie, Neuroticism-stability, and Extroversion-introversion scales of the Eysenck Personality Inventory[5] were added to the 26 variables along with their scores on the Profile of Mood States'[6] Tension-anxiety, Depression-dejection, Anger-hostility, Vigor-activity, Fatigue-inertia, and Confusion-bewilderment factors.

Point-biserial and phi correlations were calculated between the 35 variables and whether or not the patients had completed detoxification. Since the study was exploratory, it was decided to set alpha at the .10 level of significance, two-tailed test. Variables with correlations significant at less than the .10 level were then selected for inclusion within a discriminant analysis, and the hit rate for correctly assigning the 115 persons to whether or not they had finished treatment was computed.

The discriminant weights derived from the first sample were then used with the same variables in the second sample to predict whether or not the subsequent sample's patients would or would not complete detoxification. The hit rate was again computed and compared to the rate that had been achieved with the first cohort of patients.

Results

Only five variables had significant product-moment correlations with not completing (scored as 1) and completing (scored as 2) detoxification; these were race (1 = white, 2 - black), years of education, number of arrests, psychoneuroticism as measured by the Eysenck Personality Inventory, and the frequ ncy with which other opiates had been used for two months prior to admission, besides heroin and methadone. The correlations were .20, .16, -.17, -.20 and -.31, respectively. The second and third correlations were significant beyond the .05 level; and the fifth correlation was significant beyond the .01 level. All of the levels of significance were based on 113 degrees of freedom.

The five significant correlates were next used in a discriminant analysis. The correlations of the five variables with the linear sum differentiating between the patients were .45, .38, -.40, -.46, and -.75 for race, education, number of arrests, psychoneuroticism, and other opiate use, respectively; these loadings indicated that other opiate use was approximately three times more powerful in discriminating between completers and dropouts than any of the four variables which were about equally discriminating.

The discriminant function that was calculated was then employed with each patient to determine whether or not he or she would be expected to complete detoxification or not. Thirty-two of the patients had actually dropped out, whereas 83 had finished detoxifying. The discriminant analysis had correctly assigned 24 patients as dropouts and 65 patients as completers. The odds ratio for correct assignment was, therefore, 11 to 1; the percentage of correct assignment (hit rate) was 77 percent.

To determine whether or not such a high rate had arisen by chance, it was decided to employ the same five variables and their discriminant weights with the second sample and then compare the predictions with what the patients eventually did. The odds ratio for correct classification was again 11:1. Twenty patients had actually failed to stay, and only 11 had been predicted correctly; 10 did stay, and 9 had been predicted. The hit rate dropped to 67 percent.

Discussion

Within the inpatient detoxification unit described here, the patients who stayed were more educated, black, had fewer arrests, had not been abusing other opiates prior to entering, and displayed less psychoneuroticism. The relative importance of using other opiates over the four remaining variables that were found suggested that the psychopharmacological properties of methadone for achieving detoxification may not afford a 'smooth' enough withdrawal for patients who had been using pharmaceutically produced opiates such as dilaudid.

The present research has demonstrated that the patients' psychosocial characteristics could predict completing inpatient detoxification rather well. However, additional variables, such as ward environment that has been studied by Teasdale et al.[7], may significantly improve predictability. The interpersonal relationships developed between the patients, themselves, would also seem to be very important. For example, there often appeared to be a contagion effect among the dropouts in which groups of patients who had developed friendships would simultaneously ask to leave.

References

1. F. Baekeland and L. Lundwall, Dropping out of treatment: A critical review, Psych. Bull., 82: 738-783 (1975).

2. A. E. Raynes, A. Fisch, M. E. Levine, G. J. McKenna and V. D. Patch, Evaluation of hospital detoxification using various outcome criteria, Proceedings of the Fifth National Conference on Methadone Treatment, 1: 675-681 (1973).

3. M. Fortunato, R. LaVine, S. Feldstein and E. L. Richman, Predicting type of discharge from a narcotic detoxification service, Int. J. Addict., 1: 124-130 (1966).

4. T. T. Lin, Use of demographic variables, WRAT, and MMPI scores to predict addicts' types of discharge from a community-like hospital setting, J. Clin. Psych., 31: 148-151 (1975).

5. H. J. Eysenck and S. B. G. Eysenck, Manual for the Eysenck Personality Inventory, San Diego, Calif., Educational and Industrial Testing Service, (1968).

6. D. M. McNair, M. Lorr and L. F. Droppleman, Manual for Profile of Mood States, San Diego, Calif., Educational and Industrial Testing Service, (1971).

7. J. D. Teasdale, J. Evans, S. Greene, C. Hitchcock, H. Hunt and P. H. Connell, Ward environment in an inpatient drug dependence treatment unit: II. Attempts to improve ward environment, Int. J. Addict., 10: 539-555 (1975).

OUTPATIENT HEROIN DETOXIFICATION WITH
ACUPUNCTURE AND STAPLEPUNCTURE

Forest S. Tennant, Jr., M.D., Dr. P.H.

The Division of Epidemiology
UCLA School of Public Health
UCLA Center for Health Sciences
Los Angeles, California 90024

ABSTRACT

Eighteen heroin addicts were treated with acupuncture, electrical stimulation, and staplepuncture on an outpatient basis.
Treatment outcomes were compared to two similar groups of 18 subjects who were detoxified with methadone and propoxyphene napsylate.
Withdrawal symptoms were relieved for about two hours in the majority of patients after a treatment episode of acupuncture and
electrical stimulation. Staplepuncture, which is the handmanipu-
lation of a surgical staple implanted in the concha of the ear,
was reported to at least partially relieve withdrawal symtoms in
approximately 40% of subjects. Only one acupuncture/staplepunc-
ture subject was able to completely detoxify compared to 13 and
10 subjects respectively in the methadone and propoxyphene napsylate groups (p < .001). Use of acupuncture and staplepuncture
in outpatient clinics may be limited unless techniques can be
found that will relieve withdrawal symptoms for a longer period
than that observed in this study.

INTRODUCTION

Observations by Wen and Cheung and others indicate that acupuncture and electrical stimulation will relieve opiate withdrawal
symptoms for a few hours. (1-4)Sacks has attempted to develop a
"built-in" acupuncturist by inserting a surgical staple into the
concha, or inner wall of the ear, and by teaching the heroin addict
to simply move the outer edge of the staple sev eral times daily
when heroin withdrawal symptoms become difficult to bear.(5)By use
of this technique, called staplepuncture, the addict can remain
ambulatory and carry on normal social functions. Reported here is
a clinical trial of 18 heroin addicts who requested detoxification
by acupuncture and staplepuncture on an outpatient basis. Treatment outcomes of these subjects are compared to two similar groups

of 18 subjects who received methadone or propoxyphene napsylate (Darvon-N[R]) for outpatient detoxification.

METHODS

This study was conducted between February and April, 1975 at Community Health Projects, Inc., which is a health center located in West Covina, California. West Covina is a community in East Los Angeles County which is central to a heterogenous population of low and middle income white and minority families. Community Health Projects, Inc. provides a multimodality drug and alcohol treatment program in which heroin addicts may select from a variety of outpatient treatment approaches including the administration of methadone or propoxyphene napsylate.

In preparation for this study, Sacks, who developed the staplepuncture technique (5), trained the research staff to perform ear acupuncture, electrical stimulation, and staplepuncture. An information notice was sent to referral sources in the clinic's catchment area and posted in the clinic to inform the addict population of the availability of acupuncture/staplepuncture treatment. Eighteen patients were admitted to the study who requested heroin detoxification by acupuncture and staplepuncture, and who met the following requirements: morphine sulfate in the urine; history of three months of daily heroin use; presence of fresh needle marks on the extremities; non-pregnant; and no medical or psychiatric conditions requiring immediate treatment. (Table 1) Patients were informed that they could receive daily acupuncture, electrical stimulation, and staplepuncture for a maximum of 21 days. On the day the patient entered detoxification, a stainless steel surgical staple was inserted with a staplegun into the concha of each ear just posterior to the extermanl auditory meatus. Patients were instructed, when away from the clinic, to move the staple up and down vigorously by hand when heroin withdrawal symptoms or heroin craving occurred. Each day when the patient attended the clinic he was given a 15-20 minute treatment with electrical stimulation which was applied to the staple by means of a constant-current stimulator which delivered byphasic square-wave pulses of 7 Hertz and 0.2 milliampere. Additionally, acupuncture needles were inserted into the web between the thumb and second finger of both hands and into the occipital ridge behind both ears. Needles remained in place for the duration of electrical stimulation treatment.

Each day the patient answered a questionnaire about the effectiveness of acupuncture and staplepuncture. A morphine withdrawal score similar to that of Himmelsbach was recorded each day just before and after acupuncture and electrical stimulation (6). Withdrawal scores were determined by assessing the severity of the following signs and symptoms: gooseflesh, yawning, perspiration,

323

lacrimation, rhinorrhea, myalgia/arthralgia, chills, nausea/vomiting, insomnia, anorexia, depression, diarrhea. Scoring was: 0= absent; 1+=mild; 2+=moderate; 3+=severe. A urine specimen was collected under observation when the patient began detoxification and four days later. Specimens were analyzed for morphine sulfate in order to determine if the patient had ceased heroin use and successfully detoxified.

Outcomes of these 18 patients were compared to 18 consecutive patients detoxified in the same clinic by the same staff with methadone and with propoxyphene and napsylate. The patients in the comparison groups had the same admission criteria as did those in the acupuncture/staplepuncture group. (Table 1). Principal measurements evaluated in the acupuncture/staplepuncture and comparison groups were: daily withdrawal score; days retained in treatment; and number of patients who converted their urine from morphine sulfate positive to morphine sulfate negative.

RESULTS

Patients began to seek admission to the study within 10 days after availability notices were distributed. Four of 18 (22.2%) subjects stated they sought acupuncture/staplepuncture treatment because they did not accept or would not enter a residential program or one which administered methadone or propoxyphene napsylate.

Retention of acupuncture patients was low. Only three (16.7%) patients remained in treatment on the fifth day compared to 17 of 18 (94.4%) methadone and 16 of 18 (88.9%) propoxyphene napsylate subjects (P < .001), Figure 1). One (5.5%) subject converted his urine from morphine positive to morphine negative. This compares to 13 of 18 (72.2%) in the methadone group and 10 of 18 (55.5%) in the propoxyphene napsylate group (P < .001).

All 18 (100%) subjects felt that acupuncture and electrical stimulation provided at least partial relief of withdrawal symptoms on a temporary basis. Patients reported that acupuncture and electrical stimulation relieved withdrawal symptoms from 30 minutes to 18 hours with a mean of 6.94 hours and a mode of 2.0 hours. Relief from withdrawal symptoms was substantiated by morphine withdrawal scores recorded before and after acupuncture and electrical stimulation. The overall mean, daily withdrawal score for the first five days, before acupuncture and electrical stimulation, was 9.5 compared to a score of 2.3 immediately after treatment (P < .001). Mean withdrawal scores each day were significantly reduced at the P < .05 level after treatment. The overall mean withdrawal score (9.5) before electrical stimulation, however, was significantly higher than the overall mean daily withdrawal score before daily medication administration in the propoxyphene napsylate (7.6) and methadone (6.6) groups (P < .05), Figure 1. Since only one patient remained in acupuncture/staplepuncture treatment

on the sixth day, no reliable statement regarding withdrawal
scores can be made after the fifth day.

Sixteen of 18 (88.9%) subjects returned to the clinic at
least one time to report on the effects of staplepuncture. Hand
manipulation of the inserted staple while the patient was out of
the clinic was reported to at least partially relieve withdrawal
symptoms by 7 of 16 (43.8%) subjects. Twelve of 16 (75.0%) subjects found the staple manipulations to be somewhat painful. No
ear infections were observed. Interestingly, 6 of 13 (46.2%)
patients who reported using heroin during staplepuncture felt
that heroin euphoria was less than normal. Two subjects never
returned to the clinic after day one and staples were therefore
not removed by the clinic staff. Whether these subjects experienced any positive or negative effects is not known.

COMMENT

This study indicates that acupuncture and electrical stimulation will significantly relieve symptoms of heroin withdrawal
for a temporary period. Some reports have previously reported
this with human subjects and Ng and co-workers have demonstrated
this in a controlled laboratory study with animals. (7) The physiological basis for these observations is entirely unknown. Staplepuncture may also have relieved heroin withdrawal since 7 of
16 (43%) subjects reported at least some positive effects, although it is possible that similar results could have been accomplished by placebo. Acupuncture has recently been shown to probably be a placebo in treatment of chronic pain. (8) Placebo effect, however, may be a positive asset in patient care. (9) If
our subjects had been in-patients and acupuncture and electrical
stimulation had been administered more than once per day, the majority of these subjects would undoubtedly have successfully detoxified since all subjects reported at least temporary relief
of withdrawal symptoms following acupuncture and electrical stimulation. Only one outpatient in this study, however, detoxified as
indicated by urine test conversion from morphine sulfate positive
to morphine sulfate negative. It is usually difficult for patients
to attend an outpatient clinic more than once per day to receive
treatment, and this fact appeared to primarily account for the
poor patient retention and the low detoxification rate observed
here. Unless an acupuncture/staplepuncture technique can be
found to extend the time of relief of withdrawal symptoms, it is
unlikely that acupuncture/staplepuncture will achieve widespread
use in outpatient clinics. Acupuncture and electrical stimulation
appear to have more potential for inpatient use since treatments
can easily be given more than once per day.

It is not possible to conduct a double-blind study using acupuncture and staplepuncture on humans so the subjects in this study

were compared with 18 subjects who were detoxified with methadone and propoxyphene napsylate in the same clinic by the same staff. Nevertheless, all non-blind studies made it possible for staff bias to influence subjective observations and treatment outcome. Retention rates, morphine withdrawal scores, and urine conversions from morphine sulfate positive to morphine sulfate negative were superior in the methadone and propoxyphene napsylate groups. Four (22.2%) subjects, however, sought acupuncture/staplepuncture treatment because they did not accept methadone or propoxyphene napsylate as treatment agents. For this reason, acupuncture and staplepuncture may be considered an outpatient alternative for addicts who do not accept available chemotherapeutic agents. Acupuncture, electrical stimulation, and staplepuncture were administered to subjects in this study by a physician and nurses who were briefly trained and not particularly expert in the techniques utilized. It is possible that outcomes of patients may have been improved if treatment had been given by clinicians who were more skilled in the art of acupuncture and staplepuncture. Furthermore, treatment outcomes may have been better if acupuncture and electrical stimulation had been administered for a longer period or given at more body sites.

TABLE I

Similarity of Acupuncture,
Propoxyphene Napsylate, and Methadone Groups

	Acupuncture N=18	Propoxyphene Napsylate N=18	Methadone N=18
Male	83.3%	77.7%	83.3%
Female	16.7%	22.3%	16.7%
Mean Age, in Years	29.7	28.5	27.1
Mean Highest Grade Completed	9.9	11.3	11.6
Mean Length of Heroin User Years	8.6	9.1	7.8
Mean Length Current Daily Heroin Use in Months	9.8	7.0	8.8

There was no statistically significant difference for any variable between the acupuncture, propoxyphene napsylate, and methadone groups.

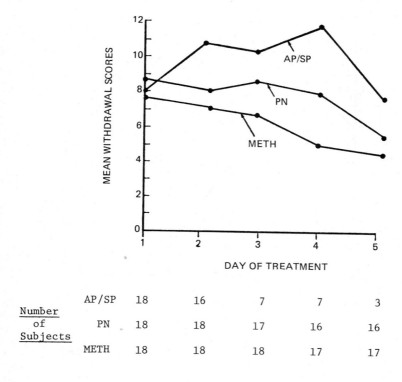

Number of Subjects		Day 1	Day 2	Day 3	Day 4	Day 5
	AP/SP	18	16	7	7	3
	PN	18	18	17	16	16
	METH	18	18	18	17	17

Figure 1. Mean opiate withdrawal scores for three treatment groups. AP/SP is acupuncture/staplepuncture group; PN is propoxyphene napsylate group; METH is methadone group. Withdrawal scores are shown only for the first five days of a scheduled 21-day program since only one subject remained in AP/SP treatment on day 6. Mean withdrawal scores for the AP/SP group was significantly higher at the $p < .05$ level on days 2-5.

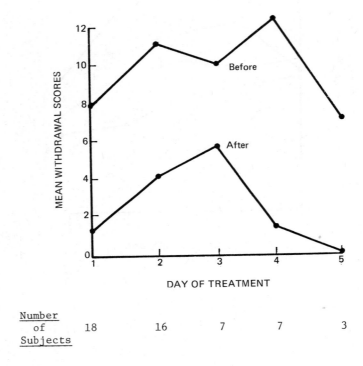

Number
of   18   16   7   7   3
Subjects

Figure 2. Mean withdrawal scores before and after acupuncture treatment. Withdrawal scores are shown for only the first five days of a
scheduled 21-day program since only one subject remained in treatment
on day 6. Mean withdrawal scores for each day were significantly reduced at the p < .05 level after treatment.

REFERENCES

1. Wen HL, Cheung SYC: Treatment of Drug Addiction by Acupuncture and Electrical Stimulation. Asian J Med 9:138-141, 1973.

2. Sainsbury MJ: Acupuncture in Heroin Withdrawal. Med J. Australia 2:102-105, 1974.

3. Kao AH, Lu LTC: Acupuncture Procedure for Treating Drug Addiction. American J Acupuncture 2:201-207, 1974.

4. Low SA: Acupuncture and Heroin Withdrawal. Med J Australia 2:341, 1974.

5. Sacks LL: Drug Addiction, Alcoholism, Smoking, Obesity Treated by Auricular Staplepuncture. Amer J Acupuncture 3:147-150, 1975.

6. Himmelsbach CK: Studies of Certain Addiction Characteristics of (a) Dihydromorphine ("Paramorphan"), (b) Dihydrodesoxymorphine - D ("Desomorphine"), (c) Dihydrodesoxycodeine - C ("Desocodeine"), and (d) Methyldihydromorphinone ("Metopon"). J Pharmacol, and Exper Therap 67:239-249, 1939.

7. Ng CKY, Douthitt TC, Thoa NB et al: Modification of Morphine Withdrawal Syndrome in Rats Following Transuricular Electro-stimulation: An Experimental Paradigm for Auricular Electro-acupuncture. Presented before the North American Congress on Alcohol and Drug Problems. San Francisco, Calif. Dec. 15, 1974.

8. Lee PK, Andersen TW, Modell JH et al: Treatment of Chronic Pain with Acupuncture. JAMA 232:1133-1135, 1975.

9. Benson H, Epstein MD: The Placebo Effect: A Neglected Asset in the Care of Patients. JAMA 232:1225-1226, 1975

T.C. - WHERE ARE WE GOING?

David H. Kerr, M.A.

President
Integrity Inc.
Newark, N.J.

Prior to 1958 the treatment of the drug addict was primarily in the hands of clergy or the professional world. The psychotherapists agreed that their techniques had little effect in dealing positively with the drug addict. In 1958 with the founding of Synanon, certain concepts like peer pressure and self help began to emerge during the development of the original "therapeutic community concept". This concept derived from a basic alcoholics anonymous approach and has been modified, revised, and refined over the years to be called the "therapeutic community" (T.C.). Dederich's model was one of survival, where every individual in the community must "pull his own weight" whether it be helping one of the brothers or sisters therapeutically, or acquiring food for the house, cleaning the bathroom, or preparing and cleaning up after meals. There were no outer limits set on anybody and everyone was expected to do the maximum for each other and the community.

Until 1975 the T.C. movement was allowed to evolve slowly and cautiously into its own model of treatment, which apparently began showing some success with individuals other than the drug addict. In 1975 however, with the national economic recession coupled with growing inflation, the federal government began cutting back funds in all areas including drug treatment. The concept of third party payment emerged as the possible solution to maintaining T.C.'s at the present treatment level, while continuing to decrease direct federal treatment dollars. Since T.C.'s were already funded under H.E.W., and since the T.C. model seemed to fit most appropriately under a residential or hospital type setting, the Joint Commission on Accreditation of Hospitals began developing standards for the accreditation of all T.C.'s along with other drug treatment programs. Adherence to these standards would then justify the receipt of third party payments through funding sources such as insurance companies, Medicaid, social security, etc.

While there was a great deal of concern and time spent in involving grass roots treatment people in the development of these standards, there may be no way to avoid the fact that the standards apply to a hospital setting. The medical model is the backbone of the standards and the T.C. has little relationship to the medical model. In fact, many concepts which have been evolving as basic to the T.C. model are in direct opposition to the medical model. The following describes some of these concepts and how the present Standards either do not address them, or directly or indirectly work in opposition to them.

Can The Therapeutic Community Continue Freely Evolving Its Own Treatment Model If The Present Proposed Standards Are Applied Rigidly?

It is very clear that survival always takes precedence over all else and it is most likely that the Standards will have to be strictly followed. Second and third generation T.C.'s being developed now and in the future are liable to be limited by adherence to these Standards and diverted in the direction of the medical model. The independent and free flowing evolution of a new concept in group or community treatment will begin to merge with, and may finally be co-opted by the medical service model.

It should be noted that these Standards are written very liberally. On the other hand, the paper work and adherence to certain specific procedures are liable to buttonhole the T.C. more and more in the direction of the medical model. With regard to paper work, the Standards are requiring every client or resident to be given a thorough social history, psychological history, medical history, psychiatric reports when indicated, etc. This Intake Summary can then be used in the development of the individual Treatment Plan. This Treatment Plan according to the Standards, focuses on the psychosocial needs of the resident, the vocational needs, the legal needs, medical needs, etc. There must be Goals set at this time where the treatment program will see to it that the individual arrives or achieves certain progress relative to his Treatment Plan. For example, John Doe comes in with a problem of no job skills. The Treatment Plan should indicate when and how John Doe will be placed into some type of skills training program and prepared for some type of career. This would be called the Vocational Treatment Plan. John Doe may also be very withdrawn and the Psychosocial Treatment Plan should show this and the Progress Notes in the individual's personal file should reflect group or individual counseling toward the goal of more openness and perhaps more aggressiveness in groups, etc. To summarize, the Intake Summary leads to the development of a Treatment Plan. The follow-up of these Treatment Plans is seen in the Progress Notes which may be reviewed on a regular basis at some sort of Multidisciplinary Case Conference where a person's individual progress is noted in relation to his treatment objectives or goals. Certain progress or lack of same is noticed and the Treatment Plan may be revised or adjusted in accordance with the experience of both the resident and the staff.

So far, this sounds innocuous enough, but strict adherence to these forms, i.e. Intake, Treatment Plan, Progress Notes, Case Conference, may cause the gradual elimination of important T.C. concepts (not required for financial survival). The Intake Summary, Treatment Plans, Follow-up, Progress Notes, and Case Conferences all focus on the individual and his progress. This is not nearly as relevent to the proper function of the T.C. as is the progress of the group and community. In fact, emphasizing an individual's progress can cause staff to put themselves above an individual in that they (staff) are developing a Treatment Plan and seeing that he adheres to it once he agrees on it. Staff then only encourages him to progress within the limits of his potential as described in the Intake Summary. A dichotomy can easily form here between staff and their statements of what's right for a resident, and the resident and what he feels is right for himself. The professional will counter that the resident has maximum input in the development of his own Treatment Plan. The T.C. worker will argue that the community decides the resident's progress within the context of that community, perhaps with little consultation with that individual resident, but rather in line with the expectations of the community and his need to fit into that peer structure. It's not what's best for him as decided by him, especially at the time of intake, or as decided by staff. The point really is that he enters into a community of people living together with certain expectations and constraints and he develops within the context of this community first, and individually, second. Classification material required by the Standards sets limits on a resident's capabilities either implicit or explicit while the T.C. has great expectations of an individual addict coming off the streets, and sets very few limits. Chuck Dederich's Synanon had to survive, people had to be relied on to work with each other toward their survival, and the spirit created by this was the same type of spirit that's in jeopardy here with the infusion of the medical model and the emergence of individual treatment needs versus the community needs and the individual within this context. These forms and reports may move in the direction of reflecting an individual's progress regardless of the community, based on the insight he shows in individual counseling and in groups, rather than his actual behavior and attitudinal progress within the context of the community.

The demands of a certain formula of staff functioning over a specific T.C., encourages the attitude of an administrator covering his T.C. according to some carefully devised formula on which his funding is based, rather than on the needs of the community. From this can develop shift work and attitudes of nine to fivers who are there doing the job in accordance with certain procedures and standards rather than working towards community spirit and belonging.

As mentioned above, the emphasis on the individual and the limits of the classification and diagnostic material might create an attitude of limited staff and resident expectation. This is in direct conflict with the T.C. "model" also, in that an individual is not expected to do good work, but excellent work, whether it be dusting the staircase, painting woodwork, repairing a chair, etc. All jobs and functions are quality work which reflect high staff and resident expectations with no limits. If a resident shows that he has limits in certain areas, then these will be recognized and his function modified accordingly. But past social history and classification material does not need to be so relevent here. Again, the concept of limits and potential described in the Intake Summary or Treatment Plan might be contradicted by the T.C. philosophy of "act as if".

Traditional psychotherapists may take a dim view of the "act as if" concept if the classification material indicates that he has failed at this function in the past. Here also, the Standards seem to suggest that the written material initiates and guides decision making while in the T.C. the "community" guides decisions as it interacts with the individual. Based on this observation a different tact can be taken which might coincide with previous classification information or might not.

With the strong emphasis on _individual_ progress and Treatment Plans, the future T.C.'s might begin ignoring the need for a resident experiencing bonified success by moving up in the status heirarchy of the T.C. The status system in the T.C. might be eliminated entirely since it has no relation to funding criteria. Giving a resident the taste of success month after month in the T.C. helps him to begin to combat the many years of failure he may have constantly experienced prior to entering that community. The success felt by a resident in seeing himself move higher and higher in the structure of the community may be one of the strongest encouragements for an addict, once he has left the community, to keep moving in a positive direction. Insight and cognitive knowledge are cheap compared to the experiences of success and achievement by a resident: "If I can make it to such a rank in the T.C., I can make it out here". The T.C. concept of oversimplification and overgeneralization of rules, regulations, and directions for new residents, works directly against the concept of individual treatment plans.

The emphasis on the individual, Treatment Plans, Goals, Objectives, etc., however, will be extremely beneficial later on in the program, especially when a resident is moving in the direction of re-entry and career, but initially, learning the mores and concepts of the community are far more important. T.C.'s should spend more time emphasizing concepts such as "this is right, this is wrong, these are the rules, this is how you behave, this is how to act as if, this is how and when to express your feelings, etc." rather than "what do you personally think you need as an individual?"

The Standards movement toward individuallizing treatment also works against the T.C. concept of the spirit of _belonging_. People must feel they belong and work toward the goal that "there's something bigger than myself here" rather than "what's in it for me" and "am I getting what I came here for according to my treatment plan?" The spirit of belonging discourages the selfishness that often accomp-

anies traditional psychiatric treatment and always follows the narcissistic addict. Supporting this concept (belonging) the T.C. emphasizes
self responsibility to combat a resident's excuses. Individuallizing
treatment encourages a resident to talk about himself and the drug addict has a habit of becoming involved in the syndrome of hundreds of
rationalizations or mechanisms to defend himself and to blame others
for what he has done to himself. The T.C. has a heirarchiacal structure with both democratic and authoritarian mechanisms. The Standards
encourage equal decision making by all of the Activity Coordinators,
again focusing on what is best for the individual rather than what is
best for the community and therefore the individual. Sometimes crises
occur in the community that need to be solved through the authoritarian mechanism and hierarchy rather than a group decision of Activity
Coordinators.

The need for cultishness in a therapeutic communtiy also works against the implicit direction of the Standards, i.e. that of professionalization. Therapeutic communities have found certain cults or
rituals to be effective community motivators.

Generally, the above comments are not directed at those who wrote
the Standards since they were well researched with a tremendous
amount of input from the community. But there may be no way to avoid
implicit concepts of the medical model dictated by the Standards
which may in the future subvert the direction of the T.C. Also, the
above comments are not meant in any way to derogate the professional
or the input of the professional, nor are they meant to diminish the
need for standards that can be objectified. But professionalism, paper work, individualized treatment, and the need to survive through
third party mayment may destroy concepts that have been developing
in another direction, i.e. that of the therapeutic community. The
Standards could be revised so that the emphasis during treatment
weighs toward the community, and the emphasis during rehabilitation
weighs toward the individual.

THERAPEUTIC COMMUNITIES
AND
INTERFACE HEALTH DELIVERY SYSTEMS

Sidney Shankman, M.D., Moderator

Second Genesis, Inc.
Bethesda, Maryland

Dave Mactas, Participant

Marathon House
Providence, Rhode Island

Alan M. Rochlin, Ph.D., Participant

Second Genesis, Inc.
Bethesda, Maryland

Introduction

The therapeutic community is a highly structured setting
which serves as a pragmatic system of social learning, a modality
providing suitable intervention into a resident's previously irresponsible life style. The individual's conflicts with society
usually resulted in punishments which neither affected nor educated
him. In the residential house, peer group pressure, censure, and
support are operating as a consistent 24 hour a day process, a
"university" for self-awareness, self-realization, and resultant
behavioral change. To make choices and to accept the consequences
of those choices is primary to the development of responsibility
in each resident. He has entered a new and demanding social
system in which he functions as an integral part with a definite
role. He can eventually transfer his sense of belonging to the
larger community and society outside the T.C.

The broad scope of services of the therapeutic community
effecting the modification of those previously irresponsible life
styles towards rehabilitation and self-actualization do not exist
in a societal vacuum. These services must involve interaction with
interface health delivery systems offered through city, county,
state, and federal health departments and agencies. The co-operative nature of the relationship between the T.C. and aligning
social services cannot be undervalued during the total period of

assessment, treatment, and re-entry, from the valueless street
world, through residence in the T.C., to transition back into the
community at large. That working relationship is defined and outlined with emphasis on the innumerable benefits to both the individual and society from programs of mutual assistance between therapeutic communities and interface health delivery systems. Panelists
from Marathon House and Second Genesis address themselves to that
relationship.

Discussion

In the early days of the therapeutic community development
there appeared to be a theme "We can do it alone." T.C.'s found
they were dealing with a population quite unresponsive to the
traditional techniques used by mental health agencies. Initially
there was the grandiose notion that the unique environment was so
powerful it could assist anyone to positive functioning without the
aid of anyone outside the residential setting. Obviously necessary
institutions, funding sources, referral agencies, etc., were adjuncts to allow the treatment process. The T.C.'s were "takers,"
without formally conceptualizing the positive integrative requirements of the T.C. working in the community of health service providers.

It is imperative that there is a re-examination of how T.C.'s
fit into the complex of mental health delivery systems if they are
to provide more beneficial assistance to the clients whom they
serve. Description of that client ranges from such categorizations
as "dope fiend," "hard-core addict," character disorder sociopath,
etc. Demographic data support that he may be from any race, religion, economic class, either sex, or varying ages from early adolescence through the forties. The client may be a volunteer or
forced by the judicial system into the T.C. as an alternative to
jail. He may come with some varying combination of inner and external motivation.

Today's polydrug abusers are complicated and demanding, whose
symptoms in the treatment process may cause them to be dropped
because they cannot readily cope with that therapeutic regimen.
Many may have severe underlying psychopathology which was not associated with the "old time dope fiend." The overwhelming impact of
the data suggest that the T.C. functions as an agency of the "last
resort" to its clients. Referrals come to the T.C. with an average
of two or more overdose treatments at emergency rooms. They have
experienced a number of other mental health agencies and have lengthy involvement with the law. It is essential to understand the
importance of the T.C. relationship with other agencies in the
mental health complex from the very start of its association with
the client. If the T.C. were able to select rationally the time
of involvement with the client, would the T.C. be the institution
of the last, first, or middle resort?

Referrals could be facilitated if research could precisely define who will benefit from the unique setting of the T.C. Ludicrous referrals could be eliminated if T.C.'s could explicitly describe the characteristics of those appropriately served and effectively helped by the T.C. approach. It is the responsibility of the T.C. to find alternative agencies for those deemed inappropriate candidates for T.C.'s, working in conjunction with other agencies to plan resources which may more adequately deal with a client's particular needs. The individual unsuited for a T.C. modality, unless intelligently placed, may wander into the ultimate referral, i.e., jail, chronic hospitalization, overdose death. It is as much the T.C.'s responsibility to create services which currently do not exist to assist with the "misfits" as any other group. It is naive or irresponsible to assume that he will be suitably handled by some other agency. It is equally naive for the other agency to assume suitable treatment for all at a T.C.

T.C.'s must avail themselves of the services of other resources to their fullest. Parole and probation officers should be involved in their respective cases and understand the rehabilitation by continuing contact with the client even after he has completed the residential treatment thus reinforcing selectively those behaviors that T.C.'s have tried hard to modify. They must know more about the client than whether he has remained clean or law abiding.

Greater emphasis must be placed on educational institutions. Abusers tend to be under-achievers, extremely afraid to attempt to approach activities at the level of their ability. Many have learning disabilities which have helped create feelings of poor self-worth and low self-esteem. The T.C. can fuse aspects of education and treatment, helping to overcome emotional blocks and negative feelings associated with the educational process, along with techniques to enhance the learning process itself. Work with school officials to explore characteristics of the T.C. population and the utilization of improved and specialized techniques of instruction should have great advantages in the rehabilitation efforts.

There also must be a fusion of the efforts between the services of vocational rehabilitation counselors and job placement specialists and the T.C. staff. More often than not, clients cop out on their abilities and interests. They sell themselves short and select the most available, least threatening, non-demanding job opportunities. Often they choose the same job they had before they entered the T.C., openly admitting boredom with it. To find, plan, and secure the best vocational/educational goal can be one of the hardest tasks involved in the rehabilitation.

Recreation specialists can offer guidance in the meaningful use of recreational time, a problem which usually confronts the

re-entry level resident. Ways of solving the dilemna, finding
positive steps that an individual must take to enhance his worth
through acquiring new acquaintances and activities is in no way
easy. Special techniques and exercises could greatly assist in
this extremely important area of the client's development.

There should be greater use of traditional mental health and
family therapy agencies who could be effective in working with
marital partners, parents, siblings, etc. Too often there is a
tendency for the T.C. to either take the total family responsibility under its aegis or, at the other extreme, leave the family
entirely out of the picture. Here selectivity as to the needs of
each individual family may very well dictate which agency is in
the best position to provide the most meaningful service and intervention. Obvious implications for prevention can occur at this
level of service.

After graduation, residents of T.C.'s may be ready for a
different type of therapy. This may be the time to stress the
applicability of traditional services for the client. Some residents may have achieved the ability and internal motivation to
profit from such treatment.

Residents at Second Genesis are required to participate in AA
meetings whether or not alcoholism has ever been a part of their
previous life styles. The general concern is that one chemical
not be substituted for another. Experience has shown that attendance at AA meetings, even at a minimum, points out another level
of dependency and temptation that must be looked at and guarded
against.

If the T.C. is to provide more beneficial assistance to its
clients, it most assuredly cannot do it alone. It requires the
use of the old and the new, the practical and the still to be discovered. The task is greater than the combined effort of the resources currently on hand, both in terms of theory, funds, manpower, and ability. Under such circumstances, to be an island is
absurd.

Self-evaluation for Therapeutic Communities

Each therapeutic community has evolved specific relationships
and agreements with the health delivery systems in each of their
jurisdictions. Obstacles have been encountered and must be addressed and ameliorated. Analysis of the answers to these questions might be helpful:

1. With limited dollars, how much does competition between
    agencies interfere with appropriate referral and services?

2. What role should local government play in interface?

3. Should there be a multi-agency screening and referral service? A central intake?

4. Do other agencies understand the therapeutic community operation and process?

5. What biases are prevalent regarding other agencies' views of the therapeutic community?

6. What are the prevalent views held by the therapeutic community regarding other health delivery systems?

7. To what extent is the therapeutic community utilizing the services of other health delivery systems?

8. To what extent could the therapeutic community increase its use of services from other agencies?

9. Is there fragmentation or duplication of services in the interaction of all the services?

10. Should there be one central agency responsible for following the progress of a client from referral source to the therapeutic community to society?

Summary

Not everyone is a candidate for a therapeutic community; however, for those who are able to adhere to its basic concepts, it is a most effective setting in which an individual can turn his life around. T.C.'s cannot exist in a vacuum. Interface with other health delivery systems is a necessity. There is little room for elitism or infighting. There must be give and take with health agencies. Residents in a therapeutic community learn the importance of a sense of community and rapport and co-operation with others. It is time that T.C.'s adhere to these concepts themselves. Particularly now that there is so much to do with such limited funding, interface with other health delivery systems is an imperative. Uppermost it must be remembered that the T.C. must serve its clients needs with all its resources and that those resources are not boundless. The therapeutic community cannot afford delusions of omnipotence. Such distortions of its self-image can only obscure its vision and subsequently its effectiveness.

HYPOTHETICAL CLIENT RETENTION FACTORS IN RESIDENTIAL TREATMENT

Daniel Heit, M.A. and Kenneth Pompi, Ph.D.

The Abraxas Foundation, Inc.
Marienville, Pennsylvania

Why do clients stay in treatment programs? This question has primacy for program administrators, evaluating committees, funding agencies, and client referral sources. When different programs are compared, inevitably client retention rates are examined. Residents, particularly in early stages of treatment, express the same concern from their own perspective: "Why should I stay?" There is a felt sense that the ability to hold clients reflects overall program quality.

It would be of value if factors which induce clients to remain in treatment could be discretely articulated. Towards this end, we hypothesize two factors extrinsic and eleven factors intrinsic to the treatment environment which influence client retention. These factors are an abstraction of the authors' involvement in all aspects of the Abraxas Foundation's residential rehabilitation program since its inception in 1973. The program, not-for-profit and funded in part by the Pennsylvania Governor's Council on Drug and Alcohol Abuse, is an alternative to incarceration for court-committed youthful offenders. The primary residential facility is in Marienville, Pennsylvania and two re-entry houses are located in Pittsburgh and Erie respectively. Total client population is about 120. We will not detail the Abraxas treatment program as that has been done elsewhere (1).

I. EXTRINSIC FACTORS

These factors are visible primarily in the referral process but continue to impact during treatment.

(1) PERSONAL ENVIRONMENT. Some people have no place to be. Adults who are estranged from their families often come to and stay in treatment because they have no alternatives. These people lack food and shelter; they are tired of being hassled by the

police or "street" enemies and tired of repeated institutionalization; they are exhausted by street hustling. Such clients comprise
a large proportion of urban program populations.

Others may be juveniles without family support for a variety
of reasons: the nuclear family no longer exists; the home environment is intolerable due to alcoholism, incest, violence, parental
psychiatric disturbance or poverty; or the adolescent by his drug
usage and other unacceptable behavior is disowned.

Some people are forced into treatment by their parents or
spouses in order to maintain affiliation with them. These people
accept treatment in order to return to a supportive family rather
than permanently escape an unsupportive one.

(2) AUTHORITARIAN AGENCY. This refers to pressure by an
agency that has some control over the client. Criminal and juvenile
offenders are increasingly being committed to programs by the
courts. The alternative to treatment for these people is jail, or
the juvenile equivalent. In other cases, mental health or welfare
agencies, schools, or other programs with authority insist on
placement.

II. INTRINSIC FACTORS

These are inherent to treatment communities either by explicit
design or result from certain events within the treatment environment.

(1) PERSONAL RELATION. Some clients develop personal
relationships with particular staff members which are outstanding
in intensity and meaning. These relationships tend to carry clients
through personal or program crises.

(2) COMMUNITY. Clients experience a powerful sense of
"tribal" affiliation to a community of peers. This differs
dramatically from previous peer affiliations on the streets in that
it is based on more in-depth personal understanding whereby
individual differences are not so arbitrarily subject to group
ostracism and retribution. The unattractive, the unintelligent,
and others who have been excluded through prejudice may for the
first time experience community acceptance.

(3) CATHARSIS. Another influence in client retention is
relief of personal distress. Some clients enter treatment in
severe, visible pain. These clients often find relief in early
clinical interactions, particularly group therapy. Surcease of
pain is a powerful positive reinforcement--clients thereby identify
the program as a place where they occasionally find respite.

(4) INSIGHT. In treatment, clients get information about
themselves which helps them understand personal difficulties, and
raises the possibility of solving them. For instance, a client
who has been rejected by women learns that his self-deprecation,
not his appearance, is the cause.

(5) SELF-ESTEEM. Therapeutic communities are structured so that clients quickly sense progress as they become involved in community functions. As program expectations are met and clients rise in community status, they begin to see themselves as estimable.

(6) HOPE. People in treatment often learn that they can fit into "straight" society in a role which may suit long-standing, suppressed, or new ambitions. Early but significant educational and vocational achievements within the program are seen as building blocks for future success. For instance, the dyslexic client who begins to read sees brand new possibilities opening up for him.

(7) NATURAL HIGH. Programs encourage clients to suspend inhibitions so that they may find new ways to enjoy themselves and the world. Sports, meditation, reading, handicrafts, yoga, sensitivity exercises, games, and music all are pleasurable "hooks" that keep people in programs.

(8) IDENTITY. Programs are laboratories in which identities crystallize through introspection, feedback, and the ability to safely test new roles. For many, time for self-development is a desirable alternative to the harried demands of living in the outside world.

(9) STRUCTURE. Clients appreciate an orderly, safe, and comprehensible environment which is governed by a clear and cogent authority. For brutalized adolescents, this authority is particularly welcomed as an alternative to the arbitrary or cruel punishments inflicted by parents and parent surrogates.

(10) LOVE. In programs, people find others who treat them with warmth, giving, and a respect for their personal uniqueness. Once experienced, this is very hard to give up.

(11) DEPENDENCY. Residential programs take care of basic human needs for those who can not or will not provide for themselves. Clients tend to stay as they become dependent on the program to meet these needs.

III. DISCUSSION

Our thirteen hypothetical factors have yet to be validated; also, we need to determine if they are actually distinct, and whether fewer (or more) would have greater utility. Although we have done no research, we have found that these factors are useful in distinguishing Abraxas' thirty-three graduates from one another and from those who have left prematurely. The present scheme, in a sense, has formalized our clinical intuition about these clients.

Are these intrinsic factors the "change agents" in the rehabilitative process? At least one, DEPENDENCY, would seem to be anti-rehabilitative. Others such as SELF-ESTEEM, INSIGHT, and IDENTITY seem very essential to the process of change. Thus it is probably true that those aspects extrinsic or intrinsic to a treatment milieu which keep people in treatment differ markedly in their impact on the actual rehabilitative process. For example, treatment at Abraxas is initiated through an AUTHORITARIAN AGENCY, namely criminal or juvenile court. This extrinsic factor, as personified by probation officers in their periodic visits to their clients, remains a retentive influence throughout treatment. This is rarely sufficient to keep people in treatment, however, as a great deal of personal investment is demanded by the program. Various intrinsic factors must visibly come into play for even those clients with heavy jail sentences hanging over their heads to remain and progress. The more clearly we can articulate these factors which bind clients to programs, particularly in the ways they interact with the differing personalities of individual clients, the better will be program retention and program effectiveness.

REFERENCE

1. A. Lissner, J. Gilmore, and K. Pompi, Contemporary Drug Problems, Winter 457 (1974).

THE THERAPEUTIC COMMUNITY AND METHADONE:
A WAY OF ACHIEVING ABSTINENCE

Edward Kaufman, M.D.

Medical Director, Chief Psychiatrist
Lower Eastside Service Center
New York, New York

Presently there are 33,000 individuals in New York City who are
receiving methadone maintenance treatment. Many of these individuals have changed their behavior substantially and are leading
productive lives. Others are not so fortunate and are still
abusing alcohol and other drugs or continuing antisocial patterns
of behavior. Many of the latter group of patients will respond to
forms of intervention used by methadone programs, i.e. hospital
detoxification for drugs or alcohol, crisis therapy, medication
changes, etc. Many will not.

It is the long-term methadone failure for whom a combination of
methadone and the TC is so essential. Su Casa, the residential TC
of the Lower Eastside Service Center (LESC) in New York City, is a
program which combines a modified Phoenix House model TC with
gradual methadone withdrawal over 2-6 months. Following withdrawal
from methadone, the resident is asked to continue his/her pursuit
of interpersonal change for about one year.

Initially, we received several patients who were not treatment
failures, but who were highly motivated to get off of methadone and
to change their lives. However, even in our first year of operation most of our patients (86%) were multiple drug and alcohol
abusers. More recently we are seeing an even higher percentage of
multiple drug abusers who tend to be "methadone failures." These
clients are more anxious, depressed and psychotic than our previous
admissions or than most residents of drug-free TCs in New York
City.

Within the past year we have seen substantial shifts in the ethnicity of our clients from Black and Puerto Rican to White. Since the
majority of our patients are now white and/or multidrug abusers,
they could not tolerate any treatment program which would require
rapid withdrawal of methadone. Many of our referrals are methadone
habituated patients who have recently undergone a 21-day detoxification from methadone, who could not tolerate withdrawal symptoms

and/or find themselves using heroin or methadone immediately after discharge.

Many patients who seem well integrated develop symptoms of serious mental illness as their methadone dose is lowered. In addition, our patients have been receiving methadone treatment for an average of 34 months prior to their coming to Su Casa. Since they are so disturbed and have been on methadone so long they would not tolerate a rapid detoxification from methadone. Thus, we currently take an average of 17 weeks to detoxify residents from methadone. From March, 1974 to March, 1976, 260 clients were admitted to the residence. Of these, 242 were started on methadone and 18 were admitted as methadone free. During this time, 205 residents have "split" (78.5%), 14 "splittees" have returned, and of these 14, 7 (2.7%) are still in the program. Thus, our net split rate is 75.8%. Of the 210 residents admitted on methadone, 65 were fully detoxified (31%), and of these, 4 have graduated and 25 have remained in the program.

A crucial factor leading to our high split rate is the program's demand for intrapsychic and behavioral change from a group of methadone patients who are not accustomed to such demands. Most methadone programs, particularly those under the New York City Health Department, have a definitive policy that no patient can be coerced into any form of rehabilitation or psychotherapy. Methadone in the TC tends to keep many residents from splitting who would otherwise leave after a few days or weeks. However, after detoxification, many of these potential early splittees leave the program. Of detoxified residents who split the program in the past 10 months, the average stay after detox was 3.8 months. Forty per cent of residents who split after detox did so in the first 2 months and 66% in the first 4 months. Many patients enter the program with the idea they will leave after they have slowly detoxified from their methadone. Although these patients are considered splittees, we have accomplished an important task with them, particularly with those who leave to return to jobs and non-destructive social relationships.

This program is in a unique position for a TC in that immediate follow-up contact must occur with those splittees who are still on methadone. Such patients must remain in contact with the program to receive their methadone until other arrangements can be made. These splittees are mainly referred to LESC methadone programs. This mitigates the effect of the stress of the "street" which causes patients to rejoin TCs. On the other hand, it keeps them in other treatments which in some cases may be more appropriate for them than a TC. All patients who stay more than a few weeks will have their methadone dosage lowered to some extent (generally 10 mg. a week after the first 1-2 weeks). Many of these splittees return to methadone treatment programs and stay on lower doses which permit greater functioning or a more gradual detoxification.

Program Description

All patients are evaluated individually to establish a treatment plan. This plan draws from directive individual, group and family therapeutic techniques, psychotropic drugs and Phoenix House or TC-type techniques.

The TC is run as a modification of a traditional Phoenix House TC. The house structure is typical with coordinators, expediters, department heads, etc. More individual therapy is required than at most TCs. Morning meetings, encounters and seminars are held daily. Shaved heads and signs are used rarely and only as a last resort when they are the only alternative to dismissing the resident. We have learned that the less intensive therapy we do, the more we must utilize punitive measures. Psychotropic drugs are used sparingly but occasionally to supplement or substitute for methadone and to treat depression, insomnia and psychotic symptomatology. Many patients have experienced severe documented insomnia for several weeks or months after detoxification.

In our middle class patients, drug abuse tends to be quite related to familial patterns. Thus, early family evaluation and therapy is essential with these patients. A core aspect of the program is a multiple family group which meets weekly with an average of eight families for a three-hour session. The techniques of our family approach are described elsewhere in these proceedings.[1]

TC techniques are determined by the Supervisor who is a graduate and former long-term employee of Phoenix House. Other therapies, such as "Primal," Gestalt, and psychodrama, have proved to be most helpful in achieving personal change. A first level "primal" is used mainly for rage reduction.

We do not feel that we reach a level of primary primal pain as described by Janov. However, we use peer pressure and the urging of the therapist to reach the deepest levels of emotional expression possible at each point in therapy. The resident is therefore urged to experience emotion by screaming progressively louder and by tapping feelings which are physically locked deeply in the abdomen and chest. These techniques are not used artifically but only when the resident is beginning to express genuine emotional pain.

The major force in getting patients to give up methadone has been peer pressure. The patients themselves push and support each other to give up methadone, often long before the staff would exert this kind of pressure. At times this pressure backfires and patients who are suffering crippling anxiety or depression are unwilling to go back on the methadone which would facilitate their treatment.

To help obviate the problems of detoxification patients were originally offered the choice of a "blind detox," in which they do not know their dosage after 40 mg. We found that this minimized anxiety during the process so that we have made "blind detox" mandatory.

Both counselors and advanced peers who have already detoxified from methadone are important role models for the residents to become drug free. The giving of the "nurturing" drug, methadone, enhances a dependent transference rather than inhibits it. This transference must be understood with intense reconstructive therapeutic exper- ience such as "primals," marathons, and intensive individual therapy before the individual gives up methadone. We dispense methadone towards the end of the day (5:00 p.m.) in order to diminish its sedative effects in the therapeutic situation. Some individuals require methadone at varying dose levels in order to deal with painful material as it emerges in therapy. Such patients need methadone to diminish anxiety and preserve homeostasis as insights are revealed to them. Other patients cannot even begin meaningful therapy until their dose of methadone is lowered below 40 mg.

The principles of crisis theory are most relevant with detoxing methadone patients. These patients are under a stress where the dynamics for change are mobilized and they are most accessible to intervention.

Previous studies on the efficacy of helping methadone patients detoxify and stay off of drugs and alcohol have emphasized how difficult a process this is. A literature review reveals that the overall ability to detoxify the general population of methadone patients is very poor (10% or less), particularly when there is an absence of intensive therapy as exists in most programs.[2,3,4,5]

There is little published on the combination of methadone and the TC. Most programs who have used this combination have not had abstinence from methadone as a goal as we have had at Su Casa.

What has been described here is a combination of methadone and the TC in a difficult patient group. We feel that for these patients the combination of methadone and the TC has been a necessity although occasionally an incompatability. Many methadone mainten- ance treatment patients will do well on methadone for 5, 8, 10 years, or the rest of their lives. Many will find that methadone treatment has helped cripple them more than their previous heroin addiction. It is this latter group of patients whom we are mainly dealing with at Su Casa. Many motivated patients can detoxify in a standard methadone program. Many more cannot. Many patients can detoxify successfully when modalities such as family treatment, day programs or intensive individual therapy are added to their therapeutic regimen. However, we have established that there is a small but important group of patients who require a combination of methadone and the TC if they are to turn the failures of their

lives into successes. Obviously, we are not stating that methadone
to abstinence programs are the answer for all narcotic addicts or
even all methadone patients. Many patients cannot or will not be
motivated to accept this type of demanding experience. We are
stating that a combination of methadone and the therapeutic
community is a necessary part of providing total services to
narcotic addicts, particularly those who have become problematic on
methadone.

TABLE I. ETHNIC BREKADOWN BY AGE - April, 1975

Residential Program, MTAR (41 Males, 4 Females)

Age Group	Black	White	Puerto Rican	Other	Totals
20 & Under	-	-	2	-	2
21 - 25	2	9	2	2	15
26 - 30	3	6	4	1	14
31 - 40	3	3	5	-	11
41 & Over	2	-	-	1	3
Totals	10	18	13	4	45
Ethnic Groups	22%	40%	29%	9%	

ETHNIC BREAKDOWN BY AGE - January, 1976

Residential Program, MTAR (40 Males, 5 Females)

Age Group	Black	White	Puerto Rican	Other	Totals
20 & Under	-	3	-	-	3
21 - 25	2	10	3	-	15
26 - 30	3	11	2	-	16
31 - 40	1	6	3	-	10
41 & Over	1	-	-	-	1
Totals	7	30	8	-	45
Ethnic Groups	15%	67%	18%		

348

References

1. Kaufman, E., Kaufmann, P., The Family Treatment of Drug Abusers.

2. Lowinson, J., Langrod, J., Berle, B., "Detoxification of Long Term Methadone Patients," Proceedings of the Fifth National Conference on Methadone Treatment, Schenkman, Cabbridge, Massachusetts (1973), pp. 256-261.

3. Cushman, P., "Detoxification of Rehabilitated Methadone Patients: Frequency and Predictors of Long-Term Success," American Journal of Drug and Alcohol Abuse (1974), Vol. 1, No. 3: 393-408.

4. Stimmel, B., and Rabin, J., "The Ability to Remain Abstinent Upon Leaving Methadone Maintenance: A Prospective Study," American Journal of Drug and Alcohol Abuse (1974), Vol. 1, No. 3: 379-391.

5. Brown, E.M., Benante, J., Greenberg, M., MacArthur, M., "Study of Methadone Terminations," British Journal of the Addictions, (1975), Vol. 70, No. 1: 83-88.

EFFECTS ON TREATMENT COMPLETION OF A MEDICAL *VS.* A
PSYCHOTHERAPEUTIC MODEL FOR METHADONE MAINTENANCE

Peter Janke

Oregon Methadone Treatment Program
Portland, Oregon

In 1971 the F.D.A. ruled that methadone programs were to begin
adding counseling and related support services to their existing
medical treatment of opiate addicts. This paper studies the implementation of this ruling in one program and its ramifications on
treatment effectiveness. In doing this, the paper tries to cast
some light on differences between a purely medical model and a med-
ical/psychotherapeutic model in the rate with which clients complete or interrupt treatment.

I.   METHOD

The Oregon Methadone Treatment Program has treated opiate addicts with both purely medical and medical/psychotherapeutic models
at different periods in its history. The rapidity and thoroughness
of the change permit a division of the Program's history into two
distinct evaluation periods. Within each period the reasons for
every termination are categorized, and frequency and rate of return
to treatment after each type of termination are computed. The two
periods are then compared as to the frequency with which maintenance
clients complete treatment by voluntary withdrawal from methadone,
taking into account the number, sex, race, age, and length of treatment of clients in treatment during each period.

II.   EVALUATION PERIODS AND SAMPLES

PERIOD A extends from the Program's inception in April, 1969,
through December, 1972, when the shift in emphasis began. During
the first 26 months of operations, Program caseload rose rapidly
and steadily to nearly 350 clients in June, 1971. By this time,
Program staff consisted of the medical director, a clerical assistant, and a part-time physician, with another clerical worker added
a few months later. Client services were limited to medication with
methadone and monitoring of dose level and its effects. Seven
E.E.A. administrative and clerical positions were filled from Dec-

ember, 1971, to April, 1972, when the first social worker was hired. After expansion of the medical and clerical staff, the caseload again began to rise. By the end of Period A the Program was medicating nearly 400 clients. Only at the very end of this period, however, was any counseling or supportive service available to Program clients, and even this was restricted to two evening groups with small and diminishing attendance. The Program followed an essentially medical model of addiction treatment throughout Period A.

PERIOD B extends from January, 1973, to the present, though for purposes of this study and comparison with Period A it ends at the close of 1975. The transformation began with implementation of a $300,000 O.E.O. grant during 1973. Within the first months of the year the Program had four full-time counselors, the number rapidly growing to 12 by the fall of 1973. Each new admission was assigned a counselor on a one-to-one basis. The counselors, professionals and trained paraprofessionals, worked in four treatment teams of three members each, supervised by a treatment coordinator and supported by a job developer and a vocational rehabilitation counselor. In-house training of staff was implemented on an on-going basis. The amount and style of formal counseling varied widely according to client need and circumstances but averaged between one and two hours per week. According to annual evaluations of all active clients, the great majority of persons in treatment during Period B report receiving as much counseling as they desire; 76% evaluate the quality of their counseling as excellent to quite good, and 72% feel it has helped them.

Objectively and subjectively, Period B represents a very different program from Period A. Treatment philosophy had shifted to a strongly psychotherapeutic model, and the staff, once exclusively medical/clerical, was suddenly transformed into one in which counselors outnumbered medical personnel by a ratio of three to one.

Period A consists of 45 months during which 887 clients were in treatment. Period B consists of 36 months during which 878 clients were treated (including 481 clients also receiving some treatment during Period A). The difference between sex ratios for the two periods is statistically insignificant (70.5% males in Period A, 72.8% in Period B), as is the difference in mean age (29.1 years for clients in Period A, 28.4 years in Period B). No difference in mean length of narcotics use before admission was found between samples. Ethnic minority groups, however, particularly blacks, are much more strongly represented during Period A than during Period B (28.7% non-whites in Period A, compared with 21.8% in Period B, with X^2 significant at the .999 confidence level).

III. HYPOTHESIS AND DEFINITIONS

This study tries to test an assumption of considerable importance for methadone treatment: that the introduction of a non-medical treatment component contributes significantly to increased treatment effectiveness. Since information on client status during treatment is largely missing for Period A, this study focuses on the proportion of clients who terminate because they have completed treatment

(by voluntary detoxification from methadone per physician's schedule), *vs.* those who terminate by interrupting treatment (through incarceration, death, medical or punitive terminations, or simply dropping out). Viewed in light of this index of effectiveness, the assumption becomes a testable hypothesis: Period B (psychotherapeutic)
will produce significantly more completed treatment terminations than
will Period A (purely medical) and significantly fewer drop-outs, incarcerations, deaths, and other interrupted treatment terminations.

IV. RESULTS AND DISCUSSION

The proportions of terminations differ significantly between the
two evaluation periods in nearly all categories (including transfers). Comparative percentages are shown in Fig. 1. Period B produces significantly more treatment completions than does Period A,
and significantly fewer drop-outs, incarcerations, and terminations
for medical and punitive reasons. All differences have been tested
by X^2 analysis of the number of persons terminating and not terminating in each category. Only for deaths is the hypothesis not supported. Here the difference, though in the predicted direction,
falls short of statistical significance.

A more detailed look at the pattern of treatment completion
within both periods is obtained by plotting the percentage of all
maintenance terminations each month which are treatment completions,
as has been done in Fig. 2. In Period A, 25.3% of all terminations
from maintenance treatment are voluntary detoxifications from methadone per physician's schedule. In Period B, 47.7% of the terminations fall in this category. The number of terminations involved
are summarized in Table I. Because of readmissions to treatment,
the 239 and 348 terminations with completed treatment in Period A
and Period B, respectively, represent 201 and 307 separate persons.
Whether we consider terminations or persons terminating, however,
the data document a remarkably significant difference between the
two periods. Clients treated under the psychotherapeutic model complete treatment by successful detoxification from methadone with
nearly twice the frequency of clients treated under the purely medical model.

These differences hold for males as well as females, whites as
well as non-whites, as documented in Table II. Females and whites
are more likely to complete treatment in both periods than are males
and non-whites, but the proportion of clients in all four categories
who complete treatment is significantly higher for Period B than for
Period A.

These data establish conclusively that clients in treatment under the medical/psychotherapeutic model complete treatment and leave
the Program withdrawn from methadone at a significantly greater rate
than do clients treated under the purely medical model. But how
successful are these withdrawals? Lacking good follow-up evaluations of Program graduates from either period, we can report here
only the negative index of returns to maintenance. Tabulations have
been made of the numbers of clients in each evaluation period who
return to treatment any time up to two months after the close of

that period, thus allowing comparison of return rates for the two periods. No significant difference was found in the rates with which persons who complete treatment return to the Program readdicted to narcotics. Within both periods, about 30% of treatment completions return to maintenance while 70% do not.

Clients completing treatment in each evaluation period take nearly the same amount of time to do so. Under both models, median length of treatment before completion is 11 months. Nor is there any appreciable difference in retention rates between the two periods, for long-term clients (26% of clients treated under each model remained on the Program without interruption through the end of their evaluation periods). The only significant difference in termination statistics between the two periods, therefore, appears to be the widely different proportions of clients completing and interrupting treatment.

An important problem remains unsolved by this evaluation design, however. Studying one program over time and across changes in philosophy and staffing permits comparison of treatment results with similar addict populations, but it cannot answer speculation as to what the original medical model might have looked like after three additional years. Would the completion rate for the first three years have nearly doubled during the next three (as Fig. 2 shows it did) even without the change in treatment models? Is a roughly even completion/interruption ratio equally possible under either model? These questions cannot be answered conclusively here. Simply continuing a line of best fit for the first section of Fig. 2 would not be an accurate projection, since part of the initial absence of completed treatments in a beginning program must be attributed to the period of stabilization and treatment necessary before successful withdrawal from methadone is possible. Taking this into account, the completion rate for Period A appears more stable about the mean of 25%. It seems unlikely that it would leap spontaneously to nearly 50% for an additional three year period of medical treatment only, but this cannot be proved.

Nevertheless, confirmation by these data of the hypothesis under test provides strong circumstantial evidence supporting the assumption that a psychotherapeutic model is more effective than a purely medical one in helping addicts complete rather than interrupt methadone treatment. The study also supplies *prima facie* evidence that an apparently growing proportion of methadone clients *can* complete and leave treatment with a greatly improved prognosis, at least, for a life of greater independence and personal freedom.

To investigate the relationship between psychotherapeutic services and successful treatment completion more fully, comparable studies from programs which have undergone similar transformations should be undertaken. These should be coupled with careful study of the detoxification process itself (including its relationship to maintenance dose levels) and with rigorous long-term follow-up studies of the increasing population of persons who have completed methadone treatment by voluntary withdrawal and not returned to maintenance programs.

Table I

Completed *Vs*. Interrupted Treatment During Two Evaluation Periods

Category of Termination	Period A 1969-1972 Medical		Period B 1973-1975 Psychotherapeutic		Total	
	N	%	N	%	N	%
Terminations with completed treatment	239	(25.3%)	348	(47.7%)	587	(35.0%)
Terminations with interrupted treatment	707	(74.7%)	381	(52.3%)	1088	(65.0%)
Total terminations	946	(56.5%)	729	(43.5%)	1675	100.0%

$$(X^2 = 91.2931; \ df = 1; \ p = .0001)$$

Table II

Treatment Completions, by Sex and Race

Category of Client	Period A 1969-1972 Medical Only	Period B 1973-1975 Psychotherapeutic	Statistical Significance of X^2 Value
Males	136/625 = 21.8%	207/639 = 32.4%	p = .0005
Females	65/262 = 24.8%	100/239 = 41.8%	p = .0005
Whites	156/632 = 24.7%	255/687 = 37.1%	p = .0005
Non-whites	45/255 = 17.6%	52/191 = 27.2%	p = .025
Total	201/887 = 22.7%	307/878 = 35.0%	p = .0005

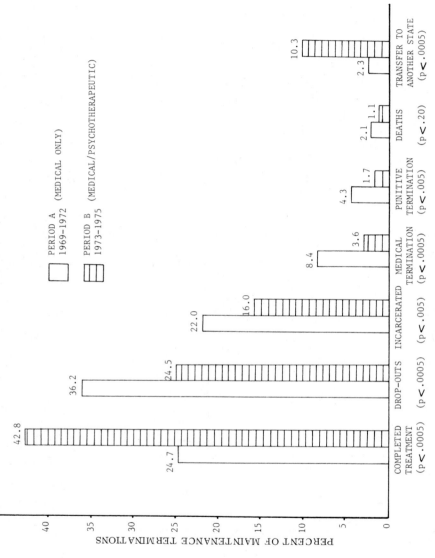

FIG. 1 This graph shows the proportion of terminations in each category for both evaluation periods. All terminations from maintenance treatment are included.

355

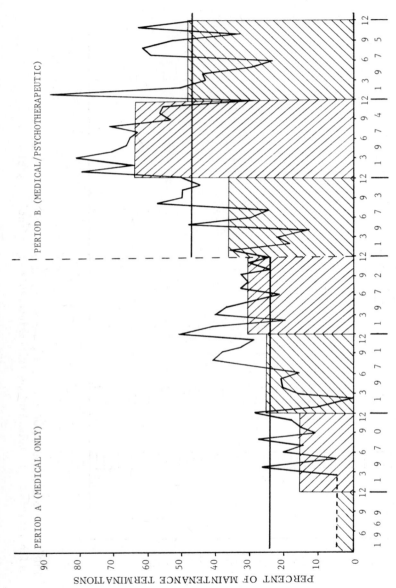

FIG. 2 The line graph shows changes in monthly completion percentages over the Program's history. The superimposed bar graph gives annual rates of completed treatment. The horizontal lines indicate comparable percentages of completed treatment for each evaluation period. Transfers out to other methadone programs are excluded since they represent neither interruption nor completion of treatment.

356

COUNSELING ISSUES IN
METHADONE MAINTENANCE PROGRAMS

Louise Meister, A.C.S.W.

Drug Dependency Program
Sinai Hospital
Belvedere at Greenspring
Baltimore, Maryland 21215

There has been a proliferation of programs that offer methadone maintenance and detoxification to the drug addict in the past
five or six years. However, there remains a scarcity of information to assist professional counselors in developing effective
techniques for working with a client who is addicted to narcotics.
This paper will attempt to explore three facets of the counseling
process with the drug addict: 1. the personality dynamics which
most frequently occur in the addicted client; 2. the initial reaction of the drug addict to the counseling component of a methadone program; and 3. a philosophy of counseling which can lead
to effective intervention in the rehabilitation process.

The drug addict has developed a long-standing pattern of
dealing with anxiety by running away from it rather than facing up
to the problems that it creates. This pattern was, in many cases,
established long before he abused drugs. Having developed this
type of coping mechanism during childhood, the potential addict is
quick to discover, when he is exposed to illicit drugs by his
peers, that drugs offer an instantaneous and pleasurable means of
escape. The user is relieved of the anxiety produced by whatever
problems he is facing and with which he doesn't feel able to cope.
The problem doesn't seem like a problem any more as long as he is
"high". Often the drug addict, after he has been admitted to
treatment, still attempts to run away from his problems with a
number of escape mechanisms. These include continued illicit narcotic use (even though methadone blocks the high), substituting
other drugs of abuse which "boost" the methadone and make him high,
nodding out (even though his methadone dosage is stabilized),
sleeping a great deal of the time or rationalizing (making excuses
for) his behavior.

The drug addict is searching for love, security, self-esteem,
autonomy, recognition and acceptance. He frequently feels

incapable of achieving these goals through his own efforts and has learned through repeated, painful experience that he can seldom trust others to consistently assist him. He stops trying to develop internal coping mechanisms and begins to rely more heavily on "easier" (drug-induced) solutions.

The addict is plagued with family, enviornmental and legal problems. The magnitude of these problems often stems from being overindulged, excessively controlled or neglected. Thus his social development has been impaired by the lack of a healthy concern and respect shown for him in his early interpersonal relationships. He frequently has a limited ability to master inner conflict or enviornmental frustration since early socialization experiences did not provide him with a stable personality organization. Then when he latches onto drugs as an "easy" solution to overwhelming problems, his socialization and consequent maturation is further impaired.

The drug addict is impulsive and pleasure-oriented due to a lack of skills for facing up to and mastering conflict. His ability to deal with stress or frustration is impaired, he becomes discouraged easily and experiences great difficulty postponing gratification. Drugs, which bring instant relief, have reinforced this striving for immediate gratification until the addict is unwilling to voluntarily postpone any pleasurable impulse. The mass media with its insistent message that there is a drug, cigarette or alcoholic beverage to provide quick satisfaction for every need, reinforces this idea that no one should have to experience discomfort or pain.

The drug addict experiences alternating tendencies toward despair and anger as a result of the inability to find long-range solutions for any problem. There is also a tendency to rely heavily on temporary solutions through drug use, which creates still more problems. On the one hand, the drug addict feels guilty about not adequately handling his responsibilities, which cause him and the important people in his life additional pain and suffering.

On the other hand, the drug addict also experiences considerable anger and rebellion against his family, friends and society. This reaction stems from the realization that they have not provided him with the skills to establish a life for himself which brings some measure of serenity and satisfaction within the context of socially acceptable behavior. This anger is exhibited both chronically and in episodic rages, and he can often find no better way to express it than through the anti-social behavior and delinquency which is an inevitable by-product of addiction.

The drug addict tends to have overwhelming unmet dependency needs as a result of inappropriate parenting. These are rarely

expressed directly but can frequently be recognized in his behavior. Much of his antisocial behavior can be seen as a bid for
attention and controls at the same time that he is exhibiting
rebellion and anger.

There is also a marked tendency for the drug addict to be
emotionally isolated at the same time that his dependency needs
are much in evidence. He may have many acquaintances as a result
of his drug-related activities and he may be married, living with
his family or with a friend. But he experiences an intense fear
of emotional intimacy based on early interpersonal relationships
that were painful, rejecting or overwhelming. These early relationships have led to a basic mistrust of others. Once again
drugs are used as an attempted solution to this problem in order
to reduce anxiety and help the user to feel more relaxed in social
situations. They also provide a substitute internal stimulation
and pleasurable experience that is in some ways comparable to the
internal satisfactions that can otherwise be realized through
intimate interpersonal experiences.

The drug addict generally presents himself to a clinic highly
motivated to receive methadone but with some degree of resistance
to a counseling relationship. He may express a willingness to
engage in counseling if he feels that it will assist his chances
for admission to the program. However, the assigned counselor
soon discovers that he is, to some extent, reluctant to become
involved in this facet of the program.

There is a tendency not only in the addict himself but also in
society in general to define drug addiction as the problem rather
than as an overt symptom of underlying emotional and/or social
problems. If the addict does recognize that he has emotional
problems, he may be overwhelmed by the implications of having such
problems. Or he may be disconcerted by a recognition of the difficulties that he will encounter in attempting to resolve these
problems. Thus he may be very reluctant to define and confront
them. Even if he has tentatively taken this step, he still may be
very fearful of sharing this information with his counselor whom
he sees as a representative of the "straight" (drug-free) world
that has so frequently rejected and punished him rather than
offering acceptance and effective assistance.

There may be some merit to the argument that a client has the
right to self-determination where counseling assistance is concerned. However, there seems to be even greater validity to a
recognition that the client has come to the clinic for assistance
in overcoming his drug problem. Since the staff, with its considerable experience and training, recognizes that confronting and
resolving some of the related psychosocial problems is essential
to permanent rehabilitation, they have an obligation to involve
him in this service as well. Because the initial impetus for

counseling more often comes from the staff than from the client, the burden is on the counselor to make the counseling relationship meaningful and to help motivate the client to become genuinely involved.

There is a further issue to resolve in establishing an effective counseling relationship. This is related to the addict's reluctance to trust the counselor because of the authority position the counselor has within the clinic structure. The counselor often shares this sense of uncertainty about being a warm and empathic person while at the same time engaging in limit-setting and disciplinary behavior as a significant aspect of the therapeutic process.

It is not easy to motivate a client who is suspicious of people from the "straight" world to become involved in an open relationship with a counselor who is in a position of some authority. A trusting relationship between client and counselor in this setting rarely develops quickly. It takes time and a great deal of persistence on the part of the counselor to win the client's confidence and to encourage him to begin to define and resolve some of the psychosocial problems in his life.

The issue for the counselor in recognizing the importance of limit-setting in the rehabilitation of the client is in understanding that in some significant ways he acts in a substitute parent role for the client. Similar to parenting, an important part of helping the person establish a healthy value system and effective behavior patterns is setting limits through external control. By so doing, it is hoped that the client will eventually internalize these controls by making them a part of his own value system. In order to effectively exercise discipline with a client without at the same time damaging the counseling relationship, it is helpful if the client has already begun to develop some confidence and trust in the counselor. This facilitates the client's recognition and understanding that the counselor's disciplinary behavior is motivated by a concern for his well-being and is an important part of the therapeutic process. If such a rapport has not already been established with the client, the counselor runs the risk that his behavior will be interpreted by the client as punitive and rejecting in its intent. Therefore, when the counselor takes on a disciplinary role, it is important that he takes the time to explain patiently and in some detail why he feels that he must take this stand.

Building a warm, genuine and empathic relationship is the basis of effective counseling. Whereas it may provide the means toward some other goal in another counseling situation, it becomes an important goal in itself in working with the drug addict. It is important to offer the client an emotionally close, trusting, helping relationship that gives him a sense of self-esteem. Such

a relationship also gives him an opportunity to be temporarily
dependent, increasingly open and secure while he is developing
internal adaptive skills. Through this experience of closeness
and openness the client learns to share himself and express his
needs and desires at the same time that he learns to be sensitive
and responsive to the reactions of the counselor. In this manner
he learns through actual experience how to form similar relationships outside the counseling situation which have the potential
for greater intimacy and longer duration.

Such a relationship is very difficult to form with a drug
addict as a result of some of the personality characteristics
already discussed. When it does genuinely occur, it is only after
many months of working together. It is also a relationship that
places a very heavy responsibility on the counselor since it demands infinite patience, consistency and an unfailing commitment.
It also demands a greater degree of active participation than
might otherwise be required of the counselor. It is only by
continual feedback, sharing of feelings and support that the
client learns how to effectively interact so that a genuine
emotional closeness is possible.

A not infrequent by-product of such a relationship is the
client's "falling in love" with the counselor and/or misinter-
preting the counselor's feeling toward him. Perhaps because the
drug addict has had more experience with sexual activity than with
emotional intimacy, he tends to confuse the two. And, as the
counseling relationship fosters an emotional closeness, there is
a tendency for the client to interpret it sexually. The counselor
at this point must possess a great deal of self-awareness and
understanding lest he or she reject the client because of his
misinterpretations and/or sexually seductive behavior. The counselor, long before he allows such emotional closeness to occur,
needs to be able to clearly differentiate not only for himself
but for his client as well, the difference between loving someone
and being "in love" (desiring a sexual relationship) with him.

If the counselor can effectively and appropriately develop
this type of relationship, he will find that the client will accept and respond positively to a greater degree of confrontation
and insight than he would have otherwise allowed. Even with the
most intensive efforts by the counselor, not all counseling relationships will reach this level of emotional involvement.

Within this general philosophical framework, there are many
other important services that the counselor should offer. As
discussed earlier, limit-setting and disciplinary measures are
important within the context of genuine respect and concern for
the client and his well-being. Since the drug addict often has
considerable difficulty relating positively to authority figures,
the counseling relationship offers an excellent opportunity to

deal with this issue. Although the client may initially rebel against any limits or punishment which the counselor feels he must recommend, he can be helped to understand and respect the wisdom of such measures. The client may impulsively want all his desires satisfied and to avoid any discomfort. However, he can be assisted to recognize and accept the fact that many of the mistakes he has made in his life have been the result of improper limit-setting by others at a time when he didn't have the wisdom or self-control to set proper limits for himself. At the same time, it is equally important that the counselor recommend appropriate rewards when the client has demonstrated an ability to exert proper self-control for a stipulated period of time.

Reality testing is another important function of the counseling relationship. The client frequently has distorted impressions of himself, of important others in his life and of the world in general. The counselor needs to continually feed back to the client information that will provide him with a more realistic impression of himself and others. Frequently this takes the form of encouraging him to attempt tasks that he had been fearful of previously. The counselor must be careful to only encourage him to undertake potentially successful activities and behaviors since another failure would be a major setback and might produce a feeling of betrayal. The counselor must be prepared to give continual encouragement along the way in order to ensure success as well as to offer whatever practical supports seem helpful.

Since the drug addict suffers from low self-esteem, it is important to help him find activities and interests that will increase his respect for himself through the mastery of the skills involved. At the same time, such activities will increase his pleasurable experience in life. Along with this, the counselor needs to help the client establish clear-cut goals and values for his life and then help him develop a plan for their achievement. This is especially important with the drug addict whose life style has been antisocial and delinquent. He must now view society and his place in it from an entirely different perspective and develop new values and goals that are consistent with this altered viewpoint.

The counselor must also facilitate the growth of the client's adaptive skills. Since he is asking the client to give up drugs as his principle means of coping with problems and the resultant anxiety, he must assist him in developing alternative coping mechanisms. Encouraging and sharing insight into the client's personality dynamics is an important part of this process. If the client can begin to understand why he thinks, feels and behaves the way he does, then he can also begin to see that these thoughts, feelings and actions are within his control and can be changed. Once the client begins to perceive that self-mastery is possible, the counselor can begin to work with him on developing the appropriate adaptive skills for promoting change and more effective functioning.

In this process, the counselor becomes an important role model for the client both in terms of attitudes and behavior. We all learn best by example and the counselor, as an important agent in the change process, becomes one of the client's foremost models. This was already discussed in the context of building the relationship, but it is important to reiterate here how extensively the client watches the counselor for inconsistencies between what he says and what he does and for examples of how situations can be dealt with effectively.

Finally and most importantly, the counselor must continue to care and show respect for the client and be able to continually express it. It should never be taken for granted that the client knows how much the counselor cares for, respects and is committed to his growth and well-being. The counselor must share this information openly, genuinely and continually as an important reinforcement to a client who is struggling against very heavy odds and formidable obstacles to reshape his life so that he may finally become drug-free.

RELATIONSHIP BETWEEN METHADONE DOSE
AND ILLICIT HEROIN USE

Murry J. Cohen, M.D., Ray Hanbury, M.A..
Barry Stimmel, M.D.

Departments of Psychiatry and Medicine
Mount Sinai School of Medicine of
The City University of New York
New York, New York

Although methadone maintenance treatment for opiate dependency has been recognized as an accepted modality in rehabilitation of the heroin addict, controversy still exists as to the optimal methadone dose that should be utilized in persons on chronic maintenance therapy. Initial clinical studies conducted by Dole et al (1) to determine the effects of an acute dose of heroin or other narcotic superimposed on oral maintenance revealed that when maintained on 80 mg. per day of methadone, a heroin addict was unable to distinguish the amount of heroin present in a $5 or $10 street bag from that of a placebo. In addition, the intravenous injection of 80 to 200 mg. of pure heroin was detected either as a faint sensation of a narcotic effect unaccompanied by euphoria or was not detected at all. For this reason 80 to 100 mg. of methadone per day was considered to be the optimal maintenance dose. Subsequently, evidence was presented by other investigators (2,3) that doses of methadone as low as 30 mg. could be associated with successful methadone maintenance with respect to program retention and cessation of heroin use. This dosage was also unaccompanied by any increase in withdrawal symptoms. This work had a great influence on programs, many of which subsequently lowered their methadone maintenance levels.

In order to once again review the relationship between methadone maintenance dose and illicit heroin use, the following study was performed.

This study relates to a program funded by the New York State
 Office of Drug Abuse Services

I. METHOD

The study took place at the Methadone Maintenance and Aftercare Treatment Program at The Mount Sinai Medical Center. Analysis of heroin use, as detected by thin layer chromatography of the urine, performed on a weekly basis, was reviewed over a three-month period and correlated with daily dose of methadone in patients maintained on 1) less than 50 mg.; 2) 50 mg.; 3) 80 mg., or 4) 100 mg. The clinical course of those persons found to be using heroin was followed for a six-month period. A comparison of these persons' subsequent heroin use with respect to alterations in methadone dose was performed. At the end of six months the survey was repeated to determine the overall use of heroin in the clinic for a comparable three-month period.

II. RESULTS

During the initial period (Group 1), 77 (15%) of the 506 patients studied were found to have at least one urine positive for morphine. The dosage distribution of all persons enrolled in the MMATP during this time period is illustrated in Table I. The majority of persons were maintained on 50 mg. daily dose of methadone, with 18% being maintained on 80 mg., 12% on less than 50 mg., and 6% on 100 mg. The frequency of weekly urines positive for morphine in the 77 patients during this three-month period is shown in Table II. It can be seen that most persons had only one urine containing morphine over the three-month period. Two or more positive urines were noted in 44%, with 12 (16%) persons having four or more positive urines.

The relationship between methadone dose and the presence of morphine in the urine is illustrated in Table III. Although the distribution of persons using morphine once in a three-month period did not differ from the dosage distribution of the entire clinic, in those individuals having two or more urines positive for morphine, a difference was noted. No one maintained on 100 mg. was found to use morphine more than once over this time period (p=0.001). In addition, if extensive heroin use is defined as the presence of heroin in the urine, on four or more occasions none of the persons maintained on 80 mg. or 100 mg. of methadone per day exhibited this frequency of illicit heroin.

Six months later an analysis of heroin use, as determined by the presence of morphine in the urine, was performed over a comparable three-month period. The results of this analysis are described in Table IV. A total of 71 (14%) of 502 persons enrolled in the MMATP had morphine in their urine. The dosage distribution of all those having positive urines on one or more occasions was comparable to the dosage distribution for the entire clinic population. However, once again no individual maintained on 100 mg. of methadone per day used heroin on more than one occasion for the three-month period.

Of the 77 persons using heroin during the initial three-month period, 27 (35%) agreed to have their methadone dose increased. This represented 81% of all persons using heroin on two or more occasions. Six of the 27 (22%) had their dose increased to greater than 80 mg., with 21 persons increasing their dose between 60-80 mg.

Use of heroin occurred in only one of the six (17%) persons maintained on greater than 90 mg. methadone a day, 5 of the 21 (23%) maintained between 60-80 mg. a day, and 16 of 50 (32%) persons maintained on 50 mg. per day or less. The overall prognosis of these 77 persons with respect to program retention was found to be quite poor, with 25 (32%) no longer on the program and four (6%) currently being detoxified from methadone. The reason for detoxification in 20 (80%) was either violation of program rules or consistent drug abuse.

III. DISCUSSION

There are several distinct advantages to maintaining persons on the lowest effective dose of methadone. Side reactions due to intermittent injection of the drug will be minimized as will interaction with agents -- most prominent seen in the alcohol/barbiturate group of drugs. In addition, should the medication be ingested by one not on methadone maintenance, the chance of a fatal pharmacologic reaction is lessened if a low methadone dose is employed.

Previous work by Goldstein and Garbutt (3) has indicated that a well-motivated person can stop using heroin and successfully enter rehabilitation just as effectively on a maintenance dose of 50 mg. as well as 100 mg. Evidence has even been presented that persons may be able to be successfully maintained on 30 mg. of methadone a day although subjective symptoms have been noted to increase in such patients.

These findings are not surprising and are consistent with the pharmacology of tolerance and dependency. Providing an individual's dependence upon heroin or any other narcotic is not great, low dose methadone maintenance will be able to maintain him at an appropriate tolerance level without any difficulties in functioning. The ability of an injection of street heroin to overcome this tolerance level, however, is related not only to the degree of individual tolerance but to the amount of heroin injected. Thus, if the potency of street heroin is considerable or the amount injected unusually high, it is not at all unlikely that euphoria will be experienced by persons maintained on a daily dose of 30–70 mg. of methadone. For this reason conclusions concerning the optimal dose of methadone to be used in maintenance must take into account the availability and potency of heroin on a regional basis as well as requirements based on individual tolerance.

The findings in the present study, although involving relatively small numbers of persons, are suggestive that at the present in New York City doses of greater than 80 mg. might be more effective in preventing illicit heroin use by those individuals who exhibit a tendency to inject this drug while on lower levels. This does not imply that all persons in methadone programs need have their dose increased to 100 mg., but rather that when heroin use is detected in persons maintained on lower methadone doses, one should not be hesitant to raise the maintenance level to 100 mg.

TABLE I: DOSAGE DISTRIBUTION

Dose	June–August 1975		November–January 1975–1976	
	No.	(%)	No.	(%)
Less than 50 mg.	63	(12)	60	(12)
50	324	(64)	320	(64)
80	91	(18)	91	(18)
100	28	(6)	31	(6)
TOTAL	506	(100)	502	(100)

TABLE II: FREQUENCY OF URINES POSITIVE FOR MORPHINE

Positive Urines	PATIENTS	
	No.	(%)
1	43	(56)
2	11	(14)
3	11	(14)
4 or more	12	(16)
TOTAL	77	(100)

TABLE III: RELATION BETWEEN METHADONE DOSE AND POSITIVE URINES

-- Frequency of Morphine In Urines --

Dose	1 No. (%)	2 No. (%)	3 No. (%)	4 or More No. (%)	Total No. (%)
Less than 50 mg.	5 (12)	2 (18)	0	0	7 (9)
50 mg.	32 (74)	8 (73)	8 (73)	12 (100)	60 (78)
80 mg.	4 (9)	1 (9)	3 (27)	0	8 (10)
100 mg.	2 (5)	0	0	0	2 (3)

TABLE IV: RELATION BETWEEN URINES POSITIVE FOR MORPHINE AND
METHADONE DOSE (PERIOD 2)

--- Frequency of Morphine in Urine ---

Dose	1 No. (%)	2 or More No. (%)	Total No. (%)
Less than 50 mg.	3 (6)	5 (23)	8 (11)
50 mg.	31 (63)	14 (63)	45 (64)
80 mg.	10 (21)	3 (14)	13 (18)
100 mg.	5 (10)	0	5 (7)
TOTAL	49 (100)	22 (100)	71 (100)

REFERENCES

1. V. P. Dole, M. E. Nyswander, and M. J. Kreek, Arch. Int. Med.,
    118: 304 (1966).
2. G. J. Berry, Proc. 4th Natl. Conf. Meth. Treat., Natl. Assoc.
    Prev. Addict. Narc., New York, 1972, p. 9.
3. G. D. Garbutt and A. Goldstein, Proc. 4th Natl. Conf. Meth.
    Treat., Natl. Assoc. Prev. Addict. Narc., New York, 1972,
    p. 411.

SOME THERAPEUTIC RAMIFICATIONS OF PICK-UP SCHEDULING IN METHADONE MAINTENANCE TREATMENT

Paul R. Cassarino, M.A.

Health Services Administration
Methadone Maintenance Treatment Program
New York, New York

Currently in methadone maintenance treatment, a patient's pick-up schedule is generally determined by the patient's length of time in treatment, the patient's having or not having employment, and, at times, the results of urine testing. Much of the restraint placed on giving take-home medication comes either from certain Federal Regulations or from pressure exerted by the community in which the clinic is located. The issue of the clinic's responsibility to the community is certainly important. It is ironic that people who have become addicted to street methadone often go for help to the very clinic from which their illicit methadone has been inadvertently supplied as take-home medication to a clinic patient. Yet, as important as Federal Regulations and community pressure may be, clinic personnel must now begin also investigating the therapeutic ramifications of issuing take-home medication.

In determining pick-up scheduling, little discussion or attention has been given to the therapeutic significance of either the take-home medication itself or the change in pick-up schedule. If one were to examine the psychological ramifications of take-home medication in relation to the population with whom we are working, it would become clear that (1) take-home medication is actually in many cases detrimental to the rehabilitative process, and (2) that the program's expectation that the patient will not manipulate the take-home medication in some way, indicates a lack of knowledge and insight among staff as to the psychology of the patient. To begin with then, it is important to examine certain aspects of the nature of drug addiction in general and of the drug addict specifically.

In methadone maintenance there seems to be a
lingering allegiance to the concept that in drug addiction the central problem has been the addict's taking of
the drug. Consequently the response has been that if
the drug is provided the problem has been essentially
solved. Evolving from this concept was the philosophy
that methadone was some sort of "cure"; that the
methadone, in and of itself, was the "answer". This
response followed a kind of traditional medical model
in which the disease is identified and the drug administered. Those of us who have worked in the clinics
over a period of years have seen that this model has,
except for a very few patients, failed. What has
emerged in the clinic setting is a population of
patients with problems and personality disorders that
exist independently of the drug addiction. We have
found we are confronted with a group of people with
problems and for whom the use of heroin was not the
problem but an attempt at self-help that failed.

In a review of twenty-one studies on the personality of heroin addicts conducted between 1925 and 1974
undertaken by Richard Fulmer at Teachers College, it
was found that "all the studies see the addict population as suffering from various mental disorders other
than the addiction itself."[1] Further, "the subsample
seen as 'normal' or without psychopathology was always
very small or non-existent."[2]

While many may be skeptical of results indicating
the addict population having "traditional" psychological
disorders, numerous personality studies using varying
techniques, (psychiatric interview, life history interview, MMPI Test) yielded the same result: that drug
addicted persons had psychological problems other than
addiction and that the addiction resulted as an
"adaptive function" to whatever the psychological
function was.[3]

Gerard and Kornetsky investigating the adaptive
functions of heroin addiction found that "the problems
of living as a drug addict in our society facilitate
the denial and avoidance of the patient's underlying
problems."[4]

The general implications for treatment based on
the above-mentioned studies are that the overt addiction
and the chemical treatment of that addiction (i.e. methadone) should be de-emphasized and that the psychology
and psychodynamics of each patient should be the main
concern of counselling personnel. The methadone, in

fact, should become almost peripheral to treatment. The patient must come to understand that the methadone is not a cure-all, but rather that the methadone is a way of "buying time" while the patient works through the feelings, fantasies, and negative behavior patterns from which he sought refuge in drugs. Quite clearly, a patient coming to a clinic twice a week, picking up methadone and waving at his counselor as he goes out the door has neither an idea of what the underlying problem may be nor is dealing with it at the clinic. The very same patient will eventually decide to detox with the staff's blessing and then turn-up, strung out, two months later, to re-apply. The fact that everyone on staff will be surprised to see the patient re-apply indicates that the concept of drug addiction as essentially a physiological problem which can be solved by detoxifying a patient over a long period of time still permeates the drug treatment field.

The practice of scheduling patients so that they are given take-home medication fits well into the concept of the medical model in which the drug cures the disease. As long as drug addiction is seen as essentially a physiological problem it is assumed that the patient will take his or her methadone home, drink it as prescribed and eventually "get better". Personnel who staff the clinics know however that methadone is constantly sold, bought, halved, doubled, traded, mixed and generally manipulated extensively. Patients who have good jobs and good salaries are found to be selling methadone as well as patients in difficult economic circumstances. Patients who are raised from coming to the clinic from two or three days a week to five days a week often feel high because they haven't been taking (ingesting) their take-home medication. Staff members become upset at the patient and at themselves because they feel that their judgment and trust have been betrayed.

What has actually happened is that the staff member has failed to understand a very important psychodynamic relationship; the relationship between the patient and the drug. While the drugs in general do not have any particular significance to the non-addict, except that drugs help relieve pain and cure disease; to the addict, that small bottle of methadone in his pocket has enormous symbolic significance. It often represents to the patient the only means he has for dealing with the problems of daily living. It is important therefore that we separate the psycho-social significance of the drug from its physiological effects. When this is done, the drug can be seen as having a symbolic meaning and the taking of the drug (or not taking of it) serves as a way of manipulating others and self.

The take-home methadone becomes like the heroin before it. It is powerful and life-giving; it can easily become entangled in the compulsive ritual of trading, selling, and manipulating narcotics. It is difficult for the patient to deal with the methadone just as it was difficult to deal with the bags of heroin; difficult in terms of the patient's own ego and difficult in terms of the environment.

The staff member who gives a patient take-home medication and then turns around and chastises the patient for not properly taking the medication is as much responsible for the problem as the patient. The staff member fails to understand the significance of the methadone to the patient and also is guilty of giving the patient the very thing in his life that the patient has the most trouble dealing with - narcotics. People who would think it cruel to bring the compulsive eater a dozen cupcakes or the alcoholic a bottle of scotch, do not seem to see how similarly unfair it is to consistently give the addicted person narcotics "to go".

Issuing take-home medication also has the important ramification of increasingly lessening the contact of a patient with his or her clinic. While patients and staff alike may respond to this question with a perplexed "so what?", it has been the experience of persons working in methadone that the clinic itself probably serves as the single most therapeutic agent in methadone maintenance treatment. A good clinic can offer a patient perhaps the only non-chaotic daily life situation the patient may know. The clinic can subtly provide the patient with a knowledge and feeling of what it is like to experience structure in day to day existence.

Looking at the relationship of the patient and the clinic from a psychological perspective, it can be seen that the clinic community does in fact replicate the family for the patient. Frequently, for patients who have never experienced the familial objects or who have felt in terms of their own egos to have lost family objects, the well-run clinic can provide a surrogate family. This not only gives the patient the experience to some extent of feelings associated with the positive family situation, it also affords him or her the opportunity to work out difficulties which may have arisen in the actual family.

Counselors and counselling is certainly important in the rehabilitative process in the methadone clinic, but the counselor is only one element of the total clinic family. The patient is most effected by the dynamic relationship among staff members and the feelings he or she receives from the clinic as a totality.

Persons on pick-up schedules drift away from dealing with the clinic and their relationship to the clinic diminishes. By placing the patient on a two day schedule the clinic surrenders its very important responsibility of providing structure and patterning in the patient's daily life. In that the clinic itself is emerging as an important therapeutic agent, the absence of the patient from the clinic is itself detrimental to rehabilitation.

REFERENCES

[1]Richard H. Fulmer, Personality Characteristics of Heroin Addicts and Their Professed Motives for Heroin Use (New York: Columbia University Dissertation, 1975), p. 29.

[2]Ibid., p. 30.

[3]Ibid.

[4]D.L. Gerard and C. Koretsky, "A Social and Psychiatric Study of Adolescent Opiate Addicts" in Psychiatric Quarterly (1954:28), p. 122.

THE PROBLEM WITH URINE SURVEILLANCE IN METHADONE MAINTENANCE PROGRAMS

Iradj Siassi, M. D.
Burleigh P. Angle, M. A.
Dominick C. Alston, B. A.

Comprehensive Drug Abuse Treatment Program
Western Psychiatric Institute and Clinic
University of Pittsburgh
Pittsburgh, Pennsylvania

Some two years ago in our clinic, problems arose when many urine surveillance results reported by the toxicology laboratory were vigorously questioned by patients. Many of the staff were skeptical about these protests, in part, because the laboratory used was federally approved and a participant in the Federal Proficiency Testing Program. Enough doubt, however, was raised to move some staff members to submit their own urines in patients' names. The more than occasional reported presence of drugs in the staff specimens, convinced us of the need for a systematic evaluation of the urine screening procedure. Our first evaluation revealed an unusually high degree of inaccuracy. Feedback of this information to the laboratory resulted in a significant decrease in the frequency of erroneous reports. Two subsequent evaluations were carried out at two months intervals, each leading to improved precision and accuracy in the reports received subsequently.

The results were reported in a previous paper [1]. This paper reports on the exact replication of that study and evaluates the same laboratory 18 months later.

METHOD

The urine surveillance being evaluated in this study is the thin layer chromatography (TLC) procedure. The evaluation process used in this study was similar to that employed by [2], and was developed by Dr. Herbert D. Kleber, Director, Drug Dependence Unit, Connecticut Mental Health Center, New Haven, Connecticut, and supplied to us by personal communication.

Urine specimens are collected at the clinic 3 days a week, Monday, Wednesday, and Friday. During the time of the evaluation, they were picked up and delivered by the laboratory on Tuesday, Thursday, and Saturday.

The preparation of the drugs in a stock solution was supervised by a pharmacologist and provided to the clinic on the day of each trial. The concentration of each drug was non-analytic, (i.e., in the commercial product form with a $\pm$ 5% limit, USP, as generally supplied by the drug company). A (1 cc^3) syringe was used to draw the drug from ampules and mixed with distilled water to obtain the required amount of stock solution with the appropriate microgram (mg) per cubic centimeter (cm^3) concentration of drugs, the prepared stock solutions were then divided into dispensing bottles of measured amounts to be mixed with specimens yielding the required microgram per cm^3 concentration of each drug, i.e., morphine and/or methadone in urine.

The specimens for the divided patient urines were collected from different patients for each trial. In a few cases, specimens were used from patients not receiving methadone at the time of the trial. The "clean urines" for mixing with drugs and for false specimens were collected from a variety of non-patient donors. Occasionally, it was reported that certain donors were taking cold preparations or tranquilizers; these were so noted and accounted for in considering the results.

The specific procedures were as follows: 1). The divided client samples were prepared by randomly selecting 10 specimens, stirring well and pouring even amounts in specimen cups. One set of 10 was submitted in the patients' names and the other set was submitted using aliases. 2). The drugged samples were prepared by first measuring a determined amount of clean urine which when mixed with the prescribed amount of drug in stock solution would yield four 40 cm^3 specimens. Three of these preparations were submitted for each sample category of mg per cm^3 concentration of drugs. The urine was measured in a standard 50 ml beaker and poured into a large beaker where the drug was added. This mixture was stirred and then poured into measured specimen cups, 40 cm^3 per cup. The donor's identity was concealed by using an alias for each specimen submitted. 3) The "false" samples were prepared by simply measuring clean urines in 40 cm^3 amounts in the specimen cups. These were submitted as a confounding factor. Again, the use of aliases protected the donor's identity.

The procedures for each trial were carried out at the clinic with no difficulty. For each trial the same researcher was responsible for measuring specimens and another for recording the samples as prepared.

RESULTS

The results of the present study are presented along with those of the first three trials that constituted the first study. Figure 1 illustrates a definite difficulty in reporting morphine in the first and second trial, which was markedly reduced by the third trial. However, as can be seen in the retest 18 months later, the error has again reached a 75-83% level of inaccuracy.

A similar rate of improvement is shown in (F. 2). Difficulty appears in Trial 1 for the divided specimens, but improves with Trial 2, and is gone in Trial 3 (F. 2). The retest error is equal to that in Trial 2 (5%).

Similarly, disagreement between divided specimens while present to some degree in Trial 1, improves with Trial 2, and is not present in Trial 3 (F. 3). Again, the retest error equals that found in Trial 2. An interesting reversal appears in reporting methadone in clean specimens. There is no problem in Trials 1 and 2, but an increase occurs in Trial 3 (F. 4). The retest reveals proficient testing, with zero percentage of failure in detecting methadone. However, in the specimens where methadone is mixed with morphine, the now familiar error pattern from Trial 1 to Trial 3 reoccurs (F. 4). This trend toward accuracy continues in the retest with 0% of failure.

Figure 5 illustrates that difficulty in reporting false positives was evidenced in all 3 trials for some drugs (methadone and others). However, by the third trial, this error fell within the usual range of accuracy acceptable to HEW. In some cases, the false reports improved or disappeared in Trials 1 and Trials 2 and 3 for methadone. Unfortunately, the retest shows that for quinine and methadone the error is much greater than any of the other previous trials. In addition, that percentage of error (quinine, 9%; methadone, 21%) is outside the acceptable range of error. For other drugs, the retest error does not exceed 1%.

SUMMARY

The retest shows a return to the high levels of inaccuracy, operating in the first 2 trials studied. In the earlier 3 trials, the frequency of error was reduced by each trial. Eighteen months later, the inaccuracy level of drug abuse detection has climbed back to 44%. It is clear that auxilliary services like laboratories need to be monitored constantly by programs to insure acceptable levels of accuracy. In fact, there seems to be a need for constant re-appraisal.

DISCUSSION

Routine use of urine surveillance in the methadone maintenance program has been from the beginning an integral part of this treatment modality [3].

The results of urinalysis were used to determine patient motivation and success [4, 5], and the use of urinalysis was an important part of the decision-making regarding disciplinary actions. However, with the proliferation of the methadone maintenance clinics, and the subsequent slot funding of the programs, continuing abuse of chemicals no longer plays an important role in whether a patient is retained or discharged [6]. In many clinics, both patient and staff have developed a nonchalant attitude towards the procedure; and urine surveillance is primarily used for meeting the requirements of regulatory agencies.

Sohn, et. al. [7] report that, in 427 examinations of labs participating in 3 surveys, perfect scores were achieved in only 44% of the examinations. Sohn reports further that of 146 labs tested, 37% passed; 16% were conditional; and 45% obtained failing scores. These results of the proficiency tests represent maximal efforts by the labs. It would not be unreasonable to assume then, that their routine performance would be poorer.

Furthermore, many of the drugs abused by patients are not identified by the routine urine screening process. Kokoski, et. al. [8] for example showed that methaqualone and benzodiazepines and similar non-narcotics are not usually identified; although they might alter the stabilization effect of methadone. Geiger [9] makes a similar observation about cocaine.

From Rohrbaugh [10] we learn that the large scale use of urinalysis testing, a major part of the army's drug abuse program was a failure. His investigation showed that the use of widespread unannounced screening procedures, underestimated the true army adddict population. In fact, it fostered a "beat the system" reaction from the soldiers. Lewis [11] in a study of 53 former addicts found that they considered routine urine surveillance a "demeaning" procedure which fostered a "contest" spirit in the patients to outsmart the supervisory staff.

Recently, the routine use of this procedure has come under criticism, primarily on a cost/benefit basis. Questions have been raised as to whether the estimated 16-20 million dollars spent each year [12] on this procedure is justified. Weinberg [13] has reported that the clinical value of urine testing is highly questionable. He further argues that the impact the urine screening procedure has on the patients' drug abuse rate is minimal. Goldstein [14] supports this view in reporting that monitored and unmonitored patients showed inconclusive results as to whether testing affected their abuse of illicit drugs.

Our data suggests a reassessment of the financial investment and investment of clinic time associated with this process, as well as the important issue of whether or not the money spent for urinalysis could be used for other more fruitful services.

ACKNOWLEDGEMENT

Funded in part by NIDA Grant #5-H80DA01356.
Special thanks to Mrs. Jacqueline Moye for her kind assistance.
Requests for table data and reprints should be directed to either Burleigh P. Angle or Dominick C. Alston.

NOTES

1. Trellis, E., Smith, F. F., Alston, D. C., and Siassi, I., The
   Pitfalls of urine surveillance: The role of research in eval-
   uation and remedy. Addictive Behavior, Vol. 1, pp. 83-88.
   Pergnor Press, 1975.

2. Riordan, C. E., Slobetz, F., Wall, S., and Primm, B. J., A com-
   parison study of thin-layer chromatography urinalysis results.
   Paper presented at the Fourth National Conference on Methadone
   Maintenance. San Francisco, January, 1973.

3. Dole, V. P., Kim, W. K., Eglitis, I., Detection of narcotic drugs,
   tranquilizers, amphetamines, and barbituates, in urine. J. of
   the American Medical Association, 198:115, 1966.

4. DeAngelis, G. G., The role of urine testing in heroin treatment
   programs. J. of Psychedelic Drugs, 1971, 4, 186-197.

5. Schut, J., Wohlmuth, T., Naglin, B., and File, K., Identification of successful patients in a methadone program, based on
   weekly urinalysis reports. Proc. Fifth Nat. Conf. on Methadone
   Treatment, Washington, D.C., 1973. National Association for
   the Prevention of Addiction to Narcotics, New York, 1973, pp.
   1066-1072.

6. Newman, Problems of methadone maintenance treatment: A program
   director's perspective. Drug Forum, 1973 (Summer), Vol. 2 (4),
   pp. 371-376.

7. Sohn, D., and Sohn, S., Drug Screening: Techniques and applications. Drug Forum, 1972, 1, 275-282.

8. Kokoski, R. J., Detection of the use of methaqualone and benzodiazepines in urine screening programs. Proc. Fifth Nat.
   Conf. on Methadone Treatment, Washington, D.C., 1973, National Association for the Prevention of Addiction to Narcotics,
   New York, 1975.

9. Geiger, W., Cocaine with speed, Proc. Fifth Nat. Conf. on Methadone Treatment, Washington, D.C., 1973. National Association
   for the Prevention of Addiction to Narcotics, New York, 1975,
   pp. 1064-1065.

379

10. Rohrbaugh, M. and Press, S., The army's war on stateside drug use: A view from the front. Journal of Drug Issues, 1974 (Winter), Vol. 4 (1), 32-43.

11. Lewis, S., Petersen, D. M., Geis, G., and Pollack, S., Ethical and social psychological aspects of urinalysis to detect heroin use. British Journal of Addictions, 1972 (December), Vol. 67 (4), pp. 303-307.

12. Goldberg, P., The uses and abuses of urinalysis, Developments in the Field of Drug Abuse, Schenkman Publishing Company, Inc., cooperation with National Association for the Prevention of Addiction to Narcotics, Cambridge, Massachusetts, 1975, pp. 931-938.

13. Weinberg, J. A., and Grevert, P., A controlled study of the clinical effectiveness of urine test results in a methadone maintenance program. Above and Proc. Fifth, pp. 1052-1059.

14. Goldstein, A. and Brown, B. W., Urine testing schedule in methadone maintenance treatment of heroin. Journal of the American Medical Association, 1970-214, 311.

THERAPEUTIC BENEFITS OF TRAVEL FOR NEWLY ENROLLED METHADONE PATIENTS

Arleen Richman, Judith Freeman, Diana Berek

Treatment, Referral, Information & Placement Services
Washington, D.C.

TRIPS is an acronym for Treatment, Referral, Information & Placement Services. The project initially was funded in August, 1973, by SAODAP to serve as a coordinated communications network that would assist members of methadone maintenance Rx programs to travel or relocate. Since February, 1975, TRIPS has been funded through a contract with the Division of Community Assistance of NIDA.

TRIPS' primary function is to arrange temporary methadone Rx in an approved methadone maintenance program which is most convenient to the travelling client's destination. After discussing any restricting regulations or program policies, TRIPS works with the client's counselor or medical staff person at the client's program to obtain the information necessary for the Trip Plan. Receiving programs are under no obligation to accept any transients and they may require clients to meet specific criteria before they will extend courtesy medication. TRIPS, however, imposes no eligibility requirements for client travel.

After TRIPS locates and contacts a convenient receiving program, we notify the sending program of the client's acceptance. The sending program is informed of the name and address of the program, the contact person, hours of medication, and any special requirements, such as fees, or the necessity of having a locked box for take-home. A follow-up package then is sent to the receiving program. The follow-up form asks the receiving program to indicate whether the client was medicated as scheduled: this is known as a "verified visit." If a client does not appear for medication, and has not cancelled the arrangements in advance, the receiving program checks the "no-show" box on the form.

Travel by Newly-Enrolled Clients Increased

Within six months of the project's inception, staff began noticing a high incidence of "no shows" for clients who had been en-

rolled in methadone maintenance Rx for less than 30 days before deciding to travel. Discussions with both sending and receiving programs revealed that these newly-enrolled clients tended to encounter
major difficulties when they travelled. In the comment section of
the follow-up report, receiving programs noted that newly-enrolled
clients were not familiar or comfortable with clinic routines, had
not yet reached stable doses, and failed to report for medication as
scheduled. Some receiving programs were convinced that clients
entered Rx simply to assure themselves of an adequate legal drug
supply just prior to departing on an anticipated journey.

During the period August through December, 1973, only 6% of all
Trip Plans processed were for clients in Rx for less than 30 days.
However, by December, 1974, newly-enrolled clients constituted 22%
of TRIPS' travelling population.

In order to test our hypothesis that clients admitted to methadone maintenance Rx programs for less than 30 days before deciding
to travel do not avail themselves of temporary medication arrangements, TRIPS decided to follow up all newly-enrolled clients utilizing our services between March 15 and April 15, 1975. During this
period, sending programs asked TRIPS to arrange temporary methadone
medication for 102 clients. Twenty-five (or slightly less than 25%
of the total) had been enrolled in Rx for less than 30 days. None
of these 25 clients was a transfer or a readmit.

TRIPS staff phoned both the sending and receiving programs involved in each of these 25 cases. Verification was made of the
following two aspects of each case: 1) did the client receive temporary methadone medication at the receiving program as scheduled;
and 2) did the client return to the sending program as expected. We
then compared the results of this two-phase follow-up with the results of a larger study (93 cases) we had concluded on a general
population sample travelling during August, 1974. The findings were
dramatic. Whereas 72% of the general population travelling during
August, 1974, completed their trips and returned home without incident, the survey of newly-enrolled clients revealed that in 72% of
these cases, major problems ensued. Only 7, or 28%, of the newly-
enrolled clients were medicated in the correct receiving program and
returned on schedule to their home programs.

Reason for Travel

Of the 25 clients studied, 13 travelled for vacation purposes;
5 travelled because of employment; 3 travelled because of illness
or death in the family and 2 gave personal business as the reason
for travel. The two remaining clients were enroute to permanent
relocations. Interestingly, both these clients arrived at their
destinations and have become permanent members of the receiving
programs.

With the exception of the two permanent relocations, only 5 of the remaining 23 clients completely followed procedures and were medicated as per prior arrangements. The reason for travel -- pleasure vs. necessity -- appeared to bear little correlation with the client's appearing for medication. Twenty-three % (3 of 13) vacationers did as instructed, as opposed to 30% (4 of 12) who travelled out of necessity.

Reports on the 18 clients who did not follow procedures reveal the following: 3 clients or 12% of the total sample, cancelled their travel plans without notifying either the sending programs or TRIPS. One client, travelling on vacation only three days after being admitted to Rx, experienced difficulties with dosage. Because this person's dose was not stabilized, the dosage constantly needed to be changed, necessitating numerous phone calls between receiving and sending programs.

Another client requested a permanent transfer upon arrival at the receiving program. The receiving program was annoyed and felt that the client was trying to circumvent that program's long waiting list. Two clients, not travelling together, were medicated the first day, did not show up for two or more days, returned to the receiving programs for their last doses, but never returned to their respective sending programs.

One client requested that the temporary receiving program arrange for a permanent transfer to still a third clinic, which is contrary to established protocol because it places both programs at a disadvantage. Still another client appeared at the wrong receiving program. One receiving program refused to medicate a travelling client who appeared "stoned" and refused to drop a urine. One client appeared at the receiving program but never returned to the sending program. Finally, the remaining 7 clients, approximately 30% of the total sample never, to our knowledge, reappeared at any methadone program. No further word was available because the sending programs had completely lost touch with these individuals.

Although the sample of cases studied was relatively small, TRIPS believes that the results presented a valid indication as to the probability of a newly-enrolled client's adherence to a pre-arranged travel itinerary. TRIPS immediately began urging sending programs to thoroughly evaluate the prospective travel plans of newly-enrolled clients. All programs that requested temporary medication arrangements for clients in Rx for less than 30 days were cautioned as to the findings of our study.

Within three months, travel requests for newly-enrolled clients sharply declined. Between August 15 and September 15, 1975 newly-enrolled clients constituted 18% of TRIPS' total travelling

population. This figure contrasts sharply with a high of 28% reported for April 15-May 15 in the same year.

Second Follow-up Study

In January, 1976, TRIPS again conducted a two-phase telephone
follow-up study on all newly-enrolled clients who utilized our services between October 15 and November 15, 1975. Of the 140 clients
TRIPS processed during this period, only 17 persons or 12% had enrolled in methadone maintenance Rx within the last 30 days. This
represents a 50% reduction in travel by newly-enrolled clients compared to the statistics compiled during the first study period.

Although travel by newly-enrolled clients had decreased significantly, the track record of these newly-enrolled clients was even
worse than their predecessors. Only 4 clients, out of 17 total,
were medicated as requested at receiving programs and returned to
their sending programs without incident.

Five clients travelled due to illness or death in the family;
5 were on vacation, 2 were enroute to permanent relocations, 2
travelled in connection with employment, 2 cited personal business
and the remaining client needed to travel for a court appearance.
Again, no significant correlation was found between reason for travel and the "show" or "no show" factor at medication sites.

The 13 clients who did not comply with prior medication arrangements broke down into the following categories: 6 clients, 4 of
whom felt the nearest receiving programs were too far from their
intended destinations, decided at the last minute not to travel.
Except in one instance, neither TRIPS nor the sending programs
was notified of the client's decision to cancel. Two clients decided to skip medication entirely. One receiving program refused
to medicate a client who appeared "high" and who insisted on carrying beer cans into the clinic. Two clients did appear at the receiving programs but never returned to the sending programs; their
whereabouts today are unknown. Two clients, not together, were
supposed to transfer permanently to different receiving programs.
However, within a relatively short stay at the receiving programs,
both clients decided to return to their original programs. The receiving programs were annoyed at all the wasted paperwork involved.

TRIPS believes it would be useful to further investigate the
reasons why clients do not appear for temporary medication services
and/or return to the home programs. Further project studies will
concentrate on the factors contributing to the "no show" phenomenon.
Among these are: 1) availability of nearest receiving program; 2)
number of days a client is scheduled to receive temporary service;
3) dispensing hours and convenience of receiving program regulation;

4) availability of heroin or other drugs of abuse in the city of destination; and travelling companions whose plans differ from the client's.

Evaluating Travel Plans

TRIPS is committed to the philosophy that clients enrolled in methadone maintenance Rx programs should be permitted to exercise the rights of mobility enjoyed by other citizens. At present we have not set any criteria regarding the length of time clients must be in Rx before TRIPS will handle the service request. However, based on the results of these two studies, TRIPS urges all sending programs to determine whether the therapeutic interest of the newly-enrolled client would best be served by travel at this point in the client's Rx plan. Unless the travel is for emergency purposes, a client's travel plans should be incorporated into the Rx plan and be evaluated on the basis of the client's stability and effort in achieving rehabilitation.

TRIPS recommends these guidelines for evaluating the travel plans of newly-enrolled clients:
1. A counselor should determine the client's reason for travel and decide whether the trip is therapeutically beneficial.
2. The counselor and the client should determine the feasibility of the travel plan. Upon request, TRIPS will inform the counselor of the distance the client must travel to the nearest medication site. (Our experience indicates that clients rarely travel more than 100 miles round-trip daily to receive methadone.) TRIPS also will be glad to supply information regarding dosing hours, fees, etc. After weighing all the available information, the counselor and the client can determine if the trip really is feasible.
3. The counselor should obtain a signed copy of the release of information to TRIPS and place this in the client's file. Counselors also should make certain that all data in the client's record is complete and up-to-date. With the client's record and travel plans before him, the counselor should call TRIPS to initiate the Trip Plan. TRIPS will request dosage information and does not recommend that the client "sit in" during the call if the clinic follows the blind dose policy.
4. TRIPS then will process the travel plan as explained earlier. The counselor, however, should stress the importance of having the client notify him in advance of any changes or cancellation of the pre-arranged travel itinerary.

A CLIENT EVALUATION OF INVOLUNTARY DETOXIFICATION FROM METHADONE MAINTENANCE

Paul Attewell, Lewis L. Judd, and Dean R. Gerstein

Department of Psychiatry
University of California, San Diego
La Jolla, California 92093

This paper reports findings of an independent follow-up and evaluation study of San Diego's Narcotic Treatment Program (NTP). A stratified random sample (N=100)of admissions to NTP from 1970-1974 were interviewed using our Lifestyle Inventory Schedule, which assesses the impact of treatment in the context of the subject's life history. Interviews were tape-recorded and transcribed. The interview included elicitation of client's views on each aspect of program structure and rules; this report focuses on responses concerning the involuntary detoxification procedure in methadone maintenance.

Detoxification is used when a program discontinues treatment of a client physiologically dependent on methadone. This is achieved by gradual reduction to zero of the maintenance dose. The federally mandated minimum "detox" in approved methadone programs is 14 days; the San Diego program had a 21-day minimum for its involuntary "detox", used for terminating clients who violated program rules or treatment contracts. Yet 45% of our sample objected specifically to the length (21 days) of detoxification.

> "That's not long enough. I know cause I've gone
> through it twice. That's not long enough. Even
> after the detox it took a good two or three weeks
> after that. At first I'm not sleeping, I'm aching
> in my bones, my back and my legs mostly. Second of
> all there's too much stomach habit to methadone and
> I get cramps in my stomach a good two weeks after
> I've had methadone. That's what took me to using
> again."

> "I don't like that. I think it should be longer...
> Something with medication might come out of it.
> The detox should be more like about 45 days, 30-45
> days. In turn, they should give you Librium or

Valium or something to help you sleep and all
that; give you something to relieve your nerves,
and give you something to help you sleep. It's
very unpleasant especially the 21 day detox; the
person that's been on methadone for a couple of
years, 21 days is an awfully short period of time
to come off...You give a person a 21 day detox on
the street and they get sick, they're gonna fix...
That's where the habit starts all over again."

The first thing that should be noted is that involuntary detoxification occurs to a distinct minority of patients. Only
twenty-two percent (22%) of NTP patients between 1970 and December
of 1974 were detoxified by staff decision. In general, this occurred as a result of continued heroin use after entering the program. An elaborate warning system was devised. After the program
detected three "dirty urines" (heroin or other illegal drugs found
on urinalysis), following the initial several-month stabilization
period, a patient was asked to sign a "contract" which stated that
future urines found "dirty" would result in the patient being detoxified and terminated from the program.

From the outsider's perspective this seems fair and adequate
warning. However, a significant proportion of patients (21%) felt
that such detoxification was wrong in principle:

"No human being should have to go through something
like that. And there's no need in it. People lose
their tempers and do things that they are sorry
for. But to punish them like that is inhuman, that's
my way of thinking, 21 days especially..."

"To me, it's childish...If a person is messing up,
whoever his counselor is oughta get with the dude
and find out what's happening...I mean the program's there to help people not to threaten them."

In contrast, other patients (11%) indicated their approval of
punitive detoxification:

"If they didn't detox you when you came up dirty
there wouldn't be any purpose in taking drops,
there wouldn't be any purpose in anything."

"It's a good rule, they have to have some way to
control people otherwise they'd be fixing all
the time."

How are we to interpret the considerable concern (and hostility) that revolves about the detoxification issue? Some additional
data from our interviews is useful in this regard. A large proportion of our sample (as in other programs) stated that they used

387

heroin after entering the program: 33% occasionally and 12% daily. This is to be expected; people do not change years of conditioning and lifestyle overnight. Psychosocial impetus toward heroin continues even when methadone prevents physiological craving (withdrawal symptoms). The difficulty for the program is to distinguish sporadic heroin users, the majority of whom cease using after a period of time in treatment, from the small minority who continue regular use. This latter group has a very low likelihood of gaining anything therapeutic from the treatment program.

Urinalysis is the basic screening device to detect illegal drug use in patients. Urine samples are taken from each patient once a week; the day is randomized. Since urinalysis only detects heroin used in the previous 72 hours at best, and is only moderately sensitive under most clinical conditions, one could use heroin occasionally and never show "dirty" if one could guess in advance more or less when one would be asked to give a sample.

Given these stipulations, patients using heroin play a form of "Russian Roulette". The decision of the program when to ask for a sample will affect whether use is detected or not. Since detection is not inevitable, when one is "caught", it comes as an annoying shock, which in turn is laid at the feet of the counselor who was ordered that day to command a urine. Secondly, in the face of large-scale sporadic heroin use, mixed with a minority of continued steady users, it takes many weeks of regular urinalysis to really distinguish between a sporadic and a regular user. Three dirty urines as a threshold for action is clearly too few - a sporadic user with bad luck could accumulate three while a luckier person who uses heroin much more regularly might not.

In response to this, the staff at NTP informally developed a considerable flexibility in ordering involuntary detoxification. Examination of a cross section of patient records indicated that sometimes as many as 5 dirty urines in a 12 week period went unremarked, while other patients were detoxified for less. The process, seen from the patient's perspective, therefore involved a mixture of bad luck and unequal treatment. He or she felt singled out for punishment, while other patients went untouched.

It appears that the clinical meaning of involuntary detoxification became distorted and lost. The original intention was to suspend those patients from treatment who were clearly not adapting to methadone maintenance, and who were therefore not helping themselves, were taking up desired clinical slots, making the program look bad, and were a bad example to others. But the emphasis shifted,at least as seen by the patients, from termination of treatment as a clinical measure, to detoxification as itself a form of punishment.

Methadone detoxification was not originally intended to be punitive. It is by and large a medically humane way to prepare a

388

patient, whom the staff feels should be removed from the program, for termination. In contrast, the 21 day withdrawal is such a rapid deescalation in the eyes of the patients that it is a punishment in itself. The program, as well, did not behave as if termination from treatment was a simple clinical response to continued counter-therapeutic behavior. The program protocols indicated that a detoxified patient could not reenter the program before 30 days elapsed. But we were able to identify a significant number of cases where detoxified patients reentered treatment after only two weeks. In other words, exceptions were made. Thus, treatment termination was viewed as a temporary inconvenience, and the focus shifted to detoxification (rather than termination of program contact) as a primary punitive response.

Clearly this sort of situation led patients to view detoxification as punishment. And this conjured up the image of the program using an addict's physical withdrawal pains as a control device. Open patient hostility to this is clearly understandable.

RECOMMENDATIONS

A more consistently applied policy of responses to dirty urines would have to be instituted to avoid this phenomenon. If urine tests are to be used in making termination decisions, then a larger number of "dirty urines" should be necessary before a client is terminated. This number should be totally standardized and exceptions not be made. Detoxification itself should be modified so that the process is less painful. But more importantly, patients who are discharged from the program because they show no indication of adapting to the program rules, or benefitting from the program, should be discharged with the intention of remaining discharged. The expectation of a "30 day reentry" discharge should be stopped. Discharge should be for a longer minimum period of time, and should be a matter of careful clinical consideration rather than an automatic process dependent primarily on the patient's documentation.

In our research we discerned a group of patients who revolved in and out of the methadone program, and who constituted a large proportion of involuntary detoxifications. This group of patients treatment careers developed into a new variant of the street addiction lifestyle. While on the program they begin regular heroin use, are detected, detoxified, go back to the street, and simply reenter the program when the pressures are such that they need a legal habit again. Program practices and rules regarding detoxification and reentry at the time of this study allowed for the continued existence of this type of patient career, which paralleled exactly the stereotypical street use of heroin: periods of addiction, interspersed with short periods of abstinence. The changes suggested above would actively discourage this type of career.

METHADONE MAINTENANCE: THE NUMBERS GAME

Phillip E. Jacobs, Ph.D.

Ellen B. Doft, MPH

Athan Karras, Ph.D.

James Koger, MA

Long Island Jewish Hillside Medical Center
New Hyde Park, New York

Discovered by the Germans during WW II, methadone was put to
its current clinical use as a heroin substitute by Drs. Dole and
Nyswander. They reported that methadone had two main effects upon
heroin addicts; it prevented withdrawal symptoms, and, when administered in sufficiently high doses, it constituted a "blockade"
which prevented the addict from experiencing euphoria following the
injection of heroin. Their solution to the addict problem was,
therefore, simple: give the addict the opiate he craves to "get the
monkey off his back" and he would then be able to lead a normal
life. He would no longer constantly find himself in trouble with
the law, would be able to land and hold a job, and of course, would
no longer be on "drugs."
     As a result of this point of view, Drs. Dole and Nyswander
claimed near miraculous results with the use of methadone. Lukoff
noted that if their claims were true, this approach would represent
a quantum leap in the treatment of social problems virtually un-
heralded in the history of contemporary society.(1) Drs. Dole and
Nyswander said that in one of their experiments the criminal behavior of addicts had been "virtually eliminated" through the use of
methadone; and that they derived a 94% success rate in ending their
patient's criminal behavior.(2) Methadone thus seemed to have
joined the ranks of other wonder drugs such as penicillin and
sulfa.
     If Drs. Dole and Nyswander could be accused of being somewhat
partial in their support of methadone, Dr. Frances Gearing could
not. Dr. Gearing, a public health epidemiologist from Columbia
University, was engaged by New York State to do a scientific,
impartial evaluation of methadone maintenance in New York City to
confirm the wisdom of this modality of treatment.

Dr. Gearing largely confirmed the Dole and Nyswander view of maintenance as a most effective treatment for heroin addicts. In a report published in the American Journal of Public Health (1974), she clearly implied that methadone maintenance treatment caused the unemployment rate for addicts in treatment to go from 64% to 28%, for only 15% of the addicts to be arrested, and for social productivity to rise from 36% to 72%. (3)

Dr. Gearing identified, but failed to put to rest, the major criticism of her evaluation of methadone maintenance treatment. Briefly, the criticism was that her results were doomed to success from the start because the performance of the program dropouts while they were in the program was not measured. The purpose of the present study was to shed light on the criticism that there was a methodological error in this type of methadone treatment evaluation in that it ignored the experience of program dropouts.

The Study

Under contract with the City of New York, Long Island Jewish-Hillside Medical Center operates a methadone maintenance treatment program. This study was initiated as a result of a series of discussions with clinic treatment personnel. Repeatedly the idea expressed was that while the program worked for some patients, there was a sizable group that appeared to derive little benefit from it. In fact, this group always appeared to be in trouble with a variety of authorities including their family, friends, and clinic personnel. Based on Gearing's findings, we did not expect these clinical impressions. Therefore, we were interested in pursuing these impressions from a practical as well as a theoretical point of view.

In her study, Dr. Gearing looked at the 1,230 patients admitted to methadone maintenance treatment in New York City from 1964 to 1968. By December 31, 1973, 770 patients (63%) were still in treatment. Unfortunately, performance data were only analyzed for these 770 patients. Equivalent data on the performance of the 460 patients (37%) who, for different reasons, were terminated from treatment were not presented. As a result of this approach, there are two possible interpretations of the data. First, the patients could look better year after year due to the effectiveness of the treatment; or secondly, they could look better merely because the success rates for the group as a whole went up as the "rotten apples" were tossed off the program.

Substantial support would be imparted to the latter hypothesis if it could be shown that two different types of patients enter methadone maintenance treatment programs; those who possess the pre-program characteristics associated with success, and those who do not. In this case, it appears that Dr. Gearing may have mistakenly identified the attrition of poor-performance patients as the efficacy of methadone maintenance treatment programs.

The purpose of the study, then, emerged as an effort to see whether the discrepency between Dr. Gearing's findings and the treatment personnel perceptions could be reconciled in terms of the second hypothesis. If it could be shown that, along variables affecting methadone maintenance treatment program performances patients were not randomly distributed between "active" and "terminated" categories, then Dr. Gearing's conclusions could not be supported from the data she presented.

Our clinic belongs to the same system as the one studied by Dr. Gearing. Therefore, forms used to collect data were the same for both studies. Data sources included pre-admission screening forms, urine analysis results, counselor's notes and the unit director's bi-monthly reports (UDR's) all of which were done for each patient. The data from these sources were validated by Dr. Gearing in her study.

In contrast to Dr. Gearing's study, which only measured the performance of patients who were active from the beginning to the end of the observation period, the present study measured the performance of anyone who had been a patient during the entire period of observation. If a patient was terminated, rather than removing his experience from the data pool, his experience was included in the overall final analysis of patient performance. Thus data were gathered on all of the 496 patients who were admitted to the program from its inception in March, 1971 through June, 1975.

The present study presents data on three areas which have generally been identified as key outcome areas for methadone maintenance treatment: employment/social productivity, criminality and drug abuse. Patients were divided into two groups - those who were active and those who had been terminated as of September 30, 1975. Terminated patients were then subdivided into positive, (advised detoxification and transfers), and program failures, (detoxification against advise, "splittees", behavior problems, etc.). As was expected, the performance of the positive patients fell in between that of the active and the program failure patients. Therefore, only the results of the active and the program failure patients will be presented.

The Results

As a whole, our population was predominantly suburban, male (84%), white (75%) and Catholic (54%). The mean age at which both the active and program failure patients began taking heroin daily was 18 years. The mean age at admission for active patients was 27 years. For program failure patients, it was 25 years. This difference and any other difference between the demographic and addiction characteristics of active and program failure patients were not statistically significant. These findings were contrary to our early hypothesis that there would be significant differences between program performance, as was measured by the outcome variables, and these types of variables.

The performance of all patients, both active and terminated, on the outcome variables can be summarized as follows: 36% were un-employed; 69% were socially productive; 46% were abusing drugs and 30% were arrested while in treatment.

The differences in performance on these same variables between active and program failure patients were highly statistically significant. Twenty-six percent (26%) of active patients were unemployed; 62% of program failure patients were unemployed. While 20% of active patients were arrested while in treatment, 49% of program failure patients were arrested while they were in treatment. The same trend was true for drug abuse. In this case, 34% of the active patients were abusing drugs; 72% of program failure patients were abusing drugs.

Next, we looked at performance on outcome variables by active and terminated patients in terms of the number of months patients were on the program. For active patients, it was measured as the number of months that an individual was in treatment at the time of his termination. At _every_ time interval for _every_ outcome variable, active patients out performed terminated patients.

Discussion

By looking only at those patients who were not terminated from the program, Dr. Gearing has not provided us with sufficient proof that her patients improved as a result of methadone maintenance treatment. It would be safer to say that some persons seem to do well on admission and continue to do well while others do not. The addicts who do improve cannot, with any certainty, be said to be improving because of methadone maintenance treatment. The ones who do not improve tend to be terminated from the program. It is possible that the good addicts would have done just as well without methadone maintenance treatment; the bad addicts do, in fact, seem to do poorly in spite of methadone maintenance treatment.

In summary, we have shown that for every outcome variable in every time interval of length of treatment, active patients did better than terminated patients. When we broke the terminated patients down further into positive terminations and program failures, the differences in the findings were even more dramatic.

On the basis of these data, we feel that the next question that needs to be answered is why do some patients succeed with methadone maintenance treatment while others fail with the same treatment?

Our data has shown that we cannot explain this difference by expected differences in demographic and/or addiction characteris-

tics in our patient population. The only appropriate means to
determine that treatment caused improvement is to have a randomly
chosen control group. Using the patient's pre-admission history to
infer future behavior has limited value and is no substitute for an
appropriately conducted study.

Our next step then will be to explore pre-admission variables
such as arrests and employment. In addition, we hope to test
whether the addict typology developed by Stimson (4) in England can
be used to explain the difference in success and failure in our
clinic population. Stimson found that treatment performance could
be predicted on the basis of a measurement of the degree to which
an individual adhered to either a "junkie" or a "straight" life-
style prior to his admission. Addicts, therefore, cannot be
viewed as a homogenous group.

To face the reality of diversity among addicts, it is necessary
for there to be different types of methadone maintenance treatment
programs. The programs should have varying goals and expectations
to meet the needs of the different types of addicts. Almost any
addict is better off obtaining his opiate supply under sanitary
conditions from a clinic which provides comprehensive medical care
than from a street peddler. Therefore, it may be necessary for
some clinics to drastically restructure their goals away from
"success" and "rehabilitation" and towards simply keeping the
patient in contact with the clinic and out of the hands of the
black-market peddler.

Bibliography

1. Lukoff, Irving, "Issues in the Evaluation of Heroin Treatment,"
    in Drug Abuse Epidemiological and Sociological Approaches
        ed. by Josephson, Eric and Caroll, Eleanor, (Washington,
        D.C.: Hemisphere Publishing Corporation, 1974). pp.129-157.
2. Dole, V.P., Nyswander, M.E., and Warner, A., "Successful
        Treatment of 750 Criminal Addicts," Journal of American
        Medical Association, 206:2708-2711, 1968
3. Gearing, Frances, "Methadone Maintenance Treatment Five Years
        Later - Where are They Now?" American Journal of Public
        Health Supplement Vol. 64; pp. 44-50, December, 1974.
4. Stimson, G.V., Heroin and Behavior, (New York: John Wiley &
        Sons, 1973.)

METHADONE MAINTENANCE: A NEGATIVE
SELF-FULFILLING PROPHECY

Thomas Edward Bratter, Ed. D. , Consultant

Pelham Narcotics Guidance Council

Matthew C. Pennacchia, Staff Coordinator

Daytop Village, Inc.

We do not claim that detoxification from methadone can be accomplished easily. When programs, however, establish effective treatment alliances with patients, we agree with Lowinson, Langrod, and Berle (1975) "that a drug-free state can be achieved." The senior author formerly directed a small private methadone clinic which stressed detoxification as a viable treatment goal (Bratter, 1975). The junior writer, a member of that program, is living proof that detoxification can be achieved. He required, in addition, a referral to a therapeutic community to help him internalize further the optimistic growth and development orientation of that program (Raubolt and Bratter 1976 and 1974). Inasmuch as the program director and a former patient have collaborated to amalgamate their experiences, the intensely humanistic orientation of the program should be evident. Length restrictions will prevent us from describing the habilitative/ rehabilitative process which will permit our critics to claim this is a simplistic presentation. We will examine what we consider to be the most neglected variable of the treatment relationship-- i. e. , the impact of both the negative and positive self-fulfilling prophesy on recovery.

The literature is replete with studies which extol the therapeutic virtues of methadone maintenance. Chambers, Babst, and Warner (1971), in fact, have provided the clinical rationale by stating "the retention power of the methadone maintenance modality is without equal in the addiction field." Despite almost total support by the Medical-Psychiatric establishment in 1972, the Department of Health Education and Welfare made it mandatory for all programs to adopt detoxification as their primary treatment goal. Cattes (1973), Chappel, Skolnick, and Senay (1973), Novick (1973), Riordan and Rapkin (1972), Gearing (1970) et al remain pessimistic about the probability of a long-term successful detoxification. Newman (1974) rhetorically proposes "no one has the temerity to question the medical or empirical basis for concluding that detoxification must be the universal goal." There remains a dearth of data which correlates the successful detoxification from methadone with the treatment goals of the program and the attitudes of the staff. Dole and Nyswander (1965), indeed, viewed the indefinite administration of methadone as the only legitimate treatment goal. The later works of Dole and Nyswander (1968 and 1967) contained no provisions for any detoxification from methadone. Dole's reasoning has been well documented. When asked to clarify the point that "people cannot be taken off methadone without a reversion to heroin," Dole (1970) responded:

> I did not say that a person taken off methadone is sure to
> revert to heroin. What he does with this compulsion is,
> of course, another matter. There are a number of people
> who are able to live with drug hunger and remain abstinent.
> Withdrawal of methadone, therefore, is not the same thing
> as dooming them to relapse to heroin. But in our experi-
> ence the return of heroin hunger is a consistent phenome-
> non of the withdrawal of methadone. What they return to
> pharmacologically after withdrawal of methadone is the
> status they had prior to treatment with methadone.

Clearly, any program which adopted the Dole and Nyswander methodology would be most reluctant to detoxify any patients. When patients inquired about the possibility of detoxifying from methadone, Berger and Schwegler (1973) reveal a curious negative self-fulfilling prophesy that "no one was advised to pursue this course; in fact in many instances the opposite tack was used. Each patient who requests detoxification is told at once that he may have this privilege, but he is warned that it is a difficult task and one that all too frequently fails." The explicit message which the staff inadvertently communicates to patients is that they not only are "sick" but also require more methadone to feel "normal." Bowen and Maddux (1972) contend "responding to missed doses by reducing the dosage gives the message that the main aim of the program is continued dependence on methadone. Responding to a patient's emotional distress by increasing his dosage of methadone furthers his drug dependence. Instead, such circumstances should be used as opportunities to help the person understand and perhaps modify his own reaction patterns and coping skills."

Unfortunately, the majority of methadone practitioners remain pessimistic about the possibility of a successful detoxification. Dumont (1972) suggests that the medical-psychiatric establishment believe "addicts are not in control of their own behavior and are not curable by any known treatment. Until one is found, the best we can hope for is to block the addict's craving, monitor his social behavior and reduce the profit of an illegal market in heroin." Patients, tragically, internalize this nihilistic view.

Freud (1953), the first to appreciate the impact of the psychotherapist regarding treatment outcome, writes that "fear expectation is certainly not without its effect on the result...in all our attempts at treatment." Freudenberger (1971) is more explicit when he warns about the negative "self fulfilling prophesy with the teenager. If we (therapists) believe that he cannot be helped, then usually he turns out not to be 'amenable' to therapy." Whenever the Dole and Nyswander concept of a metabolic deficiency is followed--i.e., dispense methadone indefinitely--methadone maintenance is viewed as a legitimate treatment goal. Bourne (1975) reports the goals of these programs are to rehabilitate socially the addict by a continued dependence on methadone. Responding to a patient's emotional distress by increasing his dosage of methadone furthers his drug dependence." Gould (1971) discusses a more counter-therapeutic patient reaction when he raises the issue. "Do not some of the patients on methadone interpret this treatment as a final judgment--society's way of telling them, in effect, 'You are a hopeless addict who is so weak (psychologically) and so destroyed (physically) that you must remain an addict all your life."

Meltzoff and Kornreich (1970) define the positive self-fulfilling prophesy as a "prognostic expectancy...that is looked for with belief, faith, confidence, or conviction of being found. It is essentially a prediction anchored in belief that may or may not be warranted. Therapeutic expectancy...brings about the anticipated goal." The impact of the positive self-fulfilling prophesy has been documented by Sloan, Cristol, and Pepernik (1970), Goldstein (1962), Lennard and Bernstein (1960), Merton (1958), and Phillips (1956). Frank summarizes the research by suggesting that "favorable expectations (by the treatment agent) generate feelings of optimism, energy, and well-being and may actually promote healing."

Whether or not it will be possible to predict the probability of detoxification <u>before</u> a person enters into a program based on the attitudes of the treatment staff needs to be subjected to rigorous double blind research studies. It is likely that in programs reported by Casriel and Bratter (1975), Mezritz, Slobetz, Kleber, and Riordan (1975), and Razini, Chrisholm, Glasser, and Kappeler (1975), and Raynes and Patch (1973) who believe that detoxification from methadone is both a realistic and attainable goal, more treatment successes would occur than in traditional programs which stress maintenance.

It is assumed, therefore, that when either the psychotherapist or the program maintain positive expectations for improved behavior performance and detoxification from methadone, patients are more likely to become autonomous (abstinent) and responsible. Krasner (1962) remains explicit regarding this issue when he reports that

> Most therapists are uncomfortable in a role labeled as a "controller" or "manipulator" of behavior. The evidence, however, is that this is an accurate description of what the therapist role actually is... The therapist... has the power to influence and control the behavior and values of other human beings. For the therapist not to accept this situation and to be continually unaware of influencing effects of his behavior on his patients would in itself be "unethical."

In a democracy, where free choice is protected by the Constitution, all citizens are guaranteed the right to be drug-free. All programs have been mandated legally to provide the conditions to help all patients become abstinent. Unfortunately, there have been abuses. The Fellows of the Drug Abuse Council (1974) denounces the mechanism for controlling addiction--i.e., the health system because:

> It can impose its demands on citizens in the name of health, often bypassing the established safeguards of due process that are inherent in criminal justice procedures. We believe that there are many traditional benefits the health professions can provide in the treatment of addiction, such as those functions specific to restoring persons to a state of physical health. But when physicians act as agents of

social control, we fear that those traditional functions are seriously compromised.

If there is to be an effective treatment for heroin addiction, those personnel who are working in the field must believe that recovery is possible and abstinence is desirable.

Nowhere in the field of treatment does the dichotomy between negative and positive self-fulfilling prophesies appear more dramatically than with the methadone issue. The programs which dogmatically accept the Dole and Nyswander "no exit" from heroin addiction theory of a metabolic disorder, can show few patients who have detoxified. Tragically, a significant number who have achieved abstinence report they have done so "against medical advice!" In contrast, programs which dispense methadone as an interim chemotherapeutic technique not only to motivate but also to stabilize patients can document significant numbers who currently remain abstinent from all chemicals. These programs' clinical experiences parallel those of the Therapeutic Community which stress abstinence as a realistic and attainable goal!

BIBLIOGRAPHY

Berger, H., and Schwegler, M.J., (1973). Voluntary Detoxification of Patients on Methadone Maintenance. Int. J. Addictions. 8:6. 1043.

Bourne, P., (1975). Methadone Benefits and Shortcomings. Drug Abuse Council. 1-25.

Bowden, C.L., and Maddux, J.F., (1972). Methadone Maintenance: Myth and Reality. Am. J. Psychiat. 129:4. 436.

Bratter, T.E., (1975). Methadone: Try It, You'll Hate It! Addiction Therapist. 1:2. 48-59.

Casriel, D.H., and Bratter, T.E., (1974). Methadone Maintenance Treatment: A Questionable Procedure. J. Drug Issues. 4:4. 359-375.

Cattes, D., (1973). What is a Successful Patient and Must Detoxification be a Factor? In Proceedings of the Fifth National Conference on Methadone Treatment. R.L. DuPont and R.S. Freeman (Eds.) NAPAN. 17-20.

Chambers, C.D., Babst, D.V., and Warner, A., (1971). Characteristics Predicting Long Term Retention in a Methadone Maintenance Program. In Proceedings: Third National Conference on Methadone Treatment. 140-145.

Chappel, J., Skolnick, V.B., and Senay, E.C., (1972). Techniques of Withdrawal from Methadone and Their Outcome over Six Months to Two Years. In. Proceedings of the Fifth National Conference on Methadone Treatment. R.L. DuPont and R.S. Freeman (Eds.) NAPAN. 482-489.

Dole, V.P. (1970). Research on Methadone Maintenance Treatment. Int. J. Addictions. 5:3. 372.

Dole, V.P., Nyswander, M.E., and Warner, A., (1968). Successful Treatment of 750 Criminal Addicts. J. Am. Medical Assoc. 206:12. 2708-2711.

Dole, V.P. and Nyswander, M.E., (1967). Addiction--A Metabolic Disease. Arch. Internal Medicine. 120. 19-24.

Dole, V.P. and Nyswander, M.E., (1965). A Medical Treatment for Diacetylmorphine (Heroin) Addiction. J. Am. Medical Assoc. 193. 646.

Dumont, M.P., (1972). Methadone Maintenance? Med. Insight. 4-11. 41.

Fellows of the Drug Abuse Council (1974). Disabusing Drug Abuse. Social Policy. 4:5. 45.

Frank, J.D., (1975). Persuasion & Healing. Johns Hopkins University Press. 200.

Freud, S., (1953). The Complete Works of Sigmund Freud Volume 7. J. Strachey (Ed.) Hogarth Press and Institute of Psychoanalysis. 289.

Freudenberger, H.J., (1971). New Psychotherapy Approaches with Teenagers in a New World. Psychother: Theory, Res., Prac. 8:1. 27.

Goldstein, A.P., (1962). Therapist-Patient Expectancies in Psychotherapy. Pergamon Press.

Gould, R.E., (1971). Methadone Reconsidered. Drug Therapy. 1:8. 22.

Krasner, L., (1962). The Therapist as a Social Reinforcement Machine. In Research in Psychotherapy Volume II. American Psychological Assoc., 45.

Lennard, H.L., and Bernstein, A., (1960). The Anatomy of Psychotherapy. Columbia University Press.

Lowinson, J., Langrod, J., and Berle, B., (1975). Detoxification of Long-Term Methadone Patients. In Developments in the Field of Drug Abuse. E. Senay, V. Shorty, and H. Alksne (Eds.) Schenkman Publishing Co. Inc. 336-343.

Meltzoff, J., and Kornreich, M., (1970). Research in Psychotherapy. Atherton Press, Inc. 258.

Merton, R., (1958). Self-Fulfilling Prophecy. Van Nostrand.

Mezritz, M., Slobetz, F., Kleber, H., and Riordan, C., (1975). A Follow-Up Study of Successfully Detoxificated Methadone Maintenance Patients. In Developments in the Field of Drug Abuse. E. Senay, V. Shorty, H. Alksne (Eds.) Schenkman Publishing Co. Inc. 132-142.

Newman, R.G., (1975). Methadone Maintenance: It Ain't What It Used To Be. In Developments in the Field of Drug Abuse. E. Senay, V. Shorty, and H. Alksne (Eds.) Schenkman Publishing Co. Inc. 54.

Novick, M., (1973). The Role of Detoxification in the Long-Term Treatment of the Drug Abuser. In Proceedings of the Fifth National Conference on Methadone Treatment. R.L. DuPont and R.S. Freeman (Eds.) NAPAN. 456-463.

Phillips, E.L., (1956). Psychotherapy: A Modern Theory and Practice. Prentice-Hall.

Raubolt, R.R., and Bratter, T.E., (1976). Treating the Methadone Addict: A Reality Therapy and Confrontation Orientation. In The Reality Therapy Reader. A.Bassin, T.E. Bratter, and R.L. Rachin (Eds.) (in press).

Raubold, R.R., and Bratter, T.E., (1974). Games Addicts Play: Implications for Treatment. <u>Corrective and Social Psychiatry.</u> 20:4. 3-10.

Raynes, A.E., and Patch, V.D., (1973). Improved Detoxification Techniques for Heroin Addicts. <u>Arch. Gen. Psychia.</u> 29. 417-419.

Razini, J., Chisholm, D., Glasser, M., and Kappeler, T., (1975). Self-Regulated Methadone Detoxification of Heroin Addicts. <u>Arch. Gen. Psychia.</u> 32:7. 909-911.

Riordan, C., and Rapkin, R., (1972). Detoxification as a Final Step in Treating the Successful Long-Term Methadone Patient. In <u>Proceedings of the Fourth National Conference on Methadone Treatment.</u> A. Goldstein (Ed.) NAPAN. 219-223.

Sloan, R.B., Cristol, A.H., and Pepernik, M.C., (1970). Role Preparation and Expectation of Improvement in Psychotherapy. <u>J. Nerv. Ment. Dis.</u> 150. 18-26.

AMITRIPTYLINE (ELAVIL) ABUSE IN PERSONS ON
CHRONIC METHADONE MAINTENANCE

Murry J. Cohen, M.D., Barry Stimmel, M.D.

Departments of Psychiatry and Medicine
Mount Sinai School of Medicine of
The City University of New York
New York, New York

Amitriptyline (Elavil) is frequently utilized in treating mild to moderate depressive states. A survey of 346 persons enrolled in a methadone program revealed 93 (27%) to have taken amitriptyline without prescription within a three-month period, with 92% of these persons ingesting the drug with the sole purpose of achieving euphoria (Table I). An euphoric state, described as similar to that produced by barbiturates or heroin, was readily able to be achieved in 75% of persons ingesting three or more tablets in a single dose (Table II). Amitriptyline abuse, previously unreported, is not an uncommon phenomenon and should be carefully considered prior to prescribing this agent to narcotic-dependent persons.

This study relates to a program funded by the New York State
Office of Drug Abuse Services

TABLE I

FREQUENCY OF AMITRIPTYLINE ABUSE WITHIN PAST SIX MONTHS

Frequency	No.	(%)
1	8	(16)
2	11	(22)
3-5	10	(20)
6-9	1	(2)
10-19	4	(8)
20 or	16	(32)
TOTAL	50	(100)

TABLE II

TYPE OF EUPHORIA EXPERIENCED WITH AMITRIPTYLINE

	No.	(%)
Similarity of Euphoric State		
Barbiturates and Related Drugs	24	(42)
Heroin	22	(39)
Alcohol	5	(9)
Marijuana	3	(6)
Amphetamines	2	(4)
Total Persons Experiencing Euphoria	56	(60)
No Euphoria Experienced	37	(40)

404

COMMITTEE OF CONCERNED METHADONE PATIENTS AND FRIENDS, INC.: OUR HISTORY AND OUR FUTURE

John Orraca
President, CCMP

Daniel Cattes
Board of Directors, CCMP

David Patterson, B.A.
Board of Directors, CCMP

Methadone maintenance programs have long been attacked by groups and individuals from one end of the political spectrum to the other, with conservatives, liberals, radicals and even middle-of-the roaders voicing strident objections. Such opposition has begun to emasculate methadone maintenance treatment and appears to be threatening its very existence. However, methadone programs do not experience the pain, frustration and suffering which results. Rather, it is the methadone maintenance patient who bears the brunt of the anti-methadone sentiment. It is the patient who has had nothing for most of his/her adult life, but who now strives to live the "normal life" society proclaims he/she should lead. However, being fired from a job one is qualified and competent to perform simply because one has chosen a particular mode of treatment, is most definitely not "normal". Nor is it "normal" to be denied life insurance, access to public housing or the right to hold certain licenses. Neither can it be "normal" for hospital administrators, business executives or law students, long free from illicit drug abuse, to have to "report" to a methadone maintenance clinic two or more times a week because federal and local regulations have applied the lowest common denominator to all patients - defining them as UNTRUSTWORTHY! However, simply recounting more obvious ways in which methadone maintenance patients encounter discrimination, does not tell the full story.

Methadone patients who are doing well must also accustom themselves to that common refrain, "When are you going to get off that stuff?". Unfortunately, those close to methadone patients cannot seem to make the perceptual connection between the program they criticize and the person they have come to love and admire or accept the chemotherapeutic orientation of the methadone maintenance program. The patient's friends and relatives read newspapers, watch television and listen to public figures who all seem to agree that methadone maintenance is something which should be eliminated, though research studies contain overwhelming evidence to the contrary, Therefore, it is not difficult to understand why patients are subjected to intense pressures. However, understanding a cause does not negate its effects. For example, the result of such pressures can often be an attempt at premature detoxification with disastrous consequences. Some patients live their lives under the constant fear of being "discovered". Such a situation presents a strange paradox as the former heroin addict should feel nothing but pride and dignity!

Finally, patients experience tremendous feelings of despair as they view the passivity of the methadone maintenance treatment programs and their reluctance to take up the banner of patient advocacy. For example, it seems easier for programs to contest governmental regulations that are economically burdensome than those which are oppressive to patients. As patients, we feel alone, exploited and at the mercy of any agency or individual bent on controlling or further restricting our lives.

Councils, coalitions and committees of every description abound, but rarely is the patient offered any meaningful position within such groups, or given the opportunity to be heard regarding his or her needs. The Committee of Methadone Patients and Friends, Inc., was born as a necessary vehicle whereby patients could regain their self-respect – the respect no one seems willing to afford us as a matter of right.

CCMP officially began its existence early in 1974, when several patients met to explore its possibilities. Within a few weeks, a Board of Directors had been named and an attorney had set in motion the mechanisms to obtain non-profit, tax-exempt status. The original members got down to the slow arduous task of building a viable, efficient and effective organization.

Methadone patients were several years older, wiser and more experienced in 1974, and were being very careful to learn from the mistakes of the past. Similar groups had made attempts at patient organization, but all had eventually failed. The Committee's Board of Directors realized that only by concentrating on first building a solid organizational structure, and by putting in the consistent hard work that this requires, could we hope to realize our long range goals. Therefore, throughout the two years of our existence, the focus of our energies has been in building a strong organizational structure. We did not undertake a massive membership drive, although the Committee membership has continued to grow. However, we did not neglect existing problems as we nurtured our organization. Thus, the C.C.M.P. has already accomplished many things which were not thought possible just a few short years ago.

Since its inception, the C.C.M.P. has made its influence felt and has been mentioned and discussed on television news programs, radio interview shows, various newspapers, Governor Carey's Task Force Report on Health (1975) and in the Community Service Society's report, Methadone Maintenance Treatment in N.Y.C. (S. Todd, NYS Committee on Youth and Correction, June 1975).

The Committee has organized and conducted a voter registration drive in selected areas of the City, which proved successful and has provided volunteers to help elect a public official in Brooklyn.

We have been successful in convincing New York City's public libraries not to purchase an "educational" film which presented a totally distorted view of methadone maintenance programs and patients, and provided substantial support to the plaintiffs in the important anti-employment discrimination landmark decision of Carl Beazer vs. New York City Transit Authority, 399 F. Supp. 1032 (1975). In addition, we have worked closely with an attorney associated with the A.C.L.U. to draft a Methadone Patient's Bill of Rights and have working arrangements with attorney groups including the Legal Action Office to whom we refer cases of alleged discrimination.

The Committee has members working closely with various federal and local officials including a State Senator's panel on penal reform and the Advisory Board of the National Drug Abuse Center for Training and Resource Development. In addition, we have submitted position papers to panels studying the New York State Drug Abuse Control Commission (now ODAS) from providing premixed medication to selected methadone maintenance clinics. This preparation often became unstable and caused nausea and other negative side effects. During the court proceedings, we received a committment that the preparation in question would not again be dispensed until proper adjustments in the formula had been made.

In February 1976, C.C.M.P. held its first annual social affair in a New York City nightclub which was attended by several hundred members and friends, and which was a tremendous success as attested to by an article in one of the community papers.

Although C.C.M.P. intends that patients continue to be its moving force, many members are not former addicts and associate membership and full participation is available to all concerned persons. The Committee has included in its membership and on its Advisory Board, a Federal Judge, a New York City Councilman, a State Senator, various medical professionals, including the directors of some of the major methadone maintenance programs, the Legal Action Office and Community Service Society.

The Committee is now looking to the future and to what we have left undone. Though we are limited by the constraints of this paper, we will briefly mention some of the areas on which we have begun concentrating. We hope to soon reach our goal of having patient and staff delegates in every methadone maintenance clinic in New York City, both to strengthen our City-wide structure and to act as our communications network and provide an efficient mechanism to deal with discrimination against patients. We hope to sit down with the supervisory staff of each methadone clinic in the City and persuade them to adopt some form of our Bill of Rights for patients and to endorse the concept of patient input into clinic policy. In addition, we have incorporated a sister political group, COMPEL, which will work for the election of candidates who are sympathetic to the needs of patients.

Now that our organizational structure is functioning efficiently, the C.C.M.P. will be launching a massive membership drive to encompass all of New York City's methadone patients and concerned citizens. We also hope to encourage ex-addicts from other treatment modalities to join hands with us to fight discrimination, which negatively affects all of us. We envision the creation of supportive, community-based groups for methadone patients similar in concept to Alcoholics' Anonymous.

Finally, we hope to launch an offensive to redirect the priorities of treatment programs, which now appear to be dictated by funding agencies, towards policies which give priority to patient rights and minimize the pressures which regulatory agencies now exert upon the programs. We hope to challenge the role of the regulatory agencies whose primary function is now unclear and encompasses the areas of funding, regulation, data collection and research.

We feel that the Committee's goals are complimentary to the interests of administrators of the various methadone maintenance programs and hope they will continue to work with us as many have in the past.

However, we will no longer leave our fate to others and will do what is appropriate and just regardless of whether others disagree with our point of view.

Perhaps, in the not-too-distant future, most of New York City's approximately 35,000 methadone maintenance patients will be able to proclaim their success openly and without fear of negative consequences.

USE OF ANTIDEPRESSANT MEDICATIONS IN
ADDICTS ON METHADONE MAINTENANCE

Francis Mas, M.D.

Unit Director, OPD 2-C
Beth Israel Medical Center
Methadone Maintenance Treatment Program
New York, New York

It is a common observation that many drug addicts use narcotics or "pills" or alcohol for relief of anxiety and/or depression.
Going further, as many as 20% of patients on methadone maintenance
seem to be afflicted with a chronic affective disorder severe e-
nough to interfere greatly with any form of counselling.

Only a minority of these patients present clear cut psychotic
symptoms, but it is not rare to find many on some form of antipsy-
chotic drug, if they are given anything. Consequently, many patients receive no treatment at all or end up fighting both the effects of a crippling illness and the side effects of anti-psychotic
drugs, not relieving them in the first place. They rarely remain
on any form of legal medication and predictably are often discharged from the clinic for chronic polydrug abuse and/or behavioral problems.

Given the fact that non-addicts suffering from depression of
various types: bipolar, unipolar, or neurotic have been known to
benefit from antidepressant medications we decided to explore their
use in a methadone maintenance clinic.

We were initially confronted with several questions:
1). Would the medication interfere with the methadone?

2). Would the additional use of a "pill" increase the sense of
chemical crutch and if successful defeat the purpose of counselling?

3). One common feature of all antidepressant medications is
their need to accumulate in the body long enough (usually three
weeks) before they become effective on the mood. Fortunately some
of them can stabilize sleep right away and we made use of that advantage. But, would heavy secondary abusers treated after a dry
out period, wait several weeks until the full effects of the medication could be felt?

4). Many staff members had ideological reservations as to the
use of "pills" in addition to methadone. How would their initial
attitude interfere with the therapeutic program?

We decided to limit ourselves to the Tricyclics antidepressants, using their secondary characteristics: of sedation as in Sinequan and Elavil; mild activation as in Tofranil and clear activation as in Norpramin and Vivactil; this in relation to patients initial symptomatology. We also added Triavil whose combination of a Phenothiazine and a Tricyclic could be useful in agitated cases.

Dosage range was flexible, 25mg. to 200mg. a day for Doxepin, Amitryptiline and Imipramine; 2mg to 20mg. a day for the Trilafon.

In order to be eligible for receiving a Tricyclic, a patient had to be:
        -medically healthy
        -free of addiction to drugs other than
        narcotics
        -Significantly and chronically troubled
        by symptoms interferring with and not
        responding to counselling.
Most frequently they were:
        -marked insomnia, chronic anxiety,
        depression(particularly early morning
        depression), chronic irritability with
        outburst, apathy and chronic fatigue; either
        alone or in combination.

In order to evaluate the outcome each patient was rated initially and after at least one month of treatment. The patient's counsellor, the clinic nurse and the medicating physician made independent evaluation using clinical criterias. Patients were rated as either "Not improved," "Somewhat improved" or "Improved." "Not improved" meant there was no perceived change in the initial syndrome. "Somewhat improved" showed partial results with an initial improvement of symptoms and social adjustment followed by a plateau. "Improved" signified a clear cut improvement with the patient remaining free of the initial symptomatology and responding well to counselling.

Each patient who had been on a Tricyclic for more than a month was given a self evaluating questionnaire.

All patients who had to be discontinued within one month of treatment due to persistent secondary abuses or for any other reasons were recorded as dropouts.

Altogether 55 patients were initiated on a Tricyclic. Eleven dropped out which leaves 44 patients who had been in treatment for more than a month.

The patient's subjective feelings as reported in the self rating questionnaire showed to be surprisingly positive in more than 80% of the cases but the objective appraisal of the staff was much more sober.

The counsellors found 25 patients "improved," 11 "somewhat improved" and 8 "not improved."

For the nurses 27 patients had improved, 6 were "somewhat improved," and 10 "not improved."

The treating physician rated 26 "improved," 8 "somewhat improved," and 11 "not improved."

Averaging those results, one finds that after at least one month on a Tricyclic 59% of patients were evaluated improved, 18% somewhat improved, and 23% not improved.

If we include the initial drop outs and consider the whole population, 47% of patients have improved, 14% have somewhat improved, and 39% remain not improved.

We did not find an apparent interaction with the given dosage of methadone. If anything, Tricyclics seemed to stabilize patients who tended initially to interpret their symptoms as "withdrawal symptoms" and requested an increased dosage of methadone.

No particular side effects were noted with the exception of some cholinergic symptoms that remained well within the tolerable limits.

Few attempted abuses of the Tricyclics occurred. Surprisingly (particularly to some staff members) several patients requested to be taken off the Tricyclic medication once stabilization had occurred.

No dependence on Tricyclics was noted.

We are aware of the limitations of the present study which does not involve a double blind evaluation and uses non-standardized clinical rating scales. Nevertheless, we feel that it has some practical value.

Based on our present experience we reserve the prescription of Tricyclics antidepressants to severe symptoms interfering with the patient's life and not responding to counselling alone.

Usually most of these patients when untreated are either subsequently discharged or are a chronic problem mobilizing counsellor's time and energy for only marginal results.

At this point, we still lose or are unable to help 1/3 of these patients but are able to work with the remaining 2/3, more than half of which responding very well.

TRANSFERENCE PHENOMENA IN THE TREATMENT OF
ADDICTIVE ILLNESS

Virginia Davidson, M.D.

Baylor College of Medicine
Houston, Texas

Wilfred Bion observed that "society, like the individual, may not want to deal with its stresses by psychological means until driven to do so by a realization that at least some of its distresses are psychological in origin." (1) After more than a decade of experience in methadone maintenance, there is now widespread acknowledgmend that attempts to treat heroin addiction by chemical means alone have failed. (2). Even so, the introduction of each new chemical is associated with an eagerness to discard the previous experience gained concerning the need for psychologic intervention, and hope emerges for a brief time that the new drug alone will produce a cure. This cycle has now operated through the introduction of methadone, long acting methadone, and each one of the narcotic antagonists. The wish to locate the cure for the addictive illness outside the patient's psyche is very strong in the persons who have been engaged in drug abuse research and treatment over the past ten years.

In this paper I shall describe certain recurring patterns of behavior which I observed in methadone maintenance patients in a clinic setting. I shall relate these patterns to the descriptions in the psychoanalytic literature of ego defense mechanisms, and draw certain parallels between the behavior I observed in the clinic with the descriptions of transference phenomena which have been observed in the psychoanalysis of patients with boderline personality organization. (3). Other writers (4,5) have called attention to the primitive nature of the defenses in addicted patients. Wurmser, (6) has added much to the understanding of compulsive drug use by relating it to "narcissistic crises" in the lives of the individual drug abuser. Yet most of the psychological treatment of addicts is left to persons who have little knowledge and experience in psychotherapy. The best forms of psychotherapy are not available to addicts, partly because of the process that involves denying that addictive illness has psychological origins, but also because of the extremely trying nature of therapy with borderline patients whether or not they are not addicted to heroin.

Transference is a term which implies that the patient's behavior at a given moment in treatment is determined more by his very early experiences with significant others than by the reality stimulus of the present setting. Whenever there are rapid shifts in the way patients perceive others, whenever strong affective states such as love or hatred are predominant, (and especially when there is rapid alternation between the two), and whenever there is a powerful projection of hostile, aggressive impulses from the patient to someone else, it is likely that transference phenomena are present.

The behavior of methadone patients in the clinic setting is remarkable in several respects when compared with the behavior of other groups of psychiatric patients whose treatment utilizes the out-patient format. I shall focus on three observable differences in the clinic behavior of the methadone patients, and shall comment on the difficulties each one presents for staff management in the out-patient methadone maintenance clinic. I believe that these patterns of behavior are related to the ego defense mechanisms of splitting, projective identification, and denial which have been described in the psychoanalytic literature dealing with the treatment of borderline patients, even though the behavior described here is occurring in the context of an out-patient clinic.

The first pattern of behavior involves the <u>manifestation in the clinic setting of extreme affects</u>, which appear to be inappropriate to the reality stimulus of the moment. These affective states are usually characterized by extreme rage; for example, murderous hatred can be expressed by a patient toward a dispensing nurse who does not ready the medication as soon as the patient expects it. This expression of rage is limited to the situation in which it emerged; the patient does not carry the feeling over to everyone else he/she encounters. Feelings of contrition and remorse are likely to follow closely the expression of hatred and rage. What is familiar to workers in methadone is the rapidity with which patients can oscillate between extreme states of feeling. The patient has diminished capacity to modulate feelings, so must swing back and forth between strong positive and negative affects.

Problems for staff in relating to this aspect of the addicted patient's personality are enormous. Expression of strong hostility, anger, and blamefulness in patients arouses equally strong emotions in staff, whose common response is to retaliate - overtly or covertly - against the patient. In physicians, this is most commonly expressed through the dosage of methadone, since this is the medium through which most patient-physician contacts occur. All of us know patients who manage to alienate the staff one-by-one, then find themselves removed from the program for violations of one sort or another. The staff may not be aware of this process, and may

deny feeling hostility and suppressed rage toward the patient.   In
a well-run program this process of retaliation can be minimized by
enlightened supervision, ideally by someone <u>outside</u> the treatment
system.   Related to retaliation as a means of coping with the patient's tendency to experience strong emotions separately and intensely (splitting), is pairing. Patients "select" a staff member
with whom they establish a dependent, demanding, and clinging relationship. Few negative emotions are channeled into this relationship, but rather are expressed in strong dislikes for and refusals to deal with other staff. The "chosen" staff person becomes
the patient's advocate in all matters relating to progress and
performance, and may at times jealously protect the patient from
having contact with other staff. While patient'staff pairing may
be less destructive for the patient than retaliation, in that it
allows some patients to remain in treatment through thick and thin,
it cannot be therapeutic for the patient unless it carries some
generalizability to other relationships. As long as the therapist
is obtaining gratification from the "specialness" of the relationship, this is not likely to occur.

    Second is the <u>expectation on the part of patients that they
will be unfairly dealt with by treatment personnel, and an associated tendency to perceive the external environment as hostile and
threatenting</u>, regardless of what the actual circumstances are. Because addicts live dangerous lives, and because they are frequently incarcerated or are being implicated in criminal activities, we
assume it is reasonable for them to behave in a suspicious, guarded,
and untrusting manner when they come to treatment. While this kind
of explanation might possibly account for the addict's initial
problems in relating to the staff, it cannot begin to account for
the persistent incapacities in forming trusting relationships that
exist for years after the patient has begun treatment.

    The task of providing the necessary ingredients for a thera-
peutic alliance to be established with the patient is difficult
when the patient's problems are manifest in qualities that appear
to make this primary task impossible. Effective staff must maintain the capacity to be empathetic toward the patient; the patient,
however, behaves in such a way toward "helping" people that this
empathic quality in staff is always undermined and jeopardized.
All therapists must maintain a sense of their own worth and value;
they must have self-esteem and a sense that the work they do with
patients "matters." Yet when the patient's style of relating involves projecting onto others the intensely aggresive, hostile, and
negative impulses felt inside, the therapist receives constant messages that he/she is being aggressive, hostile, and unsympathetic
toward the patient. With problems of this magnitude, not to become
locked into an equally hostile countertransference relationship is
a monumental task for the best-trained therapists; for the untrained
and unskilled, it is impossible.

Last, is the <u>denial of entire segments of reality, especially involving behavior concerning drug usage; related forms of denial are evident in the need patients demonstrate to appear impervious to the impact methadone maintenance has on their lives</u>. Patients commonly express the belief that <u>they</u> are in control of their drug usage; they actually believe that they will be able to withdraw from methadone at the future time of their own choosing, even if previous attempts have resulted in quick relapse to heroin. Denial, in the psychological sense, is most often confused by staff with conscious lying and manipulation. While addicted patients certainly have in common with other patients the habits of lying and manipulation, it is impressive to what extent the latter explanations are used by staff members to account for patients' behavior. The gruff, loud, and complaining behavior that patients exhibit toward appointments often covers up the desperate fear patients have about emotional contact with another person. Their apparent superficial involvement in counseling is often interpreted by staff as "low motivation." Grumbling about having to keep appointments, complaints about the time lost in the clinic, and especially assertions that the counseling relationship is a waste of time, may mask the patient's terror of involvement. What masquerades as a devil-may-care attitude toward the clinic may represent massive denial of the importance of the clinic in the patient's life. Much of this "difficult" behavior is seen as part of a constellation of undesireable social characteristics attributed to addicted patients. Staff may try to eradicate this behavior through elaboration and enforcement of clinic rules with the hope that the patient will become more compliant, and then amenable to therapy. This is somewhat akin to stating that if the patient did not have psychological problems he/she would be easier to treat.

The behavior we see in the patient is the manifestation of his/her problems in living, and is not an artifact of either the clinic setting or of the addicted patient's socio-cultural background. The problems which this behavior presents for the treatment of addicted patients are considerable, and are similar to the problems encountered whenever the treatment of any borderline patient is undertaken. Understanding negative transferences can lead to effective management, and to the prevention of transference psychoses. It is crucial to protect and nurture the positive transference relationships that develop; for many patients it is easier first to establish a positive bond with the clinic than with a counselor. Whenever clinics are structured in such a way that this is an unreasonable expectation, treatment prospects remain glum.

REFERENCES

1. Bion, W. (1949). <u>Experiences in Groups</u>. Basic Books, N.Y., p.22.

2. Goldstein, A. (1976). Heroin Addiction. <u>Arc. Gen. Psyc.</u> 33,353-358.

3. Kernberg, O. (1975). <u>Borderline Conditions and Pathological Narcissism</u>. Jason Aronson, N.Y.

4. Khantzian, E., Mack, J., and Schtzberg, A. (1974). Heroin Use As An Attempt to Cope: Clinical Observations. Amer. J. of Psy. 131:2, 160-164.

5. Vaillant, G. (1975). Sociopathy As A Human Process. Arc. Gen. Psyc. 32, 178-183.

6. Wurmser, L. (1974). Psychoanalytic Considerations of the Etiology of Compulsive Drug Use. <u>J. Amer. Psychoanal. Assoc</u>. 22:4, 820-843.

HUMANISTIC MANAGEMENT OF THE TREATMENT OF NARCOTIC ADDICTED PERSONS: THE HEALING PARTNERSHIP

Robert B. Kahn, Ph.D.

Deputy Director, Narcotic Abuse Treatment Program
San Diego County

N. T. Schramm

Program Director, Narcotic Abuse Treatment Program
San Diego County

In 1965, Vincent Dole, an internist and biochemist, and Marie Nyswander, a psychiatrist, offered a "progress report" of their treatment of a very select group of 22 patients previously addicted to diacetylmorphine (heroin), stabilized with oral methadone hydrochloride using dosages ranging from 50 to 180 milligrams. They further reported that this treatment resulted in the "disappearance of narcotic hunger" and "induction of sufficient tolerance to block the euphoric effect of an average illegal dose of diacetylmorphine" (Dole and Nyswander, 1965).

Ausubel (1966) subsequently criticized Dole and Nyswander's report stating, "There is no pretense of simply using a maintenance dose, which by definition is the smallest dose necessary to prevent withdrawal symptoms" when patients are "stabilized" at 100 to 180 mgms. daily. Furthermore, "If they truly consider this only a 'progress report' how do they explain the unqualified conclusions stated at the end of the article and how do they reconcile the three feature articles in Look (1965) and the New Yorker (1965) obviously prepared with their consent and cooperation, with the tentative nature of a progress report?" And finally, "Millions of people throughout the United States have been led to believe by these mass circulation journals that the menace of drug addiction is now comparable to that posed by poliomyelitis after the discovery of the scrupulously tested oral vaccine against that latter disease".

In part, as the result of the Dole and Nyswander study, reinforced by the lay literature, heralding the panacea for the eradication of heroin addiction, the treatment communities' expectations as to what might be accomplished with methadone have been totally unrealistic.

We have been attempting to treat persons chronically addicted to a narcotic believing these persons to be statistically psycho-dynamically deviant from the "normal" society when some data suggests otherwise (Leighton, 1956, and Strole, 1962) and do the impossible, extinguish the dependency on narcotics of these persons "afflicted".

This paper addresses what the authors feel is a more practical and reasonable approach to the handling of the narcotic abuse problem.

The program where this approach has been implemented is located in San Diego, California, where a change of administration has taken place within the last nine months.

HISTORY OF THE SAN DIEGO NARCOTIC TREATMENT PROGRAM

Methadone treatment in San Diego County was initiated by the Department of Psychiatry, University of California, San Diego, in 1969. Initially, the program operated out of the University Hospital. In 1970, the University entered into an agreement with San Diego County to operate the County's first and only methadone maintenance program. The program had an original capacity of 298 clients (48 residential and 250 outpatient). The residential treatment facility closed in October 1974.

During the month of January 1975, Touche Ross & Co., a certified public accounting firm, completed a management review of the San Diego County Narcotic Treatment Program. The management review reports that clients were offered services at four clinic sites, including a central intake-stabilization facility, and three outpatient methadone maintenance clinics. Additionally, "During our review, we found that the program's static matrix capacity was uncertain. We contacted NIDA personnel in Los Angeles. They indicated that currently there is a verbal agreement between NIDA, San Diego County, and the University that the client capacity is 420 outpatient clients."

Funding was from two sources - the National Institute on Drug Abuse and the County. $1,055,598 was earmarked for clinical programming, $54,048 for program evaluation, and $165,000 for administrative costs." The total was $1,274,646. "During our review, we analyzed the cost per client year. The average client census figures for the review period, July through December 1974, were divided into annualized costs to arrive at an annual cost per client of $2,574 which is substantially above the NIDA guideline cost per client ($1,700). We included the costs from the residential facility which was open a short time. We do not consider the effect of these costs to be material."

THE NARCOTIC ABUSE TREATMENT PROGRAM TODAY

The administrative responsibility of the Narcotic Abuse Treatment Program was assumed by Teledyne Economic Development Co., July 1975, who successfully responded to a request for proposals from San Diego County. At present, the budget is $999,847. There exists three outpatient methadone maintenance clinics with a matrix of 480 clients, a 10-client detoxification treatment modality, and a Residential Treatment Facility with 20 residents.

The administration of the Narcotic Abuse Treatment Program has been involved in methadone treatment long enough to recognize some unique problems confronting this particular modality, setting it apart from other health delivery systems. First and foremost, the unrealistic expectation placed upon this modality to "cure" the afflicted. Most dramatically, we are mandated to treat persons who are legally and morally unacceptable and who may or may not be medically or psychiatrically dysfunctional and yet we are armed only with only medical and psychological technology to deal with them.

It is our position that if an individual were to commit a crime, that individual should be dealt with by the criminal justice system. Therefore, it is our position that any individual whom we come in contact with is ours to deal with in ways which we feel are consonant with his and the community's best interests. Our society, at this point, may choose one of two alternatives when considering what to do with those dependent on narcotics: (1) to murder them or (2) to handle them in a way consonant with the present attitudes and concerns of society. The first alternative being unacceptable, we are then left with the second alternative.

Any discussion of medical or psychotherapy with regard to this population is academic, if we do not have the facilities and staff to offer services. The community at large is fed up with anyone on the dole, their feeling being that they are as entitled as anyone to some benefits. Their taxes are high, the prices confronting them in the supermarkets are outrageous, and their patience is on the wane. Therefore, our first priority is economics.

As indicated previously, the University of California at San Diego spent $2,574 per methadone maintenance client per year. By contrast, if we subtract $100,000 from the $999,847 budget, which includes the Residential Treatment Facility, a balance of $899,847 is the actual annual budget for the outpatient clinics. Using a matrix of 480 outpatients receiving services, the cost per client year is $1,875, or a savings of $699 per patient per year, or in other words, an overall annual savings to the community of $335,520.

It is our position that all we need to say at this point in our history when comparing ourselves to the expense of penal institutions, rehabilitation centers, residential treatment facilities, inpatient services, detoxification treatment modalities, is "We do no worse than any modality and we do it for less money." The second priority is community relations.

After all the community taxpayer is concerned with (1) getting the most for his dollar, and (2) to be satisfied with the type of service offered. Specifically, a service that does not disrupt his or her normal existence. To this end, the Narcotic Abuse Treatment Program has done several things. First of all, when individuals are diagnosed by the criminal justice system and being served by the medical/psychological community, it is no wonder that methadone programs are characterized by an air of hostility and ongoing confrontation.

Often, methadone staffs are forced into the position of being custodians and extensions of the criminal justice system. So-called patients appear to be victims coerced into "treatment", the alternative being the coroner's roster or incarceration. Since this modality in and of itself promotes a suppressive condition, we reduce negativity to its minimum. We decided rather than setting arbitrary parameters, i.e., an individual being positive for opiates so many times would be terminated from the program, or that we would decide what amount of methadone an individual needs, etc., that (1) we would ignore urinalysis for all practical purposes. After all, for a person to meet the requirements for this type of treatment, we are assured that he or she is chronically abusing narcotics and to spend millions of dollars reaffirming the fact that dope fiends shoot dope is wasteful. Secondly, to discuss how much methadone we should give an individual makes us more akin to the dope dealer than to the treater. Therefore, individuals adjust their own dosages, as has been shown to be appropriate (Goldstein, 1974). The only way in which an individual will be denied services from the Narcotic Abuse Treatment Program in San Diego is if he sells or uses heroin on the clinic premises or engages in an overt violent act.

Treatment

The staff matrix of the Narcotic Abuse Treatment Program in-corporates as many people at various levels of expertise as is economically feasible. We have hired both degreed and non-degreed professionals. The female/male mix reflects the 70% male, 30% female addict population in treatment. Additionally, naive individuals (relative to substance abuse treatment experience) asking those embarrassing questions, and persons with primarily formal education and discipline who can offer theoretical positions to compliment the ex-addict's street experience are recruited. This mix offers clients the opportunity to select a person with whom they can most easily relate to to begin the therapeutic process.

In addition, there are specific procedures that we follow to encourage a healthy environment. We attempt to spread the dosing schedule over the day as much as possible. We are open 11 hours a day. We have a physician in attendance eight hours a day. We try to reduce paperwork to its absolute minimum. We have a computer statistics form that is incorporated into the ongoing activity of the clinic. The form allows the counselor the opportunity to record all of the variables pertinent to his or her caseload. The form is submitted on a monthly basis to the administration who returns a printout to the individual counselor, reinforcing and encouraging reliable reporting. We have the capability of sorting information requested by staff. For example, we can sort time in treatment by opiate positive rates, etc. This inexpensive (less than $2,000 a year) capability supplies us with a unique data base that is reliable and saves valuable time when preparing monthly and quarterly reports. This is an example of what we are doing to create a supportive milieu, allowing the time for healthy therapeutic involvements.

A client is entitled to services. Clients coming in for service receive the best medical, legal, and psychological counseling we can offer. Contrasted to mental health settings where at times it is necessary to create hurdles for individuals to better demonstrate their motivation, we attempt to seduce our clients into utilizing our services. The milieu created encourages individuals to contact persons they have a high degree of affinity for and gradually reach out to others who were at first less acceptable.

Tentative results of research underway suggests that this population is no more deviant than the community at large. We concluded that the hiring of psychiatrists and psychologists is economically wasteful and possibly undermines the intent of this service system. After nine months of operation with no psychiatric or psychological staff per se, we have only referred one client for psychiatric consultation. Our belief is that the environment is crucial with regard to encouragement or discouragement of psychopathology and that if psychopathology is not tolerated, its manifestation will be minimal.

We do not neglect the client. We have staff meetings around particular cases and we devise reinforcement systems that might encourage clients to take risks and involve themselves more fully. However, at the administrative level, we do not coerce or otherwise pressure the counselor to shrink or even squeeze the heads of their clients or to "clean 'em up". As a result of this, staff morale is high and their availability is maximized by their lack of frustration which often characterizes the staff of most facilities attempting to do the impossible.

General Discussion

The Narcotic Abuse Treatment Program in San Diego is administered by a team of managers who believe that a safe environment need be created and that persons who are presently dependent on narcotics are not necessarily mentally ill and who may be in treatment primarily because they are found to be legally and morally unacceptable. It is our responsibility to serve the community in a way consonant with their expectations: (1) economically, (2) minimally disruptive, and (3) offering the best services available, in that order.

We are treating a single client for almost $700 less than that client was treated for one year ago and a substantial waiting list exists as well. The community at large feels that they now have a viable alternative to incarceration and the revolving door court/ treatment scene characterizing the community for many years because of a program unwilling to accept the addicts' behavior or tolerate their continued use of illicit substances. The treatment program is characterized by an organization that decentralizes administration, has specific lines of communication, and a healthy interaction of paraprofessionals and professional staff both degreed and non-degreed. De-emphasizing urinalysis and methadone dispensing has allowed individuals to become more interested in themselves and discuss issues more relevant to their health and progress.

Within the milieu, the individual counselor has a caseload of 40 persons. Initially, twenty of these are interested in counseling, ten are ambivalent, and ten might best be characterized by a "go to hell" attitude. In time, as those persons in the original 20 group find that they are gaining information, those who are ambivalent enter into that group, and those that were initially totally resistant become ambivalent. We are beginning to realize a shift from the "go to hell" group into the wanting counseling group because we show respect for each individual and offer information that they are asking for and can utilize immediately. This is now taking place in each clinic and as the program expands this notion, it becomes more of a force in the community at large, attracting more and more persons.

It is our belief that there exists approximately 100,000 persons in California presently addicted to narcotics. We have data suggesting that over $5 million could be saved in California a year if we were to provide a proper service system for narcotic dependent persons (Sackman, 1975). All we claim is that we are doing no worse for less money than the program that was previously operated in San Diego County. In addition, we offer the following for your consideration.

Final Statement

Dole and Nyswander offered counseling but reported "No specific psychiatric treatment was provided... There has, however, been very little need for psychotherapy, and no indication that structured group therapy would contribute to rehabilitation." (Dole and Nyswander, 1967). Without it they reported 94% success in ending criminal activity of former heroin addicts (Dole et al., 1968) rivaling our outcome today.

Additionally, Dole and Nyswander reported a theory of the
existence of a metabolic basis for heroin addiction (Dole and
Nyswander, 1967) which might be assumed was their rationale for
de-emphasizing psychotherapy. Today, evidence suggests the existence of what has been called "endorphin" which is reported to be
"a normally occurring morphine-mimicking chemical in the brain"
(Snyder, 1976) re-introducing the biochemical or physiological
feature of the addiction pattern.

It seems that we still do not know if we are dealing with an
"addictive personality" or a metabolic disorder, but we do know as
Blachly (1970) demonstrated that equally successful outcomes can
be the result when psychotherapy is not emphasized.

In any case, are we not working in an emergency room as contrasted to an operating room? Should we not just stop the bleeding
and quit worrying about building a new person? And finally, if
there is no place to treat this person even after you stop the
bleeding, where is he going when you involuntarily terminate him?

Discharges

University of California, San Diego
Administration
(July 1 - December 1974)

Reason	#	%
Staff Decision	69	22
Split	151	47
Patient request	19	6
Jail	39	12
Left Area	22	7
Hospitalized	7	2
Graduated	9	3
Death	3	1
Total	319	100

Teledyne Economic Development Co.
Administration
(July 1 - December 1975)

Reason	#	%
Violation of Rules	1	.7
Split	55	40
Patient Request	8	6
Jail	41	30
Left Area	3	2
Hospitalized	0	0
Completed Treatment	25	18
Death	4	3
Total	137	100

REFERENCES

Ausubel, David P., "The Dole-Nyswander Treatment of Heroin Addiction," JAMA, Vol. 195, No. 11, March 14, 1966.

Blachly, Paul H., "The Simplest Methadone Blockade Treatment Program," presented at the A.P.A. Meetings, San Francisco, May 1970.

Dole, Vincent P. and Nyswander, Marie, "A Medical Treatment for Diacetylmorphine (Heroin) Addiction, A Clinical Trial with Methadone Hydrochloride," JAMA, Vol. 193, No. 8, August 23, 1965.

Dole, Vincent P. and Nyswander, Marie, "Heroin Addiction - A Metabolic Disease," Arch Intern Med, Vol. 120, July 1967.

Dole, Vincent P. et al., "Successful Treatment of 750 Criminal Addicts," JAMA, Vol. 206, No. 12, December 16, 1968.

Goldstein, Avram et al., "Control of Methadone Dosage by Patients," Proceedings, First National Drug Abuse Conference, New York, 1974.

Leighton, D. C., "The Distribution of Psychiatric Symptoms in a Small Town," American Journal of Psychiatry, 112, 716-723, 1956.

Sackman, Bertram S. and Sackman, M. Maxine, "The Incidence and Prevalence of Nonmedical Drug Use in Los Angeles County." Study conducted for the County of Los Angeles, Agreement No. 24033, March 17, 1975.

Sackman, Bertram S., "The Public Cost of Treating Heroin Addicts," presented to the California Conference of Methadone Programs, Oakland, June 12, 1975.

Snyder, Sol H., The Journal, Vol. 5, #1, 1976.

Strole, L. T. et al., "Mental Health in the Metropolis: The Midtown Manhattan Study." New York: McGraw-Hill, 1962.

Touche Ross & Co., "San Diego County Narcotics Treatment Program Management Review," January 31, 1975.

INTERPERSONAL TRUST AND HEROIN ABUSE

James C. Ungerer,[1] Robert J. Harford,[1] Bruce Kleinhans,[2]
Randall S. Coloni[2]

[1]Department of Psychiatry
Yale University School of Medicine
100 Park Street
New Haven, Connecticut   06511

[2]Addiction-Prevention Treatment Foundation, Inc.
100 Park Street
New Haven, Connecticut   06511

I.   INTRODUCTION

Interpersonal trust has been defined as the expectancy "that the word, promise, verbal or written statement of another individual or group can be relied upon" (1). Trust may be important to therapeutic outcomes. According to Carney (2), "the therapeutic relationship is a trusting relationship," and many clinicians believe that trust between therapist and client is essential for therapeutic success (3, 4, 5).

If interpersonal trust is necessary for successful therapy, rehabilitation of individuals who are predisposed to low trust might be especially problematic. In rehabilitating criminals, Rappaport (6) found that trust was the most persistent obstacle in his therapy groups. Criminals were predisposed to discuss safe and nonproductive topics because they did not believe either the therapist's promises of confidentiality or his therapeutic communications. Rappaport concluded that effort and ingenuity were required to establish the essential atmosphere of interpersonal trust with criminals.

Several clinical and anecdotal reports characterize opiate abusers as distrustful and untrustworthy (7, 8, 9, 10). If this view is accurate, opiate abusers pose especially difficult treatment problems because an essential element for rehabilitation is absent. In fact, treatment for opiate dependence has had disappointing results (11, 12, 13). The therapeutic recalcitrance of opiate abusers may be partly due to their reluctance to engage in trusting relationships.

Empirical evidence also suggests that opiate abusers are low in trust. Capel and Caffrey (14) compared attitudes of heroin addicts with those of other deviant and non-deviant comparison groups. Although it was not directed at this issue, their study suggested that the heroin abusers were more distrusting.

We investigated trust in opiate abusers using the Rotter Interpersonal Trust Scale (1). This instrument measures the generalized expectancy that the oral or written promises of others are reliable. It has been used in laboratory settings, peer groups ratings, and questionnaires. Low trusters distrust experimenters (15) and peers in experimental games (16, 17). They are less trustworthy (tell more lies) in experimental debriefing sessions (18), and are rated by their peers as less trusting and less trustworthy (1). This evidence suggests that the Rotter scale is a valid instrument for measuring interpersonal trust. We compared the levels of interpersonal trust in opiate abusers, abusers of other drugs, and college and non-college comparison groups.

II. METHOD

A total of 310 persons seeking treatment for drug dependence completed the Interpersonal Trust Scale. Testing was conducted during intake to the Drug Dependence Unit of the Connecticut Mental Health Center in New Haven. Applicants who had participated in treatment programs or who had been incarcerated during the preceding six months were excluded from this study. The testing procedure was presented as voluntary research directed towards helping the clinics improve the quality of treatment. Applicants were assured confidentiality and were told that their performance would not influence their treatment status. Five applicants refused to participate.

III. RESULTS

The majority of the respondents were White (62.9%), males (75.2%) and dependent on opiates (60.6%). Their mean age was 23.2 years. The group of 188 opiate dependents differed significantly from the group of 122 who were not dependent upon opiates with respect to race and age but not sexual composition. A total of 49% of the opiate dependents were White as compared with 80% of the non-dependent comparison group ($x^2 = 27.4$; $df = 1$; $p < .001$). The opiate dependents were significantly older than the comparison group (24.8 years versus 20.7 years; $t = 8.09$; $df = 308$; $p < .001$).

Race and sex differences in trust scores were not statistically significant. The correlation between age and trust was small but statistically significant ($r = -.133$; $p < .01$), suggesting that older applicants were likely to be less trusting than younger applicants. Since age was related to both trust and opiate dependence, it was necessary to assess the separate effects of age and opiate dependence upon trust. A 4-way factorial analysis of variance was performed in which Age, Opiate-dependence, Sex and Race were entered as independent variables. The latter two variables were included in order to investigate the possibility of interaction effects with Race and Age. Age was dichotomized at the median for each of the eight Sex X Race X Opiate-dependence cells of the design. The analysis of variance indicated a significant Opiate-dependence main effect on trust (F = 7.99; df = 1,294; $p < .01$) such that applicants who were dependent upon opiates were less trusting (61.4) than those who were not dependent upon opiates (64.6). This relationship was not related to differences in age and racial composition between the two groups, since none of the interactions was statistically significant.

Relative to opiate dependents, the mean trust score of non-opiate abusers was closer to those of four college samples (66.4, 64.4, 63.8, 65.8) recently reported (19). Furthermore, the mean trust score of opiate abusers would be included in the lowest one-third of the college trust distribution while the mean trust score of the non-opiate drug abusers would be included in the middle-third of that distribution (20). Opiate abusers also were lower in trust than delinquent girls (66.4) reported by Karoly (21).

IV. DISCUSSION

Opiate abusers were significantly lower in trust than applicants who abused other drugs. They also were less trusting than samples of college students and delinquent girls. Non-opiate abusers were similar in trust to the college and delinquent comparison groups.

The reasons for the relationship between trust and opiate abuse are unclear. Our analyses suggest that, despite a low negative correlation with trust, age is not an important explanatory factor. One possible explanation is that low trusters are predisposed to opiate use. Perhaps low trust results in heightened anxiety, and low trusters find the anxiety-reducing effects of opiates rewarding. High trusters may find opiates less rewarding and either discontinue use of these drugs or limit usage to non-addictive levels. Another explanation is that heroin dependence decreases interpersonal trust. Kamstra (9) observed that:

> Heroin. . . always seems to involve a lack of trust.
> Perhaps it's the nature of the drug itself; anything
> that creates such a need in the body, a need that has
> to be satisfied at all costs, is inherently dangerous.

One way to investigate this possibility would be to compare trust scores with duration of use. Decreases in trust with increased use would support the hypothesis that opiate abuse itself generates low trust. Another approach would be to conduct longitudinal studies with high risk adolescent populations. If low trust predisposes individuals to opiate abuse, low trusters might be more likely to begin using opiates than individuals who are high in trust.

Regardless of the reasons, low trust in opiate abusers has rehabilitative implications. Therapy depends upon communication. If communication is hampered by distrust of therapists, chances for successful rehabilitation are low. Opiate abusers may be especially likely to view therapy merely as an opportunity to provide relief from legal pressure, medical and financial assistance, and accessible chemical substitutes for opiates. This cynical perspective may shield opiate abusers from the difficult alterations of attitudes and behaviors which may be necessary for their rehabilitation.

Low trust in opiate abusers also may have adverse implications for the validity of their communications to treatment personnel. They may be more suspicious of ulterior motives and be more likely to falsify information in order to protect themselves against suspected risks. This possibility implies that important information should be corroborated by other sources wherever possible.

Our findings have implications for theories of drug abuse, since they support the hypothesis that opiate abusers are lower in trust than non-opiate drug abusers as well as other segments of the population. The reasons for this relationship are not well understood and suggestions presented here are rudimentary. Because the traditional viewpoint has found empirical support, however, more effort should be made to investigate the relationship between interpersonal trust and opiate use. These investigations may improve our understanding of the psychological dynamics of addiction and, perhaps, lead to more effective therapeutic interventions.

This research was supported in part by grants from the National Institute of Drug Abuse: DA 01097 and DA 16356.

REFERENCES

1. J. B. Rotter, J. Personality, 35:651 (1967).
2. F. Carney, Amer. J. Psychother., 220 (1975).
3. M. Deutsch, J. Conflict Resol., 2:265 (1958).
4. F. Friedlander, J. Applied Beh. Sc., 6:387 (1970).
5. C. Rogers, Harv. Educ. Rev., 32:416 (1962).
6. R. Rappaport, Int. J. Psychother., 21:489 (1971).
7. E. Brecher, Licit and Illicit Drugs, Tittle, Brown, Boston, 1972.
8. H. Christian, Osler's Principles and Practice of Medicine, 15th Edit., Appleton-Century, New York, 1944.
9. J. Kamstra, Weed: Adventures of a Dope Smuggler, Bantam Books, New York, 1975.
10. L. Kolb, in Drug Addiction: A Medical Problem, Thomas, Springfield, Illinois, 1962.
11. B. Fangenauer and C. Bowden, Amer. J. Psychiat., 128:41 (1971).
12. B. Levy, Amer. J. Psychiat., 128:868 (1972).

13. M. Perkins and H. Bloch, Amer. J. Psychiat., 128:47 (1971).
14. W. Capel and B. Caffrey, Psychol. Rep., 35:859 (1974).
15. M. D. Roberts, Unpublished Masters Thesis, University of Conn., 1967.
16. B. R. Schlencker, B. Helm, and J. T. Tedeschi, J. Personal. Soc. Psychol., 25:419 (1973).
17. T. L. Wright, Unpublished Doctoral Dissertation, University of Conn., 1972.
18. J. D. Geller, Unpublished Doctoral Dissertation, University of Conn., 1966.
19. T. L. Wright and R. G. Tedeschi, J. Consult. Clin. Psychol., 43:4 (1975).
20. D. J. Hochreich, J. Personal., 42:543 (1974).
21. P. Karoly, Psychol. Rep., 36:571 (1975).

VARIABLES RELATED TO LENGTH OF STAY IN A
PSYCHIATRIC DRUG REHABILITATION PROGRAM

Melvin Cohen, Ph.D.
Athan Karras, Ph.D.

Hillside Division
Long Island Jewish-Hillside Medical Center
Glen Oaks, New York 11004

INTRODUCTION

Before any drug treatment program can be studied for its effectiveness in helping clients, it must be effective in retaining
those clients in treatment for a reasonable period of time. One
of the purposes of studying length of stay is to determine which
types of clients will stay in which programs. Although there have
been previous reports on variables related to length of stay in
different types of treatment programs, few, if any, have allowed
for the random assignment of clients into different programs.

The study reported in this paper was based on a random assignment of psychiatric patients with moderate to heavy poly-drug abuse
and addiction histories into one of two inpatient treatment modalities - a therapeutic community type vocational rehabilitation
program specifically for drug abusers or a traditional milieu
therapy psychiatric program for a mixed population of drug abuse
and non-drug abuse patients.

The Strauss Cottage drug abuse program is an 8-9 month inpatient-to-aftercare treatment program, which requires only a
three month hospitalization period. It is based on three essential principles: the use of intensive social modeling procedures,
basic to the programs of Synanon and Phoenix House; the urgency
of continuity of treatment from the hospital to the community; and
the emphasis on vocational-career evaluation, guidance and placement service to stress the general goal of a successful and active
return to the community.

Patients who met the criteria for study subjects were randomly assigned either to the Strauss Cottage experimental group

which was comprised only of drug users or to a control group, where subjects were placed with drug and non drug use patients in traditional in-hospital treatment and aftercare programs. There were 175 Strauss patients and 104 controls. Study subjects were males and females between the age of 16-33 years, half of whom were moderate to heavy "soft" drug abusers, the other half being opiate addicts. Subjects were detoxified of physically addicting drugs prior to entering the program. One third of the study subjects were diagnosed as psychotic, primarily schizophrenia, the majority of patients diagnosed as having a character disorder. About 50% of all patients had been previously treated in other drug rehabilitation programs.

METHODOLOGY

Patients in the Strauss and control units were interviewed during their first week of hospitalization by a research assistant, using a comprehensive structured interview to elicit information concerning their educational, work and drug history, current living arrangements, arrest record, convictions and previous treatment experience. Follow-up interviews were conducted at 6 & 12 months following discharge from the hospital to determine the patient's post-hospital adjustment in terms of work and school functioning, drug use, and overall social adjustment.

Optimal program length of stay for Strauss patients was 90 days inpatient plus an additional 180 or more consecutive days in continuous after-care services with the same Strauss treatment team. For control patients optimal hospital stay ranged from 60-90 days inpatient, plus a maximum of 1-2X per week non-continuous after-care services for an indefinite period of time. However, for the controls, after-care was not a continuation of their inpatient services, the regular hospital after-care program being independent of the inpatient program.

The distribution of actual length of stay for the two groups, including both inpatient and after-care days in treatment, indicated that 44% of the Strauss patients were still in treatment after 90 days (13 weeks) whereas only 19% of the controls were still in treatment that long. However, 50% of the controls were still in treatment after 60 days (8½ weeks).

Different criteria were therefore used for dividing Strauss and control patients into short and long stay groups. Strauss patients who stayed in treatment over 90 days and therefore made the commitment to continue in Strauss aftercare, were considered as long termers, whereas the criteria for long term stay was 60 or more days for controls. Patients staying less days than these criteria were considered as short termers. All statistical analyses, comparing long & short term patients, are based on a 2x2 chi-square design.

RESULTS

Strauss

None of the variables relating to psychiatric factors such as diagnosis and previous hospitalization nor to socio-demographic factors such as sex, age, family intactness, education and social class significantly differentiated between short and long term Strauss patients. The variables which did significantly differentiate related to patients' previous history of employment, drug use immediately prior to hospitalization and history of criminal-sociopathic behavior (Table I).

Strauss patients who had a history of having worked, but mostly in semi-skilled and laborer type jobs, stayed in treatment longer than those patients who had never worked as well as those patients who had worked in more skilled mechanical, artistic or clerical type jobs. The Strauss long-term clients had also more often been fired from their job(s) and did not get along as well with their fellow workers.

Thus, the employment variables indicate that patients who had more difficulty maintaining low level jobs stayed in treatment longer in the Strauss program than those who had more skilled jobs which they left on their own volition. None of these employment variables were significant for controls. In addition, Strauss patients who had used drugs less than daily, if at all, prior to admission to the hospital, stayed in treatment longer than those who used drugs daily prior to admission. Since there were no significant differences in history of severity of drug use between the length of stay groups, it appears that diminished drug use prior to intake is an indication of higher motivation for treatment. There was no significant difference between the control groups on this variable.

The arrest and legal status data indicate that Strauss patients who had a greater number of arrests and who had a legal status at intake (i.e., on probation, parole, etc.) stayed longer in treatment. This suggests the addition of an external motivating factor to remain in treatment, to satisfy legal authorities that one is enrolled in a drug treatment program.

Interestingly, the arrest data was also significant for the controls, but in the opposite direction. Control patients who had never been arrested stayed in treatment longer than those with a history of arrests.

Controls

Among controls, there were several variables which significantly differentiated between short and long stay patients but showed no relationship to length of stay for the Strauss population (Table I). The first of these variables, diagnosis, indicates that patients diagnosed as psychotic, specifically schizophrenic, were more likely to remain in treatment longer. Those control patients diagnosed as non-psychotic, primarily neurotic and character disorder, did not stay as long. Though the trend was similar for Strauss patients, the differences were not significant.

Socioeconomic status, based on the Hollingshead and Redlich two-factor score of parental education and occupation, showed that controls from higher social class levels (1,2,3) stayed significantly longer than those from lower social class levels (4,5). The findings for education are similar to those for socio-economic status, the higher the educational level achieved by the client, the longer they remained in treatment.

A most interesting finding is that relating to previous drug treatment. Significantly more of the control patients who had never been involved in a treatment program specifically for drug users, stayed in treatment longer. Conversely, those who had been in at least one drug treatment program prior to hospitalization, stayed for a shorter period of time. In addition, as indicated previously, control patients who had never been arrested also stayed longer in treatment.

DISCUSSION

In summary, Strauss patients who remained in treatment longer tended to be those who had had unsatisfactory work experiences in low level jobs, were not using drugs regularly prior to admissions, and had been previously arrested and many of whom were on probation or parole at intake. These patients may have found the Strauss goals of vocational rehabilitation as more relevant to their needs than those patients who terminated treatment earlier.

Control patients who stayed in treatment longer were the psychotic, higher socioeconomic status and higher educational level individuals who had never been arrested and had not previously been in a drug treatment program. This type of patient is more representative of the "typical" psychiatric patient than of the drug abusing patient.

Table 1. Variables Significantly Differentiating Length of Stay
Among Strauss and Control Patients

Variable	Strauss			Control		
	Short Stay	Long Stay	P	Short Stay	Long Stay	P
Employment history:						
Never worked	54%	46%	<.05	56%	44%	NS
Worked	30%	70%		42%	58%	
Type of employment:						
Mech., cler., arts	58%	42%	<.05	37%	63%	NS
Semi-skilled, labor	37%	63%		45%	55%	
Prime reason for leaving job(s):						
Fired	26%	74%	<.10	31%	69%	NS
Quit	47%	53%		40%	60%	
Relationship with fellow workers:						
Very good	61%	39%	<.01	54%	46%	NS
Average-poor	28%	72%		40%	60%	
Drug use 1 month prior to admission:						
None-non daily use	34%	66%	<.05	46%	54%	NS
Daily use	55%	45%		45%	55%	
Number of arrests:						
None	69%	31%	<.05	30%	70%	<.05
One or more	43%	57%		55%	45%	
Legal status at admission:						
None	57%	43%	<.10	41%	59%	NS
Prob., parole, etc.	40%	60%		43%	57%	
Diagnosis:						
Psychotic	40%	60%	NS	38%	62%	<.05
Non-psychotic	54%	46%		60%	40%	
Socioeconomic status:						
Upper to middle class (1,2,3)	45%	55%	NS	39%	61%	<.10
Lower classes (4,5)	51%	49%		62%	38%	
Education:						
Some college	44%	56%	NS	27%	73%	<.01
H.S. grad. & below	52%	48%		58%	42%	
Previous drug treatment:						
No	51%	49%	NS	33%	67%	<.02
Yes	45%	55%		62%	38%	

SYSTEMS THEORY APPLIED TO
TREATMENT OF HEROIN ADDICTS

Eva Fogelman, M.A., C.R.C., Bruce Binette, M.S.W.
Vernon Patch, M.D., Anthony Raynes, M.D.

Boston Drug Treatment Program, Boston, Ma

Drug treatment in America has been differentiated more according to program modality rather than to psychological theory and its application towards treatment of the individual. Much has been written on the effectiveness or non-effectiveness of established programs such as methadone and self-help groups, but very little has been written on an established psychological theory of treatment. The authors feel that the modality may not be as important in treatment of the individual as is the theory behind the treatment itself. Systems theory is a conceptual model which offers a more holistic approach in analyzing the problem and in determining the patient's individual treatment needs.

What the authors have found is that addiction is not only the problem of the addict, but also the problem of everyone involved with this person. Without their involvement, substantive or lasting change is unlikely. Drug treatment programs generally work with the addict alone towards change in treating only the addict, programs often identify the patient as the only problem in much the same way as does the family system of the addict. Altering components of the system in which the addict is enmeshed (family and/or helping agencies) rather than trying to directly influence change in the addict's personality structure is the better method in dealing with addiction.

This paper will consider systems theory as applied to the understanding of the etiology and treatment of heroin addiction. The causes of the addiction will be explored by examining past and present systems in the addict's life beginning with the family of origin. Innovative treatment methods based on systems theory will be discussed.

ETIOLOGY OF DRUG ABUSE

Just as treatment modality philosophies have been polarized so have been ways in which etiology of the individual's addiction oversimplified. In the early 60's when addiction was primarily a problem of the ghettos, there was a general philosophy that poor social conditions and a vague notion of absent father/possessive mother caused the widespread use of drugs in this environment. When drug addiction spread to the suburbs, the validity of these general notions was questioned. Not being able to blame social environment or broken families, it was then assumed that individual psychological problems were at the root of addiction. What emerged were general assumptions such as environment vs psychiatric problems in looking at etiology as applied to treatment.

One of the basic tenets of systems theory has been in taking all systems, past and present, into consideration in the treatment of the individual. The importance of etiology from a systems approach is that each patient should be examined individually. Some of the factors to be considered are: (1) family of origin and past generations, (This would include, repetition of patterns of behavior in several generations, family myths, family rules, family secrets, early trauma, losses, parent's relationship, parental dealings with conflict and other identified patients in the extended family.), and, (2), social environment (This would include peer groups, educational and vocational patterns, living conditions, crises and socioeconomic norms.).

After examining these factors, what emerges is a clearer sense of the pattern of behavior that the addict has learned in his family of origin and how he uses these patterns similarly in all aspects of his life. Dealing with problems in a maladaptive way, such as taking drugs, often originates from similar patterns from the past generations. Parents may have dealt with conflicts by abusing alcohol or by running away and children turn to drugs as an indirect means of handling their situational or emotional difficulties.

In conjunction with understanding the etiology, the criteria for developing an appropriate treatment plan include two major factors. One is all of the systems that the addict is emotionally involved with, including helping agencies, and the other is what is causing the greatest distress at the present time.

The multiple problems that so often beset the addict are many times presented to the therapist in an overwhelming manner as the addict's means of resistance to treatment. It is necessary for the therapist to help prioritize these problems in such a way that the addict gets a better sense of just what is causing the most pain at the present time. In assessing the systems and the pain, one can then decide on an appropriate treatment plan and with whom one can work.

TREATMENT METHODS CONSIDERED AND RECONSIDERED

There are criteria used for assessing whether one should be treated individually or in a group. Good prognosis for individual treatment would include, (1) a patient who has a capacity for insight and a high level of motivation, (2) that there are no systems that are drastically affected or that impede the progress of the individual while in treatment, and (3) that the patient is not too dependent on other social agencies which often complicates and affects the treatment effort.

Groups are a very good method for people who have a hard time learning how to express feelings in a socially acceptable manner. Feedback and support from others are often helpful for the more isolated patient. The most important criterion in assessing group candidates is some latent capacity to trust. At times one may want to see a patient individually at first to help build a sense of trust before entering a group.

In working with individuals and with groups, treatment centers have characteristically tried to perceive the individual intra-psychically rather than interpsychically. Often the therapist is left wondering why these efforts have failed.

When a systems approach is not used, there may be several reasons why treatment has not been successful. Systems are static only if there is no change. When one individual attempts change, the equilibrium of the system is affected. Often this unbalances the system. When the system becomes unbalanced, there is an inevitable loss of secondary gains to someone or to several people in that system. Some examples of loss of secondary gains are:
   (1) Needy parent. Mother often complains about son's addiction, but often fosters dependence on her by providing funds, keeping him home etc.. When son attempts to become more independent, mother is threatened that he will leave and often unknowingly sabotages his efforts to change.
   (2) Masking family conflicts. The family focuses on the addict as primary problem in an effort to avoid the real problem. Often mother and father fight about child's addiction rather than their own personal conflicts.
   (3) Scapegoating. Often a family system operates by having a scapegoat who is conveniently the addict. If the addict changes, the family will have to find another scapegoat and there is usually much pressure to keep the addict in the scapegoat role.
   (4) Getting close while high. The illusion of closeness is often a secondary gain of being high on drugs. If one, or both partners stop taking drugs, the problem of interpersonal

relationships becomes more apparent.
(5) _Peer pressure_. Addict peer group is invested in patient's addiction as part of a collective self esteem. There is much pressure to keep the peer an addict because they are one down if the addict leaves their system. They are one down literally and one down emotionally.

In deciding who to involve in the treatment of the addict, an important point to consider is who is the most ready to change. At times there may be no one who is ready to change. There may be treatment alternatives to this. For example, the so-called "easy rider couple". This usually consists of a pimp and his woman who are both benefiting from each other's roles - she, emotionally and he, financially. Seeing them individually or as a couple, the therapist would not have much success in change; however, placing several such couples in a group together may provide a less threatening way of getting them to make changes in their lifestyle. In mirroring each other as couples, it is often less threatening to see someone else's problems than one's own.

When the patient is not ready to change there may be other identifiable people in the system who are ready to change. For example, parents may be tired of their daughter's addiction and problems surrounding this and they may want to be involved in therapy. At times, a non-addicted spouse may threaten to leave and may want to be involved in the spouse's treatment as a final act of reconciliation.

At times the addict may not be ready to change but is often forced to change as the result of a crisis caused by an outside intervention. For example, a child abuse agency may petition to take a child from the home, or a spouse may go to jail. The addicted individual is then more apt to get actively involved in treatment.

The treatment program itself should assess its idiosyncrasies in treating individual patients. In treating the addict, sometimes the clinic unknowingly mirrors the addict's family of origin. Workers may be responding to a patient in much the same way that the family does, and this itself can be a clue to understanding and treating the repetitive maladaptive interactions with the patient.

There are two major problems that one encounters in treating the addict -- _trust_ _and_ _resistance_. This can be because of many reasons, which may or may not be traced to early losses and oral conflicts. Basically, however, the addict environment fosters mistrust and certainly one who cannot trust himself will have a hard time trusting others. Because of this lack of trust, resistance to treatment will be high in allowing the therapist to bring in even more people who do not trust the addict. An alliance with the patient must be developed before bringing in other family members or agencies.

There are many strategies which one can use in treating an addict using the systems approach;
    (1) Couples systems - One may want to see couples individually or in a group.
    (2) Family systems - An addict may be seen with his family of origin or nuclear family. Multiple family groups may be less threatening to some fmailies.
    (3) Networks - Bringing family members, friends and other agencies together in an effort to facilitate the patients' efforts to change and reintegrate.
    (4) Multiple Impact Therapy - Bringing together other agencies and sharing information to provide a consistent mode of interaction for a corrective and therapeutic experience in itself.

In conclusion, people in general repeat systems that go back to family of origin and that system repeated a previous system. It is not by chance that one gets addicted. People unknowingly choose spouses who repeat their parents' relationship and addicts choose drugs as an indirect way of masking conflicts as had the family of origin used other indirect responses to handle conflicts. Drug programs often mirror families of origin. The patient interacts with them as he does with his family of origin.

REFERENCES

Ackerman, Nathan, ed. "Family Therapy in Transition" International Psychiatry Clinics, 17, 4, Boston, Little & Brown, 1970.
Alexander, Bruce K. & Dibb, Gary S. "Opiate Addicts and Their Parents," Family Process, 14:499-514, 1976.
Attardo, N., "Psychodynamic Factors in the Mother-Child Relationship in Adolescent Drug Addiction: A Comparison of Mothers of Schizophrenics and Mothers of Normal Adolescent Sons," Psychother. Psychosom., 13:249-255, '65.
Bateson, Gregory, Steps to an Ecology of Mind. New York, Ballantine Books, 1972.
Berger, M.M., "Multifamily Psychosocial Group Treatment with Addicts & Their Families," Group Process, 5:31-45,73.
Fram, David, Hoffman, Howard, "Family Therapy in the Treatment of the Heroin Addict," Proceedings: 5th National Conference on Methadone Treatment, 1973.
Haley, Jay, Strategies of Psychotherapy. New York, Grune & Stratton, 1963.
Harbin, Henry T., & Maziar, Howard M. "The Families Drug Abusers: A Literature Review," Family Process 13:411-431, 1975.

Hirsch, Robert, & Imhof, John, "A Family Therapy Approach to the Treatment of Drug Abuse and Addiction," Journal of Psychedelic Drugs, 7(2):181-185, 1975.

Mead, Eugene & Campbell, Susan, "Decision Making and Interaction by Families With and Without a Drug Abusing Child," Family Process, 11:487-497, 1972.

Minuchin, S. Montalvo, Guerney, B., et al. "Families of the Slums, New York, Basic Books, 1967.

Minuchin, S. Montalvo, "Families and Family Therapy," Cambridge, Harvard University Press, 1975.

McGregor, R., "Multiple Impact Therapy with Families," Family Process, 1:15-29, 1962.

Randall, H., "Drug Use and Abuse and the Family," Woman Physician, 27:70-74, 1972.

Rosenberg, C.M. "The Young Addict and His Family," British Journal of Psychiatry, 118:469-70, 1971.

Satir, Virginia, Stachowiak, James & Taschman Harvey A., "Helping Families to Change," New York, Jason Aaronson, 75.

Schwartzman, John, "The Addict, Abstinence and the Family," American Journal of Psychiatry, 132:2 154-7, 1975.

Seldin, Nathan, "The Family of the Addict: A Review of the Literature," The International Journal of the Addictions, 17(1):97-107, 1972.

Steinglass, Peter. "Experimenting with Family Treatment Approaches to Alcoholism, 1950-1975: A Review," Family Process, 15(1):97-121, 1976.

Wellisch, David, Gay, George & McEntee, Roseann, "The Easy Rider Syndrome: A Pattern of Hetero- and Homosexual Relationships In A Heroin Addict Population," Family Process, 9:425-30, 1970.

Wolk, R.L. & Diskirk, M. "Personality Dynamics of Mothers and Wives of Addicts," Crime and Delinquency, 7:148, '61.

SEX DIFFERENCES IN PSYCHOLOGICAL CHARACTERISTICS OF APPLICANTS FOR DRUG ABUSE TREATMENT

James C. Ungerer,[1] Patricia Tenerella-Brody,[1] Robert J. Harford,[1]
Wilma Wake[2]

[1]Department of Psychiatry
Yale University School of Medicine
100 Park Street
New Haven, Connecticut   06511

[2]Addiction-Prevention,
Treatment Foundation, Inc.
100 Park Street
New Haven, Connecticut   06511

I. INTRODUCTION

Recent investigations of sex-related personality differences in drug-abusing treatment populations have found a greater degree of psychological maladjustment among female clients than is evident in males. For example, Ellinwood, Smith, and Vaillant (1) found that females were more attention seeking, more erratic, and visited medical clinics more frequently than their male counterparts. Doyle and Levy (2) reported that, compared to males, the females in their sample were more likely to report: (a) bad feelings about their bodies; (b) poor physical health; (c) an inability to express feelings; and (d) poor relationships with members of the opposite sex. Peak and Glankoff (3) reported that women seeking treatment felt guilty because they rejected the sex roles that society assigns to them, and Schultz (4) concluded that female clients view themselves as sexual objects with poorly defined egos and low self-esteem.

These findings suggest that some of the differences between male and female clients in treatment for drug dependence pertain to feelings of control, self-esteem, anxiety, guilt over sex role performance, and poor interpersonal skills. Because the number of studies is small and some of the interpretations are based more upon clinical impressions than upon empirical evidence, the conclusions suggested by these studies must be considered tentative.

As part of our research program, we administer six personality inventories that are suitable for indicating sex-related psychological differences. These scales include: the Rotter Locus of Control Inventory (5); the Rotter Level of Aspiration Board (6); the Taylor Manifest Anxiety Scale (7); the Eysenck Personality

Inventory (8); the Mosher Forced Choice Sex Guilt Subscale (9); and
the Rotter Interpersonal Trust Scale (10). The Locus of Control
Inventory measures the expectancy that significant life events are
controlled either by personal efforts or by external factors such
as luck or powerful others. The Level of Aspiration task assesses
the degree of confidence characterizing achievement behavior and
may be interpreted as an index of self-esteem. The Taylor Manifest
Anxiety Scale measures "trait" anxiety. The Eysenck Personality
Inventory measures a neuroticism-stability dimension as well as
introversion-extraversion. The Mosher Sex Guilt Subscale measures
"a generalized expectancy for self-mediated punishment for violating,
or anticipating violating, internalized standards of proper (sexual)
conduct" (11). The Interpersonal Trust Scale indicates the extent
to which an individual believes the communications of other people
or institutions. According to Rotter (10), this belief may be a
prerequisite for the development of skills necessary for meaningful
interpersonal relationships.

II. METHOD

A total of 80 females and 246 males seeking treatment for drug
dependence completed the test battery during intake at the Drug
Dependence Unit of the Connecticut Mental Health Center in New
Haven. Applicants who had participated in treatment programs or
who had been incarcerated during the preceding six months were excluded from this study. The testing procedure was presented as
voluntary research directed towards helping the clinics improve the
quality of treatment. Clients were assured confidentiality and
were told that their performance would not influence their treatment status. Five clients refused to participate.

III. RESULTS

A. UNIVARIATE FINDINGS

1. PERSONAL CHARACTERISTICS

The majority of the 326 applicants were male (75.4%), White
(62.9%), heroin dependents (60.7%) who were experiencing some
degree of involvement (57.7%) with the criminal justice system.
Their mean age was 23.2 years. A total of 30.5% were referred by
the criminal justice system with 12.6% of these being stipulated to
treatment as an alternative to incarceration. Litigation was pending for 32.6% while 26.2% were on probation and 8.1% were on parole.
2. SEX-RELATED DIFFERENCES IN PERSONAL CHARACTERISTICS

Males were more likely than females to have cases pending in
the courts (x^2 = 8.04; $\underline{df}$ = 1; $\underline{p}$ < .005). Sex differences in age
were marginally significant ($\underline{t}$ = 1.82; $\underline{df}$ = 324; $\underline{p}$ < .10) such that

443

the male applicants were approximately one year older than the females (23.4 years versus 22.3 years). None of the other applicant characteristics were related to their sex.

3. SEX-RELATED DIFFERENCES IN PSYCHOLOGICAL CHARACTERISTICS

According to univariate analyses, compared with males, females were significantly more guilty about sex (t = 2.21; df = 316; p < .05), more neurotic (t = 6.18; df = 316; p < .001), more anxious (t = 5.44; df = 313; p < .001), more cautious in their goal setting behavior, (t = 5.04; df = 255; p < .001) and had more atypical shifts in aspiration (t = 2.54; df = 255; p < .05). In addition, their Lie scores were marginally lower than were the males' (t = 1.84; df = 315; p < .10).

B. MULTIVARIATE FINDINGS

The fact that sex differences occurred in correlated variables suggested that the dimensionality of the sex differences could be reduced by a multivariate analysis. For example, the largest sex differences were obtained for neuroticism and anxiety, but the high correlation between these two measures (r = .80) indicated that they measure similar dimensions. We used Rao's stepwise method of discriminant analysis to derive the linear combination of measures that maximally distinguished males from females. According to the criterion of relative size of the standardized discriminant co-efficients, two variables, the Eysenck Lie score and the Taylor Anxiety score, did not contribute sufficient unique discriminative power to be retained. The resulting 4-variable function for 234 males and 76 females showed that neuroticism contributed the most unique discriminability (.82) followed by cases pending (-.48), age (-.35) and sex guilt (.31). The canonical correlation associated with this function was .42, and the function correctly classified 67.9% of the males and 73.3% of the females. This procedure was repeated with the addition of three aspiration variables for the subset of applicants who completed the aspiration task. The resulting 5-variable function for the 191 males and 56 females showed that mean level of aspiration also contributed significant unique discriminability. Neuroticism again received the highest standardized discriminant coefficient (-.68), followed by mean aspiration (.47), cases pending (.37), age (.31), and sex guilt (-.21). The canonical correlation associated with this function was .49, and the function correctly classified 72.3% of the males and 73.2% of the females.

The three most discriminative psychological variables, then, were neuroticism, level of aspiration, and sex guilt. The mean neuroticism score obtained by the males (11.9) resembled the means obtained by male and female samples of "normal" individuals reported by Eysenck (8). The mean neuroticism score of females (16.1), how-ever, was well outside this range and even exceeded the range of scores (13.7 - 15.8) obtained by "abnormal" and "neurotic" samples.

444

The mean level of aspiration score for males (M = 1.8) also approached the average scores for males (2.0 - 2.5) in college populations (12, 6). While Rotter (6) observed that level of aspiration scores might be lower for women because of less experience with motor tasks, he also noted that a negative score, such as that obtained by these women (M = -0.1), indicates extreme caution and deflated self-esteem.

Males and females were guiltier than recently reported college samples (13). The mean guilt score of males (M = -16.8), however, more closely resembled that of the combined college samples (M = -19) than did the mean guilt score of the females (M = -12.3). The females were guiltier than either the female college or the male applicant groups.

IV. DISCUSSION

The findings suggest that male and female applicants for drug abuse treatment differ on three psychological dimensions. Females were significantly more neurotic, more cautious in achievement situations, and more guilty about sex. Females also were more maladjusted than female comparison groups in the general population. They were more neurotic than even the "abnormal" samples of females and males reported by Eysenck. With respect to achievement aspiration, female applicants were more cautious than previously reported college samples. Finally, with respect to sex guilt, they were more guilty than recent female and male college samples. Males, on the other hand, resembled the male comparison groups along all three psychological dimensions.

The etiology of these differences is a matter for speculation. Perhaps female applicants for treatment are more maladjusted because maladjustment predisposes women to abuse illicit drugs. Women more frequently than men may resort to unprescribed drug use in order to cope with their emotional difficulties or they may use drugs simply because drug abuse is an extention of their atypical psychological perspectives.

Perhaps females seemed more maladjusted because maladjusted female drug abusers are more likely to apply for treatment. Males and females may abuse drugs with equal frequency. Males, however, may become involved in treatment more frequently because the nature of their crimes is more likely to attract the attention of police. In fact, the males in this sample more frequently had legal pressure than the females.

We should note that these explanations assume that maladjustment precedes drug abuse. A plausible alternative is that drug abuse may induce psychological maladjustment. Neurotic conflict, deflated self-esteem, and guilt over sex-role behavior may be the consequences of violating normative substance-abuse standards for women in our society.

In view of the large number of alternative explanations, the etiology of psychological maladjustment in female clients should be

investigated. One approach would be to study case histories. Careful case history investigations may clarify the reasons that women
enter treatment and whether psychological maladjustment is an ante-
cedent or consequent condition of drug abuse.

In addition to etiological investigations, efforts should be
made to implement rehabilitative approaches that improve the psychological status of women in treatment. For example, since female
clients may be low in self-esteem, effective career counseling
should be stressed. Preparation for useful employment could help to
bolster feelings of low achievement and raise their level of self-
esteem. Since they serve as role models for the clients, female
staff members should be trained in dealing with the specific problems
facing women in treatment. Identification with a respected and
accomplished team of women could help to modify a client's negative
perceptions of herself and other women. Female clinicians should be
skilled in both individual counseling and group therapy for women.
Group sessions could address common problems and individual sessions
could focus on unique problems of individual female clients. Day
care centers would provide a necessary, supportive service for members who have young children. This type of facility also could provide a forum for members who are ambivalent regarding their role as
mothers. These suggestions are hardly comprehensive but, if implemented, could be helpful in alleviating the neurotic conflicts, the
deflated self-esteem and the guilt which may afflict women in
treatment.

This research was supported in part by grants from the National
Institute of Drug Abuse: DA 01097 and DA 16356.

V. REFERENCES

1. E. Ellinwood, W. Smith, and S. Vaillant, The Int. J. Addic.
    1:2, (1966).
2. K. Doyle and M. Levy, Annual Meeting of the American Psychological
    Association, Chicago, Illinois, August 31, 1975.
3. J. Peak and P. Glankoff, in Developments in the Field of Drug
    Abuse, Massachusetts: Schenkman Publishing Company, 1975.
4. A. Schultz, in Developments in the Field of Drug Abuse,
    Massachusetts: Schenkman Publishing Company, 1975.
5. J. Rotter, Psychol. Monogr., 80: (1 Whole No. 609) (1966).
6. J. Rotter, Social Learning & Clinical Psychology, Englewood
    Cliffs, New Jersey: Prentice Hall, 1954.
7. J. Taylor, J. Abn. Soc. Psychol., 2, (1953).
8. H. Eysenck and S. Eysenck, Personality Structure and Measurement.
    Knapp, California, 1969.
9. D. L. Mosher, J. Consult. Psychol., 30:25 (1966).
10. J. Rotter, J. Person., 35:651 (1967).
11. D. L. Mosher, J. Consult. Clin. Psychol., 32:690 (1968).
12. D. Crowne, J. Person. Soc. Psychol., 3:641 (1966).
13. P. R. Abramson and D. L. Mosher, J. Consult. Clin. Psychol.,
    43:4 (1975).

EXPLAINING LENGTH OF TIME IN TREATMENT FOR DRUG ABUSE CLIENTS

Angelo Bardine, B.S.

Chief Analytical Studies Section, DSPI
National Institute on Drug Abuse
Rockville, Maryland 20852

Wayne H. Ferris, Ph.D.
Bradford T. Greene, Ph.D.

Research Associates
Richard Katon and Associates, Inc.
11300 Rockville Pike
Rockville, Maryland 20852

I.   INTRODUCTION

The purpose of this analysis is to examine whether certain social and demographic characteristics of clients admitted to drug abuse treatment programs are associated with length of time in treatment. Time in treatment is an important variable in the drug abuse treatment process. If select client characteristics are systematically related to length of time in treatment, and if these can be identified, it may be possible to plan more realistically for the kinds and amount of resources required to meet future treatment demand.

II.   SCOPE

A random sample of 13,268 drug abuse clients out of 146,681 clients discharged during the period from November 1, 1974 to September 30, 1975 was analyzed.

The data file is the National Institute on Drug Abuses' Client Oriented Data Acquisition Process (CODAP) Historial Clients' File.

(More information on CODAP can be obtained from the authors). It
contains information on clients who were discharged from treatment
in federally-supported drug abuse treatment programs on or after
November 1, 1974. The file links information recorded on clients
at both time of admission to and time of discharge from treatment
during discrete treatment episodes within particular programs. The
file contains matched records for 88.6% of the clients admitted to
treatment.

III. RESULTS: BASIC RELATIONSHIPS

The analysis is based on eleven contingency tables. (The tables
are available upon request). Examination of a percentage distribution for length of time in treatment shows one-fourth of all
clients are in treatment for less than one month, nearly one-fifth
are in treatment for one month, and 44% of all clients are in treatment for less than two months.

Cross-tabulating time in treatment by primary drug of abuse at time
of admission to treatment indicates the existence of a relationship
between the two variables. Thirty-two percent of all opiate abusers
are in treatment for less than one month, compared to only 10% of
marihuana/hashish abusers. Differences among the other drug types
(alcohol, barbiturates/sedatives, amphetamines/cocaine, and hallucinogens), however, are few and generally small.

Examination of time in treatment by number of prior treatments revealed that the two variables are somewhat related. Twenty-one
percent of those clients with no prior treatment experiences are in
treatment for less than one month compared to 43% of clients who
have had more than two previous treatment experiences. In general,
clients with more prior treatment experience tend to spend less
time in treatment.

Analysis of time in treatment by frequency of use of primary drug
and number of years continues use yields results quite similar to
those for time in treatment by number of prior treatment experiences, i.e., clients that abuse drugs more spend less time in treatment.

Time in treatment cross-tabulated by age suggests that length of
time in treatment diminishes as age increases, although the relationship is weak. Twelve percent of clients from the 10-17 age
group are in treatment less than one month, compared to 30% of
clients in the over 30 age group.

IV. ANALYZING TYPE OF DISCHARGE AND OTHER FACTORS

Thus far the relationship between length of time in treatment and other variables has been examined without considering type of discharge. It is quite possible that the reason for discharge affects the relationships involving time in treatment.

This study differentiates three types of discharges: (1) the client completed treatment in the judgment of the treatment staff; (2) the client left or "split" before completing treatment; (3) the client was discharged for non-compliance to program/clinic rules.

Some important percentage differences are evident if we compare time in treatment by reason for discharge. They type of discharge evidencing the clearest trend is that of non-compliance -- increasing from 14% for the less than one month category through 27% for the four to ten months category. The greatest percent of clients who split before completing treatment do so in less than one month, whereas the largest percentage who complete treatment stay in treatment four to ten months.

If length of time in treatment by reason for discharge is studied for the two primary drugs of abuse -- opiates and marihuana/hashish, it is found that not only are there important differences between these abusers with respect to length of time in treatment, but also with respect to the reason for discharge. For example, nearly 36% of opiate abusers complete treatment in less than one month, compared to only 4% of the marihuana/hashish abusers. It is noteworthy that most of the opiate abusers who complete treatment in less than one month do so within a detoxification modality. It is a requirement that detoxification cannot exceed 21 days if methadone is being used. This and the fact that a considerable number of opiates abusers are assigned to the detoxification modality helps account for the relatively large percentage (36) of opiate abusers who complete treatment in less than one month.

Considering opiate abusers only, 15% of those discharged for non-compliance occur in less than one month of treatment, compared to nearly 32% for the three types of discharges combined. Of those completing treatment, nearly one-fifth remain in treatment for more than 10 months. Only 6% of the opiate abusers who split before completing treatment stay in treatment this long.

Analysis of time in treatment by reason for discharge for opiate abusers only, and comparison of maintenance and drug free modalities, shows considerable differences for length of time in treatment between the two modalities. Nearly one-quarter of all drug free opiate discharges leave treatment in less than one month and another fifth leave after one month in treatment. In contrast, less than 10% of the opiate abusers in the maintenance modality leave treatment in less than one month and 15% after one month in treatment.

Almost 61% of the opiate abusers discharged from maintenance stayed in treatment four or more months (not considering type of discharge). In comparison, only one-third of the drug free discharges stay in treatment for four months or longer.

In the drug free modality nearly 31% of the opiate abusers split or leave before completing treatment in less than one month, compared to only 12% in maintenance. Only 10% of those in a drug free modality and 4% in maintenance complete treatment in less than one month.

Looking at the longer time in treatment categories, the distinctions are considerably different. Almost 50% of the opiate abusers in maintenance who complete treatment are in treatment for more than 10 months, but only one-fourth do so in the drug free modality. A fifth of those in the maintenance modality leave before completing treatment after more than 10 months in treatment, compared to about 6% in the drug free modality. Similarly, more than one-third of those in maintenance are discharged for non-compliance to program rules after more than ten months in treatment, compared to 10% in the drug free modality.

Comparing marihuana/hashish and opiate abusers in terms of reason for discharge and for the drug free modality, important differences are evident between the two primary drugs of abuse. Proportionately, opiate abusers are in treatment for a shorter period of time than marihuana/hashish abusers. Close to one-fourth of the opiate abusers are in treatment for less than one month, compared to only 8% of the marihuana/hashish abusers.

However, if opiate and marihuana/hashish abusers in the drug free modality are compared not only in terms of length of time in treatment but also in terms of type of discharge, it is found that some of the differences are explained by the reason for discharge. Opiate abusers split and are discharged for non-compliance to program rules at a faster rate than marihuana/hashish abusers. Nearly 11% of the opiate abusers complete treatment in less than one month across the other time in treatment categories, however, the differences are less pronounced. Fifty-seven percent of the opiate abusers who complete treatment are in treatment four or more months compared to about 60% of the marihuana/hashish abusers staying in treatment four or more months.

Based on treatment regimens normally assigned one would not expect to find marihuana/hashish abusers in treatment for periods of time as long as those for opiate abusers. This seems to be partly explained by the faster rate at which opiate abusers split or are discharged for non-compliance to program rules. Overall, opiate abusers experience more difficulty in staying in treatment in a drug free modality than do marihuana/hashish abusers.

V.   CONCLUSIONS AND IMPLICATIONS

In a short presentation on a complex topic, it is not possible to provide an exhaustive analysis. The data discussed have pointed to relationships between length of time in treatment, primary drug of abuse, number of prior treatment experiences, age, reason for discharge, and modality.   (And the other variables which measure extent of drug abuse).

Without attempting to summarize all of the findings mentioned in the discussion, some of the more salient ones will be considered. First, with respect to the relationship between primary drug of abuse and length of time in treatment, the most distinct patterns were evidenced for opiates and marihuana/hashish. With respect to variables measuring extent of drug abuse, the data indicate that clients with more treatment experiences and abuse tend to stay in treatment for shorter periods of time. Concerning age, the data show that drug abusers in the younger age categories spend somewhat more time in treatment than do older abusers.

When reason for discharge and modality were introduced into the analysis along with primary drug of abuse, the understanding of length of time in treatment was improved. The maintenance modality appears to be more conducive to staying in treatment regardless of whether or not the client completes treatment. For example, of clients completing treatment proportionately more opiate abusers in the maintenance modality than in the drug free modality stayed in treatment for the longest time period. The data also show that opiate abusers are particularly vulnerable to leaving treatment during the first month of treatment.

When opiate abusers are compared in terms of type of discharge and for the drug free modality alone, it becomes evident that opiate abusers who split or were discharged for non-compliance to program rules were, proportionately, in treatment for shorter periods of time than were opiate abusers who completed treatment. This explains why proportionately more marihuana/hashish abusers stay in the drug free modality for longer periods than do opiate abusers.

451

IMAGES OF THE OPIATE USER AND THERAPEUTIC REGIMEN:
THEORETICAL CONSIDERATIONS

Thomas V. Rush

Governor's Council On Drug and Alcohol Abuse (PA)

Thomas J. Keil

University of Louisville

John Busch

University of Louisville

If there is one general theme which is apparent in the drug
treatment literature, it is a notable ineffectiveness in "curing"
the clients. The explanation for this "ineffectiveness" has
generally taken one of two forms: the liberal view or the conservative view. The liberal view holds that the problem can be
explained by inadequate program operation. If the programs could
be made more rational and if services were more comprehensive and
integrated, there would be dramatic improvements in program
effectiveness. Meanwhile, the conservative approach holds that
some public problems cannot be solved through public policy.
Causation is so inextricably bound with the nature of man and the
nature of sociocultural forces that they cannot be readily handled
(Miller and Ratner, 1972).

We propose that both conservative and liberal interpretations are erroneous insofar as they are based upon incomplete
theories of behavior. What is demanded is a reconceptualization
of the phenomenon. Ideally, such a reconceptualization should
break through the conceptual barriers of existing theories and
propose alternative intervention strategies. In other words, what
is needed is a full paradigm revolution, in the sense in which
Kuhn (1970) uses the term.

This publication was prepared independent of the professional status of the author as an employee of the Governor's Council on Drug
and Alcohol Abuse, Commonwealth of PA, and the conclusions and interpretations contained herein are solely those of the author.

A.   An Alternative Paradigm

Allport (1960) has distinguished between behavioral theories
that view an organism as a quasi-closed system and those that view
it as an open system. We hope to show how the prevailing interpretations of drug use employ quasi-closed models, and how these
models are built into efforts to control and treat drug use.

There can be little question that the biological person is a
clearly bounded system; however, there does remain a high degree
of "openness" (Von Bertalanffy, 1962) as opposed to "closedness."
Here "openness" is used in the same sense as Buckley when he states
that an open system means "...not simply that it (the system)
engages in interchanges with the environment, but that this interchange is an essential factor underlying the system's viability,
its reproductive ability or continuity, and its ability to change"
(1967, 50). In other words, the very nature of the organism and
the future properties it will have is related to the content of its
environment.

The psychological dimension hears a strong relationship to
the biological system, with each system entering into exchanges
with the other (e.g. the literature on psychological stress and
physiological reaction, Kosa, et al., 1969). Because of the
above relationship it is easy to assume a priori that they are both
open to the same degree.

While little genetic change has occurred in humans over the
past 15,000 years, significant alterations have occurred in man's
adaptation to and modification of his environment. Mankind's
capability for adjusting to and transforming the environmental
context is to be found in his capacity to communicate reflexively
through symbols (Lenski, 1974), which permits the accumulation and
across-generation transmission of knowledge about the environment.
Furthermore, while communication and the coordinated action it
makes possible serve to facilitate adaptation, they also play
major roles in enhancing the complexity of the very environment
within which they operate.

Man, as an open psychological system, is capable of experiencing greater internal structural elaboration than are the quasi-
closed system animals, which results from environment-person transactions. Therefore, any attempt to explain the behavior of an
open system organism must emphasize environmental factors to a
greater extent than is the case if one is dealing with quasi-
closed organisms. Empirical evidence is accumulating that can be
interpreted in ways showing the importance of situational influences on behavior, Raush, Dittman and Taylor (1959), Raush,
Farbman and Llewellyn (1960), Zimbardo (1971), Argyle and Little
(1972) and Moos (1974) are but a few such studies. Argyle and
Little (1972) provide a comprehensive review of the evidence on

traits of social behavior with the goal of summarizing the relative effects of person and environment on behavior. They state:

> "...ask what are the relative effects of Persons,
> Situations, and their interactions on different
> kinds of behavior... Person and Situation inter-
> action account for more variance than either
> Situations or Persons alone. With the passage
> of time and in more adequately functioning
> groups, Situations are relatively more important
> sources of variation than are Persons" (15-16).

Argyle and Little's (1972) empirical results are consistent
with their interpretations of the direction of effects in previous
research.

B.   Implications Of The Open System Paradigm

Generally, if one perceives the human actor as a quasi-
closed system and if one finds that the person is engaging in
conduct disturbing to others in ways that call forth negative
sanctions, the greatest efforts to change the undesirable behavior
will be directed at modifying the internal organization of the
person. From an open system paradigm, one can predict that such
treatment efforts are bound to have only limited success in large
numbers of the cases where they applied. Failure is guaranteed
insofar as these treatment efforts are person-based and neglect
the role of person-environment transactions in developing and
stabilizing behavior. If one accepts Argyle and Little's (1972)
experimental results, one is directed away from the person as the
cause, and is led to a focus on the nature and extent of person-
environment transactions. Therefore, difficulties in "curing"
drug use are traceable neither to the intractability of human
nature nor to organizational non-rationality, but, rather, are
linked to deficiencies in the basic paradigm structuring the
current treatment efforts.

It can mostly be said that a quasi-closed system paradigm
permeates the treatment modalities. One of the largest modalities
for handling heroin users is methadone maintenance. Arthur Moffett,
et al. (1974) analogized methadone for a junkie to insulin for a
diabetic. Operating under a closed system paradigm, it assumes
heroin use can be curtailed by merely working on the particular
user. Psychotherapy is another modality which is frequently
adopted, and its thrust is toward restructuring the psychological
organization of the user so the individual internalizes "appropriate" control over his/her behavior. As Adler, et al. (1974) said,
"While total abstinence from drugs may be a highly desired goal, a
commitment to self improvement is the overriding concern of this
modality" (59). On the surface, therapeutic communities would
appear to be environmentally based modalities, but upon close

analysis, we find them to be quasi-closed systems. Ultimately, the stated objective of the therapeutic communities is to re-structure the person so as to remove those individual defects that lead to drug use, which implies that only certain types of persons are susceptible to deviant pressures emanating from the environment.

C.   Toward An Open System Paradigm

The alternative conception that we have sketched stresses understand variables not only specific to the person, but also to the environment, as well as the interactions between the person and the environment. Before examining what a policy for dealing with drug use would look like using such a paradigm, some addition comments on the paradigm are in order.

In Western culture, the person as an etiological source is so thoroughly ingrained in our perceptions of a definition of reality that it is difficult to suggest alternative models, and it is even more difficult in the field of drug use. In part, this difficulty can be traced to the model dominant in this field. Expertise in the field of drug use, ultimately, is seen to be linked to the physician role. The difficulty is that the totality of the physician's experience and training leads to an adoption of an illness model, which focuses on a quasi-closed system. The very word "treatment" connotes strategies of change that are person-oriented. Even researchers such as Moos (1974), while noting the effects of various organizational properties of the treatment system, continue to emphasize personal reorganization. Moos' research is interesting in this context in several respects. He takes what he calls a "social ecological" approach, which is "the multidisciplinary study of the impacts of physical and social environments on human beings" (1974, vii). This approach is con-sistent with an open systems conceptualization. However, Moos has used the approach sparingly, concentrating on the operation of "treatment environments" per se. Having such a focus, the study did not challenge the treatment goal of matching individual to environment by reorganizing the internal psychological structure of the person; and it neglected the possibility of reorganization being "undone" once the individual leaves treatment. Effectively, these two points display Moos' implicit reliance on a quasi-closed system model.

It is hoped that our analysis will lead the reader to one important conclusion: while it is important to recognize the role of environment in the genesis and maintenance of behavior, it is just as critical to design "treatment" systems that focus on envi-ronmental change. Recognition of the role of environment is mean-ingless if one is interested solely in person-based ameliorative interventions. At least two related points may be made. First, the contributions of macro systems (the environmental context) can

take many forms. For example, the distributive system of any
society, in combination with various cultural conceptions of
morality, may affect the legitimate and illegitimate opportunity
structures existing within the society (Cloward and Ohlin, 1960).
To fully understand the way macro systems impinge on behavior, one
must also appreciate the interactions that they have on various
micro systems within the society. One might hypothesize that removing some of the contribution to drug use that originates in
macro systems and their interrelationships with micro systems will
result in lowering both the incidence and the prevalence of drug
use. Secondly, from an open system paradigm, one might hypothesize
that there is no intrinsic relationship between personal characteristics and types of deviance. The contributions of macro and
micro systems to forms of "deviance" such as drug use may not be
in their generating specific patterns of deviance, but, rather, in
generating structural possibilities for "deviance" in general. In
other words, these systems produce the structural parameters within which probabilities for choice develop. If these points are
correct, one might conclude that massive programs directed to
controlling and treating various forms of "deviance" will come to
nought so long as their target is the individual deviator. More
effective programs would entail working directly on the properties
of the social system that are deviance producing.

D.   A Summation

     In suggesting that contemporary theories of drug use have
neglected the environmental factor, we are interested in the
environment insofar as it becomes subjectively meaningful to the
individual. Thus, it is the person himself, who is a crucial variable mediating the influence of the environment; he is not merely
the passive recipient of environmental pressures to conform or to
deviate (Matza, 1969; Taylor, et al., 1973). At the same time,
deviance is not to be understood as totally person generated, in
the sense suggested by psychotherapeutic imageries. As Mead (1934),
Simmel (1950), and Berger and Luckmann (1966) suggest, person-
environment transactions must be viewed as dialectical relations.
In both micro and macro contexts, dialectical interaction between
self and situation is where the meaning of the self and its behaviors are generated. Similarly, the meaning of the environment
is constructed in its interactions with socially organized selves.

     Such a paradigm has major implications for public policy.
Current government efforts are directed to subsidizing treatment
programs that seek to establish a "healthy" balance within the
person so that he/she is adjusted to present circumstances in ways
minimizing deviance and/or of giving the person skills to move to
a new environment where he/she will not be exposed to deviant
motivations. The new environment, coupled with the new personality
organization, supposedly will insure that the person will construct
and maintain conventional behavioral patterns. Nowhere is public

456

policy geared toward changing directly the patterns of social organization within which deviant motivations emerge and within which deviant choices are differentially distributed. In cases where policy is oriented to "prevention," rather than, or as a supplement to treatment, the former is defined in terms of working upon the individual or upon small groups, rather than the society at large. If drug use is to be controlled, however, a broader focus for intervention efforts is demanded.

References

Adler, Frieda, et al.
1974 A Systems Approach to Drug Treatment, Philadelphia: Dorrance.

Allport, Gordon W.
1960 "The Open System in Personality Theory," Journal of Abnormal and Social Psychology, 61, 301-11.

Argyle, Michael and Brian R. Little
1972 "Do Personality Traits Apply to Social Behavior?," Journal of Theory and Social Behavior, 2, 1.

Berger, Peter L., and Thomas Luckmann
1966 The Social Construction of Reality: A Treatise in the Sociology of Knowledge, Garden City, New York: Doubleday.

von Bertalanffy, Ludwig
1962 "General Systems Theory - A Critical Review," General Systems, VII: 1-20.

Buckley, Walter
1967 Sociology and Modern Systems Theory, Englewood Cliffs, New Jersey: Prentice-Hall.

Cloward, Richard and Lloyd Ohlin

1960 Delinquency and Opportunity: A Theory of Delinquent Gangs, New York: Free Press.

Kosa, John, et al.
1969 Poverty and Health: A Sociological Analysis, Cambridge, Massachusetts: Harvard University Press.

Kuhn, Thomas
1970 The Structure of Scientific Revolutions, 2nd ed., Chicago: University of Chicago Press.

Lenski, Gerhard R.
1966 Power & Privilege: A Theory of Social Stratification, New York: McGraw-Hill.

Matza, Davis
    1969 <u>Becoming</u> <u>Deviant</u>. Englewood Cliffs, New Jersey: Prentice-
    Hall.

Mead, George Herbert
    1934 <u>Mind</u>, <u>Self</u>, <u>and</u> <u>Society</u>, edited by C.W. Morris, Chicago:
    University of Chicago Press.

Miller, S.M. & R.S. Ratner
    1972 "The American Resignation: The New Assault on Equality,"
    <u>Social</u> <u>Policy</u>, 3(May/June).

Moffett, A., <u>et</u> <u>al</u>.
    1974 <u>Medical</u> <u>Lollipop</u>, <u>Junkie</u> <u>Insulin</u>, <u>or</u> <u>What</u>?, Philadelphia:
    Dorrance.

Moos, Rudolf H.
    1974 <u>Evaluating</u> <u>Treatment</u> <u>Environments</u>, New York: John Wiley &
    Sons.

Raush, H., Dittman, A., and Taylor, T.
    1959 "Person, Setting, and Change in Social Interaction," <u>Human</u>
    <u>Relations</u>, 12: 361-378.

Raush, H., Farbman, I., and Llewellyn, T.
    1960 "Person, Setting, and Change in Social Interaction: A
    Normal Control Study," <u>Human</u> <u>Relations</u>, 13: 305-322.

Simmel, Georg
    1950 <u>The</u> <u>Sociology</u> <u>of</u> <u>Georg</u> <u>Simmel</u>, translated and edited by
    Kurt H. Wolff. New York: Free Press.

Taylor, Ian, <u>et</u> <u>al</u>.
    1973 <u>The</u> <u>New</u> <u>Criminology</u>. New York: Harper Torchbacks.

Zimbardo, P.G.
    1971 Hearings before Subcommittee No. 3 of the Committee on the
    Judisiory House of Representatives Ninety-Second Congress
    First Session on Corrections, Part II, <u>Prisons</u>, <u>Prison</u>
    <u>Reform</u>, <u>and</u> <u>Prisoners</u> <u>Rights</u>: California. October 25, 1971.
    Serial No. 15. U.S. Government Printing Office, Washington.

PERSON PERCEPTION IN DRUG ABUSE COUNSELING

Don C. Des Jarlais

Bureau of Social Science Research
New York State Office of Drug Abuse Services
New York, New York

The importance of person perception has been emphasized under a variety of rubrics in the literature on psychotherapy and counseling. Accurate perception of the client by the counselor has been discussed in terms of making diagnoses [1] and in terms of the need for empathy with the client[2]. Accurate perception of the counselor by the client has been discussed in terms of the "transparency" and "genuineness" of the therapist[3].

Given the importance generally accorded to the accuracy of person perception among counselors and clients, sources of systematic misperception have been frequently studied. Usually systematic misperception is attributed to the individual personality dynamics of the perceiver[4].

There is considerable evidence, however, that person perception is also influenced by the relationship between the perceiver and the perceived person [5]. The present study is an exploratory study of systematic misperceptions that may be attributable to the role relationship between counselor and client rather than to the personality characteristics of individual therapists and clients.

Drug counselors and clients were selected as subjects for several reasons. First, there has been relatively little study of person perception in drug treatment; and secondly, the mixture of intrapersonal, interpersonal, legal, and cultural factors in drug "abuse" [6] would make accurate person perception particularly problematic.

METHODS

Subjects

Subjects were 10 counselors (7 male, 3 female) and 19 clients (12 male, 7 female) from a drug counseling center in a medium sized city. The center provided both individual and group counseling but did not provide either residential treatment or chemotherapy. Clients were young (median age 18 years) and are best described as "poly-drug" users. The most frequently used drugs were marijuana, hashish, amphetamines and hallucinogens. Only 3 of the clients reported ever having regularly used heroin and all of them reported using more than one drug.

The counselors were older (median age 25 years) and had bachelor's degrees in social science and/or were doing graduate work in the field. While the counselors had not developed an "orthodox" theory of drug abuse treatment, transactional analysis was the theory they discussed most frequently at staff meetings and reported as most useful in their work.

Instruments

Clients and counselors were presented with a 28 item list of "reasons why people might or might not use drugs" and asked to check those that "relate to your own use/non-use of drugs." The use of such a check list format was found to have both concurrent and construct validity in previous research on drug education[7]. Clients were then asked to complete the instrument as they imagined a "counselor in a treatment program" would, and counselors were asked to complete the instrument as a "client in a treatment program" would.

Data Analysis

Frequency counts of the motives checked by clients and counselors were compiled to indicate shared motivations toward drug use within each group. Chi square tests were used to test the significance levels of differences in frequencies of reported and perceived reasons. Two-tailed tests and the .05 level of significance were used throughout.

RESULTS

Comparison of the predicted self reports of the other (perception of the other) with the actual self reports is a standard way of measuring the accuracy of person perception. As Table I shows, significant differences were found on 7 reasons for counselors' perception of the clients and on 5 reasons for clients' perception of the counselors. Counselors' misperceptions of clients were generally in the direction of expecting more interpersonal reasons for drug use. Counselors expected clients to report more concern with having a good time at parties, showing independence from authorities, avoiding hassles with parents, being cool, and greater concern with how drugs would affect members of their families.

Client perceptions (expectations) of counselors differed from counselor self reports on 5 reasons. The direction of these perceptual inaccuracies was in terms of an idealized picture of the counselors. Clients expected that counselors would report greater concern with the effects of drugs on society as a whole, on family members, the effects on mental health, and lesser concern with doing things with friends and lesser curiosity about new experiences.

DISCUSSION

The misperceptions of counselors and clients can be related to the role aspects of the client-counselor relationship [8]. The counselor - client relationship is heavily asymmetrical. The counselor has greater power in the relationship, having the moral (and sometimes the legal) authority to change the drug usage of the client. Concomitant with this greater power, the counselor is expected to have a greater understanding of the problem of drug abuse and the technical expertise to induce behavior change. That the clients perceived an idealized picture of the counselors would specifically support the legitimacy of the counselor's greater power in the relationship.

The role requirement for a drug counselor to have an understanding of drug abuse and the technical expertise to reduce drug abuse necessitates that the counselor adopt some "theory" of the "problem" and how behavior change occurs. The theory used by the counselors in this study was transactional analysis. The systematic errors in the counselors' perception of the clients were in the direction of a greater interpersonal determination of drug use. This specific error may be an example of "logical error " [9, 10] resulting from using transactional analysis which emphasizes interpersonal determinants of problem behavior.

Given the relatively small number of subjects, the results of this study must be considered preliminary. The findings suggest that the role requirements of counselor and client roles contain limiting factors on the accuracy of person perception in a therapeutic encounter. These issues need to be considered in the assessment of treatment planning, clinical records and therapeutic outcomes.

TABLE 1
ACCURACY OF EXPECTATIONS ABOUT THE OTHER[1]

	Counselor Expectations	Client Reports	Client Expectations	Counselor Reports
1. How drugs might affect society as a whole.	10	21	63	20*
2. Decreased effectiveness in studies or work.	20	21	53	20
3. Escape from problems.	40	58	47	30
4. Put down people interfering with my life.	40	21	21	0
5. Curiosity about new experiences.	50	58	32	90*
6. Like being high.	100	74	16	40
7. Avoiding boring situations.	80	48	21	20
8. Feeling more alert, stronger or more powerful.	50	21	16	20
9. Moral reasons against using drugs.	10	37	42	30
10. Might lose my job.	30	16	79	70
11. Doing things with friends.	80	58	21	60*
12. Loss of control over thoughts, feelings and actions.	50	37	53	20
13. How drugs might affect my friends.	30	26	37	10
14. Legal penalties for possession of drugs.	50	32	63	70
15. How drugs might affect member of my family.	70	26*	63	20*
16. Self-awareness & consciousness expansion.	30	37	37	40
17. Not becoming dependent upon drugs.	40	37	63	30
18. Having a good time at parties.	70	32*	21	10
19. Being cool.	80	26*	21	20
20. Showing independence from authorities.	80	10*	20	0
21. Dangers to mental health.	40	37	69	30*
22. Relaxation, feeling calmer.	70	68	26	30
23. Becoming a burden on others.	10	26	21	0
24. Allows me to be alone when I want to be.	40	16	16	0
25. Avoid hassles with parents.	30	42	68	50
26. Dangers to physical health.	60	10*	16	0
27. Wanting to learn about drugs.	50	10*	53	50
28. Increased awareness of music, sights, tastes, etc.	80	32*	26	50

[1]All figures are percentages; N=10 for counselors; N=19 for clients
*Significant difference in frequency of reporting, $P > .05$.

REFERENCES

1. F. Redlich and D. X. Freedman, The Theory and Practice of
   Psychiatry. Basic Books, New York, 1966.

2. C. R. Rogers, Client-Centered Therapy. Houghton-Mifflin,
   Boston, 1971.

3. C. B. Truax and R. R. Carkhuff, Client and therapist transparency in the psychotherapeutic encounter. Journal of
   Counseling Psychology, 12: 3-9 (1965).

4. O. Fenichel, The Psychoanalytic Theory of Neurosis. Norton,
   New York, 1945.

5. D. M. Pedersen and K. L. Higbee, Self disclosure and relationship to the target person. Merrill-Palmer Quarterly 15: 213-20
   (1969).

6. J. V. DeLong, Treatment and rehabilitation. In: Drug Abuse
   Survey Project, Dealing with Drug Abuse. Praeger, New York,
   1972.

7. D. C. Des Jarlais, Socialization, social influence and social
   power in a cross-age drug education project. Doctoral dissertation, University of Michigan, 1971.

8. T. Parsons, The Social System. Free Press, New York, 1951.

9. J. P. Guilford, Psychometric Methods. McGraw-Hill, New York,
   1936.

10. R. Tagiuri, Person perception. In: G. Lindzey and E. Aronson
    (eds.), The Handbook of Social Psychology. Vol. 3(2nd ed.).
    Addison-Wesley, Reading, Mass., 1969.

PATTERNS OF TREATMENT UTILIZATION IN A MULTIMODALITY DRUG ABUSE TREATMENT PROGRAM

Iradj Siassi, M.D.
Burleigh P. Angle, M.A.
Dominick C. Alston, B.A.

Comprehensive Drug Abuse Treatment Program
Western Psychiatric Institute and Clinic
University of Pittsburgh
Pittsburgh, Pennsylvania

INTRODUCTION

Appropriateness and acceptability are the critical factors in any comprehensive approach to the problem of drug dependence [1]. To argue the merits of one type of treatment versus another in the absence of data about what type of treatments the patients are eligible for, and the treatments they actually chose, would be a sterile debate. Generally, the focus has centered around the superiority of one type treatment over the other on such marginal issues as applicant screening [2]; simulation of decision making processes regarding referral of multimodal patients [3]; "treatment boards" [4]; or multimodality treatment impact [5, 6]. However, there has been a dearth of studies analyzing the patterns of treatment utilization in multimodality drug abuse treatment programs. Precise investigation into the interaction of delivery systems and patient needs have not been thoroughly formulated.

In this paper, (A) analysis is made of a year's experience in a program whose resources included: 1). an inpatient detoxification unit; 2). a methadone maintenance clinic; 3). a choice of therapeutic communities; and 4). a wide range of outpatient therapies, and (B) an examination is undertaken of the fate a year later of the patient admitted in the first month of the study.

In examining the patterns of utilization of these services by patients, this initial effort considers the appropriate pairing of treatment services to patient eligibility.

SETTING

The Comprehensive Drug Abuse Treatment Program (CDATP) of the Western Psychiatric Institute and Clinic has been in operation since October 1973. Its component members consist of 2 therapeutic communities, a methadone maintenance program, a family therapy unit, and a core unit of "drug specialists" who carry out the initial screening evaluation on all patients, as well as providing a variety of psychotherapies.

METHODOLOGY

This report on patterns of utilization consists of 2 studies. The first is a description of the treatment eligibility and selection of services by all patients of the CDATP during 1975. The second study is a one-year follow-up of those patients who applied for treatment in January 1975.

From January 1, 1975 to December 31, 1975, 648 patients applied to the CDATP for treatment, and were evaluated by a core unit of drug specialists (masters and doctorate level mental health professionals). This procedure included a psychosocial evaluation as well as filling out state forms on sociodemographic variables, drug abuse history, medical history, and personal background. On the basis of this intake evaluation, the patients' eligibility for treatment was established. The patients were then informed of the available services, and reference was made on the basis of both their eligibility and their choice to: methadone maintenance; an inpatient detoxification unit; one of two residential therapeutic communities; a family therapy unit; or to outpatient psychotherapy.

The first study consists of reviewing the intake records and disposition reports of all 648 patients who applied for treatment during 1975. The patients were divided on the basis of their abuse of opioid or non-opioids, and were socio-demographically compared.

The second study examines the fate a year later of the 81 drug abusers who applied for treatment during January 1975.

RESULTS

A). The first study illustrates 4 variables on which substantial difference existed: sex, age, race, and previous treatment. As can be seen in Table I, the opioid abusers are predominantly male, whereas the non-opioid abusers are equally divided between male and female. The non-opioid abusers tend to be younger than the opioid abusers. Racially, the greatest number of opioid abusers are black, while the greatest number of non-opioid abusers are white. And finally, the opioid abusers have had previous treatment experiences more often than the non-opioid abusers. These differences in demographic variables are consistent with our studies of other urban area drug abuse treatment programs. The two questions that we posed were: a). what services are these patients eligible for?; and b). given their eligibility, what services do they choose to utilize? The answers to these questions are presented in Table II.

As noted, there were 648 applicants for treatment. Of these, 376 (58%) indicated that they abused opioids, while 272 (42%) indicated that they abused non-opioids (i.e. barbiturates, amphetamines, benzodiazepines, hashish, marijuana, etc.). It should be noted that 100% of those opioid abusers who were eligible for methadone maintenance chose to go into methadone maintenance treatment. Of those 280 opioid abusers who were not eligible for methadone maintenance, 160 (57%) chose outpatient psychotherapy and 8 (1%) chose to enter a therapeutic community. The remaining 42% of the opioid abusers not eligible for methadone treatment either refused service (29%); were jailed before receiving service (8%); chose referral to another program (2.5%); or chose inpatient detoxification (2.5%). Nearly all of the latter, 116 patients, were those who demanded entry into methadone maintenance; and failing that, were reluctant to seriously consider other treatment modalities.

As noted, there were 272 applicants who were non-opioid abusers. Of these, 56% chose outpatient psychotherapy, an overwhelming preference above either therapeutic communities (chosen by 13%), inpatient detoxification (chosen by 13%), or family therapy (chosen by only 9%). Of this group, 12% refused service.

In summary, those patients with a history of opiate abuse who were eligible for methadone maintenance, all chose to enter this treatment modality. Those who were not eligible, either chose outpatient psychotherapy or else failed to enter into treatment. The non-opioid abusers tended to choose outpatient psychotherapy far above any other treatment modality.

B). There were 81 applicants for treatment in January 1975. Table III shows a demographic analysis of the patient characteristics. Table IV shows the treatment selected by opioid versus non-opioid abusers. Table IV also shows what became of these patients by the end of 1975.

There were 47 applicants who were abusers of opioids. Of these, 12 were eligible and entered methadone maintenance. At the end of a year, 10 were still in methadone maintenance, one had died of an overdose, and one had transferred to another program. Of the remaining 35 opioid abusers who were not eligible for methadone maintenance, 20 (57%) chose outpatient psychotherapy; and by the end of the year, 12 of them (60%) were still in treatment. The other 15 opioid abusers either refused service (28%); were jailed before receiving service (9%); chose inpatient detoxification (3%); or were transferred to another program (3%).

There were 34 non-opioid abusers who applied for treatment in January 1975. All 34 applicants entered into outpatient psychotherapy; but by the end of the year, only 9 (37%) were still in treatment. Of the 5 who entered into a therapeutic community, 2 (40%) were still in treatment at the end of a year. The family therapy service was chosen by 5 applicants; and at the end of the year 4 (80%) were still in treatment.

CONCLUSIONS

The two preliminary conclusions that can be drawn are: 1). The observed differences between opioid and non-opioid abusers suggest that these two groups represent different populations with different expectations and different degrees of motivation for treatment. 2). The either/or positions on therapeutic communities versus methadone maintenance; inpatient detoxification versus outpatient psychotherapy; family therapy versus individual therapy, etc. are simply irrelevant. In the absence of legal restrictions that compel the patient to accept a given treatment modality, we expect that opioid abusers who are eligible for methadone maintenance will continue to seek this treatment modality; and those who are not eligible, will either opt for outpatient psychotherapy or refuse treatment. And, the overwhelming majority of non-opioid abusers will continue to choose outpatient psychotherapy.

ACKNOWLEDGEMENT

Funded in part by NIDA Grant #5-H80DA01356.
Special thanks to Mr. Terry Piper for his kind assistance. Requests for table data and reprints should be directed to either Burleigh P. Angle or Dominick C. Alston.

REFERENCES

1. L. Brill and L. Lieberman, Major Modalities in the Treatment of Drug Abuse, Behavioral Publications, New York, 1972.
2. M. Greenberg, Proc. 5th Natl. Conf. on Methadone Treatment, National Association for the Prevention of Addiction to Narcotics, New York, 1973, pp. 143-150.
3. L. D. Savitz, K. Tile, and T. U. McCahill, Proc. 5th Natl. Conf. on Methadone Treatment, National Association for the Prevention of Addiction to Narcotics, New York, 1973, pp. 158-168.
4. W. Moton, J. Sall, U. Petros, Proc. 5th Natl. Conf. on Methadone Treatment, National Association for the Prevention of Addiction to Narcotics, New York, 1973, pp. 151-157.
5. B. S. Brown, R. L. Raport, V. F. Boss, et. al., Comp. Psychiatry, 13(4), 1972, pp. 391-397.
6. J. H. Jaffe, M. S. Zaks, and C. M. Washington, I. J. of Addict., 4:481-490, (1969).

RURAL DRUG TREATMENT WITHIN A
COMMUNITY MENTAL HEALTH CENTER SYSTEM

Gwendolyn A. Hayes, M.P.H.

Division of Drug Misuse
Department of Mental Health
Jackson, Mississippi

This study is an examination of the utilization of drug
misuse services provided by Community Mental Health Centers within rural Mississippi. It has been demonstrated that several
demographic variables which systematically describe characteristics
of living conditions of populations residing in specified geographic units are an important determinant affecting the utilization of mental health services. The variables examined were
age, sex, ethnicity, employment status, educational level, and
type of drug misused.

Historically, in community mental health centers in Mississippi, the clientele are mostly white, and middle class. The
failure of these centers to meet the needs of the lower socio-
economic and minority groups is of paramount concern. This paper
addresses the following questions: What are the characteristics
that describe persons receiving drug misuse treatment within the
centers?; Is the group receiving drug treatment services of the
center indicative of the total catchment population of these
centers?; How well are rural populations needs met by the delivery
of drug misuse treatment services within the centers in Mississippi?: and How do centers in Mississippi comply with federal and
state standards and criteria?

Socio-economic status shows a strong positive correlation
with the utilization of service. Other pertinent socio-environmental factors include the cultureal and ethnic patterns that
determine which behaviors are defined as problems. When a minor
is the client his reference group, the functioning of his family
or guardian affects the outcome of care. The organization and
design of services affect utilization. Factors such as the
location and cost of services and the presence of impediments,
such as "waiting lists," are of major importance. Other factors
which influence the use of services are the interests and background of the staff, the use of outreach and advocacy techniques.

469

Eight community mental health centers were scrutinized for this paper. The communities served by these centers vary in size. The minimum size of the centers catchment areas is 75,000 persons with a maximum of 245,00 persons.

All centers face at least two of the traditional barriers of utilization of services—financial and geographic accessibility. Mississippi is basically a rural state, therefore, many clients have problems with transportation. As an aid to the transportation problem, many centers have mental health workers located in some or all of their catchment counties or they use another alternative, rotating of clinics which are set up frequently throughout the center's catchment area. Most of these centers serve from 2 to 10 counties. The centers are centrally located in the catchment community and offer transportation where possible.

Drug services within the center are integrated into the center's mental health system where access to the center's physicians, psychologists, social workers and other treatment personnel is readily available.

Clients usually enter the system by referrals from other agencies and institutions, (including but not limited to schools, churches, social services agencies) walk-ins, courts, parents or guardian, peers. Referrals are also made by the center to other agencies such as Vocational Rehabilitation and hospitals. Affiliation agreements exist for hospital care, etc.

Most centers offer a broad range of services, though some centers are more comprehensive in their capability for services. Among the treatment modalities most frequently used are outpatient, inpatient, partial hospitalization and detoxification. Services available are individual, group, and family counseling, psychiatric examination and evaluation, consultation and education, biofeedback, transactional analysis and emergency services.

Data Collection, Results and Discussion

The study group was comprised of all patients who received drug treatment services from the eight centers during the period of February 1, 1975 - January 31, 1976. Data were obtained from CODAP admission forms completed routinely upon each client's initial visit to the center. Table 1 represents the age distribution, sex, and ethnic group of the drug clients seen. A total of 318 persons were seen during the study period. The predominance of white males is evident and also of clients within the age range of 18-24. Only 16% of the drug clients seen by the centers are black. The total % of the black population of the centers catchment area with drug problems is 41%. Assuming that the drug problems are equally distributed among the population, blacks with drug problems are under-represented by a ratio of 3:1.

Table 2 examines general characteristics of the state with
specific emphasis on those eight centers which had a drug program.
All of the programs examined were of recent origin and have been
in operation for less than a year.

As indicated in an Incidence and Prevalence Survey conducted
in 1974, Mississippi has a relatively low rate of drug use as
compared to other states. The recent history of drug misuse in
the state has been characterized by a marked rise in treatment
programs.

The data reflects the classic findings that males outnumber
females in receiving drug misuse services at community mental
health centers. It further reflects the disproportionate high
use of these services by the white population. Of the 318
patients in treatment, 193 or 61% were males and 125 or 39% were
females. The males were most likely to be receiving treatment
at these centers for drug misuse than females. The number of
drug misusers in treatment in Mississippi is higher for whites
than blacks. Of the 318 drug misusers treated, 265 or 84% were
white and 53 or 16% were black. Most of the patients were polydrug users. The highest peaks of drugs used were 11% barbiturates, 32% hashish and marijuana, 18% tranquilizers and other
sedatives, 5% heroin, 7% amphetamines, 5% hallucinogens, 8%
morphine and other opiates. The other 14% was spread between
illegal methadone, alcohol, cocaine, inhalents, over the counter
and prescription drugs. The secondary and tertiary drug of
choice were also obtained. The secondary results were more
significant. 28% of the patients had no secondary drug of choice.
19% used marijuana and hashish, 12% used alcohol, 8% tranquilizers, 9% hallucinogens, 7% amphetamines, 6% barbiturates, 4%
morphine and other opiates, 3% cocaine. The remaining 2% was
spread between illegal methadone, inhalents, over the counter and
prescription drugs.

The drug misusers in treatment were a youthful population.
The range in age of all patients in treatment were from 10-70.
Some 6% were over 50 years of age, 25% were between 25-49, 47%
were 18-24 and 21% were below 17 years of age. The youthfulness
of the population in treatment is related to the early age at
which onset of drug misuse commonly occurs. In Mississippi, as
nationally, the onset of drug misuse is now an adolescent
phenomenon. The years of highest risk is quoted as 15-18 years
of age. Most of the drug misusers in treatment were not gainfully employed. 239 or 75% were not employed. Only 16 or 5%
were either in school or employed part-time and 63 or 20% were
employed full-time. 189 or 59% had less than a high school
education with 40% of this group having at least a ninth grade
education and 54 or 17% had educational levels beyond high school.
These findings support the interpretation that persistent misuse
of drugs is usually incompatible with steady employment or long
term academic achievement.

471

The greatest disparity as evidenced by the data is the black underserved populations. There are several conjectured reasons for this. Among these are the historical impact of systematic discrimination, the resulting lack of knowledge and experience on the part of the minority community in utilizing public services, the ineffective means of outreach techniques used to attract minorities, the limited number of black professionals and other personnel employed by the centers which limits the ability of the program to attract and deal with problems of the minority population. There is a great feeling of disillusionment among minorities and in some cases, hostility and distrust toward the proliferation of predominantly white run, white oriented programs. The criminal justice system is frequently utilized to deal with minority problems. Treatment alternatives are not made as available in the majority of cases for minorities. This indicator also contributes to the negligible number of blacks treated at these centers. There are cultural and social variations in which persons define drug problems, therefore, it impacts on utilization of these services.

The third issue addressed in this paper is how well are rural needs met by the delivery of services within the centers in Mississippi. Services are provided rural populations by extending center services into rural communities, by the establishment of satellite clinics in the counties at least one day a week and by placing mental health county workers in the surrounding rural counties. This is one means of ensuring the accessibility of community mental health services to all residents of a catchment area. It is not without problems. In rural communities, transportation is still a barrier to utilization. There are no public transportation systems established.

In order to maximize participation in the Center's programming, there is a need for continuous involvement of all groups within the community in the planning, development, and operation of the program. This ensures that the Center's program will be responsive to the needs of the community, have visibility, optimal utilization by all subgroups, and a public base of support.

The fourth issue explores the degree of centers in the state compliance with federal and state standards and criteria.

The federal funding criteria mandated by NIDA, coupled with several state requirements have been used in Mississippi for state programming standards and criteria for treatment programs. While much drug programming follows the traditional medical model, most mental health centers follow the community mental health model. It is very difficult to develop standards which are truly applicable to all programs in all circumstances. The basic underlying intent of these federal funding criteria is to assure continuity, quality and a degree of consistency of services within treatment programs. Before the federal criteria were made more flexible, allowing for more local program discretion concerning the applicability of these criteria, programs were facing some difficulties. Among these were the requirements for routine physical examinations which included certain prescribed tests regardless of the patient's presenting needs or drug(s) misused; and the hours of the program's operation. The difficulty in compliance with the requirements for physical examination is the inherent problem of available health resources in rural areas. Many of the patient's drug problem(s) had no parallel importance to their medical histories. Thus, most of the programs applied for exception to this requirement. The federal funding criteria states that each outpatient drug free program shall provide services at least six days per week. Most centers official service hours are from 9-5 with answering services after hours to answer emergencies. Since most of the centers follow this same regimen, most applied for exception to this requirement though many have scheduled evening and weekend clinics.

The state devised a mechanism to assign static capacity slots to centers based on the amount of federal and local match dollars. The total amount of federal and local monies per program was divided by $1700 which gave the number of matrixable slots, $1700 being the maximum amount that NIDA used to compute outpatient cost. In order for a client to be counted as a static slot, the program has to provide the level of services as specified in the criteria and must render person to person services at least once per month on a regularly scheduled basis. Other state requirements include the establishment of advisory councils, provision of in-service training and participation in the state's planning effort for the state plan.

Conclusion

A statewide study of drug misuse programs and the population of drug misusers in treatment has limitation and advantages. The major limitation of this approach is that it is restricted to those who seek treatment. The representativeness of this population with respect to true incidence and prevalence is questionable since this data is now dated within the state. The advantage of this approach is that it provides detailed information on a sizable portion of the statewide population of drug misusers and the treatment they receive.

TABLE I

Age, Sex, Ethnic Group By
Community Mental Health Centers
(CODAP – February 1, 1975 – January 31, 1976)

	REGION I				REGION II				REGION III				REGION IV				REGION VI				REGION VII				REGION XII				REGION XIII				
I.R.D	June 1975				Feb. 1975				May 1975				Oct. 1975				March 1975				Aug. 1975				Feb. 1975				Feb. 1975				
S.C.	16				28				27				14				16				14				20				27				
AGE (yrs)	BM	BF	WM	WF	BM	BF	WM	WF	BM	BF	WM	WF	BM	BF	WM	WF	BM	BF	WM	WF	BM	BF	WM	WF	BM	BF	WM	WF	BM	BF	WM	WF	TOTAL
<17	4	0	1	1	0	0	5	2	0	0	1	3	0	0	3	1	1	2	4	3	0	0	0	1	4	0	5	2	0	0	13	11	67
18 – 24	0	1	8	2	2	0	12	5	1	0	9	8	0	0	2	0	7	1	8	5	1	0	2	1	5	3	17	5	1	0	28	17	151
25 – 49	0	0	0	0	1	2	3	9	1	1	6	4	3	1	1	1	3	2	4	9	1	0	2	0	1	0	1	7	2	1	9	5	80
50 +	0	0	0	0	0	0	6	2	0	0	4	2	0	0	0	0	0	1	0	2	0	0	1	0	0	0	0	1	0	0	0	1	20
TOTAL	4	1	9	3	3	2	26	18	2	1	20	17	3	1	6	2	11	6	16	19	2	0	5	2	10	3	23	15	3	1	50	34	318

LEGEND

I.R.D. – Initial Reporting Date on CODAP; S.C. – Static Capacity (maximum number of patients who can be treated at any one time)
BM – Black Male; WM – White Male; BF – Black Female; WF – White Female

TABLE 2

Population Characteristics
(1970 Census)

Mississippi Total Population (2,216,912)

REGIONS	POPULATION TOTALS	ETHNIC COMPOSITION			
		BLACK	%	WHITE	%
Region I Clarksdale, Ms	87,527	55,142	63.0	32,385	36.7
Region II Oxford, Ms	156,004	65,366	41.9	90,638	58.1
Region III Tupelo, Ms	157,807	35,980	22.8	121,827	77.2
Region IV Corinth, Ms	78,104	8,826	11.3	69,278	88.7
Region VI Greenwood, Ms	178,618	100,026	56.0	78,592	44.0
Region VII Starkville, Ms	148,473	56,717	38.2	91,756	61.8
Region XII Hattiesburg, Ms	213,484	57,854	27.1	155,630	72.9
Region XIII Gulfport, Ms	187,872	32,126	17.1	155,746	82.9
Total	1,207,889	412,037	41.0	795,852	59.0

DADE COUNTY'S PRIDE PROGRAM

Donald J. Samuels

Pride Program
Dade County Schools
Miami, Florida

It's a feeling...
   It's a program...

Pride is a feeling.

Especially, it's a feeling of self...a sense of one's own worth, of dignity, of self-respect. It's peer counseling, Magic Circle, "Ziggy's Place." It's rap rooms, decision making, value clarification. It's parent communication, transactional analysis; it's transcendental meditation; music, yoga, leathercraft, macrame and a whole batch of alternatives. Put it all together and we're talking about the Dade County Public Schools' Substance Education Program.

PRIDE stands for Professional Resources in Developmental Education. It is a program designed to prevent students from developing self-defeating behavior. It steers students away from drugs, and other potential problem areas, and points them toward themselves-toward feeling good about themselves and those around them.

The program recognizes that young people face a myriad of potential problem areas. Drug abuse is just one. So while it includes drug information, it does so within the context of decision making, intra/inter personal skills development, the ability to distinguish alternatives and make rational decisions about one's life. It seeks to help young people develop to their optimum capability in all areas. Pride in self begins early. So does Dade's program. By use of a vehicle called the Magic Circle, elementary school youngsters are provided the opportunity for self-expression, for finding out that other people feel the same way you do sometimes but sometimes they don't and that's OK, too. Each person becomes a communicator who both gives and receives. Everyone is someone. In addition to being involved in a Magic

Circle program, elementary school youngsters can be found in a
host of other affective education programs - programs designed to
make them feel, think, express, interact, to promote personal
growth and develop that important feeling of self-esteem.

PRIDE Is Having Someone Be There

In PRIDE everyone gets into the act. It starts with the
resource specialist, trained in techniques of interaction, and
knowledgeable about community resources. There's a specialist in
every junior and senior high school in Dade County.

The specialist assists teachers in obtaining materials
necessary for the informational aspects of the program, counsels
parents, refers and assists youngsters in getting into rehabilitation agencies should that be necessary, organizes all kinds of
student involvement programs — like yoga and macrame and transcendental meditation. Having been trained, he or she now trains
others — parents, teachers, students — to enteract in a positive
way, to reach out to each other. The resource specialist recognizes that teenagers generally can relate to others better than
to anyone else, understands peer pressure and trains young people
to act as peer counselors.

More than 1,500 peer counselors have been trained in techniques of active listening, clarification of values and decision
making skills, and more join the ranks all along. Peer counselors
have worked with over 5,000 students in group situations and
hundreds more in individual exchanges helping them to identify,
clarify and work out their own personal "hassles."

Their program is a give and get one. While they're helping
others, the counselors are reinforcing their skills in interaction,
becoming more aware of their own feelings, growing as they help
others grow. Some student counselors may elect to work with
younger students at the fifth and sixth grade levels. These teen
counselors visit feeder elementary schools on a regular basis and
help youngsters to understand themselves better. They pave the
way to junior high, perhaps make some of the "heavy" problems
these youngsters will face much lighter.

PRIDE Is Having a Place to Talk and Someone to Talk To

The Lighthouse, The Yak Shack, Ziggy's Place, The Open Door,
The Way Up, The Place, Aquarius, One Step Beyond. They sound like
TV shows, but they're not. They're the names given to some of
the rap rooms located in all Dade's junior and senior highs.

Each resource specialist is responsible for having one in
his school. There's always someone there to listen. It's a place
where kids can drop in, talk about their problem, socialize, just

477

have fun. The kids design, decorate and name their own rap room.
You're likely to find bean bag chairs, colorful posters, murals-
who knows what. The rap room may be used on a drop-in basis by
individuals, on a regular schedule by a group or by entire classes
wanting to experience some different kinds of learning. It's a
get-to-know-each-other place for people who might otherwise feel
different, alone, alienated. This applies to students, teachers,
administrators and parents also.

PRIDE Is Doing Something That's Fun and Interesting

Having nothing to do ... being bored ... looking for kicks;
these are some of the things that lead to inverse behavior. The
resource specialists help to organize programs the students want.

A project might be any of the various programs mentioned,
or maybe it's getting together to help the handicapped or clean
up the neighborhood. Maybe it's making sure the rap room is open
in the evening so there's a place to go. Resource specialists
have to make things happen during school, after school, in the
evening. The plan is simple: find out what the students want,
find out how to get it, do it.

Activities run the gamut of physical, sensory, emotional,
interpersonal, social, political, and intellectual.

PRIDE Is Training Teachers and Parents to Communicate with Youngsters

Assisting teachers in working more effectively and affec-
tively with students is a part of the specialist's role. It may
be through a faculty workshop demonstrating a value-clarification,
problem-solving technique, a visitation to a teacher's class and
some on-site practice of selected skills. Once the teacher has
learned them and can go it alone, he receives professional growth
credit for his new expertise.

Inservice education for staff at all levels is an important
part of PRIDE. Parents get into the act, too. One way may be
through a workshop, available days and evenings on a regular
basis. The point is to enable parents to communicate better with
their youngsters, understand their lifestyle and needs.

Parents get help in other ways. It's not enough just to
learn how to communicate with your youngster. Suppose he's
already in trouble? To whom does one turn for advice and help?
The resource specialist can direct parents to the proper agencies,
counsel them, help them over some of the rough spots.

PRIDE Is When Your School Board and Community Support Your Program

The pride program is supported to the tune of $1.2 million dollars annually in local funds recommended by an administration and appropriated by a School Board that recognized a need and, with the community behind it, reacted to that need. Dade County has been especially fortunate in having a uniquely qualified school board member as advisor to the program - Ben Sheppard. Widely known throughout and beyond Dade for his interest and activity in drug prevention and rehabilitation, "Dr. Ben" is both doctor and lawyer - a practicing pediatrician, former juvenile judge, and a pioneer in the field of drug rehabilitation.

PRIDE is a system-wide program which must be broad enough yet individual enough to serve the diverse needs of the nation's sixth largest school system. Program co-ordinator is Don Samuels, to whom falls the direct responsibility for organization and implementation of program design, budget, staff and curricula management.

The nature and scope of the PRIDE program is shared with groups and agencies throughout the community. Thus the program acts as a liaison between students and parents and those agencies that best can assist with whatever problem may exist.

PRIDE ... Is Proud

Dade County's program has been nationally recognized by the President's Special action Office on Drug Prevention, as attuned to the national philosophy of what drug abuse prevention and education should be about. PRIDE is being emulated by other school systems - and is pleased to share its contributions to youth even as it seeks more and better answers.

The goal of education is to provide for the optimum physical, social, emotional, and intellectual growth and development of the student in the light of his needs and interests. The aim of the PRIDE program is to ensure that each student has the foundation and the spirit, as well as the skills, with which to achieve that goal — the kind of life that makes a person proud.

GREEN LAKES WILDERNESS EXPERIENCE

Richard Beals, Counselor; Joel Miller, M.A.;
Peter Janke, Researcher; Al Brundage, R.N.;
David Striar, Student

Oregon Methadone Treatment Program
Portland, Oregon

INTRODUCTION

Mental Health practitioners continue to ask the question: How do we break through the barriers that keep the opiate-addicted individual from achieving potential for satisfaction? How can the addict's social relationships be strengthened? How can we create conditions which help people realize a meaningful and creative life? And finally, can a more effective method be found to kindle the forces from within to help provide individuals with personal strength?

The Green Lakes Wilderness Experience was an experiment in expanding drug treatment into a non-conventional environment. It was hoped that this combination of therapy and the outdoors would provide some answers to the questions raised above.

The planning group decided to take ten clients and five staff members on a ten-day wilderness experience which included mountaineering and survival activities. Both components shared common elements: 1) risk-taking, 2) rigorous physical exercixe, 3) the need for integrated effort, 4) individual problem-solving, 5) unfamiliar tasks, 6) new and demanding environments. The planners felt that these two different situations would be catalysts to breaking down staff-client, staff-staff, and client-client communication barriers. In addition, they would provide the stimuli for self-exploration, assertiveness, increased competence and self-confidence on the part of both staff and clients (or, as they were later designated, support and main team members, respectively).

I. SELECTION OF STAFF AND CLIENTS

The staff selected consisted of three counselors, one researcher and one nurse. Their varied abilities, plus their skill in counseling and observation, allowed costs to be held at a minimum.

As the wilderness experience was seen as a non-institutional means to facilitate intimacy, awareness, confidence, and competence in clients, it was obvious that the people who would benefit most from such an experience would be those deficient in the above-mentioned characteristics.

II. PRE-TRIP PLANNING

Evening groups were held once a week for the purpose of procuring and organizing the necessary supplies. Group 1 priced and purchased non-personal equipment, such as camping stoves, hiking boots,
and back-packs. Group 2 organized menus, purchased and distributed
food. Group 3 ordered essential medical supplies.

III. WILDERNESS ACTIVITIES

The trip began on a Monday morning in mid-July. The first discrepancy between plans and reality appeared at once. Instead of the
eight main team members scheduled, only five appeared. The staff-
client ratio had dwindled from 10:5 to 5:5 and the trip itself seemed jeopardized. It was then decided to go ahead with the project
and depart on schedule.
From Portland the group of ten drove to the Three Sisters
Wilderness Area. Arriving about noon, they began hiking along a six
mile trail leading from the roadhead up into the Green Lakes area
at the base of the South Sister. For many of the clients and some
of the staff, this initial hike with 35 to 40 pound packs up steep
and eventually trailless terrain was their greatest extended physical exertion in years and extremely rough going. The country was
spectacularly beautiful, but progress along the trail brought with
it the second major shock of the day. Within a mile the trail itself was completely covered with snow which deepened with increasing gains in altitude. Within a few hours the group, prepared for
a summer camping trip, found itself in the grip of winter. Uncertainty and anxieties began to replace the initial exuberance of the
hike.
This second departure from expectations proved to be a major
obstacle to the group's planned activities. First of all, it increased the normal separation between fast and slow hikers on the
trail; snow and the psychological difficulties in accepting it slowed several of the hikers to a crawl. This combined with ambiguity
in selecting the project's campsite resulted in a day-long separation of two support team members from the rest of the group. Secondly, the unexpected winter conditions constituted a major psychological, as well as physical, impediment. Two of the clients became
particularly depressed and withdrawn by the discrepancy between the
totally frozen lakes and their dreams of swimming and fishing. They
refused to participate in planned activities and seriously affected
the morale of the group with their openly expressed wishes to return to the city.
Both these crises, however, were discussed openly and forth-
rightly in group sessions around evening campfires. The separated
staff members were reintegrated into the group after a long and
heated discussion about the importance of group participation and
shared experiences of the wilderness project. Similarly, the dis-
gruntled clients were able to express their anger and frustration to
a receptive group. As a result, they became full participants again
and later encouraged others with their enthusiasm and energy. These

evening group sessions helped greatly both in overcoming unexpected obstacles and in underlining the therapeutic intentions of the trip. Without them, it is quite likely that the trip would have completely disintegrated and ended in failure within the first two days.

Instead, pride and satisfaction began to develop as the group became able to transcend the unexpected difficulties of winter camping and continue the planned activities despite ice and snow. During the next three days the group separated into two halves, one of which would attempt an ascent of the 10,000 ft. South Sister, while the other set out on an overnight survival hike.

The first mountaineering group consisted of the five members who felt most capable of succeeding. Three staff members and two clients left the 6,000 ft. base camp early in the morning and worked their way on two ropes through mountainous terrain in order to establish a secondary camp at the 8,000 ft. level. They experienced winds in excess of 50 mph upon arrival, however, and spent the rest of the day and all night pinned down in their tents. Once again, some interaction around the campfire occurred, but most of the time was spent inside tents, sleeping or melting snow with which to cook meals. The final assault on the summit was scheduled for morning. Since the winds persisted, the group decided at the coaxing of the staff guide in charge to return to base camp. It was felt that an ascent of the summit could be hazardous since summit winds can exceed 100 mph.

The second mountaineering group departed two days later. The logistics were identical. The second group hiked to the secondary campsite that had been established by the first group and decided, since one of their members was suffering from altitude sickness, that they would establish a small camp for her, try to push on to the summit that day, and return to the secondary camp by nightfall. It was early enough in the day that a summit assault could be made without endangering the member left behind. This group continued, reaching with great effort the summit in the afternoon, and returned to find the remaining member not yet recovered. It was decided then that for her safety the group would descend to base camp. The entire second expedition was thus compressed into one day.

Both mountaineering groups, whether or not they made the summit, shared the same feelings of companionship, excitement, and accomplishment. Whether it was the success of reaching the camp at 8,000 feet, or the success of reaching the summit, all participants reported feeling they had pushed themselves close to their limits and reached a goal worth attaining.

The overnight survival outings were more problematic. The original plan envisaged group members foraging for edible plants, fishing, and testing their skills in the ancient craft of woodlore by constructing rude shelters against the night. With snow, ice, and winter temperatures, however, these plans required drastic revision. It was decided to take sleeping bags for safety's sake, but leave behind all tents, utensils, and food other than a few pieces of jerky.

The first survival group, which set out past the frozen lakes as the mountaineering group began its climb, soon disintegrated, com-

plaining of the purposelessness of the venture, and returned to base
camp after only a few hours. Once more, open ventilation of feelings and clarification of purposes in the evening group session
helped revitalize the participants' going. This same group later
succeeded as the second mountaineering ascent group. The second
survival group hiked from the South to the Middle Sister over snow-
covered hills and established a camp among scrub pine surrounding an
8,000 ft. lake, returning to base camp the following day. Both maj-
or components of the wilderness outing had been accomplished - not
in the manner they had been conceived, perhaps, but accomplished
nonetheless.

The most serious problem of the trip occurred the next afternoon, after six full days in the wilderness. One of the staff members, bathing in the freezing waters of a thawing stream, dislocated
his shoulder, was completely immobilized, and spent the next eight
hours in intense pain. With the exception of one client, who became completely withdrawn, the entire group rallied to his support.
The shoulder was splinted, a protective sun-screen was erected, and
two members of the group ran back out to the trailhead and drove to
the nearest town to alert a rescue team. Others ran to the trailhead for medication, while the rest stayed with the wounded member
to give him support and encouragement. Although unfortunate, the
episode evoked more unity of purpose and closeness of feeling than
anything that could have been planned. The group reacted to an unexpected and dangerous crisis with great compassion and competence.
At nightfall a rescue team of volunteers reached the campsite and
carried the wounded member out to the trailhead. Shortly after mid-
night he was admitted to a local hospital and the wilderness experience ended with a crescendo of unanticipated excitement and exertion.

IV. ASSESSMENT OF RESULTS

In assessing the effectiveness of the wilderness outing we
have listed below observed behaviors and responses during the outing
and evaluated its long-term effects. 1. The Wilderness Group, meeting once a week in the evening, had a choesiveness and energetic
quality unique in this agency. 2. Nine days of close interaction,
in camp and in tents, brought about feelings of closeness. The final accident was a culmination of this trend, bring the group (with
one exception), closer than it had ever been. 3. Client-participants repeatedly undertook and accomplished endeavors of which they
were convinced they were incapable. The three who scaled the mountain were the three who had not attempted it on the first trial because they were positive they had no chance of reaching the top. Two
of them made it, and the success gave them a feeling of satisfaction which, according to their later reports, has endured. 4. Personal differences and crises which, in some cases, threatened the
continuance of the project were aired in nightly group discussions
and in smaller sub-groups. These meetings were generally open and
productive. 5. With the notable exception of one client member, no
long-term fundamental changes in behavior or personality resulted
from the Green Lakes experience. Nor are there any current behav-

ioral indications that, with the one exception yet to be discussed, any of the clients significantly increased their assertiveness, feelings of competence, or abilities to adapt to new and challenging situations. Moreover, basic problems of obtaining employment and maintaining close and important relationships persist for most of the participants.

In one case, however, fundamental, long-term changes do appear to have occurred. At the beginning of trip planning, this man was viewed by his own counselor and at least two of the main team members, as untrustworthy and likely to require much support and supervision. As the trip planning progressed, this client began to take on increasing responsibility for organizing the group and obtaining the necessary equipment for the trip. In addition, throughout the entire experience, both support and main team members learned that he could be relied upon to provide support and direction.

To best illustrate the nature of this man's behavioral change, it should be noted that as heavy, daily user of marijuana, he brought a quantity of it with him, but left it at the trailhead at the beginning of the hike and remained drug-free for the entire experience. After returning to Portland, he estab lished a more amicable and productive relationship with his counselor, successfully detoxified from methadone and established himself in a vocational training program. Currently, he has entered into a living arrangement with a female Program client and her child. In this relationship he appears to be accepting paternal responsibilities. He is also seeking employment.

In the mountains, exposed to unexpected winter weather and unaccustomed exertion and challenge, purely role-based distinctions between 'counselor' and 'addict' eroded, leaving both counselor and addict freer, simply as persons, to work together, make decisions, solve problems, interact, and consider the significance of their actions and experience without formal constraints. The participants felt this happening. "What I got out of it the most," one of the client-participants decided, looking back on the experience half a year later, "(was) one of the best highs I had all summer long. I felt like I was on a cloud for a month after I came back." Yet another client reported of her mountain-climbing experience, "(I) really honestly didn't believe I could make it, I really didn't. It was a very satisfying thing..(to have reached the summit)." She went on to note that "part of the point of the whole thing was experiencing things as they were and coping with them." It is clear that clients were able to gain non-drug-induced payoffs for their actions, and to develop greater feelings of self-confidence. Thus, although the wilderness adventure had few demonstrable long-term effects, it does appear to have provided an enrichening experience in both staff and clients' lives.

MEASURING UNPRESCRIBED DRUG USE WITH RANDOM INTERVAL URINALYSIS SCHEDULES

Robert J. Harford and Herbert D. Kleber

Department of Psychiatry
Yale University School of Medicine
New Haven, Connecticut 06511

Federal funding guidelines stipulate that methadone programs must monitor urines of their clients for evidence of unprescribed opiate use on a random basis at least once a week. The value of urinalyses results for clinical practice, patient motivation, and evaluation of program effectiveness is reduced to the extent that use of unprescribed drugs is not detected. Except for Goldstein and Brown's (1) theoretical discussion of this topic, the effects of different methods of scheduling collection of urine samples on the validity of urinalyses results as a measure of actual client opiate abuse has received scant empirical attention. This report describes how a change in the method of scheduling collection of urine samples affected the rate of detected opiate use by members of a methadone maintenance program.

The possibility of undetected drug use is assured by urine scheduling procedures which allow the client "safe" periods (i.e., days during which there is no chance of being tested). Daily collection of urine samples eliminates safe periods and maximizes the probability of detecting unprescribed drug use, but the high costs of lab fees, demands on staff time and inconvenience to clients make this type of collection schedule impractical. The least effective urine collection schedules are periodic sampling procedures in which tests are equally spaced (e.g., every Friday). Because of their constant length intervals between tests, periodic schedules result in safe periods extending from the day of testing to perhaps 24 hours before the next scheduled testing date. If clients learn that there are safe periods in their urine collection schedules, they will be able to use unprescribed drugs without fear of detection.

Three methods for random urine collection have been proposed which produce schedules with variable lengths of intervals between tests. Goldstein and Brown (1) have suggested a constant probability (CP) scheduling method in which the client's probability of being selected for urine testing (1/k) is constant from day to day.

This scheduling system eliminates safe days but allows the possibility (P_n) of extended periods of time without tests which is described by the expression $P_n = (1-1/k)^n$ where n is the number of consecutive days without tests. Indefinite periods of time without tests are theoretically possible under this system. The possibility of long periods of time without being tested might encourage some clients to use opiates in hopes of beating the odds against being detected. There is also the danger of significant undetected relapses to opiate use.

Kleber and Gould (2) demonstrated that extended periods without testing could be eliminated by establishing maximum intervals between tests and randomly sampling from the set of all possible intervals between tests. Each randomly selected interval determines the next test date and initiates a new test interval whose length again is determined by random sampling from the set of intervals. Since the probability of being tested on any one day within the interval is $1/(k-n+1)$ where k is the length of the interval and n is the number of days since the last scheduled test, the probability of going n days without being tested is $P_n = 1-1/(k - (n-1))$. Whenever n=k, the probability of being tested is a certainty. This random interval (RI) scheduling method guarantees that every client will be tested at least once every k days with an average of k/2 days between tests. Like the CP method, RI scheduling allows a finite probability that clients will be scheduled for urine collection on any number of consecutive days. This characteristic eliminates the possibility of safe periods.

Many drug dependence treatment programs currently use neither the CP or RI method of scheduling urine tests but rather use a fixed interval (FI) method. FI algorithms randomly select a fixed number of testing dates from a set of allowable days within a predetermined time interval. Once the desired number of tests are scheduled, no additional tests are scheduled until the beginning of the next testing interval. This method limits the maximum length of time between tests but allows the possibility of safe days. For example, if clients are to be tested twice a week and Monday and Tuesday are selected as the two test dates, the client might realize on Tuesday that he will not be scheduled for another test until the following Monday at the earliest. Consequently, an FI schedule may encourage drug use by guranteeing that it will not be detected under certain conditions. Underdetection of drug use may have adverse consequences for clinical effectiveness and invalidate research or evaluation activities that depend upon urinalysis results.

METHOD

In November 1970 the Park Street methadone clinic of the Drug Dependence Unit in New Haven switched from FI to RI urine collection schedules. We investigated the effects of this change by retrospectively comparing rates of detected quinine and opiate positives during the months immediately preceding and following this change.

RESULTS

January, 1970 to July, 1975 was selected as the time period to be covered by the analyses. During this 67 month period a total of 45,982 urine samples were tested of which 1,713 (3.7%) were positive for quinine and 233 (0.5%) were positive for morphine. The average monthly rates of positive tests were 5.0% for quinine and 1.9% for morphine. The difference in the two sets of percentages is accounted for by the fact that the number of tests per month (mean = 686) was negatively correlated with the percentage of positive tests for quinine (r = -.23; $p < .05$) and morphine (r = -.31; $p < .01$). For quinine, the percentages gradually increased from 2.1% during month 1 to 9.6% during month 67. For morphine, the percentages increased from 2.4% to 3.8%. The mean absolute value of the month-to-month fluctuations in percentage of tests positive for quinine and morphine were 1.3% and 1.4%, respectively. During the FI period from 1/70-11/70 the mean monthly positive rates for quinine and morphine were 4.1% and 3.0%, respectively. The corresponding rates for the last FI month were 3.7% and 2.4%. During the first full month of the RI schedule both rates of detected drug use more than doubled to 8.4% and 6.8%. Both increases were statistically significant (χ^2 = 13.85; df = 1; $p < .001$; χ^2 = 15.82; df = 1; $p < .001$). This was the second largest monthly change in the rate of quinine positives (z = 2.24); $p < .05$) and the largest monthly change in the rate of morphine positives (z = 4.11; $p < .001$) during the period from 1/70 to 7/74. During the second month of RI scheduling, the quinine rate decreased to 5.5% (χ^2 = 4.70; df = 1; $p < .05$) while the morphine rate decreased to 3.1% (χ^2 = 11.52; df = 1; $p < .001$). These and subsequent monthly decrements seem attributable to the superiority of the RI scheduling method in detecting drug use. As detection of opiate use and clinical responses became more certain, clients evidently became less likely to risk loss of program privileges. In the next 39 months quinine positives averaged 2.9% of tests and morphine positives averaged 0.7% of tests.

DISCUSSION

There were two significant effects of the change from FI to RI schedules. On the month immediately following implementation of RI schedules the rate of positive quinines increased by 125.6% and the rate of positive morphines increased by 179.3%. These findings indicate the superior detectability of opiate use with RI schedules. For the first time, clients could be scheduled for tests on two or more consecutive days. As a result, safe days were eliminated and previously undiscovered opiate use on days immediately following urine collection could be detected causing an immediate increase in the total percentage of positive tests. As opiate use during formerly safe periods was detected, clinical sanctions such as revocation of take-home medication privileges and threat of termination from treatment were invoked. As a result of these sanctions, actual drug use decreased to the extent that, even with the superior detectability of the RI schedules, in two months morphine and quinine positives decreased below their FI baseline levels. In subsequent months the rates of detected opiate use continued to decline. During more than three years of RI scheduling quinine positives were approximately 30% less frequent and the morphine positives were 80% less frequent than during the FI period. Thus, the major effect of the RI schedules was increased detectability of actual opiate use by reducing sampling error. The increased probability of detection combined with the initiation of appropriate clinical responses to opiate use produced a significant net long-term reduction in client opiate use.

The evidence indicates that by eliminating safe days and restricting the length of maximum interval between tests, RI schedules produced greater than 100% increases in detectability of opiate use. Consequently, opiate use declined for more than three years after RI scheduling was adopted. This finding suggests that programs which do not use RI methods may be underestimating the actual opiate use of their clients by more than 50%.

We have one important reservation concerning the validity of these conclusions. The retrospective methodology for this analysis was necessarily correlational. There may be other plausible explanations for the large increase in positive urinalysis results observed in December, 1970 and for the subsequent 3-year decline. Decreased quality of street heroin or increased client acceptance of methadone as a narcotic substitute are possibilities. Verification that implementation of RI schedules caused these subsequent events requires an experimental manipulation of schedules with random assignment of clients to either FI or RI scheduling conditions. Since there are no disadvantages of the RI method as compared with either the FI or the CP methods, however, the clinical and research benefits seem to justify the minor implementation costs which would be needed for immediate adoption of RI urinalysis scheduling.

This research was supported in part by grants from the National Institute of Drug Abuse: DA 01097 and H80 DA 16356.

REFERENCES

1. A. Goldstein and B. W. Brown, Jr., J.A.M.A., 214: 2 (1970).
2. H. D. Kleber and L. C. Gould, J.A.M.A., 215: 13 (1971).

SOCIOECONOMIC FACTORS IN COMMUNICATION:
HOW THEY AFFECT COUNSELING AND REHABILITATION

William C. McKeever, Jr., M.S.
Roger Renteria, M.A.

The Mount Sinai Hospital
New York, New York

In order to achieve positive results in counselling one of the
main thrusts of therapy must be the establishment of effective
communication between the counsellor and the client. It becomes
the job of the therapist to know the client and to understand his
needs in helping to establish a good rapport. For this reason the
understanding of language and its ramifications for particular
segments of society, as well as society as a whole, is vital for
the establishment of a good therapeutic relationship.

Working with disadvantaged families in Spanish Harlem presents
a variety of problems in the area of communication. In this part
of New York the majority of the residents are Puerto Rican. In
the methadone maintenance and aftercare treatment program at Mount
Sinai Hospital, which services Spanish Harlem, 71% of the male
population and 29% of the female population are Spanish speaking.

The therapists, many of whom speak no Spanish, must find
adequate ways to communicate with their patients. But this
situation is complicated by a number of factors. Not only do many
of the patients speak only Spanish but most of the patients fall
into the category of disadvantaged or deprived--a situation which
further complicates the development of language arts. Added to
this is the fact that the drug addict has to some extent create a
language of his own in order to make himself more easily identifiable among his peers.

Because of the low educational level of many of the adults and
mixture of cultures, a combination of poor Spanish and poor English
(Spanglish) is spoken. Within a given family no one language may
be spoken fluently. This can create a breakdown of communication
with others outside ones own culture. A restricted language code
is in existence in many of these families. As the child grows to
adulthood his language grows only within the confines of this
restricted area. Because of poor training the child is never able
to use language to its fullest.

Rivera (1971) reports that most of the residents of Spanish Harlem can be placed into the category of disadvantaged. Puerto Ricans have the lowest levels of salaries and education. Sixty percent of Puerto Ricans in New York are living below the poverty level ($4,000 annually).

Tthese grim socio-economic statistics present other problems in the area of language development. Lifestyle greatly affects the training of the child and there are certain aspects of life in "El Barrio" which prevent the proper growth within children in the field of language arts.

Razran (1973) points out that a child must learn words in order to make relationships. As the child grows, his perceptions will have different meanings. His perceptions will grow and change as the child interacts and gives new meanings to words. If the child grows in an atmosphere where vocabulary is limited his vocabulary and perceptions will remain limited.

The development in the normal child, of object constancy, which is essential for a grasp of reality, requires the experience of repetitive encounters with things and people in similar situations. A child needs to develop the trust that the significant objects in his environment continue to exist and retain their basic characteristic even when they cannot be touched or seen. The child's developing sense of reality and himself in action in this reality, depends on the predictibility of his environment.

A child growing into an increasingly complex and confusing world needs for his development significant adults to process necessary information in ways that will help him in the ordering of his universe. Although, for the young child, learning of basic emotions and of simple realities can occur in nonverbal modalities, transmission of complex information to him requires the use of language and the development of dialogues (Minuchin, 1967).

Many of the patients who come to our clinic lack the constancy of lifestyle that help the child develop a sense of reality. Clinical interviews with many patients reveal a lifestyle that is often in a state of change and turmoil. Parental figures often change within the household. Absentee fathers, working mothers, common use of the "extended family," intervention of social agencies keep a child's surroundings in constant state of flux. As children, many of the patients were not taught to deal with people on a one to one basis. Communication on this level is often alien to them.

This fact can be of great importance when trying to establish a counselling relationship. For many of the patients this is a new experience and before trust can be established the mechanics of meaningful conversation must be mastered.

A child in order to communicate must have self observation as well as an ability to communicate the observed. He must experience the fact that "I am affecting my environment."

In reference to self observation, whish is so important in the development of language skills, the child of lower socio-economic and disadvantaged families learns to be inattentive in the home, in the preschool environment. The lack of expectation reduces motivation for beginning a task and therefore makes less likely the self-reinforcement of activity through gaining feelings of competence. In these impoverished, broken homes there is very little of the type of interaction seen so often in middle class homes, in which parents set a task for the child, observe its performance and in some way reward its completion (Minuchin, 1967).

It rarely happens in the ghetto home that parents orient the child toward completion of goals. The child is unable to establish feelings of self-worth by completion of a task followed by reward. In large families the parents do not individualize. Children do not have to respond to individual goals set in accordance with individual aptitudes. Individual skills and talents are often overlooked and therefore remain undeveloped.

Our patients from similar environments seem to retain this same lack of individuality. Group members seem to look at themselves as "ex-junkies" or "drug addicts" instead of individuals within a group. The group members do not look upon themselves as individuals with special needs and desires and competencies. Sessions often revolve around shared experiences within the "drug life." It become difficult to discuss and achieve individual goals or tasks or group goals as they may vary from one member to another.

This lack of individuality also creates a situation in which the child does not expect to be heard. Children can become lost in large families living in overcrowded conditions. Within the families of this milieu, "parents' responses to children's behavior is relatively random and therefore deficient in the qualities that convey rules which can be internalized; also parental emphasis is on the control and inhibition of behavior rather than on guidance." (Minuchin, 1967). To remedy this situation the child develops techniques for attracting attention to himself. The intensity of speech becomes more important than the content. Assertion of power is more important than knowledge. Other kinetic modifiers, such as pitch, also become important. In general, it might appear that in the resolution of conflict it is necessary to hear the content of what is being transacted; one can almost predict the winner by non-content clues (Minuchin, 1967).

Searching for recognition, the child soon learns that within the confines of an overcrowded slum dwelling loud noises receives the quickest recognition. Content of conversation being unimportant, a situation is soon created where conversation becomes a series of unrelated facts screamed between two or more people. Subject matter is often not carried to a conclusion. A series of monologues, thematically unrelated, can become a conversation. The result is a style of communication in which people do not expect to be heard and assert themselves by yelling.

Therapists at Mount Sinai have noted the patients' use of sound in conveying messages. Interaction with staff and other patients has, at times, resulted in "yelling" and "screaming" by patients. In order for many of the patients to feel assured that they have been understood they must yell. If they speak loudly they will be understood. In group, patients compete for the "floor" by raising their voices. Other group members can interpret the importance of a statement by how loudly it is said rather than by its content.

Patient X, a 43 year old Puerto Rican male, was seen by the counsellor in an individual session. The goal of the session was to inform the patient that, because of numerous infractions of clinic rules, he was being discharged from the program. The counsellor spoke in a moderate speaking voice and spent about 20 minutes explaining the decision. In the next session it became quite evident to the counsellor that the patient had absorbed nother of what was said in the first session. In the second session the counsellor spoke much louder and the patient seemed to absorb the message.

There are other factors that could have influenced the patients blocking the message. But as pitch increased the patient understood more of the message. This is not to say that counsellors should scream at their patients but therapist must be attuned to this fact and must engage his patients to substitute the value of content for the conditioned response of sound. Clarifications can be used by the counsellor to point out important issues of the content and patients can be taught the importance of content through positive reinforcement.

In general the formal rules that participants in a dialogue share, regulate the signaling that one has heard, understood, a agreed or disagreed. Only then is the processibility of carrying themes to conclusions realized. This closure is shared by others. There are processes for receiving and recovering information and for signaling shifts in content matter. Important in this process is the capacity to differentiate relevant information from accompanying static which may blur the clarity of information. Only when these rules have been developed does communication and reception of content become autonomous and useful for problem solving functions (Munichin, 1967).

Many clinic patients are not accustomed to closure within conversation. It is often seen in a group setting how the topice changes in contributions from member to member. Group members may not be accustomed to having topics brought to a conclusion by content. Although this is common in most groups, the problem is even further complicated by problems in language. It becomes incumbent on the therapist to introduce to the group members the importance of content and thereby create a learning experience in which they can utilize their own abilities to bring closure to a topic.

The fact that drug addicts have created a society within a society creates another language problem. Jargon has been invented by the drug addicts to create for themselves a language of their own. This jargon, although necessary for survival within the drug community, can create a stumbling block in treatment if the therapist is not aware of it. This is not to say that counsellors should use the jargon of the patients in conversation. If the counsellor has come from a different milieu the patients may consider it an affront if the counsellor uses words and phrases that are not part of his own training. However, awareness of jargon on the part of the therapist can do much to help expediate dialogue.

Added to jargon is the use of body language and eye contact. Although people of all cultures use body language, it plays a particularly important part in the conversations of Puerto Rican people. Therapists should be aware of the meanings of these sig-nals so as to be able to translate not only as meaningful affect responses but also as meaningful conversations.

The existing problems of language can and should be dealt with by the clinical staff in a positive way. Staff members can inter-act with families and, by example, indicate to parents a more constructive and beneficial way to deal with their children. Language classes can be established to help instruct clients in the art of language. Role playing can be used in groups to show the various uses of language. While linguistic improvements are being learned, better communication is being established and, hopefully, finer treatment is being achieved.

REFERENCES

Delgado, M., Social work and the Puerto Rican Community. Social Casework, February, 1974, p. 117-123.

Lewis, M., & Freedle, R., Mother-infant dyad: the cradle of meaning In P. Pliner, L. Krames, T. Alloway (eds.), Communication and Affect, New York and London: Academic Press, 1973.

Minuchin, S., Montalvo, B., Rosman, B.L., & Schumer, F., Families of the slums. New York and London: Basic Books, Inc., 1967.

Razran, G., Symboling and semantic conditioning anthropogeny. In P. Pliner, L. Krames, T. Alloway (eds.), Communication and Affect. New York and London: Academic Press, 1973.

Rivera, J.J., Growth of a Puerto Rican awareness. Social Casework, February, 1974, p. 84-89.

THE ARTFORM PROCESS:
A Clinical Technique for the Enablement
of Affect Management in Drug Dependent Individuals+

Milton E. Burglass, M.D., M.P.H., M.S., M.Div.*
David H. Bremer**
Robert J. Evans III**

*Instructor in Psychiatry, Harvard Medical School at
The Cambridge Hospital; Director, Thresholds Unit,
Polydrug Treatment Program, Cambridge, Mass.

**Associate Clinical Director, Polydrug Treatment Program

In contrast to earlier psychoanalytic theories which stressed the regressive aspects of drug dependence, more recent formulations have emphasized its autoplastic and adaptive features. Krystal has postulated that during withdrawal the dependent individual undergoes affective regression, that the affects of anxiety and depression dedifferentiate into a common precursor state, and that resomatization and deverbalization ensue.[1] Khantzian has suggested that individuals select the substance upon which they become dependent on the basis of their experience of its ability to enhance certain ego functions to cope with dysphoric internal states.[2] While these formulations have suggested the important contributory role of impaired affect management in the development of drug dependence, they have offered few proposals for the formulation of problem-specific treatment.

In this paper we shall focus on a single treatment input, the "Artform Process," its function within the system of psychotherapy known as Thresholds, and its implementation with clients in a hospital-based polydrug treatment program. We understand this to be a specific treatment input because it directly addresses the problem of affect management postulated to be pertinent to polydrug dependence.

I. AFFECT MANAGEMENT

In the Freudian neuropsychological model, internal and external stimulation is managed by the neural process of lateral cathexis.[3] In modern neurophysiology, affect is thought to be regulated through semipermanent dendritic microstructure.[4] If this process

+The conclusions expressed in this paper are based in part on work supported by the National Institute of Drug Abuse, Grant # H81 DA 01519 01.

is impaired, the organism will experience excessive excitation. In the modern neuropsychological model, emotion is modulated through cognitive structure and the cortical modification of sensory input channels[5],[6]. If there is a deficiency in cognitive structure, emotion may not be controlled, and the individual may experience disorganization of behavior and loss of autonomy, two conditions frequently manifest in our drug dependent clients.

II. SPECIFICATION OF TREATMENT

Our selection of treatment inputs was guided by a structural formulation of drug dependence emphasizing its adaptive and cybernetic aspects[7],[8]. We sought inputs which would engage, assess, strengthen, or install the cognitive structures and skills serving ego autonomy. The Thresholds system of psychotherapy was devised in 1965 for the short-term, intensive treatment of character problems associated with criminal behavior[9]. In modified form, it has been applied to problem of adolescent development[10], obesity[11], and remedial education[12]. Thresholds focuses on enhancing the client's ability to monitor and control the self-system. Two strategies are applied to this end: 1) the teaching of the cognitive skills involved in decision-making and 2) the teaching of a structure and process for on-going self-analysis. Two primary therapeutic tactics are utilized: 1) the didactic, curricular presentation of a seven-step paradigm for the analysis and resolution of internal and external situations and 2) the use of the artform process as an experientially acquired structure for the integration of experience. In this paper, we shall consider the artform process and its use in the enhancement of affect management.

III. ARTFORM PROCESS

The Artform (hereafter AF) is a structured form of conversation between client(s) and therapist around a shared experience (an art print, a movie, an interpersonal event, etc.) The therapist processes the experience by posing a structured series of questions which have as their basis a sequence of cognitive tasks designed to facilitate the abstraction and manipulation of the experience by the participants. There are no "right" answers to these questions. They are broadly constructed to allow a range of alternative answers: Yet each participant is expected to answer the question asked and not some other one. Appropriate responses are affirmed by the therapist. Participants respond individually to each question as the interrogatory process moves through six distinct levels characterized by increments in the individual's <u>involvement</u> with the process, the <u>complexity</u> of the posed cognitive demand and the <u>intensity</u> of the client's affective response to it.

495

A. Levels of the Process

1. OBJECTIVE

The process is initiated at the objective level where clients recall details of the experience or stimulus under consideration. Clients isolate and identify elements of the total experience. These simple tasks undermine the common assumption that internal or external experiences exist in an "absolute" way, as inviolable entities not amenable to re-interpretation.

2. SUBJECTIVE

Clients increase their involvement by slightly modifying the elements described in the previous level, using categories or procedures supplied by the therapist; for example: "What object would you remove from this painting if you had to remove one?" At this level clients enhance the ability to perform cognitive operations on internal representations of their experiences.

3. EXPRESSIVE

The process increases in complexity, risk, and involvement as participants modify their image of the stimulus, using categories with clear personal associations and connotations: _e.g._, "What music does this book suggest to you?"

4. INTERPRETIVE

At the interpretive level, clients integrate the modified image of the stimulus and their personal associations into an abstracted theme or narrative; e.g., "What would you title this experience?" or "How would you tell this experience as a story?"

5. CONCRETIZING

The AF reaches a peak of personal involvement and risk with the question "Where have you seen this experience in your own life?" permitting clients to objectify their own now abstracted experiences just as they are objectifying the stimulus. Objectivity of this sort allows for the intentional cognitive reorganization of previously unprocessed experience and affective energy.

6. RESPONSIVE

The responsive level completes the AF process as clients summarize the experience and respond actively to it; "What does this experience say to you?" "What do you say to it?" Having abstracted both the stimulus and the link with personal life experience to the level of dialogic engagement, participants are re-directing any remaining unbound energy back onto the original stimulus.

B. The Dynamics of the Process

The increase in cognitive structure and processing capability which is facilitated by repetition in the AF and which results in enhanced affect management, is the salient dynamic of the AF process. The process allows clients to move gradually into high risk areas of personal concern in an atmosphere of affirmation where each one's response is affirmed or returned for modification, not on the basis of its specific content, but for its appropriateness to the AF's structural demands.

IV. CLINICAL APPLICATIONS

A. Group Applications

Artforming is the primary group process employed in the Thresholds treatment method. Most groups take as their focus some tangible object or experience, often an art reproduction, a short film, or a popular song. Any mutual experience can be artformed, including events from the group's history.

The combination of a sense of strong group identity, based on mutual risk-taking and affirmation, with the experience of enhanced personal efficacy, tends to make the process intrinsically rewarding and attractive to clients.

B. Individual Applications

Artforming is used in individual counseling sessions as a technique for affect management in two circumstances: 1) when the client experiences an affective flood that impedes his or her capacity to function; and 2) when the client appears locked into a reactive pattern of behavior; that is, when able to generate only a limited repertoire of alternative responses, usually negative and disabling ones, to demanding life situations.

Clinically, we often observe how an event external to the self can precipitate a flood of affect that threatens to overwhelm the ego's capacity to bind it. Lacking sufficient cognitive structure to process the new input, i.e., not having the sufficient categories of meaning to which to assign component parts of the event, or lacking the ego skills of abstraction which would render the event more manageable, the energy of the event enters the person's self-system and, not being bound in structure, threatens massive motor discharge, manifest in "acting out" or somatization. The AF structure serves as an external template which binds the affect. As the energy of the event becomes bound in the cognitive categories and structures of the AF, the client experiences a calming, somatization ceases, and verbalization increases. The client's cognitive structure is reenergized and s/he is again able to act upon, i.e. control, both the internal ane external situation.

The AF structure can also be submerged in a conversational context. The therapist pays close attention to the flow of the interaction and integrates the demands for cognitive processing and clear response into casual but directed dialogue.

C. Crisis Intervention Applications

The submerged AF can be an effective crisis intervention technique useful to foster increased cognitive processing facility in the face of massive affective floods. In crisis management the therapist must dwell upon simple, often seemingly irrelevant, objective level tasks until the client can negotiate them; for example: "These are nice pants, where did you get them?" After this level of functioning has been established, the therapist may, if the situation allows, concentrate on the objective elements of the experience itself and slowly begin the standard AF process.

A final word: in artforming, the sole concern is to enable the client to gain self-control through the performance of increasingly complex cognitive tasks. The AF offers a simple, easily delivered, structured means for accomplishing this end in minimal time.

References

1. Krystal, H., *Psych. Quart. Suppl.*, 36:53-65, 1962.
2. Khantzian, E.J., *Psychiatry Digest*, 36:19-22.
3. Freud, S., "Project for a Scientific Psychology," appendix in the *Origins of Psychoanalysis: Letters to Wilhelm Fliess, Drafts and Notes 1887-1902*, Basic Books, New York, 1954.
4. Pribham, K.H., *Languages of the Brain*, Prentice Hall, Englewood Cliffs, New Jersey, 1971.
5. Spinelli, D.N., and Pribham, K.H., *Electroencph. Clin. Neurophysiol.*, 20:44-49, 1966.
6. Nobel, K.W., and Dewson, J.H., *J. Aud. Research*, 6:67-75, 1966.
7. Burglass, M.E., Evans, R.J. and Bremer, D.H., *Sedative-Hypnotic Dependency Cycle*, Correctional Solutions Foundation, Cambridge, Mass. 1975.
8. Burglass, M.E., Evans, R.J. and Bremer, D.H., *The Opiate Dependency Cycle*, Correctional Solutions Foundation, Cambridge, Mass. 1975.
9. Burglass, M.E. and Duffy, M.G., *Thresholds Teachers Manual*, Correctional Solutions Foundation, Cambridge, Mass. 1974.
10. Van Utt, G., *Fostering Autonomy in the Female Adolescent*, Correctional Solutions Foundation, Cambridge, Mass., 1975.
11. Milligan, J.E., *Decision-Making and Weight Control in the Female Adolescent*, Correctional Solutions Foundation, Cambridge, Mass., 1975.
12. Milligan, J.E., and Taylor, J.G., *Genesis: Manual for the Teacher*, Correctional Solutions Foundation, Cambridge, Mass. 1975.

IMPROVED SEDATIVE-HYPNOTIC DETOXIFICATION
USING BARBITAL, SODIUM

Lionel G. Deutsch, M.D.

Queens Hospital Center Affiliation
Long Island Jewish-Hillside Medical Center
Jamaica, New York 11432

Athan Karras, Ph. D.

Hillside Division
Long Island Jewish-Hillside Medical Center
Glen Oaks, New York 11004

Approximately one-third of the admissions to the Queens Hospital Center Drug Detoxification Service have been, at least in part, for treatment of Sedative-Hypnotic dependency. Initially, we used phenobarbital or nembutal for detoxification but were unsatisfied. The reason was that we needed an agent with a longer duration of action to smooth out the troublesome nadirs and zeniths produced by both detoxification agents. After a year with pento- and phenobarbital we tired of seeing the minimally intoxicated whimper how sick they were (and wanted more) and were annoyed with the 'stoned' gorillas roaring how sick they were (and wanted more).

Barbiturates in general take a fearsome toll of ego functions: perception, reality testing and cognition are grossly impaired, especially during the early days of detoxification. We now saw that, in addition to longer action, we needed a drug which produced minimal disinhibition at a dose which effectively prevented withdrawal. Moreover, we were concerned with how well our liver-damaged patients would metabolically degrade the pento- or phenobarbital we gave them. We realized that induced hepatic enzymes would shorten the duration of action of the agents we already thought too short. In addition, pentobarbital powder settled out of the Tang we served it in.

We decided to reintroduce Sodium Barbital into clinical use. Fischer and von Mering had originally introduced it in 1903 but the drug gradually fell into disuse due to its excessively long action.

Although it had found successful use in treating alcoholic delirium tremens fifty years ago in this country and is currently in use in Denmark for this purpose, in the United States the drug is virtually relegated to making Veronal buffer for serum protein electrophoresis.

Barbital's prolonged action is due in great part to its resistance to degradation by the liver into inactive forms. Ninety-five percent of the administered dose escapes hepatic metabolism in the naive individual and scarcely less in the barbiturate-dependent patient. The only route of excretion is via the kidney, providing a duration of action of 12 to 24 (or more) hours. The drug is highly water soluble, making it easy to prepare and dispense and it is quite inexpensive. In experimentally sedated subjects, much less analeptic is required for arousal than with phenobarbital or pentobarbital. This translates into the fact that milligram for milligram, barbital sedates less, thereby causing less disinhibition.

METHOD

1.   Patients

Of 100 recently admitted sedative-hypnotic abusers detoxified with Barbital, 67% has been using barbiturates, nearly 50% were using diazepam and nearly 40% alcohol. Twenty percent of our patients were dependent upon other drugs such as methaqualone, ethchlorvynol and meprobamate. Fifty-five percent were dependent on narcotics. These figures indicate multiple dependencies.

The age range of our group was from 16 to 73 years, with a mean of 24 years. The ratio of males to females was 2.5:1.

2.   Detoxification Procedures

     a.   Titrate patient to signs of minimal cerebro-cerebellar dysfunction with pentobarbital. These signs include diminution of superficial reflexes, lateral nystagmus, positive Romberg, gait ataxia and dysarthria. We depend upon the drug history of our initial estimates regarding tolerance. Patients are permitted to become normal but not to go into withdrawal. We challenge with 200 mg. of pentobarbital suspension in juice and observe one hour after ingestion. Excluding those who become grossly intoxicated, we divide patient responses into three groups: a) mild cerebro-cerebellar dysfunction; b) no effect; c) withdrawal beginning despite the test dose. Group a) usually stabilizes when treated with 200 mg. of pentobarbital q6h or 400 mg. of Barbital q12h. Group b) requires an additional 100 mg. of pentobarbital and another hour of observation. If mild cerebro-cerebellar dysfunction appears, this patient should stabilize with 300 mg. of pentobarbital q6h or with 600 mg. of Barbital q12h. However, if the patient is still normal, we give an additional dose of 100 mg. of pentobarbital and observe. Experience with this group shows that after 400 mg., total, they will develop the signs of mild cerebro-cerebellar dysfunction even if they are still unintoxicated when examined. Treatment with 400 mg. pentobarbital q6h or 800 mg. of Barbital q12h suffices. Group c) patients require 200 mg. of pentobarbital more and observation for one hour. If withdrawal continues to the next examination, we double the dose, that is, give 400 mg. of pentobarbital. We continue to double the dose of pentobarbital hourly so long as withdrawal persists. The total amount of pentobarbital given minus that which has worn off (we assume a 4-6 hour effect) is administered q6h. Twice that amount q12h as Barbital would likewise stabilize this patient.

b. Maintain this dose, one day for every year of uninterrupted abuse, up to four days. Adjust dosage during this period, if necessary, to provide minimal cerebro-cerebellar dysfunction.

c. Detoxification proceeds safely at 100 mg. decrements daily, at least in the beginning. Smaller decrements are advisable for the last 150-300 mg. A three or four day period using placebos allows us to follow the patient while the long-lasting Barbital levels fall by renal excretion. Acting-out may occur at any time; irritability and insomnia are most frequent below daily Barbital doses of 300 mg. In such instances, one can either increase the Barbital or employ moderate doses of major tranquilizer, e.g., chlorpromazine. In either case, we reduce daily Barbital decrements, e.g., to 50 mg. daily or every other day.

The reduction schedule may proceed evenly with morning and evening doses declining approximately together (see Table I, Schedule I); or the morning dose may be progressively reduced to zero while holding the evening dose constant (see Table I, Schedule II). The resultant once-daily Barbital regimen provided by Schedule II has shown itself to be entirely sufficient to prevent withdrawal signs and symptoms.

RESULTS AND DISCUSSION

Barbital can substitute for the entire gamut of barbiturates, sedatives (except ethchlorvynol), alcohol and benzodiazepines. It is less sedating, so that counseling and psychological evaluation can start earlier in the detoxification process. In addition, management of the more difficult polydrug patient is easier. It is safer

501

for the all-too-frequent liver-damaged patient. It is easier and less expensive to prepare and administer. It is very long lasting, eliminating the dips in sedative effect which usually act as grist for the abuser's manipulation mill.

Barbital replaces methaqualone only modestly well but it is satisfactory. Meprobamate has never been the only drug of abuse in our series but those using it have been comfortable on Barbital. Patients whose major abuse is with glutethimide have a smoother detoxification when only half their "Doriden" is replaced with Barbital and the other half given as "Doriden". Patients dependent on ethchlorvynol fare best when treated with phenobarbital and valium although an occasional patient has done satisfactorily with Barbital.

TABLE I

Alternative Barbital Detoxification Schedules

Schedule I:	9 a.m.	9 p.m.	
	600 mg.	600 mg.	
	.	.	Period of Stabiliza-
	.	.	tion and Maintenance
	.	.	
	550 mg.	550 mg.	
	500 mg.	500 mg.	
	450 mg.	450 mg.	
		etc.	

Schedule II:	600 mg.	600 mg.	
	.	.	Period of Stabiliza-
	.	.	tion and Maintenance
	.	.	
	500 mg.	600 mg.	
	400 mg.	600 mg.	
	300 mg.	600 mg.	
	200 mg.	600 mg.	
	100 mg.	600 mg.	
	---	600 mg.	
	---	500 mg.	
		etc.	

THE FREE CLINIC APPROACH TO COMMUNITY MEDICINE AND DRUG ABUSE TREATMENT

David E. Smith, M.D.

Haight-Ashbury Free Medical Clinic
San Francisco, California

In October of 1973, I had the opportunity to travel to several western European countries to study both their health care delivery systems and their drug treatment programs in an attempt to analyze and reflect on these and other questions relative to free clinics. The purpose of this paper, then, is to present my historical perspective on the national free clinic movement, including an evaluation of its current status, and to speculate on the role of the free clinic in America's changing health care delivery system. One cannot understand the current status of the free clinic movement and its role unless the historical origins and sociocultural evolution of the free clinic movement are appreciated.

Evolution of the Free Clinic Movement: In the past nine years, over 500 free clinics have opened across the United States and at the present time serve over two million client visits a year, treating a wide variety of health problems ranging from venereal disease to drug abuse. The people served by the burgeoning free clinic movement are primarily alienated, dropped-out youth, although the recent appearance of the third world free clinic has broadened the scope of the free clinic movement to include an increasing number of minority youth, as well as older inner-city ghetto dwellers.[1]

With the evolution of the multi-faceted variety of free clinics scattered across the U.S. and the parallel development of a whole series of innovative community-based human services such as hotlines, crisis centers and drop-in counseling centers, it has become progressively more difficult to define exactly what constitutes a free clinic. The word free means more than no charge per patient visit. The original philosophy of the free clinic was that free was not an economic term but rather a state of mind. It was felt that health care was a right, not a privilege, and that medical institutions should recognize a culturally pluralistic consumer population. In the origins of the free clinic movement, a major issue was freedom from "bureaucratic tangles" and freedom to treat people as human beings rather than criminals, a particularly important issue in regard to the drug abuse population. The free clinic people wished to carefully differentiate their program from "charity facilities" and thus emphasized that no proof of financial need would be required, feeling that a human being should not have to qualify for something that should be a basic right. The free clinic philosophy implies a minimum of red tape and other barriers between doctors and patients, and also freedom from applying conventional labels and value systems to individuals regarded as "deviant" by the dominant culture. In contrast to traditional medicine, with its focus upon the disease process, free clinics attempt to relate to the entire individual. This difference, though subtle, is immediately apparent to the patient, and is conveyed by the attitude of the clinic staff. Essential to a somewhat elusive free clinic philosophy is the fact that there is no fee and no patronizing or moralizing attitude.[2]

The National Free Clinic Council, which is giving grants to individual free clinics for drug abuse training, initially defined a free clinic as:

> Any non-governmental administered agency whose purpose is to provide free health care without financial, geographic, or eligibility requirements for its clientele.

Smith, Bentel and Schwartz[3] attempted to be specific in their definition by stating that a free clinic operation must include the following:

1. Direct delivery of either medical, dental, psychological or drug rehabilitation services.
2. Presence of a professional relevant to the service provided.
3. Service available to everyone without a means test.
4. In general, no direct charges (although small charges for specific services such as pregnancy tests or donations may be requested).
5. Specified hours of service.
6. Care provided from a specified facility or location.

In addition to providing direct medical, dental, psychological and drug rehabilitation services, free clinics are active in a variety of other areas. For example, they serve as an important source of credible drug information for the young user who feels that "establishment drug education" is essentially dishonest.

Free clinics also serve as social institutions where alienated youth can find a place to participate in meaningful work experience. Many young people have acquired skills as medical paraprofessionals or drug counselors, administrators of medical programs, apprentices to lab technicians, and in a variety of other jobs that have helped them re-enter the dominant society in a constructive way after leaving the free clinic. Free clinic staff, by going out into the community and discussing a variety of health and neighborhood issues, has served as a valuable source of public health education and preventive street medicine.

The Health Policy Advisory Center, a radical health care delivery evaluation and publication organization in New York City, analyzed the National Free Clinic movement, and felt its guiding principles could be summarized as follows:[4]

1. Health care is a right and should be free at the point of delivery.
2. Health services should be comprehensive, unfragmented and decentralized.
3. Medicine should be demystified. Health care should be delivered in a courteous and educational manner. When possible, patients should be permitted to choose among alternative methods of treatment based on their needs.
4. Health care should be deprofessionalized. Health care skills should be transferred to worker and patient alike; they should be permitted to practice and share those skills.
5. Community-worker control of health institutions should be established. Health care institutions should be governed by the people who use and work in them.

Free clinics did not come about as a consequence of Federal government initiatives as did neighborhood health centers, but were almost entirely a grassroots people's movement that started in opposition to the established health care delivery system.

The first free clinic opened its doors in the Haight-Ashbury District of San Francisco in June, 1967, during a time described by thousands of young people from all over the country as the "summer of love".[5] Many had rejected their traditional middle-class upbringing in search of a new future. Unfortunately, in their effort to get "high" on this new way of love and sharing, they also rejected common-sense rules regarding cleanliness, sanitation, and nutrition. The results were hepatitis, venereal disease, upper respiratory infections, and other communicable diseases which spread rapidly as more people crowded into already overcrowded quarters, while the Public Health Department and local hospitals refused to offer health services to this new generation.

The Haight-Ashbury Free Medical Clinic, as originally conceived, was basically an outpatient medical clinic with a "calm center" for persons experiencing "bad trips" from LSD. Soon after opening, it became apparent that more was needed since this population was encountering great difficulty in securing treatment and was denied service when attempting to follow traditional medical channels for mental health services. Meetings were held, more volunteers recruited, and the "calm center" became the psychiatric annex of the Haight-Ashbury Free Clinic.

In the free clinic the demystification of the physician appealed to both patients and young health care professionals. These young professionals were oriented more to the health team concept than to the traditional model wherein the doctor need not explain practices to patients or involve the patient in his/her own treatment. Also, the health professionals in a free clinic environment dress casually and are culturally sympathetic with the views and feelings of alienation in the youth culture.

In addition, free clinics have long been used as a resource for drug education. This service is becoming more organized and effective as clinic staff members move into their communities with information about drugs, nutrition, first aid, etc. Speakers Bureaus, set up and staffed by clinic personnel, work in schools and other institutions with programs for civic and community groups. Information about impure street drugs, which is basically unavailable in the open media, is collected and distributed through the free clinics. Pamphlets and papers on nutrition and sanitation are written and developed by free clinic staff for use by their patients. First aid and health care prevention classes are conducted for community education as well as for in-service training.

Some Unresolved Political-Community Free Clinic Issues: As described by Smith and Wesson[6], within the past decade the concept of community has achieved ubiquitous prominence. The return to a smaller unit of social interaction was psychologically appealing to those who felt overwhelmed by the megalopolis composed of growing governmental bureaucracies and conglomerate corporations. The theory rapidly became politicized, however, first in the community mental health movement of the early 1960's and soon after in the rapidly developing drug abuse industry. A whole new cadre of expressions such as "catchment areas," "community representation" and "community advisory panels" came into existence. The concept invaded the university in terms like "community involvement." The medical schools were required to provide services which were "relevant to the community." Washington, particularly the National Institute of Mental Health, became even more enamored with the idea. Individuals skilled at obtaining federal monies learned to couch their requests for financial aid in community terms. Washington in turn developed more and more criteria to determine ways in which monies would become available for these communities.

Government, as the provider of financial resources for most drug abuse treatment services, has greatly shaped the delivery of those services, and as a result, is viewed with great suspicion by many free clinics who wish to shape their own destiny and philosophy. Herein lies one of the greatest paradoxes in drug abuse treatment including federally funded drug treatment programs in free clinics. On the one hand the government insists on representation from the communities served and ostensibly requests the community to design the type of services it needs. On the other hand, by setting up guidelines, selectively funding and making special monies available for "special interest" projects of the government, the government has controlled almost entirely the nature of delivery of services. Our intent, however, is to point out the inherent conflict between funding agencies with guidelines and funding criteria and "community" self-determinism.

Community representation can be confused easily with representative democratic community self-determinism. In practice, the community "representative" often is a negotiating agent acting as a buffer between Washington policy and community needs. If the community representatives have the respect and support of their community, compromises are more likely to be accepted from these individuals than from government officials. At best, this is an expedient substitute for social democracy and, at worst, a form of sophisticated cooptation of local power via the mechanism of neocolonialism. Furthermore, in practice, community representation is weighted in favor of community non-drug residents and drug treatment personnel. The drug abuse industry's consumer, the "drug abuser", rarely has more than token representation.

Of the various types of communities, the only community which could muster enough independent political clout to be heard would be either the geographic community of approximately catchment area size, or one held together by common ideology but not geographic boundaries. In practice, this latter community is too scattered, transient, anarchic and just plain disinterested to muster any meaningful services on its own behalf. More stable geographic communities, however, have developed political weight and have formed coalitions to gain additional political leverage.

In the last few years federal health and drug abuse policy has decentralized community funding under revenue sharing and the "new federalism." This process together with an explosion of social and political activity at the neighborhood level has brought many drug programs into crisis with their community. Certain alternative agencies such as free clinics have worked for a long time developing strong community representation in their organization. Other federally initiated efforts such as community mental health centers and neighborhood health projects have also seen similar work.

However the question becomes: Outside of an overall community coordinating body, should the specific community efforts be purely advisory or, as many free clinics and radical health workers have suggested, should the community control the health service agencies in their community including the community-based drug abuse treatment and rehabilitation efforts? A great deal of the rationale for such community control is that the agency would be more responsive to the needs of the community if such community control is in effect. The community control has much more impact than the often superficial community advisory board.

Unfortunately, such community control often produces major conflict with the workers in that agency, particularly if the workers in the community have a different view of what the primary problems are. Drug abuse treatment, which is a service provided by many free clinics, is a very unpopular issue at the neighborhood level. Most people want drug abuse treatment services of some sort but not in their area. Vigorous citizen protests are very often organized to get community treatment and rehabilitation efforts out of the neighborhood, particularly if these services are based in a free clinic which is viewed as threatening to the existing sociopolitical order.

During my brief trip to Europe in October of 1973, I found that the best resolution of this community-clinic conflict occurred in Sweden where there are street-front facilities that resemble American-style free clinics. These programs are state initiated and funded and are called "open clinics." They deal primarily with the psycho-social problems of non-university students who have in essence dropped out or are alienated from the social system in Sweden. The major problems with these young people revolve around drugs and include difficulties with alcohol, hashish, intravenous amphetamines and morphine-based drugs. The emphasis is primarily on psychological counseling and social rehabilitation as this group has a great deal of difficulty finding jobs.

Under the health care delivery system in Sweden, all medical care is free and is provided by the State, so there is no need for extensive adolescent facilities. The primary purpose of these clinics is to contact a difficult-to-reach population and refer these patients whenever necessary to specialized mental health and drug treatment facilities that are located in the community. They also provide some aftercare.

An interesting observation is that although a team approach is used in these open clinics, the staff is highly professional and no ex-addicts or street people are employed. In contrast, free clinics in the U.S., serving similar populations, have almost half of their staff made up of ex-addicts and street people. All clinics in Sweden have to be licensed, with the professional staff receiving certification. An ex-addict or street person cannot receive such certification in most cases unless s/he has returned to school and received appropriate education and certification. Again, it appears that the American-style free clinic is unique to the United States and is born out of unmet neighborhood health needs. In other countries with comparable population, the basic medical services are taken care of free of charge by the State health care system.

508

Free clinics in this country serve as substantial documentation to the gross inadequacies of our approach to health care which are observed in no other industrialized country. The many Europeans with whom I talked during this three-week trip expressed amazement that the U.S. is still the only industrialized country that does not have a national health insurance plan covering all of its citizens.

If the health care delivery system changes dramatically in the U.S. toward a socialized medicine similar to Sweden's, it is apparent that much of the impetus for the large free clinic movement in the U.S. will be removed. However, certain elements of the free clinic approach to health care delivery will continue to be valuable under any outcare delivery system. In addition, free clinic workers must realize that an alternative agency has room for flexibility and creativity, e.g., hiring of ex-addicts, street people, and para-professionals, which may be lost if these institutions are incorporated into a changed health care delivery system in the U.S.

As emphasized by Taylor,[7] consumer control has often been confused by free clinics with the issue of community control. Unfortunately the free clinics in the United States have not dealt adequately with this issue, relying primarily on the staff of former-consumer employment model. However, in my visit, I was not able to find any successful alternatives to this dilemma revolving around community and consumer conflicts which could be adapted to American free clinics. Further work needs to be done in this important area if free clinics are to maintain an effective community approach to health care and drug abuse.

References:

1) Smith, David E.; Wesson, Donald R. & Ciceri, Rod. "The National Free Clinic Movement: Historical Perspectives." Adit. Vol. II (3) 1, 2, 12-16. (Oct. 1973).
2) Smith, David E. & Bentel, David J. "A New Phenomenon Has Appeared on the American Health Care Scene." Calif. Health (4/1970)
3) Smith, David E.; Bentel, David J. & Schwartz, Jerome (Eds.), The Free Clinic: A Community Approach to Health Care and Drug Abuse. (Beloit, Wisconsin: STASH, 1971). 206Pp.
4) Bloomfield, C.; Levy, H.; Kotelchuck, R. & Handelman, M. "Free Clinics." Health Policy Advisory Bulletin No. 34; 1-16 (Oct.1971).
5) Smith, David E. & Luce, John. Love Needs Care: A History of San Francisco's Haight-Ashbury Free Clinic. (Boston, Mass.: Little Brown & Co., 1971). 405 P.
6) Smith, David E. & Wesson, Donald R. "Editor's Note" in "Community Approaches to Drug Treatment and Rehabilitation", Journal of Psychedelic Drugs. Vol. 6(2). (Apr.-Jun., 1974).
7) Taylor, Rosemary. "Consumer Control and Professional Accountability in the Free Clinics." Paper presented at the Society for the Study of Social Problems. (New York: August, 1973).

PSYCHOACTIVE DRUG USE AND ASSOCIATED DRIVING BEHAVIOR AMONG
16 - 49 YEAR OLD LICENSED DRIVERS

George W. Appenzeller, M.S.W.

South Carolina Commission on Alcohol and Drug Abuse
Columbia, South Carolina

The South Carolina Alcohol Safety Action Program (ASAP) is a
special project of the South Carolina Commission on Alcohol and
Drug Abuse. The program places driving under the influence
offenders in appropriate education and treatment services. During
the first two years of operation, researchers and clinical workers
noted that many ASAP clients admitted to using psychoactive drugs
in addition to or rather than alcohol prior to their arrests. An
incidence and prevalence study of drug use and driving was conducted during the summer of 1975 to confirm these observations.

The survey instrument and the sampling technique were designed to
provide data on the demographic characteristics, alcohol and
psychoactive drug use, driving behavior and knowledge and attitudes
about drugs and driving among a representative sample of licensed
drivers in the 16 through 49 age group. A series of reports and
papers based on this data are planned. This paper focuses on two
areas of interest--the incidence of psychoactive drug use before
driving within the sample and the incidence of traffic tickets and
vehicular crashes among persons using certain categories of drugs
before driving.

I. INCIDENCE OF DRUG USE

Of the sample of 488 drivers, 292 (59.8%) had used psychoactive
drugs during the previous year, exclusive of over-the-counter
drugs, and 190 (38.9%) had driven afterwards. This compares with
351 (71.9%) who had consumed alcohol and 255 (52.3%) who had
driven afterwards.

Relatively low percentages of the sample combined alcohol with
over-the-counter or prescription psychoactives. However, illicit
drug users exhibited a different behavior pattern. Illicit drugs

had been used by 121 (24.8%) of the sample during the previous
year, and 88 (18.0%) had driven afterwards. Eighty-seven (17.8%)
had used an illicit drug with alcohol and 64 (13.1%) had driven
after using that combination.

II. INCIDENCE OF TRAFFIC TICKETS AND ACCIDENTS

The incidence of traffic tickets and accidents over the previous
three years was higher for every category of drug use before
driving than in the total sample, as can be seen in Tables I and
II.

The category prescription psychoactives in combination with alcohol exhibited the highest significant difference for accidents when
compared to the total sample (N=488,x^2=4.0901, p=0.05). Alcohol
alone exhibited a lower significance (N=488,x^2=1.8354, p=0.2), as
did prescription alone (N=488,x^2=2.6048, p=0.2). The lowest significance for accidents was exhibited by illicit alone (N=488,
x^2=0.9960, p=0.3) and illicit in combination with alcohol
(N=488,x^2=0.4008, p=0.6)

Significance for traffic tickets in the last three years by drug
category was considerably different. Alcohol, illicit in combination with alcohol and illicit alone exhibited a highly significant
difference when compared to the total sample (N=488, ^{2}=21.0519,
p=0.0005) (N=488, ^{2}=29.4384, p=0.0005) (N=488, ^{2}=31.7183,p=0.0005)
Prescription in combination with alcohol exhibited a fair degree
of significance (N=488, ^{2}=1.6507, p=0.2) and prescription alone
slight significance (N=488, ^{2}=1.2189,p=0.3).

III. SUMMARY

Driving after using psychoactives appears to occur nearly as often
as driving after using alcohol. Those who use illicit drugs more
often drive after use than those who use other categories of drugs.

Persons who use psychoactive prescriptions alone or in combination
with alcohol appear to be the most likely of all groups to have
accidents, yet are stopped for traffic violations the least often.
Users of illicit psychoactives, alone or in combination with alcohol, are the least likely to have accidents but are most likely to
be stopped for traffic violations. Persons who use alcohol and
then drive are more likely to be stopped for traffic violations
than they are likely to have accidents.

The effort in substance use and traffic safety has heretofore been
concentrated on alcohol. Future programming should place part of
this effort on psychoactive drug use.

TABLE I. Frequency of accidents in the previous three years by category of psychoactive drug used before driving.

	Total Sample		Over-the-Counter		Over-the-Counter & Alcohol		Prescription	
	#	%	#	%	#	%	#	%
No Accident	359	73.6	148	71.8	22	73.3	93	68.4
One Accident	103	21.1	45	21.8	7	23.3	33	24.3
Two Accidents	17	3.5	7	3.5	1	3.4	8	5.9
Three or More Accidents	9	1.8	6	2.9			2	1.4
Total	488	100.0	206	100.0	30	100.0	136	100.0

	Prescription and Alcohol		Illicit		Illicit and Alcohol		Alcohol	
	#	%	#	%	#	%	#	%
No Accident	18	58.1	61	69.3	45	70.3	181	71.0
One Accident	9	29.0	21	23.9	14	21.9	56	22.0
Two Accidents	3	9.7	5	5.7	4	6.2	12	4.7
Three or More Accidents	1	3.2	1	1.1	1	1.6	6	2.3
Total	31	100.0	88	100.0	64	100.0	255	100.0

TABLE II. Frequency of traffic tickets in the previous three years by category of psychoactive drug used before driving.

	Total Sample		Over-the-Counter		Over-the-Counter & Alcohol	Prescription	
	#	%	#	%	#	%	#	%
No Tickets	334	68.4	130	63.1	20	66.7	88	64.7
One Ticket	106	21.7	50	24.3	5	16.7	29	21.3
Two Tickets	31	6.4	20	9.7	4	13.3	11	8.1
Three or More Tickets	17	3.5	6	2.9	1	3.3	8	5.9
Total	488	100.0	206	100.0	30	100.0	136	100.0

	Prescription and Alcohol		Illicit		Illicit and Alcohol		Alcohol	
	#	%	#	%	#	%	#	%
No Tickets	18	58.1	38	43.2	25	39.1	151	59.2
One Ticket	7	22.6	32	36.4	27	42.2	66	25.9
Two Tickets	2	6.4	8	9.1	7	10.9	25	9.8
Three or More Tickets	4	12.9	10	11.3	5	7.8	13	5.1
Total	31	100.0	88	100.0	64	100.0	255	100.0

IS GROUP THERAPY REALLY AN EFFECTIVE PART OF DRUG ABUSE PROGRAMS?

Jerry P. Flanzer, DSW, ACSW

Assistant Professor
University of Wisconsin-Milwaukee
School of Social Welfare

Floyd A. Aprill, MSW, ACSW

Psychiatric Social Worker
Milwaukee County Mental Health Center
Drug Abuse Program

Group therapy is being increasingly used on an outpatient basis for the treatment of drug addicts. Yet, a review of the literature points to fragmentary knowledge and paucity of information covering group treatment of drug addicts. Is it because we do not report failures? Much of the literature simply describes existing multi-modality programs. Few evaluate the effectiveness of the group modality being used, describe the rationale for using group therapy or even delineate its clientele. Group therapy alone has not shown the promise of group therapy in conjunction with methadone maintenance for the treatment of narcotic addicts.

Methadone by itself is an extremely important treatment modality. Therein lies both its advantage and its disadvantages. Because it is so powerful and works so swiftly to remove the addict's craving for heroin, receiving methadone brings about major disruptions in his life. A methadone maintenance client is obliged to give up two strong coping mechanisms: (a) the time-limited "narcoticizing" effect of the drug itself for dealing with intrapsychic, interpersonal and physical pain; (b) the twenty-four-hour-a-day, seven days a week addiction lifestyle characterized by its "ripping and running." This behavioral repertoire provides a coping mechanism to avoid responsibility, to minimize interpersonal intimacies, to defend self-concepts, to mask failures, and to "narcoticize" stress and pain through activity. The blocking effect of methadone maintenance makes it impractical to continue using illicit narcotic drugs for euphoria (a). Such programs make as their first demand the ceasing of the addict's lifestyle (b). This creates an immediate conflict as it is impossible to continue rationalizing a continued addiction lifestyle to support their narcotic dependency. These disruptions require swift supportive and wise treatment if narcotic addiction patients are to choose to remain in their respective program.

Group therapy offers some distinct therapeutic additions to changing lifestyles which methadone maintenance cannot do alone. Methadone maintenance does not produce significant positive change in self-concepts, group therapy does. It does not liberate rebellious behavior or externalization of negative feelings, group therapy does. Methadone maintenance is successful in behavioral adjustment and adjustment to societal needs. Group therapy deals with the basic underlying assumption of methadone treatment that asocial behaviors are associated with drug addiction and that drug-taking may be a function of underlying interpersonal, social and/or intrapsychic problems.

The treatment rationales for group therapy vary widely; they include the client need for peer socialization, the client need for consensual validation and behavioral feedback, and the client need to distance himself from the authority figure(s). Group therapy allows the individual to work toward these goals without first placing himself in what he experiences as completely helpless and dependent positions to the therapist/parent. The variety of persons in a group upon whom transferences might be projected increases the possibility of maintaining at least some positive feelings toward some group members. Also, there is a reinforcement effect which allows for an easier time in breaking through defense mechanisms, as well as the component of more easily introducing social reality.

An important rationale, seldom cited, is the therapist's need for diffused strong dependent relationships away from himself and toward the group members. Another important rationale never found in print is the agency's need to "balloon" payments and/or client contact time. Rationales for group treatment, however, must correspond to client-problem need (drug addict type), goals for treatment and the type of group therapy being offered. The authors present a beginning typology for this differential diagnosis and treatment strategy. This typology is an adaptation of McBroom's (1972) socialization classification to apply to narcotic drug addiction.

1. THE CLIENT SOCIALIZED TO THE SPECIFIC DRUG CULTURE: This presumes that the drug addict has learned behaviors endemic to the drug subculture, primarily for reasons of group identification. (This includes basically normal individuals without any pre-existing psychopathology.)
2. THE CLIENT WHO HAS BEEN INADEQUATELY SOCIALIZED: The drug addict who has missed the teaching and opportunities to learn from adequate role models that normally occur early in life.

515

(This includes neurotic psychotic problems often masked by a pseudo-sociopathic behavioral overlay.)

3. UNSOCIALIZED CLIENTS: The unsocialized clients are those that have been severely neglected and deprived as children and who consequently internalized few social values. (This includes sociopathics and character disorders.)

4. PRESOCIALIZATION: The presocialized clients are those who are in serious trouble with their drug problem, but have not yet succumbed to the drug culture.

The authors suggest the following group treatments to correspond to the above-mentioned socialization models:

SOCIALIZED TO THE DRUG CULTURE clientele have roles adequate to the drug community but are inadequate to the societal integration. Treatment may be seen in two phases:

In the first phase, treatment focuses on the rehabilitation and reconstruction of the damage done by the addictive lifestyle. This would include any treatment format aimed at re-establishing family and peer group functioning, developing work records and job skills, completing educational needs, as well as learning new non-chemical ways of coping with stress. An educative group aimed at correcting specific behaviors, teaching new styles and ways of handling interpersonal relationships and day-to-day problems, giving direct information for access to community resources, including vocational skill learning would be appropriate. Much time may be spent in this type of group with direct interpretation reasoning and explanation of their behavior, demonstrating to the abuser the irresponsible and self-defeating aspects of his behavior.

In the second phase, treatment focuses on the reintegration of the patient into the community. Much time is spent discussing fears and anxieties about re-entrance into the community. Heterogeneous growth groups at this time could produce a safe social milieu for risk-taking with straights.

INADEQUATELY SOCIALIZED clientele are in need of developing competence and mastery over their impulses and of developing ego strength, in general. Traditional social group work and psychotherapy through the group process with their focus on building ego strength in interaction with group members, and psychoanalytic group therapy with its focus on insight and transference are the group treatments of choice for the inadequately socialized drug addict. In addition to these therapeutic groups, the educational and integrative groups outlined for the drug culture patients are also needed.

UNSOCIALIZED clientele are represented by the sociopathic personality. It is suggested that highly structured milieu or therapeutic communities focus on personality reorganization and massive behavioral change may be the treatment of choice. On an outpatient basis, group therapy using a behavioral model may be the most viable. If we are asking individuals to make choices and changes in their behavior, supportive educative and rehabilitative services must be available to make such choices amenable. Sociopathic individuals can benefit from psychotherapeutic groups, particularly after having gained the necessary nurturance and internalization of self often developing through the other group modes.

One of the most important aspects to structuring a group for the treatment of drug addicts, however, is the degree of homogeneity or heterogeneity. The authors are primarily referring to grouping members by problem issue or underlying psychopathology. Placing a drug addict in a group of drug addicts increases the likelihood of "contacts" in the deviant subculture. Placing a drug addict in a group with non-drug addicts may be ill-advised, for the drug addict may not be accepted, or he might be destructive.

Thus the educative and behavioral model group preferably should be homogeneous for drugs. The social group work, group psychotherapy and psychoanalytic-oriented groups should preferably be heterogeneous for drugs. Reality factors such as time and expense and therapist training and experience and the lack of acceptance of drug abuse clients by agencies often dictate homogeneous drug abuse groups. Many a drug addiction program can attest to the problem of getting interagency and intraagency funds to come their way. Staff/patient cost ratios of drug abuse programs rarely are allowed the same considerations as in the mental health arena, particularly when referring to methadone maintenance programs. Thus, many programs cannot afford professionals with intensive group treatment training. Poor ratios have led to rapid staff turnovers. In many programs, heavy reliance is upon the least trained. This has greatly limited many group treatment success possibilities, let alone the differential diagnosis-treatment plan advocated by these authors. The problems in distance between the layers of training between staff members, the difficulty in maintaining meaningful staff development and interagency collaboration often tend to neutralize positive effects of any group therapy program.

Careful reconsideration of the design of drug abuse programs offering group therapy are in order. Addicts themselves vary in terms of personality, social and psychological patterns, as well as in preaddictive personalities. Group therapy is effective when treatment relates to the needs of the individual patient rather than attempting to apply one group treatment modality to all. Consideration must be given to differential diagnosis linked to specified treatment strategies. The authors offer one diagnostic group treatment typology in the hope that differential research and evaluation will develop to clarify the issues further.

BIBLIOGRAPHY

Baider, Lee (Fall, 1973). Group work with addicts and therapists: Observations in a drug addiction clinic. Drug Forum 3: 91-102.

Battegay, V., and Ladewig, G. (1970). Gruppen therapie und gruppenarbeit mit suechtigan frauen (Group therapy and group work with addicted females). Brit. J. of Addiction 65: 89-98.

Boslow, H. M., Rosenthal, D., Kandel, A., and Manne, S. H. (1961). Methods and experiences in group treatment of defective delinquents in Maryland. J. of Soc. Therapies 7: 65.

Bratter, T. E. (1972). Group therapy with affluent, alienated, adolescent drug abusers: A reality therapy and confrontation approach. Psychotherapy, Theory, Research and Practice 9: 308-313.

Brown, Vivian Barnett (Fall, 1971). Drug people: Schizoid Personalities in search of a treatment. Psychotherapy, Theory, Research and Practice 8: 213-215.

Danceau, Paul (1973). Methadone Maintenance and the Experience of Four Programs. The Drug Abuse Council. Washington, D.C.

Furst, W. M. (1963). Homogeneous vs. heterogeneous groups. Group Psychotherapy and Group Function: 408-410.

Konopka, Gisela (1949). Therapeutic Group Work with Children. University of Minnesota Press, Minneapolis.

Lowinson, Joyce and Zwerling, Israel (1972). Group therapy with narcotic addicts. Groups and Drugs: 25-44.

McBroom, E. (1970). Socialization and social casework. In Theories of Social Casework, R. Roberts and R. Nee (Eds.). Columbia University Press, New York, pp. 315-351.

Sabbath, G. (1964). The treatment of hard-core voluntary drug addict patients. Intern. J. of Group Psychotherapy 14: 307-317.

Spotnitz, Hyman (1972). Comparison of different types of group psychotherapy. In Sensitivity Through Encounter and Marathon, Harold I. Kaplan and Benjamin J. Sidock (Eds.). Jason Aronson, Inc., New York, pp. 27-58.

Whittaker, D., and Lieberman, M. (1964). Psychotherapy Through the Group Process. Atherton Press, New York.

MEDICAL COMPLICATIONS

MEDICAL COMPLICATIONS OF NARCOTIC DEPENDENCY:
A CHANGING PATTERN

Barry Stimmel, M.D.

Department of Medicine
Mount Sinai School of Medicine of
 The City University of New York
New York, New York

The medical complications associated with illicit heroin use are
well known. The severity of such complications has also been
emphasized in recent years through statistics released by the
Office of the Medical Examiner of the City of New York. In 1969
and 1970, heroin was found to be the single leading cause of death
in young men between the ages of 15 and 35, including nonaddicts.
(1)

It is less frequently realized however that, with the exception of
an actual pharmacologic overdose, almost all of the medical complications in heroin dependency are related not to the narcotic properties of heroin but to the contaminants with which the drug is
mixed, as well as to the unsterile methods attending its injection.

In 1964, Drs. Vincent Dole and Marie Nyswander introduced the concept of oral methadone maintenance in the therapy of chronic heroin
dependency. (2) From 1964 to 1968, 1,230 persons were admitted to
methadone maintenance (MM) to study the effectiveness of this therapeutic modality. Demand soon exceeded supply and although many
programs were established from 1969 to 1972 in New York City, there
were waiting times extending to six months' duration. Responding
to this need, increased funding for MM programs became available
with subsequent expansion of treatment facilities. In 1973 and
1974, approximately 35,000 to 40,000 persons were on methadone
maintenance in the greater New York area. (3)

The actions of methadone to comfortably maintain a narcotic dependent person as well as permit a level of tolerance to the euphoric
effect of narcotics not able to be overcome by injection of street
heroin have been well described. This "blocking" of the heroin

---

This study relates to a program funded by the New York State
 Office of Drug Abuse Services.

euphoria has resulted not only in a marked decrease but, in most instances, a complete cessation of injection of street heroin by those participating in MM. The elimination of behavior centering around "heroin seeking" activity hopefully results in a major change in lifestyle, allowing the former heroin addict to achieve realistic goals and objectives. Another less publicized but equally important effect is the elimination of the severe medical complications previously attending heroin use. The following study was undertaken to assay the effects that expansion of methadone maintenance programs have had on the medical complications of illicit heroin use.

I. MATERIALS AND METHODS

Admissions of narcotic users to the General Medical Service at The Mount Sinai Medical Center between 1971 and 1972 (Period I) were compared with those ocurring during the following two years, 1973-1974 (Period II). The division of admissions between the two periods represents the approximate point at which positions in methadone programs in New York City began to expand, with the demand for such therapy being less than the number of positions available. This was felt to indicate that MM was now readily available on a citywide basis to all persons desiring this therapeutic modality.

All admissions were classified both as to narcotic used (heroin or methadone) as well as the type of organ system disorder requiring entry into the in-patient service. All admissions in narcotic users relating to elective procedures were eliminated from the study. Individuals admitted on several occasions during each period were counted as single admissions if the admission was related to the initial disorder. In instances of more than one admitting diagnosis, only the primary ones were used for purposes of this classification.

II. RESULTS

In 1971 and 1972 (Period I), there were 223 admissions in narcotic users, with heroin use seen in 86% and methadone use in 14%. This represented 3.5% of all admissions to the General Medical Service (GMS). This can be compared to 100 admissions of narcotic users over the ensuing two-year period (Period II) which represented 1.5% of all GMS admissions ($p < 0.01$) during this period. During this latter period, heroin was the main narcotic used in 75%, methadone in 25%.

The reasons for hospitalization during both periods are illustrated in Table I.

During Period I infectious complications represented the single most common reason for hospitalization, being responsible for 35% of all admissions in narcotic addicts. The type of infections encountered ranged in severity from abscesses and cellulitis secondary to injection of heroin to endocarditis, septic pulmonary emboli, and tetanus.

Endocarditis was present in 13 persons, representing 17 admissions. Complications occurred in 16 of the 17 admissions (94%), with surgery required in four instances. Three patients expired from their disease.

The relationship between infectious complications and type of narcotic used was reviewed. Heroin use was responsible for 94% of all infectious admissions and was the only drug used in every one of the more severe complications.

Hepatic disease was the next largest single diagnosis made during Period I, being responsible for 43 (19%) of narcotic addict admissions. Heroin was the predominant drug in 77% of cases, with acute or chronic viral hepatitis occurring in 38 of 43 admissions (88%) due to liver disease.

Admissions occurring during Period II reveal a somewhat different pattern (Table I). Infections were responsible for only 19% of admissions, with hepatic dysfunction being the single leading cause of entry into the hospital (22%). Infectious complications noted during this period, however, differed greatly from those seen over the preceding two years (Table II). While the percent of persons hospitalized with abscesses, cellulitis, or pneumonia was comparable during both periods, there were no cases of endocarditis, septic emboli, arthritis or osteomyletis during Period II. Heroin use was seen in 18 (86%) of persons admitted with infectious complications and was responsible for all five admissions due to abscesses and three of the four admissions due to pneumonia.

Although the incidence of admissions due to liver disease did not change between the two study periods (19% v. 22%), only one case of severe acute viral hepatitis was admitted. Chronic hepatitis or cirrhosis was noted in 17 of 22 persons (77%), with alcoholic hepatitis being seen in 4 (18%). Heroin use was present in 82% of these persons.

The number of overdose reactions admitted during Period II increased greatly over the two cases occurring during Period I. Of the 15 admissions relating to overdose reactions, heroin was the only drug taken in 6 (40%), methadone in 2 (13%), with multiple drug ingestion being found in 7 (47%).

III. CONCLUSIONS

The review of admissions of narcotic users to a GMS revealed the
medical admissions secondary to narcotic use to decrease markedly
with respect to both absolute number and relative proportion of
all admissions to the in-patient service between 1971 and 1972 as
compared to 1973-1974. Although heroin injection still represented
the major drug abused in persons admitted during both periods, the
type of admission has changed greatly with respect to infectious
complications and hepatic dysfunction. Few severe infections
occurred over the second two-year period, without any cases of
endocarditis or septic pulmonary emboli being noted. Similarly,
admissions due to hepatic disease now appear to reflect the
presence of chronic hepatic dysfunction rather than acute viral
hepatitis.

TABLE I. CLASSIFICATION OF HOSPITALIZED
NARCOTIC USERS

COMPLICATIONS	PERIOD I		PERIOD II	
	No.	(%)	No.	(%)
Cardiovascular*	6	(2.6)	5	(5)
Endocrine	7	(3.1)	5	(5)
Gastrointestinal	13	(5.7)	7	(7)
Hematological	8	(3.5)	2	(2)
Hepatic Disease	43	(18.9)	22	(22)
Infections	80	(35.3)	19	(19)
"Overdose" Reactions	2	(0.9)	15	(15)
Renal	7	(3.2)	6	(6)
Respiratory*	4	(1.8)	3	(3)
Miscellaneous	57	(25)	16	(16)
TOTAL	227	(100)	100	(100)

* Noninfectious

TABLE II: COMPARISON OF ADMISSIONS DUE TO
INFECTIONS: PERIOD I V. PERIOD II

	PERIOD I		Period II	
	No.	(%)	No.	(%)
Abscesses or Cellulitis	20	(25)	5	(26)
Endocarditis	13	(16)	0	
Pneumonia	17	(21)	4	(21)
Septic Pulmonary Emboli	4	(5)	0	
Septic Arthritis/Osteomylitis	10	(12)	0	
Tetanus	1	(1)	0	
Other	16	(20)	10	(53)
TOTAL	81	(100)	19	(100)

REFERENCES

1. M. Halpern, Hum. Path., 3: 13 (1972).
2. V. P. Dole and M. E. Nyswander, JAMA, 193: 646 (1965).
3. F. R. Gearing, Am. J. Pub. Health Supp., 64: 44 (1974).

THE LONG-TERM TREATMENT OF HEROIN ADDICTS WITH CHRONIC DISEASES

Edward Shollar, Ph.D., Helene Finkelstein, M.A., Lee Hoffman, M.D.

Van Etten Drug Treatment Program
Albert Einstein College of Medicine
Bronx, New York

In June 1966 a methadone program was begun on the Chest Service of Van Etten Hospital. It was established for in-patients with tuberculosis who were known to be hard-core heroin addicts. Subsequently, the scope of the Van Etten Drug Treatment Program has been expanded to include hard-core addicts, whether in-patients or out-patients, who have any chronic disease requiring long-term medical supervision. Among the diseases currently being treated are: tuberculosis, asthma, chronic obstructive pulmonary disease, bacterial endocarditis, Hodgkin's disease, epilepsy, and diabetes.

VEDTP services are delivered through three major organizational sections; medical, counseling, and vocational. A therapeutic approach is maintained through regular team meetings and patient-centered consultation among members of each section. The Program's school offers classes in basic education while vocational specialists provide hands-on skills training in the clerical and shoe repair areas. Vocational skills classes and vocational counseling are also available to patients.

Program results were initially reported on the 63 patients in treatment in March 1969.[1] The current census (10/75) is 287.

Of the 63 who were on the Program in March 1969, 20 remain active patients. Of those 20, 14 are maintained on methadone and 6 who have been successfully detoxified from methadone, are drug-free. 43 are no longer Program members.

The 20 patients currently on the Program had a total of 107 prior convictions. Since membership, which for these patients now ranges between 80 and 112 months, the total number of convictions for the entire group is 4.

16 of these patients have had no opiate use since a methadone maintenance level was reached. The remaining 4 continue to use opiates to some degree but all less than 1% of the time.

9 of the 20 are employed full-time and 2 are homemakers. 17 have a stable home life and 8 among them are raising children.

10 of this group have TB. Since joining the Program, 8 of them have completed a two year course of chemotherapy. This treatment could not be delivered to any of these patients prior to admittance to VEDTP.

Data in Table I illustrates the current rehabilitation status of patients treated in March 1969.

Of the 43 patients no longer receiving treatment at VEDTP, 15 currently are considered to be successfully rehabilitated or were so at the time of their deaths. 19 of the 43 do not, or did not at the time of their deaths, meet the criteria for successful rehabilitation which includes: the absence of opiate use and alcoholism, no criminal activity, and adequate ongoing medical supervision of the patient's chronic illness. The whereabouts and status of 9 former patients are unknown.

Of the 63 patients in treatment in March 1969, 32 (51%) are, or were at the time of their deaths, successfully rehabilitated; 22 (35%) are not; and the status of 9 (14%) is unknown.

The Program's initial aim was to reduce the number of irregular hospital discharges of seriously ill heroin addicts. In the 33 months prior to the opening of the Program, 49% of heroin addicts were irregularly discharged from the Chest Service at Van Etten Hospital. In the 33 months after the Program's opening, the percentage of irregular discharges of our patients was only 5%.

Providing good medical follow-up was another of the Program's objectives. Table II illustrates the medical treatment history of 196 of the Program's current patients. They kept 54% of their medical appointments prior to admittance to the Program and 89% since admittance. Total medical care delivered on an emergency basis has dropped from 41% of the time to 8% since joining VEDTP, and emergency room use as the facility providing the treatment was reduced from 32 to 7%. In-patient treatment has dropped from 19 to 4%.

Prior to admittance to the Program, pregnant women had their first prenatal doctor's visit in the 26th week of pregnancy and averaged 4 doctor's visits per pregnancy. Since admittance, the first doctor's visit for prenatal care is in the 11th week, and there are an average of 16 visits during the pregnancy.

Current Problems

Alcoholism and "pill" abuse represent major obstacles to the medical and social rehabilitation of former heroin addicts.

9% of the Program's patients have debilitating alcoholism and an additional 32% have some problem with alcohol. In a recent test for valium and librium, we found that 33% of all patients were positive for valium and 8% for librium. While some of these individuals use these drugs as part of a well-monitored treatment and others use them infrequently, many are genuinely addicted. Additionally, patients using these so-called minor tranquilizers also tend to use alcohol excessively.

It is our impression that the majority of those who abuse the minor tranquilizers and alcohol are individuals whose experience of anxiety significantly interferes with their functioning. The level of their self-medication of valium and alcohol tends to be beyond their actual needs, which contributes to the serious difficulties they ordinarily have in engaging in productive activities.

Alcohol abuse is a major problem for many ex-heroin addicts. We found alternating periods of heroin and alcohol use among a number of our patients. 33 of our current patients followed a particular pattern of substance abuse. They had no drinking problems while they were addicted to heroin prior to coming to the Program but developed a drinking problem when they stopped using heroin. These 33 patients also began using heroin heavily again and did so for at least one month. 24 of these 33 patients, when using heroin again, stopped drinking completely. Of these 24, 2 were terminated from the Program before their heroin use stopped a second time, 22 remained on the Program and when their heroin use stopped a second time, all 22 went back to having significant problems with alcohol. The notion that heroin and alcohol addictions are mutually exclusive is contradicted by these preliminary findings.

Conclusions

Delivering adequate health care to drug addicts seems greatly facilitated by employing a hospital based clinic that simultaneously treats medical illness and drug addiction. The clinic staff provides drug counseling, primary medical care, and when necessary, acts as an effective conduit for other medical and social services.

At least 51% of VEDTP patients in treatment in March 1969, are currently, or were at the time of their deaths, successfully rehabilitated. This group of patients had an average of 16 years of addiction and 49 months of incarceration prior to admittance to VEDTP. These results support the earlier findings[1] that methadone maintenance treatment can be a major vehicle for the medical and social rehabilitation of heroin addicts.

Notable among the current problems in the treatment of drug addiction is the general increase in valium and librium abuse and the frequent occurrence of alcoholism in former heroin users.

Our preliminary findings indicate that for many individuals alcoholism and heroin addiction may represent alternating periods of a continuing cycle of addiction. Ascertaining the exact nature of this addiction cycle, and determining the effect of methadone in this cycle, should be the aim of further investigations.

The suggestion that individuals have been cured of their heroin addiction and should be transferred to an alcohol abuse program for their current alcoholism may be short-sighted. Such transfers are contraindicated unless a cyclical heroin-alcoholism addiction is ruled out.

TABLE I

CURRENT (10/75) REHABILITATION STATUS OF PATIENTS
TREATED AT VEDTP IN MARCH 1969

	SUCCESS *	FAILURE *	UNKNOWN
Active VEDTP patients (20)	17	3	- -
Terminated from VEDTP (43)			
Graduated - now drug free	6	- -	- -
Transferred to other drug programs	2	4	- -
Dropped from VEDTP for in-attendance or violation of program rules	- -	5	- -
Died while on VEDTP -			
non-drug related cause	7	1	1
complication of alcohol	- -	3	- -
Died after terminated from VEDTP	- -	2	1
Incarcerated	- -	4	- -
Whereabouts unknown	- -	- -	7
Total (63)	32	22	9
	(51%)	(35%)	(14%)

* Rehabilitation is considered successful if: there is no opiate use, no criminal activity, and adequate ongoing medical supervision of patient's chronic illness(s).

529

TABLE II

MEDICAL TREATMENT OF VEDTP HEROIN ADDICTS WITH CHRONIC DISEASES

	PRIOR TO VEDTP (%)	DURING VEDTP (%)
Where Treatment Received		
VEDTP	– –	80
Other hospital clinic	28	5
Private physician's office	12	3
Emergency room	32	7
Hospital (in-patient)	19	4
Other	9	1
Medical Appointments Kept	54	89
Form of Treatment		
Emergency	41	8
Routine	59	92
Received at Least One Annual Checkup	22	98
Prenatal Care		
Time of first physician's visit	26th wk.	11th wk.
Number of prenatal visits	4.1	16.0

REFERENCE

1. Hoffman, L.: A methadone program for addicts with chest disease. JAMA, 211: 977–987 (February 9) 1970.

METHADONE ILEUS SYNDROME: FATAL CASE REPORT*

Richard B. Rubenstein, M.D.
William I. Wolff, M.D.

Department of Surgery
Beth Israel Medical Center
New York, New York

In 1975, we described five methadone maintenance patients who presented with a syndrome of fecal impaction associated with impaired colonic motility (methadone ileus) (1). We wish to present an additional case, one which was untreated and proved to be fatal.

FATAL CASE REPORT

A 24-year-old Puerto Rican male became addicted to heroin at age 16 and started methadone maintenance four years later. At age 18 (5/22/69), he underwent an exploratory laparotomy and suture of a diaphragmatic laceration resulting from a stab wound.

In May 1975, four weeks prior to his second admission (6/7/75), the patient developed constipation. He passed flatus frequently and had several episodes of diarrhea, never passing formed stool. Progressive abdominal distension ensued and this eventually became massive. During the week prior to presentation, the patient took several enemas to no avail. Despite the fact that several relatives urged him to seek medical advice, he refused. Six hours prior to hospitalization he had an episode of vomiting, followed by progressive dyspnea. He was rushed to our medical center via ambulance.

On admission, the patient was cyanotic, apneic, and pulseless, with fixed, dilated pupils. Efforts at reresuscitation were fruitless. The degree of abdominal distension was extraordinary. The marked respiratory compromise, resulting from the diaphragmatic elevation, was evident from the admission chest x-ray. The diaphragm was elevated to the level of the second inter-

*As presented at the 1976 National Drug Abuse Conference held in New York City.

costal space. An autopsy was performed. The entire large bowel was packed with firm stool; the circumference of the ascending colon measured 36 cm.

DISCUSSION

Methadone and other morphine congeners increase intestinal tone, diminish the amplitude of contractions, and produce a marked decrease in propulsive activity (2,3). The resultant slower passage leads to increased absorption of water, producing hardened feces. This is the pharmacological basis of the methadone ileus syndrome.

Patients with methadone ileus present with intestinal obstruction. Symptoms include crampy abdominal pain and distension, frequently accompanied by a recent onset of constipation. Vomiting can occasionally occur. Examination reveals abdominal distension with generalized tenderness. Abdominal x-rays are compatible with colonic obstruction - multiple air-fluid levels are the rule. However, fecal material may be prominent throughout the colon. This, coupled with a clinical history of methadone maintenance, should lead the physician to suspect the methadone ileus syndrome.

Treatment is non-surgical. Initially it includes the administration of intravenous fluids, nasogastric suction, repetitive high colonic enemas and bisacodyl suppositories. After the patient's general condition has improved and some stool is passed, laxatives should be given.

We have previously presented five cases of methadone ileus, and have subsequently treated several additional cases successfully. However, as this case exemplifies, if left alone or treated improperly, the syndrome can be fatal. As methadone maintenance therapy becomes more widely used, and since it may be a lifetime program, we believe that the methadone ileus syndrome will be seen with increasing frequency.

REFERENCES

1. I.A. Spira, R.B. Rubenstein, D. Wolff, and W.I. Wolff, Ann. Surg., 181:15 (1975).
2. E.E. Daniel, W.H. Sutherland, and A. Bogoch, Gastroenterology, 36:510 (1959).
3. L.S. Goodman and A. Gilman, The Pharmacological Basis of Therapeutics (4th ed.), The Macmillan Company, New York, 1970.

ADEQUACY OF SEXUAL PERFORMANCE IN MEN
MAINTAINED ON METHADONE

Ray Hanbury, M.A., Murry J. Cohen, M.D.,
Barry Stimmel, M.D.

Departments of Medicine and Psychiatry
Mount Sinai School of Medicine of
The City University of New York
New York, New York

The clinical effects of narcotics on the metabolism and the behavioral implications of such effects with respect to heroin dependency have only recently begun to be studied intensively. It
has been a common assumption that the effect of opiates on sexual
activity is consistently detrimental.

With the advent of methadone maintenance as a recognized modality
in rehabilitation of heroin addicts, problems associated with sexual function in men maintained on methadone rapidly emerged.
Methadone has been considered to be a cause of impotence, ejacula-
tory disturbances, and lack of desire for sexual relations in a
considerable number of individuals on methadone maintenance. Most
of these studies have been uncontrolled, describing only those
persons coming forward with symptoms of sexual dysfunction.

In an attempt to determine the prevalence of sexual dysfunction
amongst men enrolled in a methadone maintenance and aftercare
treatment program, as well as to identify correlative factors with
respect to etiology of this dysfunction, the following study was
undertaken.

I.   METHODS AND PROCEDURES

A random selection of 50 men from a population of 355 men (14%)
enrolled in a methadone maintenance and aftercare treatment program who were without evidence of any serious underlying medical

---

This study relates to a program funded by the New York State
Office of Drug Abuse Services.

disorder was obtained. All persons readily agreed to complete a questionnaire concerning their sexual activity while drug free, on heroin, and on methadone maintenance. This questionnaire was a modification of one previously described by Espejo et al (1) and could be completed by the subject within a fifteen-minute time interval. At the end of the interview, if sexual dysfunction was found to be present, the subject was asked why this information was not brought to the attention of his therapist at an earlier date. A comparison of data obtained between those individuals experiencing sexual dysfunction and those individuals without sexual dysfunction was made in an effort to determine whether any correlations could be made between persons susceptible to sexual dysfunction on methadone therapy.

II. RESULTS

All subjects readily completed the questionnaire without difficulty. Thirty-three persons (66%), (Group I), reported normal sexual functioning on methadone therapy, whereas 17 (33%), (Group II), reported varying degrees of sexual dysfunction.

The demographic characteristics of patients in both of these groups revealed no apparent difference with respect to ethnicity, marital status, age, or length of addiction to heroin. Those persons experiencing no sexual dysfunction had a slightly longer duration of methadone maintenance therapy than those persons experiencing sexual difficulties (29.9 months v. 24.1 months, respectively), but this was not statistically significant.

Classification of the sexual dysfunction described by the 17 persons can be seen in Table I. Failure to achieve orgasm was the most frequent complaint, being seen in 14 (88%) of all persons. Failure to achieve an erection was noted in eight persons, with six individuals experiencing a lack of sexual drive and two with delayed ejaculation. Approximately one-half of the persons started to experience sexual difficulties within one month of initiating methadone therapy. Only one individual experienced difficulties after chronic methadone maintenance.

A comparison of methadone dosage and ingestion of other drugs of abuse between Group I and Group II revealed no difference in consumption of alcohol or presence of polydrug abuse between those persons experiencing sexual dysfunction and those reporting adequate sexual activity while on methadone. Similarly, the methadone dosage was comparable in both groups. The mean methadone dosage of those persons with sexual difficulties of 62.4 mg., although slightly higher than that seen in persons without dysfunction (59.49 mg.), was not statistically significant.

The presence of diagnosed psychologic disturbances was also found to be comparable in both study groups. The percentage of persons exhibiting depression and/or insomnia was somewhat greater in Group II (47% v. 24%); however, the small numbers involved make it difficult to adequately interpret these data.

Not unexpectedly, the frequency of sexual relations while on methadone was found to be different between the two groups of patients, with no individual in Group II reporting daily sexual relations as compared to daily sexual activity present in 12 (36%) persons in Group I. When a comparison was made, however, between the presence of sexual dysfunction on heroin and in the drug-free state, a marked difference was noted between the groups. Twelve of the 17 individuals with sexual difficulties experienced similar problems on heroin as compared to only one person (3%) in Group I. None of the individuals with adequate sexual performance on methadone maintenance experienced any problems in the drug-free state as compared to two of 17 (12%) persons experiencing sexual difficulties on maintenance therapy.

Although the numbers are small, a comparison of the types of sexual dysfunction seen during narcotic and drug-free states revealed that the problems reported by patients on methadone closely parallel the problems seen while on street heroin.

Since adequate sexual function is a relative term, the frequency of sexual activity in the drug-free state was studied in those in Group II (Table II). Only three individuals (17%) reported daily sexual activity as compared to 36% of persons in Group I. Sexual activity among patients in Group II occurring weekly was approximately equal when drug free, on heroin, or on methadone.

Since individual changes in sexual frequency while on narcotics as compared to that seen while abstinent from narcotics may be masked by group comparisons, the frequency of sexual activity in each individual was reviewed. Ten persons (59%) had no change in frequency of sexual activity, as compared to the drug-free state, while on heroin and/or methadone. Similarly, decreased frequency was noted in seven (41%) persons.

The patients were asked to indicate their degree of concern by classifying their difficulty as minimal, moderate, or severe. Minimal was defined as being a lack of concern, moderate as being associated with anxiety but not of sufficient degree to consider dose reduction. The dysfunction was considered severe if of sufficient intensity to have the patient request dose reduction or detoxification. Utilizing this classification, five (30%) felt minimally concerned, 10 (59%) had moderate concern, with only two (12%) persons considering altering their methadone dose or detoxifying. It is, however, important to emphasize that the reason given by 10 of the 17 patients for not bringing this problem to

the attention of the staff was related to a feeling of embarrass-
ment rather than a lack of concern.

III. DISCUSSION

Although the population sample in this study is not large and the
information received self-reported, it is nonetheless apparent
that sexual dysfunction is of importance in men maintained on
methadone maintenance, being seen in approximately one-third of individuals under study. In considering the etiology of this dysfunction, it is essential to attempt to define associated parameters. Equally important is to attempt to ascertain if these symptoms are not underlying signs of maladjustment that would be
present in the drug-free state and indeed might lead an individual
to turn to narcotic use for relief of anxiety. In this regard it
is of interest that the frequency of sexual activity, while drug
free, in persons experiencing sexual dysfunction on methadone was
not high. In fact, this frequency was unchanged from that existing during both abstinence and heroin dependence in 59%.

It is therefore conceivable that despite the pharmacological effects of the drug, the actual patterns of sexual dysfunction seen
in certain individuals on methadone maintenance may be related to
preexisting patterns of sexual behavior, in some instances perhaps of sufficient intensity to have become a prime factor in
initiating heroin use. In such cases it would be expected that
methadone maintenance would not only fail to alleviate this dysfunction but, unaccompanied by the euphoria seen with heroin use,
might serve to intensify the symptoms of sexual inadequacy.

TABLE I: CLASSIFICATION OF SEXUAL DYSFUNCTION

	No.	(%)
LACK OF SEXUAL DRIVE	6	(38)
FAILURE OF ERECTION	8	(50)
DELAYED EJACULATION	2	(13)
FAILURE OF ORGASM	14	(88)

TABLE II: ANALYSIS OF PAST AND PRESENT SEXUAL ACTIVITY

	Drug-Free No. (%)		Heroin No. (%)		Methadone No. (%)	
DAILY	3	(17)	1	(6)	0	-
SEMIWEEKLY	2	(12)	0	-	2	(12)
WEEKLY	10	(59)	8	(47)	8	(47)
BIWEEKLY	1	(6)	5	(29)	5	(29)
MONTHLY	1	(6)	3	(18)	2	(12)

REFERENCES

1. R. Espejo, G. Hogben, and B. Stimmel, Proc. 5th Natl. Conf. Meth. Treat., Natl. Assoc. Prev. Addict. Narc., New York, 1973, p 490.

ISSUES

CHALLENGING EMPLOYMENT DISCRIMINATION AGAINST
FORMER DRUG ABUSERS:
BEAZER v. NEW YORK CITY TRANSIT AUTHORITY

Eric D. Balber
Mark C. Morril

Legal Action Center
New York City

INTRODUCTION

A recent court decision represents a major breakthrough in
efforts to secure equal employment and rehabilitation opportunities for former drug abusers. A United States District Court
judge in New York City ruled on August 6, 1975, that the New York
City Transit Authority's policy of excluding from employment all
methadone maintenance patients violated the United States Constitution. Under the opinion, the Transit Authority (TA) is required
to consider methadone maintenance patients for job positions on
an individualized basis.

The plaintiffs in the action were represented by the Legal
Action Center, a public interest law firm located in New York City.
The Legal Action Center has focused substantial resources on the
rights of former drug abusers since its formation two years ago
and acts as a clearinghouse in this area, providing legal advice
and assistance, or, where appropriate, referral to other resources.

The significance of the decision is evident. For the first
time, virtually all of the existing data on the employability of
methadone maintenance patients has been compiled and embodied as
extensive formal findings of fact by a federal court. Thus the
substance of these findings can now be conveyed to potential employers, both public and private, indicating that the employability of methadone maintenance patients has received extensive scrutiny and a stamp of approval by the federal judiciary. Particularly useful in persuading potential employers to hire former addicts should be the Court's findings of fact with respect to the
general experience of employers in this regard.

541

Moreover, moving beyond the negotiation stage, the Beazer decision can now be regarded as having the force of law on this issue. Thus a program's vocational rehabilitation staff or counsel
can responsibly represent that it is illegal to exclude methadone
maintained patients from employment solely on the basis of their
present or past participation in a methadone maintenance program.
Furthermore, although Beazer was brought on behalf of methadone
maintained patients, it would appear to have wide ranging ramifications for the employment prospects of drug-free patients as well.

Excerpts from the Court's opinion follow. The full decision
is published in volume 399 of the Federal Supplement, at pages
1032-1058.

* * * * * * * * * * * * * * * * *

"This is a class action against the New York City Transit Authority ("TA")...

"The action challenges the blanket exclusion from any form of employment in the New York City subway and bus systems of all former
heroin addicts participating in methadone maintenance programs,
regardless of the individual merits of the employee or the applicant. Plaintiffs also allege that there is a similar exclusionary
policy even against former heroin addicts who have successfully
concluded their participation in a methadone program.

"The amended complaint alleges that this policy violates the due
process and equal protection clauses of the Fourteenth Amendment
....The claim is that there is no legal basis for classifying all
present and former methadone maintenance patients as unemployable
for any position in the TA.

....

"Basically the class represented by the named plaintiffs consists
of all those persons who have been, or would in the future be,
subject to dismissal or rejection as to employment by the TA on the
ground of present or past participation in methadone maintenance
programs.

....

"It is the general policy of the TA that no person using narcotic
drugs may be employed.

....

"Methadone is regarded as a narcotic....It is stipulated that no
written permission has ever been given by the (TA) Medical Director
for the employment of a person using methadone.

"The effect of this policy is that, if it is revealed that a current employee of the TA is a user of methadone he will be discharged, or if an applicant for employment is a user of methadone,
he will not be employed. This policy applies to all positions in
the TA regardless of whether they are operating or non-operating
positions. Moreover, the policy operates as an absolute exclusion
-- no consideration being given to individual factors such as recent employment history, successful adherence to a methadone program, or evidence of freedom from heroin use.

. . . .

"The reasons given by the TA as a basis for this policy....can be
summarized....as follows. Methadone maintenance, as a treatment
for heroin addiction, has been developed relatively recently. The
TA contends that the use of methadone in place of heroin is merely
the substitution of one narcotic for another. The TA asserts that
methadone maintenance treatment fails to a significant degree in
remedying the basic problems of heroin addiction -- with the result that a methadone maintenance patient embodies the underlying
character defects which caused him to turn to heroin in the first
place, and that there is a substantial risk that such a person,
while on methadone, will revert to heroin or turn to other drugs
or alcohol abuse. The TA contends also there are significant adverse physiological effects from methadone itself, which would impair the performance of such person as an employee even if he
faithfully refrained from heroin or other illicit drugs or alcohol
abuse. The TA further contends that its operations involve such
serious problems of safety, both with respect to the public and to
the employees, that they cannot prudently employ present or past
methadone patients. Finally, the TA argues that there is no satisfactory way of screening the reliable methadone patient from the
unreliable, so that it is administratively necessary to have a
blanket exclusionary policy.

"I have concluded that the blanket exclusionary policy of the TA
against methadone maintenance patients is constitutionally invalid.
Plaintiffs have more than sustained their burden of proving that
there are substantial numbers of persons on methadone maintenance
who are as fit for employment as other comparable persons.

"No one can have the slightest doubt about the heavy responsibility of the TA to the public, including their duty respecting the
safety of millions of persons who are carried on its subways and
buses. However, in my view, the blanket exclusionary policy a-
gainst persons on methadone maintenance is not rationally related
to the safety needs, or any other needs of the TA.

"I have concluded that the policy is the result of a misunderstanding by the TA regarding the nature and effects of methadone
maintenance. I do not say this in any spirit of criticism.

543

The information about methadone maintenance in the public domain
is all too fragmentary and confusing. Myths and misconceptions
abound. On the other hand, the trial of this case has afforded
a unique opportunity to explore in depth the somewhat controversial issues surrounding methadone. A balanced and realistic
view of the subject is possible as a result.

. . . .

"The picture which emerges from all the evidence is basically
this. There are some 40,000 persons in New York City on
methadone maintenance. It is, at present, the most widely used
method for rehabilitating heroin addicts. Among these 40,000
persons on methadone maintenance there is a great variation
(as there is in the population as a whole) with regard to
characteristics such as educational qualifications, employment
skills and background, anti-social behavior, alcohol usage,
and abuse of illicit drugs. But the crucial point made so
strongly by plaintiffs' witnesses was never convincingly
challenged--that methadone as administered in the maintenance
programs can successfully erase the physical effects of heroin
addiction and permit a former heroin addict to function normally
both mentally and physically. It is further proved beyond any
real dispute that among the 40,000 persons in New York City on
methadone maintenance (as in any comparable group of 40,000
New Yorkers), there are substantial numbers who are free of anti-
social behavior and free of the abuse of alcohol or illicit drugs;
that such persons are capable of employment and many are indeed
employed. It is further clear that the employable can be
identified by a prospective employer by essentially the same type
of procedures used to identify other persons who would make good
and reliable employees. Finally, it has been demonstrated that
the TA has ways of monitoring employees after they have been
hired, which can be used for persons on methadone maintenance just
as they are used for other persons employed by the TA.

"This proof applies with equal, if not greater, force to those
former heroin addicts who have successfully completed participation
in a methadone program.

"I have therefore concluded that the present blanket exclusionary
policy of the TA against employing, or considering for employment,
any past or present methadone maintained person regardless of his
individual merits, is unconstitutional (as a violation of the
equal protection and due process clauses of the Fourteenth Amendment.)"

MODEL PROCEDURES
FOR
INVOLUNTARY TERMINATION FROM
METHADONE MAINTENANCE TREATMENT PROGRAMS

Eric D. Balber
Risa G. Dickstein
Attorneys

Legal Action Center
New York City

The involuntary, summary termination of patients from methadone maintenance treatment programs has recently become a matter of
increased concern to patients' groups, treatment programs, attorneys and governmental agencies.

Reports received by the Legal Action Center indicate that
patients face three basic problems in connection with summary terminations. First, the termination decision itself may be arbitrary
and without adequate and systematic review procedures it cannot be
corrected. Second, programs may fail to offer terminated patients
an adequate detoxification regimen and an acceptable transfer to
another treatment source. Thus the patient is often left with the
unattractive alternatives of extreme medical discomfort or the illicit purchase of drugs. Lastly, patients often experience serious
dislocation when they are forced to precipitously sever ties that
they have developed over the course of a long period of time when
a particular treatment program, and they may be permanently lost to
the treatment process.

The countervailing consideration is, of course, the genuine
need of programs to deal with patients who are unruly or dangerous
or who fail to comply with essential program norms.

In an attempt to deal with the summary termination problem,
attorneys at Legal Action Center have undertaken a variety of efforts. These efforts have included investigation of specific cases
and, in a few instances where negotiated relief was impossible to
obtain, temporary relief was sought and obtained from the Federal
court. But for the most part we have directed our energies toward
assisting programs in developing termination procedures, and in

545

working with regulatory agencies in an attempt to formulate comprehensive termination standards, which will both protect the rights of patients and place a minimal burden on programs.

Set forth below are some of the model provisions that the Legal Action Center believes should be included in any termination procedures. Individual programs should, of course, develop their own protocols to meet their individual needs. The following provisions are necessary, however, to provide the minimal due process guarantees to which patients are entitled.

I. Specific criteria or grounds for termination. These criteria should be developed in consultation with the program's staff and may include medical as well as non-medical reasons. The criteria should involve patterns of conduct rather than single instances of unacceptable behavior, with the exception that a single instance of unacceptable behavior may constitute adequate grounds for termination if it involves substantial risk of physical injury to persons, or the destruction of property of significant value.

II. Prior warning of termination. Except for reasons involving substantial risk of physical injury to persons, or the destruction of property of significant value, it is improper to make termination recommendations without a prior warning to the patient by a program staff member. The warning must consist of a written confirmation informing the patient that he or she has engaged in unacceptable conduct, and that if such conduct is repeated or continued, termination from treatment may be considered.

III. Notice of termination recommendation. Written notice of a program's intent to terminate a patient must be given to the patient expeditiously after a termination recommendation has been made and the program intends to approve it. The notice should be signed by the program sponsor and must include a specification of the program standard violated, a description of the patient's conduct believed to have violated such standard, the proposed date of termination, and the fact that the patient may request a hearing to contest the termination decision. The notice must also describe the patient's rights pertaining to a termination hearing.

IV. Termination hearing. The hearing, if requested, should be held as expeditiously as possible, but the patient must be given reasonable access to his or her treatment records and a reasonable period of time to prepare his or her case. The hearing must be conducted by a neutral and detached hearing board, which, if possible, should be comprised of two or more members. At the hearing the patient must have the right to be represented by counsel or a law advocate of his or her choice. The client must also have the right to present his or her case by making a written or oral statement, introducing documentary evidence (including material from his or her program record), and presenting and cross examining witnesses.

V. <u>Termination decision</u>. A decision to involuntarily terminate a
patient must be based solely on the specifications contained in
the notice of termination recommendation, must be made in written
form and must contain a statement of reasons underlying it. Such
statement of reasons must include an indication of which of the
specifications contained in the notice of termination have been
sustained and what behavior alleged has been found to be true.
The program sponsor should sign the termination decision and must
be responsible for it. A patient being involuntarily terminated
must be given a copy of the decision relating to his or her termination, and the decision must be made part of the patient's treatment record.

VI. <u>Appeal of the termination decision</u>. All patients should have
a right to appeal to the program sponsor for reconsideration of a
termination decision. The program may fix a reasonable time period within which such right to appeal must be exercised and may establish procedures for such an appeal. Patients exercising their
right to appeal must be maintained without change in treatment
status pending the outcome of the appeal.

VII. <u>Implementing the termination decision</u>. Patients must not be
terminated on the day immediately preceding a weekend or a Federal
or state holiday. Patients must not be terminated without being
offered both a detoxification regimen and, if possible, a referral
to another methadone maintenance treatment program. Detoxification
scheduled must be in accord with sound medical practice and in no
case must they occur in less than a twenty-one day period.

A number of programs which have adopted due process termination procedures similar to the above report that they enable them
to deal more fairly and expeditiously with problem patients.
There have been virtually no reports of due process procedures resulting in a loss of program integrity.

PATIENT PRIVACY RIGHTS IN DRUG AND ALCOHOL ABUSE
TREATMENT PROGRAMS

David C. Lewis, M.D.

Deputy Chairman
Massachusetts Security and
Privacy Council

Associate Clinical Professor
of Medicine
Harvard Medical School

New Federal regulations safeguarding the confidentiality of
patient records in drug and alcohol abuse treatment programs have
raised anew issues concerning the desired limits of client privacy
rights and the necessity for special attention to record confidentiality.

In the general health care system, most patients still assume
that implicit in the doctor-patient relationship is absolute confidentiality, an assumption buttressed by years of ethical tradition. Moreover, some states have put legal teeth into medical
custom by enacting laws to establish a doctor-patient privilege.
Whatever the legal status, the patient still assumes that the
personal information he surrenders for purposes of treatment is
held strictly in confidence. The assumption is often contravened
in actual practice, and the patient has usually been the one least
informed about the scope of the disclosure of his personal health
information.

Medical information, coupled with personal identification,
is routinely released by both private and institutional providers
for claim payments, medical and fiscal audits, utilization review,
and for research. Ever rising costs of care, particularly as
they dig deeper into the taxpayer's pocket, demand accountability
--accountability to assure that services are in fact delivered at
a level of care commensurate with high standards. Given this need
for accountability, it necessarily follows that the purchaser of
services, whether it be the government acting on behalf of the
taxpayer in administering the Medicare and Medicaid programs or
the private insurer acting on behalf of the consumer/client, must
have access to information sufficient to hold the provider accountable for costs incurred. Inevitably then, some personal health

information must be examined. Now the possibility exists that
these disparate data bases will share personal health information.
Not infrequently, personal information is provided to those claim-
ants beyond that necessary to accomplish the task for which the
information was requested. Given the efficiency of computerized
records and the current lack of planning to define the uses to
which the recorded information may be put, the potential for widespread and systematic abuse of privacy is greatly increased.
Specialized drug abuse and alcoholism treatment programs present
additional problems in that they may not be directly under the
sponsorship of health facilities. Therefore, their patients may be
even less protected by tradition and law against abuses of patient
confidentiality rights.

The contention here is that the cherished principles of
privacy need not--indeed must not--be abandoned in our quest for
cost accountability and efficiency. To the contrary, the greater
the demands for health data, the greater must be the vigilance of
health professionals to assure that, notwithstanding the legitimate
needs for accountability, the client's privacy rights are preserved.

Some general guidelines for protecting client privacy rights
follow:

First, no personally identifying data should be released to
another agency, whether private, Federal, or state, or to any research group unless such release is properly and legally mandated
or obtained with the specific informed consent of the individual.
In practice, this means that the patient has the right to know
who, other than the provider of services, has seen his record or
any abstract of it and for what purpose. This recommendation is
premised on the recognized fact that data collected for one purpose
--for example, treatment--should not be used for another--for
example, law enforcement. Aggregate statistics, however, can and
should be made available, provided no identification of individuals
is possible.

Second, the security with which personal health information
is collected and stored must be rigorous and specified. Any individual who collects, processes, or stores data must be trained
regarding the issues of confidentiality and made sensitive to
privacy issues. Sanctions for inappropriate disclosure of information should be well articulated and enforced for both providers
of service and monitoring government agencies.

Third, personal date extracted from a client's record must
be kept at an absolute minimum. At present, unnecessary demographic data, income statistics, and social histories wend their
way into treatment summaries. An individual need not even be
personally identified for the purpose of making a medical or FDA

program audit. What is necessary is the ability to retrieve an
individual's health history for verification and further information. Therefore, any information that becomes part of a data
base for program audit should include neither the name of the individual, nor the social security number, nor any other personal
identifier that can interface with other data systems. If data
must be maintained with either name or social security number, it
should not be released with this identifying information.

The providers of care, as well as their clients, have privacy
rights. These rights are even less clearly defined because they
seem to conflict with both the patients' rights to privacy and
whatever rights the public may have to know about the care that is
provided. What, for example, are the provider's rights with respect to data collected on those services performed by the provider? To what extent does the public have a right to know about
the efficacy of provider care? How can this right be balanced with
the provider's rights to privacy? Does the act of being a provider
foreclose per se any privacy rights? These issues cannot now be
answered for neither legislation, nor case law, nor precedent in
health practices yields ready answers. It is clear, however, that
in a conflict over rights to privacy, government as the representative of the public interest has the overwhelming advantage over
the individual and the provider.

I. New Federal Regulations for Alcohol and Drug Abuse
    Patient Records

New Federal regulations have attempted to define both the
individual's privacy rights and the rights of the government regarding record confidentiality. They represent a major advance in
the protection of clients' rights and serve as a viable model for
general application in the health and social services field. A
general analysis of these Federal regulations may be found in an
article by Dennis J. Helms in Contemporary Drug Problems, Fall
1975, 259-283.

The purpose of these regulations is to "implement the
authorizing of legislation in a manner that, to the extent practicable, takes into account two streams of legal thought and social
policy. One has to do with enhancing the quality and attractiveness of treatment systems. The other is concerned with the interests of patients as citizens, most particularly in regard to
protecting their rights of privacy."

Implementation has been slow and difficult. Some programs
which had professed strong opinions on the need for increased
recognition of clients' rights are not yet following the new
regulations. Other programs are following the new regulations,
and all programs have a heightened sensitivity to the issues of
record confidentiality. No doubt, there will be some modifica-

tions of the regulations to solve some of the practical problems that have been encountered.

The keystone of the regulations is in the area of the client's right to know--the informed consent and the concept that the client shares control of the personal information collected about him. This is the area where programs encounter the greatest difficulty in implementation because the regulations impede the previously free and informal exchanges of personal client information among programs. There is no shortcut to implementing these provisions, if primary rights are to be preserved.

An interesting line of argument against the need for these regulations is that clients do not care if violations of their record confidentiality occur. As was discussed earlier, the tradition of privacy rights in the health field comes from the doctor-patient relationship, which does not have its roots in poverty health care systems and is more a reflection of a middle and upper class value system. To the extent that addiction treatment programs serve clients who may not hold to a middle-upper class system, clients may not be affronted by the violation of such rights, as they have never felt that they had these rights in the first place. While alcohol addiction spans the entire socioeconomic spectrum, there are disproportionate numbers of programs which attend to the skid-row group. The skid-row alcoholic has, in many ways, already given up any degree of privacy by the overt declaration of his alcoholism. Drug addicts too, particularly heroin addicts, often have relinquished their privacy by multiple arrests and incarceration. With the important exception of juvenile offenders, privacy rights are not well preserved in the criminal justice system. They are legally surrendered along with other freedoms, as a consequence of breaking the law.

Many drug addicts have difficulty in separating the treatment system from the street experience and from their experience with enforcement. Some even expect the treatment personnel to act like police authority figures. Most programs try to distinguish themselves from the street culture and enforcement and to provide a special place where rehabilitation can be facilitated. Skid-row alcoholics and heroin addicts are not likely to complain if confidentiality is violated; on the contrary, they are used to it, and the fact that they are used to it has been used as an argument that the new Federal regulations are unnecessary. Rather than being an argument against the regulations, this is a strong argument for the special need to promulgate confidentiality regulations on behalf of this group of patients.

A further incentive for the regulations is the strong possibility that violation of confidentiality rights discourages treatment. While it is difficult to obtain data to prove this contention, it is impressive that many drug users who were able to

seek care at free clinics tell the staffs that one major fear of
going to hospitals or other organized treatment programs is that
they feel they would be reported automatically to some authority
such as schools, employers, or police. Particularly in the first
treatment contact for the early drug or alcohol abuser, the reputation that a program has for protecting client confidentiality
may be important.

In summary, in spite of the fact that the new confidentiality
regulations are difficult to implement and that many clients of the
programs involved will state that they have little concern about
such violation of their rights, it is important that these regulations be attended to. They will bring drug and alcoholism treatment programs into the tradition of the general health and social
service delivery system. In addition, as client confidentiality
becomes the tradition in addiction treatment programs and known in
the client community, they will encourage the early treatment of
individuals who might otherwise be reluctant to seek help.

PROTECTION OF INDIVIDUAL RIGHTS
IN ADDICT DIVERSION PROGRAMS

by

James C. Weissman
Department of Health and Hospitals
Denver, Colorado

I. INTRODUCTION

In recognition of the integral relationship between addiction
and criminal behavior, the federal government has attempted to
facilitate the coordination of activities between the criminal
justice and drug abuse treatment/prevention systems. During the
late 1960s, several state and local jurisdictions developed criminal justice and drug abuse interface programs which served as
models to the federal planners.

In 1971 the President's Special Action Office for Drug Abuse
Prevention (SAODAP) initiated a national program designed to
stimulate the interfacing of local criminal justice and drug abuse
treatment resources. That program, TASC (Treatment Alternatives
to Street Crime), has sponsored projects in over thirty cities at
a cost of more than $20 million.

The TASC process involves the screening of municipal jail
populations to identify drug addicts, diagnostic testing of identified addicts, and referral of the addicts to community-based
treatment facilities. TASC staff monitors the treatment progress
of the referred addicts and feedback is routinely provided to the
referring criminal justice agencies, i.e., courts, prosecutor, and
probation and parole departments. Some TASC projects also feature

vocational rehabilitation, client escort, and client advocacy services. Although TASC-like programs existed in many communities prior to the advent of the TASC funding mechanism, the generous availability of federal discretionary funds for TASC projects stimulated growth of the community-based interface model. Parallel to that phenomenon has been the emergence of the pretrial diversion concept. Diversion of selected offenders has always occurred through the vehicles of police and prosecutorial discretion, but the last decade has witnessed a formalization of the diversion process. Implementing the recommendations of the 1967 President's Commission on Law Enforcement and the Administration of Justice and other blue-ribbon committees, many communities have initiated juvenile and adult pretrial diversion projects.

Funding of diversion programs has also attracted generous support from the federal government. The Labor Department and the Law Enforcement Assistance Administration have both channeled millions of dollars into pretrial diversion programming. Development of TASC projects has been intertwined with the diversion concept. Nearly every TASC grant application has specified pretrial diversion tracts for its addict target population. Indeed, TASC is categorized by various government documents, most notably the 1975 Presidential White Paper on Drug Abuse, as the leading federal initiative in addict diversion. The 1975 Federal Strategy for Drug Abuse and Drug Traffic Prevention recommended at least one TASC project in every state demonstrating a significant drug abuse problem and major population center.

Legal controversy has consistently plagued the pretrial diversion concept, particularly addict diversion. A range of personal liberty issues endemic to the operation of criminal justice-drug abuse intervention programs has been identified. Two years ago, at the First National Drug Abuse Conference, Richard Atkins presented a thoughtful paper concerning the role of defense counsel in addict diversion proceedings (1). Other commentators have addressed the same subject from slightly varying perspectives (2-4).

In this paper the author presents his views on the topic from yet a different frame of reference, that of a legally trained former diversion program administrator and current treatment program director. The brevity of the format mandated for this paper, however, limits the scope of the investigation. A full analysis of the salient moral and legal issues is eschewed in favor of a delineation concrete programmatic recommendations. The recommendations seek to protect the rights of the addict divertee while permitting the efficient and effective operation of the diversion process.

II. THE RECOMMENDATIONS

The following suggestions regarding addict diversion program features and legal representation of the addict divertee are offered:

1. The deferred prosecution adjudicatory model, in preference to the deferred judgment and sentencing model, should be employed for effecting diversion. This would avoid 'constructive coercion' of the addict defendant to irremediably enter a guilty plea in order to participate in the diversion program.
2. The addict should be entitled to expungement of his instant arrest record upon successful completion of the diversion program. The successful divertee earns this privilege which serves as a powerful incentive toward successful diversion participation.
3. Diversion programs should offer a comprehensive multi-modality range of treatment services. The availability of limited options, e.g., only methadone maintenance, does not meet the diverse treatment needs of the pluralistic criminal addict population.
4. Diversion agreements between the prosecutor, court, treatment program and divertee must be specific; the divertee's responsibilities toward the other parties, the criteria and

procedures for revocation, and the criteria and procedures for granting and refusal of successful termination must be definite and unambiguous. This will avoid the undesirable situation of unchecked discretion lying with the prosecutor, court and treatment program.

5. Eligibility criteria for diversion of addicts should be expansive rather than restrictive. Only 'dangerousness' as demonstrated by prior violent antisocial conduct and diagnosed lack of treatment suitability are valid exclusionary criteria.

6. Diversion screening interview data should not be made available to the prosecutor and court until defense counsel has had an opportunity to examine the information and advise his client regarding release of the data.

7. The diversion program should insure that screening interview data are never used as a basis for prosecution. Careful safeguards should be instituted to avoid this possibility.

8. Fundamental due process guarantees should be provided to the divertee charged with violation of his diversion agreement. At a minimum, the client should be afforded the following guarantees: notice, hearing, right to cross-examine the witnesses against him, right to counsel, and the privilege against self-incrimination.

9. Defense counsel should advise the client to carefully consider all relevant factors before agreeing to participate in a diversion program. At a minimum, counsel could make his client aware of the following variables and assist him in their analysis as regards the client's decision:

   a. the strength of the evidence against the client in the instant case;

   b. the probability of the client benefitting from the treatment offered by the diversion program;

   c. the nature and impact of the other options available to the client, e.g., the probable sentence the client would receive if diversion is refused and the client is convicted and sentenced;

d. the nature and impact of the legal benefits offered by the diversion program.

e. the nature of the risks imposed by the program's procedures relating to revocation and determination of successful program completion;

f. the track record of the prosecutor, court and treatment program with regard to handling of divertees.

REFERENCES

1. R. Atkins, Proceedings of the National Drug Abuse Conference, 1: 829-833 (1975).

2. Note, Addict Diversion: An Alternative Approach for the Criminal Justice System, Georgetown Law Journal, 60: 667-710 (1972).

3. H. S. Perlman, Legal Issues in Addict Diversion, Drug Abuse Council, Inc. and American Bar Association, Washington, D.C. (1974).

4. U.S. Department of Justice, TASC Legal Analysis, Government Printing Office, Washington, D.C. (1973).

DILEMMAS OF DRUG ABUSE CONTROL:

SOME UNRESOLVED ISSUES

James C. Weissman

Department of Health and Hospitals
Denver, Colorado 80204

I.   INTRODUCTION

In this paper I have attempted to construct a paradigm for
drug abuse control which reflects both my experiences in corrections and drug abuse treatment programs and my internal value
system. The paradigm suggests a new "reform" approach to the
legal regulation of drug abuse behaviors, i.e., consumption,
ancillary to consumption, and trafficking offenses. The paper
adopts a sectionalized design including a brief historical overview,
identification and examination of selected major issues, the goals
of sentencing, and the paradigm. For purposes of the brevity
mandated by the format of these proceedings, the historical overview and the goals of sentencing sections are eliminated entirely
and the other materials are shortened drastically.

II.   SELECTED MAJOR ISSUES IN DRUG ABUSE CONTROL

Three interrelated issues dominate drug abuse regulation
lawmaking. These doctrinal issues are:
   (1) Is drug abuse an illness or a crime?
   (2) How do we distinguish between the 'user' and the 'pusher'?
   (3) Is the criminal law effective in deterring drug use?

Although these questions deserve a great deal of discussion, space restrictions permit only summary responses herein. With regard to the first issue, drug abuse is both an illness and a crime. It is a crime since we have chosen to so define it and in all probability will retain this status in the forseeable future. However, drug abuse is also a health matter, as evidenced by the $200+ million allocated annually by Congress to drug abuse prevention activities. It is not a prototype medical disease, but a behavioral health problem with significant public policy implications.

The 'user' vs. 'pusher' dichotomy is without substance. There are many non-user profiteers who have garnered substantial pecuniary gain from trafficking activities, but the average illicit drug seller is also a user. Commentators have suggested a number of replacement classification schemes which take into account the offender's social characteristics instead of focusing exclusively upon the offender's conduct.

All available evidence indicates that the criminal law is an utter failure at deterring drug usage. Statistics reveal several hundred thousand opiate addicts and several million marijuana users. In 1974 the FBI reported 642,000 drug law arrests. Nevertheless, the scientific evidence is sparse and the issue demands rigorous evaluation efforts.

III.   THE PARADIGM

This is an initial model-building exercise and should not be assessed as a final product for adoption or rejection. The purpose of the exercise is to stimulate the reader to thoughtfully consider the values and goals of drug abuse regulation.

The initial inquiry is what types of drug abuse behaviors are to be examined. The universe of relevant drug abuse behaviors may be divided into four discrete categories:

(1) consumption offenses, i.e., possession and use.

(2) trafficking offenses, i.e., sales, distribution, dispensing, etc.

(3) ancillary to consumption offenses, i.e., possession of narcotics paraphernalia, loitering, disorderly place, etc.

(4) property acquisitive offenses committed to raise funds for the purchase of drugs.

What harms are attached to these classes of offenses? The following schematic indicates the major harms to which society is exposed as a result of commission of the offenses:

OFFENSE CLASS	HARM
(1) Consumption offenses	(1) User's loss of self control and risk of adverse medical consequences; society's loss in decreased productivity of the user; depreciation of the prohibition against drug use
(2) Trafficking offenses	(2) Pecuniary gain by the offender through unsanctioned means; loss of possible taxes imposed on the illicit activities; promotion of illicit drug usage, particularly among the unwary innocent
(3) Ancillary offenses	(3) same as (1)
(4) Property acquisitive offenses	(4) Invasion of the property rights of the victims

With these harms in mind, the task is fashioning alternatives to the current system which will obviate those evils within the parameters of the goals of the criminal law. Those goals, retribution, incapacitation, rehabilitation, and deterrence, are critical elements to the paradigm.

Consumption offenses are committed by two types of individuals, the drug dependent and the experimenter or casual user. The predominant goals of the criminal law with respect to the former are rehabilitation and specific deterrence. The solution, therefore, is that proposed by the Uniform Drug Dependence Treatment and Rehabilitation Act. The individual will be offered treatment in lieu of the otherwise available sentence, but the treatment period cannot exceed the possible period of punishment. Since retribution and incapacitation are not applicable, the outside limit should be no more than a year. This solution does not denigrate the harms but seeks to be responsive to their existence. With regard to the experimenter or casual user, the goal is specific deterrence and prevention of his escalation to drug dependency. A pretrial diversion disposition with the availability of drug education in lieu of probation-type supervision would be an appropriate vehicle.

Trafficking offenses operationalize the goals of retribution, incapacitation, and deterrence. The primary dimension to be considered in evaluating the phenomenon of drug trafficking is the offender's motivation. If he is a user engaging in trafficking activities in order to raise funds for the purchase of drugs, the alternative of treatment in lieu of punishment will be suitable. However, if calculated financial gain underlies commission of the offense, a more punitive approach is appropriate. In that situation, the best solution would be to levy a fine proportionate to the offender's illicit earnings. This will punish and deter (by removing the gain) and therefore render the expensive isolation alternative unnecessary. The harms will be properly addressed and revenues will be generated for more socially useful purposes.

Ancillary consumption offenses are subject to the identical analysis provided the consumption offenses. Yet, I must question the very existence of these lesser offenses. The harms are one step removed from actual consumption and these offenses are generally used only as a plea bargaining device where proof of the consumption offense itself is difficult. If my suggestions for consumption offenses are implemented, the lesser-included ancillary offenses will lose their raison d'etre.

More difficult questions may be posed with respect to the property acquisitive crimes. For the first time, there is a classic victim who suffers a tangible loss as a direct result of the offense. Society generally perceives the drug dependent offender as functioning under an overriding compulsion to commit the offense; courts have been unwilling to recognize a pharmacological duress defense as a total exculpation device, but the concept of impaired responsibility of the drug dependent has generally been recognized sub rosa for this class of offense. This should be formalized by once again offering the offender treatment in lieu of the otherwise imposable sanction. Restitution to the victim should be mandated if treatment is selected, insuring society of its due by directly responding to the harm arising from the conduct. The higher degree of harm contained in this offense may justify a slightly longer period of criminal justice jurisdiction or treatment alternative, as society may wish to exact retribution under this circumstance.

As noted at the outset, this is only a skeleton of a paradigm. Some important threshold issues, e.g., the propriety of continued criminalization of the consumption offenses, and emerging constitutional doctrines are ignored. However, it is hoped that the model-building exercise has been able to accomplish its purpose of intellectual stimulation.

VALIDITY OF PRETRIAL DIVERSION FOR DRUG ABUSERS

Nancy A. Wynstra, Esquire

D.C. Superior Court
Washington, D.C.

Discussion centered around key issues--programmatic and legal--
facing treatment programs which formally interface with the criminal justice system. Panelists were three individuals (Martin J.
Mayer, Esq., former Director, Criminal Justice Program, New York
City Addiction Services Agency; Andrew M. Mecca, MPH, Director,
Marin County Substance Abuse Program; John P. Bellassai, Esq.,
Director, D.C. Superior Court Narcotics Diversion Program) with
substantial experience in planning and operating drug diversion
programs.

The programs represented differ procedurally and, in consequence,
have great variations in their client populations. Thus the New
York City Program acts as a "broker for services," identifying eligible defendants to the court and the prosecutor, making recommendations as to the appropriate treatment modality, escorting or referring defendants into appropriate treatment programs when and if
diversion is approved, and coordinating progress reports and follow-
up from the receiving treatment programs back to the judge and prosecutor. Both felons and misdemeanants are eligible for diversion,
although most cases in which prosecution is deferred pending treatment are misdemeanors.

The Marin County Program, a TASC project, also works as a conduit
to funnel drug-dependent defendants out to various in-patient and
out-patient treatment programs, and to receive and forward to the
criminal justice system urine surveillance and other progress data.
The program has an in-house employment assistance unit. The typical Marin County TASC defendant in the early years of the program
was white, adolescent, and a "speed-freak." By 1975 the TASC population was more racially mixed, with heroin the drug of choice for
a sizeable percentage of clients. Everyone arrested for any offense in Marin County, except sale of narcotics or violent crime,
is eligible for the program. The majority of program participants
now are charged with felony property crimes.

Both the New York and the Marin County programs arrange for drug
services to defendants who are not diverted as well as those who

are. Both programs are under the administrative control of an executive branch, non-criminal justice system, agency.

The Washington, D.C. program differs markedly from the other two models: It was set up by the CJS, run by the CJS (D.C. Superior Court) and is a "pure" pretrial diversion model, i.e. every defendant enrolled is guaranteed the dismissal of pending charges upon successful completion. Participation is limited to drug dependent defendants charged with non-violent misdemeanors and with no prior felony convictions. In contrast to the other models, the project does all its own treatment--individual and group counseling, urinalysis, job development and placement, except for methadone detoxification and maintenance. All participants are required to plead guilty as charged at entry; after six months of successful participation without rearrest, defense counsel can move to have such guilty pleas withdrawn, and after four more months in treatment, making 10 months in all, the charges will be formally dropped by the prosecutor.

Summary statistics on the 127 participants serviced during Calendar Year 1975 indicated that most were black (91%), male (84%), average age 25.5 years, first offenders (61%), highschool dropouts (52%), unemployed at enrollment (60%), heroin abusers at enrollment (68%) and, by their own choice, abstinence clients (61%) once enrolled.

The following areas of concern were addressed by the panelists during the discussion:

1. What is the appropriate or required role of defense counsel in diversion cases? Is it a good or bad idea for programs to interview defendants concerning enrollment without counsel present? In what ways, at a minimum, should defense counsel be involved?

2. Is offering a drug-dependent defendant the option or "choice" of diversion vs. going to trial (and possibly remaining in jail pretrial in lieu of bail) inherently coercive? If not, how can diversion programs develop safeguards to minimize the chance of coercion or unintelligent choices by defendants?

3. Is there an inherent role conflict (for those diversion programs which offer their own treatment) between the therapeutic function and the authority/surveillance function (i.e. reporting progress or lack of progress to the court or prosecutor)? If so, does this necessarily compromise a program participant's due process rights, if he is performing poorly and faces unfavorable termination?

4. Who really is the diversion program's client, the defendant/participant or the criminal justice system? Can a drug diversion

program serve two masters? What compromises--programmatically and legally--does the nature of drug diversion (a mixed medical/legal model) force upon program personnel and how should these be handled. How does the dual nature of the program impact on such things as reporting progress; defining success and failure criteria; records confidentiality; the problem of re-disclosure of prejudicial data on clients forwarded by the program to court or prosecutor.

5. What are legal due process requirements (both substantive and procedural) for entry into or removal from diversion? Does a potential participant have a right to a hearing or appeal if excluded from diversion at the initial intake stage? Does a program participant have a right to a hearing before termination, and if so, what form should such a hearing take?

6. Can and should drug diversion programs limit the categories of drug-dependent criminal defendants eligible for enrollment? If so, under what circumstances?

7. Is conditioning entry into a diversion program on pleading guilty to pending charges legally permissable? Is it desirable or undesirable from a rehabilitation perspective? If legally permissable, what procedural safeguards should programs employ to protect themselves and their client's rights where required guilty pleas are involved?

The panelists agreed that it is desirable--and wise, in view of an increasing number of legal challenges nationwide--to maximize defense attorney involvement, certainly to get counsel to read, explain to clients, and sign speedy trial waivers, program enrollment "contracts", etc. where applicable.

The need for written waivers and to reduce eligibility criteria and mutual rights and obligations in a diversion program to writing was stressed by the panelists, especially when the issue of the inherent coerciveness of diversion in lieu of prosecution or incarceration was considered. There was some disagreement over whether offering a defendant the "choice" of diversion vs. regular prosecution was inherently coercive or only whether it often was coercive in fact. All agreed that test cases in this area are bound to arise and that programs would now be well advised to devise procedures and written guidelines, and client "contracts", and to maximize defense attorney involvement so that courts, when ruling on such cases in the future, can at least see evidence of good faith efforts on the part of diversion programs to address and solve these problems.

Extended discussion centered on the seeming collision between new federal drug abuse patient confidentiality regulations and the requirement that diversion programs monitor and forward client performance data to the criminal justice system. It was pointed out that those regulations, in their revised form, allow for written blanket releases to be signed by diversion program participants at entry, authorizing the release of any and all client performance data to CJS decision-makers for the duration of program involvement. All panelists expressed unease at such broad release authorization, and it was suggested that this is a vital area for defense attorney consultation.

All recognized the potential dilemma of drug diversion programs in obtaining and keeping the confidence of their clients while acting as monitors for the criminal justice system. All agreed, however, that programs, to maintain their credibility with the system, must be perceived as willing to report poor performance or non-performance, as well as success in treatment.

On the broad due process questions, all panelists agreed this is sure to be an area for upcoming court test cases. Consequently, programs were urged to install basic due process features—published eligibility criteria, defense attorney involvement at intake and outtake and hearings before termination decisions—out of fairness to participants and in anticipation of inevitable court challenges.

Generally the panelists were enthusiastic about diversion programs for drug users. All were concerned, however, that there has been insufficient evaluation and analysis to answer many of the questions concerning the desirability for and structure of such programs. Although such programs seem to hold promise we do not yet know, on a long-term basis, whether they work more or less well than routine criminal justice processing.

ETHICAL ISSUES IN RELATING TO
THE CRIMINAL JUSTICE SYSTEM: A PANEL DISCUSSION

Milton E. Burglass, M.D., M.Div.
Gerald J. McKenna, M.D.
Richard Bickford
Norman Shostak, M.Ed.

Cambridge Hospital Department of Psychiatry
Polydrug Treatment Program
Cambridge, Massachusetts

I. REMARKS OF MILTON E. BURGLASS, M.D., M.Div.

It would seem that the first ethical issue to be faced by a treatment program is that arising from a conflict of agency. Whose agent is the therapist--the client's, or the system's? Traditionally, in the medical model, the physician, as healer, is unequivocally the advocate of the patient/client, and acts without exception in his/her interests. What obtains in the instance of coerced or enforced treatment? The client is infantilized by the assumption that some person or institution knows better than does he/she what is "best." Such assumptions compromise the ethic of autonomy and the principle of self-determination. The former provides for the freedom of the individual to be who he/she decides to be. This perforce includes the freedom to be the addicted one. Development of an individual along lines chosen by another or in accordance with principles and values dictated by another individual, a social collective, or a culture--declarations of the "absolute" validity of definitions of normalcy and deviance notwithstanding--clearly violates the ethic of autonomy. Subtleties of clinical theorizing may postulate the nature of the client's "illness" as being precisely manifest in his/her loss of proper perspective about what is best, but such ultimately dehumanizing, self-justifying fabrications must fall when confronted with the principle of self-determination, a value widely proclaimed as immanent in this socio-political system. This principle holds individuals to be responsible for their own lives, and capable of determining them through their decisional acts. Clinical sophistry which serves to support coercion via the assumption of infantilization is inimical to our cultural experience. Yet, for the moment such ideologizing rules the day. Supported by the pseudo-scientific "revelations" of the social sciences, this distorted and alienating mode of thought succeed neither in explaining nor excusing human beings from responsibility for their lives. Rather, it accuses them of being less than fully human by holding them to be hopeless, helpless, and hapless victims of invisible, internal forces and external pressures.

Our culture is threatened by a near-militant, smugly self-righteous par-psychiatricism. Clearly, our institutions of justice are not beyond its reach. When criminals were criminals and not patients, when parties to a crime were either perpetrators or victims, and not abulic pawns in some fictional intrapsychic drama; human liberty and justice were living concepts. There can be no clean relationship with the criminal justice system for one who stands with another person as healer or therapist. Finally, it is we as individuals, not as members of collectives, programs, or departments that must decide on which side we stand. And, surely, "not to decide is to decide."

II. REMARKS BY GERALD J. MCKENNA, M.D.

In addressing the ethical questions of the relationship of drug treatment programs to the criminal justice system I will comment briefly on four areas: the laws pertaining to drug use in this country; the accountability of individuals for their behavior; the behavior of criminal justice personnel in enforcing laws; the role of drug treatment programs in effecting changes.

All of us on this panel believe that there is no rational basis for existing laws regarding drug possession and use. Their existence at all would appear to be grounded in a puritanical heritage rather than logic. Existing laws clearly offend an individual's freedom of choice, since even if possession and use of drugs were definitely harmful, the harm would be solely to the individual. There is no current medical rationale for supporting existing drug laws. In fact, if medical standards solely were applied, drugs such as alcohol and nicotine would be outlawed, while cocaine and marijuana would be legalized, in light of existing knowledge about these drugs.

We would hope, then, for a reappraisal of laws affecting drug possession and use and for changes to be made which would be in keeping with an individuals right to choose for himself.

Currently, drug related crimes fall into four major categories: 1) possession and use of illicit drugs, 2) sale of illicit drugs, 3) crimes committed in obtaining licit and illicit drugs, 4) crimes committed while in a drug intoxicated or withdrawal state. The first two categories pertain to behaviors which I view as ethically neutral and victimless. The latter two categories involve behaviors secondary to drug use and for which the individuals should be held responsible. It is important for treatment programs to be aware of these differences since they should influence the contact between a treatment program and the criminal justice system. For example, I would consider it inappropriate for a drug treatment program to accept someone sent by the court who had been charged with or convicted of drug possession but whose drug use, if any, was not considered by the individual to be a problem. On the other hand, I would accept a person who had committed repeated violent acts, for example, while intoxicated with alcohol, barbiturates, etc., and who had a desire for treatment to control drug use or deal with some underlying problem and who was offered the choice between treatment and incarceration.

It has been my experience in working with the probation officers and judges in the courts in Massachusetts that they are not seeking criminal prosecution in drug related cases but are genuinely seeking to avoid miscarriages of justice. It should be an important role of personnel in drug treatment programs to continually educate criminal justice personnel, legislators, and the general public in the facts about drug use and drug dependence, dispelling common myths and misconceptions and hopefully effecting meaningful change.

III. REMARKS BY RICHARD BICKFORD

This discussion focuses on issues which arise after screening, evaluation and diversion from the court have taken place. At this point, the patient enters into a contractual agreement with the program. Ideally the formulation of this agreement would involve the program representative, the court representative (usually the probation officer) and the client. Specific areas regarding treatment progress and communication between the court and the program would be discussed at this time, disagreements worked out, and a common understanding would be reached. In reality, little discussion takes place and all parties usually act according to their own assumptions. This often results in two phenomena which eventually create an atmosphere which allows the patient to easily and conveniently avoid his responsibilities to both the court and the program.

The first of these I call the "Let's make a deal" phenomenon. Here the court and the program say to the client,"O.K., we've done this for you and given you a break, now show us your gratitude by doing well in treatment." This statement is rarely verbalized and remains unstated. The problem is that the client is rarely able to live up to these expectations. Consequently, when the client does not do well, feelings of anger, failure, and guilt develop which further block communication.

The second phenomenon that takes place often evolves from the first. This is called the "Who's the bad guy?" phenomenon. When the client does not do well in treatment or terminates, a real breakdown in communication between the court and the program ensues.

The court does not want to be saddled with the responsibility of violating the client's probation and possibly having him sent to jail. The program does not want the responsibility of reporting to the court information that could be used to violate the client's probation. For the first time, issues of confidentiality arise all over the place, blame is assigned liberally by all parties, and the client is back in the street, having successfully avoided his responsibilities. In psychiatry this is known as a successful T-A aplit. The client has successfully manipulated therapist and administrator to his own advantage.

Ethically, two considerations arise: On the one hand, possibly the client should not have been involved in the court process at all, since the criminalization of drug-related crime is of questionable validity. On the other hand, one must consider that the client has once again successfully avoided responsibility for his actions; hence, the behavioral pattern is reinforced. An ethical dilemma ensues.

IV. REMARKS BY NORMAN SHOSTAK, M.Ed.

Despite the considerable advantages to the accused, addict diversion retains parallel characteristics of other criminal justice programs: This parallel reflects both the court and treatment programs continued acceptance of a naive belief system.

Both continue to accept cultural definitions of acceptable substance use, translate these beliefs into laws, and continually expand in its efforts at regulation, when often the beliefs are misbeliefs and some of the laws unconstitutional, and many of the regulatory efforts in vain.

It is not my intention to contribute to the discussion on this ethical dilemma. Rather, the following will describe the situation in which the client, the program, the court and the community find themselves when they agree to participate in 'addict-diversion.'

The court referred client remains under the control of the criminal justice system, his/her community liberty being dependent on conformity with the rules and program requirements.

The court referred client remains fully subject to prosecution and criminal sanctions for alleged criminal conduct if he/she 1) fails to meet the program requirements for successful termination, 2) in some cases, fails to convince the court that "positive change" warrants dismissal of the prosecution, upon termination from a program.

The program, often flexing their professional autonomy, require controversial examinations. The existing use of urinalysis
examination, when before the court, could be found in violation of
the Fourth Amendment, a provision which requires the court to determine the reasonableness of searches conducted without warrants,
not to mention requiring a definition of a legal search. A search
warrant can only be issued by a judicial officer when probable
cause (taking of substances?) can be proven. This legal question
raises others. The Fifth Amendment protects against self-incrimination. If the program terminates a client for successive "dirty
urines" the client is then found in violation of the courts, which
has already stipulated its conditions for diversion. Is this not
self-incrimination?

These legal questions warrnat each program to consider its
participation in this "legal process." Accordingly, future programmatic efforts should be directed toward minimizing the "damage
done by drugs." Clearly, chemistry is far less significant than
the impact of the imprudent ways in which they are used, the settings in which they are used, the laws punishing their use, society's attitudes toward users, and so on. A series of drug
classifications and misclassifications and congressional reactions
have built the foundation of our judicial view of addictions. It
is my position that each treatment program should review and re-
consider its unethical participation in a process which has proven
true to form: unethical, illegal and allied with a false belief
system.

THE DILEMMAS OF COORDINATING TREATMENT WITH CRIMINAL JUSTICE: A TWO-YEAR EXPERIENCE

Arlene Lissner, B.S., John Gilmore, A.B., and Kenneth Pompi, Ph.D.

The Abraxas Foundation, Inc.
Marienville, Pennsylvania

To satisfy the courts' increasing demand for alternatives, existing drug programs seem more and more attracted to the possibility of accepting court-stipulated clients. They should be forewarned that in doing so they will also be accepting a new set of demanding problems.

The Pennsylvania Governor's Council on Drug and Alcohol Abuse chartered the Abraxas Foundation to implement an experimental project that would accept youths convicted of drug and drug-related crimes in lieu of incarceration. The Abraxas treatment program began operation in Fall 1973. After a short-lived experiment with a token economy system, the Foundation adopted a treatment format based on therapeutic community (TC) practices. This changeover has been described in detail elsewhere (1). We would like to share our experiences at Abraxas regarding the difficult mutual accomodation of the TC and the criminal justice system. It will become clear that although we have resolved some problems intrinsic to this accomodation, many can be resolved only on an ad hoc basis, and some are perhaps insoluble short of major legislative or judicial decisions.

Several interrelated, overriding issues quickly developed in our experience with court-stipulated clients. First, we realized that many TC procedures and expectations designed for volunteers driven by their own desperation to seek help are simply inapplicable to non-volunteers compelled by the courts to undergo "treatment." Second, we found ourselves both accountable to the courts for information on clients' progress and restricted from divulging much real information by stringent federal laws protecting clients' confidentiality. Finally, we were cursed with our own resentment of what we saw as the courts' and other justice agencies' incursions into our affairs. We initially partook of traditional TC secretiveness--the attitude that courts need not and should not be privy to the treatment of their clients, that the courts are benighted antagonists.

These three issues soon emerged when we were confronted with residents who were difficult to handle. If volunteer programs hope to be more extensively utilized as alternatives to incarceration, they should anticipate a more recalcitrant population, for they will probably have to give up screening "prospects" as rigorously as traditional TC's. Most our residents were polydrug users; well under fifteen percent were heroin addicts. Although the majority of our referrals have used drugs, given their current mean age of eighteen it would be surprising if they had not. In general, they do not feel they need help, and the most they usually expect at first is that Abraxas will be a more palatable injustice than others that have been dealt them. Clearly, the standard demands made by volunteer programs are inappropriate for the vast majority of such court-stipulated prospective clients.

Moreover, typical sentencing procedures do not permit lengthy, intense scrutiny of candidates. A court simply cannot afford the time and expense of transporting large numbers of those awaiting sentence to tryouts which most would fail. This would be especially impractical for Abraxas as we are a statewide program, and our primary facility is physically isolated from the predominantly urban areas we serve. Our typical intake process thus consists of a single two-hour, at most, interview conducted by an individual staff member or, in especially distant areas, someone who is simply familiar with the program. Thus, our intake procedure will probably remain more a matter of eliminating the few who are overtly violent or psychotic than of selecting the few who are strongly committed.

The various sentences under which residents arrive often affect at least their initial motivation. Stipulations in sentences differ, for Abraxas accepts both adjudicated juveniles and convicted young adults from over two thirds of Pennsylvania's sixty-seven counties. Sentences generally include one or more of these stipulations:

1. sentenced to Abraxas for a specified period of time or until successful completion of treatment, whichever comes first;
2. sentenced to Abraxas until successful completion of treatment (indeterminate sentence);
3. suspended commitment to county prison or state correctional institution, committed to Abraxas;
4. commitment to Abraxas as a condition of parole or probation.

Reactions to the various types of sentences are unpredictable, but the condition of being under sentence influences nearly all residents. If they were volunteers, they could leave without repercussions. Were they sentenced to traditional incarceration, they would have to plot an escape and become fugitives in order to leave. Abraxas, however, is an alternative, so they can be returned to court at any time for reconsideration. In a sense they are "sentenced volunteers," and their freedom of choice--even if they initially view it as a choice of poisons--helps induce most to consider leaving at some point before completing the program. To help residents through these crises and to understand an important factor in their lives, staff at Abraxas must be aware of a variety of sentencing procedures, a further complication of their already difficult job.

While most of our residents do not initially make the personal commitment required at the outset in traditional TC's, they must make it at some point if they are to profit from Abraxas. Thus, the community has to and does tolerate a good deal of jailing, testing, and general acting out--sometimes for months at a time-- from its newer members. Although such behavior is dealt with, it seldom results in immediate expulsion, as it might elsewhere. It was difficult for many of our staff, particularly those trained in TC's, to realize and accept this fact of Abraxas life.

Besides being unfair for clients whose initial commitment is more legal than personal, frequent expulsions--whether expulsions for infractions of peculiarly program norms or arbitrary expulsions of individuals suspected of wrongdoing--would be intolerable to the courts. Expelling a court-stipulated client is a complicated process. First we must notify his probation officer, who then must procure a court order from the sentencing judge. Just making these contacts often takes days because the officer, judge, or both may be simply unavailable. Court order in hand, the probation officer next has to arrange the client's transportation back to the home county and his detention until a replacement hearing can be held. Transportation is usually not immediately forthcoming, as it depends on law enforcement officials' schedules. People rarely act out to the extent that we must call the police to get them off grounds and into a local jail, at our expense. Thus, we generally must keep our persona non grata on grounds as discharge procedures are being completed. Although we isolate them with resident advocates, they can and sometimes do conspire, act out, run away, and otherwise disturb the community before they are picked up. The process does not end once the resident has been removed. We must also send the court a final report which includes recommendations for further disposition. Some judges require written explanations of why we want a resident expelled before they will initiate procedings to remove him. Staff have also had to appear at the hearings of discharged clients, occasionally to defend our progress and final reports in a hostile courtroom.

At the beginning we exacerbated matters with our independent posture. Although we expected probation officers to convince judges that clients had to be removed, we had not previously warned them that the residents were even having trouble. Our written progress reports to court officials were infrequent and sparse: We used a rating scale to indicate the client's general posture and added merely one sentence of explanation.

The reports were vague not only because of our fancied independence, but also because we were genuinely confused about the extent of constraints imposed by federal laws protecting the confidentiality of clients in drug treatment programs. The Foundation's lawyers and administrators and the Governor's Council have spent considerable energy trying to interpret these regulations.

Whatever the reasons for their inadequacy, our initial progress reports drew criticism quite apart from early crises around discharges. Officials complained that they simply were not being informed of what was happening at Abraxas. One county threatened to pull out its clients and made invidious comparisons between Abraxas' reporting and that of certain traditional institutions.

Since then we have expanded our written reports to provide more and more detailed information on client progress. Reports describe the resident's current general attitude, performance on passes, openness to groups and counseling, ability to discharge responsibility, and apparent current problems. Recently we have also been implementing written treatment plans for all residents to give them a greater share in their treatment, ensure treatment continuity, and refine our reporting and self-examination. Summaries of those plans are being added to progress reports. Residents read their reports and sign waivers for release of the information they contain. Furthermore, we have also come to use court officials' phone calls and visits not only to warn them of impending trouble with their clients, but also to solicit their advice and support. Thus, having begun by simply placating court officials in order to survive, we have moved to a genuine partnership in which they have a share in the treatment program. This arrangement is natural to us but may seem anathema to staff of programs which do not deal with many court-stipulated clients.

Worse yet, mutual support now exists between Abraxas and the local police where at first there had only been mutual antipathy. This change came about largely because of our occasional runaways. Staff in other programs need take no special action when a volunteer leaves, but we must immediately notify court officials and the police when one of our court-stipulated clients absconds. At first when police came to investigate these incidents, we were reluctant to cooperate, citing strict interpretations of the federal confidentiality regulations. It seemed that the police had deliberately harassed out-of-state staff about getting Pennsylvania drivers licenses, and some staff felt generally hostile toward police anyway. We feared that they might in some way resent having to bother with our runaways or even use them as an issue to arouse our neighbors. However, after a few contacts our fears were unrealized. When some runaways stole cars and broke into cabins, the police handled matters with professional discretion. They did not want our neighbors unnecessarily alarmed any more than we did. With further communication we began to understand many of their problems and the pressures on them to maintain law and order. In turn, many of the State Police have visited Abraxas and attended sessions at our Training Center.

The Abraxas Training Center has facilitated exchange between Abraxas and other elements of the greater community besides the police. Probation and parole officers, youth groups, prevention and treatment workers, personnel from penal institutions, educators, students, and social workers have also attended Training Center workshops. Although the workshops provide training in treatment and counseling techniques, they primarily serve as a forum for criminal justice and treatment personnel to share perspectives and insights. It seems that their experiences at these workshops have influenced some criminal justice workers to send more offenders to treatment programs.

Clearly, having primarily court-stipulated clients from an entire state has required Abraxas to make many adjustments that are unnecessary for local programs with volunteers. Traditional intake, treatment, and discharge operations were all affected. Additional staff were required solely to supervise reporting procedures, oversee interviews and other intake processes, maintain contact with numerous criminal justice personnel, satisfy demands for statistics and other information, and manage often idiosyncratic payment and other administrative procedures of well over fifty agencies. Expert legal advice has been an ongoing necessity to survive, among other things, the sometimes contradictory pressures of local, state, and federal regulations. Clinical staff had to become aware of the many legal and apparently external factors which often affect the traditionally most routine treatment decisions. Staff in the re-entry facilities learned to do interviews and maintain continual liason with court officials in addition to fulfilling their more traditional roles.

However difficult it has been for us to implement a TC-based program for court-stipulated youth, we hope that the future will see more such efforts and more alternatives to incarceration in general. Abraxas has already helped young people who, although in great difficulty with the law, had no history of drug use. Hopefully the courts will be encouraged by such successes and will continue to expand their use of treatment rather than confinement for people in trouble.

REFERENCE

1. A. Lissner, J. Gilmore, and K. Pompi, Contemporary Drug Problems, Winter 457 (1974).

576

MARIN COUNTY TASC: THREE YEARS

OF SUCCESS AND WHY IT WORKED

Andrew M. Mecca, MPH

Director, Substance Abuse
Community Mental Health
Marin County, California

Doris J. Pick, Ph.D.

Director of Research
Equinox Systems, Inc.
Marin County, California

The Treatment Alternatives to Street Crime program (TASC) developed by the Special Action Office for Drug Abuse Prevention
(SAODAP) to identify drug abusers shortly after their arrest and
refer them to appropriate treatment modalities. It was created as
a means of attempting to break the typical drug user's "street
crime--to arrest--to street crime" pattern--a costly and self distrusting vicious circle. The various federally funded TASC programs use the leverage available through the criminal justice system to move the arrested addict into treatment. This responsibility of TASC is best summed by the following goals:

> GOAL I: To reduce drug abuse and addiction.
> GOAL II: To reduce drug related crime.
> GOAL IIIa: To increase educational level.
> GOAL IIIb: To increase employment level.

The creation of the federally funded TASC programs is a product of the belief held by many individuals and professional groups
that "the traditional process of trial, conviction, and incarceration has failed to rehabilitate drug dependent defendents and to
stop the revolving door of crime" (Bellassai and Segal, 1971).
Thus, TASC programs are created in response to the apparent need to
find new alternatives to deal with the current, seemingly hopeless,
drug problem.

A Systems Approach to The Marin TASC Evaluation:

Since a new and changing program was being assessed, the evaluation process needed to be flexible in design and implementation. The evaluation design for the Marin TASC program, therefore, was framed within a theoretical construct of systems theory, in the following manner:

Objects: The parts or components of the TASC System are its three programs. They are (1) the Core Program, (2) the Diversion Program, and (3) the Volunteer Work Program.

Attributes: The properties of the TASC System are selected behavior of the staff, such as competencies, skill, knowledge, etc.

Relationship: The key relationship that ties the TASC System together is its decision-making process.

The evaluation procedure was conceived in four stages. The first three stages represented the major focus of the evaluation. Stage I was devoted to assessing the Core Program in terms of its three goals: (1) reducing drug usage, (2) reducing drug-related crimes, (3a) increasing the educational level and (3b) increasing the employment level of TASC clients. Determining the Core Program outcomes represents one indicator of TASC's overall effectiveness. Also included in Stage I was the development of a client profile designed to understand better the dynamics of clients participating in the Core Program. Stage II (attributes of the system) was devoted to evaluating staff behavior through other individuals' perceptions of them (vis-a-vis questionnaire). Stage III (system relationship) represented a study of the system itself. This was another way of assessing the TASC level of effectiveness, for what goes on within a system has a bearing on staff performance. Whatever data TASC routinely collected on the three programs since each of their inceptions was deemed to be Stage IV. Because of limited space for this publication, Stages II, III and IV are summarized in the summary.

Stage I: The Core Program Evaluation

A. Development and Analyses

From approximately 150 clients seen between October 1, 1973, and December 30, 1974, 80 client sheets were randomly drawn for mean and percent score analyses, but there was one exception to this procedure. Since the number of clients who completed the program was so few, all cases (N-7) were incorporated into the study. All the data were grouped to elicit certain information about the sample group.

The same data collected were re-arranged into client groups and analyzed with mean and percent scores in terms of time sequences divided into four phases.

B. Findings

GOAL QUESTION I: Is TASC, an alternative approach to incarceration, effective in reducing drug abuse?

Looking at the client group drug history, the mean age for using a primary drug is 19 years and 5 months. At the time the cli clients entered into the TASC program, the average age was 26 years, indicating a drug history, mainly of heroin, of approximately 7 years.

The analyses of the data indicate a trend in favor of the treatment process as having a positive effect on reducing drug use. Therefore, an affirmative answer can be given to GOAL QUESTION I. Is TASC, an alternative approach to incarceration, effective in reducing drug use?

The evidence for GOAL QUESTION I is strengthened when it is assessed concurrently with GOAL QUESTION II (reducing drug-related crime), since a majority of those who return to drugs also show a high re-arrest record. GOAL QUESTION II: Is TASC, an alternative approach to incarceration, effective in reducing drug-related crimes?

The results of a research study conducted by Mecca (1974) in the Marin County Jail during the month of November 1972 showed that the recidivism rate of opiate-dependent burglars was seven to eight times that of any other category. The results of this current study indicate that the TASC client population not only has an average number of seven arrests with an average number of five convictions, but the crime history is long: the average age of first juvenile arrest is 15 years and the average age of first adult arrest is 20 years and 5 months. This historical client profile when compared to the results of this evaluation reveals a most impressive picture: Over 90% of all TASC clients show a pattern of no re-arrests, regardless of whether they have completed treatment, are currently in treatment, or have dropped treatment. In fact, over 80% of the drug offenders in the client dropped group fall into the category of "no re-arrests".

The present evidence clearly indicates strong, positive trend in favor of treatment as being effective in comparison to incarceration in reducing drug-related crimes. This positive, effective approach leaves its impact elsewhere: for example, in cost savings by taxpayers. It costs $18.00 per day to keep drug offenders in jail. This is in contrast to $6.00 per day for treatment care. Also, property owners would appear to save approximately $4,325,000 in lost property. This is based on a federal cost matrix for a two year period.

Thus, the answer to GOAL QUESTION II is affirmative: Is TASC, an alternative approach to incarceration, effective in reducing drug-related crimes?

GOAL QUESTION IIa: Is TASC effective in increasing the educational levels of drug offenders?

According to data analyses, over one-third of the clients have at least a high school diploma with 40% having education beyond the twelfth grade at the time of their involvement with TASC. As treatment progressed, the majority of the clients showed no educational changes. However, looking at clients by group, the data suggests that only those clients who completed the treatment made any educational changes. A tentative conclusion is made that this goal is not being achieved.

GOAL QUESTION IIIb: Is TASC effective in increasing the employment status. However, looking at clients by group, those who dropped treatment reflect a work record of less than three months as compared to clients who remained in treatment and had completed treatment. These two groups showed a working record of between 11 and 12 months.

Summary of Findings

Measuring the TASC success against current research, which indicates the extreme difficulty in rehabilitating drug users, conclusions from this investigation unquestionably justify the continuation of TASC as an intervention system for drug-dependent individuals. However, in the opinion of the evaluators, it is also important to realize that the etiology of our contemporary drug problem should be explored and that programs should be designed which emphasize the prevention aspects of the problem. Although the Core Program represented the major focus of the evaluation, some mention should be made of the TASC staff's efforts in implementing the concept of prevention, with the Diversion Program Model --a program for first-time drug offenders--and the Volunteer Work Program--conceived for other types of legal offenders.

To date, TASC has admitted a total of 362 individuals to one of several Diversion Programs. Of this total, 240 persons or over 80% have either completed a program or are currently in one.

Even though no major conclusion can be drawn from these figures alone, they do suggest that the Diversion Program is somewhat successful in inducing clients to complete the program, and they may lend some support to the supposition that the earlier a problem is detected, the greater is the probability for effecting a change.

TASC has extended the notion of prevention through its efforts of coordinating the Volunteer Work Program. This program is a vehicle through which misdemeanants and felons are selectively channeled into community service work for a stated number of hours or days. For example, between April, 1975 and September, 1975, TASC has assisted in placing a total of 166 individuals in various types of agencies, such as convalescent hospitals.

All the data collected and analyzed from studying the components of the system (the three programs), the attributes of the system (staff performance), and the relationship that ties the system together (decision-making processes) have been synthesized to complete the picture of TASC as a system.

The major conclusion drawn from the syntheses of all information is that TASC is a highly effective system. From its effective internal decision-making processes emerge effective program outcomes This based on staff performance, its competency level and its ability to work effectively with other professionals and their clients.

INTERFACE OF CLINICAL AND CORRECTIONS STAFF
IN A MULTI-MODAL DRUG ABUSE PROGRAM
(THE MILWAUKEE MODEL)

Floyd A. Aprill, M.A., M.S.W., ACSW

Psychiatric Social Worker
Milwaukee County Mental Health Center
Drug Abuse Program
Milwaukee, Wisconsin

Gary J. Parker, M.S.S.W.

Probation and Parole Agent
Wisconsin State Department of
Health and Social Services
Division of Corrections
Bureau of Probation and Parole
Milwaukee, Wisconsin

Jerry P. Flanzer, DSW, ACSW

Assistant Professor
University of Wisconsin-Milwaukee
School of Social Welfare
Milwaukee, Wisconsin

Large numbers of drug abusers, particularly heroin addicts, have active or past involvement with the criminal justice system.

Although there is disagreement as to the extent and causal association of criminal behavior and narcotic addiction, there is a general consensus of opinion that a relationship
does exist. Narcotic addicts have a far greater risk of criminal involvement than non-drug abusers, particularly in relation to specific revenue-producing crimes.

Based on patient self-reports, the Milwaukee County Drug Abuse Program has found that over two-thirds of its patients have supported at least a portion of their habits by illegal means. Fifty per cent of the patients have an adult criminal record. Over one-third of the current patient population have an active involvement with the criminal justice system (probation or parole).

Although drug abuse treatment programs and the criminal justice system frequently deal with the same individuals, each has traditionally evolved a separate model for working with drug abuse clients. Each system has fundamentally different goals and objectives. Furthermore, roles of professional staff differ significantly in these two parallel systems.

The primary goal of the criminal justice system is the protection of society. The "social control" aspects of the criminal justice system are primary. Innovative corrections programs have striven for the dual objectives of rehabilitation of the offender and protection of society. Such programs must nevertheless be limited by their "primary responsibility" to protect society from victimization. In cases of role conflict, it is to society that the probation officer must owe his primary allegiance.

In the treatment system the primary goal is to assist the individual drug-abuse patient in maximizing his optimal bio-psycho-social functioning. Given this therapeutic and remedial objective, the "primary responsibility" of the clinician is the interests and well-being of his patient.

Maintenance of the traditional dichotomy between the treatment and criminal justice system may be unrealistic given the current realities of these two systems.

Clinical treatment programs in their efforts to promote therapeutic change in drug-abuse clients can not afford to ignore the political reality of the inherent power and authority of the criminal justice system.

In order to provide effective treatment, drug abuse programs must be able to retain clients. The confidence of key people in the criminal justice system is necessary to insure that patients with criminal justice involvement are not prematurely removed from treatment. In addition to direct removal of a patient from treatment, criminal justice personnel can subtly subvert treatment efforts by ordering specific treatment modalities or methodologies inappropriate to an individual client. The criminal justice system in its effort to protect society through mechanisms of social control can also substantially benefit from interfacing with the treatment system.

The "punitive approach" including criminalization and incarceration of addicts for punishment and deterence has been a dismal failure. Seemingly more progressive criminal justice treatment utilizing solely the "rational authority approach" of probation and parole has not produced significantly better results. Neither has civil commitment programs provided the answer. The widely documented failure of the traditional "revolving door" criminal justice handling of narcotic addicts has produced a frustration largely responsible for the growing linkages between the criminal justice system and treatment systems. It has also prompted development of new and innovative treatment-oriented criminal justice programs.

Many large communities with massive drug-related crime problems have implemented correspondingly large methadone programs operated or parented by the criminal justice system. Whatever the aegis, all of these programs have reported highly significant results in reducing criminal behavior and producing other therapeutic changes.

These reports have not been welcomed by all observers. Serious ethical and philosophical issues concerning linkages and interfaces of the criminal justice and treatment system have been raised. This is particularly true in regard to criminal justice operated methadone maintenance programs.

Perhaps a model for effective C.J./treatment system interface and linkage which can minimize these potential dangers is that of a medical/mental health model treatment program interfacing with the C.J. system (instead of vice versa). This alternative to the C.J. system based model has been developed by the M.D.A.P. and is presented in the remainder of this paper.

The MDAP is a clinical unit of a comprehensive community mental health center. Program elements include inpatient, outpatient, and detoxification services. The outpatient treatment component includes 300 methadone maintenance and fifty abstinence clients.

From the inception of the program, clinical staff have been aware of patient involvement with the C.J. system.

This initial dialogue with the criminal justice system was not an organized interface or linkage but merely informal communication on an individual case basis. As program size increased, the ineffectiveness of this type of response to the criminal justice system became increasingly clear. Lacking post-adjudication feedback to the criminal justice system, courts were reluctant to permit treatment alternatives to incarceration. It was feared that if treatment proved ineffective and the patient continued to victimize society that the court would have no handle on this situation. In addition, the logistical problem of coordinating services with large numbers of probation and parole agents, each with separate attitudes and biases, was approaching the impossible.

It became apparent that the best alternative was to develop a formal coordinated linkage with the criminal justice system. A probation-parole-interface agent from the Wisconsin Division of Corrections, Bureau of Probation-Parole, was assigned to the MDAP Program in March, 1974. After approximately four weeks of discussions and meetings between the agent and staff, the agent cross-

referenced the methadone patient master list and the master list of
Milwaukee County Correction clients. Prior to this time, the
clinic had irregularly furnished a list of correction clients to
the Bureau of Probation-Parole. In March, 1974, the list contained
the names of 23 patients. The cross-reference revealed that 89 of
180 MDAP clients were probation/parolees supervised by 68 agents.
Due to the larger number of shared clients, a probation-parolee
caseload was established at MDAP.

The agent was furnished office space within the clinic proper
for the following reasons: (1) client/agent accessibility is facilitated as clients must regularly report to the clinic for their
methadone; (2) closer supervision of the client; (3) agent awareness of client problems; (4) the agent's close association with
patient allows him to be constantly familiar with the "street
scene."

The development of the interface required the resolution of
certain key issues: The most critical issue was that of confidentiality, e.g., how to approach the clients and their respective agents in relation to their transfer to the "Meth Caseload."
One outstanding fear of the clients was that of having their supervision revoked when their agent became aware of their participation
in the methadone program without having first sought their agent's
permission. A second fear was that their agents, utilizing the
threat of revocation, would make them cease participation in the
program rather than transferring their case to the "Meth Caseload."

These fears were resolved in the following manner: (1) a
verbal agreement was that clients now on the program would not be
revoked due to their participation; (2) the agent activated client
involvement by discussing the transfer with each client; (3) a Release of Information was obtained; (4) the chief of the Milwaukee
Region of Probation-Parole then sent a memo to all offices stating
that the agents would be contacted in relation to client transfers
to the "Meth Caseload" and the transfers would then be initiated.

Confidentiality with new patients is currently handled in the
following manner: (1) all incoming patients are informed of the
fact that an agent is assigned to the program; (2) a release of
information authorizing a check of criminal justice involvement is
required of all incoming clients; (3) the agent checks the master
lists; (4) identified correction clients are requested to sign a
Release of Information allowing the Bureau access to the program
files; and (5) the correction client is transferred to the "Meth
Caseload." Refusal to sign the release precludes involvement by
the agent assigned to the program. In the one instance when a
client refused to sign a release, the agent was not involved in his
supervision. He was subsequently revoked for probation violations.
The agent would not become involved prior to or during revocation
proceedings. Subsequent to that time, there has not been a single

instance where a client has refused to sign the Release of Information.

The clients view the agent's role not only as a punisher but also as a potential advocate representing their rights in the criminal justice system. The agent assumes the role necessary to keep the individual client's attendance and adjustment on a satisfactory level. The use of authority in supervision varies. In an unsatisfactory adjustment situation, i.e., dirty urine, poor attendance, etc., a confrontation transpires between counselor, client, and agent, thereby eliminating manipulation of the agent and counselor. The roles are clearly defined. The counselor is not involved in the decision to revoke and does not share the agent's responsibility. Likewise, the agent is not a therapist and does not have treatment responsibility. Discussion also revolves around the resources available that are associated with the program plus those associated with the Bureau. Additionally, the continuous communication that exists between methadone staff and the agent allows each to be fully aware of the resources of the other.

Having a parole agent part and parcel of the Milwaukee Program lends to cooperation on a day-to-day basis. The differential roles of the two systems is seen daily. Their working together guarantees a continuum of care. Clients can no longer play one against the other. The two organizational groups begin to see gaps between the two services and use each other's resources to fill them. Both staff groups begin to stop blaming the other, not permitting further client manipulation and in effect freeing the client to take responsibility. This becomes, then, a counterdependency move by the agencies. The clear differential role pattern serves to decrease interorganizational role ambiguity, conflicts and gaps.

Some people have argued that rehabilitation and social control of the drug abuser are dichotomous goals which cannot be successfully integrated. The authors believe that they can be integrated in most cases. However, they cannot be integrated in the same staff member. Authority may be shared between staff, but responsibility must ultimately remain with the appropriate staff, i.e., C.J. responsibility with the agent, treatment responsibility with the clinical staff. Sharing responsibility can lead to blurring of roles and ineffectiveness of both agency systems.

The Milwaukee Model provides an alternative to previous treatment interfaces based primarily in the C.J. system. Treatment-oriented personnel working with drug addicts fearing (1) possible co-option and loss of identity to the system and (2) frustrated by conflictual treatment and social control plans might consider the model presented here. Reality dictates that treatment programs cannot ignore the criminal justice system. The authors present here a model for this "marriage of necessity" where both parties can retain identity and grow together.

THE CONFLICT BETWEEN THE CRIMINAL JUSTICE SYSTEM
AND ADDICTION REHABILITATION IN A SPECIFIC URBAN
SETTING - NEW ORLEANS

Dr. Edwina D. Frank
Albert L. Juniel, Jr.
Vernon J. Shorty

INTRODUCTION

It is generally agreed that drug addiction is an illness.
The abnormalacy of addiction for a given person or group can be
expressed in physiological, psychological and sociological terms.
When we in the treatment and rehabilitation field speak of addiction, we speak of curative or preventative measures, further
agreement of the fact that drug addiction is an illness can be
found in many instances, in various umbrella agencies under which
addiction services are housed, funded and developed. Yet, there is
also evidence of a persistent attitude which continues to view
drug addiction as a crime requiring punishment rather than as an
illness requiring treatment. (It may be noted here that the
clear cut delineation of alcohol addiction as a seperate entity
from drug addiction, further projects this position).

It is agreed that the illegal drug traffic associated with
certain drugs, and the high cost of maintaining a habit more than
often leads to criminal acts which gets the addict into frequent
encounters with the court. The irony of it all is that the "drug
addict" like the alcoholic and food addict has the same pattern
of psychological and physical behavior. The difference is the
social behaviors which derives primarily from the efforts to
maintain a habit; or the function of the social setting in which
the addiction is generated. We are not suggesting here that
illegal drugs be sanctioned or legalized. We are however suggesting that certain addicts are penalized for the symptoms of
their addiction, especially ghetto and proverty groups, or heroin
addicts. We are further suggesting that the social incompetency
associated with the addiction is in many instances a part of the
illness. The focus of this paper is on analyzing the area of
conflict in the criminal justice system which operates against
the concept of treatment and rehabilitation. This discussion
will deal with three areas of impact: the law enforcement system,
the penal system and the judiciary system.

THE LAW ENFORCEMENT SYSTEM

The first area in which there is obvious conflict between
treatment and criminal justice processes is that of law enforcement. Most of the specific problems here arise from efforts of
law enforcement which focus on eliminating drug traffic or the
arrest of the addict for criminal activity.

The illness of the addict, his need to attain drugs, and his
vunerability makes him a good candidate for being used in an
undercover investigation.

As a result of undercover investigations, a given addict
may be arrested and charged with possession of drugs as much as
a year after the incident. He may by this time be doing well in
a treatment program. His arrest for prior involvement more
than often interrupts treatment with incarceration.

THE PENAL SYSTEM

Prisons, as institutions, has traditionally been custodial
in their focus. This is especially so as it relates to the
addict, in that once the addict is sentenced, all too often,
there is total seperation from any thing that resembles treatment
or rehabilitation. If an addict has been in a treatment program
prior to commitment, all treatment ceases. If an addict has
not been treated prior to commitment, he does not begin treatment
with his prison sentence. Specific problems evolving from the
conflict between the penal system and treatment are as follows:

1. The psychological impact of incarceration without
treatment tends to increase dependency for the addict to return
to drugs on release (this is especially true for the addict
who comes from proverty circumstances).

      (a)   immediate unplaned seperation from the drug
           by incarceration accomplishes physiological
           withdrawal but does not permit the addicted
           person to develop coping mechanisms or the
           dissonance reduction needed.

      (b)   there are no equally attractive alternatives from
           which to select between drug taking and prison
           activities. The prison experience is so deficit
           that their is a tendency to glorify drug seeking
           and related activities that were engaged in prior
           to incarceration.

2. In today's prison, all too often the exposure, encounters,
social system of the prison, not only reinforces behaviors of
social incompentency but introduces the addict to a new repertoire

of criminal behavior, i.e. which in prison, the person becomes
a part of the prison subcultural social system by adapting
appropriate behavior to survive homosexuality, power struggle,
wheeling and dealing, and etc. Also, for the neophyte, an
introduction to the various criminal methodologies which increases
his knowledge of criminal behavior.

THE JUDICAL SYSTEM

Specific contradictions to rehabilitation lie in the laws
and interpretation of laws, which has an impact on the addict.
Most of the addicts encountered with the laws relate to possession
of drugs or crimes associated with attainment of drugs.

1. Governmental efforts to reduce the crime rate in most
major cities have accelerated the development of new rigid laws.

2. In the state of Louisiana, penalty for drug possession
range from suspended sentences, probation and fines to life
imprisonment with out probation or parole.

SUMMARY

It is our position that addiction is an illness and thus
the treatment and rehabilitation of addicts should lie within
the society system set up to treat.

1. There is a difference in eliminating illegal drug
traffic, eliminating conditions conductive to the development
of addiction; and the treatment of the addict. These should
not be confused.

2. Present efforts which deny treatment once the addict
has made contact with the criminal justice system are not only
inadequate, but do noting to treat the person who is addicted.

3. Representatives of the criminal justice system are
involved on the boards of rehabilitation and treatment programs
and therefore play a role in the decision making process; the
reverse is not true in that representatives of the treatment
sector do not participate in decisions regarding law making
and other judiciary processes related to the addict.

CRIMINAL JUSTICE/DRUG TREATMENT PROGRAM
INTERFACE CONFERENCE: THE ST. LOUIS MODEL

Harvey W. Feldman

Saint Louis University

George Friesen

Drug and Substance Abuse Council
of Metropolitan St. Louis

G. Jon Yaffe

St. Louis Area Drug Abuse
Coordination Council

On July 18 and 19, 1974, a group of representatives of the major drug treatment programs in the
Metropolitan St. Louis area met with key representatives of the criminal justice system. This meeting
did not come about as a result of any single crisis
situation. In fact, overt conflict between the
criminal justice and drug treatment systems had not
taken place to any significant degree. There had been
consistent recurring evidence that coordination between these two systems was far from optimal. Personnel from the treatment sector showed an incomplete
understanding of the functions and potential of criminal justice programs, and criminal justice personnel
did not appear to be aware of the range of services
offered by treatment programs or of the methods utilized by these programs. While overtly friendly, each
system looked on the other suspiciously.

Biased attitudinal problems existed within both
systems. To a degree, criminal justice people viewed
treatment personnel as naive idealists who misunderstood both their clients and the nature of crime.
Likewise, treatment people viewed criminal justice

personnel as uncaring, hostile representatives of an
essentially mechanistic system.

Despite these limiting factors, it was also evident that St. Louis presented a unique opportunity for
achieving an effective interface between criminal
justice and drug treatment programs. The key actors
in both systems had, over time, established working,
if tenuous, relationships. By participating in the
July 18 and 19 discussions at Saint Louis University
they had also evidenced their willingness to confront
those problem areas where their responsibility for
drug users overlapped.

Based on these observations, participants in this
meeting made a series of key operational decisions.
These were:

1) to hold a series of conferences bringing together the key groups of actual and potential
   interface situations;
2) to produce working agreements: written memoranda of understanding and policy directives
   regarding criminal justice system and treatment roles and responsibilities;
3) to establish clearly defined and mutually
   acceptable interface procedures and evaluative
   criteria as well as a mechanism for continued
   interface negotiation so that these conferences could serve as a model for ongoing
   interface negotiations in the St. Louis region.

To meet these goals, it was determined that program activities would occur in the following sequence:

1) Implementation level activities, involving
   line-workers from both systems and intended
   to describe and make more precise the procedures needed to insure maximum inter-system
   coordination;
2) Policy development activities, with agency
   chiefs developing precise policy guidelines
   which would reflect as well as support the
   procedures described by the line-workers;
3) Policy-making activities, which would involve
   the major governmental units in the Metropolitan St. Louis area in adopting and
   implementing policies developed through this
   interface program.

Implementation Level Activities

Immediately following the initial discussions at
Saint Louis University, an Ad Hoc Steering Committee

was established which took responsibility for planning a "Lineworkers' Conference." Thirty-six representatives of the drug treatment and criminal justice systems were invited to the conference. Conference participants were pre-assigned to one of three groups which were composed of judges, prosecutors, probation officers, police, clinicians, para-professionals, public defenders, and clients. Each small group was assigned a facilitator/consultant whose major tasks were group leadership and processing, task maintenance, and feedback.

Two major documents, developed prior to the Lineworkers' Conference, were intended to serve as the dual focal points of conference activities. These documents included:

1) an interface schedule developed by the Ad Hoc Steering Committee in which a hypothetical client was tracked through the criminal justice and drug treatment systems where points of interface were specifically located;

2) a listing of major problem areas relating to Criminal Justice/Drug Treatment interface as developed prior to the conference by criminal justice and drug treatment personnel working in separate groups.

After developing some group cohesiveness, each group compared the idealized Interface Schedule developed by the Steering Committee and compared it with the actual on-the-street perceptions of group members.

In addition, reflections on the problem statements--and suggested solutions--developed discreetly by both systems were solicited. The groups were offered a conflict resolution process that involves the acceptance of roles and boundaries as well as an emphasis on clear and distinguishable areas of impact. Consensually, the groups were to decide on the appropriateness of certain actors solving specific problems and where collaborative problem-solving can and/or should occur.

The basic question to be confronted was: how shall we best manage existing or potential conflict between these two systems?

One type of problem, for example, of which both systems were acutely aware was, as stated by Treatment System representatives:

"Police periodically arrest clients of treatment programs on the premises of these treatment programs,"

and, as stated by Criminal Justice System personnel:

591

"Drug treatment programs, on
occasion, knowingly harbor wanted
persons."
Through negotiation, one of these conference
groups developed the following negotiated memorandum
of understanding:
1) As a matter of policy, police will not
make arrests of clients of drug treatment
programs on their premises except where
compelled by:
a) The seriousness of the crime involved, or
b) To prevent serious crime, or
c) When the wanted person is confined to
the drug treatment program for a significant period of time.
2) As a general principle, drug treatment
programs will not knowingly harbor wanted
persons.
The Lineworkers' Conference met its major goals
which were to develop recommended solutions which were
written in the above format and called Written Memoranda of Understanding. These memoranda would serve
as the basis for the next Conference of Agency Chiefs,
whose responsibility it would be to refine and ratify
them.

Policy Development Activities

The next step was to plan for an Agency Chiefs'
Conference at which the memoranda of understanding
would be refined and ratified. This conference,
entitled the "Forum for Creative Change" was held on
December 13, 1975.
The program brought together the region's foremost
representatives of the Criminal Justice and Drug Treatment systems. Utilizing agreements developed at the
Lineworkers' Conference as well as other materials,
these individuals were to strengthen mutual understanding and create a groundwork for developing innovative approaches to bettering working relationships
between the two groups. Fully aware that the outcome
of this effort would affect both citizenry-at-large
and those persons directly involved with either or
both systems, civil rights experts and citizen representatives constituted a third body of participants.
Participants were assigned to one of three groups,
roughly organized on the basis of concern with (1)
Juveniles, (2) St. Louis City adults, or (3) St. Louis

County adults. Recommendations developed in the small groups were presented to a final plenary session.

The following recommendations were developed at this conference:

1) Workers in both systems need to be informed of federal legislation entitled, <u>Confidentiality of Alcohol and Drug Abuse Patient Records</u>, and its application to the activities of both groups;

2) There is a need for the support and expansion of drug abuse prevention efforts in the areas of primary prevention, early intervention, and treatment;

3) There is a need for the creation of a new TASC (Treatment Alternatives to Street Crime) program to provide for the pre-trial diversion of drug dependent arresters into treatment;

4) Precise memoranda of understanding concerning the proper nature of criminal justice and drug treatment system relations were developed, with special emphasis on a) client rights, and b) the necessity of treatment programs to maintain a position of client advocacy;

5) More attention should be given to providing full health care services for substance abuse within the existing health care delivery system.

Although the ultimate impact of a program such as the one we have described is always difficult to assess, we would see outcomes such as the following as indicators of success:

1) A set of written memoranda of understanding which covers current and potential areas of conflict;

2) A permanent structure for resolving conflicts either not covered or not sufficiently clarified by existing memoranda (i.e. a conflict management team);

3) A mechanism for developing and refining memoranda of understanding as need for them arise;

4) A structure of cooperation between the two systems which maintains respect but does <u>not</u> blur the boundaries of the system: a conscientious effort to avoid a medical/criminal justice system collaboration against drug users.

THE AUSTIN, TEXAS TASC EXPERIENCE

James A. McDonough, O.P., M.A.

TASC Administrator
Adult Probation Department
Travis County Courthouse
Austin, Texas 78767

A. Introduction

Since my colleagues on the panel have pretty well explained the
TASC concept as it relates to a national strategy and their local
situation, I will limit my remarks to what I consider unique to the
Austin experience. Therefore I will speak on five specific areas:
1. sponsorship by an agency within the criminal justice system,
2. alternative to sentencing before alternatives to prosecution,
3. importance of urinalysis screening and surveillance, 4. cooperation with State parole, and 5. evaluation.

    1. Historically, SAODAP approached Austin Mayor Roy Butler
with the TASC concept. He found it exciting and referred it to
the Austin Police Chief, Bob Miles. A large meeting was called
with County and District Judges along with representatives from
Drug Abuse Treatment Agencies. The upshot of the meeting was to
recommend that Mr. Giles Garmon, Chief Adult Probation Officer, be
contacted and solicit his interest. Mr. Garmon was indeed interested and appointed me to develop the program.

I share the opinion of other officials in our criminal justice
system that this "historical accident" was probably the most important reason for the survival and growth of Austin TASC. The
relationship of our agencies to drug treatment was distant, hostile, and certainly distrustful. Because of sponsorship within
our agency many doors were open at the police department, courts,
and prosecutors offices that would have been closed or slightly
ajar if "treatment types" were attempting to work with hard drug
users prior to adjudication. Austin TASC moved slowly and with
many problems; credibility with criminal justice was not one of
them!

    2. Alternative Sentencing vs. Alternative to Prosecution.

Our community was not and is not ready for diversion of hard drug
abusing offenders from the system. It is ready for a pre-trial

intervention which can identify the drug problem and seek treatment assistance while prosecution proceeds and after sentencing if the person is found guilty. This is what we developed. Frankly, I still feel this is best in the long run. Self initiated requests for assistance is just not typical of our client profile. Furthermore, a continuing treatment program is unrealistic in the relatively few instances of self referral. The coercive treatment referral and treatment tracking of Austin TASC is admittedly a difficult referral for a drug abuse treatment agency to work with: motivation is not a given. But coercive referral is a start and you don't get to your second step until you have a first.

Hopefully Austin TASC will develop alternatives to prosecution in the future. My thought at this time is that it won't happen until we wxpand our intervention to working with offenders with a much more community tolerated problem: alcohol.

3. Importance of Urinalysis

Austin TASC has its own urinalysis laboratory. This operation is used both for mass screening at the City jail and the surveillance of TASC clients under probation supervision (including those supervised while on "Conditional Personal Recognisance Bond"). Treatment people are quick to point out the limitations and over reliance on urinalysis usage. I generally agree that it of limited value in treatment: especially in the achievement of long term treatment goals. However, I cannot stress the importance that urinalysis has for criminal justice types, especially the Courts. Among the many advantages we see are: it provides us with objective evidence; it cuts out a level of "conning" that we expect from hard drug users; and its effective in analyzing the drug-crime problem in the local community.

4. Cooperation with State Parole

Austin TASC has taken the initiative in offering urinalysis screening and surveillance services to State parole officers. This not only gives them an effective tool in working with their parolees which they haven't had before, but, we feel, protects our community from the illegal behavior that parolees with newly acquired heroin habits may represent for our community.

Only parolees who have been previously involved in heroin use are eligible for TASC services. Also, I feel our involvement with drug abuse treatment agencies and personnel has helped overcome a strong resistance on the part of local parole officers dating back to the establishment of these services in our community. Parole officers have told me that they feel more confident in making a referral to a certain agency because they know that we are working with them.

5. Evaluation

I feel that most program evaluations are constructed by academicians for academicians. They are usually insensitive to the pragmatism of local political leaders and Court officials. The Austin approach has been designed to measure our effectiveness as it relates to the cost of crime and the recidivism rate of persons under probation supervision.

On intake, but after detox, all opiate abusing clients are asked to give us the daily amount of heroin they were using just prior to being "busted." The street price in Austin is estimated at $50 per gram. They are also interviewed to determine their method of supporting their habits: property-theft type crimes and/or non-theft type crimes. Most come out with a formula which is a combination: e.g., 40% theft; 60% non-theft.

The above information is reported monthly and a cumulative total is kept. Thirty months of Austin TASC offers our local officials the following:

   a. Daily heroin consumption potential of TASC
       clients: $16,460.00

   b. Daily criminal activity potential of TASC
       clients:

       1) Property-type crimes $22,702.00
       2) Non-property   45,820.00
           Total $68,522.00

   c. Total heroin consumption potential
       while under supervision: $12,236,149.00

   d. Total criminal activity potential
       while under supervision: $35,081.201.00

I do not expect to find my evaluation design to be written up in a distinguished academic journal. But, frankly this does not bother me.

We have reduced our recidivism rate for known heroin and hard drug using probationers from 90% to 21%. I won't elaborate on that other than to tell you that our TASC recidivism rate for felons is equal to our department overall revocation rate for felons.

I will conclude with simply an expression of thanks to you for listening and to Mr. Regner and Jim Weissman for the opportunity to be here. Also, to the Texas Corrections Association who paid my way!!!

TREATMENT ALTERNATIVES TO STREET CRIME (TASC): HOW WELL DOES IT WORK?[1]

Mary A. Toborg, Raymond H. Milkman, Lawrence J. Center

The Lazar Institute
Washington, D.C.

The Treatment Alternatives to Street Crime (TASC) program evolved from observations that many drug-dependent persons engaged in street crime to support their habits and were recurringly arrested, released and rearrested. To break this cycle, the first TASC project was established in 1972 to help channel criminally involved drug abusers into treatment, in order to rehabilitate them into productive, law-abiding citizens. As of October 1975, a total of 36 projects had been funded, at a Federal cost of $21.8 million. The projects had enrolled approximately 17,000 clients, including almost 5,000 who were still in treatment. In addition, approximately 15% of the TASC entrants had successfully completed the program's requirements.

In order to assess the present state of knowledge concerning the operations and effectiveness of the TASC program, three major data collection activities were undertaken: a review of existing literature and work in progress, telephone interviews with the 22 TASC projects which were operational as of February 1975, and site visits to ten projects. Major findings are summarized below for project operations and program outcomes.[2]

I. PROJECT OPERATIONS

Although TASC projects share similar goals, they vary in their operational response to attaining those goals. Individual projects may provide different sets of services to different types of clients within varying environmental settings. Moreover, projects may intervene in routine criminal justice system processing in several ways, including pretrial intervention, in which normal judicial processes occur but information on treatment progress is provided to the courts for use in sentencing, if the client is found guilty; diversion, in which the client does not come to trial if treatment progress is satisfactory; and posttrial processing, in which the client is identified and referred to treatment after the case has been adjudicated.

Despite this diversity, most TASC projects serve five major functions:

. identifying drug abusers in contact with the criminal justice system and offering those eligible the opportunity to participate in TASC;

. diagnosing the drug abuser's problems and recommending appropriate treatment;

. monitoring the performance of TASC clients and returning the violators of TASC requirements to the criminal justice system for appropriate action;

. counseling clients, by meeting treatment needs, assisting with ancillary services, or providing crisis intervention services; and

. managing the project, including conducting research and evaluation studies of performance.

The costs of these activities vary considerably for different projects. For example, the cost per client served at sixteen TASC projects ranged from $214 to $2055 and averaged $932. However, such a calculation is of limited value, since the same budget level may support vastly different sets of services (in some cases including treatment) at different projects.

A number of evaluation studies have been conducted of individual TASC projects. However, these analyses are of little use in assessing the overall TASC program, due to the lack of comparability among the studies. The type of evaluation may vary from project to project; the definitions used for the same types of evaluation may differ; or similar basic data may be collected, but categorized in ways precluding cross-project analysis. Indeed, the absence of standardized information in TASC projects imposes major limitations on the analysis which can be conducted with existing data. However, some findings recur in the various analyses of TASC projects. These include:

. The use of mass urinalysis testing of all arrestees is not essential for identifying potential clients. Interviewing arrestees selectively or relying on referrals from judges, probation officers, defense attorneys and others appears to be as effective and may be less costly.

. There is some indication that TASC's formalized mechanism for referral to treatment is more effective than informal referral procedures.

. TASC's monitoring of clients, and prompt reporting of
violations, appears to improve client performance.

. criminal justice system representatives often report
that TASC's monitoring of clients is one of the most
important features of the program and greatly enhances
its credibility.

II. OUTCOMES

TASC participation is assumed to influence clients to enter
and remain in treatment. Successful completion of treatment is in
turn assumed to be associated with such outcomes as reduced criminality, lessened drug abuse, improved economic status and revita-
lized health. These outcomes will materialize because successfully
treated clients will no longer be drug dependent, or need to commit
crimes to obtain funds to purchase drugs. Moreover, they will be
better able to hold a steady job or otherwise participate in the
economy through legal means and will no longer be prone to a variety of drug-related illnesses.

Although this chain of reasoning underlies the TASC concept,
little information is presently available to test its validity.
Individual TASC projects do report monthly on clients who are
rearrested on new charges. As of October 1, 1975, eight percent of
the TASC clients at 22 reporting projects had been arrested on new
charges while in TASC. However, little analysis has been done of
the recidivism of different groups of TASC clients, such as those
participating in TASC for varying lengths of time or having different characteristics. Nor has the recidivism of former TASC clients
been systematically analyzed for periods after leaving the program.
Moreover, outcomes of TASC clients have not been compared with
those of otherwise similar persons who did not participate in TASC.

In addition to arrest data, several TASC projects have analyzed other types of outcome information. However, these data are
usually quite limited in scope, often consisting of the percentage
of clients retained in treatment or the percentage of positive
urine tests during treatment participation. As in the case of
recidivism data, little outcome analysis has been done for different groups of TASC clients or for periods after leaving the program. Nor have TASC client outcomes been compared with those of
otherwise similar non-participants.

Besides their effect on client outcomes, TASC projects may
have a number of other important impacts. For example, persons
interviewed in TASC communities sometimes commented that TASC had
reduced the criminal justice system processing burdens, improved

599

the handling of criminally involved drug abusers and improved communications between the criminal justice and treatment systems. In some cases the TASC concept was also being considered for use with other groups of arrestees, such as alcoholics.

An additional impact sometimes considered for the TASC program is whether projects succeed in becoming institutionalized, that is, whether they obtain State or local funding to replace the initial Federal support. As of November 1975, six projects had completed their maximum Federal funding period of approximately two years. All had been institutionalized. In addition, three projects had been terminated before completion of the Federal funding period. These projects had been unable to obtain sufficient clients to warrant continuation.

Aside from reporting projects' success or failure in achieving State or local funding, little else can be said about the institutionalization process. No analyses have considered whether institutionalization reflects the locally perceived value of the projects or merely the local financial situation. Nor have any analyses assessed the operations of TASC projects before and after institutionalization.

Another type of TASC impact occurs from projects' identification of drug abusers lacking prior treatment. A variety of information indicated that approximately 55% of TASC's clients were receiving treatment for the first time. However, in the absence of outcome data on the long-range effectiveness of the TASC intervention, the importance of this "outreach" function cannot be adequately assessed.

The lack of data on client outcomes after completion of the TASC program, especially as compared with otherwise similar groups of non-participants, precludes defensible statements regarding TASC's long-range impact on drug-related crime or the associated processing burdens of the criminal justice system. Although TASC's short-term effects include an eight percent rearrest rate while clients participate in the program, the inducement of a large number of people to enter treatment for the first time and impressionistic information that TASC's activities have improved the interface between the criminal justice and treatment systems, such findings cannot substitute for analysis of a program's long-range impact. Without such analysis, few definitive statements can be made regarding how well TASC works.

NOTES

[1]The research upon which this article is based was supported by grant number 75 NI-99-0062 from the National Institute of Law

Enforcement and Criminal Justice, Law Enforcement Assistance
Administration, U.S. Department of Justice. Points of view or
opinions stated in this document are those of the authors and do
not necessarily represent the official position or policies of the
U.S. Department of Justice.

[2]A more detailed discussion of findings is available in
Treatment Alternatives to Street Crime (TASC), National Evaluation
Program Phase I Report, Series A, Number 3, Law Enforcement
Assistance Administration, Washington, D.C., February 1976.

THE DECRIMINALIZATION OF URINALYSIS

Robert B. Kahn, Ph.D. and N. T. Schramm

Narcotic Abuse Treatment Program
San Diego, California

LAW

The rules and regulations governing the operation of maintenance treatment are as follows:

A. Schedule of Testing; Substance Tested For

In maintenance treatment random urinalysis will be performed at least weekly for morphine and monthly for methadone, barbiturates, amphetamines and other drugs as indicated. Those patients receiving their doses of the drug from medication units will also adhere to this schedule. The urine should be collected at the program's primary facility or at the medication unit.

B. Method of Collection

Urines should be collected in a manner which minimizes falsification of the samples. The reliability of this collection procedure shall be demonstrated.

C. Laboratories

Laboratories used for urine testing shall participate in and be approved by a proficiency testing program designated by the Food and Drug Administration. Any changes made in laboratories used for urine testing shall acquire approval of the Food and Drug Administration.

We are now saddled with a law which requires, overtly and covertly, the operation of methadone maintenance treatment in a punitive manner.

To indicate the absurdity of this legislation, consider the following example:

If you seek treatment for an upper respiratory infection from
a physician, he tells you that you are to follow the regimen
of drinking liquids and taking certain medications. In a
relatively short period of time (10 days or 2 weeks) you should
show improvement. You take your medication and try to the best
of your ability to follow those instructions. If (perhaps due
to your schedule or the lifestyle you lead) your condition
deteriorates because you do not take the medication in the
manner in which it was prescribed, and at the end of the 10-day
or 2-week period you return to the physician in a worse physical
condition, you are not punished as a result of your body fluids
indicating the presence of the disease which the physician is
treating.

In accordance with the Food and Drug Administration we are
remanded, and in the State of California, required by implication, to terminate you if your cold does not get better.

Carrying the example to its logical absurdity, it is then the
responsibility for the physician to tell you that because you
did not follow this course of treatment properly, he will no
longer treat you. The next time he sees you, you will be in
the emergency ward of a hospital with acute pneumonia.

At that time, or in case of a flexible readmission policy, you
may be readmitted for treatment only under the condition that
you guarantee that you will follow the treatment regimen as
prescribed by the physician.

Therefore, we take a body fluid test and punish the client population for not getting well, based almost solely on that information.

COST

In a recent monograph published by the Drug Abuse Council entitled
"Methadone Benefits and Shortcomings", it is indicated that there
are approximately 135,000 patients in methadone treatment programs.
At an average cost of $3.00 per screen 52 times/year, the methadone
maintenance treatment budget nationally for urinalysis is
$21,060,000. According to our rough calculations, that is approxi-
mately 8.8% of the treatment dollars allocated to each client.

In California, the regulatory agency - Department of Health,
Substance Abuse Branch - is even more specific in its requirements.
It has only been until recently that we did not also have to test

for methadone weekly, instead of monthly. But in California the
regulations are such that each urinalysis result that indicates a
positive presence of a drug must be confirmed by using a different
methodology, which naturally increases the cost per screen.

There seems to be quite a market for the processing of urines for
drug treatment programs. If, in fact, the urinalysis industrial
complex must exist in accordance with Federal and State regulations,
it should necessarily follow that the dollars be expended in the
best interest of the client and program effectiveness.

USE OF THE RESULTS

In California, take-home dosage privileges are tied specifically to
positive urinalysis results. The California law requires that if
there are two positive tests for illicit drugs in a 60-day period,
or three positive tests for illicit drugs in a 90-day period, the
individual must be reduced one step level in his or her take-home
dosage privilege. There is also an implication that a client's
tests must be negative for illicit drugs for a period of 6 months
prior to being placed on a take-home status. Very little or no
latitude for clinical judgment is permitted.

How often have you heard "is he/she clean?" How many times are
judgments made about individuals based solely on the constancy of
the opiate positive? How much significance is given to the fact
that if a client must use heroin 3 times a day, 7 days a week for
many months prior to admission to a methadone maintenance treatment
program, why isn't the significant reduction of the use of heroin a
satisfactory indication of effective treatment? How many of you
are aware that if a client who has been using 21 times a week (as
criteria for admission) now only uses heroin 3 times a week, his or
her random urinalysis will always be positive for morphine? Does
the staff really understand the duration of barbiturate metabolites
and barbiturate indications? Does the staff really understand the
thin layer chromatography procedures and intricacies, the sensi-
tivities of the various mechanisms and processes that are used?

If, in fact, we are punitively concerned about the illicit use of
drugs, why isn't there a mandatory test for alcohol?

EFFECT ON CLIENT

I trust you. Now let's make sure - I want to watch you pee.

In unsophisticated programs no effort is made to correlate the use
of drugs to significant events. Working with the UCLA Drug Treatment Program, Bert Sackman and Jerry DeAngelis, Ph.D. have written
a paper which indicates that there is a significant correlation
between adverse activities in the client's life and the use of
drugs. It appears that it is mandatory for those of us in the

treatment of substance abuse to begin to accept the basic premise
that the use of illicit drugs while in a treatment program is an
indication of adversity and anxiety-producing situations in a
client's life.

It is then appropriate for the treaters to intervene to assist the
client population in dealing with these issues, rather than to
punish them for utilizing a drug which has been substituted for the
treater's inability to deal with the situation as it is presented.

I don't, by any sense of the imagination, intend to indicate that
the counselors and staff members of substance abuse programs are
responsible for the actions of the client population. I do, however, strongly suggest that unless we begin to assist the clients
in developing an understanding of methodology to be used as an
alternative to drug use, we are nothing more than our critics say
we are.

If a test comes back from the lab indicating a single woman is
pregnant, do we treat her, or do we send her to the nearest federal
institution to be imprisoned? If a positive VDRL comes back from
the lab, do we treat the disease, or do we punish the person? If a
positive urinalysis is entered in the client's chart, do we then
punish the client, or do we treat them in the same way we treat the
pregnant woman or the client with venereal disease?

Some will argue that using drugs is against the law, therefore, we
must maintain continuity by conforming with the criminal justice
system by reacting to this illegal activity. I suggest to you that
punishment should be reserved for the political system which
fosters a socio-economic environment that affords substance abuse
as the only alternative to some people. The funds allocated to
treatment programs are for treatment, not punishment!

Should we not begin to assume that drug abuse needs good treatment?
And should we not begin to assume that when an individual is
utilizing an illicit substance while under the umbrella of a treatment program, it is our responsibility to respond to that deficiency?
May not the punitive approach to body fluid testing ultimately result in the concealment of unmanageable personal problems?

Should we, as treatment professionals, begin to observe the phenomena of drug abuse in the controlled clinical settings rather
than punish the phenomena of drug abuse in the treatment setting,
much like the criminal justice system punishes the drug abuser?

OPTIONS

It appears that it would be far more beneficial to begin to utilize
urine testing as a means of indicating adversity in conjunction
with other behavior. You hear it argued that it is possible for

the adequately experienced counselor to detect drug abuse without the use of urinalysis. If we are going to use urinalysis as some sort of indicator of progress or success, would it not be more appropriate to utilize the urinalysis in a real time situation? That is, specifically, by reverting to using onsite testing devices which give immediate feedback.

Many of us realize that for the heroin addict on the run and in trouble, tomorrow will not come, and yesterday didn't happen. It therefore behooves us to reach out to the individual in treatment in a real time "now" situation. Then the crucial questions must be asked - what for and how do I use the urinalysis results?

The authors contend that urinalysis results should be utilized specifically, in the same manner as chest X-rays, VDRL, CBC, SMA12, pregnancy testing, pap smears, etc., are used, i.e., in a professional treatment way and in no way to bring discredit or punitive action on the part of the program toward the individual that abuses the substance. If it is absolutely mandatory for some to have an objective indication of client progress or success, let that indication be employment, family stability, involvement in psychotherapeutic or counseling situations, and let it not be based solely on 30 cc's of urine.

Let us begin to look at patterns and behavior in the person as a whole rather than the person's urine.

Let us begin to adjust our concepts toward effectively ameliorating a disease, which is the use of illicit substances, rather than punishing a person for using a substance which we can't control.

It is time for substance abuse treatment programs to begin to treat the clients and not to punish them. It is time to separate ourselves from the criminal justice system. It is time to begin to view our enterprise as a professional treatment modality - not a professional extension of the criminal justice system which requires some objective means to continue to punish a person for the varied abuses which we tell the public we are treating.

606

A SURVEY OF STATE REGULATIONS GOVERNING
THE DISPENSING OF METHADONE

Bonnie Stone

Methadone Maintenance Treatment Program
New York City Department of Health
New York, New York 10013

In December, 1972, the U.S. Food & Drug Administration (FDA)
published special requirements for the regulation of the use of
methadone. Along with numerous application, reporting and record-
keeping requirements, it sought to govern even the specific amount
of the drug administered or dispensed to the patients by medical
practitioners. This, it was argued, was "because of the hazards
known to exist from diversion and misuse of methadone."[1] Limits on
dosage and take-home days of medication were proscribed by the regulations over the objections of many practitioners across the
country. Since authorities and local programs could further
restrict take home medication policies to conform to local needs,
some practitioners argued, there was no need to impose such limitations on a national basis. The cost of administering programs on a
daily basis would severely limit the use of methadone, and the
restrictions would produce an increased drop-out rate and subsequent
relapse for thousands of addicts. In fact, when the regulations
went into effect, the drop-out rate was reported to have increased
dramatically in the country's largest program.[2]

In brief, the FDA restricted the dosage level to 100 mg. for any
single dose to be consumed away from the clinic's immediate control.
In addition, patients would be allowed to have only limited amounts
of take-home dosages as shown in Table I.

Three years have passed since these regulations went into effect
and the argument continues. While the regulations are quite
restrictive as written, they are minimum standards only; and State
authorities are free to further restrict the dispensing and administration of methadone as they see fit. The purpose of this short
survey was to examine what if any, subsequent actions the fifty-five
State Methadone Authorities[3] may have taken with regard to these
restrictions.

A mail survey was conducted in the fall of 1975 with the results
shown in Table II.

Thirty-three authorities reported that they have incorporated the FDA regulations in full and have not made any additions to them.

Twenty-two authorities have developed additional regulations governing the use of methadone. Not all of these have the force of law (i.e. Missouri), but they all in practice, govern methadone usage in their state. (see Appendix 1)

Only six of these twenty-two authorities have developed regulations governing take-home methadone which are more stringent than those of the FDA. Table III lists the six states and describes the restrictions more completely.

Ohio and Puerto Rico do not allow any methadone to be taken out of the clinic by their patients.

California, Colorado, Georgia and Idaho have somewhat stricter limits on the time in treatment required for-take home privileges. In addition, Colorado limits the dosage allowed to 50 mg. for those patients for whom take-home medication is permitted.

Since State Authorities also set only minimum standards, there are numerous individual programs and localities throughout the country which restrict take-home medication beyond the limits set by the FDA and the individual State authorities, but an exhaustive study of individual programs was not conducted at this time. Two large and well-known programs have restricted take-home medication completely and are noted below:

1) Washington, D.C. Narcotic Treatment Administration
2) City of Boston Methadone Maintenance Treatment Program

Both of these programs service most of the methadone patients in treatment in their respective cities, and thus their policies in practice govern their respective environments.

Thus, with the exception of six state authorities and a number of individual programs, the FDA regulations governing take-home medication remain as the national standard.

Table I

FDA Regulations Governing Take-home Dosages

Time in Treatment	Number Take-home Doses / Week
0 - 3 months	1
3 months - 2 years	4
Over 2 years	5

Table II

Take-home Policies of State Methadone Authorities

	State Regulations	
No State Regulations	Same as FDA	More Restrictive
33	16	6

Table III

State Authorities with Stricter Rules
for Take-home Medication

California

Time limits	# Take-home days/week
0 - 90 days	0
91 - 180 days	1
181 days - one year	2
One - two years	4
Over two years	5

Colorado
I. No take home dosages over 50 mg./day

II. Time limits	# Take-home days/week
0 - 6 months	0
Over 6 months	4

Georgia

Time limits	# Take-home days/week
0 - 3 months	0
Over 3 months	Same as FDA

Idaho

Time limits	# Take-home days/week
0 - 3 months	1
3 months - 18 weeks	2
18 - 24 weeks	3
Over 24 weeks	4

Ohio
No take-home medication permitted

Puerto Rico
No take-home medication permitted

Appendix 1

State Authorities with Additional
Regulations Governing Methadone Treatment

Alaska
California
Colorado
Florida
Georgia
Idaho
Illinois
Indiana
Michigan
Missouri
New Mexico
New York
Nebraska
Nevada
Ohio
Pennsylvania
Puerto Rico
Texas
Utah
Virginia
West Virginia
Wisconsin

Notes

1. "Methadone: Listing as New Drug with Special Requirements and
   Opportunity for Hearing," HEW, FDA. Federal Register Vol. 37,
   No. 242, Part III. December 15, 1972.

2. "Retention of Patients in the New York City Methadone
   Maintenance Treatment Program," Robert G. Newman, MD, MPH,
   Alex Tytun, M.S., Sylvia Bashkow, M.S. (mimeo, 1974)

3. The designated fifty-five authorities include one in each of
   50 states and one each in the District of Columbia,
   Commonwealth of Puerto Rico, Virgin Islands, American Samoa,
   Guam.

THE DILEMMA OF THE ASIAN AMERICAN DRUG ABUSER

Tommy Chung and Ron Wakabayashi

Asian American Drug Abuse Program, Inc.
Los Angeles, California

The dilemma of the Asian American Drug Abuser is paradoxically manifested in the general lack of visibility of its symptomology. The invisibility of the Asian American Drug Abuser, both within the ethnic community and by the society at large, has, historically and currently, operated to reinforce the illusion equating lack of visibility with lack of a problem.

The perceptual tools normally utilized to define a drug abusing population, have, in large part, been instruments developed by majority culture institutions. The application of these measuring instruments to the Asian American communities in the United States fail to analyze significant social indicators appropriate for specific cultural and ethnic populations. Commonly, data gathering and retrieval systems exclude the incorporation of devices to isolate data on these populations. The Census activity, the major population data gathering effort in public view, is an obvious example of this exclusion.

The failure to segregate and analyze empirical data on Asian American populations, creates a situation where human need expressions from these communities are either unknown and ignored, or subject to controversey. In either case, clear barriers to needs identification and, subsequently, service delivery exist.

I. HISTORICAL BACKGROUND

According to the 1970 Census, there are approximately two million Asian Americans in the United States. Of this number about 600,000 were Japanese; 450,000 were Chinese; 350,000 were Pilipino; and the remaining populations of Asian Americans were not differentiated in the Census. This figure, enlarged since the Census, because of the large immigration influx, represents a hundred year plus history of an Asian American presence.

Although Asian American populations are composed of a variety of cultures, value systems, traditions and language, a number of historical similarities and relationships are shared. Under labels such as Oriental, Asiatics or Gooks, Asian Americans have been viewed in an undifferentiated manner. Customs and practices of a particular ethnic groups have often, inappropriately been assigned in a generalized form to an entire racial population. Similarly, stereotypes and prejudices have been historically experienced by these populations as though they were a single monolithnic population.

Early Asian American immigrants arrived on American shores during the course of the Civil War. These first Chinese immigrants were met with harsh and demeaning treatment. Beatings and lynching were not uncommon. The Japanese immigration began shortly after the Chinese, and the focus of discrimination and exploitation transferred to them. These early pioneers came to America in search of sharing in the wealth and plenty, that characterized the early descriptions of America that reached Asia. The United States was described as a "Mountain of Gold" in China.

Instead of sharing in the riches of new opportunites, these early immigrants faced menial employment, were forbidden citizenship, forbidden the right to own land, segregrated in the public schools, and generally maltreated. The early immigrant populations of Asian Americans endured over 600 pieces of anti-Asian legislation, while making major contributions to the development of the Intercontinental Railroad, Agriculture, Fishing industry and assorted small businesses. The largely male population of Asian Americans that constituted the large part of the ethnic communities, were denied an opportunity to bring wives, and, in that way, were prevented from establishing families. The isolated and traumatic early exposure to the United States was a prelude to the development of later social concerns of succeeding generations.

Through a disciplined attitude toward economy, and the invention of various devices to circumvent to anti-Asian sentiment of the time, visible and organized communities of Asian Americans developed. A system of "Picture Brides" arranged for the immigration of women. Ethnic community institutions were created to parallel those of the government, and meet the needs of community members. Family, Church, Prefectural, and Fraternal organizations were erected to respond to the interests and needs of members. Complete colonies of Asian immigrants were organized, nearly independent of the majority culture.

The development and relative prosperity of Chinatowns and Little Tokyo's were viewed as evidence of the clannishness of Asian Americans. The congregation and concentration of these ethnic minorities was not understood to be a survival strategy response to the objective conditions of the period. Rather, ethnic enclaves, was viewed as indicative of the non-assimilation characteristic assigned to this population.

The particular history of Asian Americans became a major ingredient in the formulation of characteristics of following generations. The attitudes of distrust and fear of public institutions was subtly transferred from one generation to the next, perpetuating an interdependece within the ethnic community. Concurrently, following generations had this view reinforced by events and circumstances that took place and are taking place to this day. During World War II, 110,000 Japanese were incarcerated. Most of these were born in the United States and citizens of the country. Experiences such as this reinforced a self image among Asian Americans, that their status in the citizenship hierarchy of the nation was lesser than other citizens. Consequently, Asian Americans were made to feel inferior to their counterpart citizens.

Responding to the effects of this history, Asian American community members adopted a strategy for acceptance through accomodation. Accomodation translated to mean presenting a model image of the community to the larger society. Asian Americans developed a value system that placed great emphasis on discipline and achievement in order to gain favor with the majority society. Characteristic of the operation of this value system was the deemphasis, and sometimes, denial of any community elements, activities or behavior that may become viewed negatively and distinguishingly by the majority culture.

This behavior, over a course of time, provided a basis for a new interpretation of the stereotypic characteristics assigned to Asian Americans. Phrases such as the "Quiet American", "Silent Minority", and "Model Minority" develop as synonyms for Asian American. A myth develops that Asian Americans are a model for assimilation, evidenced by the levels of educational achievement, strong family structure, lack of deviance and passivity.

II. THE DILEMMA

The historical circumstance of the Asian American provided a basis for conflicts in the self concept (identity) and related conflicts in social role. The adoption of the strategy of accomodation provided multiple reinforcements to the concealment of human needs within the Asian American pouulation. Under this colonized mentalality, members of the community maintain high personal, family and peer expectations to achieve, greatly reinforcing existing cultural expectations in the same direction. Under this kind of value set, any activity short of extraordinary, was not given recognition. Deviant or underachieving behavior was treated by rejection toward the individual, and active denial of any deviant pattern of behavior within any element of the population. The activity of active denial provided an internal control within the ethnic communities, to maintain an idealized image of the community.

The myth of a model minority is perpetuated from two arenas. The stereotypes held by the dominant culture, and the unrealistic implementation of a self image by the ethnic community, tend to support a dynamic concealing deviant problems within the Asian American communities. The result of this psychological set has been exemplified in a pathology of invisibility, until most recent times.

The problem of drug abuse in Asian American communities varies from ethnic group to ethnic group. Each ethnic community has its own unique characteristics and developmental pattern. Generalizing the experience gives some insight to the dilemma, but fails to comment on detailed culturally specific manifestations of the snared experience. For example, in Los Angeles County a caseload in a treatment program may include fourteen or more distinct ethnic groups that commonly relate to the Asian American operational definition.

Commonly, experience in related human service delivery activities provide population characteristics that parallel the experience in drug abuse. The admission rate of Asian Americans in California in 1971 to State Mental Hospitals was recorded at a level significantly lower than the corresponding population percentage. A cursory analysis might conclude that this would be evidence that this population has lesser needs than others. A further review finds that this same population has the longest average duration of institutionalization in the state hospitals, implying a greater severity ration in the admission population. The lower rate of admission is additionally evidence of early historical learning, the distrust of public service delivery agents, and a preferred alternative service delivery system within the community, itself. This experience was repeated in the investigation of utilization of Federal Catagorical Aids by Asian consumer populations. A use rate lower than the corresponding population percentage was experienced, until familiar community based service deliverers interfaced with the County operated Catagorical Aid program.

The experience in drug abuse is confronting a similar dilemma. In the 1960's, the Japanese community in Los Angeles experienced a large number of deaths among its youth population. The obiturary column in the ethnic vernaculars identified causes of death in phrases such as respitory collapse, pneumonia, and heart failure. While the majority of these deaths were directly drug related, the community attitude of accomodation acted to deny the existence of a drug abuse problem within its youth. Problems of this sort were concealed by families in order to protect family name and community image. This concealment coupled with the model minority view held by most major service delivery institutions, allowed the problem to develop and fester, until the problem reached a large magnitude. In 1970, Japanese American Community Services, Inc., had identified 31 deaths of youths in the community that were related to drug abusing behavior.

Asian American youth are faced with a myriad of influences that have greatly likelihood of resulting in drug abusing behavior. Subtly, a self image (identity) that has been badly damaged has been transmitted to them. The incidence of cosmetic eye surgery to remove the characteristic epicanthic fold, breast enlargement surgery, hair coloration and other minor indicators of racial-ethnic deprecation has been evident within the population. Concurrently, cultural and psycho-social pressure to deny and conceal drug abusing behavior, precludes any external early intervention. Racial and ethnic stereotypes have tendencies within public service delivery systems to return an acting out youth to the family, which tends to statistically validate a lack of service needs in the Asian American communities. Finally, even when protracted deviant behavior of a particular Asian American youth is involved with the juvenile justice or service delivery system, little appropriate, culturally specific resource is available. Consequently, little attention is given to those Asian American youths.

The expression of the Asian American dilemma parallels the experience of other drug abusing populations. However, specificity of treatment and prevention efforts to these communities, must include culturally specific vehicles in the planning and delivery of service. Clients may range from an elderly Chinese male, who has a 50 year history of drug abuse, to a 13 year old Japanese, Cambodian, Lao, Samoan, or Indonesian girl. Family, Tribal, Cultural, Nutritional, Linguistic, and myriad other considerations in service delivery must focus at the most basic service, assessment and policy considerations related to addressing the dilemma of the Asian American Drug Abuser.

TECATOLOGY:

A TREATMENT PERSPECTIVE CONCERNING THE CHICANO ADDICT

Ramon Adame

President, Chicano Alliance of
Drug Abuse Programs
Executive Director of
Aliviane, Inc., El Paso, Texas

There is much experential knowledge in the field of drug
abuse. This knowledge that has been experentially learned has
never really been tapped to its fullest. The intention of this
paper will do just that. A booklet has been compiled and published
on the Chicano tecato (addict). The booklet deciphers addict
pathology from a Chicano perspective, interprets the material,
then comments on treatment direction. This is presented in the
published booklet by touching on such factors as: types of
tecatos (addicts), tecato dynamics, different treatment phases,
one treatment approach vs another, the tecata (female addict), the
tecato family, a tecato glossary of terms, etc. The booklet
touches on almost every factor that is considered of some importance in the pathology of the tecato (addict). Some of the factors
might be considered very liberal and perhaps radically different
from the traditional. One of these negates the entire concept of
changing or modifying the addict's behavior by dealing with the
application approach. Overall the booklet is written in such a
way that it provides a practical point of view rather than a
theoretical one. The booklet expands TECATOLOGY (Addictology) to
the art that it is.

Mr. Adame (Monchi) writes "In this booklet I wish to declare
that it is an impossibility to change and/or modify the ways of
the tecato (addict). We must face the fact that we have been
working against the grain.

The above quote is taken directly from the Introduction of
his booklet entitled TECATOLOGY. It can certainly be translated
as an out-front challenge to the multitude of drug abuse workers.
It is certainly more than a gesture at providing the so terribly
needed vitality to the field of drug abuse. The above challenge
that he poses is answered from his perspective as he writes, "The
key word here is continuation. Yes, continuation. We must

encourage the tecato to continue with his personal characteristics. We must allow him to continue being manipulative and slick. How many of us, ex-addicts, really left all this behind? None of us! If we had done this, we would not be here. Instead of grabbing the syringe and cotton, we grabbed the lunchbox and the alarm clock."

In general, what Mr. Adame believes, is that many drug programs have the notion that addicts' lives are so totally negative that none of the traits, schemes and survival techniques of their street backgrounds can be employed in structuring and living a positive life-style. He challenges this, turns it completely around and plainly communicates that no one really has the right to change anybody else. It is a matter of simply providing the person with two packages of life. These packages are basically the same with the exception of their application. Yes, the tecato (addict) has a multitude of skills and it is up to him or her to apply them in a negative way or positive. One merely orients the individual to both and then he or she must be allowed to be free to choose. Again it is simply a matter of the tecato (addict) choosing between the packages of life after they have been presented to him by the counselors in therapeutic communities.

The application of Tecatology in most Chicano TC's may be considered negative, in that in many situations the counseling staff may lose the controls. This is precisely why when the reins are tightened, the staff gets defensive and the growth process stops.

"The staff react by threatening the tecato. Whether the tecato is a parolee, probationer, or volunteer, the staff continually jumps into a negative cycle and plays either a very defensive or apologetic role. The counselor replies with such phrases as "I'm just doing what I'm told;" It's not my doing;" or, "If you don't get it together, we'll..." Unfortunately out of this negative interaction, the tecato in most cases leaves anyway.

The above is precisely why it took many years to develop TC's for the Chicano tecatos. Still, nowadays, many people feel that it is impossible to operate TC's for Chicanos. The excuses are usually the cultural differences, etc. However, most people never have stopped, translated these unique differences and applied treatment direction to them.

Tecatology takes into account the natural processes that determine leadership roles and other social dynamics among tecatos. It defines and fully explaines the roles of the tecato MACISO, the SLIKA and the CHAFA, and contends that the addict (tecato) does not have identity problems as is commonly assumed. "The tecato knows where he is at.

617

Mr. Adame (Monchi) feels that it is the responsibility of treatment workers to identify the natural, basic lifestyle of the individual, and to encourage him to continue using whatever survival techniques he has developed. Helpful treatment is the process of guiding the addict (tecato) to use his talents toward things that will benefit his life, not ruin it.

In a very specific manner Tecatology is described in terms of the types of tecatos, tecato treatment, the family and women issues. A glossary of tecatological words and phrases is included with Spanish and English translations.

Mr. Adame (Monchi) feels that there are really no conclusions concerning Tecatology at this time. Many individuals might say that the addiction problem within Chicanos is not that unique. However, the attempt has been to point out certain factors that distinguish the tecatos from other addicts.

In essence what was discussed in the National Drug Conference in New York and what was written in Tecatology is only a pebble in a beach of knowledge concerning Tecatology. Mr. Adame (Monchi) hopes that people will expand on his attempt to decipher addict (tecato) principal, thus creating addiction to the science that it is.

To receive a copy of Tecatology: A Treatment Perspective Concerning the Chicano Addict, or a copy of this paper send a check or money order in the amount of $2.00 to:

Tierra de Sol Publishers
P.O. Box 200
El Paso, Texas   79942

If preferred, send a letter of request or purchase order to the same address.

THE BLACK ADDICT: A NEW LOOK AT A CURRENT POPULATION

James A. Halikas MD
Harriet S. Darvish BA
John D. Rimmer   PhD

From the Department of Psychiatry
Washington University School of Medicine
4940 Audubon Avenue
St. Louis, Missouri 63110

No one knows how many active heroin addicts there have been in the United States between 1970 and 1975, nor what proportion of them were black men. Among eastern large city public treatment programs most treatment clients are black men. In St. Louis, more than 3/4 of the client populations of narcotics treatment programs are black men. The natural history of narcotics addiction in this population has only scantily been described.

Based on 98 black men admitted to the Lexington treatment facility from New York or Chicago in 1965,Chambers and Moffett[1,2] described some of the characteristics of the population at that time. Their mean age was 30.5 years. Most had come from broken homes in childhood(65%). About 40% had completed high school; about 80% had been at some time involved in a marital situation. Virtually all had been arrested(97%) at some time in their lives, and, of those arrested,79% had also had a narcotics arrest. Arrests prior to the age of 18 had occurred for 39% of the group. The mean age of first arrest for their population had been at 19.8 years, and the mean age of first opiate use had been at 20.7 years. Chambers and Moffett concluded that"official detection of criminal deviancy precedes opiate experimentation".

Robins and Murphy[3]at about the same time interviewed a population of 221 normal black men from whom they culled a group of 22 heroin addicts. Every addict in this sample, they discovered, had had a narcotics arrest. Juvenile records existed for 73% of the addicts. Only 4 of the 22 addicts(18%) had completed high school compared to their normal population of black men where 64% had completed high school.

This current report presents more extensive descriptive findings on a large population of current black male heroin addicts one decade later.

METHODOLOGY

Four groups, each containing two subgroups, of narcotics addicts who fulfilled research criteria for various stages of treatment or non-treatment were sought: 1) Addicts new in treatment within their first two weeks at either a methadone program or a therapeutic community for their first treatment attempt; 2) Friends, associates, contemporaries of these new in treatment addicts who had themselves never been in treatment and who were currently active addicts on the street; 3) Addicts retained in treatment at either a methadone program or a therapeutic community for more than six months but less than one year; 4) Friends of these successful treatment clients who had themselves been in some form of past narcotics treatment, but who were again currently active addicts on the street.

Each of the subjects was studied by means of an extensive systematic structured interview. The research was done in St. Louis, Missouri. The outpatient methadone clinic of the St. Louis State Hospital is the largest of the three methadone facilities available in the metropolitan area and the only one available to Missouri non-veterans. The clinic population is approximately 600 of whom 85% are black and 80% are male. Two therapeutic communities also cooperated in this research, the in-resident TC, Archway House, and an out-patient TC, The Narcotics Service Council (NASCO). The Archway House in-resident population averages between 35 and 70, consistently around 70% black, 80% male and all drug free. The client population of NASCO is approximately 220 with an average of 25 live-in residents at any one time. Of the clients, 85% are black, 95% are male, and all are in drug free treatment.

All subjects were 18 years or older; all were males; all were volunteers; all were paid for the interview. Ultimately only blacks were included in the study sample because of the client populations of the treatment facilities utilized. Records were used extensively to determine potential subjects from among the treatment populations. A record check at the other metropolitan area facilities was made as part of the screening of all potential subjects. An elaborate clinical screening procedure was used to select subjects.

RESULTS

There were 192 addicts included in the final population, of whom 25 had never been in drug treatment, 48 were newly enrolled in their first treatment attempt, 68 had been retained in successful treatment for between six months and one year, and 50 were past treatment dropouts who were currently active addicts again. The mean age of the entire population studied was 28.7 years old with a range of 18-50 years of age (median age 26). The addicts who had never sought treatment were the youngest group with a mean age of 24.3, somewhat younger than their most similar parallel group, those new in treatment for their first attempt, with a mean age of 26.5. This contrasted with the two older clusters, those in treatment more than six months, mean age 29.1, and treatment dropouts, who were the oldest, mean age 31.9.

The chronology of addiction will be presented for the entire population of 192 since the results do not differ significantly between the source groups. The age at which they first tried an illegal drug was about 14, with the youngest occurring at age 5 and the oldest occurring at age 35. For the 81% who dropped out of school, this first occurred at 16.2 years of age. Shortly thereafter, at a mean age of 16.5 years, their first arrest occurred. There was some tendency for the two younger groups to have somewhat earlier arrest contact (15.6) than for the two older groups (16.9). First use of heroin occurred at a mean age of 18.4 (range 10-35) and first addiction to heroin occurred at 19.9 years of age (range 13-35). This seems to have been followed promptly by their first drug related arrest at a mean age of 20.4 years. For those 166 who have attempted treatment, this first occurred at age 26.

The number of different drugs tried by this population to date varied from 3 to 34 different drugs with the mean being 13.3 different drugs ever tried. At some time, 77% of the sample had used drugs in at least 4 of the generally recognized pharmacologic categories of illicit drugs used.

The arrest history of the entire group seems to indicate that no heroin addict is anonymous. Only 4 subjects, or 2% had no arrests ever of any sort; thus 98% had at some time been arrested for some offense. The mean age at which this first occurred was 16.5 years; the age range was 6-37 years of age (median age 16). Approximately half of the group (52%) had had at least one juvenile arrest(under age 17). At some time in their lives, 94% had been arrested for a drug related offense; the mean age at which this first occurred was 20.4 years of age; the youngest age for this having occurred was 14 and the oldest 37(median age 19).

The experience of the population in formal schooling is revealing. Only 28% completed formal high school. The mean number of years of completed formal schooling for this group was 10.4 years, though the range varied from 5 years to 19 years. School was not easy for this group as indicated by the fact that more than 80% acknowledged at least some school problems prior to the age of 12 and 90% acknowledged problems from ages 12-14. Truancy was acknowledged by 90%, having begun at about the seventh grade(6.8). Also, about 80% of the group dropped out of formal schooling at some point during their childhood. School changes on the basis of disciplinary problems occurred to about 1/3 of the population. Of the entire group, 81% acknowledged trouble in school with author- ities, and these troubles led to suspensions for 65% of the entire group.

Their problems were not limited to the classroom. Non-school related misbehavior prior to age of 12 was acknowledged by 95% of the group, and beyond the age of 12 by everyone in the sample. In fact, for the period of age 12-14, over 3/4 of the group acknow- ledged 5 or more different types of misbehavior and antisocial

activities. These misbehavior and antisocial activities included
running away from home, stealing, reputation as a bad child,having
friends with bad reputations, staying out after curfew, fights
outside of school situations, impulsivity, fighting with weapons,
recklessness, lying other than to cover misbehavior, sexual
intercourse by this time, homosexual relations, non-parentally
sanctioned alcohol use, getting drunk, and using aliases.

The biologic mother and father in an intact family unit raised
43% of the subjects through the age of 16. An additional 35% were
raised by the biologic mother as the only continuous parent figure.
Of the sample, 15% had some first degree family member with a drug
problem. While children, about 44% of this population indicated
that they had admired some adult addict.

The adult experiences of this population indicate continuous
problems. By the time of this interview, about 77% of the sample
had had at least one legal marriage or one common law relationship
lasting at least 6 months, though for only 20% of that portion did
the relationship help motivate them towards treatment at any point.
More than 95% of the sample studied indicated some past or current
social drinking and 58% of that group indicated having had at
least some alcohol related problems in the past.

Attempts were made to characterize this population by their
usual occupational rank as determined by the Otis Dudley Duncan
(O.D.D.) socioeconomic score,[4] which ranges from 02 to 96.
However, 104 of the subjects did not have an occupation which
they and/or the interviewer were willing to characterize as a
usual one. For those who did have such a usual occupation (46%),
their mean O.D.D. was 22.9 as contrasted to the general population
with a mean of 36; for those subjects who did have a usual
occupation, O.D.D. score ranged from 4-67. Regarding their recent
work history, 54% indicated that they had during the past 12 months
worked at least 3 full months in a full time regular job. It is
also of note that while 92% of the group indicated having worked
at some time during the past 5 years, 57% experienced no work
related problems from their drug use.

DISCUSSION

The findings seem remarkably consistent across the three
studies. This is even more noteworthy when it is considered that
the present study was done a decade later, reports on addicts who
are presumbably part of the more recent epidemic of heroin use and
who were collected in a wholly different way from the previous
projects. The chronology of addiction presented in this report
indicates the similarity of the four groups here interviewed. It
appears that the two younger groups are walking in the identical
footsteps previously trod by the older addicts, those retained in
treatment and the treatment dropouts. Thus, the cycle of truancy,
illicit drug use, school dropout, arrest, heroin use, heroin
addiction, drug arrest, treatment attempt, is a general and
consistent finding.

Looking more closely at the entire population reveals much additional information. That these addicts have tried 13 different drugs in at least 4 pharmacologic categories is remarkable. In light of this,however, it is not surprising to find that almost 60% have already had some alcohol related problem even though they are only 28 years old. This population clearly has a propensity to significant polydrug experimentation, and, given heroin addiction as an indicator, they appear to not be able to cope with any drug use.

Poor adjustment and antisocial behavior has been a problem for the study population since childhood. In school they were clearly difficult youngsters beginning prior to age 12 and predating first drug use with school problems, truancy, disciplinary actions, suspensions, transfers, and finally dropping out in the 10th grade. Outside of school, also, they were early on involved in a variety of deviant progressively more antisocial activities before drug experimentation began. In this context, first drug use probably ought to be considered just another antisocial event in a sequence of such events, rather than being any triggering or causative event.

In summary, therefore, it would appear that the current black male heroin addict began antisocial activities in childhood which included school problems and non-school related misbehaviors, began illicit drug use at age 14, dropped out of school at age 16 and shortly thereafter was first arrested, began heroin use at age 18 and within about 18 months became addicted, soon thereafter began having drug related police problems, achieved a marital situation but often did not achieve a usual occupation, and was ready to attempt drug treatment for the first time at age 26.

This study was supported in part by Public Health Service Grants MH 12984 (DA 00023), DA 01110, MH 13002, MH 05804, DA 4RG008. Dr. Halikas is the recipient of a National Institute of Mental Health Career Teacher award in Narcotics and Drug Abuse, MH 12984 (DA 00023).
Dr. Rimmer is presently Instructor in Mathematics in Psychiatry, Harvard Medical School, Department of Psychiatry.

REFERENCES

1. C.D. Chambers and A.D. Moffett, Negro Opiate Addiction, 11:178-201, in J.C. Ball and C.D. Chambers, The Epidemiology of Opiate Addiction in the United States, Charles C. Thomas, Springfield, Ill. 1970.
2. C.D. Chambers, A.D. Moffett, J.P. Jones, Demographic Factors Associated with Negro Opiate Addiction, Int. J. Addict., 3(2):329-343 (1968).
3. L. Robins and G. Murphy, Drug Use in a Normal Population of Young Negro Men, Am. J. of Public Health,57:1580-1596 (1967).
4. P.M. Blau, O.D. Duncan, The American Occupational Structure, John Wiley and Sons Inc., New York, 1967.

IDENTIFYING INDIVIDUALS AT RISK AMONG PUERTO RICAN ADOLESCENTS[1]

Ronald L. Nuttall   Ena Vazquez Nuttall[2] Carl Ostermann

Yolanda Zayas   Raúl A. Muñoz

Laboratory for Statistical and Policy Research - Boston College
and
Health and Social Studies, Inc. Hato Rey, Puerto Rico

This study is part of a larger project concerned with developing predictive models for adolescent use of heroin and other drugs.
The aim of the research is to develop a set of empirically validated
models which will enable us to predict which adolescents are in
greatest risk of later developing drug abusing behavior patterns.
In 1968 Nuttall and Nuttall (1) gathered data from students attending seconday schools in the Bayamón Norte school district in Puerto
Rico. In 1975 documentary and reputational data were obtained to
determine educational status, drug abuse and other deviant behavior
recorded for these 5,000 some young people. This paper describes
the results of our first model using discriminant function procedures to predict four levels of risk groups.

Theoretical Background - Researchers in the field of drug abuse
have devoted a great amount of their attention to studying the
relationship between family structure and family dynamics and drug
use and abuse. Structural factors such as completeness or incomple-
tness of the family is one of the areas most commonly studied. Many
of these studies have found that addicts are more likely to come
from one-parent families than are non-addicts (2,3,4,5). However
the comleteness of a family does not assure that it will provide
the quality of parent-child interaction which will keep a young
person out of drugs.

We expected that there would be three main realms of variables
which would be related to abuse of heroin and other deviant behavior.
These realms were: Family Structure and Dynamics, Personality of
the Child, and Social and Peer Group Influences. In the Family
Realm it was predicted that individuals lacking one or more parents

---

1. This research was supported by Grant Number 3 R01 DA00738-01S1
    NAD from the National Institute on Drug Abuse.
2. Also at University of Massachusetts, Amherst

would be more vulnerable to heroin use than were people who came from complete families.

Among those young people with their parents present, the degree of drug use has been associated with the quality of the parent-child relationships, especially with the same sex parent. In the 1968 study parent-child relationships were measured by the Spanish adaptation of the Children's Report of Parent Behavior Inventory (CRPBI) of Schaefer (6). Three factors of the CRPBI were identified: Acceptance vs. Rejection, Hostile Psychological Control, and Firm Discipline vs. Lax Discipline. These factors were similar to those found in similar investigations in this country (6). It was predicted that students who perceived their parents as not very acceptant, controlling in a hostile way, and lax in their discipline would be at greater risk of later becoming users of heroin.

In the personality realm, 14 dimensions of personality were measured in 1968 using a Spanish adaptation of Cattell's High School Personality Questionnaire (HSPQ).

In the realm of social factors, it was predicted that the lower the socio-economic status of the students's family, the more likely he would become a heroin user.

Risk Groups - Group membership was developed from examination of records during 1975. Four risk groups were developed for this research. The highest risk group consisted of young people who were in the 1968 data base and were also found to have records in the police files (96 people), in the files of drug prevention centers (35), drug treatment centers (31), Narcotics and Drug Addiction Division (17), or in newspapers articles of drug related arrests (5). The total for this high risk group was 162 people since some people were found in more than one source.

The medium risk group consisted of those people who were in the 1968 data base, were not in the high risk group, and who were recorded in the files of the school social workers as needing help with social, psychological, educational, or financial problems. Also included in the medium risk group were people who were siblings of any person in the high risk group. There were 214 people in this medium risk group.

The third group, called the high school dropout group, consisted of those people in the 1968 data base who were not in the high risk group nor in the medium risk group and who were not recorded as having graduated from high school. This group totaled 2,119 people.

The fourth group, the high school graduate group, consisted of those people in the 1968 data base who were not included in the high or the medium risk groups and who were recorded as having graduated from high school. There were 2,808 people in this group.

Statistical Treatment - The assignment of groups was made in 1975 from an examination of records and then this group membership data was merged with the 1968 data base using the Statistical Package for the Social Sciences (SPSS) system of computer programs.

The purpose of this research was to develop a statistical model which allowed the discrimination among these four groups. The procedure used is called Discriminant Function Analysis. Discriminant function analysis can be looked at in two ways, as a practical approach and as a theoretical tool. The practical aspects lie in that using an established statistical discriminant function model it should be possible to predict which students are most likely to belong to which of the four risk groups some six years later. This would allow counseling and other early intervention procedures to be targetted at those students most in need. Such focussing of efforts should be more effective than developing broad based counseling or drug education programs for students who are highly likely to be low risk anyway.

The theoretical aspect of the approach comes in when it is expected that certain variables or aspects of a child's life will lead to high risk. The discriminant function analysis may, or may not, find empirically that these variables or aspects are indeed relevant to risk prediction.

A discriminant function analysis is a specialized form of multiple regression analysis, where the dependent variable is group membership rather than a continuous variable. When only two groups are being discriminated , a discriminant function is identical to a multiple regression where the dependent variable is 1 if the unit is in Group A, and 0 if the unit is not. When there are more than two groups, as in the present study, a set of linear functions is developed which maximizes the between groups variance relative to the within groups variance.

Within each realm of variables a step-wise discriminant function analysis was run. This required the elimination of those people for whom complete data was not available. After the best predictors in each realm had been found, they were combined into one set of predictors. It is this final analysis which is reported.

Results

With four risk groups it is possible to generate three discriminant functions. However only two discriminant functions were found to be statistically significant. Table I and Figure 1 give the results of the positions of the four risk groups on these two functions. The high risk group was low on both functions while the high school graduate group was high on both functions. The medium risk was low on the second function but medium on the first. The first function contrasts the high school graduates, who score

high on this function with the high school dropouts and the high
risk group who score low on it. The second function contrasts the
high and medium risk groups (who score low) with the high school
graduates and high school dropouts (who scored high).

Table II presents the variables forming these two functions.
This table gives the standardized weights necessary to produce the
functions. The first function is seen to be highly related to the
grade level the student had achieved in 1968. Generally those
students who had been able to make it into the 12th grade were more
likely to be able to graduate from high school and to keep out of
trouble than were children who were only in the seventh or eighth
grade.

The second discriminant function, which contrasts the high and
medium risk groups with the high school graduates and dropouts, is
more interesting. The high function values (Good) end of this index
goes to those children whose parents did not use hostile psychological control measures and who used firm discipline. These low risk
children also tended to be more "Tenderminded" and to hope for high
levels of education. They also tended to live in a family owned
home and to have moved to the community rather recently. On the
other hand the high risk and medium risk students tended to have
parents who were lax in their discipline and who used hostile
psychological control methods. These children at higher risk also
tended to be "Toughminded" rather than "Tenderminded". While
this personality trait is the major difference in personality
between boys and girls, it is the psychological trait rather than
the sex of the child itself, which was predictive. The children
at high risk were more likely to live in housing projects or rented
apartments than were low risk students and also were more likely to
have had a father absent when they were younger than seven years.

Discussion

It has been found to be possible to develop a discriminant
function model distinguishing among these four risk groups. The
Wilk's Lambda was .81 indicating that about 19 percent of the
between groups variance was accounted for in the model, leaving
81 percent not accounted for. Most of the expected relationships
were found, except that high risk group children did not differ
from low risk children in parental Acceptance.

Cautions must be used in relation to this study since it was
conducted in only one district in Puerto Rico and may not hold in
other areas. Also the assignment of students to risk groups was
by means of records only. Some people may have committed crimes
or been involved with drugs and yet have escaped having their names
listed in police or drug treatment agency files. Also the police
files include many people whose alleged crimes had nothing to do
with drugs. Even records of high school graduation may have errors.

Table I

MEANS OF RISK GROUPS ON TWO DISCRIMINANT FUNCTIONS

Risk Groups	Function One	Function Two
High Risk (Police & Drug Lists)	-.48	-.57
Medium Risk (Social Workers Lists)	-.05	-.47
High School Dropouts	-.53	.06
High School Graduates	.35	.02

Table II

STANDARDIZED WEIGHTS OF VARIABLES FORMING TWO DISCRIMINANT FUNCTIONS

Variables	Function One	Function Two
Family Related		
Hostile Psychological Control	-.10	-.40
Lax Discipline	-.07	-.45
Father Home First Seven Years	-.17	.08
Personality Related		
HSPQ Factor I - Tenderminded	.10	.37
Amount of Education Hoped For	.06	.33
Social Conditions Related		
Live in Family Owned Home	-.12	.13
Time in Present Community	.21	-.24
School Related		
Grade Level Achieved (1968)	.86	-.25

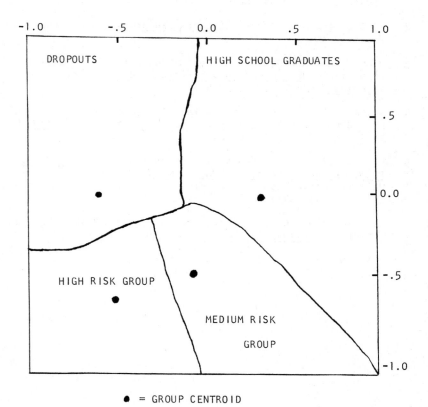

● = GROUP CENTROID

Figure 1. Territorial Map of Discriminant Score 1 (Horizontal) vs. Discriminant Score 2 (Vertical)

References

1. R.L. Nuttall, D.H. Smith, M. Siegelman, E.V. Nuttall, G.H. Smith, and P.W. Holland, Predicting Grade Point Averages. Report No. 1, Study of Factors Affecting Student Achievement. Laboratory for Statistical and Policy Research, Boston College Chestnut Hill, Mass. 02167 (1968).

2. R. Blum and Associates, Students and Drugs. San Francisco: Jossey-Bass, (1970).

3. J.M. Weiner and J.H. Egan Heroin Addiction in an adolescent population, Journal of the American Academy of Child Psychiatry, (1973), 12, 49-58.

4. N. Tec, Family and differential involvement with marijuana: A study of suburban teenagers. Journal of Marriage and the Family, (1970), 32, 656-664.

5. C.S. Garcia and J.A. Rossello Estudio de la Magnitud del Problema de las Drogas en Puerto Rico. Depto. de Psiquiatria, Esc. de Medicina, U. de Puerto Rico, San Juan, Puerto Rico (1971).

6. E.S. Schaefer, Children's reports of parental behavior: an inventory, Child Development, 1965, 36, 413-424.

SPANISH DRUG REHABILITATION RESEARCH PROJECT

Jose Szapocznik
Mercedes Arca Scopetta

Department of Psychiatry
Division of Addiction Sciences
University of Miami School of Medicine
Miami, Florida

Dade County contains large clusters of Cuban and Puerto Rican populations. A large proportion of these Latino populations reside in underpriviledged areas where poverty and high levels of social disorganization, as well as the desintegration of the traditional extended families' supportive network, combine to create special problems. A crucially detrimental aspect of this social situation is the reported high incidence of drug abuse among both Cubans and Puerto Ricans. Yet, because of the limited availability of physical and mental health services within these communities, and the unwillingness on the part of the Spanish-American to become involved with Anglo-operated programs, these populations have been highly under-represented in drug treatment programs. In recognition of this situation, the University of Miami Division of Addiction Sciences, in collaboration with Dade County's comprehensive Drug Program, established the program described in this paper. Its purpose was to serve the Spanish speaking community by attending to their mental health needs. However, the major focus was on individuals experiencing problems associated with the use and abuse of drugs.

Philosophy

The treatment of persons from a Latin cultural minority requires a specially trained bilingual and bicultural staff familiar with the problems of clients who are linguistically and/or culturally handicapped and who are experiencing the stresses of acculturation. Cultural relativity and sensitivity to ethnic diversity is a requisite to bridge the communication gap which otherwise becomes an obstacle to effective detection, client involvement and treatment. Essentially an immigrant minority, most Latinos in Dade County have sought to retain as much of the familiar as possible. Since most Anglo programs have been built around cultural characteristics that differ to a large extent from those

of the Spanish-speaking people, then those programs are in effect
unavailable to Latinos.

Our programs are built upon the premise that detection, involvement and treatment of the Latin clients necessitates a culturally sensitive approach which incorporates: (1) in-depth knowledge of the language, culture and acculturation problems of the
client population; (2) conceptualization and treatment of the
problem in a family framework; (3) intervention in those systems
which are contributing to, or affected by the problem: (4) an intensive outreach component to identify and engage potential service users; (5) development of community support systems around
the client in treatment; and, (6) case identification and early
intervention by collaborating with other relevant community programs.

Although there is really no conceptual framework at this
time that will provide all the answers to the many problems that
are arising in the acculturation process, it is through the study
of ecological adaptation and interaction that the behavioral
scientist can gain a clearer understanding of the changes occurring
among the Latins in the Miami area, and from a socio-clinical viewpoint, of the conflicts that are being experiencd by Latin families,
and particularly those of Cuban extraction. These conflicts and
their relationship to psychosocial dysfunction constitute the
emphasis of our services. Our conceptual theoretical framework
for a treatment population is alcoholistic model of social ecological phenomenology and the general systems approach. These
terms refer to a way of thinking and style of operation rather than
to a well formed theoretical structure, but it offers the counselor
the flexibility needed to design innovative treatment approaches
in an effort to meet his client's needs at many ecological levels.
Furthermore, this approach takes into consideration families as
well as nonfamily systems, and is easily adapted to all social
classes. It is our aim to emphasize the counselors' activities on
concrete action and involvement in the client's entire ecological
field.

The Developmental History of Services

In 1972, when the Drug Rehabilitation and Referral Services
in Spanish Neighborhoods was established under an OEO grant, its
primary purpose was to provide grassroot services to poverty level
Cuban and Puerto Rican drug abusers. Following the OEO model,
services were provided by paraprofessionals and young professionals
in inviting storefront locations. The emphasis was on the provision of comprehensive drug rehabilitation referral services,
functioning as a bridge between the community and the established
social service system. Clearly the emphasis was on attending to
the client's total social ecology.

Within an ecologically oriented mental health delivery service model, the local populations were engaged through a variety of activities such as high school equivalency classes, softball, and football games. Counselling was provided to youngsters identified as serious behavioral problems by the school system. Delinquent and unemployed youngsters frequently "dropped-in" to "rap" with the counselors in the clinics' open ambiance. In addition, outreach programs provided reality oriented counseling and family outreach programs for many incarcerated individuals. Through all these means, it became possible to provide services to populations which had traditionally avoided formal mental health services. In this way, we fulfilled our earliest mandate to act as a bridge between hitherto neglected Latino populations and the social service delivery system.

In July 1973, as a result of the abolishment of OEO, the total project was transferred to the National Institute of Drug Abuse (NIDA). The programs continued to develop in the direction of ecological, systems oriented therapeutic interventions. By the time a continuation application was submitted to NIDA for F'75, we had developed an innovative approach to the treatment of Latino drug abusers. This treatment model was based on systems theory, and an ecological scope. Hence, its name Ecological Systems model.

In order to make a contribution at the national level it will be necessary to test not only the effectiveness of our innovative treatment model, but also its effectiveness relative to traditional methods in the treatment of Latino drug abusers. For this purpose a scientific study was designed under the new NIDA funded project, the Spanish Drug Rehabilitation Research Project. This study submits our innovative and exciting Ecological Systems model to a rigorous experimental investigation. Within an experimental design, it compares the relative effectiveness of an Ecological Systems model to one based on more traditional intra-client approaches to therapy.

The Project and its Functions

The Spanish Drug Rehabilitation Research Project has been established to: (1) determine the needs of the drug abusing Spanish speaking population of Dade County; (2) develop and evaluate culturally sensitive mental health care delivery systems for the treatment of these individuals; and, (3) to investigate the causes and correlates of psychosocial dysfunction, including substance abuse, in the local Spanish speaking populations. For this purpose the National Institute of Drug Abuse has awarded a three-year research demonstration grant to Mercedes A. Scopetta, Ph.D., Assistant Professor, and James N. Sussex, M.D., Chairman of the Department of Psychiatry at the University of Miami School of Medicine.

Organizationally, the project consists of six units: Administration, Research and Evaluation, Training and Clinical Coordination, the Family Therapy Research Unit, and two clinical research units, Encuentro and La Casa Abierta. The first five units are located (2121 S.W. 27th Ave., Miami, Florida) in the Little Havana area, a heavily Cuban section, and La Casa Abierta is located (3240 N.W. 2nd Ave., Miami, Florida) in the Wynwood area, a section identified as a Puerto Rican political and cultural center. These interrelated units were developed for a single unifying purpose: to demonstrate the relative effectiveness of a variety of mental health services with the local Latin drug abuse population, while taking advantage of the most advanced scientific knowledge in the areas of psychotherapy and behavior change, cross-cultural psychology, research and evaluation.

The clinical research endeavours of the Spanish Drug Rehabilitation Research Project are extremely complex and elaborate, requiring a staff competent to provide mental health services as well as to conduct clinical research in drug abuse. Therefore, all of the staff must undergo extensive and intensive training in the development of necessary specialized clinical and research skills. It has been necessary to provide training to most of the clinical/research staff in the areas of interviewing skills, crisis intervention, psychopathology, data collection, research design and methodology, as well as in the use of specific research instruments such as the Psychiatric Status Schedule, the Goal Attainment Scale, and the Client Information Form, among others. Furthermore, it has not been sufficient to provide general training in these clinical/research areas, but training adaptations and modifications which permits the administration of these instruments in a culturally sensitive and appropriate fashion also had to be taught. In addition to the clinical/research inservice training program, the staff has been involved in a series of inservices as well as extramural workshops and seminars to improve clinical skills and knowledge about family centered psychotherapeutic approaches, the latter representing the major focus of all of our projects. Perhaps, the most crucial function of our training program has been to rekindle in our Anglo-American trained, bicultural staff, their skills in relating to the Latin people.

Following such an explanation, it becomes clear that most of the program's resources are devoted to the rigorous processes involved in research and data collection, leaving a limited amount of time and resources for non-research related direct services. Nevertheless, frequently it becomes necessary to provide services to individuals who cannot be included in the research studies. Such services as crisis intervention, short term therapy and referrals are provided routinely. Because of the Latino community's serious underutilization of drug programs other than our own, and because of the lack of available mental health facilities for the Spanish minority, our project also feels the responsibility of providing at least these minimum community services.

CLINICAL ISSUES IN PSYCHOTHERAPY RESEARCH WITH LATINS

Mercedes Arca Scopetta, Ph.D.

Cecilia Alegre, M.S., M.A.

Department of Psychiatry
University of Miami School of Medicine
Miami, Florida

Throughout the past fifteen years some 750,000 Cuban nationals have emigrated to the United States. More than half have remained in the Miami area. Many after first settling somewhere else have returned to Dade County. Presently, 55% of the City of Miami population are of Spanish origin. The Spanish Drug Rehabilitation Research Project addresses itself to the Latin population of the city, mainly the Cuban population.

When families are dislocated from one culture to another adaptation to the new environment must take place in order to obtain a new ecological balance between the family systems and non-family systems. This is known as the acculturation process. In the process of acculturation the families use their native culture in an effort to cope successfully with the demands of the new dominant culture. Only certain aspects of the native culture of the immigrants can make a positive contribution to the process of adaptation, while other values, customs, attitudes and traditions must be discarded for they become obsolete in the new milieu. During this process of acculturation, in which the family discovers the values, attitudes, traditions, and behavior that are functional in the new culture, as well as those that are no longer operative, conflicts and anxieties arise at many levels that have to be dealt with and resolved.

It must also be recognized that any group makes use of only certain parts of the environment. These parts are selected on the basis of its technology, social systems, and value orientation. At the same time certain aspects of the new environment influence strongly the life style of the new group, so that it is a two way process of interaction and mutual influences that is operative in the acculturation process, and that account for, not only the changes in the individuals, but also the transformations that are occurring in an area such as Miami during the last fifteen years.

Though there is really no conceptual framework at this time that will provide all the answers to the many questions that are arousing in the acculturation process and in the existing systems, it is through the studies of ecological adaptation and interaction that the behavioral scientist can gain a clearer understanding of the changes occurring in the Miami area due to the Latin influence, and from a socio-clinical viewpoint, of the conflicts that are being experienced by the Latin families, particularly those of Cuban extraction. These conflicts and their relationship to drug abuse constitute the core of our investigation.

Many Cuban families have now been in the United States for as long as fifteen years. Others have arrived through the Freedom Flights within the last years. A large number of adolescents and young adults have attended American schools through the formative years of their life and have been socialized to some degree by American institutions.

The American school environment, the peer system, mass media, movies, etc., have a tremendous impact on the growing child, accelerating the acculturation process of the Cuban youth. Even in families of more recent arrival, an assymetrical acculturation process is seen to be taking place, for young people more readily assimilate the values of the new culture, while their parents are slower to acculturate. When compared to non-immigrant families the assymetrical acculturation process taking place in the families of Cuban exiles and their adolescents increases the gap existing between the two generations. It is to be expected then that more serious intergenerational conflict and stress exist in the Latin family than in American families.

When a family mobilizes itself to seek treatment, it normally comes to our program, with an adolescent or young adults, as the indexed patient.

In many treatment facilities through out the country, the family unit is seen as the patient rather than the individual. In families of Spanish origin, this is a critical issue that must be considered, for treatment of the young frequently fails because the family, its needs, its values and traditions are not given sufficient and adequate attention.

Traditionally the Spanish family has consisted of a closed and extended system. Family values and ties are deep and all-pervasive. Family values and roles are socialized by the family and reinforced by other ecological systems to which individual members may belong (social, educational, legal, financial, and even political). Family influence encompasses alsmost all aspects of an individual's life. The family thus becomes an individual's strongest supportive system. The family not only rears the child, but also continues to

determine his position in society and subsequently his sense of
self and family identification. The family works to supply his
emotional, religious, financial and political needs to such an extent that the individual often does not, or cannot, escape family
dependence. Whether living at home with his family or separated
from it, his relationship to the rest of the family members seem
to carry a great deal of emotional weight.

The Spanish Program originally focused its attention on the adolescents and young adults with drug related problems. As family dys-
functionality and its effect on the young people became apparent,
parents and families were invited to come and participate in, and
take advantage of, the services offered. An attempt was made to
bring the whole family into therapy. Parents often came by themselves while adolescents worked in group or individual counseling.
More often, whenever the family (or parents) came to, and remained
in therapy improvement in the adolescent's behavior was faster than
in those clients seen without the parent's intervention.

Family Therapy seems to foster a therapeutic climate at home which
contributes to the outcome of therapy for the individual identified
as patient.

Though some of the Latin families have been in this country for
longer periods, many remain unacculturated, have language problems,
and belong to a low socioeconomic class, so that problems are experienced at many levels.

Major issues then that must be taken into consideration in treatment with a Latin population have been delineated in our program
as follows:

1. Intergenerational conflicts within the family as children
   acculturate more rapidly than the parents.
2. Value conflicts that emerge between other societal institutions, such as the schools, churches, government agencies and the family.
3. Problems of language barriers and communications deficits
   within the family, as the children begin to forget Spanish
   and the parents have not learned English.
4. Language barriers due to which the family members experience increased tension and anxiety as they attempt to interact with the dominant culture.

Though it can be said that American families experience similar
problems, it is evident that the Spanish family has some unique
problems that pertain to its special condition as it attempts to
survive, adapt, and function in a new and foreign environment.

To deal with these unique issues the Spanish Drug Rehabilitation
Research Project has designed a mental health care delivery system

that takes into consideration the acculturation process, the strong family ties and emotional dependence of Spanish families, the language difficulty and the proliferation of problems at many levels that these families frequently experience.

In order to do this, the program has sought and employed bilingual and bicultural staff members, familiar with the language level, the culture of origin of the client and the dominant culture. These counselors serve as models for the client, for they themselves have adapted and are functioning in the new environment in an effective manner, without having lost their identity nor cultural heritage. Thus, these mental health professionals and paraprofessionals can serve as cultural brokers for the clients and the different systems with which they interact.

In addition to the utilization of bilingual bicultural mental health workers, the program conceptualizes problems according to the theoretical framework of family systems theory.

Briefly, systems theory assumes that all significant people in the family unit play a part in the way the family members function in relation to each other and in the way the symptom is chosen and finally erupts. Misuse or abuse of drugs then, is seen as a symptom of family anxiety, disruption, etc.

Change then in the functioning of one family members is automatically followed by compensatory change in another family member. Systems theory then focuses on the functioning of a system and its component parts. (Bowen, 1973).

In this framework then, a family therapy approach conducted by bilingual bicultural counselors would be the treatment of choice for this population.

In order to attend to the multiproblems these families experience, frequently an ecological family systems approach is implemented. In this model, the therapist works at the interface between the systems, gathering meaningful data, restructuring the family transactions, and the interaction of the family members and significant members of other systems that are of relevancy in the life of the client.

Bibliography
Bowen, M. Alcoholism and the family system. The Family. The Center for Family Learning. New Rochelle, N.Y. Vol. 1, No.1, Nov. 1973.

INNOVATIVE TREATMENT MODELS WITH LATINS

Jose Szapocznik
Mercedes Arca Scopetta

Department of Psychiatry
Division of Addiction Sciences
University of Miami, School of Medicine
Miami, Florida

The staff of the Spanish Drug Rehabilitation Research Project deve-loped an innovatvie approach to the treatment of Latino drug abusers. This treatment model was based on systems theory within an ecological scope; hence, its name Ecological-Systems Model. In order to test the effectiveness of this model compared to more traditional mental health models, an experimental study was de-signed. This study evaluates the relative effectiveness of the Ecological-Systems treatment approach and another treatment model based on traditional intra-client approaches to therapy, referred to as Intramural. These two treatment philosophies hypothesize different locus for the etiology of dysfunction, and consequently, they also differ in their locus of therapeutic interventions. In the Intramural model, both problem assessment and therapeutic interventions take place within the relationship of the therapist and the client; hence, the name Intramural: within the "wall" of the therapist-client relationship. However, within Ecological-Systems theory, problem assessment and therapeutic interventions take place at the interface between the client and those systems in the client's ecology impinging upon the client.

Treatment Models

1. Intramural Therapy. Intramural therapy allows the therapist to use most traditional psychiatric and psychological modes of counseling and therapy as long as therapeutic interventions are confined to the therapist-client relationship. In this category can be included most Psychoanalytic, Regerian, Gestalt, Reality Oriented and other intra-client approaches to therapy.

2. Ecological-Systems Theory. According to Ecological-Systems theory, the etiology of dysfunction is in the nature of the interactions between a dysfunctioning individual and relevant ecological systems impinging on the individual. Therefore, it

is postulated that dysfunctional behavior is maintained and supported to some extent by the total ecology, including the client and other systems in the client's ecology for which there is some kind of a "pay-off" in maintaining the status quo. Further, it is postulated that both, the dysfunctional client and his ecological systems contribute to the labeling processes which eventuates in the identified patient label. Finally, it follows that the responsibility for dysfunction is shared by the total ecology, including the client.

The first step of an ecological evaluation is to identify the relevant systems impinging on the dysfunctional client. Diagnosing the etiology of dysfunction includes evaluating what the different systems "do" and "how" they contribute to the maintenance of dysfunctional behavior in the client. Therefore, relational issues at the interface between the identified patient and the immediate ecology are assessed, such as: (1) the clarity of boundaries between systems; (2) the delientation of lines of authority; (3) the existence of incompatible demands; (4) the patterns of relationships between systems; (5) the intensity of relationships between systems along a continuum of overinvolvement at one extreme to disengagement at the other extreme; and, (6) the relational patterns within and among systems most ameanable to restructuring.

Following an assessment of the interactions between the relevant systems and the dysfunctional client, tensions at the interface between the systems are identified. In the process of evaluating the relationship among systems, the ecologically oriented therapist also makes a series of hypotheses about the kinds of relationships necessary for effective functioning. Subsequently, a process of testing the different systems begins in order to identify the systems which are most ameanable to intervention and change. Finally, the therapist intervenes in order to restructure the systems' interactions so as to create a set of systems' relationships that will permit the more effective functioning of the client.

Methodological Issues
With an understanding of the nature of the treatment studies conducted by the Spanish Drug Rehabilitation Research Project, some of the methodological issues and concerns that have arisen are briefly discussed below. These issues involve the development of a clinical/research staff, the monitoring of experimental conditions, cultural and clinical considerations, the development of appropriate assessment instruments, and the research program's relationship to the community.

1. Development of a clinical/research staff. Perhaps, crucial in the implementation of our research studies has been the development of research skills and interests in a primarily clinical

staff. The clinical research endeavors of the Spanish Drug
Rehabilitation Research Project are extremely complex and elaborate, requiring a staff competent to provide mental health
services as well as to conduct clinical research in drug abuse.
Therefore, staff members must undergo extensive and intensive
training in the development of necessary specialized clinical
and research skills. It has been necessary to provide training
to the staff in the areas of interviewing skills, crisis intervention, psychopathology, cultural relativity, psychotherapy,
family therapy, systems analyses, data collection, research design and methodology, as well as in the use of specific research instruments such as the Psychiatric Status Schedule (5,
6), the Goal Attainment Scale (3), and the Client Information
Form, among others. Furthermore, it has not been sufficient
to provide general training in these clinical/research areas,
but training adaptations and modifications also had to be
taught which permit the administration of these instruments in
a culturally sensitive and appropriate fashion.

2. Monitoring the experimental conditions. In order to compare
the relative effectiveness of two different treatment models,
it is necessary that the clinical research staff implement each
treatment model accurately and that the distinguishing differences between the two models be maintained. However, it has
been difficult for the counsellors to adhere exclusively to the
Intramural mode of therapy when clients assigned to that experimental condition were perceived as benefiting from ecological
interventions. Paradoxically, the staffs' interventions in
ecological systems have in many instances not attained the level of sophisticated conceptualization and practice which this
model requires. Consequently, a comprehensive program of training and supervision has been instituted to further improve adherence to the experimental treatment conditions, as well as to
continue to improve the quality of services.

3. Cultural and clinical considerations. Cultural and clinical
considerations are discussed by Scopetta & Alegre (4), King (2)
and Gonzalez-Reigosa (1).

4. Assessment instruments. Evaluating change in a Latin population introduces a variety of methodological problems. When
most measures and instruments available have been developed in
English and tailored to non-Latin populations, it becomes necessary to identify and/or build measures and instruments that not
only have cross-cultural validity but that are also acceptable
to our client/subject population. Several such instruments have
already been identified to be used in the evaluation of the
client population of the Spanish Drug Rehabilitation Research
Projects. Perhaps the cornerstone of our treatment evaluation
is the Psychiatric Status Schedule (5,6). This instrument is
designed to improve the research value of clinical judgments of

psychopathology, psychosocial functioning and role functioning.
A Spanish standardized version of the instrument is available.
In addition, its cross-cultural validity is enhanced by the fa
fact that a Latino group was included in the validation and
standardization sample. Another measure of treatment effectiveness used in our studies is the Goal Attainment Scaling procedure (3). This instrument is designed to evaluate the outcome
of treatment along change criteria that are specifically tailored to each client's needs. The instrument and appropriate
instructions have been translated into Spanish by our staff.
Since the Goal Attainment Scaling procedure is a "process of
evaluation" actually divorced from any content per se, it has
not raised serious problems of cross-cultural validity. Various other measures of family treatment effectiveness are under
consideration. These will be discussed in a subsequent report.

5. The Research project's relationship to the community. Develop-
    ing a working relationship with the community to enable the im-
    plementation of the studies has been an extremely complex task.
    For one, clients are likely to reject participation in a re-
    search study in which the specific treatment assignment is ran-
    dom. Consequently, the project's image among the target client
    populations must be that of a service treatment program. How-
    ever, a service image becomes detrimental when the community
    complains that the project's cost per client in treatment is too
    too high, without an understanding of the complexities of clini-
    cal research. Another problem emerged when it became apparent
    that both treatment models under investigation and the rigorous
    evaluation of their effectiveness seemed inappropriate for some
    target client populations. Thus, in a clinical unit located
    in a small, poverty-ridden Latino ghetto, clients who perceived
    their needs in terms of social and economic crises found our
    intake procedure irrelevant. Further, as a result of their
    crisis orientation to social services they failed to become en-
    gaged in treatment, and consistently failed to return for post
    treatment evaluations.

Conclusions
The five areas of methodological issues discussed are a sample of
the problems that can be expected whenever rigorous research studies are implemented in a community setting with Latino clients.
They are indicative of the multi-dimensionality of the task of conducting clinical research in applied settings.

REFERENCES

1. Gonzalez-Reigosa, F., Levels of acculturation and psychosocial disruption in the Cuban-American family. In Proceedings: Second National Drug Abuse Conference, NAPAN, New York, 1975.

2. King, O.E., Staff in-service training: a module for professional upgrading and socialization. In Proceedings: Second National Drug Abuse Conference. NAPAN, New York, 1975.

3. Kiresuk, T.J., and Sherman, R.E., Goal Attainment scaling: A general method for evaluating comprehensive community mental health programs, Community Mental Health Journal, 4 (6) (1968).

4. Scopetta, M.A., Clinical issues in psychotherapy with Latins. In Proceedings: Second National Drug Abuse Conference, NAPAN, New York, 1975.

5. Spitzer, R.L., Endicott, J., and Cohen, G.M., Psychiatric Status Exam. Department of Psychiatry, Columbia University, 1968.

6. Spitzer, R.L., Endicott, J., and Cohen, G.M., The Psychiatric Status Schedule: A technique for evaluating psychopathology and impairment in role functioning, Archives of General Psychiatry 23: 41-55, (1970).

FORMAL THEATER AS A NATIVE AMERICAN DRUG
PREVENTION/ALTERNATIVE PROGRAM

Shirley E. Ehn
Jay C. Whitecrow

Tulsa Indian Council on Alcoholism and Drug Abuse

The Problem

There is a recurring pattern from generation to generation of
alcoholism and drug addiction among Native Americans. The Tulsa
Native American population is characterized by: Low socio-economic
status, low educational level, high alcoholism rates among parent
group, and lack of long term community ties.

The 1970 census figures show the heaviest concentration of Indian people to be in the downtown/West Tulsa area. The 1975 City
of Tulsa figures show the heaviest geographic distribution of low
income families to be in the exact same areas. The Tulsa School
System rank order charts for subsidized lunch programs for low income students name schools with the highest percentage of low income
students. These schools are located in the same areas as the low
income, high Indian population area.

The substance Abuse Among Native Americans in Oklahoma report
presented to the Joint Criminal Jurisprudence Committee in 1975
cites a dropout rate for the Oklahoma Native American juvenile of
10-15% higher than for the rest of the population and states that
49% plus fail to finish their education. The Tulsa school population figures show a decline of 316 Native American students from
junior to senior high school. The total junior high school enrollment figures for Native Americans is 771. The total senior high
school enrollment figures for Native Americans is 455. The Tulsa
Public School Research and Planning Department assumes this decline
to be the result of dropouts. Dropout figures are not kept racially in the Tulsa Public School System.

The high incidence of alcoholism among Native Americans in
Oklahoma is supported by data which reveals that death rate from
cirrhosis of the liver is nine times that of the white population

644

and six times greater than that of the black population. The Substance Abuse Report states that 30,000 to 40,000 Native Americans
in Oklahoma are affected by alcoholism. Our personal observations
are that 100% of Native American families are affected by the
disease of alcoholism. The Tulsa Public Drunk arrests for Indian
adults went up from 842 in 1974 to 985 in 1975 while the total arrests for public drunk went down. NIAAA data confirms that alcoholism rates among school youth are highest for Native Americans
(16%). Client Oriented Data Acquisition Process shows that 65%
of Indian Admissions to State Drug treatment programs are 17 years
and younger. The INCOG Juvenile Data Analysis shows the high den-
sity-low income Native American areas in Tulsa to be the areas of
highest delinquency for Indian juveniles.

The increase in Tulsa Native American population from 1973 of
11,041 to 1976 of 15,000 to 16,000 and the corresponding rise in
school age population from 1,707 in 1970 to 2,791 in 1975 show a
large influx of Indian people into the Tulsa area so that the
Indian community in Tulsa is without long term roots or cohesiveness.
For the Native American juvenile this urban migration presents a
dual problem of being cut off from his traditional heritage and
adapting to an urban inter-tribal setting.

It is in these low income areas, where destructive substance
abuse patterns already exist that the Indian young person, lacking
the educational skills for positive communication, reaches for a
sense of community in circle drinking and toxic inhalants, a group
activity.

Program Plan

As no Native American Drug Prevention/Alternative program existed in the Tulsa Area, it was the intention of the Tulsa Indian
Council on Alcoholism and Drug Abuse to initiate a program that
would affect the participants in the following ways: Increase the
participants' self esteem, increase the ability to verbalize concerns and emotions in a socially acceptable way, enable the participants to communicate those concerns to and gain approval from
the larger community, enable the participants to focus on attitudes toward drug abuse, attract the potential, experimental and
chronic drug user, and provide a socially acceptable high.

In March, 1975, after a survey of our records had shown that
we were receiving few inquiries from non-users, and early users of
drugs/alcohol, we designed a formal theater project because we projected it would best meet our goals. Structured theater would offer
the protection of form better than improvisation which places great
demands upon the participants with no assurance that they succeed.
We were able to locate an Indian director, and an Indian script of
good quality which dealt with substance abuse. In our search for
workable scripts we discovered that Indian dramatists were dealing

with drug/alcohol abuse more than any other subject. There are no published Indian scripts. We held tryouts, advertising then in Indian neighborhoods. Since formal Native American theater had never occurred in the Tulsa area, we anticipated a vigorous outreach effort for participants. Twenty-five Indian persons appeared for tryouts with no effort on our part other than posting flyers. The play was cast from this initial group and crew was selected. We raised funds from the majority community to determine receptiveness and the business community responded with donations of $1,331.50. In kind contributions totalling $830.00 were received. All staff, technical and artistic, volunteered their efforts. A $300.00 Oklahoma Arts and Humanities grant was obtained. The total expense of the project was $2,492.14. Performances were given in the Indian community in a gymnasium converted to auditorium as it was felt the Indian community would respond more favorably in familiar setting.

Rehearsal time was four weeks. During that time, rigid rehearsal schedules were adhered to as participants had never before appeared in a play. This schedule allowed for the building of team spirit and cooperation. The activity demanded group interdependence. Channel 24 agreed to video tape the process in order to establish in the participants minds the importance of the venture and to aid in evaluation. Characterization allowed participants to explore emotions, problems, and solutions.

There was some concern that the Indian community would not respond to so new a venture. Nine-hundred Indian persons attended the three performances. Community response was so favorable that an All Indian Theater Board has been established to develop a professional Indian Theater in the Tulsa area.

Of the 24 participants in production, three were chronic abusers, eleven were experimental users, seven were moderate users (where use is not a necessary part of social functions and has not caused personal or family problems), and three were non-users. All participants had one or more family members who are substance abusers (here defined as persons whose drug/alcohol use has caused personal, family or physical problems).

Of these active participants, five are now enrolled in group counselling sessions at T.I.C.A.D.A. One is enrolled in family counselling sessions at T.I.C.A.D.A. The three non-users claimed participation further strengthened their attitude against substance abuse.

Six of the participants were over thirty. The remainder (18) were in the 15-24 year age group.

Since the end of the production, nineteen inquiries concerning family substance abuse have been received from the Native American

establishment (middle-to-upper middle class Indian persons). The
production has had the effect of removing stigma from the agency.
Eight of these inquiries have led to one to one counselling sessions at the agency and two of these persons have joined the family group counselling sessions, lending an acceptability in the
Indian community to seeking help for drug/alcohol related problems.

One-hundred percent of the participants stated that the experience did increase their ability to verbalize concerns and emotions, increase self esteem and increase self esteem as a Native
American.

Sources of Data

To collect the necessary information, two members of the staff
of the Tulsa Indian Counsel on Alcoholism and Drug Abuse were involved nightly in play production to allow for informal interview
as we intended to collect data in an unobtrusive way. For objective interviews, we asked Channel 24 to ask key questions regarding participants' attitude toward self and involvement in the program. The video tape is the record of this interview. The tape
was played nine times over local cable television allowing the
production to serve as a further drug education/prevention effort
as well as allowing participants a further experience in community
approval.

Conclusions

The Tulsa Indian Council on Alcoholism and Drug Abuse assessed
the experiment as the most successful of our drug prevention/al-
ternative programs. We are seeking to establish performance oriented performing arts training as a permanent drug prevention program of the agency.

INHALANT ABUSE AMONG MEXICAN-AMERICANS OF THE SOUTHWEST

Stevan R. Lund, D.O.
Richard P. Johnson, M.A.
Gary B. Purvines, B.S.

Drug Counseling Service
Bernalillo County Mental Health/Mental Retardation Center
Albuquerque, New Mexico

I. INTRODUCTION

Deliberate inhalation of volatile solvents tɔ achieve a state of intoxication and euphoria has become a widespread phenomenon among socio-economically deprived youth, with a disproportionately high representation of ethnic minority groups, notably those of Mexican-American and Puerto Rican extraction (1 - 8). A preliminary investigation conducted at the Bernalillo County Mental Health/Mental Retardation Center of the University of New Mexico revealed that N=65 of 80 (81%) solvent abusers enrolled in the drug treatment program were of Mexican-American ancestry.

This study was undertaken to assess: /1/ the demographic characteristics of this group, including age, sex, and geographical distribution within the county; /2/ the socio-economic and psychological characteristics of users and their families; and /3/ their patterns of drug use. Observations and theoretical considerations of developmental and cultural factors which may have etiologic or therapeutic significance will be discussed.

II. METHODS

From a total of 80 inhalant abusers of a mixed ethnic background, 65 Chicano inhalant abusers were selected. All were considered to have a primary drug problem of chronic inhalant abuse. For comparison of the parameters of age, sex, and geographical distribution within the county, a control group, comprised of N=65 Chicano multiple-drug abusers who did not abuse inhalants, was randomly chosen. The inhalant abusers and the control group enrolled in the drug program of the Bernalillo County Mental Health/Mental

Retardation Center during the period from January 1975 through
September 1975. Census tracts were prepared to identify the location within the County of Bernalillo of both the study sample and
control group. Permission was obtained from the District Court to
review the arrest records of juvenile offenders in the study population. Data collection was accomplished by means of direct interviews with patients and families, conversations with drug counselors, and chart review.

Every effort was made to confirm the veracity of patient reports by conferring with those people considered to be objective
sources of information. In general, these efforts were thought to
be successful, but this of course cannot be proven. The methods
utilized were deemed adequate for the purpose of this descriptive
study.

III. FINDINGS

Census tracts revealed that of the 59 of 65 inhalant abusers
living in the county, 94.9% were concentrated in the barrios of
the Rio Grande Valley, an older, socio-economically depressed area
with the highest minority group representation. The control group
of Chicano multiple-drug abusers were more evenly distributed
throughout the city. The age range of the inhalant-using group was
11 to 26 years, with a mean age of 16.9, as opposed to 15.8 for the
control group. Male sniffers outnumbered females by a ratio of 3.3
to 1, whereas in the control group, there were approximately equal
numbers of males and females.

By far, the most popular inhaled intoxicant used was toluene-
containing aerosol spray paint, usually of the clear acrylic variety. N=49 (75%) of the patients used this substance alone, whereas only four used glue, and one used gasoline as their sole intoxicant. N=11 patients (17%) used a combination of either glue, gas
or paint; there was no mention of the use of other substances for
purposes of inhalation. The duration of inhalant use ranged from
one month to sixteen years, with a mean duration of 2.7 years.
The frequency of use was difficult to accurately assess, but
ranged from approximately once weekly to several times daily, with
an average usage of approximately 2 to 3 times per week.

The vast majority of inhalant abusers were found in addition
to abuse other drugs. N=48 (74%) used two or more drugs in addition to inhalants, and N=60 (92%) used marijuana and alcohol,
either alone or in combination. All patients reported they were
introduced to the practice by their peers, and most continued to
use inhalants in the group setting.

A. Characteristics of Users

The psychological characteristics of the sniffers in the present study sample were highly uniform. As mentioned in former

studies (1, 2, 4, 9, 10, 11), they manifested marked personality disorganization and were noted to exhibit non-specific manifestations of ego weakness as described by Otto Kernberg (12) as suggestive of borderline personality organization, consisting of inability to tolerate anxiety, poor impulse control with low frustration tolerance, and decreased sublimatory capacity. This latter trait was demonstrated by their poor school adjustment and performance. N=38 (60%) of the sample were school dropouts, the average grade for dropping out being the eighth.

Perhaps the most outstanding feature of sniffers in this sample was chronic depression, with low self-esteem and impoverished self-image, making the individual psychologically dependent on the inhalants and other drugs to alter his affective state. Patients were noted to be oriented almost exclusively to the present and were basically unaware of the future consequences of their actions. These traits, in combination with fear and resentment of authority figures, led to antisocial forms of behavior, which were further exacerbated by relaxation of inhibitions in the intoxicated state and positive reinforcement by the sniffing peer group. N=34 (52%) of patients in the study had records with the Office of Juvenile Probation. The offenses committed consisted mostly of disorderly conduct, assault and battery, intoxication with paint or alcohol, and a various assortment of property crimes, including residential burglary, shoplifting and auto theft.

B. Characteristics of Families

The families of inhalant abusers were large, averaging 5.8 siblings per family. Lack of cohesive family structure was the rule, with one or more parents absent from the home by reason of death, divorce, separation, or abandonment in N=42 (65%) of the cases. In addition to absence from the home, varying degrees of marital strife and inadequate parenting were encountered. Alcoholism was reported in one or both parents in N=37 of 65 families (57%), and drug abuse was present in N=9 (14%).

IV. DISCUSSION

When interpreting the results of cross-cultural studies, one must be particularly cautious about assuming that any given set of personality or cultural variables have etiologic significance or are unique to the group under scrutiny. In Kaufman's study of gasoline sniffers in a Pueblo Indian Village (13), he demonstrated that the observed psychosocial characteristics of the gasoline sniffers and their families did not differ appreciably from that of non-sniffing controls; he believes that economic and social factors which prevailed in the tribe were the determinants and he could not isolate factors which were limited to the sniffers.

A conglomerate of dynamic, psychological and social factors have been enumerated in this study and former studies as correlates of inhalant abuse (1, 2, 4, 8, 9, 11, 14, 15), including family disorganization and alcoholism, absence of a father figure, chronic depression and delinquency, inability to deal with hostile and aggressive impulses, emotional deprivation and disturbance, to mention but a few. The relative importance of these factors for determining the specific nature of substance abuse appears uncertain. They seem to interact with cultural factors and this seems to be responsible in part for a greater prevalence in some ethnic groups. Nor can it be assumed that these characteristics are specific for the present study sample and not applicable to youth from depressed areas in general.

The high rates of family disorganization encountered in the study sample apparently lead to serious developmental disturbance when viewed in the cultural context of a "lineal" (16) or family-based Chicano society, the child being deprived of his most vital and socially valuable support system. It appears that the sniffing peer group fills the void created by family deprivation and serves as a surrogate family providing acceptance, support and a source of identity for the sniffers. This group eventually develops a subcultural autonomy of its own and functions as an alienated social microcosm possessing a unique value system which positively reinforces antisocial activities and inhalant abuse among its members. The inhalants are particularly attractive for this group because they are inexpensive, readily accessible, easily stolen, and of sufficient potency to allow the user to escape from an unpleasant reality while intoxicated (13, 17, 18).

An alarming trend noted in the present study was the increased mean age of chronic users and decreased male/female ratios as compared to former studies. The 10:1 ratio reported in other studies was derived from juvenile authorities' statistics. Press and Done believe that "the apparent underrepresentation of females may simply relate to a lesser likelihood that girls would engage in associated activities which would be likely to bring them to the attention of authorities" (19).

The lower male/female ratio found in this study may more accurately reflect the sex differences of sniffers than were found by the juvenile justice system. If not, then this finding, in conjunction with the longer duration of use, higher mean age and greater specificity of inhalant choice, may indicate greater overall acceptance of the inhalants by barrio youth of both sexes, with its ominous portent for the future.

REFERENCES

1. Ackerly, W. C., and Gibson, C., "Lighter Fluid 'Sniffing'", Am. J. Psychiatry, 120: 1056 (1964).
2. Brozovsky, and Winkler, E., "Glue Sniffing in Children and Adolescents", N. Y. State J. Med., 65: 1984 (1965).
3. Glaser, H., and Massengale, O., "Glue Sniffing in Children: Deliberate Inhalation of Vaporized Plastic Cements", JAMA, 181: 300 (1962).
4. Massengale, O., Glaser, H., LeLievre, R., Dodds, J., and Klock, J., "Physical and Psychologic Factors in Glue Sniffing", New Eng. J. Med., 269: 1340 (1963).
5. National Drug Education Center, Norman, Oklahoma, "Solvent Inhalation Fad, Spreading Rapidly", Introspect, 4: (1974).
6. Report Series, National Clearinghouse for Drug Abuse Information, "The Deliberate Inhalation of Volatile Substances", Series 30 (1974).
7. Medina, M., and Archibeque, "A Survey of Paint and Glue Inhalation Among Phoenix Inner City Youth", conducted for Valle Del Sol, Inc.
8. Dodds, J., and Santostefano, S., "A Comparison of the Cognitive Functioning of Glue Sniffers and Non-sniffers", J. Peds., 64: 565 (1964).
9. Chapel, J. L., and Taylor, D. W., "Glue Sniffing", Mo. Med., 65: 288 (1968).
10. Cohen, S., "Glue Sniffing", JAMA, 231: 653 (1975).
11. Sokol, J., and Robinson, J., "Glue Sniffing", Western Med., 4: 192 (1963).
12. Kernberg, Otto, "Borderline Personality Organization", J. Am. Psychoan. Assn., 15: 641 (1967).
13. Kaufman, A., "Gasoline Sniffing Among Children in a Pueblo Indian Village", Peds., 51: 1060 (1973).
14. Barman, M., Sigel, N., Beedle, D., and Larson, R., "Acute and Chronic Effects of Glue Sniffing", Calif. Med., 100: 19 (1964).
15. Easson, W. M., "Gasoline Addiction in Children", Peds., 29: 250 (1962).
16. Heller, Celia S., Mexican-American Youth: Forgotten Youth at the Crossroads, Random House, New York, 1966.
17. Silberberg, N. E., and Silberberg, M. C., "Glue Sniffing in Children: A Position Paper", J. Drug Ed., 4: (1974).
18. Cohen, S., "Inhalant Abuse", Drug Abuse and Alcoholism Newsletter, 10: (1975).
19. Press, E., and Done, A. K., "Solvent Sniffing: Physiologic Effects and Community Control Measures for Intoxication from the Intentional Inhalation of Organic Solvents, I and II", Peds., 39: 451 and 611 (1967).

REHABILITATION OF ADDICTS WITHIN A CULTURAL CONTEXT

Pedro Ruiz, M.D.

Joyce Lowinson, M.D.

John Langrod, M.A.

Lois Alksne, M.A.

Albert Einstein College of Medicine
Bronx, New York

One out of every 14 persons of Spanish origin in the New York
City metropolitan area is either a drug addict or a drug abuser.
This indicates that drug addiction has assumed major proportions
in this segment of the population. At the present time, while
Hispanics represent only 12 percent of the entire population of
New York City, they account for approximately 20 percent of the
estimated 125,000* addicts in the area. Of this number, only a
little more than half have become involved in treatment programs.
The situation calls for a close examination of Hispanic patterns
of addiction and a critical reassessment of current addiction
treatment programs and personnel, as they relate to people brought
up in the cultural norms and value systems of Hispanic tradition.

We would like to present an analytical description of the
Puerto Rican patients in the drug addiction program of the Lincoln
Community Mental Health Center in the southeast Bronx of New York
City. This is one of the clinics of the Albert Einstein College
of Medicine Methadone Maintenance Treatment Program. A number of
supportive services are offered, such as: counseling and job placement; educational assistance involving remedial instruction; referral to vocational and educational programs; family and individual
counseling; referral to welfare; and legal services for those who
have cases pending at the time of entry into treatment. In addition, those who become addicted to other drugs or alcohol can be
detoxified on the inpatient unit. The program stresses community
involvement in the delivery of services. The staff of the program
is composed of: a Medical Director, three nurses, one social worker, and three paraprofessionals. Although leadership is in the

---

*According to the New York City Narcotics Register, 1975

hands of the Medical Director, non-supervisory staff have considerable influence in the decision-making process.

Of the 231 patients admitted to the program between March and November, 1971, and followed up two years later, 162 (70%) were Puerto Rican. One hundred thirty seven (85%) of the Puerto Rican patients were males; 25 (15%) were females.

One parameter of successful treatment outcome is the absence of secondary drug abuse. An examination of urinalysis records for a six-month period (October 1972 to March 1973) reveals that 25 percent of the patients were using or had used some drug other than methadone. Barbiturates (35% of drugs taken) and cocaine (41% of drugs taken) were the most frequently used drugs. There was very little use of amphetamine (3%) or heroin, as represented by quinine (15%) and morphine (5%).

One area in which methadone maintenance treatment is said to be beneficial is in the reduction of criminal behavior after entry into treatment. Cushman (1) and Gearing (2) found a sharp reduction in arrests following admission to a methadone maintenance program. While we do not have figures for arrests of Puerto Rican patients before they entered the program, we know that heroin addicts commit many crimes in an effort to gain the means to satisfy their craving. Thirty-one Puerto Rican patients (19% of the patient population) accounted for 45 arrests following admission to the program. Twelve arrests were on drug charges (possession or sale); eight were of a minor nature; and there is no information for then of the arrests. Seven of the cases were dismissed. However, this figure of 31 arrests after entering the program is much higher than that found in another study which reported only six percent of arrests over a 12-month period after entering a methadone maintenance program. (3)

Another parameter of treatment success is retention in treatment. Seventy-one percent of the Puerto Rican group was retained in treatment over the two-year period, and this is comparable with retention in treatment for the non-Hispanic patients of our program. The reasons for discharge of Puerto Rican patients over the two-year period were as follows:

Dropouts	31	(65%)
Incarcerated	10	(31%)
Deceased	4	(8%)
Voluntarily detoxified	2	(4%)
Hospitalized	1	(2%)
Total	48	(100%)

In comparing the characteristics of retained patients with those who were discharged, we found remarkably little difference. The mean length of time spent in treatment for those patients who

were discharged before March 1973 was ten months. Males and Females had almost the same retention rate (70% for males; 72% for
females).

Altogether, findings clearly indicate very little, if any,
correlation between age, sex, education or employment at admission
and the probability of retention in treatment. It is of considerable concern to us that 65 percent of all of our discharged Puerto
Rican patients have dropped out of treatment, usually with no explanation.

Analysis of Dropouts

The discharge rate for Puerto Rican patients is not appreciably different from that of other ethnic groups in other clinics.
The difference comes in the "reasons for discharge" which shows
65 percent of Puerto Rican patients discharged simply as walking
away from the program. Even allowing for the possibility that
some of the voluntary dropouts in this program might, in a more
discipline-oriented clinic, fall into a category of "discharged
for drug abuse or disruptive behavior," the dropout rate is high
enough to warrant further investigation.

It is difficult to acquire follow-up data on dropouts, but
with patient profiles so similar for retained and discharged patients, one can perhaps explain the high rate of dropouts by looking at ways the Puerto Rican culture differs from the expectations
of many of those who run the clinics in the United States.

Culturally speaking, time has a different meaning to those of
the Hispanic culture than it does to most harried Americans. Also,
if immediate results are not obtained -- no matter what type of
treatment is being considered -- one may simply "give up." There
is undoubtedly some alienation from American institutions among
Hispanics, who may perceive institutional "efficiency" as hostile
and humiliating.

The experience drawn from our study has made us advance certain basic programmatic changes to be implemented for services
where there is a large number of Hispanic patients. They are as
follows:

1. Socio-Cultural Recommendations:

With all the good will in the world, a clinic staff which
does not understand the salient cultural values and sex roles that
play an important part in the behavior and personality of Hispanic
patients will be limited in efforts to help them. More than once
in our program, we observed that female patients seen by male
staff were labelled as "uncooperative" because they were reluctant
to discuss their problems with them, thus not getting the help

they needed. In traditional Hispanic custom, women do not confide
intimate details of their lives to men other than clergy or their
husbands. In effect, they were being asked to negate principles
they lived by in order to receive help. In other cases, we observed females getting off methadone at their husband's request.
In those cases, the staff apparently unaware of the authority
vested in the male head of a Hispanic household, did not understand the clients' motivation and was at a loss to provide counsel
which would help solve the dilemma.

In another case, a Puerto Rican patient who did not understand English very well was asked for a urine specimen by a nurse
who did not understand Spanish at all. When the patient claimed
he could not urinate just then, the nurse accused him of lying.
Nobody likes to be accused of lying, and such behavior is generally unacceptable from a member of one of the "helping professions."
To a Puerto Rican, such a lack of respeto can challenge his cultural value of dignidad. Staff ignorance of the overriding importance of such matters may interfere with or destroy his rehabilitative opportunities. He may prefer to drop out rather than cope
with attitudes which seem to him downright offensive.

Cultural attitudes, beliefs and values which are strong in
those who have migrated to New York are also to be recognized to
some extent among New Yorkers of Puerto Rican ancestry as well,
although considerable acculturation has taken place in New York
born Puerto Ricans who have been through the City's school system
and who have made greater adjustment to the dominant way of life
in this City.

2. Training Recommendations

Employees working in programs servicing Hispanic populations
must understand the problem of drug addiction as it relates to the
Hispanic addict and abuser, including the effects of drug abuse on
the family structure, the community, and the addicts themselves.
Participants must learn how to design a "clinical" program that
will relate more positively and effectively to the Hispanic addict.
In order to do this, the staff must understand not only the Spanish
language and cultural traditions but also the historical aspects
common to Spanish speaking countries, such as the Spanish colonial
period, struggles for independence, nationalism, migration, and
current political issues. In addition to therapeutic skills, Hispanic staff should be trained in communication skills, the planning
of strategies for working with the families of the Hispanic addicts and with the community. In the Hispanic code, the quality
of personalismo should be encouraged in order to earn the trust of
the community, and to attract and hold the Hispanic addict in
treatment.

3. Staffing Recommendations

Ideally, Hispanic drug addicts should be treated by persons who share their language, background and experience. Although we call ourselves a pluralistic society, there are strong social and institutional pressures to conform to what is deemed good by the majority. There is a need for drug addiction programs run by and for Hispanics, partly because they prefer it, and partly because they feel that successful rehabilitation can only take place within the context of the addict's cultural heritage.

The negative self-image induced by discriminatory practices against Hispanics can be improved and made positive by providing therapists from within their own culture in a treatment program. This must be coupled with educational and training opportunities which prepare trainees for productive livelihoods rather than the menial dead-end jobs now open for them. In order to build self-confidence and restore hope for a life beyond survival, therapy and training should take place among peers in a non-threatening atmosphere created by staff and addicts who share the same cultural heritage. In effect, "drug sub-cultures provide avenues to success, to social admiration and to a sense of well-being with the world, which the members feel are otherwise beyond their reach."

Summary and Conclusions

The patients we have described constitute a hard-core addict group, and it would appear at first glance that they would be difficult to rehabilitate. We have seen, however, that according to commonly used criteria for success in treatment, a substantial number have been rehabilitated during the period under study.

The program reported on here is now providing specialized assistance in English, and high school equivalency in Spanish is being planned as well as classes in Puerto Rican history and culture. Taking into account the cultural restraints on women in discussing personal problems with male counselors, a female counselor has been hired. Because of its relatively high incidence among Puerto Rican patients, more should be learned about treatment for cocaine use. Factors which depersonalize a program, such as making it necessary to wait for medication, restrictions on taking home medication, and the implication that patients are not to be trusted when urine samples are taken, must be balanced against the need to prevent the illicit spread of methadone and the necessity to protect the patient from the consequences of drug abuse while on methadone. There is no easy answer to such problems, but it is possible that steps could be taken to minimize what Hispanics perceive as callous or punitive treatment on the part of the staff.

It is important to have a staff that is representative of and has empathy with the patients it serves. If this is not possible, staff should be knowledgeable about and respectful of patients' cultures and life styles which do not fit expected or familiar patterns. Although patients must be assisted in the program's goals of self-sufficiency, economic independence and abstention from drugs and criminality, precautions must be taken against using methadone as a means of social control. Hispanic patients will not be as likely to walk away from a program where treatment builds on acknowledged strengths, values and folkways of thier own cultural and social experience.

References

1. Cushman, P.: Arrests Before and During Methadone Maintenance: Analysis of N.Y. City Police Records, Proceedings Fourth National Conference on Methadone Treatment, NAPAN: New York, 1972, pp. 481-488.

2. Gearing, F.: A Road Back from Heroin Addiction, Proceedings Fourth National Conference on Methadone Treatment, NAPAN, New York, 1972, pp. 157-158.

3. Lowinson, J.; Alpeorin, L.; Langrod, J.: Legal Services As A Tool in Treating the Addict, American Journal of Psychiatry, 130 (5): 592-595, 1973.

A TAVISTOCK STYLE WOMEN'S
GROUP IN A METHADONE CLINIC

Ann H. Rose, M.S.

Texas Research Institute of Mental Sciences
Houston, Texas

Virginia Davidson, M.D.

Baylor College of Medicine
Houston, Texas

As a result of the women's movement and the upsurge of interest in
the special problems of women in treatment, there has been a fair
amount of attention in the literature regarding approaches to
treatment which emphasize how women's status in society at large
affects the type treatment settings. In these therapies, the
locus of the problems that women experience is placed outside the
psyche of the individual woman. Consciousness-raising groups
typically help the woman realize how she has been victimized by
society, and give her strength (through understanding her plight)
to change her life. Closely related to these groups are "self-
help" groups which offer supportive services to women in the
process of change, such as lodging and vocational counseling.
Alternatives to traditional therapy are being increasingly studied
in an attempt to gauge their effectiveness as alternative
treatments. (6) (7) We believe that these alternatives have much
to offer women patients, including patients with addictive illness.
We recognize that women addicts experience special problems
because of the social roles their addiction tends to emphasize
such as extreme dependence on men, participation in debasing and
degrading activities like prostitution which are exploited by men.

Since methadone patients have not, in our experience, participated
well in therapy groups with traditional structures, and since they
are often reluctant to attend groups which rely on investigative,
interpretative work, we felt that a model which relied on
interpreting the moment-by-moment behavior of group members might
have more applicability to this group of patients. By almost any

standard, methadone patients demonstrate deficiencies in their ability to assume responsibility for their behavior. Also, because of the stormy (and often negative) transference responses these patients establish in therapy (1), we hoped a model which relied on "neutral" consultants would help dilute the interactions between patient and therapists. When we initiated the Tavistock style group in our methadone clinic, we hoped to give women patients an educational exercise in learning how to deal with authority relationships in a supportive, all female group. We had an interest in making ourselves available as role models to the women patients in a therapeutic setting. We believed this model might be especially useful for women patients who have poor images of themselves as women, and who might be able to profit from the role-modeling effect of women therapists. (2) (8)

The A.K. Rice "Tavistock" Group Relations model is an educational concept for defining and dealing with "reality" in group work. According to the Tavistock model of group functioning, the leader or leadership role can be thought of as representing the major function of the group, which is considered its "primary task." The leadership role can rotate between individuals and/or groups who may or may not be in positions of formal authority. Closely related to the concepts of leadership and authority is collective responsibility. The ability to work effectively in a group is largely determined by the way authority is entrusted in the individual by others, and by the way the individual exercises this authority, for and over others. By focusing on the problems of leadership and authority, one sees patterns develop in the groups regarding these concepts. The process of giving authority, exercising leadership and assuming responsibility can best be understood while it is happening. (5) It is basic to the approach of this group to work in the "here and now" contrasted with traditional group therapies which attempt to explain behavior of the group by examining and interpreting the past of its individual members.

Little has been written about the use of this model or its variations in therapy groups. (3) The authors, both trained psychotherapists with knowledge and some experience in the Tavistock model, adapted this model for use in a women's group in a methadone maintenance clinic. The major modifications were the events offered the group, and the role of the consultants. Initially, the Tavistock model in our clinic was limited to the small group exercise. It was the feeling of the authors that the introduction of a women's group along with a new approach to group work would best be assimilated into this clinic on a slow and gradual basis. This would allow time for evaluation and modification.

The number of methadone patients this clinic serves is approximately 85. Of this number approximately 25% are women.

Prior to each of the twelve week sessions, the consultants
invited each of the women patients in the clinic to join the group.
They were informed in a letter who the group consultants would be,
where the group would meet, and when. They were informed that this
was a voluntary group, but were asked to make a commitment for the
twelve-week cycle. The group ranged in size from two to six
members, composed almost exclusively of women separated from their
spouses due to incarceration or a recent unresolved crisis in their
lives concerning their relationship with their spouse. At the
initial session, the consultant stated that the task of the group
would be to study their behavior in the "here and now," and that
the task of the consultants would be to observe and interpret to
the group their behavior as they were engaged in their task. The
consultants were in no way responsible for rounding up the members
for group, beginning group discussion or in any other way solving
the group's problems. Fifty-minute sessions were held once a week
for the twelve-week cycle. This paper covers the first three
cycles of 36 weeks of the group's existence.

Initially both consultants assumed the traditional Tavistock
consultant role model. Within the first few sessions it became
apparent that the members could not sustain the stress that this
model produced and at the same time deal with the "here and now."
The authors decided that one consultant would remain in the
traditional consultant's role while the other consultant assumed
a more "supportive" role. To prevent casting of roles and images
into "friend vs. foe" by the group, and becoming trapped in that
discussion, the consultants assumed each week their role on a
spontaneous basis. It was based on the needs of the group as
observed by the consultants during the initial interchanges of the
members. Once a consultant assumed her role, she attempted to
maintain it throughout that session. Rigid adherence to the
principle of time (when the consultants were available to group)
and the voluntary nature of the group were maintained in typical
A.K. Rice tradition.

Certain themes recurred in each cycle, although with varying
intensity. Security and dependency were prevalent. These
themes were reflected in issues concerning their relationship
with men, jealousy toward other women, request for the consultants
to validate the members feelings as females, and membership and
commitment to the group. The concensus of the group was that
most of their lives had been spent in trying to please men. Most
of the members felt they had been "let down" by women early in
their lives, and that they turned to men for understanding. The
women doubted they knew how to get along with each other; they
explored how men keep women apart, and how women usually agree to
it.

The size of the group and the commitment each member had to
attending group regularly occupied a significant amount of the

group's time. They were concerned most with exploring ways the group could be restructured to attract a larger membership. The issue seemed not to refer to the sex composition of the group but rather to the style and type of leadership. This was done despite the fact that the consultants reiterated to the membership that the boundaries and tasks of the members and consultants had been established.

Responsibility was a theme that affected most issues discussed. There was an ambivalence toward accepting responsibility for one's own behavior and an inability to exercise control over one's own behavior. This theme was carried out in the members' relationship with the consultants. Every attempt was made by the members to seduce the consultants out of their role of observers and interpreters of the group's behavior into a role of responsibility for "running" the group. Simultaneously, the members would state that they resented the control the medical director (one of the consultants) had over their lives. Issues concerning resentment toward both program and medical director in carrying out their responsibility in their respective roles to the clinic (as interpreted by the patients as having control over their lives) were covertly handled by the membership; yet overtly they became frustrated when these same women would not take control over the group. The same theme was evident in their relationship with men. Some members concluded that their unsatisfactory relationship with men resulted from their inability to assume responsibility for their own lives, and from the worthlessness they felt as female addicts.

It is difficult to assess the effect this particular group has had on the members of the group, the clinic membership in general, and on the staff. (4) Over the 36 weeks that the group has been in progress, we have seen women patients gradually assume more and more responsibility for their behavior in the clinic. The need to find excuses in the external environment which "cause" behavior has decreased. Some of the patients have assumed leadership roles not only in the group, but also outside the group. The women who have been able to come to grips with the task of the group most effectively and assume leadership roles have been on daily methadone dosages of 30 mgs., or less, are not living with a man, and have attended at least two of the three cycles.

A high degree of interest in the "Tavistock" approach has been generated among the staff. Focus in the clinic is on the "here and now" and issues of responsibility, authority and leadership. This focus has permeated staff/patient interaction. The patients who heretofore had a "careless" attitude concerning counseling of any kind, are absorbed in the work of the group. Some evidence is already at hand of increased responsibility and leadership in the clinic among these patients also.

The impact of initiating a "Tavistock" style women's group in a
methadone maintenance clinic has had widespread implications for
the total functioning of the clinic. Patients and staff are
assuming greater responsibility in their work roles, and are
enjoying greater self-respect. Leadership and authority roles are
seen as rotating between individuals and groups who may or may not
be in positions of formal authority. We conclude that a modified
"Tavistock" approach is a useful adjunct to traditional therapy in
a methadone clinic; however, more experience in modifying this
Group Relations work is needed.

1) Davidson, V. "Transference Phenomena in the Treatment of
   Addictive Illness: Love and Hate in Methadone Maintenance"
   Paper presented at the Third National Drug Abuse Conference;
   New York, N.Y. March 25-29, 1976.

2) Davidson, V., Rose, A. "When Women Work Together: A Study in
   Authority and Role Conflict." in NDAC for Training and
   Resources Development (Ed.) Alternative Approaches in Women's
   Treatment: In Press.

3) Hausman, W. "The Application of Group Relations Methods and
   Concepts to the Psychiatric Clinic" in Colman, A.D. &
   Bexton, W.H. (Eds.); An A.K. Rice Series Group Relations
   Reader; San Rafael, Calif., Associates Printing & Publishing
   Company. pp. 181-184.

4) Menninger, R. "The Impact of Group Relations Conference on
   Organizational Growth," International Journal of Group
   Psychotherapy, 1972, 22, 415-432.

5) Rice, A.K. 1965 "Learning for Leadership" in Colman, A.D. and
   Bexton, W.H. (Eds.) An A.K. Rice Series Group Relations Reader
   San Rafael, Calif., Associates Printing & Publishing Co.,
   pp. 71-158; 1975.

6) Weissman, M. "Depressed Women: Traditional and Non-Traditional
   Therapies." Paper presented at the Texas Research Institute of
   Mental Sciences' Ninth Annual Symposium: Effective Psycho-
   therapy" Houston, TX., Nov. 19-21, 1975.

7) Wolman, C.S. "Therapy Groups for Women." American Journal
   Psychiatry, March, 1976 133:3, 274-278.

8) Wright, F. "Sex and Style of Consultants As Variables in
   Self-Study Groups." Unpublished Doctoral Dissertation; The
   City University of New York, New York, N.Y. 1972.

THE PSYCHOLOGICAL UNDERSTANDING AND
TREATMENT OF PREGNANT DRUG ADDICTS

James Moriarty, Ph.D.

Hutzel Hospital--Wayne State University
Program for Pregnant Drug Addicts
Detroit, Michigan

The Pregnant Drug Addict! This is an emotionally loaded
label that frequently brings to mind many negative .images of the
women so labeled. They are seen as irresponsible, hedonistic,
selfish, psychopathic, unfeminine, unproductive (except for children), and parasitic. Instead of being given the emotional support that is usually given to pregnant women they are often the
recipients of self-righteous indignation for daring to bring a
child into the world. They are judged before they can present
their case and are often sentenced to suffer.

The widely held negative stereotypes are very damaging to
the treatment of the pregnant drug addict. They ignore the individuality of each woman and the unique set of circumstances and
life experiences that brought her to this pregnancy. They do not
respect her identity as a person apart from her drug dependence.
If she is treated as a thing, she soon begins to feel like one and
may seek further drugs to alter her consciousness. When she is
condemned and rejected for her behavior, her belief in her own
worthlessness is reinforced and her despair intensified. To overcome these feelings she is tempted to use narcotics. If she is
humiliated or insulted she reacts with frustration and hostility
and the self-fulfilling prophecy that she is antisocial is fulfilled.

Who then is the woman beneath the stereotype and how can she
receive appropriate treatment from the psychological point of
view? I shall now attempt to give some answers to these questions
based on my observations and experience as a psychologist with

over 300 pregnant drug addicts at the Hutzel Hospital--Wayne State University Pregnant Addict Program. Contact with these patients consisted of either interviews, psychological testing, group, individual, or family therapy. Only 12 percent of the pregnant drug addicts in our program are married. Sixty-two percent have annual family incomes of less than $5,000. Seventy percent have not graduated from high school. Ninety-eight percent are currently unemployed. Ninety-two percent are black.

Pregnancy is a stressful time in the life of any woman, even when she has environmental support. There are mood swings, doubts, fears, identity problems, and difficulties with body image and desirability. For most of the women in our program pregnancy was only one of many stresses in their lives. Poverty, lack of stable and supportive relationships, drug addiction, lack of vocational and educational skills, and discrimination due to sex, poverty or race had to be dealt with while they were pregnant. To simultaneously contend with all of these stresses was a tremendous strain on their psychological coping ability. They were in great need of emotional support, guidance, and relief from environmental pressures to help them adjust successfully to pregnancy and its consequences. Despite the many stresses in their lives they coped remarkably well.

Beneath the stereotype of the pregnant drug addict, there exists individual women who are now pregnant and who at one time became dependent on drugs. They are not strange and alien beings but women who apart from their drug dependence and its consequences are no different from other woman. Instead of turning to drugs for solutions they might, in other circumstances, have turned to religion, philosophy, material security, psychotherapy, friendship, a career, or prescription tranquilizers. Their reasons for turning to drugs varied. Each brought to her drug dependence a unique combination of life experiences, needs, and expectations. Some became dependent on drugs because they were looking for immediate gratification and had poor tolerance for frustration. Others were curious about what it felt like to be "high." Many were bored by their lack-lustre or meaningless existence and they started to take illicit drugs for the excitment of it. There were also those who became dependent on drugs because of peer or boyfriend pressure and a need to belong. Some turned to drugs following the example of parents or siblings who were drug abusers. Others became dependent as a means of manifesting their independence from their parents and their value systems. Some women also started taking narcotics to relieve physical pain and became addicted. More sought in drugs an escape from the emotional pain of anxiety,

depression, rage, disillusionment, loneliness, or estrangement.
There were also those who used narcotics as psychotropic agents to
cope with the fear of becoming psychotic. The easy availability
of narcotics was a prime factor in establishing drug dependence in
most of the women.

Whatever their reasons for becoming addicted, once they
developed physical dependence and tolerance, new reasons for
taking narcotics emerged. They needed to take the drugs to feel
normal, to feel like they were before taking the drugs. Avoiding
the pain of withdrawal became a great reinforcer for the continuation of their habit. To ensure an adequate supply of narcotics,
many were obliged to do things they found debasing or alien to
their nature. Some had to steal, others had to prostitute. Many
had to do without needed food and clothing for themselves and their
children, their bodies often disfigured from needle marks and
wasted from malnutrition, their chances of finding a decent job or
husband almost nil. It is little wonder that they frequently
referred to heroin as the "worst pimp of all."

Their drug taking habit was also reinforced by euphoric feelings, the loss of awareness (however temporary) of their helplessness or isolation, the sense of belonging and acceptance in a
group which gave them an identity, the job of hustling, making
connections, injecting the narcotic, providing for the next "fix,"
and outmaneuvering the police--all of which occupied their time
and provided them with a structure and a purpose in their lives.
Their drug dependence despite its many hardships became a way of
life that was in many ways satisfying, a way of life that beckoned
enticingly when the doors of alternative life styles were closed
to those who bore the stigma "drug addict."

Reactions to their pregnancies varied with the individual
women. Many were glad they were pregnant because their pregnancy
gave them a sense of pride in themselves that they could make a
baby in contrast to their usual feelings of impotence or helplessness. The pregnancy caused others to be treated with more respect
by their men as opposed to being treated as mere things or junkies.
The pregnancy also assured many of their feminine identity when
they badly needed reassurance. It gave them a role as mother to
look forward to when they seemed to have nothing to live for.
They would have a baby who would depend on them and give them a
sense of importance and of being needed. Others perceived their
pregnancy as a means of making their man happy when they felt
incapable of pleasing him. There were also those who became

pregnant to overcome their loneliness and isolation and wanted someone to whom they could relate.

There were also negative reactions to being pregnant. There were fears that their baby would be addicted, have withdrawal symptoms and suffer or be physically or mentally abnormal. Many also experienced guilt and fear that their man would always resent them for having an addicted or deformed baby. Many in very poor financial circumstances worried about being able to get proper food, clothing, and shelter for their baby and felt very ambiva- lent about bringing a new child into the world. There were also those who were emotionally troubled and had difficulty coping with their existing children and wondered where they would get the strength to cope with another child who was often perceived as an added burden. Some were under pressure from family members to have an abortion but chose not to have one. Others wanted to have an abortion but chose not to have one because of family pressure.

There was also resentment about the restriction of their freedom during pregnancy and their inability to act out their anxiety through activity to the extent that they were accustomed when they were "not tied down." Ambivalence or emotional rejec- tion was also present in women who had broken up with or were alienated from the fathers of their babies-to-be. Pregnancy was also a difficult time for the women who did not have the emotional support of their parents, particularly their mother. Coping with pregnancy was also made more difficult for all patients by having to lower their daily intake of methadone as pregnancy advanced. As they were reduced to 20 milligrams or less, the emotional rea- sons for first taking narcotics frequently emerged. Feelings of depression, anxiety, hostility, and boredom came to the fore. It was difficult for them to substitute the physically acceptable or pleasurable symptoms of addiction for the painful symptoms of withdrawal.

Psychological care for these pregnant addicts consisted of helping them to resolve their conflicts, adjust to their pregnancy, follow the guidelines of the program, relieve environmental stress, enhance their self-esteem, realistically anticipate and prepare for the future, detox and be vocationally rehabilitated where pos- sible and accept responsibility for their lives.

Efforts are made to treat each woman as a unique individual. The staff does not presume to know all about them or expect them to be carbon copies of other drug addicts. Great emphasis is placed on listening to them in order to understand them more fully.

Their observations and opinions are respected and their behavior is not morally judged. This emotional support and attentiveness to their needs gives them the feeling that they are being respected as persons. It causes them to open up more fully about their feelings and develop trust in the staff. They also become more receptive to the recommendations and guidance of the staff.

Because many of them have low self-esteem the staff tries to help them form a better self-image. They are given positive reinforcement for whatever they do well, e.g., careful about their appearance, dress attractively, further their education, seek vocational rehabilitation, taking care of their children, getting involved in hobbies or community activities, detoxing, coping with their problems, expressing their ideas or feelings. They are also helped to see themselves as persons separate from their drug dependence. Their many negative experiences in life; their failures have conditioned many of them to expect failure in whatever they do. This often gives them a feeling of hopelessness. The staff tries to instill hope in them by pointing out constructive things they have already accomplished by pointing out that they are in control of their destinies to a great extent no matter what their circumstances are and are not passive victims of their environment. They are also given the example of women in the program with similar life circumstances who have overcome many hardships and obstacles and now lead satisfying and productive lives.

They are provided with other means than drugs to cope with feelings of depression, hostility and anxiety. In coping with depression they are given the opportunity to share their feelings with other pregnant women. They begin to see that depression moods are common during pregnancy and they accept them more as a part of pregnancy. The women who are more chronically depressed are encouraged to keep themselves busy and occupied, plan activities, go on group outings, express their feelings directly, talk to their friends, replace repetitious depressive thoughts with thoughts that open up new possibilities and more favorable outcomes. They are given emotional support and are helped to avoid disappointment with themselves by setting more realistic and attainable goals. They are encouraged to talk out rather than act out their hostile impulses. In coping with anxiety about pregnancy and its consequences they are guided in anticipating as realistically as possible what will happen. Pregnancy, labor, delivery, and parenthood are presented as stages of growth over which they can have much control and from which they can derive much satisfaction by preparing for them.

WOMEN IN MANAGEMENT: ISSUES FOR DISCUSSION

Virginia Borrok

Alcoholism Services Consultant
Northeast Florida District Mental Health Board
Jacksonville, Florida

The following are issues that have been raised time
and again when anyone discusses women in management
positions. They must, however, be reiterated again
and again to constantly remind women (and men) of the
recurring problems which women face consciously and
unconsciously when they assume a role in society different from that which is traditionally expected of
them. By bringing these issues once more to the attention of everyone concerned, perhaps there is a chance
that something can be done about them to help the
women who are beginning the process of finding their
places in management and leader roles in their chosen
field.

I.   ATTITUDES ENCOUNTERED BY WOMEN IN MANAGEMENT

A.   From Others

Women are not taken very seriously when they embark
on a career because their dedication is not supposed
to be to a career but to marraige and family. It is
often assumed that a job for a woman is just a temporary stop gap on the road to the traditional role of
wife and mother.

Women may be more competent and committed to a particular position than a man in a comparable position but
often is paid less and is expected to do more. It
very often appears that a woman has to prove herself

over and over again to maintain her position. A man
generally does not experience similar problems.

Women in management positions are consistently treated as sex objects and become the butt of various sexual inferences in business meetings. Another indication that they are not taken seriously as competent,
committed individuals capable of doing a good job.
They are put in a stereotyped box of what a woman is
supposed to be from past societal programming.

B.   From Themselves

Women, particularly those in their 30's and 40's today,
have been the objects of programming and see themselves
in the traditional wife and mother role. If they deviate from this role there are guilt feelings with
which they must contend. As a result a woman very
often is unable to take herself seriously in a management position and becomes her own worst enemy.

A woman may be afraid to demand what a man would in
salary and recognition (it's not good to be an agges-
sive female!) for the same work. Again, her programming has been to be the subservient person, the one
who takes direction from men. There is always her
underlying fear that she may really not be as good as
the man or deserve equal pay and recognition.

The sex object role is a difficult one to handle with
the proper balance. Too many women allow themselves
to be used by men, made fun of by men, and as a result
fall back into the role of being a flirtatious female
when it is totally inappropriate in a business setting.
Once again women are forced into becoming their own
worst enemies.

II.   TRADITIONAL BEGINNINGS

Because women are so hampered, both from outside and
within themselves, by the attitudes discussed above,
they tend to start out in the "traditional" jobs for
women, particularly the secretarial, clerical, receptionist positions. This happens even when women have

the education and training to begin in positions leading up the managerial hierarchy, but men get the beginning management jobs and women come in the back door
through the secretarial or other equally subservient
route. Women tend to consider themselves lucky to get
their foot in the door any way they can.

Women who from the beginning of their education and
training embark on a particular profession (i.e., law,
medicine) do not usually go through having to start
their career as a secretary. They do, however, have to
contend with the same attitudes. They also find themselves in a minority in school and later in their chosen
profession.

III. MAKING CHANGES HAPPEN

A. Women's Organizations

There is a real need for women in like professions to
be able to have a forum in which they can get together
to discuss their problems and develop action plans to
counteract prevailing attitudes and injustice. The
Women's Movement is an example of change that can occur
through organization. Those women who never really
participated in the movement actively and who apparently have never felt strongly about being "liberated",
have reaped the benefits of the changes in public and
private policies that have occured as a result.

Professional women involved in delivering services to
women should develop organizations to heighten awareness of the needs of women. In drug and alcohol abuse
treatment programs, services are generally geared unconsciously, and in some cases deliberately, toward
men. In residential facilities, bed space for women is
either non existant or very minimal. Because of societal expectations of women, a woman in treatment has
much more difficulty in overcoming her past problems
than does a man. It is the responsibility of concerned
professional women to make the changes necessary for
women to receive at least equal concern in treatment.

B. Specialized Training and Education

Training which is unique to the special problems that
women encounter in management should be included in
managerial training for both men and women working together within organizations. Women members of the organization can be in a position to assure that the
special training is included. The understanding that
can result on the part of both will provide a setting
for changes in attitude and behavior. Only when men
and women are aware of what they are doing to each
other and to themselves while working together, will
it be possible for women to begin to realize their full
potential in management.

Women in management are in a unique position to provide
help to other women. Education is needed for women
who have not yet had the opportunity to realize their
potential. It can take many forms, from a personal one
to one educational process within an organization to
the process of setting up special programs for the
management training of women in local educational institutions. Materials which are developed specifically
for women, to address the issues they are concerned
about in their jobs, is a way in which many women managers and potential managers can be reached.

Training for men and women who deliver services to
women clients is a desperate need. Women managers in
organizations are again in a unique position to assume
responsibility for training to be provided which will
sensitize and upgrade the care given to the female
clients they serve.

Finally, women who have management responsibility must
speak out, they must write, they must educate, they must
train, they must give advice, they must consult, they
must do whatever they can to generate attention at all
levels to the unique problems of women in management
and to the unique problems faced by women who enter our
service delivery systems.

THE FEMALE NON-OPIATE DRUG ABUSER

Cynthia Musillo, M.A.

Creative Socio-Medics Corporation
Arlington, Virginia 22209

Audrey Milgrom, M.S.

Creative Socio-Medics Corporation
New York, New York 10022

I.   INTRODUCTION AND BACKGROUND

One of the most frequently quoted findings from NIDA's Polydrug
Study is a prevalence estimate setting the number of non-opiate
abusers in this country at two million. Using the polydrug data
and the same prevalence estimating technique, we found that fully
780,000 of these individuals, or over 3/4 million are women. We
believe this is the first estimate of female non-opiate abuse to
be based on an extensive national data base. As such, it is significant in two regards. It indicates the extent of female non-opiate
abuse; and, it suggests that the female drug abusing population is
probably far larger than has previously been suspected.

A notion that has traditionally confounded estimates of women's involvement with drugs is the theory that the female polydrug population is largely hidden. Support for this theory derives partially
from CODAP statistics which report a fairly consistent ratio of 1
female for every 3 males in treatment. Additional support stems
from the popular assumption that the female contingent consists
principally of housewives, who are therefore far less visible than
their male counterparts.

An examination of the theory of the hidden abuser is thus critical
to an informed interpretation of our prevalence estimate. Furthermore, it holds particular significance for treatment planners and
providers since treatment approaches cannot appropriately be designed for a population presumed to be largely invisible. The

673

present study therefore focuses on the theory of the hidden female drug abuser and provides a first step in examining some of the premises underlying this theory.

II. METHODOLOGY

The data analyzed for this investigation were collected as part of the National Polydrug Abuse Study conducted by NIDA as a collaborative research project from 1973 to 1975. During that period as many as 15 research centers collected information on more than 2300 non-opiate drug abusing subjects. Data were collected and reported to the central computer system on a wide range of variables, and included demographic, behavioral, family history and psychological test data.

For the analysis reported in this paper we constructed the following operational hypothesis:

> That, if a hidden population of female drug abusers exists, and if this hidden population is chiefly comprised of housewives, then the number of interactions with the health care delivery system exhibited by this hidden group should be significantly lower than the number of such interactions exhibited by other female drug abusers.

To test this hypothesis, the data on two groups of female drug abusers were analyzed. The first group were married women who lived with their families and who had worked less than six months in the two year period prior to their admission to the research centers (i.e., the housewife group). The second group was selected as a comparison group and was matched with the study group on marital status and living situation, but were working more than six months in the two year period prior to their admission (i.e., employed women).

Using these criteria we selected a group of 58 females from the data base as the study group (i.e., housewives) and a comparison group of 50 employed women. Data on these groups were then accessed from the data base and analyzed using the SPSS statistical analysis program. The groups were compared on a wide range of variables, including demographic and socio-economic indicators, drug taking patterns and behaviors, and interaction with facets of the health care system.

The control variables for the study were marital status, living arrangements and employement status. Three variables -- psychiatric treatment episodes, emergency room episodes and drug treatment episodes -- were used as dependent variables to test the hypothesis.

We expected that if the hypothesis was correct as formulated, statistically significant differences would exist between the two groups. Chi-square tests were used to determine the significance of the differences. The three dependent variables were used as measures of the interaction of the two groups with facets of the health care delivery system, i.e., the mental health system, the drug treatment system and hospital emergency care system.

If the hypothesis was not proven to be correct, we could not simply conclude that the hidden population of drug abusing housewives does not exist. Rather, we would call into question the premises for such a theory. Proof that such a population is more myth than fact will require experiments more complex than the one we could conduct with the limited data available.

III. FINDINGS

Our findings indicate that, at a 90% confidence interval, there are no statistically significant differences between the housewives and employed women in either age or racial composition. The majority in both groups are over thirty years old and white. We do note significant differences ($P < .01$) between the groups' level of education and source of income, but this might well be expected given the rather strong connections between employment, education and income in our society. Fully twice as many of the employed women have completed an education beyond the high-school level. Also 38% of the employed group have not completed high-school as compared to 61% of the housewives. As might be predicted, almost twice as many of the housewife group are dependent upon spouses for their financial support. It is interesting to note, however, that only 2% of either group report reliance on illegal sources of income.

Neither group has a particularly high rate of arrests or unexpected number of suicide attempts given the degree of drug abuse exhibited. Seventy-eight percent of the housewives and 84% of the employed group reported no arrests within the two years prior to polydrug center admission. Likewise, the majority of both groups (74% and 76%, respectively) reported no attempt at self destruction during the same period. On both variables group differences are not statistically significant at a 90% confidence interval.

The kinds of drug classes abused by these women, their situations of use and drug sources are presented in Table I. We note that both groups primarily abuse the opiates, barbiturates and psychotropics. In addition, the housewives and employed women alike tend to use these drugs in solitary situations and to obtain them via prescription.

Table II summarizes data on both groups' interaction with three facets of the health care delivery system. We note that fully 47% of the housewives and 42% of the employed women received drug related emergency room treatment one or more times during the two years prior to intake at the polydrug centers. Also, over half of each group reported at least one episode of psychiatric treatment during that same period. From the chi-square comparisons, it was found that the groups are not significantly different in terms of their degree of interaction with either the hospital emergency care system or the mental health system. Nor are they different to a statistically significant degree in their level of interaction with the drug treatment system.

IV. SUMMARY AND CONCLUSION

To summarize briefly, at a 90% confidence interval there are no statistically significant differences between the housewives and their employed counterparts except for level of education and source of income. These differences are not only understandable, but are also to be expected, given that employment status was used to discriminate between the groups.

Our hypothesis stated that if housewives do in fact represent a hidden group, they would differ from the more visible employed group in their degree of interaction with health care facilities. However, our analysis suggests that the groups are not only alike in terms of certain health services received, but further, there are no significant differences in their demographic characteristics or in their drug taking patterns and behaviors. On 11 variables housewife drug abusers are neither different from nor less visible than their employed counterparts. However, neither group is very visible at all, if we look for them in the drug treatment population. While over 50% of these women had sought psychiatric attention and nearly as many appeared in emergency rooms for drug related treatment, three quarters had not received services from a drug treatment program during that same two-year period.

Our findings do not disprove the theory of a hidden population, but they certainly do suggest that female drug abusers in general, and female housewife drug abusers in particular, are no less visible than their male counterparts. While male drug abusers have a higher arrest rate, appear in drug treatment programs more frequently and have more dramatic patterns of drug use than females, the female drug abuser is nonetheless highly visible in the health care system.

676

Theorizing a hidden female population is one way of rationalizing the low proportion of women in drug programs. It is also a mechanism which conveniently masks the need for specially designed services directed toward women. Therefore, we conclude that as long as the concept of the "hidden abuser" persists in lieu of its subjection to rigorous, objective analysis, treatment responsive to the special needs of the female will not be available within the drug abuse treatment system.

TABLE I

HOUSEWIVES AND EMPLOYED WOMEN
BY PRIMARY DRUG OF ABUSE,
SITUATION OF USE AND SOURCE OF DRUG

Primary Drug Class	Housewives N =58	Employed N=50
Opiates	30%	22%
Alcohol	7%	10%
Barbiturates	26%	20%
Amphetamines	5%	12%
Marihuana	5%	8%
Psychotropics	23%	24%
Other	4%	4%
Situation of Use		
Not used	3%	10%
Alone	69%	65%
With Others	28%	25%
Source of Drug		
Prescription/OTC	52%	44%
Street Buy	12%	14%
Illegal Source	5%	0%
Other	7%	18%
No Answer	24%	24%

TABLE II

HOUSEWIVES AND EMPLOYED WOMEN BY
HEALTH CARE DELIVERY SYSTEM INTERACTION

Emergency Room Episodes	Housewives N=58	Employed N=50
None	53%	58%
One or more	47%	42%
Psychiatric Episodes		
None	45%	42%
One or more	54%	58%
Prior Drug Treatment		
None	74%	84%
One or more	25%	16%

SPECIAL NEEDS OF WOMEN PATIENTS AT THE DRUG ABUSE SERVICE,
BRONX PSYCHIATRIC CENTER - ALBERT EINSTEIN COLLEGE OF MEDICINE

Suzanne M. Mondo

and

Lawrence Santora, M.A.

Drug Abuse Service
Bronx Psychiatric Center
Albert Einstein College of Medicine
Bronx, New York

American women have been the primary users of legally available psychoactive substances, except alcohol, since the nineteenth
century.[1] Now their use of alcohol is rising and they are consuming more psychoactive prescription drugs then ever before.[2]

The increased use of all licit psychoactive substances by
this country's women is, in itself, a matter of general concern.
But the appearance of large numbers of women in treatment across
the country demands that this nation's substance abuse treatment
community develop effective and attractive rehabilitation programs
for female addicts and substance abusers. This requires the cultivation by the treatment community of a sensitivity to these women's
specific needs and problems sufficient to pursue productive research and develop effective treatment.

The Drug Abuse Service of Albert Einstein College of Medicine
Bronx Psychiatric Center, where more than 1/3 of those in treatment are female, has taken a step in this direction by conducting
an in-depth survey of 147 representative female patients. The
survey has provided the Drug Abuse Service with data which not
only indicates where further research is needed but also suggests
modifications of an adjuncts to existing treatment services.

The Drug Abuse Service, begun in 1967 under the direction of
Dr. Joyce Lowinson, currently treats more then 2,200 Bronx residents over 700 of whom are women. Treatment is provided through
seven out-patient clinics geographically dispersed throughout the
Bronx. A small in-patient ward is maintained for detoxification
and the treatment of multiple addictions. Patients have available
to them at their clinic location, a wide range of specialized

support services: educational, vocational, legal and social. The results of the survey provide a preliminary picture of the female treatment population.

The data was gathered by personal interview in each women's clinic. A questionnaire was completed by the interviewer in the presence of the women being interviewed in order to ensure the accuracy of responses. Every attempt was made to be sure that the women understood the question and that her response accurately reflected the facts about herself.

The women surveyed were mostly young and non-white. The mean age of the group was 27.6 with 80.2% of them between the ages of 18 and 33. Seventy-one percent were black or hispanic. For further information on the ethnicity see table #1.

The women were questioned about the amount of their income. Forty-five percent, 44.9%, report an income of less then $5,000 and 62.2% relied upon welfare as sole support. For further information see table #2 and #3.

Two facts emerged from the income and personal data; one disturbing, the other curious. While 56 of the women reported being presently married, only 13 of them reported receiving any support at all from their spouses. While this may not be surprising, it does remain disturbing.

The curious and somewhat difficult finding to interpret concerns the number of women willing to report the source of their income compared to those willing to report its amount. Sixty-two women refused to report the amount of their income but only 18 refused to report its source. One would normally expect the reverse. What is difficult to determine is whether this unexpected disparity is due to a deficiency in the questionnaire (income and source were combined into one question) or underlying socio-legal factors.

There are several possible socio-legal explanations. Welfare fraud and income derived from illegal activities come most easily to mind. But perhaps the real explanation is somewhat more subtle: a sense of shame or actual ignorance of the amount of yearly income.

The response of the women to questions concerning their level of sexual activity, use of birth control and desire to become pregnant produced some noteworthy results. A large majority (107) stated that they did not wish to become pregnant. But, 53 women maintained a level of sexual activity (intercourse more than once a week) while using no birth control at all. These women clearly having children they neither want nor can support.

These women certainly give us good reason to be concerned about their future and that of their families. Of course, treatment programs have neither the legal nor the ethical right to interfere without invitation in the personal or family affairs of their patients. But we do have the clear cut obligation to help women avoid having children they do not want.

It is tempting to explore the reasons for such irrational and destructive behavior. It is, however, more useful to ask ourselves what can we do, what services can our programs offer to help these women avoid unwanted children. Medical, especially gynecological, services are not the answer. Almost all of these women regularly consult physicians and gynecologists. According to the data collected there is however, some hope that this vicious cycle can be broken. As the educational level of the women rose the use of birth control increased sharply. Only 37 of the women surveyed practice birth control but of these more than 3/4's (38) had at least completed high school. Furthermore, of the 19 women who were attending or had graduated college only two were engaging in sexual intercourse while not practicing birth control. While the emergence of rational behavior in this better educated group is by no means unexpected it is certainly welcomed. Clearly, this area offers opportunities for fertile research.

TABLE #1

N=147

	Number	Percent
Black	60	40.8
Hispanic	45	30.6
White	40	27.2
No Response	2	1.4
	147	100.0

TABLE #2

INCOME	Number	Percent
Under $5,000	66	44.9
5 - 10,000	13	8.8
Over 10,000	6	4.1
No Response	62	42.2
	147	100.0

TABLE #3

SOURCE OF INCOME	Number	Percent
Welfare Only	92	62.6
Welfare & Spouse	7	4.8
Welfare, Employment	1	.7
Employed	11	7.5
Supported by Spouse	6	4.1
Unemployment Ins.	3	2.0
Other	9	6.1
No Response	18	12.2
	147	100.0

REFERENCES

1. Edward M. Brecher, et al, Licit and Illicit Drugs, Little Brown and Company, 1972, page 484.

2. ibid.

682

NARCOTIC DEPENDENCY IN PREGNANCY

Methadone Maintenance Compared to Use of Street Drugs

Barry Stimmel, M.D.
Department of Medicine
Mount Sinai School of Medicine
City University of New York
New York, New York

Karlis Adamsons, M.D., Ph.D.
Department of Obstetrics and
    Gynecology
Brown University School of Medicine
Providence, Rhode Island

Over the past year, increasing attention has been given to the problem of chronic intake of various narcotics during gestation and their effects upon mother and child. Particular emphasis has been placed on methadone. The concern is understandable in view of the large number of pregnant women currently enrolled in methadone programs. In New York City alone, approximately 33,000 persons are registered with methadone maintenance programs; of these, 25% are estimated to be women of chile-bearing age. (1) Recent reports regarding the effects of methadone on the neonate have been controversial. Some consider methadone therapy relatively innocuous; others have associated it with serious hazards including severe withdrawal symptoms and even crib deaths. (1-4) With few exceptions most of the published studies involve poorly defined populations and lack adequate control groups.

The present study was undertaken to elucidate the relationship between methadone maintenance therapy and outcome of pregnancy. The course of gestation was closely followed in patients enrolled in a comprehensive methadone maintenance treatment program and was compared with that in women taking narcotics under essentially uncontrolled conditions and with that in women not exposed to narcotics agents during the antepartum period.

PATIENTS AND METHODS

All women who gave birth while enrolled in the methadone maintenance program from March 1968 to May 1974 at The Mount Sinai Hos-

This paper is an adaptation of a paper published in JAMA, March 15, 1976, vol. 235, pp. 1121-1124, copyright 1976, the American Medical Association.

pital formed the first group of patients (group 1). These 28 women
had 31 pregnancies and were followed closely with respect to methadone dose, use of other drugs, and medical complications. Urinalysis for mood-altering drugs was performed at least weekly, during
the time that the women were enrolled in the program, by thin-layer
chromatography, by a modification of the method described by Dole
et al. (5) The following are the drugs capable of detection by this
method, with their lower limits of detection (μg/ml);

Heroin	
(detected as morphine)	0.2
Morphine	0.2
Cocaine met	2.5
Cocaine metabolites	
Ecgonine	2.5
Benzoylecgonine	2.5
Codeine	1.0
Methadone hydrochloride	0.1
Glutethimide	2.5
Phenothiazines	1.0
Amphetamines	1.0
Barbiturates	1.0
Quinine	0.1

The second group consisted of women known to be users of various narcotic agents of their own choice (heroin or methadone) whose
infants were born between July 1971 and April 1974. The records of
these persons were reviewed, and only those cases in which an adequate data base concerning drug use could be obtained were included.
The 57 women in this group (group 2) were further subgrouped into
30 persons who used mainly heroin (group 2A) and 27 women who used
only methadone (group 2B), obtained either on the street or in
other methadone programs. Analysis of urine for drugs could be
performed only rarely, since most women were seen infrequently before delivery.

A third group of women (group 3) were selected from the population of women whose infants were delivered in the obstetrical
service from January through October 1972. The records of 30 women
between the ages of 18 and 35 residing in East Harlem and without
a recorded history of drug abuse were selected. Analysis of urine
for mood-altering drugs was not performed. The obstetrical records
of the women in all three groups were carefully reviewed with respect to past obstetrical history, coexisting medical problems, and
duration of pregnancy, labor and delivery.

The records of the 118 infants born to women in all groups
were reviewed to determine the incidence of fetal distress, Apgar
scores at one and five minutes, birth weight, neonatal complications, and the presence of withdrawal symptoms. All infants born
to those mothers of group 1 have been followed up through May 1974

for periods ranging from 1 to 55 months. Follow-up information could not be obtained with any consistency in the other two groups of patients. Tests for statistical significance in group comparisons were performed by use of the χ^2 and the Student t test.

RESULTS

Maternal Profile

The daily dose of methadone in group 1 ranged from 20 to 100 mg, with 65% being maintained on a daily dose of 50 mg. Use of other drugs was documented in four women in group 1.

The great variability in potency of "street" heroin and the large number of women on "street" methadone of uncertain dose in groups 2A and 2B made it impossible to estimate with any degree of accuracy the average narcotic dose taken during pregnancy.

None of the women in group 3 have a history of taking mood-altering medication.

Approximately one third of the women in groups 2 and 3 were pregnant with their first child. The percentage of primiparous women in group 1 was slightly but not significantly less. Multiparous women were more frequent in group 3 (36.7%) as compared to group 1 and 2 (19.4% and 8.7%).

Coexisting medical problems were seen in 16.1% of the patients in group 1 (P=.025), 36.6% of those in group 2, and 46.6% of those in group 3. Anemia (detected on the initial obstetrical clinic visit by the finding of a hemoglobin level of less than 10 gm/100 ml) was the most frequent problem encountered in each of the groups (12.9%, 26.3% and 23.3%, respectively).

Characteristics of Newborns

The mean Apgar scores at one and five minutes were essentially the same in all groups. Fetal distress (as manifested by tachycardia, bradycardia, or meconium detected at delivery or stillbirth) existed in 16.1% of group 1 infants, 42.1% of group 2, and 23.3% of group 3. This difference was significant (P=.05) for babies in group 2 as compared to those in group 1. One of these infants was stillborn.

The mean birth weight of infants in group 1 was 170 gm greater than that of those in group 2 (2,933 gm vs. 2,763 gm) and 376 gm less than that of group 3 infants whose mothers were not exposed to narcotic agents (P=.01 and P=.001, respectively, when compared to group 3 infants). The incidence of low birth weight (less than 2,500 gm) was essentially the same in groups 1 and 2 (22.6% and 26.3%) and much greater than the 3% incidence noted in group 3 (P=.01).

Neonatal Complications

With the exception of the signs of fetal distress mentioned earlier, infants in group 3 were relatively free of problems in the early neonatal period. Similarly, if withdrawal symptoms are excluded, no major problems existed among the infants in group 1, except that three newborns exhibited transient respiratory distress. In contrast, respiratory distress was noted in nine infants in group 2, and there were congenital defects in four infants (microcephaly, polydactyly, and two cases of hydrocele). One infant was stillborn, having died prior to onset of active labor. One infant died six hours after birth.

Withdrawal Symptoms

Narcotic withdrawal was diagnosed in 18 infants (58%) in group 1 and in 29 (51%) of those in group 2. The symptoms of withdrawal were essentially the same in both groups, consisting mainly of irritability. The onset of symptoms occurred in less than 24 hours in 28% in group 1, as compared to 59% in group 2 ($P=.01$), and 82% in group 2A ($P<.001$).

In group 1 women in whom the methadone dose was known, the mean maternal dose of methadone was greater in those whose children did not evidence withdrawal (71.5 mg vs. 47.2 mg; $P=.005$).

COMMENT

Illicit heroin use has long been associated with dysfunction of the reproductive system in women. (6) It has also been associated with an increase in complications during gestation, particularly in respect to the fetus, with 50% of newborns weighing less than 2,500 gm. (7) Considerable concern and controversy has developed about morbidity in infants born to mothers maintained on methadone. In most instances, the patients comprising the study series have been a heterogeneous group, consisting of multiple-drug users rather than of women using methadone only. The current study differs from previous series in that it attempts to define more clearly the outcome of pregnancy in mothers who are on a methadone maintenance program under close medical supervision.

The ethnic composition and average age of the three groups of women were not quite comparable. The women without a history of drug abuse (group 3) were somewhat older and of higher parity than those of groups 1 and 2.

Although it might be expected that women using illicit drugs would have the greatest incidence of coexisting medical problems, the greatest incidence was, in fact, found in the so-called drug-free group (group 3). This was due nearly entirely to the arbitrary definition of "coexisting medical problems" that included anemia (defined as a hemoglobin level) less than 10 mg/100 ml. The greater degreee of medical supervision given to group 1 women prior to the onset of their pregnancies while they were enrolled in the methadone maintenance program and their lower parity appear to account for the discrepancy.

Fetal Distress
    The incidence of fetal distress was lowest in babies born to women in group 1, being less, but not significantly so, than that seen in group 3. Forty-two percent of infants in group 2 gave evidence of fetal distress ($P<.05$), with the greatest incidence seen in infants of women taking heroin (47%) rather than methadone (37%). This finding is similar to that of Naeye et al, (8) who observed that 60% of placental specimens of heroin users showed meconium histiocytosis, indicating passage of meconium prior to onset of labor.

    The incidence of low birth weight in group 1 and 2 infants (22.6%) is comparable to that reported by other investigators. (1, 9). The precise effect of narcotic dependency on fetal development has not yet been elucidated. It has been shown, however, that the reduction in cell number is more substantial than that in cell size. (6) The effects of smoking, frequently seen in drug users, may also play a contributory role, as might poor nutrition, anoxia, and diminished placental blood-flow occurring during intermittent maternal withdrawal. Maternal anxiety, also associated with a reduced birth weight, may be another contributing factor. (10)

    The presence of neonatal complications, exclusive of withdrawal, was most prominent among group 2 infants, with serious problems, including two deaths, noted only in this group.

    The effects of methadone and other narcotic agents with respect to teratogenicity remain controversial. Falek et al, (11), in a cytogenic study of 16 opiate users maintained on methadone, found that opiate users had an unusual number of chromosomal aberrations when compared to a control group. However, in vitro studies, performed to eliminate other factors such as multiple-drug abuse, did not demonstrate an increased frequency of damage. In laboratory animals teratogenic effects of methadone in toxicologic doses (100 mg/kg) have been reported by Greber. (12) However, when the dose administered was reduced to levels more approximating the maintenance dose, no drug-related defects were observed in the fetuses. (13) In the current study, the only congenital abnormalities observed occurred in group 2 women who were using mostly heroin during their pregnancies.

    Respiratory distress was present in 9.6% of infants in group 1 and 15.7% of infants in group 2. Tachypnea and alkalosis have previously been reported in narcotic-dependent infants, and it has been suggested that these protect the newborn against the respiratory distress syndrome. (14)

Withdrawal

The incidence and severity of withdrawal symptoms in infants whose mothers have been maintained on methadone has varied greatly. (2,4,15,16) In considering this problem, it is essential to define clearly the issues. Methadone, like any narcotic agent and most pharmacologic compounds, freely crosses the placental membrane and can be found in the fetal blookstream. Therefore, it is expected that infants born to methadone-dependent women will be dependent and undergo withdrawal. However, only in a varying number of cases will the clinical signs of withdrawal actually be evident. Administration of methadone during pregnancy, therefore, is not to prevent withdrawal in the neonate but rather to decrease the incidence of maternal and fetal complications occurring during illicit heroin use.

When women on maintenance, regardless of methadone dosage, are followed up carefully with routine urinalysis to detect multiple-drug use, the incidence of clinical withdrawal approximates 60%, (1,3) the neonatal complications are minimal, and the infants usually do well. When inadequate supervision exists and when other drugs are likely to be taken by the pregnant individual, attendant complications are likely. This pertains particularly to use of barbiturates, which is quite prevalent among narcotic users. Maternal barbiturate dependency can produce severe symptoms in the neonate, practically identical to those of opiate dependency. (17) The relative frequency of patients ingesting other depressive agents might be even higher since alcohol, certain hypnotics, and tranquilizers are not always detected by thin-layer chromatography of the urine.

The symptoms of withdrawal noted in the infants in the present series were rather mild, with severe signs being more frequent in the heroin-dependent infant. Not unexpectedly, the onset of withdrawal was delayed in those infants whose mothers were maintained on methadone, in some instances for as long as four days. It is, therefore, important to watch such children closely during the first week of life so as to detect clinical signs of withdrawal.

A correlation could not be made between maternal dose and presence of withdrawal. Some infants whose mothers were maintained on a dose of 20 mg/day experienced symptoms while some of those whose mothers were maintained on higher doses remained symptom-free. This is similar to the finding of Newman (1) and may represent observer variance in diagnosing withdrawal.

Treatment of withdrawal symptoms was necessary in 87% of all infants. In the current series, phenobarbital at a dose of 10 mg/ kg was the agent most frequently used. Satisfactory effects were obtained in all but four children. In those four, paregoric was administered, with subsequent relief. The use of barbiturates, although not contraindicated, has been shown by Kron et al (18) to result in a depression of neonatal sucking response considerable greater than that seen when paregoric was used to treat the withdrawal. Since little or no cross reactivity exists between narcotic agents and other mood-altering drugs, paregoric (or other mild opiates) is probably the drug of choice in treating withdrawal. These narcotics have been used hesitantly for fear of perpetuating opiate dependency. The fallacy of this thinking is apparent. The infant is already narcotic-dependent, and use of a mild narcotic agent in diminishing doses can provide prompt, effective, and safe relief. Other depressant drugs, such as chlorpromazine, have also been advocated as effective agents. (2) Chlorpromazine offers no advantage over paregoric and in addition, chlorpromazine is known to remain in the body for 16 to 18 months following discontinuation of use.

Prognosis

The subsequent benign course of infants whose mothers had been under careful medical supervision while on methadone therapy has been confirmed by several investigators. (1, 3) However, others have reported less favorable findings with instances of sudden death. (4, 16) In many of these cases, the mother had been on methadone maintenance for a relatively short period of time prior to delivery. No urinalyses had been performed to detect the presence of multiple drug abuse, and the infants died after a period sufficient for methadone to have been eliminated from the system. The absence of objective findings in these cases makes it hardly tenable to implicate methadone as a contributing factor.

All infants in group 1 have done well following discharge from the hospital, and no abnormalities in growth have been noted. One child has had repeated episodes of pneumonia requiring hospitalization. These children, ranging in age from 6 months to 5 years, are still being followed up by the pediatric clinic, and their progress is carefully monitored.

References

1. Newman, R: Pregnancies of methadone patients. N.Y. State J. Med 74:52-54, 1974.
2. Zelsen C, Jalee S, Casalino m: Neonatal narcotic addiction. N Engl J Med 289:1216-1220, 1974.
3. Blinick G, Jerez E, Wallach R: Methadone maintenance, pregnancy, and progeny. JAMA 225:477-479, 1973.
4. Pierson PS, Kleber HP: Sudden death in infants born to methadone maintained mothers. JAMA 220:1733-1744, 1972.
5. Dole VP, Crowther A, Johnson J, et al: Detection of narcotic, sedative, and amphetamine drugs in urine. N.Y. State J Med 72:471-476, 1972.

6. Stoffer SS: A gynecologic study of drug addicts. Am J Obstet Gynecol 101:779-783, 1968.
7. Stone M, Salerno LJ, Green M, et al: Narcotic addiction in pregnancy. Am J Obstet Gynecol 109:716-723, 1971.
8. Naeye RL, Blanc W, Leblanc W, et al:Fetal complications of maternal heroin addiction: Abnormal growth, infections and episodes of stress. J Pediatr 83:1055-1061, 1973.
9. Lipsitz PJ, Blatman S: The early neonatal period of 100 live-borns of mothers on methadone. Pediatr Res 7:404, 1973.
10. Shaw JA, Wheeler P, Morgan DW: Mother-infant relationship and weight gain in the first month of life. J Am Acad Child Psychiatry 9:428-444, 1970.
11. Falek A, Jordon RB, King BJ, et al: Human chromosomes and opiates. Arch Gen Psychiatry 27:511-515, 1972.
12. Greber WF: Blockade of teratogenic effect of morphine, dihydromorphinone and methadone by nalorphine, cyclazocine and naloxone in the fetal hamster, in Keup W (ed): Drug Abuse: Current Concepts and Research. Springfield, Ill, Charles C Thomas Publishers, 1972, pp. 117-122.
13. Markham J, Emmerson JL, Owen NV: Teratogenicity studies of methadone HCl in rats and rabbits. Nature 233:342-343, 1971.
14. Glass L, Rajegowda BK, Evans HE: Absence of respiratory distress syndrome in premature infants of heroin addicted mothers. Lancet 2:685, 1971.
15. Rajegowda BK, Glass L, Evans HE, et al: Methadone withdrawal in newborn infants. J Pediatr 81:532-534, 1972.
16. Harper RG, Sla CG, Blenman S: Observations on the sudden death of infants born to addicted mothers, in Proceedings of the Fifth National Conference on Methadone Treatment, Washington, D.C., March 17-19, 1973. New York, National Association for the Prevention of Addiction to Narcotics, 1973, pp. 1122-1127.
17. Desmond MM, Schwanecke RP, Wilson GS, et al: Maternal barbiturate utilization and neonatal withdrawal symptomatology. J Pediatr 80:190-197, 1973.
18. Kron RE, Litt M, Finnegan LP: Behavior of infants born to narcotic addicted mothers. Pediatr Res 7:292, 1973.

DOES METHADONE DURING PREGNANCY AFFECT

NEONATAL OUTCOME?

Loretta P. Finnegan, M.D.
Dian S. Reeser, B.A.
James F. Connaughton, M.D.
Jacob Schut, M.D.

Departments of Pediatrics, Obstetrics and
Psychiatry
Philadelphia General Hospital and
The University of Pennsylvania School of
Medicine
Philadelphia, Pennsylvania

This manuscript reports clinical research on infants born to women on a program which utilizes a comprehensive approach of intensive obstetrical and psychosocial care combined with methadone maintenance at Philadelphia General Hospital (PGH).

Comparative groups of 488 pregnant women (303 heroin or methadone dependent and 185 non drug-dependent) who delivered at PGH between 1969 and 1975 were studied. They were divided into five groups: Group A (N=63), heroin dependent/no prenatal care; Group B (N=88), methadone dependent/inadequate prenatal care (avg. 1.8 visits); Group C (N=152), methadone dependent/adequate prenatal care (avg. 8.3 visits) / psychosocial counseling; Group D (N=85), non drug-dependent/no prenatal care; Group E (N=100), non drug-dependent/adequate prenatal care (avg. 9.1 visits). Both of these groups delivered at PGH and included women who were of the same socioeconomic and ethnic class as our drug-dependent patients.

Table I describes the heroin habit and methadone dose and duration in Groups A, B and C. In comparing groups A/B, A/C, and B/C, a significant difference is found in the amount of heroin used when groups A/B and A/C are compared but not when comparing B/C. There is no significant difference in duration of heroin usage between any of the group comparisons. Heroin use and duration in Group A have been calculated from initial heroin use to delivery and in Groups B and C, it was calculated from initial use until enrollment in the methadone maintenance clinic. Groups B and C are compared in regard to methadone dose and duration. Average daily methadone dose in Groups B and C is not significantly different but duration is.

All groups were compared in regard to obstetrical complications.
Group A, had the largest percentage of obstetrical complications.
Groups B and C were not significantly different from Group E. Striking differences were seen in the incidence of low birth weight (LBW)
i.e.,the percentage of infants who weigh less than 2500 grams or
5 1/2 pounds. The largest percentage of LBW infants was in Group A
followed by Group B in which there were 34.9%, three times the national average. The incidence of LBW is markedly decreased in Group
C in comparison to Groups A and B. For the complication of pre-
eclampsia, Group A had the highest incidence with the two methadone
dependent groups having less than the non drug-dependent groups.
Birth weights of the 303 infants born to drug-dependent women and
the 185 controls were compared. The average weight in grams was
much lower in Group A than all other groups and, as duration of
methadone usage increased, birth weight increased.

In Table II, birth weight, gestational age and Apgar scores in
Groups A, B and C are compared. There is no significant difference
in birthweight and gestational age when comparing Groups A/B. When
comparing Groups A/C, and B/C, there is a significant difference in
birth weight and gestational age. In comparing Apgar scores at 1 and
5 minutes in the various groups, the only significant difference is
found between Groups A and C.

In Table III, the incidence of prematurity, LBW, and morbidity, in
groups A, B and C are compared. Infants were defined as premature
if their birth weight was appropriate for gestational age of < 37
weeks. In comparing Groups A/B there is no significant difference
in regard to these three variables. When comparing Groups A/C, significant differences are seen in the incidences of prematurity and
low birth weight but none in morbidity. There is a trend in Group C
toward a lower percentage of morbidity in comparison to Group A.
Significant differences were found in all parameters when comparing
Groups B/C.

Severity of withdrawal symptomatology was evaluated for 287 infants
of drug-dependent mothers: mild, no pharmacotherapy; moderate, pharmacotherapy for 14 days or less; severe; pharmacotherapy for more
than 14 days. Over 80% of the infants in Groups B/C, the methadone
dependent mothers' infants, had mild or moderate withdrawal in comparison to 70% of infants in Group A. Severe withdrawal was seen in
25% of the infants of heroin dependent mothers in comparison to 11%
in both methadone dependent groups.

In conclusion, when comparing a group of infants born to heroin dependent women and two groups of methadone maintained women, one with
inadequate and the other with adequate prenatal care, striking differences are found. Both groups of methadone maintained women in
comparison to the heroin dependent women had decreased obstetrical

692

complications including pre-eclampsia, a decreased incidence of low birth weight and prematurity and an increased average birth weight, gestational age, and Apgar scores. There were no significant differences between overall infant morbidity, but withdrawal severity was greater in the infants born in the heroin dependent group than those in either methadone dependent groups.

When comparing the two methadone dependent groups, the incidence of LBW, prematurity and morbidity was greater in the group receiving inadequate prenatal care. Even though obstetrical complications were seen less in the methadone dependent/inadequate prenatal care group, average birth weights were decreased in comparison to the methadone dependent/adequate prenatal care group. There was no significant difference in Apgar scores and withdrawal severity between the methadone dependent groups. It appears that short-term methadone maintenance and inadequate prenatal care do not significantly improve infant outcome but that longer methadone maintenance during pregnancy with adequate prenatal care can significantly improve infant outcome in regard to the parameters listed above.

TABLE I

HEROIN HABIT AND METHADONE DOSE/DURATION IN GROUPS A,B,AND C

(N=303)

PHILADELPHIA GENERAL HOSPITAL

1969-1975

GROUP COMPARISONS	HEROIN BAGS/DAY	HEROIN DURATION (MOS)	METHADONE DOSE (MG/DAY)	METHADONE DURATION (WEEKS)
A (N=63)	6.1	52.7		
			N.A.*	N.A.
B (N=88)	10.1	45.4		
	p < 0.001	N.S.**		
A (N=63)	6.1	52.7		
			N.A.	N.A.
C (N=152)	10.9	46.9		
	p < 0.001	N.S.		
B (N=88)	10.1	45.4	29.5	14.2
C (N=152)	10.9	46.9	33.3	28.5
	N.S.	N.S.	N.S.	p < 0.001

* NOT APPLICABLE

** NOT SIGNIFICANT

694

TABLE II

COMPARISONS OF BIRTH WEIGHT, GESTATIONAL AGE AND APGAR

SCORES IN GROUPS A, B, C. †

PHILADELPHIA GENERAL HOSPITAL

1969-1975

GROUP COMPARISONS	BIRTHWEIGHT (GRAMS)	GESTATIONAL AGE (WEEKS)	APGAR SCORE 1"	5"
A (N=63)	2511	37.4	7.0	8.3
B (N=88)	2663	37.6	7.8	8.9
	N.S.*	N.S.	N.S.	N.S.
A (N=63)	2511	37.4	7.0	8.3
C (N=152)	2900	38.9	7.8	9.1
	$p < 0.01$	$p < 0.01$	$p < 0.04$	$p < 0.03$
B (N=88)	2663	37.6	7.8	8.9
C (N=152)	2900	38.9	7.8	9.1
	$p < 0.01$	$p < 0.06$	N.S.	N.S.

† ALL OF THE VALUES REPRESENT AVERAGES FOR THE SPECIFIC GROUP

* N.S. - NOT SIGNIFICANT

TABLE III

COMPARISONS OF INCIDENCE OF PREMATURITY (AGA, < 37 WEEKS),

LOW BIRTH WEIGHT (< 2500) AND INFANT MORBIDITY IN

GROUPS A, B, AND C

PHILADELPHIA GENERAL HOSPITAL

1969-1975

GROUP COMPARISONS	INCIDENCE OF PREMATURITY (%)	INCIDENCE OF LBW (%)	INCIDENCE OF MORBIDITY (%)*
A (N=63)	38.1	47.6	74.6
B (N=88)	30.2	34.9	80.2
	N.S.**	N.S.	N.S.
A (N=63	38.1	47.6	74.6
C (N-152)	10.5	17.1	65.8
	p < 0.001	p < 0.001	N.S.
B (N=88)	30.2	34.9	80.2
C (N=152)	10.5	17.1	65.8
	p < 0.001	p < 0.01	p < 0.03

* Infants were considered to have morbidity if they had one or
more of the following conditions: asphyxia neonatorum, aspiration pneumonia, congenital syphilis, intrauterine growth retardation, prematurity, hyperbilirubinemia, septicemia, hemolytic
disease, transient tachnypea, hypocalcemia, hypoglycemia, or
hyaline membrane disease.

**NOT SIGNIFICANT

THE EFFECTS OF HEROIN AND METHADONE USED DURING PREGNANCY ON INFANT GROWTH STATUS AT DELIVERY

Dian S. Reeser, B.A.
James F. Connaughton, M.D.
Loretta P. Finnegan, M.D.
Jacob Schut, M.D.

Departments of Obstetrics and Gynecology,
Pediatrics and Psychiatry
Philadelphia General Hospital and
The University of Pennsylvania School of
Medicine
Philadelphia, Pennsylvania

In our previous studies at Philadelphia General Hospital (PGH), we have found that infants born to heroin dependent women who seek no prenatal care during pregnancy have decreased birth weights when compared to infants of methadone maintained women, or to specific control populations. The infants of the heroin dependent women also had an increased incidence of intrauterine growth retardation when compared to infants of methadone maintained women, and, moreover, infants of methadone maintained women with adequate prenatal care have approached the statistics seen in non drug-dependent popula-tions.

This manuscript will discuss the effects of heroin and methadone, used during pregnancy, on three different growth status categories. Three-hundred and nine live infants were classified into three growth status categories based on gestational age and weight at birth: full term appropriate for gestational age, ≥ 37 weeks gestation with birth weight ≥ 2500 grams; premature, weight appropriate for gestational age of < 37 weeks; intrauterine growth retarded, birth weight not concordant for gestational age.

Within each growth status category, infants were further classified as to the drug and prenatal histories of their mothers: Group A, heroin dependent with continued heroin intake throughout pregnancy, no prenatal care; Group B, methadone maintained during pregnancy, ≤ 3 prenatal visits; Group C, maintained on methadone during preg-nancy, ≥ 4 prenatal visits. All women delivered at PGH and received prenatal care in the obstetrical clinic of the hospital. The fol-lowing maternal and infant variables were computed for each growth status class: daily heroin habit and duration of intake, daily methadone dose and length of maintenance, infant birth weight and gestational age, Apgar scores at 1 and 5 minutes, incidence of ob-stetrical and medical complications, and severity of neonatal abstinence. Neonatal abstinence was classified into four categories and defined according to severity. Class I, no withdrawal; Class II, mild withdrawal; Class III, moderate withdrawal necessitating detoxicant therapy for ≤ 14 days; and Class IV, severe withdrawal necessitating detoxicant therapy for ≥ 14 days.

Table I contains the data for the 216 full term infants. The women who had adequate prenatal care and methadone maintenance for 30 weeks of pregnancy (Group C) delivered infants with the highest birth weight. The women in Group C, although having an incidence of obstetrical and medical complications similar to Group A, had the advantage of having these complications identified and treated.

Data for the 68 premature infants are listed in Table II. It is noted here that short-term methadone maintenance, even when combined with adequate prenatal care (Group C), did not improve birth weight or gestational age of infants but did decrease the incidence of severe withdrawal. There was an increase in obstetrical complications for all groups which probably contributed to the premature birth of these infants.

The 25 intrauterine growth retarded infants are described in Table III. In this category, infants of women with methadone maintenance throughout pregnancy and inadequate prenatal care (Group B) produced the lowest birth weight infants.

In summary, when describing two groups of low birth weight infants and one group of full term infants, the birth weights of full term infants born to women maintained on methadone with adequate prenatal care were significantly higher than the weight of those born to heroin dependent women, and somewhat increased over the weight of those born to methadone maintained women who had inadequate prenatal care and significantly less daily dose and duration of maintenance.

Within the premature and intrauterine growth retarded groups, birth weights of infants whose mothers used heroin or methadone, regardless of prenatal care, were not remarkably different; furthermore, there were no significant differences in any of the other variables within these two growth status categories.

It is interesting to note that the methadone dose and duration of mothers of full term infants with improved outcome was comparable to one of the groups of methadone maintained women who delivered growth retarded infants-the difference between these two groups was that the mothers of the full term infants had four times more prenatal visits than those of the growth retarded group.

In general, within infant growth status categories as defined by birth weight and gestational age, infants of heroin and methadone maintained women, regardless of prenatal care and incidences of obstetrical-medical complications, were not significantly different in regard to the infant variables described.

698

TABLE I

MATERNAL AND INFANT VARIABLES FOR 216 FULL TERM
INFANTS OF DRUG-DEPENDENT WOMEN
1969-1975

GROUP	A N=35	B N=56	C N=125
HEROIN			
Bags/day	5.4	8.9	11.3
Use/months	51.0	44.6	42.6
METHADONE			
Daily dose	N.A.*	25.3	33.5
Use/weeks	N.A.	13.5	29.9
BIRTH WEIGHT (grams)	2873	2962	3039
APGAR			
1 minute	7.9	8.4	8.0
5 minutes	9.1	9.4	9.3
GESTATIONAL AGE (weeks)	39.6	39.8	39.8
PRENATAL VISITS	0	1.9	8.6
COMPLICATIONS			
Obstetrical (%)	28.6	14.3	22.4
Medical (%)	37.1	53.6	38.4
NEONATAL WITHDRAWAL CLASS			
I	5.7	5.4	8.2
II	42.9	42.9	28.7
III	28.6	41.1	50.8
IV	22.9	10.7	12.3

*Not applicable

TABLE II

MATERNAL AND INFANT VARIABLES FOR 68 PREMATURE
INFANTS BORN TO DRUG-DEPENDENT WOMEN
1969-1975

GROUP	A N=24	B N=28	C N=16
HEROIN			
Bags/day	6.7	11.8	9.8
Use/months	58.2	49.0	65.5
METHADONE			
Daily dose	N.A*	35.7	29.3
Use/weeks	N.A	17.0	14.4
BIRTH WEIGHT (grams)	2000	2037	2003
APGAR			
1 minute	5.7	6.2	7.0
5 minutes	7.3	7.0	8.8
GESTATIONAL AGE (weeks)	34.0	34.5	34.5
PRENATAL VISITS	0	1.6	6.5
COMPLICATIONS			
Obstetrical (%)	37.5	39.3	37.5
Medical (%)	41.7	50.0	43.8
NEONATAL WITHDRAWAL CLASS			
I	4.8	0.0	6.3
II	28.6	57.9	18.8
III	42.9	26.3	75.0
IV	23.8	15.8	0.0

*Not applicable

TABLE III

MATERNAL AND INFANT VARIABLES FOR 25 INTRAUTERINE GROWTH
RETARDED INFANTS BORN TO DRUG-DEPENDENT WOMEN
1969-1975

GROUP	A N=8	B N=6	C N=11
HEROIN			
Bags/day	8.3	7.6	7.0
Use/months	38.6	118.8	63.1
METHADONE			
Daily dose	N.A.*	31.5	30.9
Use/weeks	N.A.	35.5	14.7
BIRTH WEIGHT			
(grams)	2300	2216	2274
APGAR			
1 minute	8.0	7.8	7.1
5 minutes	9.5	9.2	8.4
GESTATIONAL AGE			
(weeks)	38.8	38.6	38.2
PRENATAL VISITS	0	2.2	6.3
COMPLICATIONS			
Obstetrical (%)	25.0	33.3	27.3
Medical (%)	50.0	66.7	18.2
NEONATAL WITHDRAWAL CLASS			
I	0.0	0.0	10.0
II	50.0	33.3	40.0
III	37.5	66.7	40.0
IV	12.5	0.0	10.0

*Not applicable

MATERNAL HEROIN AND METHADONE DEPENDENCE
AND DIFFERENCES IN SEVERITY OF
NEONATAL NARCOTIC ABSTINENCE

R.E. Kron, MD, S.L. Kaplan, MD and M.D. Phoenix, RN
Department of Psychiatry

M. Litt, DEngSci
Department of Chemical and Biochemical Engineering

L.P. Finnegan, MD
Department of Pediatrics
University of Pennsylvania
Philadelphia, Pennsylvania 19174

I. INTRODUCTION

The epidemic increase in use of opiates among women of childbearing age, and the high incidence of disturbed states of CNS arousal reported among infants born to such mothers [1], have led us to utilize objective methods for monitoring the effects upon newborn behavior resulting from maternal addiction and neonatal withdrawal. In this report we shall describe findings with regard to (i) differences in sucking behavior between infants born to street addicts on heroin and those born to methadone-dependent women, and (ii) the influence upon newborn sucking behavior of the maternal dose of methadone and the length of time that methadone was ingested during pregnancy.

II. EXPERIMENTAL METHODS

A. Sucking Measurements

An apparatus for measuring nutritive sucking behavior has been developed which consists of a reservoir for the nutrient, a metering device to regulate nutrient flow, a pressure transducer to record the sucking pulses, and a nipple from which the infant withdraws milk formula. The apparatus is designed to record sub-

atmospheric intraoral pressure (sucks) while simultaneously rewarding the infant with a quantity of nutrient
proportional to the area under the time-pressure curve
of its sucking. Test feedings lasting 10 minutes each
are carried out with this apparatus just prior to the
routine nursery feedings. A number of variables including sucking rate (sucks per minute), pressures (mm
Hg per suck), and amount of nutrient consumed (ml per
minute) are recorded and measured with automated compu-
tational methods. The details of this apparatus, the
standard operating procedures, and the methods for analyzing the sucking data have been described elsewhere
[2-6].

III. STUDY 1

A. Population

Thirty-three infants born to narcotic-dependent
(methadone or heroin) mothers were studied. Twenty-
seven mothers had been attending the methadone and prenatal care clinics associated with the Philadelphia
General Hospital (PGH), where a daily dose of methadone
was administered. Six mothers were street addicts who
received little or no prenatal care and negligible
amounts of methadone prior to delivery. During labor,
the addict mothers received no general obstetric sedation or analgesia. Local anesthesia was routinely administered during the delivery.

The 33 infants born to the addict mothers were
closely observed in the high-risk nursery at PGH where
the pediatric staff prescribed medication for each infant in accordance with a clinical scoring system for
rating the severity of the neonatal narcotic abstinence
syndrome [7,8].

B. Procedure

Measures of infant sucking were performed according
to our standard operating procedures, and statistical
analyses of the data were carried out. Sucking behavior
was correlated with the dose of methadone that the mother
was taking at the time of delivery, and also with the
length of time that the mother was taking methadone
during pregnancy.

C. Findings

Infants were grouped in accordance with the narcotic drug history of their mothers. The mothers included in the study tended to fall into three distinct groups: Group 1, consisting of six mothers, had either received no methadone treatment at all (n=4) or received only a few small doses (<15mg/day) for a few days prior to delivery (n=2). Group 2 included those who were initiated into a methadone maintenance program during pregnancy. These 15 mothers had been receiving methadone for a period of 1-4 months prior to delivery, with an average dose of 28 mg/day. Group 3 (n=12) consisted of long-term patients in the methadone clinic who had begun methadone maintenance prior to pregnancy and who in some cases had been receiving methadone for over 3 years at an average dose of 52 mg/day. The average sucking rates for the infants born to these 3 groups of mothers are given in Table I. The sucking rates are representative of the other sucking measures.

The length of time that the mother was in the methadone program correlated with the maternal dose of methadone at the time of delivery at the $p < .05$ level, indicating that those who were in the program for the longest period of time tended to receive the highest doses of methadone.

The correlation between the sucking measures and maternal dose of methadone at the time of delivery was significant at the $p < .05$ level, while the correlation between sucking measures and length of time mothers received methadone was significant at the $p < .01$ level.

IV. STUDY 2

A. Population

Sixty-two infants born to narcotic-dependent mothers were studied on an "as you come" basis as they were admitted to the PGH high-risk nursery. Forty-five were born to mothers who were enrolled in the methadone maintenance clinic and 17 were born to street addicts on heroin. All infants were closely observed, and medication for withdrawal symptoms was prescribed in accordance with a clinical scoring system for rating the severity of the neonatal narcotic abstinence syndrome.

704

B. Procedure

Sucking measures were performed and analyzed according to our standard operating procedures. Also, a two-way statistical analysis was carried out on the number of infants treated for abstinence symptoms vs. untreated within the heroin and methadone groups.

C. Findings

Sucking measures indicated that infants born to methadone-dependent mothers are more behaviorally depressed than their heroin-dependent cohort ($p < .05$). In regard to pharmacotherapy for abstinence, Table II is a two-way breakdown of the 62 infants. Of the 45 methadone babies, 12 were deemed not to require pharmacotherapy (27%), while of the 17 heroin infants 11 did not receive drug treatment (65%). These differences are significant at better than the $p < .01$ level. The findings suggest that infants born to mothers who do not attend the methadone clinic may have less severe withdrawal symptomatology. They suck better and do not require pharmacotherapy as often as the infants born to methadone clinic clients.

V. DISCUSSION

These results raise questions about a number of a priori assumptions regarding the safety and efficacy of current treatment methods for maternal and neonatal addiction. The common assertion that infants born to street addicts are at greater risk than cohorts born to mothers obtaining addictive and prenatal care has not been verified in this study. Indeed, our objective behavioral measures indicate that maternal addiction to even moderate daily doses of methadone may be associated with a more complicated neonatal narcotic withdrawal syndrome than that found in infants born to street addicts. Our findings are in contrast to a previously reported study which indicated less severe withdrawal in infants born to methadone-treated mothers and which also favors methadone maintenance because of other associated advantages such as improved prenatal care [9,10]. Evaluation of these data is complicated, not only by uncontrolled and self-selected differences in obstetric and addictive care between the addict groups, but also by the fact that many methadone addicts may be supplementing their drug intake with heroin or additional methadone.

Supported in part by Research Grants HD-06009
(NICHD), DA-00325 (NIMH) and MH-19052 (NIMH), and also
a Research Contract #1674 from the Commonwealth of
Pennsylvania Governor's Council on Drug and Alcohol
Abuse.

TABLE I

Sucking Rates Arranged by Duration of
Maternal Methadone Treatment and Average Dose

Treatment Duration	Rate, sucks/min	Average Daily Methadone Dose (mg)
Group 1 (< 2 wks) (n=6)	32.6	<15*
Group 2 (1-4 mos) (n=15)	24.3	28
Group 3 (> 9 mos) (n=12)	21.6	52

* 4 received no methadone and 2 received only
a few small doses prior to delivery

TABLE II

Infants Born to Narcotic-Dependent Mothers:
Differences between Methadone and Heroin in
Severity of Neonatal Abstinence Syndrome as Measured
by Need for Pharmacotherapy During First Week of Life

		Mothers	
Pharmacotherapy for Neonatal Abstinence Syndrome		Dependent on Methadone	Dependent on Heroin
Infants	Treatment Given	33	6
	No Treatment	12	11
	TOTAL	45	17

VI. REFERENCES

1. M.J. Goodfriend, I.A. Shey and M.D. Klein, Amer. J. Obstet. Gynecol., 71: 29 (1956).

2. R.E. Kron and M. Litt, Med. Biol. Eng., 9: 45 (1971).

3. R.E. Kron, M. Stein and K.E. Goddard, Psychosomat. Med., 25: 181 (1963).

4. R.E. Kron, M. Stein, K.E. Goddard and M.D. Phoenix, Psychosomat. Med., 29: 24 (1967).

5. R.E. Kron, M. Stein and K.E. Goddard, Pediatrics, 37: 1012 (1966).

6. R.E. Kron, J. Ipsen and K.E. Goddard, Psychosomat. Med., 30: 151 (1968).

7. L.P. Finnegan, R.E. Kron, J.F. Connaughton and J.P. Emich, Intl. J. Addictive Dis., 2: 141 (1975).

8. L.P. Finnegan, R.E. Kron, J.F. Connaughton and J.P. Emich, Intl. J. Clin. Pharmacol., 12: 19 (1975).

9. D.X. Freedman and E.C. Senay, Ann. Rev. Med., 23: 153 (1972).

10. S. Blatman, Pediat., 48: 173 (1971); Medical World News, July 21, 1972, p. 16.

THE LOW BIRTH WEIGHTS OF BABIES IN DRUG DEPENDENT WOMEN

Joan C. Stryker, M.D.

Associate Professor
Wayne State University School of Medicine
Department of Gynecology & Obstetrics
Chief of Hutzel Hospital's Outpatient Dept.
Medical Administrator of Hutzel Hospital's Program for
Pregnant Drug Dependent Women & Addicted Neonates

James N. Wardell, M.D.

Clinical Assistant Professor
Wayne State University School of Medicine
Department of Gynecology & Obstetrics
Director of Hutzel Hospital's Program for
Pregnant Drug Dependent Women & Addicted Neonates

James E. Markin, B.S.

Lay Administrator of Hutzel Hospital's Program for
Pregnant Drug Dependent Women & Addicted Neonates

A retrospective study was undertaken to ascertain if there were any pertinent factors which might be contributing to the high number of low birth weight babies among pregnant addicts (Table I). If there are consistant factors then these might be eliminated or modified to prevent low birth weight babies in pregnant addicts. At Hutzel Hospital the rate for low birth weight infants from pregnant drug addicts is 3 times greater than that for Detroit. Statistically the newborn mortality is 40 times greater among infants who are of low birth weight (1). Mental deficiency, cerebral palsy and visual and hearing defects have an increased incidence with devastating consequences in the low birth weight infant. (Henceforth "LBW" will designate low birth weight in this article.)

For correct interpretation it is important to know if the infant is premature or small. Because the exact gestational age is sometimes difficult to determine the following data was accumulated from the patients' records. From the date of the last normal menstrual period the date of expected confinement was calculated and recorded. Unfortunately many women who are drug dependent are oligomenorrhagic or are unable to accurately remember the date of their last normal menstrual period. "Quickening", the time when life is first felt, varies greatly. Most patients who are in the drug scene are in and out of withdrawal so that quickening and gastrointestinal peristalsis may be mistaken for one another. Although, if the patient states she felt quickening on such and such a date, this was noted using the 4-1/2 months as the average time for feeling fetal movement. The date was noted on the chart when the fetal heart tones were first heard and by what method. The series of fundal heights as recorded with each prenatal visit was also noted. Very few x rays were taken but, if an x ray was taken and the epiphyseal centers noted with an estimation of fetal age, this to was noted on the chart. Ultrasound has been extensively utilized at Hutzel Hospital for the past 6 years but ultrasound was utilized only in about 1/4 of these patients. The cephalic biparietal diameter is an accurate measurement and correlates well with the gestational age. If amniocentesis had been performed the values of creatinine, bilirubin, L-S ratio and fat cells were noted and the approximate fetal age then recorded. This procedure was infrequently used unless fetal maturity and/or evidence of fetal stress was of prime concern. Radio immune assay of estradiol or progesterone was not routinely ordered nor was vaginal cytology (3). Starting in 1974, at the time of birth, all babies under 2,500 gms. were observed by the Dubowitz (4) scale assessing fetal maturity. The gestational age arrived after these observations was noted on the chart. The calculated gestational age from these observations was used to formulate Table II. The shaded area in Table II is the "normal weight" for a specific gestational age. The dots represent the individual cases (115) whose birth weights were under 2,500 gms. Of the 115 cases 35.6% were classified as premature (less than 36 weeks of gestation) and the remainder as small for gestational age (over 36 weeks of gestation). The patients' total history, physical examination, laboratory results and performance in the clinic was also studied. A modification of Doctor Nesbitt's (7) antenatal high risk score sheet has been utilized. The average score for the low birth weight mothers is 6.5. Add 3 points for drug addiction and the score is 9.5 or extra high risk. In Hutzel Hospital's Outpatient Clinic patients with a score of 10 or higher usually have either a severe neonatal morbidity or even mortality.

In comparing maternal pathology of the pregnant drug addict vs. maternal pathology in the United States there is a 3.6% incidence of breech deliveries in both groups. Here the similarity ends. Preeclampsia, pyelitis, hypertension and premature separation have twice the incidence in the pregnant drug addict patients. Subscribing to the philosophy that all 4 of these medical conditions are increased by stressful living, then this increase is a rational result. Placenta previa is 5 times more frequent, why is not known. 45.8% of our patients had an admission hemoglobin of less than 10.0 gms. This is 4 times the national average. Anemia may not only be caused by low iron intake but also by chronic infection which prevents absorption of iron. Rates of infection, malnutrition, Rh factor and abnormal cervical paps is not available from national data so that the following comparison is with Hutzel Hospital's Outpatient Clinic. A state of poor nutrition was decided if the patient's weight for height and age was 10 lbs. below or 20 lbs. above the Metropolitan Life Insurance Company's scales at the time of conception. The preconception weight was by history and the height by clinic measurement. 65% in the program were malnurished. The venereal disease rate was twice that of the general clinic (5). Incidently the venereal disease rate in the low birth weight mothers was 4% higher than in the other pregnant drug addicts. 38.5% incidence of local infection includes cellulitis, abscesses, pyorrhea, cystitis and thrombophlebitis. 14.4% rate of general infection includes subacute bacterial endocarditis, pneumonia and sepsis. 17.7% of the patients with a history of previous "premature" deliveries is compatible with a long drug history. 11% of the patients with a Rh negative blood factor is lower than the norm. Sickle cell is also somewhat lower than the norm for the predominately black population of Detroit. There is a very high rate of severe cervical dysplasia to carcinoma insitu in the pregnant drug addict population.

The social-economic situation of all the Hutzel Hospital's Outpatient Clinic's patients is comparable. Most of the patients were from inner city Detroit; most were black and unmarried. If they were married they were either separated or divorced and on welfare. The pregnancies were unplanned and the emotional stress was, understandably, severe. The only factor which was not equal was the little or no prenatal care in the low birth weight mothers. The low number of prenatal visits by the low birth weight mothers attests to the poor motivation on the part of the patients to obtain health care services. Early enrollment into a comprehensive prenatal clinic is mandatory for early diagnosis and prompt medical treatment. This includes adequate nutritional counseling with food stamps and instruction in food processing. Comprehensive medical care cannot be accomplished overnight, therefore, it is only reasonable to state that frequent prenatal visits are necessary in the prevention of maternal or neonatal pathology.

The low birth weight mothers were analyzed from the standpoint of years of drug habit, dollar per day on admission to the program, methadone dosage at delivery, and the number of dirty urines (5). This data was contrasted to 100 random drug addict patients who had normal weight babies (Table III). 86% of the LBW mothers were involved with drugs for over 2 years in contrast to 50% of the normal birth weight mothers. 64% of the LBW mothers' dollar per day cost was $40. 65% of the normal birth weight mothers' drug habit was also that expensive. 78% of the LBW mothers' daily methadone dosage at delivery was 20 mg. or less but, even at this dosage, 71% had dirty urines. This means they were chipping heroin at fairly regular intervals. 40% of the normal birth weight mothers were on tang 6 weeks before delivery and 57.5% on less than 20 mg. of daily methadone. Even though the dollar per day cost was equal, twice the number of mothers were able to detoxify predelivery (realizing that 35.6% of the LBW mothers were not pregnant as long and thus they have as much time to accomplish detoxification).

710

The patients were knowingly placed on a fairly low dose methadone and an attempt made to gradually detox them. The maintenance level must be that which does not give a "high" but does prevent withdrawal symptoms, then, gradual detoxification. "Cold turkey" and "21-day wonder" detoxification does not work with pregnant women because they are 2 individuals, both of whom must be considered. The ideal goal is complete detoxification 8 weeks before delivery. Only 22% of all our drug dependent women reach that goal. If the daily methadone dose is less than 20 mg. a satisfactory result can be anticipated.

SUMMARY

In the clinic of the low birth weight babies 35.6% are truly premature and 64.4% are small for gestational age. The contributing causes are maternal pathology and maternal drug habits, both of which influence neonatal growth. The pregnant drug addict is at high risk due to a multitude of pathological conditions. Malnutrition and anemia head the list at 65%, while 38.5% have local and/or systemic infection. Preeclampsia, hypertension, premature separation of the placenta, and placenta previa account for another 20%. Some patients will have 2 or more conditions. As an example: Cellulitis, malnutrition and anemia, thus accounting for the 123.5%. Even if the baby's mother does not have major pathology, a long history of maternal drug use with a high dollar per day habit is a causative factor of LBW babies.

For the addict who finds herself pregnant and wants her baby it is strongly recommended: (1) That she enroll early into a prenatal clinic for early diagnosis and prompt treatment, (2) and be given instruction and assistance to assure regaining of nutritional balance; (3) that she instantly discontinue all street drugs, (4) and follow a low dose methadone maintenance. Patients admitted early into Hutzel Hospital's Pregnant Drug Addict Program who are thus motivated are delivering full term, normal weight, healthy, nonaddicted babies.

TABLE I

Comparison of Pregnancy Outcome

	Hutzel Hospital P.D.A. Clinic	Detroit P.H.D. Statistics-1973	
Pregnancy Outcome	Number (931)	(Ratio per 1000 live births)	
Low Birth Weight	115	131	44

711

TABLE II

Addicted Neonates' Weight and Estimated Uterine Gestation

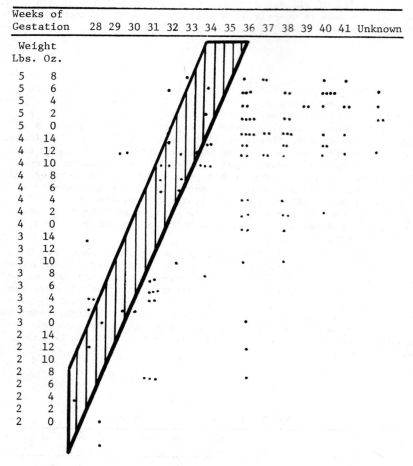

(Shaded area: Normal weight for gestational age)

TABLE III

	"Low birth wt." mothers (115)	"Normal wt." mothers (100)
Prenatal Clinic Visits:		
Little or none	40%	25%
Drug Habit:		
Less than 1 year	3%	17.5%
1 to 2 years	11%	32.5%
2 to 5 years	56%	32%
Over 5 years	30%	18%
Dollar/day:		
Under $20	10%	5%
Over $40	64%	65%
Methadone Dosage: (6 weeks before delivery)		
Tang	18%	40%
5 to 20 mg.	78%	57.5%
Over 20 mg.	4%	2.5%
Urines:		
Clean	29%	40%
Dirty	71%	60%

REFERENCES

1. B. S. Babson and R. C. Benson, Management of High Risk Pregnancy & Intensive Care of the Neonate, C. V. Mosby Publ. Co. (1971).

2. W. M. Crosby, Trauma During Pregnancy: Maternal & Fetal Injury, Obstetrical & Gynecological Survey, Williams & Wilkins Publ. Co., 29: 10 (1974).

3. A. I. Csapo, O. Pohanka, H. L. Kaihola, Progesterone Deficiency & Premature Labour, British Medical J. (1-26-74).

4. V. Dubowitz, C. Goldberg, Clinical Assessment of Gestational Age in the Newborn Infant, J. of Pediatrics, 77: 1, (1970).

5. S. R. Kandall, S. Albin, E. Dreyer, M. Comstock, J. Lowinson, Differential Effects of Heroin & Methadone on Birth Weights, Addictive Diseases: an International Journal, 2(2): 347-355, (1975).

6. R. L. Naeye, W. Blane, W. Leblanc, M. A. Khatamee, Fetal Complications of Maternal Heroin Addiction: Abnormal Growth, Infections & Episodes of Stress, J. of Pediatrics, 83: 6 (1973).

7. R. E. Nesbitt, Jr., et al, High-risk Obstetrics II (Value of semiobjective grading system in identifying the vulnerable group), Am. J. of Obstetrics & Gynecology, 103: 972-985 (1969).

PROGNOSIS OF INFANTS BORN TO DRUG DEPENDENT MOTHERS:
ITS RELATION TO THE SEVERITY OF WITHDRAWAL AND MANNER OF
TREATMENT DURING THE NEONATAL PERIOD

Cleofe J. Chavez, M. D.

Research Associate, Obstetrics & Gynecology
Associate in Pediatrics
Wayne State University School of Medicine
Detroit, Michigan

Enrique M. Ostrea, Jr., M. D.

Assistant Professor of Pediatrics
Wayne State University School of Medicine
Director, University Nursery Service
Hutzel Hospital
Detroit, Michigan

Milton E. Strauss, Ph.D.

Associate Professor of Psychology
Wayne State University
At present, Associate Professor of Psychology
The Johns Hopkins University
Baltimore, Maryland

Joan C. Stryker, M. D.

Associate Professor of Gynecology/Obstetrics
Wayne State University School of Medicine
Chief, Out-Patient Clinic
Department of Gynecology/Obstetrics
Hutzel Hospital
Detroit, Michigan

A one year follow up of 103 infants of drug dependent mothers
was done. This was to determine the effects of the severity of
withdrawal and type of treatment during the neonatal period on the
infants subsequent growth and development.

The infants studied were all delivered at Hutzel Hospital and
were born to heroin addicted mothers on methadone treatment during
pregnancy. The infants were subsequently followed up at our combined Infant-Maternal Methadone Clinic at 2, 4, and 8 weeks and at
3, 6, and 12 months of age.

715

RESULTS:

Based on our criteria, the severity of withdrawal was assessed as minor to mild or MM in 79 infants (77%) and moderate to severe or MS in 24 infants (23%). Only 7 infants all belonging to the MS fulfilled our criteria for the use of drug treatment to control their withdrawal manifestations. The rest were conservatively managed.

The characteristics of the study population are shown in Table I. There was a significantly higher birth weight ($p < 0.01$) in the infants in the MS group as compared to the MM group (3167 vs 2913 grams). However the length, head circumference and sex ratio were essentially similar in the two groups. Because of our demographic location, there was as expected more black than white infants in the series.

The infants were observed for a minimum of 5 days in the nursery. The 7 MS infants who received drug treatment for their withdrawal stayed in the nursery longer than the non-drug treated MS group (25 ± 8 vs 8 ± 2 days, $p < 0.05$). There was no neonatal death. At the time of discharge, 80% of the infants still showed some mild withdrawal signs such as tremors and mild irritability.

At 2, 4, and 8 weeks of age, there was a significantly higher incidence of persistent withdrawal in the MS as compared to the MM group (94 vs 57%; 59 vs 29%; 19 vs 5%, $p < 0.02$, Figure 1). The manifestation consisted of mild irritability, tremors, loose stools fist sucking, sneezing, stuffy nose and hiccups.

There was however, no significant difference in the incidence of persistent withdrawal manifestations in the MS group when comparing the drug treated vs the non-drug treated infants. (Figure 2). This indicates that the persistence of the withdrawal symptoms in the infants is directly related to its initial severity and is not significantly altered by drug therapy.

At 2, 4, 6, and 12 months of age, the mean weight of the infants belonging to the MM and MS groups was not significantly different (Table II). However, during the first 4 months, the mean weight gain of the infants in the MM group was significantly greater than in the MS group (3283 vs 2855 grams, $p < 0.05$). This is explained by the fact that infants with moderate to severe withdrawal have significantly higher birthweights to begin with, but then suffer from a much greater postnatal weight loss due to their withdrawal and regain the weight loss less readily.

The mean head circumference of the infants belonging to the MM and MS groups was not significantly different at 2, 4, 6, and 12 months of age and the head circumference stayed within the 10th to the 90th percentile throughout. (Table III).

The mean body length of the infants in the two groups was not significantly different on follow up, although it can be seen from Table IV, that from birth to 2 months, the body length of the infants in both groups were initially below the 10th percentile

716

but then advanced and stayed between the 10th and 90th percentile thereafter.

At 3, 6, and 12 months of age, the infants mental and psychomotor developmental indices (MDI and PDI) were assessed by the Bayley Scales (Table V). It is noted that there was no significant difference in the scores of the infants in the 2 groups.

Some medical problems, besides withdrawal, were encountered in the infants during the first 6 months of follow up. (Table VI). These consisted of gastrointestinal, respiratory, cutaneous, infectious, trauma, and neurologic problems. The incidence of occurrence of these disorders was not significantly different in either group. However, 5 out of 19 or 26% in the MS had to be hospitalized as compared to 7 out of 66 or 11% in the MM group (p<0.02). Futhermore, 3 of the infants in the study died as a result of sudden-infant-death syndrome.

SUMMARY:

In Conclusion:

1. Our study shows that in the first 8 weeks of follow up, a significantly higher incidence of withdrawal persists in infants who initially showed moderate to severe withdrawal as compared to those who only had mild withdrawal during the neonatal period.

2. There was no significant difference in the mean weight, body length and head circumference of the infants on follow up. However, the mean weight gain of the infants in the MM group was significantly greater than those in the MS group during the first 4 months.

3. There was no significant difference in the mental and psychomotor developments of the infants in the series up to the age of 1 year.

4. The medical problems most frequently encountered during the first six months are those involving the respiratory, skin and gastrointestinal systems. Although the frequency of these problems did not significantly differ in the MM and MS groups, more infants in the MS group were hospitalized.

5. The increased incidence of the sudden-infant-death syndrome in infants of drug addicted mothers should be investigated more closely.

717

TABLE I: CHARACTERISTICS OF THE STUDY POPULATION (N=103) OF INFANTS WITH MINOR TO MILD OR MODERATE TO SEVERE WITHDRAWAL

	Minor to Mild Withdrawal (N=79)	Moderate to Severe Withdrawal (N=24)
Birth weight	2914.0 ± 448.4	3167.0 ± 454.3*
Head Circumference (centimeters)	33.6 ± 1.7	33.8 ± 1.4
Length (centimeters)	48.1 ± 2.2	48.9 ± 2.6
Sex: Male	47	15
Female	32	9
Race: White	4	3
Black	75	21

*p<0.01 (Student "t" test)

TABLE II: MEAN WEIGHT (GRAMS) OF INFANTS OF DRUG DEPENDENT MOTHERS DURING 12 MONTHS OF FOLLOW-UP

	Minor to Mild Withdrawal	Moderate to Severe Withdrawal	p*
Birth	2914 ± 448 (79)	3167 ± 545 (24)	<0.01
2 Months	4818 ± 639 (49)	4670 ± 576 (15)	N.S.
4 Months	6197 ± 722 (34)	6063 ± 571 (14)	N.S.
	(3283 ± 809)	(2855 ± 669)	<0.05
6 Months	6940 ± 810 (20)	7140 ± 500 (07)	N.S.
12 Months	9904 ±1739 (09)	9856 ±1251 (06)	N.S.

* Student "t" Test

TABLE III: MEAN HEAD CIRCUMFERENCE (cm) OF INFANTS OF DRUG DEPENDENT MOTHERS DURING 12 MONTHS OF FOLLOW-UP

	Minor to Mild Withdrawal	Moderate to Severe Withdrawal	p*
Birth	33.6 ± 1.7 (78)	33.8 ± 1.4 (23)	N.S.
2 Months	37.9 ± 1.2 (39)	37.3 ± 0.8 (15)	N.S.
4 Months	40.8 ± 1.2 (33)	40.1 ± 0.9 (13)	N.S.
6 Months	42.4 ± 1.3 (20)	42.0 ± 0.9 (06)	N.S.
12 Months	46.0 ± 1.8 (09)	45.3 ± 0.9 (06)	N.S.

* Student "t" test

TABLE IV: MEAN LENGTH (cm) OF INFANTS OF DRUG DEPENDENT MOTHERS DURING 12 MONTHS OF FOLLOW-UP

	Minor to Mild Withdrawal	Moderate to Severe Withdrawal	p*
Birth	48.1 ± 2.2 (76)	48.9 ± 2.6 (21)**	N.S.
2 Months	54.5 ± 2.0 (42)	54.9 ± 2.1 (15)**	N.S.
4 Months	60.0 ± 1.9 (31)	60.2 ± 1.9 (13)	N.S.
6 Months	63.4 ± 1.9 (20)	63.8 ± 3.8 (07)	N.S.
12 Months	72.6 ± 3.3 (09)	73.8 ± 1.9 (06)	N.S.

* Student "t" test
** 10th percentile

TABLE V: BAYLEY SCALES OF INFANT DEVELOPMENT: (MDI-mental development index; PDI-psychomotor developmental index)*

3 months:

MDI: MM(37) = 114.8 ± 10.3
      MS(8) = 117.2 ± 7.3

PDI: MM(37) = 117.8 ± 9.1
      MS(8) = 115.8 ± 12.4

6 months:

MDI: MM(20) = 117.9 ± 9.9
      MS(5) = 122.0 ± 12.9

PDI: MM(20) = 109.9 ± 10.8
      MS(5) = 116.2 ± 13.3

12 months:

MDI: MM(8) = 117.3 ± 8.0
      MS(6) = 109.2 ± 6.9

PDI: MM(8) = 112.1 ± 9.2
      MS(6) = 105.5 ± 11.8

* No statistical significance in all the differences.

TABLE VI: MEDICAL PROBLEMS ENCOUNTERED DURING THE FIRST SIX
MONTHS OF FOLLOW-UP IN INFANTS OF DRUG DEPENDENT MOTHERS

	Moderate to Severe Withdrawal	Minor to Mild Withdrawal
Gastrointestinal (diarrhea, vomiting, colic and feeding problems)	13 (54.2%)	36 (45.6%)
Respiratory (colds, croup, bronchio-litis, pneumonia, asthma)	10 (41.7%)	24 (30.4%)
Skin (seborrhea, moniliasis, diaper rash, pustules)	2 (8.3%)	4 (5.1%)
Infections (conjunctivitis, viral meningitis, otitis media)	2 (8.3%)	3 (3.8%)
Inguinal Hernia	1 (4.2%)	4 (5.1%)
Trauma (ecchymoses, petechiae, cigarette burns, fractured clavicle, hematoma)	1 (4.2%)	2 (2.5%)
Neurologic (nystagmus, hyperactivity)	1 (4.2%)	2 (2.5%)

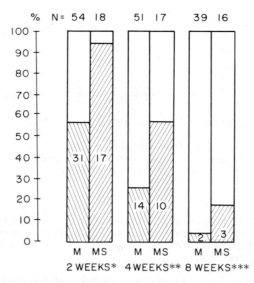

Figure 1. Incidence and Duration of Withdrawal Signs Comparing
Mild (M) and Moderate to Severe (MS). (Statistically significant
difference: *P=<0.005; **P=<0.020 ***P=<0.025.)

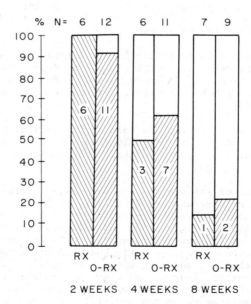

Figure 2. Incidence and Duration of Withdrawal Signs Comparing the
Treated and Untreated MS Group of Infants. (No statistical significance between the differences.)

721

METHADONE, PREGNANCY AND CHILDREARING

Josette Escamilla-Mondanaro, M.D.

Marin Open House
Director of Pregnant Addicts Program
San Rafael, California

Information presented in this paper was collected from
working with pregnant heroin addicts and addicted mothers in the
San Francisco Pregnant Addicts Program and the Marin Open House
Drug Treatment Program.

The heroin addict is often a product of battering. She is
initially battered in the home and secondarily battered by society.
The woman is groomed for failure in her own family. In taking the
early family histories of these women, it becomes clear that they
were deprived of nuturance and warm, loving care. (1,2) Their
parents had either premature or totally unrealistic demands and
expectations of them. When they could not satisfy these demands,
they were criticized and punished.

Strict sex role socialization also typifies the family of
origin. Girls were to be girls; passive, dependent, feminine,
coy, non-assertive. It is known that high feminity in females
"...correlates with high anxiety, low self esteem, and low self
acceptance." (3)

This triad of strict sex role socialization, emotional
neglect as an infant, and untimely premature expectations of performance by parents appears to typify the family of origin of
these women.

The sense of failure and low self esteem derived from the
home experience is reinforced by society at large. Coming from
low socioeconomic backgrounds, and often being non white reinforced
this initial sense of alienation and failure. The results of
societal and familial battering appear to be reflected in a recent
study which demonstrates a striking psychological mood difference
between drug abusers, and drug users. In general "...abusers feel
left out, alienated, lonely, and they have much more trouble at
home and at school..." (4) than users and nonusers. In this
schema, abnormal parenting and societal pressures have left the

individual with low self esteem and a fear of risk taking. Drug abuse becomes both a way of coping with life and a life of its own. These women have both cognitive and affective needs which will impair their parenting ability. The cognitive needs include not knowing how to care for the child, not knowing what to realisticly expect for the child at various ages. The affective (emotional) needs of the mother include role-reversal: needing the child to love and care for her: needing the child to give her the warmth and nuturance she did not experience as a child.

Children of Addicts

If the drug abuser is seen as a product of battering, a product of abnormal, dysfunctional parenting, what hope is there for the children of the drug addict? Unless the cognitive and affective needs of the parents are properly dealt with in a comprehensive program, the parents will go on to reproduce their family of origin.

It has already been demonstrated that there is a higher incidence of emotional and behavioral problems in children of alcoholic parents. (5,6) It should not be surprising that..."these youngsters have a poor self concept, are easily frustrated, often perform poorly in school, and are more likely than their peers to suffer from adjustment problems, particularly during adolescence." (7) Children of alcoholics are also twice as likely to become alcoholics than their peers of non alcoholic parents. (8) Clearly the children of drug addicts must also be at a high risk.

Bonding: The Mother-Child Relationship

When a pregnant addict is maintained on Methadone, the normal pattern of bonding between the mother and child is disrupted in two ways. First the baby is in the intensive care unit experiencing withdrawal and is seen as sick by the mother. She in turn withholds her affection, love, and warmth until she knows that he will be alright. She is preparing herself for the possible death of the child. The ramification here is that the mother may not be able to make up for lost time once she feels safe in loving her child. A wedge has been driven between the natural bonding of mother to child which may have long lasting effects on their relationship. The second disruption in this bonding occurs because the baby is experiencing the withdrawal syndrome. The irritable child responds negatively to normal coddling. The mother feels that her attempts at mothering are inadequate and that the baby rejects her. Often the mother places emotional distance between herself and the rejecting infant. This emotional distance gets translated to the baby via physical distance. The mother may hold the baby loosely or place the baby on a bed during bottle feedings. Distant and cold mothering may lead to irritable "collicky" babies whether or not the infant experienced narcotic withdrawal.

Methadone babies are described as hyperactive, irritable and "collicky" for three or more months after delivery. (9) This "collicky" syndrome may be the result of both the narcotic withdrawal and the distant mothering demonstrated by these women. This mothering is the product of the mother being rejected by her withdrawing infant as well as a reflection of the lack of warm mothering she herself experienced as an infant.

The newborn may demonstrate this irritability and hyperactivity for months after delivery. During this time, pediatricians frequently give the mother donnatol to quiet the infant. (10) This medication certainly does make the infant less irritable. The circle is completed. The mother rejected by her irritable, inconsolable child withholds her love and mothers coldly, indifferently and distantly. Her own mothering attempts are seen as inadequate. The baby becomes irritable and now where she has personally failed to console her child, a drug will do the trick. Once again, human resources take a back seat to a drug. The addict's original belief that drugs are superior to human resources has been reinforced.

Conclusion

In view of the needs of the pregnant addict, and the detrimental effects of methadone on pregnancy and parenting, pregnant addicts should be maintained on methadone only if the program is prepared to deliver comprehensive treatment. Comprehensive treatment includes: Psychosocial support dealing with both cognitive and affective needs, prenatal care, neonatal intensive care unit, pediatric follow-up, and developmental studies on children. Cognitive (informational) needs can be dealt with by: Group Teaching, nutrition, pregnancy, labor and delivery, child development, how to handle the irritable withdrawing newborn; Age Specific lending toy libraries; and child care center in which the parents participate. Affective (emotional) needs can be approached through individual and group therapy, setting warm environment, respect rights of these individuals, enjoy working with these people, set realistic goals, acknowledge even small gains, and the staff being appropriately supportive. Only programs which actively meet the needs of both the pregnant addict and her children will have a positive impact on the generational cycle of abused neglected children becoming needy and dependent adults. Methadone alone will enhance the pattern of deficient and abnormal parenting by diminishing the women's ability to reality test, and by causing the passively addicted newborn to be a highly irritable and difficult child.

The state and federal governments must begin to fund for the treatment of both the mother and child. To allow more pregnant women easy access to methadone maintenance is tantamount to poisoning more women and children unless this loosening of regulations is coupled with a comprehensive approach to the family.

A special note of thanks to Jeannine Thornton, Florence Keller, Ph.D., Grace Damaan and Esta Soler for their much appreciated technical assistance.

BIBLIOGRAPHY

1. Mondanaro, Josette, Women: Pregnancy, Children and Addiction. Monograph written for National Drug Abuse Council, Women and Drug Abuse Training Program, Oct. 1975.

2. Carr, Jack, N., "Drug Patterns Among Drug-Addicted Mothers: Incidence, Variance In Use, And Effects on Children," Pediatric Annals, Vol. 4, pp. 408-417, 1975.

3. Bem, Sandra Lipsitz, "Androgyny Vs. The Tight Little Lives of Fluffy Women And Chesty Men," in Phychology Today, pp. 56-62, Sept. 1975.

4. Yankelovich, Daniel, "Drug Users Vs. Drug Abusers: How Students Control Their Drug Crisis," in Phychology Today, pp. 39-42, October, 1975.

5. Chafetz, M.E., et al, "Children of Alcoholics: Observations in a Child Guidance Clinic," O J Stud Alcohol, 32, 687-689, 1971.

6. Fine, Etal, "Behavior Disorders in Children with Parental Alcoholism: paper presented at annual meeting of National Council on Alcoholism, Milwaukee, Wis., April, 1975.

7. Hindman, Margaret, "Children of Alcoholic Parents," in Alcohol Health and Research World, p. 2-6, Winter 75-76.

8. Globetti, Gerald, "Alcohol: A Family Affair," paper presented at the National Congress of Parents and Teachers, St. Louis, Mo., 1973.

9. Lodge, Ann, and M.M. Marcus, "Behavioral and Electrophysio-logical Changes of Addicted Neonates," in Addictive Diseases: An International Journal, Vol. 2, pp. 235-255, 1975.

10. Ramer, Cyril and Anne Lodge, "Neonatal Addiction: "A Two Year Study," paper presented at the National Drug Abuse Conference Chicago, Illinois, March, 1974 and reprinted in Addictive Diseases: An International Journal, Vol. 2, 1975.

BRAZELTON NEONATAL ASSESSMENT AT THREE AND
TWENTY-EIGHT DAYS OF AGE: A STUDY OF
PASSIVELY ADDICTED INFANTS, HIGH RISK
INFANTS, AND NORMAL INFANTS

S. L. Kaplan, MD, R. E. Kron, MD and M.D. Phoenix, RN

Department of Psychiatry
University of Pennsylvania
School of Medicine
Philadelphia, Pennsylvania 19174

L. P. Finnegan, MD

Department of Pediatrics
University of Pennsylvania
School of Medicine
Director of Nurseries
Philadelphia General Hospital
Philadelphia, Pennsylvania 19104

I. INTRODUCTION

As part of a longitudinal study of infants born to drug dependent mothers, infants were examined at 3 and 28 days of age by means
of the Brazelton neonatal assessment scales. The Brazelton is a
26-item examination coded on a nine-point scale that measures a
wide range of infant behaviors (1). The exam emphasizes cortical
and adaptive behaviors such as the infant's ability to alert to a
stimulus or to return to a quiet state after having been subject
to an irritating stimulus. This contrasts with the standard new
born neurological exam which emphasizes subcortical reflex functioning (2).

Horowitz has reported studies of the normal newborn using the
Brazelton at 3 and 28 days of age. In normal newborns, she has
found high test-retest reliability between 3 and 28 days of life
with the Brazelton (3). Using the Brazelton examination we, as
well as other investigators, have demonstrated significant differences on the third day of life between passively addicted infants
born to drug dependent mothers and control infants (4-7). The
present study examined a group of infants born to mothers enrolled

in a methadone maintenance clinic at 3 and 28 days of age with the
Brazelton to determine the persistence of the behavioral abnormalities previously found at 3 days of age. In addition, two control
groups of infants were concurrently studied: a normal control
group and a group of high risk, but non-addicted, infants. All
infants studied were delivered and cared for at the Philadelphia
General Hospital (PGH), a large urban institution. This provided
a control for social class. All infants were re-studied between 26
and 30 days of age in the pediatric outpatient department at PGH.

At PGH the passively addicted infants are routinely admitted
to the high-risk nursery to be observed for evidence of the
neonatal narcotic withdrawal syndrome. If the narcotic abstinence
syndrome develops, the infants are treated pharmacologically. Of
the 26 passively addicted infants studied, 14 received pharmacotherapy; 12 did not.

Twelve high-risk infants were studied. These infants were
only admitted to the high-risk nursery for observation as a
result of obstetrical or neonatological complications. They were
not obviously ill, but merely required more careful observation
than is available in a newborn nursery. Illustrative of the conditions that led to admission to the nursery are one low birthweight
infant (1980 grams), 3 infants delivered by Caesarian section, one
infant with mild respiratory distress syndrome and 4 infants with
physiologic jaundice. Those infants who were acutely ill were
excluded from the study by a neonatologist. Twenty-five normal
control infants were also studied. The control infants and their
mothers were free of any medical or obstetrical complications that
might lead to admission to the high-risk nursery. After spending
12 to 24 hours in the normal newborn nursery, these infants roomed
with their mothers for the remainder of the hospital stay, as is
the practice at PGH.

II. METHODS OF PROCEDURE

The experimental and control groups were examined by one of
two examiners who had previously attained an inter-rater reliability of $r > 0.85$. Frequent reliability checks during the time that
the assessments were performed enabled the examiners to maintain
high inter-rater reliability. Both examiners learned the scale
during a period of training with T.B. Brazelton and have performed
over 150 examinations. The examiners were blind to the group to
which the infants belonged.

III. DATA ANALYSIS

Two clinically meaningful groups of items were analyzed:
alertness and irritability. The Brazelton items included in these
two groups had been shown in previously reported studies from our
laboratory to be significant variables (3,4). Brazelton alertness

items studied include: item 5, visual pursuit of a red ball; item 6, visual pursuit of a ringing bell; item 7, visual pursuit of a human face; item 8, visual pursuit of a human voice; and item 10, a general estimation of the infant's capacity to alert and sustain alerting behavior. Irritability items studied include: item 16, the ease with which an infant can be brought from a crying state to a quiet state; item 17, a measure of the infant's greatest level of excitement; item 18, the rapidity with which the infant reaches an agitated state; item 19, the number of times an infant cries in response to specific stimuli during an exam; and item 21, tremulousness.

The alertness scores were arithmetically summed to generate a combined alertness score for each infant at each examination. An identical procedure was followed for the scores of irritability items. The higher the alertness score, the more alert the infant, and the irritability score, the more irritable the infant. The data were analyzed for differences between the passively addicted group and the two control groups at 3 and 28 days of age.

IV.   RESULTS (See Tables I and II)

There was a high degree of stability in normal infants for alertness and irritability scores between 3 and 28 days of age. These findings in our normal newborns are in essential agreement with those reported by Horowitz (3). Table I and Table II contrast the behavioral consistency at 3 and 28 days found in normal infants with the changes in behavior found in the high risk control group and the passively addicted group.

The passively addicted group became more alert between 3 and 28 days of age (p $<$.001) as did the high risk control group (p $<$.01). At 3 days of age the normal control group was more alert than the high risk control group (p $<$.001) and more alert than the passively addicted group (p $<$.005). There were no significant differences between the alertness scores of the three groups at 28 days of age. The normal population maintained its high alertness scores while the passively addicted group and high risk group alertness scores rose to the levels of the normal control group.

The irritability scores are consistent with the behavior that is expected clinically from the groups we are studying. An important clinical manifestation of the neonatal narcotic withdrawal syndrome is an increase in irritability. The passively addicted infants are more irritable than both control populations at 3 days of age, although the differences are not significant. At 28 days of age the passively addicted infants are more irritable than high risk controls (p $<$.1) and normal controls (p $<$.05). The normal infants did not change their irritability scores during this period, but the high risk infants and the passively addicted infants tended to increase their irritability scores.

V. DISCUSSION

That the irritability score of the passively addicted infants is significantly higher than that of the normal controls ($p < .05$) at 28 days of age suggests that the passively addicted infants continue to experience subclinical withdrawal and might benefit from further therapy for their narcotic withdrawal syndrome.

There are several possible explanations for the depressed alertness scores at 3 days of age in the passively addicted infants and the high risk control group comparet to the normal control group; two of these possible expalnations will be considered briefly. The first is that mothers of the high risk infants with low alertness scores at 3 days of age may have received more medication prior to delivery than the normal control group. However, obstetrical analgesia does not account for these findings, since none of the mothers of the infants in our study had more than 50 mg of Demerol during labor. It has been reported (8,9) that pre-delivery medication in this dosage has no measurable effect upon the Brazelton. A second explanation is that 14 of the 26 passively addicted infants were under treatment for the neonatal narcotic withdrawal syndrome at the time of the 3 day Brazelton examination and none was in treatment for the neonatal narcotic withdrawal syndrome at the 28 day examination; thus the depressed alertness scores at 3 days of age might represent the effect of treatment rather than the effect of the withdrawal syndrome. However, a comparison of the alertness scores of treated and untreated passively addicted infants did not reveal significant differences between the two groups (treated $\bar{X}$ = 27.9, S.D. = 9.9; untreated $\bar{X}$ = 27.4, S.D. = 9.5). Therefore, the low alertness scores in the passively addicted infants are not attributable to the therapy of the neonatal narcotic withdrawal syndrome.

Supported in part by Research Grants HD-06009 (NICHD), DA-00325 (NIMH) and MH-19052 (NIMH), and also a Research Contract #1674 from the Commonwealth of Pennsylvania Governor's Council on Drug and Alcohol Abuse.

Table I: ALERTNESS

Group	N	3 days X	3 days SD	28 days X	28 days SD	$p <$
Addict	26	18.8	10.5	25.3	11.9	.001*
High Risk	12	15.6	11.2	27.0	12.0	.01
Normal	25	28.4	7.7	26.0	11.7	NS

*paired two-tailed t test

Table II: IRRITABILITY

Group	N	3 days X	3 days SD	28 days X	28 days SD	p<
Addict	26	23.7	9.1	26.7	9.0	NS*
High Risk	12	18.8	9.1	22.8	10.0	.1
Normal	25	21.5	6.3	22.7	7.9	NS

*paired two-tailed t test

VI.   REFERENCES

1. T.B. Brazelton, Neonatal Behavioral Assessment Scale, Spastics International Medical Publications, London, 1973.

2. E. Tronick and T. B. Brazelton, "Clinical Uses of the Brazelton Scale," unpublished manuscript.

3. F. D. Horowitz, "Newborn and Four Week Retest on a Normative Population Using the Brazelton Newborn Assessment Procedure," paper presented at the 1971 meetings of the Society for Research in Child Development, Minneapolis, Minnesota.

4. S. L. Kaplan, R. E. Kron, M. Litt, L. P. Finnegan and M. D. Phoenix, in Aberrant Development in Infancy: Human and Animal Studies (N.R. Ellis, ed.), Lawrence Erlbaum Associates (Wiley), Hillsdale, New Jersey, 1975, pp. 139-148.

5. R. E. Kron, S. L. Kaplan, L. P. Finnegan, M. Litt and M. D. Phoenix, Intl. J. Addictive Dis., 2: 257 (1975).

6. A. B. Soule, K. Standley and S.A. Copans, "Clinical Uses of the Brazelton Neonatal Scale," paper presented at the 1973 meetings of the Soceity for Research in Child Development, Philadelphia, PA.

7. M. E. Strauss, J. K. Lessen-Firestone, R. H. Starr and E. M. Ostrea, Child Dev., 46: 889 (1975).

8. F. D. Horowitz, J. Ashton and S. Levin, "The Effects of Maternal Medication on the Behavior of Israeli Infants," paper presented at the biennial meeting of the Society for Research in Child Development, Denver, Colorado, April 1975.

9. H. Bakow, "Relation between Newborn Behavior and Mother-Child Interaction at Four Months," paper presented at the 1973 meetings of the Society for Research in Child Development, Philadelphia, PA

SCREENING OF PREGNANT WOMEN FOR DRUGS AT DELIVERY

John Eric Jacoby, M.D., M.P.H.
Medical Director

Boston Polydrug Unit
249 River Street
Boston, Massachusetts 02126

Introduction

The abuse of drugs in prenancy has been long known. Narcotic addiction in infants has been reported in medical literature since 1875.[1] Barbiturate use in pregnancy has been thought to be associated with neonatal withdrawal symptoms.[2] Hill[3] asked pregnant women at term what medication they had taken. They stated they took an average of 10 drugs. Zelson[4] reports an increase in prevalence of opiate addicted gravida in a city hospital from o.5% in 1960 to 4% in 1972.

Most drug abuse literature has been of the retrospective type describing symptoms in babies of mothers known to be using drugs.[5,6] The present research aims at studying the actual extent of drug abuse in a pregnant population, and determining if there was a significant amount of clinically inapparent drug abuse.

Methods

Over a two-month period at a large voluntary hospital, urine was collected from women at term admitted to the labor floor. The nurses were requested to obtain specimens from all admitted patients; however it was not possible to obtain urine from all patients. During this period there were 479 deliveries, and eighty-six urines were analyzed for drugs. This represented a 17.9% sample of the deliveries. There is no apparent bias in the sample, as both "sample mothers" and "all mothers" showed an almost identical ward-private ratio - (50% : 50% vs. 51% : 49%) and mean age (25.3 vs. 24.7).

The urine specimens in the sample were taken without the knowledge of the patients and were frozen and stored. A code number only to the investigator was written on the urine container, thus assuring complete confidentiality. The study in no way

affected the usual medical procedure and thus no consent was
thought necessary. Furthermore, it was felt that consent would
bias the study. The samples were analyzed by the Bureau of
Laboratories, New York City Department of Health. Thin layer
chromatography was employed to detect amphetamines, barbiturates,
phenobarbital, diphenylhidantoin (Dilantin), quinine, diazepam
(Valium), Chlordiazepoxide, (Librium), methadone, meperidine
(Demerol), codeine, morphine, and phenothiazines. The urines
were also analyzed as a check by Enzyme Immuno Assay for amphetamines, barbiturates, cocaine, methadone and opiate. A Ferric
Nitrate test for salicylates was performed.

Results

Nineteen of the 86 samples, or 22% showed the presence of
barbiturates, salicylates or quinine. Quinine is used to "cut
heroin," but may also be in tonic drinks. No other drugs were
detected in the study. Since during the study several methadone
patients gave birth, failure to detect methadone is based on
sample size. Seventeen patients (20%) showed barbiturates and/or
salicylates. Nine samples (11%) showed barbiturates and 11
samples (13%) showed salicylates. Five samples (6%) showed
quinine.

Of the patients with urinary barbiturates, one was known
to be taking phenobarbital for pre-eclampsia, but no other patient
was known to be taking barbiturates.

The characteristics of the cohort of patients whose urines
were analyzed seem to agree with the characteristics of the
population of mothers giving birth. Those patients taking a drug
represented a cross section of all types of patients. Those
taking drugs included ward patients as well as private patients,
and white, Spanish named and black patients. However, the mean
age for the barbiturate users was lower than the cohort (not
significant statistically). And the salicylate users tended to
be married, multiparous, private patients (also not significant
statistically) in contrast with the cohort of patients whose
urine was tested.

Conclusion

The use and abuse of drugs in the United States is a major
health and social problem. During pregnancy the fetus as well as
the mother is exposed to pharmacologic agents and, because of
this, pregnant women are cautioned against all medical except on
the advice of their physicians. The thalidomide tragedy is well
known. Milkovich and van den Berg[7] report on increased incidence
of birth defects associated with chlordiazepoxide (librium) and

meprobamate (Miltown, Equanil, etc.). The epidemiology of the
exposure of fetuses to drugs is not fully understood and little
is known about the abuse of drugs by a cross section of pregnant
women.

In the small cohort in this study a significant portion of
the urine samples tested at one point in the pregnancy revealed
barbiturates or salicylates. This may reflect on the widespread
availability of drugs in our society and a widespread attitude
amongst patients that drugs are safe.

Pregnant women are screened for cervical cancer, tuberculosis, anemia and syphillis. Similarly, drug abuse may be
present in a patient who may show no signs of drug abuse on
physical examination. If a physician wishes to uncover hidden
drug abusers a urinary screen for drugs might be indicated.
There is not enough experience to state whether early detection
of "sub-clinical" drug abuse would be helpful.

ACKNOWLEDGEMENT

I should like to express my thanks to Dr. Paul May of the
Buerau of Laboratories, New York City Board of Health, who
arranged to provide without charge the analyses for this study
and also provided useful advice.

TABLE I

Types of Drugs Found in Urine of 86 Patients

Drug or Combination	Number of Patients
Barbiturates (only)	6
Salicylates (only)	6
Quinine (only)	2
Salicylate & Barbiturates	2
Salicylate & Quinine	2
All Three (S., @. & B)	1
Total Showing Drugs	19 (22%)
Total Drug Free	67 (78%)

REFERENCES

1. Cobrinik, R.W., et al. The Effect of Maternal Narcotic
    Addiction in the Newborn Infant. J. of Pediatrics, 24:
    288, 1959

2. Desmond, M.M., et al. Maternal Barbiturate Utilization
    and Neonatal Withdrawal Symptomatology. J. of Pediatrics,
    80:190, 1972

3. Hill, R.M. Drugs Ingested by Pregnant Women. Clin. Pharmacol.
    & Ther. 14:654

4. Zelson, C. Infant of the Addicted Mother. N. Engl. J. Med.,
    288:1393, 1973

5. Reddy, et al. Observations on Heroin and Methadone With-
    drawal in the Newborn. J of Pediatrics, 48:353, 1971

6. Stone, M.L., et al. Narcotic Addiction in Pregnancy. Am. J
    of Obstet. and Gynecol., 109:716, 1971

7. Milkovich L. and Van den Berg, B.J. Effects of Prenatal
    Meprobamate and Chlordiazepoxide Hydrochloride on Human
    Embryonic and Fetal Development. N. Engl. J. Med., 291:1268,
    1974

ATTITUDES TOWARD ABORTION IN THE PREGNANT ADDICT

Tina Morrow Back, M.A.,CRC; Ping-wen Hou, M.D.; Frances
Labinger, R.N.

Morris J. Bernstein Institute
Beth Israel Medical Center
New York, New York

Introduction

For many women in the United States abortion represents a highly charged issue with many moral, religious,
and legal implications. For the pregnant addict, the
issue of abortion is further complicated by her life-
style, which may hamper her decision making abilities.

The female addict is often naive and egocentric. Of
primary importance to her is obtaining and using drugs.
She often does not know that she is pregnant until many
months have gone by and, even then, she may show a pronounced lack of concern for the fetus or her own health.

This research was conducted on the Female Drug Detoxification Ward of Bernstein Institute. It is a thirty-
seven bed unit provided for detoxification from opiates,
barbiturates and other habituating drugs. The duration
of hospitalization is from two to four weeks. The population is ethnically mixed with an average age of
twenty-five. Counseling and medical services are provided to enable the patient to make aftercare plans for
her discharge from the hospital.

From our sampling of three hundred patients in 1975,
thirty-four were admitted in their first five months of
pregnancy, the period in which most legal abortions are
performed. Five of these patients chose to terminate
their pregnancy and twenty-nine did not.

Before a realistic treatment plan can be developed
with the patient, her pregnancy status must be ascertained. Pregnancy tests are administered to all suspect cases. The medical and counseling staff work as
a team to explore the patient's feelings about her
pregnancy. Arrangements for an abortion can be made

during the time of detoxification. If an abortion is chosen, intensive counseling is provided before and after the procedure. If the patient wishes to remain pregnant, appropriate aftercare referrals are provided.

Views Against Abortion

The majority of our patients are opposed to abortion. There are a number of often-heard arguments which are employed to support this point of view.

Many state that they have religious or moral prohibitions. It is sometimes stated, "If God wanted me to be pregnant then I should stay pregnant."

Many patients are of the belief that motherhood affirms their womanhood. Being pregnant is status that she doesn't wish to be deprived of.

Lonliness is one of the most commonly expressed feelings of addicted women. Many feel great relief believing that the baby will be their constant companion and therefore cure their lonliness.

Some women like the secondary gains of pregnancy such as being special and being fussed over. They also feel that it may help to get the attention of an indifferent partner.

Having a baby helps support the fantasy that the pregnancy will slow her down and help her to control her impulses. Having a baby will also make everything all right and they will be like any other mother and child in our society. The mother feels that she isn't all bad if she produces a baby.

Due to feelings of emotional and financial deprivation in some of the patients, pregnancy is sometimes viewed as a bonanza in finally having something that belongs to them. For this reason, many are adament about keeping the child.

It appears that many of the patients who decide against abortion have a backup resource, such as a relative who can assume responsibility for the child if something goes wrong. This arrangement is often utilized and sometimes exploited.

One of the most important factors in an addict's continuation of her pregnancy is her attitude of passive

acceptance of life, that is, an inability to accept the
notion that she has some control over her destiny and
environment and is not merely a helpless pawn.   She
often shows no desire to manipulate her environment to
terminate her pregnancy or, in fact, to prevent it.   In
essence, this is just another aspect of her life that
she "just lets go".

Views In Favor Of Abortion

Although in the minority, several patients decided in
favor of abortion. As expected, their reasons reflect
their individual life situations. However, we have made
some observations about this group which distinguish
them in several ways from the others.

Many of the patients in this category have either
completed high school, gone to a treatment program in
the past or have worked. These factors were rare in the
other group.

Backup resources seldom exist in this group. If the
child is born, full responsibility would have to be
assumed for it, which some do not want.

Some of these women are prostitutes. An unwanted
pregnancy by an unknown man is undesirable for them and
they are anxious to have an abortion as soon as possible.

Some patients have the ability to recognize the responsibilities of motherhood and do not wish to be further burdened with the care of additional children. Some
women acknowledge negative or suicidal feelings about
themselves and find the responsibilities of motherhood
to be overwhelming.

At times, medical problems have an impact on the decision to terminate pregnancy. Drug abuse, venereal
diseases, anemia, toxemia and liver disease are often
conditions to be reckoned with.

Problems With Sexual Identity

Low self esteem, apathy and depression, hostility toward males, homosexual activity and lack of heterosexual
satisfaction are phenomena noted in the Odyssey House
study[1] They have found that these factors are responsible for the attitudnal foundation of "poor sexual
identity" which influence the behaviors regarding birth
control and abortion in addicted women.

737

They have found that there are two recurrent themes regarding attitudes toward sexuality in female addicts. First, there is a profound apathy and lack of motivation to take positive action toward controlling their futures. Second, there is a fundamental desire to become pregnant in order to be considered a normal woman with someone to love her.

Psychiatric Implications

Legalized abortion has made it possible for a woman to decide whether and if she will bear children and,for the first time, to make the decision with societal sanctions. It appears that early abortion does not produce severe emotional sequelae in most women. It has been suggested that among women undergoing this procedure that short term unhappiness and guilt may be a part of the normal response. The proportion of women with serious psychiatric complications is probably less than 10%.

Attitudes Of Staff Toward Abortion

The staff of the unit respects the right of all women to decide whether or not they wish to bear children. However, the staff feels that of primary importance is the health and welfare of the unborn child. We have formulated some opinions regarding why we feel that more of our patients should have abortions.

It is felt that the lives of most of our patients are extremely disorganized,(hence the need for inpatient detoxification), and that having a child will further complicate their lives. There is often no income or housing. There is often no person who can provide emotional support for the mother. Many pregnant patients are not involved with a treatment program which can provide medical and psychological services. Most of the patients have difficulty dealing with the fact that drug abuse is hazardous to their health and may cause fetal damage.

The most prevalent attitude we have observed in pregnant addicts is that of magical thinking. They appear to view their pregnancy in unrealistic terms. They fantasize that the baby will change their lives by forcing them to stop using drugs.

We have observed that most of these women have a lack of future orientation. Their dependency needs, insecurities and egocentricity make it difficult for them to relate to the needs of the child, which may eventually result in child neglect or abuse.

738

Summary

Each pregnant addict studied had a unique reason to accept or reject abortion. However, there seem to be several recurrent themes which appear to point toward the hazards of childbirth during the time in which our patients are involved in substantial drug abuse. It is essential that serious discussion take place with all pregnant addicts to determine whether or not they wish to remain pregnant.

Recommendations

The following are recommendations to improve the care and treatment of the pregnant addict:
1) Continued research in the field of addiction.
2) Improvement in the education of women regarding abortion, contraception, sterility, adoption and prenatal care.
3) Comprehensive and unprejudicial medical care for female addicts.
4) Greater sensitivity of rehabilitation programs toward female patients.
5) Appropriate counseling and reality testing by treatment personnel.

Reference

J. Densen-Gerber, M. Wiener and R. Hochstedler, "Sexual behavior, abortion, and birth control in heroin addicts: legal and psychiatric considerations" in Contemporary Drug Problems, 1(4) 783 (Fall, 1972)

PARENTING - PROBLEMS AND POSSIBILITIES

Carolyn Goodman, Ed.D.

PACE Family Treatment Centers
Bronx Psychiatric Center
New York, New York
              and
Department of Psychiatry
Albert Einstein College of Medicine
New York, New York

The subject of this paper is parenting, a role which many of us have, or will assume, one which is often perceived as a natural function, intuitively acquired. This, I believe, is a myth. As a parent myself, and as one who has worked with parents and children for many years, I know too well, the perils and pleasures, the frustrations and hardships, and yes the pain, which all parents face and try to cope with.

In this presentation I would like to touch upon some of the conditions which make parenting one of the most difficult of tasks and suggest directions we may take which could foster the parenting endeavor.

Let me begin with a definition. The function of parenting is an effort to rear a healthy child to maturity and independence. More specifically, to help a child cope effectively with his/her world, develop his/her intellectual powers to the greatest extent possible, and experience a satisfying relationship with his/her parents. Not an easy task.

When I read the theme of this plenary session, "Children, Our Most Precious Resource", I wondered if there had been a printing omission, because I would have placed a question mark after the title. Then it occurred to me, as it may to you, that we live with many myths, one of which is a belief that we are a child-oriented society which cares deeply about the well-being of our children.

What evidence do we have to the contrary? If we accept the fact that parenting is affected by the attitudes, values, and policies of our social and political institutions, as well as our national goals, a different scenario emerges.

The welfare system, which is responsible for many of the seventeen million children (one in four) who live under poverty

conditions, illustrates a societal cause for child abuse and
neglect. Parents who receive recently reduced benefits from
welfare, and who reflect conditions of poverty and prejudice, are
expected to be loving, patient, and generous to their children.

Legislation reduces elegibility for Day Care, and parents of
the "near poor" are forced to leave their jobs, and return to the
welfare rolls.

State Legislators, "with reckless disregard for rational and
compassionate priorities ... cut deeply into state programs for
mental health, drug addiction and corrections" (New York Times,
March 18, 1976).

The United States Supreme Court which is often perceived as
a mirror of our national purpose, upheld a decision which sanctioned corporal punishment in the school system.

Political favoritism, rather than human need, becomes the
yardstick for budgetary decisions and we learn that it is better
to be healthy and rich than sick and poor (and a dependent child),
in a fiscal crisis.

The family itself, which at one time embraced three
generations, and unmarried relatives, lives in nuclear isolation.

These stresses of parenting are felt by rich and poor alike,
who must live in a society where social relations may be more
affected by economic and self serving values, than by need and
mutual assistance.

If we are to become a society in which children are truly our
most precious resource, where can we direct our energies? I assure
you, I am far from having all the answers, but I have pondered
this question for many years. My thinking led me to design a
treatment and education program in which parent/child development
is the primary objective. The development of this program was
influenced by observations I made during a recent visit to a
country which seems to address itself in earnest to the well-being
of children and their parents. Let me share some of my thinking
and experiences with you.

Parenting, according to my definition is a care-oriented
relationship which revolves around the needs of a growing child.
This assumes that the parent understands these needs, and pre-
supposes that such parents are able to respond by providing a
nurturing environment. For many parents, a first child is an awesome experience. Here it is! A beautiful, demanding, unpredictable, image of ourselves. How do I hold it? I'm not sure I love
it. Why is it crying? Where do I look for help?

It is a reflection of our values that parenting is not considered as important as a profession, or a trade. If so, there
would be opportunities to learn about this complex function.
Parenting is also, (and this is changing somewhat), a woman's
responsibility and is not held in high esteem even though we
cherish the role of motherhood. However, parenting can be learned
in a variety of ways which I shall touch on when I describe the
PACE program at Bronx Psychiatric Center. It is difficult for a
parent to create a nurturing environment, because it involves the

capacity to give of oneself. A parent who, as a child, rarely felt
safety, succorance, and warmth has little to give. Nor can we expect parents to be nurturant when economic and emotional stress of
daily life drain so much of their energy. We must begin to think
about developing supportive networks for parents, so they can raise
their children with the help of caring others.

For some parents, understanding and nurturance are beyond
their experience. Their lives are marked by deprivation and lonliness and their "survival kit" is withdrawal into a dim world of
their own. It is for these parents that the PACE program was
designed. The program is a family centered intervention system
which tries to meet the needs of the parent, teach mothering skills,
and foster the development of the child. In four outpatient clinics
known as PACE (Parent and Child Education), located on the campus
of Bronx Psychiatric Center, two community based clinics, and a
public health station, mothers and their six month to five year old
children gather one to three times a week.

The program is focused on workshops for the mother/child, on
parent education discussions, and parent group meetings in which
more personal and family problems are discussed. In workshops,
mothers work alongside their children, and with the help of
teachers they learn the value and use of materials, and how to
construct toys from "primary" objects such as cans, bottles,
fabrics, and boxes. In the process, parents learn child development concepts such as age variations in span of attention, or a
child's need for self expression and exploration. The workshops
are designed to be mutually satisfying learning experiences for
mother and child. They take place in the PACE nursery school and
infant/toddler development rooms which are designed primarily for
children and are equipped with age appropriate learning and play
materials.

In parent education groups various aspects of child rearing
are raised by mothers and staff. The topics dealt with through
discussion, films, printed materials, and role playing, are the
growth and development of young children, discipline and limits,
children's play and toys, creative work, health and nutrition,
emotional development, and cognitive growth. For mothers who have
very young children (six months to two years) these parent education groups are an opportunity for primary prevention. Significant
gains can be made with mothers and young children before destructive patterns of child rearing become rigid and behavioral or
language lags make intervention more difficult.

The goals of parent education groups are:

To provide the mothers with a chance to talk with other
mothers and staff members about the very real problems and issues
of raising children in urban New York City in the 1970's.

To help the mothers learn from staff and from each other
how to handle the day to day problems of child raising.

To help mothers gain confidence in themselves as adults
who are capable of identifying and meeting their children's
emotional, physical, and cognitive needs.

To encourage each mother to develop her own mothering style and to recognize her own needs as a person as well as a mother.

In less structured groups, mothers discuss problems related to their personal needs, family difficulties and conditions of living which create stress in their lives. The goal of these groups is for staff and peer to work toward understanding the problems, reach constructive resolutions, and offer mutual support. While these groups deal primarily with problems, others are planned around social and recreational activities which are designed to build supportive networks for women who have few available family, or community resources.

The heart of the PACE program is the growth and development of mother and child through group learning and interaction. At times this involves a coming together of the entire family as in multiple family therapy. When it is not necessary to involve the family in this manner, every effort is made to enlist the active participation of father, children, and close relatives in a joint endeavor to create a mutually satisfying family environment. For many families, this therapeutic/learning community experience is an alternative for a system which separates disturbed mothers from their children.

The PACE staff is a multidisciplinary group of clinicians and teachers who along with the parents and children become the family. In an atmosphere which fosters trust and friendship, parents can develop relationships which generate nurturance and sensitivity to others. As their sense of adequacy and well-being emerges, so does their ability to assume responsibility for their lives and the growth of their children.

Finally, a few observations about a society from which we can learn, where parenting is enhanced by the accessibility of a vast system of supportive networks and the involvement of people in their own destiny. Traveling through the People's Republic of China, I visited creches, nursery schools, children's palaces (after school programs), urban neighborhoods, and communes, where children are cared for by young women as well as grannies. In the cities and industrial areas, day care units are often attached to work units so women can leave during the day to nurse their infants and visit their young children. Homemaking is facilitated for working parents who can call upon older men and women to help with shopping, meal preparation and other household chores. On their part, the elderly know they are making a necessary contribution by assuming these tasks.

No one asks child care workers how much schooling they have had, or how many degrees they have earned. As with many other jobs such as medical care, skills are developed in seminars and in-the-field training. (Apprenticeship is an old Chinese custom). Professionalism is not the sine qua non - people are involved because they care.

I would like to close with a quotation from Ruth Sidel's book called _Families of Fengsheng: Urban Life in China_ which reflects

743

my ideas and feelings about the possibilities of parenting and the value of men, women and children.

> "What can we learn from the Chinese as we try to build bridges to one another, to form a new sense of community? We can learn that we need not rely solely on professionals in order to care for one another, that ordinary untrained people can reach out if permitted and encouraged to do so, and that they can help to provide health care, emotional support, physical attention, and above all the feeling that someone cares. We can learn that giving is as important, perhaps, as any other human need and that by providing mechanisms for people to give to one another we humanize all of us".[1]

1. R. Sidel, _Families of Fengsheng: Urban Life in China_, Penguin Books, Baltimore, Maryland, 1974, p. 158.

COMPREHENSIVE SERVICES TO DRUG-DEPENDENT WOMEN AND THEIR CHILDREN

Loretta P. Finnegan, M.D.
Patricia R. Bookhart, M.S.W.
Lottie Moten, B.S.N.
Claudia Cohen, M.S.N.
Nellie Goodman

Family Center
Philadelphia General Hospital
Philadelphia, Pennsylvania

Although we have seen increasing numbers of pregnant addicts presenting themselves to hospitals over the past decade, in most cases they do not seek medical assistance until the onset of labor, therefore addiction in pregnancy has become an important health problem. The use of heroin carries the high risk of repeated infections, foreign body reactions, continued illegal activity, fatal overdose, inadequate nutrition, obstetrical problems such as premature labor, potential neonatal narcotic withdrawal, other serious neonatal conditions and difficulty in learning adequate mothering practices (1,2). Therefore, the clinical management of these clients is difficult because of the complications which generally result from their tendencies to neglect health care and to avoid seeking prenatal care throughout pregnancy. Social and emotional problems add to the overall difficulties of the pregnant addict. The following is a description of a program for pregnant drug-dependent women at Philadelphia General Hospital (PGH).

Family Center was developed at PGH in 1970 in an attempt to solve the overwhelming problems of this patient population (3). The method of patient management in Family Center is one of intensive prenatal care, supported by psycho-social intervention for the individual's drug-dependent state with an outreach service provided by public health nurses and community workers. During the initial visit the obstetrician meets each patient and a complete medical work-up and laboratory tests, including a urine for toxicology are performed. She is then admitted to the in-patient obstetrical service for evaluation for approximately three to four days. The patient who is less than 20 weeks pregnant is offered an abortion option. After substantiation of her addictive status, she is offered methadone maintenance or detoxification. If methadone is requested, 10 mg is given daily and increased only if she requires a higher dosage to prevent withdrawal symptomatology. The maximum dose is kept, if possible, below 35 mg of methadone per day. Through experience we discovered that high dose maintenance is unnecessary and withdrawal will not occur on carefully scheduled lower doses. Other drugs, such as tranquilizers and barbiturates are avoided unless the patient is dependent on these medications (3). During the patient's hospital evaluation, she is assigned a social worker, a public health nurse and community worker. She also receives psychiatric evaluation. If the patient's husband or consort desires treatment for opiate addiction, he is admitted to the program through the normal out-patient channels. This is encouraged by the program because involvement of the entire family has been shown to be most successful (3). This manuscript will describe the program's functions and the roles of the staff.

Role of the Social Worker

The social worker in the Family Center Program has a two-dimensional role: one in the clinical area and the other in research. The research area is designed to develop modalities of treatment related to women. Most drug treatment programs were developed to serve the needs of male addicts and those females who enrolled were treated very much like the male population. A program such as ours addresses itself to the special needs and problems of the female addict.

The direct service delivery role was designed to help introduce the client to the medical and social service aspects of the program. It also facilitates coordination of the efforts of the many disciplines involved. The way in which the worker responds to this role depends largely on the approach to social work practice. Our approach to service delivery is an environmental or structural approach. This approach begins with the assumption that individuals are rational and competent, and if provided with the proper environmental supports, they are capable of utilizing their own resources to provide for basic human needs. When the individual is unable to function effectively, the responsibility is placed on her environment and the lack of supports. This approach permits the client to define her own needs and priorities and defines the task of the social worker.

Within this framework the social worker chooses one of the following practice modalities. In individual therapy, the worker confers with the client and gets a clearer understanding of the client's needs and problems. The client is encouraged to build upon her own personal strengths and begins to consider the reality of her future plans for herself and her unborn child.

Group therapy is used to diminish social isolation among the clients and provides an arena for the discussion of common issues. All clients are encouraged to involve their families in the treatment process and Family Center has begun to stress the use of family therapy as the most desirable treatment modality. The family is viewed as the most important and influential system in the addict's life. In therapy, the family is aided to respond to the addict as a competent individual who plays a part in a family system that is dependent on the women's addiction to maintain family stability. Educational and vocational training and employment are also used as alternative forms of therapy.

Even with the availability of such comprehensive care and use of a treatment team to serve the client, there are still several factors that create problems for the social worker and the client. While the social worker is trying to carry her role as a member of the help- ing profession, at the same time she is part of a system that con- trols release of the client's methadone. The distribution of meth- adone is often viewed as a police function and confusion arises when the client sees that the social worker is also involved in this process.

It is then difficult to get the client to agree to accept the ser- vices that are available, and the worker may feel frustrated by the client's lack of motivation and involvement. If the client decides that methadone is the only aspect of the program that she wishes to utilize, it clearly places the worker in a dilemma. We must respond to the client's right to refuse treatment and also the agency's re- fusal to be merely a methadone dispensing station. These two roles conflict.

In summary, in a treatment program for pregnant drug-dependent wom- en, the social worker should: 1) respond to the client's needs and priorities - as defined by the client, 2) research and investigate new methods for treatment, and bring about structural change within the system that responds to the drug-dependent woman. This can be done by setting small tasks to achieve small goals and assuring that the client and her family take responsibility for achieving these goals. The worker needs to keep in mind that all change is incre- mental.

Role of the Public Health Nurse

The Public Health Nurse (PHN), is a vital member of the team caring for the pregnant addict and her infant. She has the unique opportu- nity to be present in all the areas encompassing patient care: hos- pital, clinic and home settings. The nurse supports the patient through pregnancy, labor, delivery and then assists her with the care of her newborn child.

After the patient's admission to the obstetrical intensive care unit, the initial meeting between the patient and the PHN takes place. By simply introducing herself in a friendly and open manner, the PHN begins to gain the patient's confidence. At the same time, the nurse explains her own role in the program and takes a nursing history. When the first encounter between the patient and PHN has been completed, the nurse proceeds to develop a plan with the obstetrician. A working relationship with the entire obstetrical staff is crucial so that problems concerning the patient's care are filtered through the PHN. During this prenatal period, nursing objectives include: 1) encouraging prenatal clinic attendance, 2) providing education regarding nutrition, basic anatomy, labor and delivery and the danger signals of pregnancy. This teaching is done in both individual and group sessions. We hold a prenatal group meeting every week, which, in addition to providing necessary information for the patients, affords them the opportunity to socialize in a non-drug related setting.

Prior to the birth of the baby, a home visit is made which allows the nurse an opportunity to assess the mother's degree of preparation for the expected child while offering her practical assistance and support in infant care. At times, many mothers express guilt about the passive addiction of the infant. Such discussions are often the first step in resolution of some of the many problems which the patient faces. In addition, the valuable information which the PHN has gained at the home visit must be shared with the rest of the staff.

After delivery of the baby and having reviewed the post partum care, the nurse begins to teach the mother some basic principles of infant care emphasizing the particular needs of the passively drug-dependent child. A formal home evaluation is made prior to the infant's discharge from the hospital. The results of the home evaluation are communicated to the nursery staff. At times, it has been necessary to maintain an infant in the nursery. This visit is an opportunity to offer the mother assistance with her infant related problems. Additional home visits are made as needed to support the mother in infant care.

In addition to the assessment criteria mentioned, we are beginning to develop a "risk assessment" scale. This will provide a method of evaluating the risk of sending an infant home with a drug-dependent mother. For those mothers with high risk scores a program of intervention will be developed. Identification of the high risk mother and the planned intervention program may hopefully help us to prevent future neglected and abused children.

Another function of the Public Health Nurse involves pediatric follow-up. The mother is urged to bring her infant to the Special Pediatric Clinic at PGH. Here, a specially trained pediatrician sees the infants and follows them on subsequent visits ensuring continuity of care. Developmental and neurological testing is performed at 6 months, one, two and three years of age. The nurse attends this clinic to reinforce the physician's instructions and to convey the mother's concern to the physician. Her presence serves as a check-up mechanism for clinic attendance. The nurse is also able to provide the hospital based physician with valuable insight into the patients home environment by giving a more realistic picture of the patient's situation.

Role of the Community Worker

The team approach includes the community worker who is involved in
direct service to the client, either in the hospital, in her home
or in the community. The services that this team member provides
to the client encompasses not only assistance with homemaking, budgeting and child care, but also help in directing the client to
community resources that will improve her living conditions. Further, the community worker encourages on-going participation in the
program's collaborative services and, when necessary, provides
transportation so that the client will have the opprotunity to
utilize them. Attempts are made to locate children born on the
program, even though their mothers no longer seek our services,
and at that time to assess the current status of the family.

In summary, the community worker is an integral component of the
Family Center Program in its total effort to meet the specific
needs of each client, and to give optimal social and medical services to these women and their children.

REFERENCES

1. L.P. Finnegan, J. of Psychedelic Drugs 7:299 (1975).

2. R.C. Davis and J.N. Chappel, Proc. Fifth Methadone Conference,

   Washington, D.C., 2:1146 (1973).

3. J.F. Connaughton, L.P. Finnegan, J. Schut and J.P. Emich,

   Addictive Diseases: an International Journal, 2: 101 (1975).

OUR ABUSED CHILDREN - CAN WE STEM THE TIDE?

By

Dr. Judianne Densen-Gerber, J.D., M.D.
President, Odyssey Institute

and

David N. Sandberg, State Director
Odyssey House New Hampshire

Chairman, N.H. Commission on
Children and Youth

Jonathan, age 16 came to Odyssey House New Hampshire as an alternative to reform school where he had been once previously for
theft. He is the second oldest child in a large lower middle
class family.

When Jonathan was 6, his parents took him and his 7 year old
brother to a Catholic orphanage where they remained for four years.
Neither boy was given an explanation as to why they were removed
from the family. Jonathan's strongest memories of this period are
his continually getting into mischief and having to stand in the
corner, and wondering why his parents had left him and his brother
at the orphanage. Due to the orphanages' policy of grouping
children according to certain age ranges, Jonathan and his brother
were separated throughout the four years.

Just as abruptly and inexlicably as their going to the orphanage,
their parents arrived one day to bring them back home. Within a
week of their return, their alcoholic father, a barrel-chested
brute of a man, began to beat them. The first incident was
"punishment" for the boys camping in the living room using lighted
candles under his hand, then his brothers.

The worst of the beatings occured when Jonathan was 12 years old.
He recalls being in the basement in his underwear one morning when
his father came to punish him for disobeying his mother. His
father first used the strap part of his belt, then beat Jonathan
with the buckle end until the buckle cracked after striking him
just above the eye. His father began to beat him with a 36" baseball bat.

The assault continued for one hour. At one point, Jonathan's
father forced him to clean the kitchen striking him whenever he
did not work quickly or efficiently enough to suit him. Jonathan
was next made to stand on a chair in the living room and wash the
walls with his arms fully raised. His father then rammed the butt

end of the baseball bat into Jonathan's stomach causing him to vomit.

Jonathan finally managed to escape from this sadistic rampage and made his way to a hospital three blocks away. His entire body was covered with blood, and he passed out shortly after being admitted.

Upon regaining conciousness, he was interviewed by the police. He told them what had happened and they filed charges against Jonathan's father. His mother, who was in the same hospital having just given birth to a daughter, came to visit him and persuaded him to recant his story about being beaten by his father. Jonathan eventually lied in court and recalls the prosecutor questioning him sternly about the consequences for committing perjury.

At the conclusion of the trial, Jonathan's father was placed on one year of probation and the whole family returned to the home where the beatings resumed. They stopped only when Jonathan's mother finally threatened to go to the police.

Jonathan's drug history began as soon as he returned home from the orphanage and consisted of "getting drunk on weekends." He was 10 years old at the time. At 11, he started sniffing glue, and at 13 began smoking marijuana regularly as well as popping pills. At 14, he used LSD for one consecutive year. At 15 and until the time he came to Odyssey House, Jonathan injected methedrine and barbituates. He was high every day. (A postnote concerning Jonathan is that today he is very happy and doing very well. He just turned 21. He now knows what it means to love and be loved, and believes his journey to health was made easier by his clear, unconflicted hatred of his father.)

Mary is 14 years old. She was referred to Odyssey House's adolescent program from a small New Hampshire district court. She had been on probation following a series of attempts at foster and childrens' home placements over the previous 3 years. Her mother was an alcoholic who died when Mary was 11. She says her real father is either dead or in jail (she thinks for murder.) She has never met him.

Mary believes that the beginning of her difficulties was a falling out with her foster parents due to her having gotten involved with drugs. She ran away, was apprehended by the police, but refused to return to her foster home saying that her foster father would abuse her.

Following several subsequent placements in foster care settings, more running away and continued drug use, Mary came to Odyssey House in lieu of being sentenced to reform school.

In reviewing the past several years, Mary indicates she was raped twice (she did not say by whom) and fears she may be damaged in-

ternally. In late 1975, she overdosed on amphetamines after leaving a group home. She explains the overdose as partly an attempt
to relieve frustration and partly an attempt to end her life.

The other representative case is Bobby, age 15, whose mother gave
birth to him very late in life. The next oldest sibling was 15
years his senior and all the other children had left home by the
time Bobby was 5.

When Bobby was 8, his mother told him that he was an unwanted child.
She also told him that he would have to start fending for himself
as his parents were old and would not be around much longer. His
father died less than two years later at which time his mother began to drink heavily. She also started bringing a series of boyfriends into the home which upset Bobby greatly.

Within a year following his father's death, Bobby began committing
burglaries for which he was sentenced to reform school for one
year. He also began sniffing glue at this time and shortly thereafter progressed to use of marijuana and hallucenogenics. His
world rapidly shrank to his room, his pet hampster and his stereo.
The one outside contact he maintained on a regular basis was a
homosexual relationship with an older man in the neighborhood, a
family friend.

These three youngsters represent in whole or in part many of the
adolescents we see at Odyssey House New Hampshire. Several re-
occurring themes stand out:

1. childhood abuse in one form or another - some violent, some
sexual, and some via extreme emotional neglect such as Bobby
experienced.

2. major family disruption experienced during childhood - divorce,
desertion, death of a parent.

3. high incidence of alcoholism amongst parents.

4. absence of ongoing nurturing from a strong, older member of the
family.

5. not surprisingly, the early development of antisocial life
style by these youngsters with drug abuse one symptomatic feature.

It is interesting to note that similar data was gathered in the
earlier days of treating heroin addiction during the 1960's. Yet
such revelations from the adult sociopath produced little sympathy. The older patients were hardened and far removed from their
abusive past. Therapeutic emphasis was on the here-and-now. But
when we began to hear from the 14 and 15 year olds - the Jonathans,

Marys and Bobbys - in 1972 and '73 we had great difficulty attempting to integrate their stories of an abusive past. These were children and their "abusive past" was still so much a part of who they were that the great majority of their "acting out" behavior including drug use was an immediate response to their incredibly destructive family situations. This was not the adult sociopath's cold self-gain at the expense of society. This was a crying out against an extraordinary societal and parental betrayal.

Once our young residents forced us to take a close look at causative factors in their budding anti-social life style, there was no turning back. By the end of 1974, Odyssey as a national organization under the leadership of Dr. Judianne Densen-Gerber had concluded that child abuse was the major cause of addiction among society's less affluent citizens.

In 1975, Odyssey Institute, the parent organization for all Odyssey service units, undertook a major research project in quest of more specific data about child abuse. The study reviewed the family history of all the women (118) in Odyssey programs to determine the prevalence of prior incestuous relationships. The women came from 26 states and were being treated for a variety of anti-social behavior.

52 of the 118 women or 44%, ranging from 13 to 42 years of age, reported being involved in an incestuous relationship. Over one-third of these sexual contacts involved intercourse. The remaining two-thirds involved attempted seduction, fondling of genitalia and exposure. The most frequent partners were fathers, uncles and quasi-family (e.g., mothers boyfriends). Others included stepfathers, grandfathers, siblings, cousins and in-laws.

Three-quarters of the women were 12 years old or younger at the onset of incestuous activity. Almost half were 9 years old or younger when they experienced their first incestuous relationship, strongly suggesting that incest is a major type of child abuse.

The 1975 incest study was followed up by Odyssey Institute's Research Department in January of 1976. Of 237 residents (152 males, 85 females) interviewed in Odyssey programs nationwide, 32 (38%) of the females and 38 (25%) of the males had some kind of incestuous relationship.

The value of this research can be better understood in light of Dr. Lee Robins' "Deviant Children Grown Up." Dr. Robins' study was based on a clinical study of 600 children between the ages of 8-14 who had abusive parents. A follow-up study when these children reached adulthood without any significant therapeutic intervention revealed that 50% were sociopathic. Suffering no physical disabilities, they tended to multiply freely thus ensuring a self-perpetuating process and a new generation of sociopaths. Of the other 300, 80% had serious diagnosible psychiatric illnesses. Only 10% were healthy.

Several years ago, Odyssey coined the solgan "Today's Abused/ Tomorrow's Addicted." It is more than a mere catchy phrase. It speaks of the high correlation between abuse suffered in childhood and subsequent antisocial behavior including addiction in adulthood. And contrary to what we might expect, those who have been abused in their early years are very apt to abuse their own offspring. This chain of abuse from one family generation to the next has been the focus of Odyssey's Mabon Parents' Program on Wards Island in New York. Both the parent and child are treated to break the abuse cycle.

With the near disappearance of the extended family and the erosion of the nuclear family, we can expect child abuse to be on the increase. This will be paralleled by an ever increasing number of anti-social young people. One thing that can be done is to increase direct service programs such as Odyssey's adolescent centers which provide intensive therapeutic intervention. A treatment investment now will cost us, but nothing in comparison to what these young people will cost us if allowed to go untreated. It is also important to acknowledge that in treating one young person today such as Jonathan, Mary or Bobby we are greatly reducing the likihood that they will be abusive toward their children.

From our work with abused individuals, we derive the incentive to wage the larger battle against public ignorance concerning child abuse. We are in great need of awareness campaigns designed to alert the general citizenry to the horror and tremendous cost of child abuse. Odyssey Institute's campaign entitled the Concerns of Children, calls for the creation of a babinet level position in the federal government to protect the needs and rights of children. Governmental decisions must be weighed in terms of their effect upon this and future generations of children if we are to flourish as a people and nation.

At the local level, we need educational courses in parenting and human relations beginning at the elementary school level and continuing through junior and senior high school. We should not leave to chance that some of our children may come to know the values of human respect for self and other people while others are kept in the shadows of life. A growing number of our children make up the ranks of the latter and it is they who so often turn to anti-social behavior including drug abuse.

If, as we say, children are our most important resource we need to commit ourselves in earnest to the proper nurturing of all our children. Only then will we have come to grips with the drug abuse phenomenon which has become so much a part of our culture.

THE RELATIONSHIP BETWEEN OPIATE ABUSE
AND CHILD ABUSE AND NEGLECT*

Rebecca M. Black, Ph.D.
Joseph Mayer, Ph.D.
Alice Zaklan, M.Ed.

Washingtonian Center for Addictions
41 Morton Street
Boston, Massachusetts

I. Child Abuse/Neglect and Opiate Abuse

The terms child abuse and child neglect are sometimes used
separately and sometimes combined. Together they are defined in
the Child Abuse Prevention and treatment Act of 1974, P.L. 93-247,
as "the physical or mental injury, sexual abuse, negligent treatment, or maltreatment of a child under the age of eighteen by a
person who is responsible for the child's welfare under circumstances which indicate that the child's health or welfare is
harmed or threatened thereby."

Definitions of child abuse and neglect often are vague since
it can be difficult to distinguish between acceptable cultural
norms, of discipline for example, and child abuse or neglect.
When Kempe (1962) first described the "battered child syndrome"
he was describing an extreme of physical abuse. Since then the
use of the term child abuse has been expanded.

Although children have always been removed from parents by
the courts, recent interest in child abuse/neglect has resulted
in new laws about adjudication of unfit parents. Heroin addicts
are particularly prone to be singled out by these laws. In New
York State, for example, one of the legal definitions of an
abused child is any child of an adjudicated heroin addict. In
other states, Massachusetts for example, an infant born addicted
is considered an abused child and required to be reported as such.
Thus, out of many groups of parents who may have difficulty in
caring for their children, the heroin addict is singled out and
assumed guilty of being a neglectful or abusing parent.

It is important to know if this assumption is valid. Apart from
shocking individual examples, little actual evidence is available
associating heroin abuse and child abuse/neglect.

*This investigation was supported in part by Grant 90-C-427,
National Center on Child Abuse, Office of Child Development,
Department of H.E.W.

Studies of child abuse and neglect have attempted to identify situations in which abuse and neglect occur, personality
characteristics of abusing parents, and characteristics of children which may contribute to the occurrence of abuse. Situational
factors associated with child abuse and neglect include: a
parental history of abuse or neglect as a child, stressful life
circumstances including poverty, chronic illness, unemployment
and social isolation, young parents, unwanted pregnancy, and
absence of one parent (Smith, et al, 1974). Many of these factors
occur in families in which a parent is a heroin addict (Braucht,
et. al., 1973).

Personality characteristics associated with child abuse/
neglect include: low frustration tolerance, low self-esteem,
impulsivity, dependency, immaturity, retardation, psychosis,
severe depression, role reversal, difficulty in experiencing
pleasure, and lack of understanding of the needs and abilities of
infants and children (Spinetta and Rigler, 1972). Many of these
have been reported as characteristic of addicts (Braucht, et. al.,
1973).

Characteristics of children which detract from their accept-
ableness or responsiveness to the parent are also associated with
child abuse/neglect. These factors include retardation, deformity,
illness, behavioral problems including hyperactivity, disobedience,
delinquency and emotional difficulties characterized by withdrawal and lack of responsiveness (Caffey, 1972). Several of
these factors may be related to opiate abuse insofar as infant
withdrawal from opiates may make the child irritable and unpleasant. This unattractiveness may interact with anxiety, inexperi-
ence, and guilt in the mother to disrup their relationship.

In summary, some child abuse/neglect can be expected to
occur in families in which a parent is addicted to heroin. However, few child abuse/neglect studies have attempted to assess
the extent to which drug addiction is involved and the results
of these studies vary and are difficult to interpret. In addition, definitions of drug addiction often are unclear and data on
drug and alcohol addiction combined.

Fitch et. al. (1975), in a prospective study of child abuse,
reported that 21.4% of mothers of abused children, 37% of fathers
of abused children and 37% of persons committing the abuse used
drugs dysfunctionally; dysfunctionally defined as "having caused
trouble with spouse, family, friends, employer, police, and the
user's own health one or more times." These percentages were
higher than for persons of the same social class in the area
studied. Another study (Kent, et. al., 1975) indicated that 41%
of mothers and 50% of fathers of abused or neglected children
under court protection were substance abusers, although only 31%
of the substance abusers were judged to need treatment. No distinction was made between drug and alcohol abuse. In many studies
drug addiction has not been included as a variable for study.

Researchers now assume that there is more than one distinct group of persons who abuse children and that child abuse and neglect may be somewhat different phenomenon. Kent, et. al. (1975) differentiated several distinct abuse and neglect clusters; preliminary results suggest that: 1) excessive alcohol or drug use is related to some, but not to all, child abuse, 2) the most severe child abuse is not associated with dysfunctional use of alcohol or drugs, and 3) dysfunctional use of alcohol or drugs is more frequently related to child neglect than to child abuse.

It is clear that factors associated with child abuse and neglect are present in the personalities and situations of drug addicts, but the connection between child abuse/neglect and opiate addiction may not be with addiction per se, but rather with the social, psychological, and situational factors often associated with addiction.

II.   A Study: Initial Results

At the Washingtonian Center for Addictions, a private, voluntary, multi-modality treatment center for drug addiction and alcoholism in Boston, Massachusetts, we are engaged in a study designed to 1) investigate and compare frequency and types of child care, abuse and neglect associated with alcoholism and opiate addiction, 2) examine the relationship between stages in the cycles of drug and alcohol abuse (acquisition, ingestion, withdrawal, and abstinence), and child care/abuse/neglect, and 3) determine the extent to which social and situational factors associated with child abuse/neglect are operative among alcohol and drug addicts.

In this study 100 alcoholics and 100 opiate addicts caring for children under 18 are being interviewed for information on: 1) demographic data, 2) history of drug and alcohol abuse, 3) childhood history, 4) care/abuse/neglect of children, and 5) the relationship between stages in the cycle of alcohol or opiate abuse and child care/abuse/neglect. Additional measures include: 1) Minnesota Multiphasic Personality Inventory, 2) Survey on Bringing up Children (Helfer), and 3) The Schedule of Recent Experience (Holmes).

Initial results indicate that not all opiate addicts seriously abuse or neglect their children, although many appear to have difficulties in childrearing similar to those we might expect in a sample of low-income parents, parents from disturbed backgrounds, or chronically ill parents. Many of the addicts are concerned about their children and have made attempts to obtain help with child care. Most mothers are aware of the dangers of drug use during pregnancy and have attempted to limit or eliminate their drug use during this period.

The treatment process sometimes interferes with care of children, since treatment may involve separation, exposure of children to the drug subculture, or risk of the child being taken away by the courts.

Addicts report that they present themselves to their children as "sick" and report consequences in their children such as preoccupation with illness, guilt, and attempts to care for the parent. Secrecy, especially with younger children, blocks discussion of problems, while older children are frequent recipients of parental confessions. The child care activity most disrupted is play. Addicts report that they are not able to pay the attention to their children which play requires, or that play is severely limited by heroin addiction.

Finally, we find that our patients are eager to participate in the study and interested in helping their own children and the children of other addicts. They point out that their relationship to their children has only infrequently been mentioned in their treatment and they welcome the opportunity to discuss their children and their relationship with their children.

References

Braucht, G.N., B akarsh, D., Follengstad, D., Berry, K. (1973). Deviant drug use in adolescence: a review of psychosocial correlates. Psychological Bulletin, 79, 92-106.

Caffey, J. (1972). The parent-infant traumatic stress syndrome: (Caffey-Kempe Syndrome), (Battered Babe Syndrome). American Journal of Roentgenology, Radium Therapy and Nuclear Medicine, 114: 218-229.

Fitch, M.J., Cadol, R.V., Goldson, E., Wendell, T. and Swartz, D. (1975). Prospective study in child abuse: Unpublished Report. (Preliminary)

Kempe, C.H., Silverman, F.N., Steele, B.F., Droegemuelle W. and Silver, H.K. (1962). The battered child syndrome. Journal of the American Medical Association, 181, 17-24.

Kent, J., Weisberg, H. Lamar, B., Marx, T. (1975). Understanding the etiology of child abuse: a preliminary typology of cases. Unpublished Report.

Smith, S.M., Hanson, R. and Noble, S. (1974). Social aspects of the battered baby syndrome. British Journal of Psychiatry, 125, 568-582.

Spinetta, J.J. and Rigler, D. (1972). The child-abusing parent: a psychological review. Psychological Bulletin, 77, 296-304.

CHILDREN OF DRUG DISTURBED PARENTS

Helen Lardner Foster
Maridee Broadfoot

Family Crisis Center
San Anselmo, California

> For every child, understanding and the guarding
> of his personality as his most precious gift. (1)

Children of drug disturbed parents learn to control their personal attitudes and behavior, their relationships to parents, friends, and teachers in order to survive the negative home environment.

> ### Why did they have us at all if they weren't going to care about us?

> The intensity of the parent's obsessive involvement with one another and the presence of alcoholism had led to considerable rejection and virtual neglect of their children. (2)

These children suffer continuous, not just occasional, family and life disturbances. Crisis is a way of life.

> It has been recognized for some years that the children of alcoholic parents are subject to a high risk of developing alcoholism in their adult years. More recently, attention has focused on the alarmingly high incidence of emotional and behavioral disorders among this group (Chafetz et al 1971, Fine et al 1975). This is not hard to understand, since life in the home of an alcoholic parent can be

759

chaotic, confusing, and unpredictable, and
frequently involved parental neglect and
even physical abuse of the children. (3)

A veneer is applied by these children to cover responses to self
and surrounding.

As Bowen (4) has emphasized, family systems
theory provides a different framework for conceptualizing alcoholism. System theory assumes that all important people in the family
unit play a part in the way family members
function in relation to each other. From this
viewpoint alcoholism exists as a common
human dysfunction in the context of an imbalance in the functioning of the total system.
From a theoretical viewpoint, every important
family member plays a part in the dysfunction
of the dysfunctional member. (5)

Many studies specifically focused on the importance of
looking at the relationship between husband and wife. However,
there are few programs specifically for the children from these
devastated households, and little focus on what can be done to
prevent disruption in a child's development and identity process.

A review was made of 52 children (ages 8-18) from counselor
reports over a period of 18 months with at least one parent who
abused or was addicted to alcohol/drugs. Of the 52 children, 75%
had mothers in the program (Group A), 25% had no mother in the
program (Group B). None of the children had fathers in the program.
The alcohol abuse by mothers in Group A was 8%, other drug
abuse 5%. For mothers in Group B alcohol abuse was 67%, other
drug abuse 6%. The abuse of alcohol by fathers in A was 100%,
33% in Group B. Other drug abuse by fathers in A was 3%, 20%
in Group B.

For such children, a parent's alcoholic behavior may be direct, swift, and devastating
in its effects, or indirectly destructive
through the attitudes and communications
of the nondrinking parent, who is often tense,
angry, afraid, exhausted, and worried about
the abnormal family climate. (6)

In Group A, 65% of the mothers physically abused their children, 35% in Group B. Of the children in Group A, 49% abused others, 60% in Group B. Self abuse was 84% in Group A, 93% in Group B. Depression in Group A was 68%, 87% in Group B. Anxiety in Group A was 46%, 73% in Group B. Ratings of fair and poor were average for both groups in school academic performance. Obvious from written stories, poems, and play activity sessions were the children's poor sentence structure, spelling, and formation of letters. Of the total number of children, 10% dropped out of school. Seventy-five percent of the children had never received any treatment previously. In Group A, 33% of the mothers were on welfare, 20% in Group B.

Of the three areas--home, school, friends--the child felt more isolated at home than any of the other two categories in both groups. A recent study by Scientific Analysis Corporation of children of nonalcoholics and children of alcoholics from similar social/economic backgrounds indicates . . .

> . . . there is a statistically significant difference in the number of serious family problems perceived by children of alcoholics and children of nonalcoholics; the control group reported an average of approximately two family problems each, whereas the children of alcoholics reported an average of six problems per family, three times as many . . . we can now see that whatever else was wrong with these families, an alcoholic parent increased the degree of misery for the children. (7)

Parents are confused and unable to provide children with nurturing and guidance. Therefore, at an early age, children are forced to assume parental roles because of the parent's inadequacy. This premature responsibility leads to confusion for the child. Self esteem and role motivation are stifled and depression sets in. Consequently, the child sets up a broad based denial system. The child does not want to realize the addiction of his parent and the emotional disturbance of the non-addicted parent. This results in impediments in the general acquisition of information and effects his perception of overall reality. Finally, confusion and denial spawn negative peer relationships.

Clinebell (8) has listed four factors that may
produce emotional damage in children of alcoholics. First, the shift or reversal of the parent's roles causes confusion and complicates
the task of achieving a strong sense of sexual
identity. Second, an inconsistent, unpredictable relationship with the alcoholic parent is
emotionally depriving. Third, the nonalcoholic
parent is disturbed and therefore inadequate
in the parental role. And fourth, the family's
increased social isolation interferes with peer
relationships and with emotional support from
the extended family. (6)

Offered in the Rainbow Project, the youth component of the
Family Crisis Center, is treatment to impact and prevent further
damage to children of parents who abuse or are addicted to
alcohol/drugs. The average length of treatment for a child is 5
months, but treatment varied from 2 days to 17 months with a median age of 12 in Group A and 15 in Group B. The focus of treatment
was centered around an environment that was safe, supportive,
and provided guidance. The children began to experience success
on an emotional level.

Each of the younger children, ages 8-14, participated in a
creative play or project activity for 2 hours weekly. The use of
art therapy in the Rainbow Project is an integral part of the program. This therapy is used as a means of encouraging self realization and enhancing self esteem.

Creative arts therapy concerns the use of
the arts--music, writing, painting, sculpture,
dance--as a process which furthers the emotional and physical integration of the individual. Creative arts therapy may function
either as primary treatment modality or as an
integral part of an overall treatment program. (9)

The older children, ages 15-18, met in group sessions for 2
hours weekly. Individual counseling was provided once a month
for 1 hour to each child. Additional counseling sessions were
available to the child when requested. Drop-in and crisis counseling was accessible 24 hours a day. Appropriate contact with
parents, school staff, and involved social agencies was an ongoing provision to each child in the program.

The child experienced being accepted as an individual with adult and peer support, perhaps for the first time in his life. With this encouragement, the child began to develop self awareness and confront his fears. Positive changes became evident in 5 areas: (1) self esteem was generated; (2) the children were able to interact successfully with children and adults; (3) academic performance and achievement improved, depression and anxiety were reduced; (4) understanding of the addiction process and its effects in the child's total family was realized; (5) the child was guided to positive alternatives for handling fears, hostilities, and self conflicts in his every day life.

REFERENCES

1. White House Conference on Child Health and Protection, Washington, D.C. (1930).
2. R. Margaret Cork, The Forgotten Children, A Study of Children with Alcoholic Parents, Addiction Research Foundation of Ontario, Canada (1969).
3. Margaret Hindman, "Children of Alcoholic Parents," Alcohol Health and Research World, Winter (1975/76).
4. Murray Bowen, "A Family Systems Approach to Alcoholism," Addictions, Summer (1974).
5. A. J. Rice, "Unilateral Education of the Family in Crisis with Alcohol," Pre-doctoral Seminar on Alcohol and Drug Research, January (1976).
6. Sharon B. Sloboda, "The Children of Alcoholics: A Neglected Problem," Hospital & Community Psychiatry, September (1974).
7. "Family Problems, Social Adaptation and Sources of Help for Children of Alcoholic and Non-Alcoholic Parents," Scientific Analysis Corporation, February (1976).
8. H. J. Clinebell, "Pastoral Counseling of the Alcoholic and His Family," Alcoholism (1968).
9. Lone Mountain College Class Description Catalog, December (1975).

IMPACT OF THE ECONOMIC RECESSION ON EMPLOYMENT OF HEROIN ADDICTS IN METHADONE MAINTENANCE TREATMENT

Frances Rowe Gearing, M.D.
Dina A. D'Amico, B.A.
Freida Thompson, B.S.

Division of Epidemiology
Columbia University School of Public Health
Methadone Maintenance Evaluation Unit
New York, New York 10032

The Methadone Maintenance Treatment Program in New York City (originally referred to as The Beth Israel or Dole-Nyswander Program) celebrated its 10th anniversary in February 1975. It had many reasons to celebrate, because its "successes" have far outweighed its "failures" by any reasonable criteria. Marked changes in the patients' anti-social behavior as measured by involvement with the Criminal Justice System, as well as substantial increases in social productivity as measured by employment and schooling have been reported previously.

Since its onset one of the major goals of this Methadone Maintenance Treatment Program in the rehabilitation of the former heroin addicts has been to assist them in becoming employable, which either involved additional schooling for a high school equivalency certificate, or more often involved learning a skill which involved job training programs. Involving these patients in job training programs assumed that job openings would be available for them, following their training period. This was a valid assumption, on the whole, until the advent of the recession.

Among the men, in the first two years after admission to Methadone Maintenance Treatment the rate of increase in social productivity for each cohort was dramatic and steady. A leveling off of the rate after the second year occured in each cohort, but at a lower level for each successive admission cohort. However, the decrease in the rate of social productivity for the 1969 and 1970 cohorts in the 6th and 5th year respectively was an unexpected development as was the early leveling off of the rate in the 1971 and 1972 cohorts. This phenomenon is even more dramatically demonstrated among the women who demonstrate this "fall off" in each cohort, with only the 1964-1968 cohort achieving a level of 50% social productivity.

The above observations coupled with what appeared to be a marked increase in the number of patients reported to be collecting unemployment insurance led us to ask the following questions:

1. Is this pattern merely the result of the rapid expansion of the size of the program, or
2. Is this the result of the economic recession? Or Both?

In order to attempt to answer these questions, we did several things. First, we plotted the data with date of first admission on the horizontal axis and percentage employed or in school on the vertical axis. We did this for each cohort from 1965 through 1972 both for men and women. The results for the first four cohorts (1965-1968) are shown in Figure 1 where it can be noted the rate of increase in social productivity in the first year after admission is dramatically high and similar for the four cohorts. This rate continues to increase through 1969 when a leveling off or a slight fall off occurs in 1970 through 1972. For the first two cohorts this trend reverses in 1973 and 1974 but the curve remains flat from 1972 on for those patients admitted in 1967 and 1968.

Among the women in the lower part of Figure 1 admissions in 1965 and 1966 were combined since there were fewer than 10 women in the 1965 cohort. The pattern is much the same but more pronounced, and the leveling off at a lower rate. The data for the later cohorts shows the same "leveling off" phenomenon at a lower rate of social productivity for both the men and the women.

To further elaborate on the question of employment and the current economic situation, patients who were either 1) Employed full-time or 2) In a job training program in 1972 were followed through 1973 and 1974 in order to determine changes in their employment status. This sample included 1,715 persons of which 91% were men and 9% women, and included patients from each admission cohort.

Figure 2 illustrates the changes in employment status in our sample. The rate of unemployment increased from 1973 to 1974. This proportion in 1973 was 12% and rose to 21% in 1974. Although the sample of women was small the rate of unemployment among the women who were employed in 1972 is greater than among the men. By 1974, 21% of the men had lost their jobs as compared with 28% of the women. Since the overall rate of social productivity as mentioned previously is substantially lower for the women than for men, the impact of the higher unemployment rates becomes even greater. Women in Methadone Maintenance Treatment appear to be less likely to become employed, and likewise they are less likely to be able to maintain their employed status.

Since our sample included patients from the Beth Israel, Harlem and the Bronx programs, we were able to obtain some indication of the impact of the recession on each ethnic group. As shown further in Figure 2, the impact of unemployment was less among the

the White patients than among the Black or Hispanic. In 1974 over
21% of the previously employed Hispanics were unemployed as compared with 23% of the Blacks and 15% of the White patients. Updating the data to 1975 increases the total unemployed to 28%; the
men to 27%, the women to 37%; the Whites to 22%, Blacks to 34% and
Hispanic to 30%.

It is evident that in this period of recession, the Black and
Hispanic population have been more severely affected than the
White. These findings are not surprising, and only tend to highlight the continued problems in a shrinking economy of obtaining
and maintaining equal opportunity for employment among minority
groups.

Table I shows the change in employment status in our sample
for each admission cohort. The earlier admission cohorts seem to
have suffered the least unemployment. In particular the 1965 admission cohort demonstrated a 3% loss of employment between 1972
and 1973 but rose to 11% in 1975. In contrast the later admission
cohorts show an increase of approximately 14% in unemployment from
1972 to 1973 and an additional 14% in reduction in employment by
1975. In total, of the 1740 patients who were employed full-time
or in school as of the end of 1972, 484 (28%) were unemployed at
the end of 1975.

These findings are undoubtedly the result of at least two factors; the number of years in treatment and the highly selected nature of the patients in the early cohorts. Not only were the early
patients given unusual and individualized personal treatment, but
they also have the added factor of having the "cushion" of having
been steadily employed for several years prior to 1972. Whereas
the patients from the later years had less opportunity to establish
themselves in their jobs, and therefore have suffered under the
"last hired, first fired" rule.

Table II shows the difference in employment trends between men
and women. For the men, full-time employment goes from 94% in 1972
to 61% in 1975, whereas for the women the range is 90% to 47%, and
unemployment rises to 27% for the men and 36% for the women. The
proportion of patients remaining in school or job training is fairly constant; (6-5%) for the men, (10-7%) for the women. The 484
people (414 men and 70 women) who were self-supporting in 1972 are
currently either collecting unemployment insurance or are back on
welfare.

A sample of 100 (85 men and 15 women) of these unemployed patients were given a one page self-administered anonymous questionnaire with an enclosed postage-paid return envelope where we asked
specifically (1) whether their employer did or did not know that
they were taking methadone, and (2) why they thought they had been
let go, and (3) did they attribute their loss of job to the fact
that they were taking methadone. The results were interesting and

somewhat surprising. Among the 62 men and 11 women (73%) who responded, approximately one-half thought that the employer knew that
they were taking methadone, but only the women felt that this fact
contributed to their job loss. The men, on the whole, felt that
their being laid off was the result of general cutbacks and the recession. The majority of the respondents mentioned both their
desire to get another job and the difficulties in finding work.

In Conclusion:

"The best laid plans of mice and men" and Methadone Maintenance Treatment Programs can go down the drain in the face of an
economic recession, if one of the major goals of the program is
gainful, meaningful employment.

In the face of a shrinking economy, the impact has been felt
unequally among the three ethnic groups, and for that large "minority" group known as women, the impact is even greater. However it
has produced an unemployment rate among previously self-supporting
patients in Methadone Maintenance Treatment for heroin addiction
far in excess of the reported figures for any other group in the
New York City population of the same age and ethnic composition.

Therefore, our answer to the original question we posed is,
"the economic recession has had a large and serious impact on the
rehabilitation of patients in Methadone Maintenance Treatment where
one of the major goals has been to become employed and remain employed, and this impact has been felt disproportionately by the
Blacks, the Hispanics and the women."

Supported under Grant No. DA 5PG004 from Special Action Office for
Drug Abuse Prevention; Grant No. 8H81 DA 01777-01 and Contract No.
271-76-1107 from the National Institute on Drug Abuse.

Table I

Percentage of Methadone Maintenance Patients Considered Socially
Productive as of December 31, 1972 Who Have Become Unemployed
By Year of First Admission

Date of Admission	Number Employed December 31, 1972	Percent Unemployed December 31, 1973	N	December 31, 1975	N
1965	37	3.0%	01	11.0%	04
1966	91	12.0	11	21.0	19
1967	153	14.0	21	21.5	33
1968	147	22.0	32	20.0	30
1969	314	9.0	29	30.0	94
1970	303	14.0	42	33.0	99
1971	526	14.0	76	32.0	167
1972	169	15.0	26	22.0	38
Total	1,740	14.0%	238	28.0%	484

Table II

Changes in Percentage of Patients in Methadone Maintenance
Treatment by Employment Status and Job Training for Men
And Women From 1972-1975

	Employed Full-Time	Employed Part-Time	In School or Job Training	Unemployed
MEN				
1972	94.0%	--	6.0%	--
1973	63.0	19.0%	6.0	12.0%
1974	62.0	15.0	5.0	18.0
1975	61.0	7.0	5.0	27.0
N=1,546				
WOMEN				
1972	90.0%	--	10.0%	--
1973	68.0	13.0%	8.0	11.0%
1974	48.0	17.0	8.0	27.0
1975	47.0	10.0	7.0	36.0
N= 194				

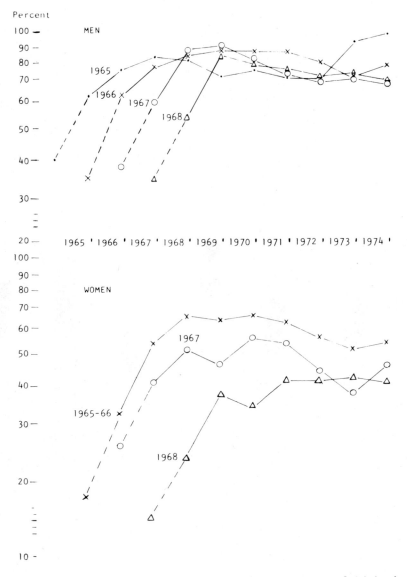

Fig. 1   Rate of Change in Social Productivity by Year of Admission
          for Patients Admitted to Methadone Maintenance Treatment
          Between 1965 and 1968

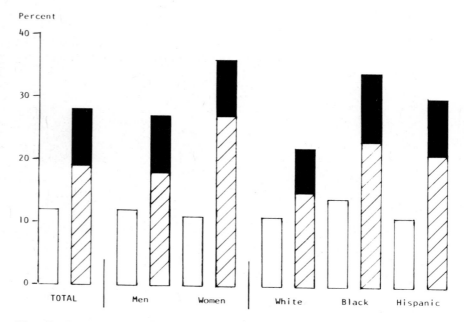

Fig. 2   Percentage of Men and Women in Methadone Maintenance Treatment Employed in 1972 Who Became Unemployed from 1973-1975

RECEPTIVITY OF LARGE CORPORATIONS TO THE HIRING OF EX-ADDICTS

Louis Lieberman

Project Director
Graduate School and University Center
City University of New York

One of the difficulties we experienced in the past, in helping addicts who were in treatment, was a general reluctance of employers to hire known ex-addicts. Although concealment of one's addiction history was always a possibility, this presented problems, not only in terms of the ex-addict's self-image and fears of discovery, but also in making contacts with prospective employers. Fortunately, the last decade has seen considerable progress in increasing the willingness of employers, particularly the larger corporations, to hire the drug-free ex-addict or those in methadone maintenance programs.

This paper reports on some aspects of the willingness of large corporations to hire ex-addicts. It is part of a larger study of drug abuse within industries located in New York City, funded under a grant from the National Institute of Drug Abuse. The three major components of this study consist of interviews with over 500 addicts who worked full time while addicted to heroin; questionnaires filled out by well over 1,000 union apprentices; and, finally, presented here, interviews with corporation executives. All told, we interviewed executives in 113 corporations. Through using various directories we tried to reach the largest firms in each industry. We asked questions only about the on-site work force about which our executive informant was most knowledgeable. This total on-site work force covered in our sample amounted to almost 280,000 employees. The industries were selected so as to reflect a wide range of blue and white collar skills. They were: Advertising Firms, Department Stores, Insurance Companies, Banks, The Mass Media, Brokerage Houses, Manufacturing, Construction, Hospitals, Utilities, Airlines, Trucking, Garment, and Maritime.

During initial contacts with the firms by mail and phone, we requested that an interview be arranged with the management person most knowledgeable about the existence of drug use and drug problems at the company. Consequently, we were referred in almost half the firms, 52 (46%), to the personnel manager, while in 35 firms (31%) a president or other high level executive was seen. In the remaining 26 corporations, we were told to speak to a medical person (physician or nurse). In a number of interviews with the executive or personnel manager, a physician was present as a resource person.

The two broadest aspects of willingness to hire the ex-addict are first --- whether the firm has already done so, and second --- if they have not, would they be willing to hire if an ex-addict was referred to them.

Almost half, 51 (45%), of the firms did employ ex-addicts; an additional forty (35%) said that they would or at least might if the right person came along, while only 15 (13%) stated they would not and an additional 7 would not answer this question.

The industries most likely to employ ex-addicts (i.e. more than three-fourths of the largest firms in that industry employ ex-addicts) were hospitals, banks and the utilities. Those industries least likely to employ (one-third of the firms or less) were insurance, construction, mass media, securities, airlines, trucking, garment and maritime. Although the actual number of companies in each industry was comparatively small, since we were interviewing the largest firms, our impressions gleaned from management were that the problems and practices around drug use of the other firms in their own industry were quite similar.

What are some of the characteristics of firms which now employ the ex-addict? Most strikingly, these tend to be the larger companies. The larger the corporation, the more likely they are to now employ ex-addicts. Twenty-one of the twenty-three firms (91%) with over 5000 workers each in the New York City office or factory employ ex-addicts, compared to 5 of the 27 firms with work forces of up to 500 (19%), 7 of 29 (24%) with a firm size of 500 to 1499, and 18 of 31 (58%) for those in the 1500 - 4999 range.

The most important dynamic aspect of firm size in this regard, we believe to be the presence of the medical officer. The relationship between company size and the presence of a physician was evident from our data: only 22% (13) of the smaller firms (under 1500 workers) had a physician available full or part-time, while 85% (46) of the firms with 1500 or more employees did have them.

When we compare the firms which have a physician on duty with those that do not, we learn that almost three-quarters of those that do have physicians (74%) now employ ex-addicts, while only 20% of those without medical officers do. Even where there is only a

part-time physician present there is greater likelihood of
employment of ex-addicts than where no physician is present.

In our discussions with the medical officers, they frequently
pointed out to us either by way of self praise when successful or
complaint when they failed, that they were instrumental in changing
the attitudes of executive management in the direction of an
increased willingness to hire the drug free or methadone stabilized
ex-addict. The positive influence of the medical officer was often
supported by anecdotal material from the president and vice-
presidents when they were interviewed. The medical directors also
influenced the hiring policy of the ex-addict by emphasis on the
pre-employment physical for all new prospective employees, as well
as company physicals when an employee is ill. As one corporate
medical director told us in summary, requiring a pre-employment
physical, which for his company included urinalysis for the
presence of drugs, indicated to existing, as well as new employees,
the company concern about drug abuse as well as the health of its
workers. The ex-addict can, therefore, be tested to see if he is
drug free, at the time of employment or, for the methadone patient,
the existence of other drugs. This company physician also
indicated a greater feeling of security by management about hiring
ex-addicts because the medical staff could, upon suspicion, require
a physical to determine if a worker were ill or had returned to
drug abuse. As our data indicated, 58% (40) of the firms that
required physicals employ ex-addicts compared to 27% (11) of the
firms which did not require them.

Another aspect of firm characteristics which appears in our
data may be related to discriminatory practices toward a number of
groups within the labor force. It seems that as management may be
reluctant to employ blacks, Hispanics and women, it also appears
reluctant to hire ex-addicts. For example, 17% of the firms with a
small percentage (10% or less) of blacks and Hispanics in the
company employ ex-addicts compared to 69% of the firms with over
half their work force from these minority groups.
Similarly, a quarter of the firms with 10% or less women in the
work force employ ex-addicts while 63% of the companies with over
half of their workers female do.

While our data is only suggestive rather than conclusive, it
appears that reluctance to hire the ex-addict may form part of a
larger pattern of discrimination in which the addict is
stereotypically seen as black or Hispanic. Certainly, the links
between racist and sexist attitudes should not surprise us. (While
there is no term for drug substance prejudice, the presence of such
prejudice was clearly visible to us in the different attitudes and
behaviors of corporate management toward present and past heroin
abusers compared to alcohol abusers.) Perhaps a more encompassing
pattern of discrimination may be involved which does not exclude
the addict because of racial stereotypes but informal company

policy which seeks to restrict workers most closely to new employees who would be acceptable to current employees, or to a company _image_ of the kind of work force it has particularly where new business is based upon seeking contracts for its services.

Although the focus and scope of this study could not permit a more intensive analysis of this issue, counselors trying to place ex-addicts and agencies attempting to open more doorways in industry to the ex-addict should be alerted to the possibility that a key barrier may be company policy to hold down the numbers of minority group and female workers as part of a general discriminatory hiring practice of the firm, and that pressures to fail may be built in when such firms agree to hire a token ex-addict.

A different aspect of prejudice or perhaps a lack of knowledge may be involved, due to management's unwillingness or inability to distinguish between current and ex-addicts. Only a quarter of the firms who reported that they never had a problem with heroin use by their employees, hire ex-addicts, while more than three-quarters of the firms with current heroin problems nevertheless do. Since it is in the larger firms where we find both current heroin use as well as a greater willingness to employ the ex-addict, we believe that, again, it may be due to the influence of the medical directors in larger firms and their more accurate perception of, e.g., methadone stabilization. We certainly _did not_ get any indication of any contagion process suggested by anyone that ex-addicts were turning on new ones.

The same relationship of drug problems and having employed ex-addicts also holds true for illegal pill use, marijuana use and over use of prescription drugs. (See TABLES I - IV.)

We also wanted to know if having fired workers for drug abuse on the job would severely prejudice management from employing ex-addicts. This did not appear to be the case. Two-thirds of the firms which have fired workers for drug abuse in the past employ ex-addicts now.

In general, management seems satisfied with the job performance of the ex-addict. For the forty-four firms where management could give an impression of their experiences with the ex-addict as worker, two-thirds (29) of the firms said that they were as good, if not better than, the other workers. Similarly, management was impressed with their turnover rate: Again, two-thirds (29) said it was the same or lower than comparable non-addict workers.

A final point: Contacting firms and talking with top level management, particularly medical directors, and making them more aware of the suitability of the ex-addict and MMTP person for employment can be a very fruitful endeavor. A case in point: We

asked our management informants if they ever heard of P.A.C.T.
(now P.A.C.T./NADAP), a private organization geared toward opening
up industry for jobs for ex-addicts as well as helping
rehabilitation agencies to prepare the addict for employment. Of
the 46 firms who had heard of P.A.C.T., 74% (34) employ ex-addicts.
Where P.A.C.T. has talked to management (in 28 firms), 86% (24)
employ ex-addicts and 15 of these 24 firms have employed the
P.A.C.T. referrals. Organizations such as P.A.C.T. appear to have
a vital role in the employment of the ex-addict since, even for
those which have employed ex-addicts, the continuance of this
practice is a high level policy matter and subject to change.
Certainly, as the labor market remains tight, there is always the
tendency to avoid hiring groups which some executives may consider
to be popularly unsuitable for employment. Efforts must be kept up
so that the drug-free and MMTP ex-addict in particular and all
drug abusers in general are not forced back in to the junkie-dope
fiend stereotype, thereby making them expendable in the labor
market during this crunch.

TABLE I — Heroin Use on Job

Employs Ex-Addicts	Current	Past Only	Neither, D.K.
Yes	17 (77%)	22 (56%)	12 (24%)
N =	22	39	49

TABLE II — Illegal Amphetamines and Barbiturates Used on Job

Employs Ex-Addicts	Current	Past Only	Neither, D.K.
Yes	16 (84%)	13 (54%)	22 (33%)
N =	19	24	67

TABLE III — Marijuana Use on the Job

Employs Ex-Addicts	Current	Past Only	Neither, D.K.
Yes	28 (70%)	10 (36%)	13 (31%)
N =	40	28	42

TABLE IV — Overuse of Prescription Drugs on Job

Employs Ex-Addicts	Current	Past Only	Neither, D.K.
Yes	25 (66%)	11 (61%)	15 (28%)
N =	38	11	54

CORPORATE EMPLOYMENT AND THE METHADONE PATIENT

Robert B. Yankowitz, M.A., and Joan Randell, M.A.

Department of Vocational Rehabilitation
Methadone Maintenance Treatment Program
Beth Israel Medical Center, New York City

To date, the ability of people in methadone maintenance treatment to perform adequately as employees has not been documented. The purpose of this research was to study the employment experience and potential of methadone maintained office workers and skilled laborers by examining their work adjustment. Work adjustment is conceptualized as the combination of job satisfaction and job satisfactoriness.(1) We hypothesized that:

1. The attendance rate, punctuality, job performance, and job satisfaction of employees in methadone maintenance treatment are the same as those of similarly employed personnel not in methadone maintenance treatment.

2. The job performance and job satisfaction of office workers in methadone maintenance treatment is the same as those of skilled laborers in methadone maintenance treatment.

I THE PROJECT

Beth Israel Medical Center's (BIMC) vocational rehabilitation counselors evaluated patients to determine their present job readiness. Objective criteria were met if the patient 1) had been in MMTP for at least one year, 2) had shown no evidence of illicit drug use for at least nine months determined by urinalysis or clinical observation by program staff, and 3) had been recently employed for at least nine months, or actively engaged in the vocational rehabilitation process. Subjective evaluation of job readiness and suitability was based on the individual's appearance and demeanor, skill and education level, and willingness to work in the corporate environment. Thirty individuals were referred to the personnel departments of corporations with headquarters in New York City. Twenty-six of them were hired.

II SAMPLE

The sample consisted of twenty-three of the twenty-six patients hired who were employed at the time of the study. (Three employees had voluntarily resigned from their jobs prior to the study. Two accepted other employment. The status of the third remains unknown because he terminated treatment, and contact ended.) This group included twenty-one males and two females, of whom thirteen were Caucasian, five were Spanish surnamed, and five were black. The subjects fell into two occupational groups: eleven skilled laborers (seven general utility mechanics and four machine attendants) and twelve office workers (nine office clerks, a claims analyst, a technical assistant, and an expediter). This sample appears typical when compared to the entire BIMC-MMTP patient population (N=6575) on basic demongraphic, drug abuse, and criminal history characteristics. Information on vocational backgrounds for the entire MMTP population was unavailable.

III MEASUREMENT AND ANALYSIS

A questionnaire was developed to rate subjects' job performance, attendance, and punctuality. It was completed either by the personnel department staff, based on their records, or by the subjects' immediate supervisor. The respondents categorized the subject's attendance and punctuality as either above average, average, or below average compared with similarly employed individuals not in methadone maintenance treatment. They also described the subject's job performance in a narrative statement, and compared it to the performance of similarly employed individuals not in methadone maintenance treatment. To quantify these descriptions of job performance, three BIMC Personnel Department interviewers independently rated each narrative statement. They used a nine point scale which ranged from unacceptable (1), through average (5), to exceptional (9). The mean of the ratings for each narrative description was used as the job performance measure for each subject. The reliability of the average ratings was .90, calculated by intraclass correlation. (2)

Each subject completed the Minnesota Satisfaction Questionnaire (MSQ), which was developed to measure job satisfaction. (3) The general satisfaction sub-scale score was used as the measure of overall job satisfaction. The internal consistency reliability (coefficient alpha) of this sub-scale for the sample population was .94.

The data were analyzed by means of chi-square goodness-of-fit tests (two-tailed) and t-tests (two-tailed). In those comparisons where sample sizes and variances were different, degrees of freedom were corrected and variances were not pooled.

IV RESULTS

The subjects' attendance and punctuality were better than those for similarly employed personnel not in methadone maintenance treatment. The mean job performance score of the subjects was not significantly different from the hypothetical average on the job performance rating scale. The job performance score of the methadone maintained office workers was not significantly different from the job performance score of the methadone maintained skilled laborers.

Comparison of the subjects' MSQ scores with normative data (3) showed that the methadone maintained employees were dissatisfied with their employment. Further analysis of the data according to occupational categories shows a difference in the job satisfaction level of the methadone maintained skilled laborers and office workers. Although the difference is not statistically significant, the percentile ranks suggest that the office workers were dissatisfied with their jobs, while the skilled laborers were satisfied.

V DISCUSSION

Our results indicate that, relative to their non-methadone maintained co-workers, the methadone maintained employees had comparable job performance and superior punctuality and attendance. Corporate employers should evaluate methadone maintained applicants according to the same criteria applied to others: the ability to do the job. In addition, methadone maintnenance treatment programs should develop job readiness criteria for screening their patients prior to formally referring them to corporate personnel departments. This would prevent treatment staff from mistakenly using job placement as a panacea for the former addict's immediate problems. When a methadone maintenance patient is referred prematurely for employment, a negative experience usually results for both the patient and the employers. The treatment program's credibility inevitably suffers. Therefore treatment efforts should focus on developing job readiness through pre-vocational, and more work experiences, before making formal referral to corporate personnel departments.

Appraisal of job satisfaction is important because it enables clients to identify and deal with sources of dissatisfaction. Expression of job dissatisfaction does not indicate poor job performance, as it is commonly assumed. The different job satisfaction levels of the methadone maintained office workers and skilled laborers may be due to differences in the nature of their work, and the physical and social environments of the two occupational groups. The milieu of the typical corporate office is more structured than the work setting of the skilled laborer; the ambiance is more formal, stricter dress and behavior codes prevail, and freedom of movement is more limited. Jobs in skilled labor may be more familiar, less threatening, and, thus, more satisfying to former drug abusers whose typical previous subculture is the antithesis of the structured office setting. Although both methadone maintained skilled laborers and office workers perform adequately in corporate jobs, the latter, due to the likelihood of their job dissatisfaction, may require counseling to facilitate their optimal work adjustment. In addition, it would be fruitful for MMTP's to concentrate their job development activities on blue collar, skilled, or technical jobs which may be more satisfying for their patients.

Unfortunately, counseling frequently terminates once a methadone maintained employee is established in a job and performing well. However, the employee may be dissatisfied with the job, and this may preclude optimal work adjustment. The assessment of job satisfaction used in conjunction with counseling can help methadone maintained corporate employees improve their work adjustment. The counselor can help the employee analyze and explore sources of job dissatisfaction, develop strategies for correcting difficulties, and perhaps encourage the employee to seek additional or alternative sources of reward outside the work setting. Employees may be confused about the source of their negative feelings, and incorrectly label them as job dissatisfaction. Exploration in counseling may reveal that the actual problem is indirectly related to the job. For example, the employee may be experiencing stress in family or social relationships due to new routines and responsibilities; long-held self-images may be challenged and subsequently require adjustment; accustomed dress and speech patterns may begin to seem unacceptable or even deviant; or, the employee may feel uncertain about whether to reveal past history or current status in methadone maintenance treatment. Thus, to enhance rehabilitation, counseling after job placement is often desirable.

To our knowledge, this study is the first attempt to empirically evaluate the work adjustment of methadone maintained corporate employees. Despite the small sample size and the crudeness of the measurement instruments, the results support the compatability of methadone maintenance and corporate employment. In light of the importance of job performance and job satisfaction to the corporate employer, the drug treatment program, and the methadone maintained employee, further research in this area is warrented. To enable adequate research, cooperation in follow-up should be secured from employers prior to placement.

N.B.: This paper is a condensed version of the original prepared for the conference. Readers who are interested in more specification, including a review of relevant literature, more detailed data analysis and results, and three tables, should contact the authors.

VI REFERENCES

1. Dawis, Rene' V.; Lofquist, Lloyd H.; and Weiss, David J., A
    theory of work adjustment (a revision). Minnesota
    Studies in Vocational Rehabilitation, April, 1968.
    XXIII, (Bulletin 47).

2. Ebel, Robert L., Estimation of reliability of ratings.
    Psychometrika, 1951, 16, 407-424.

3. Weiss, David J.; Dawis, Rene' V.; England, George W.; &
    Lofquist, Lloyd H.; Manual of the Minnesota
    satisfaction questionnaire, Minnesota Studies in
    Vocational Rehabilitation. October, 1967. XXII
    (Bulletin 45).

A STUDY OF THE CHARACTERISTICS AND CONDITIONS
ASSOCIATED WITH THE SUCCESSFUL JOB PLACEMENT
OF RECOVERED DRUG ABUSERS

Harold Alksne
Director of Research and Program Planning PACT/NADAP
And Assistant Professor C.W. Post College
New York, New York 10017

Ronn Robinson
Research Associate
PACT/NADAP
New York, New York   10017

INTRODUCTORY STATEMENT

   Addicts appear to go through a process which finally enters
them into the life cycle of addiction. The treatment and rehabilitation of drug abusers must similarly involve a process which
helps the addicts move from the central life interests which are
focused around drug addiction. It is generally recognized that
treatment and rehabilitation must support the addict's movement
away from the addiction system. The final phase or movement from
the addiction to abstinence systems involves a reentry phase to
community living and its economic life. Work defines our social
role in this culture and similarly, it must help redefine the social role of those moving away from the addiction system.

   This study examines the experiences of 1,000 applicants to a
New York organization, PACT/NADAP, which has had as a major concern
the opening up of industries for the employment of recovered drug
abusers and the placement of such clients in jobs. The material
which follows will concentrate on examining the characteristics of
individuals who are placed on jobs and those who are not, in an
effort to test the vulnerabilities of the system which is designed
to assist the addict. In addition, it will present preliminary
data concerning the ultimate success of a small sample of the
placees on the job.

AGE AND EMPLOYABILITY

   One may assume that as individuals grow older they may have
more potential in terms of the employment market as compared with
the younger job applicant. The assumption may be based on the

781

belief that, at least until the early thirties, the accumulated experience should be viewed as an advantage in the placement of an individual. Our data on addicts referred to PACT as being job ready after treatment indicates that this assumption does not hold.

Of those who are 18 years old, 48%, or almost half, are placed in jobs after they are referred to PACT. As our clients grow older, we find that it becomes increasingly difficult to place them in the jobs. Only 14% of those who are over 40 are placed by PACT/ NADAP. The older addict may be less attractive to business and industry because they may view them as having less of a potential Some industries may believe that the older addicts are not worth training and supporting in an entry-level job. In addition, these clients have a much longer period to develop a very "spotty" kind of employment record.

SEXUAL IDENTIFICATION, RACE AND EMPLOYABILITY

The most of PACT's clients are male, with three out of ten so classified. This reflects the male-female ratio in the general population of addicted individuals. The placement experience of men and women is similar with a slight advantage shown for females. We find that more women are placed in manufacturing situations by a slight margin, and more men are placed in entry level banking jobs. When it comes to sales, there is an almost identical pattern for men and women.

PACT serves a predominantly minority population, with 28% being white, 51% black, and 21% Spanish. As one would expect, blacks tend to be more difficult to place, when compared to whites and Spanish-speaking clients. However, once the recovered addicts are placed on jobs, industries rate them equally despite their racial characteristics. Hispanics are more likely to find jobs in manufacturing as compared to the other two racial groups, and whites are more likely to be involved in sales activities, as compared to Hispanics and blacks.

Interestingly, one of the most successful areas for placing addicts has been in banking. About a quarter of our addicts find jobs in this area. We discover that the Spanish-speaking and white clients are most likely to be employed by banks as compared to blacks. It should be pointed that these are trend figures and do not represent statistically significant differences.

EDUCATION AND JOB PLACEMENT

Fourteen percent of those with an education of grade school or less were placed, as compared with 30% of those with a college education and more. Education was also associated with the kinds of placements that our clients received. The poorly educated recovered addict ended up in manufacturing. Those with a completed high school education were somewhat more likely to move into banking.

TREATMENT EXPERIENCE AND SUCCESS ON THE JOB

These materials concerning length of time in treatment prove interesting as possible predictors of job readiness. Generally, the less time in treatment, the less likelihood of being placed in a job through PACT. This follows until the eighteenth month of treatment, after which longer periods of time in treatment are predictive of poorer experience in the employment market. It appears that the cutting point for success is at the eighteenth month of treatment. As one is retained in treatment for periods over eighteen months, it is less likely that the individual will be placed.

TYPE OF TREATMENT AND PLACEMENT EXPERIENCE

When we examine treatment modality, we discover that patients who come to us from methadone maintenance treatment programs are the most difficult to place. We were unable to place 81% of this group of clients as compared with 67% of those who came from drug-free residential centers. Our experience with industries is that many of them still have negative attitudes toward methadone maintenance treatment programs, feeling that it remains an addiction, and therefore, the client is not fully recovered from his problem. One of the central concerns we have is bringing about changes in such attitudes to achieve greater acceptability of the methadone passing industry we deal with.

PRIMARY DRUGS USED

It appears that the kind of pre-treatment drug orientation, as expressed in the kinds of drugs used, is predictive of later employability. Those rehabilitated addicts who demonstrated an addiction history that was focused primarily on heroin were the least likely to be placed; those with a polydrug abuse focus followed with a better chance; and, the peripheral heroin user who had been involved less intensely with heroin demonstrated the best possibilities. We may note that the primary drugs abused are not predictive of subsequent involvement in manufacturing. It is predictive of later employment in banking, where the non-heroin oriented individual has four times the chance of being employed than the heroin-oriented individual. It appears that this variable as well as others indicate that the past clearly follows these clients.

WELFARE STATUS AT THE TIME OF INITIAL INTERVIEW AND EMPLOYABILITY

Clients were asked whether they were receiving welfare at the time of the interview, as an indicator of dependence on outside sources. It appears that those clients who had been receiving welfare were more likely to be unemployable than those who were not receiving welfare.

WORK-SCHOOL STATUS

The work-school status of the client at the time of their interview with us was also reviewed for its predictive value. It appears that those clients who were employed or in a school at the time they came to PACT were easier to place than those who showed no employment or school at the time they applied for work through PACT/NADAP. This reinforces the notion that those who are successful in work are likely to continue with the equity they already had in the system.

PREVIOUS INCOME FROM EMPLOYMENT AND EMPLOYABILITY

Clients were asked in their initial interview what was their highest weekly income from a legitimate work experience. Seventeen percent of our population never earned in excess of $99.00; 10% indicated that they had earned over $200.00 a week at some time prior to coming to PACT. There is a clear and statistically significant relationship between whether a person is placed through PACT and their previous success in work as measured by income. The more they made, the easier they were to place.

Those with past low incomes seem to be more amenable to placement in banks than those with past high incomes. Although banks do have a high status in the community, this does not accrue to the entry level pay offered workers. Both sales and manufacturing follow a similar pattern. However, those with earlier higher incomes tended to be more likely to be placed in such jobs as communications, insurance, special business services, and a variety of areas in which the majority of our clients stand little chance.

PACT'S RATING OF CLIENT AND SUBSEQUENT EMPLOYABILITY

Pact workers are asked to rate clients as to their potential on the job. The workers indicate whether they feel the client is excellent, above average, average, or below average. Our data indicates that there is an expected and direct correlation between the excellence of the rating and the probability of being placed. One can view this as an indication of the skill of the worker in predicting and analyzing potential of the client and predicting the outcome of subsequent activity. Or we might explore the possibility that a self-fulfilling prophecy may be operating in which the worker's impression of the client leads to action by him which justifies his original prediction of the client's potential.

REFERRAL SOURCE OF CLIENT AND LATER SUCCESS

PACT receives its clients from a variety of sources. We discovered differences in the success rates of clients coming to us from the various agencies. It seems to us that the quality of screening that agency members do prior to sending the client to

PACT/NADAP makes a difference to PACT's ability to place such clients.

EMPLOYER'S JOB RATING AND SPECIAL CHARACTERISTICS OF OUR REFERRAL POPULATION

The material we present now represents highly provisional data on our population. What follows represents a preliminary follow-up of early PACT cases.

In the course of a follow-up we asked the employer who hired the client to rate the client's performance in relation to other workers in his job category. The employers rated these recovered addicts as follows:

Excellent	29%
Above Average	36%
Average	23%
Below Average	7%
Unsatisfactory	5%

It seems to us impressive that fully 2/3 of the clients referred by PACT to work were rated excellent or above average by their employers. Although these data are preliminary, they do compare favorably with the information generated by the Citibank in connection with addicts employed by them. Citibank reports that the recovered addicts employed by them at entry-level jobs perform more efficiently and earn more promotions than a random population of non-addict employees also at entry-level positions.

RACE, EDUCATION, AND LENGTH OF TIME IN TREATMENT, TREATMENT MODALITY AND EMPLOYMENT RATING

The employer's rating of clients were examined in terms of employee's age. It should be noted that despite the previous findings that older addicts are less employable, the ratings of the older addicts tend to be superior after they are employed. We can only speculate that this suggests that prejudice against the older employee is vacated by the subsequent demonstration of competence on the job.

Other variables were examined in connection with employer ratings. There is a tendency for more whites to be rated as excellent, and more blacks to be rated as above average. When we combine the two ratings of excellent and above average, these positive evaluations seemed to range between 54% for Spanish-speaking, 65% for blacks, and 72% for whites.

Education was also examined, and here we found that there was a more positive response to the better educated.

785

Employer evaluations were examined for the effect of length of treatment periods on the part of the client. Longer treatment, as reflected in months in treatment, appears to be associated with better ratings in work. Twenty-three percent of the clients who were in treatment for less than two years were rated excellent in their job performances compared with 35% of those who were in treatment for more than two years. We might recall that those clients in treatment for extended periods of time did not do as well as those in lesser periods of time with regard to getting a job. However, when the client is given an opportunity to perform, this factor does not apply.

The data were further examined as to treatment modality, the two largest represented being methadone maintenance treatment and drug-free residential, or therapeutic communities. The findings show that the ratings are very close as regards excellence on the job. There is a margin of about five percent of the methadone patients who were rated as excellent, as compared to 33% of those coming from therapeutic communities.

SUMMARY COMMENTS

We have observed that a number of factors seem to affect whether a recovered addict is employable. Young people, women, whites, the better educated, those retained in treatment a specific period of time, those with less of a criminal record, those with more education and less welfare involvement, are likely to find jobs more easily than those not sharing these characteristics.

We discover that for those who do get jobs the presence of the previously noted factors is reduced as predictors of success or failure.

At least one program implication can be drawn from this analysis. It seems that a number of socio-cultural definitions of the addict's background affects his employability.

This analysis illustrates that the factors determining the employability of a client, and the factors determining the performance of a client are not always parallel. Prejudice may prevail in the hiring of recovered addicts and performance in their subsequent ratings. The challenge defined by this study is to encourage employers to become more accepting of the recovered addict as a worker, and to minimize employer bias against client characteristics that often have no effect on job performance.

THE WORKING ADDICT

David Caplovitz

Professor of Sociology
Graduate School and University Center
City University of New York

The common image of the addict is that of someone who has dropped out of normal society, who moves within a highly deviant street culture of crime and drugs. It is widely assumed that the heroin addict is too unstable to hold a full-time job. But in the past decade, a number of firms have discovered that just as they are not immune to alcoholism, so they are not free of drug problems. In industry after industry, firms have found that some of their employees were using and abusing drugs. To shed light on this overlap, I have carried out a survey of addicts who held full-time jobs for an extensive period while they were addicted. Under a grant from the National Institute for Drug Abuse, we were able to interview some 555 addicts now enrolled in treatment programs in New York City who held full-time jobs for at least three months while they were addicted. Today I wish to share with you some of the findings of our study.

I. THE SOCIAL CHARACTERISTICS OF WORKING ADDICTS

To study working addicts is to study a group that is doubly deviant, for most addicts do not work full-time and, of course, most full-time workers are not addicts. It is important to keep in mind that our sample is not representative of all working addicts, for we were limited only to those addicts we could find in treatment programs who once worked full-time while addicted. A very important group about which virtually nothing is known is omitted from our research, addicts who work full-time but are not in treatment programs. These secret addicts surely must exist, for almost all of the people we interviewed were once such secret addicts, that is, they worked for months or years while addicted without participating in any treatment program. There are, then, four groups of people that it would be desirable to compare, but unfortunately, I have information on only three of these groups. These are 1) the addict population in treatment, most of whom did not work full-time for any length of time, 2) addicts in treatment who did work full-time, the people I have sampled, 3) working addicts not in treatment (the missing group), and 4) the non-addict population.

One set of important findings emerging from our study is that which shows that working addicts have social characteristics more like the non-addict population than do addicts in general. In short, having had a normal social role of a full-time occupation, working addicts were more likely to have other social characteristics of the normal population than were addicts who did not work.[1] In making these comparisons, we used 1970 census data on the general population of the three boroughs from which we sampled addicts, Manhattan, the Bronx and Brooklyn, and we further limited the general population to the age range of the working addicts which was 17 to 49. In terms of age, ethnicity, education, marital status, and even sex, the working addicts fall in between all known addicts and the general population. Thus, of those 17 years of age and older, only 18 per cent of those in the general population are between 17 and 24, compared with 39 per cent of the working addicts and fully 55 per cent of all addicts. The majority of all addicts is thus under 25, whereas a majority of the general population over 17 is over 40, and working addicts fall between these two extremes in terms of age. They are older than the group of all addicts, but younger than the general population.

For the general population of Manhattan, the Bronx and Brooklyn in the age group between 17 and 49, 59 per cent are white, 26 per cent, black and 15 per cent, Puerto Rican. The addict population, in contrast, turns out to be 50 per cent black, 27 per cent white and 23 per cent Puerto Rican. Thus, the figures for whites drop from 59 per cent in the general population to 27 per cent of the addicts. But whites turn out to be quite prevalent among the working addicts; in fact, they are the single largest ethnic or racial group. They constitute 42 per cent of the working addicts, blacks are 40 per cent and Puerto Ricans, 18 per cent.

In the general population, 43 per cent of those between the ages of 17 and 49 failed to graduate from high school and 24 per cent not only graduated but had at least some college. Among all addicts, fully two-thirds (68 per cent) failed to graduate from high school and only 9 per cent had some college. Again the working addicts fall in between, in that 53 per cent of them failed to graduate from high school and 20 per cent had at least some college. In fact, in terms of education, the working addicts look a lot more like the general population than the total addict population.

The same pattern holds for marital status. In the general
population 17 to 49, 34 per cent were single and 55 per cent
married; among all addicts 59 per cent were single and only 23
per cent married. Among working addicts, 43 per cent were single,
that is, 9 points more than in the general population but 16 points
less than in the addict population, and 38 per cent of the working
addicts were married.

Addiction is very much a male phenomenon as fully 77 per cent
of all known addicts in the city are men and only 23 per cent
women. In the general population, women tend to outnumber men, 54
per cent compared to 46 per cent. Among working addicts, 26 per
cent are women.

Were information available on the missing group, working
addicts who are not in treatment programs, we can be fairly certain
that they would look even more like the general population than the
working addicts we found in treatment programs. In short, our data
tend to support the conclusions emerging from the studies of heroin
use among Vietnam soldiers and veterans. Those studies showed that
a great majority of the soldiers who used heroin in Vietnam were
able to give up the habit once they returned to civilian life,
contrary to the picture of addicts emerging from studies of addicts
in treatment programs. Addicts in treatment may well be the
losers, those who cannot shake their habit and who in many respects
are highly deviant from the general population. Working addicts,
like the ex-GIs, may be more like the general population, better
able to integrate their drug habit with normal routines including
work.

II. JOB WORK CHARACTERISTICS OF THE WORKING ADDICTS

Hardly any of the working addicts had high level professional
or managerial jobs, perhaps because hardly any of them were able to
graduate from college. (Although 20 per cent of them had some
college, only 1 per cent were college graduates.) But some of the
working addicts had quasi-professional or para-professional jobs,
as counselors, medical para-professionals and social workers. In
all, we classified some 8 per cent of the working addicts as
employed in higher white collar jobs, almost all of whom were
para-professionals. In contrast, 20 per cent of the general
population between the age of 17 and 49 had higher white collar
occupations. Similar proportions of each group worked as sales and
clerical workers (the lower white collar group), 32 per cent and 31
per cent. However, in the blue collar world, the working addicts
had somewhat better occupations on the average than did the general
population. Thus 11 per cent of the working addicts were
craftsmen, compared with 7 per cent of the general population
and 26 per cent of the working addicts had semi-skilled jobs

compared with only 14 per cent of the general population.
Proportionately more of the general population were at the bottom
of the occupational hierarchy, 28 per cent being unskilled laborers
and service workers compared with 23 per cent of the working
addicts. In short, working addicts, while excluded from the top of
the occupational hierarchy, were by no means clustered at the
bottom; rather, their occupations were similar to, and often better
than those of the general population.

Just as the working addicts had rather typical occupations, so
their earnings compared favorably with the general population.
Unfortunately, the census data on income stems from 1970 and our
income data on working addicts probably refers to 1973 and 1974,
and inflation was no doubt a major factor in income growth during
that four and five year period. Even so, the working addicts
in 1973 and 1974 earned so much more than the general population
did in 1970 that we can safely conclude that their drug habit was
in no way a handicap to their earnings. Thus, fully 42 per cent of
the general population earned under $5200 in 1970 compared with
only 15 per cent of the working addicts in 1973 and 1974. Only 18
per cent of the general population had earnings over $10,000
in 1970 compared with 24 per cent of the working addicts in 1973
and 1974.

Not only did they have jobs very much like the general
population and earn as much if not more than the general population
but many of these addicts were able to hold on to their jobs for a
fairly long period of time while they were addicted. Thus, while
thirty per cent held on to their job for less than one year, 40 per
cent had the same job from one to almost three years and 30 per
cent worked on the same job three or more years. These figures
suggest more stability of employment than we are accustomed to
associate with addiction. Clearly not all addicts lead an unstable
life. Some are able to stay married and hold onto a job for a
fairly long period of time.

III. THE IMPACT OF DRUGS ON WORK

Almost all of the working addicts in our sample had been
addicted to heroin and many of them were polydrug users in that
they used other hard drugs along with heroin. In all, 39 per cent
of the sample used but one illegal drug (almost invariably heroin)
while 51 per cent were polydrug users (39 per cent used two hard
drugs and 22 per cent used three or more on a regular basis). The
great majority of these working addicts (82 per cent) used drugs
while they were at work. Thus, these working addicts did not
succeed in segregating their drug habit from their work life. On
the contrary, most of them brought drugs to the work place and took
drugs during the working day.

When asked why they took drugs at work, 43 per cent replied
that they took drugs to avoid sickness, 17 per cent said they took
drugs to get high and 40 per cent said they took drugs for both
reasons. In all, 83 per cent took drugs at work to avoid sickness
and 57 per cent took drugs to get high as well. Inasmuch as
feeling sick at work would interfere with one's work performance,
the use of drugs at work can be viewed more as an aid to work than
as a hindrance to it. In short, rather than drugs at the work
place being a sign of the deterioration of the work situation, it
may be more correct to view drug use at work as a positive factor
contributing to productivity.

But drug use on the job is not without its costs. When asked
whether using drugs at work ever caused them to fall asleep on the
job, almost a third (31 per cent) answered affirmatively and more
than half (53 per cent) said that their drug habit caused them to
miss days of work. Absenteeism is thus quite high among working
addicts.

The respondents were asked two questions relating to their job
performance: how good a job did their supervisors think they were
doing and how did they rate their own job performance. To each of
these questions they could respond very good, fairly good or not
too good. Somewhat surprisingly, these working addicts assigned a
high rating to their performances. Fully 64 per cent felt that
their supervisors thought they were doing a very good job, and
almost all the rest, 32 per cent, thought that their supervisors
would rate their job performance as fairly good. The working
addicts were somewhat harder on themselves than they thought their
supervisors would be as 62 per cent rated their performance as very
good, 29 per cent as fairly good and 9 per cent as not too good.
(Only 4 per cent thought their supervisors would give them the
lowest rating.) Granted that people tend to overestimate themselves
these findings are nonetheless of considerable interest. Most
working addicts think they do their jobs very well and they think
their employers would rate them highly as well. Were their drug
habit to create problems for them at work, this would undoubtedly
have come to the attention of their supervisors and they would have
difficulty believing that their supervisors would give them good
ratings. Thus, the safest conclusion to be drawn from these
findings is that their drug habit did not undermine their job
performance during most of the time that they worked while addicted.
Integrating a drug habit with the world of work may be much easier
than is commonly supposed.

This picture of substantial harmony between the world of work
and the world of drugs must be seriously qualified. For almost all
of the people in our sample, the marriage eventually broke down.
Their drug habit became such a burden that they entered a treatment
program, and at the time we interviewed them, only 45 of the 555,
or 8 per cent, still were working at the same job. When asked why
they left the job they held for the longest time, a variety of

791

reasons were given. The largest number, but only 15 per cent of the total sample, said they were fired. The next most frequent reason was that their drug habit interfered with their work to the point where they had to quit their job, a reason given by 13 per cent, and 10 per cent said they had to quit because they were arrested. These three most frequent reasons account for only 48 per cent of the cases. Other reasons ranged from laid off, to marital difficulties to illness to pregnancy to, believe it or not, the desire to spend more time on criminal activities.

The very fact that some addicts left their jobs because they were arrested and others because they wanted to spend more time on criminal behavior calls attention to the major obstacle to the harmonious marriage of drugs and work. Because drugs are illegal, they are very expensive and even working addicts who have a fairly good income do not make enough to support their habit from their earnings. Fully 74 per cent of these working addicts told us that they had to resort to crime to maintain their habit and an even larger percentage, 81 per cent, reported that they had been arrested. Some 16 per cent said they stole money from their employers and 30 per cent said they stole merchandise from their work place. This need to become involved with crime in order to maintain their habit was a major obstacle to the efforts of these addicts to blend their drug habit with a normal work life.

The common stereotype is that drug use is so debilitating that addicts cannot lead a normal life and hold on to and perform well at a job. The data of our survey suggest that this stereotype is in error. Drugs themselves are not so much an obstacle to a normal work life as is the fact that drugs are illegal and even working addicts must resort to crime. Were drugs decriminalized and made legal, these working addicts would probably have had little difficulty holding on to their jobs and meeting the expectations of their employers.

1. Information on addicts in treatment in New York City as of 1975 was provided by the State Drug Addiction Agency and data on the general population were obtained from the 1970 census covering the three boroughs from which we sampled addicts, Manhattan, the Bronx and Brooklyn.

GRADUATE OUTCOME IN A MULTI-MODALITY
DRUG TREATMENT SYSTEM

Mark A. Quinones, Ph.D., M.P.H.
Kathleen M. Doyle, B.A.
Donald B. Louria, M.D.
Lywanda Thompson

Division of Drug Abuse
Department of Preventive Medicine & Community Health
New Jersey Medical School
Newark, New Jersey 07103

The effectiveness of drug treatment programs has traditionally been evaluated by program retention rates, completion rates and
rates of patient "success" in post treatment social adjustment,
"success" being generally defined as the absence of drug abuse and
criminal activity and the presence of full time employment,
homemaking or schooling. (1,2,4,5) In recent years, studies have
proliferated that seek to measure the post treatment success of
both graduates and drop outs of therapeutic communities, outpatient
drug free programs, and long term methadone maintenance programs.

Studies by Collier and Hijazi (1) at Daytop Village, Chambers
and Inciardi (2) and De Leon, et al. (3) at Phoenix House, and
Rohrs et al. at Odyssey House report success rates of 80% and
higher for therapeutic community graduates on the 3 criteria listed
above, and success among 40% to 50% of program drop outs.

In evaluating methadone maintenance programs in New York City
over a 10-year period Gearing (5) found a consistent pattern of
decrease in arrests rates and rise in employment for persons remaining in treatment for at least a year. Newman et al. (6)
reported similar findings in a New York City program, arrests
plummeting 57% in the first 6 months. Krakowski and Smart (7)
found that, in Canada, employment among methadone patients rises
substantially in the first year.

These and other studies show a strong correlation between
time in treatment and later success in terms of employment, avoidance of drug use and reduction in criminal activity and suggest
that those persons who graduate or complete treatment are more
likely to experience such success. Since this is so, it should be
possible not only to measure a given program's effectiveness by

the success of its graduates but also, by using standardized methodologies, to compare effectiveness of different programs by comparing their graduates.

The New Jersey Medical School's Department of Preventive Medicine and its Division of Drug Abuse, have since September 1969, overseen a treatment system composed of six individual treatment programs (1 methadone maintenance , 3 therapeutic communities and 2 outpatient) plus a central intake, a registry, and a detoxification unit. During that time the Division collected data on patients entering the system as part of an overall evaluation of retention, process and patient outcome. One part of this evaluation has been an analysis of the system's graduates. Preliminary results of this study are summarized below.

Methodology

The four treatment programs considered here are a state run methadone maintenance program offering minimal supportive services (MM); a very rigid therapeutic community characterized by the messianic leadership of an ex-addict (TC1); a behaviorally oriented therapeutic community (TC2); and a psychiatrically oriented therapeutic community, with more rigidly defined levels of achievement (TC3).

In January 1975, efforts were begun to follow up 242 graduates of these programs. Criteria for selection of the sample were: (1) person was defined by the program as a graduate between January 1, 1972, and December 31, 1974, (2) pre-admission data on the person were present in the Division's data bank, (3) in the case of methadone maintenance, the person had been in treatment 18 months or longer prior to December 1974. He may or may not have been still in treatment.

Graduates were contacted and a questionnaire composed of 150 items designed to elicit psychological, behavioral and sociological information was administered. Eighty-one percent of the sample was interviewed. When the interviewing was nearly complete, a 20% random sample of those interviewed was drawn and an ex-addict counselor never before involved in the study was sent to reinterview and obtain urine specimens from those persons for purposes of verification. Employment was verified by calls to the person's employer and police records checked for recent arrests, if any. Findings so far indicate that 95% of the graduates told the truth in the sensitive areas of employment, drug use, and criminal activity. Items measuring the three basic success criteria were analyzed, using the Chi-Square and t-test of significance, within programs by sex, age, race, education and work status. Results were also compared across programs.

Results

Demographic breakdown of clients by programs revealed no significant differences except the tendency of therapeutic communities to serve more white clients while the methadone programs tend to serve more black clients.

In terms of employment, the graduates have not had striking success. Table I illustrates graduate employment 12 months prior to the interview. Neither race, sex, age nor education had a significant influence on work status. The overall low percentage may be partially explained by the fact that 1974-5 were recession years and jobs were difficult to find even for those who were not former addicts. There remains, however, the significantly lower employment rate in the methadone program when compared to the therapeutic communities ($X^2 = 19.9$, p $< .001$).

Table II illustrates graduate use of alcohol and illegal drugs. It is difficult to interpret the meaning of the high percentage of alcohol use, since the questionnaire did not include breakdowns of drinking by amount or type of alcohol. Therapeutic community graduates admitted to more illegal drug use than other clients and the admitted drug use among methadone clients is suspiciously low. Although these data were obtained by interview, the results appeared valid when compared with urine tests in a 20 percent sample. As with employment, race, age, sex and education had no influence on drug use.

Self reported criminal activity is shown on Table III. It has been found that criminal activities are usually underreported by addicts and former addicts (9). Nevertheless, assuming that the proportion of underreporting is the same for all program graduates, there is a striking difference between crime reported by TCl graduates and others. Again, race, age, sex, and education were not significant.

From these findings, some preliminary points can be made. First, compared to other studies, this analysis reveals much lower percentages of employment among graduates and long term maintenance patients. This may be partly a function, as previously noted, of the recession or it may be that, since this was an extramural evaluation, the graduates had no stake in attempting to impress the interviewers and were more truthful in their responses. Or, it may be that the programs in the Newark system provide their clients with fewer salable skills than do other programs studied. Further study is needed here.

Secondly, the astonishing differences between TCl graduates and others, particularly other therapeutic community graduates, on all criteria demonstrates the importance of leadership and atmosphere. TCl was characterized by unstable leadership, which placed greater stress on patients' unswerving loyalty to the program than on educational, vocational or therapeutic achievement. This situation deteriorated in 1974 to the point that open drug taking by staff, physical abuse of patients and questionable management of funds led the Division to close the program.

Finally it is important to note that the results shown here, especially for therapeutic communities, for a large treatment system evaluated over a considerable period of time, show only small numbers of graduates. Thus the fact that 59% of TC2 graduates are working full time must be considered in the context that this percentage represents only 11 people.

These findings, although preliminary, must lead to a reconsideration of the importance of retention and of the need for predictor models of program success which will enable us to refer patients to programs in which they are most likely to remain for the full period of treatment. We are currently examining the effects of limited treatment on program dropouts. Simultaneous studies of retention, graduates and dropouts should permit valid evaluations of individual programs and comparisons among programs, thus providing guidance for expenditure of scarce local, state and federal funds.

Table I
Graduate Employment

	Worked 12 months	Worked 7-11 months	Worked 2-6 months	Did Not Work
MM	34%	7%	18%	41%
TC1	47%	27%	7%	19%
TC2	59%	23%	0%	18%
TC3	54%	16%	15%	15%

Table II
Graduate Use of Alcohol & Illegal Drugs

	Heroin	Barb.	Cocaine	Mar.	Alcohol 4-7 Days Weekly
MM	1.1%	1.1%	1.1%	0.0%	27.6%
TC1	14.6%	7.6%	16.9%	14.6%	26.2%
TC2	4.8%	0.0%	0.0%	4.8%	10.0%
TC3	9.3%	0.0%	0.0%	9.0%	23.1%

Table III
Graduate Self-Reported Crime

	Mugging	Fencing/ Stealing	Forgery	Drug Offenses	Other*
MM	0.0%	2.1%	2.1%	2.0%	11.4%
TC1	7.2%	11.9%	7.2%	21.4%	20.2%
TC2	4.5%	0.0%	0.0%	0.0%	9.1%
TC3	0.0%	0.0%	0.0%	0.0%	0.0%

* "Victimless" Crimes (e.g., gambling, prostitution)

References

1. Collier, W. and Hijazi, Yasser, International Journal of Addictions 805-826: 9 (6) (1974).
2. Chambers, C. and Inciardi, J., Developments in the Field of Drug Abuse. Cambridge, Mass. 124-131 (1975).
3. De Leon, G., Holland, S., Rosenthal, M., JAMA 222:686-9 (1972).
4. Rohrs, Charles C., Goldsmith, Bernard, and Densen-Gerber, Judianne, New York, N.Y., Odyssey House, 1970.
5. Gearing, Frances and Schweitzer, Morton, American Journal of Epidemiology, 100:101-112 (1974).
6. Newman, R., Bashkov, S., and Cates, M., Contemporary Drug Issues 2 (3): 117-130 (1973).
7. Krakowski, M. and Smart, R., Canadian Journal of Public Health 63:397-404 (1972).

EMPLOYMENT PATTERNS OF EX-ADDICTS
IN TREATMENT

Steven Belenko, Ph.D.

Vera Institute of Justice
292 Madison Avenue
New York, New York   10017

I.   INTRODUCTION

Employment is an important rehabilitative tool for ex-addicts
in treatment (1,2), who face many obstacles in obtaining employment. Normally closed off to many jobs because of addiction,
criminal, and sporadic employment history, the problem for the
ex-addict becomes even more acute in a job market greatly reduced
by recession.

The present report focuses on employment data for a group of
203 ex-addicts in treatment in New York City who are being
followed up as part of a four-year controlled study of the impact
of supported work on the lives of ex-addicts (3). This sample
includes 74% of those assigned to a control goup in 1972 and 1973
those for whom two years of follow up data were available through
October 1975. At the time of entry into the study, participants
had to be at least 18 years old, in treatment for at least 3
months, collecting welfare, and with a sporadic work history.
Eight-five percent were referred from methadone maintenance and
15% from drug-free programs (mainly outpatient). The sample
averaged about 30 years of age at entry, was 92% male, 60% black
and 33% Hispanic; participants had been in treatment for an
average of 13 months at the time of entry into the study. The
present sample represents neither the most stable/employable nor
the more unstable/not-job-ready ex-addicts.

One focus of this report will be the type of jobs obtained
by ex-addicts, how the jobs were obtained, average salaries, and
job retention. A further analysis of those who were able to
secure and maintain jobs is also included: What are the characteristics of successful ex-addicts, and how does successful
employment interact with other rehabilitative variables?

Data were obtained from 1) initial, first and second-year follow-up interviews and 2) official New York City Police Department arrest records, covering through the participants' first year in the study. Details on interviewing and data collection procedures have been described previously (3).

II. BASIC EMPLOYMENT DATA

About half the sample found work in each of the first two years; both the number of weeks worked and annual earnings increased in the second year (Table I). During the last quarter of the second year, 41% of the sample worked at some point.

Cumulatively, 129 respondents (64%) worked at all during the first two years, in a total of 149 jobs. Average weekly salaries increased somewhat, from $96 a week in the first quarter to $105 at the end of the second year.

Although salaries were low and job turnover was high, there was a gradual increase in the proportion employed over time. At the time of entry, only 25% of the group had worked at all during the prior six months. With the gradual rise in percent working over time there was a concomitant decrease in the proportion receiving welfare, from 100% at the time of entry down to 65% in the last quarter of the second year.

III. TYPES OF JOBS, SOURCES AND SALARIES

Those participants who found work did not generally obtain good jobs: 94% of the jobs were entry-level clerical, blue-collar unskilled, or semi-skilled, with the average salaries ranging from $90 to $111 per week (Table II).

As expected, salary levels generally followed skill levels, with blue-collar unskilled jobs paying the lowest ($90) and skilled jobs the highest ($185). Semi-skilled ($111) and clerical jobs ($105) paid similar intermediate salaries, and professional/managerial jobs paid the next-to-highest salaries ($135).

The majority of jobs were obtained through a friend (34%), by self-referral (21%) or through a relative (5%). Forty percent of jobs were obtained through various public and private agencies: 13% through a drug program, 9% through New York State Employment Service, 6% through private employment agencies, and 12% other.

IV. JOB RETENTION, TERMINATION RATES

While the five participants who held skilled jobs worked longer on the average than those working at other jobs, generally there were only small differences in the number of weeks worked by job type (Table II).

The job turnover rate was fairly high, with 62% of working participants leaving their job during the period: Most participants who lost a job reported leaving for neutral (24%) of negative (14%) reasons. Twenty percent left jobs for unknown reasons, and only 3% left for positive reasons. Thirty-eight percent of working participants were still on their jobs at the end of the two-year period.

The high proportion of participants reporting neutral reasons for leaving jobs (e.g., laid off, illness, project folded) may reflect that respondents tend to report more socially desirable, neutral reasons for job loss rather than reasons which may reflect negatively on themselves.

There was no relation between reason for job termination and either job type or length of time employed.

The termination data point up an apparent lack of upward mobility on the job market for ex-addicts; if employees do not remain at one job, they tend to be fired, quit, or get laid off. This could either reflect the poor state of the New York City job market for ex-addicts, or the ex-addicts' lack of previous employment experience and difficulty holding onto a job.

V. CORRELATES OF EMPLOYMENT

A number of demographic, background, and outcome variables were examined to determine differences between employed and unemployed sample participants.

A. Sex was significantly associated with employment: females were much more likely to work fewer weeks compared to males (78% working 13 weeks or less, compared to 53% of males). Also, the longest time ever held a job prior to entry was positively correlated with the number of weeks worked during the two years (r=.156), p $<$ .05).

There was some association between age and employment, with successfully employed participants somewhat younger, but the relationship was not significant.

Employment was not significantly associated with age first addicted, longest period off heroin prior to entry, or time in treatment. Self-reported illicit drug use over the two years was associated with number of weeks worked. The proportion of respondents reporting use of illicit drugs (excluding marijuana) was lower for those who worked at least 52 weeks (17% the first year, 22% the second) compared to those who worked 0-13 weeks (31% first year, 30% the second). The first-year difference was significant with p=.05; second year difference was not significant with p > .25. Alcohol use was not related to weeks worked.

Criminal history was related to weeks worked, with those working the fewest weeks having a greater number of arrests prior to entry. This relationship was independent of age at entry.

B.   Two subgroups were identified and compared to other participants to determine characteristics for the most successful employed ex-addicts: 1) those who had worked at least 3 months steadily at one job: 33% fell into this category, and 2) those who had worked steadily for most of the two year period (at least 78 weeks); 9% fell into this category. The first subgroup includes those in the second subgroup.

Those who worked 3 months or more had an average age of 28.4, compared to 30.6 for the whole sample, and had fewer arrests prior to entry (mean of 6.5 compared to 8.6). There were no other demographic differences between the 3-month group and the other participants; addiction and employment history were similar.

In terms of follow-up data, illicit drug use rates were not affected by 3 months steady employment (about 20% reporting use the first year, 30% the second. However, the 3-month subgroup had a somewhat lower arrest rate in the first year (24% arrested compared to 33% for the rest of the sample, n.s.). Since they also had fewer prior arrests, there is some indication that criminal activity is related to employment for ex-addicts.

The second subgroup (those who worked steadily for at least 78 weeks) also were distinguished by being yojnger (mean age 28.2) and having fewer prior arrests (5.9 - compared to 8.6 for entire sample). In addition, this steadily employed subgroup reported having held a job prior to entry for a longer period of time (33 months) than the sample as a whole (24 months). Other demographic variables were similar. Other data indicated some reduction in drug use compared to the sample as a whole. Cocaine use was lower in both years (11% compared to 25% for the whole sample the first year, 16% vs. 24% during the second year). Overall illicit drug use was lower the second year (16% compared to 30% for the whole sample) but not the first (21% vs. 24%). Arrest rates, however, were the same for the 78-week group and the rest of the sample (about 30% arrested the first year).

VI. DISCUSSION

In general there is some evidence that employment is associated with lower rates of drug use and criminal activity, but the relationship is neither large nor consistent over the two years. It is not clear whether those who are able to secure and maintain employment also tend to reduce their drug use and criminal activity, or whether employment results in decreases in these indicators.

Although intake variables were not strong predictors of employment success or failure, those who were male, younger, with fewer prior arrests, and longer length of time previously held a job were more likely to find employment.

Even the most successfully employed participants had average annual earnings of less than $7,000, and the overall employment data confirm that ex-addicts are on the lower rungs of the employment ladder. Those that are able to find jobs generally get jobs with little future and low salaries. Turnover rates were generally high, and few participants left a job for positive reasons.

TABLE I
First, Second, and Combined Years Earnings,
% Worked, and Weeks Worked (N=203)

	First Year	Second Year	Years 1 and 2
% worked at all	50	48	64
Mean weeks worked*	12.2	17.2	29.3
Mean annual earnings*	$1060	$1827	–

TABLE II

Types of Jobs, Average Salaries, and Retention

	N	%	Weekly Salary	Mean # Weeks Worked
Clerical	(40)	27	$105	30 weeks
Unskilled	(56)	28	90	26
Semi-skilled	(45)	30	111	34
Skilled	(5)	3	185	49
Professional/ Managerial	(5)	3	135	24

REFERENCES

1. F.R. Gearing, Paper presented at Treatment Evaluation and Outcome Studies in Alcoholism and Drug Abuse Conference, Seattle, Washington, July 1974.

2. P.B. Rothenberg, and P.H. Kleinman, Center for Socio-Cultural Studies in Drug Use, Columbia University School of Social Work, New York City, June 1975.

3. Wildcat: The first two years - Second Annual research report on supported work. Vera Institute of Justice, New York, New York, November 1974.

SECOND FOLLOW UP REPORT ON A VOCATIONAL
REHABILITATION PROGRAM FOR DRUG ABUSERS

Athan Karras
Melvin Cohen

Hillside Division
Long Island Jewish-Hillside Medical Center
Glen Oaks, New York 11004

The concept of vocational rehabilitation for the drug abuser is not
new, but it has not been cultivated to realize its importance or
potential. Unfortunately, much of the discussion in this area is
speculative. Only an occasional institution has sponsored a study
which employs control groups to test the effect that such a program
might have on its patients.

The Strauss Cottage Drug Abuse Program is such a program. The program is part of a study funded by both the Social and Rehabilitation Services of the Department of HEW, and the Hillside Division.
As a contrast to traditional psychiatric treatment, Strauss Cottage
is an 8-9 month inpatient-to-aftercare program, which entails only
a 2-3 month period of hospitalization. The program offers all
necessary services to its patients (social, psychological, psychiatric and medical), but concentrates, right from the start on resuming an active life in the community through vocational-career
counseling, training and placement.

The efficacy of this program was tested experimentally. An attempt
was made to assign potential subjects randomly to either the
Strauss Cottage experimental group or to the conventional in-
hospital and aftercare services control group. All study subjects,
both males and females, were between 16-30 years of age and were
moderate to daily opiate and nonopiate users. Most males had
arrest records, while only 40% of females had ever been arrested.
Only a quarter of all subjects were self-supporting. Around one-
third of all subjects were diagnosed as having schizophrenia or a
depressive reaction, with schizophrenia predominating. Seventy per
cent of all subjects had previously received psychiatric help
either inpatient or outpatient. Over half of the subjects had
previously been in other drug rehabilitation programs.

The Strauss Cottage Drug Abuse Program, which initially was founded
on harsh encounter and intensive social modeling and personality

restructuring procedures, introduced by the Synanon and Phoenix House programs, has evolved toward a more behaviorally oriented one. Along the lines of Sarason and Bandura, procedures such as the token economy, role modeling and assertiveness training have been integrated into the program.

METHOD

There are 175 Strauss patients and 104 controls. Patients are considered as study subjects regardless of their length of stay in their assigned programs. An earlier report dealt with the community adjustment of 67 Strauss and 38 controls six months after post-inhospital discharge. The areas of adjustment reviewed were criminality, drug use and career adjustment. This report deals with the community adjustment of 110 Strauss and 48 controls, representing 72 and 75 percent of each group, respectively, of all patients who were eligible for follow up at this time. The same three areas are reviewed for patients who were discharged from the inpatient service for six months and in addition no longer received rehabilitation services in aftercare for six months, except on an as needed basis, not exceeding monthly contacts with staff.

RESULTS

A. Comparison of Six Month and Later Follow Up

The results in general for both follow up periods are remarkably similar in all three areas for both groups:

1. Criminality: this was measured by arrests, which are very few for both groups for both time periods.

2. Drug Use: for both time periods we find that the Strauss group claimed around 40% as being drug-free, whereas the control group had around one-quarter claiming to be drug free. Daily drug use, which for these analyses combines opiate and nonopiate use remains stable for the Strauss and control groups at around 20-25%.

3. Adequate Work Adjustment: this measure was rated on a five point scale from extreme efficiency and commitment to a job, school or training program to non-functioning during the follow up satisfied period. The first three categories, the worst of which rated the subject as mostly working with short periods of incapacity, were combined to form the adequate work adjustment group. There may be a tendency for more of the members of both groups to fall into the adequate category for the second follow up. Both edge over the 50% mark. The difference between the Strauss and control groups appears trivial, although for both follow ups the Strauss group tends to be better.

B. Later Follow Up

We will now examine in detail certain factors that may be related to two of the outcome variables at the later follow up.
Criminality will not be reviewed further because of the low
incidence at follow up. Drug use and work adjustment will be
examined as they are affected by the sex of the person, pre-
hospital work adjustment and drug use and psychiatric diagnosis.

1. Drug Use

We find no differences in drug use between the sexes or
between those with an adequate and poor work history prior
to hospitalization. There are however potential differences
related to prior drug use and to diagnosis.

There is an interesting trend regarding prior drug use and
future drug use. For both treatment groups there is a trend
for those who used drugs daily before being hospitalized to
use drugs daily at follow up. However, the Strauss group has
more of this group not using drugs at all (44% vs 0%). We
did not separate the daily users at follow up into opiate or
nonopiate groups because the cell sizes would be very small
for each group.

With regard to psychiatric diagnosis and drug use, those who
are schizophrenic or have an affective disorder are less
likely by half to use drugs daily. Both findings apply
equally to both treatment groups, although for Strauss non-
drug use was greater and daily drug use was less; moderate
drug use was the same for both groups.

2. Work Adjustment

Reviewing work adjustment, we find many more interactions
than for drug use at follow up. For the Strauss group we
find that as we progress from less than daily drug use to
daily opiate use prior to admission, the subject is more
likely to have an adequate work adjustment at follow up.
The reverse is true for controls (57% to 68% for Strauss,
and 62% to 54% for controls).

Turning to the effects of work adjustment prior to hospitalization on later work adjustment, we find that for Strauss
and controls alike those with a prior adequate work history
are more likely to have an adequate work record at follow up
than those with a poor prior work history (74% and 50%, respectively, for Strauss; 70% and 53%, respectively, for
controls). Males in both groups tend to have a better work
adjustment than females (a 10% advantage for Strauss and a
6% advantage for controls.)

There is an interaction among treatment group, work history and sex. For Strauss males, prior work history is not associated with later work adjustment, whereas it is for control males, those with an adequate history doing better by 21%. Women in both treatments do better at follow up if they did well before hospitalization, especially Strauss women (85% vs 60% for controls). Strauss women with a poor work history have very few with an adequate work adjustment (9%), whereas comparable control women do better (50%).

There is an interaction between psychiatric diagnosis and treatment with work adjustment. Both treatment groups have approximately half of their schizophrenic and affective disorder patients with an adequate work adjustment (50% for Strauss and 47% for controls). The percentage increase with an adequate work adjustment for those with other psychiatric diagnosis is 22% for Strauss and 11% for controls. There is also a triple interaction between sex, diagnosis and treatment as it affects work adjustment (see Table I). The Strauss schizophrenic-affective group, regardless of sex, do not do as well as the "other" group. Regardless of diagnosis males tend to do better than females, especially for the "other" diagnostic group. Diagnosis interacts differently with sex in the control group. Schizophrenic women have the worst adjustment, well below 50%, whereas the remaining three groups do equally as well, hovering around the 50% mark, indicating that there is no difference in adjustment for males with different diagnoses, as there is for females, favoring "other" diagnosis.

DISCUSSION

Conclusions at present are tentative for two basic reasons. The first is that very few of our differences attain statistical significance. The second is that we have not yet been able to follow up a significant portion of our subjects on any one outcome measure.

Currently we find that only drug use at follow up tends to show an overall advantage for the Strauss program, which is nonetheless modest. Analyses of interactions however show more encouraging trends and also suggest that outcome measures may not covary highly with each other.

Criminality at follow up appears infrequently. Without obtaining rap sheets it is difficult to determine how valid this information is. However, we tend to accept it because of the validity of our intake data. We found a very high correspondence between the patient's report and his probation officer's.

807

Drug use and work adjustment at follow up appear to interact in a complex manner with several variables, especially with work history. We cannot estimate the impact of the recession on our patients getting jobs, although it may be slight for the Strauss group because of the number of vocational staff helping patients to find jobs and because most of the patients were oriented toward job readiness training programs.

With some exceptions, the best way to summarize the data is to note that those with the greatest liabilities benefit least from treatment. For example, those with a history of heavy drug use are more likely to be the ones to use drugs daily at follow up if they do use them. Those with a poor work history are more likely to continue to have a poor work adjustment at follow up; schizophrenics and those with affective disorders are less likely to have an adequate work adjustment, as are women. Those with compound liabilities are helped the least. For example, women with poor work histories or women who are schizophrenic or have an affective disorder have an especially poor chance of being helped by either treatment. It may also turn out that the Strauss program, by comparison to the control program, has an adverse impact on women with poor work histories.

Some exceptions are that the former heavier drug user in the Strauss program is more likely to have the better work adjustment, and not use drugs daily; the reverse is true for controls. Also, schizophrenics and affective disorders, regardless of treatment, are less likely to use drugs daily at follow up, suggesting that they are not self-medicating themselves at follow up.

TABLE I

ADEQUATE WORK ADJUSTMENT AT FOLLOW UP (IN %)
AS RELATED TO SEX AND PSYCHIATRIC DIAGNOSIS

Psychiatric Diagnosis	STRAUSS		CONTROL	
	Male	Female	Male	Female
Schizophrenic and Affective	52	44	54	33
Other	77	63	58	50

MARKETING THE REHABILITATED FORMER ADDICT TO THE
CORPORATE COMMUNITY: FEARS AND MYTHS ABOUT
FORMER ADDICTION

H. Daniel Carpenter, M.A.
President of PACT/NADAP
New York, New York

Frank W. Gunn, Ph.D.
Director, Employment Project
PACT/NADAP
New York, New York

The genesis of PACT/NADAP may be traced to the concern of a
group of business and labor leaders in 1972 about the exodus of
business from New York City. Having identified the drug-crime
problem as a major cause, they concluded that job development and
placement of the rehabilitated former drug addict was the most
glaring inadequacy in community response to the drug-crime problem.

Thus, in July, 1973, an employment project formally was
launched. Its specific objective is to place rehabilitated drug
addicts in permanent, full-time jobs with upward mobility. On the
one hand, PACT/NADAP has been oriented toward treatment programs,
dealing presently with approximately 135 in New York City. To be
interviewed at PACT/NADAP, ex-addicts must satisfy the "Guidelines
for Referral" which require that an applicant be at least 18 years
of age, a resident of New York City, in a drug treatment program
for at least six consecutive months, and job ready, according to
the standards of the treatment program from which the applicant is
referred. In telephone prescreening, PACT/NADAP staff also ask a-
bout the applicant's skill and work history to determine whether
they are marketable. Following a positive prescreening, drug
treatment counselors prepare a letter of introduction, verifying
the information provided in the telephone prescreening, which the
applicant brings to the scheduled interview.

PACT/NADAP serves the business sector with the same commitment
it demonstrates in the drug treatment community, providing a highly screened source of skilled and unskilled job-ready applicants.
It is assumed that placees will be expected to conform to requirements in personnel policies of the employer and to the work performance standards or be terminated. Conversely, it is requested

that employers treat ex-addict employees the same as other employees. A "plus" of PACT/NADAP's service is the support system available when any difficulties are encountered by the employee in the
work context, utilizing counseling expertise at the placee's treatment program as appropriate. Regular follow-up of placees for a
full year insures that PACT/NADAP becomes cognizant with problems
and successes on the job.

In mid-1975, two other non-profit organizations with related
goals merged with PACT which became PACT/NADAP, the National Association on Drug Abuse Problems, Inc. The impact was the addition of two executive positions to the staff. A Director of Education has given PACT/NADAP a greater capacity and diversification
in educational efforts aimed both at improving the process of vocational rehabilitation in treatment programs, and sensitizing the
business community to the need, capability, and stability of the
ex-addict for full-time employment. A Director of Research has
made the Management Information System (M.I.S.), a process of collecting data on all applicants, referrals and placements, more sophisticated and begun analysis and evaluation of that data.

PACT/NADAP, a non-profit organization, has a broad financial
base. A growing roster of supporters from the business community,
together with private foundations, have made regular financial
contributions to PACT/NADAP. In some cases, support has been designated for special projects. One of these is a study of company
experience in the employment of up to 1,000 ex-addicts from various sources in the City of New York. About 60% of PACT/NADAP funding has been from a contract for services rendered with the New
York City Department of Employment, based on the number of placements in unsubsidized jobs each fiscal year.

In its first 32 months of service, PACT/NADAP has been busy at
its chosen task. As of March 1, over 1,800 companies have been solicited, followed by more than 500 initial meetings with company
representatives with over 600 job orders for one or more positions
each growing out of these efforts. Over 1,700 ex-addicts have
been interviewed, followed by more than 1,000 job referrals to potential employers. Of these, 374 persons were hired by 111 companies. Thus, it requires an average of 3 company solicitations to
produce 1 job order, and an average of 3 referrals for every
placement made. Another observation is that it requires an average of 16 company solicitations to find a company which hires ex-
addicts. Of those companies which hired, 55% later have hired
again.

PACT/NADAP applicants have a diverse background. About 51%
are black, 26% white, 21% Hispanic, and 2% fall into other categories. Educationally, 69% have a high school diploma or equivalency certificate; 4% have a bachelor's degree. The male/female
ratio is 71/29. With respect to modality of drug treatment, 48%

have utilized methadone, 50% are drug free, and 2% other or unidentified.

Job development technique is crucial to the success of an employment project for ex-addicts. This core component is an ongoing process, beginning with a marketing letter, written by the
chairman of PACT/NADAP's board who is also the president of a well-
known savings bank, addressed to the president of the company,
briefly describing the services of PACT/NADAP. The letter includes the name of a member of our staff who will be contacting
the Director of Personnel, to whom a copy of the letter is sent.
In a subsequent telephone call, our employment specialist sets a
date with the Director of Personnel or someone designated for a
face-to-face meeting to tell the story of PACT and its service to
industry.

Given the context of an economic recession and the concomitant
competition for jobs, the rationale for hiring ex-addicts must be
well organized and convincing. In addition to the services outlined earlier, persons with criminal records which will present
bonding problems are screened out as necessary, according to company policy. A large percentage of ex-addicts who do have criminal records were convicted on drug-related charges which do not
present bonding problems. Employers are informed of applicant's
criminal background.

Fears of employers which may be traced to myths about drug addiction must be dealt with obliquely or confronted, according to
the situation. The low frequency of recidivism among ex-addicts
placed by PACT/NADAP is cited -- about 1-2%. Hesitancy about
methadone maintenance is met with facts, including research findings that this mode of treatment has not been found to impair motor or mental function to any measurable degree. Reference is
made to the employment project's placement record of persons maintained on methadone, compared with those who are drug free, corresponding favorably with the intake ratio of this modality to
drug free treatment.

Emphasis is placed on the high stake the rehabilitated ex-addict has in the first job after treatment. There is a determination to be successful in this supportive situation in which the
prospective employer already has expressed willingness to hire ex-
addicts who also may be ex-offenders.

The job development meeting, whether or not it produces job
orders on the spot, is followed by regular telephone contact from
the employment specialist assigned to that company. Referrals are
either in response to job orders or are interviews of an exploratory nature, based on known typical skills needs of the company.
Such a practice also demonstrates to the company the high calibre
of applicants available.

Some financial incentives for employing addicts are available to business. On-the-job training programs (O.J.T.) feature reimbursement from government funds for a portion of salary during the period when an employee's skills are being raised to meet requirements of the job. Funding sometimes has been obtained for employer reimbursement during an employment/training phase through cooperative efforts with other manpower development agencies. Companies which hire persons who have been receiving Aid to Families with Dependent Children (AFDC) may claim a temporary income tax credit of 20% of the wages paid to the worker. Maximum credit is $1,000 per year per employee.

Corporate resistance to employment of ex-addicts also may be dealt with by involving company representatives at various echelons in group activities and even in the on-going work of PACT. "Satisfied" companies are encouraged to sponsor policy-sharing meetings to which "newer" or "problem" companies are invited. Corporate visiting teams are recruited to participate in dialogs with ex-addicts and counselors at drug treatment programs, focusing on the occupations most frequently utilized in the industries represented. Job requirements and the personnel department's perspective are high on the agenda. Personnel representatives are invited to be resource persons in PACT/NADAP's six-session training programs for counselors, "Preparing the Ex-addict for Employment."

In addition to these now-established vehicles for corporate involvement in PACT/NADAP's work, there are three new experimental programs. In January PACT/NADAP launched two pilot programs. The first was called "The Me They See," a three session series in which ex-addicts were coached on personal appearance and behavior during a job interview. Personnel representatives from the business community ran mock interviews, followed by evaluations, to familiarize the applicants with the characteristics of a successful interviewee. The second pilot program, begun in January, was the "Drug Data Seminar," a two session series in which business management participants are sensitized about drug abuse so that they are better prepared to work with ex-addicts and also become alert to emerging drug problems among employees with no known drug abuse history. A third experimental program was held early in March, a luncheon conference called, "Methadone Maintenance: Myths and Facts," sponsored jointly by PACT/NADAP and Beth Israel Medical Center. Over 20 companies participated, including a panel of business representatives who described successful experiences with the employment of persons on methadone maintenance.

The counterproductive behavior and job-related deficiencies of some ex-addicts pose difficult problems. The three most frustrating are: lack of job readiness, manifested in attitude -- especially not keeping appointments at PACT/NADAP or at a company, unrealistic goals and absence of skills -- both technical and

812

academic; work history which is spotty or nonexistent; and bonding problems. Bonding problems, caused by a history including crimes of dishonesty or breach of trust are being dealt with in four ways: several New York banks are negotiating with the Federal Deposit Insurance Corporation (FDIC) to revise its regulations in Section 19; at least one bank is taking an aggressively positive posture towards the employment of ex-addicts with these convictions; ex-offenders are encouraged to obtain a Certificate of Relief from Disabilities which helps in some bonding situations. The larger, long-range goal of PACT/NADAP is to act as a systems change agent in metropolitan New York. When companies contacted inform PACT/NADAP that they are in a job freeze, or are laying off employees, we respond that we are "planting seeds" so that when the economic weather warms up, the seeds will germinate, referrals will follow, and ex-addicts in need of jobs will reap the harvest. Positive impact on one company will be shared with another which has greater placement potential. One receptive department which begins employing PACT's referrals will help convince others within the same company to hire ex-addicts. Official company policy is not so much a concern as actual company practice and increasing openness to the hiring of rehabilitated ex-addicts.

Where do we go from here? PACT/NADAP's history is brief, but reveals a continuous growth in components and programs which directly or indirectly support the placement of rehabilitated ex-addicts in permanent, full-time employment with upward mobility. In the immediate future, PACT/NADAP hopes to develop a reentry component administered cooperatively with local treatment programs which would vastly strengthen the vocational rehabilitation phase of drug abuse treatment in New York. This would deal with the present inadequacy in a large portion of metropolitan drug treatment programs due to their financial inability individually to support professionals in this area. Finally, PACT/NADAP is seeking channels for closer cooperation with other organizations in the field of manpower development to eliminate duplication of efforts in job development and placement.

EX-ADDICT RE-ENTRY: STRATEGIES FOR
MAXIMIZING THE USE OF COMMUNITY SERVICES

Raymond H. Milkman, Lawrence J. Center and Mary A. Toborg

The Lazar Institute
Washington, D. C.

This paper is an outgrowth of analyses of the vocational services
available to drug treatment program clients in four cities: Richmond and Alexandria, Virginia, and Austin and Houston, Texas.[1] In
each city, the authors assessed procedures utilized both in-house
and by referral for providing vocational services to drug treatment program clients and developed strategies for maximizing client
access to such services.

Because similar problems tended to recur in all the cities studied,
it was concluded that a methodology should be developed which would
enable officials in any community to analyze and improve, if necessary, the vocational services available to drug clients.

I. NEED AND FEASIBILITY ASSESSMENT

Many factors can be considered by a planner or other community
official deciding whether to undertake an effort to improve drug
treatment clients' access to vocational services. Such factors are
of two different types: attitudinal and service-related. Each type
considers a different kind of potential problem which may face the
planner. Attitudinal factors to be assessed include: the interest
of drug treatment programs in improving vocational services for
their clients and whether existing relationships among treatment
programs would permit cooperative efforts to improve clients'
vocational services. Service-related factors to be considered
include: employment rates of treatment program clients and treatment programs' knowledge and utilization of existing vocational
resources.

II. TREATMENT PROGRAM ASSESSMENT

The purpose of a treatment program assessment is to analyze the
current approach of that program toward providing vocational ser-

vices for its clients. Through this effort, the planner conducting
the analysis and treatment program personnel can identify the
strong points and weak points of a program's approach. By performing similar analyses at all major drug treatment programs, the
planner can compare results across programs and obtain a city-wide
picture of both the vocational needs of drug treatment program
clients and the extent to which those needs are being met. The
methodology developed enables planners to compare data across
treatment programs to indicate: (1) the vocational services being
provided to treatment program clients on a community-wide basis;
(2) the programs which are relatively stronger or weaker in terms
of vocational services provision; (3) the percentage of clients
needing but not receiving specific vocational services; (4) the
extent to which vocational services are integrated into the overall
treatment process; (5) the level of the specific vocational services provided on an in-house basis; and (6) the experiences of
treatment program clients in receiving services from community
vocational programs.   .

The primary areas of concentration chosen as focal points for an
assessment of vocational services provided by a treatment program
to its clients are: in-house services; services offered by referral; considerations related to potential approaches for maximizing
client access to vocational services; integration of vocational
services into treatment; and clients' unmet service needs. Data on
these subjects can further acquaint a planner with the role of
vocational rehabilitation in a program's treatment philosophy and
bring into sharper focus the specific service areas in which treatment client access needs to be increased. This can lead to an
analysis of the vocational situation in the drug treatment community as a whole, which can include identification of the most
serious problems existing among treatment programs and can assist
the planner in the development of priorities for maximizing client
access to vocational services. With limited resources available,
such priority development is critical.

III. VOCATIONAL PROGRAM ANALYSIS

The premise behind an analysis of vocational programs is that
greater knowledge of these resources will lead to more appropriate
referrals of clients by treatment programs. Experience has shown
that often treatment programs refer clients to vocational programs
where those clients are not served, for a variety of reasons. If
a treatment staff member possesses comprehensive knowledge about
the objectives, services, requirements, etc., of a vocational
program, it is far more likely that a client referred there will
not experience difficulties or disappointment, but will rather
receive appropriate services.

The vocational program analysis can lead to the development of a
resource manual for use by drug treatment program staff responsi-

ble for referring clients to such programs as CETA, State Vocational Rehabilitation, training schools, educational institutions, or work training programs.

Additionally, a community analysis showing the overall characteristics of the vocational program community will assist in assessing the current access treatment clients are receiving to vocational programs and planning ways for improving that access. The community-wide analysis can assess: (1) which vocational programs provide the best individual services; (2) which programs are most and least willing to serve more drug treatment clients; (3) which programs are most experienced in providing services to ex-drug abusers; (4) which programs currently provide special services to ex-drug abusers; (5) which programs are most and least likely to accept drug clients or experience drug client drop-outs; and (6) which programs have the most serious problems in relationship with community drug treatment programs.

The analysis of vocational programs can also include consideration of those programs' perceptions of the utility of various potential approaches for maximizing drug treatment client access to vocational services. This information can be compared with similar data collected during the treatment program assessment to assist in developing a feasible approach for improving clients' vocational services.

IV. STRATEGIES FOR INCREASING CLIENT ACCESS TO VOCATIONAL SERVICES

Problems that impede better vocational servicing of drug treatment program clients can be addressed in two ways. Specific problems, evident through collected data, can be focused upon and gradual steps taken towards maximizing drug treatment client access to vocational services. In contrast, an organized, structural model, involving the participation of several drug treatment programs and/or vocational programs, and aimed at solving many existing problems and increasing drug treatment client access on a community-wide basis, could be designed and implemented.

Many considerations affect this choice. They include: (1) size of the drug treatment community; (2) current level of vocational services being received by drug treatment program clients; (3) time and staff available to the planner; (4) the planner's relationship with the community's drug treatment programs; and (5) the severity of perceived problems in the current provision of vocational services to drug treatment clients. If a decision is made not to improve access on a program or problem-specific basis, an alternative is to develop an organized, structural model involving several drug treatment and vocational programs designed to speed and

improve the delivery of services to clients from all concerned
treatment programs.

There is a wide range of structural models which can be utilized
to ensure that the clients receive appropriate vocational services.
Four of these models are described below.

A central intake, counseling and referral unit would place the
responsibility for provision of vocational services to drug treatment clients outside of the individual drug treatment programs.
Under this service model, it would be the responsibility of drug
treatment counselors to refer clients both desiring intermediate
vocational services and deemed ready for such services to the unit.
The staff of the unit would then work with the client, providing
services such as vocational assessment and counseling and, based
on their knowledge of community resources, make referrals to
appropriate vocational programs or agencies.

A mobile team of vocational specialists can serve as an adjunct to
the drug treatment community, sharing responsibility for vocational
services with drug treatment program staff. Under this service
model, vocational specialists would visit the treatment programs
in a community, consult with clients and counselors, and make
referrals and recommendations regarding appropriate vocational programs for clients. The services made available to each treatment
program through this model need not be identical. This approach
offers all programs the benefit of a vocational specialist without
subsuming any vocational services the program may already offer,
and without necessitating that the treatment programs themselves
establish any additional services or hire additional staff members.

If an institutional linkages approach is adopted, primary control
of a client's vocational plan would remain with the client's treatment program. Although various options for design of these linkages could be pursued, all linkages would ultimately provide drug
treatment programs with direct institutional access to available
and appropriate vocational resources. Purposes of the linkages
approach are to provide maximum utilization of the identifiable
strengths of a variety of social service agencies which often
serve similar target populations and to minimize client loss or
drop-out that often occurs during the referral process or in the
course of service delivery. This approach to providing drug treatment clients with vocational services maintains the influence of
a participating drug treatment program. Linkages may be established to complement services already provided by a given program,
or may result in a series of arrangements by which complete vocational services can be provided to the client outside the treatment program. This model does not necessitate that the drug
treatment community work as a united group, although in some
communities this may be to the advantage of the involved treatment
programs in the negotiation phase of the effort.

A community education effort could complement each of the service models discussed above or could constitute an independent effort. Such an effort would concentrate on improving the relationship of a community's drug treatment programs with vocational programs and area employers. By conducting an extensive, lobbying effort directed at employers and vocational program administrators, a community's drug treatment programs can increase local receptivity toward hiring former drug abusers as well as develop understanding of the needs of drug abusers on the part of vocational program personnel. Lobbying with individual vocational programs can be undertaken by the planner, but an organized effort would likely be more persuasive.

The planner who has decided to develop and implement one of the models must consider many variables during the model selection process. The data collected during treatment program assessments and vocational program analyses play a crucial role in assisting the planner to select an appropriate model for implementation in the community. Six criteria the planner can use to evaluate the likelihood that each of the four models presented here will suc-ceed are:(1) relationships among area drug treatment programs; (2) relationships between area drug treatment programs and vocational programs; (3) resources available for model development and imple-mentation; (4) receptivity of treatment programs to the various approaches; (5) receptivity of the vocational programs to the various approaches; and (6) the level of in-house vocational ser-vices being provided to drug treatment program clients and clients' unmet service needs.

In order to implement an improved service model successfully, the support of the treatment programs must be obtained. The planner cannot impose a model on the treatment programs and expect it to succeed. Nor can the planner merely present data on vocational services and allow each treatment program to pursue its own voca-tional goals in a different way. The ideal result is to have the participating treatment programs agree to undertake design of a model. This can only be done through a series of meetings at which the planner presents recommendations, receives comments and suggestions from the treatment programs, and makes necessary changes in the recommendations as a result.

Even if the treatment programs reject the planner's recommenda-tions and cannot adopt any other models, coming together to dis-cuss the vocational aspects of drug treatment can have a benefi-cial effect. It may lead to new ideas, to a sharing of knowledge, to the eventual development of another organized effort. In fact, if the planner finds that treatment program vocational representa-tives are interacting well, the suggestion can be made to continue the group as a "vocational treatment caucus" to meet regularly for duscussions of programs' vocational needs and problems.

1. Supported under HEW (NIDA) Grant 1-H81-DA-01704-01.

FACILITATING VOCATIONAL DEVELOPMENT: USE OF VOCATIONAL REHABILITATION GROUPS IN METHADONE MAINTENANCE TREATMENT

Rita Horn, M.Ed., senior author
Michael Cetrangol,M.A.,Joan Randell,M.A., Eileen Wolkstein, M.A.

Vocational Rehabilitation Department
Methadone Maintenance Treatment Program
Beth Israel Medical Center, New York City

I INTRODUCTION

Successful rehabilitation of the methadone maintained patient has been a challenge to the many disciplines which comprise
the treatment team. Vocational rehabilitation is one of those
clinical elements participating in the treatment process. This
paper seeks to describe one method of service provided by the
Vocational Rehabilitation Department in the Methadone Maintenance
Treatment Program (MMTP) at Beth Israel Medical Center (BIMC) to
help meet this challenge.

In 1968, when vocational rehabilitation counseling was introduced at BIMC, the traditional view of addiction held by the
treatment program was that once the drug dependency was clinically
controlled the patient was cured. He/she was then expected to
attain normal functioning within the community. However, after
more careful examination of the vocational progress of patients, it
became evident that many ex-addicts lacked the concrete skills
necessary to function as expected. This group of patients seemed
to lack either the educational or vocational training and/or the
life skills necessary to compete for their places in the world of
work. Vocational groups were introduced to supplement the individual vocational rehabilitation counseling already available. The
groups were designed to enhance the personal resources of the
patients through interaction with their peers. Patients were carefully evaluated in terms of readiness to participate in well-
defined vocational groups. The groups focused on helping people
to enter training, to continue their education, and/or to secure
employment. For a large proportion of the patients these groups
presumed a vocational sophistication and readiness that was later
found not to exist.

Continued interaction with patients highlighted the extent to
which the realities and the requirements of work contrasted markedly with their fantasized expectation. Lacking identity as workers,

their main sources of identification related to addiction. This often overshadowed their ability to develop any other self concept.

As the understanding of the vocational needs of the patients improved, they were recognized as individuals characterized by various developmental deficiencies. This new awareness was consistent with the views of drug addiction and vocational development as discussed by Dr. Donald E. Super (1). Super's life stage theory identifies five major stages of normal vocational development and describes the developmental task required of each. The stages include: growth, exploration, establishment, maintenance, and decline.

The stages of exploration and establishment are of primary relevance here since these characterize the developmental level of many MMTP patients. Exploration consists of learning about society and oneself; discovering one's role and function. The individual's tasks at this stage are the crystallizing and specifying of vocational preferences. Initially, this is a trial period; it is not until success and satisfaction are experienced that commitment to the choice develops. At the subsequent stage of establishment, the tasks are to implement the vocational choice and consolidate one's position within a vocation.

As this theory is applied to the addict, it becomes evident that during the period of addiction many individuals are removed from reality. They are isolated from the mainstream, and remain largely unaware and unexposed to the developmental tasks required for normal vocational growth. They are frequently not available for opportunities to explore, learn, or grow. Although physically adults, the ex-addicts' arrested development makes them adolescents vocationally. As Super states, the ex-addict "needs to be provided with the vocational exploratory behaviors appropriate to adolescence without being made to feel that he is being treated as an adolescent". (1)

II THE GROUPS

Groups were viewed as a means to provide corrective developmental experiences to those needing them. Although varying in goals and methods, underlying all vocational groups is the need for participants to develop an interest in themselves and their futures. This is a prerequisite for approaching all other tasks of vocational development. Many ex-addicts enter treatment lacking a concept of the future; their lives have been oriented to the present. With the support of a treatment program, the patients' involvement in a vocational rehabilitation group helps to develop a fututre orientation. More immediate gratification is derived from relationships with other group members, support from the leader, and a commitment to the group's goals. The ability to plan for the future is fostered as the patients participate in, and accomplish their goals within the context of the group setting.

The types of groups that evolved at BIMC fall into three categories, each accomodating different levels of vocational devel-

opment. 1) Pre-vocational activity groups. These include various
craft groups, and structured activities. 2) Personal adjustment
groups. Among these have been homogeneous groups of women and
adolescents, as well as more heterogenous mixtures of patients with
similar developmental deficiencies. Also included have been
assertiveness training skills and multi-media programs designed to
stimulate vocational exploration. 3) Vocational groups. These
have focused on skills needed to get a job, job up-grading, vocational problem solving, resources and occupational information.
Other vocational groups have specifically dealt with needs of
patients in transitional employment and/or training, and educational programs.

III ORGANIZATION AND IMPLEMENTATION

     Given the hypothesis that vocational rehabilitation groups
are of value to the patients, the implementation of these groups
within the individual clinics has often been difficult to accomplish. Sources of resistance are often presented by the treatment
staff and the patients. Treatment staff, willing to make referrals
for concrete services such as placement and training, are often
hesitant to refer their patients to vocational rehabilitation
groups. This reluctance may reflect a tendency of the counselors
to equate their effectiveness with their ability to be the only
counseling resource for the patient. In addition, counselors often
protect their already anxious patients from a group which may be
perceived as a potential source of additional anxiety.
     Many patients find group counseling more threatening than a
one-to-one approach. Since many ex-addicts have been removed from
normal patterns of socialization, a group often highlights their
deficiencies in this area. Afraid, or unable, to confront issues
of social interaction, they do not initially attend, attend
sporadically, or become early dropouts.
     A crucial prerequisite for establishing and maintaining a
successful vocational rehabilitation group is a positive clinic
atmosphere and enthusiasm among the staff. The vocational rehabilitation counselor can work most effectively when he/she is able
to enlist the cooperation and acceptance of other staff members.
Additionally, a sense of teamwork among all staff members is
necessary for any clinic endeavor to meet with success.
     The vocational rehabilitation counselor must establish per-
sonal rapport with clinic staff. Without this, the likelihood of
engaging patients is diminished. Secondly, the staff must view the
group as a clinic project, an undertaking in whose success they
have an investment.
     When group leadership is to be shared, the co-leading by a
vocational rehabilitation counselor and one clinic staff member can
be helpful. For example, when the ex-addict counselor is co-

leader he/she presents a role model of life style change and is
someone with whom the patient can most easily identify. This is
especially important during the initial anxiety arousing period of
group establishment. Similarly, a female nurse or other female
staff member may be an effective co-leader for a women's group.
If co-leadership is not feasible, and the vocational rehabilitation
counselor has established credibility among patients and staff, as
a group leader, it is possible to lead a successful group alone.

The size and composition of vocational rehabilitation groups
are usually flexible, unless there are clear reasons for controlling
these, such as with a group for women, adolescents, working or non-
working persons. Requirements for participation tend to be basic
ones: no drug abuse or acting out behavior, and some indication of
interest. These are especially true for the personal adjustment
groups and the vocational groups. The pre-vocational activity
groups tolerate more extremes in behavior and levels of motivation.

Various methods of recruitment of group members have been
successful within differing clinical structures. When a vocational rehabilitation group has been proposed to meet specific patient
needs, such as a "career planning workshop", counselors may be
requested to select patients according to the specific criteria.
For example, criteria for a career planning workshop would be:
participants have had recent work experiences but are currently
floundering; they may, or may not, be presently employed; and they
are all dissatisfied with their occupational status, and seek
vocational stability. Patients would be contacted by the clinic
counselor. A prescreening interview has been found to be super-
fluous. On other occasions, recruitment would not depend solely
on the counselor; an announcement would be distributed to all
clinic patients, inviting self-selection. General experience has
indicated that patients respond best to the least formal process
of referral. Elaborate processes often become obstacle courses.
Often patients are encouraged to attend, and told date, time, and
location. Some may need to be accompanied to the first meeting
by a staff member.

The facilities and locations of all groups should be readily
accessible and provide adequate space and privacy.

The duration of the groups varies with the rationale of the
group. Personal adjustment and vocational groups are usually time
limited; goals are identified and plans pursued within the given
time. Groups dealing with the needs of patients who are exploring
vocational preferences may be longer or even open-ended, since the
process is often a lengthy one and subject to individual variations.
In such cases, a periodic evaluation is recommended to enable
members and leaders to examine and redefine goals and progress. To
maximize and integrate treatment, feedback, both verbal and written,
is provided to clinic staff regularly.

IV CONCLUSION

To be complete, this description of BIMC vocational rehabilitation groups must reflect the degree to which these groups facilitate vocational development. The work with groups, to date, has not been subjected to statistical analysis. However, clinical experience and impressions may be of value to the reader. The interest in groups has been evidenced by sustained patient participation and staff support. Qualitative changes in patient functioning have been indicated by clinical observation, patient self-report, and concrete life style changes. A large proportion of patients has moved on to transitional employment, educational and training programs, as well as to competitive employment and job upgrading.

Many patients express a new found sense of hopefulness. As their isolation is diminished and their vocational development progresses, they are able to move forward to implement meaningful life style changes.

These observations suggest that empirical investigation is warrented. Clearly defined experimental techniques will allow for more accurate assessment of vocational growth and development.

V REFERENCES

1.   Super, Donald E., "The Career Development of the Drug
      Abuser: A Theoretical Exploration", The State of the
      Art: Vocational Rehabilitation of the Drug Abuser,
      Vol. 1, H.E.W., Washington, D.C., 1973.

EARLY VOCATIONAL REHABILITATION
ASSESSMENT OF ALCOHOLIC OUTPATIENTS

Marcie Gerber Burros, M.A.,
Stephanie M. Bozzone, C.S.W.

Alcoholism Treatment Program
Beth Israel Medical Center, New York City

I   INTRODUCTION

The clinical procedure to be described was developed to demonstrate the potential for vocational rehabilitation as an integral part of the initial assessment of individuals beginning long-term treatment for alcoholism.

The hypothesis was that vocational assessment and planning as part of the intake process would serve to facilitate patients' involvement in a more structured life-style earlier in their treatment. It was also felt that this procedure would enhance patients' involvement in the treatment process.

II   THE SETTING

The Beth Israel Alcoholism Treatment Program consists of an inpatient unit, an outpatient clinic, and a Halfway House. The outpatient service is the major component of the program, serving 700 patients residing on the Lower East Side of Manhattan. The program has a multi-disciplinary staff which includes psychiatrists, internists, nurses, social workers, vocational rehabilitation counselors, counselors (most of whom are recovered alcoholics) and a recreation worker. The O.P.C. is open six days a week from 9:00 a.m. to 9:00 p.m. with patients spending an average of four hours a day in the facility.

Since the catchment area includes the Bowery, 80 percent of the patients can be classified as "Skid Row" alcoholics when they enter the program. National statistics indicate that the "Skid Row" alcoholic comprises only 3 percent of the total alcoholic population. Therefore, this population is not a representative sample.

Patients come to the program with extensive medical and psycho-social needs. Upon admission, a majority require detoxification from alcohol, before they can be considered for long range planning. They have few outside support systems, most are undomiciled and have no families. Although a majority have worked in the past, their histories have been sporadic and reflect nagative work experiences.

III   REASON FOR PROJECT

The program's approach to treatment reflects the philosophy that sobriety cannot exist in a vacuum. There must be an alternative to alcohol in order to help the person maintain sobriety in a consistent and stable manner. Sobriety can only be achieved when the alcoholic begins to derive some gratification out of being sober, when he begins to feel productive, useful, and better about himself. To help an alcoholic maintain sobriety, other areas of his life must be sufficiently developed to raise self-esteem, offer pleasure and hence provide a reason to stay sober. Vocational rehabilitation as a major component in treatment is directed to stimulating the patient's awareness of the need for such alternatives to alcohol as well as to help him/her move in a productive direction.

However, there was difficulty in involving patients in structured activities and vocational planning. A number of factors contributed to this.

1. The population is generally passive and does not seek help. This couples with the fact that many have negative self-concepts with regard to work.

2. An alcoholism counselor is the primary counselor and coordinator of all patient services and is responsible for referring the patient to a vocational rehabilitation counselor when it seems appropriate. The counselor often had difficulty in assessing goals for patients. Likewise he experienced difficulty in assessing readiness for vocational counseling.

3. The counselor and the patients tended to view the vocational rehabilitation counselor as a job finder. There was initial uncertainty about the use of vocational rehabilitation in early sobriety. The counselor tended to be protective of the patient's anxiety level and resisted encouraging new challenges.

4. There was uncertainty as to whether patient's needs were being met by the vocational activities already developed in the clinic and whether appropriate patients were not being referred.

IV PROCEDURE

The design of the study was developed by the vocational rehabilitation counselor, the O.P.C. social service supervisor, and the
two participating alcoholism counselors. In addition, the directors of the O.P.C., the vocational rehabilitation department and
C.I.S. for the medical center, provided valuable guidance and
assistance.

Twenty-five patients comprised the experimental group and became part of the project upon referral to the vocational rehabilitation counselor by the counselor at the time of intake. To integrate this procedure into clinical process, the counselors told the
25 patients that as part of the intake procedure, they would be
referred to a vocational rehabilitation counselor.

The comparison group consisted of the 25 patients assigned to
the same two therapists prior to the implementation of this
procedure.

For the experimental group only, a structured interview form
(See Attached) and a semantic differential (See Attached) were
utilized during the initial interview with the vocational rehabilitation counselor to facilitate formulating a patient profile and
assessing vocational needs. The counselors utilized the same
semantic differential in order that both the counselor and the
vocational rehabilitation counselor might compare their attitudes
and responses toward individual patients.

Treatment plans were then developed in a joint meeting of
patient, counselor and vocational rehabilitation counselor following both initial interviews. Since the orientation was vocational,
the focus of these plans was on vocational development. Other
bio-psycho-social needs were dealt with by the counselor in the
standard clinical manner. The vocational focus was implemented by
the referral of patients to prescriptive dayroom activities, referral to outside agencies for additional socialization and vocational
services, and/or to ongoing vocational counseling within the O.P.C.
All referrals were consonant with the work both the counselor and
vocational rehabilitation counselor were doing with the patient.
In addition, ongoing joint meetings were arranged to review progress, revise plans, and maintain the communication between
patient, counselor and vocational rehabilitation counselor.

V RESULTS

Results indicate that of the 25 patients in the experimental
group, sixteen established an initial contact with the vocational
rehabilitation counselor, while continuing to see their alcoholism
counselor, eight never returned to the clinic after their initial
contact with the counselor, and one remained in treatment but was
evaluated to be psychiatrically unable to be involved in vocational
planning. Of the sixteen who became engaged in vocational rehabil-

itation counseling, five maintained ongoing counseling with both
the alcoholism and vocational rehabilitation counselors; seven
were referred to prescriptive dayroom activities within the clinic,
in addition to ongoing counseling with their counselor and periodic
joint meetings with the vocational rehabilitation counselor; two
were subsequently referred to outside community agencies for
vocational services and two became gainfully employed as a result
of ongoing counseling with both the counselor and the vocational
rehabilitation counselor.

However, in examining the vocational rehabilitation involvement of the 25 patients in the comparison group, no patients were
referred to the vocational rehabilitation counselor, nor had any
become engaged in vocational activities in the clinic or the
community.

There appear to be no major demographic differences between
the comparison and experimental groups, nor between those experimental patients who did and those who did not establish the initial
contact with the vocational rehabilitation counselor.

VI DESCRIPTION OF PATIENTS WHO PARTICIPATED

Of the 16 patients who initially established contact with the
vocational rehab counselor, the mean age was 43.4; 15 were male, 1
was female; 11 were white, 3 black, and 2 Spanish; 1 was living
with a spouse, 7 were separated or divorced, 7 had never married,
and 1 was widowed; 7 had less than a high school diploma, 6 had at
least a high school diploma, and 3 had graduated from college.
Perhaps one of the most striking findings occurred in the employment category. It was found that 2 had worked in 1975, then had
worked in 1974, 1 in 1973, 2 in 1972. Only 1 had not worked since
1965, due to physical disability. The average length of the last
job was more than 3 months. This picture of recent work experience
and employment lasting more than days, contradicts the "day work,
spot work" conception usually used to describe the work experience
of the "skid row" type of alcoholic.

VII CLINICAL IMPRESSIONS OF PATIENT RESPONSE

The treatment staff involved in the project discussed their
impressions of the patients through examination of the semantic
differential and less specific case review. Both the vocational
rehabilitation counselor and the primary therapist found that patient response to the early vocational rehab involvement did arouse
feelings of importance as a result of increased staff contact.
However, feelings of anxiety seemed to stem from an uncertainty as
to what expectations the program held for them regarding work.
Some individuals actually manifested feelings of discomfort when
having to talk about negative work histories, and at times embar-
rassment about this was evident. Some of this anxiety was allayed

when alternatives to work, i.e., prescriptive day program activities were explored in counseling with the therapist and/or vocational rehab counselor, and patients were able to consider viable options regarding their treatment. Participating staff concurred that patients seemed generally pleased that the "work" area of their lives would be incorporated into their rehabilitation.

VIII STAFF INTERACTION

With the increased sharing of responsibility for patient care, the quality of project staff interaction improved. The counselor's stereotype of the vocational counselor as a job developer was broken down; they began to view him/her as a clinician able to work with patients on a variety of levels. The counselors became more available to suggestions and plans offered by the vocational counselor and better able to assess readiness for vocational planning. Both the vocational rehabilitation and counseling staff members found that they engaged in treatment planning sessions with more concurrent plans than had appeared during the initial phase of the project. Initially, the vocational rehab counselor was duplicating many of the services provided for by the counselor, and it became necessary to narrow the focus and become more attuned to the specific vocational needs of the patient.

It was felt by both the vocational rehab and counseling staffs that the project was beneficial in improving communication among staff members.

IX PRESENT ASSESSMENT PROCEDURE

At intake, most patients do not voluntarily express interest in returning to work or to becoming involved in vocational counseling. However, when given the opportunity to consider options regarding work and/or alternatives to work, there was positive response. As an outgrowth of this pilot project, the B.I. Alcoholism Treatment Program has implemented a procedure whereby all new patients are referred to a vocational rehabilitation intake group, during their first or second week of program involvement. The results of this intake group are communicated to patients' counselors and become integrated into treatment planning.

As a result of this wide-range participation of vocational rehabilitation in the intake process, patients are becoming engaged in structured activities and/or vocational services both within the clinic as well as in the community with more frequency, and earlier in treatment. In the first three months of the intake group procedure, approximately 1/3 of the patients, who attended the group, have been able to sustain involvement in these activities. In addition, treatment planning reflects an increased awareness of, and sensitivity to, the vocational rehabilitation needs of all patients, even at very early stages of treatment.

PRIVATE EMPLOYMENT AND THE EX-DRUG ABUSER: A PRACTICAL APPROACH

William G. Double and Lee Koenigsberg
Institute for Policy Analysis
Lincoln University
Lincoln University, Pennsylvania 19352

A comparatively low-cost job development and placement mechanism can successfully bridge the gap between the ex-drug abuser and productive employment. This conclusion is derived from the recent experience of a federally funded demonstration program.

The program, JOBS for Rehabilitated Drug Abusers of (JOBS), was implemented in Boston, Detroit, Chicago and Philadelphia by SAODAP and NIDA. In Boston and Detroit the projects were sponsored by local OIC chapters; in Chicago and Philadelphia by agencies of city government.

The demonstration was initiated in response to difficulties encountered by treatment programs in trying to complete the rehabilitation of former drug absuers: namely, the ex-addicts' need for work and the often demonstrated reluctance of private employers to hire individuals with a drug history. The program was designed to test an approach which combined centralized job development, placement, counseling and follow-up. The demonstration assumed that a job was a necessary ingredient in the rehabilitation process. Although not much conclusive evidence exists to support this assumption, it seems clear that many recovered drug addicts express a strong desire to work.

The JOBS program was evaluated by the Institute for Policy Analysis of Lincoln University. The evaluation team collected data from program staff, enrollees, employers and drug treatment programs in the four cities. This paper is based upon the evaluation.

The JOBS program adopted a straightforward approach to the job placement of ex-drug abusers. The program had three basic functions: (1) to explain its objectives to employers and obtain from them pledges of job openings for enrollees, (2) to screen and counsel job-ready drug treatment clients prior to placement in these positions, and (3) to follow up for one year to assist both enrollees and employers with problems. The primary focus of JOBS

was job placement -- that is getting enrollees into jobs and keeping them employed. Traditional manpower programs, on the other
hand, tend to concentrate their efforts on pre-employment services
such as basic education, coaching, training, day care and medical
aid.

The program placed approximately 400 enrollees in jobs over a
two-year period, with each of the four projects placing about 100.
The number of participating employers ranged from about 20 in
Detroit to more than 50 in Philadelphia. In addition, about 100
enrollees were placed in training programs. Some of these were
later placed in jobs.

Program enrollees were placed most often in entry-level
positions; laborer or semi-skilled positions, usually in manufacturing. Nearly one-fourth of the enrollees were placed in clerical
occupations. About 15 percent were placed as craftsmen and
foremen and about the same percentage as professional/technical
employees, many as drug treatment counselors. The average starting wage for enrollees placed by the four projects was $3.31 an
hour. Wages ranged from a high of $4.64 an hour in Detroit, with
its relatively high paying auto industry jobs, to $2.80 in Boston.
The median wage of the last job clients reported holding before
enterering the program was $3.12. Thus, the program increased
client wages an average of 19 cents an hour. This increase does
not seem significant, especially considering the effects of inflation over the intervening period. However, enabling clients to
hold their own in earning power might be considered an accomplish-
ment--in view of their recent drug experiences and employer
skepticism about hiring ex-addicts.

As expected, initial efforts to develop private sector jobs
for enrollees met with strong employer resistance. Their typical
job development strategy was to canvass employers by phone or mail,
seeking interviews to explain the program. Initially, three or
four employers were contacted for everyone who agreed to a presentation by the project staff. For example, the Boston project
contacted 180 employers and received four responses to its initial
mail campaign. Meanwhile, the projects were innundated with client
applicants referred by drug treatment programs. Contrary to
expectations, the majority of those referred were not "job ready".
Some applicants had serious medical disabilities or were poorly
motivated to go to work; others appeared to be still addicted or
in an unstabilized condition. It became clear that many drug
treatment programs were not accurately identifying those clients
who were job ready--that is sufficiently motivated, able to work
and far enough along in treatment to hold a full-time job. The
overwhelming thrust of drug rehabilitation, it should be noted,
has been directed to treating the client's addiction. Until
recently little attention has been devoted by treatment programs
to the vocational rehabilitation or employment of clients. Few

drug treatment personnel have received training in these areas.
In fact, drug counselors are frequently temselves ex-addicts
with limited work experience outside the treatment program setting.

The success of the program's early placements was invaluable
in encouraging later employer receptivity. Many of these early
program enrollees--admittedly carefully selected by the projects--
proved to be capable workers. These enrollees and their employers
were then used by the projects as success stories in selling the
program to other companies. Moreover, project job developers
learned to tailor their approaches to the vital interests of
potential employers. They discovered, that appeals to social
consciousness were not a strong selling point. Despite corporate
rhetoric to the contrary, employers were more concerned with what
the ex-addict could do for them than with what their companies
could do for society. Employers were primarily interested in two
things: the projects' ability to (1) carefully screen applicants,
and (2) provide post-employment follow-up.

The problem of poor referrals by drug treatment programs was
approached from two directions. The JOBS projects began working
with treatment center personnel in an effort to improve their voc.
rehab. skills. Treatment counselors were oriented on employer
requirements and indicators of job readiness. The Chicago project
went so far as to develop a voc. rehab. curriculum for drug
counselors that was subsequently adopted as a credit course by the
city college system. Simultaneously, the JOBS projects began to
improve their own capability to handle clients not ready for
immediate referral to jobs. The projects established working
relationships with state voc. rehab. agencies and local supported
work and sheltered workshop programs. After second-year funding,
they began to hire special counselors with vocational rehabilitation skills.

Most JOBS Program enrollees performed well. About 80 percent
of employers interviewed said that enrollees were performing at
least as well as other employees doing similar work. This finding
indicates that most of the ex-addicts placed by the program were
capable of meeting the normal requirements of the work place.
Employer complaints centered on poor work habits rather than on
inability to carry out the functions of the jobs. Employers were
willing to accommodate lapses in performance by providing on-the-
job training or shifting enrollees to less demanding positions.
However, they were generally unwilling to tolerate excessive
tardiness or absenteeism. The majority of employers interviewed
said they preferred drug-free to methadone-maintained enrollees.
However, little difference was noted in the performance of the two
types of enrollees. Generally employers could not identify their
enrollees by treatment type. For example, an enrollee on methadone
was rated superior by an employer who avered he would never hire a
methadone-maintained client. The labeling of enrollees as ex-

addicts actually seemed to improve their chances of job retention. While all employers were told enrollees were ex-drug addicts, it was up to management whether to reveal this to supervisors. Some chose to inform supervisors; others declined. Enrollees retained their jobs longer when their supervisors were informed of their addiction histories. It appears that supervisors who were familiar with an enrollee's addiction history were more likely to be supportive and understanding when problems arose on the job.

Despite the occasional problems employer satisfaction with the program ran high. Almost all said they would participate again in JOBS or a similar program. By and large, they were favorably impressed with the enrollees they hired and with the professionalism and frankness of the project staffs.

The evaluation indicated that most employers are poorly informed about drug addiction and treatment. This conclusion is based on interviews with employers who participated in the program as well as those who refused. Their information about drug abuse came primarily from the news media: their views were marked by stereotypes and emotion rather than fact. The drug abuser was typically perceived by the employers as a heroin addict from a minority group--seldom as the experimenting teenager, the bored suburban housewife or the middle-aged white alcoholic. Few employers had any policy--other than exclusion or firing--toward hiring ex-drug users or dealing with drug abuse among their workers. Only those employers, such as auto companies, who had experienced major drug problems, had programs for helping the employed drug user. Furthermore, employers were largely uniformed or dubious about drug abuse treatment resources existing in their communities.

Interviews with clients raised intriguing questions about the relationship between drug abuser and employment. The architects of the JOBS Program were convinced that a job was vital to the rehabilitation of the drug addict. And most enrollees themselves viewed work as necessary to help them remain off illegal drugs and to return to a "normal" way of life. (This finding was not unexpected since motivation to work was a prime requisite for referral to the program). Yet, a considerable number of enrollees had been addicted to drugs while employed--prior to entering drug treatment or the JOBS Program. Indeed, evidence exists that assembly-line workers and those in other repetitive jobs may actually turn to drugs to relieve the tedium. And how many executives rely on uppers, downers or martinis in order to get through the work day? Thus, work in itself does not appear to be a strong disincentive to drug use. Research is needed to determine what, _if any_, factors related to work may discourage recidivism among former drug abusers. How important, for example, are the type of job, job security, family situation, peer pressure and continued counseling? JOBS Program data were not sufficient to shed light on these questions.

Most enrollees interviewed commented favorably on the Program.
They were generally satisfied with the services and jobs they
received. Analysis of enrollee job experience showed that the
JOBS projects were most successful in placing those with moderately
good work histories. Those enrollees with the best work histories
were most likely to be dissatisfied with the jobs the program
offered and attempted to find their own jobs. Those with the
poorest work histories were least often placed by the program. An
effort was made to quantitatively compare the results and costs
of the JOBS Program with those of other employment programs for
the disadvantages. JOBS compared favorably in terms of both
costs per placement and enrollee wages.

Perhaps the most important lessons to be drawn from the program are that private jobs can be developed for the ex-addict at a
reasonable cost...and that individuals placed in these jobs can
perform satisfactorily. The manner in which these placements
were made also is significant. Employers were fully informed of
the applicants' drug histories, and persuaded to hire them by
appealing primarily to self-interest rather than altruism. Informing employers about client backgrounds had two positive
results. First, it relieved the ex-addict of the burden of fear
and guilt which exists when this information is concealed.
Second, it made employers aware--many for the first time--that the
ex-addict can become a productive worker.

The JOBS Program also demonstrated the feasibility of a
centralized job development and placement service for the rehabilitated addict. This configuration displayed distinct advantages
when compared with the traditional decentralized job referral
service provided by drug treatment programs.

Because of their specialized nature, the JOBS projects were
able to assemble personnel skilled in vocational rehabilitation
and job development. These skills are notably lacking in many
treatment programs. At the smaller programs each drug counselor
may assume responsibility for referring his clients to jobs. At
larger programs, a single staff member may be assigned part or
full-time to this task but this individual often lacks training
or relevant experience. Also in contrast to the typical drug
treatment program, the JOBS projects became keenly aware of
employer interests and the realities of the job market place.
Whereas treatment programs tend to focus almost entirely on the
welfare of their clients, JOBS was forced to balance client
needs against those of employers. The projects soon learned that
referring clients who were unmotivated or not job ready could do
nothing but damage chances for future placements. Sensitivity
to employer needs was a key reason for the success of the program.

THE RUBICON GREAT PFLAT TIRE COMPANY

"Worn-Out Minds Re-treaded"

Stephania Munson

Office of Program Development
Rubicon, Incorporated
1208 West Franklin Street
Richmond, Virginia

> Jack says to Jill, "I didn't say you wanted to!"
> Jill: "I didn't say you said I wanted to!"
> Jack: "I didn't say you said I said you wanted to!"
> Jill answers, "Fuck You!"

Where are we? Utopia? Trapped in the pages of an absurd version of Mother Goose? We're at the Great Pflat Tire Company, where 30 adolescents live, work, play, learn, fight, and try to cross the bridge from childhood to adolescence, or from a premature adulthood to adolescence, depending on the experiences each kid brings with him.

At Pflat Tire almost anything can happen, and often does. It's a vital, volatile crucible, an alternative to juvenile detention home, to running away or hanging out on the street, to living at home with parents who are sick and tired of trying to understand.

Pflat Tire is co-ed, with a static capacity of 20 males and 10 females, bulging at the seams, understaffed, and funded for just the bare essentials. But, during the past four years of program operation, Plat Tire has been an enormously successful experiment in providing humanistic therapy to young drug abusers.

AN HISTORIC OVERVIEW

Rubicon, Inc., began in 1970 in Richmond, Virginia, as a treatment and rehabilitation program for adult heroin addicts. By 1972 a sudden upsurge in adolescent drug abuse hit the city, and Rubicon requested funding for a separate adolescent treatment component,

(1) to investigate the characteristics of drug abuse in an urban
youth population, and (2) to design, develop, and implement an experimental model for the effective treatment of the adolescent.

Many changes have occurred during the four years of Pflat Tire's
existence. Originally, the catchment area was the City of Richmond,
but referrals are now accepted from all areas of the Commonwealth
of Virginia, North and South Carolina, Maryland, Tennessee, and
Florida. Since 1972 Pflat Tire has provided services to over 400
clients, both residential and outpatient. At that time, 35% of the
clients were narcotics addicts (heroin, morphine); the remaining
65% were classified as polydrug abusers with an average of 2.6
years of experimentation (glue, heroin, amphetamines, hash, barbiturates, cocaine, LSD, marijuana, alcohol, methadone, THC, metha-
drine, in a variety of exotic combinations). In 1972 the average
client was 17.7 years of age, with an 8th grade education.

In early 1976, 20% of the Pflat Tire clients are heroin addicts
while 20% are potential alcoholics, and the remaining 60% are polydrug abusers. The average age has dropped to 15.6 years, and the
average grade completed remains at the 8th.

PFLAT TIRE AND ITS STAFF

The Pflat Tire is a large old house located on Richmond's Northside.
There are rooms with bunk beds, one kitchen with dining rooms,
study areas for education classes, a clinic staffed by a full-time
nurse and half-time physician. The staff consists of Facility Director, two Treatment Specialists, Social Worker, Cook, and a
Teacher. In-house education is conducted Monday through Friday by
the Pflat Tire Teacher, in concert with one Homebound Teacher from
the Richmond City Schools.

In addition, Rubicon's Psychiatric Social Worker, Senior Social
Worker, and Senior Teacher work with Pflat Tire kids on an as-need-
ed individualized basis, augmented by other members of Rubicon's
72-member, NIDA-funded staff. We speak of the Rubicon Family, and
in none of our treatment facilities does that concept become more
important than at the Great Pflat Tire Company.

THE APPROACH/PROGRAMMING

The Pflat Tire structure is modeled on that of a surrogate family.
The therapeutic emphasis in on a humanistic but non-permissive
approach to treating the adolescent, male and female, usually characterized as "delinquent' or "incorrigible", who exhibits a number
of behavioral/adjustment problems of which drug abuse is only one
symptom. There are times when the staff must "come down" on the
kids in an authoritarian-parent manner, but that response is kept
to an absolute minimum. The preferred relationship between staff
and adolescent is that of a low-key, supportive big-brother type

climate. This staff attitude, coupled with constructive peer-group pressure, has been successful.

The goal is to help the Pflat Tire kid learn how to relate to people, how to enjoy life, how to cope with problems without having to use drugs.

Given the average age range of the clients -- from 12 to 17 -- education plays an integral role in the therapy administered there. Most of the kids arrive at Pflat Tire with an aversion toward anything which smacks of education; many are drop-outs, flunk-outs, or tune-outs. A few never learned how to read, most think of themselves as "stupid", and a fair percentage have learning disabilities. Cajoling a Pflat Tire kid into an academic learning situation and keeping him there is therapeutic in itself. A certain discipline is implicit in learning, and the challenge is how to dissolve the repetitious patterns of failure.

The classes are small, and the kids grouped into small clusters and worked with individually. Special projects are assigned; a variety of texts and materials are utilized, based upon individual interest. The Pflat Tire kid discovers that learning can be fun, after he has successfully mastered a few pieces of academic knowledge, but he also finds out that some learning is dry and not very exciting (such as memorizing multiplication tables), but that that is expected of him, too. The goal educationally is to assist each adolescent in improving his academic functioning level, hopefully so that each kid can at least earn the G.E.D. Not a few Pflat Tire kids have gone on to college, and others to technical training or vocational schools.

In addition to education, group encounters, and frequent individual counseling, Pflat Tire kids have daily chores around the house, free time, rap sessions, family meetings. They go to the movies, concerts, sports events, and the circus. The Cook takes some of the kids to church, where several have joined the youth group and sing in the choir.

THE KIDS

If asked to point out one reason why the Great Pflat Tire Company is unique, that reason would have to be the kids who live there. Each has brought his or her own unique history, problems, and personality, but a unique potential, as well. Nearly every adolescent admitted to Pflat Tire has been brutalized in some way, an old story. But the reality of each kid's situation tends to make him lovable, and to make us, however case-worn or weary, respond to his uniqueness and want to help him find his own way. Here are just a few of the Pflat Tire kids:

Bobby - who lived at Pflat Tire, split, was sent to prison for possession of LSD, subsequently raped by an adult inmate. When he

836

returned to Pflat Tire, we kept wondering why he cried in groups
whenever sex was mentioned. When asked to sit for a while and
ponder a sign which read "Don't Blow This Chance", he punched his
fist through a wall, but then he copped to being afraid he would
always seem "like a woman", marked for life. Bobby remained at
Pflat Tire for a total of two years, graduated, is now employed as
an auto mechanic, and has a girlfriend.

Karen - a pretty honors student from a comfortable home, whose
brother and sister were on heroin. Karen said she began using
heroin "for the sheer hell of it". At sixteen, the thrill of sex
was already gone, so "what was left but to shoot up and space out?"

Darleen - who was admitted to a mental institution at the age of
12, placed on high dosages of Thorazine, and learned how to use
an intricate system of defenses, especially total withdrwal.
During her five years at the institution, Darleen became involved
in a Lesbian relationship with a hospital employee. She came to
Pflat Tire at age 17, refusing to trust anyone, unable to communicate. During a psycho-drama session, Darleen broke down, admitted
her loneliness and desire to change. After a total of three years
of off-and-on Pflat Tire residence, Darleen is now 21, has her own
apartment, an office job, and attends college classes two nights
a week.

Cubby - who has been associated with us for five years. He and
his two brothers were kicked out of the house, just 3 of 13 children of an illiterate rural couple. Today Cubby is in the Job
Corps, training to be a social work aide, and soon to receive his
G.E.D.

Annette - one of our favorites, who has been our legal child for
three years. Annette is one example of a kid who had no place to
go. She is now 17, at an exclusive boarding school, doing very
well, and comes home to us at Christmas.

SPECIAL PROBLEMS

To enumerate only a few problems encountered on a regular basis in
the operation of a residential adolescent treatment facility, there
are problems with sex in the facility, racial flare-ups from time
to time, and the constant dilemma of where to place an adolescent
when he is ready to leave Pflat Tire. There are also difficulties
with parents, and family counseling is an inevitable adjunct service which the staff must be trained to administer.

FUTURE PLANS

At present, Rubicon, Inc., is investigating several avenues by
which Pflat Tire's services might be extended to greater numbers

of adolescents. An ideal situation would be to operate two houses, one for kids 12 to 15, and the second for those ages 15 to 18. A supervised group home, a sort of quarterway or transition house for adolescents who leave Pflat Tire but are still underage and have no strong family situation to return to, is yet another highly desirable feature.

It has been said that the quality of a culture can be determined by the way in which a society treats its children. In that regard, Pflat Tire has an obligation to stay in business.

ALCOHOL ABUSE

THE N.I.A.A.A.:
PAST, PROBLEMS, AND PROGRESS

Marc Hertzman, M.D.

Director of Inpatient Services
George Washington University
Department of Psychiatry

On December 31, 1975, just three months ago, this nation
marked the fifth anniversary of the creation of the National
Institue on Alcohol Abuse and Alcoholism. In those five years
the NIAAA blossomed forth from a tiny center to a complex of
programs extending into every state of the Union. From a modest
research and demonstration base, the NIAAA burgeoned to support
treatment for more than 140,000 clients annually, by far the
largest single source of funding for assisting alcoholics this
country has ever known. Training programs of the Institute have
reached thousands of professionals and other citizens. The prevention and education components of the national alcoholism effort
have reached into every nook and cranny of this Continent, Puerto
Rico, Hawaii, and the Pacific Island. Notable contributions to
scientific research have come out of the Institute's research
program, culminating in two reports to the U.S. Congress on
Alcohol and Health.

Is this hyperbole? If you have every heard anyone from the
NIAAA staff speak in public, or if you have ever read any of the
publications put out by the Institute, you are undoubtedly
familiar with the rhetoric of alcohol abuse and alcoholism. We
are justifiably proud of what has been accomplished from modest
beginnings in half a decade. You will, therefore, be so polite
as to excuse us if we are prone to exaggerating the positive side
of achievement. Painting a rosy picture of how things are going
is a chronic disease of civil servants and administrators only
slightly less addictive than alcoholism.

This paper will be different. That is a promise. For,
since the time I made the committment to speak at the National
Drug Abuse Conference, I have left the NIAAA. And, while I am
sympathetic to the difficult tasks which face the competent,
hardworking staff there, I also feel that it is worthwhile to
pause and take a critical view of what the Federal government has
done, is doing, and will undertake to do in alcohol abuse and
alcoholism.

Times have changed and so has the environment in which
health and social programs function. The economy has been hard
hit recently. This overwhelming reality is reflected in the hold-
the-line budgets of many Federal social welfare programs, including those in Health. Congress is in a money saving mood, too,
and is striving to emulate the President by keeping the Budget
within the ceiling set by the Congressional Budget Act of 1974.
Even if economic conditions improve over the next few years, in
many quarters a mind set is developing to hold programs accountable for what they do; to define standards of quality and measure
tangible outcomes; and to proceed cautiously about involving
the central government in areas which have been traditional responsibilities of states, local government and the private sector.

Throughout the rest of this paper I would like to highlight
four salient issues. Of course, there are others which press upon
us. However, I am convinced that if we can deal with these four
principal challenges, the rest of the pieces will fall into place
more easily. They are: (1) We must give substantially more than
lip service to the prevention of alcohol and drug abuse problems,
however difficult they may be to define and measure. (2) The
insularity of professionals in our field must be overcome. We
must impress ourselves upon professionals in related health and
social services work who can help the alcoholics and addicts.
(3) Efforts to encourage the integration of alcoholism and drug
abuse with other services must be redoubled and must be made
meaningful. (4) The specific, individual requirements of high
risk populations must be taken into account in program planning.
The question is, can this be done without permanently isolating
particularly minority groups from the mainstream of care?

Prevention: Lip Service is a Liability

We argue among ourselves all the time about what prevention
is. As a practical matter, it is defined in a very straightforward way. Prevention of alcohol and drug abuse problems means
a measurable decrease in the incidence of new cases that appear
in a year's time. The fact is that we have the tools to tell what
the major problems are, and we have the means to count and
quantify them. If we need more data and we are not collecting it,
why are we not doing so? Lack of money? I doubt it: How can you
square pleas of penury with the twelve-fold increase in the NIAAA
budget since 1971?

I suggest that there is a need not to know. We have an
investment in not knowing whether we are preventing alcoholism.

Our professed philosophy of prevention in alcoholism is one
of "Responsible Drinking and Non-Drinking," the God-given right to
choose our own behavior pattern by thinking it out ahead of time
and planning our own actions. Now, I have a confession to make.

842

I have changed my mind about "Responsible Drinking." Responsible
Drinking" as an approach to prevention rests on the cornerstone
of certain assumptions, the truth of which is shaky at best. One
is that a small or moderate amount of alcohol may be good for your
health. "Responsible Drinking" was based on studies such as the
chapter in Alcohol and Health: New Knowledge about alcohol and
heart disease. If you read them carefully, they do not unequivocally conclude that you live longer or better from drinking some
alcohol than if you drink none.

Drinking any alcohol may be bad for your health. We know,
for example, that cirrhosis of the liver and fatty livers show
many gradations of degeneration from the mildest to those which
kill. It is quite reasonable to assume that alcohol is one of
the main causes of cirrhosis, and that a little alcohol causes a
little increment towards cirrhosis. We speak abou the healthy
drinking practices of Italians and stress the contribution that
such practices could make to preventing alcoholism in America.
But Italians also have one of the highest rates of cirrhosis in
the world. What it boils down to is, if there is doubt, should
we not take the course that is safest for the public's health,
given the current state of our knowledge of the illness? Probably
the major issue facing us is the role which alcoholic beverage
and drug manufacturers (in some instances they are one and the
same) play in promoting alcoholism and drug abuse. We have known
that we were going to have to take on these powerful industries
at least since Rupert Wilkinson wrote his addendum on prevention
to the Alcohol Commission Report back in 1967. Yet we have failed
even to study the effects of industry practices, much less
considered appropriate regulatory practices which would contribute
to primary prevention. Instead, we find certain alcoholic beverage advertisers actually picking up on NIAAA public service
advertisements, and redoing them in their own inimitable formats.
Collusion with the major beverage manufacturers would, perhaps,
be too strong a term to apply. However, there can be little
doubt that such may appear to be the case to some critics, so
long as the possibility of a contribution to the problems of abuse
is not at least entertained by present and former Federal
Officials.

No Pro Is an Island

The second problem we have to deal with is even more
elusive than that of prevention. It is the isolation within which
live and work the professionals of alcohol and drug abuse treatment, And under the rubric of "Professionals," I am including all
para-professionals, non-degreed professionals, counselors,
recovery workers, ex-addict workers, whatever you want to call
them.

Not long ago I had the pleasure of participating in a seminar on training physicians in alcoholism.[1] LeClair Bissell summarized the day's remarks very succinctly. One point she made left a deep impression on me. "We've passed the age of evangelism now in alcoholism." I think that we're past the age of being able to throw out statistics and expect that will convince people to take action. They want to know what to do next? How do we do it and what's in it for us? We need to provide answers. We have to stop pretending that there is any lack of interest in either alcoholism or sex. These are sure-fire topics for everybody because everybody is interested in them. If people won't come to hear about them, or won't pay attention to what we say, it's because we have so threatened them or they so threaten themselves that they can no longer hear. It is not because there's anything intrinsically disinteresting in the topic, in fact quite the contrary." What I want to stress is the last part. Alcoholism and drug abuse professionals can stop being defensive. We have made positive steps. Why do we always feel the need to justify ourselves again, retreading the same old ground until the tracks are deep?

The time has come to knock on the doors of other professionals with what we have that ought to be important to them. Rather than being defensive about working in our field, and thereby putting others on an equally defensive footing, we can begin to assume professionals should know about alcohol and other drug abuse as a matter of course.

Integrating Services: Or, the Reluctant Radicals

In essence, then, what we have created by isolating ourselves—always with the willing cooperation of the rest of the health specialists, who are only too happy to leave it to us—are a series of lonely islands of care. Two years ago at the National Drug Abuse Conference in Chicago, I put it this way: "The intent of the NIAAA is to stimulate support within the total community service system that will, first, help to enlarge community capability to provide comprehensive services for all, and, second, ensure adequate appropriate services for every alcoholic person. In this way, a truly comprehensive alcoholism program, fully integrated into the human services system, can make a major contribution to its community as it satisfies the total needs of alcoholic clients."[2] Here I stand, in the resuscitated metropolis of New York, two years later, and I could reiterate my words without changing an "i" or "t".

The urgency of the problem is, however, much more acute now than it was two years ago. For example, issues of what will be covered in a National Health Insurance scheme, if they have not already been settled, will be very shortly. And if alcohol and drug abuse services are covered only in very restricted categories, treatment could be drastically curtailed in this country.

Target Population Programs: Trying to Hit the Bull's Eye by Shooting the Bull?

The fourth problem I would like to deal with is the question of who deserves to receive project grant money for the treatment of alcoholism. That is easily answered, you will say: Everybody who needs it.

The present policy of the NIAAA Division of Special Treatment and Rehabilitation Programs is to target money to specific high risk groups. Such groups are defined by high incidences and prevalences of the illness, as well as specialized problems in meeting their human needs. The rationale for setting up the DSTRP policy originally had to do, among other things, with the limitation of the Alcoholism Treatment Centers program, the ATCs. Specifically, the amount of community participation, and the attention to minority groups problems by the ATCs, were considered to be somewhat limited.

Although it is probably still too soon to pass judgment on the new policy, the early returns are promising in several senses. First, the effectiveness of the target population treatment programs appears to be at least in the same range as that of the ATCs. They may even be less costly. Second, they are clearly more acceptable to the people at the local level who want and demand services.

New Directions: Or, Where I Shall Stand Depends on Where I sit

All who have had occasion to scrutinize the Institute programs closely would agree that basic and applied research on the questions of causation in alcoholism are needed. Although there are outstanding scientists working on such problems now, it has been a slow process attracting them to alcoholism which has been viewed most often as a backwater of science. I therefore, expect that efforts will redouble to try to make some headway into such questions as how alcohol affects the brain. Little is known and many feel the most is to be gained through such research.

Finally, the question of what quality of care we are ultimately delivering to people will become more and more pertinent. In fact, I believe that issues about what are minimal standards of care. What is good treatment practice, and how these are being observed are laced throughout the four major issues I have highlighted. The NIAAA recently conducted a follow-up study of people who had contact with or were treated by its funded grant programs. Those who completed treatment did well.

Those who had minimal contact with the program also did well.
The question then becomes, is the output worth the dollars it costs
us to mount such a treatment program? I would like to end on an
upbeat. The preliminary results of cost/benefit analyses of
various alcoholism programs indicate that, in the long run, it is
at least a break-even proposition to treat an alcoholic.

Notes

[1] Bissell, L. "Reaction," in Involving the Physician through
Alcohol Education and Training, published proceedings Eastern
Area Alcohol Education and Training Program, Inc., Bloomfield,
Conn., 1975, p. 76.

[2] Hertzman, M. Speech before the National Drug Abuse Conference
Chicago, Illinois, March 31, 1974.

PROMOTING ALCOHOLISM EDUCATION IN THE UNDERGRADUATE AND GRADUATE CURRICULUM

Toby Thierman, M.A.; Joseph C. Kern, Ph.D.

Nassau County Dept. of Drug and Alcohol Addiction
1 Station Plaza No., Mineola, New York 11501

Stewart R. Paul
Brunswick Hospital Center, Amityville, N.Y.

Despite the growing realization that alcohol and alcoholism is a public health problem, there is an absence of alcoholism education in the undergraduate and graduate curriculum (Eddy 1974).

Doctors, teachers, social workers, nurses and other helpers will encounter many alcoholics and their families during their careers. Yet, all of these groups lack a basic grounding in this field. Knox (1973) has reported that social workers and other professional groups hold inconsistent and negative attitudes toward the alcoholic.

The lack of alcoholism curriculum fosters misconceptions and ignorance, with the result that the alcoholic and his family continue to be stigmatized and rejected by society, in general, and by the helping professions, in particular. The recognition of this deficiency prompted the Alcohol Addiction Services Unit of the Nassau County Department of Drug and Alcohol Addiction to sponsor the development of an undergraduate curriculum on alcohol and alcoholism at Molloy College, Rockville Centre, N.Y. and a graduate curriculum at State University of New York at Stony Brook, Stony Brook, N.Y.

Undergraduate: "Aspects of Alcoholism Intervention"
          Molloy College

It was decided to utilize Molloy's "Mini-Mester" format (two weeks of daily intense class involvement) and
to allow two levels of student involvement: 3 credits
for 30 hours of classroom instruction plus 15 hours of
outside work or 2 credits consisting of the same
course excluding the outside work. The two level
course offering permitted students to attend the
course who could only manage a morning commitment.
Several outstanding features of the course structure
were:

1. Use of treatment staff as teachers: Since the
course was offered in the context of the Alcohol Unit,
treatment staff was available to conduct various
sessions. Hence students had the unique experience of
being in touch with practitioners who could directly
transmit the ethos of alcoholism treatment within a
treatment setting. Additional instructional sessions
were held in area alcoholism agencies where students
met with treatment personnel and experienced the
vitality, dedication and extent of their commitment to
client care.

2. Field trips and exposure to patients: The students
were exposed to a sampling of various alcoholism
treatment modalities. Field trips were scheduled
which included: Outpatient facility, short term detoxification unit, long term inpatient rehabilitation
unit and attendance at an open meeting of Alcoholics
Anonymous.

A primary goal of this education program was to produce
attitudinal changes away from the moralistic, judge-
mental view to one which accepts the alcoholic as a
sick person in need of understanding and supportive
treatment. The didactic sessions delivered by treatment staff being integrated with direct experience with
clients provided a potent combination to affect this
amelioration of attitude.

3. Assessment techniques: The course assessment techniques were designed to further affect positive
attitude change. Students were required to keep daily
logs recording their reactions and evaluation to that
days session. Students were also expected to choose 4
readings from the suggested reading lists provided, and
submit a written evaluation according to a presribed
outline.

During the second week, students were divided into 4 groups and instructed to develop a program on alcoholism which they would present to the class during its final two sessions. Although general guidelines were provided, the theme, depth and manner of presentation were left to the group to determine. Each group met outside of class for approximately 10 hours to complete its presentation. The rationale for the use of this technique was to facilitate the students integration of the material on a cognitive, affective and practical level. It has been shown that involvement of the student is essential in the achievement of this integration of attitudes (Piorkowski 1973). One group role played a situation of a female alcoholic in a hospital and the reactions of a nurse to the patient's provocative behavior. It highlights the changed behavior of the nurse after she had been given some insight into alcoholism by a fellow nurse on duty.

The curriculum was constructed with 4 basic goals: (1) To enable the students to understand and deal with their own attitudes and misinformation regarding alcohol and alcoholism; (2) To give them accurate information on the nature of alcohol, its effects on the human body and the disease of alcoholism; (3) To give them an understanding of intervention techniques and treatment modalities; and (4) To integrate thi information through a combination of various participatory experiences.

Graduate: "Understanding Alcoholism: Psychosocial
          Aspects of Alcoholism" SUNY at Stony Brook

This program differed from the Molloy Mini-Mester in that it was a full semester 3 credit course on the graduate level. Many of the students were teachers at all levels of education, but others ranged from housewives to employees of drug or alcohol programs. Some of the techniques used at Molloy were utilized again. Those repeated were the use of guest lecturers, all of whom are experts on their topic as well as having experience in the direct treatment of alcoholics and their families. Field trips again consisted of treatment facilities to gain exposure to alcoholics, as well as visiting A.A. meetings. The reinforcing mechanisms of the class log with personal reactions and evaluation forms were again used. Each student was required to attend one open meeting of A.A. and submit a paper describing his reactions to what occured. Tests were eliminated to allow the students to

concentrate on developing an interest in the course
material rather than an emphasis on rote memory.

Grades were based,in part, on class participation.
Primarily, however, a term paper which each student
developed based on a topic of interest to him was the
major grading factor. Teachers were encouraged to
develop a lesson plan based on the needs of their students and subject, and many excellent lesson plans were
developed. During the course many of the students
brought up material which reflected concern as to their
own drinking habits or those of a relative or close
friend. Since this was a graduate level program, technical aspects of alcoholism such as criteria for
diagnosis and techniques for intervention were covered
in depth. However, the primary goals of the course
remained the same as those of the Molloy program: (1)
Amelioration of attitude; (2) Integration of didactics
with experiential situations including role playing
and and site visits to Nassau County Dept. of Drug and
Alcohol Addiction facilities; (3) Use of "assessment
techniques" as a reinforcement of both attitudinal
changes and retention of course material; (4) to enable
the student to have accurate information about alcohol,
its effects on the human body and nature of the disease
of alcoholism; and (5) To enable the students to integrate this information into their personal lives and
careers.

The evaluations and students comments in their daily
logs clearly indicate the value of this type of program
at both the undergraduate and graduate level. A 42
item knowledge test regarding alcohol and alcoholism
was administered on a pre and post test basis to both
the undergraduate and graduate students. A repeated
measures analysis of variance indicated that there was
a significant shift toward a more accurate and thorough
knowledge of this field ($P=<.005$).

Attitudes were measured using Tolor's "Attitudes
Toward Alcoholism Scale". Analysis of pre and post
tests revealed that there was a directional shift away
from a "moral weakness" and "social rejection" view
toward a more"humanistic" and "disease oriented" view.
This data confirmed our belief that undergraduate and
graduate courses on alcoholism are needed and can be
effective in imparting to students knowledge about
alcohol, and showing the relevance of this knowledge
to their personal lives and professional careers.

REFERENCES

EDDY, John, KNODERER, Barbara. Need for College Drug
    Education Courses. Journal of Drug Education, Vol 4,
    No. 4, pp. 385-387, Winter, 1974.

KNOX, Wilma J. Attitudes of Social Worker and Other
    Professional Groups Toward Alcoholism. Quart. J.
    Stud. Alc. 34:1270-1278, 1973.

PIORKOWSKI, Geraldine K. Drug Education At Its Best -
    The Shaping of Values and Anti-Drug Attitudes.
    Journal of Drug Education, Vol 3, No. 1, pp. 31-37,
    Spring 1973.

POLLACK, Bernard. Decision Making - A Key to Preven-
    tion of Drug Abuse. Journal of Drug Education,
    Vol 2, No. 4 pp. 383-389, Winter, 1972.

STUART, R.B. Teaching Facts About Drugs: Pushing or
    Preventing (in press). Journal of Abnormal Psych-
    ology, 1974

TOLOR, Alexander. "Attitudes Toward Alcoholism Scale".
    Paper presented at 1974 Eastern Psychological
    Association Meeting.

PATIENT CHARACTERISTICS ASSOCIATED WITH SUCCESS
IN TREATMENT OF ALCOHOL ADDICTION

Daniel P. Sternberg, Ph.D.

Raleigh Hills Hospital

The following study was conducted to determine if certain selected patient variables were associated with successful treatment
outcome of alcoholism. It was felt that this would aid in predicting potential relapses more accurately and help indicate which program resources are being effectively utilized, and in what manner.
For potential successes, then, these resources might be emphasized
in order to reinforce gains and improvements.

I. METHOD

A. Subjects

Forty-six patients who had been hospitalized for alcoholism
during March and April, 1975 served as the subject pool for this
retrospective study. From this sample of 46 patients, 26 male and
female patients were selected to form two groups: one group consisted of 13 patients who had been "successful" for a six-month
period following discharge from the hospital, whereas the other
group consisted of 13 patients who had relapsed; each group consisted of 9 males and 4 females. Success was defined as abstinence at the end of the six-month period following discharge with
little or no known intermittent drinking. Recidivism, or relapses,
was defined as known continual and/or heavy drinking, or return to
prior drinking patterns (such as binges), and/or evidence of any
kind of drinking at the end of the sixth month following discharge.

B. Program Description

A brief description of the program will help to clarify some
of the mechanisms available to maintain contact with patients, and
assess patient progress. A more complete description of the treatment program is presented elsewhere. (1) The program is basically inpatient (averaging between 12 and 14 days) with follow-up and
aftercare. The basic treatment is aversive conditioning to alco-

hol. The aversive stimuli (unconditioned stimulus) is chemical, and nausea is the unconditioned response. Following the detoxification period of 3 days, the patient is exposed to five aversion conditioning treatments. A rest day occurs between each of these treatments, during which individualized needs assessment and identification occur along with development of a discharge and aftercare plan. During rest days and evenings of treatment days, patients are exposed to education about alcoholism (medical, psychological, and sociological), counseling services as indicated (individual, family, and group), and a good deal of facilitative interaction with other patients and staff.

Following discharge from the hospital, the patient is given a date to return for a single day reinforcement session of the aversion conditioning, usually within two weeks. Each patient's program includes approximately six returns to the hospital for reinforcement treatments over the course of a year, with the following intervals (from discharge): 2 weeks, 6 weeks, 14 weeks, 24 weeks, 36 weeks, and 48 weeks. The actual intervals of time between reinforcements are tailored to each patient's needs. The necessity of these reinforcement treatments for maintaining aversion to alcohol and for subsequent success has been well documented in the literature. (2) The patient may also return to the hospital between reinforcement treatments for otherpsychosocial services. If the patient lives within a reasonable distance of the hospital, he is invited to return for injections of Vitamin B (Thiamin) at least twice a week. Appearances for these injections, for reinforcement treatments, for other ongoing functions (roundtable discussions, graduate association functions such as Bingo games, AA Meetings, etc.), and for scheduled and unscheduled psychosocial services allow an opportunity for evaluation of patients' progress. Relapses, and even intermittent drinking are detected in a number of ways: 1.) nonappearance for reinforcement treatments, 2.) self-report of drinking at the time of reinforcement treatment, 3.) calls to the hospital for "help" from patient, family, or friends between reinforcement treatments, and 4.) the "grapevine" network of patients who are graduates of the program. All relapses in this study have been accounted for, i.e., returned for treatment, entered treatment elsewhere, or are still drinking.

C. Dependent Measures

The following psychological tests were used to determine differences between successes and relapses: 1.) Minnesota Multiphasic Personality Inventory (MMPI), and 2.) Graham-Kendall Memory-for-Designs test (MFD), a test for memory deficits related to "organic impairment". (3).

Several other kinds of data were also used as dependent measures: 1.) demographic data including age, marital status, number of years of drinking, number of children, and employment status,

2.) frequency of return to hospital for vitamin shots, and 3.)
number of reinforcement treatments attended.

II. RESULTS

A two-tailed t-test was employed to compare successes' and relapses' mean scores on "age" (Successes=53.9 years; relapses=49.3
years.) and "number of years drinking" (Successes=32.3 years; re-
lapses=25.7 years.). Neither "age" ($\underline{df}$=23; $\underline{t}$=1.0576) nor "number
of years drinking" ($\underline{df}$=21; $\underline{t}$=1.5350) were found to be significantly different for successes and relapses. A Chi-Squared test of
statistical independence was conducted on marital and employment
status. Seventy-six and nine-tenths percent (76.9%) of successes
and 58.3% of relapses were married; 85% of successes and 77% of
relapses were employed. The non-significant results for marital
status (χ^2= .995; $\underline{df}$=1) and employment status (χ^2= .248; $\underline{df}$=1)
indicate that successes are no more likely to be married and em-
ployed than are relapses. Results for the demographic data then
indicated no significant differences between successes and relapses; however, successes tended to be older, had been drinking
longer, are more often married with fewer children (successes have
2 children, whereas relapses have an average of 2.4 children) and
tend more often to be employed than relapses.

An observation of data collected on numbers and frequency of
vitamin shots and Reinforcement Treatments indicates that successes tend to keep in more constant contact with the hospital between reinforcement treatments, and in general adhere to the program rules more than relapses. These data give some indication
that closer monitoring of all patients should occur for at least
the first two months following discharge from the hospital.

Two-tailed t-tests were conducted on scales where mean scores
between successes and relapses appeared to be large. Results indicate that successes differ little from relapses, except on one
subscale of the MMPI, i.e., Depression. Even though results of
the two-tailed t-test demonstrated marginal significance ($\underline{df}$=24;
$\underline{t}$=1.7500; p $<$.10), the difference between successes and relapses
on the Depression Scale is 11 (successes had average standard
scores of 76.9 whereas relapses had a score of 65.9). It was also
interesting to note that the average patient profile is relatively
"normal" when compared to any norm group (i.e., all other clinical
scales were between 50-70). There was little difference between
successes and relapses on the MFD, which indicates that relapses
do not tend to show more organic impairment than successes.

III. DISCUSSION

The purpose of this pilot study was to determine differences
between alcoholics who were successes and relapses following

treatment. The success ratio for the patients included in this study was found to be 65%. Generalizability of these results are limited by 1.) the characteristics of the sample utilized in this study, 2.) a relatively small sample, 3.) the unique patient characteristics which may be associated with self-selection of the kind of treatment program described in this paper, and 4.) evaluation after a relatively short period of time. Given these considerations, certain conclusions can be drawn from the results of this study.

It does not appear that certain factors always believed to be related to successful outcome (e.g., being married and employed) were actually related to successful outcome, at least not in the present study. More subjective information would be needed about the quality of marriage and one's job satisfaction in order to further clarify these results.

It appears that the main differences between successes and relapses are the score on the Depression Scale of the MMPI, and behavior related to returning for vitamin shots and reinforcement treatments. The Depression Scale appears to be quite sensitive to transient emotional states, and persons with this scale elevated usually recognize their own self-depreciation, moodiness, and disposition to worry even over small matters. (4) However, "to the extent that it reflects an unhappiness with one's self-concept and an attendant willingness to change, or to try to change, it may be a prognostically hopeful sign."(5, p.24) This motivation to change may definitely be incompatible with the denial observed in alcoholics, and could result in 1.) the patient being more suggestible to goals identified in treatment, and 2.) a more potent aversion to alcohol as a result of exposure to aversion conditioning. Given the fact that successes tend to be older, and have been drinking longer than relapses, it could be hypothesized that successes are more agitated and therefore more motivated than the relatively younger relapses to do whatever is necessary to control their apparently uncontrollable drinking. Perhaps this agitation and seeming despair over uncontrollable drinking provides the necessary motivation for an individual to adhere to program rules, to undergo reinforcement treatments, and to stay in close contact with the hospital in order to continually maximize any gains made. Relapses, on the other hand, appear to be less agitated and more resistant than successes in accepting the fact that they have a problem in controlling their drinking. Useful corroborative information, now being collected to evaluate this hypothesis, includes numbers and kinds of previous attempts to quit drinking.

Useful information has been provided by this study in helping to identify patients who tend to be successful, and in suggesting alternative treatment strategies for persons who might relapse. For instance, persons who taper off contact with the hospital too rapidly (after 2-3 weeks) may be contacted and encouraged to continue receiving vitamin shots on a weekly basis (if they live relatively close to the hospital). Patients who start giving excuses for missing or postponing reinforcement treatments, especially the second reinforcement treatment, could be made the targets of extensive outreach either by staff, by other program graduates, or by a combined effort. Those patients who present an "overconfident front" may need to be confronted more often and with greater intensity than other patients. The purpose of this would be to urge these patients to more realistically question their present life-style and motivation for treatment.

In the light of the results of this study, the old belief that "the best predictor of success is past behavior" (i.e., if there have been many previous attempts to quit or control drinking with subsequent failure, the best prediction of outcome in present treatment would also be "failure") may have to be re-examined. Undoubtedly, this belief could possibly contribute to relapse, since the expectation of failure may be subtly broadcasted by treatment personnel. However, if the best prediction of success is repeated failure in the past, then predictions based on past behavior may take a new slant which would subsequently affect expectations of treatment personnel.

In conclusion, the results of this study suggest that additional data be collected to expand and verify the hypotheses suggested above, as well as replicate some of the present findings. A prospective study will also be conducted on the basis of the results of this study to predict success over at least one year and five year intervals following discharge from treatment.

IV. REFERENCES

1. Wiens, A., Montague, J., Manaugh, T., & English, C. Pharmacologic aversive counterconditioning to alcohol in a private hospital: One year follow-up. Manuscript submitted for publication, 1976.
2. Bandura, A. Principles of behavior modification. New York: Holt, Rinehart & Winston, 1969.
3. Graham, F., & Kendall, B. Memory-for-Designs Test: Revised general manual. Perceptual and Motor Skills, 1960, 11, 147-188.
4. Dahlstrom, W., Welsh, G., & Dahlstrom, L. An MMPI handbook, Volume 1: Clinical interpretation. Minneapolis: University of Minnesota Press, 1972.
5. Marks, P., Seeman, W., & Haller, D. The acturial use of the MMPI with adolescents and adults. Baltimore: The Williams & Wilkins Co., 1974.

IS CRISIS IN THE ALCOHOLIC BLACK FAMILY DIFFERENT FROM THE
CRISIS IN THE AVERAGE ALCOHOLIC WHITE FAMILY?

Lillian Frier Webb, MSW, CSW

Nassau County Department of Drug and Alcohol Addiction
Mineola, New York

In the helping profession, delivery of services to the black family
is divided. On one extreme there are those who view the black family as a variant of the norm. On the other hand, there are those
who see no difference in the black family when compared to the
white family of equal class status. Both black and white families-
particularly those in crisis-share what Milton Gordon (Assimilation
in American Life) calls "participational identification." The
similarity of the two families ends however, with the existing
caste system in America. Blacks have always been aware of this;
however, there has been a "white washing" of the concept and social
service agency's have planned programs which have prevented the
black from feeling free to recognize it, make it explicit, define
it, or to build on it.

The black man has lived through slavery, Jim Crow, discrimination,
segregation and is perhaps experiencing now a sophistocated
stereo-typing. Those who espouse the concept that "Black is
beautiful therefore all black people are beautiful" courts a concept as damaging as "for whites only." Society, including many
in the helping profession, denies the right of the black person to
be.

All black families-low, middle and upper class share a "peoplehood"
or a "historical identification which middle class Negroes share
with other middle class Negro families, including those in the
lower classes...They are indeed in the same boat." (1) The middle
class white and black fantasy is: I have no racial problem "yet
to the extent to which either the Negro or White believes this and
behaves accordingly, the psychological distance between Negro and
White is increased even if it may, on the surface, appear to be
otherwise." (2)

It is the scope of this paper to introduce a program for the black
alcoholic family in crisis which relates to the strengths of the
black family and which builds on the "peoplehood" of the black

nation. Poor blacks are faced with poverty, but also, with the problem of prejudice and of historical second-hand citizenship. No matter how he rises on the financial rung, he is faced with the latter two problems. Middle and upper class families are faced with "how can we grow in a society that is alien and distant?" Their immediate ethnic systems lack the resources that the larger white society can offer. The larger white society, in turn, treats the problems of the family: alcoholism, separation, delinquency, etc. instead of the family. There is a need for a study and treatment of the black family as a unit within an ethnical structure. There is a need for a visible black society to the white world. There is a need for agencies within the black society, such as the church, the school, etc. to become resourceful to the black family by developing and encouraging black scholars.

Research ignores the black family and the black experience. Norms are developed and used to prove the black family deviant. Programs are developed and implemented "to help" the deviant black family. Family members in their struggle to assimilate, accept this concept and try to adopt a white image. In doing so, the family becomes ineffective and helpless.

Reuben Hill equates the family in stress to "A (the event) interacting with B (the family's crisis-meeting resources) interacting with C (the definition the family makes of the event) produces X (the crisis)" (3). The "B" and "C" factor of the average American family come from within the family structure. The crisis-prone family has less of the "B" and "C" factors than the crisis-proof family. The resources of the family and the family's definition of the stressor event are important in the family's adjustment to the crisis. The family looks beyond itself--to the larger society for help in time of trouble. There is an ever-growing need for family service agencies to help the family keep intact, to offer counsel and to treat the family as a unit.

THERE IS NO SUCH SERVICE TO THE BLACK FAMILY IN AMERICA. Provocative? Examine these three vignettes: All attitudes are in praise or criticism of the black society structure:

Vignette I
"That's one reason so many of our girls don't even get through high school. They get knocked up and have a baby before they are in their teens good. And the boys all want to be pimps and gangsters, so they quit school and buy clothes to look sharp." (4)

Vignette II
"It may not sound right to speak about this on Sunday, but it is something that we suffer for on Monday. Unless the Negro churches will get busy and help to save them, you--as a race--are damned forever. Get out in these alleys and get these children who need guidance and help."(5)

Vignette III

"Physically, Martin was healthy. Intellectually, he was slightly
ahead of his age group. Socially, he was enjoying the threshold
years of self discovery and the companionship of the opposite sex.
He wore good clothes, had a little money in the bank--and was
willing to work for more. Martin was aware of mean policemen and
curt clerks, but there were friendly white teachers at the Lab
School. He was happy in his family, his neighborhood his school
and most of the time, his Atlanta. The church was almost a part
of the home." (6)

In the white family, according to Reuben Hill, there is a difference of vulnerability when families "are assessed on a class basis
alone." (7) The middle and upper-classes have money to pay for
resources that the poorer class lacks. Family services are middle
and upper-class oriented---oriented toward the families that reach
out toward them. The black family that reaches out for help to the
larger white society is normally labeled "deviant," in spite of
his class structure in the black world. The white society views
the black family as having a weak "C" factor, or poor definition
of the problem. I should like to explore a weak "B" factor.

The black family does not feel a part of the larger white society—
neither implicly or explicitly. It must, for its own survival and
stability, relate to a smaller black society for identity. "Common
to the ethnic group is the social-psychological element of a
special sense of both ancestral and future-oriented identification
with the group. These are the 'people' of my ancestors, therefore,
they are my people, and will be the people of my children and their
children. With members of other groups, I may share political
participation, occupational relationships, common civic enterprise,
perhaps even an occasional warm friendship, but in a very special
way, which history has decreed, I share a sense of indissoluble
and intimate identity with this group and not that group within the
larger society and the world." (8) The white world has excluded
the black man from his subcultures: his church, his fraternities,
his schools, his funeral societies and other systems. Yet, his is
an integral part of these systems. Apart from etymology, "Black
is Beautiful": is a movement toward "belonging-ness,"--toward
"peoplehood."

In its struggle "to be," the black alcoholic family appeals to existing programs and attempts "a cure" within the white framework.
It is this author's concept that help from the alcohol family can
come from the family itself in helping it to relate to the resources within itself and its immediate society- its ethnicity.
There is strength within the black family when it views itself as
a norm within itself. All attempts toward integration of services,
without this consideration is futile.

Andrew Billingsley writes, "social work scholars have almost ignored the family as a field of studies. Most of social work research is focused on social workers, their agencies, and their attitudes toward a variety of objects, including their clients; a
few studies have inquired into the orientations and problems of
foster parents and adoptive parents. But, with the conspicuous exception of an imaginative series of studies by Geismar and his
associates, the social work literature is barren of research based
knowledge of families. And if the family in general has been ignored by social work scholars, the Negro family has been even more
ignored. For there is a strong belief among social work scholars
that there is nothing special about Negro family life which cannot be surmised from studies of other low income and lower class
families.

The education series for the black alcoholic family seen at the
Roosevelt Counseling Center (Department of Drug and Alcohol
Addiction) spans 13 weeks. After a week of orientation (meeting
the client where he is and exploring the particular needs of the
group), the family members are exposed to the immediate resources
available to them with emphasis on their rights as first-class
citizens. The program which follows is a spin-off on the authors
concept of family strength. The event of alcoholism can effect
strength. The spouse is shown that the family structure foreign
to the white world has been the determining factor for black survival. Effort is spent to help the spouse see herself/himself as
a person capable of dealing with alcoholism as he/she is capable
of dealing with many other stresses that occur within the black
family. The role of family members is identified and stressed.
The role model is based on the present need of the family and not
on existing white models.

As with white families, black members tend to blame alcoholism
when there is family destruction. This program tends to help the
spouse unhook alcoholism and see the family as a unit. Effort is
spent to help the family members to communicate with each other
with great emphasis placed on seeing themselves as blacks.

It is the hope of this program to help the black family see that
it is an important part of American life and that the struggle of
alcoholism is merely part of the black family's struggle in white
America.

Hopefully scholars will begin to conduct studies that include the
"peoplehood" of the black and focus on the effect that this has
with the black alcoholic family.

Crisis intervention, with its emphasis on the current life situation of the client, places a new premium on the caseworkers involvement in the community to understand the person in a crisis and
to improve his social situations. (9)

Notes

1
Andrew Billingsley, Black Families In White America, (Englewood Cliffs, New Jersey, Prentice Hall, 1968) p. 10.

2
Ibid, p. 11.

3
Reuben Hill, "Generic Features of Families Under Stress," in CRISIS INTERVENTION: SELECTED READINGS, ed. by Howard J. Parad, (New York: Family Service Association of America, 1965), p. 40.

4
This vignette is recorded comments from adults about their teenagers or teenagers in their socio-economic class: I, lower class; II, middle class and III, upper-class blacks.

5
Ibid.

6
Ibid.

7
Reuben Hill, "Generic Features of Families Under Stress," in CRISIS INTERVENTION: SELECTED READINGS, ED. By Howard J. Parad, (New York: Family Service Association of America, 1965), p. 41.

8
Andrew Billingsley, BLACK FAMILIES IN WHITE AMERICA, (Englewood Cliffs, New Jersey: Prentice-Hall, Inc., 1968) quoting Milton Gordon, ASSIMILATION IN AMERICAN LIFE, (New York: Oxford University Press, Inc., 1964) p. 6.

9
David M. Kaplan, "Observations on Crisis Theory and Practice," in SOCIAL CASEWORK, Volume XLIX, Number 3, (March, 1968) p. 155.

EVALUATION OF A COMMUNITY ALCOHOLISM CENTER*

John L. Davis, Ph.D., Roberta G. Carlisle, M.S.,
and Harry E. Emlet, Jr., A.B.

Analytic Services Inc.
5613 Leesburg Pike
Falls Church, VA   22041

Since September 1974, we have been conducting an evaluation of a community alcoholism treatment center located in Fairfax County, Virginia. The center provides group education and therapy sessions for persons with alcohol abuse problems and education services for relatives of problem drinkers. The purpose of this study is to investigate cost savings accruing to the county as a result of reduced demands on county law enforcement and social services agencies by the clients of the alcoholism treatment center. Since the center is 98% supported by grants at almost no cost to Fairfax County, any such savings are realized by the county. Cost savings were estimated as the costs of those services the center's clients would have been expected to use on the basis of their use prior to treatment less the costs of the services they actually used after treatment. Implicit in this evaluation approach is the assumption that any difference in costs is due to services provided by the center. The study did not investigate the validity of that assumption.

Our study concentrated on two areas of county services, law enforcement services and welfare services. Our first step was to identify appropriate direct services. We considered the complete

*This study was carried out by Analytic Services Inc. (ANSER) in cooperation with the Division of Alcoholism Services, Commonwealth of Virginia, Department of Health, located in Fairfax County, Virginia, Peter Fleming, Ph.D., Coordinator. We wish to express our appreciation to the DAS personnel for their active participation in this study. Particularly, we wish to thank Mrs. Grace Schoner, A.C.S.W., for her extensive assistance throughout the course of the study. We also appreciate the assistance of Mr. Ronald L. York of Informatics, Inc., who provided us with a computer tape containing the NIAAA data we used.

sequence of events that might occur in processing an offender for a minor offense through the criminal justice system. First is arrest, the apprehension of an offender by the police department; second, arraignment in the violations bureau before a special justice; third, confinement by the sheriff's office; fourth, trial, which, for minor offenders, takes place in the county court; and fifth, when part of the punishment, a jail term, which is administered by the sheriff's office.

In our study of the Department of Social Services (DSS), the county welfare agency, we identified nine direct services. However, our data indicate that the use of these services by the client population is extremely limited and that the impact of the center's activities on the use of these services is also limited. The combined effect is to make the changes in DSS costs so small as to be negligible for the purposes of this study, and thus, the DSS results are not discussed further herein.

Our next step was to determine the costs of the direct services. We analyzed the budgets of the agencies involved and identified the items in those budgets as either directly related to the services we had identified or indirectly related to them. We assigned the costs of the direct items to the appropriate services. Indirect budget items were distributed according to their use by the providers of the services. Finally, a unit cost per case was calculated by averaging the costs over the number of cases handled. For the law enforcement agencies, the resulting costs were $17.28 per arrest, $9.25 per arraignment, $16.00 per day in jail, $6.25 per criminal trial, and $2.07 per traffic court trial. These costs are based on the fiscal 1974 budgets of the agencies involved. All these are costs to the local government only. In Virginia, a significant portion of the costs of the court system is borne by the state. Those costs are not included in these figures.

The personnel at the alcoholism center collected data for the study by means of questionnaires. They completed the questionnaires during interviews of the clients, at the time that they administered the more extensive intake and followup questionnaires of the National Institute for Alcohol Abuse and Alcoholism. Thus, the questionnaires used for the study were termed "Supplemental." A "Supplemental Intake Questionnaire," was completed at the time the client entered treatment at the alcoholism center. It contained two questions for the client. The first was whether the client had used services of the welfare department during the year prior to intake. The second question asked whether the client or a member of his family had been arrested during the previous 12 months.

Clients were asked to complete a release form allowing access to their Department of Social Services records if they indicated they had used social services during the year prior to intake. If a client indicated that he or a family member had been arrested, he was asked to complete an "Offense Disposition Questionnaire." The questions on this form enabled us to determine which of the law enforcement services he had used.

In addition to the intake questionnaire, a "Supplemental 180-day Questionnaire" was administered 6 months after the client entered the program. This questionnaire was similar in content to the intake questionnaire except that the time period involved was the 6 months between intake and followup. If the client had been arrested in this interval, he was also asked to complete an "Offense Disposition Questionnaire" relating to that arrest.

The data that were collected are, in all cases, self-reported by the clients. Thus, they are subject to error, both from imperfect client memory and from an unwillingness to report embarrassing incidents such as arrests. While we expect lapse of memory to be present both at intake and at followup, we expect it to cause more underreporting at intake than at followup. This is because the time period about which a client is being questioned at intake goes twice as far back as the time period about which he is questioned at followup. If we could correct for this bias, we would expect the correction to entail a larger increase in arrest rate in the year prior to inatke than in the six month period between intake and followup. This would show a greater reduction in services used after intake than the actual data indicate. Thus, as far as memory lapse affects the result, we assume our data indicate a lower bound on the reduction in services used.

The second factor is reluctance to report unpleasant or embarrassing incidents. This tendency affects both intake and followup data. However, by the time a client's followup interview occurs, he has known the center and its personnel for at least 6 months whereas, at intake, he may be seeing the center and meeting its personnel for the first time. We expect that this extended association with the center reduces a client's reluctance to discuss potentially embarrassing uses of county services. Therefore, we expect that this underreporting of the use of county services is more pronounced at the intake interview than at the followup interview. This will distort the results in the same direction as lapse of memory: the data collected will indicate a lower limit in the reduction in use of law enforcement services. Therefore, we assume that the post-intake reduction in the rate of using services is at least as great as the data indicate and may be larger if these kinds of reporting errors are important.

From September 1974 through August 1975 the center collected data on clients as they entered the alcoholism treatment center. During that time, usable intake questionnaires were completed by 632 clients. Followup questionnaires were completed by clients returning for a 6 months' followup interview, from March 1975 through March 1976. During that time, the center collected followup questionnaires from 292 clients. From 225 of them they had also collected intake questionnaires. These 225 clients will be referred to as the "followup group."

The followup group of clients reported 25 arrests in the year prior to intake and four in the six month period after intake. This difference is statistically significant at about the 1 percent level.

We analyzed the "Offense Disposition Questionnaires" for all persons reporting arrests and calculated an average cost per arrest of $126.47. This figure is dominated by the cost of imprisonment for those few individuals who received punishments of up to 4 months in prison. Further, a number of the cases were reported as still pending, and our results only include costs reported at the time the questionnaire was completed. The average of the fines collected per arrest was $18.54. Thus, the average net cost per arrest is $107.93 and the net savings per client in the followup group is $4.08 for the 6 month period. If one assumes these savings will continue for 26 years, they will be sufficient to pay for the $212 cost of the program for such a client. Testing this assumption is outside the scope of this study. Furthermore, these costs are only those of Fairfax County law enforcement agencies and do not reflect any of the benefits to other organizations or to private individuals.

Because the followup rate in this study was relatively low, we wished to determine whether there are significant differences between the group on which we had followup questionnaires and the group on which we did not. If the characteristics of the two groups are the same, there is some justification for assuming that the group on which data are missing used county services after intake at the same rate as the group on which we have data. We examined client data collected by the alcoholism center for the National Institute for Alcohol Abuse and Alcoholism (NIAAA). We obtained these data primarily on clients of the alcoholism center who entered the treatment between January and April 1975. The client characteristics studied are shown in Table I in order of decreasing level of statistical significance.

While the level of statistical significance at which one concludes that the two groups differ in a characteristic is arbitrary, .05 is often used. The difference in the first characteristic is significant at this level. We concluded that the two groups are different and that we cannot assume without reservation, that the post-intake use of services by the no followup group is the same as the followup group. However, the differences in the characteristics are not large and we tend to expect that the differences between the two groups in the use of county services would also not be large. Therefore, we expect that cost savings for the two groups would not be widely different.

Summary. For those clients on whom we have both intake and followup data, the reported rate of use of law enforcement services is 69 percent less in the six months after intake than in the 12 months prior to intake. This difference is statistically significant at about the 1 percent level.

The analysis of the law enforcement services used indicates an average net cost per arrest of $107.93, a reduction in law enforcement services cost over the six months following entry of $4.08 per client in the followup group. If one assumes that these savings would continue for 26 years, they would be sufficient to pay for the costs of the program for that client. Testing this assumption or the assumption that the reductions in the use of county services are due solely to the activities of the community alcoholism center is beyond the scope of this study.

A comparison of the characteristics of the clients for which followup data were not available with those of the clients for which such data were available indicate differences, significant at the 5 percent level, only in mean number of persons in the client's household. Thus, the two groups differ somewhat and we would expect some differences in their actual post-intake arrest rates but we would not expect them to be widely different.

TABLE I

Characteristics of Followup and No Followup Groups

Characteristic	No Followup	Followup	Statistical Significance
Mean Persons in Household	3.37	3.93	.038
Pre-Intake Arrest Rate	16%	11%	.055
Married, Living with Spouse	48%	60%	.063
Percent White	92%	85%	.077
Full-Time Job	63%	73%	.084
DWI Related Entry	77%	85%	.088
Percent Male	86%	92%	.123
Educational Level (coded)	6.72	7.25	.180
Attended Alcoholics Anonymous	22%	17%	.184
Years of Heavy Drinking	11.17	12.61	.320
Interview Perception (coded)	3.11	3.00	.400
Client Perception (coded)	2.36	2.37	.95
Income (coded)	12.24	12.23	.98
Age	36.86	36.87	1.00

THE ROLE OF WORK
IN A
HALFWAY HOUSE FOR ALCOHOLICS

Steven S. Manos

Formerly Administrative Director
Manhattan Bowery Project
New York City

Work works--that could well be the motto of a variety of rehabilitation programs. From Wildcat Service Corporation which
provides supported employment to drug addicts to Project Second
Chance which places ex-offenders in jobs to a Job Corps program
for drug-using adolescents, social programs are using work experiences to help troubled individuals to return to a normal life.

But "work works" is a calling-card phrase; introduction not
analysis; ideology not confirmed datum. Two questions must be
answered. First, what is the conceptual base for the assumption
that work redeems or rehabilitates. Second, given adequate
theory, is it borne out by experience.

As is often the case with social programs, practice precedes
philosophy and, in not too far-fetched a sense, existence precedes
essence. This paper is a preliminary effort to elucidate philosophy and theory by exploring the role of work in a halfway house
for alcoholics.

Perhaps the best place to begin is with some understanding of
the meaning of work itself. C. Wright Mills, a supreme general-
izer, makes it clear that work has no single meaning.

> Work may be a mere source of
> livelihood, or the most significant part
> of one's inner life; it may be experienced
> as expiation, or as exuberant expression
> of self; as bounden duty, or as the develop-
> ment of man's universal nature. 1

Mills' statement refers primarily to the intrapersonal
meaning of work. There is another area of meaning, usually,
the interpersonal. To work is to honor a commitment to society,
to confirm one's non-deviance.

These meanings of work are realized, and utilized in Project
Renewal, the offspring of perhaps the first program to be formally organized as a supported work program. Its progenitor
was a program for Bowery alcoholics who have been detoxified
by the Manhattan Bowery Project. Six men, working under
supervision, spent six weeks removing trash from Bowery lots.
All remained sober.

The symbolism of the work performed by that first group of
six was appropriate (and reinforcing?). Starting anew was initiated by a cleaning out, a purification of the past. It was an act
both of contribution and commitment.

The success of this first effort led, after an abortive attempt
to develop a sheltered workshop, to the founding of Project Renewal. Project Renewal is an arm of the Manhattan Bowery
Project, a nonprofit corporation, which operates one of the first
detoxification and care programs for public inebriates.

Project Renewal, located in Brooklyn, New York, is a halfway house with a required, structured, and supported work experience. First ten men, and now fifteen, residents of the Project live together in two adjoining brownstones and participate
in a year-long program of community living, work, group
therapy, recreation, and education.

The work program consists of the cleaning of about 100
community playlots in the five boroughs of New York City.
Prior to Project Renewal New York City had no efficient way to
clean these small, often out-of-the-way, urban areas. They did
not fit easily into the schedules or plans of existing agencies.

Participants in Project Renewal are alcoholics from
Manhattan's Bowery. Most have been sober for a month or
longer; some are taken almost right from detoxification. All
have convinced staff and participants of the Project that they
are eager to stop drinking.

What is their work experience? A mixed bag. Traditionally, Bowery employment has been "spot" jobs: catering,
kitchen work, loading trucks. In the summer, many men have
gone upstate to work in the resorts or the fields. But the modal
work history would record no steady job for many years,
limited job skills, loss of even temporary jobs through
drinking.

Their past may be different, however. Some, a few, have
had high level skills. Participants in Project Renewal have included a teacher, an engineer, and an accountant. Most,
though, have been blue collar workers. Thus participants do
come to the Project with a work history and habits, a remem-

bered past which can be drawn on as a source of pride and as a model for desirable behavior.

The men in Project Renewal are organized into three work crews. Each crew of five is managed by a crew leader, a senior member, who is responsible for resolving disputes, and making on-the-spot decisions about problems that arise in the course of the day.

The men work only four or five half days. For two reasons, the work experience is not rigorous. First, the experience is regarded as transitional. The light work load is intended both to attract men to the Project and to ease them back into a work set. Second, the Project requires all of the men to engage in required activities: group therapy, recreation, individual educational efforts. These activities take up the other half of the "work week."

There is a staff which organizes the activities of the house, but an effort is made to avoid paternalism, instiutionalism, and fatalism. Instead, the work experience is considered to be a major element in the residents' discovery that they can be responsible for their own lives, and an effort to foster independence and responsibility is made through self-controlling work crews, a house committee, and resident control of house funds. The staff is at the house only during working hours.

The Meaning of work

Ceremonial acts are often used to mark transitions. While entry into a halfway house involves a whole series of events comrpising rites de passage, work is one major element of those rites. The purpose of drawing a temporal line is to denote a significant change in rights and duties: undergoing the rites represents both the individual's acceptance of the duties and readiness to assume the responsibilites and also signals the group's (or society's) willingness to extend the rights and duties to the individual.

It is, thus, not far-fetched to compare the work "ordeal" to the several-month trial undergone by youths of the Thonga in South Africa in which beatings, exposure to cold and extreme thirst, eating of unsavory foods, punishment, and the threat of death are endured. Work thus becomes a statement: "I am prepared to undergo the hardships that independent living entails; I do not require the special institutional ministrations I once required; I am prepared to forego immediate pleasure for future gain."

Work as suffering, even punishment, may have another function: relief of feelings of guilt. It is unlikely that there

is an alcoholic in a treatment program who does not feel some
guilt about his past behavior. Treatment programs necessarily
engender it--even if excusing alcoholism as a disease--by in-
sisting that the alcoholic can control his behavior if he wants to.
Work can hlep to ease those feelings of guilt. Conformity to
norms and acceptance of imposed rigors is, appropriately,
treated as excusing past deviance.

But there is a far more prosaic role for work. In their
former mode of living, alcoholics in Project Renewal filled
their time with drinking, with the stupor of intoxication, or
with the activities of sheer survival. Sobriety does not permit
such easy erasure of time. Thus, work has a positive role
in eating up long hours, warding off boredom, providing
material for thought other than the next drink.

Although recent literature on work has stressed the feelings
of boredom, alienation, and meaninglessness that work may give
rise to, work can satisfy needs for affiliation, responsibility,
creativity, and self-expression. Project Renewal attempts to
stress the latter aspect. Skid Rowers are, contrary to accepted
opinion, not loners. The "bottle gang" is evidence of this. The
work group of Project Renewal offers an opportunity for day-
to-day companionship, among peers, who need not be feared
because they will condemn past behavior.

The desire for responsibility is satisfied and encouraged
through promotions and work opportunities of progressive
difficulty following graduation. Although cleaning playlots
does not necessarily satisfy needs for creativity and self-
esteem, the repair group to which the men may graduate does
offer opportunities for skilled work, where the work product
is visible and visibly useful. Further, the playlots have a
symbolic value: the renewal of life that youth represents and
the possibility of pleasure in life, without alcohol.

Work, in the context of the overall Project Renewal program,
has another important function: it generates grist for the group
therapy mill. Halfway houses permit therapy or education or
rehabilitation to take place in an environment which approximates reailty.

Residents are not acculturated to an articifical institutional environment. Instead, they are compelled to face up
to the demands that interpersonal relationships, holding down
a job, and successfully managing one's life make. When problems or conflicts do arise, they are discussed in group
sessions. Then what is learned and worked out in Project
Renewal carries over after graduation.

Over the years--Project Renewal goes back to 1970--the
Project has graduated between 20% and 25% of its entrants.

The year which ended on June 30, 1974 was a banner one. 35% of the entrants graduated. Relapses have not been frequent. It appears that the majority do not slip, and most of those that do rebound quickly.

Reference

1. Mills, C. Wright. White Collar: The American Middle Class. New York: Oxford University Press. 1951, p. 215.

ONE APPROACH TO THE TREATMENT OF THE "SKID-ROW" ALCOHOLIC

George Gubar, Ph.D.* and Edward G. Reading, S.T.M.**
Mount Carmel Guild Social Service Center, Inc.
Paterson, New Jersey***

The treatment of alcoholism in the U.S.A. has either concentrated on the blue collar worker in industry, or the results of drinking and driving. With the lowering of the drinking age in most states, teenage drinkers are receiving much more attention. Historically, the "skid-row" alcoholic (SRA) has been submitted to study, statistical analysis and a great deal of conjecture concerning the etiology of his drinking patterns. Involvement in the criminal justice system as an offender has also been discussed but, unfortunately, treatment for the SRA has been ignored, in most cases non-existent.

Other than jails, missions, transportation across county lines or enforced residence on skid row, the SRA's have never been involved in in-depth rehabilitation programs. Several years ago, New York City attempted to "rehabilitate" the SRA on the Bowery and under the heading of Operation Bowery (O.B.) alcoholic residents of the Bowery were placed in centers, missions and homes throughout N.Y., N.J. and Conn. Because a rehabilitation program must include detoxification, psychological evaluation, medical supervision, intensive therapy (psychological, nutritional and vocational) and then referral to an appropriate halfway house, O.B. failed. This program made no provisions for the above. In a sense O.B. could be equated with a highway beautification program, or an anti-litter campaign, which did not consider the SRA as a person, but only as garbage, or litter to be removed from the streets of N.Y.C.

The Mt. Carmel Guild Social Service Center, at Straight and Narrow Streets, Paterson has been the primary treatment agency for alcoholics in N.J. for over 21 years. As the problems of alcoholism has come more to public attention, treatment and assistance increased in recent years. Among persons not treated were SRA having regular contact with police/courts in connection with vagrance, disorderly conduct and other alcoholism related offenses. Handling of untreated alcoholics has been punitive rather than therapeutic. This is not due to design. Occurrence is due to limited facilities,

---

*Administrator of Mental Health Services, Mount Carmel Guild and Associate Professor, Psychology, Seton Hall University, South Orange, New Jersey

**Deputy Director, Mount Carmel Guild

***Corporate title as of 1 January 1976: Straight and Narrow, Inc., . . . a Service Guild

misinformation, helpless/hopeless attitude toward SRA by society
and law enforcement agencies.
Recent surveys and extimates place the number of alcoholics in the
U.S.A. at between 10-12 million persons. The SRA is a "mere" 2-5
percent. Most practitioners in the area of alcoholism, including
A.A. members, quickly point this fact out and then callously dis-
miss this minority from any ensuing discussion. Unfortunately,
this means that we are completely eliminating between 200,000-
600,000 SRA people from any treatment or rehabilitation programs.

In December 1971, the Mt. Carmel Hospital instituted a program for
SRA's. One of the original problems encountered was the lack of
motivation by the SRA to enter voluntarily into a rehabilitation
program. This was overcome by contracting with the sixteen municipalities and county agencies of Passaic County, N.J., for the
placement of SRA in the Mt. Carmel Program as an alternative to
incarceration for various terms in the county or municipal jails.
The eligible SRA is in the position of being processed by the criminal justice system for an alcohol related offense and may gain
entry into the program by pretrial release, bail, release on his
recognizance, or post-conviction alternative to incarceration as a
condition of probation.

The approach of the program in treatment of the SRA may be viewed
as having 3 phases: detoxification, diagnosis and placement/re-
sidential rehabilitation Halfway House treatment.

DETOXIFICATION, DIAGNOSIS AND PLACEMENT: Within a 10-day phase,
basic identification material is gathered; if possible upon admission. A complete medical examination, including blood and urine
analysis is given to detect any crisis condition which might necessitate special or immediate care. This examination also indicates the course of medical and nutritional therapy for the duration of this phase. The SRA is then assisted in bathing, and assigned a bed in the 40 bed unit where his activities can be monitored by the staff. After the initial 24-hour period the SRA is
assigned a social worker and staff psychologist. The Social Worker
initiates and helps the SRA establish contacts with Community agencies which may include referral for dental work, opthamology pros-
theses, legal aid, jobs, relocation agencies, contact with Social
Security and/or welfare agencies with regard to benefits for which
the SRA may be eligible, etc. Based on experience, a battery of
psychological tests are administered for screening. They are
administered at least 4 days after the last drink. Psychological
tests administered during alcohol intoxication, or shortly thereafter may produce results similar to psychosis. This battery includes MMPI, Bender-Gestalt, House-Tree-Person, and Rotter Sentence
Completion Test. These are of particular value since they require
minimal verbal or written responses by the patient. This factor
is relevant due to the functioning level of the SRA at that time.
The primary purpose of the battery is diagnostic and when severe
pathology is indicated, recommednations for further specific testing is made. If organicity is ruled out, but other gross

pathology is indicated, then major projective tests such as the Rorschach and the TAT are administered.

Over a period of 2½ years of testing, an interesting pattern has emerged. Approximately 20% of those treated are diagnosed as having functional psychoses, organic brain syndromes (psychotic and nonpsychotic) and mental retardation. These patients drank alcoholically, but it is the opinion of these authors that the mental health disorder was the primary problem. Referral to Psychiatric facilities for these SRA is recommended after consultation by the Administrator of Medical Services, the Administrator of Mental Health, and the Director of Social Services. Another interesting factor which became apparent is that a small undetermined number of SRA are not alcoholics, but in essence are "skid-row" personalities who choose to live the life of a SRA. This group should become the subjects of subsequent investigation to determine those personality dynamics which lead them into this life style.

For most patients, group psychotherapy of an encounter reality type is required. Five 2-hr. group sessions are held during this phase with daily individual therapy, unless pathology indicates otherwise. Some may be directed to more intensive individual psychotherapy based on their tests and/or clinical observations.

Patients are exposed to educational material concerning alcoholism including audio-visuals geared to help the patient develop insight into his problems. There are also lectures and discussions by the Staff, A.A. members are available to conduct meetings with SRA. T.V. viewing is not permitted during this initial phase, as it allows the patient to escape the reality of a structured situation. Based on individual needs/progress, each patient is referred to an appropriate phase upon completion of his 1-day period as determined by the Staff. The possible placements are a psychiatric facility, return to society or residential rehabilitation.

RESIDENTIAL REHABILITATION: In an attempt to bring about complete rehabilitation, a multiplicty of treatment modalities are employed. A)- Work Education Therapy: Many of the SRA were not able to compete with their peers scholastically, or hold a meaningful job for significant periods of time. Because the SRA has had few, in any, successes in his past due to active alcoholism, these opportunities have been lost and a poor self-image develops. Work therapy consisting of work adjustment/vocational training in areas of radio, T.V. repairs, auto mechanics, carpentry, upholstery and food preparation instills a sense of accomplishment and dignity. Some are employed as hospital orderlies in the Mt. Carmel Hospital, while others work on the general maintenance of the facilities. A GED Program is available for those who have not received high school diplomas. Special preparation is available for those who are interested in applying for admission to colleges. B)- Community Living: Since the SRA tends to have little concern for others, the program attempts to change this by having the residents housed in a 50-bed dormitory. This sharing of common space and equipment and 8 hours per day of working with others, ideally inclines the SRA toward socialization. He must accept the fact that there are others in his own society with whom he has to live and work. C)- <u>Alcoholics Anonymous</u>: Regular attendance at A.A. meetings is recommended for all. To assist the SRA in this, 2 meetings a week are held at the Center where outside speakers are invited to discuss alcoholism. Many SRA become involved in A.A. and continue after they leave the Center. D)- <u>Psychotherapy</u>: Because most SRA are symptomatic alcoholics, group and/or individual therapy and counselling are utilized to attempt to effectively reconstruct the "addicted personality" into a stable and mature individual, who is better able to cope with the demands of society. This therapy is also of a reality type and the therapist attempts to tailor it to the needs of the individual. After a minimum of 6 monthst of residential treatment, the SRA either returns to society or is referred to the Halfway House.

<u>HALFWAY HOUSE</u>: The goal of the program is not to develop a prolonged dependence on the program. It permits a gradual re-entry into society rather than the trauma of a complete and sudden return to a world which the SPA either rejected or found intolerable. The Halfway House, only 4 blocks away houses 10 men. Upon transfer to the Halfway House, the new resident immediately becomes aware of a change from the institutional life style of the past six months. He is now in a "home like" atmosphere in a house which has 3 bedrooms, 2 bathrooms, therapy and T.V. rooms, kitchen facilities, 2 sitting rooms and a dining room. As a condition of transfer, each individual secures full time employment. His salary will partially support him at the house, the rest is used to help the "recovered" SRA to return to society with not only a job but also the means for establishing a stable life style. Four months in Halfway House is recommended during which time he has a curfew from Sunday to Thursday. Weekends from Friday to Sunday evenings are free. A midnight return to the Halfway House is suggested.

<u>OVERVIEW OF ADMISSIONS</u>: From 1 July 1972 to 31 December 1974, 784 persons were interviewed as potential admissions. These were the result of daily trips to municipal jails and referrals from Superior Court Judges, Probation Officers, etc. Of this number 457 persons were accepted for a total of 620 admissions. 164 persons did not enter the program for following reasons: 1)- Did not have an alcoholic problem; i.e. first offenders 15%, 25 persons; 2)- Severe psychiatric problems were referred to other relevant agencies 13%, 24 persons; 3)- Alcohol related motor vehicle offenses 20%, 33 persons; 4)- Referred to outpatient programs, including A.A., 25%, 41 persons; 5)- Refused the program 15%, 24 persons; 6)- Medical problems required hospitalization approximately 10%, 17 persons. Of the 457 persons who were accepted into the program: 1)- 343 rebased in society after the 10day phase with no subsequent arrests; 2)- 58

referred to the Mt. Carmel Residential Rehabilitation Program,
3-6 months with no subsequent arrests; 3)- 114 persons recidivated
and were again received in the program (recidivism rate is 114/57
or 24.9% of persons treated) giving the program 75.1% success-rate
based on number of persons treated.

LIAISON ESTABLISHED: Various referrals were contacted during the
thirty-month period to establish an effective referral pattern for
this program. Over 200 private and public services are utilized
on a regular basis each year. By utilizing these ancillary services while affording the client more comprehensive health, and
psycho-social services, duplication of services is avoided.

As the scene turns from narcotics to alcohol, the population of
skid-row all over the country will increase. Information gained
from programs such as the one described will help workers in the
field of alcoholism to better serve their clients. The obvious
weakness in this program which must be considered is the lack of
facilities for SRA women beyond detoxification, classification,
referral and follow-up. Perhpas the smallest minority in the world
of alcoholics are the SRA women who number between 10-15 thousand
in the U.S. and are almost non-existent in literature.

Regardless of results, the Mt. Carmel Program is an attempt to determine whether or not skid-row alcoholics can be rehabilitated
and returned to a productive life - or must they continue to be
ignored by society as human derelicts to be tolerated but not
treated.

David I. Canavan, M.D. Administrator of Medical Services of the
Mount Carmel Hospital has divided alcoholics into categories:
The simple Alcoholic whose problem is alcohol and alcoholism,
and the symptomatic alcoholic who suffers from underlying psychological problems. In the latter group, alcoholism is only a
symptom or a manifestation of the underlying problems.

EARLY SOBRIETY TREATMENT OF ALCOHOLICS

By: Joseph C. Kern, Ph.D.

Nassau County Department of Drug & Alcohol Addiction
Mineola, N. Y.

The purpose of this paper is to present an outline of early sobriety treatment for alcoholics. There is considerable confusion in agencies regarding treatment priorities in the early weeks and months of sobriety of alcoholics. This paper offers a rationale and methodology for focusing priorities in treatment during early sobriety. This rationale is based on the treatment of over 2,000 alcoholics in this treatment setting.

Early sobriety treatment is unique to the needs of the alcoholic during the initial stages of continuous sobriety and ranges from six months to two years. The uniqueness of early sobriety treatment is built around nine concepts:
1. Identification of a single priority -- sobriety -- during the first year of treatment.
2. Supporting the existing defensive structure of alcoholics in denying problems in other life areas (family, etc.).
3. Using the obsessional fascination with alcohol as a tool to transfer this obsession in the service of sobriety.
4. Use of confrontation techniques only around alcoholic episodes and not confronting other life areas.
5. Use of the group modality as the preferred mode of treatment.
6. Use of pre-treatment motivational groups to equip alcoholics with group skills before entering the formal phase of therapy.
7. Use of educational lectures and discussions regarding alcohol and alcoholism prior to group therapy.
8. Use of structured groups where each session is pre-planned.
9. Teaching of an "early detection system" for alcoholics to warn them of impending alcoholic episodes.

The balance of this paper shall describe in more detail each of these principles.

1. Sobriety. During early sobriety treatment there is only one focus or treatment plan: that is to assist the alcoholic in

achieving continuous sobriety. All other considerations are secondary and the therapy should be geared to focus principally on
the client's drinking behavior. A complete and thorough psychosocial intake or psychological testing is not completed during
this period of time. The rationale for this is that data about
the client's life -- other than his drinking behavior -- is of
limited value in helping the client achieve sobriety. The elicitation of information regarding family and inter-personal relationships only serves to feed the alcoholic's preference for projection onto others for his drinking behavior in the belief that
there are forces outside himself which propel him to drink. A
broadly based psychosocial evaluation is appropriate only after
some weeks or months after the individual has achieved a measure
of sobriety.

2. Defensive Structure. In this regard, we support the existing
defensive structure of the alcoholic in the service of sobriety.
Statements by the client that he cannot deal with his children,
spouse and other problem areas are supported by the counselor in
the respect that this helps him focus on sobriety to the exclusion
of working on all life problem areas simultaneously. Defenses are
seen as positive in that the use of them is strengthened by the
counselor to help the alcoholic simplify his life and postpone
dealing with other anxiety laden areas until a later point in
treatment. It is obvious that we are particularly sensitive to
the alcoholic's anxiety level. We do not wish to raise anxiety
around other life areas other than sobriety because we feel that
by doing so we may be indirectly setting the stage for a relapse.
This is significant departure from treatment provided in many
Mental Health clinics.

3. Obsessions. Rather than attempting to reverse the alcoholic's
obsessional fascination with the drug, we utilize this obsession
in the service of maintaining sobriety. The alcoholic is encouraged to attend as many AA meetings a day or week as he feels comfortable with; to work as a volunteer in alcohol treatment settings; to read and talk to others in the field as much as is necessary. Rather than attempting to restructure the defensive system
to eliminate this obsessional characteristic, it is encouraged and
utilized to learn about alcohol and alcoholism in the service of
sobriety.

4. Confrontation. In general, the group structure for alcohol
therapy is of a supportive nature. When confrontation techniques
are used, it is only around drinking episodes. When the alcoholic
denies the impact of alcoholism on his functioning or minimizes his
involvement with the drug, the counselor may directly or indirectly
encourage the group to confront him regarding the reality of his
drinking behavior. In contrast, other life areas are not confronted. For example, the alcoholic may be projecting or rationalizing
away problems in his marriage or work situation. These are passed

over by the counselor and not confronted since we do not want to raise anxiety around these areas that should be deferred for solution to a later time in treatment.

5. Group Modality. It is our experience that alcoholics exhibit greater improvement in treatment in group as opposed to individual therapy. That is not to say that individual work is not appropriate, but we feel that it must be co-existent with the group. Manipulation and denial can quickly be dealt with in the group since many group members had in the past utilized these defenses. In addition, the identification of mutual experiences helps to alleviate the guilt and remorse the alcoholic secretly harbors about his past behavior.

6. & 7. Pre-treatment Motivational Groups and Education. Prior to entrance into a closed group therapy session, alcoholics at our facility attend a five session education/discussion series on alcohol and alcoholism. This serves several functions: it begins to prepare the alcoholic for being in a group situation and in a casual manner begins to equip him with the skills needed for working in group. The education lectures on alcohol and alcoholism are important, prior to therapy, in order that certain issues regarding the illness be clearly examined and processed prior to therapy in order that they not be the subject of great controversy when group begins. For example, the definition of an "alcoholic"; the progressive nature of the illness and other basic issues regarding the illness concept are dealt with during this five session pre-treatment motivational lecture series. Hence, clients have a common base of information and knowledge regarding these issues prior to beginning of their regular therapy sessions.

8. Structured Groups. We believe that group therapy, once begun, should be structured in a way that it is a living experience on how to stay sober. With this objective, we have then eliminated insight therapy as a consideration and "rap" groups. They tend to be unstructured and open-ended and are counter-productive in helping the alcoholic achieve sobriety. We believe the alcoholic in early sobriety requires a structure with discipline and needs to learn how to structure his life in a coherent manner. The group therapy is based on this principle and each session is pre-planned with a format and homework assignments. Each session is related to the previous and future ones and is structured in such a way that each group member is drawn into the discussion process.

9. Early Detection System. One of the major focuses of our group therapy is the teaching of an early detection system for alcoholics so that they may learn those signs and signals both in the environment and within themselves that precede drinking episodes. This enables the therapist to help the client learn about those feeling states which are troublesome for the client and which lead to increased anxiety and tension. Learning takes place regarding how to

deal with these states once they are identified so that they can be coped with in a way that does not eventually lead to the use of alcohol. Anger and depression are commonly reported as internal feeling states which often precede drinking episodes. We teach the alcoholic how to detect the early onset of these states and to take swift measures to cope with them before they overwhelm him. Being overtired, hungry or overworked are also commonly reported as states which precede drinking episodes and the importance of proper rest and diet are stressed.

The other central concept in the early detection system is self-esteem. Lowered self-esteem is routinely reported as pre-condition for a drinking episode and we stress the importance of the alcoholic identifying the slippage in his self-esteem and the swift performance of responsible acts which will elevate it. We have found that dwelling on etiological factors from the past, which are presumed to have led to low self-esteem, is counter-productive. Instances in the "here and now" which are related to lowered self-esteem are only dealt with and specific ways of quickly elevating it by responsible behavior taught. The relationship of this to sobriety is that with techniques at hand for raising self-esteem and identifying uncomfortable feeling states the alcoholic then has an essential tool to use to cope with these states without the use of alcohol.

I have presented here a brief sketch of the philosophy of early sobriety treatment. I strongly believe that this is an identifiable treatment modality of fairly short duration but of high relevance in assisting alcoholics achieve the initial stages of sobriety. It is only some months or perhaps years after sobriety is well in hand that more traditional modalities are appropriate. It is only then that questions of etiology and a more broadly based evaluation of the alcoholic's entire needs can be undertaken.

CONTROL OF ALCOHOL ABUSE BY USE OF THE
POCKET BREATHALYZER: A TECHNOLOGICAL
ADVANCE IN ALCOHOL TREATMENT

Forest S. Tennant, Jr., M.D., Dr. P.H.
James E. Ruckle, B.A., M.P.A.
Judy S. Jackson, R.N.
Claude R. LaBrosse, B.A., M.S.

Community Health Projects, Inc.
West Covina, California 91790

ABSTRACT - SUMMARY

A major reason for the relatively poor record of outpatient
alcohol treatment has been a lack of a cost-effective means to monitor alcohol use, abuse, and relapse. While drug abuse can be
monitored by rapid-screen urinalysis for a cost of about $3.00 per
test, a breath, blood, or urine alcohol screen costs at least $12-
$15 which is too expensive for routine clinical use. A pocket-size
breathalyzer has recently been developed which is commercially
available and very accurate. It can analyze alcohol content of
breath in about one minute at a cost of less than 10¢-15¢ per test.
This new technological advance has been found by us to have great
use in the treatment of alcohol abuse. We have found it useful in
the following clinical situations:

1. Ambulatory treatment of alcoholics;
2. Long-term monitoring of persons arrested for drunk driving
3. Management of acutely intoxicated persons;
4. Detection of occult alcohol abuse in methadone maintenance
    patients.

In particular, the use of the pocket breathalyzer in our outpatient
alcohol treatment program has resulted in longer patient retention
and enhancement of the therapeutic process.

INTRODUCTION

Alcohol abuse treatment has been hindered by lack of a cost-
effective technology to monitor alcohol consumption in persons who

seek treatment. In contrast, many drugs of abuse can be rapidly and inexpensively detected in the urine, and this technological capability has helped promulgate drug treatment efforts and upgrade the effectiveness of treatment.

During the past year we have attempted to utilize a portable, pocket-size breathalyzer in a variety of alcohol treatment situations. This instrument can quantitate breath alcohol in less than three minutes for a cost of approximately $.10-.15 per test. The clinical utility of this instrument has been so impressive that some of our preliminary clinical results and observations are presented.

BACKGROUND

In an attempt to find a portable breathalyzer that was cost-effective for clinical work, we contacted law enforcement agencies and clinical laboratories in Los Angeles, California in 1975 who advised us on various available methods. It was learned that a standard alcohol breath test which is admissable as court evidence costs $30 to $50 per test and a blood alcohol determination costs $10 to $18. One laboratory conducted a urine alcohol assay for $12. In contrast, the cost of a qualitative urine assay to simultaneously detect morphine, amphetamines, barbiturates, methadone, codeine, and propoxyphene was approximately $3.25. During this inquiry it was learned that some Los Angeles County law enforcement agencies were exploring the use of portable devices for pre-arrest alcohol screening. One of these devices was the pocket breathalyzer (Alcolmeter[R]) manufactured by Lion Laboratories of England.

The cost of the device is approximately $250, and it can conduct about 3,000 breath tests. After this the breathalyzer must be rebuilt at a cost of around $50.

METHODS

Between November 1, 1975 and February 29, 1976 (4 months) we have used the pocket breathalyzer on 61 patients in a variety of clinical situations which are described below. The breathalyzer is used by all clinical personnel and test results are recorded on an "Alcohol Monitoring Form" which is kept in the patient's chart. Recently we have begun to compare its readings with blood alcohol determination. Although our numbers of cases are small, they show a fairly close correlation. Most importantly, all the tests which showed greater than zero by breath showed greater than zero by blood.

MONITORING ALCOHOL ABUSERS IN OUT-PATIENT TREATMENT

Community Health Projects, Inc. has an outpatient alcohol treatment program. Patients attend the clinic one or two times per week at which time they participate in individual, group, or family counseling. Some patients concomitantly attend Alcoholics Anonymous or take Antabuse. About half are volunteers and about one-half are mandatorily referred by the Courts or the Calif. Dept. of Motor Vehicles. Between Nov. 1, 1975 and Feb. 29, 1976 thirty (30) new patients have been admitted to the program and breath-tested with the pocket breathalyzer during each visit.

During the initial interview they are informed that they will be breath-tested at each visit, and patients have accepted this procedure very willingly.

During this period 246 breath bests have been done, and 14 (5.7%) have shown alcohol. Eight (8) of the 30 (26.7%) alcohol patients have demonstrated alcohol on their breath at least once which indicates that alcohol abusers did not usually attend the clinic following recent alcohol consumption.

We have had three major positive outcomes of monitoring patients in outpatient alcohol treatment:

1. Greater retention in treatment. Volunteers who attended our clinic prior to the use of the breathalyzer were retained on the average for less than three visits. Following institution of the breathalyzer our retention rate has markedly increased.

2. A better therapeutic relationship between staff and patient. All counselors have expressed the opinion that a negative breath test prior to a counseling session enhances dialogue about issues other than whether the patient is still drinking.

3. Increased credibility with the Courts and California Dept. of Motor Vehicles. Community Health Projects, Inc. is similar to many alcohol programs in that it has a diversion program for intoxicated drivers. We have found that the courts and the Calif. Dept. of Motor Vehicles has been most appreciative and respectful of the practice of monitoring their clients with the breathalyzer.

INITIATION OF DISULFIRAM (ANTABUSE^R)

Since disulfiram (Antabuse^R) can only be initiated when alcohol is not systemically present in the patient, the pocket breathalyzer helps determine the safety of administering the drug. Our clinic policy is to begin Antabuse^R on an outpatient basis when:

1. The patient gives no history of alcohol consumption for at least 12 hours;

2. There is no alcohol detected on the breath by breathalyzer.

We have administered an initial dose of Antabuse^R to 15 patients using this procedure, and we have observed no adverse reactions.

MANAGEMENT OF ACUTE ALCOHOL DETOXIFICATION

When an alcohol-intoxicated patient attends a medical facility, the staff must under ordinary circumstances rely solely on clinical judgment as to when it is safe to release the patient to return home. The pocket breathalyzer has proved to be a great adjunct in the management of our acutely intoxicated patients. In a few cases we have retained intoxicated patients in the clinic until their breath registered zero. In patients who have had breath readings of .15 or higher we have not administered any psychoactive drug, and we have arranged for someone other than the patient to drive the patient home.

DETECTION OF OCCULT ALCOHOLISM IN METHADONE PATIENTS

The problem of alcohol abuse among methadone patients is well recognized.[1] Between Nov. 1, 1975 and Feb. 29, 1975 (4 months) we used the pocket breathalyzer to help detect occult alcohol abuse in 31 methadone maintenance patients. On Wednesday of each week the patients were breath-tested. Breath-testing was also done whenever a patient appeared sedated. Out of 219 breath tests, 43 (19.6%) were found to contain alcohol. Six of the 31 (19.4%) patients demonstrated repeated, positive alcohol breath tests and daily alcohol abuse was confirmed in all of these patients by history after the patient was confronted with the results of the breath tests.

Once alcohol abuse was detected in these patients, all consented to begin Antabuse^R and/or be breath-tested daily and be counseled about their problem. Patients have accepted this practice very well and it appears to have had the effect of essentially eliminating daily alcohol abuse in our patients.

DISCUSSION

The use of the pocket breathalyzer is inexpensive and it has many clinical uses.

We are only aware of one other study in which a portable breathalyzer was used for clinical purposes. Barton, Bennett, and Clarke[2] found in an unreported trial with methadone maintenance patients at the Addiction Research Corporation in Brooklyn, N.Y. that 174 of 329 (53%) breath test opportunities showed no alcohol. We found that 176 of 219 (80.4%) breath tests showed no alcohol which indicates that alcohol abuse is apparently very high among methadone maintenance patients. The portable breathalyzer used in the Brooklyn study was one produced by Borg-Warner and called A.L.E.R.T. (Alcohol Level Evaluation Road Tester) which sells for approximately $525, and which is about twice the size of the pocket breathalyzer.

Since an outpatient alcohol patient may only be breath tested once or twice per week, he/she can obviously drink between tests and not be detected. Even though this probably occurs in some cases, physiologic, alcohol dependence appears to be prevented by once or twice per week monitoring. A person who is physiologically dependent upon alcohol must drink alcohol several times per day so this condition can be detected and prevented by the pocket breathalyzer. Overall the pocket breathalyzer is a significant technological advance in alcohol treatment and prevention.

REFERENCES

1. Liebson I, Bigelow G, Flamer R: Alcoholism Among Methadone Patients: A Specific Treatment Method. *Am J. Psychiatry* 130:483-483, 1974.

2. Barton FE, Bennett M J, Clarke W M: Approaching Alcohol Problems in a Methadone Maintenance Program. Unpublished. Addiction Research and Treatment Corporation, Brooklyn, N.Y.

DRUGS AND ALCOHOL

TREATMENT OF DRUG ADDICTION AND ALCOHOLISM
IN THE SAME FACILITY: EXPERIENCE AND ISSUES

Joseph Mayer, Ph.D.
David C. Lewis, M.D.
Norman E. Zinberg, M.D.

Washingtonian Center for Addictions
41 Morton Street
Boston, Massachusetts

I.   Background

Several arguments have been cited for combining treatment
of alcoholics and drug abusers. Among these are the theoretical
and dynamic unity of addiction (Gerard, 1955), the enhancement
of research (Popham et. al. 1968), the increase in polydrug abuse
(Freed, 1973) and cross tolerance (Valliant, 1966) among addicting
substances. In opposition is the argument (Pittman, 1967) that
from a sociological perspective, addiction to alcohol and opiates
involves legal, cultural, lifestyle, racial and age differences,
and are therefore qualitatively and quantitatively different and
should be kept separate.

Turning specifically to treatment, some (Ottenberg, 1971)
recommend combining treatment and others (Neumann, and Tamerin,
1971) tend to oppose. Arguments supporting combined treatment
emphasize the "human" similarities between patients while arguments supporting separate treatment cite cultural and age differences between the groups. Discussion of these issues has
centered more on whether combined treatment can work than on the
more significant issue of whether it will work more or less effectively than separate treatment.

II.   Washingtonian Center for Addictions

The Washingtonian Center for Addictions is a private,
voluntary, non-profit, hospital in Boston, Massachusetts, specializing in the treatment of drug abuse and alcoholism. The Center
was established in 1857 and treated primarily alcoholics from
then until 1968, when treatment of a larger number of drug addicts
was initiated. From 1968 to 1976, more than 9,000 patients have
been treated, approximately 60% of these addicted to alcohol and
40% to other drugs. Of the 40% addicted to drugs other than

889

alcohol, approximately 30% are addicted primarily to opiates and 10% to a variety of other drugs.

A therapeutic community treatment modality, combining drug and alcohol patients, was used and abandoned since drug abuse patients tended to dominate the therapeutic environment and the alcoholic patients chose to leave rather than "fight." At other periods combined and separate wards, combined and separate group therapy and combined and separate staffing patterns have been established.

For the past several years the Center has conducted a multi-modality treatment program which includes two inpatient services and a number of outpatient programs. The Treatment and Evaluation Service is a 2 to 4 week inpatient program for evaluation and diagnosis, detoxification, medical services and post-hospital planning, with drug and alcohol patients on separate wards on the same floor. Treatment programs are separate while dining and recreational facilities are combined. Some staff members work with both groups of patients while others work with only one patient group.

The Extended Inpatient Service is an 8 to 10 week, abstinence, inpatient rehabilitation program offering a sheltered workshop, and educational and vocational services. Drug and alcohol patients are both housed together with the same dining and recreational facilities and are treated by the same staff.

The Outpatient Service includes individual, group and family therapy, methadone maintenance treatment, an Antabuse clinic, an alcoholism drop-in clinic, and naltrexone treatment. Treatment programs have generally separate staffs although senior supervising staff often serve more than one program.

In summary, at the Washingtonian Center alcoholics and drug addicts are treated in the same facility, usually in separate treatment programs, with combined housing, dining and recreational facilities creating a considerable amount of social contact and are sometimes, but not always, treated by the same staff.

III. Staff and Training

The Center inservice training program covers alcoholism and drug addiction, although staff working in particular programs which treat one or the other group receive training primarily for their specialization, unanimously desire training in both drug addiction and alcoholism.

One of the striking advantages of treating both groups of patients in the same facility is the enhancement of training. Diagnostic and treatment skills are sharpened since staff see many types of addiction. This leads them to view addiction from many perspectives, since they see different kinds of treatment for different types of patients and they more clearly comprehend both a chronic disease model of the addictions and the need for a multiplicity of treatments. The diagnosis and treatment of all kinds of poly-drug abuse is, of course, more easily understood and carried out.

Many new staff members begin believing that they can only work comfortably with one or another group of patients. As they are trained and gain competence, many find that their original interest may not hold up and that they prefer working with a different goup of patients. A minority of clinical staff end up working equally well with both groups. However, there are important differences between staff members. Staff who can tolerate passivity comfortably, sympathize easily and have the energy to motivate patients, do better with alcoholics. Staff who can tolerate overt anger directed toward them, can comfortably set limits, avoid being manipulated and manage their own desire to retaliate, do better with drug abusers. Further, we find that recovered alcoholics and recovered drug addicts tend to work most effectively with their own group, although, generally speaking, recovered alcoholics function more effectively than recovered drug addicts. Recovered alcoholics tend to take more personal responsibility for their alcoholism rather than to blame the drug, alcohol; recovered drug addicts, on the other hand, tend to blame the heroin, feeling that no one can go near drugs without becoming addicted, thus making them more rigid with patients and at odds with other staff.

Contact with both groups of patients generally decreases staff biases. Staff members are more able to see similarities as well as differences in these groups of patients, thus minimizing their original, often prejudiced, view of one or the other group and increasing their capacity for empathy.

IV. Treatment and Rehabilitation

Whereas the drug addict tends to turn passive into active, the alcoholic tends to turn active into passive. These differences lead to different styles of ward behavior, interpersonal behavior and problems in living. One advantage of the social contact in simultaneous treatment is that each group observes that which is so terrifying for them, namely the behavior of the other group. They begin to see that differences from their own behavior need not be so frightening. However, these same characteristic differences lead to discomfort for both groups in combined group therapy, and it is a time consuming therapeutic task to work through this discomfort in a short period. Therefore, group therapy, which we view as the therapy of choice in most instances, is separate for both groups.

Turning to overall rehabilitation, the groups again exhibit differences. The alcoholic requires rehabilitation, since usually he has a previous work history and vocational skills. Many drug addicts, on the other hand, have worked only a minimal amount of time, if at all, and need to learn how to work before they can develop more specific skills.

Finally, simultaneous treatment of both groups enhances the concept, as well as the reality, of a multi-modality treatment system and continuity of care. Since a variety of treatment approaches are used for each group, the multimodality concept is made manifestly clear to staff and patients. In a word, they see that no single treatment approach is appropriate for all patients. Continuity of care for all patients, especially for poly drug abuse patients, also is made easier since abuse of any mind altering substance is treated at the Center. If a patient receiving maintenance methadone abuses alcohol, for example, he does not become "different" and get referred to another treatment setting.

V.   Summary

This paper has briefly described eight years of experience in the simultaneous treatment of drug abusers and alcoholics in the same facility, usually in separate treatment programs but with considerable social contact between the groups. This work indicates that training is enhanced by simultaneous treatment, staff tends to work more effectively with one or the other group, most treatment programs are more effective when kept separate, treatment of poly drug abuse is enhanced in this setting and continuity of care is made easier and more effective.

References

Freed, E.X. (1973), Drug abuse by alcoholics. Int. J. Addict. 8: 461-473.

Gerard, D.L. (1955). Intoxication and addiction. Psychistric observations in alcoholism and opiate drug addiction. Quart. J. Stud. Alc. 16: 681-699.

Neumann, C.P. and Tamerin, J.S. (1971). The treatment of adult alcoholics and teenage drug addicts in one hospital; a comparison and critical appraisal of factors related to outcome. Quart J. Stud. Alc. 32: 82-93.

Ottenberg, D.J. (1975). Combined treatment of alcoholics and drug addicts: a progress report from Eagleville. Contemp. Drug Prob. Spring, 1975: 1-21.

Pittman, D.J. (1967). The rush to combine: sociological dis-
similarities of alcoholism and drug abuse. Brit. J. Addict. 62:
337-343.

Popham, R.E., DeLint, J.E. and Schmidt, W. (1968). Some comments
on Pittman's "rush to combine." Brit. J. Addict. 63: 25-27.

Valliant, G.E. (1966). A twelve year follow-up of New York
narcotic addicts: IV. Some characteristics and determinants of
abstinence. Amer. J. Psychiat. 123: 573-585.

EXAMINING THE DRUG/ALCOHOL/PSYCHIATRY INTERFACE

Gerald J. McKenna, M.D.

Instructor in Psychiatry,
Harvard Medical School at the Cambridge Hospital
Associate Director, Drug Problems Resource Center

Over the past fifteen years there has been a proliferation of treatment programs to respond to the problems of alcohol and drug dependence. Individuals with alcohol or drug dependence were formerly treated in psychiatric hospitals, general hospitals, or were sent to jail. As drug and alcohol use has become more common, there has resulted an increased confusion among persons seeking treatment and among the staffs of specialized units as to which treatment service is applicable for which individual. This paper will explore some aspects of the drug/alcohol/psychiatry interface, especially as these three areas merge on a Multiple Substance Abuse Unit.

Between 1970 and 1972, a new pattern of drug use, called polydrug abuse, was observed and there were efforts to delineate the nature and scope of this new problem (1). Because much of the polydrug problem involved the use of short-acting barbiturates and other sedative hypnotic drugs special units were established for detoxification and treatment. The National Polydrug Study pointed out significant differences between the populations of polydrug users and heroin users. As a group, it was shown that there was more psychopathology among the polydrug users, and they tended to do poorly in the "concept" style residential treatment centers, where confrontation was the accepted mode or group interaction (2). In our own program, we agree with this observation of increased psychopathology among polydrug users, and have collected new data which we feel support it.

In February, 1975 we opened a 14 bed in-patient Multiple Substance Abuse Unit at Central Hospital in Somerville, Massachusetts, under the auspices of a National Institute on Drug Abuse Demonstration Grant. The purposes of this unit were to provide detoxification and treatment for individuals dependent on sedative-hypnotic drugs, to further define patterns of multiple substance use, and to compare two treatment modalities: Thresholds, a modality which is cognitive in origin and curricular in format, and Multimodality, an approach primarily psychological and based on an interactive process between counselor and client to achieve its aims. These treatment methods are quite different and not in the scope of this paper to explore except to present a minimum background of our unit.

As patients were admitted, we noticed that the life problems presented were not uniform and that some of the patients had been "through the system". That is, they had at various times been treated in a psychiatric in-patient unit, an alcohol treatment unit, and other drug treatment facilities. While each of the other units had some awareness of the multifaceted nature of the individual's problems, they often ignored those aspects felt to be inappropriate for their particular setting, and the patient, in the end, became confused.

Figure I reviews the first 97 patients admitted to the Multiple Substance Abuse Unit. Eighteen percent (N19) had previously received treatment for alcohol problems, 27% (N20) had previously been detoxified from drugs and/or alcohol, 33% (N32) had been in other drug treatment programs. Thirty-five percent (out of a sample of 94, N37) had previous in-patient psychiatric hospitalization. With this wide mixture of problems and persons with varied previous treatment histories, we began to view the Multiple Substance Abuse Unit as a true drug/alcohol/psychiatry interface. We compared patients in our unit with psychiatric in-patients, psychiatric out-patients, and a community control group using the Psychiatric Status Schedule of Spitzer & Endicott. This instrument is administered to all patients once they are stabilized on the unit (as well as at the end of a 30 day stay and at intervals during the follow-up phase of treatment).

Figure II shows the mean scores on the Psychiatric Status Schedule of the first 56 patients admitted. This figure also shows themean scores of psychiatric in-patients (N=770), psychiatric out-patients (N=55) and an urban community sample (N=130). The mean scores for psychiatric in-patients have been standardized and arbitrarily set at 50 so that other groups can be easily compared. In examining the scales for persons entering out unit, we can see that in nearly every category they are at or above those for hospitalized psychiatric patients with the exception of denial of illness. In the categories of anti-social impulses, impulse-control disturbance and drug/alcohol use, they are markedly higher than the mean. The peak for drug/alcohol use is obvious since that represents the presenting complaint. The other two peaks are more complicated. It could be argued that anti-social impulses and impulse control disturbances are typical in individuals with character and behavior disorders. But then, one would also have to postulate that elevations of the other scales in the PSS are also typical in character and behavioral disorders. It could also be argued that, at the time one enters a drug treatment program one's life is so disorganized that all scales would be elevated. We think, though, that it is striking that most of the scales correspond to those of hospitalized psychiatric patients and believe this reflects the high degree of psychopathology to be found in the multiple substance abuse group. It is possible that the peaks for anti-social impulses and impulsive control disturbances are secondary phenomena. The manipulations and behaviors necessary to maintain an illegal drug habit would foster anti-social behavior. Impulsive behavior, furthermore, is very common as a result of intoxication with sedative-hypnotic drugs, whether alcohol, barbiturates, minor tranquilizers, or non-barbiturate sedatives.

One obvious problem in evaluating this data is the difficulty in determining character or ego traits which precede drug involvement. One cannot be sure if evidence of psychopathology preexisted or was consequent to involvement with drugs. Unfortunately, good longitudinal studies are lacking to help us with this problem.

A. Drug Dependence: Cause or Result

We believe in a multi-etiological basis for drug use and drug dependence. The notion that drug dependence is solely a result of character pathology or is, in itself, a character disorder is to ignore the myriad of other reasons why people use and become dependent on drugs. In our treatment program, comprising an in-patient multiple substance abuse unit and an out-patient narcotics treatment program, we have found individuals whose use of drugs is aimed at relief of anxiety, depression and symptoms of major psychoses (3, 4, 5, 6). We have also seen significant character pathology in both the narcotics and polydrug populations, but it has been as a result of our larger clinical experience that we reject any single etiology for drug dependence.

In our treatment approach, we view substance use as one aspect of a person's life and do not limit our treatment solely to issues of drug abuse. We attempt to help people understand the role that drug use plays in their lives as a homeostatic mechanism, a means of coping with stress, as self-treatment for a variety of emotional problems, or as supporting some of their primary ego mechanisms of defense. We do not foster the belief that cessation of drug use, per se, will solve some or all of their problems in adjusting to a complex world. In this sense, detoxification and control of drug use becomes one preliminary step in understanding the problems they face and in seeking more adaptive solutions. Attention is paid in causes of depression or anxiety. If problems of psychosis are identified, they are treated with appropriate medication; severe depressions may be treated with tricyclic antidepressants. We have hesitated to use the anti-anxiety medications because of their similarity to the drugs on which people have often found themselves dependent. The entire treatment process is aimed at helping the individuals regain control of their lives.

B. Need for Comprehensive Training

In a multiple substance abuse program where individuals present problems which cross the drug/alcohol/psychiatry interface, there is a need for more comprehensive training of counselors than we previously envisioned. Ideally, staff would receive training in the physiological and psychological problems associated with alcohol and drug use, methods of diagnosing and treating various psychiatric disorders, methods for dealing with various behavior disturbances. One wonders if counselors can be adequately trained in all these areas and whether individuals with such varied problems can be treated on a single unit. The alternative to such an attempt, however, is the fragmentation of services and the rotation of patients to psychiatric, alcohol treatment and drug treatment facilities. The latter solution, we feel, is least satisfactory for all concerned. We have attempted, therefore, to provide as broad a training base as possible for our staff. This includes an intensive orientation phase and weekly case conferences, teaching seminars, and individual supervision. We do refer patients with psychiatric problems when we feel unable to provide a safe environment for them -- i.e., acutely suicidal individuals. While many difficulties remain, most staff have developed to where they are reasonably comfortable in dealing with problems of depression, psychosis, alcoholism as well as problems associated with drug use per se.

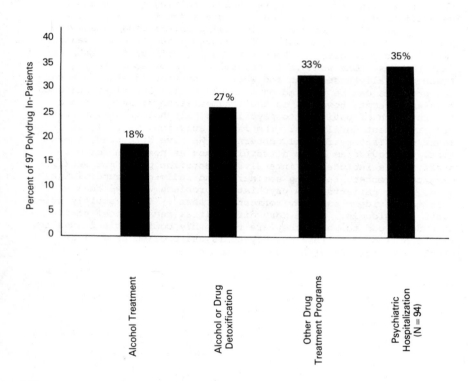

Figure I. Percentage of Polydrug In-Patients Who Have Previously
Received Various Types of Treatment

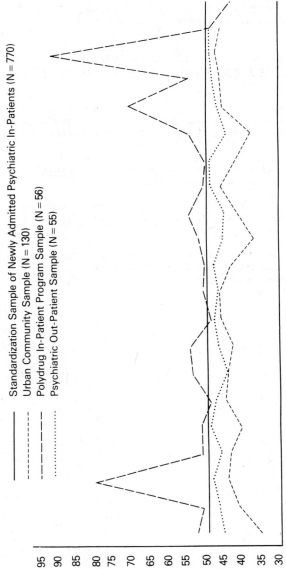

Figure II

REFERENCES

1. McKenna, G.J., Fisch, A., Levine, M., Patch, V., & Raynes, A.:
The Use of Methadone as a Psychotropic Agent, Proceedings of the
5th National Methadone Treatment Conference, Washington, D.C.,
March, 1973.

2. Benvenuto, J., & Bourne, P.G., "The Federal Polydrug Abuse
Project: Vital Report", J. of Psychedelic Drugs, April-June, 1975,
pp. 115-120.

3. McKenna, G.J., Fisch, A., Levine, M., Patch, V. & Raynes, A.:
Problems of Mixed Addictions on a Detoxification Unit, Proceedings
of the 5th National Methadone Treatment Conference, Washington, D.
C., March, 1973.

4. Wishnie, H., Opioid Addiction: A Masked Depression, in Masked
Depression, S. Lesse, Ed. J. Aronson, New York, 1974.

5. Khantzian, E.J., Mack, J., et al., "Heroin Use As An Attempt
to Cope: Clinical Observations", Am. J. Psychiatry, Vol. 131,
February, 1974.

6. Wurmser, L., Methadone and the Craving for Narcotics: Observation of Patients on Methadone Maintenance in Psychotherapy, Proceedings of the Fourth Annual Methadone Conference, pp. 525-528,
San Francisco, 1972.

MANAGEMENT PROBLEMS IN DRUG AND
ALCOHOL TREATMENT AND PREVENTION SYSTEMS

John E. Riggan
Coordinating Office for
Drug and Alcohol Abuse Programs
Philadelphia, Pennsylvania

I. INTRODUCTION

Drug and Alcohol Treatment and Prevention Systems arrived relatively late to public health and human service fields. Although
there have been treatment responses developed over a longer period
of time, attempts to approach substance abuse problems systematically at federal, state and local levels are new and, therefore,
experience many of the developmental problems of any new undertaking.

However, there are unique factors which make these new systems even more problematical than what might be expected. These
factors have to do with the nature of the problem itself and the
history of the response to the substance abuse problem. It will be
useful to detail these factors before discussing some current
management issues. Although perceived primarily as a large and
difficult public health problem, chemical substance abuse is also
categorized as belonging to a variety of other fields: law enforcement, corrections, judicial, human services, youth, education,
welfare, urban renewal, etc. Depending on the orientation, substance abusers could be sick people, socially deprived reflecting
their environment, disabled needing an opportunity, ignorant and
misguided, or willful law breakers. This has lead to a wide variety of approaches, largely led by very dedicated people who all
had to possess one common trait in order to persevere and survive.
That trait was total belief in their particular approach to this
problem. Hence, schools of philosophy were developed around the
treatment of drug addicts and particularly the heroin addict.
Respected professionals became strong advocates for a particular
approach and were seen to be competitive with other professionals
advocating other approaches. This led to strong competition for
limited funds then available and the general mistrust of each
other's approaches. Doctrinaire disputes over the best therapeutic
approach -- confrontive versus supportive versus behavior modification, and later on between all of these groups and the chemotherapeutic approach utilizing methadone in an outpatient treatment setting.

This varied and competitive environment also led eventually to other major questions concerning purpose. Debates were undertaken on the subject of cure rates, the hope for permanent solution to the addiction problem. Arguments concerning the effect of treatment on reducing crime and particularly the issue of recidivism, whether addicts in treatment did in fact return to the streets to continue in a life of crime; control theories questioning whether a major purpose of treatment should not be to maintain the addict rather than seek a drug-free state. These debates concerning the long range purpose of addiction treatment involved many approaches. However, these early programs accomplished much by furthering the state of the art and focusing national attention on effective treatment responses to addiction problems which c caught the public imagination. Their efforts led to a realization by the public and government of the seriousness of the problem and that a wider ranging treatment and prevention response was needed.

More recently, serious moves have been made towards accreditation and licensing of drug and alcohol treatment programs and certification of treatment personnel. The long range funding of these programs has also become a major concern as third party mechanisms including Medical Assistance and insurance coverages are explored.

These developments have occured over a relatively short period of time. They have led to numerous management problems which will be discussed as issues in the balance of this paper.

II. MANAGEMENT ISSUES

These developments: New treatment methodologies, rapid expansion, new agencies -- occurring over a short period of time and dealing with a highly complex, chronic public health problem have raised a number of issues in managing Drug and Alcohol Prevention Systems.

A. Issues Around Planning

In a sense, almost every function of a human service agency should be a function of planning: funding, evaluation, service delivery, research, etc. Yet with regard to medium to long range planning (2-5 years), there is very little effort being extended at any level. Everyone is concerned with the question of funding for the current fiscal year and, possibly, the one just following. This leads to a myopic view. Further, planning methodologies and approaches are missing. The absence of this planning framework leads to a number of problems:

1. - information and data currently available is not fully utilized.
2. - demands for new data are not clearly articulated and structured.
3. - planning activities are too centralized while service delivery
   is de-centralized.
4. - major demographic trends are not properly taken into account.
5. - topical environmental factors such as current economic conditions, changes in laws (decriminalization) are not anticipated.

There are also specific questions for planners to deal with:

a. Scope of the Problem

Substance use and abuse is a fact of American life. How much
of a problem is it? Additional information is needed regarding incidence and prevalence of chemical substance use.

There is growing support to decriminalize public drunkeness
and simple possession and use of marijuana. This follows the
"victimless crime" trend seen in no-fault automobile insurance legislation. These are important trends but must be studied for their
impact on the treatment system in the future. As the emphasis is
placed increasingly on treating sick people, the question of how
much treatment can society afford arises. For example, it is
roughly estimated there are over 155,000 alcohol imparied persons
in Philadelphia. There are less than 4% of that number in a badly
overfilled treatment system. This system is currently almost totally subsidized by public monies. It is apparent that there is a
limit (we may have already reached it) to funds available from the
public sector. Therefore, the importance of third party sources
are paramount to expanding the treatment system. This immediately
raises questions of mandatory or voluntary health insurance coverage, National Health Insurance plans, accreditation of treatment
facilities, and certification of treatment personnel as well as the
role of proprietary efforts. It is also apparent and now recognized that government and society will be involved in the drug
treatment business for the foreseeable future. There is no "corner"
to turn in dealing with a chronic, disabling health and social
problem. This awareness is new at the Federal level and only recently articulated in a Domestic Council White Paper. It, hopefully, will assist in dealing with the skeptics who have insisted
that any effort which leads to results short of a "cure" (defined
as a state of living which is drug free, law abiding and productive, i.e., employed) is obviously a failure. Few, if any, medical
or social-based programs could tolerate the "cure-or-fail" standard.

b. Primary Prevention Strategies

Everyone wants to believe in preventive approaches to public
health problems. The fact is that prevention is given a large
amount of lip service and a small amount of the budget. It is not
hard to understand why this is so. The practical reasons are that
the problem is presented to us and demanding a response -- treat
the individual -- and this generally requires all available time
and resources. There are other reasons: prevention efforts tend
to bog down and grow inward looking; or they quietly slip into early intervention and referral roles; or they lose themselves in
struggling with global causative factors (urban blight, illiteracy,
poverty, crime, gangs, etc.); or they become humanitarian and general in theme and lose any sense of impact. There are a number of
public administrators who flatly do not believe in prevention. A
skeptical position is not merited given the newness and promise of
some of these efforts. However, a number of planning issues are
raised as this effort continues:
  - The issue of impact - how to impact on a school system,
    and the community? What level of effort is needed? At
    what cost? How to measure the results - changed atti-
    tudes? Improved behavior indicators?
  - The issue of coordinated prevention activities - Primary
    prevention focuses on an "at-risk" population prior to
    the occurrence of a problem. These populations, pre-
    sumably, are shared with public health, mental health,
    criminal justice, welfare, youth and recreation agencies,
    and essentially the entire human service delivery system.

If prevention strategies can be agreed upon, then support for
them must come from a variety of interested agencies.

B. Evaluation Issues

Considerable emphasis has been placed increasingly on evaluation and data systems at all levels of government. Management
information systems, client data systems, fiscal management, program performance audits, case management, client tracking, cost
effectiveness studies, systems and unique evaluations are expressions with which every administrator must become familiar. These
innovations are all designed to render program activities more
accountable and to improve services and support systems in general.
However, there are serious issues raised concerning the desirability and practicality of some of these innovations as applied to
the drug and alcohol treatment system.

1. CONFIDENTIALITY
Rising above all other issues is the legal requirement of
Federal (and often State laws) to safeguard the rights of clients
in treatment by treating all client related and identifiable information as confidential. The importance and need for these legal

904

safeguards are obvious. However, efforts to monitor or evaluate program performance are severely hampered when client files and records are not available. In Pennsylvania under state law, this regulation applies to government officials in a need-to-know situation even with clients' consent. The problem is even more evident when permission is sought to perform research using client data. This regulation is currently being debated in Pennsylvania and hopefully will be modified appropriately.

2. ADMINISTRATION NEEDS VS. CLINICAL NEEDS

   An increasingly common complaint from treatment service providers these days is the number of forms they are subjected to: client in-take forms, progress forms, medical assistance eligibility and billings forms, SRS forms, etc., etc. Treatment people are sure there is no satisfying the ever growing demands to feed the paper eating monster of government. The companion to each new form is meetins to explain, to discuss, to chastise and maybe to feed back information. The highly relevant claim is made that valuable time is taken away from treating clients -- leading inevitably to the charge that the "system" is only interested in maintaining clients in treatment, not in seeing them get well. The "system" does have a number of legitimate needs:

a. Basic client data is needed to provide information on the people receiving services: socioeconomic information; substances abused, patterns, and previous treatment efforts, progress reports and turnovers, etc.

b. Forms must be filled out to obtain third party payments for services rendered.

c. Then, specific evaluation and research efforts may necessitate the collection of still more data. Obviously, management, planning, funding and evaluation efforts all require substantial amounts of information.

   A key problem is the lack of systematic management of these multiple demands for information. Treatment programs vary in sophistication from store front to multi-million dollar operations, and even the larger programs have experienced rapid growth with the emphasis placed on improving their treatment methodologies and, only infrequently, their management capabilities. This situation must change and, to some degree, it has begun, e.g., computerized billings for medical assistance is a common practice now in Philadelphia programs. However, in programs where some functions are computerized, others are managed manually, creating a mish-mash. The longer range goal must be to establish information systems which meet legitimate data needs and, rather than interfering with the work of treatment staff, provide therapists with additional information and time saving tools to enhance their performance. This will require understanding and collaboration by administrators and clinical staff.

3.   CONTROL OF INFORMATION

There is always concern in any system with the uses of information. There is open suspicion, for example, when a management information system is imposed on an organization as to whether the information will enable authority and decision-making to become further centralized. Certainly, information systems can support such a trend and furthermore, may be used to measure performance (program and individual). Whether governmental management chooses to apply such information judgmentally and negatively, reducing options at other decision-making levels, or as positive tools to be used at all levels, is obviously an important question of providers of services.

There are several systems-wide applications of client centered information. One important application is tracking clients manadated for treatment by the criminal justice system in lieu of incarceration. A similar use is following clients arrested for drunk driving who, after a careful diagnostic evaluation, are mandated for outpatient alcoholism treatment. These systems must be accurate and up-to-date. Another application are case management systems which provide follow-through from intake to aftercare to facilitate a continuum of services for a given client.

DRUG AND ALCOHOL REFERRALS FROM THE GENERAL
HOSPITAL I: A MULTI-HOSPITAL PROGRAM

Marc Galanter, M.D.

Department of Psychiatry
Albert Einstein College of Medicine
Bronx, New York

Brendan Sexton

and

Anne Fried

Addiction Services Agency
New York, New York

In 1971, the Addiction Services Agency of the City of New
York initiated a Hospital Referral Program directed at facilitating
placement in long-term treatment for addicted and alcoholic patients
who were seen for acute care in general hospitals. This program
was expanded to include teams in eight hospitals, and in 1975 provided consultation on 10,907 patients of whom 3,525 were referred
to treatment. This first paper will describe the nature of the
overall program. Specifics of the program's operation in relation
to one particular hospital will be presented in the second paper.

Context of the Program

The importance of effective referral services for addictive
disorders has been met with increasing interest in recent years.
In relation to alcoholics, for example, organized programs for
referral into treatment have been established in both non-medical
and medical contexts. Pattison (1) reviewed the operation of one
such system, the Alcohol Information and Referral Centers, which
were promoted in the last two decades as major nonmedical resources
for referral. The AIR centers are staffed principally by recovered
alcoholics and refer to a variety of community resources. In his
study, though, Pattison found only 20% of AIR referrals were successful, despite the fact that 60% of the alcoholics did eventually
seek out a treatment facility. He pointed to the importance of
having access to personnel with clinical skills, and emphasized
that the referrals are actually the first stage of treatment.

The latter point indicates the important potential role for referral from the medical context, since so many alcoholic and drug-abusing patients come there for treatment of the sequelae of addictive disease. The prevalence of alcoholism on general medical wards, for example, is striking. Barchha and associates (2) reviewed three studies and reported one of their own, concluding that alcoholism is a problem for 20-25% of male and 6-7% of female patients on general hospital wards. McCusker and associates (3) reported 60% and 34% respectively, as comparable figures male and female patients in Harlem Hospital, reflecting the higher incidence of alcoholism in a poor, center-city minority group population. At Bronx Municipal, one of the affiliated hospitals in the Hospital Referral Program, we found 21% of the beds on general medical wards occupied by alcoholics. Whereas only 12% of the white population was alcoholic, the incidence was three times as high for the black and Hispanic population (32% and 43% respectively); 29% of the alcoholic patients were 65 or over.

Given these findings, the legitimacy of a massive attempt directed at assuring further treatment for alcoholic and addicted patients is quite clear. One might well wonder why this major medical problem has been so long neglected. Our second paper will deal with some of the reasons for this lack of attention. We should note, however, that it was only twenty years ago that alcoholism was classified as a disease by the American Medical Association (1).

The establishment of comprehensive treatment for previously neglected medical problems, of course, occurred in other areas. The profound changes which came about following the advent of the community mental health movement in the mid- and late sixties illustrate the rapidity with which such transformations can be achieved. In those locales where active community mental health programs were established, previously available facilities became accessible to many persons who had been unaware of where to turn before. Accessibility itself, as well as institutional willingness to acknowledge a need for treatment, served to undercut the shame and denial associated by many with acknowledging psychological problems.

The Hospital Referral Program which we shall describe is in many respects similar in purpose, insofar as it represents an attempt to assure access to treatment for a large number of patients who were otherwise unaware or frightened of making use of such treatment. It bears similarity to a comprehensive approach toward drug abuse treatment described for Dade County (4), but places emphasis on the entry phase, in the context of a large variety of modalities already available.

STRUCTURE OF THE PROGRAM

There are five functional elements in the program:

1. Clients who are hospital patients
2. Hospitals at which field units are placed
3. Field units constituted of addiction counsellors and on-site supervision
4. Central administrative personnel
5. Treatment programs to whom patients are referred

The nature of the client population varied among hospitals, reflecting the respective neighborhoods. 74% of the patients in the overall program were men. The overall ethnic breakdown was 69% black, 14% Hispanic and 15% white, but there was a considerable range for different hospitals. Whereas 92% were black at Harlem Hospital, only 36% were at Bronx Municipal. The modal patient was 31 years old and had completed the 12th grade.

In one patient survey, the primary drug of abuse was designated as that one which was most often used and carried with it great risk. In terms of risk, for example, heroin, methadone and alcohol were rated highest in that order, followed by sedatives and stimulants. Using this system, the incidence of primary drugs of abuse was as follows: heroin 39%; Methadone 6%; alcohol 52%; sedatives, 3%. Here again there was considerable variation between hospitals. At Harlem Hospital heroin was 2.2 times as common as alcohol as the primary drug, whereas, at Bronx Municipal it was only 0.8 times as common among patients evaluated.

The typical field unit consists of three counsellors with professional supervision from one member of the medical staff. Units typically include two male and one female counsellor. Of these three, two had generally abused drugs previously and had been enrolled in a treatment program for this pattern of abuse. This latter fact is quite helpful for both patients and staff at the hospital in illustrating the potential for successful treatment of the current abusers. The similarity in ethnic distribution between counselling and patient population provided similar advantages.

Although any given activity of the counsellors may fulfill more than one function, their time allotments may be roughly broken down as follows: clinical work 35%; training exercises for hospital staff, 10%; counsellors' own in-service training, 10%; clerical work, 35%; and agency personnel activities, 10%. As can be seen, a reasonable balance is achieved between clinical, administrative and educational activities.

The central administration of the program is based in downtown Manhattan, and regular visits are made to each of the units.

it serves to facilitate liaison with hospital administration, and provides spot-checks on field team operation, as well as reviewing data collection procedures. Regular meetings are held which include the administrative personnel and members of all the units. These serve to develop a sense of common purpose and an understanding of how to deal with problems which arise in similar form in the different units.

The large numbers of alcohol and drug abuse treatment programs available in the city is reflected in the target agencies to whom patients were referred. In one six-month period, for example, referrals were made to 16 residential therapeutic communities and 55 ambulatory programs for drug abuse, as well as 24 methadone maintenance clinics, and 21 drug-detoxification programs. In addition, 22 alcohol detoxification units and 35 ambulatory alcohol programs received referrals. Altogether 3,525 referrals were made in year 1973 and, as indicated in Table I, 56% of these were to alcoholism and 44% to drug programs.

Of all patients referred in the year 1975, 81% appeared at the treatment agency to which they were referred within one week of referral. Retention in treatment varied considerably depending on the modality. For example, only 29% of patients placed in ambulatory drug-abuse programs remained in active treatment until thirty days, whereas 83% of patients completed their couse of alcohol detoxification.

Another approach to assessment of effectiveness is to ascertain the cost of services. Table II indicates the results of such an approach utilizing costs and services for the year 1974. As indicated, on the basis of evaluating the number of patients seen, each evaluation costs $58. If only referrals are included in a cost analysis, the cost of each referral is $89. The cost of each placement could be similarly computed at $116.

TABLE I: 3,525 REFERRALS FOR TREATMENT IN 1975

	% of Drug Referrals
Ambulatory counselling	18%
Methadone	8
Ambulatory detoxification	36
Inpatient detoxification	32
Residential treatment	6

Total for drugs: 1,554, of whom 90% were placed

	% of Alcohol Referrals
Inpatient detoxification	50%
Ambulatory treatment	50

Total for alcohol: 1,971, of whom 78% were placed

TABLE II: COST PER SERVICE

Central Office Staff $ 29,000
25 Field Workers   291,000

Total, with supplies and
fringe benefits $376,000

Services	Number (1974)		Cost
Patients seen	6679		$ 58
		-or-	
Referrals	4214		89
		-or-	
Placements	3228		116

References

1.   E.M. Pattison in The Biology of Alcoholism (B. Kissin and
     H. Begleiter, eds.), Vol. 3, Plenum Press, New York, 1974.

2.   R. Barchha, M.A. Stewart, and S.B. Guze, Amer. J. Psychiat.,
     125: 681 (1968).

3.   J. McCusker, C.E. Cherubin, and S. Zimberg, N.Y. St. J. of
     Med., 751 (1971).

4.   R.S. Weppner, and D.C. McBride, Am. J. Psychiat., 132: 734
     (1975).

DRUG AND ALCOHOL REFERRALS FROM THE GENERAL
HOSPITAL II: THE CLINICAL CONTEXT

Marc Galanter, M.D.

Department of Psychiatry
Albert Einstein College of Medicine
Bronx, New York

This paper describes an approach to hospital-based consultation directed at the following problem: How can addicted and
alcoholic patients in the general hospital be enlisted into long-
term rehabilitation treatment? Addictive diseases are chronic
disorders with frequent relapse. Patients, however, exhibit a
reluctance and confusion in seeking help. While this is partly
generated by patient ambivalence, it is also affected by a long
history of exclusion of addiction treatment from the mainstream of
medical care.

This highlights the importance of entry into treatment as a
crucial aspect in the rehabilitation system, but the numerous and
diverse resources now becoming available for long-term treatment
necessitate an increasing degree of sophistication for making
referral. We will consider one approach to this problem undertaken
at the Albert Einstein College of Medicine-Bronx Municipal Hospital
Center.

Hospital Treatment as a System

Most social and organizational contexts can be viewed as
groups of functionally interrelated units. These units and the
relationships between them constitute a "system," in the theoretical model developed by von Bertalanffy (1). Closed systems are
considered to operate in isolation from their environment. Open
systems take into account the effect of interactions with the environment as well as internal variations. Although it may be possible to view a particular processes as a closed system, this may
not represent all the forces which affect it.

The most·frequently used model of medical treatment can be
conceptualized as a closed system. This model may be applied to
treatment of a disease such as appendicitis. In this case, current
knowledge of those factors which may alter the morbidity in the

general population is principally limited to the specific treatment techniques which may be utilized. Since the factors one considers in approaching the treatment of such an illness can be circumscribed, the system may be viewed as a closed one: The medically ill are admitted to the hospital, receive medical treatment, and then rejoin to the healthy population.

It is this model of medical care which is generally applied to the treatment of addiction in hospitals: Medical sequelae of addiction or problems of withdrawal are treated. This pathology is regarded as if it were the primary disease process, and when it is resolved, patients are at best given the name of a drug treatment program or told to go to AA. The possibility of active involvement in the addict's problem on a long term basis is not considered a part of this closed system, and the issue of rehabilitation treatment per se is not seen as related to the operations of the general hospital.

A different model is generally applied to infectious diseases in order to deal with factors which directly affect the natural history of transmitted illness. If the closed system in the initial treatment model were applied, medical intervention would be directed solely toward infected probands. Such treatment would be inadequate, as the potential for spread of the disease requires consideration of the medical system in relation to its environment, that is, as an open system. In order to achieve optimal efficacy, issues such as quarantine and asepsis must be introduced into the medical treatment system to limit the effects of contagion and prevent disruption of function within the hospital system. If this model is applied to addictive illness, such patients would be isolated from others; separate medical services would be established specifically for them, so as not to contaminate the remainder of the hospital's operations. In matter of fact, such an approach perpetuates the exclusion of addiction from consideration as a medical illness which merits treatment.

It becomes clear that effective intervention requires examination of a subsystem within the model just described. "Medical treatment" cannot be taken for granted as a distinct entity. In the case of a "social disease" such as drug abuse and alcoholism. It must be viewed as a complex subsystem which interacts with its own environment so the operations of one can affect the definition of the other.

Within the subsystem of "medical treatment," the following areas require examination: staff-patient communication, coordination of treatment planning, continuity of care and staff education. Effective intervention in these four areas is necessary to yield optimal results. Improvement in these areas serves as the goal for the consultation program. It is anticipated that by this means, the drug abuse "problem" in the hospital can be approached such that medical management of the addict and alcoholic will include consideration of the primary addictive illness, as well as its medical consequences.

The Consultation Program

The staff includes a psychiatric director and three paraprofessional counsellors. When a request for consultation is received, a counsellor is dispatched to assess the clinical situation. After review of the case and consultation with the ward staff, plans are formulated regarding management and referral to long-term treatment.

The source of referral for the first 950 patients evaluated is indicated in Table I. At that time, two-thirds of the consultation requests came from the wards, and one-third from the emergency room. A chart review of patients revealed:

1. Sex distribution: 75% male, 26% female

2. Ethnic distribution: 40% white, 23% black, 37% Hispanic

3. Primary drug of abuse (including non-alcoholics): 65% alcohol, 16% heroin, 8% methadone, 11% other

4. Reasons for hospital visit or admission: 41% medical, 49% medical and directly related to substance abuse; 11% detoxification.

Of 873 patients on whom consultations were performed in 1975, three quarters (662) were referred for alcohol or drug abuse treatment prior to discharge, as indicated in Table II. Follow-up revealed that 84% of those referred appeared for treatment within one week of the referral. Given the general reluctance of addicted patients to participate in treatment, as well as the mutual distrust generally experienced between such patients and hospital staff, this represents in our opinion an appreciable rate of success.

The following case vignette illustrates clinical aspects of the service's operation: A 24 year-old single unemployed black woman was hospitalized for hepatic complications of alcoholism. She began drinking more heavily after her common-law husband left her a year before and she moved in with a relative who was herself an alcoholic. The patient was at first adamant in refusing treatment for her alcoholism. Before consultation was called, she denied having a drinking problem, and, as is typical with patients exercising denial, minimized her alcohol intake. Her resident and the nursing staff regarded her prospects for sobriety as negligible. Over the course of hospitalization, however, the counsellor maintained regular contact with her, while the ward social worker began seeing the patient's mother. Two meetings were held with all four parties and with the ward resident. The patient ultimately accepted referral to a residential setting for treatment of alcoholic and drug-abusing patients. This option had been chosen because it was felt that the patient did not have the emotional resources to undertake ambulatory treatment.

Numerous treatment agents operate within the hospital complex and, although they may deal directly with the patient, their efforts are often not coordinated. This is particularly true with the addict and alcoholic, where physician, social workers, and nurse may relate to different facets of a complex social issue. In the case described, the availability of a single party who works to facilitate communication within the treatment subsystem is most valuable. The presumption of effective coordination of all treatment entities cannot be made without careful nurturance of a coordinated treatment plan. We attempt to enlist the assistance of the ward's staff in disposition planning, utilizing the specialized knowledge they may provide. This also serves to educate the staff to the issues involved in drug abuse treatment, and contributes to undercutting the frustration and consequent resentment which had previously been more typical of their response.

TABLE I: SOURCE OF CONSULTATIONS REQUEST (1973-4)

Service	Number	Percent
Emergency Rooms (324, 34%)		
1. Medical/Surgical	106	11
2. Psychiatric	218	23
Wards (614, 65%)		
1. Medicine	182	19
2. Surgery	186	20
3. Obstetrics	128	13
4. Psychiatry	22	2
5. Other	96	10

Clinics (12, 1%)

TOTAL: 950 Consultations

TABLE II: TARGET AGENCY FOR 662 REFERRALS (1975)

	% of Drug Referrals
Ambulatory counselling	45%
Methadone maintenance	13
Ambulatory detoxification	17
In-patient detoxification	14
Residential treatment	11

TOTAL for drugs: 279

	% of Alcohol Referrals
In-patient detoxification	35%
Ambulatory care	45

TOTAL for alcohol: 383

REFERENCE

1. L. von Bertalanffy, General Systems Theory: Foundations, Development, Application, George Braziller, New York, 1968.

RATIONAL DRUG THERAPY FOR THE ALCOHOL
AND DRUG DEPENDENT PATIENT

Ralph M. Stanzione

Chief Pharmacist
Hartford Dispensary Methadone
Maintenance Treatment Program
Hartford, Connecticut

This will provide drug therapy information for the treatment of conditions experienced by the alcohol and drug dependent patient with emphasis on a rational approach. We are aware of and concerned about therapeutic treatment rendered to this patient population for conditions other than his/her primary illness.

The health community is generally fearful, unconcerned, undereducated, and/or undermotivated where treatment of these secondary conditions is involved while the patient is concurrently being treated for his/her primary illness. It is, therefore, our responsibility as treatment specialists to remove these walls of fear and undermotivation by utilizing informational and educational in-service programs.

It is my hope that the information provided herein will be used as an educational tool to promote sound drug therapy at all levels of the health care system. Current prescribing habits and therapeutic approaches lend themselves to much criticism because they foster the need of both prescriber and patient to seek a quick response and results. Consequently, we are faced with a trend which has significantly increased the medical management problems associated with adverse reactions, drug-drug interactions, introduction to or potentiated abuse patterns, careless drug selection, and ineffective dosage regimens. It must be emphasized that the alcohol and drug dependent patient has the sophistication to select conditions that perpetuate dependency under the guise of "it's a legal prescription." Therefore, only through the extensive use of drug information and education in the health community at large can we hopefully minimize the impact and avoid the serious consequences of these practices.

The specific areas of health care delivery requiring the immediate attention of drug abuse specialists are:

1) Community Health and Mental Health Clinics.

2) Hospital facilities, including emergency room, surgical units, medical units and maternity facilities.

This is not to say that drug abuse specialists should not make attempts to provide in-service education to all clinical hospital personnel. In addition, we must stimulate local and state medical, nursing, and pharmacy societies to undertake ongoing drug informational efforts informing their respective members in private practice at the community level. This can be accomplished by providing drug information monographs, bulletins, or alerts to these societies for reprint in their publications.

In order for therapy to be rational it must be emphasized that an accurate diagnosis is essential and drug therapy matched to this diagnosis at the lowest therapeutic dosage levels possible. It the highest levels or the most potent drugs in a class are used and fail therapeutic management becomes increasingly difficult. By starting at the lower levels the prescriber allows himself/herself the luxury of more therapeutic flexibility and minimizes the possibility of adverse drug reactions and drug-drug interactions. It is imperative to emphasize "therapeutic dosage levels" because often underdosing regimens are employed which can lead to as many serious complications as a high dose regimen. The drug selection process should proceed in an orderly fashion paying close attention to the use of the narrowest range of drugs of choice with the widest margin of safety.

Discussion

The tables presented herein are designed to assist drug treatment specialists in their attempts to communicate knowledgeable information to community health service institutions. In the poly-drug abuse attitudes of today, differentiation of diagnosis is difficult. It is hoped that this information can ease this burden as well as provide therapeutic information to insure beneficial care to the drug and alcohol dependent patient.

It should be noted that recent studies show (Greenblatt, et al) that treatment of the withdrawal symptoms of alcoholism would be greatly facilitated if Chlordiazepoxide (Librium) could be given orally. The onset is faster and peak blood levels higher. Therefore, oral administration should be initiated as soon as absorption improves.

The current standards of post-surgical and medical management of narcotic analgesic requirements of a methadone maintained patient in a community or general hospital are fair at best. In the past year this area of treatment rendered to our patients has created increased concern on the part of our entire staff. To remedy this, efforts are being made to conduct in-service education sessions with all medical and surgical ward personnel.

Summary

The current trend of drug and alcohol abuse is increasing at a faster pace than ever before at all levels of society. If we are to stem this onrushing tide of human destruction, drug information and education presented <u>factually and without bias</u> may be our only hope. Currently national mortality statistics indicate that nearly 10% of all deaths can be directly or indirectly linked to alcohol and drug abuse. Actual figures may be higher. A candid educational approach is necessary to restimulate public interest and enhance community involvement to abort the efforts of a society which increasingly attempts to solve its problems through chemical means.

The necessity for brevity in this publication prevents me from fully incorporating the entire paper as presented. Additional information will be provided upon written request.

The following tables are presented to update this information and introduce new information for use in drug informational and educational services.

TABLE I - DIFFERENTIATION OF WITHDRAWAL SYMPTOMS

Symptoms	Alcohol*	Barbiturates	Valium	Methadone	Heroin
Withdrawal (Onset)	2-4 hrs.	12-16 hrs.	24-72 hrs.	36-72 hrs.	8-12 hrs.
Autonomic	3-6 hrs.	12-24 hrs.	24-72 hrs.	2-5 days	18-36 hrs.
Nausea	+	+	+	+	+
Vomiting	+	+	+/-	+	+
Diarrhea	-	-	-	+	+
Seizures	1-3 days Usually prior to DT's	24-48 hrs. (3-7 days long acting barbs).	3-7 days If at all	None	None
Delerium Tremens	2-4 days	4-7 days	None Evident	None	None
CNS Psychosis (Drug Associated)	After 2nd day to weeks	After 3rd day to weeks	After 7th day to weeks	None	None

*It should be noted that treatment of withdrawal from alcohol can often cause hypoglycemia which can be fatal because of liver complications, and inability of the liver to manufacture glycogen in sufficient quantities for conversion to glucose. Therefore, sugar and/or glucose nutritional supplements may be necessary.

It should also be noted that all patients who smell like alcohol have not necessarily only consumed alcohol. Alcoholics notoriously couple sedative-type drugs with the alcohol which includes barbiturates, Doriden, Noludar, Placidyl, Quaalude, etc.

TABLE II - DRUG RELATIONSHIPS - OPIATES

Methadone - 1 mg. is equivalent to:
Heroin   - 1 - 2 mg.   Pantopon - 4 mg.
Morphine - 2 - 3 mg.   Paregoric - 7-8 cc (Approximately -
Dilaudid - 1/2 mg. (one-half)   poorly absorbed)
Codeine   - 30 mg.   Laudanum - 3 cc
Demerol   - 20 mg.   Dromoran - 1 mg.
Levo-Dromoran - 1/2 mg.   Leritine - 8 mg.
            (one-half)

Post-Surgical Narcotic Analgesic Management of Methadone Patients

Recent experience has shown this to be a major stumbling block in
the treatment of the drug dependent patient at the community and
general hospitals. The following are some suggestions to facilitate therapeutic management:

1) Any narcotic may be used to achieve the desired analgesia on
   a drug equivalent basis (see equivalent chart previous). The
   important consideration is not to mix narcotic analgesics,
   thereby managing the patient's analgetic requirements with
   one drug entity only which minimizes possible drug interactions.

2) The stabilized methadone maintained patient will usually
   have the same analgetic needs as the non-addicted patient
   for the surgery being performed.

3) It is usually recommended that if methadone is being used,
   the oral dose (or I.M. equivalent) be administered after
   completion of surgery to avoid complications with anesthesia.

   a) Consideration should be given to avoiding the use of
      Halothane as a general anesthetic on this patient popu-
      lation because of possible compromised liver function.

4) Lower analgetic requirements can be achieved by combining
   the stabilization dose requirements and the lowest therapeutic analgetic dose requirements and dividing them into 2 or 3
   doses per day.

Acknowledgements

The author wishes to express gratitude to James O'Brien, M.D.,
Ph.D. for his technical assistance.

References

1) Goodman, Louis S.; Gilman, Alfred: The Pharmacological Basis of Therapeutics, 4th Edition, 1970.

2) Facts and Comparison, Revised 1974 and 1975.

3) Kleber, Herbert D.: Withdrawal Techniques - A Training Paper, 1967.

4) Ray, Oakley S.: Drugs, Society, and Human Behavior, 1972.

5) American Pharmaceutical Association, Evaluations of Drug Interactions - 1973, 1st Edition, April 1973.

6) Hartshorn, Edward A.: Interactions of CNS Drugs: Psychotherapeutic Agents, Drug Intelligence and Clinical Pharmacy, Vol. 9, Oct. 1975, 536-552.

7) Greenblatt, David J.; Shader, Richard I., Koch-Wesner, Jan: Slow Absorption of Intramuscular Chlordiazepoxide, New England Journal of Medicine, 291:21, Nov. 21, 1974, 1116-1118.

921

ALCOHOL USE DURING THE METHADONE PHASE
OF ADDICTION TREATMENT
WITH SPECIAL REFERENCE TO MALE AND FEMALE DIFFERENCES

Lawrence Zelic Freedman, M.D.

Foundations' Fund Research Professor of Psychiatry
Co-Chairman, Institute of Social and Behavioral Pathology
University of Chicago

Paul M. Lin, Ph.D.

Department of Anthropology
Wichita State University
Wichita, Kansas

Georgetta Vosmer, B.S.

University of Chicago

In this and previous papers (1) (2) we have demonstrated
that increased use of alcohol among patients at the clinic of the
Behavioral Action and Research in the Social Sciences Foundation,
Inc. (Chicago), while under methadone maintenance treatment, is
extensive. Our investigation implies that the problem is more
complex than the explanation of drug substitution and experimentation offered by Fudge and Penk (3).

A retention rate of less than 40% has been cited, over a
twelve month period, for methadone clinics nationwide; and of the
remaining 40% who choose to continue treatment, many find themselves merely substituting a bottle for a hypodermic needle. The
indices which we have used, as well as clinical interviews and
group therapy sessions, show that emotional disturbances are present in the majority of clients. Males and females within the .
population have different emotional disturbances. A belief in the
necessity of treating the whole patient if a genuine cure of his
addiction is to be effected demands that these differences be
taken into account.

A study by Arnon, et al (4) has shown that males are subject
to stronger environmental pressures to use drugs than are women.
As in the case of alcohol use, this probably due to the fact
that drug use is considered less of a deviancy among males than
among females. Women, however, may be drawn to drug use as a means
of resolving internal conflicts, rather than due to environmental
pressures.

As a population, heroin addicts are a group who experience varying degrees of psychic pain for a wide range of reasons. Taking steps to avoid experiencing this pain has been a long-term modus operandi for the majority of this population. If the source of the pain -- be it physiological, psychological, or sociological -- is not contended with during treatment, the client will seek the least expensive legal means of alleviating it, if not return to his or her heroin habit.

We found in our study that over 50% of the sample population had increased its alcohol intake since entering methadone treatment programs. The proportion of men who had increased their alcohol intake differed from the proportion of women who had altered their drinking habits since entering treatment. The ratio of males to females is approximately 3:1. This indicates that sex may be an important factor in distinguishing potential alcohol abusers from non-abusers.

Factor analysis of the Cornell Index, alcohol questionnaire, and methadone dosage has shown that male and female patients are characterized by different constellations of psychiatric symptoms. Among male subjects, the dominant problems are fear and inadequacy feelings, depression, nervousness and anxiety, and neurocirculatory symptoms. Among the females, psychosomatic symptoms, hypochondriasis and asthenia, gastrointestinal symptoms, and sensitivity and suspiciousness are the most prominent problems. Initial work with the MMPI indicates that the diagnoses based on the Cornell Index have a high degree of reliability.

Analysis of Cornell Index and alcohol variables (Table I) yielded no significant psychiatric symptoms which differentiate males who have not changed their drinking habits -- since usually minimal alcohol is consumed by those addicted to opiates -- from those males who have, under methadone treatment, increased their alcohol intake, often to levels of abuse. However, the high incidence of feelings of depression and inadequacy among the male patients, and the correlation between time on medication and increased alcohol use imply that internal and external frustrations must be important causal factors. The man who has been in methadone maintenance treatment for two years, is still unemployed, and continues to feel that his life is of little worth, selects the most accessible means of relieving his anxieties.

However, females who have increased their alcohol intake are distinguished from women whose drinking habits have remained static since entering treatment. The women in our study were characterized, in general, as suffering from somatic and psychosomatic complaints. Increased alcohol useage is correlated only with those women who also evidence depression, underlying elements of anger (as indicated by three questions in the troublesome psychopathology category), and low methadone dosages. The information available at present leads one to infer that this small number of women may have turned to alcohol for the purpose of self-medication. It would be beneficial if we could determine whether lowering dosages of methadone produces some sort of hormonal upset which results in depression, or whether this depression is the result of other causes.

Thus, low-level methadone dosages are correlated with increased alcohol intake among female clients. Women who are taking 20 mg or less of methadone daily are more likely to have increased their alcohol consumption than women taking over 20 mg of the drug. There is no comparable relationship between length of time which a client has been on medication and probability of increased alcohol intake, among female clients.

However, among male clients, length of time on methadone maintenance medication is correlated with increased alcohol intake; those men who have been in treatment over 100 weeks are more likely to have increased their alcohol intake than those men who have been in the program less than 100 weeks. No correlation, for males, was found between dosage and increased consumption of alcohol.

TABLE I

Cornell Index Factors, Alcoholic Beverage Consumption Habit,
and Methadone Treatment Dosage

(Variables Used in Study)

1. Fear and Inadequacy
2. Depression
3. Nervousness and Anxiety
4. Neurocirculatory Symptoms
5. Startle Reactions
6. Psychosomatic Symptoms
7. Hypochondriasis and Asthenia
8. Gastrointestinal Symptoms
9. Sensitivity and Suspiciousness
10. Troublesome psychopathy
11. Cornell Index Total Score (Variables 1-10)
12. Was a non- or social drinker during heroin addiction
13. Was a moderate drinker during heroin addiction
14. Was an excessive drinker during heroin addiction
15. Has become a non- or social drinker since joining methadone program
16. Has become a moderate drinker since joining methadone program
17. Has become an excessive drinker since joining methadone program
18. Quantity of methadone dosage

REFERENCES

1. Lawrence Z. Freedman, M.D., in The Journal of Nervous and Mental Disease, 132:(1) (1961).

2. Lawrence Z. Freedman, M.D., in Annals of the New York Academy of Science (1976).(In Press: "Methadone and Alcohol")

3. Fudge and Penk, in Sciences, 181:702 (1973).

4. Arnon, D. Kleinman, K., and Kissin, B., in The International Journal of the Addictions, 9:(1):151-9 (1973).

MEASURING PATTERNS OF ALCOHOL CONSUMPTION IN A METHADONE MAINTENANCE PROGRAM

Robert J. Harford,[1] Frank Slobetz,[2] Izola Hogan,[2] Marjorie Mezritz,[2] Arthur Africano[1]

[1]Department of Psychiatry
Yale University School of Medicine
100 Park Street
New Haven, Connecticut   06511

[2]Addiction-Prevention, Treatment Foundation, Inc.
100 Park Street
New Haven, Connecticut   06511

Prevalence estimates of alcoholism in methadone programs range from 10% to 60% (1, 2, 3) and some observers believe that the problem is increasing in severity. Alcoholism presents at least two adverse therapeutic implications. Alcohol abuse may seriously compromise rehabilitative efforts to such an extent that alcoholism is the principal reason for treatment failure (1, 2, 3, 4). In addition, alcoholism seems to develop after admission to methadone programs (1, 2, 4). Since the long-term physiological effects of alcohol may be more severe than those of other commonly abused drugs, the therapeutic efficacy of methadone as a treatment for opiate addiction may be reduced to the extent that methadone maintenance results in increased alcohol consumption (4).

Research on development of alcoholism in methadone programs has been hampered by the lack of valid methods of measuring the longitudinal changes in alcohol use and absence of unequivocal criteria for diagnosing and classifying alcoholics. Most investigators have relied on client self-reports of alcohol consumption for which the validity is unknown. Even perfectly valid information concerning amounts of alcohol consumed would not be sufficient evidence for diagnosing alcohol abuse or alcoholism. Individual tolerances may vary and some consideration of individual differences in disfunctional effects of drinking is necessary for meaningful diagnosis. Most studies of alcohol abuse in methadone programs have measured only the amount consumed and have not considered effects of alcohol on the client's psycho-social functioning. Since these studies have adopted different, and usually unspecified, criteria for alcoholism, their results may not be comparable and their applicability to other settings is limited.

We attempted to solve the validity problem by using one physiological measure of alcohol use, breathalyzer analysis (BA), to corroborate self-reports of alcohol consumption. We also administered two brief alcoholism diagnostic instruments, the abbreviated MAST (5) and the CAGE questionnaire (6).

BA may be more valid than self-reports as a measure of alcohol consumption, but the period during which alcohol use is detectable by this method is limited to between 12 and 24 hours. Among other factors, validity also is affected by differences in amount consumed, recency of consumption and metabolism rates. Consequently, single administrations of BA alone cannot yield valid information concerning longitudinal changes in alcohol consumption patterns. Repeated physiological measures are obtrusive (i.e., affect the phenomenon being measured), expensive to administer and inconvenient to clients and, for these reasons, are impractical for use on a regular basis.

The limitations of physiological techniques with respect to longitudinal information and doubtful validity of self-reports led us to conclude that a combination of both methods might be more useful in accurately assessing longitudinal drinking patterns than either method by itself. To verify this possibility, we experimentally examined the usefulness of a single BA in increasing the validity of self-reports of alcohol consumption.

METHOD

This experiment was conducted in the Park Street methadone clinic of the Drug Dependence Unit of the Connecticut Mental Health Center. Ninety consecutive clients admitted to this clinic were interviewed concerning their drinking habits. They were assigned randomly to one of three experimental conditions. Those in the Breathalyzer-Questionnaire (BQ) group underwent BA and then completed the Alcohol Consumption Questionnaire. Clients in the Questionnaire-Breathalyzer (QB) group completed the questionnaire prior to, but with foreknowledge of, subsequent BA. Clients in the Questionnaire-Only (QO) group merely completed the questionnaire with no mention of BA. A Smith and Wesson Model 900A breathalyzer was used.

The questionnaire contained items concerning beer, wine and liquor consumption during both a typical day in the previous month and the preceding 24 hours. The total amount of alcohol (measured in absolute ounces) consumed during a typical day and during the 24 hours immediately preceding testing were calculated from responses to these items. In addition to these two measures of alcohol consumption, the questionnaire also contained the 10-item abbreviated MAST and the 4-item CAGE scale. Preliminary scanning of the CAGE revealed that item two is double-barrelled. A less ambiguous reworded version of this item also was included in the questionnaire.

Because clients may give more accurate responses if they believe that their reports will be verified, we hypothesized that the two groups which received BA would report higher levels of alcohol consumption during the preceding 24-hour period. We also expected that BA would increase a) reports of typical daily alcohol consumption undetectable by BA (i.e., during the previous month) and b) the frequency of positive responses to other questionnaire items diagnostic of alcoholism.

RESULTS AND DISCUSSION

Two statistically significant differences between the three groups were found. As predicted, clients in the BQ group more frequently gave positive responses to CAGE items and indicated greater alcohol consumption in the previous 24 hours than did clients in the other two groups. Since clients were assigned randomly to the three groups, there is no reason to believe that the BQ group was comprised of heavier drinkers than the other two groups. This finding shows that administration of BA before the questionnaire caused clients to give more accurate responses, which indicated greater alcohol consumption and alcohol-related problems.

The fact that the BQ and QB groups differed in their responses to the two measures was unexpected. This finding suggests that BA must precede the questionnaire in order to produce the effect of increased validity. Evidently, direct experience with the BA procedure, rather than anticipation of BA, encourages more honest responses, despite the fact that the BA results were not known by the BQ clients when they completed the questionnaire. This conclusion is consistent with the finding that anticipation of BA by QB clients did not influence their responses in the direction of greater alcohol consumption as compared with the QO group. This interpretation also suggests that passive monitoring methods (e.g., alcohol urinalysis in a program that routinely analyses urine specimens for drugs) would not influence self-reports of alcohol consumption.

Predicted differences in self-reported typical daily alcohol consumption during the previous month were not statistically significant. This finding has disappointing implications for the problem of measuring longitudinal patterns of alcohol use. BA in the BQ group produced increased reports of alcohol consumption during the time period in which the alcohol could have been detected but it did not affect the self-reports of undetectable alcohol consumption. This finding suggests that the possibility of detection is necessary to increase the validity of self-reports. For the time periods in which underreporting could not be detected, BA was ineffective in increasing reported alcohol use. However, the mean typical daily alcohol consumption reported by these clients (2.56 absolute oz.) was more than twice the amount (1.07 absolute oz.) reported by the group of successfully detoxified clients (4) during their pre-treatment addiction career. Whether these differences are attributable to the method or client-related differences cannot be determined.

Differences in responses to MAST items also were not statistically significant, although they were in the predicted directions. Two MAST items which permit false positive responses may have contributed to the failue of significant differences to emerge on this scale. Three participants responded negatively to MAST items "Do you feel you are a normal drinker?" and "Do friends or relatives think you are a normal drinker?", but did not give positive responses to any other CAGE or MAST items, and all reported drinking no alcohol during the previous month. Evidently, they considered themselves not to be normal drinkers because they did not drink at all. These two items, therefore, seem to encourage false positive responses which could lead to misdiagnosis of non-drinkers as alcoholics. We recommend that these items be revised or eliminated from the instrument.

Two clients responded negatively to the double-barreled CAGE items, "Have people annoyed you by criticizing your drinking?", but responded positively to an item worded "Have people criticized your drinking?". They reported drinking 2.4 and 4.8 absolute ounces of alcohol the previous day and 8.9 and 7.3 absolute ounces on a typical day during the previous two months. These results suggest that this item does not identify heavy or moderate drinkers as well as the substitute item.

In summary, administration of breathalyzer prior to self-reports seems to increase both reported amount of alcohol consumed and the frequency with which alcohol related problems are acknowledged on a diagnostic questionnaire. The effect depends upon the order in which the measures are administered and may be limited to the period of time in which alcohol consumption is physiologically detectable. Although clients and methodology differed from those of previous studies, mean alcohol consumption prior to program admission was more than twice the amounts reported by clients in this same methadone program (4). This finding suggests the possibility that the reported increase in alcohol consumption during methadone maintenance may be at least in part an artifact of underreported consumption at the time of application for treatment.

This research was supported in part by grants from the National Institute of Drug Abuse: DA 01097 and H80 DA 16356.

REFERENCES

1. B. Bihari, Proceedings. 5th National Conference on Methadone Treatment, (1973).
2. F. Gearing, Proceedings. 5th National Conference on Methadone Treatment, (1973).
3. N. R. Scott, W. W. Winslow and D. G. Gorman, Proceedings. 5th National Conference on Methadone Treatment (1973).
4. C. E. Riordan, M. Mezritz, F. Slobetz and H. D. Kleber, J.A.M.A. (in press).
5. A. D. Pokorny, B. A. Miller and H. B. Kaplan, Amer. J. Psychiat. 129: 3 (1972).
6. D. Mayfield, G. McCleod and P. Hall, Amer. J. Psychiat., 131: 10 (1974).

PROBLEM DRINKING DRUG ADDICTS: PSYCHOLOGICAL CHARACTERISTICS*

Henry Steinberger and Arie Cohen

Eagleville Hospital and Rehabilitation Center
Eagleville, Pennsylvania

Researchers in the field of alcoholism have long sought those characteristics which differentiate problem drinkers from non-problem drinkers. The purpose of this study is to investigate some psychological characteristics that might differentiate between heroin addicts with drinking problems and those without such problems.

The sample in the present study includes 753 heroin addicts whose drinking histories had previously been categorized (1); 179 addicts who report heavy alcohol consumption, drunkenness, bad physical effects from alcohol and loss of control over their drinking at some time in their histories (i.e., problem drinkers), and 574 who range from heavy drinkers without problems to abstainers. All these subjects either listed heroin as the primary drug for which they sought treatment or reported using heroin once a day or more during the two months prior to treatment; they constitute 89% of the drug abusing subjects previously reported.

All subjects were interviewed upon admission to treatment. Fifty-two items dealing with feelings, emotions and self-image were extracted from the interviews and factor analyzed, yielding eight scales containing 37 items. The four scales related to feelings are "depression", "mistrust", "phobic-anxiety", and "happiness". The other four scales deal with the subject's self-image and include "sociability", "dependency on others", "ability to cope", and "resistance to authority".

Table I includes the means for each group on the eight scales and the $\underline{t}$-test values. The problem drinking addicts scored significantly higher than the other addicts on "depression", "phobic-anxiety", "dependency on others", "resistance to authority", and "sociability", and significantly lower on "happiness". These findings are compatible with the literature on alcoholism which is replete with descriptions of the problem drinker as dependent, anxious, depressed, and resistant to authority. There is inconclusive evidence as to the sociability of problem drinkers (2,3,4).

Another variable studied, also shown in Table I, was worry. During the interview, subjects rated the extent to which they

*This work was conducted under National Institute on Drug Abuse Demonstration Grant H81 DA 01113.

worried about 14 items including money, jobs, sex, drugs and life
in general. Worry was measured as the sum of the ratings and a
t-test demonstrated that the problem drinking addicts report worrying significantly less than their non-problem drinking cohorts. It
seems unusual that the group that reports more problems would worry
less. While the effect of drugs and alcohol may supress worry,
these subjects were in treatment and sober when interviewed. One
possible explanation is that the problem drinkers denied their
worrying. This reasoning is supported by the literature on alcoholism which indicates that denial is the characteristic, major
defense mechanism of problem drinkers.

One final characteristic studied was the frequency with which
suicidal thoughts and attempts were reported, summarized in Table
II. A greater proportion of the problem drinkers reported that
they (a) had thought about taking their lives (36% vs 26%), and
(b) had actually attempted suicide (20% vs 10%). These differences,
evaluated by the chi-square test, were significant at the 0.025 and
0.01 level respectively.

Many clinicians and therapists, especially in methadone clinics,
have noticed with concern the heavy drinking of some of their patients. The results of the present study suggest that these
patients are different from other heroin addicts. Their therapy
might be improved by the therapists' awareness of these psychological differences, particularly their propensity towards suicide.
Possibly, the added support, intensive therapy and opportunity for
more thorough surveillance found in a therapeutic community would
prove a more adequate shelter for the problem drinking heroin
addict.

Table I

SUMMARY OF DIFFERENCES ON VARIOUS SCALES

Item	Mean for Problem Drinkers (N=179)	Mean for Others (N=574)	Standard Deviation (N=753)	t	p
Depression	18.18	16.90	4.73	4.68	.01
Phobic- Anxiety	14.98	13.67	4.88	4.34	.01
Happiness	13.46	14.03	3.76	2.46	.01
Dependency	9.11	8.24	3.25	4.34	.01
Resistant to Authority	9.57	9.04	3.00	2.80	.01
Sociability	8.65	8.09	2.45	3.25	.01
Ability to Cope	19.82	20.05	3.27	1.17	N.S.
Mistrust	5.57	5.59	2.27	.17	N.S.
Worry	27.25	29.31	7.39	4.54	.01

Table II

SUMMARY OF DIFFERENCES IN THE NUMBER OF SUBJECTS
CONTEMPLATING AND ATTEMPTING SUICIDE

Item (refering to suidide)	Problem Drinkers (N = 179)		Others (N = 574)		Chi-Square	p
	N	%	N	%		
"... thought about..."	66	35	149	26	5.82	.025
"... actually tried..."	37	20	62	10	10.79	.01

REFERENCES

1. H. L. Barr, Problem drinking by drug addicts: an empirical typology. These proceedings.

2. E. Hanfmann, The life history of an ex-alcoholic with an evaluation of the factors involved in causation and rehabilitation. Quarterly J. of Studies on Alcohol, 12: 405, (1951).

3. M. C. Jones, Personality correlates and antecedents of drinking patterns in adult males. J. Consulting and Clinical Psych., 32: 2, (1968).

4. E. Singer, H. Blane and R. Rasschau, Alcoholism and social isolation. J. of Abnormal and Social Psychology, 69: 681, (1964).

PROBLEM DRINKING DRUG ADDICTS: CHILDHOOD
AND SOCIAL CHARACTERISTICS*

Patricia Hannigan and Harriet L. Barr
Eagleville Hospital and Rehabilitation Center
Eagleville, Pennsylvania

Eight hundred and sixty-four drug addicts were questioned at
their admission to treatment regarding their use of various drugs,
including alcohol. The addicts were also interviewed extensively
about their childhood experiences and family backgrounds. On the
basis of their drinking histories, six types of drinkers were identified; five groups reporting various patterns of drinking and one
group of abstainers (1). Sixteen people were not classified and
were eliminated from the analyses. These six types were then collapsed into two groups: those who give clear evidence of a drinking
problem, either past or present (N=209), and those who report never having had such a problem (N=639). The social and familial
backgrounds of those two groups were compared. There were no significant differences between the two groups in general measures of
social class while growing up, such as parents' education and
parents' occupation, or in race, sex, or age.

When asked about their school experiences, the problem drinkers' responses indicated that they had experienced significantly
more difficulty concentrating on what the teacher was saying than
the non-problem drinkers ($p < .01$), they more often made mistakes
through doing things too fast ($p < .001$), they more often got into
fights at school ($p < .01$), and they more often skipped school
($p < .01$). There was no difference between problem drinkers and
others in more objective, external statements about difficulty in
school, such as being expelled, having to repeat a grade, or being
suspended. In other words, the problem drinking drug addicts in
our sample seem to have had significantly more internal and behavior problems with school than the non-problem drinkers, though
they do not seem to have experienced any more official negative
sanction for these difficulties.

While there is no significant difference between the groups
with regard to parents separating or divorcing, the problem drinkers claimed significantly more often than others that they had had

*This work was conducted under National Institute on Drug Abuse
Demonstration Grant H81 DA 01113.

unhappy childhoods. There is no difference between the groups on their reports of how close they were to their mothers while growing up, both groups claiming maternal closeness. There is, however, a significant difference between the groups on the issue of closeness to father; the non-drinkers claim to have been significantly closer to their fathers than the problem drinkers do (t=2.63, p < .01). These data suggest that the problem drinkers come from less cohesive, close families than the non-problem drinkers.

The problem drinkers report significantly more deaths in the family during their childhoods, especially death of mother (p < .01). They significantly more often report that someone in the family was often violent (p < .001), that they were abused or beaten as children (p < .01), and that someone in their childhood home had a mental breakdown, or exhibited bizarre behavior of some kind (p < .02). In other words, within a sample which comes largely from broken, unstable homes, and whose early childhood experiences are poor by the general standards of the society, those who abuse alcohol in addition to other drugs have had even more chaotic childhoods than their non-alcohol abusing counterparts.

The subjects were then asked about attitudes toward alcohol in their childhood homes. Problem drinkers were significantly more likely than other addicts to have come from homes where parents either clearly approved or clearly disapproved of alcohol; in other words, from homes where alcohol was an issue. The non-problem drinkers tended to report that they either didn't know their parents' attitudes, or that their parents neither approved nor disapproved of alcohol. Furthermore, problem drinkers were significantly more likely than other addicts to have mothers, fathers, sisters, and brothers who used alcohol excessively during their childhood. Thus, it seems clear that more of the problem-drinking addicts had alcohol abusing role models than non-problem drinkers.

Assessment of the subjects' adult lifestyles indicated that the alcohol abusing addicts have significantly less stable lives. They have, on the average, moved more often in the last two years, and are significantly more likely than the other addict group to report having been "on the bum", with no regular place to live (p < .001). When queried about their sources of support, the problem drinkers significantly more often than non-problem drinkers report income from selling drugs and other illegal activities. Their arrest records reflect this differential involvement in criminal activities; problem drinkers are significantly more likely than other addicts to have been arrested at all (p < .02), they display a significantly greater average number of charges (p < .02), they have spent more time in jail (p < .001), have been charged with more crimes against individuals and crimes against property, as well as more charges of drunkenness and disorderly conduct (p < .001),

935

driving under the influence (p<.01), and other motor vehicle violations (p<.02).

The final issue investigated under the rubric of adult life-
style was their social interaction. Predictably, all the addicts
who reported current problems associated with drinking reported
significantly more often than the other groups that they now have
friends who drink excessively. All in all, the adult lifestyles
of the problem drinking drug addicts are even more deviant and unstable than that of their non-problem drinking counterparts.

In summary, these data on a large sample of drug addicts indicate that those addicts who have a drinking problem in addition to
their primary addiction to a drug have had more chaotic childhoods
than those addicts who do not report a drinking problem, and that
the problem drinking addicts have more deviant and unstable lifestyles as adults.

It is not surprising that people who abuse more than one substance should be the most extreme cases within a population of substance abusers. However, these data support the notion that the
excessive use of alcohol over and above another addiction is not a
result or symptom of heavier involvement with a drug abusing subculture. Instead, the problem drinking appears to be associated
with factors which predate involvement with such a subculture.
Further investigation is necessary to discover whether the real issue here is specifically alcohol abuse in addition to abuse of
another substance, or whether the issue is simply the fact of
multiple addiction. The larger question which must be addressed is
whether the addict who abuses more than one substance is somehow
a different kind of addict from a single substance abuser, or if he
simply has more of the same problem.

References

1. H. L. Barr, Problem drinking by drug addicts: an empirical
   typology. These proceedings.

PROBLEM DRINKING BY DRUG ADDICTS: AN EMPIRICAL TYPOLOGY*

Harriet L. Barr

Research Department
Eagleville Hospital and Rehabilitation Center
Eagleville, Pennsylvania

The phenomenon of problem drinking by drug addicts and its
implications for treatment is closely related to two issues of
national concern. One is the problem of alcohol abuse by methadone
maintenance patients, viewed by many as the greatest single cause
of treatment failure in that modality (cf. 1,2). The second,
broader issue is that of multiple substance abuse, either of alcohol and other drugs or of more than one drug. The accumulating
evidence supports a generic approach to the problem of substance
abuse, that is, a concern with the person's addictive problem whatever
the substance of abuse, rather than a focus on the particular substance of abuse.

These issues are the central concern of a NIDA-funded prospective study of problem drinking in drug addicts and its implications
for treatment outcome conducted by Eagleville Hospital and Rehabilitation Center. This report documents the extent of problem drinking in the histories reported by drug addicts at the time they
enter treatment, and presents an empirically derived typology of
drinking histories. Preliminary data on the ability of the typology to predict problem drinking at the time of a 12-month followup
will also be presented in this paper. The papers following report
relationships between the typology and drug abuse variables, family
and social background, and personality measures.

Subjects, Data and findings

Each subject entered the study at the time he or she was admitted to treatment for drug addiction and was followed for at least
12 months thereafter. The sample includes 864 drug addicts, of whom
274 entered an abstinence residential therapeutic community that
treats drug and alcohol abusers together (Eagleville), and 590 entered one of ten methadone maintenance programs in the greater
Philadelphia area. In addition, for purposes of comparison and
establishing criteria for alcohol abuse, intake interviews were

*This work was conducted under National Institute on Drug Abuse
Demonstration Grant H81 DA 01113.

obtained from 243 alcoholics entering Eagleville Hospital. This
report is based entirely on selected items from the intake and
12-month followup interviews.

The drinking history typology is based entirely on items from
the intake interview that represent the respondent's personal behavior, experiences and attitudes related to drinking. A number of
the items are taken from Cahalan's studies (3,4) of problem drinking in general population samples, enabling us to compare our data
with his. A preliminary report of our data (5) has shown that the
drug addicts in this study report levels of alcohol intake and problems associated with drinking greatly in excess of those found by
Cahalan and his associates in the general population. The measures
on which the typology is based are:

1. <u>Alcohol Consumption</u>. Subjects were asked separately how
often they drank liquor, wine, and beer, and the quantity of each
consumed on a typical day of use. The daily average amount of pure
ethanol consumed was calculated and summed for the three beverages.
A logarithmic transformation was used in the analyses; quantities
reported here are expressed in terms of the appropriate equivalent
amount of whiskey. <u>Q-F Current</u> refers to the two months prior to
interview; <u>Q-F Ever</u> to the period when the respondent's drinking
was at its maximum, which may or may not be the current period.

2. <u>Loss of Control</u> is a 4-item scale including: tried to cut
down drinking but failed; kept on drinking after promising yourself
not to; worried about your drinking; finding it hard to stop before
getting high. Scored for <u>Current</u> and <u>Ever</u>.

3. <u>Bad Reactions</u> to drinking is a 12-item scale including:
blackouts, "shakes," tremor, anxiety, depression, anger, fighting,
visual distortion, hallucinations, D.T.'s, loss of emotional control
and seizures. Scored for <u>Current</u> and <u>Ever</u>.

4. <u>Consequences</u> of drinking is a 7-item scale of problems in
work, school, family and social relationships caused by drinking.
Scored for <u>Current</u> and <u>Ever</u>.

5. <u>Intoxication</u> is the number of times that the respondent reports having been intoxicated for a full day or more, <u>Current</u> (in
the last 3 months) and <u>Ever</u>.

A two-stage process was used in developing the typology. First,
a D^2 cluster analysis, based on 16 variables, was performed by computer (BMD Computer Program P2M, cf.6), using every third case from
the combined drug addict and alcoholic sample (N= 369). Six
variables in addition to the ten described above (i.e., 5 <u>Current</u>,
5 <u>Ever</u>) were used in this analysis: Social Reasons for Drinking
(4-item scale); Psychological Gains from Drinking Current and Ever
(18-item scales); number of times drunk in the last three months;
how much you would miss drinking if you had to give it up; and probability of substituting alcohol if narcotics are unavailable.

The computer analysis grouped the sample into five clusters.
The next step was to examine the mean profiles of each cluster on
the 16 variables. The first observation was that, of the variables
that were multi-item scales, those representing problems or negative effects of drinking sharply differentiated the clusters (<u>Loss</u>

of Control, Bad Reactions and Consequences), while those representing positive effects or motives for drinking were less differentiating (Social Reasons, Psychological Gains). The latter were accordingly dropped as a basis for the typology, as were three single
items whose meaning duplicated other variables.

The five clusters were differentiated along three dimensions,
which were then used as the basis for a logically-derived typology:
(a) alcohol consumption, (b) symptoms, or problems associated with
drinking, and (c) whether the person's maximal level of consumption
and symptoms was still current at the time of admission to treatment. The criteria on which the typology is based are:

(a) Q-F Ever was divided into three levels. "High" represents
the range in which most of the alcoholics fall, and corresponds to
a daily average of 4 oz. of whiskey or more. It includes 99% of
the alcoholics (with a daily average = 36.61 oz.) and 49% of the
drug addicts (with a daily average of 17.56 oz.). "Moderate" is a
level below that cut-off point, but greater than zero, and includes
1% of the alcoholics and 26% of the drug addicts. "Zero" drinking,
or claimed lifetime abstinence from alcohol was reported by no alcoholics and 25% of the drug addicts.

(b) Symptoms Ever was derived by combining the four variables
of Loss of Control, Bad Reactions, Consequences and Intoxication,
as scored for Ever. The mean product-moment intercorrelation among
these measures is .70. To equalize their influence, each was converted to a four-point scale, ranging from 0 to 3, and they were
then summed to yield a possible score range of 0 to 12. A score of
5 or more is considered "High Symptoms Ever"; 97% of alcoholics and
26% of drug addicts fall into this range. The mean score of those
in the high range is 9.0, and that of all others is 1.0. (The mean
for all alcoholics is 10.3; for drug addicts it is 2.6.)

(c) Current vs. Past. To simplify the analysis, the decision
was made to identify this dimension solely on the basis of alcohol
consumption. Accordingly, those subjects identified as "High Q-F
Ever" were classified as either "High Q-F Current" or not. To be
classified as no longer "High Q-F", a subject had to meet two criteria: (1) that Q-F Current be less than half Q-F Ever, and (2)that
Q-F Current be below the cut-off point for "High Q-F" as defined
above. Of those who were "High Q-F Ever", 80% of the alcoholics
and 51% of the drug addicts were also "High Q-F Current." Of those
not drinking at a high level currently, current moderate drinkers
and current abstainers are grouped together in this analysis.
Whether reported current abstinence was voluntary or not is also
not taken into account. It should be noted that, while change in
symptoms was not used in the "current vs. past" categorization, it
did drop as consumption dropped. For those with "High Symptoms
Ever" whose current consumption remained high (Type I), the mean
current symptoms score was 6.8, while those whose consumption had
dropped to a low level (Type II) had a mean current symptoms score
of 1.7.

It should be noted that not all combinations of these three
criteria are possible, since "High Symptoms Ever" cannot occur with

zero consumption, and the current vs. past distinction is applied only to those with "High Q-F Ever." As a result, seven types are logically possible. These are presented in Table I, with the percentages of drug addicts and alcoholics falling into each type.

Types I and II represent those with a history of problem drinking, past or current, and include 24.2% of the drug addicts and 95.6% of the alcoholics. Types III and IV report high alcohol consumption (past or current), but few or no symptoms, and include 24.9% of drug addicts and 3.1% of alcoholics. The presence of a few alcoholics in these two groups (7 cases) suggests that some subjects in these groups do in fact have symptoms, but either deny them to themselves or merely fail to report them in the interview. Types V and VI, representing moderate drinkers and abstainers, include 49.0% of the drug addicts, and one alcoholic. Type VII consists of a small number of subjects whose consumption of alcohol falls into the moderate range, but whose symptoms are in the high range. Examination of these cases shows that most of them are close to the cut-off point on one or both variables, and they may be considered tentatively to be cases misclassified by the cut-off points. Since they are so few, they are dropped from subsequent comparisons among the types. When these types are compared with the clusters yielded by the computer analysis, we find that the five clusters correspond to Types I, II, III and IV combined, V, and VI.

Overall, the distribution of drug addicts and alcoholics over the types supports the interpretation that Types I and II indicate a history of problem drinking and that, at a minimum, about a quarter of the drug addicts in this sample have at some time resembled alcoholics in their drinking behavior and its effects. At the time that their drinking was at its maximum, they drank an average of 22.8 oz. of whiskey daily, or close to 1½ pints. Of those in these two types, 58.4% of the drug addicts and 81.2% of the alcoholics were drinking at alcoholic levels at the time they entered treatment. Some of the rest were involuntarily abstinent, but the data show that a number of the drug addicts had reduced or stopped their drinking as they became addicted to other drugs. The same is true of the drug addicts in Types III and IV; that is, over half of those who once consumed large quantities of alcohol but deny symptoms had reduced or stopped their drinking, most often on becoming addicted to drugs. One might expect that drug addicts who once drank excessively would be at higher risk for developing drinking problems during or after treatment for their drug problem than those without such a history. This issue will be explored by examination of the 12-month followup data.

The types were compared in regard to age, race and sex, and no significant differences were found. In comparing the drug addicts admitted to methadone maintenance with those entering Eagleville, no significant differences appeared in the proportions with "High Symptoms" (Types I, II, vs. III, IV, V, VI) or "High Q-F Ever" (Types I, II, III, IV vs V, VI). The Eagleville sample had a significantly lower proportion with "High Q-F Current" (Types I and III: 19.4% vs. 28.8% for methadone subjects), which is a result of the fact that more of the Eagleville subjects entered treatment directly from prison and thus were involuntarily abstinent. There were, however, statistically significant and substantial differences among the methadone clinics in the proportions falling into the six types.

Predictive Ability of the Types and Discussion

To test the typology's ability to predict problem drinking after admission to treatment, the 12-month interviews of 100 methadone subjects were compared with the same subjects' intake interviews. At 12 months, 19 reported symptoms of problem drinking, and 13 reported drinking in the alcoholic range (i.e., High Q-F) without symptoms. In all, therefore, 32% could be considered as actual or potential abusers of alcohol at 12 months. When we group them according to the drinking history typology identified on admission, the percentage of each type with evidence of problem drinking at 12 months was:
Type I: 9/15 = 60%;   Type II: 5/10 = 50%;   Type III: 11/15 = 73%;
Type IV: 1/10 = 10%;   Type V: 4/26 = 15%;   Type VI: 2/24 = 8%.
Thus, Types I, II and III were likely to be abusing alcohol 12 months after entering methadone maintenance, while Types IV, V and VI were unlikely to be. While these results are very preliminary, and the data are highly summarized here, they make it clear that problem drinking during and after treatment for drug abuse is to a large degree predictable from the pre-treatment drinking history. In the 100 cases examined, of the 32 who could be considered problem drinkers at 12 months, 25 (or 78%) came from Types I,II and III, while only 22% of the remaining cases did so. These findings serve to validate the usefulness of the typology. It must be kept in mind, however, that the few cases that run counter to expectation are of special interest, particularly the 6 cases from Types V and VI who appear to be exhibiting a drinking problem for the first time at 12 months. They will be the object of special study.

We have, then, demonstrated that an empirically derived typology of drinking histories reported by drug addicts is descriptively useful and has predictive value. The following reports demonstrate its ability to sharpen our understanding of the phenomena of substance abuse. Perhaps the most striking finding reported here is the high incidence of problem drinking in the histories of individuals whose presenting problem on entering treatment is identified as drug abuse. A quarter report histories that could be taken as sufficient evidence of alcoholism, past or present. An additional quarter have ingested excessive quantities of alcohol, although they deny symptoms. For these people, the problem seems to be substance abuse as such, not the abuse of a particular substance.

The types are quite broad, and we plan to examine them in detail to determine whether some or all of them consist of sub-types that can be usefully differentiated. Types II and IV, for example, represent former heavy drinkers who have cut down or stopped. Are there important differences between stopping and cutting down? In particular, are those whose abstinence is involuntary, e.g., because of imprisonment, improperly classified by these types? These issues will be pursued in subsequent analyses of the data.

Table I

EMPIRICAL TYPOLOGY OF DRINKING HISTORIES

TYPE	ALC. CONSUMPTION		SYMPTOMS	% OF DRUG ADDICTS	% OF ALCO- HOLICS
	EVER	CURRENT	EVER		
I	High	High	High	14.1	77.6
II	High	Mod,O	High	10.1	18.0
III	High	High	Low,O	11.2	1.8
IV	High	Mod,O	Low,O	13.7	1.3
V	Mod	Mod,O	Low,O	23.8	.4
VI	O	O	O	25.2	--
VII	Mod	Mod,O	High	1.9	.9

(N=864)   (N=228)

NOTE: The N for alcoholics is reduced by 15 cases for whom
there was insufficient data for classification.

REFERENCES

1. B. Bihari, Alcoholism and Methadone Maintenance, Amer. J. Drug
& Alcohol Abuse, I(I), 79, (1974).

2. G. W. Jackson & A. Richman, Alcohol Use Among Narcotic Addicts,
Alcohol Health & Research World, Spring, (1973) p. 25.

3. D. Cahalan, Problem Drinkers: A National Survey, Jossey-Bass,
Inc., San Francisco, (1970).

4. D. Cahalan, I. H. Cisin, & H. M. Crossley, American Drinking
Practices, Rutgers Center of Alcohol Studies, (1969).

5. H. L. Barr, D. J. Ottenberg, & A. Cohen, Drinking by Addicts,
presented at: The North American Congress on Alcohol and Drug
Problems, San Francisco, December 16, (1974).

6. W. J. Dixon (ed): BMDP: Biomedical Computer Programs, Univ. of
California Press, Berkeley, (1975) p. 323.

PROBLEM DRINKING BY ADDICTS: CHARACTERISTICS OF DRUG USE*

Arie Cohen

Eagleville Hospital and Rehabilitation Center
Eagleville, Pennsylvania

The purpose of the present paper is to discuss further the typology of drug addicts in regard to their drinking previously described (1), and to present some preliminary findings about alcohol and drug use by these types.

The typology of drinking patterns developed by Barr (1) can be conceptualized by the following three facets mapping sentence (2):

Heroin addict who drinks

Amount
1. heavily
2. moderately   in the
3. not at all

Time
1. past and present
2. past only

and

Problems
1. has
2. has not

drinking related problems ———→

Type 1
⋮
Type 6

Of the 12 theoretically possible combinations, Barr identified 7 in her data. One type, however, occurred so infrequently that it was excluded from subsequent data analysis.

Table I presents the six types and includes the code for each type. By utilizing this technique, it becomes possible to identify certain combinations of the facets that did not occur in the present sample. Some of these combinations cannot exist, such as $A_3T_1P_1$, which denotes an addict who has never drunk but has problems associated with drinking. However, some other combinations that have not yet been identified may exist in the general drinking population. For example, the type $A_2T_1P_1$ denotes a person who drinks only moderately but still presents alcohol-related problems. This type of person, who rarely appeared in the sample, might be one who is highly sensitive to alcohol. Further investigation of this type might throw more light on the issue of constitutional predisposition to alcoholism. In addition to its conceptual value, the mapping sentence technique is useful in data analysis. The implications of this issue in regard to the present data will be discussed elsewhere.

*This work was conducted under National Institute on Drug Abuse Demonstration Grant H81 DA 01113.

This preliminary analysis will be limited to heroin addicts only. Within this group, analysis will focus mainly on differences between the addicts who have alcohol related problems and addicts who have not experienced such problems; namely a comparison between types 1 and 2, and types 3, 4, 5 and 6. First, in order to examine the validity of the typology, differences between the types in alcohol related variables that were not part of the criteria for creating the typology will be examined. Then, differences between the types in drug use variables will be presented, and finally some implications of the results will be discussed.

The present sample includes 753 addicts in treatment for heroin addiction. The data was obtained through a structured interview of approximately two hours duration. Within this sample, 179 heroin addicts were identified as problem drinkers (types 1 and 2), and 574 heroin addicts were identified as non-problem drinkers.

First, a comparison was made between reasons for using alcohol and reasons for using drugs within each group of addicts. The responses to 12 items adopted from Cahalan, Cisin and Crossley (3) were used for this analysis. The items were: I use it because "it helps me to relax", "people I know use it", "it helps me to forget my worries", "on certain occasions this is the thing to do", "it helps cheer me up when I'm in a bad mood", "I need it when tense and nervous", "it helps me to relate to people better", "it helps my mind work better", "I like to get high"; "to be sociable", "to celebrate special occasions" and "when I want to forget everything". The subjects were asked to indicate how important each item was as a reason for using alcohol. The set of items was then repeated, this time requiring the subjects to respond to the items as reasons for using drugs, and the amount of differentiation between the reasons for using alcohol and the reasons for using drugs was computed for each type (the formula for the differentiation score is:
$\Sigma \ d^2 = \Sigma$ [reasons for using alcohol - reasons for using drugs]^2).
The means of the differentiation scores between alcohol and drugs for types 1,2,3,4, and 5, were 10.10, 13.22, 13.92, 16.44 and 15.95 respectively (F=5.74, p<0.01). The means of the differentiation scores across the types increase as the type's involvement with alcohol is decreased. In other words, the more an addict is involved with alcohol, the less he differentiates between his reasons for using the two substances. In order to further investigate this relationship, the rank order correlation between the means of the reasons for using alcohol and the reasons for using drugs was computed for each type. For type 1, the group reporting highest involvement with alcohol, the correlation is 0.53 (p<0.05) and for type 5, the group reporting least involvement with alcohol but still responding to the items, the correlation is -0.04 (p>0.05). These two correlations again demonstrate the lack of differentiation between the reasons for using alcohol and drugs in problem drinkers and the existence of such differentiation in non-problem drinkers.

This lack of differentiation between alcohol and drugs is not limited to reports of reasons for use; it is expressed in behavior, too. When presented with the question "when you could not get

944

heroin or another narcotic, how likely would you be to use alcohol as a substitute?", the problem drinker is significantly more inclined to respond "usually" or "sometimes" than the non-problem drinker (t=10.58, p<0.01). Furthermore, when asked how much they would miss alcohol if they had to give it up all together, types 1 and 2 were more willing to admit than the other types that they would "miss it a lot". In addition, the problem drinking addicts indicate more frequently than the non-problem drinkers that alcohol was the first drug they ever used (χ^2=14.24, p<0.001).

The above results, indicating that the problem drinking addict is different from the non-problem drinker in various measures related to alcohol use, support the face validity of the proposed typology.

For the proposed typology of drug addicts to be of any predictive value, its types should be differentiated by variables that are not related to alcohol. In the following section, differences in drug use between the problem drinking and the non-problem drinking addicts will be presented.

In regard to use of specific drugs, the problem drinking heroin addict reports more frequent use of amphetamines than the non-problem drinking addicts during the two months prior to his admission to treatment (t=3.24, p<0.01). On the average, the problem drinker is older than the non-problem drinker when he starts to use amphetamines (the mean ages were 22.05 and 19.47 respectively). The problem drinking addict also smokes, on the average, 29 cigarettes per day, while the non-problem drinker averages only 24 (t=2.03, p<0.05). Furthermore, the problem drinking addict uses marijuana more frequently than his non-problem drinking counterpart during the two months prior to his admission to treatment (t=2.29, p<0.05). However, the two groups do not differ in age of first use of marijuana, or in the age of first use and frequency of cocaine, hallucinogens, tranquilizers, barbiturates, inhalants or number of cups of coffee or tea drunk per day.

In regard to drug use in general, the problem drinkers and the non-problem drinkers perceive similarly their reasons for using drugs; the rank order correlation between the means of the reasons for using drugs in types 1 and 5 is 0.93 (p<0.01). However, the problem drinkers perceive the following items as significantly more important as reasons for using drugs than the non-problem drinkers: "it helps me to relax", "to forget everything", "need it when tense and nervous", and "helps my mind work better". Furthermore, the problem drinking addict is higher than the non-problem drinking addict on the four scales that measure problems associated with drug use. These four scales - psychological gains, bad reaction, loss of control and consequences - include the same items as the four alcohol related scales with the same names (for the listing of the items see (1)). Table II includes the means and standard deviations of these scales for the problem drinking group and the non-problem drinking group. Finally, the problem drinker experiences more frequently than the non-problem drinker accidental overdoses, crashes and bad trips.

All these measures which differentiate between problem drinking heroin addicts and non-problem drinking addicts constitute a

945

complete cycle of addiction. First comes the expectation that the drug will satisfy personal needs (e.g. "need it when tense and nervous "); then, following the use, the psychological gains are obtained. However, as drug use continues, bad reactions to the drugs occur and loss of control over the use is experienced, followed by the serious consequences in everyday life. This creates a stronger need for psychological relief via drugs and the vicious circle is completed. The problem drinking addicts' high scores on all these variables indicate their deeper involvement in all stages of the cycle.

The first question that comes to mind in view of the above findings is why is it that drug addicts who are involved in problem drinking report greater need and stronger effects from drugs. Is it possible that the joint use of drugs and alcohol has a synergetic effect? If so, one would expect no psychological or socio-demographic differences between problem drinkers and non-problem drinkers. However, further data do not support this assumption. Steinberger and Cohen (4) report that problem drinkers have more disturbed psychological profiles and more suicidal attempts than the non-problem drinkers, and Hannigan and Barr (5) have found that the problem drinking addicts have had more chaotic childhoods, and more deviant lifestyles than the non-problem drinking addicts. These additional findings suggest that the problem drinking addict is a different type of addict to begin with, whose addiction is more diffused and general in nature and is possibly rooted deep within his total personality structure. If this speculation is correct, then the prognosis for the problem drinking addict is likely to be poor, unless he receives treatment designed to meet his special needs. Furthermore, chemotherapy, such as methadone maintenance, which is oriented toward the chemical dependency per se, would be the least effective form of therapy for this type of addict.

The data for testing these speculations have already been collected and their analysis and interpretation will help clarify some of the issues pertaining to addiction to chemical substances.

Table I

THE SIX TYPES AND THEIR CODES

TYPE	AMOUNT	TIME	PROBLEMS	CODE
1	heavy	past & present	yes	$A_1T_1P_1$
2	heavy	past	yes	$A_1T_2P_1$
3	heavy	past & present	no	$A_1T_1P_2$
4	heavy	past	no	$A_1T_2P_2$
5	moderate	past & present	no	$A_2T_1P_2$
6	no use	past & present	no	$A_3T_1P_2$

Table II

THE MEANS AND STANDARD DEVIATIONS OF THE PROBLEM DRINKER
AND THE NON-PROBLEM DRINKER ON THE FOUR DRUG-RELATED
PROBLEMS SCALES

THE SCALE	PROBLEM DRINKER		NON-PROBLEM DRINKER		t	α
	M	S.D.	M	S.D.		
Psychological gains	13.08	3.84	11.36	4.29	4.26	0.01
Bad Reactions	5.45	2.82	4.37	2.71	4.08	0.01
Loss of Control	3.78	0.55	3.59	0.77	2.71	0.01
Bad Consequences	5.22	1.86	4.67	1.96	2.93	0.01

REFERENCES

1. H. L. Barr, Problem Drinking by Drug Addicts: An Empirical
   Typology. These proceedings.

2. I. M. Schlesinger, and L. Guttman, Smallest space analysis of
   intelligence and achievement tests. Psychological Bulletin,
   71, 95 (1969).

3. D. Cahalan, I. H. Cisin and H. M. Crossley, American Drinking
   Practices, Rutger's Center of Alcohol Studies, New Brunswick,
   (1969)..

4. H. Steinberger and A. Cohen, Problem Drinking Drug Addicts:
   Psychological Characteristics. These proceedings.

5. P. Hannigan and H. L. Barr, Problem Drinking Drug Addicts:
   Childhood History and Social Characteristics.
   These proceedings.

THE USE OF ALCOHOLISM SCREENING TEST TO IDENTIFY THE POTENTIAL FOR ALCOHOLISM IN PERSONS ON METHADONE MAINTENANCE

Aaron Cohen, M.S., William McKeever, M.S.,
Murry J. Cohen, M.D., Barry Stimmel, M.D.

Departments of Psychiatry and Medicine
Mount Sinai School of Medicine of
The City University of New York
New York, New York

The diagnosis of alcoholism, particularly in its early stages, confronts the health professional with an exceedingly difficult problem. Not infrequently, through denial on either the part of the patient or therapist, an advanced state of alcoholism is allowed to occur prior to its recognition.

The prevalence of alcoholism in patients enrolled in methadone maintenance programs has been well described. Unfortunately, although these individuals are seen daily by treatment staff, in most cases the diagnosis of excessive alcohol intake also goes unnoticed until drinking patterns have been firmly established and functioning impaired. In an attempt to develop a method of early identification of an individual at high risk of becoming alcoholic once enrolled in methadone maintenance, the following study was undertaken.

I. DESCRIPTION OF STUDY

A modification of a self-administered alcohol screening test (SAAST), developed by Swenson and Morse (1), was utilized to assess an individual's potential for alcoholism. The test as originally formulated by these investigators was able to differentiate alcoholics from a non-alcoholic group of patients drawn from a general medical population. The SAAST was modified by the insertion of questions to provide a measure of validity with respect to an individual's response to the overall questionnaire. A validity score was felt to be quite important in an effort to overcome the

This study relates to a program funded by the New York State
Office of Drug Abuse Services

defensiveness frequently seen in alcoholics concerning admission of drinking patterns. The subtle changes in the items were made so that the patient would most likely be unaware that the same answer was expected.

The SAAST was given individually by a counselor to each patient, with a yes or no answer required for each item. Total score was obtained by a summation of the number of questions answered in the alcoholic direction,with the higher scores indicating a greater potential for the existence of alcoholism. Utilizing this system, excluding the five validity questions, the highest possible score obtained by any individual would be thirty-four.

The SAAST was administered to the following groups:

1) Thirty patients enrolled in the MMATP who currently exhibited signs of severe alcoholism (Alcohol Group);

2) Thirty patients enrolled in the MMATP who were stabilized on methadone maintenance and exhibited neither signs nor symptoms related to alcohol intake (Control Group);

3) Eighty consecutive admissions to the MMATP over a six-month period (Admission Group).

Tests for significance between groups were performed using the Student t test. A level of significance was considered to exist if p values were less than 0.05.

II. RESULTS

A demographic analysis of the Alcohol and Control Groups revealed no significant differences with respect to sex, ethnicity, age, and years of narcotic addiction. The Alcohol Group had a mean score of 14.03, the Control Group a mean score of 3.00 ($p < 0.001$). The validity score was derived on the basis of whether the same answer was given to a test question and its corresponding validity question. Complete agreement between the five test questions yielded a maximum score of 5, while complete discordance a score of 0. It was hoped that this measure would, to some extent, reflect alcoholic defensiveness.

The Alcohol Group had a mean validity score of 3.3 v. a score of 4.3 with respect to the Control Group ($p = 0.01$). No one in the Control Group had a validity score of less than 3.

The scores on the SAAST of the 80 persons in the Admission Group are illustrated in Table I. It is important to emphasize that all persons in this Group were already screened during intake to eliminate those who were thought to have a problem with alcohol use. Part of the intake procedure consists of obtaining a drinking history from the applicant. Any person indicating an existing difficulty in controlling his/her alcohol intake is referred to treatment facilities that are better prepared to treat alcoholics than our program.

The mean score of persons in the Admission Group was 5.17 compared to 3.00 for the Control Group (p=0.01). It was felt that the higher scores in this Group might be explained by the presence of either hidden alcoholics or individuals with the potential for developing alcoholism at some time in the future. In order to test this hypothesis, this Group was subdivided based on SAAST scores of 0-7 and 8 or above. A score of 8 was selected as a cutoff point indicative of potential alcoholism as it represented a value greater than 2 standard deviations from the Control Group. Twenty-one patients of the 80 (26%) in the Admission Group had scores indicative of potential alcoholism. It should be emphasized that some of the primary therapists of these patients were completely unaware of the individual's risk for developing alcoholism.

A follow-up of three to seven month's duration of the Admission Group was performed to determine the frequency of excessive drinking once enrolled on methadone maintenance. A diagnosis of excessive alcoholism was made on the basis of 1) a history of consuming increasing quantities of alcohol since enrollment in the program and 2) frequent evidence of excessive alcohol intake when appearing for medication. The relationship of excessive alcohol intake with SAAST scores is illustrated in Table II. Of those persons scoring below 8, 5 of 59 (8%) had difficulties with excessive alcohol intake. One of these two individuals initially had a low validity score suggesting excessive denial. Of the 21 patients with test scores of 8 and above, 12 (57%) were found to consume excessive amounts of alcohol within seven months of enrollment in the MMATP.

III.   CONCLUSIONS

1)   A SAAST is able to differentiate a group of alcoholic patients from a control group of nonalcoholics.

2)   The inclusion in the SAAST of questions to determine validity of an individual's response are valuable as an indication of defensiveness. A low validity score, when accompanied by a low SAAST, was found to be useful as an indicator of the potential to develop alcoholism.

3)   The SAAST can be used not only as an indicator of existing potential to become alcoholic but also to identify the hidden alcoholic.

4)   This test is therefore considered to be a valuable addition to existing intake procedures as an aid to the early diagnosis and perhaps prevention of alcoholism.

TABLE I

COMPARISON SAAST SCORES BETWEEN EXPERIMENTAL
AND CONTROL GROUPS

Group	No.	Mean Score	S.D.*	Range
CONTROL	30	3.00 ± 1.72**		0-7
ADMISSION	80	5.17 ± 4.64		0-22

  * S.D.=Standard Deviation
** P < .01

TABLE II

FOLLOW-UP STUDY OF EXCESSIVE DRINKING
IN ADMISSION GROUP

Score	No.	Excessive Drinkers No.	(%)
Below Eight	59	5	(8)
Eight & Above	21	12	(57)
TOTAL	80	17	(21)

REFERENCES

1. W. M. Swenson and R. M. Morse, Mayo Clin.Proc., 50: 204, (1975).

POLYDRUG ABUSE

POLYDRUG ABUSE AND COMPREHENSIVE TREATMENT INTERVENTION

David E. Smith, M.D.; Donald R. Wesson, M.D.,
and Grace M. Dammann

San Francisco Polydrug Project
527 Irving Street
San Francisco, California 94122

I. INTRODUCTION

Implicit in many discussions of drug abuse treatment is the assumption of an "ideal" treatment modality for each patient. Accordingly, research studies are designed to demonstrate the effectiveness of the modality, and assessment is viewed as the technique of collecting information to match the patient to the most appropriate modality. This "ideal modality" approach can be faulted on two counts. First, it fails to recognize that a given treatment modality may be effective at one time in the patient's treatment, and be ineffective, or even contraindicated, at another. Second, it tends to restrict treatment to the use of a single modality. There is the possibility that several modalities used in combination may be effective, whereas any one of these modalities used alone, may not.

We propose in this paper a pragmatic framework for designing treatment interventions which is sensitive both to temporal considerations--by dividing treatment into clinically useful phases-- and to the necessity of integrating medical, psychological and social interventions in providing effective care. An outline of our schemata is shown in Table I.

While many patients enter treatment at phase 1, others may enter for detoxification (phase 2), or even following detoxification (phase 3). Some patients will proceed sequentially from phases 1 through 4. For others, crisis intervention, such as treatment of an overdose, may be required while they are in phase 4. The importance of the model is not so much in defining "steps" for the patient as in Alcoholics Anonymous, but rather in giving the clinician a conceptual framework for applying various treatment interventions. This paper will examine three forms of intervention which are useful at different points during the comprehensive treatment process.

II. TREATMENT MODALITIES

A. Individual Psychotherapy

Individual psychotherapy, or the process of meeting on a one-to-one basis with clients for the purposes of discussing problems, offering advice and examining the clients' various human relationships, is likely to be called psychotherapy when done by a psychologist or psychiatrist, and counseling when done by other individuals. In general, individual psychotherapy has not been highly regarded as an effective treatment modality in the drug abuse field, whether done by ex-addicts or psychologists. This is an example of a modality which, in our opinion, is useful in all phases of treatment, although a modality which, by itself, is rarely sufficient. For example, during crisis periods, it can be used to help relieve the client's feelings of extreme isolation, fear, and anxiety. During the detoxification phase, it can be used to support the detoxification process by providing the client with a framework in which to discuss some of the feelings emerging as a result of decreased drug use. Regular psychotherapeutic sessions serve to establish rapport and trust, and to keep the individual in treatment. After the therapist-client relationship is firmly established, (in phase 3) and important to the client, the relationship can become a powerful influence. In addition, the sessions can be used to identify new problem areas and offer an opportunity to assess the impact of other treatment interventions. The therapeutic relationship can be an opportunity for the client to modify behavior either through identification with and modeling of the therapist, or through insight into the consequences of current behavior. When viewed in light of what can be accomplished through individual psychotherapy, we believe that psychotherapy is an important part of any treatment plan.

B. Pharmacotherapy

While the judicious use of psychotropic medication can be an effective intervention at any stage of treatment (e.g., Narcan^R-- to reverse the effects of opiate overdose), pharmacotherapy is an extremely useful treatment modality in helping to achieve stabilization during phases 3 and 4. Pharmacotherapy can be considered under three non-mutually exclusive categories. While all three forms involve the long-term administration of psychoactive drugs, the mode of action of the drugs and the therapeutic rationales are sufficiently diverse that they are best considered separately.

We conceptualize drug maintenance as the use of prescribed amounts of the drug of abuse, or a drug with similar properties. In the treatment of heroin dependence for example, methadone has received considerable attention. The use of the long-acting methadone is feasible because the individual develops tolerance to its narcotic effects which are cross tolerant with heroin. Since this

tolerance blocks the effects of heroin, the individual's incentive
for using heroin is greatly reduced. No comparable tolerance-
producing agent exists to block the effects of sedative-hypnotics
or stimulant drugs. Because of the tendency to escalate dosage,
maintenance on the drug of abuse is generally not feasible,
although there are individual exceptions.

Treatment of the individual with drugs which reverse the
effects of the drug of abuse is called antagonist therapy. With
the treatment of heroin dependency, cyclasozine has been used
experimentally. Its routine use has been hampered by its propensity to produce side effects. A variant of antagonist therapy
is the use of Antabuse^R in the treatment of alcoholism. Ingestion
of alcohol after ingesting Antabuse^R results in nausea, vomiting,
and other unpleasant and sometimes dangerous, signs and symptoms.
Unfortunately, no practical antagonist drugs exist for amphetamines
and the commonly used sedative-hypnotics.

A third use of psychopharmacological drugs in the treatment
of drug abuse is psychotropic drug therapy. Here the goal is
treatment of underlying psychopathology which may be contributing
to the individual's drug abusing behavior. Unfortunately, such
therapy is not feasible with many drug abusers because their
inconsistent and unreliable usage of prescribed drugs and their
intermittent use of illictly obtained drugs. While the use of
certain psychotropic medications may be clearly indicated from
a psychological diagnostic perspective, the hazards of such
therapy may contraindicate its use. Sometimes, with careful
administration of the drug at a half-way house, drug abuse
treatment staff can circumvent the problem of inconsistent or
unreliable usage, although concurrent abuse of illicitly obtained
drugs may still expose the individual to the risk of adverse drug
interactions. The following are our observations on the use of
psychotropic medications in the treatment of drug abusers.

1. TRICYCLIC ANTIDEPRESSANTS

Tricyclic antidepressants for relief of depression and associated symptoms such as insomnia, are frequently useful. Pharmacotherapy with tricyclics is particularly valuable in treating the
rebound depression amphetamine abusers experience after detoxification. Progress is enhanced by a balanced approach using a tricyclic antidepressant for relief of depression while involving
the client in other forms of treatment such as psychotherapy and
residential treatment. Elavil^R, (amitriptyline hydrochloride) and
Tofranil^R, (imipramine hydrochloride) 100 to 150 mg at bedtime for
a period of three to six months, with careful monitoring of any
side effects, has proved effective.

Clients with suicidal depression should be given tricyclics
in limited quantity because of the medication's potential as a
suicide agent.

2. LITHIUM CARBONATE

Lithium carbonate has been particularly effective as a treatment modality for individuals with affective disorders, including manic depressive illness, unipolar mania, and unipolar endogenous depression. It has also been effective in treating symptoms which are associated with depression such as insomnia. In addition, it has been effective in treating major affective disorders at serum levels of 0.8 to 1.0 meg/L. Clients with suicidal depression should be given the medication in limited quantities because of its low therapeutic index. As with the use of tricyclic anti-depressants, lithium is most effective when used in conjunction with psychotherapy and, if needed, residential placement.

3. PHENOTHIAZINES

Phenothiazines and butyrophenones have been extremely effective in treating thought disorders which are either precipitated by drug use, or masked by heavy drug abuse. Phenothiazines should not be used in the period of post-drug exposure because of the possibility of idiosyncratic reactions and additive effects with the drugs the client may have taken. Phenothiazines should not be used where PCP use is suspected because of the possibility of cardio-respiratory depression. Phenothiazines should not be used where sedative-hypnotic withdrawal is suspected to be the precipitant of psychosis, as they lower the seizure threshhold. With persons withdrawing from sedative-hypnotics, Haldol[R] can be used and withdrawal should proceed at half the normal rate. Finally, anti-psychotic medication is necessary in the treatment of amphetamine induced psychosis as the thought disorder clears quickly upon cessation of amphetamine use. For psychotic-like symptoms which emerge with the ingestion of hallucinogenic substances, excessive doses of amphetamines, or PCP, the best therapy is non-somatic supportive counseling in the immediate post-drug exposure period, with removal from an over-stimulating environment.

For the clients who manifest thought disorders in the post-detoxification period, anti-psychotic medication is generally effective in both eliminating the psychotic symptoms and in alleviating the anxiety which the client was attempting to medicate. Again, drug maintenance on phenothiazines is effective only insofar as it is supported by other treatment modalities. If residential placement is required, the policy and attitude of the program towards anti-psychotic medication should be explored. Similarly, it is important that therapy be provided by a professional who supports the use of the medication. Finally, it is often helpful to have the drug administered on a daily basis, during periods of crisis for clients who have difficulty taking the medication as directed.

C. Biofeedback

Biofeedback has received recent attention as a therapeutic modality for drug abuse. Several years ago, the San Francisco Polydrug Project began using biofeedback with polydrug abusers. We developed a number of impressions based on individual case studies. Because of changes in equipment and changing patterns of applications as we gained more experience in the technique, we have not used consistent procedures. Therefore, we emphasize the impressionistic nature of our results.

With biofeedback, physiological functions such as electrical activity of muscles, hand temperature, or brain waves, are electronically measured and electrically processed to convert the function to an auditory or visual signal which is feedback to the client. The most widely known form of biofeedback is electroencephalogram (EEG) in which the frequency and amplitude of brain waves are processed electronically to detect frequencies in the range of 8-13 Hz, commonly known as alpha. Electromyolography (EMG) converts muscle electrical activity to a tone which is proportional to the amount of muscle electrical activity. The individual attempts to reduce muscle activity by reducing the frequency of the tone. With temperature biofeedback, the individual's temperature (usually measured by a thermistor on the fingers) is made proportional to a tone. As anxiety and unpleasant emotions activate the limbic system of the brain with consequent vascular constriction, teaching the individual to warm his hands is a method of teaching affective control. In addition, temperature biofeedback is used for treatment of migraine headaches. Other physiological functions can be used in biofeedback but are not as common as the three just described.

Biofeedback as a treatment modality can have two distinct kinds of therapeutic effects. When used with a client who experiences chronic pain such as migraines, and who attempts to medicate with analgesics, biofeedback can have a specific effect. It is possible, with such clients, to alter physiological function--contraction of vessels--by teaching them how to warm their hands or dilate the vessels. Dilation of the vessels, in turn, can result in a reduction of the frequency and/or duration of migraines, thus limiting or removing both the symptom for which the drug was being taken, and overall drug use. In such cases, the effect is specific to the symptoms which the client self-medicated.

Often, however, the effect of biofeedback training is nonspecific. For example, for clients whose primary reason for taking drugs is anxiety, the acquisition of control to reduce muscle tension may lead to reduced drug use. In addition, however, such control may generalize to other areas of interaction with the self and the world. In such instances, the biofeedback training--with the acquisition of muscle control--results in an internal "placebo effect", with control in one area becoming transferred to other areas. The effect is non-specific; it makes no difference what modality the client has learned.

Biofeedback probably has its greatest application in the later phases (3 and 4) of treatment. Biofeedback should not be introduced so early in treatment that the client is unable to be successsful. Failure only increases feelings of hopelessness and further lowers the individual's self-esteem. Individuals who are in crisis or undergoing the stresses of withdrawal have difficulties in learning control over their EEG or temperature. EMG is generally the easiest modality to learn, and can sometimes be useful during withdrawal in reducing muscle tension.

To achieve maximum therapeutic benefit, biofeedback sessions should be given daily, for 30 minutes a piece. A series of at least 30 separate biofeedback sessions is generally necessary for the acquisition of physiological control. Clients should be encouraged during biofeedback sessions to express their feelings about the various sensations they experience while learning control. Such expression allows input from the staff which can circumvent the client's feelings of displeasure or discomfort. For example, stimulant users often have a different idea of relaxation than decreased muscle tension. Some may report the feeling of reduced muscle tension to be an unpleasant state and they may describe it in terms of being dead or sleepy. Such sensations can be interpreted by staff as a change in psychological state which will pass as they continue to use the equipment.

Biofeedback is most appropriate with clients whose target symptoms are pain syndromes, particularly those which are vascular related, or chronic anxiety and insomnia. However, biofeedback can be useful with a wide variety of clients.

The knowledge that the individual is able to acquire control over physiological processes alone is frequently of importance in increasing the individual's self-esteem and feelings of mastery over his environment. We believe this control to be of great symbolic importance to an individual who has relinquished control of his feeling states and physiology to drugs.

Except, perhaps, in clients who are using drugs to self-medicate pain, anxiety, or affective distress, biofeedback alone would not be expected to "cure" drug abuse. Like psychotherapy, regular biofeedback sessions maintain regular contact with the client. The newness of the procedure and the impressive equipment may serve to mobilize hope, and may exert prominent placebo effects. The modality deserves further consideration and one should not despair. While biofeedback alone is insufficient therapy for the majority of patients, the modality may have some role in the therapy of most patients. The goal of biofeedback is the acquisition of physiological control, and its utilization has been successful when the patient acquires control. Psychotherapy and biofeedback are frequently complementary. Biofeedback serves to build self-esteem, a feeling of mastery, and the acquisition of non-drug control of feeling states. Psychotherapy, on the other hand, can serve to modify human interactions--a change which cannot be acquired through biofeedback.

III. SUMMARY

Comprehensive treatment of the polydrug abuser generally requires the strategic use of a variety of treatment modalities and techniques. The use of a particular modality is effective only when adequate consideration has been given to the needs of a particular client and the appropriate timing of the intervention. We have presented a conceptual framework which indicates a range of possible interventive techniques, given client needs and status.

TABLE I

GRID OF DRUG ABUSE INTERVENTION

Categories of Service:	No Patient Change	Restore Patient Base Potential		Improve Patient Potential
	1 Identify and Evaluate — Crisis Services	2 Short-term Stabilization	3 Long-term Stabilization	4 Rehabilitation
Medical	Treatment of: 1) OD 2) Withdrawal 3) Infection	1) Detox 2) Treatment of acute medical problems	1) Treatment of chronic medical problems 2) On-going medical care 3) Well-body care, i.e., exercise, nutrition, etc. ⟶	
Psychological	Short-term Rx for: 1) Suicidal thoughts 2) Panic	1) Psychological support for detox 2) CMHC involvement 3) Short-term Rx	1) Long-term psychotherapy ⟶ 2) Relationship Rx 3) Pharmacotherapy 4) Biofeedback, T.M., etc. ⟶	
Legal	Legal assistance for: 1) Arrests 2) Foster-care placement	1) Legal aide 2) Private atty. 3) Court interact a. probation/ diversion b. foster-care placement	1) Probation 2) Diversion	
Social				

GRID OF DRUG ABUSE INTERVENTION

Categories of Service:	No Patient Change		Restore Patient Base Potential		Improve Patient Potential
	Identify and Evaluate	1 Crisis Services	2 Short-term Stabilization	3 Long-term Stabilization	4 Rehabilitation
Residential		1) Missions 2) Emergency crash pads 3) Churches	1) Inpatient 2) Day hospital 3) CMHC	1) Half-way house 2) Foster home 3) Live-in job 4) Day programs 5) CMHC	1) Apartment 2) Satellite housing of: (a) drug programs; (b) half-way houses
Economic		1) Emergency relief from general asst. 2) Emergency relief from churches	1) Welfare—county state, federal 2) private missions 3) Unemployment ins.	1) SSI 2) State disability 3) Federal disability 4) Job	1) Job placement
Occupational			1) Voc. rehab. 2) Emp. comm. 3) Work pool	1) Voc. rehab. 2) Emp. comm. 3) Work pool 4) Apprenticeship programs	1) Voc. rehab. 2) Job placement 3) Apprenticeship programs
Education	Drug Education		Aide in school re-entry	Educational planning ————→ Special learning ————→	
People			1) Family and other support system intervention 2) Day-treatment groups	1) Family-grief-work 2) Family referrals 3) Support groups	1) Growth groups

WHAT TREATMENT TECHNIQUES WORK
WITH TODAY'S POLYDRUG ABUSER

Edward Kaufman, M.D., Panel Chairperson

Medical Director, Chief Psychiatrist
Lower Eastside Service Center
New York, New York

Polydrug abuse unfortunately is a term which conveys different
meanings to different workers in the field. This term was originally introduced to describe the simultaneous abuse of more than one
drug.[1] However, when the Federal Government funded polydrug programs the term came to be defined as what NIDA (National Institute
of Drug Abuse) considered "polydrug" for funding purposes, i.e.
dependence on a psychoactive drug or drugs in which the primary
drug dependence was not heroin, methadone or alcohol. Other workers continue to use polydrug to describe other types of multiple
drug use. To simplify this confusion this author has divided
mutliple drug abuse into four categories.[2]

Type I.   Narcotic abuse, with the abuse of other psycho-
           active drugs and alcohol

Type II.   Methadone maintenance with the abuse of other
           drugs and alcohol

Type III. Alcohol abuse with the abuse of other drugs

Type IV.   The abuse of more than one non-narcotic drug.

Type IV is what is usually referred to as "polydrug." In this
paper we will deal with the problems of treating all four types of
multiple drug abuse. Many treatment principles apply to all four
types and many to specific types.

The author has previously described the causes of drug abuse as
multiple with an emphasis on many psychodynamic and social factors.

Since there are so many possible causes of drug abuse in each given
individual it follows that any treatment plan must be tailored to
the specific causes in each individual.

Individuals who abuse drugs to a point where intellectual functioning is frequently impaired during therapy sessions or their lives
are totally preoccupied with obtaining drugs are virtually un-
treatable as outpatients. Frequently an individual can be detoxified from multiple drug abuse in a hospital and can then engage in
meaningful treatment. At times this detoxification must be repeated several times before treatment can occur. Multiple drug abusers
who are not habituated to any drug can be treated as outpatients,
particularly if they are capable of building up a therapeutic
alliance and transferring their attachments from drugs to a therapist or therapeutic team. Patients who continue to abuse drugs or
revert to dependence after detoxification can, in the author's
experience, only be treated in a residential setting. One answer
to the problem of multiple drug abuse among methadone patients is
to first get them to give up methadone. Peer pressure exerted
through the therapeutic milieu of the program is a crucial factor
in helping patients give up any drug, particularly maintenance
methadone.

The first step and the common denominator in the successful treatment of drug dependent patients is to get them to give up their
pattern of drug abuse. Once this is accomplished, be it through a
TC, drug maintenance, transference, or self-determination, there
must be an individualized treatment plan which offers a full
range of therapeutic and vocational services. Psychoanalytically-
oriented therapies, particularly those in which the therapist maintains a passive role, are not generally successful with multiple
drug abusers. This is because individuals who are used to "the
immediate effects of drugs frequently find the slow tedious
process..." of such therapies "to be excruciating."[3] Thus,
therapies such as Gestalt, Primal, Encounter, and Transactional
Analysis tend to be more successful because they are more
immediately rewarding. However, if these therapies are not based
on individual need and psychodynamic principles, they tend to be
of only short term benefit. What makes any psychotherapy successful with these patients, including psychoanalytic, is the therapist's active use of his own experiences and emotions. He or she
must use a variety of directive techniques to break through
emotional barriers.

Psychotropic drugs, in the author's experience, tend to be of little
use in the majority of drug abusers. Minor tranquilizers (Valium[R],
Librium[R]) tend to be abused no matter how judiciously they are
prescribed. Mellaril or other major tranquilizers with minimal
side effects can be used to relieve neurotic anxiety or psychotic
symptoms. Drug abusers tend to have a very low tolerance for the
side effects of phenothiazines. They also dislike the non-euphoric
effects of these drugs. When patients can be persuaded to take
them regularly they can be very helpful.

Antidepressants are of value in only the most serious of overt
depressions where vegetative symptoms are present. The recent

abuse of Elavil^R for its sedative and synergistic properties
have made it extremely difficult to use this antidepressant in the
New York City area. In addition, other antidepressants may only be
useful in a residential setting as such patients are unable to
tolerate the frustration of waiting two or three weeks for such
medication to work. We have recently used Lithium Carbonate in two
multiple drug abusing patients with overt schizoaffective disorders
and achieved moderate success. We would suggest further use of
Lithium in carefully selected cases with definite mood cyclic
disorders underlying or accompanying drug abuse. When drug abuse
is the result of underlying neurotic anxiety or depression or of
psychosis, every effort must be made to maintain the patient on
appropriate chemotherapeutic agents.

Treatment must be geared to specific causes in specific individuals
as well as to type of multiple drug abuse. When social factors
are prominent as in urban ghettoes, a treatment approach should
emphasize educational, vocational, recreational and housing factors.
In the past five years, ghetto bred addicts have become more
involved with Type IV drug abuse. However, once their pharmacologic dependence is treated, they can still be treated by an
approach that uses the above modalities. Ghetto addicts also do
quite well in a TC when there are appropriate role models for
identification. The lower an individual's basic motivation for
change, the more he should be placed in a low intervention program
with emphasis on drug treatments such as methadone maintenance or
narcotic antagonists with little emphasis on psychotherapy. Such
programs should provide for shifts to higher intervention modalities when motivation increases.

The degree of psychopathology in multiple drug abusers is directly
proportional to:

    1. higher social class
    2. drug use patterns which are unusual in a social system
    3. severity of multiple habituation
    4. shifts from one pharmacologic category to another

As psychopathology rises, the need for psychiatric participation
in treatment increases. Sicker patients do not do well in
traditional TC's as they are unable to tolerate confrontation and
punishment, separation from family and friends, or early responsibility. Since most serious abusers of multiple drugs tend to be
the sickest of drug abusers they do not do well in TC's unless
there is substantial psychiatric treatment and input as to modifications of traditional techniques.

In middle class patients drug abuse tends to be quite related to
familial patterns. Thus, early family evaluation and therapy is
essential with these patients. Multiple family therapy is

particularly effective with this group and is described elsewhere in these proceedings.

Individuals should be offered a variety of relaxation techniques and recreational activities to help deal with their problems and anxieties in a drug-free manner. To this end, baseball, basketball, volleyball, gymnastics, charades and theater and concert attendance are available and encouraged. Yoga, chanting and breathing exercises are also helpful in providing patients with drug-free alternatives as well as relief from the anxiety of detoxification. Rage reduction techniques are particularly necessary and helpful as patients are detoxifying.

The Federal Government, through NIDA, has helped unearth and delineate the extent of the multiple drug problem, particularly of the Type IV or "polydrug" pattern. It is most unfortunate that with the discovery of need has come a shrinking of funds for treatment. Despite the commonality of multiple drug use and abuse the individual who has become addicted to one or more multiple drugs is quite difficult to treat. He or she requires many modifications of present mental health and TC approaches. In all cases these modifications require more intensive therapy by more highly trained personnel. Thus, we have the paradox of having determined the need for new, expensive treatment centers at a time when there are insufficient funds to support vital existing programs. Hopefully, funds will soon be made available to treat this needy and growing group of multiple drug abusers.

REFERENCES

(1)   Bourne, P.G., Polydrug Abuse -- Considerations in a National Strategy, Amer. J. Drug and Alcoh. Abuse, Vol. 1, No. 2: 141-158 (1974).

(2)   Kaufman, E., The Abuse of Multiple Drugs, Amer. J. Drug and Alcoh. Abuse, Vol. 3, No. 2, in press.

(3)   Smith, D.E., Wesson, D.R., The Federal Approach to Polydrug Abuse, Journal of Psychedelic Drugs, Vol. 7, No. 2:111-114 (1975).

(4)   Wesson, D.R., Personal Communication, 1975.

MULTIFACTOR DETERMINANTS OF
TREATMENT INVOLVEMENT IN POLYDRUG USERS

Edward Deaux, Susan Case, John Phin, and David Speck

Philadelphia Psychiatric Center
Philadelphia, Pennsylvania

This report presents a methodological model for the isolation of variables differentiating non-patient drug users (those who were not enrolled in a drug or alcohol treatment program, were not involved in psychotherapy, and were not seeking treatment at the time of testing) from patient drug users (those who were in treatment or who were seeking treatment). It must be emphasized that the methodology and the model are relatively more important here than the data which were used to test the model.

The purpose of the model was to predict the status of a subject as patient or nonpatient. As tested on our data, however, the model's function is more accurately described as "postdicting" in that each $\underline{S}$'s status as a patient or nonpatient was known.

Sample. The Philadelphia Research Center tested approximately 400 polydrug users during the course of its involvement in the National Polydrug Study. The first 253 paid-informant $\underline{Ss}$ tested from December 1974 through March 1975 comprised the sample included in this report. Of these $\underline{Ss}$, 189 (74.7%) were nonpatient drug users and the other 64 (25.3%) were patients.

Instrumentation. The model was tested with items from three widely used instruments, as well as an intake form which obtained demographic and drug use data. Two instruments were self-administered: the Minnesota Multiphasic Personality Inventory (MMPI) (1) and the Profile of Mood States (POMS) (2). The third instrument was the Current and Past Psychiatric Scales (CAPPS) (3) which is an interviewer completed schedule of 112 items.

Model. Because some drug users decide to enter treatment and others do not, it is important to determine what variables are involved in that decision and how those variables interact. Further, the identification of these variables and their interrelationships might help in developing a model which could predict anyone's propensity to seek treatment. Clinically, the idea that drug use *per se* is not the sole factor in a person's entering a drug-treatment program has gained wide acceptance, but the question of which fac-

tors are involved in that decision still needs to be addressed
through statistically sound methodology.

The approach involved five steps: 1. Three mutually exclusive
dimensions were specified: Personal Functioning, Social Functioning, and Drug Use (both current and historical). 2. Items which
related clearly to only one of the three dimensions were chosen
from the POMS, CAPPS, MMPI, and intake form. 3. Intercorrelation
matrices and factor analyses were utilized to reduce the number of
variables within each dimension to approximately 25. 4. Each set
of variables was subjected to a computerized statistical technique,
the Automatic Interaction Detector (AID) *(4 and 5)*. The outcome
was a "tree" which began with the total sample of 253 and divided
and subdivided that sample into groups of decreasing size. These
groups were defined by their scores on predictor variables which the
AID had found to relate to differences in the dependent variable.
The process ended with small groups in which the homogeneity was
maximized and further splitting was not advantageous. Since the
dependent variable was dichotomous (patient or nonpatient) the ideal
result of the use of the AID was to isolate subgroups composed exclusively of all patients or all nonpatients. 5. The model was
evaluated relative to its success in predicting patient/nonpatient
status and in explaining the variance in the dependent variable.

Results.

1. Personal Functioning: Among the personal functioning
variables, the eighth clinical scale of the MMPI, Schizophrenia,
was identified by the AID as best splitting the total sample of
253 Ss. The subgroup of 101 Ss with scale scores above 72 were
split from the group having lower scores (n = 152). The high
score group contained 42.6% patients while the low score group had
13.2% patients. The next predictors were "number of suicide attempts," splitting those with none from those with one or more, and
the CAPPS past scale of Depression/Anxiety, splitting those with
scores over 2.18 from those with lower scores. In all, 13 variables were used to split the sample into 15 subgroups. Twenty-three
patients and 106 nonpatients were isolated. The variance accounted
for was 46.46% ($F_{14,238}$ = 14.45).

2. Social Functioning: The first predictor variable to
split the sample was the CAPPS past scale dealing with the S's
friendship patterns and sexual adjustment. This variable split
the initial group into two subgroups, 90 having higher scores
(41.1% of whom were patients) and 163 with lower scores (16.6% of
whom were patients). The next predictors selected were "number of
months employed" and CAPPS past item "nonacademic school difficulties." Ten variables were used to split the 253 Ss into 16
subgroups. Eleven patients and 90 nonpatients were isolated; 58.39%
of the variance was explained; and the F ratio for the final subgroups was 23.25, df = 15,237.

969

3. <u>Drug Use</u>: The first split was made on the basis of the
S's motivation for using drugs on his <u>first</u> drug experience, splitting 33 <u>Ss</u> (66.7% patients) who were motivated by self-medication
or iatrogenic reasons from the remaining 220 <u>Ss</u> (19.1% patients)
who cited social-recreational use as their motivation. The next
variables selected were drug preference—high risk vs. low risk
drugs, and CAPPS past items "problems with drugs"—moderate to
severe from minimal or none. Ten variables were used to split the
<u>Ss</u> into 18 subgroups which isolated no patients but isolated 97
(51.3%) of the nonpatients. The percentage of the variance accounted for was 55.35% and the F ratio was 17.14, df = 17,235. Two
criteria were used to evaluate the differential success of these
three sets of variables in predicting patient/nonpatient status.
The first was the proportion of the dependent variable's variance
which was accounted for by the AID's assignment to successive subgroups. The second was the success of each set in isolating subgroups composed of only patients and nonpatients. The three sets
of variables did not differ to any great extent on these indicators,
with the important exception that the set of drug-use variables was
less successful at isolating exclusive groups and was the only
variable set which failed to isolate a group composed exclusively
of patients.

Acknowledgement

This research was supported by Grant H81 DA01657 from the
National Institute on Drug Abuse, Dr. John Benvenuto and George
Beschner, Project Officers. The Project Director was Dr. Alfred
S. Friedman, Director of Research, Philadelphia Psychiatric Center.

References

1.   S. R. Hathaway and J. C. McKinley, *The Minnesota Multiphasic
Personality Inventory Manual*, (rev. ed.), New York: The
Psychological Corporation, 1967.

2.   D. M. McNair, M. Lorr and L. F. Dropplemann, *EITS Manual for
the Profile of Mood States*, California: Educational and Industrial
Testing Service, 1971.

3.   J. Endicott and R. L. Spitzer, Psychopathology Scales,
Archives of Gen. Psych., 31:414-418 (1974).

4.   J. A. Sonquist, *Multivariate Model Building*, Michigan:
Survey Research Center, The University of Michigan, 1970.

5.   J. A. Sonquist, E. L. Baker, and J. N. Morgan, *Searching for
Structure*, Michigan: Survey Research Center, The University of
Michigan, 1973.

CASE FINDING PROCEDURES IN
A STUDY OF POLYDRUG USE

Mark Morein, John Phin, Arlene Tirabassi, and Samuel Patterson

Philadelphia Psychiatric Center
Philadelphia, Pennsylvania

This report presents the sampling strategies that were developed by the Philadelphia Polydrug Research Center (PPRC), during the Center's participati   in the National Polydrug Project (1). The National Polydrug Project was initiated to determine the nature of and the need for special treatments for abusers of the non-opiate substances that are grouped under the rubric "polydrug." The major focus of the National Polydrug Project was medical management and treatment of the most "dysfunctional" abusers.

PPRC was established as a diagnostic evaluation and referral agency. PPRC intended to study "hidden" abuse of licit and illicit substances and the referral process in the metropolitan area.

Procedure. Over 400 drug users were tested with a clinical research battery. Money rather than access to treatment was the inducement for drug users to participate in the study. Within this paid informant sample, 74% of the first 253 subjects denied interest in receiving treatment from any of the available treatment agencies. The recruitment of our subjects was based on substances used, the duration of use and reported dosage. For qualification in our polydrug study, an applicant must have been using a non-opiate, non-alcoholic substance (e.g., barbiturates, amphetamines, hallucinogens, etc.), at least once per week, and for a period of three months prior to screening. Primary users of heroin or alcohol were not included in this study. However, we were interested in all substances used by qualified subjects. (2 and 3)

Priorities were generally agreed to be:

1.   The collection of accurate clinical data on qualified informants.
2.   The recruitment of a large number of informants, regardless of their intention or desire to enter treatment.
3.   The creation of a social network contact system among small groups of drug users to insure a continuous flow of subjects

and to establish "trust" thereby enhancing the accuracy of the self-report data.

    4.   The collection of data quickly to avoid confounding the results given the ever changing drug scene, especially among youth.

PPRC Goals were:

    1.   To insure reliability and validity of self-report data including data collected on drug use.

    2.   Solicitation of a large enough sample so as to provide meaningful results and to increase the impact and generalizability of the results of the National Polydrug Project *(1)*.

We sought to achieve our goals through the use of posters, newspaper and radio ads, and the implementation of these preconceived strategies.

Strategies.

    1.   A nonjudgmental attitude among staff about drug use.

    2.   The selection of a professional staff based on speculations about who would be best able to extract accurate information from the client-target population.

    3.   The selection of the most "discrete" and "neutral" research site available in order to dissociate ourselves from both traditional and nonconventional treatment centers, and to provide an atmosphere that did not suggest any particular drug using scene.

    4.   An attempt was made to conceal our interest in any particular substance-use pattern to minimize the formation of a response set.

    5.   An explanation, in detail, of our procedures and security system designed to insure confidentiality.

As indicated by a breakdown of the referral sources of the first 253 subjects, most were referred by friends (52%). Street posters and newspaper notices were the next two most frequent sources of referral (15% and 12% respectively). Advertising ceased after the first few weeks of data collection and although the influx of qualified subjects varied from time to time, we were quite satisfied by the quality and quantity of our informants. Given the results of our sampling technique, we consider our strategies to be successful.

Subjects.

The study was designed to attract establishment-type drug users — housepersons and businesspersons using drugs secretly, and to focus on the causes and spread of abuse within the middle-class community. Two percent of the first 253 subjects were housewives, 1.2% were of the business managerial level, and 0.8% were higher executives. High school and college students accounted for 32.4% of the sample.

Occupationally, the subjects were spread over the major census categories. Unskilled labor, 12.6%; administrative personnel, 12.3%; clerical and skilled labor, 11.9%; and semi-skilled labor, 9.5%, were the most frequently reported occupational categories.

Eighty-seven percent of the first 253 subjects were white, 11.9% black, and 0.8% (two cases) were Puerto Rican. The mean age was 24 years.

We had greater success in developing networks of eligible polydrug users among whites than blacks. The black sample was not large enough to make any significant comparisons. However, informal discussions with black subjects about their impressions of the data collection technique surfaced the following theme:

    1.   Suspiciousness, a reluctance to talk with "strangers" about family, life experiences and drug use.
    2.   Initially thought the law or narcotic enforcement officials were linked with the research.
    3.   Students from predominately black colleges had too far to travel for the amount of money offered.

It follows that social analysts and researchers seeking entry in the black community would require a different approach and technique. It is clear that the Latino or Spanish-speaking youth are underrepresented, pointing attention to cultural and ethnic disparities in the research project. Our findings are consistent with Winnett, Fuchs, and Moffatt (1974) *(4)*, who also found that monetary compensation alone would not induce participation by blacks.

Implications: Comparison with Other Procedures and Populations.

    The DARP system *(5)*, with an $\underline{N}$ of over 40,000, is probably the most complete source of information currently available on demographic and background variables of contemporary drug users in treatment. DARP data were collected from reports from treatment agencies funded by NIMH (later by NIDA), and represented drug users who 1) desired a service, and 2) were "filtered" by the admission requirements of the treatment agency. While not limited to polydrug users, DARP should be viewed in light of methodological considerations raised by the Wynne Associates' *(6)* extensive review of the literature (on the nature and treatment of non-opiate abuse) for NIDA. "We do not know whether or not clients coming to treatment are truly representative of the drug-using class as a whole."

    Kirschner Associates *(7)* implemented a statewide household survey of The Prevalence and Intensity of Drug and Alcohol Use in Pennsylvania with an $\underline{N}$ of approximately 3,000. At the same time similar statewide household surveys were conducted in South Carolina and Minneasota with N's of 2,000 (8). Although these surveys provide data where none previously existed, the 61-item, multiple-choice questionnaire used by Kirschner in the study sought only limited demographic data and no information on the respondents' backgrounds, and no "clinical" or "in depth" material. PPRC's battery, by comparison, elicited extensive demographic, background and clinical data, i.e., some 2,500 separate pieces of information (3).

The Hennepin County Polydrug Research Project (9) was the closest to Philadelphia's research design both in data collected and in seeking a "hidden" population of drug users who were not seeking treatment. However, there are important methodological sampling differences such as Hennepin County's use of "sociological gate-keepers," i.e., paid peer interviewers who surveyed drug-use networks in the field. While there are similarities in the populations, the background and data collected by PPRC are significantly more in-depth and clinical in nature.

The foregoing presentation illustrates the particular value of the PPRC effort compared to other relevant research. Coupling a survey of an essentially unidentified, nonpatient polydrug-using population with an extensive battery adds impact and depth to the present state of polydrug-use data and the National Polydrug Study (1). More specifically, as PPRC contributed 189 out of 215 or 88% of the total national nonpatient sample, between-group, (patient v. nonpatient) comparisons are now possible (2 and 3). Further, PPRC's large, nonpatient cohort sample, alone, could be used as a control group for demographic, historical, and clinical studies, thus adding power to current multiple drug use data.

Acknowledgement.

This research was supported by Grant H81 DA01657 from the National Institute on Drug Abuse, Dr. John Benvenuto and George Beschner, Project Officers. The Project Director was Dr. Alfred S. Friedman, Director of Research, Philadelphia Psychiatric Center.

References.

1.   J. Benvenuto and P. G. Bourne, The Federal Polydrug Abuse Project: Initial Report.

2.   E. Deaux, S. Case, J. G. Phin, and D. Speck, Multifactor Measures of Drug Use Severity, Functioning, and Treatment Involvement in Polydrug Uses, Paper presented at National Drug Abuse Conference, 1976.

3.   J. G. Phin, S. Case, and M. J. Morein, The Philadelphia Paid Informant Sample: A Suggested Comparison Group for Polydrug Studies Paper presented at National Drug Abuse Conference, 1976.

4.   R. A. Winett, W. L. Fuchs, and S. A. Moffatt, Personal and Impersonal Methods of Recruitment for Social Research, *J. of Comm. Psych.*, 2:(4), 376-379 (1974).

5.   S. B. Sells, The DARP Research Program and Data System, *Amer. J. of Drug and Alcohol Abuse*, 2:(1), 1-14 (1975).

6.   Wynne Associates, *The Nature and Treatment of Non-Opiate Abuse: A Review of the Literature*, Division of Research, NIDA: (1974).

7.   Kirschner Associates, *The Prevalence and Intensity of Drug and Alcohol Use in the Commonwealth of Pennsylvania*, Report Preparation: E. Schaps and E. Rubin (1973).

8.   W. A. Glenn and L. G. Richards, *Recent Surveys of Nonmedical Drug Use: A Compendium of Abstracts*, National Institute on Drug Abuse (1974).

9.   Hennepin County Polydrug Research Project, *A Study of the "Hidden" or "Unidentified Polydrug Abuser*," Prepared by: Aries Corporation (1975).

THE PHILADELPHIA PAID INFORMANT SAMPLE: A
SUGGESTED COMPARISON GROUP FOR POLYDRUG STUDIES

John G. Phin, Susan Case, and Mark Morein

Philadelphia Psychiatric Center
Philadelphia, Pennsylvania

This paid informant sample was gathered by the Philadelphia Psychiatric Center—Polydrug Research Center as part of its contribution to the National Polydrug Study (1). Signs offering money in exchange for information and a peer-network referral system were used to induce participation in the study (2). This procedure sampled the general population of non-opiate, "polydrug" users as well as the dysfunctional abusers that are usually described in studies of drug use.

Results.

These results were obtained from the first 253 of over 400 subjects to complete the research battery which included the Polydrug Pilot Project - Intake Form (1), the Current and Past Psychopathology Scale - CAPPS (3), the Profile of Mood States - POMS (4), the Minnesota Multiphasic Personality Inventory - MMPI (5), and a local battery supplement.

Sample Demographics.

The sample of Philadelphia polydrug users was a youthful group with a mean age of 24 and a median age of 22. Two-thirds of the sample were male and 87% were white. Eighty percent had never married. Fifty percent live with their family and 35% live with friends. The mean number of school years completed was 12 and more than one-third of the sample were still attending school.

Two-thirds of the sample were unemployed but only 15% of the sample had not worked in the last two years. Nineteen percent were primarily supported by unemployment, social security, or public assistance and only 2% were supported by illegal activities. One-third of the sample had been arrested, 13% had attempted suicide, 39% had had non-drug related psychiatric treatment, and 18% had had related emergency room treatments.

Sample Drug Use.

In order to qualify for the study, a subject had to have reported at least weekly use of a substance other than alcohol, marijuana, or an opiate for at least three months prior to his participation. Table I shows the portion of the sample using each substance by frequency of use. Social-recreational use of substances obtained from illicit sources predominated. The mean number of drugs used at least weekly was 2.57; single substance use was rare. Almost two-thirds were at least somewhat motivated to be drug free. Twenty-two percent had had at least one drug overdose and 15% had been treated for a drug problem.

Comparisons between Patients and Nonpatients.

Of the 253 subjects included in our study, 189 (75%) were neither applying for nor receiving any mode of treatment and were classified as nonpatients. The remaining 64 were patients. Differences between the two groups on demographic variables were minimal. Patients and nonpatients were also compared on the MMPI, POMS, and CAPPS. Table II shows high MMPI scores for nonpatients on the Psychopathic Deviance, Schizophrenia, and Hypomania scales. Patients were also high on these scales and in addition, were high on Depression and Psychasthenia.

Mean POMS scale scores for male and female patients and nonpatients are shown in Table III. All groups scored low relative to their respective norm groups on the Tension, Depression, Anger, Confusion, and Fatigue scales.

Mean CAPPS summary scale scores for male and female patients and nonpatients showed relatively low ratings on current and past symptomatology. The highest rated scales were: Impulse Control for male patients; and present and past Depression/Anxiety, and Phobic Reactions for female patients.

Discussion.

The age, sex, and race of the paid informant and National Polydrug (1) samples are similar. Both samples contain more white and female subjects than do the DARP and CODAP samples. The paid informants were better educated and had lower incidence of unemployment.

Barbiturate/sedative-hypnotic and psychotropic use was more prevalent among National Polydrug patients than among paid informants on DARP or CODAP patients. Amphetamine, cocaine, marijuana, and hallucinogen use was more prevalent among paid informants than among the other groups. Paid informant opiate use was low since heavy opiate users were diverted from the program.

977

CAPPS ratings of paid informants suggest minimal dysfunction rather than the "surprising" levels of dysfunction of the Polydrug patients reported by Benvenuto and Bourne (1). POMS self-report results indicate that the paid informants are relatively satisfied with their affective state. On the other hand, MMPI results are consistent with the impressions of Benvenuto and Bourne. The high MMPI results should be considered in light of the counter culture identities of the paid informants.

Within the paid informant sample, 96% of the patients and 36% of the nonpatients would have been referred to treatment by their interviewer. Ninety percent of the paid informants reported having at least one problem resulting from their drug and alcohol use. The majority of the paid informants had stopped using drugs at least once and also felt that they were or had been dependent on drug use, but few wanted to discontinue their drug use. Furthermore, they expressed little interest in any available drug treatment program. The stigma of drug programs that "turns off" older more middle-class drug users is apparently felt by the youthful paid informants.

Many of the paid informants chose low stress, low risk lifestyles. Considering their MMPI results, if problems increase, i.e., the economy worsens or drug law enforcement tightens, the paid informants may show more dysfunction associated with their drug use and greater utilization of treatment programs.

Acknowledgement

This research was supported by Grant H81 DA01657 from the National Institute on Drug Abuse, Dr. John Benvenuto and George Beschner, Project Officers. The Project Director was Dr. Alfred S. Friedman, Director of Research, Philadelphia Psychiatric Center.

TABLE I: Percentages Using Each Drug by Frequency of Use

Drug Used	Daily	Sev.Times/Wk.	Weekly	Less than Wkly
Heroin	0.40%	1.58%	1.19%	4.74%
Illegal Meth.	0.40%	0.40%	0.40%	0.40%
Other Opiates	1.19%	1.98%	1.58%	9.88%
Alcohol	11.07%	20.95%	7.51%	5.14%
Barbiturates	7.91%	20.55%	9.49%	24.90%
Amphetamines	5.14%	16.60%	10.67%	28.06%
Cocaine	0.79%	5.14%	5.53%	25.69%
Marijuana	57.31%	23.32%	2.77%	5.92%
Psychotropics	0.40%	4.35%	7.11%	31.23%
Hallucinogens	7.11%	7.51%	2.37%	9.09%
Inhalants	0.00%	0.79%	0.79%	2.77%
Non-Prescription	0.79%	0.00%	0.40%	0.00%
Other (usually PCP)	0.79%	4.74%	5.14%	7.91%

TABLE II: Summary MMPI Results

MMPI Scale	Nonpatients			Patients		
	X̄	S. D.	% Over T = 70	X̄	S. D.	% Over T = 70
Hypochondriasis	54.34	10.37	8%	57.78	10.00	11%
Depression	58.84	12.41	17%	65.80	14.87	37%
Hysteria	58.18	9.48	9%	59.70	9.04	11%
Psychopathic Deviate	68.96	11.16	43%	75.41	10.83	59%
Masculine/Feminine	61.98	15.10	34%	59.54	12.49	26%
Paranoia	60.87	12.18	16%	65.22	12.32	30%
Psychasthenia	60.24	11.42	19%	67.43	13.68	51%
Schizophrenia	67.41	14.78	35%	77.15	14.19	69%
Hypomania	71.23	10.96	47%	71.87	11.41	50%
Social Introversion	50.99	9.32	2%	56.94	9.21	7%

TABLE III: Summary POMS Results

POMS Scale	Patients				Nonpatients			
	Males		Females		Males		Females	
	X̄	T*	X̄	T*	X̄	T*	X̄	T*
Tension	10.70	41	13.04	41	8.66	43	9.42	44
Depression	11.00	42	15.85	42	6.87	44	7.33	44
Anger	7.55	45	11.93	47	6.04	45	5.11	44
Vigor**	18.55	61	13.78	57	17.64	53	17.70	53
Fatigue	5.58	44	8.67	44	5.25	42	5.92	43
Confusion	8.33	44	9.56	44	6.13	41	6.81	42

* The T distribution has a mean of 50 and a standard deviation of 10. Patients are compared to outpatient norms, nonpatients to college student norms (McNair, et al., 1971).

** The higher the score, the more vigorous.

References.

1. J. Benvenuto and P. G. Bourne, *The Federal Polydrug Abuse Project: Initial Report.*

2. M. J. Morein, J. G. Phin, A. Tirabassi, and S. Patterson, *Case Finding Procedures in a Study of Polydrug Use.* Paper presented at National Drug Abuse Conference, 1976.

3. R. L. Spitzer and J. Endicott, *Current and Past Psychological Scales*, Columbia University, 1968.

4. D. M. McNair, M. Lorr, and L. F. Droppleman, *EITS Manual for the Profile of Mood States*, Educational and Industrial Testing Service, 1971.

5. S. R. Hathaway and J. C. McKinley, *The Minnesota Multiphasic Personality Inventory Manual*, (rev. ed.), New York: The Psychological Corporation, 1967.

POLYDRUG GRAND ROUNDS-
The Best of the Worst

John Eric Jacoby, M.D., M.P.H.

Harvard Medical School
Boston, Massachusetts

Betsy S. Comstock, M.D.

Baylor College of Medicine
Houston, Texas

Michael D. Cox, Ph.D.

Lafayette Clinic
Detroit, Michigan

CASE I - THE BOSTON UNIT

Virgil H., a 30 year old black male, was first admitted to the Boston Polydrug Unit on October 20, 1975 via transfer from an alcohol detoxification unit.

Virgil has a long history of drug abuse, beginning with codeine cough syrup at the age of eleven. Prior to admission he was drinking 3 quarts of wine per day, smoking marijuana occasionally, using 3 to 4 bags of heroin per day (when available) and taking 130 to 140 mg. of diazepam (Valium) per day. He has never overdosed but had one seizure 1 1/2 years ago, associated with barbiturate withdrawal. Virgil has been drug free only once while serving a one year jail sentence. At the time of admission he had undergone three detoxification programs. He failed to remain "straight" for longer than three day stretches.

His father, an alcoholic, died when he was sixteen. His parents were divorced. He has had little contact with his mother. Virgil has two older brothers who are both alcoholics; they also have criminal records. Before coming to the clinic, Virgil was living with his grandmother in another state. Virgil was married for approximately two years. He has two sons by this marriage and a daughter by his girlfriend. He has had little contact with his children.

Virgil was expelled from school for car theft in the eleventh grade and has since passed his high school equivalence test. In June of 1972 he attended rehabilitation school and received training in electronics.

The patient was diagnosed as being addicted to alcohol and diazepam, and being a heroin abuser. He was given a 10 day gradual diazepam detoxification.

Initially, Virgil was fairly quiet and rarely socialized on the ward. He stated that he had always been alone and always would be. He appeared very depressed with little feeling of self-worth, saying that he should leave the Unit to make more room for people more worthy.

Before he left the Unit, some progress was revealed through a general opening up which allowed him to discuss his negative feelings. He became very productive at the workshop and accepted increasing responsibility on the ward. Also he began to relate more openly toward the other patients.

The staff primarily focused on Virgil's inability to recognize and express his emotions. The staff made a constant effort to confront Virgil about his complacent attitude. Virgil decided to enter a halfway house. Five weeks after admission he was transferred there and that night obtained alcohol. He was transferred to a therapeutic community which he left after 2 hours.

Comment - Dr. Jacoby

This case illustrates the confluence of Social and Psychiatric origins of multiple drug abuse. This is a black patient who fails to fit into the alcoholic or opiate addict category exclusively. His diazepam addiction is possibly a secondary problem caused by attempts to refrain from alcohol and heroin. His depression/anxiety is to him overwhelming and his limited ego strength allows him to find relief of these symptoms only with drugs.

He has "failed" in treatment in several modalities. He is also choosy about his treatment, preferring life on the street to the perceived hardships of a therapeutic community. This choosiness can be described by many Psychiatric professionals as "lack of motivation" or "inappropriateness for therapy". That constitutes circular reasoning and helps us professionals to project the cause of our failure to the patient.

One paradox illustrated here is the addiction to diazepam which to some extent does afford relief to the patient from his psychiatric symptoms. This intertwining of "cure" and illness makes the use of drug therapy in these patients extremely difficult.

To summarize the issues in this case we see the confluence of social problems, psychiatric problems, as well as opiate, alcohol and minor tranquilizer addiction. We note many therapeutic dilemmas caused by lack of appropriate facilities and a lack of curative therapy.

CASE II - FROM THE HOUSTON PROGRAM

J.T., a 40 year old professional woman recently divorced, entered the Houston Polydrug Program for treatment of excessive use of pentazocine (Talwin) and phenobarbital. She stated she wanted treatment "for survival", stating she understood her life was endangered by the extensive cold abscesses, and necrotic ulcers, with staph infections involving her arms, legs and buttocks. She reported a 5 year history of drug abuse, having become addicted after introduction to analgesic and sedative drugs by her physicians. She obtained her drugs through illegal prescriptions, and at the time of admission was injecting 25 cc. of pentazocine daily (750 mg.), as well as using variable amounts of phenobarbital.

The patient reported four previous hospitalizations for drug withdrawal. Each withdrawal had been complicated by excessive gastro-intestinal cramping, vomiting, and finally by intestinal obstruction. She had had 3 laparotomies for obstruction. During one a bezoar was found obstructing the small bowel. Mrs. T. was convinced that further withdrawal would precipitate another abdominal crisis. However, she also knew she was at risk for a life-threatening sepsis. In addition, she had exhausted all available injection sites, and had given up working several weeks prior to admission.

Past medical history was significant for pre-addiction surgery, first an oophorectomy, then a gastrectomy for peptic ulcer disease. Addiction began following the gastrectomy.

Psychiatric history was remarkable for its negativity. Mrs. T. described herself as always happy, interested in people, devoted to her three children and their home, and vitally interested in her work. She denied emotional problems even though her marriage had ended unhappily and she had few or no friends.

Mrs. T. was an only child. She recalled her father as a wonderful man, her mother as distant, and both as not understanding her. After the death of her mother, she moved to care for her father in his home for a number of months. Her father is diabetic and has leg ulcers. Mrs. T. was described as an over-achiever, eager to please, outstanding in school and in her professional career. She felt duty bound to provide for her parents and for her elderly husband until he divorced her.

At the time of admission, Mrs. T. was extremely cooperative and courteous, although she had put off admission 3 times before she finally entered the unit. She appeared pale and malnourished. Significant physical findings included necrotic ulcers and scar tissue replacing virtually all the skin over her forearms, lateral upper arms, buttocks, thighs and lower hips. There was generalized edema, especially involving the lower legs, and purulent exudate over much of the involved areas. There was loss of muscle tissue underlying the involved skin, with significant contractures at most joints.

Laboratory evaluation was unremarkable. The blood and urine contained pentazocine and phenobarbital. The skin lesions consistently contained coagulase positive staph aureus resistant to antibiotics.

Psychological testing revealed an MMPI with a neurotic slope, elevated depression and psycopathic deviant scores. POMS, CAPPS, BPRS, and HDS all were consistent with depressive symptoms. Projective tests indicated strong use of denial and of somatization, severe body-image distortions, with suggestion of potential for cognitive disorganization. Intellectual functioning was in the superior range. Neuropsychological testing was normal.

In-hospital treatment lasted 6 weeks. Gradual drug withdrawal accomplished a drug-free state without any significant abstinence symptoms. Physical therapy with associated use of antibiotics and debridement resulted in appreciable granulation of the ulcers and stretching of contractures.

Psychotherapy was supportive, and succeeded to the extent that it helped Mrs. T. accept her treatment. Post discharge she has had multiple skin grafts which have restored epithelial integrity. After 12 months she remains drug-free.

However, no appreciable change has occurred in her psychological status. Mrs. T. has shown uncertainty and marginal ability to cooperate in the protracted medical care she is requiring. She has gained no insight into the masochistic nature of her addiction.

Comment - Dr. Comstock

This case is presented because it demonstrates several important features of management of drug addiction. First, the detoxification process was complicated in the sense that numerous previous tries had failed. A very slow withdrawal in a highly supportive environment was indicated.

Second, this patient is representative of those whose drug abuse is self-punitive and reflects a masochistic postion where physical illness or self injury are linked with inability to tolerate success. Rehabilitative issues are extremely complex for such individuals. They have an uncanny ability to sabotage their own treatment. This patient has succeeded in antagonizing most of the people who have tried to help her (she probably holds the all time record for missed appointments).

The third issue of importance is that this patient reflects a constellation of personality features which are encountered as an important typology in drug abuse. Mrs. T. states she took drugs any time she felt low or "felt herself sinking". She used drugs for relief of her chronic personal psychological discomfort.

She meets criteria for the diagnosis of borderline personality, with psychological features including failure of object fusion, establishment of a mirror transference, marginal social adjustment, with a rigid defensive posture utilizing primitive defenses which periodically were observed to fail. A chaotic and bizarre quality

in her interpersonal process was illustrated when she first presented for admission wearing a see-through blouse and stating, "I know
you can't stand to look at me. My husband left me because drugs
have made me so ugly."

We have been successful in helping this patient to become
drug-free and to allow her skin to heal. The task of fostering the
psychological growth she will need in order to sustain these gains
remains an imposing challenge.

CASE III - FROM THE DETROIT POLYDRUG PROGRAM

Frank, a 15 year old white male, was referred to the Program by
his probation officer. Frank was at that time a ward of the court
following a long history of antisocial behavior including drug dealing, chronic truancy and breaking and entering. He had been arrested 25 times in the last five years, but convicted only four times.

Frank presented a five year history of multiple drug abuse beginning with alcohol at age ten. In the two years previous to this
hospitalization, Frank had been primarily dependent on various
hypnosedatives including barbiturates, five to six capsules six to
eight times per month, and 30 mg. of Valium on a daily basis. In
addition, his drug intake included phencyclidine (PCP), marijuana,
alcohol, and various opiates and hallucinogenic substances.
Frank supported his drug abuse by pushing a wide variety of drugs
at several Detroit area schools.

Frank is the youngest child in an upper middle class family of
six. His siblings were reportedly also abusing various drugs.
Frank's parents were involved in divorce proceedings. This marriage was the second for both parents. Frank's father was described as an aloof,domineering, professional man, while the mother was depicted as passive and unable to set limits. Frank va-
cillated between living with either of his parents and rooming with
friends.

Psychological test results indicated a personality disorder.
Frank possessed insufficient impulse control, deficient judgment,
poor frustration tolerance and limited capacity for self evaluation.
Frank had little capacity for interpersonal trust and consequently
manipulated others for his own gain. The evaluation also revealed
a remarkable absence of guilt or remorse concerning his trans-
gressions as well as high levels of denial, projection of blame,
and acting out. Despite his chronic truancy which left him with at

best a sixth grade education, Frank obtained an IQ of 123 plus above average scores on the neuropsychological test battery.

The Detroit Polydrug Program featured a four week in-patient program including group, individual and family therapy. The unit operated a therapeutic community in which all staff members regardless of orientation assumed an active role in the treatment process. Incorporated within the milieu was a strongly supported form of patient government which had as one of its primary responsibilities the handling of patient behavior problems. The focus of the therapeutic approach was group therapy utilizing a transactional analysis base.

Since Frank had been in police custody for several weeks, detoxification was not required. Upon admission, Frank tried to project a tough-guy image and responded to the community orientation with a disrespectful, hostile, uncooperative attitude. The unit responded by setting firm yet reasonable limits on his behavior. The patient government enforced these limits by granting or withdrawing privileges contingent upon Frank's behavior. He was confronted with his denial and projection. This intervention was accomplished in two ways, first by discussing the psychological test results and his family background with him in a "formulation" session, and secondly, during the group sessions by pointing out his attempts at interpersonal manipulations. Family therapy, though clearly indicated, could not be attempted due to the fragmented family situation and parental resistance.

Gradually, he adjusted to the limit setting and a sense of trust began to develop between Frank and the staff. He was discharged as improved although with a guarded prognosis due to the chronicity of his problems and the seriously disturbed family situation. Frank failed to return for follow-up as well as his out-patient therapy which had been arranged prior to discharge. Attempts to recontact Frank were unsuccessful.

Comment - Dr. Cox

The preceeding case study serves to illustrate the following factors frequently observed in the polydrug population:

1. The presence of moderate to severe psychopathology in the individual abuser.
2. A high incidence of current and past drug abuse in the families of the abusers.
3. The presence of significant familial or marital dysfunction.

Frank also felt emotionally shunned by his parents and his acting out behavior may have served initially to provide increased attention. His drug involvement and delinquent activities compelled the environment to respond to him. Too often the only response by family was to get him "off the hook" legally. His success in avoiding legal punishment further reinforced his disregard for society and its rules. What had originated as a response to family conflicts now was rapidly developing into an ingrained life style.

GENERAL COMMENTS - DR. JACOBY

The Polydrug problem is the third large class of the addictions. It was recognized long after alcoholism and opiate addiction were known. The cases presented today show the diversity of the patients who fit into this category. The cities represented show the geographical ubiquity of polydrug abuse; the age range presented is 15 to 40, but in Boston we had patients from 14 to 62 years of age. Each of the patients presented here have underlying psychological difficulties and compared to opiate addicts, polydrug patients have more severe psychiatric problems. The varying social classes illustrated are representative of our experience; thus, just as the availability of medications is widespread in our society, the abuse of these drugs is a widespread phenomenon.

We have observed some unifying concepts in the pathology and therapeusis of the polydrug patients.

Chronicity and Recurrence: The polydrug patient may be helped briefly but often returns to a pattern of drug abuse. The search for a "cure" may be illusory and indeed this hypothetical "cure" has blinded us to the need for "care". Most patients improve their functioning during treatment and in this sense are helped.

Rejection of these Patients - These are persona-non-grata.
Most Psychiatric facilities simply refuse to treat these patients
even if they have severe psychiatric illness.

Patient Rejection of Treatment - Patients underestimate their
need for treatment. They feel that a 2 week detoxification has them
cured. They cannot conceptualize a year of therapeutic community
treatment, of 3 years of psychoanalysis, or a year of day care.
Indeed, many patients fail to seek treatment altogether and while
those in treatment are undoubtedly the most seriously ill, the patients know others equally ill who fail to seek any treatment.

Patient Duplicity - As professionals, we are obliged to be honest and fair with our patients. With polydrug patients we must entertain no expectations that these qualities will be returned. This
is a fact and not a moral issue.

Inappropriateness of Certain Therapy - Care of polydrug patients
involves 3 elements: 1) Medicine, 2) Psychiatry, 3) Security. Attempts to fit these patients indiscriminately into therapy is dangerous and results in reinforcing failure in the patient. Most alcohol
programs do not have the medical back-up needed for polydrug patients. They are often limited to 5 day detox and this is too short.
Psychiatric facilities often don't have the experience to detoxify
patients, nor is the security adequate for these clever drug smugglers.

Therapeutic communities with their "You can help yourself if you
try" attitude were developed in response to opiate addiction. They
are useful for this problem and possibly personality disorders. The
self-help staff however normally cannot cope with severe depression or frank psychosis which are common in polydrug addicts.
Care of polydrug patients requires real expertise and planning their
treatment is no place for amateurs.

We hope that you in the audience have gained some understanding from this presentation. Our comments should add some of our
perspective on the problems, but it is these cases - real human
beings - who best illustrate the need for further work in this field
and the need for adequate treatment programs which are able to
care for polydrug patients.

FACTORS ASSOCIATED WITH DETOXIFICATION
AND REFERRAL OF SEDATIVE-HYPNOTIC AND OPIATE ADDICTS

Athan Karras, Ph.D.   Beny J. Primm, M.D.
Bernice Siegel, B.A.   Ernest Boston, D.D.
                             Sherman W. Patrick, MA, M.P.H.

Long Island Jewish-   Addiction Research & Treatment
  Hillside Medical Center   Corporation
New Hyde Park, N.Y. 11040   22 Chapel Street
                             Brooklyn, N.Y. 11201

In 1973 the National Institute on Drug Abuse sponsored a nationwide coordinated effort to locate and offer nonnarcotic addicts
detoxification and referral services for continued treatment. Two
institutions in New York City, the Addiction Research and Treatment
Corporation and the Long Island Jewish-Hillside Medical Center and
its affiliate, the Queens Hospital Center, participated in this
effort. ARTC developed contractual arrangements with four hospitals in Manhattan for detoxification services to be performed for
referrals sent to them. Two hospitals accounted for less than five
percent of its subjects. ARTC drug counselors interviewed and
counseled patients with regard to future rehabilitation plans and
made referrals for continued treatment. In contrast, the Queens
Hospital Center already had a detoxification ward established for
males; women were detoxified on open medical wards of the Center
by the same physicians assigned to the detoxification ward.
Counseling services for both sexes were provided by drug counselors
assigned to the central screening drug unit of the Center, to which
the addict patient had originally presented himself.

There are obvious striking differences between the two New York
programs: ARTC served the inner city, and with its contractual
partners had to develop the expertise in detoxification and referral matters, in addition to mounting an advertising campaign
and informing the public of the service. Detoxification seldom
exceeded ten days. QHC already had a smoothly functioning manifold
drug service program, ranging from screening for appropriate disposition, to a variety of drug and non drug rehabilitation services, in addition to the detoxification service already mentioned.
There was often a waiting list for detoxification and a highly
developed referral network with other programs. Detoxification for
sedative-hypnotic drugs seldom lasted less than two weeks. Its
drug patients were unlikely to be the inner city kind.

This report reviews some of the salient background characteristics of the two patient populations and some of the determinants of successful detoxification and referral for continued treatment.

METHOD

Background data on patients, such as demographic information, past and current drug use, past and current work adjustment and living arrangements, criminal activity, psychiatric and psychological examinations, and so on, were obtained by trained research interviewers. Initial interview data were obtained within the first 2-3 days of hospitalization for detoxification. Psychiatric and psychological data were obtained later to minimize confounding from drug action. Follow up interviews were obtained at time of referral as well as at six weeks, three months and, for a handful, at six months.

The ARTC group provided the research interviewers for the Manhattan-based program. The Queens group had research assistants assigned to it from the department of psychiatry of the Long Island Jewish-Hillside Medical Center. The ARTC group started collecting data nearly a year earlier than the Queens group, which accounts for its noticeably larger number of subjects.

There are 123 patients in the ARTC pool and 40 patients in the Queens Hospital pool. All were detoxified from nonopiate drugs, the predominant ones being overwhelmingly of the sedative-hypnotic class. A fair number were also detoxified from opiates, which most often was illegal methadone.

RESULTS

Seven patient variables are considered here: age, sex, ethnic group, education, previous detoxification episodes, previous drug or psychiatric treatment and the type of mixed addiction, that is, legal or illegal methadone. The four Manhattan facilities are combined, since there were no differences in successful detoxification among them.

A. General Descriptors of Subjects

We find only two descriptors out of the seven which significantly differentiate the two programs from each other, ethnicity and mixed methadone addiction. The Queens program had 80% whites, whereas the Manhattan programs had nearly half of its sample white. There were fewer subjects in the Queens program on illegal methadone (10% as against 42%) and more of them in methadone pro-
~ams (45% as against 17%).

For both programs males predominate, as do whites; the modal age group for both is 25-34 years and the modal educational range for both is 9-12 grade. Around two-thirds of the subjects in both programs were previously detoxified and the majority in both had previous drug or psychiatric treatment. Whereas both programs have the same percentage of subjects who are on methadone (around 55%), there is an interaction between the two programs regarding methadone use, as noted above.

All reported differences are statistically significant at $p < .05$, using the chi square or Fisher exact probability test.

B. Descriptors of Those Successfully Detoxifying

Minority groups were pooled, as were ages, forming an under 35 and over 35 group, and educational levels, collapsed into eighth grade or under and ninth grade or more. Statistical analyses showed no difference in outcome between the combined subgroups at probability levels exceeding .20. Both programs have the majority of its patients detoxifying successfully, but the Queens program has an additional 19% who do so (82% vs. 63%). There are four descriptors which distinguish successful candidates between programs, all indicating greater success for the Queens program. These are sex, ethnicity, age and rehabilitation experience. All these differences are significant at $p < .05$.

Within the Queens program, there are no differences among any of the descriptors. For the ARTC program we find that minorities do better than whites, as do those whose educational level is above the eighth grade.

There are no significant interactions between descriptors for the Queens group but there are for ARTC. Ethnicity interacts with age and illegal use of methadone. Another interaction is found between previous detoxification experience and education.

There is an ethnicity-age interaction. Almost all Black-Hispanics 35 and older detoxify (94%), compared to Black-Hispanics under 35 (66%), whites under 35 (46%) or over 35 (72%). The three latter groups are not statistically different from each other, as they are from the older Black-Hispanic ($p < .05$, in each instance).

The Black-Hispanic group which uses no methadone or is on legal methadone does conspicuously better than Black-Hispanics on illegal methadone or whites combined (87% vs. around 50% for the three others; differences are significant at $p < .01$ in each instance.)

Subjects with low educational status and no previous detoxification experience are not likely to detoxify (12%) as compared to those with previous detoxification, regardless of educational level (63%) or those with no experience but more education (73%). Differences are significant at p< .05.

C. Descriptors of Those Successfully Referred

The number successfully referred for further treatment was 54 (44%) for the Manhattan group and 18 (45%) of the Queens group. Excluding those who left AMA, too soon to have referral plans made, no plans were made for 26 of the ARTC group and 6 of the Queens group. These represent 29% and 18% of the Manhattan and Queens groups, respectively, for whom a referral could have been made, as estimated by the length of time in detoxification. The difference between the programs is far from being statistically significant. No patient group appears to be over-represented with regard to not having a referral made.

Of those patients for whom a referral was made, all of the ARTC group appeared at the recommended facility following detoxification (54 out of 54). Of the Queens group, 18 out of 23 showed up, representing 78% of those for whom a referral was made. The difference between the two programs is not statistically significant. A greater percentage of the Queens men showed than the women (14 out of 15 (93%) and 4 out of 8 (50%), respectively.) This difference is statistically significant (p < .06., using the Fisher exact probability test).

DISCUSSION

In line with findings from the other centers in the study, polydrug users in the New York area who sought detoxification services were typically white, male, with several years of high school and in their late twenties. As with other centers, the polydrug users were immersed in the life style of the heavy drug users.

The New York group diverges from the composite picture in the frequency with which methadone was being currently used. Over half the patients were on methadone. For the ARTC group, the majority on methadone were using it illegally; the reverse was true for the Queens group. We are not certain whether the descriptors of the New York sample of patients reflect the general drug abusing population in the two locations in the metropolitan area in which we conducted the study, although it is obvious that they represent those who typically turn up for treatment in Manhattan and Queens. As with the other participating centers we failed to uncover to any significant degree the covert, respectable nonopiate addict.

The majority of patients in our sample successfully detoxified, although the Queens group had a significantly higher percentage who succeeded. It is unlikely that we will be able to determine if this difference between locales was due to patient or procedural differences in detoxification. Important detoxification differences are the fewer detoxification days for the ARTC group and the newness of the procedures for their medical and counseling staff. (Successful detoxification rates were, however, very similar for the first and second halves of the ARTC sample.)

There were no detoxification differences among various patient groups for the QHC group, but there were between the two locales. The Queens detoxification program did better with males, white, those under 35 years of age and those with a previous detoxification episode.

Differences in successful detoxification among patient groups within the ARTC program go along with the same factors found to affect differences between programs. However, unlike its companion program in Queens, important interactions between descriptors were found which either override these gross group differences or mask them. For example, the Black-Hispanic group was especially likely to complete detoxification. In contrast, two descriptors which did not show differences, namely use of illegal methadone and history of previous detoxification, actually interact with ethnicity and education.

Treatment beyond detoxification seems essential for these patients, making referral to a rehabilitation program extremely important. A small minority in each program were not referred for some reason or other, none of which is particularly salient. Of those referred, both programs had high success, the ARTC group doing especially well, having all its patients show up, probably because of its escort service. The Queens group, in contrast, did not escort its patients, except for those males who entered one of the rehabilitation programs of the Medical Center which was exclusively for males and was located on the same floor as the detoxification unit. The combination of being on a special detoxification unit and being more likely to enter a rehabilitation program across the way from the unit may account for the markedly greater success of men following through on the referral recommendation than women. The advantages of an escort service or of a close-by rehabilitation facility appear obvious.

No study would be complete without determining the ongoing adjustment of its subjects, the topic of a future report.

FAMILY THERAPY

FAMILY THERAPY WITH DRUG ABUSERS:
A VIDEOTAPE WORKSHOP

Edward Kaufman, M.D., Chief Psychiatrist
Lower Eastside Service Center

Pauline Kaufmann, M.S.W., Consultant
Phoenix House

Therapeutic communities (TC's) for drug addicts have traditionally viewed the family and familial ties as antithetical to rehabilitation. The addict was given a new family, the TC and ties with his/her own family were severed. A blackout period of three to six months during which the addict had no contact with his family was enforced.

Despite this drastic severing of family ties, subsequent recurring phenomena have demonstrated that the family is part of the solution as well as the problem, and therefore, must be part of treatment from the beginning. These phenomena include:

(1) Addicts tend to replicate old familial patterns in their new environment.

(2) Internalized feelings about family members, dealing with control, rage, and dependency inhibits the addict's growth. These feelings can more easily be worked through with the real family.

(3) Families frequently sabotage treatment through a variety of consciously or unconsciously determined mechanisms, such as encouraging elopements and use of drugs and/or alcohol.

(4) Family systems exert tremendous pull or suction upon the lives of their members. If the old system which helped produce the addict is not changed the addict will respond to the existing system suction by returning to drug use upon completing or splitting from the TC.

In the structural approach, the total family is viewed as the patient, with the addict as the symptom bearer for the family. In the traditional TC the family was urged to cast the "symptom" out. The addict was then taken into the TC to be symbolically reborn and rehabilitated. Upon release, the graduate who returned to the influences of an unchanged family system would start the cycle once more. In the few cases where he/she managed to escape the family would choose another sibling as the symptom bearer.

Whenever family therapy is used with some degree of success it has proven to be preventative as well as curative.

In a TC setting, multiple family therapy (MFT) is a useful modality. The use of a group of families provides a network of support that enables families to make positive structural changes. Family members are able to identify patterns which create and perpetuate drug abuse. With the support of the network they are able to experiment with new ways of relating that encourage individuation and role diversity. Patterns of manipulation, extraction, and coercion are identified and negated. The family's need to perpetuate this behavior through scapegoating, distancing, protection, or infantilization is discouraged and new methods of relating are encouraged and tried.

There are usually as many as thirty to forty people in the group. The group includes addicts and their immediate families as well as any relatives who have an impact on the family. There are usually two or more family therapists working with the group. An experienced family therapist works with counselors in the program as co-therapists. This provides for feedback to and from the program as well as trains counselors in the dynamics of families and the techniques of family therapy. The total group frequently functions as adjunctive family therapists. Taking their cues from the primary therapists, they will be confronting, reassuring, and supportive as well as act as change agents. They share experiences and offer help by acting as extended families outside the actual therapy hours. Residents who accompany each other on visits home also serve as therapists in the home and behavioral reporters in MFT.

Families tend to feel guilty when confronted by the addict family member with their role in the addiction cycle. This has occurred in the "streets" and reoccurs in the early phases of therapy. If the therapist does not intervene, they will frequently try to induce guilt, devastate and ultimately pull the addict out of treatment. Parents must be given a great deal of support in family sessions because of their own guilt and the tendency of patients and counselors to attack them. Addiction is viewed as a family problem. There are no scapegoats. Multiple family therapy groups help residents actualize insights about their family which they have achieved in their own therapy. Many families learn to express love and anger directly for the first time in these groups. Deep emotional pain is expressed when appropriate and other family members are encouraged to give support to such expressions rather than nullify it or deny it.

The identified patient acts as the barometer of the total family functioning. When his/her behavior in the TC becomes maladaptive or disruptive it can be assumed that the family is under increased stress and may be reverting to their former structural patterns. This is particularly true in adolescent day programs when there is frequent parental contact. The troubled family should be called in for individual sessions. They are then encouraged to bring the content of these individual sessions into the multiple family group. Thus, the identified patient's behavior is viewed as part of the family stress at the same time as it is handled as his individual responsibility by his peers in encounter groups within the TC. In the family session therapeutic homework may be assigned to reinforce the family's structural changes. This will be further strengthened by the multiple family group. Not only are family tasks assigned, but different family roles may be assigned for the same purpose.

Our approach is that drug addiction is a symptom of family stress that is exacerbated by societal stress. We are involved, therefore, with the forces within the family that maintain the symptom. On a broader basis we must also be involved with those forces within the therapeutic community that serve to maintain symptoms. The staff also has its own "family system." This system also can be dealt with in ways that are similar to those used to deal with family dysfunction.

Any number of therapeutic strategies may be useful in restructuring the family. Much will depend on the individual therapist's style. We particularly delineate individual boundaries by not permitting family members to speak for each other and by pointing our non-verbal coercive communications which tend to overwhelm family members or inhibit expressiveness. We assign tasks to family members to promote individuation. It is most important for mothers who are sole parents to find pleasure in their own lives and for couples to learn or relearn to enjoy each other. Frequently grandparents must be brought in before parents can change sufficiently.

We have found that psychodramas dealing with negotiation and resolution of disagreements, formation of positive subgroups, changing communication style, teaching verbalization of anger, affection, friendship, as well as the usual encounter techniques, are all helpful in changing the dysfunctional system. The "empty chair" technique has been used to tap deep feelings to family members who are not present--generally anger at the withdrawal of the member, but also anguish at loss.

Family work is also possible with absent families, using psycho-drama and family sculpting. Here, the resident recreates his family by using other residents and staff to enact family roles. This sculpture is mainly nonverbal and tends to tap deeply buried feelings.

Family therapy can be done through working with the individual alone once there is a knowledge of the structure and dynamics of a family. Material from family therapy provides many important concepts for individual and group therapy.

Couples groups should also be used which may include graduates and their spouses, spouses and/or lovers of residents, and in-house couples. All of the factors and techniques described in the family group are relevant here. Couples may begin their therapy in the multiple family group and be transferred to the couples group when a definitive relationship is established and when work with the primary family no longer has priority.

Videotape can also be used to confront family members with emotions which are denied. By repeated replays it is possible to have family members recognize such patterns as guilt induction and infantilization through enmeshing affection and denegration.

In this workshop a videotape of an MFT which focused on two families was shown. Many of the dynamics and techniques described in this report were demonstrated by viewing the tape. The primary family which was shown consisted of the identified patient and a younger sister and brother. The mother had been quite active in MFT but did not attend this session because the family had moved over 75 miles upstate. The father had never been present but was frequently discussed because of his pattern of severe withdrawal. The father had not left his bedroom in three years and never came out when his son visited. In this session the son realized how much he had identified with his father's emotional isolation, even to a point of duplicating his posture. He was helped to recognize and experience his rigid control system. His anger to his father will be a subject for future group work. He also realized how he had attempted to be a father to his younger siblings to a point of neglecting his own needs. The sister reached out to him and partially broke through his isolation with her poignant plea. Another resident who was attending the group with his mother identified heavily and sobbed about not being closer to his own sister. He was asked to talk to the first resident's sister as if she were his own. In doing so he reached a deep level of yearning and anguish. His mother reached out to him and began to rock him. To diminish the infantilization, the therapist asked the mother to hold him, but not rock him.

Although this session facilitated the expression of deep feelings these were not all in the direction of appropriate structural family change. The discussant pointed out that more effort should have been exerted to minimize the sister's enmeshed feelings to her brother as well as the mother's infantilization of the second resident. It was also suggested that strenuous efforts could have been successful in bringing in the father of the first resident in an effort to diminish his distance from the family.

Unfortunately, there is a paucity of reports on the use of multiple family therapy with drug abusers. The indications are that family therapy reduces the incidence of splitting, acts as a preventative measure for other family members and builds a subculture that acts as an extended "good family" after family therapy sessions have been discontinued.

OUTCOME OF FAMILY CRISIS INTERVENTION
WITH ALCOHOL AND POLYDRUG ABUSERS

Bianca Podesta, Ph.D.

and

Joyce Lowinson, M.D.

Albert Einstein College of Medicine
Bronx, New York

Family therapy is being used more and more as a tool of crisis intervention as well as for ongoing treatment with polydrug
abusers (1). The methadone-maintained ex-addict who is abusing
alcohol or sedative hypnotics usually lives alone or with his parents. This takes into account the lower marriage rate among addicts as well as the many we have seen who have had families of
their own, with children in placement, and who are estranged from
their mates. For them, a correction of their relationship with
their original families is often a goal of treatment, allowing
them to learn to function within a balanced system.

In a service where treatment goals include not only abstention from (or reduction in) the abuse of drugs and alcohol, but
improvement in the quality of life, relationships, and, wherever
possible, employment, work with the patient's original family
should begin early in treatment.

The staff of the Alcohol and Polydrug Abuse Research Project
consists of professionally trained family therapists. The other
therapeutic modalities - individual, group, and activities therapy - are seen as occurring within the context of the systems approach. The staff seeks to understand its role as a surrogate
family, and their relationships with patients provide an important piece of each patient's network. Because the patient's own
family and their cooperation are frequently unavailable, we have
developed a type of family crisis intervention to cope with problems arising from feelings of alienation, loneliness, and habitual drug abuse.

In the initial phase of the patient's involvement with the
service, the therapist and patient prepare a genogram. The standard genogram includes three generations of the family - children,

parents, and grandparents. When a patient's family is largely unknown, or deceased, and when contact with remaining family members
is non-existent, another meaningful member of the patient's network, such as a longtime neighbor or friend, may be counted as a
significant part of the patient's "family."

Crisis intervention treatment may be precipitated by an escalation in a patient's psychopathology, drug abuse and/or disturbances within the family. If the patient is willing, a number
of family and network members will attend a session or series of
sessions where the following is pursued:

1. The identification of the problem in the family; the problem can be elicited from the members of the family or network who
are present at the session. The youngest family member or the
least talkative member may be asked what the problem is. But the
therapist must never accept the designation of a person (family
member) as the problem.

2. The responsibility pattern in the family. The therapist
attempts to discover in what manner responsibility is divided
among family members. Finding the imbalance, the therapist then
leads the discussion toward a redistribution of the percentage of
responsibility each family or network member will take for the
smoother running of the system. This can be carried out through
task assignment.

3. Finding solutions to the current (probably recurrent)
crisis. Family and network members should be included in the
pooling of solutions, and here the therapist's skill and sense
come importantly into play. The solution will be most effective
that takes into account the identified problem, and the redistribution of responsibility, as well as including the best of
family members' ideas, and the therapist's firm recommendations.

As regards the outcome of family crisis intervention, I will
refer first to differentiation. Greater differentiation of self
has been seen as an important goal of ongoing family therapy (2);
and, in many cases, this can become the goal of crisis treatment.
Patients who have not been able to see themselves as distinct from
other family members often try various roles as a method of accomplishing the necessary individuation. Becoming different, that
is playing the bad guy or the drug addict may be a misguided
search for differentiation. Living alone and cutting oneself off
from relatives and friends is usually a desperate attempt to
achieve psychic separation. The feared opposing drive is toward
fusion, or undifferentiated relating.

In cases where more than one of the family members are drug
addicts, the need for separation from the parental bond may be
extreme. These patients, in identifying with another addicted

family member, become locked into undifferentiated relating. This group of patients does not live with their families: therefore, since differentiation comes about only when a person can observe, listen to, and compare himself to others he lives with, at least part of the family must be brought together several times. One such patient lived alone, but maintained regular contact with his mother, took a meal at her apartment once a day, and could be said to be unhealthily fused with her. The only way that he could separate successfully was to express anger toward her. When he began to abuse alcohol and show other signs of psychological deterioration, a family session was arranged to include his mother and his apartment house neighbor. The neighbor was chosen by the patient as the only other person available in his network. The mother who talked incessantly during the early part of the session was directed by the therapist to keep quiet for awhile, then to listen to the patient's neighbor; then to listen to her son. The problem was identified as loneliness, alcohol, and maternal crowding. Responsibility was redistributed in the following ways – the patient was assigned to attend to his own meal preparation and to resume his study of classical guitar, an interest he had given up in high school. His neighbor offered to become available to him once a week to go out to a movie or a community activity. The mother's involvement was firmly limited to two visits with her son per week – one visit could consist of a meal at her home, but the other visit must involve an activity outside her home. All contracted for three more crisis sessions. These sessions provided the first opportunity in many years for this isolated patient to learn to differentiate within a family context.

Our second outcome focus is for the patient living with his family. Often such a patient relates in a manner similar to an adolescent, a person who is, in fact, an unemployed and otherwise dependent adult. Family crisis intervention would again strive toward differentiation. But here there would be a shift in the goal to <u>corrective integration</u> within the family system. An adult polydrug abuser living in his parent's home is seldom held responsible for any part of the functioning of the household. The vicious cycle of most such families is as follows:

1. Patient is kept at home because family wants to help him to rehabilitate.

2. Patient is pressured by family to find employment, stop using pills and alcohol.

3. Patient reacts to pressure with increased anxiety and drug abuse.

4. Family threaten to throw patient out if he doesn't stop.

5. Patient overdoses, is taken to hospital, returned home.

The patient is usually contributing importantly to the dysfunctional family system. The patient may be providing the excitement or diversion that the parents' marriage lacks. Even in adulthood the patient has been able to return to his role as baby in the family (if indeed he has relinquished it at all), and it provides the glue for his parents' relationship. Corrective integration involves both the patient and the parents assuming responsibility in different ways. If son and mother, for instance are over-close, they push father away from mother. The therapist might then give an assignment to mother to go on a weekend away with father.

With these patients living at home, a specific number of family sessions should be contracted - five or ten, if possible. The resistance to change within the family system will be great, especially as the patient first begins to move toward a differentiated, more responsible self. This is something that the therapist can teach and demonstrate in the sessions. The success of corrective integration is also reinforced by group therapy work performed by our service. The patient observes and experiences that there is, indeed, a different way of doing things, another way of acting with people, perhaps a better way. The patient must try these new ways out, again and again (3). Such behavioral and experienced changes in self will require the readjustment by other family members, and the therapist must attend to them too. When a patient, long thought of as hopeless begins to change, a marriage may break up, a mental or physical breakdown may occur in another close family member.

Occasionally isolated patients will express longing to be reunited with their parents, and reunion is the third outcome we will consider. Frequently this outcome has been suitable for women in their middle years. Their longing may be seen to represent a wish to be dependent; but in certain patients for whom the toll of heavy drug abuse has included a divorce from their original family as well as from their family of procreation, a beneficial reunion may be possible. The necessity for crisis intervention usually occurs at the very beginning of treatment. In one case the patient, a woman, had aged parents who lived a thousand miles away; she had not seen them in twelve years, and had written to them several times of her troubles, asking for money. Early in her final crisis with us, she spoke with resignation of her desire to "go home." She had been receiving help from our service, and had been calling us her family. Previously we had encouraged her to work at gaining independence, while resuming communication with her parents. Her final crisis involved a fire in her apartment brought about by her carelessness when in a drugged state. She was found by a therapist on the service, sitting dazed on the hospital grounds. She was hospitalized imme-

diately on our inpatient unit. This time, crisis intervention
therapy consisted primarily of preparing the patient for the trip
back to her parents' home. We never managed to involve any but
one person who knew the patient, and this person was a neighbor
who had cared for the patient's dog during her past crises. Our
work included planning for her journey home, contacting methadone
programs, and making travel arrangements. The review of possibilities awaiting her included: a tense or rejecting atmosphere
at her parents' home (she expected this from her father); a methadone pick-up schedule that might prove inconvenient, and difficulties she might have in finding friends and employment. The
patient attributed her failure to function in New York to the bad
influence of drug-abusing acquaintances. The reunion was effectively carried out. Our communication with her since then -
approximately one year ago - consists of letters and phone calls.
There are hardships, some of which were unanticipated, such as her
parents' poor medical condition. Her role changed strikingly from
prodigal child to the responsible caretaker for her aged and ail-
ing parents. I believe that we helped her to see this as the
meaningful contribution that it is. Other successful aspects of
this outcome include the patient's living within her own family,
the great decrease in destructive behavior, specifically drug
abuse. The patient expresses longing now for the freedom of New
York, but the realities of her home situation preclude that possibility for the time being.

The three outcomes of family crisis intervention described
above - differentiation, corrective integration, and reunion - do
not represent happy endings. They do, however, represent the best
and most human solutions we could find in our patients' times of
crisis. This attempt to describe three frequent outcomes is also
an attempt to determine goals of crisis treatment with the population of alcohol and polydrug abusers that we know.

SAMPLE GENOGRAM

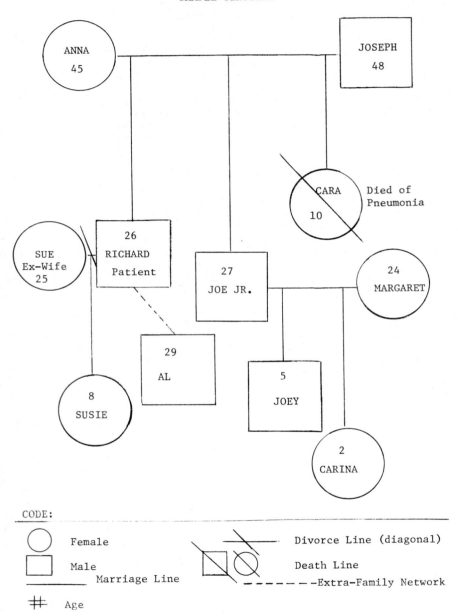

CODE:

○ Female

□ Male

———— Marriage Line

⌗ Age

✕ Divorce Line (diagonal)

□̸ ○̸ Death Line

– – – – – Extra-Family Network

REFERENCES

1. Stanton, M. Structural Family Therapy with Drug Addicts,
    Proceedings of the National Drug Abuse Conference, 1976, New
    York: Marcel Dekker, Inc. In press.

2. Mendelsohn, H. Differentiation and Individuation - A Psycho-
    analytic View, The Family, 1 (2):7-12, Spring, 1974.

3. Fried, E. Active Passive - The Crucial Psychological
    Dimension, New York: Harper and Row, Inc., 150, 1970.

A STRUCTURAL APPROACH TO FAMILY THERAPY WITH DRUG ADDICTS

M. Duncan Stanton, Ph.D.

Philadelphia Child Guidance Clinic
Philadelphia, PA.

This report will attempt to highlight some aspects of a treatment
and research program carried out by the Philadelphia Child
Guidance Clinic, Philadelphia V.A. Hospital, and the University
of Pennsylvania. The major purpose of the project is to test
the efficacy of a structurally oriented family therapy program
for treatment of drug addiction. As of April 1976 we have
completed family therapy treatment with fifteen cases and have
follow-ups of from one to eleven months. Of the fifteen cases,
twelve completed the required ten treatment sessions; a few
cases required more than ten sessions. Thirteen of the fifteen
cases (87%) are now free of illegal drugs and ten (67%) are de-
toxed and drug free. Thirteen (87%) of the cases are either
working or are in school full-time. These results are dramatically better than outcomes for a matched group of patients which
did not undertake family therapy but were given other modes of
treatment.

The patients involved are all male heroin addicts under age 36.
Half are black and half are white. All have at least some
military service, although they may have been discharged prematurely for drug abuse; most have not been to Vietnam. Patients
with pychosis or history of pychosis are excluded. They and
their families must live within one hour's drive from the clinic.
They must have two parents or parent substitutes available for
treatment (e.g., stepfather, mother's boyfriend). At intake
they must have been seeing one of these parents at least weekly
and the other at least monthly. Initially, at least, all of
them are on either methadone or naltrexone.

One area in which we have had to exert a great deal of effort is
in getting the families into treatment. Our therapists expend
considerable energy in making contact with various members
of the family and in side-stepping family coalitions which would
permit only selected members to attend sessions. It takes

from five to twenty or more contacts (interviews, telephone calls, home visits), stretching over a period of one to ten weeks to get them into the first session. However, once they have engaged in treatment, the families have tended to stay with the process.

The approach used is a very active one in which the therapist attempts to bring about change in family interactions within the sessions. Specific tasks and concrete behavioral indicators are used. It is a goal-oriented, symptom-focused approach in which urinalysis results are an integral part of the program. The therapist sets boundaries and generally tries to restructure the family, often by reinforcing generational boundaries, i.e. between parents and their offspring.

An important facet of the therapists' role is that they are given control over methadone dosages and other medications. In the early stages of the project they did not have this control and the patients would often play the therapist and the drug counselor off against each other. We do not think this treatment will succeed unless the therapists have such control.

Within a month from treatment onset the therapist can expect a family crisis of some sort. At this point he must be prepared to devote considerable time to assisting the family through this difficulty. It usually arises when change starts to occur in the addicted member and is an expected and possibly a necessary step for effective change and improvement.

It has become increasingly clear that the family treatment must deal first with the triad composed of the addict and both parents before proceeding further. If this step is skipped therapy will falter and possibly fail. In some cases with married addicts we started with the marital pair and found that it only served to stress or dissolve the marriage; thus the addict would end up back with his mother. Further, a pattern which we see repeatedly is that when the addict improves the parents start to separate. If he gets "dirty" again they reunite in relation to him. Much of our effort has gone into changing this pattern.

We believe this approach is showing tremendous promise for the reduction and elimination of drug addiction. Within the next year we will have a larger number of cases from which to draw conclusions and make statistical comparisons.

FAMILY THERAPY IN A THERAPEUTIC COMMUNITY

Katia Hope

Family Counselor
New Bridge Foundation
Berkeley, California

When a drug abuser comes to a therapeutic community, the addict often hopes to leave   family problems at the door. This paper describes some of my observations of a nine month exploratory program to introduce family therapy concepts and family counseling within a therapeutic community called New Bridge Foundation, in Berkeley, California. Here, we have attempted to incorporate the entire family into the treatment process, rather than ignore, reject,or isolate the parents, spouses, friends and children of the drug abuser.

The special population of addicts with children was the target of this project. A three generation approach evolved to include services for the children of the addicts, the resident addicts who are parents, and the parents and spouses of the residents. We look at the whole family as a system of interacting parts with roles, patterns and functions that all work to support as well as often sabotage the drug abuser. Major problems and key issues are encountered in each generational group woven around the themes of separation and loss, abandonment, confusion over affection and ambivalence about family roles. These issues are not unique to the drug abusing family, but are characteristic of many troubled families. Indeed, drug abusing families tend to be multi-problem families already caught up in the criminal justice system, unemployment, welfare, and school failures. This paper does not try to answer the elusive question of just what is the drug abusing family or unique about it. The paper presents a description of the key issues found within each generational group and the problems encountered in providing services for each group.

My role as family counselor is to co-ordinate and develop the efforts of the three generation approach to a family program, educate the staff to the necessity and sensitivity of family work, and overcome the high anxiety by the residents over involving their families into treatment. Initially, I met resistance as a non-addict professional coming into a system often antagonistic to professionals who are seen as easily conned and manipulated, insensitive to the street life, and not able to identify on human levels. The mutual testing still goes on. The first lesson I learned is that these heroin addicts are simply people who come from families with problems--one of which happens to be drug or alcohol abuse.

The population at New Bridge Foundation reflects the mixed ethnic and class makeup of the Bay Area. With over 80 residents, the ethnic breakdown is about 50% white, 45% black, 5% Chicano and Asian. Their ages range from 18 to nearly 50. About 20% are women. Nearly 30% of the total population have children. 95% are probated by the court system. This is a drug-free community which attempts to treat a wide range of drug abuse: heroin, pills, PCP, and alcohol. The focus of the family program is to concentrate on the special needs of women in treatment and drug abusers who are parents.

There is no typical child of an addict--some seem to be managing all right and some seem already on the path to problems. What is clear is that by puberty, the lure of the "glamorized street life" becomes more urgent and the problems intensify. Nearly every resident over 35 with children has at least one child on heroin. Children are often the major spoken motivation for coming into and staying in treatment.

The children show varying degrees of neglect and emotional scarring. Mostly, the children are tentative, fearful to trust adults and afraid of losing their parents permanently. Often the child appears almost parental--admonishing the adult to be good, get well and come home soon.

Bringing children into the program for visits, art activities, and outings with their parents proved to be a powder keg situation. I naively started to have kids visit every other weekend. Within six weeks, the parents' group was down from 20 to 8 members. My first lesson was crucial: go slow. Having the children visit is like touching a raw nerve--all the guilt, feelings of failure and longing for the family come to the surface. The membership of parents' group went back up as I brought in the children of parents at least two months in the program   only every 4 to 6 weeks. Now, I routinely predict at least a few residents to unintentionally sabotage their visits with their child just before the visit by breaking rules to lose privileges, or by leaving the program. Predicting such a crisis tends to minimize its effect and makes the residents more self-conscious of their attempts to sabotage themselves. Since the parents seem most fearful of answering the child's pointed questions, we role-play before each outing "101-questions- your- child- will -ask-to-stump-you." We talk about ambivalent feelings--both the positive feelings of having kids and the negative side to being a parent. Mostly, the parent learns how to not make promises, admit they don't know and how to listen to the child's voice and feelings.

The parents of these children are seen in a biweekly therapy group which provides a supportive group of other addicted parents.

The addict parent feels tremendous guilt and low self-esteem. They are often convinced they are failures as parents, and indeed, some are. Ninety percent of the parents (both men and women) had their first child in their late teens. About 50% knew about some sex education and knowledge of birth control but none used it. The child provides a source of pride, someone to love in a world of loneliness and emptiness. Being a parent connects them, if only briefly, with the world of normal activities. For most, planning and actually going on a successful zoo trip is like planning to go to the moon--viewed as overwhelming, easily sabotaged unexpectedly, a delicate operation full of hidden pitfalls and perils. The parents need desperately to relearn the fundamentals of child rearing, child development and communication skills.

Most of these fathers have no jobs, few skills, little posi- tive work experience, and rare father images to imitate. They have failed at the traditional role of the father as financial care-taker, so they tend to over-compensate with male-strutting, having lots of women, and a mock-macho pose. Often, these fathers dote on their children, belying the tough "street image".

The mothers seem often to be in rougher shape, and their children generally appear more disturbed (i.e., hyperactive, very withdrawn). Burdened often with the major, (if not sole), respon- sibility for child rearing, the mother has had to give up her child while heavily abusing drugs and now during treatment. The guilt feelings over the separations are magnified within the mothers because they, themselves, were not raised by their own mothers. Most often a grandmother parented them during their formative years. Sometimes their mother simply rejected them, or economic necessity forced these young mothers to get jobs and leave children with their relatives. This jumping of generations for parenting roles seems very characteristic of this group. In fact, the most significant predictable behavior in the drug abus- ing family is the repetition of specific patterns in the parenting process.

The grandparent generation plays a crucial and often over- looked role in these families. These resident addicts are highly attached and protective of their own mothers and fathers. Although the drug abuser is often in his/her mid to late twenties, they often live close by, work for and with their parents, and are in daily or at least weekly contact with them. Rather than iso- late the parents, we encourage their participation in our bi- monthly meetings that act as part business and part therapeutic sessions. The business group which includes spouses, parents, friends, and relatives, plans open-houses, parties for the resi- dents, raises money for emergencies and gets up-to-date information on changes within the program. The therapy groups work to educate the family members as to how they may have inadvertantly helped to continue the drug abusive behavior. Major work is done to min- imize self blame, to avoid focusing solely on the addict as the problem or to avoid feeling total responsible as failing parents. We encourage breaking the umbilical cord, especially by focusing

on the misuse of economic support to maintain dependence. Family
members are taught how their covering up, continually supporting,
or taking responsibilty for the "drug abuses" only perpetuates the
addiction.

The identified problem member of the family often acts out
the unspoken familiar conflicts. One conflict is of rebellion and
sabotage against an authoritarian parent who is now on the decline
and losing his power to coerce, frighten into submission, or
overwhelm the family. A drug addict also provides a dependent person for middle-aged mothers who now experience a severe identity
crisis with the threatened loss of the mother role as they face
an "empty nest". A family crisis can be predicted within a short
time of the identified patient leaving the family system because
the identified patient has provided the focus of the family and
often kept the parents from talking seriously about their own
relationship. These families have a glued together quality which
encourages the role reversal between grandparent and parent
generation. The grandchild may represent the second chance for a
parent who feels like a failure with their addict son or daughter.
Often, the grandparent takes over the parenting during the infancy
and then doesn't want to let go of the child. The new child is
almost like a necessary sacrifice to replace the addict who has
been the dependent child into his late 20's. The major developmental task of the family to nurture and allow the child to
leave the nest is thwarted by the overprotective and sometimes
seductive mother. The fathers are often uninvolved and have a
self-righteous sterness to them.

I've found the parents of the residents skittish of formal
settings for family counseling. I practice much of the family
counseling on the run, in informal settings, or during family
visits. Family counseling then becomes a more natural part of the
ongoing activity.

These are just a few observations about key issues faced by
each generation in this three generation approach. The need to
go slow with these families is very real. Major raw nerve endings
are exposed. Touch, even a positive one, is painful and not to be
trusted. This exploratory program continues to evolve and give
promising results. The families who have been involved have stayed
on, reinforcing each other's growth and change.

Family services are greatly needed. Working with the families of drug abusers convinces me that drug abuse and addiction
is in great part learned behavior, firmly embedded in family
patterns and often passed down in the generation to the son or
daughter who most resembles the adult addict parent. We can see
the potential continuation of drug abuse over generations, the
scarring by the separation and loss, the need to reconstruct
family communication along more positive lines while the child is
still young. NIDA needs to widen it's scope to include children
of addicts as part of the key preventative role.

CONJOINT THERAPY WITH METHADONE
MAINTAINED MARITAL PAIRS

Carl Gasta, MA

West Philadelphia Community
Mental Health Consortium, Inc
Philadelphia, Pennsylvania

Marital partners, previously addicted to heroin, who are both in methadone maintenance treatment, present special needs in their diagnosis and psychotherapy. It is not possible to treat one or both partners without treatment affecting, or being effected by their addict bond marriage. Not only two individuals, but a crucial relationship system is involved in treatment. Both partners' successes and failures are negotiated through their marital dynamic, and the relative success of therapeutic intervention is dependent upon the therapist's ability to diagnose and treat at the marital system level.

The effects of methadone maintenance treatment upon marital and family functioning has been studied by Clark, et al., (1) while O'Donnell, et al. (2) reported on the marital histories of heroin addicts. Wellisch, et al. (3) described an "Easy Rider" syndrome, a pattern of addict partnerships based upon mutual heroin addiction.

This paper reports the clinical experience of providing diagnosis and conjoint marital therapy to twenty addict marital pairs. All marriages were heterosexual and the partners considered themselves married, whether legally bound or not. They had experienced a mutual past, were living together when in treatment, and anticipated a future together. All forty persons had received a minimum of one year of methadone maintenance prior to conjoint therapy. All couples participated in a minimum of three months to as much as two years of marital therapy. Conjoint marital therapy was defined as therapy conducted with both partners present, with a therapeutic focus upon the dynamics of the marital relationship.

CLASSIFICATION OF MARITAL STYLES AND DYNAMICS

In marriage therapy literature, there exists many diagnostic and classification systems based upon marital partners' personality styles and the form of their interaction patterns. Ard and Ard (4) and Gehrke and Moxom (5) are representative. However, the twenty marriages discussed here any single category based upon psychiatric terminology. What does differentiate them from other samples of marriages is their addict bond, the construction of a marital relationship based upon mutual heroin addiction.

The parameters of the addict bond relationship are best investigated by applying three criteria described by Berman and Lief (6). First, power: who is in charge, or more accuarately, how is power exchanged within the relationship. What are the covert and overt operations of the exchange? Second, intimacy: partners must deal with their ambivalence concerning their needs for emotional clossness versus distance. The fit between two people and their changing needs creates possibilities for unity or conflict that are endless. Third, boundary: what does the marriage include and what does it exclude? What are the marital goals and activities?

Persons imbedded in an addict bond marriage have negotiated these issues of power, intimacy, and boundary according to the dynamics of heroin addiction. They demonstrate and experience all the more common marital processes, such as relatedness, sexuality, and child rearing, but are together as man and wife because heroin abuse structured and reinforced their marital relationship.

DIAGNOSING THE ADDICT BOND

During intial diagnosis of the addict marriage, two primary areas of historical data are sought. First, personality development of each partner and their psychosocial realities at time of meeting is investigated. This includes an assessment of the then current relationship between each partner and his family of origin. Second, diagnosis focuses upon the behavioral construction of the addict bond. Were one or both spouses heroin addicts at first contact, or polydrug abusers who graduated to heroin abuse, or did conjoint addiction follow months or years of non-conjoint drug abuse? Did one spouse teach the other heroin abuse? Who hustled, who copped, who shot up who? Did shooting up lead to emotional relatedness and communication? Within the addiction cycle, did partners share heroin equally, or did cheating occur? Did the couple accept or exploit assistance from either family of origin?

As the interviewer gathers this data, he also observes current personality functioning of each partner, and the behavior of the marital interaction system. Also, what are the couple's goals, and present environmental realities?

DIAGNOSTIC RESULTS

The strength and stability of the addict bond derives from its synergistic or organizing effects. Mutual addiction efficiently resolves the three structual issues faced by any marital pair: power, intimacy, and boundary. Who shall lead and give orders is decided by who hustles best, who cops the best, etc. One partner may perform all the drug activity tasks, while the other partner provides motivation and support. Or tasks may be shared. Whatever the arrangement, mutual addiction is usually a period of optimal agreement concerning leadership and followship. Intimacy issues are similarly resolved because both partners can agree that they need heroin more than affection and sexuality. And, heroin use can serve to release or allow sexual behavior by reducing anxiety and employing euphoria as foreplay. Finally, marital boundaries are clearly set. The marriage exists to gain and use heroin.

Using these three diagnostic criteria on the twenty addict marriages reported here, two general groupings, each containing ten marital pairs, was observed.

The first group can be described as symbiotic dyads, marital pairs composed to two psychologically incomplete personalities who have blended into one functional living unit. Both spouses report impoverished and destructive developmental experiences, and early, conflicted efforts at separation from families of origin. Learning drug abuse and eventually heroin addiction was central to their developing marital relationship. Heroin was usually self administered. Sociopathic defenses are prominant in the marital system and in one of the partner's personality functioning.

The most striking diagnostic feature of the symbiotic dyad is its communication behavior. As they respond to questions, partners will "cross talk," speak simultaneously without regard to the other. Also, one partner can, in mid-sentence, complete the thoughts and feelings of the other partner's self report. These acts are behavioral representations of the blended, symbiotic quality of their addict bond. Usually the history they provide emphasizes one spouse's life story. It is difficult to learn of the personal history of the other spouse. In these marriages,neither partner has demonstrated an adult work role.

The second group of ten addict pairs are labeled mixed dyads, being characterized by their variety of marital style. They can be more accurately classified according to marital interaction types, such as the "neurotic illness" syndrome (5). Marital partners describe more benign and conventional developmental histories and more mature self-differentiation is observed among individual partners. The development of the addict bond was quite variable. In five of these marriages, the wife became an addict after one or more years to a drug abusing husband. In almost all of these marriages, the husband did all the copping and regularly "hit" (injected heroin) the wife. In this group, most husbands worked satisfactorily.

TREATMENT PROCESS

The first goal of conjoint treatment of addict pairs it to demand and assist the couple to achieve drug abuse abstainance. Once gained, treatment goals and strategies can be individualized for each pair. As was found in the diagnosis of these twenty couples, there were observable differences in treatment process between symbiotic dyads and mixed dyads.

Symbiotic dyads exhibited considerably more interpersonal conflict within their marriage, more environmental crises, and less productive use of treatment resources. They experienced more difficulty at gaining or maintaining drug abuse abstainance. Together, they continuously attempted to manipulate the therapist into such roles as surrogate parent, surrogate mate, and judge and jury. Most of the males would not work. If these marital partners were parents their children were quite vunerable to neglect or abuse.

Mixed dyad couples demonstrated more marital and social stability over time, and treatment progressed along relatively specific themes or issues. They achieved and maintained drug abstainance more easily, and any drug abuse lapses could be clearly related to their marital dynamics. Marital issues concerning power were less frequent than concerns with emotional intimacy. In contrast to symbiotic dyads, mixed dyads had little difficulty with marital boundaries.

During methadone maintenance, drug abuse lapses always signaled the presence of disequilibrium in the homeostatic marital dynamic. Something was happening covertly within the marital process, and was expressed overtly via drug abuse. With symbiotic dyads, it often meant that one of the partners had made some progress in personal growth or greater intolerance of the binding nature of the marital relationship. Symbiotic dyads rarely informed the therapist that drug abuse had occurred or was imminent. Conjoint denial of urinalysis results was frequent. Mixed dyads were much more likely to admit to drug lapses, or seek help in preventing drug abuse. For them, drug lapses meant repetition of basic neurotic interaction contracts, or resistance to potential growth in the marital dynamic. Important clues as to which partner was serving as enforcer of the marital homeostasis was emergence of that partner's drug cravings, which would trigger stimulus cues and non-verbal agreements and result in the conjoint drug abuse cycle. Both partners would then succumb to their addict bond, thus surrendering personal responsibility for their drug abuse and reinforce the solidarity of their marital relationship.

MARITAL THERAPY RESULTS

Of ten addict marital pairs labeled symbiotic, eight couples no longer live together as man and wife. Of these sixteen persons, seven have completed methadone treatment and for at least one year have remained drug free. Five of these are women. Two symbiotic dyads remain married, and in conjoint treatment. For symbiotic dyads, successful treatment has meant that one partner developed sufficient personal resources to leave a stable though highly constricting and unsatisfying marriage.

Of ten addict marital pairs labeled mixed, seven couples continue to live together as man and wife, and to remain in conjoint methadone maintenance treatment. For these seven couples, progress in treatment has meant continuing psychosocial stability, little evidence of drug abuse, and an intense fear of detoxification from methadone. Excepting for the removal of drug abuse as symptoms, they exhibit little change in original marital dynamics. Of the three separated couples in the mixed dyad group, one is apart because of a mate's imprisonment. Two couples have separated by choice, and one partner from each of these marriages have achieved and maintained a drug free life.

REFERENCES

1. J. Clark, W. Capel, B. Goldsmith and G. Stewart, J.Marriage Fam., 34: 496 (1972).

2. J. O'Donnell, K. Bestman and J. Jones, Internat. J. Addictions, 2: 21 (1967).

3. D. Wellisch, G. Gay and R. McEnee, Family Process, 9:425 (1970).

4. B. Ard and C. Ard, (eds.) Handbook of Marriage Counseling, Science and Behavior Books, Palo Alto, Calif., 1969.

5. S. Gehrke and J. Moxom, Family Process, 1: 253 (1962).

6. E. Berman and H. Lief, Amer. J. Psychiat., 132: 583 (1975).

THE FIRST FAMILY COOPERATIVE

Letitia C. Lynn

Odyssey Institute, Inc.
24 West 12th Street
N.Y., N.Y. 10011

In nine years, the face of drug addiction has devolved from
that of an adult single drug abuser to the adolescent poly-drug
abuser to the teenage mother abuser with from one to four dependent
children. To recognize the existence of the adult male drug
abuser is to acknowledge a priori: the existence of the child and
parent drug abuser. Only when this is acknowledged will society
begin to confront the actual problem of which drug abuse is merely
a call for help. The problem is the moral and ethical breakdown
of positive social values as engendered by the fragmentation of
both the family unit and the collective community conscience.
There is little recognizable inter-dependence or strong family
bonding within our society, even for the purpose of survival.

Five years ago, young drug abusive parents--mostly women with
from one to thirteen children--began to appear on Odyssey's door-
step. There were no father figures and sense of family. The
women and children clung to one another. The mother knew neither
how to cope with nor how to nurture their children. They were but
children themselves. In 1971, the Parenting Program of Odyssey,
officially began its work with these mothers together with their
children. The task of the Parenting Program was two-fold:

1. To treat the addiction of the parent.

2. To teach healthy concepts of child nurturing/mothering.

The majority of these mothers were the products of abusive
and neglectful homes themselves and now they were addicted,
abusive and neglectful parents in their own right. It was clear
that there was an undeniable correlation between "Today's abused
and tomorrow's addicted." If this cycle was to be stopped, a
secure family environment had to be provided for these children.

The Motivational and Treatment phases of the Parenting
Program were highly successful, but the women were not graduating.
The financial demands of a single parent raising a family: the fear

of isolation and loneliness in an urban environment; a critical
lack of day care services; and the absence of marketable job skills
had discouraged our residents from leaving the supportive Odyssey
community.

It was therefore in the latter part of November 1974 that
Dr. Judianne Densen-Gerber and the staff of the Odyssey Parenting
Program designed an extended family re-entry plan for these single
parents, their children, and other interested single men and women
in Odyssey programs who wished to experience a family life-style.

On December 18th, 1974, eleven adults (four of whom were
parents), black and white, ranging in ages from 19 to 35, came together with their seven children from 1-½ to 7 years of age, to
begin the first Family Cooperative of Odyssey.

The immediate areas of concern included the preparation of
projected budgets, rotating child-care, cooking and cleaning
schedules. Those who preferred to seek jobs were entitled "supporters." All earned monies would be pooled and allowances allot-
ted. Those who preferred to stay at home and care for the household and children were entitled "providers." Initially, there
were three men who wished to be providers and three women who
wished to be supporters. Already, the flexibility and freedom of
role definition afforded by this kind of extended family--irrespec-
tive of traditional sex stereo-typing--was evident.

The following characteristics were observed within the first
six months of this extended family experience:

1. The mothers were highly protective and territorial of
    their children and were resistant to the idea of any
    other adult watching over their children. The children
    were aggressive, often uncontrollable, distrustful of
    most adults, clung to their mothers, and were generally
    sullen and rude.

2. Every adult member expressed their fear of the closeness
    inherent in this life-style. Subsequently, inappropriate
    male and female pairing-off ensued which provided a
    temporary sense of false security.

3. There was an exaggerated sense of psuedo-familial role-
    playing which included obvious sibling teasing and rough-
    housing among some of the younger adults, as well as the
    protective maternal and paternal attitudes of others.
    Every adult began to slowly realize the weighty responsi-
    bility of caring for and setting an example for the
    children. The needs of the children came first; the needs
    of the family as a whole followed second, then the needs
    of the individual.

The basic tenants of the family were mutual respect financial independence from Odyssey, and inter-dependence among the family members.

In February, the family moved into a two-family home in Brooklyn for a six month rental period. During this time, six of the adults chose to leave the cooperative, four of whom were wage earners. They were dating and preferred to leave the Co-op to pursue their relationships. Only one mother actually chose to leave the Co-op throughout the entire year long history of the family. The mothers seemed to understand from the very beginning the extraordinary freedom and fulfillment that this kind of life-style afforded them.

The Co-op then welcomed a few new members into their ranks and moved into their present home in Newark, New Jersey, in July 1975. Since then, one of the original members of the Co-op family married another member of the Odyssey Community and have made the Co-op their home. Their first child was born in March.

In the early fall, a 15 year old boy from the regular Odyssey Program came to live at the Co-op, as he had never enjoyed a positive, supportive family life of his own.

It has been, however, the children of this extended family who have most benefited from this life-style. They are calmer, more articulate, infinitely more trusting and joyous than before. They freely go from adult to adult with their stories and troubles. They no longer cling to their mothers as if there was no other attentive support, love or affirmation. It is for these children that alternative, mutually supportive life-styles must be developed for the supposed panacea of the nuclear family with a father, mother and 2.6 children as a practical and emotional luxury is lived successfully by a select few.

The Family Cooperative has proven to be successful for the people of Odyssey, but more importantly, could prove to be a way of life for all kinds of people: troubled adolescents; the forgotten elderly; the divorced, single, working parent.

By providing supportive, home environments for the children of these families, their chance of anti-social behavior will be reduced.

Those of us concerned with stemming the tide of social disorder by providing more services to the disadvantaged, must be committed to studying, evaluating and creating new models for living. Then, and only then will effective preventive treatment begin.

ADMINISTRATION AND MANAGEMENT

FACTORS INVOLVED IN DEALING WITH YOUR LOCAL POLITICIAN

Mary Beth Collins

Executive Director
Community Organization For Drug Abuse Control
Phoenix, Arizona

On this matter of politicians, and politics, and all kind of things like that, some of us argue against, some of us hate, some of us don't like to deal with: They are like the nose on our face and the ears on the sides of our heads, we all have them! And we are all responsible for them. If we have reached the age of franchise, we are responsible for them and the place that they play in our lives, because we either voted them in or, by not voting, we allowed them to get into the position that they presently hold.

And they have power! The most powerful position that you as an individual vote to fill is that of President of the United States. Second to that is the position of United States Senator. There are only a hundred of those. Then comes the position of United States Representative. Following that, your state legislators. Then the county councilmen. And then the individual that perhaps has the most direct effect on your everyday life, the city council-man or magistrate.

Let's think a little bit about that power, how does it affect us? First of all these individuals have the power to levy taxes. They can tax our land, our income, they can tax the purchases we make in stores. They have the power to regulate buildings and real estate, what goes where, where roads go, where parks go. They have the power to regulate businesses, and who gets a license to do what. They have the power to regulate traffic, and whether the road in front of your house is a four-lane highway or a two-lane road, or a one-way street.

But also they spend money. And they appropriate these funds on personnel to run all this business, or on things such as roads and buildings and sewers and water, and on services. And it's in this latter area that a good many of us are vitally interested. Because it's from this latter area that many of us receive the funds that keep us in existence.

We vote these people in, we put them in. Doesn't it make sense to know them? And doesn't it make sense to let them know us? How do we do this?

First of all, we start at the campaign stage. We see individuals that look attractive to us. We listen to them, on the radio, on television, and in person. We read literature on how they stand, in the newspaper, in the magazines. They think our way, and he or she becomes our kind of person. We get involved with that person. We may go down and actively campaign for him or her. We may put a bumper sticker on the back of our car. We may stuff envelopes. We may get on the telephone. Next, we vote for that individual, and we make sure that everybody else in our area votes too. We talk up that individual, our candidate, and we get the voters out to vote--hopefully, to vote for our candidate. Most of all, we get our face known--to that candidate. And we get our name known. One small hint--wear a nametag. It helps. When someone meets hundreds of people, it's quite awesome to remember everyone. And by wearing a nametag, you also not only keep your face known to that individual, but make your name easy to be spoken.

After that individual is elected, keep it up! And that is true with all elected individuals. You should deal first with the individual that you and others like you in your geographic area are responsible for voting in. In dealing with your legislator, remember you are his constituent, and the only person he is really responsible to is the voter.

If there is a legislator, a key individual that you need to get to, such as the Chairman of a member of the appropriations or the health and welfare committee, you find a constituent in their area, and contact them. Or you contact your elected representative to talk to them. You can contact that key person yourself, but again he is first responsible to his voter, then to the general public.

You keep an eye on these key people, and you keep an eye on your legislator. You do this in a variety of ways.

Often published in your local daily paper, sometimes once a week, sometimes more often, is a roster on how your federal legislator has voted. If it is not in your local paper, call the editor and ask why. For your local legislator, there quite often is a special weekly paper that is published. Your agency, if you belong to one, should subscribe to that paper. If you don't belong to an agency, or if you can't afford a subscription, go down to your local library and take a look at it. You can look up your local legislator, the one who resides in your township, your neighborhood, and you can see how they voted. By watching the voting of all of the legislators, you find some friends. By watching the voting of your legislators, you see best how to approach them, what their thinking is, what their aims and goals are.

Suppose an issue comes up. There is a particular law that you want to change, or there is a law that you want enacted. Or there is a clarification of the law that you or your agency feels is necessary. Or perhaps there is a proclamation, such as a memorial to a particularly wonderful worker, that you feel takes legislative action. How do you work to get these things done?

The first order of business for you is to learn the protocol, learn to whom to address your request, learn how to address it and where to address it. There are various ways to approach the legislature. Number one, there is a petition. There are laws in every state on petitions. There is a specified format for petitions, and for getting signers for each petition. Follow these laws. Your petitions are useless unless you do.

Secondly, you can reach your legislature through a personal letter from a group. Your agency's board can write a letter to the legislature supporting or advocating against a certain bill.

Third, a personal letter can be sent from an individual. Each member of your board can send his personal letter to his particular legislator. Point of interest: each personal letter is considered by legislators to have the backing of 100 voters.

Also in this category, if time runs short, are mailgrams and telegrams. Mailgrams can be sent overnight through Western Union. Telegrams take even a shorter period.

A fourth way to approach your legislature is via the phone. I know in our own state of Arizona there is a direct line into the senators' offices. This is a special number, and by using this number you can either contact the senator or one of his aides immediately. When time is short and you need to make your views known quickly, this is the quickest way. Generally speaking, a legislator considers a phone call as one vote.

Please remember that all decisions are made well in advance of the final reading of the bill on the floor of the senate or the house, and the final ballot. They are first heard in subcommittee hearings, and it is here you can testify and have a positive constructive voice. They are secondly heard in committee hearings. Most of your work should be done prior to a committee hearing. If you are asked to appear before a committee, or if you feel strong enough about an issue to appear before a committee, learn each member of that committee's name, who they are, what they stand for, and greet the committee members first, previous to making your presentation.

If at all possible, try to schedule meetings with individual committee members prior to the committee hearing. Try to pick a nonbusy time. Realize that your approach must be positive and constructive, and "short as a woman's skirt--long enough to cover

the subject, but short enough to be interesting"! You should present, on one page of a sheet of paper, your entire position. The
law or the bill number you are addressing your remarks on should be
listed first. Then, how it will affect you, for good or bad. Then
some changes that will help in the law or the proposed bill. It is
often said that laws are passed on amendments. You should reemphasize and reemphasize your particular choice of change. You should
set your priority as to the change you want first, and your compromise second. Lean hard on the advantages of your choice. Ask your
personal legislator how he stands on a bill. If he is with you and
agrees with you, ask him to help. If a particular legislator, or
your legislator, will be voting against the bill, see if it is the
whole bill or only a part of the bill, and perhaps you can reach a
compromise on this.

If the issue appears to be a very close one, set your machinery to
work. Find some constituents of other committee members and ask
them to talk to their legislators. Remember, this must be a very
important issue to you to work this hard on it. You can wear out
your welcome, and you must make every moment count.

If at all possible, use the staff of the legislature. When you
want mechanical information, reach the staff, ask them for particulars. Solve all problems you can with the secretary. She will let
your legislator know you called.

As you work for your agency in the legislature, or as you get involved more and more with politicians and with the legislature, or
with your city council, you may find that you have a feel for it,
or you may find that it is very necessary for you to be there a
good deal of the time. You may find that it will be necessary to
register yourself as a lobbyist. If this is your or your agency's
decision, plan to spend some real time on this. You should learn
the process inside and out.

A word of caution. If you are a staff member of a non-profit I.R.S.
501 (c) (3) agency, you are by Federal law prohibited from lobbying.
You should know exactly what is considered lobbying and what is
considered educating. However, if the field of lobbying seems
exciting to you, or if you want to explore it further as a volunteer
for your group--and you are not also on staff, read on!

What I have previously outlined for you is a brief overview of what
will be necessary to be a lobbyist. Take everything I have said
and double it!

In lobbying, remember, you are a legislative educator and an advocate for what you believe in. Be consistent, be out front, and be
truthful, and say the same thing to all. Sound different than what
you've heard of as "lobbyists"? But it is absolutely essential.
Someone who comes in there and tries subterfuge and tries to say

one thing to one person and one thing to another is soon discovered, and soon discounted and loses all their effectiveness.

Once you are registered, and read and know all the laws on being a lobbyist, step back and look at what you're doing. Set your priorities, and set your plan of action for the legislature.

Speak to small groups of people, and get these groups of people to understand your thinking and why you are advocating the way that you are. Several small groups often make up a majority. If you are asked to testify in committee hearings, keep your testimony short and factual. Do plenty of work prior to the committee work. Realize your legislature needs information, such as: This is the likely impact of this bill; and give the alternative impacts of a bill. Always keep your approach on a positive basis.

The greatest strength of any lobbyist is the friends that he has who can help him fight his battles when the going is rough. The key to good public relations is making friends when you don't need them so you can have them when you do, and realize that these friends can't be play friends--they have to be people who think like you do, believe like you do, and will fight like you do.

Make lots of friends of voters, particularly voters, people who are active, so there are workers for you when you need them. Make friends with the press. Always keep the press informed as to your thinking. Give them a synopsis of what you are advocating for. Keep them alert as to progress on your particular bill.

A few final pointers. Don't ever threaten a legislator. He won't believe you or respect you, and he won't have anything to do with you. Don't raise hell after a vote has been taken and a bill either passed or rejected, unless you've talked to your legislator beforehand. And even then it's not too good an idea. Bite your tongue. Don't ever embarrass your legislator.

Finally, if your bill gets defeated, look at where you possibly haven't done your homework. Learn from that mistake. Gain from it. Don't just sit over in a corner and pout and find people to take the blame for your failure.

How do you start? Talk to the leadership of your legislature, your city council, your county government. Be helpful to them. Work with them. Listen and be responsive. And find you can help make the changes necessary to turn the tide on this problem all of us fight.

COMMUNITY ACCEPTANCE OF ADDICTION TREATMENT PROGRAMS: A
CONTEMPORARY PERSPECTIVE

Pedro Ruiz, M.D., John Langrod, M.A., Joyce H. Lowinson, M.D.

Albert Einstein College of Medicine
Bronx, New York

This paper proposes to analyze the sources of political and
community opposition in the field of health service delivery. As
an example we will describe our experience in the field of drug
addiction. We have decided to place emphasis on this subject because of the extraordinary changes that have developed in conceptualizing the types of services that should be provided.

In recent years there has been a significant change in the
setting and location of addiction treatment services (1). This
has favored the development of programs on a local level, instead
of in isolated locations as in the past. An example of the latter
is the United States Public Health Service Hospital in Lexington,
Kentucky. These changes have come about as a result of the difficulty found in rehabilitating addicts in "large, depersonalized,
isolated institutions" (2). On the other hand good results have
been reported in the social rehabilitation of addicts, especially
hispanics, by providing locally based treatment (3). Workers in
the field of addiction now advocate treatment directed at maintaining patients in their own communities.

In addition to the change in treatment setting, there has
been an increase in the levels of addiction in recent years (5,6).
The consequences of the Korean and Vietnam Wars have undoubtedly
played a significant role in the increase of drug abuse (7)

These changes in treatment setting as well as the increase in
drug abuse have contributed to the development of unique problems
in relations between the community and the various treatment centers. There have been few studies in this area reported in the
medical literature. Our philosophy, which is oriented to a community based social view, forces us to pay the closest attention
to these problems.

Our Experience

Our study is based on the Albert Einstein College of Medicine Methadone Maintenance Treatment Program (AECOM MMTP). This program, supported by the New York State Office of Drug Abuse Services, has been in existence since 1968. It is currently operating seven community-based outpatient clinics in different sections of the Bronx serving approximately 2,300 patients. These clinics service lower as well as middle class communities. At the time of their establishment, we faced significant community relations problems, despite the fact that methadone maintenance has been well established as a treatment modality.

These community problems became manifest primarily through opposition to the opening of these clinics. Opposition has been noted not only to establishing programs in the field of drug abuse, but it has extended to other areas, such as alcoholism (8), and mental health services (9).

In general, such opposition manifests itself in the following ways:

1. Demonstrations directed against both the patients and the staff of the treatment centers.

2. Through the invocation of laws designed to prohibit such programs, especially through court injunctions designed to block the opening and/or continuation of the treatment center.

3. Through the use of economic pressure such as refusal to rent appropriate space or refusing to provide adequate maintenance services.

4. Through the use of political pressure directed against office holders representing neighborhoods where treatment programs are planned. This becomes most manifest at election time when such threats make legislators feel most vulnerable. Political leaders then may invoke threats to withhold funding from programs and/or "assist" the community by proposing or having enforced restrictive zoning laws.

5. Through the use of "peer pressure" brought against community leaders so that they will withhold approval for programs within regional and community planning boards.

6. Finally, adverse publicity through the news media, concentrating on alleged poor results of treatment as well as other stereotypes, is employed.

In analyzing opposition to the establishment of addiction treatment programs, we observe the following causes:

1. Fear that property adjacent to the site of the treatment program will depreciate in value and/or that it will be vandalized. It should be noted that these fears occur in poor communities as well as wealthy communities.

2. The expectation of an increase in the level of criminality as a consequence of the presence of a treatment center where addicts come to seek and receive treatment. Sight should not be lost of the existing difference in this regard between wealthy and poor communities. Wealthy communities are more likely to deny the presence of drug addiction in their midst than poor communities, where drug addiction is nothing more than a problem of everyday life. This leads to greater acceptance and, at times, protection of the addict in the poor communities.

3. The existence of stereotyped thinking about drug abuse, specifically the belief that the addiction is a chronic illness having little hope of successful treatment.

4. The fear, especially among the poor, that addiction programs are one more means of social control by the white majority over the black or hispanic minority. This becomes most pronounced in relation to methadone maintenance programs. This fear is exploited on occasion by individuals involved in the drug traffic who resist the establishment of successful treatment programs.

5. The existence of racist attitudes within the white majority directed against minority groups. This is most frequently observed in those geographic areas which are undergoing a state of social and economic transition.

6. The utilization in the political arena of negative publicity designed to discredit the addict patient, favoring the cutting of addiction treatment programs during the current state of fiscal crisis. This allows legislators to support funding to those areas that are most advantageous politically.

The above causes of resistance constitute a strategic design reflecting a socioeconomic basis. As far as the poorer populations are concerned, this strategy is developed through the utilization of suspicion, resentment, and possibly violence. It should be noted that these tactics are used regardless of the ethnic group involved, if the economic level is low. Examples of such extreme manifestations of resistance as violence are the Watts riots among blacks in California, or the opposition to school busing among the poor whites of Boston. Among middle class populations the strategy is less violent, with greater use of political pressure based on the power of the taxpayer and voter. This form of struggle is most often waged through civic and political associations. The fact that the planners of treatment programs generally belong to the middle class may to some extent blunt the opposition to treatment in middle class communities. Among poorer socioeconomic groups the problem becomes more complex because the opposition is directed toward the professionals who work in the programs, a vast majority of whom are white and do not live in the community, while most of the community residents are members of minority groups.

Discussion

Solutions to these problems are complex since our goal is to offer treatment to addicts who require it, yet at the same time we wish to respect community sentiments. This is of utmost importance because of the difficulty in treating addicted patients in other types of psychiatric facilities (10). It is also well known that the treatment of addicts within the framework of classical psychiatric practice presents serious problems because of the difficulties which most psychiatrists have in adequately understanding patients of a lower socioeconomic level (11).

On the basis of our experience we would like to offer the following methodology for the opening and maintenance of addiction treatment programs:

1. The participation of members of the same ethnic group toward which services are directed is essential in all phases of planning. This allows for greater identification with the proposed services by the community, thus decreasing the resentment and suspicion which always exists against agencies foreign to the community.

2. Community participation in the operation of addiction treatment programs is important. This involvement should be on both the direct service level as well as on the administrative level. This has given good results in some types of mental health programs (12).

3. The use of community education in all phases of the development and operation of addiction treatment programs is indicated. This would provide the community with greater knowledge of and sensitivity to the problem of addiction.

4. Allocation of funding for addiction treatment should be directed toward the development of programs having a community based, outreach orientation. This would enhance a greater acceptance of and identification with the programs, as well as providing higher quality of service and accessibility.

5. The recruitment and hiring of personnel from the community, who reflect its ethnic composition will make for better communication between the staff and patients, making the service more attractive.

6. The development of training and upgrading staff programs should incorporate all aspects of community life. This approach has contributed to the improvement of services provided in the field of community mental health (13).

7. Programs should not limit themselves to offering addicts treatment but should also provide comprehensive services related to other problems faced by the addict and his family. This would assure that programs will not become isolated but on the contrary will constitute a vital, integral part of the community.

8. The development of voter registration projects among staff, patients, their families and friends would create a force capable of defending the rights of the rehabilitated addict and guarantee the availability of treatment services.

9. Local vigilance directed to educating and pressuring governmental bureaucracy from interfering with the autonomy and sound development of the community must be maintained at all times.

10. Programs should be easily accessible to patients, and their location should be in commercial rather than residential areas.

11. Services should be limited to patients living or working in the community so as to allay anxiety about the influx of addicts into the community.

12. Local governmental authorities should be involved in all phases of program development so as to assure that all social services, such as access to welfare or licensing for patients, is available to programs treating the addict. This would permit optimal service delivery to all communities that require addiction treatment programs.

13. The involvement of local community organizations and leaders in ongoing program evaluation would permit the strengthening and improvement of effective programs and the elimination of the ineffective ones.

Conclusion

We have attempted to present a comprehensive analysis of the problems faced in treating the addict in the community at the present time. The diverse causes and reasons for community resistance to treatment centers have been analysed. The different ways in which community dissatisfaction is manifested have been examined. In addition, an appropriate methodology has been advanced for the planning and implementation of addiction services within a frame of local community participation around the stated problems.

REFERENCES

1. Ruiz, P., Langrod, J., Lowinson, J. Resistance to the Opening of Drug Treatment Centers: A Problem in Community Psychiatry, The International Journal of the Addictions, 10 (1):149-155, 1975.

2. Lowinson, J., Langrod, J. Neighborhood Drug Treatment Centers, New York State Journal of Medicine, 75 (5):766-769, 1975.

3. Ruiz, P., Lowinson, J., Marcus, N., Langrod, J. Treatment of Drug Addiction in Two Different Communities, New York State Journal of Medicine, 73 (18):2244-2247, 1973.

4. Nash, G. Community Response to a Narcotic Addiction Treatment Facility: The Case of Prospect Place. In De Leon, G. (ed). Phoenix House: Studies in a Therapeutic Community, New York, MSS. Information Corp., 25-41, 1974.

5. Greene, M.H., Nightingale, S.L., Dupont, R.L. Evolving Patterns of Drug Abuse, Annals of Internal Medicine, 83 (3):402-411, 1975.

6. National Institute of Drug Abuse. Heroin Indicators Trend Report, DHEW Publication No. (A.D.M.) 76-315, 1976.

7. Ruiz, P. Community Approach to Addiction Problem, New York State Journal of Medicine, 72 (8):970-971, 1972.

8. The New York Times. Neighborhood Groups Oppose Alcoholic Center on 14th Street, February 22, 1976, 41.

9. The New York Times. Flatbush Rejects a Psychiatric Facility, October 9, 1971, 36.

10. Corman, A.G., Khantzian, E.J. Psychiatric Care of a Methadone Patient, Psychiatric Annals, 6 (4):158-164, 1976.

11. Ruiz, P., Behrens, M. Community Control in Mental Health: How Far Can It Go? Psychiatric Quarterly, 47 (3):317-324, 1973.

12. Ruiz, P. Consumer Paricipation in Mental Health Programs, Hospital and Community Psychiatry, 24 (1):38-40, 1973.

13. McWilliams, S.A., Morris, L.A. Community Attitudes About Mental Health Services, Community Mental Health Journal, 10 (2):236-242, 1974.

ON BECOMING DIRECTOR: THE CLINICIAN AS ADMINISTRATOR

G. Graham Jackson, M.D.

Montgomery County Methadone Center
113 East Main Street
Norristown, Pennsylvania 19401

This paper is to be a very personal and pragmatic experiential statement addressed to clinicians. The ideas are not necessarily original but distilled from diverse sources, personalities,
and philosophies which have been meaningful and helpful to me. I
am a psychiatrist who has enjoyed being a therapist in an eclectic
but primarily psychoanalytically-oriented private practice; a Director of several medical, psychiatric, and drug programs; and a
consultant both in administration and clinical skills to medical,
mental health, and drug programs. Over the years I have observed
that the skillful clinician is often recruited for important posts
in health services, yet few prepare themselves for this responsibility and many clinicians who might function best in leadership
roles often view administration with fear or contempt or both.
(I might add that administrators who have not come from a clinical
background often view their clinicians with a similar lack of understanding.) Thus, in this presentation, I appeal to clinicians
to explore the field of administration since, theoretically, a
well-trained and experienced clinician understands the needs of
the population for whom services are delivered and should best be
able to deal with the interpersonal relationships involved in administration. No clinical discipline has a monopoly on leadership,
but the leadership must be professional, that is, knowledgeable,
ethical, responsible, and able to learn from others.

Before becoming the Director, however, it can be mentioned
that you, the clinician, go through several phases beginning with
a pre-promotion period during which you become involved in increasing teaching and organizational responsibilities. Although
vaguely aware that you are climbing the administrative ladder,
your conscious identity remains that of a clinician or a clinician-
teacher rather than an administrator. However, it is during this
phase that you may find yourself being considered as a candidate
for Director in your current or some other agency. During the
second phase, you are invited to become a candidate, meet with the
selection committee, and, while interested, ask for more information and time to think the matter over. (There is an important
difference between wanting to be the Director and wanting to do
the job of the Director!) If your decision is to seek promotion

you may then campaign for your candidacy through sponsors and credentials. After selection, negotiation, acceptance, and appointment, there is a final moment in this preliminary process: Becoming the Director-designate. This phase is brief, but an important one in the process of promotion -- your decision is now firm and your appointment has been publicly announced but you are still in transition, half out of your old job and half into the new one; leaving the old job with a mixture of regret and relief and also finding the new job a mixed blessing. The Director-designate desires the great promise that the new position offers but naturally has anxiety about the change in life goals and career directions: he looks forward to broader professional responsibilities, yet suffers doubts about his ability to manage them; he may also experience a sense of loss from becoming further and further removed from his patients.

The type of responsibilities and problems that you as Director-designate will have will vary with whether you are inheriting a program with staff, facilities, and policies already established or creating an entirely new program. In the first case, you will find many staff fearful of you and unable to adapt to your priorities, with a consequent temporary decline in morale and an increase in personnel turnover until you get your own support staff on line and policies clarified. To minimize these problems, maximize input from the existing staff: make them feel valued and important by asking for their views in terms of your role and theirs. Do not neglect the so-called lower echelon -- secretaries, bookkeepers, etc., -- since they are the oil that keeps the gears running smoothly. On the other hand, if you are requested to start a program (making your job in many cases much easier) but you then obviously must expend a great deal more effort in recruitment and meeting the preconditions necessary to implementing your ideas.

In either case, as the new Director you must develop an organizational philosophy and coordinate a senior executive staff. Decisions about this group will involve its size, formality, or informality, and whether it will be solely advisory to you or have decision-making authority. The role of this senior group and your relationship with them is of crucial importance since the Director is at the interface between the organization and the outside world and finds himself further and further removed from the "production line."

There is much than can be said about organizational theory, business and accounting principles, and other aspects of administrative skills. While some of these will be addressed in passing, the focus of this discussion of administration will be on relationship issues: Director to staff, Director to Board, and Director to community and governing bodies.

We could define "administration" as getting things done through the cooperation of others. This is based on three principles: Investigation or finding out what is needed; planning (for personnel, facilities, funds, etc.); and forecasting. The latter requires a knowledge of alternate solutions adopted elsewhere as gained from familiarity with the current literature and attendance at conferences such as this one. It also requires the ability to entertain and encourage the unorthodox which is best accomplished in a social and physical setting conducive to free expression. The ideas a minute thus garnered must later be subjected to thoughtful analysis.

My particular interest in administration is in the area of the Director's relationship to his staff. Effective administration demands a style of leadership which I chauvinistically describe as "benevolent patriarchy." Operating under this philosophy, the Director chooses the right staff and then provides them with the opportunity to get on with their jobs with a minimum of interference and a maximum of support. This staff must have both the knowledge and the feeling that you are behind them to bear the ultimate responsibility if they should find themselves in difficulty. The Director should not fear making the final decisions -- 'the buck stops here.' In choosing staff seek leaders with skills and intelligence superior to yours who can teach you something. While ready to learn, however, it is the Director who sets the pace for the staff. The Director must have not only virtue but the appearance of virtue; if he is lazy, dishonest, disorganized, etc., there is a very good chance that this will filter down and influence the character of the entire program. It has often struck me how much an agency reflects the personality of its leadership.

To retain their position, staff who work for me must be able to work well with patients _and_ get along with the other staff. I feel that technical competence is not enough. Any staff member who creates dissension or otherwise breaks down the morale and cohesiveness of the organization should be let go.

The organization retains its personnel through several means. With regard to salary versus fringes, I feel that money, although necessary and even a status symbol in terms of gross pay, may not be as important as the "freedom fringes." The freedom fringes include giving the staff the freedom to set their own hours (within limits determined by their patients' schedules, agency meetings, etc.); the freedom to select their own time off (in this, I encourage frequent, short time off rather than long annual vacations) and freedom to advance -- you will notice losses of your best staff increasing with decreased room at the top. Other freedoms are the freedom to make decisions that stand; freedom to establish their own turf; a place they can call their own, rather than shifting from office to office or sharing a space with a large group; freedom to socialize (expect six hours of concentrated work per day from your staff and understand that two hours spent relaxing with other staff, exchanging ideas and discussing problem cases, will probably result in a more productive operation than one in which the Director measures staff output by number of minutes put in). In addition, group cohesiveness is enhanced when co-workers get to know each other in dimensions beyond their professional images via social relationships outside the office at staff picnics, dinners, etc. Such cohesiveness lends itself to greater mutual support and free flowing evaluative exchange. A final important freedom is the freedom to fail -- without shame or regret if not through negligence or incompetence.

As a Director, you have to supervise. This requires communicating to your employee what you want; determining if your message is understood; teaching him how to do it; and finally, checking to see that it has been done correctly. If it has, bug off. (A mechanism for implementing this concept can be the writing by the employee of his own job description including criteria for effective performance. This role concept and its execution is then jointly reviewed periodically by you and the employee.)

Your success in the elements of administration so far mentioned will be reflected in low personnel turnover and absenteeism. Fiscal soundness and, of course, the attainment of program goals and objectives are additional and indispensable reflections of your effectiveness. I would interject here that objectives should be specific, time-limited, and measureable. Too often programs talk in terms of vague entities like 'increased personal happiness,' 'improved family relationships,' etc. Instead, if you wish to compare your performance with your objectives, you will need to state that "by such and such a date, a certain number of patients will have accomplished a certain thing which will be measured by such and such a parameter." (E.g., "by December 31, 1976, 80% of all patients active on that date will have urines free of narcotics as measured by EMIT analysis on random observed specimens collected during the preceding seven days.") Thus, you measure only the measurable. As in other aspects of administration, this requires information gathering, planning, and noting of progress or lack thereof. In the public health field, probably one of the most frequent (but not necessarily the best) measures of a Director's effectiveness is fiscal soundness (cost-effectiveness or cost-benefit ratio). This requires being harshly realistic with respect to needs, past experiences, economies that can be effected, quality control, etc. I make it a policy to underspend budget and aggressively collect revenues. Unforseen budgetary changes or questionable expenditures are brought out in the open and clarified with funding sources as soon as their existence becomes apparent.

I would like to make a few comments now about the use and abuse of power. People submit when they fear harm if they don't conform or if they expect something of value from you or the organization. Authority rests in the position or office you hold, not in your personal charisma. The office you hold gives you control through the ability to withhold or bestow gifts, favors, money, status, power, prestige (private phone lines, keys to the executive washroom, etc.) You need not lean on your authority to use it. You already have the power as Director to make final decisions and implement policy, so there is no need or place for muscle flexing. Instead, invite suggestions and advice. An when you delegate authority, do not overrule, undercut or criticize publicly those to whom authority was given. After all, if your agent has not done the job you wanted, his failure reflects on you. To avoid this kind of failure, your orders must be understood, consistent with the goals of the organization, compatible with personal interest, and capable of execution. Whatever you do, don't issue an order that can't be carried out. The habit of compliance is reinforcing. Remember, it is not what people are told, but what they accept that counts.

In addition to the Director's relationship with his staff, there is his relationship with the Board of Directors. I will make only a brief comment here. Firstly, the Director must educate and facilitate communication among the Board. Secondly, it is my view that the Boards in their role of providing wealth, wisdom, and work should decide what program they wish to support; then one individual must be designated to see it through. Thus the Board's main job (aside from securing funding) is to select that individual in whom they have confidence, and then support him fully in running the program for them. The Board should not try to rescue a badly run program by making or changing decisions the Director should have made in the first place. If the Board does not like his decisions, do not change those decisions, change the Director! On the other hand, if they want the Director to serve them efficiently they will need to give him the same kind of support-with-freedom as described for the Director's relationship with his staff and a sufficient staff and length of time to implement his ideas and bring them to fruition. (It seems too often that, having finally decided upon a Director after a long debate, Boards then expect him to produce immediate results -- perhaps as some compensation for their delay in selecting him.)

In conclusion, I throw out a few random thoughts. First, never mix a clinical position with your administrative duties so as not to undercut or be in competition with your clinical staff -- administration in or of itself will demand enough of your time. You should, however, continue to be involved in exercising your clinical skills and increasing your clinical experience -- thus, consider being a clinical consultant to some other agency or maintain a small private practice. Second, you can have either a loosely organized or tightly controlled organization, as long as it is understood that control is exercised or will be exercised. Finally, stress individual responsibility: Yours, the staff, that of the patients (to show up for appointments, pay fees, demonstrate motivation for change.)

MANAGEMENT IN A DRUG ABUSE UNIT:

A PRIMER FOR MASOCHISTS

Harvey Weiner, D. S. W.
Jacob Schut, M. D.

Drug Abuse Rehabilitation Program
West Philadelphia Community Mental Health Consortium, Inc.

Synopsis

The drug abuse field is getting around to recognizing the importance of management and administration in drug programs. There is a danger in focusing only on the clinical aspects of service, for it has been the authors' experience that good program administration is as important as good clinical services when considering the overall impact of a treatment program on the lives of individual patients.

Management refers to the overall organization of a program; i.e., do things flow smoothly, do patients experience a sense of cohesiveness, do staff interact with each other in a constructive, supportive manner, as opposed to a program in which there exists a pervasive sense of disorganization and conflict.

As the title of this paper suggests, those of us who are involved in drug program management recognize that our task is not an easy one. A common dilemma we face is the need to deliver high quality, humane services, while at the same time complying with funding criteria and state and federal regulations which overlap and sometimes contradict each other. Other common

Dr. Harvey Weiner is the Clinical Coordinator and Dr. Jacob Schut is the Director of the program.

frustrations include "no growth" budgets (a euphemism for program cutbacks in a period of unparalleled inflation),and staff "burn-out" due to the difficulties of working with a patient population where relapse is a frequent occurrence.

One of the central concerns of program administrators is the need to establish a program structure which, while in compliance with regulations and funding criteria, encourages flexibility and staff initiative in responding to the specific needs of an individual patient. Exclusive concern with regulatory detail can result in a program which is cold, inhumane, and anti-therapeutic.

A contention of the authors is the proposition that attention to the basic principles of administration helps a program run smoothly. Treatment in such a program is provided in a supportive atmosphere, where patient-staff interactions are characterized by mutual respect and an understanding of each other's roles. There is a need for program managers to involve themselves in formal management training, since most program administrators arrived at their present administrative positions through the usual route of clinician⟶ supervisor⟶ administrator.

The elements of program structure begin with clarity as to program objectives; i.e., an idea of what the program is trying to accomplish. Clear cut objectives are important for both patients and staff, since they serve as the basis for designing treatment plans to meet the specific needs of individual patients.

Organizational structure refers to the formal, hierarchical relationships of authority which exist between staff, and between the various units which comprise a program. The organizational structure establishes channels of formal communication and supervision, and reflects the division of tasks within the program. Staff supervision and administrative decision making should generally occur within the channels which have been established for this purpose. If key decisions are consistently made without regard for the established structure, this is a sign

that the formal channels are no longer functional. When communication is poor and formal supervisory channels are dysfunctional,
some staff members may attempt to further their own ends by ex-
ploiting the existing confusion. The result of such conflict is
that patient care deteriorates while staff devote time and energy
to internecene struggles. Failure to adhere to the established
organizational lines of supervision and communication is one of
the major causes of staff conflict within programs.

There is a need for multi-disciplinary cooperation in
treatment, since addiction is a disorder characterized by physical,
social, and psychological dysfunction. The difference between
success or failure often depends on the social supports which have
been built into the patient's life during treatment. These social
supports, which include a job or vocational training and improved
relationships with family and friends, will have to sustain the
patient during the difficult period following discharge from the
program. Because of the special skills needed to evaluate patient
progress in regard to social, medical, psychological, and vocational treatment goals, all staff should be prepared to participate
in multi-disciplinary team meetings and case conferences. Decisions which are made in regard to case management and therapeutic
intervention should represent the combined judgement of all staff
who are working with a particular patient.

Written job descriptions are important for each position
in that they serve as guidelines for staff performance. Job
descriptions also serve as the basis for the periodic staff
evaluations which should be a part of the ongoing supervisory
process. Also recommended is the establishment of a formal
grievance procedure for staff, to resolve occasional differences
which may arise between staff and supervisors.

There is also a need for a written document describing
the program's rules and expectations. This document should be
given to the patient as a part of the intake process. It should
clarify what the patient can expect from the program, and what the

program expects in return. By providing a common frame of reference for treatment, such a document can prevent needless patient-
staff conflict in regard to expectations which are unclear, ambivalent, or inconsistent. The rules and expectations should delineate the program's treatment goals, available services, fees
(if any), expected patient behavior and participation, penalties
for unacceptable patient behavior, and the right of patients to
appeal decisions which they consider to be unfair or arbitrary.

Throughout the paper, emphasis is placed on the need to
provide adequate structure as a means of facilitating the treatment process. It has been the experience of the authors that
attention to the basic principles of administration will ease the
burdensome task of those who are charged with the responsibility
of drug program management.

REFERENCES

How to Improve Individual Manager Performance, American Management
        Association, 1970.

Jacob Schut, Robert Steer, and Frank Gonzalez, "Types of Arrests
        Recorded For Methadone Maintenance Patients Before, During
        and After Treatment," British Journal of Addiction to
        Alcohol and Other Drugs, LXX (1975).

Ruth Smalley, Theory for Social Work Practice, New York: Columbia
        University Press, (1967), p. 166.

Richard Stephens, "The Truthfulness of Addict Respondents in
        Research Projects," The International Journal of the
        Addictions, VII, No. 3 (1972).

Harold Triggs, "Clinical Problems of Selection, Prediction, and
        Patient Failure," Proceedings of the Fourth National
        Conference on Methadone Treatment (San Francisco, 1972),
        p. 133.

TREATMENT RECORDS: ONE AGENCY'S ANSWER*

Arnold Andrews, M.A.

Director of Rehabilitative Services
Operation PAR, Inc.
St. Petersburg, Florida

On June 1, 1975, Operation PAR, Inc. was awarded a grant by the Florida Drug Abuse Prevention and Education Trust to formally develop a record-keeping system used in PAR's five programs with apparent success. Bases for the allocation were testimonials by Federal and State monitors and frequent requests for consultation by referred drug abuse agencies. A training manual and corresponding instructional film were, therefore, developed of the system.

The PAR system, which has been often termed "innovative," is, in reality, nothing more than an adaptation of traditional clinical procedures to the special field of drug abuse. However, it is unique in that it provides the trainee with detailed instruction on the essential data elements required in a "good" report and in that it sidesteps technical writing style by using "plain English."

The training manual resulting from this effort provides a narrative written in dialogue form, a list of summary points, a program learning guide, and work problems for each chapter.

Table of contents are as follows:

*Record of Treatment by Arnold Andrews was partially supported through a grant by the Florida Drug Abuse Prevention and Education Trust, Robert L. Shevin, Trustee.

1045

What follows are some excerpts from the manual which will hopefully illustrate its content.

The chapter titled "The Comprehensive Evaluation" offers, among other things, an overview of the evaluation process (Exhibit I); describes in detail what data is required in an evaluation and how it should be written (Exhibit II); and a list of the significant evaluation data elements and their significance (Exhibit III).

EXHIBIT I: EXAMPLE OF NARRATIVE STYLE

The Comprehensive Evaluation: General Description and Purpose

Can you give me a general explanation of the Comprehensive Evaluation?

> Well, in general, it is a written report on what has been learned, from all available sources, about the client and what is being assumed about him from the information. The report is composed of five sections:

> 1.) An Abstract which is a brief description of the client being evaluated and the reason for his being in treatment;
> 2.) A Medical History which summarizes the significant medical conditions or treatment that the client has experienced;
> 3.) A Social History which summarizes his social development;
> 4.) A Psychological Assessment which profiles the different components of his personality; and
> 5.) Impressions which describe the interpretation of all the information with regard to the client's condition, the problems that he appears to be experiencing, and his ability to deal with them.

The report is continuously reviewed for accuracy and corrected, as new evidence becomes available.

What purpose does the Comprehensive serve in treatment?

> As we are offering it here, the evaluation serves several purposes in treatment. First of all, it allows you to organize large amounts of normally scattered data in such a way that you can gain a more accurate and complete understanding of the client and the problems that he may be experiencing. Once this evaluation is completed it serves a second purpose of providing a continuous guide to treatment and its planning.

EXHIBIT II: EXAMPLE OF WRITING FORMAT

Format for Written Service Evaluations

I.   Abstract.   First entry is a brief <u>identification paragraph</u>.
     It should be unlabeled, single spaced, and indented.
     Essential Elements:
         a.)   demographic description (name, age, sex, race,
               marital status)
         b.)   ref·rral source
         c.)   presenting complaint
         d.)   type of treatment and admission date

II. <u>Medical History</u>.   This section is labeled and should consist
     of three brief paragraphs:

            Paragraph 1.   The first paragraph should summarize any
                           significant medical condition and treat-
                           ment occurring in client and family.   This
                           should be listed in chronological order
                           to the present medical workup at admission.
                           (Consult Set 1).

EXHIBIT III: EXAMPLE OF DATA ELEMENTS AND THEIR SIGNIFICANCE

Evaluation Element	Significance
psychiatric and drug treat-ment history	- allows for estimation of progress of disease and the gearing of intervention efforts accordingly
nature of treatment	- allows a basis for estimation of treatment approach.
treatment outcome	- if pattern exists, probability is that it will be repeated, therefore, allows for treat-ment plan modification

III. Social History

1. place of birth	- learning experiences vary with geography and size of city or town. This provides a con-text for understanding signif-icant events in client's life.

2. rearing environment   - learning experiences vary with
   a.) location   physical locations and socio-
   b.) socio-economic   economic standing within
        setting   communities. Information on
                                     possible norms learned can be
                                     obtained by knowing these
                                     factors.

The chapter titled "The Treatment Evaluation" illustrates the
"teaching through example" approach taken in the manual (Exhibit IV); the summary points found at the end of each chapter
(Exhibit V); and the accompanying program instruction (Exhibit
VI).

EXHIBIT IV: ILLUSTRATION OF "TEACHING THROUGH EXAMPLE"

    5.) Describe the progress made for each primary problem
        under each category in a coherent narrative by
        reporting:
            a.) what methods were and were not followed;
            b.) what objectives were and were not followed;
            c.) the extent to which the goal was or was not
                achieved;
            d.) the state of the problem at the time of your
                report (based on your observations and the
                client's self-reports); and
            e.) any other related significant information.
        Label each group of descriptions by their category:
        Medical, Social, Psychological and the first three
        parts of the report will be completed.

Can you give me an example of how progress is described in a
narrative?

    Sure. Why don't we try it with the shade tree example.
    Here is his Treatment Plan:

Problem	Goal	Objective	Method
No safe protection from sun	Find safe protection from sun	1. Find a nearby shade tree without apples	1. Survey area from hill for promising trees
			Select a satisfactory tree

1048

Now here is his written Treatment Evaluation:

(Methods)
After surveying the area and selecting a satisfactory
(Objective)
tree, John Doe appears to have found a nearby shade tree
(Goal)
without apples. Consequently, he now seems to be safely

protected from the sun and reports that his problems of
(Problem)
not having any such protection is greatly relieved.

(Signed)
O.J. Sigmund, Counselor

EXHIBIT V: EXAMPLE OF SUMMARY POINTS AT THE END OF EACH CHAPTER

1.) In general, Treatment Evaluation is an estimation of how
     effective treatment has been in helping the client resolve
     his problems. In other words, it is an evaluation of the
     counselor's approach to treatment and the progress the
     client has made toward resolving his problems.
2.) Treatment evaluations are conducted at the end of each
     treatment period (30-90 days) and written as a four-part
     report. The first three sections describe the progress
     made with medical, social, psychological problems addressed
     in the Treatment Plan. The fourth and last section explains
     the counselor's interpretation of the client's performance
     and the indicated changes for the subsequent Treatment Plan.

EXHIBIT VI: EXAMPLE OF PROGRAM INSTRUCTION

1.) In general, the Treatment Evaluation is an estimation of how
     effective _____ has been in helping the client _____
     his _____.

_____
                treatment; resolve; problems

2.) In other words, it is an evaluation of the counselor's _____
     to _____ and the _____ made by the client toward
     resolving his problems.

_____
                approach to treatment; progress

1049

A MODEL FOR THE CLASSIFICATION
OF JOB CATEGORIES
IN THE DRUG ABUSE FIELD

Mark A. Quinones, Ph.D., MPH
Kathleen M. Doyle, B.A.
Lywanda Thompson

Division of Drug Abuse
New Jersey Medical School
Newark, New Jersey   07103

Brendon Sexton, M.A.

Addiction Services Agency
New York, New York

During the last two decades considerable attention has been
directed to the drug user and abuser in American society. This
has prompted the development of a wide range of rehabilitation and
treatment programs, each with its own concept of care and service,
covering the full range of therapeutic modalities.

As programs have developed, job categories have been conceived to manage specific activities within each program. Those
recruited and filling these job categories have been drawn from a
pool of candidates which include "squares" as well as former
addicts. Often, the former addicts recruited are themselves
successful graduates of the respective program.

As a consequence of the multitude of new job categories,
there is no clear-cut definition as to how each job category relates to others in the particular agency, let alone to other
therapeutic agencies. Many of these categories, when compared
from modality to modality, appear to have similar functions but
different titles, similar titles and different functions or different titles and functions.

In many instances this pattern may be by design since some
programs attempt to "homogenize" the work situation in an effort
to make all coworkers feel equal. However, this often gives rise
to elements of conflict among workers, and is perceived by clients
who in effect are expected to recognize clear-cut distinctions
between themselves and the working staff.

The issue is further compounded when we compare job categories from one agency to another. Seldom is any distinction made
between an occupation, a semi-profession, a marginal profession,
or a profession. In the absence of such criteria, anyone who is
not a patient is viewed as a member of the "professional team."

Recognizing this problem, the Division of Drug Abuse, New
Jersey Medical School, and the Addiction Services Agency of New
York City examined a sample of drug programs in New York and New
Jersey. All told, 20 programs were reviewed representing a cross
section of the major treatment modalities. The following data
were collected from each program:

1. List of job titles and salaries.
2. Job description for each title.
3. Qualifications for each title.
4. Actual academic, work and drug background of
   person presently filling the position.

In view of the data collected from these programs, job titles
were classified into two general areas:

1. Administrative staff (those primarily concerned with financial aspects and the day to day operations of the program), and
2. Treatment staff (those primarily involved in patient
services).

This approach revealed that people were functioning in both
groups (administrative and treatment) under a variety of titles,
i.e. Executive Director, Program Director, Coordinator, Administrator, etc., with a wide range of duties and responsibilities. A
wide range of salary levels, educational requirements and work experiences was found. For example, salaries ranged anywhere from
$14,000 to over $30,000 per annum; educational levels ranged from
11th grade to Ph.D. and work experiences ranged anywhere from no
prior experience to 15 years of relevant experience.

In light of the above, this paper attempts to review concepts
in the world of work as a model for classifying job categories in
the drug abuse field on the basis of viable criteria. Such an
approach should help in:

1. illustrating the confusion which presently exists in the
   drug abuse workplace,
2. differentiating between work roles,
3. assisting in the structuring of work roles,
4. more accurately classifying roles on the basis of
   experience, education and training,
5. providing an understanding of work roles in relation
   to each other, and
6. providing a standardized approach useful in classifying
   work roles and categories from agency to agency.

An essential first step in handling the problems of licensure
and/or certification, this model concerns itself with four major
categories viewed in a career perspective and existing on a continuum: 1) occupations, 2) semi-professions, 3) marginal professions, and 4) the professions. Each has increasing requirements
as one moves from left to right. Thus, each work role in drug
abuse can be broadly classified within each major category.

WORK ROLES

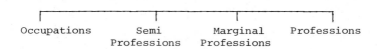

Occupations   Semi   Marginal   Professions
                Professions   Professions

Work Role - Man's very existence depends on his varied societal
roles. The work role designates him as a worker and affects all
aspects of his life, including his perception of himself. (1)

Types of work have both a market value and a social and prestige value. Often these are not strongly correlated - e.g. a
blue collar worker (sanitation man @ $18,000) may earn much more
than the more prestigious white collar worker (office supervisor
@ $11,000). In the drug field, we find the social value of the
job extremely important, particularly to the ex-addict. As a
result, these jobs are not arranged on a rational continuum which
should lead upward in terms of career perspective.

Occupations - The work role involves all levels of interaction in
the world of work and represents the framework within which all
work activities, regardless of level, take place. (1) Occupation
can be defined as a specific position which an individual holds
in relation to others in the work scenario, through which he provides a service, and for which he is remunerated.

The occupation per se is a more precise description of the
work role. It contains all the elements found in the basic work
role, in addition to others which distinguish it as an occupation.
It is central to determining individual prestige and to the allocation of social privileges. (2) It serves as a source of identification which tends to displace other status fixing attributes,
i.e. ancestry, religion, political affiliation and personal
character.

Semi-Professions - This is a special group in the world of work,
consisting of new occupational groups whose claim to the status

of a profession has neither been fully established or fully desired. They fail to meet the criteria of the professions because
their training is shorter, their status less legitimized, their
right to privileged communication less established; there is less
of a specialized body of knowledge, and they are less autonomous
from supervision or societal control. Physician assistants, lab
technicians, etc. are examples of the semi-professions. (3)

Many drug abuse roles fall into this category. The difficulty is two-fold: first, there is little difference between
occupations and semi-professions in drug abuse; they are often
confused with each other. Second, drug workers often devote more
energy to defending their status against societal limitations
than to organizing their work roles so that their members may
operate in a mobile career pattern.

Marginal Professions - Included in this category are those occupational groups which exceed the standards of semi-professions but
are lacking in all of the essential criteria of the true professions. For all practical purposes, marginal professions often
view themselves as professionals but lack community sanction and/or
sanction by other bonafide professional groups. When compared to
the traditional professions, the marginal role becomes clearer. (4)
Some examples of marginal professions are osteopaths, chiropractors, psychologists and podiatrists.

The Professions - This category functions in an intellectual work
role, requiring a long process of formal training. Essential to
the professions is the maintenance of an occupational ethic and
rules which govern the relationships between the members and
clients. The professions experience special protection by the
broader community, have clearly defined rules of conduct, a sense
of responsibility, and criteria for the recruitment and training
of their membership. In addition, the profession provides protection for its members. The profession maintains a minimum fee
or salary for service, is involved in a professional practice,
and provides the client skilled services or advice. (5) Examples
of the traditional professions are medicine, law and theology.

Discussion - The drug abuse field contains a maze of occupational
titles which are difficult to assess in terms of job role, income,
education and training. Similar titles often have different job
functions and different requirements when comparisons are made
from program to program. Because of this, it is difficult to
consider any form of credentialing or licensure until some organized system has been put forth which can equate job titles,
functions, salaries, work experience and education into a broad
but meaningful grouping.

This paper has attempted to provide a broad model, based on 4 major groupings, in an effort to explain the relationship of work roles to occupational categories within the structure of drug abuse programs.

One dilemma facing drug abuse workers is the lack of job uniformity from one geographical area to another. The above model could help alleviate this problem. Also, as new job titles are created to meet growing program needs, standardization will be facilitated. Implementation of this broad model offers drug abuse staff a career perspective and direction toward occupational goals, as well as appropriate designation for a given occupational category. Also, as new job categories are developed they can be located in appropriate relationship to each other in terms of role identity and identity and function. Therefore the model clearly recognizes that each job category in the drug abuse field has a vital task to perform, and that each is an essential link in the chain toward improved care.

The above groupings are not offered as the final step in classifying job and work roles for the purposes of credentialing. Nonetheless, we see it as an important first step in providing handles for more effectively assessing individual job functions relating to each other within the program's organizational pattern.

REFERENCES

1. L.I. Dublin and A.J. Lotka, in Length of Life, The Ronald Press, New York, 1936, p. 220.

2. T. Caplow, in The Sociology of Work, The University of Minneapolis Press, Minneapolis, p. 30.

3. A. Etzioni, in The Semi-Professions and Their Organization, The Free Press, New York, 1969, p. IV-X.

4. R.H. Hall, Professionalization and Bureaucracy, Amer. Soc. Rev., 33:92 (1969).

5. S. Nosow and W.H. Form, in Man, Work and Society, Basic Books, Inc., New York, 1962, p. 197.

FUTURE FUNDING FOR DRUG ABUSE TREATMENT

Nancy A. Wynstra, Esquire

D.C. Superior Court
Washington, D.C.

Recent cutbacks in categorical funding for alcohol and drug abuse
treatment services, combined with federal regulations requiring
alcohol and' drug treatment programs to maximize the receipt of
third party funding and to impose charges on alcohol and drug treatment patients for services received, have caused wide-spread concern in the treatment community. In response to this concern
several individuals, representing various organizations, established, in December 1974, the Funding Task Force of the North American Congress on Alcohol and Drug Problems to serve as a vehicle
for program oriented individuals to advise federal representatives
about the impact of various funding problems and funding sources
on treatment programs. In 1975 the Task Force received funding
from the National Institute on Drug Abuse to prepare a report.

The Funding Task Force operated through four regional task forces
whose work was coordinated by a Steering Committee which included
the chairpersons of the regional groups. In its report the Funding
Task Force sought to identify funding problems experienced by any
component of the Task Force and to illustrate such problems with
the specific experiences of programs represented in the group. Although the Funding Task Force makes no claim to be fully representative of the alcohol and drug treatment field, it believes its experiences with various funding sources and funding problems are
representative of generic problems.

Of primary concern to the Task Force was the necessity for funding
mechanisms for alcohol or drug treatment services to cover a broad
enough spectrum of services and service providers to insure that
individual patients or clients may be provided with the continuum
of care which is adequate and appropriate to their needs. Needed
care may include a combination of inpatient or outpatient hospital
services, direct medical care, residential care in various sheltered environments, counseling, job training and placement assistance, family assistance, and aid in dealing with various life
problems. Care may be given by a variety of personnel, some of
whom may lack traditional academic credentials. However, many

funding mechanisms, particularly traditional health care financing
mechanisms such as private health insurance or Medicaid or Medicare, frequently reimburse only for services rendered by academically credentialed health care personnel, primarily physicians and
nurses. Consequently services may be structured primarily to capture such third party reimbursements whether or not such a service
structure best fits individual treatment needs or has the best
record of treatment success. The Task Force believes that financing, especially for services like alcohol and drug treatment which
go beyond the traditional medical model, must be set up so that
care is provided on the basis of an assessment of individual needs
and not on the basis of what care is covered by a particular financing mechanism.

Funding sources for alcohol and drug treatment are generally divided between sources, usually referred to as categorical funds,
which fund complete program operations, and sources, generally
known as third party payers, which reimburse particular programs
for services rendered to individual clients. Third party payer
categories for service payment are generally categorized by the
type of service or service provider rather than by client needs.
Each funding source, whether categorical or third party, is likely
to have different policies and standards for determining what services will be covered, but the payers provide no mechanism to fund
treatment programs to assist them in meeting the standards.

The Task Force attempted to set a framework, from a community perspective, in which trends in the funding of alcohol and drug abuse
treatment services could be evaluated. In this context a concern
of the Task Force is that it appears that a growing percentage of
total program funding is currently being used to meet various over-
head requirements, at all levels of program administration, rather
than for the direct provision of treatment services. While the
Task Force recognizes the validity of funding sources developing
standards and qualifications for payment for services as part of an
effort to control the quality of such services, it is concerned
that many effective and innovative programs cannot function along
the classic health care mechanism model. Thus, care must be taken
to assure that the need for developing standards for payment is
balanced against the need to provide a full spectrum of effective
services so that an appropriate continuum of care can be provided
in individual cases. Funding must be available for traditional
and non-traditional services, including those services which cannot be financed on a client reimbursement basis and those services
which do not fall within the medical model.

The Task Force rejected the definitions and components of care
which other organizations have suggested as appropriate for alcohol and drug treatment service delivery because it felt that these
categories tended to be provider oriented or medically oriented
rather than client oriented. The Task Force identified the compo-

nents of care it felt to be necessary to provide adequate client services. These included consultation, education and prevention; outreach, assessment and referral; crisis management, both residential and non-residential; residential and non-residential primary treatment and rehabilitation; residential and non-residential transitional or aftercare; and supportive services. The Task Force felt that, as a general matter, the first two care components should be program funded but that once a client enters the crisis management stage, and thereafter throughout the treatment sequence, individual clients can be tracked so that funding should be available on a reimbursement or client basis. The Task Force noted that, although supportive services could technically be funded on a client reimbursement basis, it might be that some such services should be programmatically funded so that service provision is not disrupted by the need to determine client eligibility for reimbursement from various sources.

The Task Force analyzed all current funding sources, both public and private, for alcohol and drug treatment programs, and endeavored to indicate the problems that treatment programs have encountered in obtaining funding from the various sources. In making this analysis the Task Force noted that no national figures are available to permit a detailed analysis of sources of funding for alcohol and drug treatment services, and recommended that NIDA or some other appropriate organization undertake to obtain such information, through the use of a funding matrix suggested by the Task Force, on a regular basis. The matrix would permit any treatment program to determine which funding sources provide support for each care component and, if analyzed on a state, regional, or national basis, would facilitate an analysis of actual or potential funding of drug treatment.

Among the funding sources identified and analyzed by the Task Force are federal categorical grants, federal formula grants, Medicare, Medicaid, Title XX, supplemental security income, state funding, local funding, community mental health center funding, dedicated funds, revenue sharing, vocational rehabilitation, LEAA, armed services related funding, private health insurance, health maintenance organizations, food stamps, client fees, foundations, and local "scrounging." In each funding area the Task Force noted that there is a problem of conflicting policies or service definitions, so that there is no clear picture, on a national basis, of the extent to which funds are actually available for alcohol and drug treatment services. For all third party payment funding sources the Task Force noted that there are problems in determining client eligibility and that available funds do not address many important areas including primary prevention and the entire range of nonmedical treatment services. It was also noted that many treatment programs are unable to meet third party payer requirements for recordkeeping, credentialing and accreditation, and that it is difficult for programs which have previously operated on the basis of general grants or contracts to deal with the administrative and cash flow problems created if they shift to primary reliance on third party payments.

One reason that it is important for treatment programs to deal with the problems inherent in obtaining third party payments is the fact that dealing with these problems now will put programs in a better position to collect payments in the event a comprehensive national health insurance program is enacted. The Task Force looked at the potential coverage for alcoholism and drug treatment services under national health insurance and concluded that a national health insurance program should cover the full range of services applicable to alcohol and drug abuse treatment.

The ideal coverage package is one which would provide coverage for the full spectrum of medical care and related supportive services for the treatment of alcoholism and drug abuse in addition to comprehensive coverage for other health care problems. Such ideal coverage would include a full range of inpatient and medical services as well as outpatient and residential programs and appropriate care given by non-medical personnel. Although a full range of services should ideally be covered, it is entirely appropriate that reimbursement be contingent upon service providers, both personnel and facilities, conforming to appropriate standards of quality care. Such standards might include state or local licensure, JCAH accreditation, and state or national certification or credentialing of treatment personnel.

In the event that it is determined that coverage for the full range of alcohol and drug treatment services will not be available under national health insrrance, and that NHI will be primarily a medical reimbursement system, it is important that no exclusion be made for the treatment of such conditions. At minimum, the same services for treatment of alcoholism and drug abuse should be covered as are covered for the treatment of any other physical or mental condition.

If NHI will not be available to cover the full range of services necessary to provide treatment to an individual suffering from alcoholism or drug abuse, because many of these services do not conform to the medical model, it must be understood that NHI will have limited applicability to financing treatment for these conditions. Alternative sources of funding should be specifically identified.

The Task Force noted that many of the necessary services for the treatment of alcohol and drug abuse fall outside of the spectrum of hospital and medical care which is normally covered by private health insurance programs and which appears to be the immediate target of NHI legislation. To the extent that national health insurance continues this focus, it is unlikely that NHI will provide for the full range of necessary services. Enactment of any NHI package, even one which does not fully provide for alcohol and drug abuse treatment services, may lead to a decrease in categorical funding and, thus, may lessen the availability of resources for home care, counseling services, work-related programs, and other forms of service which have proven successful in dealing with individuals with alcohol and drug abuse problems at considerably less cost than care in hospitals or other medical institutions. Prevention programs, which are unlikely to be funded under NHI in any event, would also suffer if categorical funding is decreased because of NHI. The Task Force noted that, in all probability, a national health insurance program will have the characteristics and limitations of other third party payment mechanisms including being a reimbursement system, being medically oriented, being available only through qualified providers and eligible   programs, and being available only to eligible clients.

In addition to its recommendations relative to specific funding sources the Task Force recommended that attention should be given to the development of consistent service definitions for the alcohol and drug abuse field and that attention should be focused on assuring funding for the full continuum of services. The Task Force also recommended that total federal funding for alcohol and drug services should be increased.

In general the Task Force felt that a more thorough exploration of a number of questions about the viability of alternative funding sources for alcohol and drug abuse treatment services was needed and was concerned about the fact that programs are being required to seek alternative funding, in the face of federal cutbacks, despite the fact that such funding is not realistically available for many of the clients or services involved in drug abuse treatment programs.

THE IMPACT OF THIRD PARTY PAYMENTS
ON DRUG TREATMENT PROGRAMS

Arthur Stickgold MA

Narcotics Prevention Project
Los Angeles

Wright Institute of Los Angeles

Early sociologists viewed the problem of addiction as an inherent pathological state. Whether the result of hereditary factors or of the enviornment, the drug addict was in need of removal from society less he disrupt the moral fabric of the body politic. But later sociologists, coming from a far more liberal perspective and with a better understanding of the role of enviornment, promoted the idea that the drug addict was "sick" and in need of treatment, not incarceration. This assumption was given weight of law when the Supreme Court stated essentially the same thing: the addict should not be considered a criminal merely because of his status as an addict.

This thinking, considered progressive for its time, resulted in the provision of extensive treatment services to addicts for the first time. During the mid to late sixties and into the early seventies drug treatment facilities proliferated throughout the nation. While some of the funding for these programs came from the war on poverty, the vast majority of both federal and local funds came from the health establishment. As the option was funding to and by the criminal justice establishment, this was considered a major victory by liberal workers in the field.

For a decade these seemingly forward thinking approaches were hailed by the treatment community and by the community mental health movement. But today we are beginning to see some of the latent dysfunctional consequences of these decisions: consequences which were neither anticipated nor desired when the definition of addiction as a disease was being promoted.

What was actually being discussed in the sixties when we said the addict was sick was not a medical model but a medical metaphore. This metaphore used much of the language of the medical model and called upon the sympathies which the sick role made one eligible for. It did so to contrast the problem which addicts face with the more punative criminal justice model.

The medical model involves an exchange wherin the patient gives up some of his rights to self determination and takes on an obligation to seek treatment and to cooperate with the treatment agent. In return, he is released from certain responsibilities, both in the specific area of his illness (which is now monitored by medical authorities) and in the social sector.

This is in sharp contrast to many of the treatment programs which came out during the mid to late sixties. These programs had very little to do with a chief componant of the medical model: the use of medication. (With the exception of methadone maintenance, most programs actively avoided medicating their clients, calling all drugs crutches.) In the earliest days even medication to ease the pain of withdrawal was looked down on and "kick pads" were utilized. And while today there is limited acceptance of the use of medication for detoxification, this is seen as a short term regimen -- hardly ever more than fourteen days, and often less than seven days.

The medical model's "sick role" was also ignored. Clients (not patients) were not seen as having an obligation to seek treatment. Nobody was coerced by program staffs to enter treatment. And when courts or others pressured addicts to obtain treatment the program staff usually felt the probability of success was significantly lower than usual. Workers made their availability known to the potential client population. Help was an opportunity, never an obligation. In some programs much was made of expulsion and readmission procedures where readmission was contingent on stringent punishment -- something which would never be done to a medical patient who sought to reinstate therapy.

Perhaps the greatest conflict with the medical model was in the assumptions about the client's responsibilities. Rather than relieving the client of some of his social responsibilities, the program worked to have the client take on responsibilities which had been avoided in the past. Refusing to take on these additional responsibilities was seen as failing to cooperate in the treatment program.

The treatment which was provided for the addict generally had a well defined goal which was agreed upon by both the client and the worker. (But rarely a "treatment plan" written up by the worker as in the medical model.) For some the goal was abstinance. For others it was cutting back on the dose or frequency. For still others the goal was simply seen as survival! A key element in the treatment was the integration of the addict into a community which was not drug oriented and the establishment of new informal relationships. Financial stability was important but, while jobs became an important element in building self respect, a welfare check was often seen as being equal to a pay check in providing for the financial needs.of the client.

But more important, programs used "treatment methods" which would never be considered to be part of the medical model. Addicts, especially those who had just left jail or a detoxification ward, rarely had cars. And if getting a job was seen as an important first step in cleaning up, the worker often had to drive a client to job interviews or to the employment office.

The telephone became an important tool in treatment. Where traditional therapy requires face to face interaction, the drug treatment worker often used the phone in a highly therapeutic manner. Where the medical model expects the patient to act normally, such behavior in an addict was a sign of improvement and was rewarded. The use of the phone just to let the client know that someone out there still cared was an important part of "treatment".

In short, treatment was a hodgepodge of activity. It was giving a client a lift and talking about the weather. It was talking to relatives and lovers to help them understand where the client was at. It frequently involved talking with significant others in the client's world, including employers, parole agents, probation officers, land lords and even occasional creditors. Once in a while it was a request to the local pusher not to sell anything to the client for a while! (And amazingly, they often agreed!)

These unconventional programs were a product of the non-medical approach which the government initially took toward the problem. When drugs first became visable (not, of course, when they first became a problem which was decades prior to this) nobody could really say what the best way was to deal with them. The approach taken was the establishment of demonstration grants to various groups aimed at seeking a solution.

But over time it became only logical that the demonstrations be evaluated. A social program might be evaluated in terms of social variables, but this is difficult to do and, even more important, it becomes difficult if not impossible to assign credit to any one aspect of the social enviornment for the change which is observed. Even more important, the goals of many of the treatment programs were not always compatible with those of the larger society. While some programs might consider reduction of a habit to be a success, society looked for abstinenance. Where the program might see being on welfare and taking care of a family as a successful outcome, society looked for employment. In short, the evaluators began to look toward the success criteria of the medical model: cure.

In keeping with this new thinking is the current initiation of a funding model which is more in keeping with the medical model: the utilization of third party payments based on a fee for service system. This is the same system which is utilized by insurance companies in the private sector and by the government in public health programs such as medicaid and medicare.

Third party payment schemes typically have a series of restrictions, the first of which is generally what kinds of problems are covered. In the medical system this means that most programs do not cover such things as eye glasses or routine dental work.

Just as there is a limit on which problems might be dealt with in a third party payment scheme, so is there a restriction on the techniques which might be utilized to amiliorate the problem. With health insurance this means that psychotherapy might be allowed to help a patient deal with disfigurement, but cosmetic surgery is generally excluded; tests doen in a hospital are covered, but the same test done in a doctor's office is not.

Finally, third party payment systems generally if not always specify who are permitted to receive payment for providing services. As a rule, only licensed professionals may receive payment. In the health insurance industry this means that physicians and psychologists can receive payment if they are licensed, but that chiropractors are rarely eligable and that faith healers are never covered.

All three of these limitations: what may be treated, how it may be treated and who may do it, are crucial in thinking about the future of drug treatment programs under a third party payment system. Such limits do not restrict the programs per se, but they do restrict the activities for which the program will be paid. And as soon as a service which was rendered by a program is no longer a billable service, one of two things must happen. Either some people in the program must generate extra revenue to make up for the services which are not billed for, or the entire operation of the program must be reoriented toward those services which are considered more "legitimate" since they generate operating funds.

Limits on what may be treated are beginning already. Federal guidelines today tell us to concentrate on the hard core heroin user and give a lower priority to the poly-drug abuser who was so in vogue only a year ago. And alcoholism may not be treated under any circumstances!

How people may be treated is becoming a second problem. Non-medical treatment programs in California typically have a schedule of eligible services with two items on it: individual counselling and group counselling. No other services may be billed for. And, at least in theory, the same fee would be generated by a ten minute session as by one which took the entire day. The latent consequences here are obvious: maximize the quantity of contacts, not the quality of treatment.

Since the fee schedule stipulates that the counselling must be face to face, the traditional extensive use of the phone to remain in constant contact with a client must be curtailed as it no longer generates revenue. While conjoint counseling would be allowed, there is really no way to bill for working with the client's family unless the client is present. The same goes for contacts with the parole officer, employer, friend and relative. If the limits ever begin to state *where* the treatment must take place the restrictions might well eliminate even the family counseling.

Finally, third party payment systems might well enter the area of defining who may provide treatment services. Just who they would allow is certainly unclear at this time, but implicit is some sort of credentialing system. The confusion in this area is well documented in the Federal Funding Criteria. In attempting to spell out who should perform services it refers at different points to "a qualified mental health professional", "a duly qualified professional" and "a professional mental health consultant."

Since definitions are not yet clear, it is not certain what impact this will have. It is certainly the case that at present this
question is creating great anxiety among treatment workers. Depending on the nature of the definition and the extent to which workers
are "grandfathered" in we may or may not loose a large number of the
current treatment workers. (Current California legislation, for
example, would require all workers to become psychological technicians -- a position which requires a training program which virtually none of the paraprofessional treatment workers now have.)

Stressing the medical aspects of addiction was a good strategic
ploy during the sixties by those who wished to obtain funds to help
the addict. For the best part of a decade this produced an increase
in governmental assistance to treatment programs which might otherwise either never have been seen or, worse, might have been channeled into the efforts to incarcerate addicts.
Today we are beginning to see some of the untoward consequences
of these early efforts. Drug abuse in general is a social problem.
That it has a physiological concomitant does not in any way lessen
the extent to which this is also true of narcotics addiction.
Social problems may be ameliorated and even cured through the utilization of traditional social change measures, including attempts
to change a client's social enviornment and his participation in it.
But in defining the problem as medical, we are quickly seeing the
system moving in a direction which will greatly constrain our
ability to undertake social change activities. Certainly to the
extent that programs need to alter the attitudes of the rest of
society the medical model will all but eliminate program effectiveness.
It is necessary to come to grips with the problem as it presents itself to the treatment community and to define seperate
(but equal!) medical and non-medical approaches to treatment, both
of which have empirical validity. While strict cost/benifit analysis may not show them as equally economical, we may be hard
pressed to determine which would win out in a cost/effectiveness
contest.
Narcotics addiction is a problem with social causes and a
social support mechanism. It is defined as a problem in a specific
social system. There is certainly room for a medical model in the
treatment of addiction. But to utilize such a model at the expense
of eliminating the social treatment model would be a great mistake.
To the extent that the utilization of third part treatment models
implicitly or explicitly lead to the elimination of social models
they are highly disfunctional.

THE MAXIMIZATION OF THIRD PARTY FUNDING
SOURCES IN DRUG AND ALCOHOL TREATMENT

Richard J. Cohen

Coordinating Office for Drug & Alcohol
Abuse Programs (CODAAP)
Philadelphia, Pennsylvania

One only has to consult the Proceedings of any year's
National Drug Abuse Conference to ascertain the major areas of
concern of drug abuse practitioners at any period in the development of the field. Clearly, early volumes were filled with discussions of methadone dosages: later issues focused on ancillary
therapeutic services and non-methadone based treatment; most recent publications have seen a significant mixture of account-
ability/administrative topics dispersed among the treatment discussions. Through this evolutionary process little concern has
been directed toward consideration of fiscal issues. When support
for drug services was discussed, the gaze was sharply turned toward the Federal agencies involved in the field. There was little
talk of broad based funding schemes; there was no discussion of
shared funding responsibilities; there was no apparent consideration of the multiplicity of non-addiction based funding streams
for the support of drug services. Among the many reasons for this
situation was the fact that drug treatment was a generally new
field growing very quickly within a panicked society willing to
generously fund quick "solutions." In those early days government
agencies were often allocating more funds than rapidly developing
providers could spend. Then, as more agencies grew interested in
drug treatment and service responses become more sophisticated,
the economy tightened and the rumors of "turning the corner" went
forth from the national leadership. It is clear to all of us in
the field that the financial strings are now much tighter. For
the first time in the history of this young field, established
programs are going into bankruptcy. Increased funding levels of
government support inflation. Things are changing.

This paper speaks to one important group of responses to
this dilemma: third party funding sources. As each year in the
history of drug treatment seems to have had a theme (methadone
treatment; multi-modality treatment; special populations; polydrug services; credentialing), it is suggested that the focus or
many is now turned to funding sources. The many related

presentations at this Conference speak to this point. Further, NIDA is currently conducting training seminars in the third party area throughout the Country. These sessions follow from work done by Macros Systems, Inc. under a special consulting contract with NIDA. Also prepared by Macros Systems for NIDA's National Clearinghouse for Drug Abuse Information is a series of six bimonthly fact sheet published by the Clearinghouse as a part of its "Report Series." Without a doubt, the third party mechanism which has had the greatest impact on Pennsylvania's drug treatment system is Medical Assistance (Title XIX Medicaid). This program was established in 1965 by Public Law 89 - 97, and includes benefits for individuals determined "categorically needy" and at the State's election "categorically related - medically needy." Federally matching funds are available for both medical care to and administrative costs associated with these two groups. Such federal matching funds are provided to States on the basis of a formula which considers State per capita income. In addition of extending aid to poor persons who do not meet any categorical criteria but whose low income precludes them from meeting medical expenses. This group of individuals is termed non-categorically related-medically needy" and is not a part of the Title XIX Medicaid program. There are no Federal matching funds available for this category of individuals. Pennsylvania's coverage of the non-categorically related-medically needy with Medical Assistance benefits is most important to the drug and alcohol treatment system, since a significant number of clients are members of this group.

Officially, Social and Rehabilitation Service (SRS) known as Public Law 93-647 (Social Security Act, Social Service Amendments of 1974), Title XX ("Grants to States for Services"). The new Title XX replaced Titles IVA and VI in October of 1975. It begins a Federal/State partnership in the funding of social services programs, allowing States the opportunity to define both services and who may receive them through a Comprehensive Annual Services Program Plan (CASPP). In most categories Title XX funds are provided on a 75/25 basis, with states and/or providers responsible for the matching share. Simply stated, Title XX provides for approved social services to eligible clients at contracted facilities. The implementation of Title XX in the individual states in regard to drug and alcohol services has varied widely; therefore, this paper's discussion of realities within Pennsylvania may be unique to this State. Within Pennsylvania Title XX funds pass to the drug and alcohol system through a contract between the Department of Welfare (Title XX Single State Agency) and the Governor's Council. This contract includes a ceiling on available funds for specific services determined eligible for drug and alcohol programs. The funds resulting from this contract function as reimbursement for services already delivered and therefore already funded. As the principle source of these funds which supply SRS services, the SCA receives reimbursement for the provision of services which it has already funded. Consequently, this allows the SCA to fund new or additional services.

In considering impact on the treatment system, it is useful to compare Medical Assistance and Social Rehabilitative Services as revenue sources. As has been discussed, SRS flows in a match arrangement while MA is based on a sliding Federal share to eligible clients and all State money to another category. The drug and alcohol population, as noted, most often falls into the "non-categorically related-medically needy" group which is funded by non-Federal funds. This distinction is most important, since such locally generated funds can be used as match to Federal grants. In this way Medical Assistance can service as a prime source of matching funds. Utilizing this mechanism, agencies can use the ability to generate significant matching funds as strong support for the attraction of contract/grant support from a wide variety of sources. Another difference between SRS and MA is that MA is a "fee for service" relationship while SRS is a program funding arrangement.

Both Medical Assistance and SRS monies have had a most positive impact on the Philadelphia drug and alcohol system over the past two years. SRS funds have been used to initiate a variety of new programs. Such SRS funds contribute heavily to the total service delivery system; they are not agency focused, but rather system-wide (or city-wide) in their scope or effect. Contrasting this is the role of Medical Assistance fees which find their major influence on the individual generating provider agency. The program which generates funds has the ability to determine the use of the money, as long as it is for an approved drug or alcohol related purpose. This fact acts as a motivator to eligible agencies to maximize such funds. Further, MA income faces no ceiling limitation similar to the SRS ceiling. Within the context of SRS, a contractor agency cannot bill beyond the contracted ceiling, no matter what costs are faced for the delivery of such services. Since MA is based on a simple fee for service relationship, no such ceiling is involved.

CODAAP has worked to develop systems toward the maximization of such funding sources. In respect to SRS, CODAAP has worked closely with provider agencies as well as Department of Welfare officials. The importance of a full understanding of the legislative and regulatory base of Title XX funding is essential here. Also, the coordination and systemization or eligibility and billing procedures is of major importance. Within a large complex service delivery system, a great deal of cooperation is required in order to bring a large amount of funds which do not flow directly back to the generating program into the total system. This requires understanding, open lines of communication, and trust, as well as a means of mobilizing resources to meet the

stringent requirements of Title XX. CODAAP accomplished this
through the assignment of a highly qualitied individual to the
accomplishment of the maximization of available SRS funds within
the existing and often changing limitations.

The maximization of Medical Assistance has been somewhat more
complex, due to the fact that funds flow directly back to the
generating agency. The first step in the process is the insurance
of full information regarding the amount of MA funds obtained by
each agency. This allows the SCA to monitor the receipt of funds,
insure the availability of matching program funds, and require the
re-programming of monies generated beyond the budgeted level.
This last function is crucial. In order to expedite the maximum
impact of MA funds on the drug and alcohol system when such funds
are provider based, the SCA must have the authority to insure that
such surplus funds be placed back into an area of need within the
system. A simple understanding of motivation underscores the
importance of allowing agency flexibility in developing new
services with the money it has earned. The first step in this
total process is naturally the establishment of optimal program
eligibility for MA. The next step lies in the establishment of
yearly funding levels for particular programs. Although each
agency submits a full budget including MA projections and CODAAP
requests, these items must then be negotiated in terms of available
funds and the agreement of parameters of projections utilized. A
major factor of concern here is the level of MA reimbursement projected by the individual agency. CODAAP utilizes a simple formula
consisting of stated frequency of visits, percentage of eligible
clients, and services offered in determining an appropriate MA
projection.   In addition program history and unique features are
considered in comparing each program to the funds generated by
similar programs. While computing such realistic MA levels, the
"carrot and stick" theory is used by allowing for the flexible
use of some portion of funds generated when full effort has been
made toward the collection of all such available funds.

CODAAP makes clear, both explicitly and implicitly, that its
major concern is what the full funding of needed drug and alcohol
services is. Where efforts by providers indicate maximum utilization of potential third party mechanisms, CODAAP reinforces
such administrative practices through allowances for the establishment of new services with funds beyond the established ceiling
level. Such programmatic flexibility serves as the carrot.
Further, in calculating City/State contribution, CODAAP will not
budget funds where in-house projections of MA do not show agency
efforts at maximization; herein lies the stick. Another major
factor in the generation of full third party monies lies in the
use of computerized billing systems. Such systems, first used by
methadone treatment programs, have proven themselves most effective
in insuring complete and accurate billings.

The implementation or a well constructed client fee schedule, while still a subject of great debate, has important ramifications for the optimum generation of third party funds. First, third party agencies such as MA require the existence and utilization of a rate schedule for individuals able to pay. While the implementation of such a procedure is usually carried out as a matter of law, there are important benefits. Directly, there is the income, limited as it is, which derives from this source. Also there is the important effect of client responsibility which at least a number of workers in the field support. Probably the most important administrative impact of such client fees is quite indirect: the client fees requirement influences individuals eligible for MA to enroll, therefore increasing MA eligibility rates.

It is understood that little attention has been paid to Blue Cross/Blue Shield and other private insurers within this paper. Clearly, these are important funding sources which require full consideration. CODAAP is beginning to address increased attention in this direction. In addition, the potential role of any National Health Insurance bill must be fully understood in order to maintain an appreciation of the "state of the art" in this area.

It is clear that our field has changed significantly over the past several years. There is no doubt that it has grown a great deal in size and sophistication. Although some would say that such growth has not been of positive impact on the clients requiring service, it has been inevitable growth addressing a crucial need. During the "epidemic" phase grant funds were available to meet these needs. Time has grown harder and public opinion is not quite as excited about the demon of drug abuse. Plentiful grant funding is disappearing and growing match rates become a major concern. The field of drug and alcohol treatment must settle in for the longer haul. It seems evident that third party funds will serve an increasingly important role in the provision of drug and alcohol treatment services. In this way the maximization of third party funding sources directly relates to the delivery of the needed services to the most clients in need. Over time, this remains a consistant goal.

"Basic Concepts- Title XX - Social Services Funding." Report Series 35-A. National Clearinghouse for Drug Abuse Information, DHEW. August, 1975.

"Third Party Reimbursement." Report Series 35-B. National Clearinghouse for Drug Abuse Information, DHEW. October, 1975.

EVALUATING THE INTERVENTION SKILLS OF DRUG HOTLINE COUNSELORS

Michael P. Haines, M.S., Director

Mother Sunshine
DeKalb, Illinois

A study was conducted in fall, 1975, at Mother Sunshine, a drug program in DeKalb, Illinois. Mother Sunshine has 25 volunteers and five professional staff responsible for the 24-hour hotline. In addition, the professional staff conduct a drug education and training program, Sunlight Project, (alternative growth experiences and groups), formal therapy, and a drug information library. The hotline began in December, 1970, and currently receives about 60 calls per week. The calls range from drug information to phone counseling, and from emergency crisis intervention to life sustaining first aid. The drugs most often involved in these calls are, in descending order: depressants, psychedelics, stimulants, alcohol, cannabis and opiates. Volunteers who answer the hotline have an average age of 19.8 years, with a range of 16-26. They have little to no initial crisis intervention experience and are trained primarily by fellow volunteers and the staff (average age of 25 years, with a range of 21-29). The program has contractual back-up from a psychiatrist, psychologist and a registered nurse.

Mother Sunshine has been evaluated by the Illinois Drug Abuse Program (IDAP), the Illinois Dangerous Drug Commission (DDC) and most recently by the National Institute of Drug Abuse (NIDA). In each and every case, program methods, innovativeness, youth involvement, etc., were the criteria for evaluation rather than counselor effectiveness or intervention skills. It is perhaps asking too much for outside agencies to do such risky evaluating. In fact, the line programs would probably be the loudest critics of such techniques. Consequently, programs are evaluated in the areas of counselor competence only after a tragedy has occurred, and otherwise judge their competence by intuition and occasional feedback from consumers.

PURPOSE

This project was undertaken in order to develop a tool to evaluate the intervention skills of drug hotline counselors, particularly the skills of program-trained paraprofessionals and volunteers.

The need for such a tool became evident during an in-house brainstorming session. Professional and volunteer staff agreed that a more objective and comprehensive means of evaluating trainees should be developed. It was decided that the evaluation be a process in which both the professional staff and volunteers participate. This was done in order to maximize group cohesion. Consideration was then given to such fundamental aspects as:

a) group compatibility
b) committment and responsibility
c) ability to use program resources
d) competence in intervention skills

(To evaluate group compatibility, five point Likert-like polarity scales were employed to rate an individual's group interaction, social acceptance, etc. To evaluate committment and responsibility, records of trainee attendance at training classes, weekly group meetings, weekly shifts, and other agreed upon committments were kept. To evaluate an individual's ability to use program resources, worksheets were passed out, answered, collected and discussed.) All that remained was to develop the tool to evaluate what many considered the most important aspect of hotline work-- the actual ability to intervene effectively when a person is in crisis.

Readings in the area of evaluation of hotline skills uncovered a wealth of "how to. . ." manuals, volumes of intervention theory, studies citing the need for evaluation of paraprofessional, professional and/or volunteer hotlines, but there was nearly a total absence of evaluation tools and techniques. Those techniques described were generally limited to the counselor effectiveness scales of Carkhuff (Core Dimensions of Counselor Effectiveness, Beyond Counseling and Therapy) or Gazda (Global Scale, Human Relations Development). Both scales presented difficulties when applied to Mother Sunshine for the proposed project. Gazda's scale was entirely too limited. It inadequately dealt with unique aspects of hotline intervention by emphasizing the essentials of face-to-face, ongoing counseling. Although developed as a measure of face-to-face counseling effectiveness as well, Carkhuff's scales were applicable to hotline work due to their comprehensive nature. Two basic difficulties with Carkhuff's scales were: the jargon and concepts were too discipline-specific and Carkhuff "school" oriented; in that these were designed for ongoing, face-to-face counseling rather than hotline intervention, they provided little or no evaluation of the counselor's problem-solving skill or ability to use resources -- critical aspects of emergency work.

In response to this need, the Post Call Report (PCR) was developed. The PCR is a rating tool synthesizing Carkhuffian concepts with Mother Sunshine training theory. It evaluates the counselor's ability to handle classic drug hotline dilemmas, approximating a call-specific desired outcome. It is written with the non-professional evaluator in mind, without formal or esoteric vocabulary.

POST CALL REPORT

The PCR has two primary parts. Part A is a general hotline counselor effectiveness scale and Part B is a call-specific rating of counselor effectiveness. Part A defines the concepts of empathy, listening, problem solving and disposition. Part B is comprised of ten role play scenarios with script-specific key points and desired outcomes. The counselor is rated on a poor-to-excellent, five point scale.

The PCR, or tapes based on the role plays, could be used as training materials for both counselors and evaluators. It is an evaluation tool which requires relatively little expenditure of time or money. The PCR may be self-administered by a program, allowing, or even encouraging, honest evaluation, because the fear of external criticism is removed.

PROCEDURE

In its initial experimental run, the PCR was used to evaluate volunteer trainee intervention skills in two ways:

1) Trainees, at the completion of training (6 weeks), attended a workshop at which individuals answered role play calls and were evaluated with the PCR (Parts A and B) by the professional staff.

2) During their last four weeks of training, the trainees answered actual hotline calls while a veteran volunteer monitored the dialogue on an extension. Upon the completion of training, these veteran volunteers evaluated their peers' intervention skills with the PCR (Part A only).

POST CALL REPORT - PART A

Following are working definitions of the counselor effectiveness terminology: Empathy, Listening, Problem Solving, Disposition, as utilized within Mother Sunshine's Volunteer Training Program.

(The 1 to 5 rating scales have been omitted from Part A due to space restrictions.)

EMPATHY: Empathy is the "in touchness" of the counselor, the ability of the counselor to get into the shoes of the caller, to identify with the caller's feelings and predicament. Empathy is not sympathy. Empathy must: a) genuine - real, not forced or play acted; b) accurate - directed toward the caller's concerns and feelings, not the counselor's feelings or the counselor's projections of what the caller should be feeling; c) person-to-person - human, not mechanical, not "Dr. Freud and patient", not "hot-line volunteer and caller", but "Mike and Phil" or "you and me", "us", "we", sharing this experience; d) supportive - hospitable, communicates to the caller that it is okay to tell the counselor what's troubling him.

LISTENING: Listening is the art of "hearing" the caller in spite of personal biases and hunches. It is important that the counselor not smother the caller with his/her anxious chatter or rapid fire questions. The counselor should ask facilitative or "leading" questions and make supportive remarks which urge the caller to express himself-herself. Ideally, a listener is dynamic, a good passive hearer and a good active solicitor and provider of feedback. In listening, the importance of cue vigilance cannot be overstressed. The counselor must listen for and hear the cues which every caller provides when talking. Cues direct the counselor to key feelings, events and even solutions. Cues can be present both in the content and delivery of the caller counselor conversation.

PROBLEM SOLVING: Problem solving is a process wherein the counselor provides accurate information and discusses the various options, alternatives and consequences which are realistically available to the caller regarding this particular dilemma. In many cases, the counselor must prod the caller towards decision making and concrete action, but should not be making decisions for the caller. The counselor must confront the caller when decisions are ambiguous, unrealistic, and/or irresponsible. Failure to resolve the caller's problem is not necessarily an indication of poor problem solving technique.

DISPOSITION: Disposition is the method by which the counselor concludes or "disposes" of the call. It must include at least one of the following: a)unambiguous planning - "What will you do for the rest of the night?"; b)linking - "I'll meet you here tomorrow and we'll go to the hospital together."; c)referral - "I don't have that information here but I'll give you a few numbers you could try." d)summarizing - restating the conclusions, decisions and commitments resulting from counselor-caller interaction. Whatever the method of concluding, it should approximate the severity of the crisis. The call should not end without establishment of mutual commitment by the caller and counselor toward agreed-upon plans.

The following are two examples of the role play scripts which comprise Part B of the Post Call Report.

POST CALL REPORT - PART B

Role Play

Description - Caller is a married individual calling about spouse, whose "excessive" dope smoking (everyday) is interfering with their life. Spouse isn't getting his/her duties done nor is he/she spending any time with the caller except when he/she is wrecked. "We just don't go anywhere together anymore. Things aren't as good as they used to be for us. I want to do something about it." (There is a vibe here that the whole marriage is on shaky ground).

Opening script - "Can people get strung out on grass? You know, smoke it too much? Well, my husband/wife seems to just be high all the time lately."

Role Play

Description - (Start this call as if it is nothing more than an identification of a drug). Caller is a high school student, 16 years old. (Describes the drug in response to counselor's questions). "The cap has the work G-E-I-G-Y on it. It has a number - 45." "Is it dangerous? What happens if you drink while taking it?" Caller is emotionally alternating between agitation and feeling "down". Caller has taken three of these capsules and was going to drink with it. Caller did this dope because he/she was depressed about the dissolution of his/her relationship with girl/boyfriend. Caller can't come to Mother Sunshine nor can counselor come to him/her because the caller doesn't want his/her parents to know what is going on.

Opening script - "Can you tell me what some medicine is? It's a yellow and red capsule."

STAFF FAILURES IN THERAPEUTIC TREATMENT PROGRAMS:
WHAT CAN WE DO?

Herbert J. Freudenberger, Ph.D.

Independent Practice of Psychoanalysis
Coordinator of Mental Health; S.E.R.A.
Staff Training Consultant, Covenant House, N.Y.

This author has been engaged actively in working with real-
dents and staff of drug abuse treatment programs for the past
fifteen years. During that period, many residents of programs
have completed treatment. A significant number of those men, and
some women have become the people that staff and sometimes manage
those programs. I have made a number of observations as to what
happens to these men and women once they work in programs and
begin re-entry into society.

We, the members of treatment communities set up our staffs
for failure. The failure can be seen in the increasing number of
men and women who turn from narcotic abuse to alcoholism: in the
increasing number who are unable to maintain relationships with a
lover or mate; in the increase of signs of mental illness as well
as psychosamatic complaints by the staff and in the ongoing deterioration of values and techniques as demonstrated and practiced
in the rigid treatment approaches used with residents. Staff often does not have a clear sense of trust, honesty, morality, responsiveness and responsibility to the residents placed in their
charge. Also they have a minimal sense of what the concept of
personal responsibility implies and too many still suffer from an
inadequate sense of self.

What Do We Do Wrong?

1. In view of the reality that our residents are in treatment for increasingly shorter periods of time (some as little as
six months), often we do nor recognize that the shorter time
available means that we need to shift our treatment approaches.[1]
Programs are still caught up excessively in the encounter technique. That approach has only limited applications at this time,
because it was designed for the hard core addict. We are now no
longer dealing with the addict of the 1950's, but a poly-drug
abuser of the 1970's. The abusers are as young as twelve years

of age and do not require encounter techniques to bring about change. Rather, they need educational assistance, life restructuring and parenting.

2. We are swayed too readily into being satisfied with surface behavior modification and do not recognize that simply to adjust an addict to his society is not sufficient for the addict. The consequences are that often one of the only tasks we accomplish is to teach the addict, through negative reinforcement, not to put the needle in his arm. But <u>we do not fill in the terribly empty feelings and void</u> that exist in the addict. We build up our residents as facades with an inner hollowness. We help them take the needle out of their arm, but we do not teach them the dangers of further chemical abuse, such as alcohol.[2]

3. Alcohol abuse has become a major problem in narcotic programs. In order to alleviate the pressures of work, the staff often will use beer or hard whiskey as a way of relaxing after work. Alcohol serves as a means of easing the anxieties of socializing. It is a socially-approved as well as a personally-permissible avenue to "feeling better" when we are seeking to make contact with members of the opposite sex. We tend not to prepare our graduates as well as our staff for socializing after they leave a treatment facility. Many do not know how to mix with the "straight" members of society. They tend to seek out the former addict peer group, a group that is familiar and comfortable.

Further, the staff has not been taught that for many of them drinking is a danger, and they have not been alerted to the dangers of their reliance on a chemical substance to lessen tension, and dull feelings of depression and loneliness. Programs have devoted an insufficient amount of time in discussing whether the use of marijuana by graduates is acceptable to staff. The questions of Do you adopt a non-chemical abuse life style--or not?; How far do you go with that attitude?; Does it include cigarettes, coffee and tea also?; have not been adequately discussed.

4. Directors of programs act too quickly in shifting residents to staff positions. The resident is often still unclear as to who he is as a person when we expect them to become members of a staff who will act in a rational and objective manner. We compound the error by leaving the staff's roles undefined. In the morning they are residents, during the day they become staff, and in the evening encounter group, they are expected to act as residents once again. The absurdity of this continued split of functioning is especially intolerable to the identity confused addict.

5. We do not prepare our residents adequately for their re-entry into society and return to their families. Many male residents have been away from their mates and children for years.

1076

They may have been on the street, in prison, in mental hospitals, or in treatment. As they return to their families, they find often that their wives have become stronger, more independent and assertive, and are unwilling to relinquish their new found power as wage earners. Too often, the man believes that he can just walk back in and reassert his former position or take on a new role that he has never demonstrated within the family. To say that this is a cause for instant conflict is an understatement. There is almost no preparation on the part of anyone for the resident's return to the family.

A women's return to her family often creates other problems. She may now need to take her children back from a sister, mother or mother-in-law who has gotten used to the children and vice-versa. The woman now also needs to think in terms of a job, male companionship and finances. So much of this often is ignored in a program.[3]

An adolescent's return to his former neighborhood may mean a shift in peer group relationship, an attempt to go to school, and a shift on the part of everyone in the family. The other siblings now need to see this youngster as a _former_ drug abuser, not as the "con" person they remember. The young man may now see many things wrong with his family and seek to correct them, only to be met with hostility, resentment, fear and rejection. For many young people without any appropriate emotional support system, this is the beginning of the end once again.[4]

6. We tend not to teach the residents how to cope with life problems that they will be confronting. We do not give enough information seminars on how to handle finances, how one works with interest charges, using a checking account, the meaning of saving money, budgeting oneself on a salary, postponing the purchase of furniture or a car. Instead, we allow them to "shoot up" with a credit card and watch the residents seeking to emulate a staff member and acquire all the trimmings of success, only to lose them to a credit agency. Often this is the beginning of the road back to despair and narcotics.

7. We are derelict in our responsibilities in teaching our residents adequate hygiene. This becomes an especially serious issue for the women residents. Many have never had gynecological care. We tend not to give them facts on appropriate diets and nutrition. They do not know how to take care of their medical and dental needs. Instead, we allow them to continue their inadequate food intake and poor shopping practices.

8. They are not given sufficient vocational counseling and job alternatives. We do not convey to them the realities of the job market. They usually do not know what faces them once they leave treatment. Instead, they seek to prolong their re-entry by

staying in the program as staff members. If they leave, too many go back to the menial and unskilled jobs they had before. This lack of planning and consequent disillusion will serve only to promote their return to addiction.

9. We do not spend sufficient time to discuss the burn-out phenomenon. Our staff is not protected from this common occurrence. "We promote the dedication and commitment of our staff and do not alert them to the dangers of their psychosomatic symptoms, depression, frustration, lack of fulfillment and paranois."[5]

What Can We Do?

1. We can begin by treating re-entry seriously, initiating it as a process from the day of the resident's induction into the program.

2. Set up peer-level growth groups composed of former drug abuse residents and their counselors; recognize the needs of grappling with loneliness, socialization, the use of alcohol and how to meet people; organize sharing rap groups that will speak to these issues; use role playing to work out how one behaves in school and job interviews.

3. Organize and train teams of counselors to help the resident to return to his family and begin an active family therapy program. If need be, have the residents and family meet in the family's home, rather than in the agency.

4. Hire more "straight" men and women who have not been drug abusers. They can serve as role models for the addicts and can help them overcome their hesitancies in relating to the outside world once they leave treatment.

5. Hold information seminars on sex, finances, nutrition and body care.

6. Rethink the value system that is verbalized by the program and then see how it is practiced. Is there lip service about no alcoholism, while at the same time there is no confrontation about staff drinking? Are there statements about honesty and trust, yet confidentialities are broken constantly by counselors in their gossip with each other?

7. Set up a way that a resident can continue to have contact with a program once he leaves. Graduation should not mean final separation. Let us be a bit more human and not so rigid.

And finally, we need to shift from some of our still practiced therapeutic community treatment rigidities. For example, we still rely too strongly on group in-house treatment and do not pay

enough attention to the uniqueness of each individual resident.
The philosophies and concepts that worked for us yesterday may no
longer be applicable today. Let us also not forget that the
staff is there for the residents and that the residents are not
there for us. But also, let us remember that many of our staff
are programmed to personal failure unless we are alert to help
them avoid it. If too many of our staff return to drug abuse,
it is time to take a serious look at our own treatment philosophies.

References

1. H.J. Freudenberger, How We Can Right What's Wrong With Our
    Therapeutic Communities?, J. of Drug Issues, Vol. 4, No. 4,
    Fall, 1974, 381-392.

2. H.J. Freudenberger, The Therapeutic Community Revisited.
    American J. of Drug and Alcohol Abuse, Vol. 3, No. 1, June,
    1976.

3. H.J. Freudenberger, The Woman in Treatment in a Therapeutic
    Community, Second National Drug Abuse Conference Proceedings,
    to be published 1976.

4. H.J. Freudenberger, The Dynamics and Treatment of the Young
    Drug Abuser in an Hispanic Therapeutic Community. J. of Psy-
    chedelic Drugs, Vol. 7, No. 3, July-Sept., 1975, 273-281.

5. H.J. Freudenberger, The Staff Burn-out Syndrome in Alterna-
    tive Institutions, Psychotherapy: Theory Research and Prac-
    tice, Vol. 12, No. 1, Spring, 1975, 73-83.

HOW TO DEVELOP A PROFESSIONAL-PARAPROFESSIONAL
TEAM APPROACH IN A MULTI-MODALITY TREATMENT PROGRAM

Herbert J. Freudenberger, Ph.D.

Independent Practice of Psychoanalysis
Coordinator of Mental Health; S.E.R.A.
Staff Training Consultant, Covenant House, N.Y.

A new group of people helpers has emerged in the past ten years: the human services workers. They are the men and women who have stepped forward due to an increasing lack of available professional staff in drug and alcohol abuse programs. It has become apparent to these men and women that they need further training. Unless they receive this training, they will continue to find themselves replaced by more qualified individuals. Previously, they were the backbone of many programs, and as such have been and are, invaluable for services to continue, but funding cutbacks have made the problem even more critical because the paraprofessionals are usually among the first to be discharged.

The professional has only recently re-entered the field of drug treatment. This is due, in part, to the successes that human services workers have achieved in working with addicts, as well as the new accreditation, certification and licensing requirements that are now being implemented.

The professional has a decided advantage over the human services worker paraprofessional. Professionals are better educated, tend to have a more varied range of job experiences, often have had the opportunity to develop managerial skills and are essentially comfortable with writing reports and record keeping. All of these factors aid the professional to remain on the job and make it increasingly difficult for the human services worker to compete and do the same.

With these realities in mind, this writer sat down with the staff of a number of agencies, with whom he serves as consultant and began to work out ways of combining the skills of both groups. It was hoped that such a process would lead to mutual sharing and respect while allowing as many as possible of each group to remain employed and productive.

The first area of discussion was the similarities and differences that exist between the two groups. As indicated in a previous article,[1] "the professional's identity primarily rests on his formal education and job experiences, whereas the human services worker's identity rests basically on his clinical instincts and in those skills which have been, for the most part, street and on-the-job training acquired."

The identity of the paraprofessional rests primarily on an emotional dedication and a personal commitment in the value of the treatment that he is providing. However, the motivation of the professional rests for the most part on an intellectual commitment basis. Consequently, the two operate predominantly from distinctly different personal reference points--the intellectual vs. the emotional, the acquired, vs. the instinctual. These differences often make for conflict and confused mutual interaction.[2]

Another area of difference that became apparent in our discussion, was the barrier created by the communication process: each group used a different language to express itself. The professional thinks and talks in terms of abstract ideas, concept and language that often reflects his academic training. The human services worker thinks and expresses himself more in terms of common sense approaches, practical issues, concrete concepts and street language.

Recognizing that these are only some of the major sources of differences, we began to attempt to organize ways through which the two groups could begin to relate to each other more meaningfully. In one program, this writer suggested that three men and two women who composed the staff of the mental health component be called the "professional" members of the team. None of the five had more than a B.A. degree. Each had been trained to function as a social worker and/or case worker, and each was operating in the program within those job description categories. We then decided to have each of the "professional" members of the team seek out a human services worker paraprofessional member of the staff, and discuss with him or her the concept of working as a team within the program.

We met as a group of ten individuals on many occasions to iron out differences in terms of what we each wanted from the team, what we were seeking to do with it, and how this in turn could benefit the program. I had an important advantage in one agency, in that three of the five human services workers were graduates of a six-month staff enrichment program, and so were predisposed to learning and open to sharing. The author has discussed this enrichment program in a previous paper.[3]

We initially decided that a number of factors would be essential in order for the team concept to take hold. Each member of the team would take it upon himself to meet with the other a number of times daily. These meetings could be brief and could be held anywhere in the facility, or even by telephone. We believed this to be necessary for continuity and consistency of contact, and for an on-going check on ourselves as to how we were doing. Also, we began to define duties that could be shared by both. We decided that we would attempt to sit in on counseling sessions as a team; that case conferences and initial treatment plans would be shared, discussed and decided upon; that discussions would be held as to the functioning and ongoing treatment plan shifts as they would occur. We also requested that each keep a diary of feelings and attitudes and how, or if they were resolved. Initially, we sought to "mix" the make-up of each team; for example, have a black man and white man become a team, have a straight man work with a gay man, have an Anglo woman work with an Hispanic woman, have a non-addict professional work with a former addict human services worker. We sought to do this in order to begin to break down emotionally-charged attitudes and prejudices and to begin to open broadened avenues of communication. However, this was not totally possible because the teams fell victim to the agency's funding problems. One woman member was shifted to another job function in the agency and a male member resigned.

The duration of all teams was a minimum of six months. One lasted for approximately nine months and one for a year. A number of findings emerged:

1. Each person spoke of the importance of the support that they had received from the other. In times of stress, from client or personal problems, each was pleased that he could turn to his colleague. A feeling of mutual trust was established slowly and very real confidences and doubts were brought into the open.

A number of problems evolved for us as a consequence of sharing personal problems. The professional member of the team had to be cautioned about becoming a "therapist" to the human services worker as such behavior would confuse their respective roles in the agency, as well as their roles with each other. An issue in a second agency was the subtle covering up for each other's teammate. This resulted in certain errors or deficiencies not being brought out. Once this problem was talked about, it was dealt with by all of us, and avoided in the future.

2. The two women team members became especially supportive of each other. They began to share mutual women problems as members of a staff composed predominantly of men. Their work together ultimately led to the forming of women's consciousness-raising groups with the residents and staff of one agency, which served as the basis for a general shift of attitudes and treatment approaches within the program.

3. Another consequence of the team approach was that personal value systems were brought out and scrutinized by all members. Attitudes that had never been questioned were evaluated and discussed. One man was prone to miss appointments, forget schedules, and not submit reports as he dreaded any sort of writing. By his attitude and role model presentation the professional gave the paraprofessional a sense of what it is like to approach a task in a mature and non-manipulative manner and gave him a sense of appropriate job performance. Also, the former addict-paraprofessional had never been able to talk with either a "square" or other staff members about his job problems. In the past, the "square" had been too frightening to approach and the rest of the paraprofessional staff could not be talked to about this problem. Because to talk to them would imply a deficiency, which in turn might lower his sense of competence in his, as well as their eyes.

An issues of work were raised, the previously addicted members began to talk of their outside problems. Their re-entry into society was fraught with anxieties and conflicts. These conflicts were aired for the first time among our team members, and such basic issues as "how do you open a checking account?" "how do you get yourself on a budget?" "how do you meet people?" were brought up. This type of sharing was an important means through which former prejudices between the two groups were diminished, and in time a real sense of humaneness came into being among all of us.

4. The non-addicted professional came to learn a great deal about the professional's ways of looking at a resident. The professional initially was not aware of all the subtleties of why one resident should be allowed to remain in treatment and another not. But in time, the clinician-human services worker demonstrated the basis for his thinking and the reasons for his conclusions. A real respect for the human services worker's clinical intuitiveness emerged. An important decision that we made at the outset helped a great deal as we moved along. As a group we decided that wherever a final clinical decision was needed, then the human services worker's decision was final if there was a disagreement. This stood us in good stead and helped to raise the image of the human services worker.

During one of our meetings, one of the team members suggested that we begin to role play with each other. This technique of role shifting brought about an awareness of problems we each faced in doing our work, and brought some conflicts into the open.

Many of the conflicts emerged that the degree professional feels when working with the paraprofessional. The professional wanted to be in charge, the paraprofessional felt angry and inferior. The professional believed s/he knew more, had little to gain from the team concept, and initially behaved like a teacher. The absurd part of this was that those who were called "professional" in the team would really be considered paraprofessionals in any other agency. So it appears that titles help to make the difference in how human beings perceive themselves and each other, as they tend to behave according to the labels ascribed.

All of us who participated learned and grew from the experience. A wonderful consequence of our work was that every human services member of the team has been either promoted in his respective agency or has gone on to a higher paying, more responsible position. Because of their experience on the team, some made the decision to go back to school.

Note: We all participated in the panel at the National Drug Abuse Conference. It was both a celebration of a success and a fond farewell.

The author would like to thank Joseph Cooke, Myrna Colon, Judy Dills, John Franco, Sara Perez and Ted Rutkowski for their efforts and cooperation in helping to make this concept work.

References

1. H.J. Freudenberger, The Professional and the Human Services Worker: Some Solutions to the Problems They Face in Working Together, J. of Drug Issues, July, 1976.

2. H.J. Freudenberger, The Professional in the Free Clinic, New Problems, New Views, New Goals, chapter in The Free Clinic; A Community Approach to Health Care and Drug Abuse, edited by David Smith, David Bentel and Jerome Schwartz, Stash Press, Beloit, Wisconsin, 1971.

3. H.J. Freudenberger, Developing a Paraprofessional Staff Enrichment Program in an Alternative Institution, Professional Psychology, Vol. 4, No. 3, Nov., 1973.

ANALYSIS OF FOUR YEAR PARAPROFESSIONAL
TRAINING EXPERIENCE

Thomas C. Kauffman, M.Ed.
Henderson Hendrix, Ed.D
Ethel Revels, M.S.W.

INTRODUCTION

This study represents an effort to follow up the effectiveness
of two training programs sponsored by a large City Health Department and directed toward preparing formerly addicted persons to be
counselors in drug programs. The programs are closely related,
and the graduates are grouped together for the study. The first
trainees graduated four years ago and the most recent one year ago.

THE PROGRAMS

In August of 1971, the Detroit Health Department, under a grant
from the State of Michigan funded by the Manpower Development and
Training Act, initiated the ARC Training Program (ARC - Addict
Rehabilitation Counselor). The ARC Training Program continued for
two years and graduated four classes: March, 1972; September,
1972; April, 1973; and October, 1973. From the ARC experience a
new grant application was written and sent to the National Institute on Drug Addiction (NIMH-HEW). The agency created by the
reception of this grant is called the Detroit Institute of Addiction Research and Training (DIART): it is funded for thirty-two
months and has graduated two classes: January 1975, and February,
1976

The ARC Training program was to train and prepare former heroin
users for the purpose of better staffing the many drug abuse programs which were beginning to operate in the community and which
wished to put to use the street knowledge of ex-addicts for drug
treatment effectiveness. It was staffed by a well-trained and experienced Director and two training assistants, one a professional
from the field of education and the other a bright former addict
who has learned about therapeutic communities while incarcerated at
the Federal Penitentiary in Milan, Michigan. The training program
classes lasted for six months, and the 24 selected trainees attended from 35 to 40 hours per week. The setting was that of a modified therapeutic community which included therapy sessions, peer

pressure, and staff counseling. The training consisted of seminars, lectures and workshops, together with four half days each week devoted to clinical experience. At the close of each six-month class a fair percentage of trainees were able to find jobs immediately; 94% of the 76 graduates were able to find employment.

It was decided, at the end of the fourth class that 76 paraprofessionals graduated, and most of them employed in two years, indicated a slower rate of training. Thus, the DIART program was designed to last for one full year and it was to include courses given by a local community college for credit. Only 15 trainees were selected for each class. Funding was obtained from the National Institute on Drug Abuse, since this Manpower Development and Training Act no longer existed. The new program was to have the same objectives as the old ARC Program; training and rehabilitation. Emphasis was now being placed on the educational part of the program, and the trainees were able to earn 60 credits (enough for an A.A. degree) in twelve months. A block of twelve credits was given for the training and clinical experiences provided by DIART aside from the community college taught courses. DIART is a larger program than the ARC Training Program; besides the paraprofessional classes, this program has trained four classes of professional people since 1973. Its full time staff includes a Director, two coordinators (one for the paraprofessional program and the other for the professional); and a training consultant. The eleven graduates of the first DIART class are included in this follow-up report; the most recent class (Feb. 1976) had not graduated at the time of this study.

THE STUDY

Method:

The authors of this study wanted to secure valid follow-up information on graduates of these closely related programs. We wanted to know how many were still employed, how many had worked in the field for which they were trained, how many still worked in this field, and how many went on to further studies after graduation. For the future development of training programs by the DIART agency, two more questions relating to obtaining college credit and additional education were asked.

Questionnaires were mailed, and responded to; telephone interviews were conducted in seven instances. All graduates were asked questions relating to their feelings about their own therapeutic-social growth in the program. However, it is our intention to compare the social orientations of the members of only two classes of ARC Training Program graduates: those who graduated in March of 1972, and in April of 1973. Their employment and educational pursuits before and after are also compared.

I RESPONSES OF ALL RESPONDENTS

A. Employment of Graduates

Firm effort was made to contact all of the 87 graduates; 56 responses were obtained. Of the 56, 40 were presently employed. Of these, 33 were working in training related employment, and 51 had at some time been employed in training related jobs. (Table I)

To call attention to the significance of these figures, it must be pointed out that a review of demographic data of two classes graduating 4 and 3 years ago reveal that only 1 of the trainees was employed at the time of entrance into the program; 75% had been unemployed for more than one year.

B. Education

Of the 56 respondents to our questionnaire, 39 (70%) had continued with additional training or education after graduation. The majority listed community colleges and universities. Others enrolled in job-related (5) and non-job-related training (2). Only 16 or 56 respondents did not have any subsequent training or education. (Table II). In addition, 6 persons who listed colleges and universities also took in-service training.

C. Social Orientation

To obtain information about the way graduates feel these programs affect their social orientations, they were asked: general questions about their ability to cope with life and four subordinate questions about relationships with: a) family, b) authority, c) peers, d) money management. The respondents, overwhelmingly and in both programs, responded that they were helped in their social orientations. Question "d," about money management is the only question to which a large number replied "no" (20). Table III supplies these responses:

II COMPARISON OF TWO ARC CLASSES

Twenty-four (24) were admitted to the first and 26 to the third class, 21 and 20 were graduated. Examining the backgrounds of the graduates of the first ARC Training Program class (graduated March 1972), reveals that only two trainees were employed at all in 1971, prior to training, which began in September of that year. Our current data reveals that 9 (43%) are now employed. All (100%) respondents have been employed in the field for which they were trained since graduation. (Other, verified, sources reveal that 1 nonrespondent is employed. Also, one member of that session has died but had remained employed steadily for three years - until the time he died.)

1087

At the time of training, the ages of this group ranged from 19-43 years; range of time on drugs was from 2 1/2 to 26 years. Studies of 22 members of the class, while in training, revealed 94% were involved in crime, with 16 of them having been convicted and having served a total of 555 months in jails and prisons; range of drug costs were from $30-200/day.

The third ARC Training Program (graduated April, 1973) was generally composed of persons who were employed more recently prior to entry into training (The session began on October 10, 1972). All but one were unemployed, but 12 had been employed during that same year - 1972. Current data for this class reveals that 14 of 20(70%) graduates are still employed. Thirteen (13) of 15 (87%) respondents have been employed in training related jobs since they graduated. 85% of the total class is known to have been so employed since graduation.

This group of trainees ranged from 19 to 45 years of age while in training; they were on drugs for from 0-24 years (2 were non-users; among users, they ranged from 3 months for one person to from 2 years minimum for all the rest). Among the formerly addicted all but one person (96%) were engaged in illegal activities while addicted. Fifteen (15) of them were convicted for a total of 40 convictions. The range of drug costs for the users were from $3/day, for one who used briefly, to $150/day for the heaviest user.

A significant difference in the two classes is found between the level of education achieved by the two classes prior to entry. The first session's 24 admitted trainees averaged 11.4 years of school. The third session's 26 admitted trainees averaged 12.2 yrs. This difference affected the classes greatly because the courses taught were to be comparable to college level. The third class was screened from over 200 applicants, and the staff which screened them placed increased emphasis upon academic ability as important to continued success of substance abuse counselors.

Among the 13 respondents from the first class of graduates, 6 have acquired more education and/or training since graduation. Ten of fifteen respondents of the third class have gone on to school.

Table IV provides information comparing the two classes. It is derived from the demographic charts, answers of the respondents to our questionnaire, and data from the studies of criminal activity.

TABLE I
Employment of 56 Respondents

% Now employed	71%
% In training related jobs	59%
% Ever employed in related work	91%

TABLE II
Number of Respondents seeking more education

Type of Education Pursuit	Number Seeking
Colleges	32
Job related training	5
Non-job-related training	2
None	16

TABLE III
Social Orientations after Program

Question	Improved	Not Improved
Coping with daily life	55	1
Relationship with family	54	2
Relationship with authority	54	2
Relationship with peers	56	0
Money management	36	20 (1 undecided)

TABLE IV
Social Orientations: A Comparison of Two Classes

Factor	1st Grad. Class	3rd Grad. Class
Number of respondents:	13	15
Employment	None at entry: 2 during nine months previously. 43% - four yrs. after graduation.	1 at entry; but 12 during previous nine months. 70% - three yrs. after graduation.
Age at entry	range: 19-43 years	range: 19-45 years
Time on drugs	2 1/2-26 years	0-24 yrs (2 non-users)
Cost of drugs	$30-200/day	$3-150/day (for users)
Criminal activity prior to program	94% involved	96% involved (for users)
Education at entry	Mean years: 11.4	Mean years: 12.2
Education after graduation	Continued: 6 respondents.	Continued: 10 respondents.

PUTTING HUMPTY DUMPTY BACK TOGETHER:
THE PROBLEM OF FORMER STAFF IN TREATMENT

David Weinberg

Chicago Health Manpower Consortium, Inc.

Oliver Wilson

Illinois Drug Abuse Program

"Humpty Dumpty sat on a wall,
 Humpty Dumpty had a great fall,
 All the king's horses
 And all the king's men
 Couldn't put Humpty together again."

                    Nursery Rhyme

Viola Harwood charges toward the clinic door, "You sonof-
abitch!! None of you hypocritical bastards gives a good
goddamn about any nigger in here!Just put me on a detox!
Everyone knows you're all a bunch of dopefiends anyway,
and the sooner I get away from here the better."

Three days later Viola is in the office of the clinic di-
rector.She is crying and she is drunk.She complains that
she is lonely, sick, and scared.She has nightmares every
night. She has no skills,no family, no source of income.
She says she is too old and frightened to go back to whor-
ing. Not an unusual drama for a methadone clinic but this
client is different than most. She is the former social
service director of Umoja Drug Abuse Center.

Ronald Beaumont walks briskly to the podium.The audience
applauds and cheers warmly. With quiet dignity,tears well-
ing in the corners of his eyes,Ronald accepts an award for
outstanding contributions as a counselor of the Freedom
Clinic. A poignant scene no doubt - and how much more so
to those who know that only two weeks previously Ronald
was confronted for selling cocaine at Unity Place, where
he is now a problem client.

Ronald and Viola (not their real names) are typical of a difficult type of client - the former ex-addict counselor who has returned to heroin abuse. These individuals are in treatment for various reasons - some, because they still feel the need for a supportive environment and others, the majority, because they have returned to the use of narcotics. This paper deals with the latter.

What contributes to "the fall" of some ex-addict counselors back to heroin abuse? The pressures on the typical counselor in our methadone programs are tremendous. A counselor must cope with a myriad of regulations, reams of paperwork, long and awkward working hours, low pay scales, and an unresponsive and constantly changing client population.

To work in the harried conditions at a methadone clinic must be strenuous for a trained professional, yet most counselors in the Illinois state contractual system have little formal education and only superficial job training. For many ex-addicts a counselor position is the first "respectable" job after years of illegal or anti-social behavior. It may well provide their only opportunity to perform in a semi-professional status. Thus, the need for the ex-addict counselor to succeed is extreme, while their tools and conditions for achieving or even recognizing success are minimal.

Without adequate training, counselors do not know how to develop realistic expectations of their clients. Thus they place excessive demands on self and feel inadequate and frustrated if clients fail to reform. Under the vigorous circumstances of a methadone clinic, it is not surprising that many staff members fall, but rather that so many do manage to maintain their roles.

We interviewed eleven former counselors in treatment in the IDAP system. They included nine (9) blacks and two (2) whites, three (3) women and eight (8) men. They ranged in age from twenty-two (22) to forty-five (45), with the majority over thirty (30). A surprising number-five-came from black middle class backgrounds. We did identify some common characteristics which may have led to their failure as staff. Most of those interviewed were perceived by both themselves and others as having excessive concern for clients. Personal concerns were always secondary. These former staff also believed that they somehow shouldered special burdens; either they cared more than the other staff or held positions of unique responsibility. One ex-counselor spoke with pride of the extra hours spent rapping with his clients in the streets; another felt that in his role of deputy director he was constantly called upon to play the part of a hatchet man.A large number of former counselors in treatment were,indeed,senior staff, many of whom had assumed supervisory responsibilities after short times on the job with no preparation for management roles.Most of those interviewed felt barriers between themselves and co-workers;they felt unable to communicate their inner feelings for fear of loss of status or position.Consequently many left their counseling jobs with feelings of bitterness and anger toward other staff, especially their superiors. Though some ex-staff left because of drug problems, many did not resume narcotic usage until after separation from employment. This return to hard drugs may be viewed as something more than a return to a familiar coping pattern. Drug use may represent a slap-in-the-face to former co-workers - a way for saying "See what you made me do!" Such an attitude may persist when the former staff member re-enters the therapeutic situation.

What happens when former staff members seek assistance for their drug problems? Many look for rehabilitation from former colleagues. Several interviewers said that the presence of one-time associates reminded them of more successful days. One suspects that these associates were also reminders of present failure.

The presence of ex-drug abuse workers in treatment provides significant problems for present counseling staff. Those counselors who knew the "fallen angels" socially may draw away, uncomfortable with a changed definition of roles. Some working staff may feel threatened, may fear that "this could happen to me" and therefore seek to dis-identify themselves from the ex-staff client through scorn and ridicule.

The counselor assigned to the case of an ex-staff member faces a formidable task.Often times former workers have at their disposal a broad experiential knowledge of therapeutic techniques, with which they can play endless games to avoid disclosure. A staff counselor may easily feel intimidated and inadequate under these circumstances.

It is therefore best that former staff receive treatment in novel settings, from a clinical team with which they are unfamiliar. Such a team should be integrated professionally to include psychiatrists, psychologists, and social workers, as well as counselors.If the above circumstances are not possible, then special orientation should be provided to clinical teams on the unique problems and needs of former staff members.

Ex-staff re-entering treatment may be extra sensitive to how they are viewed by other clients.In some cases, clients will "rub it in" concerning the altered status of the ex-staff, getting even for past perceived affronts by the former counselor. While we witnessed few such instances, the fear of such among many of those interviewed was genuine.For this reason most avoided attending therapy groups. Many minimized the actual time spent in the clinic. Others went to the opposite extreme and became leaders of client protest groups against current staff policy. To create a forum where former counselors can express their feelings without fear of recrimination we have created a special peer group consisting of former counselors and those clients presently employed in human service positions.

Enthusiasm in these groups has been high, although attendance has waned greatly.

Status is a crucial factor in relationships with former staff. An ex-director, for example, may feel that she/he should be counseled only by a director. If this is not possible, the former director may become resentful.

Painfully aware of their loss of status,former staff may experience an exaggerated loss of self-esteem. They feel like utter failures, and their role as clients is a constant reminder of their loss of position. It is important to point out to such individuals that, while they may be unemployed, they still retain valuable knowledge of human relations techniques. Thus, we have implemented a program of vocational counseling designed to identify to improve the human service skills possessed by the former staff member. We hope that this will lead to training and placement in jobs related to human services,such as corrections and youth counseling. In such positions, former ex-addict staff can earn a living and contribute usefully to society, while regaining a sense of dignity and self-worth.

STAFF IN-SERVICE TRAINING:

A MODULE FOR PROFESSIONAL UPGRADING AND SOCIALIZATION

Olga E. King, MSW

Department of Psychiatry
University of Miami School of Medicine
Miami, Florida

Staff Inservice Training

The staff of the Spanish Drug Rehabilitation Research Project is composed of indigenous members of the community in that they are all bilingual and bicultural, i.e. Anglo and Latin. However, it is not sufficient for us to avail ourselves of skilled mental health workers who have cultural knowledge. Intensive training is a major component of the program so that not only the highest possible levels of professionalism are available for service and research, but also to insure a high degree of cultural relativity and sensitivity in the performance of professional activities.

We aim at integrating the professional upgrading of the staff with what might be called "professional socialization" of their therapeutic talents and interventions. From intake through termination and follow-up the program must do its clinical, research and community work in a manner which responds to the specific needs of the Spanish-speaking people and which will prove acceptable and efficacious to them.

Our health professions and institutions have, for the most part, remained notoriously unresponsive to demonstrated needs of specific ethnic groups, and are highly unimaginative when asked to develop innovative approaches to such problems. Professional training in the campuses shows clear cultural lags and academic training has to a great extent ignored the question of accomodating knowledge and skill to the idyosincratic needs and ways of our Latin population. We cannot risk success at the level of the individual therapist's way of adjusting his personal acquaintance with the culture to his professional know-how. Instead, in our training program we aim at standardizing their interventions and integrating cultural components into all aspects of their functions. For instance, we cannot afford to simply teach Family Therapy; we must teach Family Therapy with Latin families. We can't just acquaint them with community resources, we must show how they are effectively used on behalf of the alienated Latin client.

The Spanish Drug Rehabilitation Research Project training module is one which introduces the counselors-therapists to the principals

and practice of community mental health work, while providing clinical exposure to a host of situations characterized by drug involvement, acute emotional disturbance, social and personality disruptive behaviors, cultural shock and acculturational crises. In
this light the objectives of a training module are as follows:
(a) Developing in the trainees a flexible repertoire of diagnostic
    and treatment skills.
(b) Orienting trainees to the influence of socio-environmental
    factors as potential instigators of clienthood (substance
    abuse).
(c) Cultivating an awareness and appreciation of socio-economic,
    cultural and ethnic differences and commonalities in the help-
    ing process.
(d) Providing clinical experience in early detection, rapid
    assessment and prompt intervention in conditions which inter-
    fere with the capacities of individuals to function effective-
    ly in social roles and social interactions.
(e) Developing capabilities for working effectively with resources
    outside of this program and with an interdisciplinary team
    within the program.
(f) Increasing and focusing the trainees' knowledge of and rela-
    tionship with our particular cultural group so that interven-
    tions can be delivered in a culturally sensitive, acceptable
    and efficient manner.

For these objectives to be achieved, it is essential to facilitate
the trainees' acquisition of the attitudes and skills necessary for
community mental health work. They must be introduced to the body
of knowledge which serves as the theoretical basis of such work and
a medium must be provided for both work and learning that is consistent with the goals of community mental health work both in the
primary and secondary levels of intervention, as they relate to our
specific client population and needs.

In effect, from the standpoint of the program, help delivered by
our counselors must meet three criteria; (1) the job must be done
more effectively; (2) the individual members engaged in the program must grow and develop; (3) the job must be done in a culturally sensitive fashion and responsive to the idyosincratic needs of
our specific cultural groups. These three criteria tend to merge.
The program is effective only as the participants themselves grow.

The skills that are taught during the course of this module can be
classified into four categories: Clinical, negotiative, collaborative and evaluative. The clinical skills include intake assessment, psychosocial diagnosis, crisis management, and treatment.
The negotiative skills to be taught pertain primarily to the disposition and referral processes, including our expectation that
the clinician will follow up all referrals to resources in order
to guarantee that it is effective. Through assisting the alienated minority client to negotiate complex institutional mazes in
the interest of achieving appropriate health and social services,

the trainee is introduced to the roles of expeditor, facilitator, advocate and cultural bridge. The experience of serving in a consultant capacity to other agencies in the community (or vice-versa) is tied to a teaching forum that focuses on issues in the evaluation and use of community resources as alternatives to traditional clinical care.

Collaborative skills are essential for effective community mental health work where interdisciplinary teams and working groups are focusing on the same individual and/or community entity. The evaluation component of the program demands skillful administration of research instruments and analysis of research data. It also demands an effective process of feedback between frontline workers and research staff.

There is one additional aspect to the training needs of our program which is directly related to the Latin's style of seeking help. I am referring to the fact that our Latino clients come to the agency only when the situation they confront can be described as a crisis. In order then, for therapeutic interventions to be effective, the counselor must move quickly to help the client whether the crisis and permit the individual to cope more effectively with his ecological environment. In training our staff we help them to visualize a crisis as a learning dilemma, i.e., that the person is experiencing a situation for which he has no adequate coping behaviors. The strategy of the helper is then to establish appropriate behavioral patterns. All too often the behavioral pattern which emerges in crisis is the adoption of the dysfunctional role (e.g. escape thru drugs, sickness). This could be grossly reinforced by a helper who responds to this role, rewards and encourages it by asking questions which are solely concerned with drug usage, inadequacies, etc. In this manner, and to the exclusion of "let's grapple with the problem that got you to use drugs," the purpose is defeated. In order to minister completly to the non-functioning client, the helper is taught to pay attention to a problem which may not be "why am I taking drugs" or "what's wrong with my head." There may indeed be something wrong, but there is usually something wrong in the universe in which the drug user is trying to function. Instead what needs to be learned by both helper and client is a wide repertoire of functional problem-solving behaviors. We aim to teach our counselors to relegate, in the interest of time and efficacy, the usual concerns for theoretical criteria to a subordinate position in reference to the primary goal: to create constructive change in the individual-'s condition, i.e., deterioration in the capacity to cope must be halted and reversed. To achieve this it is essential to learn a diagnostic and evaluation process which arrives at understanding of the precipitating circumstances of the crisis as well as the coping potential of the client. The counselor learns to revive and strengthen coping abilities, i.e., those observable action patterns and behavioral functions enabling the client to maintain himself in his environment.

FUNDAMENTAL CONSIDERATIONS FOR TRAINING MINORITY
SUBSTANCE ABUSE PROFESSIONALS

William T. Marshall and Robert H. Eichberg

Central City Community Mental Health Facility,
Substance Abuse Training Program

In many countries throughout the world, and in many parts of
this country, people who care, and who understand human need and
suffering, often devote tremendous amounts of time and energy caring for the emotionally and physically ill. Quite often these helping agents, while being essential parts of the health care delivery
system, are not possessed of professional degrees and credentials.
They plan an indispensible role in society, but are not sufficiently
recognized and appreciated by those who are in positions of economic power--those who allocate money for health and mental health
services. Money, in the form of contracts, grants, fellowships and
fees for services, is generally routed to the most heavily degreed
individuals. In the case of health institutions and programs,
those with academically trained administrative personnel, and licensed or certified treatment personnel, are most likely to receive
federal, state or local money to provide services to their communities and to the clients who need their help.

While there are perhaps many justifications for the above
system of rewards, such a system also has inherent flaws which frequently make the best client care unlikely. This is particularly
true in "economically disadvantaged" communities, and even more
obvious in minority communities where the health professionals and
the consumers often have difficulty relating to each other. We
are probably all familiar with the highly qualified staff, housed
in the best equipped and most up-to-date facility, whose staff
meetings center around the problem of: "Why don't more people
avail themselves of our services?" If the community and the potential client population does not relate to the program being offered, even the best of staffs are likely to be ineffective and
unproductive. We ought to be particularly cognizant of this problem
in the substance abuse treatment field and make every effort not

only to assure competent client care, but to maximize the likelihood
that clients will take advantage of the services we have to offer.

Particularly in terms of drug treatment, many of the traditional treatment approaches and settings have been unsuccessful at
reaching and holding minority clients. Many of the existent programs
which appear to have good track records working with minority clients
were started by people with a high degree of personal interest,
energy and creative vitality. More often than not, these individuals were not credentialed professionals, and have come to be
called "non-professionals," "para-professionals," or more recently,
"non-degreed professionals." Some had histories of personal drug
use, abuse or addiction; others did not. Some had previous training
and experience in related health fields; others did not. Some had
academic backgrounds in areas not directly related to substance
abuse; others had no such background. Regardless of their differences in education, many of these workers have become true "professionals" in their jobs and should be recognized as such. Still
others have the potential of functioning at a professional level,
but lack some of the necessary experiences and training to function
optimally in their roles. These are the people, from a wide variety
of backgrounds, who have made drug abuse treatment programs viable
service delivery systems in minority communities, and it is these
same individuals who are in jeopardy of being pushed out of the
field as it becomes continually more sophisticated, political and
"professional". We are approaching a real dilemma in the substance
abuse treatment field in terms of the career development and potential job mobility of substance abuse workers, and we have an obligation to face this problem ethically and thoughtfully.

Several factors are currently interacting to bring this problem
to the foreground:
- Reduced availability of program support monies increases competition for existing funds. This makes maximum staff and program effectiveness essential if a program is to continue to
  receive public support for its services.
- Third party payment for substance abuse treatment is likely to
  be forthcoming with correspondent standard levels of competence
  for treatment program personnel.
- More stringent Federal and State regulations require accountability for the quality of treatment services being delivered
  and establish a standard acceptable level of program performance.
- Pending certification and credentialing requirement for substance abuse workers necessitates one's development of skills
  and knowledge to assure that he is competent to perform adequately on the job.
- Frustration and demoralization are frequently experienced by
  front line personnel as a result of increasing internal and external pressure to function at "professional" levels without
  being provided additional technical and emotional support.

These factors, taken as a whole, cause negative reactions within minority communities where their implementation is known to have several significant implications: 1) diversion of money from community programs to more traditional institutional settings, 2) loss of jobs, 3) decrease in the quantity and quality of client care. It is essential that we develop a strategy to assure that these consequences are not realized. The Central City Community Mental Health Facility, Substance Abuse Training Program is attempting to deal positively with this issue, and to implement a strategy of community organization and training which will assure high quality drug abuse treatment in the Southeast Health Region of Los Angeles County--a primarily Black community.

This substance abuse training project began in January, 1974, with a grant from the National Institute on Drug Abuse. During the first project year the program provided short-term (24 hours) training to physicians and nurses working in the Black community of Los Angeles. During the second project year the program was expanded to allow a broader range of professionals within the community to gain knowledge, enhance their understanding, and upgrade their skills in dealing with substance abuse and related problems. A thorough discussion of the rationale and development of this training program for professionals has been discussed elsewhere (Eichberg and Marshall, 1974). In the present paper we are focusing on the training of "substance abuse professionals"--those people who work diligently and consistently in drug abuse treatment programs.

In order to assure valuable and relevant training for substance abuse professionals, a training program should include an assessment process which allows it to work closely with individual treatment programs in formulating a curriculum and method of presentation. The training should address the service delivery gaps of the individual program, the needs of the treatment program staff, the pending requirements for credentialing, and regulations for federal funding of treatment programs. These elements are linked in a dynamic way, requiring on-going assessment procedures. In this way a training program can raise the level of service delivery, assuring a standard level of competence, and can facilitate the credentialing process for all concerned.

With the current limited jobs available in the field, and the possibility that this situation might become even worse, it is also important that training programs provide academic credit which might facilitate the trainee's movement into other areas of work in the human service field. Curricula should be designed to meet requirements for such credit, while still being responsive to the needs of trainees. This necessitates a training approach which stresses both experiential and didactic learning.

A training program ought to also be familiar with the nature of treatment programs and be sensitive to subtleties of the treatment process which often make these programs effective where other more traditional approaches have not been. Without recognition and appreciation of these program dimensions, a training project runs the risk of destroying essential elements of the treatment milieu.

It would also be helpful, in planning strategies for training substance abuse professionals in minority communities, to focus on a limited geographic area. This would increase contact between the treatment and training programs, minimize the trainees' travel time and time away from work, and make it possible to provide a central and comfortable meeting place. Being located on the same turf is also likely to increase the probability that the training project will be trusted by the treatment programs and their directors.

In the past, major training grants have been awarded primarily to non-minority institutions. These projects have often been unsuccessful at establishing good working relationships with minority programs and the minority community. Sometimes the projects have been unresponsive to the needs of minorities, or perhaps unaware of these needs. Other times the minority community has been reticent to become involved with these training projects out of fear of being taken over by them. In addition to the mistrust, it is often felt that the information received from these institutions is hardly transferable to a "real-life" minority community setting. It is critical that a comprehensive training project is responsive and effective at confronting this issue if it is to be accepted by community-based treatment programs.

As mentioned above, a training program which would meet the needs of treatment program staff should provide academic credit as well as curricula which will meet the requirements of credentialing and increase service delivery effectiveness. Many treatment program staff members do not hold academic degrees. A large number came to their jobs with years of street experience with drugs, and through their own treatment histories have become well acquainted with the treatment process. Many have worked in the field for years and have performed a broad variety of jobs: administrative, clerical, accounting, counseling, vocational rehabilitation counseling, fund raising and grant writing, etc. These skills, especially when enhanced through further training and supervision, make many treatment program staff members valuable on the job market. Unfortunately, however, academic degrees often increase the likelihood of being hired in most occupational settings. A credential as a substance abuse worker will not constitute a job classification or a license, nor will it carry with it the flexibility of a college degree. It is important to develop a plan which makes it possible to receive a marketable college degree while being trained in order to afford trainees the greatest potential for movement into other career areas.

This is a critical issue since we must provide training for substance abuse professionals, but cannot ethically train them exclu-

sively for jobs which may not exist in the future due to funding
cutbacks. If we train people solely for work in the substance
abuse field, we are creating a situation where a "rehabilitated"
addict, with many potentially transferable skills, must look primarily to drug programs for work. It is encumbent on us to provide
treatment staff with as many tools as possible for movement out of
the drug area, as well as for upward mobility within it. In this
way a training program can be seen as an adjunct to, or extension of,
the treatment process.

Since most training programs which would fit the strategy of
being tied closely to the community would not be accredited academically, it is important to work cooperatively with accredited institutions. Several possibilities exist for such a cooperative
venture, and new inroads are being made very day. The concepts of
a "university without walls", or a degree which is awarded for
equivalency credit based on life experience, are both important innovations in this area. Working closely with local colleges and
universities is another viable alternative to assure that credit can
be received for training in knowledge and skill areas necessary to
function as a substance abuse professional.

As trainers in the field, and ourselves "substance abuse professionals", we strongly urge that substance abuse workers get the
best support and training that they can. It is the responsibility
of the funding agencies to make sure that adequate attention is
paid to developing the creative and professional potential of many
dedicated and talented individuals who work in the treatment of
dependency disorders, and that such professional development be
aimed at both vertical mobility within the substance abuse field
and at lateral mobility into other service delivery systems.

Eichberg, R. H., & Marshall, W. T. Rationale and development
of a community-based substance abuse training program for
professionals. Paper presented at the North American Congress
on Alcohol and Drug Problems, San Francisco, December, 1974.

A WORKING MODEL FOR THE CERTIFICATION OF SUBSTANCE
ABUSE COUNSELORS

V. VERNON WOOLF, Ph.D.
Past Executive Director, Tri-County Council on Drug Abuse
Rehabilitation and Education, Provo, Utah

INTRODUCTION

Certification of substance abuse counselors has long required the development of a working model which gives administrators and other human service delivery workers an objective process
for the identification, evaluation and reporting of counselor
skills. It is widely held (North, 1975; National Association of
Alcoholism Counselors and Trainers, 1974; Steinberg, 1974) that
any such certification process must include both the "academic"
or formal educational aspects of counselor training as well as the
more practical experiential or "street level" demensions of
counselor skills. Since there was no comprehensive model available which allowed for the training, evaluating and reporting of
counselor skills, and since we had several drug rehabilitation
centers which employed a number of non-degreed specialists in
counseling, we found ourselves faced with the necessity of developing our own model for the certification of our counselors.

THE PROCESS FOR DEVELOPING THE MODEL

The development of the working model actually began six
years ago. With over two hundred identified drug abusers attempting to "get well" we selected those who seemed most able to h
others and began to train and support them in their counseling
efforts. Eventually we identified certain priority skills which
correlated with effective counseling and program development. We
arranged and received a federal grant and the program grew in its
sophistication and the need for a formalized certification process
evolved. With the help of the staff, program participants, and
other human service professionals, we eventually outlined a model
for certification and are now in the process of publishing a
human service training and certification manual. For the past two
years this model has proved workable and effective in our evaluation efforts, job placement, pay increase incentives, job security,
and has been required as part of the official administrative

monitoring process. For the purposes of this presentation two
aspects of this certification process may be of primary importance to the reader. The first is the actual skills which we
have found to be correlated with effective counseling and the
second is the developmental sequence we evolved for the measurement of these skills.

THE HUMAN SERVICE DELIVERY SKILLS

Three general areas of skill emphasis were delineated.
These included a certification for helping role skills, community
development skills and administrative skills. The experienced
human service delivery agent will recognize the common denominators which these three areas of responsibility have to all human
service agencies. A brief narrative description follows:

I. Helping Role Skills

Helping role skills relate to understanding self and communication with others in a constructive rather than destructive life
style. The skills measured include: communication and empathy,
values clarification, confrontation, medical aspects of counseling,
modeling, problem-solving, basic living skills, group processes,
crisis intervention, human growth and behavior, assessment, follow-up, professional ethics, and special program emphasis skills.
These helping role skills are essential to any program which orients itself toward human problems and their solutions.

II. Community Development Skills

In order to insure program relevance and responsiveness to
the community needs any human service program must have personnel
with community development skills. The fundamental elements of
community development skills include: community organization (theory and practice), methodology and function of boards, resource
mobilization techniques, community mobilization, community process
understanding, and social problems correlation skills. Without
adequate community development a program tends to treating symptoms rather than maintaining a perspective of jointly treating
environmental causitive factors. Awareness of community relevance
and responsiveness to community needs leads to an active growing
pain between the program and community and aids the community in
becoming more able to solve its own problems.

III. Administrative Skills and Management Profile Ratings

Administrative skills and management profile rating skills
are essential to effective program management and efficient administration. All levels of program staff and/or volunteer participation have administrative and management responsibilities and
must have the necessary skills to function on the job. The prima-

ry elements of these skills were found to be the following: information systems and fiscal management, management by objectives, organization climate management, logistical coordination, personnel management, management training, proposal reading, writing, and processing, planning and guideline sensitivity, volunteer concepts, volunteer training and management roles, and supervisory process skills. Program effectiveness and quality of services rendered will depend largely upon the administrative and management skills.

Not all job descriptions will require the same degree of skill accomplishment. Nor do all jobs require expertise in each of the above skill areas. Job certification therefore should reflect the specifics required by the particular job. Skill advancement and job advancement is also measurable when each skill level has a developmental sequence as a part of the certification process. For this reason we developed a four level sequence for each specific skill measured in the certification process.

THE FOUR STAGE DEVELOPMENT MODEL FOR SKILL CERTIFICATION

We found that the obtaining of any particular skill followed a natural sequence of development. Generally, each new staff member would progress systematically from a probationary state to full status as a staff member. Once a staff member was secure in his job he went through an expanding and integrating stage which required some supervision. At stage three the staff member was able to function without supervision and was self-motivating on the job. A final stage was evident in which the staff member became a supervisor and trainer to other staff members and community leaders. Skills which could be measured objectively by a scale or continuum were graduated into each stage of development. For example, if we wanted to measure empathy as a part of the helping role skills, we used the Truax (1970) scale which has nine graduations. It was obvious that anything below the five level on the Truax empathy scale was below the minimum for program staffing as far as the helping role job positions were concerned. In order for a person to qualify for any staff position he had to function at the five or above level of empathy. Stage one, the probationary stage, required a rating of five, stage two, the new staff member, required a stage six rating, stage three, the full status staff member had to be at least at the seven rating level and a trainer had to qualify at a rating of eight or better. Any skill rating on a scale could be applied to the four stages of certification in a similar manner.

Skills however, do not regularly lend themselves to measurement by scales. In order to certify staff members in skills such as values clarification, group leadership, and problem-solving, we used a developmental model based upon cognitive sophistication and exposure. Stage one personnel would be exposed to situations

and challenges which would give some indication of their understanding of a particular skill area. They would be required to
attend and function adequately in a values clarification workshop
and to be able to apply what they had learned to specific situations with program participants who had identified needs for values clarification. At stage two they would be expected to aid in
the conducting of a values clarification workshop and to prepare
a presentation for staff training on the principles involved in
some aspect of the skill area. At stage three the staff member
must be able to review the literature on the given skill area and
conduct the training seminars without supervision. A stage four
certification requires that the staff member develop a written
position paper which makes a contribution to the field of values
clarification (or whatever skill area being certified). This
sequence was followed for most of the skill areas contained in
the manual. A "grid" was developed which listed each skill and
the requirements necessary to qualify in each level of certification for each specific skill. Testing and measurement tools were
accumulated or developed to give a more uniform and systematic
evaluating and reporting process. These have now been put together in a human services training and certification manual.
Staff members have enthusiastically responded to this certification process for several reasons. Firstly, it measures the skill
whether it was academically obtained or intrinsically inherent in
the person. Both the school and the street experiences are valid
in this certification process. Secondly, they found that once
obtained the certification was ample demonstration of professional skill and could be obtained to get school credit, new job
placements and could be used to negotiate for higher pay, etc.
Thirdly, employer confidence in the staff increased as did the
self confidence of many staff members. Finally, it provided the
staff with specific growth incentive. Literally every staff member involved in this certification process has become involved in
further schooling or advancement in their skill training. Needless to say this personal incentive for growth has had a direct
effect upon the quality of service rendered by the staff.

SUMMARY

    A four stage developmental modality for certification of
counselors is presented. The field proven model provides objective criteria for certification and evaluation in the areas of
helping role skills, community development skills, and administration skills. A manual for certification, evaluation and training
is available by writing Dr. V. Vernon Woolf, 460 North, University Avenue, Provo, Utah, 84601, or phoning 801-377-5448.

REFERENCES

National Association of Alcoholism Counselors and Trainers, Inc.,
Roy Littlejohn Associates, Inc. (1974). Proposed National
Standard for Alcoholism Counselors. Copies available from
National Association of Alcoholism Counselors and Trainers,
Inc., P.O. Box 756, Arlington, Virginia 22216.

North, John W., (1975). Project Certification. Copies available
from Council of State and Territorial Alcoholism Authorities,
Inc., 1101 15th Street, N.W., Suite 206, Washington, D.C.
20005.

Truax, Charles B., (1970). A tentative scale for the measurement
of accurate empathy. University of Calgary, Alberta, Canada,
at Calgary, Alberta, Canada.

Steinberg, Sheldon S., (1974). Relationship of drug abuse services
to the credentialing process. Paper presented to: Single
State Agency Training Officers Conference, Ramada Inn, Rosslyn,
Virginia, Wednesday, August 14, 1974. Copies available from
Single State Agencies.

A TWO YEAR EXPERIENCE IN TRAINING FORMER ADDICTS TOWARD CERTIFICATION IN THE FIELD OF HUMAN SERVICES

Anthony Lopez, M.S.W.

Director of Training
Drug Abuse Training Program for Paraprofessionals
School of Medicine
University of Southern California

In July 1973 the University of Southern California Training Program for Paraprofessionals began. The purpose of this paper is to document the results after three years of training parapro-fessionals, as well as to describe the program characteristics that have made it successful. The program dramatically breaks from the traditional academic approach to a more intensive effort; eight months (40 hours per week) of training, with particular emphasis on human services.

Three agencies have pooled their resources to train paraprofes-sionals for substance abuse programs to enhance their effective-ness and their horizontal mobility. The agencies are: The Divi-sion of Social and Community Psychiatry which provides education and experience relevant to psychological and interpersonal prob-lems, as well as administrative problems; The Narcotics Preven-tion Project which provides instruction in social and occupational rehabiliation, client advocacy and community organization; and, The Rancho Los Amigos Drug Treatment Center where the students learn management of substance related emergencies, methadone management and in-hospital treatment. During the eight months of intensive training, the students rotate through all educational com-ponents and upon completion obtain a certificate and twelve college credits from U.S.C. The students are monitored by field work instructors, frequently assessed and individually assisted. By prior arrangement students enter employment in a community drug program immediately upon graduation. Staff devotes the four-month hiatus to program assessment and revision.

The primary objective of our program is to educate paraprofessionals so that their personal experience with substance abuse, and their social and occupational rehabilitation will be enhanced by human services knowledge and skills. A secondary objective is the creation of a training model based on the collaboration of an academic organization, a street oriented rehabilitation agency and a substance abuse emergency and treatment hospital unit. A third objective is to demonstrate the need for a permanent Training Institute for substance abuse paraprofessional workers.

The unique feature of our program is the provision of knowledge and experience with management of emergencies (overdosing), withdrawal (cold turkey and drug supported), hospital treatment of complications, counselling (individual, family, group), as well as all aspects of rehabilitation and social integration.

Applicants are screened by an Admissions Committee, and must meet the following criteria: (a) have the endorsement of a drug abuse program guaranteeing employment upon graduation; (b) no criminal charge pending, and addicts free from drugs for at least 6 months; (c) proof of graduation from high school or a GED or pending GED examination; (d) have access to an automobile and possess a driver's license and valid automobile insurance; and, (e) in good health. Preference is given to individuals from minority groups and/or poor areas.

Students receive the following: (a) full tuition for 12 college credits; (b) a stipend of $450 a month; (c) mileage of $28 a month; and, (d) a certificate upon completion of the course.

The program addresses itself to the following student needs:
(a) Clinical: (1) conducting a client interview resulting in an
        assessment, a management plan and a written record;
                (2) application of simple concepts of crisis theory
        in crisis intervention;
                (3) application of basic principles of counselling,
        both in one-to-one and group settings;
                (4) recognition of drug abuse related clinical
        emergencies with appropriate steps taken, i.e., referral
        to appropriate medical/psychiatric agencies.
(b) Academic:(1) to understand basic concepts of normal/
        pathological human behavior;

(2) to know the various forms of therapy and to participate in therapeutic management;

(3) to understand community forces and methods for community improvement, especially those related to drugs.

(c) Job Skills(1) to deal with courts, law enforcement agencies, etc., to facilitate rehabilitation of the client.

The following describes our training sites: The Division of Social & Community Psychiatry, USC School of Medicine offers didactic and clinical training. Students spend one day a week in classes at the Psychiatric Hospital, L.A. County/USC Medical Center. Classes consist of seminars, lectures, and student interviews of psychiatric patients, observed by peers and an instructor through a one-way mirror. After the interview, the student watches his performance on a video replay while the instructor and peers discuss technique and content. Rancho Los Amigos Drug Treatment Center is a multi-modality hospital dealing with patients who have overdosed or who are addicted to heroin. In their training here, supervised by a field instructor, students observe and assist in acute medical care services, participate in team discussions, are familiarized with pharmacotherapy and medical terminology, and learn to document observations. They conduct intake interviews, and function as co-therapists in group therapy. The Narcotics Prevention Project (NPP), a multi-modality street oriented program, differs from traditional services models in that services are designed around the needs of the client rather than the service system. Here, the students rotate through: (1) Hospital Intake — for detoxification; (2) Field Services — after a client has detoxified, aftercare services are available through this office; (3) Job Development; (4) Legal; (5) Group Therapy; (6) Halfway Houses — for men and women; (7) Referral Resources.

The results of our program are impressive. In the following tables, Table I describes the sex distribution of graduates and students now in training. Table II is a composition of graduates and students who were users and non-users. Table III describes graduate and student ethnic composition.

The following shows the current employment status of graduates from the first three cycles:

Employed in human service (drug abuse)	34
Employed, not in human service	3
Unemployed	3

```
Continuing studies, fulltime                         1
Deceased                                             2
                              TOTAL                  ──
                                                     43
```

Of the 54 students enrolled in the first three training cycles,
eleven were terminated when they failed to meet the program
requirements. Twenty-four students were enrolled in the
fourth training cycle; twenty-one of these will graduate on
March 15, 1976.

In recognition of the quality of our training, the University
increased the value of the course from six academic credits to
twelve (without increasing the tuition – a first in the history of
the University of Southern California). While the Certificate,
awarded to graduating students currently has no legal recognition, it has become a document highly valued by its recipients as
palpable evidence of a completed effort. It is anticipated that the
Certificate will have great practical significance if and when
certification and licensure of drug abuse treatment and rehabilitation workers becomes a legal requirement.

In conclusion, I would like to state, based upon the successes
experienced in these past two years of training, it is my contention that a nine month course of intensive training can provide
non-professionals an education that would supersede the existing
curriculum provided in the two year community college course
of study. The nine-month curriculum must be intensive and
generic, and should espouse the most contemporary trends in
human behavior. Thus, it is necessary to begin looking ahead
to the development of a Training Institute (TI) rather than to
the perpetuation of transient "training programs".

TABLE I
Sex Distribution

	Graduates		In Training		Total	
	#	%	#	%	#	%
Male	22	51	15	63	37	55
Female	21	49	9	37	30	45
TOTAL	43	100	24	100	67	100

TABLE II
Composition of Ex-Substance Abusers

	Graduates		In Training		Total	
	#	%	#	%	#	%
Former Users	29	67	15	63	44	66
Non-Users	14	33	9	37	23	34
TOTAL	43	100	24	100	67	100

TABLE III
Ethnic Composition

	Graduates		In Training		Total	
	#	%	#	%	#	%
Chicano	19	44	11	46	30	45
Black	15	35	9	38	24	36
Caucasian	6	14	2	8	8	12
Asian American	2	4.7	1	4	3	4
American Indian	1	2.3	1	4	2	3
TOTAL	43	100	24	100	67	100

1111

EDUCATION OF SOCIAL WORKERS FOR TREATMENT OF SUBSTANCE-ABUSERS

Maria Rosenbloom

Hunter College School of Social Work
The City University of New York

Because of the serious dimensions of Alcoholism and Drug
Abuse in our society, and, because an increasing number of people
come to the attention of social agencies due to difficulties related to this problem, it is imperative that all social workers
have some basic preparation in this area. A recent study by the
Council on Social Work Education recommended that specialized content in this area be taught "as long as there exists an abundance
of ignorance in this crucial problem area." (1)

This ignorance often leads social work agencies to exclusion
from serving individuals and families affected by this problem --
though social work expertise is badly needed and relevant to many
aspects in prevention - treatment - rehabilitation of alcoholism
and drug abuse.

It has been my experience in teaching graduate social work
students that once exposed to an understanding of this problem in a
focused and a comprehensive way -- within the social work perspective -- motivation develops to serve this population and, to reverse the pattern of exclusion which has been characteristic of social agencies when confronted with this problem.

At the Hunter College School of Social Work, as it is true for
many graduate social work schools across the country, some information about selected aspects of this problem is disseminated in various parts of the curriculum. In addition, the school offers an
elective course in "Alcoholism and Drug Abuse - Social Work Intervention" as well as field placements to a small number of students
in specialized agencies, namely those with primary responsibility
for alcohol and drug related rehabilitation.

I would like to share with you my experience in developing
this curriculum, namely teaching the course; establishing field
teaching centers in these specialized agencies and as Faculty Advisor to students assigned to them for their field work practicum.

I. The Course: Alcohol and Drug Abuse - Social Work Intervention

The objectives are to impart basic information; stimulate critical thinking; assist students in their efforts to integrate this knowledge into their practice, and increasing their awareness of those facets in social work theory and service delivery that have particular relevance to prevention - treatment - rehabilitation in Alcoholism and Drug Abuse. "Basic" content includes:

Facts about Drugs that are used and abused: (including alcohol and nicotine), their consequences for physical, emotional and social functioning. Public Policy and the Law.

The major theoretical orientations as to what causes and maintains substance abuse.

The major interventive approaches -- with special attention to the multiple ideologies involved; their base in theory; techniques; staffing patterns.

Special Issues in "Female Drug Abuse" -- prenatal care -- the new-born -- care of children -- the legal aspects; societal attitudes.

A variety of teaching methods are provided: an examination of relevant professional literature, including daily news in the public media; analysis of selected records of practice, presentation by instructor, students and guest lecturers.

The course reverberates with themes related to the controversial issues underlying practice in this field. They include the differential and often polarized views on: definition, causation, and solution of the problem; the goals and type of intervention; or the theoretical orientation to guide practice-decisions. (2)

Gradually students develop an atuneness to the lacunae in knowledge; to the ambiguities and half-truths pervading this field; to the impact of public values and attitudes on problem-definition, on quality and effectiveness of services.

Throughout, students are encouraged to use the social work tool of individualization to establish the meaning of drug-use for the person (its functional and dysfunctional aspects) within the context of his total life-experience and encounters with the family and community -- with consideration toward the variables of age, neighborhood, the legal system and the prevalent "social scene" which includes availability and popularity of certain "substance" and public attitudes toward its consumers.

Emphasis is placed on the importance of differentiating between experimentation, irregular use and addiction; the tragic consequences resulting from lumping them together and the potentials of differential social work intervention in these different levels of drug involvement. (3)

While there is generally a recognition that an individual "on drugs" is both influenced by and, in turn, influences his wider milieu, students become aware that these notions are rarely built into treatment approaches. Instead, intervention is usually focused solely on the drug-dependent individual -- without consideration to needed changes in the colluding, significant systems, particularly that of the family and the surrounding community. Therefore, students are encouraged to apply a multi-systems view as the unit of attention, both in problem-assessment and as a target for intervention.

In this field "anything goes." Treatment decisions are rarely individualized and are often influenced by chance, or the value-stance of professional and para-professional staff. This is particularly striking in relation to the issue of drug freedom or drug substitution -- as objectives of treatment. Drug-dependency may be viewed by some practitioners as a disease entity, by others as a deviance; by many others as a personality aspect. Consequently, the treatment focus may be solely on cessation of the drug-use without attention to the complex, perpetuating factors that maintain the problem and continually lead to relapse.

On the other hand, treatment often reveals a preoccupation with the early life experiences as the sole operating, dynamic force in the condition -- without attention to the significant and critical aspects of the "here and now" which maintains the problem.

The course aims at counteracting the use of inaccuracies as "facts" or reliance on simplistic notions and stereotypes typical in this field -- and often resulting in "fitting the case" to a singular conceptual viewpoint on interventive approach.

We badly need a theoretical and practice model that integrates the relevant psychodynamic, familial and socio-cultural dimensions with the dynamics inherent in the drug-experience itself. These experiences have a "life of their own," and in turn, shape behavior and functioning, and ultimately, personality. In the absence of such a model, students are encouraged to draw from a broad spectrum of sociological, psychological and social work practice theory -- as applicable -- rather than commit themselves to a narrow conceptual rationale or a "prescription for doing."

Highlighted is the importance, at all times, of relating to the problem of ambivalence about continuing or giving up drugs; and consideration of a wide range of possibilities inherent in the concept of "success."

Whether the substance-abusing individual is treated in a specialized program, such as a detoxification service, a Methadone Maintenance Clinic, a Therapeutic Community, or in a non-specialized agency -- the ultimate goal must be on helping him achieve a better functioning capacity and easing his integration into the community. This may call for an emphasis on strengthening the person or on sensitizing the familial and societal structures. Usually, there needs to be a combination of both.

Thus, particular attention is given to those aspects of social work philosophy and methodology that have particular relevance toward these objectives. This includes our time-honored insistence on individualization of human needs and resources; our understanding of the complex interrelationship between social reality and the individual experience; our skills in enhancing social functioning; engaging the family; mobilizing resources of the community.

The concept of comprehensiveness and continuity of service -- a traditional social work commitment -- are stressed for thier relevance to the stubborness of the problem and as a means of counteracting the typical and unsuccessful "revolving door" approach.

All social work practice models are seen as applicable. This includes the open-ended, dynamically oriented model. Certainly, it is not irrelevant to those who are willing to grapple with the task of identifying and, eventually, modifying behavioral patterns that have become ego-syntonic. Other approaches, such as those focused on "crisis" -- intervention; on "reaching out" and "developmental-socialization" tasks may carry particular relevance to a clientele whose lives are often dominated by emergencies, or those many who were stunted in their social development, either earlier or as a result of long-term involvement in the "drug life."

The social work role, in the specialized Drug Abuse programs that are dominated by psychiatrists, ex-addicts, or recovered alcoholics -- are also examined. Those aspects that enrich the social work vision as a result of these team-work experiences are identified as well as the functions and tasks that can be delineated more appropriately as within the competence of the other staff members.

II. The Field Work Practicum

Rehabilitation programs in Drug Abuse and Alcoholism have provided field work opportunities for a number of our students for many years. So far, about 200 students have had the experience in working with alcoholism and drug related situations, as part of their field practicum. This may involve the student in work on an individual basis; with the family; in groups or in some aspects of community organization.

We have had no follow-up to ascertain what meaning this experience has had for these students in their career -- following graduation. Informal communications suggest they have done well on the job market and are often sought after because of this particular experience.

There are many "bugs" in field work training, unique to this area. The greatest problem for the student is the energy which he must expend, figuratively and concretely in maintaining a regular contact with the alcohol and drug-dependent client. This is so because of the way of life customary for this population, the characteristic denial of the problem by the individual and family alike; and because we still lack solid professional skills to counteract this.

Schools must encourage the student who is strong, conceptually and attitudinally toward accepting these difficult placements. Faculty and Field Instructors must be responsive to serious frustrations of the student-learner in these settings. Indeed, the frequency of frustration is a hallmark of this area of practice and is an important though a tough part of the learning experience.

The agency must be flexible to permit the student to utilize appropriate procedures beyond those characteristic for staff, e.g. intensive, involvement of the family in the rehabilitation process.

The Field Instructor and Faculty Advisor should help the student with the transferability of knowledge -- from the specialized to the generic and vice versa. Administrative supports of school and agency are necessary for the amount of time that such teaching requires. (4)

A placement in "Drug Abuse" undoubtedly infuses the student with much knowledge about the various aspects of this problem. It offers a particular opportunity for learning how to tolerate frustration in working with the "less accessible" clients; how to accept a wide range of goals and definitions of "success;" how to maximize every opportunity to make some dent because another opportunity may not come; how to translate concern and creativity into innovation when the "know-how" is inadequate.

It is expected and appropriate that only a proportionate number of students will be placed in addiction settings for their field work courses. Yet, all schools of social work must assure that they impart on the students comprehensive knowledge and basic skills to work in the area of Alcoholism and Drug Abuse -- since this is increasingly becoming a most serious national problem. Each school can creatively design curriculum arrangements by which this mandate will be fulfilled.

REFERENCES

1. Council on Social Work Education, "Curriculum Project on Drug Abuse" 1971-1973.

2. I. Weisman, "Drug Abuse: Some Practice Dilemmas, " Social Service Review, Vol. 46, #3 (1972).

3. H. Alksne, L. Lieberman and L. Brill, "A Conceptual Model of the Life Cycle of Addiction," The International Journal of Addictions, Vol. 2, #2 (Fall, 1967).

4. M. Rosenbloom, G. Stanton and P. Caroff, "Faculty Advisement - A Proposal for the 1970's," Social Work Education Reporter, Vol. 21, #1, (December-January 1973).

IN-SERVICE TRAINING IN SUBSTANCE ABUSE:
AN ESSENTIAL COMPONENT OF INDUSTRIAL EMPLOYEE
IDENTIFICATION AND REFERRAL PROGRAMS

C. Panyard, Ph. D., K. Wolf, Ph.D., S. LePla

Detroit Health Department
Herman Kiefer Hospital
Detroit, Michigan 48202

The management of large industrial concerns is discovering
the benefits of encouraging treatment rather than termination of
substance abusing employees. It is virtually impossible to eliminate substance abusers from the work force. Given the increasing
prevalence of drug abuse in all segments of society, there is a
high risk of simply replacing one substance abuser with another.

The treatment of the substance abuser results in a savings to
both the employee and the corporation. The Kelsey Hayes Company
(1974), which has a progressive Center for Counseling and Guidance,
reported that employees identified as substance abusers had an absenteeism rate of 635 hours per year, which was five times the plan
plant average. In terms of income, this represented an annual loss
of $3,270 per employee. Those individuals who subsequently parti-
cipated in the Center for Counseling and Guidance reduced thier
rate of absenteeism by over 58% and reccovered approximately $1,627
each in annual income. Treatment of substance abusers results in a
reduction of absenteeism, better job performance, fewer labor relations problems and fewer Sickness and Accident claims (Wiencek,
1971).

The General Motors Corporation issued its first policy statement of drug abuse in 1973. George B. Morris, Jr., General Motors
Vice President, initiated formal contacts with the United Auto
Workers. He stated, "The Corporation and the International Union
have an interest in encouraging early and comprehensive treatment
looking toward rehabilitation. We are willing to undertake discussions . . . which will lead to the establishment as soon as
practicable of a joint drug abuse recovery program at a selected
location or locations on an experimental basis."

The GMC-UAW joint pilot drug abuse recovery program was implemented through the Detroit Hospital Drug Treatment Programs, a NIDA-Detroit Health Department sponsored program. The Neighborhood Services Organization - Health Resource Program (NSO), a component of the Detroit Hospital Drug Treatment Programs, was designated as the site of the GMC-UAW drug abuse recovery program. The Neighborhood Services Organization - Health Resource Program provided comprehensive care, including methadone maintenance, and detoxification, group and individual counseling and vocational and educational services on an outpatient basis. It was agreed that all GMC employees identified as having substance abuse problems would be referred to the N.S.O. clinic. The centralization of treatment for employed clients would allow for both a degree of specialization on the part of the treatment staff and would provide convenient referral mechanisms for feedback to the Corporation. Five General Motors plants were selected to participate in this pilot project.

Initial efforts were directed toward the development of a practical referral system. A Plant Committee, consisting of representatives from union, management and the medical departments, was developed in each plant. The Committee was to function as the referral agent from the plant. Both supervisors and employees had access to the members of the Committee when referral services were needed. The Plant Committee would refer the substance abusing employee to N.S.O. and receive feedback from N.S.O. on the employee's progress in treatment. Appropriate signed releases regarding confidentiality of employee/patient participation was obtained on all clinic patients.

Although the referral system appeared adequate and was approved by upper-level management, initially few General Motors employees were referred to treatment. It appeared that employees did not quite believe in the non-punitive stance of management. Supervisors, on the other hand, did not know how to approach employees suspected of abusing drugs and were often afraid of such contacts because of potential union grievances. In order to meet the objectives of the referral program - the early identification of employed substance abusers and motivating employed substance abusers to participate in treatment - a massive in-service training program was undertaken to five General Motors plants in Detroit.

Training was provided on the general nature of substance abuse, drug information, resources available, how to approach an employee and the specific referral mechanism. It became apparent, with a corporation as large as General Motors, that several different kinds of training were needed to reach all individuals involved. Six groups of individuals were identified as needing specialized training in substance abuse. Those groups were: (1) upper-level management, (2) supervisory personnel, (3) resource personnel, (4) potential clients, (5) the union, and (6) the treatment clinic staff.

The in-service training presentations consisted of the film "The Drug Memo" which demonstrated the effects of different drugs. The film's narrator was a factory foreman and it was directed specifically at line supervisors. The film was followed by role-playing by treatment clinic personnel in which the most effective methods for confronting an employee and making the referral were portrayed. Members of the audience were encouraged to participate in the role-playing. This technique always facilitated active discussion. The in-service training sessions also included an explanation of the referral mechanism. The basic information presented to each group was similar, but the emphasis was quite different.

Upper Level Management

Training for upper-level management was essential for the implementation for the identification and referral program. Their sanction and active support was necessary in order to iniitate meaningful contacts with other levels of management. With this group, the emphasis in training was on the cost benefits to the Corporation of treating rather than terminating substance abusing employees. The position that General Motors was not a social agency but a manufacturing concern was made repeatedly by some of the more conservative managers in training sessions. They were less interested in rehabilitating employees than in improving production speed and quality. This position was adopted by the trainers when working with upper-level management.

Within the hierarchial structure of General Motors, the greatest social distance existed between upper-level management and potential substance abuse referrals. The cultural and experiential differences resulted in many misconceptions and biases on the part of management. The trainers attempted to debunk the mythology of the "dope fiend" and to overcome the misinformation on which management acted. Drug referral and treatment information was presented in a manner to diminish the highly moralistic, Protestant work ethic approach of upper-level management to substance abusers.

Supervisory Personnel

The success of a referral program is dependent upon the ability of supervisory personnel and assembly line foremen to identify and to approach substance abusing employees. Supervisory personnel are the front-line contacts with potential referrals and, as such, are essential components of a referral program. Consequently, the staff of the Detroit Hospital Drug Treatment Programs devoted the most time to training supervisory personnel.

Training for supervisory personnel included basic drug information and identification of substance abusers. Supervisors were told repeatedly that they were not to diagnose an employee's problem. The supervisor's function was limited to notifying the employee that a problem existed in terms of "inadequate job performance." The supervisor was not to attempt to identify the cause of poor work performance. He was to make it clear that the employee was responsible for improving his job performance and that a variety of services were available to him for assistance. At no time was it considered appropriate for the supervisor to confront the employee about suspected drug abuse.

Attention was paid to how the supervisor should respond to an employee after the employee had enrolled in a treatment program. Supervisors were assured that special privileges were not appropriate. All employees, substance abusers and abstainers, were accountable for their job performance. If job performance did not improve after seeking assistance, then the standard disciplinary procedures were to be followed. Training for supervisory personnel functioned to alleviate the fear of approaching a substance abusing employee by providing supervisors with information about the problem, skills for confronting the employee and an alternative to termination.

Plant Committee

Employees identified by supervisors as being in need of assistance were referred to the Plant Committee for evaluation and referral to the most appropriate agency. The Plant Committee functioned as a resource for other plant personnel. It was the first level of diagnosis and the first representative of the Corporation to confront the employee about substance abuse specifically. The Plant Committee needed the most intensive training. They needed enough information to answer the questions of supervisory personnel and to explain the treatment alternatives available to the substance abuser. In addition, members of the Plant Committee needed interpersonal communication skills so that they could facilitate the employee's entry into treatment rather than turn him off to the rehabilitation process.

A three-day workshop was developed to meet the special needs of the Plant Committee. The workshop was designed to be experiential and didactic. The areas to be covered included the physiology and psychology of addiction, the cultural background of substance abusers, communication skills, treatment approaches, recognition of substance abuse in industry and the referral process. Unfortunately, Union/Management difficulties arose that forced the postponement of the workshop. The delay in implementing specialized training for members of the Plant Committee was a shortcoming of the in-service training effort.

The Substance Abusing Employee

A group that is frequently overlooked in training efforts is the group for whom the service is designed - the substance abusing

employees. Therefore, potential clients were included in this
training effort. Bulletin board announcements and payroll notices
about the program proved inadequate. They were too easily avoided
and ignored. The Detroit Hospital Drug Treatment Programs conducted a training program in an area that would insure maximum employee participation - the cafeteria. The film "The Drug Memo"
was shown during all lunch periods in all employee cafeterias in
one of the participating General Motors plants. Clinic counselors
were available at literature tables to answer questions about
drugs, treatment, and company policy. The confidentiality of program participation was stressed by employees. The commitment of
management to treatment, which was demonstrated at the training
session, resulted in many self-referrals by employees.

Union

The role of the union in implementing a referral program must
be addressed through training. Informational programs were held in
general union meetings and at meetings of committeemen. It was
helpful to emphasize that family members, as well as fellow employees, could receive services through the program. Active union
members and committeemen were instrumental in establishing the
legitimacy of the referral program with the employees. Moreover,
the employees also seem to trust their union representative more
than management statements about the non-punitive consequences of
requesting a treatment referral.

Treatment Clinic Staff

Training cannot be limited to the members of industry, but
must also be provided for the staff of the treatment program designed to accept industrial referrals. Counselors must be aware of
industry's objectives and methods of assessing if those objectives
are being met. The nature of the work environment and its implications must be understood. Counselors should be familiar with union
grievance procedures, shop rules, and management disciplinary procedures. A knowledge of the work environment should enable a counselor to better prepare the client to survive on the job without
using drugs.

An effective industrial in-service training program should not
be limited to one presentation. As supervisors became more comfortable with confronting employees and employees began to accept
the non-punitive stance of the company, many questions were raised.
Follow-up contacts were essential in order to maintain communication between the Corporation and the treatment center. The continual flow of information facilitated new referrals.

One member of the N.S.O. Clinic was designated as the Plant
Liaison and charged with the full-time responsibility of maintain-

ing contact with Corporation and Union personnel. In addition to formal monthly reports, weekly meetings with the Plant Committees were held. Employees in treatment began to trust the relationship between the plant and the treatment center. With their written consent, group sessions were held between the Plant Committee, the Plant Liaison and the employees in treatment. These joing sessions eliminated a considerable amount of game playing on the part of the employees in treatment because everyone present would know "the story" so that no one could be "conned."

In summary, approximately 6,000 General Motors Corporation employees, from upper-level management personnel to assembly line workers, in five General Motors plants in Detroit were involved in the training program. The in-service training proved to be an essential element in the implementation of the industrial substance abuse identification and referral program. It provided factual information with which management could act, reduced the level of fear and misunderstanding of substance abusers in supervisors and demonstrated to potential employee referrals the Corporation's and Union's preference for treatment rather than termination. Training was designed to meet the specialized needs of all members of the industrial community. In-service training functioned as a method of entry into industry and as a method of maintaining that relationship.

REFERENCES

Wiencek, R.G., Drug Abuse and Alcoholism in Industry, Industrial Canada, 1971, August, 21-24.

Francek, J.L., Kelsey-Hayes Company Center for Counseling and Guidance Report, March 29, 1974.

Morris, G.B., Jr., General Motors Corporation Inter-Organization Communication re: Drug Abuse - Pilot Program, November 19, 1973.

REPORT ON SUBSTANCE ABUSE TRAINING PROGRAM
GRADUATE LEVEL TRAINEES

Henderson Hendrix, Ed.D
E. John Orosz, M.A.
Thomas C. Kauffman, M.Ed (Sci)

Introduction:

The increase in addiction through the late sixties and early seventies resulted in the establishment and expansion of numerous treatment facilities. Detroit, hard hit by the abuse of substances, embarked on an aggressive counter attack involving almost every conceivable mode of treatment. Staffing of the treatment facilities with competent individuals became a serious problem. Equally as difficult was the problem facing (non-related) professionals such as nurses, teachers, school and family counselors, etc. They frequently became involved in the problems created by addiction without any knowledge either of the substances being abused or addiction itself.

This paper describes the efforts of the Detroit Health Department to establish a training program which would provide those specific areas of knowledge and those clinical skills which would enable professionals to deal more effectively with substance abusers and their problems.

As it was originally proposed, the Detroit Institute of Addiction Research and Training (DIART) Graduate program was designed for trainees who possessed Master's degrees or the equivalent in psychology, social work, nursing rehabilitation counseling, sociology or police administration. They had to be already employed by agencies dealing with drug abuse problems with the plan to be involved in the training three days per week. The proposed program called for one day of various kinds of classroom instruction and two days of "internship" or on-the-job training at treatment facilities. In addition, weekly group therapy sessions and monthly half day field trips to other facilities were also envisioned. To enable trainees of such caliber to participate in the program, a daily stipend of $30.00 was requested. This stipend was not approved. In addition, once recruitment of eligible trainees began, it was found that the Master's requirement coupled with the lack of a stipend constituted a stumbling block. Most of the eligible trainees were in the process of obtaining an advanced degree. Those who already possessed their Master's were generally too deeply immersed in their work to be able to give up the time necessary to participate in the program. This was particularly true of minority candidates, many of who desired such training. Consequently it was decided to change the Master's degree requirement to a Bachelor's degree and to make the clinical placements on an individualized basis as much as possible. The result of such arrangements was that the professional trainees schedule was reduced to two days a week. Most employed candidates gave up their days off in order to fulfill their commitment to the DIART program. The above changes enabled DIART to recruit individuals who were interested in obtaining training in substance abuse and who, in order to obtain this training, made a considerable sacrifice of both time and money.

Selection Criteria:

The acceptance of trainees was highly selective. Candidates were screened by a two member committee of the staff. Motivation, honesty, judgement and potential for learning were some of the qualities considered in accepting or rejecting an applicant. Emphasis was placed on:

1. Candidates' application which contained a biographical sketch as well as reasons for seeking training in this field.

2. Recommendations - One from present employer and two other responsible individuals.

3. Interview in which candidate's achievements, attitudes and aspirations were thoroughly explored.

As the program was implemented, several candidates who lacked a Bachelors degree (See Table I) were referred by clinics. These individuals had a great deal of practical experience, generally at least two years of college and were involved in the area of substance abuse. Such candidates were permitted to enter the program after an additional screening process and only after concurrence of other staff members.

The program graduated forty-four out of fifty trainees. Tables I and II present demographic data characteristics of the forty-four trainees at the time of admission. Tables II and III clearly show how an intensive professional program of course instruction and clinical experience prepared the students to narrow their employment from a spread of 17 different positions to six occupations:

The Training Program:

The length of the training program was six months; therefore, the above data represents four classes. The training program was designed to provide inter-action between the professional and para-professionals. The physical facility re-enforced this original concept. Classes were held for both groups in the largest class-room. The few times that groups separated, the professionals made use of a smaller room. All other facilities, lounge and offices, were shared by both groups. This constant physical contact helped in the growth of mutual understanding and appreciation. DIART provided the first opportunity for both groups to recognize each other on the human level; it helped to break down the usual "we vs. them" attitude so prevalent in such a group.

Courses presented were developed with the idea of providing basic knowledge and understanding of human behavior in general and those which provided specific knowledge and understanding into the dynamics and treatment of substance abuse. Specifically courses were presented in the following major content areas:

1.   Courses related to providing substantive knowledge in areas directly related to substance abuse such as Pharmacology, legal and medical aspects of substance abuse.

2.   Courses related to methods and techniques such as: counseling, interviewing, case work; group work, supervision, etc.

3.   Courses and training in the area of clinical training and exposure.

4.   Workshops, special case analysis and other similar conferences primarily to examine the concept of values - social, ethnic, cultural etc.

The instructors were drawn from various segments of the Academic, Professional and Service Community to provide highly specialized training for the various segments of the program. They were chosen on the basis of recognized excellence and com-petency in their respective fields as well as their ability to relate to the type of trainee with whom they would be involved.

An integral segment of the program was the clinical placement. Due to the obligations that the professional trainees had to their job and/or education, great latitude in the particular working time was granted. All trainees were to have had a minimum of eight hours of clinical experience per week. Many who had the time did consid-erably more. The purpose of the placement was to provide an oppor-tunity to implement the theories that had been presented in class. Trainees were expected to maintain an officially signed time sheet and a narrative of their experiences. Each trainee was evaluated by the clinic supervisor, the DIART supervisor and then provided a self evaluation. In this manner, the difficulties faced could be met head on and DIART had an ongoing appraisal of the progress of the individual.

Finally, each professional trainee was required to complete a term paper, (mini-research paper) on a topic involving substance abuse. Their efforts were supervised and evaluated by the Director of Research. It was his responsibility to assist the trainees and to evaluate with them the results of their efforts. Each paper is included in the individual trainee's file.

Conclusion:

The results of the training program are impressive. Forty-four trainees from seventeen different occupations and/or professions ranging from audimetric technician to a free lance writer successfully completed the program and were awarded certificates. Twenty-five are currently employed in the area of substance abuse (twenty-one in drug abuse, four in alcohol); two are vocational rehabilatation counselors; two are social workers; six are nurses; three are teachers and six are full time students, there are nine others who are working for advanced degrees on a part time basis. Those students who were interested were able to obtain between eight and twelve graduate credits for the training they received at DIART. Most of the DIART graduates now in school admit that the fact that they were able to receive credits for their DIART training provided the catalyst they needed to continue/resume their education.

TABLE I

General Characteristics (44 Trainees):

Age	Range	23-59		MEAN	34
Sex	Female	31		Male	13
Race	Black	24		White	19
			Native American		1
Marital	Single	17		Married	18
			Divorced & Separated		9
Education BA +		35	Two Years of College		+9

1127

TABLE II

Employment (before):

Audimetric Technician	-1	Nurse (Practical)	-4
Bookkeeper	-1	Secretary	-1
Clerk (Law Office)	-1	Social Worker	-4
Community Services	-2	Student	-5
Community Services Aide	-1	Teachers	-6
Day Care Worker	-1	Teacher's Aide	-1
Laborer	-1	Writer (Free Lance)	-1
Nurse (RN)	-6	Counseling	-2
		Counseling (Sub. Abuse)	-6

TABLE III

Occupation (after):

Substance Abuse	25
Vocational Rehabilitation	2
Social Workers	2
Nursing	6
Teaching	3
Students	6

CAREER TEACHERS FOR MEDICAL EDUCATION
IN DRUG AND ALCOHOL ABUSE

Marc Galanter, M.D.

Department of Psychiatry
Albert Einstein College of Medicine
Bronx, New York

Joel Solomon, M.D.

State University of New York
Downstate Medical Center
Brooklyn, New York

In 1971 the National Institute of Mental Health acted in
response to a growing awareness of the need for redefining the
scope of training in drug and alcohol abuse in American medical
schools. The resulting program now includes the support of 36
Career Teachers in Alcohol and Drug Abuse who are faculty members
at their respective medical schools, and two national training
centers for medical education in substance abuse. The goal of
this program is to contribute materially to a refocusing of the
American medical profession on the legitimacy of alcohol and drug
abuse as important and treatable medical illnesses.

The program, of course, reflects an increasing emphasis
which has been placed on medical education in this area in recent
years. This is illustrated by a report of The Council on Mental
Health of the American Medical Association in 1972 (1), which emphasized educating future physicians in alcoholism and drug abuse,
and by conferences such as that sponsored by the National Council
on Alcoholism at the New York Academy of Sciences in 1971 on professional training in alcoholism (2).

FORMAT OF THE CAREER TEACHER PROGRAM

The principal thrust of the program is directed at the
teaching of drug abuse and alcoholism in the undergraduate medical
curriculum. Each Teacher appointed was already on the faculty of
his respective school, and had shown a particular interest and experience in the area of addictive illness. Specific areas of specialization varied among the nominees, from clinical service to

research or public health. After appointment, they become actively engaged in the developing and implementing of curriculum relating to this area. It was his responsibility to evaluate the overall perspective of courses in the medical school and to develop a strategy for filling in gaps or to generate entirely new curricular programs where necessary.

The Career Teachers are usually known at the schools to have an interest and expertise in the field, and were therefore available as consultants, both within the medical school and to the surrounding community. This role proved to be a most valuable one. Once the reputation was established, a Teacher was in a position to contact members of various departments and discuss aspects of substance abuse curriculum which might be relevant to their courses. At several schools, for example, the departments of obstetrics and gynecology expressed interest on the effect of drugs of abuse on the pregnant mother and fetus. Career Teachers were in a position to work with Chairmen and faculty in arranging for related teaching.

Two major patterns emerged for altering curriculum. In one, efforts centered around a school-wide curriculum committee. Influence fairly was exerted evenly throughout various departments. The second pattern began in the Teacher's respective department where he would generate an active and sizable program. This program often carried a good part of the necessary undergraduate training. From this base he was then able to branch out into other departments, having proven the validity of his endeavor.

THE TRAINING CENTERS

The federal program was established to support the teacher for a period of three years, after which it was expected that the school would provide the resources for continued support, with the faculty member perhaps achieving tenure by then. It was important to assure that the Teachers would acquire the expertise to warrant a continuing role. Central to this goal were two national training centers established to provide supportive and training services, one at the State University of New York, Downstate Medical Center, and the other at Baylor University in Houston.

The centers undertook a variety of activities, as follows:

1. On-site Training: Both in formal courses and in exposure to ongoing research and clinical programs, the Career Teachers were exposed to a variety of innovative approaches in the field. Grant support allowed for extended periods of study at Centers when it was desirable.

2. Bibliography on Alcohol and Drug Abuse: A bi-weekly bibliography of current citations in the field annotated for easy evaluation is regularly distributed.

3.   Data-retrieval Terminal: Career Teachers have access for
        printouts on topics related to the area of substance abuse.

4.   Resource Handbook: A detailed handbook of all educational
        materials, ranging from text, review articles, films and
        videotapes, as well as listings of local resource centers
        has been prepared as a major reference for education in
        substance abuse.

5.   Regular National Conferences: Three times a year the Career
        Teachers convened to confer on curricular matters and aca-
        demic material of interest to the group. Programs were
        drawn up by the Career Teachers in collaboration with the
        Training Centers who assisted with necessary arrangements.
        Almost universally, the Career Teachers found these meetings
        to be very helpful, particularly in light of the isolated
        positions which they often occupied at their respective
        schools. Most of the Teachers had few, if any, colleagues
        actively involved in this area at their respective faculties.

CAREER TEACHER ACTIVITIES

        The activities of the Career Teachers fall mainly into two
categories:

1.   Undergraduate and Residency Curriculum: Medical students'
        courses underwent considerable change over the tenure of the
        initial group of Career Teachers surveyed in 1975. The
        amount of curriculum time dedicated to substance abuse in-
        creased by a factor of 2.1 in the pre-clinical years and 2.8
        in the clinical years. At the majority of the schools, most
        of the basic science departments had some input from the
        Career Teachers. In addition, inroads had been made into
        working with house-staff at the principal teaching hospitals.
        This group was essential in their central capacity as role-
        models. A principal vehicle for working with the house-staff
        was the consultation, since house-staff like graduate phy-
        sicians, were often perplexed in managing substance-abusing
        patients.

2.   Continuing Education: Career Teachers serve in a variety of
        capacities in organizing and teaching in continuing education
        courses. In less populated areas, they are often the only
        educational resource for such work. In addition, a variety
        of panels and programs have been undertaken by Career
        Teachers on a national level, such as one continuing educa-
        tion course organized for the 1976 Annual Meeting of the
        American Psychiatric Association. Collaborative work be-
        tween Career Teachers on a program such as this generates

models which can be subsequently applied at their respective institutions.

A CONTINUING ORGANIZATION

With many of the Career Teachers reaching the end of their three-year experiences, it became apparent in 1975 that the efforts begun at their respective schools were at a point where much of the benefit to be derived lay in the future. It was apparent that the Teachers had undertaken a major alteration in the educational and social systems in which they worked. Such systems are not rapidly changed, and without continuing involvement the curriculum structure could revert back to what had preceded.

The group therefore proposed to establish a continuing organization to achieve the following goals:

1. Further development of teaching curriculum and programs.

2. Mutual support and continued sense of purpose among this group.

3. Maintaining contact with recent developments in the field.

4. Acquainting the beginning Career Teachers with achievements to date.

5. Serving as the nucleus for a national organization on medical education in substance abuse.

The group is currently establishing such an organization, to operate in affiliation with another ongoing group, one dedictated either to medical education in the behavioral sciences, or to research and treatment in substance abuse. It is hoped that a sophisticated approach to alcohol and drug abuse will become an acknowledged part of the mainstream of medical education.

REFERENCES

1. AMA Council on Mental Health, JAMA, 219: 1746 (1972).

2. F.A. Sexias, and J.Y. Sutton, Ann N.Y. Acad. Sci., Vol. 178 (1971).

RESEARCH

OPIATE RECEPTORS - ISOLATION AND MECHANISMS

Eric J. Simon

Department of Medicine
New York University Medical Center
New York, N.Y.

I. INTRODUCTION

Research on the mode of action of narcotic analgesic drugs and the mechanism of the development of tolerance and physical dependence is one of the oldest of scientific pursuits. For many years the first step in the action of these drugs was postulated to be their binding to highly specific "receptor" sites. This specific drug-receptor interaction was thought to trigger certain chemical or physical changes leading to the observed pharmacological responses. The reason for such a receptor postulate was the striking structural and steric specificity of the action of narcotic analgesics. Rather minor structural changes have major effects on the pharmacology of the molecule, leading in some instances to the formation of antagonists, drugs whose main action consists of counteracting the effects of other opiates. While the receptor postulate dates back 2 to 3 decades, the discovery of the existence of specific opiate receptors occurred only about 3 years ago.

II. DISCOVERY OF STEREOSPECIFIC BINDING SITES IN ANIMAL BRAIN

Binding of opiates to tissue homogenates was demonstrated some years ago in our laboratory using equilibrium dialysis (1). However, attempts to measure specific binding, defined as binding of labeled dihydromorphine, sensitive to displacement by the specific antagonist, nalorphine, were unsuccessful.

More recently Goldstein et al.(2) were the first to utilize the property of stereospecificity to search for opiate receptors. A series of modifications of the Goldstein procedure led to the discovery of stereospecific binding sites in homogenates of rat brain independently and simultaneously in three laboratories (3, 4,5). In our laboratory we used ^{3}H-etorphine, a narcotic analgesic of enormous potency (about 10,000 times as potent as morphine in rats) as our labeled ligand. The hope, which was realized, was that the great potency of this drug might reflect, at least in part, high affinity for the receptor. ^{3}H-etorphine of high specific activity was incubated with rat brain homogenate at very low concentrations (10^{-10}–10^{-8}M) in the presence of a large excess of either unlabeled levorphanol or its inactive enantiomer dextrorphan. The homogenate was centrifuged and the pellet washed twice with cold buffer by recentrifugation. Radioactivity in the washed pellet was determined by liquid scintillation counting. Stereospecific binding was defined as that portion of the binding that is prevented by excess levorphanol but not by dextrorphan. Using this procedure, most of the binding (70-80%) was found to be stereospecific. More recently a more rapid filtration technique was used by Pert and Snyder (5) and this has been adopted in our laboratory.

III. PROPERTIES OF STEREOSPECIFIC OPIATE BINDING SITES

The binding sites have to date been found only in the central nervous systems of vertebrates and in the innervation of certain other tissues known to be sensitive to opiates, such as the guinea pig ileum and the mouse vas deferens. The sites are tightly bound to cell membranes. Enrichment of stereospecific binding in the synaptosome fraction (4,6,7) suggests that the binding sites are primarily present near synapses. Whether they are located post or pre-synaptically has not yet been determined.

Binding of opiates is saturable and half saturation (a measure of affinity) occurs at concentrations that are comparable to the brain concentrations at which these drugs are thought to exert their pharmacological effects. In a number of studies (3,8,9) excellent correlation has been found between the in vivo potency of a large number of opiates and their affinity for stereospecific binding sites.

The opiate binding sites are very sensitive to proteolytic enzymes, such as trypsin, chymotrypsin and pronase (3,10) as well as to a variety of reagents known to react with functional groups of proteins, the most thoroughly studied of which are reagents that react with sulfhydryl (SH) groups (11). A protein (or proteins) is therefore essential for stereospecific binding of opiates. Sensitivity to phospholipase A (10) suggests a role for phospholipids. All properties of the stereospecific binding sites so far examined are consistent with their being the recognition and binding components of pharmacologically important opiate receptors. These sites will henceforth be referred to as receptors.

IV. DISTRIBUTION OF OPIATE RECEPTORS IN THE BRAIN

The availability of human brain tissue obtained during autopsies at the Office of the Chief Medical Examiner of the City of New York permitted us to establish the existence of opiate receptors in human brain. A study of the distribution of receptor sites in over 40 anatomical regions of human brain was undertaken in collaboration with Dr. John Pearson (12). Levels of binding were found to vary greatly from region to region. High binding (0.3-0.4 pmoles/mg protein) was found in all regions of the limbic system except the hippocampus which has a rather low level of opiate binding. All regions consisting primarily of white matter, the cerebellum and regions of the brain stem were very low or virtually devoid of binding. High binding was also found in certain non-limbic areas such as the locus coeruleus and the pulvinar. Very similar results were reported by Kuhar et al. (13) for monkey brain.

V. THE POSSIBLE PHYSIOLOGICAL ROLE OF OPIATE RECEPTORS

Many investigators have suggested that in order to survive the eons of evolution opiate receptors must possess a physiological function that conveys a selective advantage on the organism that carries them. This led to a search for an endogenous ligand for the receptor. Exploration of all known neurotransmitters or modulators met with uniformly negative results. This then prompted the search for the existence of a previously unknown opiate-like molecule in the brain. Two laboratories were successful about the same time in demonstrating opiate-like activity in aqueous extracts of pig brain. Hughes et al. (14) showed that such extracts inhibited electrically stimulated contractions of isolated guinea pig ileum and mouse vas deferens. This inhibition was reversed by naloxone. Terenius and Wahlstrom (15) showed that something in aqueous brain extracts was able to compete for binding to opiate receptors. More recently Hughes et al. (16) reported that the active principle of their extract consists of two pentapeptides with the structures H-Tyr-Gly-Gly-Phe-Met-OH and H-Tyr-Gly-Gly-Phe-Leu-OH. A larger peptide with opiate-like properties was found in bovine pituitary by Goldstein and his collaborators (17,18). These opiate-like peptides or endorphins are discussed in detail by Dr. Goldstein. The question of their physiological role has not yet been answered. However, it is attractive to speculate that the endorphins and their receptors represent components of an endogenous pain-suppression system. At any rate, if a function is found for these peptides, the physiological role of opiate receptors will be clarified.

VI. CONFORMATIONAL FORMS OF THE OPIATE RECEPTOR

The finding in our laboratory (3) that increasing salt concentrations resulted in the reduction of opiate binding while no such effect was seen by Pert and Snyder (5) for naloxone binding, led us to suggest that this might reflect a difference in the manner in which agonists and antagonists bind to receptors. Evidence to support such a difference was obtained by Pert et al. (19) who also discovered that the effect was highly specific for sodium salts which reduced the binding of agonists but increased the binding of antagonists. Other alkali metal ions such as K^+, Rb^+ and Cs^+ do not exhibit this discriminatory effect, while Li^+ is partially effective. Detailed studies of the effect of sodium (20) led to the finding that the results are most readily explained by the interconversion of two conformational forms of the receptor. The conformation prevalent in media containing Na^+ has a higher affinity for antagonists and a lower affinity for agonists than the conformation that exists in Na^+-free media. Independent evidence for this interconversion was obtained by a study of the kinetics of receptor inactivation by the SH-reagent, N-ethylmaleimide (11). In the presence of sodium SH-groups of the receptors are markedly less accessible to inactivation ($t\frac{1}{2}$ of 30 min instead of 8 min). This protection shows the same ion specificity and dose-response to sodium as the changes in ligand affinity. The significance of the ability of the receptor to change its conformation is not yet known, but the great specificity of sodium in producing this phenomenon leads us to suspect that it may be important.

VII. ATTEMPTS TO ISOLATE OPIATE RECEPTORS

To study the detailed chemical composition and functioning of opiate receptors it will be necessary to solubilize them off cell membranes and purify them. Some progress in this direction has been achieved in our laboratory (21). Cell membranes from rat brain are allowed to bind ^{3}H-etorphine. The bound membranes are freed of unbound drug and concentrated by centrifugation and resuspension in a smaller volume of buffer. The membranes are then treated with a 1% solution of the non-ionic detergent Brij 36T. Ultracentrifugation of this suspension at 100,000 x g yields a clear supernatant that contains most of the radioactivity. By use of chromatography on XAD-4 resin it was determined that 25-30% of the radioactivity in the supernatant is still bound to a large macromolecule. The molecular weight of this complex, as determined by chromatography on Sepharose 6B, was 350,000. Evidence was obtained that the solubilized macromolecular moiety attached to etorphine has properties identical to those of the opiate receptor. To date, the free macromolecule obtained by allowing the etorphine to dissociate is not able to rebind opiates stereospecifically. Efforts to modify the conditions to allow us to obtain a soluble receptor capable of binding opiates in solutions are in progress.

VIII. SUMMARY

Considerable evidence has been accumulated demonstrating that stereospecific binding sites for opiates and their antagonists are the long-sought opiate receptors that mediate the pharmacological effects of these drugs. To date evidence suggests that one type of receptor can exist in several conformational states, but the question of the existence of multiple receptors for the many responses evoked by opiates is still unsettled.

The discovery of opiate receptors has recently given rise to another very exciting finding, namely the existence of polypeptides in animal and human brain that can bind to the receptors and exhibit opiate-like activities. The study of the interaction of receptors with exogenous and endogenous ligands, the reactions triggered by these interactions, and the isolation and purification of receptor molecules should within the next few years give us considerable insight into the mode of action of narcotic analgesics. An understanding of the physiological role of the receptor and its endogenous ligands may also lead to greater comprehension of aspects of brain function.

IX. REFERENCES

1. D. Van Praag and E.J. Simon, Proc. Soc. Exp. Biol. Med., 122:6 (1966).
2. A. Goldstein, K.I. Lowney and B.K. Pal, Proc. Natl. Acad. Sci. U.S., 68:1742 (1971).
3. E.J. Simon, J.M. Hiller and I. Edelman, Proc. Natl. Acad. Sci. U.S., 70:1947 (1973).
4. L. Terenius, Acta Pharmacol. Toxicol.32:317 (1973).
5. C.B.Pert and S.H. Snyder, Science 179:1011 (1973).
6. C.B.Pert, A.M. Snowman and S.H. Snyder, Brain Res. 70:184 (1974).
7. R.J. Hitzeman, B.A. Hitzeman and H.H. Loh, Life Sci.14:2393 (1974).
8. R.S. Wilson, M.E. Rogers, C.B. Pert and S.H. Snyder, J. Med. Chem. 18:240 (1975).
9. I. Creese and S.H. Snyder, J. Pharmacol. Exp. Ther. 194:205 (1975).
10. G.W. Pasternak and S.H. Snyder, Mol. Pharmacol. 10:183 (1973).
11. E.J. Simon and J. Groth, Proc. Natl. Acad. Sci. U.S. 72:2404 (1975).
12. J.M. Hiller, J. Pearson and E.J. Simon, Res. Commun. Chem. Pathol. Pharmacol. 6:1052 (1973).
13. M.J. Kuhar, C.B. Pert and S.H. Snyder, Nature 245:447 (1973).
14. J. Hughes, Brain Res. 88:295 (1975).
15. L. Terenius and A. Wahlström, Acta Pharmacol. Toxicol. 35: Suppl. 1:55 (1974).
16. J. Hughes, T.W. Smith, H.W. Kosterlitz, L.A. Fothergill, B.A. Morgan and H.R. Morris, Nature 258:577(1975).
17. H. Teschemacher, K.E. Opheim, B.M. Cox and A. Goldstein, Life Sci. 16:1771 (1975).
18. B.M. Cox, K.E. Opheim, H. Teschemacher and A. Goldstein, Life Sci. 16:1777 (1975).
19. C.B. Pert and S.H. Snyder, Mol. Pharmacol.10:868 (1974).
20. E.J. Simon, J.M. Hiller, J. Groth and I. Edelman. J. Pharmacol. Exp. Ther. 192:531 (1975).
21. E.J. Simon, J.M. Hiller and I. Edelman, Science 190:389 (1975).

SPECULATIONS ON THE NEUROCHEMICAL NATURE OF OPIATE DEPENDENCE:

AN OVERVIEW

Doris H. Clouet

New York State Office of Drug Abuse Services
Testing and Research Laboratory
Brooklyn, New York

DEFINITIONS

Opiate dependence is defined as a state of chronic opiate exposure wherein a dose of opiate no longer produces most of the behavioral responses produced by the first injection, and wherein the omission of a dose produces drug-seeking behavior and a new set of pharmacological signs termed abstinence. The difference between narcotic analgesics and other classes of drugs in producing dependence and tolerance is one of degree. Tolerance develops very rapidly to chronic opiate use and dependence is complete, as judged by abstinence signs upon drug withdrawal, and by drug-seeking behavior exhibited by chronic users, animal or man.

ANATOMICAL SITES OF ACTION

Several areas of brain (hypothalamus, medial thalamus, medulla and basal ganglia), spinal cord, pituitary gland and some neuromuscular junctions are indicated as the anatomical sites where direct opiate action has been demonstrated (1). At some neuromuscular junctions opiates act to impair neurotransmission. In the spinal cord some spinal reflexes are altered by opiate administration. In the pons-medulla vegetative functions such as respiration, blood flow, emesis are controlled, although higher centers may modulate the functions. Opiates act on vegetative functions and are presumed to act in the medulary centers. In the hypothalamus opiates alter pain sensitivity, temperature regulation and the release of pituitary releasing factors. The trophic hormones of the pituitary gland are also affected by opiate administration, presumeably by way of hypothalamic nuclei. The limbic system, including the neocortex, has been implicated in the behavioral responses to the use of narcotic analgesics. Thus, sites of opiate action are located throughout the central nervous system and in some peripheral areas.

NEURONS AS SITES OF ACTION

Attention has focused on neuronal cells and their synapses as the sites of the initial drug: receptor interaction required for opiate action as a result of neuropharmacological and electrophysiological studies (2). The sites where tolerance and dependence develop on chronic opiate use may be closely related to the sites of initial responses, either anatomically or by serial reactions. When administered to experimental animals, radioactively-labeled opiates are found in brain regions with a distribution related to physicochemical characteristics of the drug, and not to the pharmacological potency of the drug or the state of tolerance of the animal (3). Using a very potent opiate, etorphine, we have been able to show stereospecific binding of this drug to synaptic membranes of rat brain, after etorphine administration, with a decreased binding in the membranes from rats receiving the narcotic antagonist, naloxone along with etorphine (4).

OPIATE RECEPTORS

An important advance in the understanding of mechanisms of opiate action was the discovery of stereospecific opiate binding sites in brain (5, 6, 7). The receptors had high affinity for active narcotic agonists and antagonists and a saturable binding, as well as stereospecific recognition of the active isomers. Isolated synaptic membranes from many areas of brain contain opiate receptors, although their distribution is not even throughout the nervous system. After the initial drug: receptor binding the interaction must produce a transduction of the information to secondary effector processes. A tentative identification of the cAMP-adenylate cyclase system as one mediator of the transduction is supported by two general lines of evidence: (1) the nature of the adenylate (and guanylate) cyclase systems as amplifiers of the regulation of neurotransmission by ions, neurotransmitters and neurohormones (8), and (2) the changes found experimentally in the sensitivity of the cyclases in neurons in cell culture when exposed to morphine or other opiates (9, 10).

The identity of one neurotransmitter as the unique agent in the synapses containing opiate receptors has not been possible because the administration of narcotic agonists to animals produces changes in all of the well known neurotransmitter systems: acetylcholine, norepinephrine, dopamine, serotonin, histamine, GABA, etc. (11). Most of the effects on neurotransmitters are dose-dependent and reversible by narcotic antagonists, thus indicating that the effects are opiate-specific. However, most of these effects may be secondary to the initial disturbance of the synaptic membrane by the binding of the opiate to the receptor, or they may be counter-responses to the initial effects produced by the drug.

ENDOGENOUS LIGAND

Recently, naturally occurring 'morphine-like' substances have been found in brain (12, 13, 14). These substances bind stereospecifically to opiate receptors and have shown morphine-like activity in animals. The substances have been identified as small peptides, in particular, pentapeptides: methionine-enkephalin and leucine-enkephalin (15). Methionine-enkephalin is a sequence of amino acids found in a larger peptide, beta-lipotropin, a hormone of the anterior pituitary gland. Larger segments of beta-lipotropin also bind stereospecifically to opiate receptors and have morphine-like pharmacological activity (16, 17). It is possible that the neurons secrete the small peptides as neurotransmitters, or, equally, that the peptides are regulators of neuronal activity like other neurohormones.

THEORIES OF DEPENDENCE

Of all the hypotheses concerning the biochemical mechanisms of tolerance and dependence to narcotic analgesic drugs, two have stood the test of time. Tolerance by 'denervation supersensitivity' was suggested by Jaffe and Sharpless in 1968 (18). In this hypothesis, opiates interfere with neuronal transmissions, thus depriving post-synaptic receptors of stimulation. As a consequence, the receptors become supersensitive. Among the evidence supporting this hypothesis is our study of post-synaptic adenylate cyclase in the rat caudate nucleus (19). The cyclase became supersensitive to dopamine in chronically morphine-treated rats. The other hypothesis that has withstood the challenge of subsequent experimentation is one put forth by two laboratories, Goldstein and Goldstein (20), and Shuster (21), in 1961. Tolerance occurs by adaptive changes in the rates of neurotransmitter biosynthesis and catabolism, by alterations in the activity of the appropriate enzymes, to compensate for changes produced by the opiate. Again, among the evidence that supports this hypothesis is a study from our laboratory in which we found that the activity of the catecholamine biosynthetic enzyme, tyrosine hydroxylase, was increased in two brain areas after long-time morphine treatment of rats (22). The two theories are not mutually exclusive because each expresses one aspect of a general compensatory response of the type found in the nervous system after other kinds of stresses.

SUMMARY

(1) Opiate receptors are distributed unevenly throughout the central nervous system, and in some peripheral neuromuscular junctions.
(2) Opiate receptors are characterized by the stereospecific binding of narcotic agonists and antagonists in vitro.

(3) Naturally occurring ligands of the opiate receptor are peptide in nature.
(4) Tolerance develops to chronic opiate use by adaptive changes in the synaptic neurotransmitter systems.

REFERENCES

1. H.L. Borison, in Narcotic Drugs: Biochemical Pharmacology, (D.H. Clouet, ed.), Plenum Press, New York, 1971, p.342.
2. D.H. Clouet, in Chemical and Biological Aspects of Drug Dependence, (S.J. Mule and H. Brill, eds.), CRC Press, Cleveland, 1972, p. 545.
3. D.H. Clouet and N. Williams, Biochem. Pharmacol. 22:1283, 1973.
4. S.J. Mule, G. Casella and D.H. Clouet, Psychopharmacol. 44: 125, 1975.
5. L. Terrenius, Acta Pharmacol. 32:317, 1973.
6. E.J. Simon, J.M. Hiller and I. Edelman, Proc. Nat. Acad. Sci. 70: 1947, 1973.
7. C.A. Pert and S.H. Snyder, Science, 179:1011, 1973.
8. P. Greengard, in Adv. Cyclic Nucleotide Res. (G. I. Drummond, P. Greengard and G.A. Robison, eds.), Raven Press, New York, Vol. 5: 585, 1975.
9. J. Traber, R. Gullis and B.H. Hamprecht, Nature, 256:57, 1975.
10. S.K. Sharma, M. Nirenberg and W.A. Klee, Proc. Nat. Acad. Sci. 72:590, 1974.
11. D. H. Clouet, in Catecholamines and Behavior, (A. Friedhof, ed.), Plenum Press, New York, 1975, p. 167.
12. J. Hughes, Brain Res. 88:295, 1975.
13. L. Terrenius and A. Wahlstrom, Acta Physiol. Scand. 94:74,1975.
14. H. Teschemacher, K.E. Opheim, B.M. Cox and A. Goldstein, Life Sci. 16:1771, 1975.
15. J. Hughes, T.W. Smith, H.W. Kosterlitz, L.A. Fothergill, B.A. Morgan and H.R. Morrise, Nature, 258:577, 1975.
16. C. H. Li and D. Chung, Proc. Nat. Acad. Sci. 73:1145, 1976.
17. R. Guillemin, N. Ling and R. Burgus, Comptes Rendues Heb'd. Sceances Acad., Ser. D., 282: (in press).
18. J. Jaffee and S.K. Sharpless, in The Addictive States, (A. Wilker, ed.), Williams and Wilkins, Baltimore, 1968, p. 226.
19. K. Iwatsubo and D.H. Clouet, Biochem. Pharmacol. 24:1499, 1975.
20. D.B. Goldstein and A. Goldstein, Biochem. Pharmacol. 8:48,1961.
21. L. Shuster, Nature, 189L314, 1961.
22, D. H. Clouet and M. Ratner, in Reports, NRC-NAS Committee on Problems of Drug Dependence, 1971, p. 728.

NEUROCHEMICAL AND BEHAVIORAL CONSIDERATIONS ON
THE RELATIONSHIPS BETWEEN ETHANOL AND OPIATE DEPENDENCE

Kenneth Blum, Ph.D.

Department of Pharmacology
The University of Texas Health Science Center
San Antonio, Texas

INTRODUCTION

β-phenylethyl amines are known to condense non-enzymatically with
aldehydes through a Pictet-Spengler mechanism to produce a class of
compounds called TIQ alkaloids.[1] Recent demonstration of the endogenous formation of these substances in vivo[2] has provided the
basis for the hypothesis regarding biogenic amine involvement with
alcohol dependence. Cohen and others[3]   advanced the hypothesis
that the formation of endogenous alkaloids might be responsible for
the addictive properties of ethanol in vivo.

The idea that the formation of these compounds may contribute to
the addiction liability of ethanol has been supported in part by
the fact that tetrahydropapaveroline (THP), conjugate of dopamine
with dihydroxyphenylacetaldehyde, is the requisite intermediate in
morphine biosynthesis in the opium poppy Papaver somniferum.[3]
Considering the possibility that these compounds are formed after
the ingestion of ethanol and may contribute through structural similarities to the development of dependence to ethanol, it is conceivable that the opiate derivative could yield effects similar to
those seen after morphine administration. In this regard, Ross et
al.[4] reported that morphine, ethanol and the TIQ alkaloid salsolinol deplete calcium in regional areas of the brain. This effect is
selectively antagonized by the stereospecific narcotic antagonist,
naloxone. Ross, et al.[4] described in vivo evidence demonstrating
pharmacological activity of the neuroamine-derived alkaloid salsolinol, which suggested a common biochemical action for morphine and
ethanol.

Recently evidence was presented[5] for the possible role of dopamine-
derived compounds such as salsolinol and 6,7-dihydroxytetrahydro-
isoquinoline (6,7-dihydroxy-TIQ) in the ethanol-induced withdrawal

convulsion response in mice utilizing the Goldstein ethanol vapor technique.[6] These studies demonstrated that 6,7-dihydroxy-TIQ intensified the withdrawal reaction and that both salsolinol and the TIQ derivative were equipotent in producing hyperexcitability in mice which was elicited by handling. On the basis of these and other experiments,[7] TIQ-like substances were proposed to contribute to post-alcohol intoxication states.

Although previous research has provided evidence for the improbability of the commonality of addictions for alcohol and opiates[8] the work of Ross, et al.[4] along with the work done in our laboratory[4],[7] and by others[9] on the TIQ compounds prompted further evaluation of the hypothesis.

METHODS

The alcohol vapor chamber technique first described by Goldstein[10] and associates serves as a model for the production of ethanol dependence. Male Swiss-Webster mice (18 - 25 g) are utilized. Groups of 24 mice were housed in an air-tight chamber and exposed to ethanol vapor for three days. During exposure the animals receive a daily dose of pyrazole, a compound known to insure stable blood ethanol levels. Upon withdrawal from the alcohol, the animals are assessed for the severity of resultant convulsions according to scale developed by Goldstein and Pal.[10]

RESULTS

6,7-dihydroxy-TIQ at a dose of 50 µg/A i.c. injected at the 5th and 13th hour post-alcohol withdrawal significantly ($P < .001$) augmented the withdrawal score in mice. Along these lines it is important to point out that chlordiazepoxide, the known anti-anxiety agent and drug of choice in the treatment of alcohol abstinence significantly blocked ($P < .001$) ethanol-induced withdrawal and also blocks TIQ induced convulsions in mice. Further suggesting that the TIQ based alkaloids may play a role in post-alcohol intoxication states.

Furthermore, we have found a biphasic effect of salsolinol on the withdrawal convulsion response. Salsolinol at a dose of 10 µg/A i.c. produced a significant reduction of ethanol-withdrawal convulsions, whereas, higher doses of 100 µg/A i.c. resulted in an intensification of this response. The suppression effect of salsolinol may be due to the fact that this alkaloid is indeed responsible for the addictive effects of ethanol and thus, acts as an ethanol replacement agent under these experimental conditions. Intensifica-

tion with higher doses may be simply due to the convulsive properties of salsolinol as previously documented.

To further study the role of TIQ alkaloids in the ethanol dependence phenomena, we decided to administer L-dopa, a dopamine precursor amino acid, to see if this agent would intensify ethanol
withdrawal convulsions due to enhanced dopamine-derived TIQ
formation.

L-dopa at a dose of 20 mg/kg which was injected daily for four days
significantly (P < .001) enhanced the withdrawal convulsion
response. However, when the dopa decarboxylase inhibitor was included the augmenting effect of L-dopa was markedly reduced. Since
the decarboxylase inhibitor prevents formation of dopamine via
decarboxylation of dopa, this would implicate dopamine in the
L-dopa effect.

We should not leave this discussion with the idea that dopamine is
responsible for intensification of the withdrawal response. In
fact other reported studies from our laboratory show that i.c.
administration of dopamine to mice undergoing withdrawal actually
suppresses this withdrawal convulsion response. Further, the
dopamine receptor blocker haloperidol intensifies the response.
We therefore, suggest the intensification effect observed with
L-dopa was due primarily to the formation of the TIQ salsolinol
rather than due to the formation of dopamine per se.

Since it has been found that naloxone, a narcotic antagonist, can
block morphine dependence, it was decided to determine whether
naloxone and other narcotic antagonists similarly block ethanol
dependence.

Naloxone injected every six hours for four days at a dose of 2.5
mg/kg to mice exposed to ethanol vapor significantly inhibited
(P < .01) the withdrawal scores in mice.

If dopamine-derived alkaloids are indeed responsible for the addiction liability of ethanol, and since naloxone interferes with
ethanol dependence we decided to study naloxone-TIQ interactions.

Furthermore, since it has been shown in mice that dopamine-derived
alkaloids[5] intensify alcohol-withdrawal convulsions and produce
hyperexcitability[7] in this species, experiments were designed to
determine if naloxone could also block TIQ-induced hyperexcitability in mice.

The effects of intracerebral injections of either 6,7-dihydroxy-TIQ,
50 μg alone, naloxone, 2 mg/kg injected i.p. alone or naloxone, injected i.p. thirty minutes prior to 50 μg of 6,7-dihydroxy-TIQ on
the convulsive response in mice for five hours following the administration of the drugs were studied. Control subjects received
i.c. injections of artificial cerebral spinal fluid in an

equivalent volume as the TIQ injected subjects. For this experiment at least ten mice were in each group. The results indicate that naloxone significantly (P < .001) blocked the TIQ-induced hyperexcitability as measured by convulsions elicited by handling in mice.

Most recently, ethanol has been found to deplete regional brain calcium.[4] This acute effect of ethanol was blocked by naloxone.[4] To further characterize the inhibition of ethanol dependence by naloxone experiments were designed to analyze brain calcium during daily exposure to ethanol vapor in saline and naloxone treated mice.

The result of this preliminary experiment indicated that chronic ethanol exposure resulted in a significant decrease (P < .01) of brain calcium 24 hours following exposure. Ethanol under these conditions produced a decrease in total brain Ca^{2+} of approximately 30%, whereas, the depleting effect of ethanol lessened during the two days of exposure as evidenced by a 22% for day 2 and 15% for day 3 of exposure. Although, the calcium depleting effect decreased the loss was still significantly different (P < .05) from control values for the third day of exposure. However, when naloxone was administered 24 hours prior to and during exposure to ethanol vapor, the ethanol-induced calcium decrease was significantly abolished (P < .001).

To further characterize the calcium role in ethanol dependence other experiments were performed.

The effect of 45 mg/kg of calcium gluconate, injected every day prior to ethanol vapor exposure, on the ethanol induced withdrawal convulsion response was evaluated. The results show that calcium gluconate significantly reduced the initial phase of the withdrawal convulsion response.

The results of these experiments could suggest that the naloxone-induced inhibition of ethanol dependence may be due to its effect on the calcium-induced depleting actions of ethanol.

Other studies included the effects of naltrexone and naloxone in ethanol-induced narcosis. The results indicate that both naloxone and naltrexone could significantly block ethanol narcosis. However, the effects of narcotic antagonists are not simple since we have found that higher doses of naloxone and naltrexone potentiate sleep-time response.

Recently, Ross and co-workers, showed that naltrexone, at doses up to 2.5 mg/kg significantly increase alcohol consumption in hamsters given a choice of 5% ethanol and water, morphine suppressing this response and dextrorphan having no effect. This work prompted us to further explore naltrexone effects in alcohol consumption. Unexpectedly, we found in six hamsters that drinking is initially decreased and four days later significantly increased with 5 mg/kg of naltrexone, a slightly higher dose than that employed by Ross, et al.[11]

At this point in time we have no explanation of this response. However, it is tempting to speculate that naltrexone may be inducing enzymes which may alter the ethanol drinking response.

Effects of ethanol and proteins in membranes are well known. Furthermore, effects of protein synthesis inhibitors, like cyclohexamide has been shown to inhibit morphine dependence. Thus, due to the possibility that enzymes may be responsible for ethanol effects and possible commonality to morphine, cyclohexamide was utilized to study the effects of protein synthesis inhibition on ethanol dependence.

Cyclohexamide injected at 20 mg/kg daily significantly inhibited ethanol dependence.

If commonality exists between morphine and alcohol then these agents should be useful in ameliorating withdrawal reactions.

Morphine at a dose of 10 mg/kg i.p. significantly depressed ($P<.05$) the withdrawal convulsion scores of mice undergoing withdrawal from alcohol vapor exposure. Saline control scores were higher by 500% than those of the morphine treated mice at peak difference. The mean convulsion socre was 1.11, whereas, for morphine it was 0.43 showing marked suppression of ethanol withdrawal convulsions in mice. The duration of action of this effect for morphine was at least fifteen hours.

Is this suppression by morphine due to its short-term central depressant effects or to some other common specific interaction between alcohol and morphine in the nervous system (CNS)? Experiments were designed to see if morphine at 10 mg/kg would produce analgesia as a measure of its central effects for a period shorter than fifteen hours.

The method of Haffner, as modified by Bianchi and Francesehini,[12] was employed to determine the duration of acute pharmacologic effects of morphine. In this procedure, an artery clip with the branches enclosed in a thin rubber tube, is applied to the root of the tail of a mouse for thirty seconds; the animal makes continuous attempts to remove the noxious stimulus by biting the clip. In this experiment, there were two groups of ten mice each. The mice were injected intraperitoneally with either 10 mg/kg morphine sulfate or an equivalent volume of physiological saline and after thirty minutes the artery clip is applied for thirty seconds. Morphine inhibited the biting response by approximately 69% as compared to control and this effect lasted four hours. This experiment would suggest that the suppression observed on ethanol withdrawal convulsion response lasts much longer than morphine's short-term analgesic effects. Morphine suppressed ethanol-induced withdrawal convulsions by 83% at the lst hour following its injection and 15 hours later the suppression is still at the 83% level compared to its saline control in other experiments.

Administration of ethanol into the brain of mice undergoing withdrawal significantly inhibited (P<.005) the convulsion response induced by abrupt removal of ethanol.

The suppressive action of morphine on ethanol-induced withdrawal in mice does not appear to be due to morphine intoxication but due to some other common specific interaction between alcohol and morphine in the CNS.

Finally, other work[13] indicated that the dopa-based TIQ alkaloid produces analgesia and this effect is blocked by naloxone. These substances also potentially produce analgesia and ethanol narcosis.

In summary the following information supports the commonality theory.

1. Naloxone-induced inhibition of ethanol dependence.
2. Naloxone-induced inhibition of ethanol withdrawal convulsions.
3. Blockade of TIQ-induced convulsions by naloxone.
4. Blockade of ethanol-induced brain calcium depletion by naloxone.
5. Morphine suppression of ethanol-induced withdrawal convulsions in mice.
6. Intensification and inhibition of alcohol withdrawal convulsions in mice by TIQ alkaloids.
7. Calcium gluconate-induced reduction of ethanol dependence in mice.
8. Inhibition of ethanol dependence by cyclohexamide, a protein synthesis inhibitor.
9. Inhibition of ethanol narcosis by narcotic antagonists.
10. Potentiation of ethanol narcosis by TIQ alkaloids.
11. Naloxone-antagonism of TIQ induced analgesia.
12. Cross-tolerance to morphine and alcohol.
13. Similar depletion of regional brain calcium between morphine, ethanol and salsolinol and subsequent blockade with naloxone.
14. Enhancement of ethanol dependence in morphine dependent animals.
15. Suppression of ethanol preference with morphine.
16. Enhancement of ethanol drinking with naloxone.

REFERENCES

1. C. Schopp and H. Bayerle, Liebigs Ann. Chem. 513:190 (1934).
2. M.A. Collins and M.C. Bigdeli, Life Sciences 16:585 (1975).
3. G. Cohen and M. Collins, Science 167:1749 (1970).
   J.E. Davis and M.J. Walsh, Science 167:1005 (1970).

4. D.H. Ross, M.A. Medina, and H.C. Cardenas, Science 185:63 (1974).

5. K. Blum, J.D. Eubanks, J.E. Wallace, H.A. Schwertner and W.W. Morgan, Proc. Nat. Council on Alcohol., Edited by F. Seixas, New York Acad. of Science, New York (in press) (1975).

6. K. Blum, J.D. Eubanks, J.E. Wallace, and R.G. Tabor, Pharmacologist 16(2):661 (1974).

7. K. Blum, J.D. Eubanks, and J.E. Wallace, Proc. 37th Ann. Meeting Committee on Proglems of Drug Dependence, Washington, D.C., p. 551 (1975).

8. A. Goldstein and B.A. Judson, Science 172:290 (1971).

9. H.D. Brezenoff and G. Cohen, Neuropharmacology 12:1033 (1973). R. Heikkila, G. Cohen, and D. Dembiec, J. Pharmac. Exp. Ther. 179:250 (1971).

10. D.B. Goldstein and N. Pal, Science 172:288 (1971).

11. D.H. Ross, I. Geller and R.J. Hartmann, Proceedings of Western Pharmacology Society (in press) (1976).

12. C. Bianchi and J. Francesehini, J. Pharmac. 9:280 (1954).

13. A.M. Marshal, M. Hirst and K. Blum (unpublished observations).

PHARMACOKINETICS OF NALOXONE AND NALTREXONE IN RATS

Stephen H. Weinstein, Ph.D., J.M. Schor, Ph.D.

Department of Biochemistry
Endo Laboratories
Contribution No. 109
Garden City, New York

INTRODUCTION

Naltrexone [(-)-N-cyclopropylmethyl-14-hydroxy-nordihydro-morphinone] (1) is a potent narcotic antagonist when administered parenterally and orally to rats (1,2,3) and man (4,5). Its duration of action has been reported (2,3,4) to be longer than naloxone's in both species. The metabolism of naltrexone has been studied by Cone (6) and Cone et al. (7). The metabolite found in human urine was the glucuronide of the C-6-B -hydroxy analog of naltrexone [(1)-N-cyclopropylmethyl-14-hydroxynordihydroisomor-phine (II)]. Recently Cone, et al. (8) have attributed the longer duration of action of naltrexone to the long biological half-life of the free base of this metabolite. On the other hand, Fujimoto, et al. (9) have reported that the low potency of this metabolite militates against its contributing substantially to the overall narcotic antagonist action of the parent compound.

The duration of action of a drug is dependent upon its pharmacokinetic properties, i.e., the rates of absorption, distribution, metabolism, and excretion. The pharmacokinetic properties of naloxine have been reported in rats (10), and they are consistent with the observed rapid onset and short duration of pharmacological action. To determine whether the pharmacokinetic properties of naltrexone differ significantly from those of naloxone, and can account for the longer duration of action of the naltrexone, plasma levels of naltrexone in rats after intravenous, subcutaneous, and oral administration have been determined and solutions to the two compartment open pharmacokinetic model have been generated for this drug for the three routes of administration.

EXPERIMENTAL

Analytical Methods

Extraction from rat plasma, silylation, and quantitative determination by gas chromatography of naltrexone was performed as previously described for naloxone (10).

Animal Studies

Naltrexone·HCl was administered to male, Charles River CD rats intravenously and subcutaneously at a dose of 1 mg/kg. The oral dose was 10 mg/kg. Blood was obtained by cardiac puncture with heparinized syringes at specific times after dosing. Plasma was separated by centrifugation.

Metabolism Studies

Rats were dosed orally with 10 mg/kg of naltrexone·HCl. Urine collected for 24 hours was pooled, subjected to solvent extraction, and chromatographed on silica gel thin layer plates (11).

Pharmacokinetic Calculation

A computer program (COMPT) for optimizing the solution of integral nonlinear compartmental models of drug distribution, written in extended BASIC for use in time-sharing computer systems, (12) was used to generate pharmacokinetic parameters. To augment these computations a FORTRAN IV program, NLIN, for least-squares estimation of nonlinear parameters (13) was also used.

Calculation of pharmacokinetic parameters for the 2 compartment model has been extensively discussed by Wagner (14).

RESULTS

Metabolism Studies

Although the alpha and the beta C-6-hydroxy epimers of reduced naltrexone are not distinguishable from each other in the thin layer chromatography systems used, their R_f does differ from naltrexone's. Rat urine extracts yielded only unchanged naltrexone and conjugated naltrexone (presumably the glucuronide). Presence of conjugated naltrexone is assumed since the amount of unchanged naltrexone increased following hydrolysis of the urine. Nothing corresponding to either epimer of the reduced naltrexone was detected.

Plasma Levels of Naltrexone and Derived Pharmacokinetic Parameters

Fig. 1 shows the average plasma levels of naltrexone. The curves are the best fit generated by COMPT and NLIN. The data from all routes of administration fit the two compartment open model with first order absorption after oral and subcutaneous administration. The two compartment model and the definitions of the pharmacokinetic parameters are shown in Scheme I. The model provides a good fit of the theoretical curve to the plasma level data obtained following intravenous, oral, and subcutaneous administration of naltrexone.

DISCUSSION AND CONCLUSIONS

It has been reported that plasma levels of naloxone after oral administration to rats fit a one compartment model with rapid absorption and elimination (10). The plasma level data for oral naltrexone fit a two compartment model. The rate determining step in elimination of naltrexone is not K_{10} (0.16 min^{-1}), but is K_{21} (0.054 min^{-1}). The K_{10} values for the two narcotic antagonists are the same; however, K_{21} for naltrexone is three-fold slower than its K_{10}. Blumberg and Sayton (3) have reported naltrexone to be three times longer acting than naloxone in rats after oral administration. It appears, therefore, that the longer duration of action of naltrexone after oral administration is due to its retention in the peripheral compartment. This compartment may contain the drug receptor sites or it may act as a depot for release of the drug into the central compartment which, itself, may contain the drug receptor sites.

Intravenous administration of naltrexone results in pharmacokinetic constants very similar to those found after oral administration. However, differences between the pharmacokinetic properties of subcutaneously administered naltrexone and those of intravenously and orally administered naltrexone are apparent both from the curves in Figure 1 and the pharmacokinetic parameters. These differences may be attributable to the slow absorption rate constant observed after subcutaneous administration (K_{01} after subcutaneous administration is 0.19 min^{-1} while it is 0.51 min^{-1} after oral administration).

Calculation of the distribution rate constants, K_{12}, and K_{21}, and the elimination rate constant, K_{10}, was based on the assumption of absorption being essentially complete during the terminal log-linear phase of drug elimination. If absorption continues to play a role during the distribution and elimination phases of the plasma level time curve the values of the calculated constants may be greatly affected. This may be occurring in the case of naltrexone given subcutaneously. The subcutaneous absorption rate constant (K_{01}) is approximately one third of the oral K_{01}. After the bolus intravenous injection distribution is essentially instantaneous. Thus, naltrexone exhibits apparent route dependent pharmacokinetic properties.

When comparing the pharmacokinetic parameters for intravenously administered naltrexone with those reported (10) for intravenously administered naloxone, differences become apparent (Table 1). The rate of entry of naloxone into compartment 2, determined by K_{12}, is quite slow, with a faster K_{21}, i.e., faster rate of return to compartment 1. This situation is the opposite of that observed for naltrexone. The result is that very little naloxone enters and remains in the peripheral compartment. This is further reflected in the small volume of distribution in compartment two, V_2. While the duration of action of naloxone following intravenous administration is known to be short, there is, unfortunately, no data available on the duration of action of intravenously administered naltrexone. It may be predicted, however, that naltrexone's duration of action would be longer than naloxone's.

This would be due to naltrexone's greater access to and residence in the peripheral compartment.

Although the C-6-B -hydroxy analog of naltrexone (II) was not detectable in our laboratory, as a metabolite in rat urine, its presence in small quantities could not be ruled out entirely. Recently Dayton and Inturrisi (15) have reported that only a small fraction of the administered dose of naltrexone was found in rat urine and of this only 15% was II. Thus, the relatively long duration of action of naltrexone in rats appears to be attributable to its own intrinsic pharmacokinetic properties rather than to the presence of the C-6-B -hydroxy metabolite.

SUMMARY

The pharmacokinetic properties of naltrexone differ significantly from those of naloxone and appear to explain the longer duration of action of naltrexone. The C-6-B -hydroxy metabolite of naltrexone was not detected in rat urine, and, though it cannot at this time be completely ruled out, does not seem to play a role in the duration of action of naltrexone in rats.

TABLE I

Comparison of Pharmacokinetic Properties
of Naloxone and Naltrexone in Rats
1 mg/kg, intravenous

Constant	Naloxone	Naltrexone
V_1, liter	1.23	0.54
V_2, liter	0.31	1.29
V_{ss}, liter	1.54	1.83
Cl_p, liter/min	0.054	0.11
K_{12}, min^{-1}	0.017	0.13
K_{21}, min^{-1}	0.070	0.054
K_{12}/K_{21}	0.24	2.40
K_{10}, min^{-1}	0.044	0.20
a_2, min^{-1}	0.030	0.031

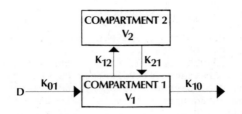

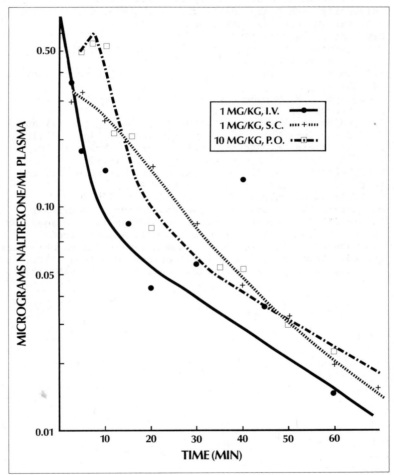

Fig. 1 - Plasma Levels of Naltrexone in Rats after Oral, Subcutaneous, and Intravenous Administration.

    1 mg/kg, I.V. ———•———; 1 mg/kg, S.C. - - + - - -;
    10 mg/kg, p.o. - - - 0 - -

Scheme I - Two Compartment Open Model for Drug Distribution

REFERENCES

1. H. Blumberg, H.B. Dayton, and P.S. Wolf, Toxicol. Appl.
    Pharmacol., 10, 405 (1967).
2. H. Blumberg and H.B. Dayton, Fifth International Congress on
    Pharmacology, Abstracts of Volunteer Papers, 23 (1972).
3. H. Blumberg, H.B. Dayton, "Naloxone and Related Compounds" in
    "Agonist and Antagonist Actions of Narcotic Analgesic Drugs,"
    H.W. Kosterlitz, H.O. Collier, J.C. Villarreal, Ed.,
    University Park Press, Baltimore, Md., 1973, pp. 110-119.
4. W.R. Martin, D.R. Jasinski, and P.A. Mansky, Arch. Gen.
    Psychiatry, 28, 784 (1973)
5. W.R. Martin, V.L. Sandquist, ibid., 30, 31 (1974).
6. E.J. Cone, Tetrahedron Let., 2607 (1973).
7. E.J. Cone, S.Y. Yeh, and C.W. Gorodetzky, Pharmacologist, 15,
    242 (1974).
8. E.J. Cone, C.W. Gorodetzky, and S.Y. Yeh, Drug Metab.
    Dispos., 2, 506 (1974).
9. J.M. Fujimoto, S. Roerig, R.I.H. Wang, N. Chatterjie, and
    C.E. Inturrisi, Proc. Soc. Exp. Biol. Med., 148, 443 (1975).
10. S.H. Weinstein, M. Pfeffer, M.J. Schor, L. Franklin, M. Mintz,
    and E.R. Tutko, J. Pharm. Sci., 62, 1416 (1973).
11. S.H. Weinstein, M. Pfeffer, J.M. Schor, L. Indindoli, and
    M. Mintz, J. Pharm. Sci., 60, 1567 (1971).
12. M. Pfeffer, J. Pharmacokin. Biopharm., 1, 138 (1973).
13. Marquardt, D.W., "Least-Squares Estimation of Nonlinear
    Parameters," a Computer Program in FORTRAN IV Language; IBM
    Share Library, Distribution No. 309401, August, 1966.
14. J.G. Wagner, "Biopharmaceutics and Relevant Pharmacokinetics,"
    1st ed., Drug Intelligency Publications, Hamilton, Ill., 1971.
15. H.E. Dayton, and C.E. Inturrisi, Fed. Proc. 34, 815 (1975).

METHADONE DOSE, PLASMA LEVEL, AND CROSS-TOLERANCE TO HEROIN IN MAN

Jan Volavka*, M.D., Karl Verebey+, Ph.D.,
Richard Resnick**, M.D., and Salvatore Mule+, Ph.D.

*Missouri Institute of Psychiatry, +New York State
Office of Drug Abuse Services, Testing and Research
Laboratory, **Department of Psychiatry, New York
Medical College

INTRODUCTION

The therapeutic action of methadone is based on
two effects: it protects the ex-addict from the symptoms of withdrawal, and it inhibits the action of
heroin by cross-tolerance. The amount of methadone
needed to provide these effects is a subject of controversy. Goldstein (1970) has reported that the
amount of heroin abuse in patients on methadone maintenance was not dependent on the stabilization dose.
Goldstein's interpretation is that the heroin blocking
effect was probably sufficiently great even at the
lower doses. Wieland and Moffet (1970) have compared
the low-dose and high-dose daily methadone maintenance
dose; the low-dose patients showed a higher rate of
heroin use than the high-dose group. These authors
felt that the methadone "blockade" was a partial deterrent for the high-dose patients (but not for those
on low-dose methadone). Contradictory assumptions
about the extent of cross-tolerance to heroin have
thus been invoked to explain clinical efficacy (or
lack of it) of low-dose methadone maintenance. Previous studies of cross-tolerance (Dole et al., 1966;
Zaks et al., 1970) used 100 mg of methadone per day
as the minimum dose; we have therefore decided to explore the doses of 80 and 40 mg per day. It is possible that the difference between the results reported
by Goldstein and by Wieland and Moffett was based on
individual variation in biological disposition of
methadone. Plasma levels might reflect such variation,

and we decided to study them in this context. Pharmacokinetic and excretion data obtained in the same subjects have already been published (Verebey et al, 1975).

METHODS

Twelve male post-addict paid volunteers were the
subjects. They had been reportedly opiate-free for at
least six weeks before the start of the study. After
admission to a closed ward, the subjects received a
"challenge". Baseline respiration rate was recorded,
a photograph of the pupil was taken, a blood sample for
methadone determination was drawn, and an injection was
administered i.v. The recording of pneumogram was then
restarted and proceeded for four minutes. The fifth
minute was used for a short interview: the patient was
asked to use a "high" scale to indicate any change. A
total of six consecutive four-minute segments followed
by one-minute interviews was recorded. Thirty minutes
after the injection, another pupil photograph was taken
and an opiate-effect questionnaire was administered.
The patient was then asked how he liked the "shot". A
scale was used to measure the "liking". The patient
also gave his estimate of the retail price of the "shot".
An experienced observer rated the behavioral effects on
another scale. Double-blind procedures were followed.

A total of five such challenges was done in each
patient. Three of the challenges used heroin (15 mg/
70 kg); placebo was given in the remaining two. The
first challenge was always with heroin. After the
first challenge, the patients were started on methadone.
Two dose schedules were used (each in six patients).
The "low-dose" schedule brought the patients up to a
maintenance dose of 40 mg per day; the "high-dose"
schedule used 80 mg per day. Both schedules reached
the top dose in 17 days. The heroin and placebo challenges during the methadone treatment were done in
pairs; the two challenges in a pair were separated by
24-72 hours. The order within pairs was counterbal-
anced. Challenges were done 24 hours after the methadone dose. The first pair of challenges was done approximately on the 9th day on methadone. The daily
methadone dose at that time was 25 or 50 mg. The second
challenge pair was done around the 19th day of treatment.

For statistical analyses, the four measures of subjective response ("liking", dollar value, number of
positive items on the questionnaire, and the averaged
"high") were combined in a single composite measure of
subjective response.

RESULTS

1) Comparison among heroin challenges: The effects of
the two methadone dose schedules on cross-tolerance was

explored by comparing the heroin responses of high vs. the low-dose methadone groups. This was done separately for the challenges performed around the 9th day and for those around the 19th day of treatment. Simple non-parametric tests were used. No significant dose effects were detected on any of the four variables tested (pupil size, breathing rate, observer rating, and subjective response). Results of more complex analyses will now be presented separately for each variable.

The effects of methadone and heroin on pupil size are displayed in Table I. Multiple regression analyses demonstrated that the pupillary response to heroin was significantly related (negatively) to the duration of methadone treatment, current methadone dose, and methadone plasma level. The effect of treatment duration was partly independent of dose or plasma level of methadone. This was demonstrated by the fact that the duration of treatment accounted for a significant proportion of the variance associated with the post-heroin pupil size (9%) even when the effects of dose and plasma level were statistically controlled.

Table I shows that the pre-injection breathing rates decreased after the start of methadone treatment and remained relatively stable when the methadone doses were increased. Heroin decreased the respiration rate. The response of the two methadone groups were different even before the methadone treatment was started. The effect of methadone dose, plasma level, or duration of treatment on the respiratory response to heroin was not statistically significant.

The observer rating of heroin effect decreased significantly as a function of methadone dose, plasma level and of treatment duration. These three effects were dependent on each other.

The composite rating of subjective response was analyzed in the same ways as the observer ratings. The subjective response to heroin declined significantly with the increasing dose and plasma level of methadone, and with the duration of treatment. As had occurred with the observer rating, these effects were not independent of each other.

2) Comparisons between heroin and placebo challenges: All challenges (heroin and placebo) given around the 19th day of treatment at the stabilization doses were used in these analyses. The results indicate that heroin elicited significantly greater pupil constriction, breathing rate depression, and subjective effects than placebo.

Analogous tests were performed for the challenges done around the 9th day of treatment. Significant differences between heroin and placebo were detected in all four variables under study.

DISCUSSION

The decrease of responses to heroin while the patients were on methadone indicates the development of cross-tolerance. The responses were not completely abolished at any point of our experiment.

The strength of cross-tolerance was related to the increasing doses of methadone, but the difference between the high- and low-dose schedules was relatively unimportant. The clinical implication of this finding would be that 80 mg offer no major advantage over 40 mg as far as the cross-tolerance is concerned.

Methadone plasma level results suggest that inter-subject differences in the metabolism and disposition of methadone do not play a major role in the development of cross-tolerance to heroin.

TABLE I

RESPONSES TO INJECTIONS OF HEROIN AND PLACEBO

RESPONSE VARIABLE	RELATION TO INJ.	METHADONE DOSE	DAYS ON METHADONE				
			0	9 days		19 days	
			HEROIN	HEROIN	PLACEBO	HEROIN	PLACEBO
PUPIL DIAMETER (mm)	Before Inj.	Low Dose	6.25	4.58	4.72	5.10	5.32
		High Dose	5.47	3.87	3.65	4.65	4.87
	After Inj.	Low Dose	2.53	2.75	4.30	3.95	5.28
		High Dose	2.68	2.90	3.53	3.88	4.63
BREATHING RATE (Breaths/min.)	Before Inj.	Low Dose	18.1	13.0	13.0	11.8	12.2
		High Dose	22.3	12.2	12.5	11.2	11.8
	After Inj.	Low Dose	13.4	10.3	12.4	9.3	12.0
		High Dose	11.7	8.0	11.4	9.6	11.1
OBSERVER RATING	After Inj.	Low Dose	3.67	2.83	0.00	2.17	0.00
		High Dose	5.33	1.70	0.50	0.17	0.00
SUBJECTIVE RESPONSE	After Inj.	Low Dose	152.2	125.5	0.0	43.7	3.3
		High Dose	138.7	40.1	15.2	11.8	0.0

Note: Each number represents the average of six patients. The range of observer rating scale is 0-6. See Text for the subjective response.

REFERENCES

1. Dole, V.P., Nyswander, M.E., and Kreek, M.J.: Narcotic blockade, Arch. Intern. Med. 118: 304-309, 1966.
2. Goldstein, A.: Blind controlled dosage comparisons with methadone in 200 patients, in Proceedings of the 3rd Natl. Conf. on Methadone Treatment, N.Y., 1970, pp. 31-37.
3. Verebey, J., Volavka, J., Mule, S., and Resnick, R.B.: Methadone in man: Pharmacokinetic and excretion studies in acute and chronic treatment, Clin. Pharmacol. Ther., 18: 180-190, 1975.
4. Wieland, W.F., and Moffett, A.: Results of low dosage methadone treatment, in Proceedings of the 3rd Natl. Conf. on Methadone Treatment, N.Y., 1970, pp. 48-49.
5. Zaks, A., Fink, M., and Freedman, A.M.: Duration of methadone induced cross-tolerance to heroin, in Proceedings of the 3rd Natl. Conf. on Methadone Treatment, N.Y., 1970, pp. 54-56.

SELF-MAINTAINED DRUG DEPENDENCE IN RATS

Edward T. Uyeno

Stanford Research Institute
Menlo Park, California

Since a forced administration technique to induce physical dependence on drugs is not appropriate in the determination of the developmental correlates of drug dependence, an increasing number of researchers are developing self-administration methods to be applied to laboratory animals. In an experiment involving oral self-administration an animal is given a choice of a drug solution or control solution (1-4). A disadvantage of the oral route is the suppressive effect of the test solutions due to disagreeable taste. In an intravenous self-administration system, an animal is trained to press a lever to activate an infusion pump in order to self-inject a drug solution through an indwelling chronic venous catheter (5-10). In the present study, a self-administration technique was used to investigate the voluntary initiation and patterns of self-injection of morphine sulfate, cocaine hydrochloride, and ethyl alcohol by rats.

I. METHOD

Male rats of the Fischer strain were maintained on a feeding schedule designed to deprive them approximately 20 hours before the initiation of the daily training to press a lever for a food pellet. After an animal had learned to press the lever and regained its normal weight, it was anesthetized with pentobarbital sodium to enable implantation of a chronic catheter, constructed according to the technique of Weeks and Collins (11). One end of the cannula was inserted into the right jugular vein, and the distal end was subcutaneously passed around the armpit to exit from the body at a skin incision on the top of the skull. Then the catheter was put into a coiled spring (50 cm in length) designed to prevent the rat from biting the polyethylene tubing. The bottom end of the spring was cemented to the cleaned surface of the skull, and the top part was fastened to a balancing bar, suspended from a swivel, located above the cage. The polyethylene tubing emerging from the top of the spring was linked to a tiny metal tube protruding from the

bottom of the swivel containing an enclosed stuffing box. Finally,
another piece of polyethylene tubing was used to connect the swivel
(via the second minute metal tube jutting from the top) to a 5 ml
syringe, operated automatically by a syringe driver. The driver
was wired to a control logic apparatus with a digital readout
device.

After the surgery each animal was housed in a special test cage
where food and water were supplied ad lib. The test cage was
provided with a lever which the rat could press to activate the
self-administration system. For a week to three weeks the animals
were allowed to press the lever to self-administer 0.9% saline
solution. Then the syringe with the saline solution was replaced
with another one containing a drug solution to permit a voluntary
initiation of drug self-injection at the rate of 0.013 ml/press.
In the first experiment the animals were initially offered morphine
sulfate solution of 2.5 mg/ml concentration. As they developed
tolerance to the narcotic, the concentration was gradually increased to 50 mg/ml. In the second investigation, another group of
rats was presented with cocaine hydrochloride solution of 0.05
mg/ml concentration. Some animals that developed tolerance and
increased their consumption were given a series of higher concentrations in a sequence of a geometric progression. In the third
evaluation a new supply of animals was offered an ethanol solution
of 1% concentration (v/v). The concentration was increased by 1%
increments every 15 to 25 days until a 5% solution was reached.
The total number of times that each animal pressed its lever during
each 24-hour period was transformed to indicate the total amount
(in mg) of the drug self-administered.

II.   RESULTS AND DISCUSSIONS

In the first experiment most of the animals initiated self-
administration of morphine and gradually became dependent on it.
The total daily amount of the drug self-administered by each subject was plotted against day to describe a pattern of self-injection. A typical pattern of morphine self-administration (Fig. 1)
shows daily fluctuations; however, an overall trend indicates that
an animal developed tolerance to the narcotic and increased its
consumption. The daily intake leveled off approximately five to
six weeks after the initiation of self-injection. The animals in
the second experiment self-administered a relatively large amount
of cocaine during one or two days and reduced their intake substantially during the next three to five days (Fig. 2). This
cyclic pattern of self-injection continued during several months.
Approximately 20% of the cocaine-dependent rats overdosed themselves, convulsed, and died. The subjects in the third experiment showed considerable variations in their daily alcohol self-
administration (Fig. 3). Once in 7 to 12 days they increased
their consumption erratically. Despite periods of voluntary

reduction in self-injection, interspersed between days of high intake, the typical graph generally indicates a gradual increase in the consumption.

The patterns of self-injection of morphine, of cocaine, and of alcohol by the rats were similar to the corresponding modes of self-administration by Rhesus monkeys described by Deneau et al. (9). The data suggest that the self-administration technique may be applied efficaciously to investigate the behavioral and environmental determinants of drug dependence.

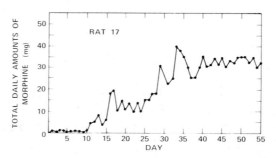

FIG. 1.   A typical pattern of morphine self-administration.

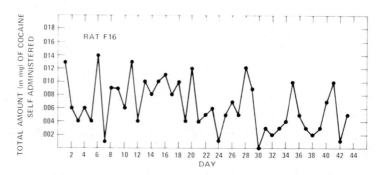

FIG. 2.   A cyclic mode of cocaine self-injection.

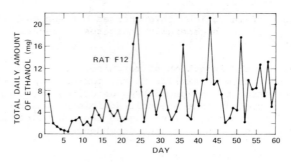

FIG. 3.   A characteristic manner of ethanol self-administration.

REFERENCES

1.   J. R. Nichols, C. P. Headlee, and H. W. Coppock, J. Amer.
     Pharm. Assoc. Sci. Ed., 45: 788 (1956).

2.   A. Wikler, W. R. Martin, F. T. Pescor, and C. G. Eades,
     Psychopharmacologia, 5: 55 (1963).

3.   D. K. Kamano and D. J. Arp, Intern. J. Neuropsychiat., 1:
     189 (1964).

4.   R. Kumar, H. Steinberg, and I. P. Stolerman, Nature 218:
     564 (1968).

5.   J. R. Weeks, Science, 138: 143 (1962).

6.   C. R. Schuster and T. Thompson, Committee on Drug Addiction
     and Narcotics, NRC-NAS, Ann Arbor, Michigan, (1963).

7.   R. Pickens and T. Thompson, J. Pharmacol. Exp. Ther., 161:
     122 (1968).

8.   R. Stretch, G. J. Gerber, and S. M. Wood. Can. J. Physiol.
     Pharm., 49: 581 (1971).

9.   G. A. Deneau, T. Yanagita, and M. H. Seevers, Psychopharma-
     cologia (Berl.), 16: 30 (1969).

10. E. T. Uyeno, J. Pharmacol. (Paris), 6: 283 (1975).

11. J. R. Weeks and R. J. Collins, Psychopharmacologia (Berl.), 6:
     267 (1964).

THE EFFECTS OF BARBITURATES ON BRAIN FUNCTIONING*

Joseph J. Tecce, Jonathan O. Cole, Joseph Mayer,
and David C. Lewis

Laboratory of Neuropsychology
Boston State Hospital

Department of Psychiatry
Tufts University School of Medicine
Boston, Mass

Washingtonian Center for Addictions
Boston, Mass

The aim of this study was to assess the influence of short-acting and long-acting barbiturates on electrical brain activity, mood, and behavior. Electrical brain activity was measured by an event-related brain potential, contingent negative variation (CNV). CNV is a slow shift in the EEG baseline (see Figure 1) appearing between the occurrence of two successive stimuli presented in a constant foreperiod simple reaction time paradigm (1). CNV amplitude appears to be a sensitive indicator of central nervous system changes produced by a variety of psychotropic agents, such as 10 mg of dextroamphetamine (2) and 50 mg of chlorpromazine (3). Based on these and other studies reporting associations between CNV changes and behavioral alertness, Tecce and Cole have proposed an attention-arousal model to explain mechanisms of drug action (4, 5). This model led to the expectation that amplitude of CNV and measures of attention performance and mood state would be useful in evaluating the influence of pentobarbital (fast-acting barbiturate) and phenobarbital (slow-acting barbiturate). In addition, an attempt was made to account for individual differences in barbiturate

*Supported by USPHS Career Scientist Development Award 1-K02-00016 (JJT) from the National Institute of Mental Health and research grants DA01032 (JM) from the National Institute of Drug Abuse and MH-19211 (JJT) and MH-16128 (JOC) from the National Institute of Mental Health.

response by studying subjects classified on the basis of two CNV
shapes (see Figure 1): Type A shape, having a fast rise time and
Type B shape, having a slow rise time (6). Previous work
indicated that Type A individuals are prone to early excitation
after recieving 10 mg of dextroamphetamine whereas Type B
individuals show early drowsiness prior to excitation (2).

Methods

Subjects. Thirty male college undergraduates and graduates,
who were screened medically and psychiatrically, served as paid
volunteer subjects. They were randomly assigned to either
pentobarbital (100 mg), phenobarbital (100 mg), or placebo groups
(10 subjects per group).

Procedure. After a 15-minute rest, the following test
sequence was administered: (a) a simple reaction time (CNV) run;
(b) the Profile of Mood State (POMS) (7); (c) the Continuous
Performance Test (CPT) (8); and (d) the measurement of blood
pressure and neurological signs of barbiturate influence. A CNV
run consisted of 16 trials of the light flash-tone-key press (see
Figure 1). The light-tone interval was 1.5 secs; the key press
terminated the tone.

A dysphoria index was developed from the POMS by pooling
anxiety, confusion, hostility, and depression items. Attention
was measured by requiring the discrimination of serially presented
visual letters (key-press to "X" and no key press to other
letters). Letters were presented rapidly appearing for .2 secs at
the rate of one every 3.20 secs (range: 2.80 to 3.60 secs).
Attention performance was measured by latency to respond to "X"
(discrimination latency). The complete test sequence lasted about
25 min and was given once prior to the oral administration of
drug and placebo tablets and then each half-hour for three hours
post-treatment.

CNV was recorded from frontal (Fz), central (Cz), and
parietal (Pz) scalp areas referenced to linked earlobes.
Electro-oculographic (EOG) recordings were made from above and
below the right eye in order to remove from off-line analyses
trials with ocular artifacts. CNV amplitude was defined by the
difference in voltage between the 256-msec epoch prior to tone
and the 512-msec period in the EEG baseline prior to the light
flash. Averaged CNVs were based on 6 to 12 trials, the number
being constant within a subject.

Data analyses. Independent t-tests based on 18 degrees of
freedom were carried out to evaluate the statistical reliability
of mean differences.

Results

In the second hour post-treatment, compared to the placebo group the phenobarbital group showed a significantly lower amplitude of CNV recorded at Pz ($p < .03$) and tended to be slower ($p < .08$) in CPT discrimination latency. The dysphoria index of the POMS showed a pattern of elevation for the phenobarbital group post-treatment with this group significantly higher ($p < .03$) than the pentobarbital group in the third hour post-treatment. In the second hour post-treatment, Type B individuals in the phenobarbital group showed significantly slower ($p < .03$) discrimination latencies than Type B individuals in the placebo group and in the third hour post-treatment showed significantly slower ($p < .05$) latencies than Type B individuals in the pentobarbital group. This difference approached significance ($p < .10$) in the third hour post-treatment. There were no drug-placebo differences in CPT latency among Type A groups. The phenobarbital group tended to be higher on the POMS dysphoria index, post-treatment, than either pentobarbital or placebo groups. This difference approached significance ($p < .10$) for the phenobarbital-pentobarbital comparison in the third hour post-treatment.

Discussion

Since the only significant drug effect on CNV amplitude involved the parietal (Pz) recording area for the phenobarbital group in the second hour post-treatment, it appears that the effects of 100 mg of either pentobarbital or phenobarbital on electrical brain activity as measured by CNV amplitude are weak ones. The finding that discrimination latencies tended to be slow for the phenobarbital group in the second hour post-treatment suggests that CNV reduction by phenobarbital was associated with attention impairment. The elevation in dysphoria scores in the phenobarbital group suggests that CNV reduction at Pz and attention performance decrement on the CPT may have been mediated by distraction from a negative hedonic mood state. Furthermore, the relation of phenobarbital administration to distraction and dysphoria may be a reason why this barbiturate is less abuse-prone than pentobarbital.

Subjects characterized by a Type B CNV shape had slower discrimination latencies and increased dysphoric mood in the second and third hours post-drug than Type A subjects, suggesting that Type B individuals are prone to distraction from a negative hedonic state, such as dysphoria, and that these characteristics are magnified by phenobarbital.

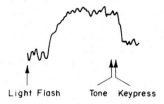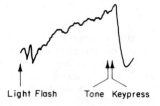

Figure 1. Two types of CNV shape based on fast (Type A) and slow (Type B) rise times.

References

1. Walter, W. G., Cooper, R., Aldridge, V. J., et al. Contingent negative variation: An electric sign of sensorimotor association and expectancy in the human brain. Nature (Lond.), 203: 380-384, 1964.
2. Tecce, J. J., and Cole, J. O. Amphetamine effects in man: Paradoxical drowsiness and lowered electrical brain activity (CNV). Science, 185: 451-453, 1974.
3. Tecce, J. J., Cole, J. O., and Savignano-Bowman, J. Chlorpromazine effects on brain activity (contingent negative variation) and reaction time in normal women. Psychopharmacologia (Berl.), 43: 293-295, 1975.
4. Tecce, J. J., and Cole, J. O. Psychophysiologic responses of schizophrenics to drugs. Psychopharmacologia (Berl.), 24: 159-200, 1972.
5. Tecce, J. J., and Cole, J. O. The distraction-arousal hypothesis, CNV, and schizophrenia. In D. I. Mostofsky (Ed.), Behavior control and modification of physiological activity. Englewood Cliffs, N. J.: Prentice-Hall, 1976, in press.
6. Tecce, J. J. Contingent negative variation and individual differences: A new approach in brain research. Arch. gen. Psychiatr., 24: 1-16, 1971.
7. McNair, D. M., Lorr, M., and Droppleman, L. F. Profile of Mood States (Manual). Educ. Indus. Test. Serv. San Diego, 1971.
8. Rosvold, H. E., Mirsky, A. F., Sarason, I., et al. A continuous performance test of brain damage. J. consult. Psychol., 20: 343-350, 1956.

METHADONE ADDICTION IN CATS:
EFFECTS OF LSD UPON WITHDRAWAL

Roy Tansill
Tom Booker
&
Althea M. I. Wagman

Maryland Psychiatric Research Center

Methadone is a physiologically and psychologically addictive compound used as a legal substitute in the management of opiate addiction. Methadone withdrawal, although milder than that associated with heroin, produces symptoms for a longer period of time (1). In addition Stimmel, et al. (2) found that 90% of 146 detoxified methadone maintained patients followed up after one year returned to narcotic use.

Therapeutic use of narcotic analgesics for the treatment of pain associated with terminal cancer produces tolerance and other symptoms of drug addiction. However, patients maintained on narcotic analgesics have manifested reductions in narcotic consumption for weeks or months following the administration of LSD in the context of psychotherapy (3). A similar phenomenon has been reported by narcotic addicts who experienced a loss of tolerance to narcotics following ingestion of LSD (4). Savage et al. (5) found that administration of LSD to addicts in a residential therapeutic setting, showed promise of reversing the psychological dependence upon heroin. These data suggest that a substance with psychotherapeutic potential which also acts as an antagonist to the withdrawal syndrome might facilitate recovery from the psychological dependence as well as mitigate the physical withdrawal symptoms.

The present study was designed to assess the behavioral aspects of methadone addiction and withdrawal in cats and the effects of LSD upon behavior during withdrawal. A two component schedule was used to assess the ability to perform responses at high rates for reinforcement (Variable Ratio, VR) and the ability to

1171

inhibit response or space responding (Differential
Reinforcement of Low Rate, DRL). The latter schedule
also provides for the assessment of response accuracy.
Recent studies indicate that cats develop addiction to
narcotics with chronic administration (6). Cats were
also selected as subjects because the half life of LSD
in cats (135 mins.) is similar to that in humans (175
mins.) (7). A cross over design was used during withdrawal to determine whether LSD modified the syndrome.

Procedure

Four adult mongrel cats (one male and three females, average weight 2.5 Kgm.) were maintained on a 23
hour food maintenance schedule with water ad libitum.
The male was housed separately in a 4' X 8' X 10' colony
cage while the females were housed together in a colony
cage of the same dimensions. The animal pens were
maintained at 50% humidity with constant illumination.

Two Lehigh Valley (LVE) small primate operant
boxes were used. These boxes were placed in ventilated,
sound attenuating LVE cubicles located in a room adjacent to the housing facilities. Reinforcement consisted of .75 ml. of homogenized canned dog food and water.
The response bar was located 6" above the floor and 8"
to the right or left of the feeder.

Ss were trained on the multiple VR 10, DRL 25 sec.
schedule of reinforcement for 30 minutes a day, five
days a week. This schedule required 18 weeks of shaping
before training began on the multiple VR 10, DRL 25.
Each component of the multiple schedule was available for
15 minutes. The VR component was signaled by the onset
of a white light over the response bar and the DRL 25
component was signaled by a tone cue. Also, to maximize
the distinctiveness of cues associated with the VR & DRL
schedule, Ss were trained in separate experimental chambers for VR & DRL components. Each day the order of
presentation of the VR & DRL components was reversed.

Daily records were kept of VR response rate, total
number of DRL responses and total number of DRL reinforcements. Also, 1/2 hr. prior to each daily run,
activity and pupillary measures were taken. Activity
levels were recorded by rating activity (on a 3 point
scale) in the home cage and traversing a 16 ft. hall to
the running room. Pupillary ratings (on a 5 pt. scale)
were recorded by observing the pupil in ambient light
(32 ft. cds) and in direct light (65 ft. cds) eminating
from flourescent tubing 3' away from the eyes. Pupils
that were totally dilated in ambient light and which

did not respond to direct light were given a score of 5. Dilated pupils which responded minimally to direct light were rated at 4. A score of 3 was given to dilated pupils which responded normally to direct light. Normal pupillary dilation and response was scored 2 while a score of 1 was given for complete miosis in response to light.

Gradually increasing dosages of methadone were administered daily over a 5 month period with the maximum dose of 5 mg. (2.0 mg/Kg) throughout the last two months preceding the first 2 week withdrawal period. During this 2 week period, 2 Ss were given LSD (40 mcg/Kg) on the second day. Following the first withdrawal period all Ss received 5 mg (2.0 mg/Kg) of methadone for 6 weeks prior to the second withdrawal period. The remaining 2 Ss received LSD (40 mcg/Kg) on the second day of the final withdrawal period.

Initially, drugs were given by combining liquid methadone with 20 gms of dry Purina Cat Chow and fed to S after the completion of the operant task and on weekends. This procedure was replaced by administration of 5 mg capsules p.o. in order to produce consistent dosage levels during the eight weeks prior to the first withdrawal period.

During withdrawal capsules containing lactose in place of methadone were administered. LSD assisted withdrawal was identical to unassisted withdrawal with the exception that LSD mixed with 8 ml. of milk was given on Day 2 of the assisted withdrawal and plain milk was given on Day 2 of unassisted withdrawal.

The order of assisted and unassisted withdrawal was counter balanced such that two Ss received LSD during the 1st withdrawal period and the other two Ss received LSD during the second withdrawal.

Results

The acute effects of methadone (.4 mg/Kg p.o.) administration were observed by the third day. Increased rate of response occurred in both VR and DRL with a concomitant decrease in DRL reinforcement. Each time the dose was increased in 1 mg. increments a similar change in response rate occurred. These changes however, were usually not present after the tenth day at any dose except the highest (2.0 mg/Kg.). At this dose, 20 days of high rate responding occurred prior to return to pre-drug levels.

The changes in behavior following chronic 5 mg. methadone maintenance during LSD assisted and unassisted withdrawal were assessed by a three-way analysis of variance with repeated measures. Comparisons were made between the measures for nine of the 10 days preceding each withdrawal to nine of the 10 days following the initiation of withdrawal.

In general, VR response rate was higher (F=5.09, p<.02) during LSD assisted withdrawal conditions. Analysis of covariance indicated that the effect was primarily due to the differences between the two methadone maintenance comparisons rather than withdrawal condition (F=.15, p>.10).

Response rate in DRL was reduced (F=13.68, p<.001) in both withdrawal conditions. Fig. 1 shows the average number of responses and the associated standard errors for each condition. Responses were reduced by 22% in the unassisted condition and 35% after LSD. Although, these differences are not significant they are in the appropriate direction.

A significant increase in the number of reinforcements obtained in DRL was also found during withdrawal (F=44.3, p<.001). In addition a significant interaction was found (F=13.1, p<.001) between drug-withdrawal comparisons during the assisted and unassisted conditions. Fig. 2 shows that the average number of reinforcements increased during each withdrawal compared to the methadone maintained state. Analysis of covariance demonstrated that LSD produced a significant increase in reinforcements when pre-withdrawal reinforcements were covaried (F=16.02, p<.05).

Response accuracy in DRL was assessed by comparing the number of reinforcements obtained to the number of reinforcements available (the maximum number was 36) (F=8.07, p<.05). Fig. 3 shows that accuracy increased from 38% to 55% during assisted withdrawal. Follow up of 2 Ss given 40 mcg/Kg LSD after 30 days of methadone abstinence showed no facilitation of DRL performance.

Pupillary size ratings are presented in Fig. 4. During the last two weeks of methadone maintenance, the median rating was 3 compared to the expected value for normal Ss of 2. During unassisted withdrawal miosis was observed in response to direct light for up to 5 days before pupillary response returned to normal. Miosis was observed only on day one following LSD administration. LSD assisted withdrawal produced more occurrences of normal pupillary response than unassisted withdrawal. Activity ratings were not significantly altered during these comparison periods.

Discussion

The acute effects of methadone resulted in increased response rates on both schedules with resultant decrease of reinforcement on DRL. These effects returned towards pre-drug levels with continued administration of the same dosage. The largest dose required the longest period for the rate increases to stabilize near pre-drug levels. Dilation of the pupil did not completely return to normal during the maintenance period.

Withdrawal from methadone produced a slight rate increase in VR but decreased rate in DRL while increasing the accuracy of response. LSD assisted withdrawal augmented these effects. Return to normal pupillary size was also facilitated by LSD.

Hine et al. also (8) found that Δ^{-9}THC administration blocked many of the behavioral symptoms of naloxone precipitated morphine abstinence in rats. These data suggest that substances with psychoactive properties such as LSD and Δ^{-9}THC, may have psychotherapeutic efficacy in the management of opiate withdrawal.

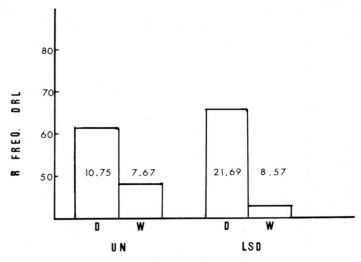

Figure 1

Average frequency of response in the DRL component of the multiple schedule. Methadone maintenance (D) compared to withdrawal (W) for the unassisted (UN) and LSD assisted (LSD) conditions. The standard error of each mean is indicated.

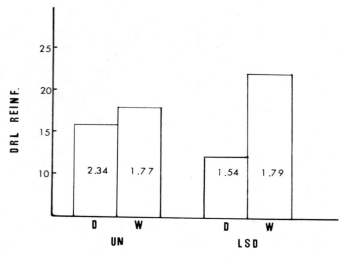

Figure 2

Average number of reinforcements obtained in the DRL component of the multiple schedule. Methadone maintenance (D) compared to withdrawal (W) for the unassisted (UN) and LSD assisted (LSD) conditions. The standard error of each mean is indicated.

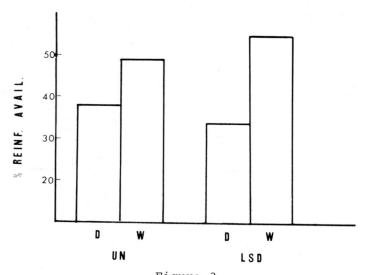

Figure 3

Percentage of available reinforcements obtained in the DRL component of the multiple schedule. Methadone maintenance (D) compared to withdrawal (W) for the unassisted (UN) and LSD assisted (LSD) conditions.

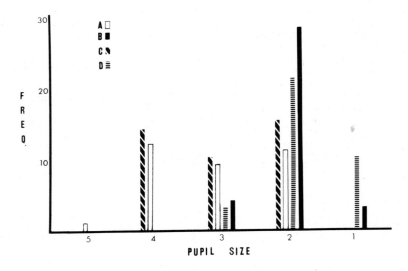

Figure 4

Frequency of pupillary size ratings during the two
methadone conditions (A & C) compared to assisted (B)
and unassisted withdrawal (D).
    Pupil size ratings given as follows: 5 - dilated,
no response to direct light; 4 - dilated, minimal
response to direct light; 3 - dilated, normal response to direct light; 2 - normal, normal response
to direct light; 1 - normal, complete miosis in
response to direct light.

References

1. O.L. McCabe, in The Drug Abuse Controversy (C. Brown & C. Savage, eds.), National Educational Consultants, Inc., Baltimore, 1971.
2. Stimmel, Robin & Engel, Prognosis of patients detoxified from methadone maintenance, a follow-up study. 5th National Methadone Maintenance Conference, Washington, D.C., 1973.
3. W. Pahnke, A. Kurland, Goodwin & W. Richards, in Psychedelic Drugs (R. E. Hicks & P. F. Fink, eds.), Grune & Stratton, Inc., New York, 1969
4. R. Tansill, Personal Communication, 1975.
5. C. Savage, O.L. McCabe, in The Drug Abuse Controversy, (C. Brown & C. Savage, eds.), National Educational Consultants, Inc., Baltimore, 1973.
6. G. Labreque & E.F. Domino, J. of Pharm. & Exp. Ther., 1974, 191, No. 1., pp. 189-200.
7. G.K. Aghajanian, & O.H.L. Bing, Clin. Pharm. & Ther., 1974, 5, 611.
8. B. Hine, E. Friedman, M. Torrelio & S. Gershon, Sci., 1975, 187, pp. 443-445.

SUDDEN TOXICITY TO METHADONE IN MONKEYS*

Edward W. Snyder
Robert E. Dustman
Richard Straight
Anthony Wayne
Edward C. Beck

Veterans Administration Hospital
Salt Lake City, Utah 84113

Despite extensive research into the nature and mechanisms of tolerance to narcotic analgesics (1) the phenomenon of sudden toxicity to a previously tolerated maintenance dose has received only passing attention (2). Such a toxic reaction, often fatal and usually occurring during periods of maximal drug administration, has been observed in dogs and monkeys (3). A recent study reports one such reaction to a high maintenance dose of methadone in an aged, ill and injured monkey who eventually died of hepatic necrosis (4). However, there is apparently no report of a sudden and temporary toxic reaction in a healthy animal maintained on moderate, fixed doses of a narcotic. The present study provides behavioral and electrophysiological description of such a reaction along with critical plasma levels of methadone in monkeys.

Twelve adult stump-tailed macaques (Macaca arctoides) were stereotaxically implanted with electrodes contacting dura and with depth electrodes inserted in critical subcortical areas. Animals were allowed to fully recover from surgery before baseline recordings began. Only visual evoked responses (VERs) recorded from occipital cortex with reference to frontal sinus will be reported in this paper.

During recording the monkey sat quietly with head fixed in a plastic restraining chair while 10 μsec light pulses presented approximately every two seconds were delivered by a photic stimulator aimed at the center of a reflecting hemisphere surrounding the monkey's face. EEG and stimulus pulses were amplified, and stored on electromagnetic tape for subsequent digitization and computer averaging of evoked responses.

Following baseline recording, six monkeys began sustained ingestion of methadone with six placebo-control animals undergoing the same recording and "dosing" procedure. All animals were weighed regularly for dose adjustment purposes. The drug, methadone HCl dissolved in water, was administered orally in cherry-flavored syrup at 8:00 A.M., 4:00 P.M., and 9:30 P.M. daily in an effort to keep the animals continually exposed to safe levels of the drug. Doses were chosen which had produced only slight behavioral depression in pilot research. The initial total daily dose of 3 mg/kg was increased rapidly to 15 mg/kg/day after the second week. During this time VERs were recorded frequently between 12:00 Noon and 1:30 P.M. and blood samples were drawn immediately after a recording session for radioimmunoassay of methadone content (5). Table I gives plasma levels of methadone on days when no toxicity was observed.

During the first week on 15 mg/kg/day Monkey 107 showed no striking changes in behavior or VER. Then, on the eighth day at approximately 2 hours after the A.M. dose, the monkey was very obviously depressed with shallow breathing, gross ataxia, fixed gaze and slightly dilated pupils. The means of four VERs collected over a six-day period prior to the reaction and the VER and plasma levels obtained at the time of the reaction are depicted in Figure 1. The VER showed a marked reduction in amplitude of early components and an increase in latencies. No changes were made in the dose and the monkey did not show the reaction again until 70 days later. This reaction required nalorphine HCl (.5 mg) to reverse respiratory depression; the animal recovered fully.

A second animal (No. 111) first showed the reaction on the morning of the 20th day of 15 mg/kg/day. See Figure 1 for the VER as compared to the mean of four records obtained over 10 days prior to the reaction. The amplitude of the early component (P1-N1) was markedly reduced and latency increased while the second component (P2-N2) disappeared entirely. One hour later P2-N2 had reappeared and the plasma level had dropped to 165 ng/ml. For the animal's protection the 4:30 P.M. dose was halved but subsequent doses were given in full strength with no signs of toxicity. After a total of 76 days at 15 mg/kg/day the monkey had another reaction with a plasma level of 130 ng/ml and a VER closely paralleling the dashed lines in Figure 1. The dose was not altered until four days later when Monkey 111 had another reaction. As a precaution, the dose for all animals was reduced to 12 mg/kg/day. Over the next three months Monkey 111 showed the toxic reaction three times with plasma levels of 420, 175 and 230 ng/ml, respectively. As the reaction recurred, twice requiring .5 mg of nalorphine HCl to reverse respiratory depression, the dose for all animals was gradually reduced. Despite this precaution Monkey 111's final toxic reaction progressed rapidly into respiratory arrest. Nalorphine restored breathing but the animal had suffered severe brain damage and died three days later.

A third monkey (No. 103) showed the reaction only once after many weeks of maintenance. Its plasma level of methadone was 250 ng/ml as compared to a mean level of 25 ng/ml (Table I). The animal recovered fully without nalorphine. However a fourth monkey (No. 104) required nalorphine after a toxic reaction to 5 mg/kg (administered twice daily) and the maintenance dose for all animals was further reduced to 3.5 mg/kg (twice daily). This dose has been maintained safely and without consequent intolerance for over five months.

Thus, four monkeys on sustained ingestion of methadone, at doses typically causing little depression, occasionally evidenced moderate to severe reactions. In all cases the reaction was sudden, temporary and occurred with no apparent precipitating factors such as illness, trauma or decrease in body weight. In all instances the reaction occurred within 3 hours following the morning dose of methadone.

One explanation for the reaction comes from recent work with mice (6) which demonstrated liver enzyme induction to result from methadone treatment. If enzyme induction accounts for tolerance to methadone, a toxic reaction could result from the disruption of this system which is apparently highly sensitive to, among other factors, changes in nutrition, ambient temperature, and general cleanliness of the environment (7). Slight changes in any of these variables might trigger inhibition of microsomal metabolism resulting in increased plasma levels of methadone.

While the behavioral signs of toxicity were unmistakable, a more quantitative description is provided by the VER. It is useful to divide the VER into "primary" (0-60 msec) and "secondary" (past 70 msec) components since there is general agreement that the primary components reflect activity of the classic afferent system ascending through specific thalamic areas to primary receiving cortex. The "secondary" components are apparently influenced by collaterals from the reticular activating system and nonspecific thalamocortical pathways. With this differentiation various drugs have been classified and described in terms of their probable site of action (8). The results of the present study indicate that methadone, at plasma levels which produce general depression without loss of consciousness, attenuates all components and increases their latencies quite unlike the effects of barbiturates, marijuana and alcohol at comparable doses (8,9). These results suggest that a plasma level of the drug sufficient to produce the behavioral signs of toxicity has a general depressant effect from brain stem to cortex in the conscious animal.

With one exception (Table I) the toxic reaction occurred whenever the plasma level of methadone reached or exceeded 130 ng/ml indicating a striking difference between human and monkey sensitivity to methadone. Human methadone addicts frequently show blood levels far in excess of those causing severe problems in our monkeys (10). In addition to an apparent difference between human and monkey sensitivity to available methadone, our results support evidence (4) that the ratio of methadone plasma level to oral dose is much lower in monkeys than man. Apparently the drug is absorbed more readily from the gastrointestinal tract of humans.

Despite possible species differences, any indication of sudden toxicity, especially given its potential lethality, has obvious implications for methadone maintenance programs. There are, however, no reports that such a reaction is responsible for methadone related deaths in humans. Such deaths are variously attributed to an acute overdose, the synergistic action of multiple drugs, causes secondary to drug use such as impaired liver function due to hepatitis, or loss of tolerance following abstinence and subsequent acute overdose (11). If sudden toxicity to a previously tolerated maintenance dose was a contributing factor in these deaths it would almost certainly remain obscure and confounded by a complex and often incomplete medical history.

*Supported by Veterans Administration Project 0864-03 and NIMH Grant 5-T01-DA00388. We thank Mr. Don Shearer and Mr. Paul Sine and the employees of the Animal Research Facility for their expert technical assistance.

Table I

Plasma Levels (ng/ml) of Methadone over the Period of Sustained

Drug Ingestion on Days when no Toxic Reaction was Seen

Monkey	111	103	107	108	113	102
Plasma Level						
Mean	44	25	44	27	29	25
Range	0-105	0-85	0-100	0-140[a]	0-123	0-120
No. of Samples	41	33	14	28	17	11

[a]140 ng/ml was the highest plasma level obtained in the absence of a toxic reaction. Animals 113 and 102 never evidenced toxicity.

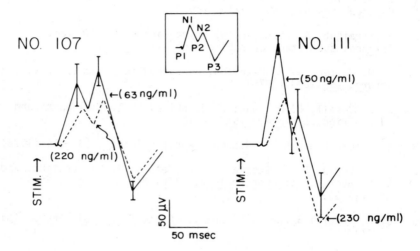

Fig. 1. VERs under various blood levels for the two animals exhibiting the toxic reaction (dashed lines). Solid lines indicate mean pre-toxic values with vertical lines indicating (±) two standard deviations from amplitude means. With the exception of P3, latencies during the toxic reaction were more than two SDs from latencies at the lower blood levels.

REFERENCES

1. D. H. Clouet and K. Iwatsubo, Annu. Rev. Pharmacol., 15: 49 (1975).

2. C. C. Hug, in Chemical and Biological Aspects of Drug Dependence (S. J. Mulé and H. Brill, eds.), CRC Publ. Co., Cleveland, Ohio, 1972, p. 316.

3. M. H. Seevers and L. A. Woods, Am. J. Med., 14: 546-557 (1953).

4. T. J. Crowley, M. Hydinger, A. J. Stynes, and A. Feiger, Psychopharmacologia, 43: 135 (1975).

5. R. Straight, A. Wayne, E. W. Snyder and R. E. Dustman, Science, submitted for publication.

6. L. W. Masten, G. R. Peterson, A. Burkhalter, and E. L. Way, Nature, 253: 200 (1975).

7. E. S. Vesell, C. N. Lang, W. J. White, G. T. Passananti and S. L. Tripp, Science, 179: 896 (1973).

8. D. L. Clark and B. S. Rosner. Anesthesiology, 38: 564 (1973).

9. E. G. Lewis, R. E. Dustman, B. A. Peters, R. C. Straight, and E. C. Beck, Electroencephalogr. clin. Neurophysiol., 35: 347 (1973).

10. C. E. Inturrisi and K. Verebely. Clin. Pharmacol. Ther., 13: 633 (1972).

11. J. Chabalko, J. C. Rosa, and R. L. Dupont, Int. J. Addict. 8: 897 (1973).

NEUROCHEMICAL EFFECTS OF METHADONE IN NEWBORN RATS

Theodore A. Slotkin, Christopher Lau,
María Bartolomé and Frederic Seidler

Department of Physiology and Pharmacology
Duke University Medical Center
Durham, North Carolina 27710

Studies in man suggest that newborn babies of opiate-addicted mothers experience disturbances in development and function of the central nervous system as well as retardation of general growth; in animals, perinatal narcotic exposure is associated with disturbances in development at the biochemical level [1-9]. Recent studies from our and other laboratories have examined the role of the polyamines in normal and drug-altered development [8-10]; polyamine levels in each organ parallel the period of most rapid cellular growth and replication, and numerous studies have shown that they are intimately involved in both protein and nucleic acid synthesis [11, 12]. The initial, and probably rate-limiting step in polyamine synthesis, is the conversion of ornithine to the diamine putrescine, catalyzed by ornithine decarboxylase (ODC) [13, 14] (Fig. 1). Subsequent steps involve the transfer of a propylamine group from decarboxylated S-adenosylmethionine to form the polyamines, spermidine and spermine. We have been interested in the role of ODC activity in regulating polyamine levels and the possible effects of opiates on this rate-limiting enzyme. ODC exhibits high activity in many tissues displaying rapid rates of growth, and levels of polyamines appear to correlate well with ODC [15-18]. Because this enzyme has one of the shortest turnover times of any mammalian protein, relatively large changes in activity can be evoked by growth stimuli [10, 19, 20].

In the central nervous system, the highest ODC levels are seen during prenatal and early postnatal life [9, 10]. At these times, the maturational pattern of ODC appears to be particularly sensitive to hormonal or drug influences, and a number of studies have shown that ODC may represent an early index of disturbed development [8-10]. In the present study, the effects of methadone on the developmental pattern of brain ODC and on brain weight have been examined in rats. One problem faced by any investigation of drugs and development is that of separation of direct effects of drugs on the fetus or neonate from those due primarily to drug effects on maternal metabolism or behavior; to dissociate drug effects on the mother from those on the offspring, we have contrasted maternal drug administration with methadone administered directly to the pup, and in addition, the effects of different periods of drug exposure and of neonatal withdrawal have been determined.

Pregnant rats were given 2.5 mg/kg of methadone subcutaneously on the tenth day of gestation, 3.5 mg/kg on the following day and 5 mg/kg daily thereafter continued through weaning. In studies with direct administration, pups were given the same doses beginning either at birth or at 10 days of postnatal age, and continued until young adulthood.

Direct chronic administration of methadone to pups beginning either at birth or at 10 days of age resulted in deficits of 10-15% in brain weight throughout the course of drug administration (Fig. 2). Pups born to controls but reared by mothers receiving methadone (postnatal group) displayed normal brain weights through 6 days of age, after which time the deficits resembled those obtained with direct administration of methadone; despite cessation of exposure at weaning (22 days), these rats still showed a deficit at 37 days of age, indicating a persistent growth retardation even two weeks after stopping methadone. In the group born to and reared by methadone-treated rats (prenatal + postnatal), brain weights were low throughout development (p<0.001 by paired t-test). However, in the group exposed to methadone only prenatally, there was a smaller change in brain weight (0-7%, p<0.01 by paired t-test).

To evaluate the biochemical correlates of these alterations in growth of the brain, ODC activity was determined (Fig. 3). At 0-2 days of postnatal age, brain ODC in control rats was greater than 2 units per gram, but declined markedly at subsequent ages and was undetectable after 17 days of age. Direct chronic administration of methadone to pups beginning at birth or at 10 days of age resulted in delays in the developmental decreases in ODC activity. In pups exposed to methadone by maternal administration, the greatest prolongation of high brain ODC was obtained with the prenatal + postnatal group. A smaller effect of shorter duration was seen with postnatal exposure only, and no delay in the developmental decline of brain ODC was seen with the prenatal group.

What do these biochemical changes mean in terms of brain development? First, continual (prenatal + postnatal) maternal methadone administration produces a "delay pattern" of brain ODC development associated with the deficit in growth of the brain in the offspring. This is a "delay pattern" because the prolongation of the period of high ODC activity indicates that the period of most rapid development is occurring later than it is supposed to. Since rats exposed to methadone prenatally + postnatally undergo withdrawal at weaning, it is of considerable importance that deficits in brain weight persist into young adulthood, indicating that the developmental lag in the central nervous system continues even after termination of drug exposure, and beyond the purely biochemical events typified by ODC.

However, it is not clear from maternal studies alone whether the effects of methadone exposure on ODC and growth reflect alterations in maternal metabolism or behavior, or whether the actions do indeed result from drug effects in the pups. These possibilities are evaluated in the studies in which pups received methadone directly. In neonates receiving direct drug administration, the effects on brain ODC and brain weight were qualitatively similar to those in pups exposed prenatally + postnatally or postnatally alone by maternal administration (that is, a delay pattern of ODC and low brain weights), suggesting that a direct action on the developing animal may be responsible for these effects of methadone. The quantitatively greater effect with direct administration might reflect the different dosage reaching the pups due to maternal drug metabolism, or to the different route of drug intake (parenteral vs. orally from milk) or the different time course of each exposure (single injection once a day vs. continually with feeding).

Since the delay in fall-off of brain ODC apparently could be produced by purely postnatal direct or maternal drug exposure, it was important to examine whether there is any role for the prenatal period of exposure. While brain ODC was within statistically normal limits in pups born to methadone-treated mothers but reared by control mothers (prenatal group), there was a consistent trend (p<0.01) toward subnormal brain weights from 10 to 40 days of age (Fig. 2), suggesting potential effects of prenatal exposure on postnatal development even after withdrawal at birth. Additionally, the prenatal period of drug exposure appeared to sensitize the pups to subsequent methadone treatment, since those exposed prenatally + postnatally showed a delay pattern of larger magnitude and longer duration than those exposed only postnatally (Fig. 3). These results indicate that although purely postnatal exposure to methadone does produce a more dramatic effect on brain development than does purely prenatal exposure, the presence of drug during the prenatal period plays an important role in the subsequent actions of methadone on development.

In conclusion, these data demonstrate that fetal or neonatal exposure to methadone delays the development of the brain as typified both by organ weight and by the pattern of ODC activity. Both the prenatal and postnatal periods of exposure play a role in the effects, and also the delays in organ growth can persist far beyond the termination of drug exposure. Most of the effects appear to be related to direct actions on the fetus or neonate, but additional actions on maternal metabolism or behavior may play ancillary roles.

Acknowledgements. Supported by USPHS DA-00465; Dr. Slotkin is recipient of Research Scientist Development Award K01-DA-00006 from the National Institute on Drug Abuse.

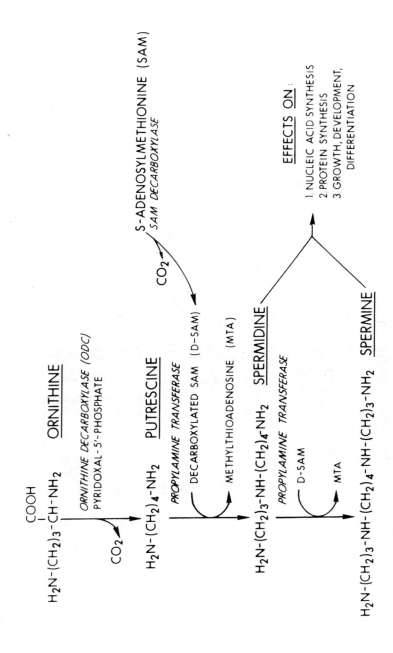

Fig. 1: Biosynthetic pathway of the polyamines.

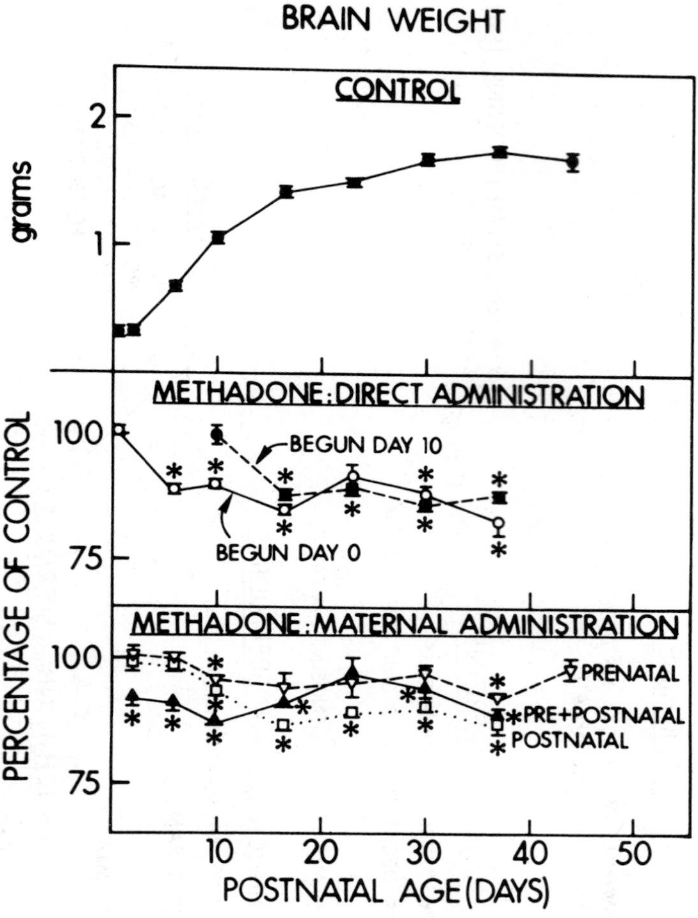

Fig. 2: Brain weights of developing rats treated daily with methadone either by direct administration begun at 0 or 10 days of age, or by administration to the mother begun at 10 days of gestation. Points and bars represent means ± standard errors of six to eighteen determinations; asterisks denote significant differences (p<0.05 or better) vs. controls.

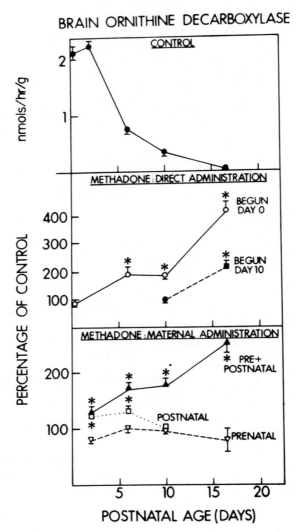

BRAIN ORNITHINE DECARBOXYLASE

Fig. 3: Brain ornithine decarboxylase activities in rats treated daily with methadone either by direct administration begun at 0 or 10 days of age, or by administration to the mother begun at 10 days of gestation. Points and bars represent means ± standard errors of six to eighteen determinations; asterisks denote significant differences (p<0.05 or better) vs. controls.

REFERENCES

1. H.S. Harpel and R.F. Gautier, J. Pharm. Sci., 57: 1590 (1968).
2. J.D. Iuliucci and R.F. Gautier, J. Pharm. Sci., 60: 420 (1971).
3. C. Zelson, S.J. Lee and M. Casalino, N. Eng. J. Med., 289: 1216 (1973).
4. C. Zelson, E. Rubio and E. Wasserman, Pediatrics, 48: 178 (1971).
5. A.M. Reddy, R.G. Harper and G. Stern, Pediatrics, 48: 353 (1971).
6. G.S. Wilson, M.M. Desmond and W.M. Verniaud, Am. J. Dis. Child., 126: 457 (1973).
7. G. Friedler and J. Cochin, Science, 175: 654 (1973).
8. S.R. Butler and S.M. Schanberg, Biochem. Pharmacol., 24: 1915 (1975).
9. T.A. Slotkin, C. Lau and M. Bartolomé, J. Pharmacol. Exp. Therap., in press.
10. T.R. Anderson and S.M. Schanberg, Biochem. Pharmacol., 24: 495 (1975).
11. L.A. Pearce and S.M. Schanberg, Science, 166: 1301 (1969).
12. A. Raina and J. Jänne, Med. Biol., 53: 121 (1975).
13. A.E. Pegg and H.G. Williams-Ashman, Biochem. J., 108: 533 (1968).
14. D.H. Russell and S.H. Snyder, Proc. Natl. Acad. Sci., 60: 1420 (1968).
15. T.R. Anderson and S.M. Schanberg, J. Neurochem., 19: 1471 (1972).
16. C.M. Caldarera, M.S. Moruzzi, C. Rossoni and B. Barbiroli, J. Neurochem., 16: 309 (1969).
17. D.H. Russell, S.H. Snyder and V.J. Medina, Life Sci., 8: 1247 (1969).
18. E.J. Herbst and A. Dion, Fed. Proc., 29: 1563 (1970).
19. D.H. Russell and S.H. Snyder, Endocrinology, 84: 223 (1969).
20. C.V. Byus and D.H. Russell, Life Sci., 15: 1991 (1974).

RELATIONSHIP BETWEEN PROTRACTED PHYSICAL SIGNS AND RELAPSE IN POST-ADDICT RATS

Arthur S. Schwartz and Patricia L. Marchok

Barrow Neurological Institute of St. Joseph's Hospital and Medical Center, Phoenix, Arizona

The phenomenon of relapse to narcotic administration after a period of abstinence remains one of the most important problems in treatment of addiction, yet there has been little systematic study of its etiology.

Current thinking concerning the sources of motivation for relapse may be divided into four categories: 1. "Euphoric" or positive reinforcement effects learned during the addiction phase (1,2); 2. Negative reinforcement due to escape from abstinence, also learned during the addiction phase (3,4); 3. Long-lasting physiological and behavioral changes induced by previous narcotic administration (5,6); 4. Hyper-responsivity to stress in association with the above long-lasting changes (7,8).

Most authors agree that more than one of the above factors may influence the tendency to relapse, but they differ in their attribution of primacy. Thus, the long-lasting biological and behavioral changes are considered by Dole (6) to generate a narcotic craving which leads to relapse, while these changes are considered only adjunctive to narcotic-reinforced, conditioned responses by Wikler (9,10) and by Goldberg (11).

It has been reported by others that, several weeks after complete abstinence, we may find: 1. reactions resembling withdrawal symptoms after nalorphine injections in monkeys (12); 2. tolerance to the analgesic effects of morphine in rats (13); 3. adrenal gland hypertrophy in rats (14); 4. increased metabolic rates and body temperature in rats (15); and 5. increased aggression, also in rats (16). Most importantly, some of these changes and others have subsequently been reported in human addicts as well (17).

Because a demonstration of an association between these long-term phenomena and relapse would have far reaching implications for treatment and theory, we examined this possible relationship in the rat. Our results lead us to conclude that the reinforcement effects of morphine, as experienced during the initial conditioning phase, are more important factors in relapse than protracted biological changes.

METHOD

Male albino rats were conditioned to acquire a preference for a formerly non-preferred goal box in a Y-maze, by associating the effects of morphine with running to and remaining in the respective goal box. Details of the procedure are described elsewhere (3,18). Different groups of at least 11 animals each were first injected with noncontingent saline or increasing doses of morphine for several days, and then reinforced in the Y-maze with either saline or 1, 5, 20, 60, 100 or 200 mg/kg morphine intraperitoneally. Acquisition of a preference for the morphine-reinforced box was tested by 16 free-choice trials at the end of a 2-week training period, after which the rats were withdrawn from opiates and laid aside for 3 weeks. The abstinent rats were then returned to the Y-mazes for 16 additional preference (i.e., relapse) tests during which no drugs were administered.

Following the relapse tests the animals were examined for signs of long-lasting biological and behavioral changes that had been reported by others. First they were administered 10 mg/kg naloxone, i.p.; body weight and temperature changes, as well as withdrawal signs such as "wet-dog" shakes, chattering, abnormal posturing and diarrhea were scored. Two days later the post-addict rats were examined for long-term tolerance by comparing the analgesic effect of 15 mg/kg morphine with that in the saline control group, using the hot plate latency technique. Two days later they were observed for aggressive responses (16).

Two further groups of rats, trained with saline or with 20 mg/kg morphine exactly like the above groups, were sacrificed 24 hr after relapse testing for measurement of adrenal weights and radioimmunoassay determina-

tion of blood plasma levels of thyroxin and corticosterone.

RESULTS AND DISCUSSION

Acquisition and relapse performance as a function
of training dose is shown in Fig. 1. All the morphine
doses proved to be effective reinforcers as shown by
significant acquisition of morphine-box preferences by
each drug-treated group. Acquisition was positively
dose-related as indicated by a correlation coefficient
of .47 between these two variables ($\underline{P} < .001$).

The incidence of relapse was also directly related
to previous training dose, but only up to 60 mg/kg.
Relapse dropped after the very high doses, which also
produced catalepsy during the training sessions, suggesting incomplete tolerance to morphine's depressing
effects at these doses. It is also possible that the
higher doses interfered with long-term memory (19).

None of the signs usually associated with acute,
precipitated abstinence were significantly or consistently increased in our post-addict rats by naloxone as
compared to its effect in the saline control group.
Some significant aggression was observed in the post-
addicts, but it bore no relationship to previous training dose or to relapse. Further, there was no evidence
of a protracted increase in metabolic rate as reflected
by thyroxin levels, or of increased endocrine activity
as reflected by adrenal weights and corticosterone
levels, in the 20 mg group, despite the fact that these
rats showed clear relapse (Table I).

The only long-term biological consequence of addiction which was significantly related to previous
dose was tolerance to morphine's analgesic effects
(Fig. 1). However, even the tolerance (hot-plate
latency) scores were not predictive of relapse since
a) the 5 mg group was not tolerant but relapsed significantly; b) the high dose groups showed significant
tolerance but hardly relapsed (possibly for the reasons
mentioned above); and c) there was no significant correlation between individual relapse scores and hot-plate
latencies. In summary, we found no evidence to support
the hypothesis that relapse is associated with any of
the protracted signs we measured.

On the other hand, again considering only those
groups which relapsed, a significant correlation was
observed between acquisition and relapse scores for

each individual rat (r = .28; P <.05). This suggests
that the tendency to relapse depended on those factors
which were operating during the chronic addiction stage
and which were responsible for the acquisition of
narcotic-reinforced conditioned behavior. Although
generalizations from the rat to man are hazardous, it
is worth considering that theories of relapse in man
based on long-term biological changes run counter to the
present results.

Table I. Comparison of behavioral and endocrine effects
          in rats trained on saline and 20 mg/kg.

	Saline N = 13	20 mg N = 12	P<:
Morphine Box Choices (%):			
Acquisition	46	78	.001
Relapse	48	67	.01
Adrenal wts (mg)	47.3 ± 2.8	47.5 ± 2.5	.50
Thyroxin (µg/100 ml)	4.6 ± 0.3	4.7 ± 0.4	.50
Corticosterone (µg/100 ml)	26.4 ± 2.9	20.4 ± 3.0	.10

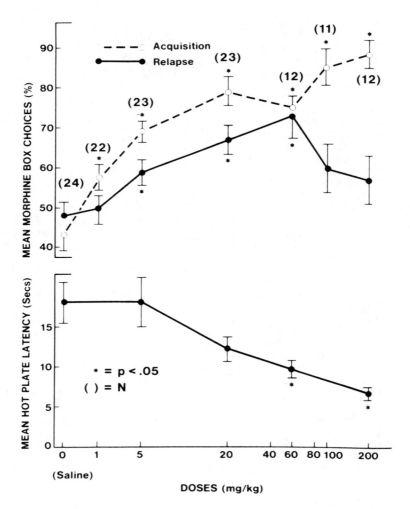

Fig. 1. Acquisition, relapse (top), and hotplate latency scores (bottom), as a function of training dose of morphine. Acquisition and relapse scores have been converted to mean percent trials of total free-choice trials in which each group selected the morphine-reinforced goal box. Vertical bars = ± SE. Significances derived by comparison with saline control group.

REFERENCES

1. N. Bejerot, *Amer. J. Psychiat.*, 128: 842 (1972).
2. W. E. McAuliffe and R. A. Gordon, *Amer. J. Soc.*, 79: 795 (1974).
3. H. D. Beach, *Canad. J. Psychol.*, 11: 104 (1957).
4. A. R. Lindesmith, *Addiction and Opiates*, Aldine, Chicago, 1968.
5. A. Wikler, in *Narcotics* (D. M. Wilner and C. G. Kassebaum, eds.), McGraw-Hill, New York, 1965, p. 85.
6. V. P. Dole, *New Engl. J. Med.*, 286: 988 (1972).
7. W. R. Martin, in *Drug Abuse: Proc. Int'l. Conf.* (C. J. D. Zarafonetis, ed.), Lea and Febiger, Philadelphia, 1972, p. 153.
8. W. R. Martin, C. G. Eades, W. O. Thompson, J. A. Thompson, and H. G. Flanary, *J. Pharmacol. exp. Therap.*, 189: 759 (1974).
9. A. Wikler, *Behav. Sci.*, 16: 92 (1971).
10. A. Wikler, *Arch. gen. Psychiat.*, 28: 611 (1973).
11. S. R. Goldberg, in *Drug Dependence* (R. T. Harris, W. M. McIsaac, and C. R. Schuster, eds.), Univ. Texas Press, Austin, 1970, p. 170.
12. S. R. Goldberg and C. R. Schuster, *Science*, 166: 1548 (1969).
13. J. Cochin and C. Kornetsky, *J. Pharmacol. exp. Therap.*, 145: 1 (1964).
14. J. W. Sloan and A. J. Eisenman, in The Addictive States (A. Wikler, ed.), Williams and Wilkins, Baltimore, 1968, p. 96.
15. W. R. Martin, A. Wikler, C. G. Eades, and F. T. Pescor, *Psychopharmacologia*, 4: 247 (1963).
16. G. Gianutsos, M. D. Hynes, S. K. Puri, R. B. Drawbaugh, and H. Lal, *Psychopharmacologia*, 34: 37 (1974).
17. W. R. Martin and D. R. Jasinski, *J. Psychiat. Res.*, 7: 9 (1969).
18. A. S. Schwartz and P. L. Marchok, *Nature*, 248: 257 (1974).
19. C. Castellano, *Psychopharmacologia*, 42: 235 (1975).

NALTREXONE PHARMACOKINETICS: EVALUATION OF A SUSTAINED NALTREXONE DELIVERY SYSTEM

R. H. Reuning, L. Malspeis, A. E. Staubus,
M. S. Bathala and T. M. Ludden

College of Pharmacy, The Ohio State University, Columbus, Ohio

I. INTRODUCTION AND EXPERIMENTAL

The purpose of this report is to illustrate the scientific and experimental aspects of applying a pharmacokinetic analysis of plasma drug level-time data to the determination of release rates of naltrexone from a sustained-release delivery system. In reviewing this work it is possible to cover only selected studies. Experimental details and the compilation of pharmacokinetic data on naltrexone will be left to other publications. The electron-capture gas chromatographic (GLC/EC) assay for naltrexone has been described (1-3). Single iv dose and constant-rate iv naltrexone infusion experiments in monkey were carried out. Naltrexone plasma level-time data were analyzed by nonlinear least-squares regression (4) to determine kinetic parameters for naltrexone.

The sustained-release naltrexone delivery system consisted of $33^{c/}$ naltrexone in rods of dipalmitin (25%)-tripalmitin($75^{c/}$) and was provided by Battelle Memorial Institute (note Acknowledgements). The rods were implanted subcutaneously in the monkey and plasma samples withdrawn periodically thereafter for 6 weeks and then assayed for naltrexone. At the end of 6 weeks the rods were removed surgically and assayed for naltrexone. Subsequently, an iv bolus dose of naltrexone was administered, multiple plasma samples obtained and assayed, and the clearance of naltrexone determined.

II. RESULTS AND DISCUSSION

A. Analytical Methods and Metabolism

The cornerstone for application of a pharmacokinetic analysis of plasma drug levels is an analytical technique that is both specific for unchanged drug and sufficiently sensitive. Since metabolites of a drug are notorious for interfering with many assay procedures, a complete knowledge of metabolic pathways and how metabolites influence the assay is essential in order to establish specificity.

A typical chromatogram obtained in the GLC/EC assay for naltrexone in monkey plasma is illustrated in Fig. 1. Naloxone is the internal standard. The sharp peaks are typical of chromatograms obtained with either 3% OV-1 or 3% OV-17 column packing (Applied Science Laboratories). Blank plasma assayed by the same procedure yielded chromatograms free of interference at the retention times for naloxone and naltrexone. This leaves naltrexone metabolites in plasma as potential compounds that could interfere with an accurate assay for plasma naltrexone. Several research groups have established that α-naltrexol, β-naltrexol and their conjugates as well as conjugates of naltrexone are the main metabolites of naltrexone in several species (2,5-7). Since conjugates are generally not extracted by nonpolar solvents such as the benzene used in this assay, the main metabolites that could interfere with the naltrexone assay are α- and β-naltrexol. The retention times of the derivatives of naltrexone, α-naltrexol, β-naltrexol and naloxone under several different GLC/EC conditions are listed in Table I. It is evident that the heptafluorobutyrate (HFB) derivatives of naltrexone and its metabolic reduction products are not separated using a 3% OV-1 column. However, the 3% OV-17 column does separate the derivatives of naltrexone from the corresponding derivatives for α- and β-naltrexol (Table I). The pentafluoropropionate (PFP) derivatives appear to yield the greatest separation between the α-naltrexol and β-naltrexol derivatives, with the best separation obtained on the 8' 3% OV-17 column. Thus, while one would be misled by assay interference from metabolites if an OV-1 column were used, the evidence indicates that a benzene extraction procedure together with the use of an OV-17 column yields an assay that is specific for unchanged naltrexone.

B. Pharmacokinetics and Sustained Release Evaluation

The plasma level-time profile for naltrexone after i.v. bolus administration in the monkey is illustrated in Fig. 2. The bi-exponential non-linear least squares fit to the data (solid curve) for this 4 kg monkey yielded an estimated half-life ($t_{\frac{1}{2}}$) of 241 min and a clearance of 60.5 ml/min/kg. Similar results have been obtained in other monkeys. However, one still is not sure of the applicability of this quantitative description until it has been demonstrated that the pharmacokinetic parameters do not change with dose. One rigorous way to test for dose-dependent clearance is to infuse the drug iv to steady-state at several different constant infusion rates so that the range of steady-state levels encompasses the levels expected in the application of the pharmacokinetic parameters. This approach has been utilized for naltrexone in the monkey and the infusion rate was directly proportional to steady-state plasma naltrexone concentration over a range of about 6 to 80 ng/ml. It thus appears that the clearance of naltrexone is independent of dose in the concentration range studied.

The procedure utilized in this study for evaluation of the sustained-release delivery system consists of (a) measurement of naltrexone clearance following a bolus iv injection and (b) measurement of plasma drug levels at periodic intervals after subcutaneous administration of the naltrexone delivery system. This method does not require measurement of drug levels in urine or feces. The single dose "calibration" of naltrexone clearance in the experimental monkey was accomplished from the data in Fig. 2. Plasma naltrexone levels obtained in the same monkey subsequent to administration of the sustained-release naltrexone delivery system are illustrated in Fig. 3. Multiplication of each plasma level by the monkey's clearance yielded estimates of apparent release rates of naltrexone from the sustained-release delivery system over the entire six weeks of the experiment (Fig. 4). Naltrexone release from this delivery system is initially more rapid and then declines in approximately a biexponential manner ($t\frac{1}{2}$ of 1.4 and 12.3 days for initial and terminal phases, respectively).

In order to validate the calculated release rates of naltrexone, a mass balance comparison was made. This served as a final check on the pharmacokinetic technique employed, the experimental accuracy, and the assumption that the monkey's clearance remained constant. The calculated naltrexone released (16.5 mg), as estimated by the area under the apparent release rate-time curve (integration of the curve in Fig. 4 from 0-42 days by the trapezoidal rule), was added to the naltrexone found in the delivery system upon removal from the monkey after 42 days (14.5 mg), and this sum was compared to the dose administered (33.5 mg). The data indicate that 92% of the dose was accounted for. This excellent mass balance confirms the naltrexone release rates (Fig. 4) estimated from the results in Figs. 2 and 3.

This report shows that a pharmacokinetic evaluation of naltrexone release rates from a sustained-release delivery system can be achieved from an analysis of plasma naltrexone levels only, provided that the assay is specific for unchanged naltrexone and is sufficiently sensitive, and provided that an appropriate experimental design and pharmacokinetic analysis is utilized.

III. ACKNOWLEDGEMENTS

The authors are indebted to Drs. D. R. Kalkwarf and M. F. Sullivan, Battelle Memorial Institute-Pacific Northwest Laboratories for providing the naltrexone delivery system, and to Mr. S. Harrigan and Mr. J. Wiley, Parke-Davis and Co., Ann Arbor, for carrying out the experiments in monkeys and Mr. B. Morrison for work on the assays. Supported by contract HSM-42-73-182 from NIDA.

Table I - Retention Times of the Derivatives of Naltrexone,
Potential Metabolites and Naloxone under Various Conditions[a]

Compound	3% OV-1 6 ft. column	3% OV-17 6 ft. column		8 ft. column
	HFB	HFB	PFP	PFP
Naltrexone	4.8	6.1	6.0	10.0
α-Naltrexol	4.7	5.5	5.7	9.4
β-Naltrexol	4.7	5.3	5.1	8.7
Naloxone	3.1	3.8	3.6	6.1

a
Values in the table are the GLC/EC retention times in minutes.

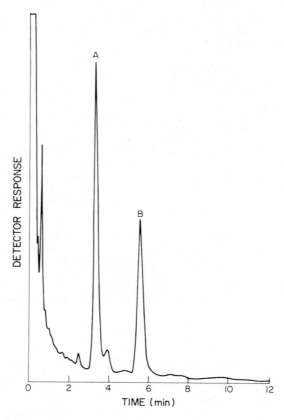

Fig. 1 - Chromatogram of extracted and derivatized monkey plasma to
which naltrexone (50 mg) and naloxone (60 ng) had been added. Key:
A, naloxone pentafluoropropionate; B, naltrexone pentafluoropropionate. The 6 ft. column was packed with 3% OV-17 on gas chrom Q.

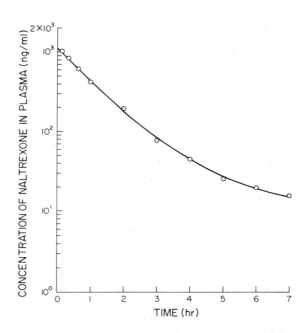

Fig. 2 - Plasma naltrexone concentration-time curve for intravenous naltrexone, 5 mg/kg bolus, in monkey 6728. Open circles are experimental data and the curve is a nonlinear least-squares fit.

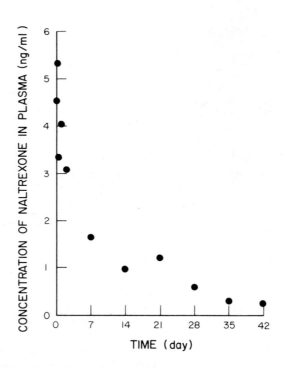

Fig. 3 - Plasma naltrexone concentration obtained during the six week period subsequent to administration of naltrexone, 8.38 mg/kg, in a sustained release delivery system to monkey 6728. Times of the first 5 data points are 3, 6, 12, 24 and 48 hr.

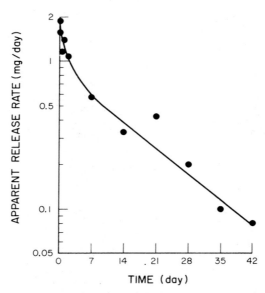

Fig. 4 - Semilogarithmic plot of the apparent release rate of naltrexone as a function of time after administration of naltrexone,
8.38 mg/kg, in a sustained release delivery system to monkey 6728.

REFERENCES

1. V. K. Batra, R. A. Sams, R. H. Reuning and L. Malspeis, Acad.
    Pharm. Sci. 4, 122 (1974).
2. L. Malspeis, M. S. Bathala, T. M. Ludden, et al., Res. Comm.
    Chem. Pathol. Pharmacol. 12, 43 (1975).
3. R. A. Sams and L. Malspeis, J. Chromatog., in press.
4. C. M. Metzler, NONLIN, Upjohn Co., Kalamazoo, Mich. (1969).
5. E. J. Cone, C. W. Gorodetzky, and S. Y. Yeh, Drug Metab. Dispos.
    2, 506 (1974).
6. ibid., J. Pharm. Sci. 64, 618 (1975).
7. N. Chatterjie, J. M. Fujimoto, C. E. Inturrisi, et al., Drug
    Metab. Dispos. 2, 401 (1974).

FECAL EXCRETION OF METHADONE AND ITS METABOLITES: A MAJOR
PATHWAY OF ELIMINATION IN MAN

M.J. Kreek, C.L. Gutjahr, D.V. Bowen and F.H. Field

The Rockefeller University
New York, New York

After oral ingestion methadone is readily absorbed and then
is rapidly and widely distributed in the body (1). Because of
this wide distribution into nonspecific reservoir sites, less than
three percent of a dose of methadone is in the total plasma volume
at time of peak plasma concentrations, which occur at two to four
hours after an oral dose, but also, plasma concentrations of methadone sufficient to prevent the onset of abstinence sysmptoms are
maintained for at least twenty-four to thirty-six hours after an
oral dose in most maintenance patients. (2, 3, 4, 5).

It has been shown in animal studies that the liver is a major
nonspecific reservoir for methadone. (6) It has also been shown,
using the isolated perfused rabbit liver preparation, that over
eighty-five percent of a single pulse dose of methadone, over a
wide concentration range, is extracted by the liver during a single pass, a phenomenon that may be of especial importance when the
drug is administered orally. (7) Methadone is also metabolized
primarily by the liver. (8)

Several pathways of methadone metabolism in man have been e-
lucidated by analyses of urine specimens from patients in maintenance treatment. (9) The major pathway of methadone metabolism in
man is first N-demethylation followed by rapid cyclization to form
the major pyrrolidine metabolite. Both the pyrrolidine and pyrroline metabolites may be hydroxylated.

Using techniques of gas liquid chromatography, it has been
shown by this laboratory, as well as by several other laboratories,
that methadone is excreted in urine primarily as unchanged methadone and the pyrrolidine metabolite. (5, 10) The ratio of pyrrolidine to methadone has been reported to range from 1:1 to 5:1.
However, in most studies reported, less than forty percent of the
daily dose of methadone has been accounted for as the sum of methadone and the pyrrolidine metabolite excreted in urine. (3, 4, 5,
10)

Minor pathways of methadone metabolism include hydroxylation
to form hydroxymethadone; oxidation followed by N-demethylation
and cyclization to form a pyrrolidone metabolite; and finally, reduction followed by N-demethylation to form N-demethylmethadol.(9)
This latter pathway is of interest since the methadol metabolites
are the only metabolites of methadone known to be pharmacologically active. In the studies in which all of these metabolites have
been looked for and semiquantitated, less than fifty percent of
the daily dose of methadone has been accounted for in urinary excretory products. (9) It has been also reported that methadone
may be excreted in sweat. (11) However, the total amount excreted
by this route is probably less than ten percent of the daily dose.

Our gas liquid chromatographic methods for quantitation of
methadone and its pyrrolidine metabolite in plasma and urine have
been modified for the quantitation of methadone and semiquantita-
tion of the pyrrolidine metabolite in feces. (10) These assays
are carried out using homogenates of twenty-four hour fecal collections. Methods for the qualitative analysis of methadone and
several of its metabolites also have been developed using gas chro-
matography-chemical ionization mass spectrometry. (10, 12) In
this technique, the relative retention times of methadone and its
metabolites using gas chromatography, and the masses of the pro-
tonated ions of each metabolite molecule are used to identify the
presence of each compound. Using these methods, the pyrrolidine,
pyrroline, pyrrolidone and hydroxymethadone metabolites have been
regularly observed in human feces. The hydroxylated derivatives
of pyrrolidine and pyrroline and also methadol have been tentatively identified in some specimens of human feces. (10)

Feces from ten patients on chronic methadone maintenance
treatment have been studied using both the gas chromatographic and
gas chromatography-mass spectrometric techniques described. These
patients were being maintained on methadone doses ranging from 30
to 100mg per day. The range of amounts of unchanged methadone
shown to be excreted in feces in 24 hours was from 0.10 to 4.32mg.
In all patients studied, the major excretory product in feces was
shown to be the pyrrolidine metabolite. The range of amounts of
the pyrrolidine metabolite excreted in feces in 24 hours was 0.13
to 63.3mg. The ratio of excreted pyrrolidine to unchanged methadone in the patients studied ranged from 1:1 up to 25:1. From 10
to 45 percent of the daily methadone dose was excreted in feces as
the sum of methadone plus the pyrrolidine metabolite.

The fecal excretion of methadone and the pyrrolidine metabolite was studied in one maintenance patient for seven consecutive
days. This patient was maintained on a methadone dose of 100mg
per day. A mean of 2.19mg of methadone was excreted in feces over
24 hours, and a mean of 42.06mg of pyrrolidine was excreted over
24 hours. Thus, the mean sum of methadone plus pyrrolidine excreted in feces was 44.25 per 24 hours or 44 percent of the daily

dose. However, considerable variation in excretion of both methadone and pyrrolidine was observed.

During a continuous, but separate, study period, this same
patient received a single tracer dose of radiolabeled (14) C methadone. Twenty-four hour urine and twenty-four hour fecal collections were carried out for nine days. The amounts of radioactivity
from methadone excreted in urine and in feces were determined using techniques of fecal homogenate oxidation and scintillation
counting. Over a nine day period, 50% of the administered dose of
radiolabeled methadone was execreted in urine and 41% excreted in
feces, with the sum of 91% of the administered radiolabeled methadone excreted by these two routes in nine days. Thus, both by
mass measurements and by the use of a single radiolabeled tracer
dose of methadone, it was shown that between forty-one and forty-
four percent of a single daily dose of methadone is excreted by
the fecal route in this patient.

Fecal excretion of methadone and the pyrrolidine metabolite
in two patients on methadone maintenance treatment who had severe
chronic renal disease was also studied in collaboration with Dr.
Arnold Schecter of SUNY, Downstate Medical Center. Patient #1 was
maintained on 40mg per day of methadone and was studied while undergoing acute peritoneal dialysis for treatment of acute decomp-
ensation of chronic glomerulonephritis. The patient was putting
out significant amounts of urine at the time that this study was
performed. Fecal excretion of unchanged methadone was 0.69mg per
24 hours, and of pyrrolidine metabolite 5.5mg per 24 hours. Fifteen percent of the methadone dose therefore was excreted in feces
as the sum of methadone and pyrrolidine metabolite by this route.
Very small amounts of methadone or metabolite were measured in the
peritoneal dialysates. Patient #2 was maintained on 50mg per day
of methadone, and was studied while undergoing chronic hemodialysis
for management of end-stage renal disease; this patient was anuric.
Fecal excretion of unchanged methadone was .75mg per 24 hours and
fecal excretion of the pyrrolidine metabolite 48.3mg per 24 hours.
Ninety-eight percent of the administered methadone dose was therefore accounted for in feces as the sum of methadone and its major
metabolite.

The final group of patients studied were patients on methadone maintenance who were also being treated for tuberculosis at
the Bellevue Chest Methadone Maintenance Program. These patients
were studied in collaboration with Dr. Jane Garfield of the Department of Medicine, New York University School of Medicine. Fifty-
six patients were treated with INH (with or without other antitu-
berculosis drugs). Thirty patients received rifampin in addition
to INH and other drugs. Of these, nine patients had no symptoms
when rifampin was added to their regimen. However, fourteen patients developed mild symptoms of narcotic withdrawal and seven
patients had severe symptoms of narcotic withdrawal when rifampin

was added to their regimen. Special studies were carried out in
six of the severely affected patients, both off and on rifampin
treatment, to determine the effects of rifampin treatment on methadone metabolism. (12) It was shown in all six patients that
plasma levels of methadone while on rifampin treatment were significantly reduced at each time point studied, as compared to
levels when not receiving rifampin. However, there were variable
changes in apparent terminal plasma half-life during rifampin
treatment in this study group, with decreased plasma half-lives in
two patients, no changes in three patients, and an increased plasma half-life in one patient during rifampin treatment. Urine excretion of methadone and the pyrrolidine metabolite, both off and
on rifampin, were studied in four patients in whom satisfactory
twenty-four hour urine collections could be obtained while off and
on rifampin treatment. Fecal excretion of unchanged methadone was
less than 1mg per 24 hours while off and on rifampin treatment.
However, fecal excretion of the primary excretory product, the
pyrrolidine metabolite, increased in both patients while on rifampin treatment. (See Table I). While off rifampin, 34% of methadone was excreted in urine and 13% in feces as the sum of methadone and pyrrolidine metabolite. Thus, 47% of the administered
dose could be accounted for as the sum of methadone and pyrrolidine excreted by these two routes. During rifampin treatment, total excretion of methadone and the pyrrolidine metabolite increased
to 52% of the dose excreted in urine in 24 hours and 54% in feces,
or a total of greater than 100% during this single day of study.
In the second patient, the sum of methadone and pyrrolidine metabolite execreted in urine did not increase while on rifampin treatment. However, the total amount excreted in feces increased markedly, with 96% of the daily dose excreted as the sum of methadone
and pyrrolidine metabolite in urine and feces during a 24 hour
period.

In these patients, rifampin effected a lowering of plasma
levels of methadone, accompanied by the appearance of narcotic
withdrawal symptoms. Increased urinary and fecal excretion of the
major pyrrolidine metabolite was observed suggesting that at least
one mechanism of rifampin action might be the enhancement of methadone biotransformation to the pyrrolidine metabolite during the
first pass through the liver.

In summary, fecal excretion of methadone and its metabolites is
a significant route of elimination of this drug in maintenance patients, and may become the principal route of excretion in some
states of altered physiology. The pyrrolidine metabolite of methadone is the primary compound excreted in feces. Unchanged methadone is excreted in amounts usually less than 1 to 5% of the administered dose. Using gas chromatography and mass spectrometry,
several other methadone metabolites have also been identified in
human feces.

Table I

Fecal Excretion of Methadone and Pyrrolidine Metabolite Off and
On Rifampin Treatment

Patient and Methadone Dose	Rifampin	Fecal Excretion in 24 Hours (mg)		
		Methadone	Pyrrolidine	Sum
#1 (60mg/d)	Off	.13	7.6	7.73
	On	.41	31.8	32.21
#2 (30mg/d)	Off	.63	10.2	10.83
	On	.44	26.5	26.94

References

1-V.P. Dole and M.J. Kreek, Proc. Nat. Acad. Sci., 70:10 (1973).
2-V.P. Dole, M.E. Nyswander and M.J. Kreek, Trans. Assoc. Am. Physicians, 79:122 (1966).
3-H.R. Sullivan and D.A. Blake, Res. Commun. Chem. Pathol. Pharmacol., 3:467 (1972).
4-C.E. Inturrisi and K. Verebely, J. Chromatogr., 65:361 (1972).
5-M.J. Kreek, N.Y. State J. Med., 73:2773 (1973).
6-E.H. Harte, C.L. Gutjahr and M.J. Kreek, Clin. Res., 24:623A (1976).
7-M.J. Kreek, M. Oratz and M.A. Rothschild, Gastroenterology, 75:88 (1978).
8-A. Pohland, H.E. Boaz and H.R. Sullivan, J. Med. Chem., 14:194 (1971).
9-H.R. Sullivan and S.L. Due, J. Med. Chem., 16:909 (1973).
10-M.J. Kreek, Ann. N.Y. Acad. Sci., 281:350 (1976).
11-G.L. Henderson and B.K. Wilson, Res. Commun. Chem. Pathol. Pharmacol., 5:1 (1973).
12-M.J. Kreek, J.W. Garfield, C.L. Gutjahr and L.M. Giusti., New Engl. J. Med., 294:1104 (1976).

BIOLOGICAL FATE OF 3H-LAAM IN THE RAT, DOG AND MONKEY

Gary L. Henderson

Department of Pharmacology
School of Medicine
University of California, Davis

l-a-acetylmethadol (LAAM) is under clinical investigation as a possible substitute for methadone in maintenance programs. It has been reported by Fraser and Isbell (1) to prevent narcotic withdrawal symptoms in humans for more than 72 hours, three times longer than methadone.

This paper describes the metabolism and excretion of ^{3}H-LAAM and its metabolites following oral and intravenous administration in the rat, dog and monkey.

METHODS

Radiolabeled LAAM (l-a-acetyl methadol-2-^{3}H·HCl) was administered by gastric lavage at a dose of 2 mg/kg to male and female beagle dogs and Rhesus monkeys and at doses of 5 and 10 mg/kg to Sprague-Dawley rats. ^{3}H-LAAM was administered intravenously to dogs and monkeys at a dose of 2 mg/kg and to rats at a dose of 5 mg/kg. Blood, urine and feces were collected for up to 96 hours after drug. Total radioactivity was determined by combusting an aliquot of each sample and then counting the resulting ^{3}H$_2$0. LAAM and metabolite levels were quantitated using a quantitative thin-layer chromatographic technique described previously (2).

RESULTS AND DISCUSSION

Fig 1 shows a comparison of the plasma levels of radioactive drug observed in the rat, dog and monkey following a 2 mg/kg oral dose in the dog and monkey and a 5 mg/kg oral dose in the rat. Fig. 2 shows the plasma decay curves for ^{3}H-LAAM following intravenous administration of the same doses.

Absorption of the drug from the gastrointestinal tract appears to be relatively rapid. Following oral administration, typical opiate-like effects could be seen within 30 min and peak plasma drug levels occurred approximately 2 hrs later.

A comparison of the areas under the curve for oral versus intravenous administration shows that LAAM is more efficiently absorbed in the dog than in the monkey or the rat.

Generally, the plasma decay curves appear to be biphasic. After peak plasma levels are reached, drug concentrations decrease until 12 hrs after drug. The t1/2 for this early phase is approximately 6 hrs in the three species studied. After 12 hrs, the rate of drug elimination from the plasma decreases and low (less than 100 mg/ml) but measurable drug and metabolite levels persist for up to 96 hrs. It was difficult to precisely determine the t1/2 of this terminal phase. The drug levels were at the lower limits of the analytical methods and quite variable, especially in the rat. However, the t1/2 of this terminal phase is estimated to be approximately 50 hrs.

In all of the species studied, LAAM is extensively metabolized. Five metabolites -- norLAAM (N-LAAM), dinorLAAM (DN-LAAM), methadol (MOL), normethadol (N-MOL) and N-acetylnormethadol (N-acetylNMOL) have been identified as metabolites in the urine of rat, dog and monkey, and in the plasma and bile of the rat. The specific radioactivity of the LAAM was not high enough to allow quantitation of LAAM and metabolites in the plasma of dog and monkey.

The hydrolysis produces, MOL and N-MOL, may be pharmacologically important metabolites. Both metabolites were found in significant amounts in the urine of the rat, dog and monkey and in the plasma and bile of the rat.

As can be seen from the data in Table 1, most of the administered LAAM is excreted in the feces. Only 24% of an orally administered dose was excreted in the urine of the dog and 14%, 8% and 10% of the dose was excreted in the urine by the monkey, rat and man, respectively. The fact that approximately 80% of an administered dose is excreted in the feces of all species studied suggests that biliary excretion is probably the predominant route of elimination for the parent drug and metabolites. In the rat, 80% of an administered dose was found to be excreted in bile. Enterohepatic circulation may be an important factor in determining the long duration of action of LAAM, particularly in the rat.

The dog demonstrated the greatest pharmacological response to LAAM. Following oral administration, the plasma drug levels (total radioactivity) were approximately five times higher in this species than in the rat or monkey. The dog also excreted MOL as as the major urinary metabolite while the rat and monkey excreted the demethylated products, N-LAAM and DN-LAAM, as the primary metabolites.

The increased levels of MOL excreted by the dog may indicate that the route of metabolism--either hydrolysis to MOL or demethylation to N-LAAM--may be dependent on the concentration of the parent drug in the plasma. The dog, which had higher plasma levels of total radioactivity, excreted MOL as the major metabolite. In the rat, increasing the dose from 5 mg/kg to 10 mg/kg caused a marked increase in the plasma levels of MOL and N-MOL, while the plasma levels of the demethylated products, N-LAAM and DN-LAAM, increased only slightly.

There also appears to be a sex-related difference in the biological disposition of LAAM in the rat. Female rats tended to have higher levels of LAAM and metabolites N-LAAM, DN-LAAM, MOL and N-AcetylNMOL at the later time periods (24 to 72 hrs). In male rats, N-LAAM and DN-LAAM levels tended to rise more slowly, reach lower peak levels, but remain high up to 48 hours. This difference in drug plasma levels was found when the drug was administered either orally or intravenously. Also, these differences in drug and metabolite levels found in plasma were observed in the lungs. There were no significant differences in either the area under the curve values or the total body clearance values for total administered radioactivity in male and female rats. Therefore, the differences in plasma drug values do not seem to be related to differences in absorption, but due to differences in drug metabolism. The data in our study might best be explained by assuming that male rats metabolize LAAM and conjugate the metabolites more rapidly than do female rats.

In summary, the biological disposition of LAAM appears to be qualitatively similar in the rat, dog and monkey. The drug appears to be rapidly absorbed from the gastrointestinal tract, extensively metabolized and excreted primarily via the bile. The dog had the highest plasma levels of ^{3}H-LAAM and also exhibited the greatest behavioral response to the drug. There also appeared to be a sex-related difference in the disposition of LAAM in the rat in that male rats excreted the drug at a faster rate than females. The long duration of action appears to be due to extensive enterohepatic recirculation and binding to tissue proteins.

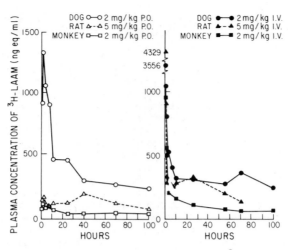

Figure 1 (left)   Plasma disappearance curves of ^{3}H-LAAM (total radioactivity) following oral administration to the dog, rat and monkey.

Figure 2 (right)   Plasma disappearance curves of ^{3}H-LAAM (total radio activity) following intravenous administration to the dog, rat and monkey.

TABLE 1

Urinary Excretion of LAAM and Metabolites

| Compound | Amount Excreted (% of administered dose) | | |
	Rat	Dog	Monkey
	0 - 48 hr	0 - 96 hr	0 - 96 hr
LAAM	0.18	0.14	0.17
N-LAAM	0.35	0.11	0.13
DN-LAAM	0.71	0.11	0.15
MOL	0.10	0.23	0.12
N-MOL	0	0.05	0.11
N-Acetyl	0	0.13	0.06
Total Free Drug	1.34	0.77	0.74
Conjugates	6.78	16.77	12.55
Total Radioactivity	8.12	17.54	13.29

REFERENCES

1. Fraser, H.J. and Isbell, H.   J. Pharmacol. Exp. Ther.
   105:458 (1952).

2. Kuttab, S.H., North-Root, H. and Henderson, G.L.
   J. Chromatog.   177:193 (1976).

FETAL HEPATIC METABOLISM OF DRUGS OF ABUSE

Barry H. Dvorchik, Ph.D., and Vincent G. Stenger, M.D.

Departments of Obstetrics and Gynecology and Pharmacology
The Milton S. Hershey Medical Center of The Pennsylvania
State University, Hershey, Pennsylvania

In contrast to fetal liver from common laboratory animals, human fetal liver possesses the capacity to metabolize drugs at an early gestational age (see ref. 1). For certain drugs of abuse, where the metabolite(s) possess significant pharmacological activity (e.g. the N-demethylated metabolites of acetylmethadol or LAAM and meperidine) the finding that the fetus can metabolize drugs raises many questions as to the significance of this activity with respect to teratology, toxicology, and clinical medicine. Recent reports from our laboratories (2,3) have shown that biochemical and ultrastructural similarities exist between livers obtained from the fetal stumptailed macaque and the human fetus. These similarities led us to suggest that the fetal stumptailed macaque may be an excellent animal model for the study of fetal hepatic drug metabolism and its significance to the developing human fetus. The studies reported here characterize the fetal hepatic N-demethylase system in microsomes obtained from the stumptailed macaque during the last trimester of gestation with respect to the metabolism of benzphetamine, ethylmorphine, meperidine, and methadone.

MATERIALS AND METHODS

Fetuses were obtained from a colony of stumptailed monkeys (Macaca arctoides) maintained by the Department of Obstetrics and Gynecology at the Milton S. Hershey Medical Center and known to have an average gestation period of 170 ± 7 days. Male and female adult monkeys were healthy and not receiving any medications. Details as to housing, determination of gestational age, delivery of the fetus, tissue preparation and assay techniques are given elsewhere (2,4).

Briefly, fetuses were delivered by Cesarean section and livers removed within 10 minutes of delivery. Sections were removed for light and electron microscopy and the remainder of the liver divided into right and left physiological lobes, based upon the distribution of blood vessels and ducts. The plane of separation between the physiological lobes runs forward from the gallbladder and the inferior vena cava, somewhat to the right of the falciform ligament. The lobes were rinsed with buffer (0.01 M HEPES, pH 7.35), weighed, minced with scissors, rinsed twice more and homogenized. Homogenates were prepared so that each ml contained 20 mg liver, wet weight. Microsomes were isolated by differential centrifugation and resuspended in 0.1 M HEPES buffer, pH 7.53 such that each ml contained 3 mg microsomal protein.

N-demethylase activity was assayed by measuring the formaldehyde produced during the demethylation process according to the method of Nash (5). Incubation mixtures contained, in addition to microsomal suspension, an NADPH generating system (NADP, glucose-6 phosphate, Mg Cl_2 and G-6 PD), substrate, and buffer. Incubation was carried out for 10 min at 37°C under air. The reaction was terminated by the addition of perchloric acid. An aliquot of the supernatant fraction obtained after centrifugation was removed and an aliquot of double strength Nash reagent B added. After incubation for 10 min at 60°C the solutions were allowed to cool to room temperature and the absorbance was then read at 412 mm. Cytochrome P-450 determinations were made on an Aminco DW-2 spectrophotometer (6) using an extinction coefficient of 100 mM^{-1} cm^{-1}.

RESULTS AND DISCUSSION

Microsomal fractions isolated from livers of the fetal stumptailed macaque obtained at the beginning and end of the third trimester of gestation were capable of catalyzing the in vitro N-demethylation of benzphetamine, ethylmorphine, meperidine and methadone (Table I). Analysis of data obtained from rat microsomes (4) indicated that at the low levels of activity (and thus absorbance) observed in fetal microsomes an error of two-fold could be expected in the apparent Km. Thus, in these studies a two-fold variation in the apparent Km was not considered significant.

Evaluation of the data in Table I indicates that during the last trimester of gestation the apparent Km for the N-demethylation of benzphetamine, ethylmorphine, meperidine, and methadone remains unchanged. The apparent Km for each substrate was similar to the corresponding apparent Km obtained with microsomes isolated from adult livers.

The V_{max} for each substrate, expressed as activity per mg microsomal protein, was fairly constant during the last trimester of gestation. As expected, the V_{max} obtained from adult microsomes was significantly greater than the V_{max} obtained from fetal microsomes (Table I). When activity was expressed per g liver the capacity of the fetal liver to metabolize drugs was observed to increase during the last trimester of gestation. This was due to an increase in the amount of microsomal protein per g liver (Table II). When the increase in the content of microsomal protein was taken into consideration, the N-demethylase activity of fetal liver (V_{max} expressed as activity per g liver) increased about 2-fold during the last trimester of gestation.

Fetal circulation contains umbilical and various other vascular shunts, absent in adults. The major portion of the umbilical venous blood perfuses the left physiological lobe of the fetal liver, while only a small fraction is shunted directly into the inferior vena cava via the ductous venosus (7). The portal vein carries blood to the remaining portion of the fetal liver, the physiological right lobe (7). Other differences between the two lobes of fetal liver include (a) differences in the oxygen saturation of the blood perfusing the lobes, umbilical venous blood having about a 2-fold greater oxygen content than portal vein blood (8) and (b) more hemopoietic foci appear in sections obtained from the right physiological lobe than from the left physiological lobe (9).

In light of the above and the observation that in fetal guinea pigs the lobe of the liver receiving umbilical venous blood contained greater concentrations of thiopental than the rest of the liver immediately after thiopental administration (10), we hypothesized that the left physiological lobe of fetal liver might have a greater capability to metabolize drugs and steroids than the right physiological lobe. Homogenates of the left physiological lobe of fetal liver obtained near-term contained more cytochrome P-450 than the right physiological lobe (8.00 ± 0.72 nmole cyt. P-450/g liver versus 4.40 ± 0.77 nmole cyt. P-450/g liver; mean $\pm$ S.E); no differences in cytochrome P-450 concentration were observed in the lobes of liver obtained from adult monkeys (left lobe = 30.67 ± 2.03 nmole cyt. P-450/g liver; right lobe = 29.00 ± 1.00 nmole cyt. P-450/g liver; mean $\pm$ S.E).

Only direct measurement of drug metabolism in fractions of liver obtained from the left and right physiological lobes can answer the question as to whether a differential capacity exists between the two lobes with respect to drug metabolism. If the development of fetal hepatic drug metabolism during the last trimester of gestation parallels the development of cytochrome P-450 then the observed differences in cytochrome P-450 concentration may be associated with differences in the capacity to metabolize drug substrates.

SUMMARY

1. Microsomes isolated from the liver of fetal macaques during the last trimester of gestation catalyzed the N-demethylation of benzphetamine, ethylmorphine, meperidine, and methadone.
2. The apparent Km for each substrate did not change during the last trimester of gestation and was similar to the respective apparent Km obtained with adult microsomes.
3. V_{max} (activity/g liver) increased about 2-fold during the last trimester of gestation due to a 56% increase in the content of microsomal protein per g liver.
4. The concentration of cytochrome P-450 in the left physiological lobe of fetal liver was 2-fold greater than in the right physiological lobe. This difference may reflect a differential capacity within fetal liver to metabolize drugs and steroids.

TABLE I: APPARENT Km and V_{max} FOR THE N-DEMETHYLATION OF
BENZPHETAMINE, ETHYLMORPHINE, MEPERIDINE, AND METHADONE BY
MICROSOMES ISOLATED FROM LIVERS OF FETAL AND ADULT MONKEYS[a]

MONKEY	AGE[b]	SUBSTRATE	APPARENT Km[c]	V_{max} [d]
FETUS	120/170	BENZPHETAMINE	0.14 ± 0.02	2.7 ± 0.8
	160/170		0.15 ± 0.03	3.7 ± 1.7
ADULT			0.08 ± 0.01	103.3 ± 20.8
FETUS	120/170	ETHYLMORPHINE	0.44 ± 0.03	2.4 ± 0.3
	160/170		0.90 ± 0.10	5.0 ± 1.5
ADULT			0.75 ± 0.16	163.3 ± 39.1
FETUS	120/170	MEPERIDINE	0.24 ± 0.01	1.6 ± 0.4
	160/170		0.26 ± 0.02	4.3 ± 1.8
ADULT			0.17 ± 0.03	131.7 ± 31.8
FETUS	120/170	METHADONE	0.48 ± 0.08	2.4 ± 0.8
	160/170		0.27 ± 0.02	2.0 ± 0.6
ADULT			0.12 ± 0.01	58.0 ± 18.2

[a] Each value is the mean ± S.E. of 3 determinations.
[b] Fetal age is expressed as a fraction of the gestational period, in days
[c] mM
[d] nmole formaldehyde/mg microsomal protein/10 min.

TABLE II: CYTOCHROME P-450 LEVELS IN WHOLE HOMOGENATES AND MICRO-
SOMES OBTAINED FROM LIVERS OF FETAL AND ADULT MONKEYS

AGE[a]	N[b]	CYTOCHROME P-450			MICROSOMAL PROTEIN[e]
		Homogenate[c] (nmole/g liver)	Microsomes[d] (nmole/g liver)	(nmole/mg protein)	(mg/g liver)
120/170	3	2.27 ± 0.63	1.20 ± 0.61	0.063 ± 0.012	36 ± 7.3
160/170	6	7.95 ± 1.11[f]	3.03 ± 0.76	0.144 ± 0.023[f]	56 ± 3.5[f]
ADULT	4	28.8 ± 4.8	9.78 ± 2.23	0.658 ± 0.079	44 ± 6

[a] Fetal age expressed as a function of gestational age in days.
[b] Number of livers studied
[c] Cuvettes contained 3-8 mg protein/ml
[d] Cuvettes contained 1-3 mg protein/ml
[e] Calculated from the amount of cytochrome P-450/g liver as determined in whole homogenates and the amount of cytochrome P-450/mg microsomal protein
[f] Difference between means statistically significant ($p < 0.05$) as determined by the Student's "t" test.

REFERENCES

1. O. Pelkonen and N. T. Kärki, Life Sci., 13: 1163 (1973).
2. B. H. Dvorchik, V. G. Stenger, and S. L. Quattropani, Drug Met. Disp., 2: 539 (1974).
3. S. L. Quattropani, V. G. Stenger, and B. H. Dvorchik, Anat. Rec., 182: 103 (1975).
4. B. H. Dvorchik, V. G. Stenger, and S. L. Quattropani, Drug Met. Disp., 4: 423 (1976).
5. T. Nash, J. Biol. Chem., 55: 416 (1953).
6. B. Schoene, R. A. Fleishman, H. Remmer, and H. F. v. Olderhausen, Eur. J. Clin. Pharmacol., 4: 65 (1972).
7. A. E. Barclay, K. J. Franklin, and M. M. L. Pritchard, in "The Foetal Circulation and Cardiovascular System and the Changes that they Undergo at Birth", Blackwell Scientific Publications, Oxford, 1944.
8. R. A. Karim, Obstet. Gynecol. Survey, 23: 713 (1968).
9. J. L. Emery, J. Anat., 90: 293 (1956).
10. M. Finster, H. O. Morishima, L. C. Mark, J. M. Perel, P. G. Dayton, and L. S. James, Anesthesiol, 36: 155 (1972).
(This work supported in part by NIDA Grant DA-001180-01 and a grant from the National Foundation-March of Dimes)

SECRETION OF ABUSED
DRUGS BY THE
RAT AND HUMAN
PAROTID GLANDS

G. John DiGregorio

Department of Pharmacology
Hahnemann Medical College
Philadelphia, Pennsylvania

I. INTRODUCTION

Several investigators have studied the secretion of various drugs in both animal and human saliva. Drugs, such as opium derivatives[1], ethanol[2], penicillin[3], and barbiturates[4,5] have been detected in salivary secretions of treated animals including the goat, dog and horse. In man, salivary secretions have been demonstrated to contain various antibiotics[6], diphenylhydantoin[7] and theophylline[8]. However, none of the above studies have attempted to study the parotid secretions of similar drugs in humans and animals.

Studies reported here have investigated the salivary secretion of various drugs from both the rat and human parotid glands. The drugs which have been studied are amobarbital, chlorpromazine, codein, glutethimide, meprobamate, morphine, pentobarital, phenobarbital, secobarbital, methadone and ethanol. These studies have been designed in an attempt to establish (1) the ability of either the rat or human parotid glands to secrete the drugs under investigation, (2) a correlation either qualitatively or quantitatively between those drugs secreted by the rat parotid gland and the human parotid gland and (3) a rat saliva to plasma concentration ratio for each drug.

II. MATERIALS AND METHODS

A. Animal Experiments

Albino Wistar male rats (150-200 gm) were anesthetized with urethane (1.8 gm/kg, intrapertoneally) and tracheotomies were performed. With a dissecting microscope (Olympus Model SZ III), both parotid ducts, femoral artery and brachial artery of each animal were surgically exposed for cannulation. Parotid ducts were cannulated according to a method described by Chernick, et al[9]. Both the femoral artery and the brachial artery were cannulated with a heparinized PE 50 cannula. The femoral artery was used for the administration of the various drugs being studied. The brachial artery was used for the constant infusion of a secretatory agent.

The secretagogue, pilocarpine (0.2 mg/ml) and acetylcholine (o.125 mg/ml) were infused through the brachial artery over a thirty minute saliva collection period at a rate of 0.2 ml/min for thirty minutes. Prior to the infusion, the drugs under investigation were administered intravenously via the femoral vein. At the end of the thirty minute collection period, whole blood (4 to 8 ml) was withdrawn from the right common carotid artery through a heparinized cannula (PE 60) into a glass syringe. The blood was centrifuged and the plasma removed. Both plasma (2 ml) and saliva (0.2 ml) samples were utilized for drug determinations.

B. Human Experiments

Human volunteers were male subjects between the ages of 21-30 years old. Complete histories and physical examinations including ECG, blood and urine chemistries were performed before the experiment and after its completion.

Parotid saliva was collected from the human volunteers by means of a modified double human Teflon-lashley cup[10] of the type described by Carlson, et al[11] and Curby[12]. Orange-flavored lozenges were used as a stimulus to induce reflex salivary flow. Saliva was collected in graduated tubes during specific time intervals so that flow rates could be measured. Each drugs was administered orally and, one hour post administration, saliva was collected for approximately 4-6 minutes. The volume of saliva collected was approximately 3-4 ml depending on the subject. Saliva was then analyzed for presence of the particular drug administered.

III. RESULTS AND DISCUSSION

Tables I, II, and III demonstrate the results of the drugs detected and quantitated in rat parotid saliva during parotid stimulation by acetylcholine and pilocarpine infustions. The mean saliva and plasma concentrations of each drug are expressed in terms of mg %. One can compare the ratios of the concentrations of the drugs in rat parotid saliva by that in the plasma (s/p). The ratio indicates the degree of salivary excretion of an agent as compared to its plasma values. In the acetylcholine induced secretions, morphine has the highest s/p ratio followed by chlorpromazine, amobarbital, codeine, secobarbital, glutethimide, phenobarbital, pentobarbital and meprobamate. In the pilocarpine induced secretions, morphine has the highest s/p ratio followed by chlorpromazine, codeine, ethanol, pentobarbital, amobarbital, meprobamate, phenobarbital, glutethimide and secobarbital. Methadone (5 mg/kg) could not be detected with either acetylcholine or pilocarpine stimulation in rat parotid saliva.

Table IV shows the individual drugs detected and quantitated in human parotid saliva. The salivary concentrations are expressed in terms of ug % one hour after drug administration. The results indicate that codeine has the highest salivary secretion per unit of dose followed by phenobarbital, pentobarbital, secobarbital, meprobamate, amobarbital, chlorpromazine, and glutethimide. Methadone could not be detected in parotid saliva of subjects taking 10 mg p.o. of methadone.

The results from this study indicate qualitatively that the rat parotid gland and the human parotid gland are similar in their ability to secrete certain drugs in parotid saliva. With the exception of morphine and alcohol, all of the drugs detected in rat parotid saliva (Tables 1, 2 and 3) which includes amobarbital, pentobarbital, phenobarbital, secobarbital, meprobamate, chlorpromazine, codeine, and glutethimide have also been detected in human parotid saliva (Table IV). Detection of morphine and ethanol in human parotid saliva has not been accomplished.

In evaluating patterns of secretion of the drugs in rat and human parotid saliva, it would seem apparent that many factors including the distribution, metabolism, plasma protein binding and pk_a of drugs play an important role in determining the relative concentration of drug that is secreted in the saliva as compared to plasma. Usually, for a drug to be secreted in saliva, the drug should be available to the salivary gland in the nonionized form and unbound to plasma proteins. If such a relation could be established then one could predict, by measuring drug salivary concentrations of various drugs. This would be of particular importance in several areas e.g. bioavailability studies where repeatedly blood samples must be taken and in establishing blood levels in individuals where blood collection is difficult, the geriatric, children, and addict populations.

IV. CONCLUSIONS

Qualitatively, a correlation exists between the rat parotid and human parotid gland secretions of the various drugs studied. The following drugs: amobarbital, chlorpromazine, codeine, glutethimide, meprobamate, pentobarbital, phenobarbital, and secobarbital have been detected in both rat and human parotid saliva. Morphine has only been detected in rat parotid saliva. Methadone could not be detected in either the rat or human parotid saliva.

In the rat parotid gland, drug secretion appears to be dependent on the method of gland stimulation. Differences in drug secretions has been found to exist between acetylcholine and pilocarpine induced secretions. In either case, morphine appears to be secreted in the highest concentration whereas methadone could not be detected in either system. Drugs such as chlorpromazine, codeine and meprobamate appear not to be influenced by either acetylcholine or pilocarpine glandular stimulation. The concentration of amobarbital, glutethimide, morphine, phenobarbital and secobarbital secreted in rat parotid saliva are decreased after pilocarpine stimulation when compared to their salivary concentrations after acetylocholine stimulation.

In human parotid saliva, quantitative comparisons with rat parotid saliva are difficult to establish due to a number of variables. Method of glandular stimulation, subject population size or subject selection may account for some of these variables. Further controlled studies are necessary to firmly establish quantitatively correlation between species as well as between volunteer subjects.

TABLE I

Drugs Detected in Rat Plasma and Acetylcholine Induced Parotid Saliva

Drug	n	Dose* (mg/kg)	Concentration** (mg%) Plasma	Saliva
Amobarbital	6	10	0.53 ± 0.13	0.63 ± 0.10
Pentobarbital	5	10	0.68 ± 0.11	0.37 ± 0.07
Phenobarbital	5	10	0.58 ± 0.05	0.35 ± 0.06
Secobarbital	5	10	0.47 ± 0.23	0.32 ± 0.04
Meprobamate	5	10	0.73 ± 0.24	0.30 ± 0.03
Morphine	5	5	0.03 ± 0.01	0.16 ± 0.07
Chlorpromazine	5	5	0.09 ± 0.02	0.20 ± 0.06
Codeine	5	10	0.08 ± 0.02	0.09 ± 0.02
Glutethimide	5	10	0.11 ± 0.30	0.09 ± 0.02
Methadone	5	5	———	———

* Doses administered intravenously

** Mean ± Standard Error. Volume of 200 ul of saliva was analyzed in each experiment. Total collection time was thirty minutes.

TABLE II

Drugs Detected in Rat Plasma and Pilocarpine Induced Parotid
Saliva

Drug	n	Dose* (mg/kg)	Concentration** (mg%) Plasma	Saliva
Pentobarbital	6	10	1.34 ± 0.23	0.79 ± 0.13
Amobarbital	6	10	1.00 ± 0.19	0.60 ± 0.04
Meprobamate	5	10	0.90 ± 0.14	0.44 ± 0.05
Phenobarbital	5	10	0.98 ± 0.08	0.34 ± 0.07
Secobarbital	4	10	0.56 ± 0.03	0.15 ± 0.02
Morphine	5	5	0.04 ± 0.01	0.12 ± 0.01
Codeine	4	10	0.08 ± 0.03	0.10 ± 0.03
Glutethimide	5	5	0.27 ± 0.08	0.10 ± 0.02
Chlorpromazine	5	5	0.02 ± 0.005	0.08 ± 0.02
Methadone	5	5	———	———

* Doses administered intravenously

** Mean ± Standard Error. Volume of 200 ul of saliva was analyzed
   in each experiment. Total collection time was thirty minutes.

TABLE III

ETHANOL CONCENTRATIONS IN RAT PLASMA
AND PILOCARPINE INDUCED SALIVA

Dose*	n	Concentration Plasma	(mg%)** Saliva
150	4	2.7 + 0.43	3.0 + 0.15
200	4	11.2 + 0.43	12.3 + 1.3
300	4	22.6 + 2.6	27.6 + 2.8
400	4	29.1 + 2.9	35.0 + 3.8
500	4	42.6 + 3.5	55.8 + 2.0

* mg/kg drug administered intravenously
** Mean + standard error at fifteen minutes

TABLE IV

Drugs Detected in Human Parotid Saliva

Drug	Dose (mg, p.o.)	Salivary Concentrations** (ug%)
Meprobamate	400	110.0 + 20.0
Phenobarbital	60	50.0 + 20.0
Glutethimide	250	40.0 + 10.0
Pentobarbital	50	24.0 + 4.0
Codeine	15	20.0 + 1.0
Secobarbital	50	19.0 + 4.0
Amobarbital	60	15.0 + 2.0
Chlorpromazine	25	6.0 + 2.0
Methadone	10	————

** Mean + standard error of three human experiments for each drug. Two to four ml of saliva was analyzed in each experiment. Saliva samples were collected one hour after the oral administration of the drug.

REFERENCES

1. J.C. Munch, J Am Pharm Ass. 24: 557 (1935).

2. K. Iribe, K. Miyazzawa, H. Nakajima, and E. Kamoshita, J Nihon Univ Sch Dent 11: 34 (1969).

3. J.F. Borzelleca, and H.M. Cherrick, J Oral Ther 2: 180 (1965).

4. F. Rashmussen, Acta Pharmacol et Toxicol 21: 11 (1964).

5. A.J. Piraino, G.J. DiGregorio, and B.T. Nagle, J Dent Res 55: 43 (1976).

6. I.B. Bender, R.S., Pressman, and S.G. Tashman, J Am Dent Assn 46: 164 (1953).

7. G.J. Conrad, H. Feffay, L. Boshes, and A.D. Steinberg, J Dent Res 53: 1323 (1974).

8. R. Koysooko, E.F. Ellis, and G. Levy, Clin Pharm and Therap 15: 454 (1974).

9. W.S. Chernick, E. Bobyock, and G.J. DiGregorio, J Dent Res 50: 165 (1971).

10. H.J. Eichel, N. Conger, and W.S. Chernick, Arch Biochem and Biophys 107: 197 (1964).

11. A.J. Carlson, A.L. Crittenden, Am J Physiol 26: 169 (1910).

12. W.A. Curby, J Lab Clin Med 41: 493 (1953).

THE URINARY EXCRETION PROFILE OF NALTREXONE AND NALOXONE IN MAN AND SEVERAL LABORATORY ANIMAL SPECIES

Edward J. Cone

National Institute on Drug Abuse
Division of Research
Addiction Research Center
Lexington, Kentucky

Naloxone (Narcan) like naltrexone (1) is a relatively pure narcotic antagonist and is used clinically for reversal of narcotic-induced respiratory depression. In addition, naloxone has been proposed for use as a therapeutic aid in diagnosing physical dependence (2). Both compounds have been employed in the ambulatory treatment of former narcotic addicts (3). The usefulness of naloxone in this regard is limited since it is relatively ineffective orally and has a short duration of action. Extremely large oral doses are required to produce a significant duration of blockade to the agonistic activity of heroin (3). Naltrexone, the N-cyclopropylmethyl congener of naloxone, has a longer duration of action and has been found to be effective orally. A single 15 mg oral dose was found to produce a significant level of antagonism for at least 24 hours (1).

These differences in narcotic antagonistic potency and duration of action may be explained in part by differences in mode of metabolism of naltrexone and naloxone. Significant differences might also occur in their respective bioavailability of active metabolites and/or parent drug. Metabolic studies of these drugs in man and laboratory animals at the Addiction Research Center have been aimed at exploring and elucidating these differences.

Conjugation

Both naltrexone and naloxone and their respective metabolites are found as conjugates in the urine of numberous animal species including man administered drug (5,6). As shown in Table I, 18% of naltrexone and 25% of naloxone administered to man was excreted in the urine as the parent drug, most of which was conjugated, presumably as the glucuronide. In contrast only 48% of the 6-β-hydroxy-metabolite of naltrexone was excreted in acid-hydrolyzable conjugate form. Extensive conjugation of naltrexone and naloxone and their 6-hydroxy-metabolites also occurs in dog and rabbit. Guinea pig is intermediate in conjugation and rat is apparently a poor conjugator of these compounds. With rat being excepted, it is evident that conjugation in man and the other species is a major bio-transformation pathway limiting the duration of action of these drugs.

Reduction

Reduction of the C_6 keto-group to the 6-$\underline{\beta}$-hydroxy-metabolite is the predominantly observed metabolic pathway for naltrexone in man. As shown in Table I, 35% of the administered dose of naltrexone is excreted in the urine as 6-$\underline{\beta}$-naltrexol, 52% of which is excreted in the unconjugated form. In contrast only 5% of naloxone is excreted as 6-$\underline{\beta}$-naloxol, most of which is conjugated. The 6-$\underline{\beta}$-hydroxy-metabolites also are found in the urine of other species adminis-tered naltrexone or naloxone. The apparent order of occurrence of these metabolites in these species are as follows: guinea pig > rabbit > rat $\geq$ dog.

Previous evidence from studies on the metabolism of naloxone (11,7) and naltrexone (6) had indicated that the stereospecificity of the drug metabolizing enzyme responsible for reduction of the C_6 carbonyl group may vary with species. As shown in Table I, small amounts of the 6-$\underline{\alpha}$-hydroxy-metabolite of naltrexone were excreted along with the larger amounts of the 6-$\underline{\beta}$-epimer in all species studied. Recent studies have shown that a similar pattern of ex-cretion is observed for naloxone administered to rat and guinea pig (7). However, it is likely that contribution of pharmacological activity arising from the 6-$\underline{\alpha}$-hydroxy-metabolite is minor unless within species variation were found to be large.

Dealkylation

Noroxymorphone, the N-dealkylated metabolite of naltrexone and naloxone, was detected in the urine of man, rat and monkey adminis-tered naltrexone and man administered naloxone (8). However, esti-mates of the concentration of this compound in the urine of man administered naltrexone indicate that the quantity was limited and did not exceed the total amount of noroxymorphone administered as a contaminant of the naltrexone (*ca.* 1%). Consequently N-dealkyla-tion of these compounds in these species does not appear to be an important biotransformation pathway.

Hydroxylation and Methoxylation

Both hydroxylated and methoxylated metabolites of naltrexone and hydroxylated metabolites of naloxone were detected in the urine of man and several animal species administered drug (8). Similar metabolites of naltrexone isolated from human blood and urine were subsequently reported by Verebely, *et al.* (9). The amounts of hy-droxylated and methoxylated metabolites of naltrexone and naloxone isolated from man are consistently low making structural identifi-cation difficult. However, somewhat greater amounts have been de-tected in the urine of rat (8) and rabbit administered naltrexone. Extraction of the acid-hydrolyzed urine of rabbit administered nal-trexone chronically (40 mg/day, sc) followed by separation on TLC

1229

of the hydroxy-metabolite region (R_f 0.05 - 0.30) provided a semi-purified mixture of 6-β-naltrexol and a new metabolite. The new metabolite when analyzed by GC/MS/CI (methane) was found to have molecular weight of 647. The addition of 4 silyl groups (4 X 72) and a molecular weight increase of 16 over that of 6-β-naltrexol was observed and was indicative of a hydroxylated metabolite of 6-β-naltrexol. Apparently the new hydroxyl group has been silylated to form the quadrasilyl derivative. Preliminary evidence indicates that the site of hydroxylation and methoxylation of these new metabolites is on the aromatic ring (8,9). However, final structural confirmation remains to be completed. The possible pharmacological contribution of these new metabolites is unknown.

Activity of Metabolites

There have been several studies on the narcotic antagonistic and agonistic activity of the 6-hydroxy-metabolites of naltrexone and naloxone. Martin *et al.* (10) reported that the antagonistic activity of the naltrexone metabolite from the guinea pig (6-β-naltrexol) was *ca.* 0.26 that of naloxone as determined in the morphine-dependent chronic spinal dog. Fujimoto *et al.* (11) and Chatterjie *et al.* (12) reported on the activity of 6-α- and 6-β-naltrexol and naloxol, finding significant antagonistic activity in both forms, albeit somewhat lower than that of the parent compound. Interestingly, Chatterjie *et al.* (12) also reported finding significant antinociceptive activity for the 6-α- but not for the 6-β-hydroxy-metabolites.

Time Course of Urinary Excretion

The pattern of excretion of free and conjugated naltrexone and naloxone in all animal species studied was similar, with the major portion of parent drug being excreted in the first 24 hours. During the 24-48 hour period excretion declined to *ca.* 2% or less for all species except dog which excreted 8% of both parent drugs. The bulk of the 6-hydroxy-metabolites of both drugs also were excreted during the first 24 hours. Man appears to differ significantly from the other species in excreting the hydroxy-metabolite in larger amounts (*ca.* 8% of administered dose) in the 24-48 hour period. The slower rate of excretion of the metabolite with respect to that of naltrexone was reflected in their respective urinary excretion half-lives. These were calculated for free naltrexone and 6-β-naltrexol from urinary excretion data obtained from a group of six human subjects administered a single dose of naltrexone (50 mg, orally) (5) and were 1.1 ± 0.2 and 16.8 ± 0.9 hours, respectively. In this study free and conjugated naltrexone was detectable to 8 and 24 hours, whereas the 6-β-hydroxy-metabolite was detectable 6 days after drug administration. It is possible that the extended half-life of excretion of the metabolite over that of the parent compound is due to conversion of the large amounts of naltrexone to metabolite (*ca.* 43% of the administered dose) (5). The amount of metabolite formed might be such that the capacity of the conjugation pathway (presumably glucuronidation) is exceeded (13). Thus, more metabolite than parent would be available for lipid storage with the resultant effect being that of delayed excretion.

1230

TABLE I. Urinary Excretion of Naltrexone and Naloxone and Their Metabolites

Naltrexone[a]

Species, N[c]	Day	Free Parent		Total Parent[b]		Free 6-β-Hydroxy-metabolite		Total 6-β-Hydroxy-metabolite[b]		Total 6-α-Hydroxy-metabolite[b]	
		1	2	1	2	1	2	1	2	1	2
Man, 4, oral		1.2	0[d]	17.6	0[d]	18.1	4.4[d]	34.9	7.8[d]	0.6	—
Guinea Pig, 6, sc		28.3	0.4	45.1	0.4	8.0	0.5	10.8	0.5	0.7	0
Rabbit, 4, sc		6.5	1.7	49.9	2.6	0.7	0.3	5.9	0.7	0.2	0
Rat, 6, sc		5.1	0	5.1	0	0.2	0	0.3	0	0.1	0
Dog, 2, sc		3.3	0	46.3	8.2	0	0	0.3	0	0.1	0

Naloxone[a]

Species, N[c]	Day	Free Parent		Total Parent[b]		Free 6-β-Hydroxy-metabolite		Total 6-β-Hydroxy-metabolite[b]		Total 6-α-Hydroxy-metabolite[b]	
		1	2	1	2	1	2	1	2	1	2
Man, 2, oral		0.9	—	25.5	—	0	—	4.8	—	—	—
Guinea Pig, 6, sc		7.6	0.1	32.4	1.5	7.2	0.3	23.1	0.7	—	—
Rabbit, 4, sc		3.7	0	36.1	0.2	0.5	0	2.5	0.1	—	—
Rat, 6, sc		1.8	0	3.3	0	0.1	0	0.1	0	—	—
Dog, 2, sc		2.5	0	57.4	8.1	0	0	0.1	0	—	—

[a] Percent administered dose as determined by gas-chromatographic analysis of the silylated derivatives using naloxone as internal standardization of naltrexone and dilaudid for naloxone analysis. The analyses were performed on a Varian GC Model 2700 using 3% OV-225. Samples unavailable for analysis are indicated by —.

[b] The samples were acid-hydrolyzed, hence the values represent both free and conjugated drug.

[c] Number of subjects and route of drug administration.   [d] Values taken from reference (5)

References

1. W. R. Martin, D. R. Jasinski, and P. A. Mansky, *Arch. Gen. Psychiat., 28:* 784 (1973).

2. W. R. Martin, C. W. Gorodetzky, and T. K. McClane, *Clin. Pharmacol. Ther., 7:* 455 (1966).

3. A. Zaks, T. Jones, M. Fink, and A. M. Freedman, *JAMA, 215:* 2108 (1971).

4. D. R. Jasinski, W. R. Martin, and C. A. Haertzen, *J. Pharmacol. Exp. Ther., 157:* 420 (1967).

5. E. J. Cone, C. W. Gorodetzky, and S. Y. Yeh, *Drug Metab. Disp., 2:* 506 (1974).

6. E. J. Cone, C. W. Gorodetzky, and S. Y. Yeh, *J. Pharm. Sci., 64:* 618 (1975).

7. E. J. Cone, Unpublished observations, NIDA Addiction Research Center, Lexington, Kentucky, 1976.

8. E. J. Cone and C. W. Gorodetzky, Metabolism of Naltrexone and Naloxone. Reported to the Committee on Problems of Drug Dependence, Washington, D. C., 1975.

9. J. Verebely, M. A. Chedekel, S. J. Mulé, and D. Rosenthol, *Res. Comm. Chem. Pathol. Pharmacol., 12:* 67 (1975).

10. W. R. Martin, P. E. Gilbert, C. G. Eades, J. A. Thompson, and R. E. Huppler, Progress Report on the animal assessment program of the Addiction Research Center. Reported to the Committee on Problems of Drug Dependence, Washington, D. C., 1975.

11. J. M. Fujimoto, S. Roerig, R. I. H. Wang, N. Chatterjie, and C. E. Inturrisi, *Proc. Soc. Exp. Biol. Med., 148:* 443 (1975).

12. N. Chatterjie, C. E. Inturrisi, H. D. Dayton, and H. Blumberg, *J. Med. Chem., 18:* 490 (1975).

13. G. Levy, *Chem.-Biol. Interactions, 3:* 291 (1971).

REVERSAL BY DIBUTYRYL CYCLIC ADENOSINE 3':5'
MONOPHOSPHATE OF AMOBARBITAL OVERDOSAGE IN THE RHESUS MONKEY

Major L. Cohn

Sidney K. Wolfson, Jr.

Felicien M. Steichen

Marthe Cohn

University of Pittsburgh School of Medicine

Pittsburgh, Pennsylvania

No previous study of drug overdosage has yet established the essential links between behavioral and pharmacologic events and anatomical sites. Such linkage is indispensable to understand the mechan-
ism(s) involved. Despite recent in-vitro findings on the effect of
putative neurotransmitters, intermediate metabolism, enzymes and
membranes on cellular functioning within systems, no correlation
has been demonstrated with in-vivo events.

Current theories of drug overdosage are inadequate for several reasons: 1) they are nonspecific and fail to identify the site(s) of
action in the brain; 2) in-vitro evidence cannot be demonstrated
in-vivo; 3) the mechanism by which brain cell dysfunction leads to
the observed behavioral events has not been defined.

Increased drug abuse has changed methods of treatment. The standard treatment for barbiturate overdosage, a leading cause of
suicidal death, used to be supportive therapy and analeptic drugs.
However, analeptic drugs are not effective against hypnotic drug
overdosage (1); they often add to the toxicity already present and
even increase mortality by producing such severe complications as
cardiac arrhythmias, hyperthermia and convulsions. In recent years
the analeptics have been rejected for supportive therapy alone.
Unfortunately, symptomatic treatment does not reverse barbiturate
poisoning in the brain; a surviving patient with irreparable brain
damage is not a desirable result.

Our previous findings that the nucleotide adenosine 3':5'-Monophos-
phoric adic (cyclic AMP) and its dibutyryl analog dose-relatedly

shorten amobarbital-induced narcosis (2), led us to investigate
their antidotal therapeutic effectiveness.

We selected rats for the first phase of our study because large
numbers of animals are required to obtain statistically significant
values. We selected the primate for the second phase because data
obtained from this species are most relevant for prognosis in man.
In rhesus monkeys we have confirmed and extended our previous findings in rats (3), that dibutyryl cyclic AMP is an effective antidote to amobarbital overdosage. Amobarbital-overdosed rhesus monkeys whose mean arterial blood pressure (MABP) fell to below 50% of
normal readings. survived after administration of dibutyryl cyclic
AMP and are now in good health, behaviorally normal, and without
any sequellae.

METHODS

Because dibutyryl cyclic AMP does not cross the cerbrospinal fluid
barrier, the drug has to be injected centrally. Two weeks prior to
the experiment, stainless steel 27 gauge cannulae (David Kopf
Instruments, Tujunga, California) were stereotaxically implanted in
the lateral ventricle of the brain of **female** rhesus monkeys of
breeding age, 4-5 Kg. in weight. Stereotaxically implanted cannulae have multiple advantages over the subarachnoid technique we
had previously reporte 94): they eliminate unnecessary manipulation of the concentrations of dibutyryl cyclic AMP reaching the
lateral ventricle, simplification of the administration of drugs,
and sampling of cerebrospinal fluids and measuring of fluid pressure (an indirect measure of brain blood flow perfusion).

On the day of the experiment, prior to the induction of narcosis,
the rhesus monkey was premedicated with atropine 0.01 mg/kg injected intravenously. Anethesia was induced with 60% nitrous oxide,
40% oxygen and intravenously-injected gallamine 2 mg/kg. Intuba-
tion was performed under direct vision. The same mixture of
nitrous oxide and oxygen was maintained, but small increments of
gallamine were given. Breathing was automatically controlled by a
Harvard Respirator small animal pump. Catheters were inserted into
the right and left femoral arteries and left vein. The catheters
on the right side were connected to transducers to permit the continuous recording of arterial and venous pressures on a multi-
channel recorder. The catheters in the left inguinal area were
used to obtain arterial blood samples for blood gases, pH, amobarbital and cyclic AMP concentrations and blood chemistries. A mid-
esophageal themistor lead was positioned to measure body temperature. Cardiac output was determined by thermal dilution. An
indwelling catheter was used to measure urinary output.

Needle electrodes inserted into the extremities permitted the recording of Lead II of the electrocardiogram, and fronto-occipital electrodes provided electroencephalographic recordings from the cortex. After the blood gases and other parameters had been stabilized for one hour, amobarbital (Amytal) (E. Lilly Company, Indianapolis, Indiana) 155 mg/kg was injected intraperitoneally into rhesus monkeys of both the control and experimental groups. The arterial blood pressure was allowed to fall to below 50% of the control values before sodium chloride 0.9% was administered centrally through the implanted cannulae to the control group, and 3 mg of dibutyryl cyclic AMP (Sigma Company, St. Louis, Missouri) to the experimental group.

RESULTS

Within six minutes of amobarbital injection, the arterial blood pressure fell to below 50% of the control value. When the 50% point was reached, ventilation with 100% oxygen was undertakne. Sodium chloride failed to control the rapid fall of the arterial blood pressure. The control group monkeys died in less than thirty minutes.

In the experimental rhesus monkeys, the similarly lowered arterial blood pressure stabilized within minutes of the injection of dibutyryl cyclic AMP, and gradually, over several hours, returned to control values (Fig. 1). The cardiac output followed a similar course. So did the heart rate, which had initially slowed by 30 or 40%. In contrast, the cerebrospinal fluid pressure recovered rapidly. The electroencephalogram, monitored with scalp electrodes, was electronically silent for over six hours and gradually returned as symptoms of arousal became evident. Mechanical ventilation was discontinued about nine hours after the injection of the lethal dose. Now, seven to eight months after their ordeal, the rhesus monkeys behave normally and do not seem to suffer any sequellae.

DISCUSSION

There is no known antidote to anesthetic, hypnotic and transquilizer drug poisoning. Our initial observations that dibutyryl cyclic AMP (2) and to seven structurally unrelated compounds: paraldehyde, chloral hydrate, diazepam, ketamine, halothane, ethanol and methanol (5) suggested an antidotal therapeutic role for the nucleotide. Injected centrally into rats overdosed with 185 mg/kg of amobarbital, dibutyryl cyclic AMP reduced the mortality rate from 100% to 23% (3). Similarly, dibutyryl cyclic AMP reduced the toxicity of the seven structurally unrelated compounds (5). Such findings suggest a true drug interaction in which one drug changes the pharmacologic effects of another through enhancement of a physiologic opposing system. Since dibutyryl cyclic AMP was administered centrally, its antagonism to the structurally unrelated depressant drugs is in the target cells of the central nervous system. Thus, we have demonstrated that without removing the barbiturate from the system by lavage, emesis, forced diuresis or dialysis and without the supportive measures of fluid therapy or vasopressors, dibutyryl cyclic AMP directly antagonized the amobarbital-induced central nervous depression and the subsequent cardiovascular collapse. In the control monkeys, the arterial blood pressure fell rapidly and inexorably until death, while dibutyryl cyclic AMP blocked the fall and gradually, over three to four hours, returned the blood pressure to control values. Thus, dibutyryl cyclic AMP reversed poisoning equivalent in monkeys to an extravagant dose of 10.85 mg given to a 70 Kg man. Despite ventilation, the control monkeys died within thirty minutes, suggesting that ventilation alone is inadequate protection against distributive, low resistance shock. Of great interest is the fact that the electroencephalogram (EEG) remained silent for six hours after treatment with dibutyryl cyclic AMP. The pupils were fixed and widely dilated for hours. Gradual constriction and slow recovery of the pupillary light reflexes were observed simulatneously with the return of minimal brain electrical activity. Because our treated monkeys survived such ominous symptomatology, we conclude that brain electrical activity recorded with scalp electrodes should not be accepted as a decisive factor in the pronouncement of death of patients overdosed with barbiturates.

Radioimmunoassay measurements of cyclic AMP concentrations in the cerebrospinal fluid of the amobarbital-overdosed rhesus monkeys are in progress to correlate biochemical facts with behavioral events, concentrations of cyclic AMP with depression and arousal (6). Though we do not understand the mechanism triggered by dibutyryl cyclic AMP, our in-vivo findings suggest that cyclic AMP is a key factor in the reversal of amobarbital overdosage.

ACKNOWLEDGEMENTS

We are indebted to Mr. Eugene Cook, Dr. Elisabeth Podoba, Mrs. Carol Phillips and Miss Anne Gloninger for their invaluable technical assistance; and we wish to thank Dr. Myron Taube and Miss Nadine Darocy for their excellent contributions to this manuscript.

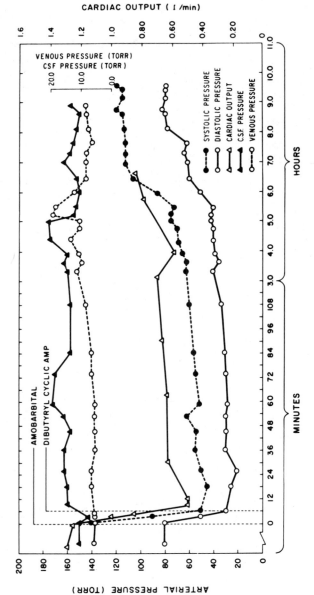

Fig. 1 -- Reversal of Amobarbital Overdosage by Dibutyryl Cyclic AMP in the Rhesus Monkey.

REFERENCES

1. B.J. Kraynack, M.L. Cohn, F.H. Taylor, and M. Cohn, Pharma-
    cology, 13: 1976 (IN PRESS)

2. M.L. Cohn, H. Yamaoka, F.H. Taylor, and B. Kraynack, Neuro-
    pharmacology, 12: 401-405 (1973).

3. M.L. Cohn, F.H. Taylor, M. Cohn, and H. Yamaoka, Res. Commun.
    Chem. Pathol. Pharmacol., 6: 435-446 (1973).

4. M.L. Cohn, Toxicol. Appl. Pharmacol., 25: #146, p. 496 (1973).

5. M.L. Cohn, M. Cohn, F.H. Taylor, and F. Scattaregia, Neuro-
    pharmacology, 14: 483-487 (1975).

6. M.L. Cohn and M. Cohn, Sixth World Congress of Anesthesiology,
    Mexico City, Mexico, #185: 91, April 24-30, 1976.

A NEW INHALATIONAL ANIMAL MODEL FOR ALCOHOL
ADDICTION AND WITHDRAWAL REACTIONS

Major L. Cohn, Marthe Cohn and Helen Baginski

University of Pittsburgh School of Medicine
Pittsburgh, Pennsylvania

Although alcoholism is prevalent in many countries, our experimen-
tatal knowledge of its cause is limited because no animal model to
date accurately mimics the major behavioral features seen in human
alcoholics. Thus, the value of data yielded by previous animal
studies is speculative. Requirements for the ideal animal model
have been reported by Falk, Samson and Winger [1]: 1) Animals
should orally ingest ethanol solution excessively and chronically
in a pattern that increases the concentration of blood ethanol analogous to that of the alcoholic; 2) Animals must demonstrate unequivocal physical dependence on ethanol; 3) Food and ethanol
should be available from sources physically separate, so that the
factors determining ethanol intake are not inextricably bound to
those primarily concerned with meeting nutritional requirements;
4) The experimental arrangement for ethanol ingestion should
retain an elective aspect by being free of extrinsic reinforcement
(for example: shock avoidance, food pellet delivery, etc).
Although Deneau et al. [2], Pieper and Skeen [3] have reported interesting results in rhesus monkeys, their animal model is: 1)
Very high in cost; 2) A slow process and time consuming; 3) Limited to few animals because of housing and handling problems. Faced
with such difficulties, we chose the rat as animal model, devised a
new inhalation method, and produced alcohol-addicted rats.

To duplicate feeding experiments described by Rawat and Kuriyama
[4], rats were housed four per cage, and fed a diet of 61% Slender,
(Mead-Johnson, Indianapolis, Indiana) to which either 6% ethyl alcohol v/v or isocaloric sucrose was added. Cannibalism in both
groups decimated the rats, and the experiment had to be discontinued. Next, we repeated the work of Goldstein and Pal [5], and
Goldstein [6], [7], [8], [9], [10], and found that while their
passive inhalational method had definite advantages, the results
did not fulfill all the requirements proposed by Falk, et al. [1].
To improve the alcohol inhalational model, we ordered an inhala-

tional chamber for toxicology studies. Such a chamber allows passive addiction of rats at reasonable costs and a wide range of experiments with minimal handling. The glass walls of the tank-like chamber permit us to freely and continually view and score behavioral events. However, the most critical improvement in our system is the use of an ultrasonic nebulizer (DeVilbiss Model 35) to deliver a homogenous high-density mist of ethanol vapors with particle sizes between 0.2 and 3 μ. These fine and nearly uniform particles make contact with the entire alveolar surface of the lungs of the rat, enabling ethanol vapors to be absorbed by a huge surface. For our needs, we converted the nebulizer to deliver the ethanol vapors at rates varying from 0 to 0.46 ml/min. The carrier gas of our inhalational system is compressed air, set at a flow rate of 3 l./min. Conventional and/or gas operated generators deliver much larger aerosol particles, which affect only the upper airway passages and have little contact with the alveolar surface of the lungs, producing much lower blood alcohol concentrations.

Our nebulizing system is so effective that pyrazole (a known hepatic toxinogen) is not needed to maintain consistently high blood alcohol concentrations (2-4 mg/ml). A graduated reservoir containing the 50/50 solution of alcohol-distilled water is located outside the inhalational chamber. The alcohol solution is continuously nebulized with minimal handling. With the flow regulated at 0.46 ml/min., saturation of the chamber is maintained at about 25 mg/l. While this concentration is twice as high as that reported by Goldstein and Pal [5], it produces very few deaths. The fine ethanol vapor mist has another advantage over the conventional system of delivery: it avoids large quantities of fluid collecting at the bottom of the cages.

METHODS

Sprague-Dawley male rats, 100-150 g (Zivic-Miller, Pittsburgh, Pennsylvania), were housed in individual cages, under constant illumination, at temperatures between 21°C and 23°C. Each rat was fed Purina rat chow dispensed in food cups and water ad lib. Every 24 hours, weight of the rats and rate of food and water consumption were recorded. After a week of acclimation, each rat was exposed in our inhalational chamber to a 50% ethanol-distilled water v/v solution. Ethanol was nebulized at 0.46 ml/min with a DeVilbiss Ultrasonic Nebulizer, Model 35 (Somerset, Pennsylvania). Control groups were submitted to the same protocol, but exposed to water vapors only. Three 100 ml Kimax drinking bottles containing either water, Slender (Mead-Johnson, Indianapolis, Indiana), or mixtures of 61% Slender and various concentrations of alcohol 12% were made available to all rats during and after treatment. Weighed amounts of Purina rat chow were placed in the cages for ad lib consumption. The amounts of water, Slender, Slender-ethanol mixture and rat chow consumed were recorded every 24 hours. Random rotation of the three drinking tubes prevented a preferential habit, and the addicted rat's preference for ethanol was clearly discerned.

Blood samples were taken three times a week and the enzymatic determination of blood alcohol followed the method of Lundquist [11], with 10 μl samples of tail blood assayed in duplicate. The blood was deproteinized with 0.09 ml of 3.4% perchloric acid. After a 90 minute incubation with the 3.0 ml of the reaction mixture, the change in optical density of 340 nm was determined. Alcohol vapor concentration was measured by the same enzymatic method.

The unstressful standardized tilt plane test was used to measure ataxia and open field behavior was assessed and scored [12]. The weight, blood pressure and rectal temperature were recorded and followed biweekly. In a selected group of animals, gross and fine motor activity was measured on a two-channel electronic activity monitor [13]. Scoring of behavioral reactions followed the grading system of Goldstein and Pal [5].

RESULTS

During the first exposure to alcohol vapors, a session of eight hours, the rats did not lose the righting reflex. They were then exposed five times, on alternate days, and experienced a progressive loss of alcohol tolerance and exhibited more severe symptoms of depression in increasingly shorter exposure times. Severity of intoxication was determined at the time of removal from the inhalational chamber by scoring respiratory depression, irritability to handling, ataxia, hyperactivity, sedation and narcosis. Tremors and convulsions were never observed in any treated rats. We found no correlation between blood concentrations and alterations of behavioral events.

The diet of the control group consisted of water, Purina lab chow and a solution of Slender-sucrose. Sucrose was added in concentrations isocalorically equivalent to the 12% ethyl alcohol given to the study group. Although they had free and unlimited access to water and Purina lab chow, the control rats showed a distinct preference for Slender-sucrose solutions. As shown in Fig. 1, their body weight increased steadily while their total caloric intake decreased progressively, reaching 43% of control values at the end of the 12 week period. Rat performance was tested twice a week in an open field and scored for the number of squares crossed, curiosity, exploration, grooming, sniffing, rearing, frequency of urinations. The tilt plane test showed that all control rats, regardless of their weight, maintained their balance at or above a 30° inclination.

The rats of the study group were similarly exposed to alcohol vapor treatment. However, their diet differed from that of the control group. Alongside the water bottle and Purina lab chow, a bottle containing a mixture of 12% ethyl alcohol and Slender was also available. Following the alcohol inhalational treatment the rats voluntarily consumed increasing amounts of alcohol (Fig. 2). Two to four weeks after the last inhalational exposure, the rats ingested alcohol in the range of 7 g/kg of body weight. The body weights of these rats increased steadily to a mean of 520 gm (100 g less than the weight of the control rats on the Slender-sucrose diet), while their total caloric intake decreased progressively, reaching 45% of control values at the end of the 12 week period. The decline in caloric intake was not significantly different in the two groups of rats. No behavioral differences between the two groups were noticeable in the open field behavior test. However, on the tilt plane, the rats in the study group were unable to maintain their balance above 25° inclination.

At the end of the 12 week period we re-exposed the rats to alcohol vaporization in order to determine whether repeating the treatment would alter alcohol consumption (Fig. 3). Following re-exposure, the voluntary alcohol consumption rose abruptly to 8 g/kg of body weight and did not significantly decline thereafter. The only alterations we found were the loss of the ability to swim and the ability to maintain balance above 25° inclination. Both of these changes suggest a locomotor deficit.

The percent of the calories derived from the alcohol intake compared to the total caloric consumption was calculated by summing up the caloric values of Purina lab chow, Slender and alcohol. Following the second inhalational exposure, the percent of alcohol consumption increased from approximately 15% to well over 40% of the total caloric intake. In contrast to the findings of Freund [14], who reported that a 45% concentration of ethanol in a liquid diet results in the death of all animals, no rats included in our study died. Our results are very similar to those obtained by Falk et al. [1], who reported a 44.8% of alcohol caloric intake in rats on a forced feeding polydipsic regimen.

DISCUSSION

Using our modified, more efficient inhalational technique, we have addicted rats so that they voluntarily, without coercion or reinforcement, consume increasing amounts of alcohol, although water and Purina lab chow are freely available. Our model meets the most critical of the requirements proposed by Falk, et al. [1].

Unlike Goldstein [9], who reported decay of physical dependence within one day, we found that lethargy, staggering, disorientation, gross tremors, hyperactive startle reactions to noise, ataxia, stereotyped locomotor behavior and weight loss lasted from several days to two to three weeks after alcohol vaporization was discontinued. These symptoms of withdrawal are more pronounced in mice than in rats. We have never observed convulsions or audiogenic seizures in any of the rats exposed to alcohol. Thus, our findings are closer to those of Mendelson et al. [15], who showed long-term alcohol physical dependence in man.

In the present study, rats passively exposed to ethanol vapors freely consumed between 7 to 8 g/kg of ethanol, a higher consumption than that reported by Heintzelman et al. [16] in rats on a polydipsic-induced feeding regimen.

Although the nature of the addictive process to alcohol is unknown, we do know that alcohol dependence in man is achieved by slow process. Because medical, environmental and emotional determinants complicate the study of alcoholism in humans, we have developed an animal model to provide behavioral, biochemical and neurophysiological data on alcohol addiction.

ACKNOWLEDGMENTS

We wish to thank Doctor Myron Taube and Miss Nadine Darocy for their excellent contributions to this manuscript.

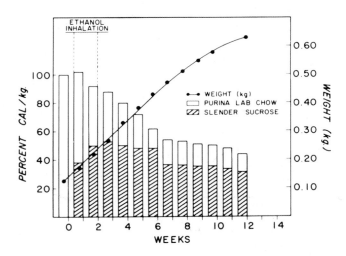

Fig. 1 -- Mean Weight of Rats and Percent of Their Calorie/kg intake of Purina Lab Chow and Slender-Sucrose Solution for a Period of 12 Weeks.

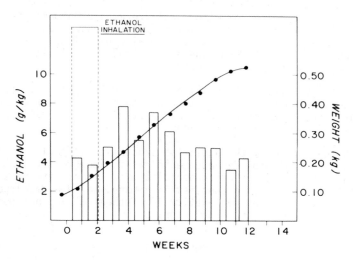

Fig. 2 -- Mean Weight of Rats and Ethanol Intake (g/kg) for a Period of 12 Weeks.

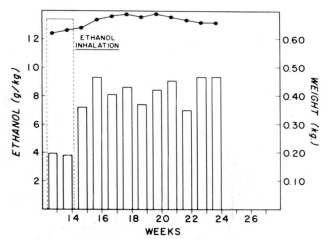

Fig. 3 -- Mean Weight of Rats and Ethanol Intake (g/kg) for a Second Period of 12 Weeks.

REFERENCES

1. J.L. Falk, H.H. Samson, and G. Winger, Science, 177: 811-813 (1972).

2. G. Deneau, T. Yanagita, and M.H. Seevers, Psychopharmacologia, 16: 30-48 (1969).

3. W.A. Pieper and M.J. Skeen, Life Sci., 2(1): 989-997 (1972).

4. A.K. Rawat and K. Kuriyama, Science, 176: 1133-1135 (1972).

5. D.B. Goldstein and N. Pal, Science, 172: 288-290 (1971).

6. D.B. Goldstein, J. Pharmacol. Exp. Ther., 180: 203-215 (1972).

7. D.B. Goldstein, J. Pharmacol. Exp. Ther., 183: 14-22 (1972).

8. D.B. Goldstein, J. Pharmacol. Exp. Ther., 186: 1-9 (1973).

9. D.B. Goldstein, J. Pharmacol. Exp. Ther., 190: 377-383 (1974).

10. D.B. Goldstein, Fed. Proceedings, 34(10): 1953-1961 (1975).

11. F. Lundquist, Meth. Biochem. Anal., 7: 217-251 (1959).

12. H. Wallgren and H. Barry, III, Biochemical Physiological and Psychological Aspects, Volume 1, Elsevier Publishing Company, New York, New York, pp. 400, 1970.

13. S.G. Holtzman and F.H. Schneider, Life Sci., 14: 1243-1250 (1974).

14. G. Freund, Arch. Neurol., 21: 315-320 (1969).

15. J.H. Mendelson, S. Stein, and M.T. McGuire, Psychosom. Med. 28: 1-12 (1966).

16. M.E. Heintzelman, J. Best, and R.J. Senter, Science, 191: 482-483 (1976).

URINARY DISPOSITION OF NALTREXONE
AND ITS METABOLITES*

Harry E. Dayton, Nithiananda Chatterjie and Charles E. Inturrisi

Department of Pharmacology
Cornell University Medical College
New York, New York 10021

Naltrexone is a narcotic antagonist having little agonist
activity. Its long duration of action and the apparent absence of
side effects have led to its evaluation and use as an opiate
blocking agent in chronic therapy (1). Investigation of the metabolism of the drug indicates that in man the 6-keto function undergoes reduction to form predominantly the 6β-alcohol. While in the
chicken the 6α-alcohol primarily results (2,3,4,5). These reduction
products, β-naltrexol and α-naltrexol are two chemically distinct
compounds which could conceivably have different pharmacologic
activities. Since they are produced metabolically in a species
stereoselective manner after naltrexone administration, it became
important (1) to examine the potential pharmacologic activity of
β-naltrexol itself and also that of α-naltrexol and (2) to quantitatively examine the urinary excretion profiles after naltrexone
administration in species commonly used in chronic drug toxicity
studies.

The development of a sensitive and specific method for the
simultaneous quantitation of β-naltrexol, α-naltrexol and naltrexone was carried out in our laboratory (6). This method involves
differential solvent extraction from the biofluid, followed by
trimethylsilyl derivative formation using bis-(trimethylsilyl) tri-
fluoroacetamide + 1% trimethylchlorosilane. Quantitation was
achieved using gas-liquid chromatography with flame ionization
detection. Of the several liquid phases tested for GLC analysis
of the compounds of interest, it was found that although 3% OV-17,
on a solid support of Gas-Chrom Q did provide some separation of

---

*Our research as described in this paper was supported in part by
SAODAP Grant No. DA-00458. Dr. Inturrisi is an Andrew W. Mellon
Teacher-Scientist for 1975-76.

the α-β epimers as TMS-derivatives, 3% QF-1 on Gas-Chrom Q, 80-100 mesh provided baseline separation for all three compounds. Figure 1 contains sample chromatograms obtained using this system, with oxilorphan as the internal standard. The left panel is a chromatogram obtained from extracted and derivatized analytical standards. The right panel is the chromatogram obtained from extracted and derivatized monkey urine to which was added only the internal standard. The range of linear response to these TMS derivatives was observed between 0.1 and 60 mcg. The lower limit of sensitivity for all these compounds as TMS-derivatives is 0.025 mcg/ml of biofluid.

The urinary excretion patterns in chronically dosed naltrexone maintanence patients who had been receiving 125 mg of naltrexone orally three times per week for four weeks reflected an average of 37% of the administered dose recovered in the 48 hours post drug administration. β-naltrexol in both unconjugated and conjugated forms was the predominant urinary excretion product with very little free naltrexone appearing in the urine. The time course of urinary excretion indicated that following oral administration of naltrexone, there was a rapid excretion into the urine of both naltrexone and β-naltrexol which was followed by a slower elimination rate consisting almost exclusively of β-naltrexol. For example, only 3% of the administered dose was recovered 24-48 hours, while 24% was recovered during the first four hours post drug administration. These patterns correspond quite well with the reports of Cone et al. after a single oral dose in man, and supported the idea that β-naltrexol might possibly be playing a part in the long duration of antagonist action seen in man following naltrexone administration (4).

The urinary excretion pattern of naltrexone in rhesus monkeys receiving 12 mg/kg of naltrexone orally every day for 8 months is somewhat different from that of chronically treated man. Like man, both naltrexone and β-naltrexol appear in the urine. But, the monkey conjugates β-naltrexol more extensively than man, excreting very little of the free β-alcohol into the urine. An apparent sex-related difference in urinary excretion patterns was observed and found to be independent of urinary pH. That is, approximately 2 - 2½ times as much of the dose administered was recovered in females as in males, with a very small percentage of the dose being recovered in feces of either sex. Less than ½ of the administered dose of naltrexone could be accounted for in the 24 hour fecal and urinary collections of these chronically treated animals. The predominant and persistant urinary metabolite, though, in both chronically treated man and the monkey is β-naltrexol.

In rabbits after multiple intraperitoneal doses approximately 18% of the administered dose could be accounted for in the 24 hour urine. The rabbit also eliminates naltrexone and β-naltrexol with conjugated naltrexone being the predominant urinary compound.

Urine was analyzed from Holtzman rats used in chronic naltrexone toxicity studies receiving 100 mg/kg of naltrexone orally every day for one year. These animals did excrete both naltrexone and β-naltrexol in the urine in free and conjugated forms, although a surprisingly small percentage of the administered dose could be recovered.

Work in a number of laboratories, including our own, leads to the general consensus that for all mammalian species, the primary reduction product appearing in the urine is β-naltrexol (3,4,5,6, 7). With more sensitive analytical techniques, it has been possible for some investigators to identify the presence of α-naltrexol in trace amounts (8).

Preliminary characterization of the pharmacologic activity of β-naltrexol and α-naltrexol was carried out in conjunction with Dr. Harold Blumberg and H. Dayton of Endo Labs (9). These studies indicated that both β-naltrexol and α-naltrexol, when administered separately to mice, appear to be much less potent as narcotic antagonists than naltrexone. β-naltrexol, like naltrexone produced no antinociceptive activity in mice while α-naltrexol doses exhibit some. Fujimoto et al. have also examined the antagonist activity of these compounds in mice and found similarly that β-naltrexol is approximately 1/50 as potent as naltrexone, and that α-naltrexol is only slightly more potent as an antagonist than β-naltrexol (10). These low potency estimates of the reduced metabolites militate against the idea that the formation of such compounds outside the CNS could contribute substantially to the overall narcotic antagonist action of naltrexone.

The species variant total base recovery from urine indicates that either other routes of elimination might be quantitatively important for this drug, or that other products of biotransformation exist. The latter idea has been recently substantiated by the preliminary identification of 2,3 hydroxymethoxy naltrexone in the laboratories of Cone and of Verebely(8,11), and the identification of trace amounts of α-naltrexol in species indicated above.

In summary, it is clear that species differences do exist in the quantitative patterns of urinary excretion of both naltrexone and its metabolites. Such differences must be taken into consideration when choosing species in which to evaluate the pharmacodynamics of a new compound.

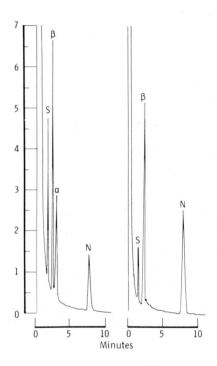

Figure 1. Chromatograms of naltrexone (N), β-naltrexol (β), α-naltrexol (α) and oxilorphan (S). The left panel represents these compounds added to urine, extracted and prepared as TMS derivatives. The right panel represents urine from treated monkeys to which oxilorphan (S) has been added followed by extraction and derivatization.

REFERENCES

1. W. R. Martin, D. R. Jasinsky, and R. A. Mansky, Arch. Gen. Psychiat., 28: 784 (1973).

2. E. J. Cone, Tetrahedron Letters, 28: 2607 (1973).

3. E. J. Cone, S. Y. Yeh, and C. W. Gorodetzky, Pharmacologist, 15: 1242 (1973).

4. E. J. Cone, C. W. Gorodetzky, and S. Y. Yeh, Drug Metab. Disp., 2: 506 (1974).

5. N. Chatterjie, J. M. Fujimoto, C. E. Inturrisi, S. Roerig, R. I. H. Wang, D. V. Bowen, F. H. Field, and D. D. Clark, Drug Metab. Disp., 2: 401 (1974).

6. H. E. Dayton and C. E. Inturrisi, Drug Metab. Disp., in press (1976).

7. L. Malspeis, M. S. Bathala, R. M. Ludden, H. B. Bhat, S. G. Frank, T. D. Sokoloski, B. E. Morrison, and R. H. Reuning, Res. Comm. Chem. Path. Pharmacol., 12: 43 (1975).

8. E. J. Cone and C. W. Gorodetzky, Fed. Proc., 35: 469 (1976).

9. N. Chatterjie, C. E. Inturrisi, H. B. Dayton, and H. Blumberg, J. Med. Chem., 18: 490 (1975).

10. J. M. Fujimoto, S. Roerig, R. I. H. Wang, N. Chatterjie, and C. E. Inturrisi, Proc. Soc. Exp. Biol. Med., 148: 443 (1975).

11. K. Verebely, M. A. Chedekel, S. J. Mule, and D. Rosenthal, Res. Comm. Chem. Path. Pharmacol., 12: 67 (1975).

SPECULATIONS ON THE NEUROCHEMICAL NATURE OF ETHANOL DEPENDENCE: AN OVERVIEW

Boris   Tabakoff

Department of Physiology
University of Illinois Medical Center
Chicago,   Illinois

The neurochemical components of the addiction syndrome referred to as alcoholism result from the interaction of this drug with neurons which under normal circumstances are tightly controlled by feedback regulatory systems. Many of the neuronal systems of brain exhibit such feedback control which is responsive to the output of the neurons. This output can be correlated with the release of transmitter. Examples of this type of neuronal control would be the striatal dopamine neurons or the alpha presynaptic receptors recently described for the noradrenergic systems. Ethanol may interact at one or more sites, and such interaction could result in a change in output from the neuron. The interaction of ethanol with neurons may be either direct, such as the membrane effects which lead to a block in conduction (1) or indirect such as those effects producing changes in input to the neuron (2). In either case the resultant change in input would activate feedback controls which would try to compensate for the effects of the ethanol. On the other hand, the feedback controls may in themselves be affected by ethanol. This model may be regarded simply as a modification of the models for the development of tolerance and physical dependence proposed by Goldstein and Goldstein (3) or Jaffe and Sharpless (4) and recently reiterated by Kaufman, Koski and Peat (5).

Such models are used to conceptualize the factors which are responsible for the tolerance to ethanol's behavioral effects and symptoms of physical dependence. The symptoms of physical dependence after withdrawal of ethanol can be separated into an early withdrawal phase and a late phase known as delerium tremens. Since the CNS of animals is more accessible to biochemical manipulation than the human counterpart, most of the studies performed in the area I am covering have been done in animals.

We have recently used a behavioral rating scale to monitor the intensity of the withdrawal syndrome in mice and correlated these measures with measures of autonomic responses such as withdrawal hypothermia during the early withdrawal period (6). In addition, French and his coworkers (7) have reported a secondary phase consisting of hyperkinesia in animals three days after ethanol withdrawal which they equated with delerium tremens.

The major question in neurochemical research in this area has been: What are the underlying mechanisms responsible for the withdrawal symptoms, and are the same mechanisms responsible for both tolerance and physical dependence. Some of the confusion which has resulted from studies trying to answer these questions is probably due to major differences in the degree of physical dependence, the methods of ethanol administration, blood ethanol levels at the time of testing, and the manifestations of the withdrawal which in many cases were not monitored and make critical comparison between different studies difficult.

Not all data is inconsistent, however, and some investigators have well correlated their neurochemical data with behavioral and physiological effects of intoxication and withdrawal. The most consistent results seem to be with regard to NE metabolism. The prominent effect of an acute dose of ethanol on brain NE metabolism is to depress the turnover of NE (8,9), although there may be an initial phase of increased turnover (10). This initial phase of increased turnover may be a response similar to that seen in the adrenal which results from the emotional excitation initially produced by ethanol.

In sharp contrast to the effects of a single dose of ethanol, it has been shown that the NE system after chronic ethanol administration is in a state of hyperactivity as demonstrated by studies showing increased NE turnover (9,10,11). Several major questions have to be asked regarding this increased activity: 1) is this activity responsible for any of the manifestations of withdrawal or 2) is it a protective response elicited by the withdrawal symptomatology and 3) could this be a neurochemical manifestation of tolerance rather than physical dependence and as such, are tolerance and physical dependence simply progressive examples of the same biochemical continuum? Prior to addressing these questions, I would like to consider the possible mechanisms by which the chronic intake of ethanol could alter NE metabolism and produce such an increase in NE turnover.

The rate-limiting enzyme in the synthesis of NE is tyrosine hydroxylase and the activity of this enzyme seems to be coupled to impulse flow (12) and also to the components which make up the intracellular milieu in noradrenergic neurons. Two mechanisms for the control of enzyme activity have been currently popularized. The first is the depletion of a small extravesicular pool of NE during impulse flow which would relieve the feedback inhibition on the activity of tyrosine hydroxylase. The second proposed mechanism is, by the action of Ca^{++} and cAMP on the enzyme (13). Both the cation (Ca^{++}) and the cyclic nucleotide increase the affinity of the enzyme (activated enzyme) for the cosubstrates and significantly decrease the affinity of the enzyme for norepinephrine and thus effectively prevent feedback inhibition of the enzyme.

Increasing concentrations of ethanol have been shown to produce a reduction in impulse conduction (4). This would lead to an accumulation in presynaptic NE and decrease in synthesis as has been seen after acute ethanol administration. Another effect which may also be correlated with acute ethanol intake was demonstrated by

Seeman (3). A significant amount of Ca^{++} was shown to be segregated from the free form onto biological membranes in the presence of ethanol and this phenomenon could remove the Ca^{++} necessary for optimum tyrosine hydroxylase activity. Ross et al. (14) have also shown that a single dose of ethanol significantly reduces the levels of Ca^{++} in various brain areas but tolerance quickly develops to this effect of a single dose of ethanol. The decreases in free Ca^{++} and total brain Ca^{++} could again be reflected in a decreased activity of tyrosine hydroxylase and the decreased NE turnover.

Since ethanol has been shown to produce a dose-dependent inhibition of transport systems in the choroid plexus (15) and the choroid plexus is also the tissue responsible for the production of CSF and control of Ca^{++} levels in brain, ethanol may lower brain Ca^{++} by its effects on the choroid plexus.

The effects of ethanol on free Ca^{++} or on impulse flow could thus explain the effects of an acute ethanol dose in decreasing NE turnover. The chronic effects would then have to include the phenomena of increased membrane tolerance to the effects of ethanol or an increase in brain Ca^{++} levels in the presence of ethanol. Interestingly, Ross and his coworkers (16) have recently reported that chronic exposure to ethanol increased the calcium content of synaptosomal membranes of animals chronically drinking ethanol compared to control animals.

Increased NE turnover after chronic ethanol intake may also result from formation of false transmitters in the CNS. Here I am referring to the formation of the TIQ alkaloids by either a direct condensation of amines with acetaldehyde (17) or the condensation of the aldehydes produced from the amines with the parent amine (18). The TIQ's could interact with either postsynaptic or presynaptic receptors and act as weak agonists or antagonists. Interaction at postsynaptic sites could induce activity in a feedback loop which would in turn activate synthesis. Such interaction of TIQ's with noradrenergic beta receptors has been demonstrated by Cohen and Dembiec (19). On the other hand, the release of TIQ derivatives into the synaptic cleft could result in an interaction with presynaptic alpha receptors which have been shown by several groups to control the release of NE into the cleft. Blockade of these alpha receptors would result in overflow release of NE from presynaptic terminals and the depletion of presynaptic stores would activate amine synthesis.

Chronic ethanol administration may alter acetaldehyde metabolism. Korsten, et al. (20) have noted that alcoholics have significantly higher blood acetaldehyde levels than non-alcoholics after ethanol administration. We have also noted (see Table I) that blood levels of acetaldehyde tend to increase during chronic ethanol ingestion by mice. Increased blood acetaldehyde if reflected in brain (21) could lead to increased formation of the TIQ alkaloids. I feel that the changes which result in altered characteristics of tyrosine hydroxylase such as those dependent on changes in intracellular Ca^{++} and altered receptor reactivity to released NE are the most promising in explaining the increased NE turnover after chronic ethanol consumption.

I would now like to return to the questions I posed as to whether the increase NE turnover during withdrawal is 1) responsible for the symptoms of withdrawal, 2) a response to the stress of withdrawal, or 3) more related to the manifestations of tolerance to ethanol.

In answer to the first two questions, two types of experiments seem to lead to opposite conclusions. The time course of the increase in NE turnover (10,12) indicates the presence of the increased turnover at times when no withdrawal signs are present. Therefore, increased NE turnover is not simply a protective response to the stress of withdrawal. On the other hand, several authors have shown that increased noradrenergic activity in the CNS protects animals from drug-, electrically- and sound-induced seizures, and three sets of authors have demonstrated that blocking noradrenergic systems and depleting NE potentiates the hyper-reactivity and seizures seen during withdrawal. Thus the questions of the exact role of NE in withdrawal symptomatology remains unanswered.

In response to the question of whether changes in the noradrenergic system may be responsible for some of the tolerance observed during chronic ethanol consumption, I have the following evidence from our laboratories.

We placed control mice and mice pretreated with 6-hydroxydopamine (6-OHDA) in a situation in which they were provided with only one source of food and water, and this source was a liquid diet containing 7% ethanol. Prior to being placed on this diet and at various intervals after being placed on the diet, the mice were injected with a 3 g/kg challenge dose of ethanol and their temperatures and behavioral responses were monitored. NE levels were significantly decreased in the 6-OHDA-treated mice. Although control animals consuming the ethanol-containing diet became quite tolerant to the effects of ethanol, the animals treated with 6-OHDA prior to chronic ethanol administration did not develop any tolerance to the temperature lowering or hypnotic effects of ethanol. On the other hand, no difference in the withdrawal symptomatology was evident between the 6-OHDA-treated animals and the control physically dependent animals, thus indicating that 6-OHDA did not affect the development of physical dependence.

I feel that a fruitful model for the development of tolerance is the following: an acute dose of ethanol, possibly by depressing transport systems in the choroid plexus, lowers brain Ca^{++} levels. This in turn decreases tyrosine hydroxylase activity which coupled with decreased impulse flow would result in a decreased amount of NE in the synaptic cleft. The hypothermia and behavioral depression concomitant with acute ethanol ingestion may be directly or secondarily coupled to this noradrenergic deficit.

On chronic ethanol administration, a tolerance develops to the Ca^{++} lowering effect of ethanol and in fact Ca^{++} levels are increased in brain. This increase in Ca^{++} could result in increased tyrosine hydroxylase activity leading to increase in NE available for release with impulse flow and thus result in a tolerance to the depressant effects of ethanol.

Our studies also seem to point to a dissociation of the mechanisms underlying tolerance and dependence. However, a great deal of further work is required in this area. Similarly, we do not feel that a single transmitter is responsible for all the concomitants of tolerance and another for physical dependence. Thus, further work should be aimed at determining neurochemical as well as behavioral profiles of tolerance and dependence.

Supported in part by grants from PHS-NIAAA(#02696), NINDS (#12759), and U. of I. Research Board. BT is a Schweppe Foundation Fellow.

Table I. Blood Acetaldehyde Levels (nmoles/ml) in Animals Chronically Consuming Ethanol

Days on Alcohol Diet:	1	2	3	4	5	6
am	- -	140 ± 13	84 ± 20	101 ± 30	50 ± 15	260 ± 115
pm	- -	76 ± 16	82 ± 33	81 ± 34	168 ± 31	182 ± 70

References

1. P. Seeman, Pharmacol. Rev. 24:583 (1972).
2. H. Kalant, Fed. Proc. 34:1930 (1975).
3. A. Goldstein and D. B. Goldstein, in The Addictive States (A. Wikler, ed.), Williams-Wilkins, Baltimore, 1968, p. 265.
4. J.H. Jaffe and S.K. Sharpless, in The Addictive States (A. Wikler, ed.), Williams-Wilkins, Baltimore, 1968, p. 226.
5. J.J. Kaufman, R. Koski and S. Peat, Life Sci. 17:83 (1976).
6. R.F. Ritzmann and B. Tabakoff, J. Pharm. Exp. Ther., in press.
7. S.W. French, D.S. Palmer, M.E. Narod, P.E. Reid and C.W. Ramey, J. Pharm. Exp. Ther. 194:319 (1975).
8. L.A. Pohorecky, J. Pharm. Exp. Ther. 189:380 (1974).
9. P.V. Thadani, B.M. Kulig, F.C. Brown and J.D. Beard, Biochem. Pharm. 25:93 (1975).
10. W.A. Hunt and E. Majchrowicz, J. Neurochem. 23:549 (1974).
11. L. Ahtee and M. Svartström-Fraser, Acta Pharm. et Toxicol. 36: 289 (1975).
12. R.H. Roth, V.H. Morgenroth and S. Salzman, N-S Arch. Pharm. 289: 327 (1975).
13. V.H. Morgenroth and R.H. Roth, Molec. Pharm. 11:427 (1975).
14. D.H. Ross, M.A. Medina and H.L. Cardena, Science 186:63 (1974).
15. B. Tabakoff, R.F. Ritzmann, W.O. Boggan, J. Neurochem. 24:1043 (1975).
16. D.H. Ross, H.L. Cardenas, S.C. Lynn, Trans. Am. Soc. Neurochem. 7:150 (1976).
17. G. Cohen and M. Collins, Science 167:1749 (1970).
18. V.E. Davis and M.A. Walsh, Science 170:1005 (1970).
19. R.E. Heikkila, D. Dembiec and G. Cohen, Finnish Foundation for Alcohol Studies 23:297 (1975).
20. M.A. Korsten, S. Matsuzaki, L. Feinman and C.S. Lieber, New Eng. J. Med. 292:386 (1975).
21. B. Tabakoff, R. Anderson, R. Ritzmann Biochem. Pharm. in press.

HISTORY OF NARCOTIC ANTAGONISTS IN
ADDICTION THERAPY--FUTURE PROBLEMS

William R. Martin

National Institute on Drug Abuse
Division of Research
Addiction Research Center
Lexington, Kentucky 40511

The history of narcotic antagonists dates to the turn of the
century when Pohl synthesized N-allylnorcodeine and found that it
antagonized some of the depressant effects of morphine. It was
Pohl's concept that allyl groups functioned as metabolic stimulants and with this thought probably in mind some 40 years later
N-allylnormorphine was synthesized and studied by two groups of
investigators, Hart and McCawley at the University of California,
and Weijlard, Erickson and Unna at the Merck Research Laboratory.
At this time, there still was divided opinion as to how nalorphine
antagonized morphine; some evidence indicated that nalorphine had
stimulant properties in its own right, while other data indicated
that it was a competitive antagonist of morphine. The resolution
of these discrepancies came (cf. [1]) when it was shown that the
competitive antagonists nalorphine and cyclazocine also had agonistic activities which partially accounted for some of their
stimulant actions, and that when these agents were administered
chronically tolerance developed to their agonistic but not antagonistic effects [2, 3]. It was also demonstrated that when
patients to whom cyclazocine had been administered chronically
were abruptly withdrawn, an abstinence syndrome emerged after a
latency of several days [2]. These observations suggested that
cyclazocine had a very long duration of action in man, a property
not present in other species. Subsequent studies demonstrated
that indeed both the agonistic and antagonistic activities of
cyclazocine persisted for over 24 hours and that when it was administered chronically in dose levels of 4 to 6 mg/day it completely
antagonized the euphorigenic actions of "street size" doses of
morphine and heroin and markedly attenuated the ability of morphine
to produce physical dependence [4]. At this time we suggested
that cyclazocine might have utility in assisting highly motivated
narcotic addicts in remaining abstinent and felt that antagonist

therapy might have several benefits to the patient: (1) It would prevent overdose deaths. In our studies we had shown that 100 mg of heroin administered intravenously in patients receiving 4 mg of cyclazocine per day produced only very modest effects. (2) Antagonist therapy would also prevent the development of physical dependence as a consequence of spree use of heroin. (3) Since it would prevent or block the reinforcing properties of morphine (production of euphoria and abstinence as a consequence of physical dependence), extinction of conditioned abstinence and drug-seeking behavior would occur if patients continued using heroin. (4) It would decrease anxieties associated with abstinence. (5) It was further hoped that blocking the agonistic effects of morphine would allow physiologic extinction of protracted abstinence to proceed without being exacerbated by intermittent "street" use of heroin.

Immediately following our experiments with cyclazocine, we were fortunate to begin our studies with naloxone. Naloxone had been previously studied by Lasagna [5] and was thought to produce analgesia with modest doses and hyperalgesia at higher doses. When administered to subjects even in large doses, naloxone did not produce subjective changes like either those of morphine or nalorphine. Further, when it was administered chronically, it likewise produced virtually no changes and when withdrawn no abstinence syndrome was observed [6]. We, therefore, concluded that naloxone must be a relatively pure narcotic antagonist. Dr. Jerome Jaffe of Albert Einstein College of Medicine and Dr. Alfred M. Freedman of the New York Medical College had begun clinical trials of cyclazocine in the treatment of addicts and found that cyclazocine's dysphoric subjective effects may have decreased its acceptability to patients. Our studies with naloxone revealed that it had a relatively short duration of action and was relatively ineffective orally and for this reason we felt that it would not be as useful in treating addicts. Zaks et al. [7] subsequently confirmed these observations and found that nearly a gram a day of naloxone was required to produce a degree of blockade that was achieved with 4 mg per day of cyclazocine. At this time we began to speculate about the possibility that a drug having certain structural properties of both cyclazocine and naloxone might be endowed with the desirable properties of both. Through the cooperation of Drs. Harold Blumberg, Ralph Jacobsen and Irwin J. Pachter of Endo Laboratories, Inc., we were able to obtain naltrexone, a congener of naloxone, which has the N-methylcyclopropyl moiety on the nitrogen. Dr. Blumberg had previously shown that naltrexone was several times more potent than naloxone as an antagonist. Studies were undertaken by Endo Laboratories, Inc. which showed that naltrexone did not cause adverse effects in large doses using accepted toxicologic methods. Following these investigations, we initiated studies in man and showed that naltrexone was approximately 2 to 3 times more potent than naloxone, that it had a duration of action longer than naloxone but shorter than cyclazocine, and that when administered orally in dose levels of 50 mg chronically it produced a degree of blockade comparable to that seen with 4 mg of cyclazocine daily. Naltrexone also appeared to be virtually devoid of agonistic activity, and we felt that it would not be aversive to patients wishing to have antagonist therapy [8]. We have subsequently studied other antagonists in both man and the chronic spinal dog. Oxilorphan was found to be approximately equipotent to cyclazocine as an antagonist in man and although its agonistic actions were less than those of cyclazocine they were qualitatively similar. Diprenorphine was studied in the chronic spinal dog and found to be slightly more potent than naltrexone as an antagonist, but had agonistic actions similar to nalorphine and oxilorphan. Continuing research with naltrexone has confirmed, I believe, most of our initial findings. It is a potent orally effective antagonist that is virtually devoid of side effects and toxicity in clinically useful dose levels.

Only a small portion of addict patients seem to accept antagonist therapy. Over some years, we have been impressed by the fact that drug abusers have a constellation of negative feeling states that we have termed hypophoria consisting of feelings of unpopularity, inefficiency and ineptness as well as a poor self-image. We have further observed that virtually all drugs of abuse are capable of diminishing feelings of hypophoria. We have also shown that these negative feeling states are exacerbated when narcotics are administered chronically, as well as during both early and protracted abstinence and that these negative feeling states may be associated with early drug use as well as relapse following treatment. As a consequence of a variety of studies, we believe that protracted abstinence, as well as possibly congenital and hereditary factors, may give rise to increased need states in the addict. These increased need states in turn give rise to impulsivity and feelings of egocentricity. The failure of the social setting to provide gratification for these exaggerated needs leads to a reactive hypophoria and sociopathic behavior. The fact that narcotic antagonists do not relieve these hypophoric feelings and that chronic maintenance therapy not only does not relieve them but exacerbates them may be the reason for the surprisingly low acceptance of these two rational therapeutic modalities. Recent studies comparing a group of alcoholics and narcotic addicts with a control population have revealed that indeed both addicts and alcoholics do have exaggerated feelings of egocentricity, impulsivity, hypophoria and sociopathy and that these subjective changes are associated with a highly significant elevation of the luteinizing hormone and testosterone levels. These findings not only support the need hypothesis for drug addiction but may give additional insight into the development of new and additional therapeutic modalities that may be useful in complementing antagonists and maintenance therapy.

References

1. W. R. Martin, _Pharmacol. Rev._, _19_: 463 (1967).

2. W. R. Martin, H. F. Fraser, C. W. Gorodetzky and D. E. Rosenberg, _Clin. Pharmacol. Ther._, _6_: 731 (1965).

3. W. R. Martin and C. W. Gorodetzky, _J. Pharmacol. Exp. Ther._, _150_: 437 (1965).

4. W. R. Martin, C. W. Gorodetzky and T. K. McClane, _Clin. Pharmacol. Ther._, _7_: 455 (1966).

5. L. Lasagna, _Proc. Roy. Soc. Med._, _58_: 978 (1965).

6. D. R. Jasinski, W. R. Martin and C. A. Haertzen, _J. Pharmacol. Exp. Ther._, _157_: 420 (1967).

7. A. Zaks, T. Jones, M. Fink and A. M. Freedman, _J. Amer. Med. Ass._, _215_: 2108 (1971).

8. W. R. Martin, D. R. Jasinski and P. A. Mansky, _Arch. Gen. Psychiat._, _28_: 784 (1973).

AN OVERVIEW OF THE USE OF NARCOTIC ANTAGONISTS
IN THE REHABILITATION OF OPIATE DEPENDENT PERSONS

Arnold Schecter, M.D.

Clinical Associate Professor
of Preventive and Community Medicine
New Jersey College of Medicine
Newark, New Jersey

It is ironic that there are 10 papers at this meeting reporting favorably on the use of two narcotic antagonists in opiate rehabilitation programs at the same time that massive cuts in drug
abuse program funds are being announced in many areas across the
country. It is also ironic that at least two of this year's papers
emphasize the usefulness of the synthetic antagonist cyclazocine
while NIDA is currently funding the development of only one antagonist, the thebaine derived naltrexone. Another partially agonistic antagonist, oxilorphan, described with some optimism by Dr.
Resnick at last year's meeting, is not being funded for development
this year. Long acting depot forms are again at this meeting almost, but not quite, ready to test in humans. What sort of patients, what sort of programs, what sort of opiate antagonists
(pure or partially agonistic), and route of administration, oral or
by injection, are still moot questions. With methadone waiting
lists absent in many parts of the country the demand of patients
for antagonists is less than in past years when Kings County Hospital in Brooklyn could draw 200 patients from its methadone waiting
list for cyclazocine to drug free program, although some patients
later elected methadone when it became available. Today the same
hospital has an average of about 2 patients in treatment with cyclazocine at any given time - and 700 plus receiving methadone.

It seems reasonable to consider the development of the concept
of using opiate antagonists to rehabilitate opiate dependent persons. The beginning of the era of applicability of opiate antagonists to addict rehabilitation began with Dr. William Martin and associates at the Addiction Research Center at Lexington, Kentucky.
In 1964 Dr. Martin became the father of the narcotic antagonist rehabilitation theory when he reported the effects of cyclazocine in
humans and suggested its use in rehabilitation therapy for opiate
addicts.[1] This coincided in time with Drs. Vincent Dole and Marie

Nyswanders' pioneering efforts in New York with methadone.[2] Abraham Wikler, a former Lexington researcher, in a series of articles beginning in 1965, became the avuncular theoretician of the narcotic antagonist conditioned abstinence school.[3] Jaffe and Brill reported on a small clinical research project using cyclazocine in a clinical setting for the first time;[4] this was performed at Einstein Medical School in the Bronx, New York. Programs were begun in New York City, Brooklyn, New Haven, Chicago, St. Louis, Detroit, Boston and California, where just recently work began employing the antagonists.

Cyclazocine's dysphoric effects, a dexedrine like high and occasional psychotomimetic effects (hallucinations), during induction especially, appeared to be responsible for patient lack of acceptance in the late 60's and early 70's which became the methadone and therapeutic community eras in drug abuse therapy in the United States - just as the 1920's had seen opiate maintenance clinics and the thirties and forties and fifties the narcotic "farms." Naloxone, a pure antagonist, was used therapeutically although, surprisingly, not prophylactically, for cyclazocine's dysphoric effects by Resnick, Fink, and Freedman, and associates at the New York Medical School.[5] Naloxone alone, by mouth, was tried by the same group.[6] This pure antagonist caused no dysphoria but in the massive amounts used, 3 gms per day, in order to obtain 24 opiate blockade, gastrointestinal distress and high cost made further testing impracticable. A pure, long acting, antagonist seemed to be the answer, if only one could be synthesized.

Naltrexone, with the cyclazocine molecule's cyclopropyl methyl group added to naloxone seemed to be the answer. It was a pure opiate antagonist, long acting (up to 3 days) and caused no dysphoria - and was available for oral ingestion. Martin reported promising (FDA) Phase I testing in humans,[7] and Resnick[8] and Schecter[9,10] independently began clinical use of the drug in January, 1973 and initially reported promising findings. On the large SAODAP, (Special Action Office for Drug Abuse Prevention) chart listing progress of narcotic antagonists, including cyclazocine, M5050, naltrexone, BC 2605, BC 2610, and many others now forgotten, naltrexone, then referred to as EN 1639A, seemed to lead the pack. The National Institute on Drug Abuse (NIDA) funded 15 naltrexone narcotic antagonist programs. One year later in 1974 NIDA held a naltrexone - not narcotic antagonist - conference in Seattle. Serious problems of patient retention and cooperation in providing safety and efficacy data were noted in most programs.

Surprisingly, one pilot program which was described by almost all principle investigators at the Seattle meeting as scientifically unsound and of dubious ethical value, an outpatient 'double blind' naltrexone - placebo outpatient cooperative study, was next funded at five sites by NIDA. The double blind feature was evidently promoted by the Food and Drug Administration. Obviously the

addicts who continued heroin usage even one time after beginning
the study (presumeably all of them if they were in fact opiate addicts in need of treatment) knew whether they were taking an antagonist or a placebo; each patient could then tell his or her physician, if he/she so elected, which medication he was receiving.
Surely this must rank as one of the more curious of the so called
double blind experiments ever conducted. One assumes that when the
code is broken the naltrexone patients will be found to have remained in treatment longer than the placebo patients even though
volunteers for this unusual program may well not be typical antagonist patients. Doubtless also, fewer opiate overdose deaths would
be expected in the naltrexone group if the 'n' were sufficiently
large to obtain the usual opiate overdose deaths, seen so frequently over time in patients in most treatment programs. (I assume a
lesser death rate exists in addicts in treatment - methadone, therapeutic communities, or day care - compared to addicts not in
treatment programs.)

Current schools of thought feel one of three things should be
done with the antagonists: Meyer and coworkers at McLean Hospital
and Harvard Medical School feel antagonists have little role to
play in opiate addict rehabilitation in their somewhat unusual
clinical setting. NIDA is convinced that Naltrexone alone is worthy of development with their limited funds. They envision this
pure antagonist, in oral or depot form, as being used in presently
structured treatment programs. They hope to channel their limited
research funds into development of naltrexone from its present FDA
classification of a Phase II drug to the new drug or NDA stage, and
then permit NIDA and other funded methadone, therapeutic community,
or day care, treatment programs to use the drug. The federal government is not funding any partially agonistic narcotic antagonists
at the present time. The third school of thought including Parwatikar, Brahen, Kissin, Schecter and possibly Fraser, has suggested
partially agonistic antagonists for some, perhaps most, antagonist
patients. It was suggested that a slight 'high', comparable to
methadone, a mild withdrawal syndrome upon abrupt cessation, and
alleviation of depression are reasons for using cyclazocine or similar antagonists including BC 2605 and BC 2610 for most patients
rather than a pure antagonist like naltrexone especially until a
depot naltrexone is available.

In addition to the type of antagonist and the type of treatment program and program staff it is necessary to examine the type
of patients with whom we work. How to retain patients while in
competition with methadone programs is also a difficult question.

Another point worthy of consideration is the essential issue
of money. With radical surgery being performed on drug abuse programs at present in many parts of the country, does the concept of
narcotic antagonist therapy have any chance of surviving, let alone
thriving? Pharmaceutical companies regard these drugs as finan-

cially not worth the risk and cost of development. Few patients
of the 276,000 patients in all drug abuse programs nationwide will
ever conceivably use them. Federal, State, and Local funding is
usually for treatment exclusively, not research nor demonstration
although some treatment modalities have not demonstrated their efficacy in as convincing manner as their strongest proponents would
suggest, in my opinion. Third, Federal, State and Local funding
for narcotic antagonist projects are at an extremely low dollar
level at present - usually they are nonexistent.

It seems reasonable to propose dropping the stipulation by
funding agencies that research not be conducted in treatment programs; this can only lead to improved outcome for out-patients.
In addition it should be remembered that until we learn more of the
natural course of "untreated" opiate dependence and compare matched
patients in treatment with controls our "treatment" programs have
no reason to be considered other than unproved experiments or at
best semi-humane attempts to deal with a complicated issue. The
relatively well funded methadone and drug free programs could probably be markedly more effective with additional modalities including narcotic antagonist, alcoholism treatment and multiple addiction treatment. Second, it seems not unreasonable for the funding
agencies, especially NIDA, to fund at least fifteen 3 to 5 year
narcotic antagonist programs across the country; these would cost
from $200,000 to $400,000 per year each, a relatively small sum
when compared to NIDA's methadone and therapeutic community funding.
Last, since we now have at least two pioneering narcotic antagonists which block the effect of opiates, the original ostensible
selling point of methadone, thus protecting patients from opiate
overdose and 'reinfection' with the disease of opiate addiction
while they are used, I would suggest that this attribute alone justifies diverting 2% to 5% of Federal, State and City methadone and
drug free funding for narcotic antagonist clinics to assist motivated addicts to become opiate free. Surely it is unrealistic to
expect methadone patients who are rehabilitated to desire lifelong
maintenance. Antagonists offer an ideal post methadone short term
program leading to a drug free state. In a similar vein, patients
ineligible for methadone because of less than two years of addiction certainly deserve a treatment alternative to continuing street
heroin (or illegal methadone) use for at least two years before
they are eligible for chemotherapeutic (but opiate to drug free)
outpatient therapy. Also, it seems reasonable to remember the history of opiate use in the United States in this century. We are
living in the third opiate permissive time in this century: "Pre"
Harrison Act of 1914, the opiate maintenance clinics of the 1920's,
and now the methadone clinics of the 1960's and 70's. Surely it is
deceiving our methadone patients to give them the impression that
public policy in the United States has long tolerated chronic
opiate use - whether legal or illegal. If narcotic antagonists and
comprehensive narcotic rehabilitation therapy is not available when
public policy shifts what will happen to our patients? Let us not

forget also that methadone is not available even today to thousands of addicts in those states which have not yet and probably will never accept the concept of (methadone opiate) "treatment."

REFERENCES

1. W.R. Martin, C.W. Gorodetsky, and T.K. McLane, Proceedings CPDD, NRC-NAS, 1965.

2. V.P. Dole, and M.E. Nyswander, A Medical Treatment for Diacetylorphine (Heroin Addiction: A Clinical Trail with Methadone Hydrochloride, JAMA, Vol. 193 80-84, 1965.

3. A. Wikler, Narcotics, D.M. Weiner & G.C. Kasselbaum eds. McGraw-Hill Co., 1965.

4. J.H. Jaffe, and L. Brill, Int. J. Addict. (1966) 1:99-123.

5. R. Resnick, M. Fink and A. Freedman, Cyclozaine Treatment of Opiate Dependence: A Progress Report, Comp. Psych., Vol. 12 #6, 1971, 491-500.

6. M. Fink, A. Zaks, R. Sharoff, A. Mora, A. Bruner, S. Levit, and A.M. Freedman, Naloxone in Heroin Dependence, Clin. Pharm. & Ter., Vol. 9, 1968.

7. W.R. Martin, D.R. Jasinski, P.A. Mansley, Proceedings CPDD, NRC-NAS, 1974.

8. R.B. Resnick, J. Volovka, A. Freedman, Short-Term Effects of Naltrexone: A Progress Report, Proceedings CPDD NRC-NAS, 1974.

9. A.J. Schecter, Clinical Use of Naltrexone (EN1639A) Part II Experience with the First 50 Patients in a New York City Treatment Program, Am. J. Drug and Alcohol Abuse, Vol. 2&3, 1976.

10. A.J. Schecter, and D. Grossman, Naltrexone in a Clinical Setting: Preliminary Observations, Proceedings CPDD, NRC-NAS, 1974.

11. R.E. Meyer, S.M. Miria, & J.L. Altman, The Clinical Usefulness of Narcotic Antagonists: Implications of Behavioral Research Findings on the Use of Naltrexone, Am. J. of Drug and Alcohol Abuse, Vol. 3, #2, 1976.

THE EFFECTS OF NALTREXONE
ON SECONDARY ABSTINENCE SYMPTOMS

Ashburn Thomas, A.C.S.W.
Richard B. Resnick, M.D.
Richard S. Kestenbaum, Ph.D.

Department of Psychiatry
Division of Drug Abuse Research and Treatment
New York Medical College
5 East 102nd Street
New York, New York

Close to a hundred thousand people are on methadone maintenance. Reports in the literature suggest that prognosis is poor for these patients sustaining abstinence after they have gotten down to a zero mg. dosage of methadone (1,2,3). Many detoxified Methadone Maintenance Treatment Program patients go back on methadone in a relatively short period of time. Following withdrawal from opiates, there is a long lasting period where patients experience feelings of lethargy, apathy, weakness, poor appetite and hypochondriasis (5). This syndrome, known as secondary abstinence, may persist for months. These symptoms may be one reason why otherwise apparently rehabilitated patients are unable to sustain abstinence. Helping patients through this secondary abstinence period would be an important public health contribution, since it might help patients to stay drug free for a longer period of time.

In our clinical experience at New York Medical College, patients who have detoxified from methadone and then received naltrexone, the narcotic antagonist, have reported feeling less lethargy and apathy, and increased appetite and energy level during the post detoxification period. These patients attributed some of this symptomatic relief to naltrexone.

Because of these clinical observations, we set up an initial double blind study, in which 19 patients who had detoxified from methadone maintenance were randomly assigned active or placebo naltrexone.

To qualify for inclusion in the study, subjects had to be adult males, 21 years of age or older who:

1) were on methadone maintenance for 6
   months or longer;
2) requested detoxification;
3) had not abused opiates for 6 months
   or longer;
4) gave their informed consent;
5) met all other inclusion and exclusion
   criteria for receiving naltrexone in
   accordance with FDA guidelines.

Nineteen subjects fulfilled these criteria and were then put onto
the double blind study. Ten received active medication and nine
received placebo. These subjects were assessed by way of a
symptom checklist. Each symptom was rated on a 4 point scale:

    0 - absence of symptom
    1 - mild symptom
    2 - moderate symptom
    3 - severe symptom

The checklist was administered on each visit to the clinic.
Symptoms on the checklist included: Loss of appetite, anxiety,
nervousness, difficulty sleeping, feeling "down," low energy or
fatigue, irritability, difficulty concentrating, lack of sex drive,
muscular or joint pain, headaches, tearing, sweating, speeding,
diarrhea, nausea or vomiting, abdominal pains, and chills.

There was a tendency for the symptom ratings to be somewhat lower
for the 10 subjects on active naltrexone, than those of the subjects on placebo naltrexone. However, the difference was not
statistically significant. We suspected either our symptom checklist was not sensitive enough to pick up the difference in clinical improvement, or that different staff members rated patients
differently.

To control for differences in raters, a psychiatric social worker,
who was blind to whether a patient was receiving active or placebo
naltrexone, administered the symptom checklist, and observed each
patient's course of recovery. In addition to the checklist, the
observer used clinical treatment interviews as part of his assessment. Six patients have been followed in this manner.

The results for this group were similar to our initial 19 patients
in that those receiving active naltrexone showed a trend towards
lower severity of symptoms compared to those who received placebo
naltrexone.

However, the blind observer found striking, and clinically significant, differences among patients during clinical interviews.
Some patients in their counseling sessions emphasixed difficulties
they were experiencing in interpersonal areas of their lives

(i.e. marital, familial, on the job problems, etc.). Somatic complaints were rarely brought up spontaneously. For other patients, the reverse was true: during clinical interviews they focused more on their somatic complaints, rather than on interpersonal difficulties. When the double-blind code was broken, these two different ways of using sessions coincided with whether patients were receiving active or placebo naltrexone.

The 4 patients who received active naltrexone reported less severe symptoms of lethargy, weakness, poor concentration and poor appetite. Clinical interviews were primarily focused around interpersonal problems. The two patients who received placebo naltrexone reported severe symptoms of lethargy, weakness, poor concentration, and poor appetite. Clinical interviews were primarily focused around these and other somatic complaints.

Although mean differences between groups on the symptom checklist were not statistically significant, the single item on the checklist that correlated best with the active or placebo medication was the ability to concentrate. None of the 4 patients on active naltrexone reported poor concentration, while the two patients on placebo reported poor concentration.

In one remarkable example, a patient who focused more on difficulties with his girlfriend and school work during his first 8 weeks on the study suddenly seemed to change in the ninth week, and began to complain primarily of severe somatic symptoms (aches in his knees, stomach cramps, chills, and excessive tearing and sweating). The blind observer noted and recorded this clinical change in the patient. After the double blind code was broken, we learned that the patient's medication had been changed for unrelated medical reasons from active to placebo, at the same time the observer had noted the clinical change in the patient's concerns.

These preliminary findings suggested naltrexone may relieve secondary abstinence symptoms and be useful as a transitional treatment for patients discontinuing methadone maintenance.

References

1. Cushman, P. and Dole, V. Detoxification of Well Rehabilitated Methadone Maintained Patients. In Proceedings of the 5th National Methadone Conference 262-269, 1973.

2. Lowinson, J. and Langrod, J. Detoxification of Long-Term Methadone Patients. Presented to the Committee on Problems of Drug Dependence at 36th Annual Meeting Mexico City, March 10-14, 1974.

3. Stimmel, B., Rabin, J. and Engel, C. The Prognosis of Patients Detoxified From Methadone Maintenance: A Follow-Up Study. In Proceedings of the 5th National Conference on Methadone Treatment 270-274, 1973.

4. Martin, W.R., Jasinsky, D.R., Haertzen, C.A., Kay, D.C., Jones, B.E., Mansky, P.A. and Carpenter, R.O. Methadone- A Re-Evaluation. Archives of General Psychiatry 23:286-295, 1973.

5. Riordan, C.E. and Rapkin, R. Detoxification as a Final Step in Treating the Successful Long-Term Methadone Patient. In Proceedings of the 4th National Conference on Methadone Treatment 219-220, 1972.

FUTURE OF ANTAGONIST TREATMENT

S. Parwatikar, M.D., FRCP (C)
J. Crawford, M.A.

MISSOURI INSTITUTE OF PSYCHIATRY
5400 Arsenal Street
St. Louis, Missouri

I. RATIONALE

As it is with other fields, drug addiction research is surrounded by controversy. Some writers pose narcotic addiction as a simple problem of physiological dependence. Advocates of this position see treatment as detoxification or, in cases where detoxification has not been followed by a drug-free state, some form of maintenance.

An alternative view is furnished by various authors (1, 2, 3). They present addiction as having a heavy learning component. The patient, being aware of tension and anxiety, seeks and obtains relief in narcotics usage. Each time such discomfort is relieved by narcotics, drug-seeking behavior is reinforced. These authors feel such reinforcement acts as an operant conditioner to drug-seeking behavior and is somewhat independent of the physiological dependence. In this position detoxification would terminate the physical dependence but would leave the psychological (operantly conditioned) dependence intact.

According to the authors, this psychological dependence manifests itself by a "craving" and a seeking for drugs. Numerous authors support this observation (4).

This suggests that the relief of tension and anxiety by the narcotic acts as a powerful operant reinforcer to drug-seeking behavior; that often, environmental factors act as eliciting stimuli to these behaviors. Presumably, the use of the antagonist drug, which prevents the euphoric tranquiling effect of narcotics, prevent reinforcement. Habits which go unreinforced become extinguished.

In late 1973 and early 1974, an antagonist drug study (Cyclazocine and Naltrexone) was conducted at the St. Louis State Hospital under the auspices of the Missouri Institute of Psychiatry. The purpose of the study was two-fold: (1) to test

the usefulness of antagonist drugs as an adjunct to the treatment
of heroin addiction and (2) to assess the medical aspects of such
treatment.

II. METHOD

Voluntary patients (113) were received on a research ward,
completely evaluated, both medically and socially, detoxified with
Methadone, allowed to go drug-free for two or three days, inducted
on an antagonist drug and then discharged from the ward and maintained on an outpatient basis. During the entire period various
supportive services were extended.

Subjects were male, at least 18 years of age without physical
or mental abnormality, meeting criteria of narcotic addiction as
evidenced by withdrawal, history of addiction, positive urinalysis
and a desire to be drug-free. Such subjects were recruited from
the following populations: (1) those asking for detoxification from
a Methadone Program; (2) those obviously addicted who did not meet
the criteria for methadone maintenance; and (3) probationers and
parolees who were not actively addicted but had a long history of
addiction.

Preparatory to entering the program, each subject received a
thorough briefing as to the expected effects of the antagonist
drugs.

III. FINDINGS AND RESULTS

Patient interviews, staff conferences, anecdotal records,
clinical charts and social histories furnished the basis for analysis and interpretation. Certain demographic variables were found
to be statistically related to retention. It was found that clients
of higher education, displaying later age of onset, identifying
with an occupational role and having an intact heterosexual relationship are more likely to remain in treatment (5). In addition,
some strong, well-founded clinical impressions emerged:

(a) In a review of the physicals and blood workups, nothing
remarkable emerged. As is the usual in addict populations, liver
profiles were somewhat elevated in terms of SGOT and LDH. Some
VDRL false positives were encountered. Upon analysis of the data,
neither Naltrexone nor Cyclazocine seemed to have had any serious
effect on blood pressure, pulse, respiration or temperature. It
appears that with good clinical practice, both Cyclazocine and
Naltrexone are toxicologically safe.

(b) Seemingly both drugs induced side effects in at least 80%
of the patients. In general, such side effects as were encountered
were similar for the two drugs; the difference being that Cyclazocine side effects were somewhat more severe. For both drugs, the
side effects included: drowsiness, increased libido, fullness of
head, weakness, blurred vision, cramps, difficulty of concentration
and coordination, itching, sweating, running nose, running eyes,
constipation etc. Additionally, some Cyclazocine patients tended

to display erratic blood pressure patterns and hallucinations (both auditory and visual). In both drugs these side effects were usually mild and transitory, abating after a few days. Only in a few Cyclazocine cases was it necessary to terminate induction; in no case was this necessary for Naltrexone. Finally, it appears that Cyclazocine side effects were more noticeable.

(c) Patient interviews indicate that some clients experienced the antagonist drug as inducing drowsiness, being mildly sedative, mildly euphoric and/or anti-depressant. This was true for both drugs but particularly for Cyclazocine.

(d) Clients under some legal or group pressure tend to remain longer on the program for both drugs.

(e) Despite the heavier side effects, patients tended to remain on Cyclazocine as long as on Naltrexone; the average stay being approximately 48 days and 45 days respectively.

IV. DISCUSSION

Cyclazocine, in spite of its greater agonistic properties and side effects than that of Naltrexone, did not show any difference in its ability to keep clients in that program from that of Naltrexone.

Several explanations of this phenomenon can be offered. One can allege that only the more motivated would have sufficient emotional stamina to overcome the vicissitudes and discomforts of the side effects and hence, by virtue of that motivation, they would have remained on the program in any case. The subjective bias of the investigator offers another explanation.

What appears as a far more satisfactory explanation, is derived from the cognitive dissonance theory; the greater the privation that one endures for a particular cause, the more likely is one to come to value it (6). Despite its seeming similarity to the motivation explanation (suggested above), this latter explanation of the phenomenon is quite different from the former; both in its logic and in its application to treatment.

In the former case (i.e. positing superior motivation as the crucial variable), those having high motivation would have the capacity to overcome the aversive character of the side effects and by such endurance to continue to take the medication until sensory adaptation had set in. Upon completion of this adaptation, the subjective symptoms will have abated and, thus, the client will continue to take the medication for the sake of its beneficial effects. Presumably, such clients will be incapable of enduring the direct discomfort of the withdrawal syndrome but able to bear the (milder) discomfort of side effects. Under this formulation, only the highly motivated would be selected for such chemotherapy. This motivation may be displayed in part by his willingness to stay on the drug, as well as tolerate mild to moderate side effects.

Further, our other clinical impressions lend collateral support for the former position. Being more centrally embedded in the social context, being under legal pressure or being more subject

to group pressure, all tend to channel behavior within institutional bounds. To the unsocialized, such pressure would result in
conflict; the privation resulting from such conflict and adjustment
results in cognitive reorganization tending toward a greater valu-
ing of the final adjustment selected. Such dynamics are analogous
to the "forced compliance" research of various authors (7, 8, 9).

Basically, there are two factors that would determine the
success or failure of the antagonist treatment. (1) The ability
of a person to continue taking drugs and (2) repeated frustration
with heroin injections while on the drug. The former is dependent
on three factors. (1) Pressure to be drug-free. This may be
either legal, familial or social. (2) Development of alternatives
to addict life style and (3) the properties of the drug that makes
the addict take it religiously.

Under pressure to be drug-free, the addict may be forced to
accept any drug. Such is the case in treatment of alcoholism with
antabuse. Development of alternatives is essential to any treatment but the seductive nature of the treatment medication also may
play quite an important part. Addicts, by their habit and conditioning, are looking for something that produces bodily change.
Granted that they are looking for euphoric, rather than dysphoric
effects, it is clinically observed that experiments with a variety
of drugs, including alcohol, while on Methadone Maintenance, is
not uncommon. It is thus felt that unless a drug has some qualities of tranquiling, antidepressant or euphoric/agonistic nature
the subjective feeling that he/she is on a medication for "treatment of heroin addiction" is not present.

Cyclazocine has agonistic properties and the side effects
during induction period are no worse than those which are observed
during the induction period of high dose antidepressants used regularly in average psychiatric practice.

The authors thus feel that the usage of Antagonists in treatment of heroin addiction needs to be looked into further. It is
suggested that Antagonists, which do not have any agonistic effects
such as Naltrexone, could be used only in restricted, therapeutic,
community-like facilities and Antagonists which show some agonistic qualities be used in outpatient settings where subjective
insight and judgment plays a greater part in the ensuing results.

It is also felt that antagonist treatment should not be
offered as a mass treatment but the drugs Cyclazocine and Naltrexone be made available to physicians interested in treatment of
narcotic addiction similar to other tranquilizers and antidepressants available on the market.

V. CONCLUSIONS

A. Antagonist therapy seems to be suitable: (1) for clients
motivated to be drug-free. Prognosis is guarded if the client
comes simply out of judicial pressure. (2) When some mechanism is
available to ensure timely taking of the medication; family or peers
could provide some pressure to do so. (3) When experimentation

with Heroin should be allowed, while on Antagonist, if not encouraged.

      B. In order to maintain the "forced compliance" pressure,
existing social structures impinging on the client's life, must be
continuously monitored and reinforced.

      C. Other things being equal, an antagonist that provides
mild but tolerable agonistic effects may provide better adjustment.
Further research of this point is needed.

REFERENCES

1. W. R. Martin, Ill. Med. J., 130: 489 (1966).
2. A. Wikler, Conditioning Factors in Opiate Addiction and Relapse (D. Wilmer and G. Kasselbaum, eds.) McGraw-Hill, New York, 1965.
3. A. Lindesmith, Problems in Social Psychology of Addictions (D. Wilmer and G. Kasselbaum, eds.) McGraw-Hill Book Co., New York, 1965.
4. D. Clouet, Narcotic Drugs Biochemical Pharmacology Plenum Press, New York - London, 1971.
5. S. Parwatikar, J. Crawford and C. Unverdi, Am. J. Drugs and Alcohol, 2: 379 (1975).
6. J. Brehm, J. Abnormal and Social Psychology 58: 379 (1959).
7. J. Brehm and A. Cohen, Explorations in Cognitve Dissonance Wiley, New York - London, 1962.
8. E. Aronson and J. Carlsmith, J. Abnormal and Social Psychology, 66: 584 (1963).
9. L. Festinger and J. Carlsmith, J. Abnormal and Social Psychology, 58: 203 (1959).

PREDICTORS OF OUTCOME WITH NARCOTIC ANTAGONISTS

Greta R. Lonborg, M.F.A., M.A.
Richard B. Resnick, M.D.
Gordon Hough, Ph.D.
Richard S. Kestenbaum, Ph.D.
Marcel Harris, A.A.

Department of Psychiatry
Division of Drug Abuse Research and Treatment
New York Medical College
5 East 102nd Street
New York, New York

A more widespread availability of narcotic antagonists for use in treatment programs is anticipated in the near future. Criteria for identifying patients most likely to respond to this mode of treatment have not been thoroughly investigated. In retrospective studies, Resnick et al. (1970, 1971) have explored factors associated with retention in cyclazocine treatment. We designed a prospective study to test the validity of intake variables as predictors of outcome in naltrexone treatment. Fourteen parameters were selected from our intake questionnaire, consisting of psychosocial and drug histories developed on the basis of clinical experience in the treatment of opiate addiction.

METHODS

Ninety-two consecutive 18-50 year old male volunteers from multi-ethnic and socioeconomic backgrounds applied for treatment with naltrexone at the Division of Drug Abuse Research and Treatment, New York Medical College, between May 1 and August 31, 1974. These patients presented at our out-patient department where a thorough intake questionnaire describing demographic, psychosocial and drug histories was administered. Medical and psychiatric examinations were given, an informed consent was executed, and patients were admitted to our in-patient unit for detoxification from opiates. They remained in the hospital for the opiate-free period required to avoid naltrexone precipitating withdrawal. While hospitalized, patients were started on naltrexone and any financial and/or living arrangements were made as necessary by counseling staff. Following discharge to the out-patient unit, they were assigned to a primary therapist. Medication was dispensed by the nursing staff, and patients were required to ingest medication a minimum of three times per week.

Selection of Study Population

```
TOTAL NUMBER OF SUCCESSIVE ADMISSIONS.................... 92

    Excluded for medical and/or psychiatric
        ineligibility...................................... 2

    Excluded because they were direct transfers
        from cyclazocine without interim periods
        of readdiction.................................... 4

    Excluded for incomplete detoxification during
        study............................................. 43

    Excluded because they had taken out-patient
        medication less than one week..................... 13

POPULATION REMAINING ON MEDICATION AT LEAST ONE WEEK.... 30
```

Of thirteen patients who were excluded for having taken naltrexone for less than one week, one had medical problems not identified at intake, and two stopped medication because of severe side effects. Ten had sought hospitalization for detoxification only, for which consent to take naltrexone was a prerequisite; they apparently had no intention of remaining on the medication.

Twelve months after their first out-patient dose of naltrexone, the study group were categorized as opiate-free (Group I, N=8) or opiate-dependent (Group II, N=22). We compared these two groups on the basis of the following parameters: age at intake; age of first opiate use; age first addicted; number of years addicted; mean amount of opiates used (measured in street dollars) during the two months prior to admission; longest period of abstinence on the streets of New York; longest time clean elsewhere in the streets; employment status at intake; longest period of continuous employment prior to admission; education level; and therapists' rating of capacity for object relationships. The latter was assessed by therapists on the basis of ongoing relationships at admission and an evaluation of the patient's self-report about prior object relationships.

RESULTS

Group I patients had sustained periods of abstinence on the streets of New York longer than Group II patients ($p < .05$). In addition, Group I remained on naltrexone a mean of 4.91 months; Group II took naltrexone a mean of 2.10 months ($p < .01$). Those whose level of opiate use was lower, took naltrexone for a longer period of time.

	X̄ $ opiates used	X̄ # mos on naltrexone
Group I	$9.75	4.91
Group II	$22.00	2.10

Since we found no substantial differences between these groups on intake variables other than the level of opiate abuse measured in street dollars prior to admission, we wanted to determine whether patients who took naltrexone (Groups I + II, N=30), differed from those who did not detoxify (Group III, N=38).

Group III spent an average of $53 on opiates during the two months prior to admission, compared with Groups I and II combined who had spent a mean of $22 daily on opiates. Group I had used a mean of $9.75, which was significantly less than Group III who used a mean of $53 (p < .01). A similar comparison of Group II ($22) and Group III ($53) was also significant (p < .05). It is interesting to note that five patients from Group III returned later for treatment, and their mean level of usage at that time was $11 daily.

During this study period, 16 patients became readdicted and returned for treatment. The mean time on naltrexone during the first admission was 30 days; the mean time during the second treatment period was 85 days (p < .06).

DISCUSSION

The purpose of this study was to determine whether selected intake variables might be useful predictors of outcome for naltrexone treatment. After comparing patients who were opiate-free with those who were opiate-dependent 12 months from their first out-patient naltrexone dose, we found insufficient evidence to define predictive variables. A lower level of opiate abuse prior to entering treatment, however, indicated a longer time in treatment. A striking observation was that patients who present for re-admission remain in treatment longer with each successive re-admission. This was, perhaps, the most important finding in this study, and has certain implications for treatment.

Because our data analysis did not find a number of clear-cut pre-dictors of outcome, we turned our attention to treatment factors, such as staff attitudes and the opportunity for interpersonal rewards, which may have affected all subjects and caused the intake parameters to be distributed rather evenly among the groups. Our staff regards treatment as a process, and addiction as a disorder with remissions and relapses, not unlike other types of behavior and/or psychiatric problems. Such a point of view is not entirely consistent with the aim of this study, namely, the identification of patients who are likely to achieve a simply defined positive or negative outcome. An outcome defined in such a bipolar way is consistent with the most common treatment expectation of the patients, but is alien to the idea of treatment as process.

The idea that treatment is process is the principal treatment factor that may have lessened the extent to which intake parameters identified and discriminated among patients in terms of outcome. Very often, patients have a sense of failure over previous efforts to combat their drug problem. Many have also experienced failure in education and work. Often they have been incarcerated. Few have a sense of self-esteem. Frequently the first therapeutic issue is the patient's ambivalence about being in treatment, where the possibility of failure causes anxiety and enforces false notions of strength to make it without medication or therapeutic support. Conveying to the patient that ambivalence is expected, that relapses are expected, and that treatment can go forward despite these regressive periods helps to create a treatment environment in which patients can feel comfortable as they learn to accept themselves and to manage their problems maturely.

The therapist keeps reinforcing the idea of process, until the patient begins to understand that he is making unrealistic demands on himself. Expressions like "I sabotaged myself," or "I feel like using and know I'm not ready to stop taking naltrexone" indicate that he is beginning to recognize the nature of his addiction. The ability to say that he knows that he still has a problem avoiding drugs but feels that other things in his life are changing is an even stronger indication that he is beginning to view treatment as a process.

The most difficult task is attempting to reward a patient for consistent appointments and medication, while creating an environment in which he can be truthful about relapses without feeling he has failed or jeopardized his relationship with staff.

Patients are surprised by the amount of attention they are given. A common statement when patients enter treatment is, "I am only a guinea pig being used for experimental purposes." This statement reflects their feeling that there is nothing important enough about them as individuals to elicit interest. They do not wish to view medical examinations as preventive or corrective measures, but feel that data is being collected for research purposes only. In this vein, it is evident that patients feel rewarded when the clinical, nursing and clerical staff show daily recognition and ask how they are feeling. Patients are frequently heard to say after being in treatment for some time, "He (or she) really cares about me."

A major problem in treatment is the patient's expectations that being drug-free will produce instant harmony in his family and social relationships. Since we know from experience that many of these relationships are based in part on opiates or dependency needs, it is essential to help family members adjust to new expectations and new dynamics. Some of these relationships dissolve, and the therapeutic process has to facilitate viewing such dissolution as progress rather than as another failure.

There are additional rewards for patients who begin to view the drug problem as one that requires him to remain in contact with his therapist. This idea requires constant reinforcement, because when the patient believes that being drug-free will solve every problem, he is unprepared to deal with his newly experienced frustrations and anxiety. This is particularly true of patients who had used opiates as "medication" to alleviate stress, and who have not internalized coping behaviors for stressful situations.

Finally, we might speculate about the predictor variables we did find. Patients who were opiate-free for a longer time in the streets in the past, and who had a lower level of addiction immediately prior to treatment, may be the ones who can learn most readily that treatment is a process. Patients who are more addicted and who are less able to function without being addicted may very well be the ones whose interest in immediate gratification most interferes with their discovering that treatment is a process and that simple solutions to problems is infantile.

SUMMARY

Our review of the data suggested that those patients whose level of addiction as measured in dollars spent on opiates is highest prior to admission will be least likely to sustain treatment. This was substantiated by an examination of each sub-group in this study, and its mean level of usage in relation to outcome. An evaluation of successive readmissions led us to conclude that with each successive readmission, patients sustain treatment longer. The implications for treatment include the necessity to educate patients about the recidivistic nature of addiction, in order to facilitate more realistic expectations about the treatment process. We cannot "undo" their earlier experiences of failure, nor can we erase their impressions. We can, however, enable patients to develop a sense of worth based on the progress they make during treatment, which can substitute for the euphoria they experienced with opiates. Finally, we can revise our own expectations about the treatment process. In light of the recognition that this problem is recurrent, we can begin to make long-range follow-up studies at five and ten years, at which time patients will, hopefully, have been able to sustain treatment sufficiently long to integrate their learning and to utilize their new adaptive behaviors without the artificial support of opiates.

References

1. Resnick, R., Fink, M., Freedman, A.M. A Cyclazocine Typology in Opiate Dependence. American Journal of Psychiatry 126: 1256-1260, 1970.

2. Resnick, R., Fink, M., Freedman, A.M. Cyclazocine Treatment of Opiate Dependence: A Progress Report. Comprehensive Psychiatry 12:491-502, 1971.

NARCOTIC ANTAGONIST (NALTREXONE) TREATMENT

David C. Lewis, M.D.
Washingtonian Center for Addictions
Boston, Massachusetts

The Washingtonian Center for Addictions in Boston has offered opioid-addicted patients the option of receiving a long-acting narcotic antagonist, naltrexone, in conjunction with their regular course of treatment since January 1, 1974. Between January 1, 1974 and March 15, 1976, twenty patients received naltrexone for varying periods of time. This paper will report findings on the first treatment course in this group of twenty patients.

I.   PATIENT SELECTION

During this study period 627 male patients between the ages of 18 and 47, hospitalized at the Washingtonian Center for Addictions for opioid detoxification, were informed about naltrexone treatment in small groups which focused on post-hospitalization treatment alternatives. If patients selected naltrexone, they were told that treatment would involve daily attendance at a clinic and counseling no less frequently than once a week. In addition, participation in a safety and efficacy study was required because of the investigational nature of the drug. After a detailed explanation of the experimental nature of naltrexone treatment, patients were given an informed consent to read. Patients then met with the Principal Investigator to discuss any questions and to sign the informed consent. This was followed by an additional discussion with the patient and signing of the informed consent by the hospital's Human Subjects Officer, who verified the subject's voluntary participation and checked on the subject's understanding of the risks involved in taking an investigational drug.

Of the 627 male patients undergoing opioid detoxification who were informed about the option of narcotic antagonist treatment, 123 expressed serious interest in the program.

Forty (40) eventually signed informed consents, but only twenty subjects actually completed the baseline evaluation phase and received naltrexone.

The three reasons most frequently cited by potential nal-trexone subjects for not participating in the study were:
1) aversion to use of any chemical support; 2) dislike of program structure (daily clinic visits and many laboratory tests); and 3) general aversion to participating and "being used" in a new and unknown treatment method.

As the study progressed another concern which emerged as a major reason for nonparticipation in the study was their fear of being unable to get high. This fear was often manifested by an intense concern about the details of naltrexone action. Specifically, potential subjects would ask how long the effects of the drug would last, what medications could be used for the relief of pain in case of an accident, and whether taking naltrexone would reduce their future ability to get high. In spite of reassurance that the project was entirely voluntary, that they could withdraw from the project at any time, and that they could still experience the opioid high 24-48 hours after stopping naltrexone, several patients with this concern decided not to participate in the study.

It was our expectation that patients would be concerned with the possible toxic and side effects of naltrexone and that this would be a major reason for avoidance of the study. How-ever, contrary to expectations, while patients were aware of the potential risk of toxicity and of side effects, few stated that such a risk would be a deterrant to participation in the study.

II.   DEMOGRAPHIC CHARACTERISTICS OF
        NALTREXONE PATIENTS

Table 1 shows the demographic characteristics of the twenty subjects. The mean age at the start of treatment was 27.9 years. The duration of addictive opioid use was 7.1 years with 20.8 years being the average age at onset of ad-diction. The average patient completed high school and was in the normal range of intelligence. The mean number of pre-vious treatment attempts was 4.1 and included psychotherapy, detoxification, methadone maintenance, and therapeutic com-munities.

The patients who volunteered for naltrexone were demo-graphically more like the patients on our methadone maintenance treatment program than the patients on our detoxification program, even though those who volunteered for naltrexone actually were on the detoxification program at the time they volunteered. Naltrexone patients are older than patients on the detoxification program, more are white, and more are working at the onset of treatment.

III. STUDY PROCEDURES: NALTREXONE INDUCTION, PHYSICAL AND BEHAVIORAL MEASURES

After detoxification was completed, baseline measures of physical status, including Symptom Check List, chest x-ray, ECG, and blood tests, were performed. Several baseline psychological tests were also obtained: Current and Past Psychopathology Scale (CAPPS); Wechsler Adult Intelligence Scale (WAIS); the Minnesota Multiphasic Personality Inventory (MMPI); and Profile of Mood States (POMS). Subjects also received naltrexone placebo daily during this baseline period. During the baseline period, seven to ten days after the last detoxification dose of methadone, naloxone challenges were performed. Following the naloxone challenge, naltrexone was substituted for placebo in increasing 10 mg. doses until a level of 50 mg. was reached. All patients were required to participate in individual or group psychotherapy and to participate in repeated measures to assess the safety of the drug. In addition to these measures, the Symptom Check List and Profile of Mood States (POMS) were administered bi-weekly.

IV. PRELIMINARY FINDINGS

As indicated in Table 2, the average duration of receipt of naltrexone was 4.9 weeks, with a range of less than one week to 17 weeks. The duration of naltrexone treatment contrasts with the duration of treatment in two other opioid-addicted populations (methadone maintenance and drug abstinent patients) who were treated in the Outpatient Service of the Washingtonian Center for Addictions at the same time as the naltrexone patients. Methadone maintenance patients remained in treatment an average of 22.4 weeks, while drug abstinent patients remained in treatment an average of 2.0 weeks.

In order to examine the parameters that might affect the duration of treatment, the demographic data was divided into subgroups according to the length of patient participation on naltrexone. No significant differences in any of the demographic measures were correlated with the length of receipt of naltrexone.

Similar analysis of patient data from the Profile of Mood States, the Symptom Check List, and the Minnesota Multiphasic Personality Inventory was limited by the small number of patients (n=20) and the sequential termination of patients from the program (n=10 after three weeks of naltrexone treatment). A preliminary analysis of these measures indicated differences in the POMS scores correlated with duration of naltrexone treatment. It appeared that patients who remained on the program the longest had an initial drop from a higher baseline total mood disturbance to a lower mood disturbance score one week after the onset of naltrexone treatment while those subjects who left the program earliest did not show such an initial reduction in mood disturbance. However, further analysis of the sequential weekly POMS data indicated a general decline in the total mood disturbance over time for all subgroups. Therefore, we are unable to identify any particular pattern of responses following the receipt of naltrexone that predicts which subjects will drop from the program early or remain on naltrexone for longer periods of time. On examining the baseline data alone there were differences that correlated to the duration of naltrexone treatment. Breakdown of patient scores on these measures according to length of stay on the program indicates that the patients who continue on naltrexone the longest show less baseline psychopathology, less baseline mood disturbance, and fewer baseline symptoms than patients dropping out within the first two weeks. Later follow-up of both groups indicates that the patients who continued in naltrexone treatment longest were more likely to be employed and less likely to be addicted as of March 15, 1976.

These findings are consistent with data on other methods of treatment, which indicate that psychologically healthier patients continue longer and have more positive outcomes in treatment than less psychologically healthy patients.

Repeated physical and neurological examinations, electrocardiograms, blood hematology and chemistries, as well as analysis of patient histories and symptom check list, do not reveal any toxic effects which can be attributed to naltrexone.

In summary, naltrexone treatment attracts a small subpopulation of the addict population who remain in treatment with the drug for a shorter duration than our methadone maintenance patients but longer than our drug abstinent outpatients. As in other methods of treatment, measures of psychological health are correlated with length of participation in this modality of addiction treatment.

NARCOTIC ANTAGONIST (NALTREXONE) TREATMENT

Table 1. Demographic Data - Naltrexone Study (n = 20)

	Mean
Age	27.9 years
Length of Addiction	7.1 years
Age of Initial Addiction	20.8 years
Previous Number of Treatments	4.1
Education	11.8 years
I.Q.	103.8

Race	Percent
White	85%
Black	15%

Religion	
Catholic	65%
Protestant	20%
Other	15%

Marital Status	
Single	40%
Married	35%
Separated/Divorced	25%

Table 2. Duration of Receipt of Naltrexone (March 15, 1976)

Number of Subjects	Interval (Days)
4	0 - 7
7	8 - 21
4	22 - 56
5	57 - 119

Mean: 34.8 days
(4.9 weeks)

Total 20   Median: 17.5 days
(2.5 weeks)

1284

NIDA'S ROLE IN THE DEVELOPMENT
OF A NARCOTIC ANTAGONIST

Demetrios A. Julius, M.D.

National Institute on Drug Abuse
Clinical Behavioral Branch
Division of Research
Rockville, Maryland

The idea of developing one or more narcotic antagonists for
their use in the treatment of narcotic addiction goes back many
years. The theoretical and practical basis for such a potential
use of these agents was formulated in the mid-60's by both
Dr. William Martin and Dr. Abraham Wikler in their work at the
Addiction Research Center in Lexington, Kentucky. Stated succinctly,
it was postulated that drug seeking behavior in the narcotic dependent individual is maintained by a set of classically conditioned
responses. The tolerance and physical dependence which eventuates
with the continued use of a narcotic, together with the subjective
experience of the narcotic "high", are assumed to contribute significantly to the drug seeking behavior of the individual. The narcotic antagonists, it was theorized, could then be used to break
the chain of events leading to this conditioned state of drug seeking behavior. By blocking the euphoria and dependence producing
properties of narcotics, the antagonists could give the addicted
individual a chance to effect a change in his life style and habits.
 With these notions in mind in 1971, the newly created Special
Action Office for Drug Abuse Prevention made the development of
narcotic antagonists one of its main priorities. In early 1972 there
were several antagonists in existence; all at various stages of
development. The purest antagonist was naloxone. It seemed to be
a potent antagonist and showed almost no agonist action of its own.
Its main drawback as a therapeutic agent in heroin addiction were
its high cost, the difficulty in synthesizing it, its short duration
of action, and its very poor oral absorption. Another potent antagonist was cyclazocine, which demonstrated a longer duration of
action of up to 24 hours with 4 milligrams of the substance. However, its drawback was also recognized - its strong agonist properties when administered rapidly to individuals. These properties
consisted of dysphoria and psychotomimetic effects. In addition, a
number of other compounds - EN1639A (which we now know as naltrexone),
BC-2605, and M-5050 (known as diprenorpine) - were still at early
stages of testing in animals and in humans. Consequently, in the
initial testing of narcotic antagonists for the treatment of volun-

teer addicted individuals, cyclazocine was chosen since it was the most developed and longest acting agent. Cyclazocine, with its above mentioned unpleasant effects, was not well received by the addict volunteers and soon acquired a bad street reputation. However, it was successful in the treatment of some individuals, and these individuals are still in fact being treated with cyclazocine in certain clinics in New York City.

In the meantime, the development of EN1639A was proceeding rapidly. This agent appeared to have a bright future for use in the therapy of opiate addicts. It had a good duration of action (50 milligrams   24 hours) and did not have any of the unpleasant side effects of cyclazocine. Consequently, by 1973, naltrexone was chosen as the antagonist of choice for further development. It was about the same time that the Division on Narcotic and Drug Abuse was separated from NIMH and expanded into the National Institute on Drug Abuse. Within the Institute, the Branch on Experimental Therapeutics in the Division of Research inherited much of the responsibility for the continued clinical testing of naltrexone. The supervision of the program of developing new synthetic long lasting preparations and delivery systems was assumed by the Biomedical Branch. That program is currently under the direction of the Research Technology Branch.

From 1973 through 1974, the clinical naltrexone program consisted of about seventeen contracts and grants that fit into a rather loosely knit system. Five of these research clinics were selected to participate in the double-blind placebo study of naltrexone that was, and is being conducted by the National Academy of Sciences. Induction of patients into his study began in mid-1974, and the clinics are now in the process of gathering follow-up data on the patients who have participated in the study. The double-blind has not yet been broken for the investigators. However, the existing data are now being tabulated and analyzed by Biometric Research Institute in Washington, D.C. Their efforts will then be forwarded to the Committee for the Evaluation of Narcotic Antagonists within the National Academy of Sciences and a final report of this particular study will be written by the end of this year. Approximately 190 subjects have taken at least one dose of study medication, about ½ on placebo, ½ on naltrexone. The results are not in yet, but it seems that naltrexone was of benefit to a certain percentage of subjects in this study.

To return now to 1974, the studies underway at that time were conceived by NIDA to represent Phase II Testing of naltrexone; that is to say, naltrexone was receiving exposure in limited clinical populations. We were especially interested in looking at the safety aspects of this drug when it was administered to humans. Consequently, a tight monitoring system had to be devised if the limited staff at NIDA was to function properly in detecting any ill effects of the drug. We therefore decided to establish the same kind of monitoring of all the other research clinics that existed for the five clinics in the National Academy of Sciences' study. Thus by early 1975, we were able to gather much information, both

1286

safety and efficacy information, into the central data bank of
Biometric Research Institute and were able to keep constant and
close watch over any potentially unpleasant or harmful effects of
the drug. Up to the present time, we have not seen any dysphoria
or other psychic ill effects from this drug. The question arose in
the past whether naltrexone caused an increase in blood pressure.
According to the collective data, there seems to be a small (2-3
millimeters of mercury), but not statistically significant, rise
in both systolic and diastolic pressure after initial administration
of naltrexone. However, by four to six weeks there is a return to
baseline and in many cases a 2-3 millimeter decrease in both systolic and diastolic pressures. The only occasional side effect with
some subjects seems to be an abdominal and gastrointestinal discomfort. When this was found at the beginning stages of treatment, it
was attributed to minor withdrawal symptoms, because opiates were
presumably still in the addict's system. However, these symptoms
have been reported later on in treatment as well. Some researchers
have found that these symptoms are sometimes relieved by antacids
or by administering naltrexone to the addict after he has eaten.
So it may be that naltrexone acts as a gastric irritant for some
addicts. An intriguing question, however, is what interaction
could naltrexone be having with the endogenously occurring opiate-
like compound that has recently been isolated by researchers? Could,
in fact, these abdominal symptoms be related to such an interaction?

To date, therefore, we have seen no serious, lasting side
effects directly attributable to the ingestion of naltrexone. This
antagonist appears to be a rather safe chemotherapeutic agent for
the treatment of opiate addiction.

This now brings us up to date. The NIDA naltrexone program
currently consists of the five National Academy of Sciences clinics,
four clinics that are using naltrexone in conjunction with different
behavior therapy techniques, and a number of other clinics that
are using naltrexone in a variety of treatment settings and in conjunction with a variety of other therapies. Aside from the N.A.S.
clinics, over 600 addicts have taken at least one dose of naltrexone in the other clinics. Total numbers of at least one time
ingestion of drug are therefore over 700. We consider the program
to be entering into the late stages of Phase II testing and are
preparing the data collected to be submitted to FDA by early 1977.
Thereafter we hope to enter into Phase III development of naltrexone which would mean more widespread usage of the drug in more
clinics. We hope this phase of development will be off the ground
by early-to-mid 1977.

Naltrexone has proven to be an interesting agent.....almost a
non-drug drug because of the lack of discernible effects other
than its opiate blocking capacity. As it has been used to date, it
seems to be a safe drug and an efficacious one in some addicts.
We are now interested in further testing out its efficacy in more
open studies and in new and innovative techniques of administration.
The question arises of how can naltrexone's efficacy best be
maximized? Should we think of this drug as another long term

maintenance chemotherapy? Or would it be more effective when used in conjunction with short term crisis - intervention techniques; or in conjunction with various behavioral techniques; or in a contingency manner so that the addict could ask to be put on naltrexone when he felt the need arise? Then, also, what factors such as attitudinal, environmental, and sociocultural variables both in the clinic personnel and in the addicts treated are crucial for the effective use of this drug? Finally, are there intrapsychic or personality variables in addicts that make some appropriate for one kind of treatment and others appropriate for another kind of treatment? These are all complex problems in the area of drug abuse treatment in general. Hopefully, further research will continue to reveal solutions to these problems, and we will be able to place the narcotic antagonists most productively into the overall treatment approach to opiate addiction.

NARCOTIC ANTAGONIST AND
THE PAROLEE-INDIVIDUAL
AND SOCIETAL CONSIDERATIONS

Thomas E. Hanlon, Ph.D. and

O. Lee McCabe, Ph.D.

Maryland Psychiatric Research Center
Catonsville, Maryland   21228

During the past twelve years, the present investigators have
carried out an extended program of evaluative research in a
community-based abstinence clinic for addicts paroled from the correctional institutions of Maryland. Earlier studies in this program afforded extensive clinical experience with the opiate abuser
in a program incorporating weekly group psychotherapy, a high level
of parole supervision, and daily urine surveillance(1,2).   The
regimen also included counseling of the addict by a member of the
clinical staff and by the parole agent after evidence of narcotic
drug use, constant monitoring of social adjustment, and vocational
assistance. The backgrounds and characteristics of the addict parolees in this program showed remarkable similarity over successive yearly samples, and the courses that the samples followed in
the program were so predictable that any positive departure from
them after therapeutic intervention was viewed with cautious optimism. It was with such a baseline as a frame of reference that a
series of studies was subsequently undertaken in the same setting
to explore the efficacy of experimental treatment procedures, primarily including the administration of narcotic antagonists on a
daily and contingent (i.e., only when indicated by evidence of
narcotic drug use) basis. Superimposed on the already existing
abstinence program, these experimental probes, extending over a six
year period, have involved both open and controlled evaluative
techniques. Detailed descriptions and interpretations of the results of this research have been presented elsewhere(3,4,5,6). The
purpose of this present report is to examine some of the ethical-
legal-research issues that have arisen during the course of the
overall research program.

I. STATEMENT OF THE ISSUES

Is the administration of a narcotic antagonist to newly released parolees an application of preventive medicine or chemical
control? Unique in the practice of medicine, such administration
often entails the treatment of individuals who do not consider themselves sick, who see no need for medical intervention, and whose
symptoms and clinical course are evaluated more in societal than in
individual terms. Why then do such individuals consent to treatment? Is their consent really voluntary, and if not, how does this
affect their participation in prescribed treatment procedures? Can,
in fact, the true worth of any new procedure be adequately evaluated under such circumstances?

II. THE EXPERIMENTAL NATURE OF THE TREATMENT

Because they are experimental, the use of narcotic antagonists
in maintenance treatment programs necessarily involves formal evaluation of safety and effectiveness and adherence to procedures designed to protect the rights and welfare of individuals involved in
human experimentation. Consent to participate in such a program
must be both voluntary and informed, stipulations which are doubly
important when applied to the case of a parolee. Although there is
little question as to the ability of most narcotic antagonists to
block the euphoric and analgesic effects produced by opiates, it
is when they are used prophylactically, i.e., administered over an
extended period of time to prevent addiction, that issues regarding
appropriateness and effectiveness arise. In this context, an
important issue relating to the use of antagonists with individuals
on parole appears to be the possible administration of medication
against an individual's will or as the sole alternative to punitive
or restrictive measures enforced by society.

There are those who argue that voluntary consent to participate in any type of experimental treatment, as far as the parolee
is concerned, is an impossibility. That even under the most benign
circumstances, subtle coercive and/or suggestive influences are invariably operative in a prison setting, where the decision to participate is made, causing the prospective parolee to agree to the reception of medication. These critics point to the undeniable pressure to cooperate that pervades institutional life, to perceived
fear of retaliation or disapproval from the prison administration,
including the parole board, and to the likelihood of continued institutionalization in the event of refusal to participate.

Considering the above, it is important to disabuse the parolee
of his doubts and fears by a fair explanation of narcotic antagonist treatment and by assuring the availability of alternative treatment should the parolee decide against the reception of a narcotic
antagonist. As indicated, in our own approach we prescribe

antagonists in the context of an ongoing abstinence program involving urine monitoring and weekly group psychotherapy. Should a
parolee refuse to participate in narcotic antagonist treatment, he
is still entitled to remain in the abstinence program. He may also
seek referral to any of several other available programs in the
community. It is thus made clear that agreeing to the reception of
experimental medication is not, and cannot be, a condition of parole
and that even if one initially agrees to receive medication, he may
refuse medication with impunity at any subsequent point in time.

III. THE ADDICT PAROLEE AS A RESEARCH SUBJECT

In view of the inconvenience and possible risk associated with
experimentation, one wonders what the inducements are that originally prompt an addict to opt for the narcotic drug approach over
such alternatives as therapeutic communities and abstinence programs. Easily implemented in an outpatient clinic, the approach
certainly offers more freedom in the community for the parolee than
that offered by a residential program. As for its advantage over
routine abstinence, the use of antagonists provides additional support to the motivated individual who is not entirely convinced he
can remain narcotic drug free on his own.

Despite its apparent supportive advantages, narcotic antagonist
treatment is not especially popular among newly released parolees,
who often express the conviction that they will never resort to
narcotics use again. For a variety of reasons, many parolees enrolled in urine monitoring programs affirm that they do not wish to
take medication of any kind. Depending on one's orientation in
these matters, such an affirmation can be regarded as either com-
mendable or devious. The intractable individual obviously refuses
medication because he wants no part of a treatment regimen that will
deny him the pleasure afforded by narcotics. Even among those who
are sincerely motivated to remain narcotic drug-free, however, many
refuse to participate in a narcotic antagonist program, preferring
to "go it alone," at least initially.

Our experience to date has also been that prior to release
from prison, prospective parolees frequently agree to the reception
of a narcotic antagonist yet refuse medication when they arrive at
the clinic or shortly after the initiation of treatment. There are
several possible explanations for this. Although the availability
of alternative programs facilitating release argues against a need
for deliberate deception, some parolees apparently agree to participate for indirect, manipulative reasons. A more generally applicable explanation, however, is that viewpoints and motivations regarding the use of narcotics that one has in a prison setting are
to a large extent situationally determined and do not necessarily
carry over to the process of reintegration into free society. For
many individuals, subsequent refusal to take medication is simply
the exercising of their option to reverse what they have come to
regard as a bad decision. For those who subsequently balk at

extended supervision of any type, it is a matter of gaining their freedom from another encumbrance of their parole experience. And, finally, for those who are more vulnerable, the stress of readjustment, peer pressure, narcotic drug availability, and habitual patterns of response to conditioned stimuli inevitably combine to undermine whatever positive motives originally existed.

IV. A POPULATION AT RISK?

Parolees directly referred to a narcotic antagonist program presumably have had little or no opportunity to indulge in narcotic drug use prior to referral. In spite of this, past procedures have been to initiate medication immediately on admission to the program. A current argument against this approach is that since narcotic antagonists have no pharmacological effect on the urge to take narcotics, their use prior to opiate involvement is not warranted. Also, those parolee addicts who do not resort to narcotics are needlessly subjected to medication involving at least some degree of inconvenience and risk. There is the counter argument, however, that if antagonist medication is routinely administered on admission to the abstinence program, there is a greater likelihood that opiate use will be avoided through the nonspecific, deterrent effects of administering an acknowledged narcotic blocking agent. There is the further argument that for some individuals who deviate the lack of reinforcement of the first few instances of narcotics use should have an inhibitory effect on continued use. Considering both this and the fact that we have no reliable means of identifying the parolee who will deviate, the utility of past blanket prescription procedures seems less questionable. This is especially so if one additionally considers the large percentage of parolee addicts who are likely to deviate within the first few months of release(2).

V. EVALUATION OF TREATMENT EFFECTS

Since the specific usefulness of a narcotic antagonist derives from its prevention of the usual reinforcement experienced when narcotic drugs are taken, the evaluative issue as far as antagonists are concerned is whether they have an extinguishing effect on subsequent narcotic drug-taking behavior once narcotics are resumed. In the case of an addict parolee, a suitable criterion of effectiveness is, therefore, the extent of narcotic drug use after the parolee's first deviation.

Regarding the typical reaction of the addict parolee to narcotic antagonist medication, results of our open and controlled studies have shown that the extent of placebo-effects are quite remarkable. The mere taking of oral medication, even though inactive, apparently has a decidedly beneficial effect in terms of program retention and outcome. For example, in our controlled comparison of a placebo and a no-medication control group(3), both of which received parole supervision and group psychotherapy, respective completion rates over a nine-month treatment period were found to be 50% vs. 25%, indicating in this one instance, at least, a two-fold advantage in favor of inactive medication.

Convincingly demonstrating the superiority of a narcotic antagonist over its corresponding placebo was a more difficult task than we had first imagined in view of the unexpectedly high placebo reactivity among our samples of parolees. However, controlling for placebo response, we were still able to identify two consistent specific responses to narcotic antagonists: 1) a slight, though repeatedly discernible, decrease in narcotic drug use; and 2) a consequent maneuvering to avoid medication, either intermittently or permanently. Although associated with less narcotic drug use, it was not possible to show any added benefit of active medication over placebo in terms of length of program participation or final program outcome in any given case, which are, admittedly, crucial criteria of effectiveness.

Our findings have also consistently suggested a relationship between avoidance, or rejection, of medication and the narcotic blocking effect of the active agent. In our most recent report on the use of the antagonist, naloxone, with the addict parolee(6), we made the paradoxical point that effectiveness as an antagonist often precludes successful treatment outcome. There was little reason to doubt that naloxone successfully blocked the euphoric and analgesic effects produced by opiates, thereby reducing the parolees' incentive to use narcotics while medicated. Rather than inhibiting the drug-taking behavior of less motivated addict parolees, however, the principal effect of naloxone (administered on a contingent basis) appeared to be that of reinforcing avoidance of medication and indulgence in otherwise uncooperative behavior.

REFERENCES

1. A. A. Kurland, J. C. Krantz, M. M. Henderson and F. Kerman, Int. J. Addict., 8:127(1973).
2. O. L. McCabe, A. A. Kurland and D. Sullivan, Int. J. Addict., 10:211(1975).
3. A. A. Kurland, T. E. Hanlon and O. L. McCabe, Int. J. Addict., 9:663(1974).
4. A. A. Kurland, O. L. McCabe and T. E. Hanlon, Int. J. Addict., 11:117(1976).
5. T. E. Hanlon, O. L. McCabe, C. Savage and A. A. Kurland, Int. Pharmacopsychiat, 10:240(1975).
6. T. E. Hanlon, O. L. McCabe. C. Savage and A. A. Kurland, submitted for publication.

PATIENT CYCLAZOCINE AND NALTREXONE
INDUCTION AND PLACEBO EFFECT VARIABILITY
AS A FUNCTION OF PSYCHOLOGICAL FACTORS

Thomas Capone, Ph.D.
Leonard S. Brahen, Ph.D., M.D.
Victoria Wiechert, M.P.S.
Gail Kalin

Medical Research and Education Unit
Nassau County Department of Drug and Alcohol Addiction
Mineola, New York

I. INTRODUCTION

Early studies with the narcotic antagonist cyclazocine documented induction drug effects such as insomnia, restless (1), weakness, irritability and somnolence (2). Brahen et al (3) reported on controlled double-blind placebo studies with cyclazocine (10 day induction) and naltrexone (5 day induction). He noted with cyclazocine that in addition to the above effects such effects as constipation and dry mouth were also significantly greater than in placebo conditions. Significant naltrexone effects included loss of appetite, somnolence, gas, constipation and abdominal cramps. He also reported significant variability of effects between subjects with each of the antagonists with significantly greater variability of effects with cyclazocine.

The effects of personality, biochemical and physiological states, and the environment, have long been recognized in psychopharmacology as factors potentially contributing to the variability of drug effects. Linderman and vonFelsinger (4) and Lasagna, vonFelsinger, and Beecher (5) have indicated that reactions determined by personality have confounded drug specific reaction patterns and urge investigative procedures aimed at separating drug specific effects and personality contributions.

An early study by Shagass and Kerenyi (6) measured the sedation threshold (amount of intravenous amobarbital sodium required to produce slurred speech and concomitant EEG changes). Of 224 patients rated by pyschiatrists in regard to degree of hysterical or obsessional symptomatology, they found higher hysteria ratings significantly associated with greater drug sensitivity (lower threshold).

Another approach to determining specific drug responses has been the use of a placebo in controlled studies. While placebo studies help evaluate the extent of true drug effect they have not been frequently conducted to clarify the multiple determinants of such reactions in the individual patient. There is some evidence (7) for the position that a placebo reactor exists at one end of the psychological continuum (intraversion, acquiescence, hysteria) and that a placebo non-reactor exists at the other.

It is of note that both studies of drug effects (6) and the study of placebo reactivity (7) have associated hysteria ratings with effects. Interestingly psychoanalytic theory (8) characterizes the hysteric as particularly amenable to suggestion, prone to conversion of unconscious conflicts into somatic symptomatology and disturbances in sensorium.

On the basis of both theory and reported findings one would therefore, expect a significant relationship between hysteria ratings and an individual's level of induction and placebo effects with naltrexone or cyclazocine. The present study sought to investigate this with the realization that if antagonists are to be used widely test findings to predict specific subject suitability will be important for individual patient selection and preparation for treatment.

II. METHODS

A. Setting
The Nassau County Department of Drug and Alcohol Addiction, in cooperation with the Nassau County Correctional Center is currently operating under NIMH Grant; the first narcotic antagonist jail work-release program.

B. Design
A total of 20 subjects were randomly assigned to either receive cyclazocine (N=10) or placebo (N=10) at the start of the study. The assignment was not known to anyone having direct contact with any of the subjects or the subject himself. The drug group completed induction on day 10 and remained on active drug throughout the study while the subjects receiving placebo for the first 10 days began drug induction on day 11 and completed induction on day 20. Drug induction involved daily increasing increments of .2 mg b.i.d. for 10 days to the maintenance dose of 2 mg b.i.d. on the 10th day of induction. Beginning on day 21 after completion of the double-blind study, all subjects were maintained with a dosage of 2 mg b.i.d.

Subsequent to the study of the 20 subjects receiving cyclazocine an additional 20 subjects were studied in double-blind fashion using naltrexone. Of these 20 subjects, 10 subjects were randomly assigned to a drug induction group involving daily increasing increments of 5 mg b.i.d. for 5 days to the maintenance dose of 25 mg b.i.d. (50 mg daily) on the 5th day of induction. The other 10 subjects received placebo the first 5 days of the study. Each of these subject subsequently either after the 5 day placebo condition (N=5) or 10 day placebo condition (N=5) went on to a standard 5 day induction with increasing increments of 5 mg b.i.d. (50 mg daily) on the 5th induction day.

C. Measurements

1. PSYCHOLOGICAL PREDICTOR FACTORS
Upon admission to the study standardized psychometric testing was conducted, in addition to clinical psychodiagnostic assessment (including Rorschach). The psychological factors selected for the present study were derived from the Minnesota Multiphasic Personality Inventory, a standardized pencil and paper test providing subtest scores for hypochondriasis (HS); depression (D); hysteria (Hy); psychopathic deviate (Pd); paranoia (pa); masculinity-feminity (MF); schizophrenia (Sc) and hypomania (Ma). Of these HS, and Hy, were selected for inclusion in the study because of theoretical and suggested empirical relevance.

2. CRITERIA MEASURES OF DRUG EFFECTS
All subjects twice daily (morning and evening) completed a questionnaire regarding the perceived effect of the drug. In this study total self reported effects (TSE), were selected for study.

III. RESULTS

A. Correlation of Predictor Factors With Induction Drug Effects

1. HYSTERIA
A significant positive correlation was obtained for hysteria scored on the MMPI and total number of self reported effects (TSE) for the combined regular cyclazocine induction condition and the cyclazocine induction after placebo condition (r=.56, P<.05, N=20). Additionally a significant positive correlation was obtained for hysteria on the MMPI and total number of self reported effects (TSE) for the combined induction condition and induction after placebo conditions for naltrexone (r=.48, P<.05, N=20).

2. HYPOCHONDRIASIS
While a suggestive positive relationship was found between hypocondriasis (Hy) and total self reported cyclazocine induction drug effects this correlation was not statistically significant r=.41,

N=10, N.S.) Hypochondriasis was significantly and positively correlated with total self reported naltrexone induction drug effects (r=.50, P<.05, N=20).

3. CLINICAL PSYCHODIAGNOSTIC FACTORS
As a group subjects treated with naltrexone had few significant adverse effects during induction. Where disturbing effects were reported they were mild and tolerance developed by maintenance. Cyclazocine effects were generally of greater intensity. Three subjects had particularly marked effects characterized by "paranoid" type ideation, "bizarre dreams", feeling isolated and experiencing things as unreal, and "feeling edgy." Clinical review of baseline Rorschach records suggested instances of percepts marked by poor form level, manifestations of fragmentation or dissolution and isolation of parts of the blot from one another, instances of attack and other signs suggestive of strong ego treats associated with castration fears. The above signs suggested weak pre-morbid ego defenses and strong super-ego injunctions.

B. Correlation of Predictor Factors
With Placebo Effects
A significant positive correlation was found in the cyclazocine fondition between total self reported effects during placebo and hysteria scores (r=.78, P<.01, N=10). Total self reported effects during naltrexone placebo were not correlated significantly with hysteria scores (r=.23, N=10, N.S.).

IV. DISCUSSION
The purpose of this study was to investigate the nature of personality factors associated with drug effect. The psychological factor most strongly implicated in drug effect for both the cyclazocine and naltrexone induction conditions was hysteria. Evidence of higher hysteria ratings being associated with stronger drug effects has been previously reported (6). Interestingly, psychoanalytic theory hypothesizes that hysterical symptoms appear when ego regression occurs and unconscious or controlled conflicts and impulses emerge as conversional somatic symptoms, disturbances in sense of reality and more generally in outbursts of feelings and ideas which are normally hidden. In the induction phase repression may be partially removed by the hallucinogenic effects of the antagonists (observed to be stronger with cyclazocine). Hysterical suggestibility would then tend to exacerbate underlying conflicts and hypochondriacal concern. Psychodynamic observations suggest that most often paranoid ideation during cyclazocine induction was associated with pre-morbid conditions of disturbed super-ego development. Specifically, parent figures were incorporated as primarily punitive without the reassuring balance of love and protection. Projections of such punitive parenting figures in the form of percieved ego attack, suspiciousness, etc. were exacerbated as ego defenses were temporarily weakened by drug. Interest-

ingly, Fenichel (8) indicates that, "the projection of feared excitements onto nature or onto particular environmental situations in anxiety hysteria, occurs in a more outspoken and obvious manner in schizophrenia."

Hysteria was significantly associated with placebo effect in the cyclazocine condition but not in the naltrexone condition thus providing mixed confirmation for evidence characterizing placebo reactors as high on the intraversion continuum associated with hysteria (7). One possible explanation for these findings relates to the generally poorer street reputation of cyclazocine while naltrexone is commonly viewed as milder (3). The stronger association of high placebo effects with the subject characterized as more highly hysterical in the cyclazocine condition may be causally related to hightened expectation with this agent interacting with hysterical suggestibility. In the naltrexone condition apprehension appeared lower thus providing less basis for exaggerating hysterical liability of reactions. These findings suggest the need to continue exploration of drug and placebo effects as a function of true drug effect level, subject psychological characteristics, and to additionally attend to levels of expectation of drug effects.

REFERENCES

1. J. Jaffe, in Current Psychiatric Therapies, Grune & Stratton, N.Y., 1967.
2. A. Freedman, M. Fink, R. Sharoff, and A. Zaks, Amer. J. Psychiat. 11:124 (1968).
3. L. Brahen, T. Capone, V. Wiechert, and D. Desiderio, Submitted Arch. of Psychiat. (1975).
4. E. Lindeman and J. vonFelsinger, Psychopharmacologia, 2: (1961).
5. L. Lasagna, F. Mosteller and J. vonFelsinger, Amer. J. of Med., 16:(1954).
6. C. Shagass, A. Kerenyi, J. nerv. ment. Dis., 126:(1958).
7. S. Fisher and R. Fisher, Psychoopharmacologia, 4:(1963).
8. O. Fenichel, The Psychoanalytic Theory of the Neurosis, W. W. Norton & Co., New York, 1945.

A COMPARISON OF CONTROLLED
CLINICAL AND LABORATORY STUDIES
OF THE NARCOTIC ANTAGONISTS
CYCLAZOCINE AND NALTREXONE

Leonard S. Brahen, Ph. D., M.D.*, **
Thomas Capone, Ph. D.**
Victoria Wiechert, M.P.S.**
Anne Babinski, B.A., R.N.**
Dawn Desiderio***

*Department of Psychiatry, State University of
New York at Stony Brook
**Nassau County Department of Drug and Alcohol Addiction
***Adelphi University, Independent Study Program

I.   INTRODUCTION

When adequate quantities of an oral non-addictive narcotic antagonist are administered to a drug-free individual, a subsequent
response to, as well as a dependence on narcotics is blocked, and
a dependence on narcotics cannot occur. (1,2).

Compared with methadone the antagonist has the advantage of
being relatively safe at high dosages in the narcotic free patient.
Additionally it is non-addicting, and possesses no "street" value.
Therefore, when the courts mandate a drug treatment program for
narcotic addicts the antagonist will provide an additional option
of narcotic blockade beyond the single drug treatment of methadone
now available.

The clinical experience with cyclazocine revealed unpleasant
(dysphoric) induction side effects, mostly limited to the first few
weeks of treatment. (3,4). Since most addicts are poorly motivated they often find cyclazocine induction side effects an insurmountable barrier to treatment. A more recent available antagonist,
naltrexone, has been reported to produce fewer side effects.

We, therefore, carried out controlled clinical and laboratory
studies in order to comparatively assess the portential for side
effects and toxicity for these narcotic antagonists. This was done
with an induction regimen designed to produce the minimum level of
side effects with the final maintenance dose providing an adequate

narcotic blockade (4 mg/day, ½ dose in A.M. and ½ dose in P.M.).
Each side effect was quantified for incidence by day of induction
(A.M. as well as P.M.).

Such data were also obtained for naltrexone (50 mg/day, ½ dose
in A.M. and ½ dose in P.M.)(2,4,5).

Medical and laboratory data were compared in the pre-drug and
post-drug period for both cyclazocine and naltrexone.

II. METHOD

A. Setting

The studies reported were carried out by the Nassau County Department of Drug and Alcohol Addiction in cooperation with the Nassau County Correctional Center, East Meadow, New York. The studies
of the individual antagonists were done sequentially. Cyclazocine
studies preceeded the naltrexone studies.

B. Patients

All patients admitted to and completing this study were essentially healthy (physically and mentally), males, 18 and over.

C. Test and Examinations

The patients admitted to this study were given a history and
physical examination as well as the following work-up: chest
roentgenogram, electrocardiogram, urinalysis, CBC with differential,
SMA 6/60, SMA 12/60, prothrombin time, platelet count, Australian
Antigen, reticulocyte count, VDRL and sickle cell tests. Vital
signs (temperature, blood pressure, pulse, and respiration) were
taken twice daily for the first five control days prior to the
starting of the antagonist and twice daily for the remainder of the
time (100 to 200 days) the patients received the antagonists. Slit
lamp eye examinations were only done on the naltrexone patients
(this examination was not required by the regulatory agencies for
the cyclazocine study). The tests and examinations noted above
were repeated at intervals as required by F.D.A. and N.I.D.A. Each
inmate also provided a urine sample nightly for routine detection
of possible drugs abused during the study.

C. Design

A classical double-blind, triple observer design was employed
with random assignment to active drug or placebo. Earlier work established that the inmates' self-report was the most reliable and
therefore, the data reported in this paper is derived exclusively
from that source. (4). Based upon data from other investigators,
a 5 day naltrexone induction regimen was used and compared with the
10 day induction for cyclazocine. (2,5).

The post-drug medical and laboratory data were compared with
the pre-drug data for both antagonists to determine any changes
related to drug administration.

III. STATISTICAL METHOD

The Analysis of Variance test (repeated measures design) was used for the statistical comparison involving measured side effects.

In the toxicology analysis, simple means and standard deviations of pre-values and post-values were computed for descriptive purposes. Inferential analysis of significance of differences between pre-test and post-test involved the use of correlated "t" tests for repeated measures on the same subject.

IV. RESULTS

A. Overall Comparison of Individual Side Effects

A comparison of the incidence of drug effects produced by each agent indicates cyclazocine produced many more side effects than naltrexone (298 vs. 67). For each side effect category except gas and loss of appetite responses, cyclazocine produced a greater incidence of side effect than naltrexone for the induction period. All effects reported for naltrexone were of a mild order and in no case was a patient ever discontinued from treatment as a result of such effects. Some of the responses reported for cyclazocine were severe and therefore, required discontinuation of treatment (3 of 20 patients).

The spectrum and ranking of side effects of one drug differed from the other. Little correlation exists in the ranking of side effects of one drug to the side effects of the other (Rho=.24, N=14, N.S.).

B. Comparison of Total Side Effects

Cyclazocine and naltrexone induction effects differ from their respective placebos. These observations were conformed statistically. Cyclazocine induction effects were significantly greater than its placebo effects (F=7.50, df=1, 18, P < .05) and this was also true for naltrexone induction vs placebo effects (F=8.60, df=1, 18, P < .01).

Cyclazocine produced more side effects responses than naltrexone. A comparison of cyclazocine and naltrexone "induction after placebo" responses shows a high level of cyclazocine responses compared to a very low level of naltrexone effects. This difference is significant (F=18.4, df=1, 18, P < .01). Naltrexone's low order of induction effects is relatively sustained through the initial maintenance phase whereas, cyclazocine higher level of induction effects appeared to drop off sharply during the initial maintenance phase. (The peak responses for cyclazocine "induction after placebo" were on days 6 and 7 of drug administration corresponding to the peak days 5 to 8 of induction).

C. Comparison of Drug Inducted Laboratory Changes

Normal ranges used were established by the Nassau County Medical Center Laboratory. The average range of time between the sampling for the pre-drug and post-drug data ranged from 100-200 days.

Cyclazocine induced a significant depression in the following (but, both pre and post drug data are within normal limits): hemoglobin, hematocrit, calcium, albumin, total protein.

Naltrexone induced a significant depression in the following (but, both pre and post drug data are within normal limits): BUN, platelets, cholesterol, systolic and diastolic mean blood pressure.

Naltrexone induced a significant rise (still within normal limits) of: uric acid and prothormbin time.

Abnormal values in the pre-drug control period were found for certain of the laboratory tests. The neutrophil values for both cyclazocine (50.3% to 47.9%) and naltrexone (52.6% to 51.4%)were below normal range (54-62%) in the pre-drug assessment and were reduced even further in the post-drug period but not at a statistically significant level (t=.67, df=13, N.S., t=.28, df=10, N.S.). The lymphocyte counts for both cyclazocine (45.2% to 50%) and naltrexone (42.5% to 45.5%) in the pre-drug control period had a mean beyond the normal limits (25-33%) and there was a statistically insignificant increase in the post-treatment period (t=1.34, df=13, N.S., t=.3, N.S., t=.70, df=12, N.S.). For SGOT both cyclazocine (81.2 to 69.7 um) and naltrexone (73.9 to 76.4 um) pre-treatment values were above normal limits (10-50 um) and although naltrexone value increased and cyclazocine value decreased in the post-treatment period neither was statistically significant (t=1.43, df=13, N.S., f=.3, df=12, N.S.). These findings regarding the reversal of neutrophils to lymphocyte ratio and the elevated SGOT value have previously been reported for heroin addicts. (6).

V. DISCUSSION

The data reported reflects the higher incidence of induction side effects for cyclazocine over naltrexone, three of the original 20 cyclazocine patients discontinued treatment because of drug side effects, characterized in these instances by paranoia, a high degree of restlessness and the feeling of loss of control. In contrast, no patient was discontinued from a naltrexone treatment prior to completion of induction because of side effects.

The data presented is in accord with our clinical impression that naltrexone produces a minimum of side effects compared with cyclazocine. The few minor effects noted on the naltrexone induction schedule can be eliminated by first administrating a placebo treatment phase. In contrast prior treatment with placebo does not reduce the high level of side effects found on cyclazocine induction. Cyclazocine produced more side effects than naltrexone, such as difficulty sleeping, nervousness, dizziness, headache, tired, dry mouth, "skin itchy", cramps and constipation.

Naltrexone has the advantage over cyclazocine of having consistent low order side effects. Further, we found the few side effects with naltrexone are primarily centered in the G.I. ystem such as: gas, constipation, abdominal cramps, and loss of appetite (without any concurrent weight loss). In regard to CNS, the naltrexone effect reported most often was tiredness.

Regarding the laboratory data, when the pre-drug control mean value was within normal limits and the post-drug control value differed significantly, such post-drug mean value always remained within normal limits. Nevertheless, some interesting suggestive trends have been noted and merit further attention. For cyclazocine, special attention should be paid to the hemoglobin and hematocrit, calcium, albumin and total protein. For naltrexone, trends are noted for uric acid, BUN, cholesterol, platelet and prothrombin time. We additionally found naltrexone diastolic blood pressure to fall a small but statistically significant degree, but without apparent clinical importance.

For neutrophils, lymphocytes and SGOT the mean pre-drug values were abnormal and remained abnormal in the post-drug period, but did not change significantly for either agent as a result of drug administration.

The controlled data reported in this paper supports naltrexone over cyclazocine as the drug of choice in the treatment of narcotic addiction.

This investigation was supported in part by the NIMH Grant #HSM 42 72 210 and NIDA Grant #1 RO1 DA 01249-ol NAD.

REFERENCES

1. W. Martin, G. Gordetsky, and T. McClane, Clin. Pharmacal. Ther. 7:(1967).
2. W. Martin, D. Jasinski, and P. Mansky, Arch. Gen. Psychiat. 28: (1973).
3. A. Freedman, M. Fink, R. Sharoff, and A. Zaks, Amer. J. Psychiat. 124:(1968).
4. L. Brahen, T. Capone, V. Wiechart, Submitted Amer. J. Drug and Alcohol. Addic.
5. R. Resnick, J. Volavka, A. Freedman, and M. Thomas. Amer. J. Psychiat. 131:(1974).
6. L. Moyron, E. Kaplan, S. Alling, and J. Becktel, Clin. Chem., 20:(1974).

STEREOCHEMICAL IDENTIFICATION AND
STEREOSELECTIVE SYNTHESIS OF β-NALTREXOL*

Nithiananda Chatterjie, Harry E. Dayton and Charles E. Inturrisi

Department of Pharmacology
Cornell University Medical College
New York, New York 10021

It is the purpose of this report to discuss some of the recent information on the chemistry and metabolism of naltrexone and congeners.

Compounds possessing narcotic antagonist activity may be of value in the treatment of opiate dependence. As a function of dose, narcotic antagonists will reverse or prevent most of the effects of narcotics including euphoria. Upon repeated administration tolerance does not appear to develop to their antagonist action and they do not induce physical dependence.

The potential usefulness of narcotic antagonists as opiate blocking agents in patients with a history of heroin abuse was first demonstrated in the mid 1960s during clinical trials of the benzomorphan derivative, cyclazocine (1, 2, 3). The undesirable side effects experienced by a significant number of patients stimulated the search for other narcotic antagonists.

One group of compounds that have received considerable attention are the N-substituted derivatives in the oxymorphone series. The N-ally noroxymorphone derivative, called naloxone (Fig. 1) was synthesized by Lewenstein and Fishman in 1960 (4).

*Our research as described in this paper was supported in part by SAODAP Grant No. DA-00458. Dr. Inturrisi is an Andrew W. Mellon Teacher-Scientist for 1975-76.

Although a potent narcotic antagonist in animals (5) and in man
(6) and relatively free of side effects, its short duration of action
and very poor oral potency limited its general usefulness for
treatment. For example, Zaks et al. (6) found that a single dose
of nearly 3 grams of naloxone hydrochloride was necessary to
produce a narcotic blockade that would persist for 24 hours. In
man the major urinary metabolite of naloxone is the pharmacologically inactive 3-glucuronide (7, 8, 9). It would appear that
the rapid metabolic inactivation of naloxone is in large measure
responsible for the relatively short duration of antagonist action
and the huge first pass effect reflected in the extremely poor oral
potency of the drug.

Naltrexone (Fig. 1) is the N-cyclopropylmethyl derivative
of noroxymorphone (10). The initial pharmacologic data on
naltrexone in laboratory animals indicated that the drug is a
potent narcotic antagonist with an extended duration of action
(11, 12). In man naltrexone is an effective antagonist at oral
doses of 30-50 mg per day. The duration of action at these
doses is at least 24 hours and side effects are minimal (13). At
present naltrexone appears to be the most promising candidate
for use in treatment.

Recent efforts have been directed toward an understanding
of the disposition of naltrexone in man and laboratory animals.
Cone (14) discovered that the major human urinary metabolite of
naltrexone was a compound wherein the 6-keto function of the
drug was reduced to the corresponding 6β-hydroxy alcohol
(Fig. 1). We obtained definitive spectroscopic evidence by use
of proton nuclear magnetic resonance techniques (Fourier
Transform) that this metabolite was indeed the 6β-hydroxy
epimer (now called β-naltrexol) (15). These studies drew
attention to the stereochemistry of the alcoholic biotransformation products of members of the 6-keto morphine series.

In collaboration with Dr. James Fujimoto of the Medical
College of Wisconsin we observed species variation in the
6-keto reduction products of naloxone and naltrexone (15, 16).
We found, for example, that the metabolite of naltrexone isolated
from rabbit urine was β-naltrexol while that from the chicken was
α-naltrexol (Fig. 1). Fujimoto and associates discovered that an
enzyme activity partially purified from rabbit liver catalyzed the
stereoselective reduction of 6-keto morphines (17).

Our interest in both the role of biotransformation of
naltrexone and naloxone and in the relatively long duration of

action of the former, necessitated a quantity of the appropriate 6β-metabolites in a relatively pure state for use as analytical standards and for pharmacologic characterization. Therefore we sought to obtain the 6β-hydroxy alcohols from naltrexone and naloxone.

Chemical methods are readily available for the synthesis of 6α-hydroxy epimers from naloxone and naltrexone, by hydride reduction of the 6-keto function of the parent compounds (18). No claim was found in the literature of a selective chemical reduction of 6-keto derivatives having the morphine skeleton to yield 6β-hydroxy epimers. Our initial attempt to obtain β-naltrexol by reduction of naltrexone with lithium tri-sec-butylborohydride (L-selectride) yielded solely the corresponding 6α-alcohol. This was not surprising, since ring C of the 14-hydroxydihydromorphinone skeleton should offer steric hindrance to a hydride, approaching from the concave side. More recently instances of obtaining mixtures of 6α and 6β-epimeric alcohols (the 6β-epimers undoubtedly being the minor component) in hydride reductions of these compounds have been reported (19, 20).

Our approach to the problem was to use a reagent which would reduce the carbonyl group of these drugs in a highly alkaline medium, wherein the enolate might be generated. Another consideration was to utilize a reducing agent which conceivably reduces the ketone function by a mechanism of electron entry via the oxygen atom. These considerations pointed to formamidinesulfinic acid as the reagent of choice for our purpose. Our objective was achieved in the reduction of naltrexone and naloxone with this reagent using a procedure modified from that of Nakagawa and Minami (21) for the reduction of various ketones. Our procedure produced β-naltrexol and β-naloxol in yields of 88 and 40%, respectively (22). Further, the metabolites obtained were virtually free of the 6α-epimers, as evidenced by GLC and proton nuclear magnetic resonance techniques. This method is clearly advantageous when compared with other lengthy and arduous methods of separation (20).

We are currently studying this process for scope and mechanism; we have also extended it to ketones in the morphine and codeine series, lacking the 14-hydroxy group (23).

An adequate supply of β-naltrexol for use as an analytical standard aided the development of a method for the separation

and quantitation of naltrexone and metabolites. The urinary
excretion profiles following naltrexone in man and several other
species have been completed (24) and the role of biotransformation in the time-action of naltrexone has been discussed in a
recent review (25).

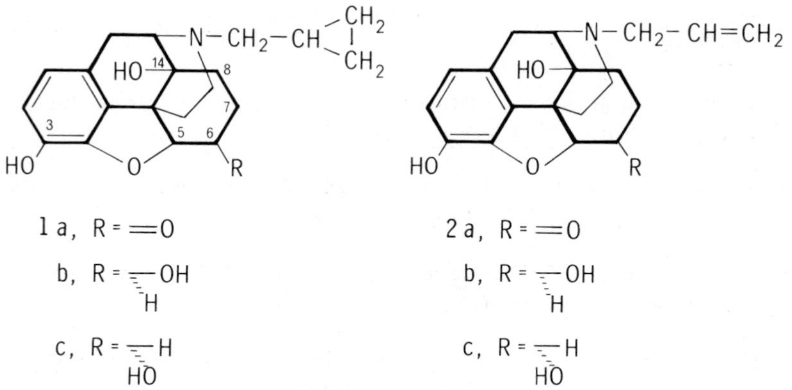

Figure 1. Structural formulae of naltrexone (1a), naloxone (1b)
and their corresponding 6-hydroxy derivatives. 1b is
designated β-naltrexol and 1c is α-naltrexol, 2b is β-naloxol
and 2c is α-naloxol. From Chatterjie et al. (22). By permission
of Journal of Medicinal Chemistry.

REFERENCES

1. W. R. Martin, C. W. Gorodetsky, and T. K. McClane, Clin.
   Pharmacol. Ther., 7: 455 (1966).

2. J. H. Jaffe and L. Brill, Int. J. Addiction, 1: 9 (1966).

3. A. Freedman, M. Fink, R. Sharoff, and A. Zaks, J. Amer.
   Med. Assoc., 201: 191 (1967).

4. M. J. Lewenstein, U. S. Patent, 3,254,088 (1966).

5. H. Blumberg, H. B. Dayton, M. George, and D. N. Rapaport, Fed. Proc., 20: 311 (1961).

6. A. Zaks, T. Jones, M. Fink, and A. M. Freedman, J. Am. Med. Assoc., 215: 2108 (1971).

7. J. M. Fujimoto, Proc. Soc. Exp. Biol. Med., 133: 317 (1970).

8. K. F. Ober and J. M. Fujimoto, Proc. Soc. Exp. Biol. Med. 139: 1068 (1972).

9. S. H. Weinstein, M. Pfeffer, J. M. Schor, L. Indindoli, and M. Mintz, J. Pharm. Sci., 60: 1567 (1971).

10. H. Blumberg, I. J. Pachter, and Z. Matossian, U.S. Pat. No. 3,332,950, July 25 (1967).

11. H. Blumberg, H. B. Dayton, and P. S. Wolf, Toxicol. Appl. Pharmacol. 10: 406 (1967).

12. H. Blumberg and H. B. Dayton, in Narcotic Antagonists, Advances in Biochemical Psychopharmacology, Vol. 8, Raven Press, New York (1973).

13. W. R. Martin, D. R. Jasinski, and P. A. Mansky, Arch. Gen. Psychiatry, 28: 784 (1973).

14. E. J. Cone, Tetrahedron Lett., 28: 2607 (1973).

15. N. Chatterjie, J. M. Fujimoto, C. E. Inturrisi, S. Roerig, R. I. H. Wang, D. V. Bowen, F. H. Field, and D. D. Clarke, Drug. Metab. Dispos., 2: 401 (1974).

16. N. Chatterjie, C. E. Inturrisi, J. M. Fujimoto, and S. Roerig, Pharmacologist, 16: 226 (1974).

17. J. M. Fujimoto, S. Roerig, R.I.H. Wang, N. Chatterjie, and C. E. Inturrisi, Proc. Soc. Exp. Biol. Med., 148: 443 (1975).

18. I. J. Pachter and Z. Matossian, U.S. Pat. No. 3,313,197, (1968).

19. E. F. Hahn and J. Fishman, J. Org. Chem. 40: 31 (1975).

20. L. Malspeis, M. S. Bathala, R. M. Ludden, H. B. Bhat, S. G. Frank, T. D. Sokoloski, B. E. Morrison, and R. H. Reuning, Res. Comm. Chem. Path. Pharmacol., 12: 43 (1975).

21. V. Nakagawa and K. Minami, Tetrahedron Lett., 27: 343 (1972).

22. N. Chatterjie, C. E Inturrisi, H. Blumberg, and H. B. Dayton, J. Med. Chem., 18: 490 (1975).

23. N. Chatterjie, J. G. Umans and C. E. Inturrisi, J. Org. Chem., in press, 1976.

24. H. E. Dayton and C. E. Inturrisi, Drug. Metab. Disp., in press, 1976.

25. C. E. Inturrisi, Ann. N.Y. Acad. Sci., in press, 1976.

URINARY EXCRETION PROFILES IN CYCLAZOCINE MAINTENANCE PATIENTS*

Robert F. Kaiko and Charles E. Inturrisi

Analgesic Studies Section
Memorial Sloan-Kettering Cancer Center
New York, New York

I. INTRODUCTION

Over the past decade several compounds possessing narcotic antagonist activity have been evaluated for the treatment of opiate dependence (1, 2, 3, 4, 5). The first of these was cyclazocine, a synthetic agonist-antagonist analgesic of the benzomorphan series.

The thorough pharmacologic evaluation and proper clinical use of many compounds have been facilitated by an understanding of their biotransformation and physiologic disposition. By use of tritiated cyclazocine it has been established in the dog that cyclazocine is biotransformed to norcyclazocine and that glucuronide conjugates of both the parent and nor compound are formed (6, 7). The purpose of our work was to develop a specific and sensitive method for the identification and quantitation of cyclazocine and its biotransformation products in the urine of patients receiving cyclazocine for the treatment of opiate dependence.

II. MATERIALS AND METHODS

A multi-step solvent extraction procedure followed by a gas-liquid chromatographic analysis were utilized for the isolation and quantitation of cyclazocine and norcyclazocine in urine from two patients after an oral dose of 1.9 mg of d,l-cyclazocine. The details of these procedures have been reported (8).

*Financial support was provided by The Narcotic Antagonists Research Program of the New York City Department of Health, SAODAP Grant No. DA-00458 and NIGMS Grant No. GM-00099.

III. RESULTS AND DISCUSSION

Our preliminary gas-chromatographic studies demonstrated that the lower limit of quantitation according to the linear dynamic range of detector response to cyclazocine and norcyclazocine was 50 and 200 ng, respectively. The expectation that smaller amounts would exist in human biofluids necessitated the development of a more sensitive method. As illustrated in Fig. 1, such a method was realized by the conversion of cyclazocine and norcyclazocine to trifluoroacetyl derivatives. This resulted, firstly, in a shift towards increased detector response; secondly, an extension of the linear dynamic range down to 10 ng; and thirdly, a greater than 10-fold decrease in the relative standard error for triplicate determinations of cyclazocine and norcyclazocine. The derivatization procedure facilitated quantitation by producing more volatile compounds resulting in less adsorption onto column packing materials.

Figure 2 shows two chromatograms resulting from the trifluoroacetylation of extracts of 4 ml aliquots of urine from a patient receiving cyclazocine for the treatment of opiate dependence. These particular aliquots were from the 8-12 hr period after an oral dose of 1.9 mg of cyclazocine. Chromatogram a represents the peaks that resulted from the trifluoroacetylation of cyclazocine, norcyclazocine and the internal standard, levallorphan, following extraction from urine. Chromatogram b represents the peaks that resulted when an aliquot of urine from the same sample was exposed to acid-hydrolysis prior to extraction and derivatization. The amounts of cyclazocine and norcyclazocine existing as acid-hydrolyzable conjugate were calculated by subtracting the quantities represented in a from those in b. The method can be used to quantitate as little as 10 ng of cyclazocine and norcyclazocine per ml of urine when using a 4 ml aliquot.

Previous reports (9, 10) of methods for the determination of cyclazocine in human biofluids have suffered in that they have failed to demonstrate the application of the method to samples of biofluids from patients receiving the drug and have been limited to the quantitation of the parent compound alone. The method reported here is both sufficiently sensitive and reproducible for the quantitation of cyclazocine, norcyclazocine and their acid-hydrolyzable forms in the urine of patients receiving cyclazocine for the treatment of opiate dependence. We have observed that both cyclazocine and norcyclazocine are present in patient plasma in their free and conjugated forms. The use of a flame ionization detector, however, does not permit adequate quantitation of plasma levels but the use of an electron capture detector would significantly increase the limit of sensitivity of the method.

The cumulative urinary excretion of cyclazocine and its biotransformation products is illustrated in Fig. 3. Following the oral administration of 1.9 mg of cyclazocine, the relative rate of excretion of each form of each base remained in the same order throughout the 12 hr dosing interval. Total cyclazocine accounted for a greater fraction of the excreted drug than did total norcyclazocine. The conjugated forms of both cyclazocine and nor-cylazocine accounted for a greater fraction than did the free forms. Approximately 60% of the administered dose was accounted for as cyclazocine and biotransformation products in the 12 hour dosing interval. The cumulative urinary excretion profile for the second patient was qualitatively similar to the one illustrated in Fig. 3. As with the first patient, 60% of the administered dose was accounted for as cyclazocine and biotransformation products.

Our observations suggest that the biotransformation of cyclazocine in man resembles that found in the dog (7), in that cyclazocine was excreted primarily as the free and conjugated parent compound with appreciable amounts of both free and conjugated nor-cyclazocine also excreted in the urine. An incomplete recovery of the administered dose of cyclazocine within the 12 hr dosing interval is consistent with several possible explanations including incomplete absorption from the gastrointestinal tract, other primary routes of elimination, other biotransformation products and the failure of the rate of elimination to match the rate of drug administration. Other significant biotransformation products have been suggested (7).

Hydrolysis of conjugated cyclazocine and norcyclazocine by beta-glucuronidase treatment of a 0-4 hr urine sample from a patient resulted in an amount of cyclazocine being released that was equivalent to the amount release by acid-hydrolysis. The amount of norcyclazocine released by beta-glucuronidase, however, accounted for only 25% of the amount released by acid-hydrolysis. In the dog, beta-glucuronidase releases amounts of cyclazocine and norcyclazocine that are equivalent to the amounts released by acid-hydrolysis (7). Thus, in man, as in the dog, cyclazocine and norcyclazocine are excreted in the urine as glucuronide conjugates following the administration of cyclazocine. Our preliminary data suggests that, unlike the dog, man may excrete norcyclazocine in a conjugated form other than the glucuronide.

The observations are consistent with the suggestion that both N-dealkylation and glucuronide conjugation (Fig. 4) are important routes of biotransformation for cyclazocine in man. The methodology presented here is applicable to the determination of cyclazocine and its biotransformation products in biofluids other than urine with little modification. Thus, these methods should provide the technical basis for understanding the relationships between the concentration of cyclazocine in biofluids and the narcotic blockade induced by cyclazocine treatment of opiate dependence.

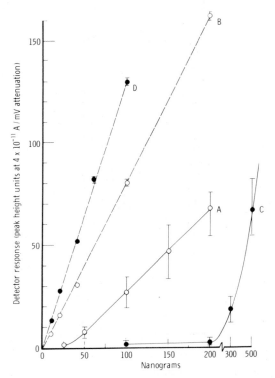

Fig. 1. Effect of trifluoroacetylation of cyclazocine and norcyclazocine on linear dynamic range. Each point represents the mean
of triplicate determinations; the brackets represent the range.
GLC conditions are as described in the text. A = cyclazocine; B =
trifluoroacetylated cyclazocine; C = norcyclazocine; D = trifluoroacetylated norcyclazocine. From Kaiko and Inturrisi (8). Reprinted with permission from the Journal of Chromatography.

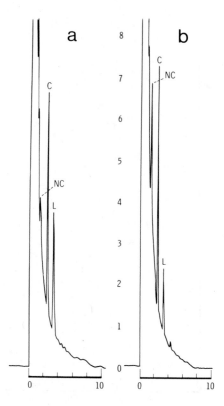

Fig. 2. Chromatograms of human urine extracts from a patient who
received an oral dose of 1.9 mg cyclazocine (C). The internal standard, levallorphan (L), was added directly to the urine and the
extract prepared. Norcyclazocine (NC), C and L present in the
extract were trifluoroacetylated just prior to GLC analysis. (a)
Free unconjugated C and NC. (b) Total free and conjugated C and NC
resulting from acid hydrolysis of the urine prior to extraction.
Retention times are NC = 1.8 min, C = 2.7 min and L = 3.6 min
GLC conditions are as described in the text. From Kaiko and
Inturrisi (8). Reprinted with permission from the Journal of
Chromatography.

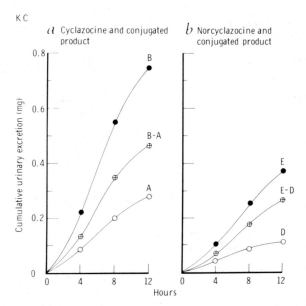

Fig. 3. Urinary excretion of cyclazocine (A), conjugated cyclazocine (B-A), cyclazocine plus conjugated cyclazocine (B), norcyclazocine (D), conjugated norcyclazocine (E-D) and norcyclazocine plus conjugated norcyclazocine (E) following an oral dose of 1.9 mg of cyclazocine to patient K.C. From Kaiko and Inturrisi (8). Reprinted with permission from the Journal of Chromatography.

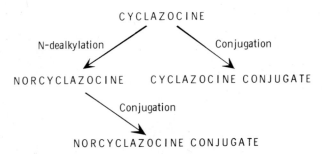

Fig. 4. Metabolism of cyclazocine in the human. From Kaiko and Inturrisi (8). Reprinted with permission from the Journal of Chromatography.

REFERENCES

1. M. Fink, A. Zaks, R. Sharoff, A. Mora, A. Bruner, S. Levit and A. M. Freedman, _Clin. Pharmacol. Ther._, 9: 568 (1968).

2. W. R. Martin, D. R. Jasinski and P. A. Mansky, _Arch. Gen. Psychiatry_, 28: 784 (1973).

3. W. R. Martin, C. W. Gorodetzky and T. K. McClane, _Clin. Pharmacol. Ther._, 7: 455 (1966).

4. J. H. Jaffe and L. Brill, _Int. J. Addiction_, 1: 99 (1966).

5. A. Freedman, M. Fink, R. Sharoff and A. Zaks, _J. Amer. Med. Ass._, 201: 191 (1967).

6. S. J. Mule and C. W. Gorodetzky, _J. Pharmacol. Exp. Ther._, 154: 632 (1966).

7. S. J. Mule, T. H. Clements and C. W. Gorodetzky, _J. Pharmacol. Exp. Ther._, 160: 387 (1968).

8. R. F. Kaiko and C. E. Inturrisi, _J. Chromatogr._, 100: 63 (1974).

9. K. Ahmad and F. Medzihradsky, _Life Sci._, 10: 707 (1971).

10. K. A. Pittman and T. A. Williams, _Pharmacologist_, 15: 167 (1973).

HISTORICAL PERSPECTIVES ON THE USE OF
LEVO-ALPHA-ACETYLMETHADOL (LAAM or LAM) IN
REHABILITATING OPIATE DEPENDENT PERSONS

Arnold Schecter, M.D.

Clinical Associate Professor
of Preventive and Community Medicine
New Jersey College of Medicine
Newark, New Jersey

The use of long acting methadone preparations for human detoxification for opiates was reported by Isbell and Wikler in 1948[1] and Fraser and Isbell in 1952;[2] the time between doses was 72 hours. In the 1960s Dole and Nyswander[3] reported the concept of methadone rehabilitation during opiate maintenance therapy. Evaluation studies by Gearing[4] helped to reestablish the concept of opiate maintenance as a therapy in a way it never really was established in the United States during the 1920s, the earlier opiate maintenance era in the U.S.[5,6]

Major problems were soon noted with methadone therapy as it was extended from the highly selected earler Dole Nyswander and then New York City Beth Israel Hospital patients. Daily ingestion in the clinic was very inconvenient for patients who were working, in school or training, or homemakers; take home methadone became a source of illegal street methadone replacing street heroin. Deaths from accidental overdoses in non tolerant individuals, especially children, caused very bad publicity to be directed to the modality. A longer acting form with no take home medication seemed desirable. Jaffe and associates in Chicago including Schuster, Blachly, Senay Renault, and DiMenza and others in a series of papers from 1970 to 1972[7,8,9,10] suggested that LAM could replace methadone in a treatment program with no decrease in safety and efficacy. Their work was later confirmed and extended by Zaks Fink and Freedman and reported by them in 1972.[11] Three day a week LAM did indeed seem to equal 7 day a week methadone, as Senay and others put it. Blachly and Irwin sounded a note of caution concerning suspicious EEG patterns and also hyperglycemia with LAM.[12] Nervousness and irritability had been noted in some LAM patients in the early clinic studies of Jaffe.

When Dr. Jaffe became director of the Special Action Office for Drug Abuse Prevention, S.A.O.D.A.P., and office of the

President of the United States, the problems mentioned previously with methadone caused him to consider extending the supposed advantages of LAM to most methadone programs. LAM was to be given three times weekly with no take home privileges. It should be noted that in at least one area, the District of Columbia, where methadone take home privileges were eliminated, the elimination of privileges was cited as one of several reasons for the decrease in methadone patients.

Two large scale cooperative studies were funded to study and develop levo-alpha acetylmethadol (LAAM): The first was a co-operative Veterans" Administration study which placed heroin addicts in rigid incremental steps during medication buildup on high (100mg), or low dose (50 mg), methadone or LAAM (80 mg) in a double blind fashion, beginning with an initial dose of 30 mg. The high dose (100 mg) methadone appeared to have the highest patient retention factor, followed by the lower (50 mg) methadone with LAAM at 80 mg in this rigid study having the lowest retention rate. Safety in the three cohorts appeared about equal. Then a SAODAP/NIDA non "blind" or open non fixed dose methadone/LAAM random patient assignment cooperative study was conducted at 17 sites. Methadone again had better patient retention or "holding" power but safety again appeared about the same in the two groups.[13] It appeared at last years meeting, the Second National Drug Abuse Conference in 1975, that patients in those cities where take home methadone was available frequently reverted to methadone, possibly because of a need for increased revenue from the sale of some of the take home methadone.

Questions which arose last year concerned irritability possibly seen in some patients, the question of the long LAAM weekend - does the drug last 3 days in most patients? - the psychological effect on patients of ingesting opiates only 3 times weekly rather than their usual daily ritual and the lack of the methadone "glow" or "mellowness" or "tranquilizing effect" of the short acting form-apparently absent in the long acting methadone. At this time an (FDA) phase 3 study is about to begin which hopefully, with the cooperation of up to 80 clinics and up to 6,000 patients will move LAAM to the new drug or NDA stage within the next 3 years. Avram Goldstein's group has begun attempting to shepard heroin addicts through LAAM followed by an opiate antagonist such as Naltrexone, and then on to a drug, or opiate, free stage in a one year, one year, one year sequential or stepwise fashion.

The following thoughts are based on our experience with the Brooklyn Downstate Medical Center - Kings County Hospital, LAAM project:

First, LAAM may stand little or no chance of patient acceptance in cities with (liberal) take home methadone privileges -

as New York - because of the many patients who need or desire
money and therefore sell their methadone - certainly the majority
of the 34,000 methadone patients in New York in any given month.
Stratification of the collaborative study data from cities with
and without take home policy with respect to LAAM drop out would
be of interest in reviewing data from the SAODAP (open) cooperative
study.

Second, LAAM should prove very useful for new patients - 3
day a week clinic visits ought to be preferred to 7, or in some
cases 6, visits weekly.

Third, the proposed compensation of $5 per patient per week
for 40 weeks presently offered by the Whysner firm for research
expenses in the Phase 3 cooperative study to participating clinics
will not cover costs and will discourage many clinics from participating - especially in areas with a higher cost of living, and
therefore higher salary levels.

Fourth, unless Medicaid agencies set a higher LAAM clinic
visit rate than for methadone or set a capitation rate for LAAM
drug clinics will lose funds in Medicaid fees when switching from
methadone to LAAM. By way of illustration Medicaid pays on a
fee-for-service basis in New York City, $4 to private physicians
for a methadone visit, $8.50 to New York City programs to ap-
proximately $15 to some hospital based programs. New York State's
backward fee-for-service rather than capitation reimbursement
mechanism will surely act as a barrier for many programs which
would otherwise wish to offer LAAM to patients.

Fifth, smaller staffing patterns, especially of medical and
nursing but also counseling staff should be needed with LAAM
clinics with their decreased patient visits - unless patients feel
the other services of the clinic are equally important and worth
coming for more than 3 times a week. This may prove a god-send
for clinics in times of financial difficulty.

Sixth, LAAM may prove useful and popular for non emotionally
disturbed patients who are not in need of methadone's tranquilizing effect of "mellow" feeling.

Seventh, the so called "LAAM irritability syndrome", safety
to women, safety to the fetus, and percent of patients for whom
LAAM will not last 3 days need further study. The active metabolites of LAAM and its metabolic pathways in man are receiving
the needed study at this time. Whether LAAM is appropriate for
patients with liver disease needs to be determined; possibly there
may be some difficulty because the metabolites rather than LAAM
itself cause the long opiate action.

Eighth, long term safety of LAAM-over one year- is not known at this time and is of the utmost importance.

Ninth, methadone diversion and illicit sale with its concomitant deaths in non tolerant individuals including children, will markedly decrease when LAAM becomes licensed as a new drug and take home methadone is not permitted (except perhaps for dosages below 30 mg in selected rehabilitated patients).

Tenth, we are now living in the third era of opiate permissiveness in the 20th Century United States. Before the passage in 1906 of the Food and Drug Act, and before the Harrison Narcotic Act of 1914 opiate use was tolerated even without physician patient contact. In the 1920's opiate maintenance clinics were frequently seen and briefly tolerated throughout the United States. Now in the 1960's and 1970's with methadone we are in this centuries third opiate permissive era. If LAAM is not widely offered and if methadone (of all kinds) does not become a clinic use only - no take home drug - throughout the country - we may well relive history because of widespread and widely publicized abuse(s) of take home methadone in addition to a general anti chronic opiate ingestion feeling in the United States. It seems to this worker in drug abuse therapy wiser to suggest a Federal Policy of no take home methadone or no take home methadone except once or twice weekly above 20 mg daily dose level - if we wish to preserve this very useful rehabilitative modality for our present and future patients' sake.

REFERENCES

1. H. Isbell & A. Wikler, A.J. Eisenman, M. Dangerfield, and E. Frank, Liability of Addiction to 6-dimethylamino-4-4-diphenyl-3-hepetone In Man; Arch. Clin. Med. 83:362-392 1948.
2. H.F. Fraser, & H. Isbell, Actions and Addiction Liabilities of alpha acetyl methodols In Man; J. Pharm. Exp. Therap. 105:458-465 (1952).
3. V.P. Dole, & M. Nyswander, A Medical Treatment for Diacetylmorphine (Heroin) Addiction; JAMA 193:646-650 1965.
4. F.R. Gearing, Successes and Failures in Methadone Maintenance Treatment of Heroin Addiction in New York City; Proceeding, 3rd National Conference on Methadone Treatment, Government Printing Office (1970).
5. D. Musto, The American Disease, Yale.
6. The Shreveport Clinic - Drug Abuse Council, Monograph 1975.
7. J.H. Jafe, C.R. Schuster, B.B. Smith & P.A. Blachly, Comparison of Acetylmethadol & Methadone in the Treatment of Long Term Heroin Users; JAMA 211:1834-36 (1970).
8. J.H. Jaffe, & E.C. Senay, Methadone & L-Methadyl acetate: Use in Management of Narcotic Addicts; JAMA 216:1303-05 1971.

9.   J.H. Jaffe, E.C. Senay, & P.F. Renault, A Six Month Pre-
     liminary Report of the Rehabilitative Efficacy of L-Methadyl
     Acetate Compared to Methadone; Proceedings, Fourth National
     Conference on Methadone Treatment, NAPAN p199-201 1972.
10. J.H. Jaffe, E.C. Senay, C.R. Schuster, P.R. Renault, B. Smith,
     S. DiMenza, Methadyl Acetate as Methadone a Double Blind
     Study in Heroin Users; JAMA 222:437-442 1972.
11. A. Zaks, M. Fink, A.M. Freedman, Levomethadyl in Maintenance
     Treatment of Opiate Dependence; JAMA 220:811-13 1972.
12. J. Klette, R. Gilles, & W. Ling, LAAM Principle Investigor
     Meetings 1975.
13. J. Klett, W. Ling, Proceedings, Second National Drug Abuse
     Conference 1975 (in Press).

PHASE III CLINIC STUDY OF LEVO-ALPHA-ACETYLMETHADOL

John A. Whysner, M.D., Ph.D.

Whysner Associates, Washington, D.C.

The purpose of the Phase III trial of levo-alpha-acetyl-methadol (LAAM) is to establish efficacy of this medication for the maintenance of persons addicted to opioids. Also during the course of the Phase III trials additional data relating to the safety of LAAM will be obtained. It is the intended purpose of the Phase III clinical trials to provide sufficient information to allow the FDA to grant a New Drug Application for LAAM.

The administrative structure which has been developed for these Phase III clinical trials is intended to provide for a centralized drug supply, data collection, and administrative system with a maximum national clinical participation. Whysner Associates is the prime contractor for NIDA and is responsible for the coordination of the study which includes filing of the IND application, medical supervision, review of results, administration of all subcontractors, and development of the final NDA application. Subcontractors include the Vitarine Company, who will be the formulator of the liquid concentrate, Friends Medical Science Research Center, Inc. who will provide data management and analysis support, and approximately 50 methadone clinics who will perform the clinical trials and provide the data for analysis. A Medical Advisory Panel has been established which is responsible for approval of the study protocol, analysis of any adverse reactions, and review of the conclusions of the study.

The subject population will be approximately 6000 men and women over the age of 18 who meet the current criteria for entrance into methadone maintenance programs or who are currently clients of such programs. The clinical trial will last up to 40 weeks for each patient. Each clinic will participate in one of two studies which are being conducted as part of these Phase III trials.

In one study all patients will be put on LAAM. In a
second study a random assignment of patients will be
made to LAAM or methadone providing a comparative analysis of efficacy and safety measures.

Measures of Efficacy

The proof of efficacy for maintenance of persons addicted to opioids may be defined as the relief of abstinence over a prolonged period of time when the drug is
given on a regular basis. There are three aspects of
the abstinence syndrome: drug seeking behavior, physiological and psychological changes. A drug such as
LAAM must prevent the development of abstinence in all
three areas. Therefore, measures of efficacy must be
aimed at measuring the signs and symptoms of the development of abstinence in these three areas.

The measure of drug seeking behavior can be attempted
through history taking, direct measurement of illicit
drugs in body fluids, or assessment of the consequences
of taking illicit drugs. During the past several years
our ability to measure illicit drugs in body fluids has
been developed to the point where these methods are both
reliable and are a regular part of the methadone program
routine. Therefore, in the Phase III studies this will
be the most important measure of drug seeking. Assessment of the use of illicit drugs through history taking
or an independent measure of the consequences of heroin
use such as number of arrests, employment, etc. is not
reliable or easy to quantitate.

Physiological signs of abstinence will be measured
through the analysis of a symptom-sign checklist. The
components of the checklist are well known parts of the
physical abstinence syndrome; for example, sweating,
gooseflesh, and rinorrhea.

For the psychological component patients may become
anxious, hostile, irritable, require other drugs such as
tranquilizers, develop other patterns of drug abuse such
as polydrug abuse, or adjust poorly to the social and
work environment. Many of these aspects of psychological abstinence may be difficult to measure; however,
measures will be attempted. The Profile of Mood States
will be used to measure anxiety, hostility, and irritability. Also questions involving hours of employment,
number of arrests, and a global assessment of client's
progress will be made.

There are no fixed scales against which efficacy can be measured. It is not known what is an acceptable level of abstinence or what are acceptable drug seeking, phy- siological or psychological changes. Therefore, a heavy reliance must be made on comparative measures with a control group.

The only applicable control group for this study would be persons who are currently on methadone maintenance therapy. Comparisons of the efficacy and safety mea- sures will be made between the methadone and LAAM pa- tients in part of the Phase III study.

Another determinant of an acceptable level of abstin- ence would be the willingness of the participant to stay on the drug. If one can make the assumption that re- maining on the drug is the equivalent of efficacy, drop- out rates are very useful. The reason for dropout and a judgment by the clinic of whether such a dropout is drug related will be determined. Only those dropouts which are drug related such as side effects, feelings of withdrawal on weekends, etc. will be used as efficacy measures. However, dropping out of the study to attempt detoxification would be viewed as a positive result.

Safety Measurements

Previous Phase II clinical studies have indicated that for a 40 week period LAAM does not cause any consistent abnormalities in the CBC, SMA-12, urine analysis, EKG, or EEG which would be cause for concern. However, these Phase II studies have only been accomplished on 170 males for 40 weeks. Therefore, it is desirable to test a large number of males and females to determine if there are any untoward reactions which occur on a low frequency basis. It is hoped that the Phase III studies will include approximately 2000 patients on LAAM for 40 weeks. This should test enough individuals to give an estimate of the incidence of adverse reac- tions to the medication.

Another problem which must be studied during Phase III is the use of other medications concurrently with LAAM. It is known that drug interactions may occur which would either potentiate or prevent the effective action of narcotics. The use of both prescription and illicit drugs may have untoward interaction effects. Although it has been suspected that certain other drugs may in- teract favorably, not enough patients have been studied

to gather any quantifiable data. In the Phase III
studies the use of all medications will be documented
and the possibility of any drug interactions will be
investigated thoroughly.

Open Versus Blind Study

The use of any maintenance drug for the treatment of
heroin addiction has a strong subjective component to
its effectiveness for both the patient and the physician. A double-blind study is designed to eliminate the
impact of these subjective effects on the outcome of
the study. Double-blind studies have been used in the
past to compare the effectiveness of LAAM to methadone
and the results of these studies have been described
elsewhere. There are several reasons for which the
Phase III study has been designed as an open rather
than a double-blind study. These are the following:

1. The primary advantage of using LAAM instead of
    methadone is the need for only three day a week
    pickup. If a double-blind study was done a schedule
    of either daily pickup or of three day a week pickup
    would be necessary in both LAAM and methadone groups.
    This would negate the scheduling effect of LAAM.

2. The large number of patients needed for the Phase
    III study and the use of multiple clinic sites makes
    the logistical problems associated with such a
    study very difficult.

3. A double-blind study may adversely effect the effi-
    cacy of either methadone or LAAM in an unpredictable
    way. The patient population is very anxious con-
    cerning the medication they are receiving and about
    participation in a clinical study. One of the
    greatest difficulties encountered in the Phase II
    study was that the efficacy results had a large
    number of patients who dropped out because of the
    nature of the study rather than the drug.

4. The blind is difficult to keep because patients and
    physicians would be able to break the code due to
    the subjective effects of the drug.

Use of LAAM in Females

The Phase III study will be the first large-scale use of
this drug in females. A small group of females were

tested before the FDA restrictions on the use of LAAM.
During the course of the Phase II studies there was a
study of seventeen females of nonchildbearing potential.
The use of LAAM in females at this stage is essential
otherwise another large-scale study in females would
need to be constructed. It is currently being decided
whether or not some females should be given LAAM
throughout pregnancy or whether all women who become
pregnant while on LAAM should be switched to methadone.
The arguments on both sides of this question are valid.
The use of LAAM through pregnancy would mean exposing
pregnant females and neonates to a new drug with which
the medical community is unfamiliar. However, LAAM
may prove to be a drug with fewer problems in the pregnant female and the neonate than does methadone. The
long duration of action of LAAM may make the neonatal
withdrawal syndrome less severe.

Current Status of the Study (March, 1976)

The current planning for the Phase III study of LAAM
has been almost completed. The final study design,
forms, data management system, formulation of the drug,
and analysis have all been in progress and should be
completed within a couple of months. It is anticipated
that the Phase III study will begin in the Spring of
1976 and that induction of these patients will be completed by the Fall of 1976. An additional 40 week
period will be needed for the follow-up of the last patients included in the study and time will need to be
available for the final data analysis and collection.
Therefore, it is anticipated that the Phase III study
will be completed late in 1977. Hopefully by that
time all of the other animal and human data will be
completed to allow the award of a NDA for LAAM. Therefore, beginning in 1978 there may be another maintenance treatment modality available for the treatment of
heroin addiction.

Clinical Safety and Relative Efficacy
of LAAM--A Collective Experience

Walter Ling, M.D.
Sepulvada (California) Veterans Administration Hospital
C. James Klett, Ph.D.
Perrypoint (Maryland) Veterans Administration Hospital

Introduction and Description of the Studies

The relative advantage of LAAM over methadone has been discussed by
previous speakers of this panel. The present report deals with the
issues of clinical safety and relative efficacy of LAAM in comparison to methadone. The data came from two multihospital studies
identified here as V. A. and SAODAP-NIDA studies respectively. The
studies are similar in basic designs but differ in several important
respects. The V. A. study was double-blind, fixed dose, and the
subjects were street addicts not previously on methadone maintenance.
The SAODAP-NIDA study, on the other hand, was open, with variable
doses, and the subjects were addicts already on methadone maintenance. Thus the V.A. study involved a period of induction while on
the SAODAP-NIDA study patients were directly switched from daily
methadone to three times a week LAAM. Four hundred and thirty-one
patients participated in the V.A. study with 146 on methadone
50 mg., 142 patients on methadone 100 mg., and 142 on LAAM 80 mg.
Six hundred and thrity-six patients participated in the SAODAP study;
308 were on methadone and 328 on LAAM. Both studies lasted 40
weeks.

A multilayer monitoring system for the patients' safety during the
study was adopted. This involved the local principal investigator
as having the primary medical responsibility of the patients. He
determines the patient's suitability for admission and continuation
in the study, and reviews all laboratory data before submission for
central processing. Once every few weeks the laboratory results of
all study subjects were reviewed by a member of the medical advisory
panel for any significant individual variations or group trends.
Every three or four months the aggregate data were subjected to statistical analyses for cross-sectional variations and longitudianl
trend development. Twice a year all the principal investigators met
to discuss their clinical impressions and review any deaths or significant adverse reactions. Twice during the study the entire laboratory listing was reviewed by an independent investigator. Finally the data was reviewed by yet another independent physician
through a NIDA subcontract.

Results of the Studies

The results of the studies will be considered under two general
headings, viz safety and efficacy.

Clinical Safety

The monitoring system mentioned above did not reveal any significant
individual abnormalities or alarming group trendes. Our confidence
in this evaluation was enhanced when several investigators independently arrived at the same conclusion. There were no deaths in the
V.A. study. Two deaths occurred in the SAODAP study, one from an
apparent overdose, and one from complication of alcohol abuse. No
other adverse reactions were reported in either study. No subject
was hospitalized for any study-drug related illnesses. Three methadone patients and eight LAAM patinets from the V.A. study and
three methadone patients and 11 LAAM patients from the SAODAP-NIDA
study dropped out for various "side effects." However, no consistent pattern emerged in the side effects reported.

Laboratory values obtained at prestudy, every four weeks during the
study and at termination, were subjected to cross-sectional and
longitudinal analyses. The only significant finding was a very
slight weight gain in all three groups in the V.A. study. The
magnitude of this weight gain was only in the neighborhood of a few
pounds and no morbid obesity was reported. This weight gain did
reach the level of statistical significance mainly because of the
large sample size. This slight tendency to gain weight was not
apparent in the SAODAP-NIDA study. In both studies there appeared
to be a very slight downward adjustment of hematocrit, and to a
lesser extent hemoglobin and red blood cells, in the early weeks of
the study with restabilization at a somewhat lower level. However,
all the values were well within the limits of normal and there was
no clinical anemia noted in any patient in either study. Although
a large number of subjects showed abnormal liver function tests on
admission, there did not appear to be any time-drug interaction
during this study. The vast majority remained stable throughout the
trial period for both the methadone and LAAM groups.

Efficacy

The primary pharmacological effect under study in both drugs is
their ability to suppress withdrawal symptoms reflected subjectively by the patient's feeling of comfort or discomfort and objectively by the presence or absence of opiates and other drugs of abuse in
random urinalysis. These are our primary measures of outcome. We
recognize these are other outcome variables such as program retention, employment and arrest rates, etc. However, we feel these
latter variables, while they may reflect the total program rehabili-

tative effort, are less desirable as indicators of what a drug
such as methadone or LAMM can be expected to do on its own merits.
We consider this latter group of outcome variables meaningful
contingent upon the patient's ability to remain drug free. An example of the imperfect nature of the contingent outcome variables
is that of program retention. In an open trial such as the SAODAP-
NIDA study, the clinician can opt to return a LAAM patient to methadone but not to reverse. Thus the study designed works in favor
of the control drug and against the study drug.

With respect to subjective discomfort, we use a 30-item symptom-
sign checklist obtained weekly for the first eight weeks and every
four weeks thereafter. Both drugs appear effective in suppressing
withdrawal symptoms and the degree of discomfort, after the initial
period of adjustment, was minimal in all patient groups.

Evidence of illicit drug use was measured by weekly random urinalysis for opiates, barbiturates, amphetamines and other drugs of
abuse. We devised a urine index taking into consideration the pattern (i.e. early vs. late) as well as the frequency of drug abuse.
This index produces a score from 0 (no positive urines) to 120
(positive on every test). In the V.A. study the means for opiate
positive urines for the three groups were: Methadone 50 mg 33.3
methadone 100 mg. 22.6, and LAAM 80 mg 20.8. The methadone 50 mg.
group clearly used more opiates than the other two groups. No significant difference was seen in the SAODAP-NIDA study and the respective scores were 15.0 for methadone and 14.9 for the LAAM group.
What this may mean is that under conditions where clinicians can
make adjustments in dosage, both drugs could achieve a significant
degree of abstinence in terms of opiate abuse.

A global assessment of outcome was also made on each patient by the
local research staff at the end of the study (at termination for
early terminators). In the double-blind V.A. study the methadone
50 mg. group was deemed less improved compared to the other two
groups. No apparent advantage for either group was noted in the
open SAODAP-NIDA trial.

Conclusion

We believe we have demonstrated under the conditions of these
studies the safety and efficacy of LAAM as an alternative agent for
maintenance treatment of chronic opiate addicts.

A COMPARATIVE ANALYSIS OF LAAM PATIENTS

IN THE INNER-CITY AND SUBURBS

A. Sidney Howe, M.D.

Suffolk County Drug Abuse
Treatment Services
5 Shore Lane
Bay Shore, New York   11706

Beny J. Primm, M.D.

Addiction Research and
Treatment Corporation
22 Chapel Street
Brooklyn, New York   11201

Joseph S. Drew, Ph.D.

Addiction Research and
Treatment Corporation
22 Chapel Street
Brooklyn, New York   11201

Roderic Gillis

V.A. Hospital
Perry Point, Maryland   21902

This study was conducted to compare the effects of LAAM (l al-pha-acetylmethadol, a long acting congener of methadone) on two disparate groups. Early LAAM programs at the Bay Shore Clinic in Suffolk County and a Harlem facility of the Addiction Research and Treatment Corporation were used.

From the Bay Shore Clinic, 41 volunteers were chosen and 30 were chosen from A.R.T.C. The study was conducted over a period of four months in 1975.

The Bay Shore program was in the suburbs of New York City. It primarily serviced a white, middle class, young (average age 27), fairly well educated (over 50% completed high school) population.

In contrast, the Harlem program serviced an almost entirely black, lower class, older (average age 35), not as well educated (less than 50% completed high school) population. In addition, the patients who volunteered from A.R.T.C. had been addicted longer, prior to treatment, than the Bay Shore volunteers. Other differences were that the volunteers from A.R.T.C. had been in treatment for a shorter period of time and were on a lower dose of methadone. Also, while the A.R.T.C. volunteers were either unemployed, earned little money or had not been working at a job for very long, the Bay Shore volunteers were generally employed full-time, earning a significant income. Seventy-eight percent of the Bay Shore volunteers were wage earners compared to the 47% of the A.R.T.C. volunteers.

Prior to undertaking this study, the authors assumed that the same kinds of factors influencing the prognosis of treatment with any drug would be in effect. In other words, the stage of addiction prior to the start of treatment would be an important factor. Thus it was believed that the A.R.T.C. patient would do better in this LAAM test since it was more likely that he would be in the third stage of addiction before he entered treatment. At Bay Shore the patients were less likely to be in the third stage of addiction.

Another important factor determining how well a patient did in the experiment, particularly when volunteers were used, would be how well patients did in treatment before volunteering for the research study. At Bay Shore, there were practically no volunteers from the patient group that was doing the best; patients who had, for the most part, been rehabilitated: holding a full-time job, being reunited with their families, no report of criminal activity or illicit drug use, and therefore who would be on an infrequent pick-up schedule.

In contrast, all of the volunteers at A.R.T.C. were on a six-time-a-week pick-up schedule of methadone. Therefore, the less frequent pick-ups of LAAM would be to these patients' advantage, even to those among the group who were doing well.

While the experiment was being conducted, there developed a feeling of elitism among the A.R.T.C. volunteers. This attitude developed as a result of the less frequent pick-ups, the amount of special attention received, the increased number of special examinations and the attitude of the staff towards these volunteers. Adding to their feelings of elitism, were the patients' own attitudes towards each other.

Although the A.R.T.C. staff was strongly in favor of the experiment, the staff at Bay Shore had some initial misgivings. They questioned the advisability of using a new drug and wondered whether a change in the routine of patients who, for the most part, had only experienced modest therapeutic improvement, would be beneficial.

Since this case study consisted of two groups of volunteers with almost diametrically opposed characteristics, several important conclusions can be drawn for the general field of chemotherapeutic approaches to the treatment of chronic drug users. The conclusions are based on the results that only 5 of the 41 volunteers completed the LAAM program at the Bay Shore Clinic. On the other hand, 10 out of 30 completed the program at A.R.T.C. Thus 12% finished at Bay Shore compared to 33% at A.R.T.C., almost three times the percentage.

These results are surprising in view of the fact that patients on methadone maintenance at the Bay Shore facility do significantly better than patients at A.R.T.C. when reviewing the factors one considers in rehabilitation such as the amount of time a patient stays in treatment, his employment, illicit drug involvement, and other illegal involvement.

Of course, the main reason why A.R.T.C. methadone-maintained patients do not do as well as the Bay Shore patients in these criteria is mainly due to the lack of support systems that are available to inner-city patients. The forces that exist among the white middle class in suburbia that lead to rehabilitation usually are nonexistent for ghetto blacks. Minority groups living in ghetto slums often do not have any family ties, or at best have only fragile ones. They are not in contact with relatives or friends who have the economic means to assist them. Therefore the very forces that often drive a black ghetto resident to drug addiction prevent him from being rehabilitated. Addiction is usually the only way he has of coping with the socio-economic environment of the ghetto. In short, we are speaking about the difference between "habilitation" and rehabilitation. The white suburban addict has the support and purpose needed for rehabilitation; the black addict does not. Why then, should A.R.T.C. patients find it easier to cross over from methadone to LAAM? Is it solely because of the easier, less frequent pick-up schedule? Or is it because the A.R.T.C. patients were on a lower dose of methadone? Is it because the elitism gave some ego-fulfillment and sense of contribution to patients who previously had low opinions of themselves and had no support systems? Is it because of the higher ratio of counselors to patients that existed at A.R.T.C.? Or, very simply, is it because the treatment grapevine, after four months, had given LAAM the seal of approval as a safe and efficacious drug?

The authors conclude that all of these factors come into play to a greater or lesser extent. This study suggests that less frequent pick-ups contribute significantly to the length of time patients remain in treatment, even though there are intrinsic disadvantages. Furthermore, drug abuse treatment programs might be unnecessarily punitive by the use of strict guidelines and frequent pick-ups. Clearly, these results suggest that LAAM would be more successful in the treatment of ghetto residents than in the treatment of suburban addicts. Therefore, LAAM might replace methadone at inner-city drug abuse programs. However, before such conclusions can be drawn definitively and put into effect, similar types of comparative studies must be undertaken.

TABLE I

Comparative Date for the Two LAAM Programs

	A.R.T.C.	Bay Shore Clinic
Average Age	35	27
Racial/Ethnic Group	96% Black	78% White
Marital Status:		
Never Married	27%	29%
Ever Married	73%	71%
Education:		
Attended College	23%	10%
Completed High School	20%	46%
Attended High School	57%	44%
Occupational Role:		
Wage Earner	47%	78%
Non-Wage Earner	53%	22%
Gross Three Months Earnings:		
Less than $500	60%	32%
$500-$1,500	17%	22%
Over $1,500	23%	46%
Overall Change in Drug Abuse:		
Improved	77%	12%
Unchanged	23%	66%
Worse	0%	22%
Completed the LAAM Program	33%	12%

1333

LAAM: AN ALTERNATIVE TO METHADONE

Jack D. Blaine, M.D.
Pierre F. Renault, M.D.

National Institute on Drug Abuse
Clinical Behavioral Branch
Division of Research
Rockville, Maryland   20852

The concept of methadone maintenance was developed in the mid-1960's by Drs. Dole and Nyswander. Methadone was believed to be an essential part of a comprehensive program of treatment and rehabilitation of chronic heroin addicts. Much research was performed and clinical experience was attained as methadone maintenance treatment achieved widespread acceptance in the late 60's and early 70's. The information gathered demonstrated repeatively that treatment programs utilizing methadone and comprehensive counseling services were effective and a safe form of treatment for many heroin addicts when performed under adequate medical supervision.

While methadone maintenance had been shown repeatedly to be the most effective treatment of opiate addiction available, several clinically and politically significant problems related to the pharmacology of methadone arose. Low doses of methadone did not suppress the narcotic craving and abstinence for a full 24 hours in many addicts. Large doses of methadone required to provide sustained relief of abstinence symptoms for these patients often produced unwanted sedation causing the patient to "nod" for the first several hours after consumption. But more important, the patient was required to attend a methadone dispensing clinic daily to consume his medication under staff supervision, an inconvenient and burdensome demand. This requirement was considered antitherapeutic when the patient was assuming responsibility and trying to engage in work, rehabilitation or education programs, or responsible home-making.   A compromise solution was reached; take-home methadone.

"Those patients whose employment, rehabilitation, education, or homemaking responsibilities would be hindered by daily attendance were permitted to reduce to three times weekly the number of clinic visits when they must ingest the drug under staff observation."

Unfortunately, the practice of permitting take-home supplies of methadone for unsupervised self-administration contributed to new problems. Accidental ingestion of methadone by non-tolerant persons, especially children, led to an alarming increase in methadone toxic reactions and over dose fatalities. Also, a market

developed for illicit sale and redistribution of methadone to
heroin addict peers suffering from withdrawal or to drug users
seeking a new euphorient.

Thus, a longer lasting medication would have many practical
therapeutic advantages over methadone and partially resolve some
of these problems encountered in clinical treatment programs.
Fortunately, chemical and pharmacological data were already available for l-alpha-acetyl-methadol (LAAM, l-methadylacetate   a
chemical relative of methadone. The early clinical work on LAAM
focused on morphine-like analgesic properties. At the Addiction
Research Center, Fraser, Isbell and co-workers demonstrated LAAM's
ability to relieve and prevent opiate withdrawal symptoms in addicts
for up to 72 hours. Their studies suggested potential clinical usefulness of LAAM because of its oral effectiveness, long duration of
action and low toxicity.

In 1968 Jaffe and co-workers in Chicago were able to substitute without difficulty D, l-alpha-acetylmethadol (DLAAM) three
times weekly for daily methadone in a small group of methadone
maintenance patients. The results of that initial pilot study
corroborated that D-LAAM could suppress opiate withdrawal symptoms
in opiate dependent patients for up to 72 hours.

Based on the positive results of this pilot study, the
Division of Narcotic Addiction and Drug Abuse, NIMH, contracted for
production of four kilograms of LAAM in 1969 and encouraged further
clinical investigation of LAAM. This ensuing research substantiated
the usefulness and safety of LAAM as a maintenance treatment of
heroin addiction. These researchers found that LAAM offers the
patients, clinician and treatment program several advantages over
methadone. Due to LAAM's long duration of action, the frequency of
visits to clinic can be reduced from daily to three times weekly
even for patients just entering treatment. Addicts find participation in treatment more acceptable and return more regularly,
especially those trying to engage in work, education or rehabilitation activities outside of the clinic.

LAAM offers the patient a smoother, more sustained drug effect
than methadone. The patients appear more alert and more emotionally level. Oral consumption even during the period of escalating
doses did not produce excessive sedation or subjective euphoria,
i.e., the patients do not report being "loaded" or "nodding." Also
LAAM frees the individual from the daily habit of engaging in drug
seeking and drug taking behavior. Thus, the individual feels less
drug dependent when daily drug taking is not necessary.

These factors are consistent with the treatment program goal
of de-emphasizing the mystique of drugs and drug taking. With LAAM,
there can be less talk, seeking, taking and relating around chemicals. More time and energy is available to patient and staff to
focus on psychological, social, educational and vocational goals
rather than biological drug stabilization.

Furthermore, LAAM offers a practical answer to the problems
related to take-home methadone. Illicit redistribution can be lessened by reducing the amount of take-home medication. If necessary,
a no-take-home policy can be established by programs where diversion.
redistribution and accidental overdose is especially prevalent.

Several pharmacological properties make LAAM less prone than
methadone for abuse. LAAM must be metabolized to attain its psychoactivity. Thus, several hours pass between taking LAAM and the
onset of psychoactivity. Therefore, LAAM is less likely to be a
reinforcer of drug taking because substances with a rapid, immediate onset of euphoric effects are much more desired by users. LAAM
has another unique characteristic which makes it less desired.
Unlike other narcotics, LAAM is more rapidly effective orally than
intravenously.

LAAM also offers treatment programs advantages over methadone
by improving the logistics of medication dispensing. Weekend dispensing hours may no longer be necessary. By reducing the required
number of clinic visits, efficiency of treatment may be increased
due to savings of staff dispensing and pharmacy services. Thus,
LAAM can potentially increase the number of available treatment
slots, without scrificing control of the medication.

In June 1971, the Special Action Office for Drug Abuse Prevention (SAODAP) was established. One of SAODAP's mandates was the
expansion of research on "long-lasting, blocking drugs." Based on
the potential advantages of LAAM over methadone, Dr. Jerome Jaffe,
SAODAP's first director, initiated in the summer of 1971 a comprehensive review of the status of LAAM utilizing experts from the
various government agencies and the private sector.

The conclusion of the review was that LAAM was the most promising compound available but that the pharmacological development
of LAAM was not proceeding rapidly enough. Several problems were
found to be delaying LAAM development. Neither Federal Agencies or
pharmaceutical industry was promoting or developing the drug. LAAM
investigation was limited to a few research centers. Quantities of
LAAM necessary for use in treatment were not available.

Furthermore, unlike methadone, which was marketed as an analgesic prior to its use in narcotic addiction treatment, LAAM was
not patented or marketed. LAAM was not patentable because it had
been in the public domain for many years. Thus, no pharmaceutical
company was interested in spending extensive research and development funds for a drug without exclusivity and with a limited market,
especially a controlled schedule I narcotic requiring special precautions and regulatory controls.

To fill the void created by the pharmaceutical industry,
SAODAP set as a high priority the creation and coordination of a
governmental mechanism for developing this type of pharmaceutical
substance using LAAM as the prototype.

Although LAAM was to be developed as rapidly as possible, it
was imperative to avoid the many problems encountered by methadone
due to inadequate and incomplete study before widespread largescale
use. Federal Agencies assumed the responsibility to be certain that
LAAM was a safe and effective drug before marketing. Therefore,
SAODAP organized and promoted interagency cooperation in LAAM
development. SAODAP effectively utilized the expertise in academic
and pharmaceutical communities for advice and monitoring the process.

In the Spring of 1972 an interagency Pharmacology Task Force was formed of representatives from SAODAP, the Veterans Administration, Department of the Army, the Food and Drug Administration, the National Academy of Sciences, and the Division of Narcotic Addiction and Drug Abuse. This group reviewed previous and ongoing work on LAAM and planned and coordinated the subsequent development toward the New Drug Application.

Further animal studies were needed to establish intermediate and long-term nontoxicity of LAAM. DNADA contracted with the Department of Army's research facilities at Edgewood Arsenal to perform the necessary studies in December 1971.

The amount of LAAM available severely limited the progress of both animal and clinical investigation. A large supply of LAAM was obtained through the cooperation of the Penick Pharmaceutical Company in 1972.

Through this coordinated effort, the necessary animal studies could be phased with the subsequent clinical studies. DNADA-Funded-Clinical Phase I Investigational New Drug studies began in June 1972. Simultaneously, DNADA initiated extensive chronic animal studies to provide required toxicological data to support safe, prolonged administration in man.

The planning and initiation of further clinical studies proceeded cautiously. To protect the well-being of potential subjects, the Medical Advisory Committee and Pharmacology Task Force wanted data from the long-term animal studies available before long-term Phase II clinical studies were initiated. By the Spring of 1973 sufficient animal toxicity data was available from the Edgewood Arsenal study. The clinical studies were to proceed in successive stages contingent upon continued evidence of lack of toxicity indicating probable safety in animals.

In April 1973, pilot clinical Phase II studies were initiated in three Veterans Administration Drug Dependence Treatment Centers to evaluate the safety and efficacy of LAAM maintenance compared to high and low dose methadone maintenance in street heroin addicts.

In the Summer of 1973 based on the updated animal data, the existing data from the pilot studies and other available clinical data, the decision was made to continue the study for a total of 40 weeks and to proceed with the addition of nine more Veterans Administration Treatment Centers in Cooperative Study. The clinical study was carried out over a 2 year period, terminating in the Spring of 1975. Four hundred thirty male heroin addicts were treated. Of these, 142 received LAAM.

Because some of the technical inadequacies in the Edgewood Arsenal Study, DNADA initiated additional chronic rat and dog studies of LAAM in 1973. At approximately this time, SAODAP began planning and organizing another larger cooperative Phase II clinical study of LAAM to provide more patient data. The study was designed to complement the Veterans Administration study.

The SAODAP cooperative study was initiated in February 1974 when the safety data from the second animal toxicity study and the clinical data from the VA Cooperative Study was adequate to support

an additional 40 week human safety and efficacy study. Sixteen (16)
outpatients drug treatment clinics throughout the country were
chosen for participation. Seven hundred sixty seven (767) male
patients, of whom 383 received LAAM, participated in this study.
When SAODAP began to phase out in the Fall of 1974, the coordination and direction of the LAAM project, were officially transferred
to the recently established Division of Research, National Institute on Drug Abuse (NIDA), successor to DNADA, NIMH. NIDA extended
the SAODAP clinical studies to perform additional investigations
including studies in women without child-bearing potential and to
continue longer data collection.

In June 1975, NIDA contracted with Whysner Associates to
conduct Phase III Clinical Evaluation of LAAM and to make appropriate arrangements for the eventual filing of the New Drug Application and marketing of LAAM. The contract is currently ongoing
and arrangements are made to formulate and distribute LAAM. The
Phase III Investigational New Drug Application has been submitted
and final approval is immenent.

Clinics are being enlisted to carry out the clinical study.
An estimated 6000 patients, including those already maintained on
methadone and heroin addicts entering treatment, will be asked to
participate in a 40 week study on safety and efficacy of LAAM. The
open study will be performed in approximately 50 cooperating methadone maintenance programs nationwide. A common protocol for medical
monitoring and evaluation of clinical efficacy will be utilized to
produce uniform patient data. The study will require approximately
two years to complete after which the New Drug Application for LAAM
can be submitted to FDA to permit its marketing to interested treatment programs.

Pending successful completion of this Phase III large scale
clinical trial, the formidable task of developing at an accelerated
pace a drug which offers considerable potential benefit to heroin
addicts and treatment programs will be accomplished.

The Task of developing a drug the private sector was unwilling
or unable to undertake has been carried out in accordance with
stringently applied Federal Regulations designed both to ensure the
kind of scientific baseline data establishing LAAM safety and efficacy and to provide a mechanism that can be a model for future drug
development in the narcotic dependence treatment field. Conjointly
the task has entailed creating the means for cooperation between
the many agencies and individuals involved in a far-flung and large
scale project.

NIDA does not currently anticipate that LAAM implementation
will lead to dramatic alteration in the current Federal opiate addiction treatment policy or philosophy. LAAM appears to be an alternative to, rather than a replacement for, methadone. For some
opiate addicts, LAAM, like methadone, may be the primary treatment.
For others, temporary pharmacotherapeutic stabilization will act
merely as a tool to engage the narcotic-dependent individual into
participation in a comprehensive treatment program, and others may
require no pharmacological support at all. LAAM provides one more
choice in tailoring treatment to each individual's needs.

THE ROLE OF ACTIVE METABOLITES IN THE DURATION OF ACTION OF ACETYLMETHADOL (LAAM) IN MAN*

Charles E. Inturrisi and Robert F. Kaiko

Department of Pharmacology
Cornell University Medical College
New York, New York 10021

The purpose of this report is to present evidence that, in man the long duration of certain of the pharmacologic effects of 1-alpha-acetylmethadol (commonly called LAAM) is a consequence of the formation and accumulation of active metabolites. We will briefly review the pharmacologic and pharmacokinetic information that supports a role for active metabolites, in particular, data obtained in our laboratory as a result of studies over the past three years directed toward the identification and quantitation in human biofluids of the biotransformation products of acetylmethadol.

Current interest in the use of acetylmethadol as a maintenance drug in the treatment of heroin dependence stems from the earliest clinical studies of the drug by Fraser and associates (1, 2). These careful investigators noted the relatively long duration of certain of pharmacologic effects of acetylmethadol, in particular the suppression of abstinence in morphine dependent subjects.

Studies in laboratory animals have suggested that biotransformation may play a critical role in determining the time-action characteristics seen following administration of acetylmethadol (3, 4). In both the rat and man the onset of narcotic

*The work was supported in part by NIDA Grant DA-00297, Dr. Inturrisi is an Andrew W. Mellon Teacher-Scientist, 1975-76.

effects is more rapid after oral than following parenteral administration. McMahon and co-workers first demonstrated in 1965 that acetylmethadol undergoes N-demethylation in the rat to noracetylmethadol (5). In addition ester hydrolysis would produce methadol and normethadol (Fig. 1). Each of these compounds has been shown to possess narcotic activity in animal test systems.

In 1973 by use of a combination of solvent extraction and gas-liquid chromatographic procedures we reported the presence of acetylmethadol, noracetylmethadol, methadol and normethadol in the urine of acetylmethadol maintenance subjects (6). These results were confirmed by the use of chemical ionization mass spectrometry (7). In addition this sensitive analytical tool provided evidence that, in man, noracetylmethadol was biotransformed to the primary amine dinoracetylmethadol (Fig. 1). Billings and associates (8) were the first to isolate dinoracetyl-methadol from rat urine and to obtain the compound by chemical synthesis. They found that dinoracetylmethadol possesses narcotic activity in rodent test systems (8).

We now have evidence for the excretion of at least four active biotransformation products. In attempting to understand the role of these metabolites in the pharmacologic action of acetylmethadol we have recently directed our efforts toward the development of an analytical method for the measurement of acetylmethadol and metabolites in plasma. We have established that acetylmethadol, noracetylmethadol and dinoracetyl-methadol are present in the plasma of maintenance subjects while methadol and normethadol are not detectable above the limits of sensitivity of the method (7, 9). An analytical method for the simultaneous quantitation of acetylmethadol, noracetylmethadol and dinoracetylmethadol has been developed in our laboratory (7). The difficulty of obtaining the required resolution by gas-liquid chromatography of noracetylmethadol from dinoracetylmethadol was circumvented by utilizing conditions during the extraction procedure that favor the conversion of noracetylmethadol and dinoracetylmethadol to stable and easily resolved amides. A representation of the proposed shift is shown in Fig. 2. At a pH of 13 and a temperature of 70 degrees both amines undergo an intramolecular acyl shift to the corresponding amides (7). Thus the method involves the extraction of the unchanged amines from plasma followed by their conversion to the amides prior to the last step of the extraction procedure. Sample chromatograms of human plasma extracts are shown in Fig. 3. Note, for example, that in Panel A the chromatogram shows the presence of peak corresponding to acetylmethadol, the added internal standard and the amides of noracetylmethadol and dinoracetylmethadol (7).

The time-course of acetylmethadol, noracetylmethadol and dinoracetylmethadol in subject plasma is shown in Fig. 4. These subjects had been maintained on an oral dose of 40 to 60 mg of acetylmethadol three times per week for 6 to 10 weeks. The initial (zero time) sample was collected 72 hours after the previous dose and just prior to the test dose. In addition a pharmacologic effect of acetylmethadol was assessed in these subjects by measuring pupillary diameter concurrently with the collection of plasma samples. As seen in Fig. 4, noracetyl-methadol and dinoracetylmethadol persist in plasma throughout the 72 hour dosing interval. The plasma level of acetylmethadol reaches a peak at 4 hours and is barely detectable by 24 hours. The mean peak of pupillary constriction occurred at 8 hours. Thus while acetylmethadol disappears rapidly from plasma two biotransformation products persist in plasma and a pharmaco-logic effect (miosis) is sustained. The time-action of the miotic effect corresponds most closely with the time course of plasma noracetylmethadol (9). These results are in agreement with the findings of Billings et al. (10). In mice the antinoceceptive potency of noracetylmethadol is approximately 10 times greater than either acetylmethadol or dinoracetylmethadol (11, 12).

We propose that following administration of acetylmethadol the drug is taken up by tissue reservoirs followed by a sequence of pharmacokinetic processes involving redistribution and, most importantly, biotransformation by the liver to provide a continuous source of active metabolites during the dosing interval. The pharmacokinetics of acetylmethadol results in a smooth and sustained level of pharmacologic activity.

Urinary excretion profiles (7, 9) indicate that approximately 28 percent of a maintenance dose appears in the urine as acetyl-methadol and known metabolites. More information is required on both the routes and extent of metabolism of acetylmethadol. Methadone, a structural congener of acetylmethadol, undergoes extensive biotransformation in man (13).

Clearly, the critical role of biotransformation in the time-action characteristics of acetylmethadol requires a

careful evaluation of the influence of concurrent administration
of drugs known to effect the enzymes of biotransformation. Also
we would expect that when patients begin to receive acetylmethadol there will be a period of time required before the active
metabolites reach steady state maintenance levels. Whether
this pharmacokinetic lag period is associated with patient
complaints remains to be determined.

We have only begun to gather the data necessary for a
disciplined pharmacologic understanding of this potentially
useful and very interesting drug.

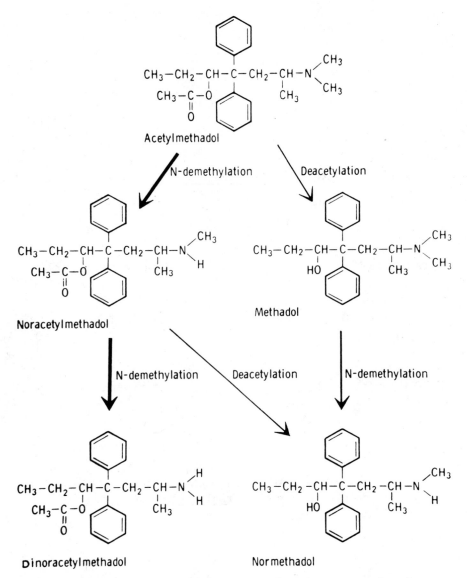

Fig. 1. Structural formulae of acetylmethadol, noracetylmeth-adol, dinoracetylmethadol, methadol and normethadol. From Kaiko et al. (7). By permission of Journal of Chromatography.

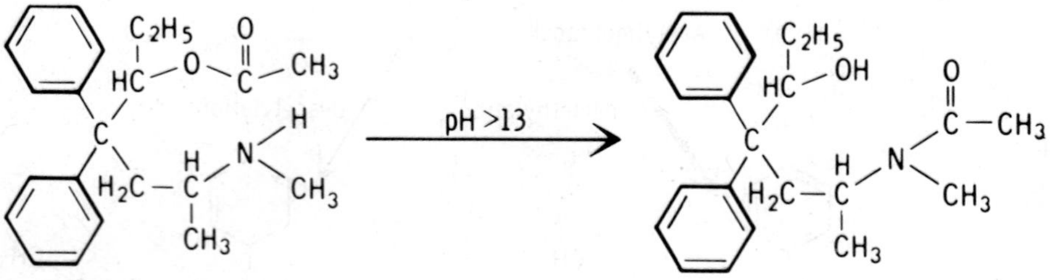

Noracetylmethadol Noracetylmethadol Amide

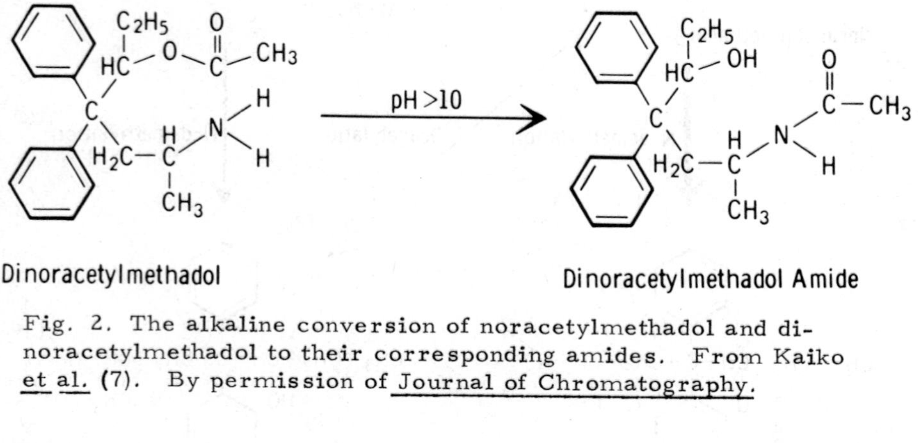

Dinoracetylmethadol Dinoracetylmethadol Amide

Fig. 2. The alkaline conversion of noracetylmethadol and dinoracetylmethadol to their corresponding amides. From Kaiko et al. (7). By permission of Journal of Chromatography.

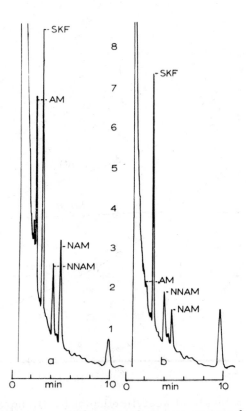

Fig. 3. Chromatograms of human plasma extracts from a
patient who received an oral dose of 50 mg of acetylmethadol
(AM). The internal standard, SKF 525-A, was added directly
to the plasma and the extract prepared. Noracetylmethadol
(NAM) and dinoracetylmethadol (NNAM) present in the extract
were quantitatively converted to their corresponding amides
just prior to the final step of the extraction procedure. (a)
4-h Post drug plasma. (b) 48-h Post drug plasma.
Retention times are: AM, 1.8 min; SKF, 2.5 min; NNAM,
3.6 min; NAM, 4.2 min. From Kaiko et al. (7). By
permission of Journal of Chromatography.

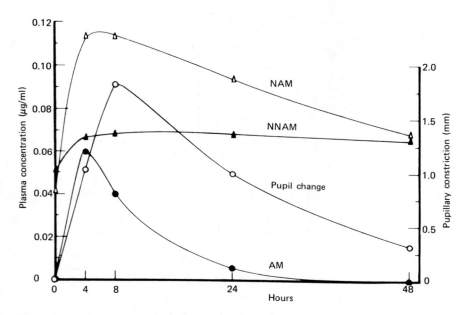

Fig. 4. Plasma levels of acetylmethadol (AM), noracetylmethadol (NAM), dinoracetylmethadol (NNAM), and pupillary
constriction in acetylmethadol maintenance subjects receiving
40 to 60 mg acetylmethadol HCl 3 times per week. The results
represent the mean of 8 subjects. From Kaiko and Inturrisi
(9). By permission of Clinical Pharmacology and Therapeutics.

REFERENCES

1. H. F. Fraser and H. Isbell, J. Pharmacol. Exp. Ther.,
   105: 458 (1952).

2. H. F. Fraser, T. L. Nash, G. D. Vanhorn, and H. Isbell,
   Arch. Int. Pharmacodyn., 98: 443 (1954).

3. C. Sung and E. L. Way, J. Pharmacol. Exp. Ther., 110:
   260 (1954).

4. R. M. Veatch, T. K. Adler, and E. L. Way, J. Pharmacol.
   Exp. Ther., 145: 11 (1964).

5. R. E. McMahon, H. W. Culp, and F. J. Marshall, J.
   Pharmacol. Exp. Ther., 149: 436 (1965).

6. R. F. Kaiko and C. E. Inturrisi, J. Chromatogr., 82:
   315 (1973).

7. R. F. Kaiko, N. Chatterjie, and C. E. Inturrisi,
   J. Chromatogr., 109: 247 (1975).

8. R. E. Billings, R. Booher, S. E. Smits, A. Pohland, and
   R. E. McMahon, J. Med. Chem., 16: 305 (1973).

9. R. F. Kaiko and C. E. Inturrisi, Clin. Pharmacol. Ther.,
   18: 96 (1975).

10. R. E. Billings, R. E. McMahon and D. A. Blake, Life
    Sci., 14: 1437 (1974).

11. S. E. Smits, Res. Commun. Chem. Path. Pharmacol., 8:
    575 (1974).

12. N. Chatterjie and C. E. Inturrisi, J. Med. Chem., 18:
    630 (1975).

13. C. E. Inturrisi, Ann. N. Y. Acad. Sci., in press (1976).

OTHER ISSUES

A STUDY OF SOCIAL REGULATORY MECHANISMS IN
CONTROLLED ILLICIT DRUG USERS

Norman E. Zinberg, M.D.
Wayne M. Harding, Ed.M.
Miriam Winkeller, B.A.

Department of Psychiatry
Harvard Medical School
Cambridge, Massachusetts

The level of hysteria and irrationality which characterized
the cultural response to the explosion of illicit drug use in the
1960's has greatly diminished. Along with this emotional change,
policy positions and strategies which were then accepted as vir-
tual articles of faith are now being questioned. Maintenance
treatment programs for opiate addicts have become socially more
acceptable as an alternative to abstinence, and universal drug
education in the schools, once looked to as a panacea to prevent
drug abuse, has become suspect as a stimulator of drug use. At
the same time, the national policy toward the use of certain
drugs--legal prohibition--has resulted in such high costs, both
financial and psychological, that "drug abuse is coming to be
seen not as a disease to be 'wiped out' but as a chronic ailment
to be managed" (Vogl, 1973). And according to a recent Harris
poll (Harris, 1976), 86 percent of the public now opposes sending
a marihuana smoker to jail, a major reversal from 1969 when 42
percent of parents indicated they would turn their own children
over to the police for using marihuana (Zinberg and Robertson,
1972).

Despite these changes in outlook, however, the public and
professional discussion of drug use remains centered on one as-
pect--the harmful pharmacological properties of the illicit substances being taken by significant numbers of people. A more
important and more promising dimension--that of the quality of
drug use, including the diversity in drug-using styles and the
corresponding differences in the consequences of use, ranging
from beneficial to deadly--has been all but ignored, except, possibly, in connection with marihuana. The belief that the social
policy regarding drugs, including marihuana, flows logically from
their chemical goodness or badness seems to have obscured the important fact that the way in which a drug is used may mitigate or
potentiate its pharmacological properties.

In 1972 the Drug Abuse Council, Inc., of Washington, D.C., began to sponsor a study of controlled drug use which was undertaken by the authors--a study designed to locate and investigate users of marihuana, the psychedelics, and the opiates who, like most social drinkers, have managed to maintain regular, moderate using patterns that do not interfere with effective functioning. From the longitudinal interview data collected up to this time, we have been able to draw one clear conclusion: that achieving controlled use depends chiefly on developing and assimilating social sanctions and social rituals (Jacobson and Zinberg, 1975; Zinberg, 1975; Zinberg, Jacobson and Harding, 1975; Zinberg and Jacobson, 1976; Harding and Zinberg, 1976).

The Nature of Controlled Use

Our sample of 99 controlled users can be distinguished from compulsive users in a number of ways. All subjects tend to maintain regular ties to social institutions, such as work-place, school, and family. At the time of their last interview, 27 subjects were in school (two of them part-time); 43 were working full-time; eight were working part-time; one had retired; and four who had regular work histories had recently become unemployed. Of the remaining subjects, only six fell into a "hustling/hanging out" category; others were involved in child care, housekeeping, and so forth. Controlled users maintained ordinary social relationships with non-drug users. None of the subjects manifested demonstrable physiological or psychological impairment attributable to their controlled use.

Drug use is of course important to controlled users. Our subjects have clearly stated that they would miss their primary drug if it were no longer available. Significantly--and this finding contrasts with the results of studies of compulsive users --our subjects demonstrate an ability to keep drugs on hand for some time without using them, and to continue their leisure activities. Controlled heroin users in our sample wait for "good" circumstances to use the drug (a social sanction), as opposed to compulsive users, who generally restrict use only when the drug is unavailable. Most subjects are deviant only by virtue of their drug use. Some have an earlier history of criminal activity or school disciplinary problems, but generally this has not overlapped with their current period of controlled use.

The data from our study challenge the prevailing tendency to regard regular, non-compulsive use (particularly heroin use) as simply a brief transition stage between abstinence and serious drug-related problems. The mean length of time of controlled use for our subjects is 4.0 years, and with heroin users alone it is 3.6 years. With some subjects (including heroin users) controlled use has exceeded ten years. But more important than the duration of controlled use is evidence indicating the stability of these

using patterns. None of our subjects has shifted toward significantly more frequent use even through such crises as divorce and
job loss. On the contrary, any long-term shifts have tended to
be in the direction of less drug involvement.

Rituals and Social Sanctions

     When the 99 subjects in our sample are viewed individually,
a variety of variables, including personality, family background,
and availability of the drug, can be identified as influencing
their controlled drug use. One crucial variable, however, applies
to all members of the sample--the acquisition of rituals and
social sanctions that reinforce but limit use.

     The term ritual refers to the stylized, prescribed behavior
surrounding the use of a drug. This behavior may include methods
of procuring and administering the drug, selection of a particular
social and physical setting for use, and special activities undertaken after the drug has been administered. The term social sanction refers to the precepts and rules regarding the circumstances
which permit use but prescribe limits.

     In our culture the paradigm for controlled drug use is the
use of alcohol, a psychoactive drug which has as great a potential
for producing profound physiological and psychological harm as any
illicit drug. The seriousness of alcoholism, while not denied, is
placed in a new light when the number of alcoholics in the United
States--some 6 to 8 million--is compared to the number of Americans who drink but avoid compulsive use--some 105 million (New
York Times, 1973). Clearly, the vast majority of people who drink
alcohol succeed in controlling their use of this powerful drug.

     The widespread, non-compulsive use of alcohol in the United
States can best be explained in terms of its socio-cultural con-
text--the rituals and social sanctions which the culture has
developed. Alcohol-using rituals define acceptable use: having
a beer with the boys after work, a few martinis at a cocktail
party, a highball before dinner, wine with dinner, a drink at a
business luncheon. This is not to say that use cannot and does
not occur at other times, but when it does, the users are aware
that they are taking special exception to the social sanctions
which govern use.

     The internalization of these social sanctions and rituals
begins in early childhood. The child sees his parents and other
adults drinking. He also learns the possibilities of excess as
well as the varieties of acceptable drinking patterns from
newspapers, movies, magazines, and television. In some cases this
socialization process is more direct--children sip wine at religious rituals and celebrations, or taste their parents' drinks.
Many authorities believe that a gradual and careful early intro-

duction to alcohol by parents contributes to restrained adult use
(Chafetz and Demone, 1962; Wilkinson, 1970).

Sources and Functions of Controlling Rituals and Social Sanctions

The rituals and social sanctions for the use of all drugs--
not just alcohol--operate at several different levels: in small
groups (for example, using only in a certain room, assigning one
group member to secure the premises); among collections or classes
of people (cocktail parties, beer at ball games, drug use at rock
concerts, wine with dinner in Italian households); and in the culture as a whole (coffee drinking and alcohol use). The Drug Abuse
Council (DAC) data indicate that controlled users adhere to those
specific rituals and social sanctions which each group develops
for itself, and that the peer using group is the prime mechanism
by which these guidelines for controlled use are developed.

The controlling rituals and social sanctions to which the
subjects of the DAC study subscribe function in five overlapping
ways.

1. They define moderate use and condemn compulsive use. For
instance, several subjects use heroin with friends every weekend
but condemn use at other times as "junkie"-like.

2. The rituals and sanctions limit use to physical and
social settings which are conducive to a positive or safe drug
experience. A maxim shared by virtually all psychedelic-using
subjects is, "Use in a good place at a good time with good people."

3. Rituals and sanctions reinforce the principle that dependence or addiction should be avoided. Subjects who use heroin
are acutely aware that they can become addicted, and they interpret increasing tolerance to drug effects as a signal to cut
back on use.

4. The sanctions and rituals assist the user in interpreting
and controlling the drug high itself. Passing a joint around provides an opportunity to gauge the effect of the drug after each
"toke" and thus to titrate dosage accordingly.

5. Rituals and sanctions support the user's non-drug-related
obligations and relationships. For example, some subjects do not
use opiates on Sunday evening because this would leave them too
tired to work effectively on Monday.

The subjects of the DAC study acquired rituals and social
sanctions gradually during the course of their illicit-drug-using
careers. The details of this process varied from subject to subject. Some had been controlled users from the outset; other went
through one or more periods of compulsive use before firmly establishing control. Virtually all subjects, however, required the

assistance of other controlled users to construct appropriate rituals and social sanctions out of the folklore and practices of the diverse subculture of drug-takers.

It is this association (often fortuitous) among controlled users which provides the necessary reinforcement for avoiding compulsive use. Virtually all DAC subjects are or have been connected with a controlled use group. Subjects rarely use drugs alone; over 80 percent of their use takes place with other controlled users.

While controlled use groups are the main source of rituals and social sanctions, there also appear to be at least four secondary sources. First, some of the precepts learned in the course of culture-based socialization in the controlled use of alcohol may be successfully adapted to the use of illicit drugs. Second, the lessons learned about controlling one illicit drug may be applicable to another. If this is so, one might expect to find, for example, that early controlled marihuana use is predictive of later controlled psychedelic use. Third, control over one drug, in the narrow sense of ability to deal with a drug high, may be transferred to another drug experience when the drugs are pharmacologically similar. For example, a user who had achieved some control over a barbiturate high might be better prepared to cope with a heroin high. Fourth, direct exposure to compulsive users who are obviously suffering from adverse drug effects may sometimes be helpful to controlled users. Such exposure may strengthen the sanctions the controlled users have already adopted by consciously or unconsciously delineating the differences between the two groups: differences in their relationships to the drug itself, in their integration of drug use into a personal and social context, and, of course, in the consequences of use.

Drug Use and the Sociocultural Context

Underlying the social and legal taboos against illicit use of the psychedelics, heroin, and, to a lesser extent, marihuana, is the conviction that because of their pharmacological properties these drugs cannot be taken on a long-term, regular basis without causing serious problems. The unfortunate condition of heroin addicts and other compulsive users is regularly invoked as "proof" of this "pharmacomythology" (Szasz, 1975). In contrast, our DAC study demonstrates that regular use of these substances on a controlled basis is possible. Moreover, the data indicate that peer group influences, which are usually considered to contribute only to the "bad" use of drugs, can provide the necessary support, in the form of rituals and sanctions, for avoiding compulsive use. These findings suggest that the management of illicit drug use by means of elaborate, culturally based, controlling social sanctions and rituals needs to be investigated as a realistic and more humane way of preventing drug "abuse" than the present method of total prohibition.

Our culture does not yet recognize, much less support controlled use. Users are declared deviant, or "sick" and in need of help, or "criminal" and deserving of punishment. Family-centered socialization for use is not available. Parents, even if they were willing to help, would be unable to provide guidance either by example (as with alcohol) or in a factual, non-moralistic manner.

Therefore, the task of educating people about controlled use rests squarely with the peer group--an utterly inadequate substitute for cross-generation, long-term socialization. To a large degree, association with controlled users is a matter of chance rather than of deliberate personal choice. Because illicit drug use must be a covert activity, newcomers are not presented with an array of using groups from which to choose.

The chief difficulty in achieving social control over drugs is that significant changes will be required in both public attitudes and social policy before effective rituals and social sanctions can develop. These social controls are not the work of a moment; they develop slowly over time in ways that fit the culture. Griffith Edwards (1973), who calls this kind of response "cultural plasticity," describes how the use of a drug can be slowly evolved by different tribes. One tribe may use the same drug as an energizer that another tribe uses as a tranquilizer, depending on how the drug fits each group's controlling rituals and sanctions. We certainly do not recommend the wholesale, immediate legalization of marihuana, psychedelics, and opiates, for such an abrupt shift in policy would make impossible the natural development of the elaborate social support and carefully defined social context of use which are needed to prevent abuse.

Three steps, however, can be taken now to develop familiarity with the drugs in frequent use and thus to lay the basis for social controls. First, the laws can be changed to encourage legitimate areas of drug research and experimentation. Second, more comprehensive and value-neutral information about licit and illicit drugs can be given to the general population. Third, distinctions can be drawn among the various degrees of drug use, thus allowing knowledge about the controlling conventions to be disseminated. All these actions will help to strengthen the existing subcultural rituals and social sanctions and to remove prevailing misconceptions about the power and danger of these drugs.

These recommendations represent only the first of many changes which would be required before coherent social sanctions could develop around illicit drug use and before more realistic legal controls could evolve. It is not possible to specify the sequence of changes with any confidence, for to do so would be to ignore the essential fact that using patterns will shift in response to these changes and to other new factors. When such shifts have begun, intensive research aimed at measuring them will be needed in order to provide data upon which to base further constructive steps.

References

Chafetz, M.E. and Demone, H.W., Jr., Alcoholism and Society, Oxford University Press, New York, 1962.

Edwards, G.F., The Plasticity of Human Response. Maudsley Hospital, London, 1973. (mimeograph)

Feldman, H., Ideological supports to becoming and remaining a heroin addict., J. Health and Social Behav. 9:131-139, 1968.

Harding, W.M. and Zinberg, N.E., The effectiveness of the subculture in developing rituals and social sanctions for controlled use, Drugs, Rituals and Altered States of Consciousness (Ed. B.M. du Toit). In press.

Harris, Louis. A lenient attitude on pot fines, Chicago Tribune, January 26, 1976.

Jacobson, R. and Zinberg, N.E., The Social Basis of Drug Abuse Prevention, Drug Abuse Council Monograph Series SS-5, Drug Abuse Council, Washington, D.C., 1975.

New York Times, April 9, 1973.

Preble, E. and Casey, J.J., Jr., Taking care of business--the heroin users' life on the street, Int. J. Addictions 4:1-24, 1969.

Stephens, R. and Levine, S., The "street addict role": implications for treatment, Psychiatry: J for the Study of Interpersonal Processes 34:351-357, 1971.

Szasz, T., Ceremonial Chemistry: The Ritual Persecution of Drugs, Addicts and Pushers. Anchor Press/Doubleday, Garden City, New York, 1975.

Vogl, A.J., Drug abuse: is the tide turning? Med Econ, p. 82-99, May 28, 1973.

Wilkinson, R., The Prevention of Drinking Problems. Oxford University Press, New York, 1970.

Young, J., The Drugtakers: The Social Meaning of Drug Use, MacGibbon and Kee, Ltd., London, 1971.

Zinberg, N.E., Addiction and ego function, Psychoanal. St. Ch. 30:567-588, 1975.

Zinberg, N.E. and Jacobson, R.C., The natural history of chipping, Am. J. Psychiatry 133:37-40, 1976.

Zinbert, N.E., Jacobson, R.C., and Harding, W.M., Social sanctions and rituals as a basis of drug abuse prevention, Am. J. Drug and Alcohol Abuse 2:165-182, 1975.

Zinberg, N.E. and Robertson, J.A., Drugs and the Public, Simon and Schuster, New York, 1972.

TOLERANCE, REPRESSION AND DRUG USE:
A COMMENT ON DR. ZINBERG'S REMARKS

Ronald Bayer

Greenwich House
50 Cooper Square, New York, New York

Out of our therapeutic impotence must come the
prophylaxis of the neurosis.
                              Freud, 1909

Having witnessed the consequences of a prohibitionist
social policy with regard to drug use, it is not surprising that the suggestion that there is a benign solution to the mess which we confront - one which avoids
both the barbarism of imprisoning those who use illicit
drugs and the only thinly veiled incarceration which is
the truth of enforced therapy - would be eagerly welcomed. When such a solution also holds open the possibility of an end to the untoward social consequences of
our current approach (the crime-drug nexus assumed to
flow from prohibition) while leaving intact the normative order's insistence on productivity and personal
responsibility (indeed, is put forth as functional for
that end) it becomes even more appealing. Finally,
when such a solution identifies the rigid, often stupid,
institutional forms we have created as the primary
source of our problems and, hence, suggests that adjustment or reform of those institutions might lead to a
more salutory state of affairs, it becomes especially
congenial to contemporary liberal social thought.

Dr. Zinberg's main lines of argument tend to steer away
from the seemingly prior questions of social and psychological etiology of drug use. Like the sociologists
of deviance and the anti-psychiatrists, Zinberg suggests
that far more important to our understanding is the
reaction to drug use, the process of labeling users, of
diagnosing them, and their consequent isolation in a

sub culture often impervious to the moderating
influences of the greater society. Thus he argues that
the legitimate public concern regarding the maintenance

of responsible social roles is subverted by the policies
we pursue. If the "setting" in which drug use occurs
permitted the development of rituals and customs designed to integrate drug use into the social fabric, then
the disruptive aspects of such behavior would be reduced significantly.

When Zinberg attempts to derive policy implications from
his more abstract formulations there is a moderation
which is quite stunning. While his arguments tend to
lead towards a "liquor store" model of control, he puts
forth a "drug store" model in which physicians would be
granted the right to prescribe or dispense drugs like
heroin to users. Hence, after discussing the possibility
of non-disruptive opiate use, after showing that with
even the assumedly most potent of pharmacologic agents
it is possible, given the appropriate "setting", to use
in a responsible fashion he calls for an experiment
with heroin maintenance clinics:

> Informal drug education centering on controlled use
> must supply the range of possibilities now available
> about alcohol...

> In order to achieve that form of early education some
> form of legalized controls would be necessary. That
> does not mean that heroin should be openly available
> at newstands, but it does mean that heroin mainten-
> ance clinics can be tried and an open discussion of
> the drug's benefits and drawbacks begun.

But why this retreat? Is it possible that Dr. Zinberg
recognizes that given the "setting" under which drug
use, but especially opiate use, occurs in the United
States that a social policy like that which prevails
with regard to alcohol would create a grave problem
involving the expansion of uncontrolled drug use,
especially in the ghettos?

Norman Zinberg's own discussion of the fate of those
who became addicted in Vietnam is instructive here:

> The determining factor in their heroin use had been
> the intolerable setting in Vietnam, and once they
> returned to the United States neither the power of
> the drug nor a susceptible personality proved to be
> decisive in keeping them drug dependent.

If the nature of drug use was "determined" in Vietnam by
the "intolerable" conditions there, what of the intolerable conditions at home, especially for the underclass?

It is probable that a relaxation of legal constraints on narcotics use would, given the conditions of our society, produce an expansion of compulsive drug use. I feel that Dr. Zinberg is aware of this possibility and, hence, retreats from the implications of his own argument.

Here it is possible to note the problematical nature of Zinberg's concept of "setting". While the effort to enforce abstinence by law most certainly has an impact on the way in which people will use drugs and upon the meaning of that behavior for the user, so too do the broader social conditions of deprivation. The effort to banish as it were questions of social etiology from the discussion of drug use makes that discussion one-sided and suggests that it is only the reaction to drug use which is a problem.

An alternative way of accounting for the moderation of Dr. Zinberg's policy proposals is suggested ironically by the very analogy he draws with alcohol use. In noting that well over 100 million Americans of every strata consume alcohol and that such behavior is well integrated into our social and commercial life, Zinberg acknowledges that there are about 5,000,000 persons for whom alcohol use constitutes a severe problem, for whom the capacity to control and limit alcohol consumption seems to be lacking. During the "heroin epidemic" of the late 1960's and early 1970's there was nothing approaching that number of persons for whom heroin use had become the overhwelming preoccupation of life. So it would appear that the use of the prohibtionist approach has in fact been fairly successful in limiting the extent of heroin involvement. A full scale relaxation of legal controls on the sale of heroin such as that which is suggested by the liquor store model, an approach supported by Dr. Thomas Szasz and elements of the American Civil Liberties Union,would thus doubtlessly result in a widespread extension of heroin use as well as compulsive use.

Our society has made the decision to tolerate the existence of 5,000,000 alcoholics and to absorb into the social fabric an incredible reliance upon alcoholic beverages. We may also make the decision to tolerate the vast expansion of other non-medical drug use because the costs of prohibition either with the threat of the penal or therapeutic sanction are too great. It is in the context of this tendency towards absorption into the social fabric of behavior that I would like to conclude.

In the 19th century a productionist ethos appropriately reflected the needs of an expanding capitalist indus-

trial order. The excessive consumption of intoxicants
was seen as incompatible with hard work and instinctual
renunciation. I think it is that which, at least in
part, accounts for the crusade-like assaults for a good
part of this century on public drunkards and drug users -
their ethnic and social characteristics resulting in
fury being added to that assault. The shift towards a
consumptionist orientation in capitalism, one which
stresses gratification rather than renunciation, has
had a marked impact on the extent to whcih abstemious-
ness is demanded or at least held to be virtuous. Consumption having become the condition of rather than the
antagonist to production, the use of alcohol and drugs
has become increasingly acceptable. Indeed, with ever
greater frequency it is argued that many persons may
require the use of intoxicants so that they can continue
to bear the stresses of everyday life, to meet the
demands of the labor process. Only that drug and alcohol use which makes the user dysfunctional, so it is
asserted, is of legitimate concern. The extent of
tolerance extends, however, with increasing frequency to
the large numbers who are made dysfunctional by their
compulsive use of drugs and alcohol, such tolerance
being seen as an unavoidable social cost for a less
repressive social policy. On an admittedly speculative
level I would argue that the willingness to absorb such
behavior is a reflection of the tendency on the part of
the American capitalist social order to produce something approaching a permanent labor surplus. With the
need for labor power reduced, the univerality of the
norms of productivity and striving has been undercut.

There is here a great irony. The various ideologies of
tolerance now current which present themselves as a
critical force in the service of liberation to free
drug users from repressive state controls actually tend
to serve a profoundly conservative function. By
focusing on the institutional nature of oppression and
upon the rights of drug users to be free of constraints,
as long as they do not harm others, these ideologies
tend to ignore the extent to which drug use like
alcoholism is a reflection of human wretchedness rooted
in the oppressive qualities of the social system. By
integrating into the social fabric that behavior which
might serve as the basis of a social critique, such
tolerance tends to mask social oppression. The
ideologies of tolerance demand the freeing of the drug
user from the oppression of legal controls which it is
argued harm the user as well as produce untoward social
consequences. The freeing of persons from the need to
rely upon drugs necessitates going beyond such tolerance
and must commence with a critique of the social order.

THE SOLUTION TO NARCOTIC ADDICTION IN THE
PEOPLE'S REPUBLIC OF CHINA

Paul Lowinger, M.D.
Associate Clinical Professor of
Psychiatry and Community Medicine
Departments of Psychiatry and Community
 Medicine
University of California School
 of Medicine
San Francisco, California

"...our struggle is not an isolated one...we
have the feeling that, when we obtain victory,
this victory will be of great assistance to
the struggle of the American people for
liberation."

Mao Tse-Tung, June 24, 1937

Narcotic addiction and other drug abuse in the United States
has been increasing during the last decade so that it is a national problem and epidemic in some communities (1,2). The effects
on health, personality, crime and community life constitute a major crisis. China was the other nation with a severe narcotic
problem in the twentieth century but the Chinese overcame their
problem in a few years after their Revolution of 1949. Why was
this remarkable accomplishment almost entirely ignored or denied
in the United States? The active antagonism between the Government
of the United States and the People's Republic of China was the major factor in obscuring this noteworthy event. This report will
examine the Chinese solution to their opium problem and look for
those elements which may have application to Americans in their
personal and national struggle with addiction.

The history of narcotics in China begins in the ninth century
with Indian opium imported by Arab traders for Chinese medicine.(3)
It was not until the eighteenth century that large quantities of
opium grown in India created addiction in China despite Imperial
edicts against opium in 1729 and in 1800. The export of opium
from India to China was a most profitable business for the British

East India Company which also imported tea and silk from China to the West. By 1850 a fifth of the revenue of the British government of India was derived from the opium trade with China. The Imperial Government of China became increasingly concerned as many people were addicted, officials were corrupted by the profits and there was a great outflow of silver from China to pay for the opium. Peasant revolts in China against the ruling Manchu dynasty were widespread after 1810 when the negative trade balance of China caused landlords and tax collectors to take a greater share of the peasant's grain crop. These factors led to a patriotic attempt at suppression of the opium trade when in 1839 a Chinese official destroyed 20,000 chests of opium weighing 150 pounds. This resulted in the Opium War from 1839 to 1842 when the British occupied parts of the Chinese coast. The Chinese lost this war and the resulting Treaty of Nanking opened China to an opium trade which remained active until 1949. The Opium War led to the British acquisition of Hong Kong, the opening of major Chinese ports to foreign trade, the limitation of Chinese tariffs on imports to five percent and the establishment of extraterritoriality which exempted British and other foreign nationals from Chinese law. (4,5) These measures were directly and indirectly responsible for the continued oppression of China by Opium. This treatment of China continued as the United States joined this pattern during the Second Opium War, and the United States representative, Caleb Cushing, negotiated the Treaty of Wanghsia in 1844, called "the smugglers delight" by one historian. (6)

The Taiping Rebellion which broke out soon after against the Manchus, lasted from 1851 to 1864. Among its demands were suppression of opium, control of foreigners and rent and land reform. (7) Nonetheless, opium use spread through all social classes and by 1906 more than 15 million were addicted. (8) By the 1920's estimates of opium use ranged from an incredible 25% of the urban population (9) to 40 million users in a population of 400 to 500 million. (10) Before World War II the estimates were that between seven and eighty million people were using opium in China. (9,11,12)

The history of the Opium War is particularly important since the "legal" import of Indian opium into China continued until 1917. Foreign nationals enjoyed official exemption from Chinese law until 1942 although in fact such law was never applied to them until 1949. Until 1929, import tariffs were limited to five percent and this prevented the development of Chinese domestic industry. The Revolution of 1911 which established the Republic of China never dealt effectively with the opium trade which remained an established and important source of illegal income for Chinese warlords and generals who were doing the producing and distributing. (4,13) Chinese grown opium for smoking had been used since 1860, with an annual crop of 22,000 tons by the early twentieth century. (14) Illegal opium trade continued to support the warlords and provin-

cial leaders of the government after Chiang Kai-shek came to power
in 1927. Local warlords sometimes demanded their taxes in opium
according to Rewi Alley who traveled in China during the 1920's
and 30's. (15) The Communists however had eliminated opium poppy
growing and smoking from their Soviets in South China between 1927
and 1935. Chu Teh, the commander of the Communist armies and himself a former addict, burned ten thousand pounds of opium at Lung-
yen in 1929. (16) There was no opium in the Communist areas after
the Long March to Yenan in 1936 according to Edgar Snow. (17)

The Japanese occupation of China which began with Manchuria in
1931, enlarged in 1937 and increased again during World War II had
the effect of greatly increasing opium use in China with the profit
to the Japanese and their Chinese collaborators. (4) The political
and economic role of opium during the last years of Chiang Kai-Shek
in Mainland China after World War II is described by Epstein (4)
and by Beldon (18) and was also observed as a health problem by an
American doctor and nurse. (19, 20) Despite the severe punishment
of a few users by the Chiang Kai-shek government, addiction remained frequent. Opium production continued to support politically
powerful warlords and corrupt Kuomintang government officials. (13,
15)

The People's Republic of China was proclaimed on October 1,
1949 in Peking. Effective control of the country took place between 1948 and 1950. In February, 1950, the Government Administrative Counsel issued a Circular Order for the Prohibition of Opium
signed by Premier Chou En-lai. (21) On October 1, 1950, the
Ministry of Public Health issued an Order for the Promulgation of
the Provisional Regulation on the Control of Narcotic Drugs. Reports in 1951 of 10,000 addicts in Canton were heard (22) but by
1952, only secret opium smokers were reported (23) in that city,
although there still were 451 opium smugglers in Hankow and
459 smuggling firms in Nanning. (24) By March, 1953, the Government's New China New Agency claimed that, "...as a result of the
immense effort of the Central People's Government in strictly prohibiting the cultivation, manufacture and sale of opium and the
strict control of all narcotic drugs in the past three years, the
main opium producing areas have changed completely and the cultivation...production and sale of opium and other narcotic drugs have
been completely eliminated." (25)

An English surgeon who worked in China for 15 years (26) reported that there was no opium addiction when he went to China in
1954. (27) Rewi Alley saw no opium in rural Kansu province after
1950. (15) Robert Williams who lived in China from 1965 to 1968
as a Black political refugee from the United States found no addiction. (28) There is a similar report from Edgar Snow who
traveled in China in 1960 without finding any narcotic problem although he had seen a severe narcotic problem during his 1936 trip
to Chiang Kai-shek's China. (27) There are also reports from

Americans about the absence of narcotics in China after 1971. (30-34)

The U.S. Government reports on opium production and distribution in China are interesting because they emanated from a source publically hostile to the People's Republic and allied with the Chiang Kai-shek government in Taiwan. The early reports from Harry Anslinger in the U.S. Bureau of Narcotics and the Nationalist Government on Taiwan said that the People's Republic of China was producing and exporting opium as national policy. (36, 37) However, by 1967 the U.S. Treasury Department Bureau of Narcotics said that there was no opium exported from the People's Republic of China. (38) In 1971 the Bureau of Narcotics and Dangerous Drugs reported that the production of opium in the People's Republic of China was 100 tons a year which was just enough for their medical use. (39) Nonetheless, accusations of opium production for export have continued from sources hostile to the People's Republic of China, including official Soviet sources, (40,41), the Taiwan press (42), right-wing columnist John Chamberlain (43), and John Schmitz who was the American Independent Party presidential candidate in 1972 after George Wallace was shot. (44)

To underline the initial success of the anti-opium drive of the new government is the fact that there was a significant drop in the number of opium users among those who left China for Hong Kong as refugees between 1949 and 1953. (45-47) In 1963, the report about health in China by Worth who interviewed refugees in Hong Kong confirmed the absence of narcotic addiction. (48) Refugees in the United States from the People's Republic acknowledge that narcotic addiction has been absent since the early fifties. (49-50)

What is the explanation for the success of this campaign after 200 years of an epidemic national narcotic addiction problem? Most importantly the value system of the young people changed so that there was no new supply of addicts. This is fundamental to the solution of the addiction problem since the national perpetuation of narcotic addiction depends on a supply of new users. Old users have less money to buy narcotics, die, go to jail, and are "clean" for intervals. New users are the major impetus to growing demand, and distribution networks, and are the prime causes of the crimes committed to get money for additional purchases.

The value transformation of the young was however accompanied by far reaching institutional change. In a country which was 90% rural, land distribution and collective farming as well as a new educational, social and vocational opportunities remain central to the solution. (29) The transformation of the Chinese village and its people is discussed by Myrdal (51) and Hinton. (52) Similar changes took place in the cities with nationalization of commerce and industry, full employment, humanized working conditions and social welfare programs. (53) The ideological transformation of the younger generation was due to the new chance to make something

of their lives. The nation and its youth had a redefinition of
their worth and role, summed up in the Chinese word <u>fanshen</u>, "...to
turn the body, or 'to turn over'. To China's hundreds of millions
of landless and land-poor peasants it meant to stand up to throw
off the landlord yoke, to gain land, stock, implements and houses.
But it meant much more than this. It meant to throw off superst i-
tion and study science, to abolish 'word blindness' and learn to
read, to cease considering women as chattels and establish equality
between the sexes, to do away with appointed village magistrates
and replace them with elected councils. It meant to enter a new
world." (52)

The mechanism by which the reintegration of Chinese society
was accomplished was the organizational leadership and ideology
of the Communist Party. Small street committees offered political
and cultural leadership and effective social pressure in many communities. The basic unit of government structure was based on a
residential group of 100 to 200 people which was part of larger
community organizations. Such a basic unit was effective in carrying out national decisions because members of every third or
fourth family in such groups were neighborhood activists. These
local cadres were responsible for propaganda, agitation and indoc-
trination in the anti-opium campaign and were also a source of information about and social censure of those who continued to use
opium. The successes and failures of this campaign were reported
to higher authority. Medical treatment of addicts was available in
the cities and difficult cases were referred to rehabilitation centers. National health campaigns against the closely related phenomena of opium and prostitution had the local support in the early
1950's of a disciplined Communist Party which then numbered six
million members.

The anti-opium campaign was closely linked with land reform
and other social changes. Distribution of the land was followed
by a change from the cultivation of opium, a cash crop, to the badly needed food crops.

The enemy in the anti-opium campaign was declared a class
enemy,
"To import opium in large quantities to China is a most pernicious means of the imperialists to destroy the Chinese
nation. The imperialists have intended to eliminate our resistance and to enslave us as their colonial people...In the
past, the reactionary governments of the various regimes
were governments representing the feudalists, bureaucrats
and compradores, who colluded with the top imperialists to
do evil and did not dare to offend the imperialists. They
therefore could not and would not dare to suppress and
exterminate the opium evil; but their actions were just
nominal. On the contrary, under the cloak of prohibiting
opium, they implemented the narcotization policy and utilized

the name of opium suppression to exploit the people.
Thus the more they suppressed the opium evil, the wider the
use of opium was extended. Chiang Kai-shek's suppression
of opium and narcotics was an explicit example." (25)

Meetings for everyone concerning addiction were part of the
new mass line. People spent an hour a day discussing political and
health topics of national importance. The testimony of former addicts was important at all levels of this discussion, which took
place in both the mass media and small community groups and rehabilitation centers. Mass meetings, slogans and flags used the words
of the ex-addicts. Addiction was denounced as anti-social and
unhealthful, a result of imperialism and capitalism.

June 3, 1951 was "Anti-opium Day" in Canton--five thousand representatives of various community circles of the city as well as
4,000 former opium addicts and 2,000 members of the families of addicts attended a mass meeting to commemorate the day in 1839 when
Lin Tse-hsu confiscated 20,000 chests of opium from the British.(54)

The success of the anti-opium campaign also relied on the fact
that the opium trade was suppressed and the land formerly used for
poppy cultivation was turned over to food crops. A Canton newspaper reported:
"Before liberation about 200 mou of land in the suburbs of
Canton were given to poppy cultivation. By the spring of
1951 the suppression of poppy cultivation was successfully
accomplished." (24)
Guidelines for the suppression of opium growing issued in March,
1951, suggested that "opium suppression should be undertaken in
conjunction with the various tasks such as the movement for bandit
suppression, against despots, and of rental reduction, agrarian reform and production..." (55) These results and the approach to the
problem which linked addiction to the wider social and economic
institutions contrasted with the ineffectiveness of the Chiang Kai-
shek government whose anti-opium organization sometimes arrested
and punished addicts but took no action against opium production or
distribution.

In the cities, the rehabilitation of opium addicts began with
their compulsory registration. Arrangements made by city-wide
Anti-opium Committees included treatment to break the habit at home
or in the clinics and hospitals. A Canton newspaper, on June 3,
1951, reported that an anti-opium clinic and hospital had been
opened on April 16, by the Canton Municipal Committee for Suppression of Opium and Narcotics. It had accomodations for more than
500 patients. The experience of addict Chang Yueh in the clinic
was described in detail in the press:

"During the days of the reactionary regime, he tried, without success to rid himself of the habit on no less than
four occasions. Before he entered the present hospital, he

was filled with doubts and anxieties. He feared the suffering he must go through during the cure, the long time
it would take, the repetition of his past failures, relapses after cure, the treatment by authorities as a criminal, the insanitary state that would be found in the hospital, the need to sleep on the floor, and a host of
other things. He found all his fears entirely unfounded.
Only a few days after entering the hospital, he became
visibly relieved and told his fellow addicts gratefully:
'There is really a difference in the Peoples Government.
The workers here are so considerate and attentive to our
needs. Fellow inmates are so friendly and helpful to one
another. Family members may visit us three times a week.
How can I but become confident in being able to achieve
my cure smoothly? The addicts live a group life in the
hospital. At 7:30 in the morning they take their first of
their medicine. They then meet to discuss the current affairs and the evils of the habit they had. Breakfast is
served at 9:00 after which patients are seen by the doctor
by rotation. Many spend their time in the cultural and
entertainment reading room. In the afternoon, two hours
are spent in studies and discussions. In the evening,
there are also social gatherings. The cure is being carried out with medical treatment supported by cultural
amenities and group discussions. In this way the addicts
found the cure more pleasant and interesting. Cures were
affected on the average in 12 days. Those physically weak
or with other complications necessarily needed a longer period,
usually more than one month. The method of gradual reduction of the habit was normally applied." (56)

In the rural areas where 90% of the people lived, withdrawal
from opium was equally successful but was "cold turkey" since medical care and hospitals for addicts were not available, according to
Alley who observed these events in Kansu province. (15)

Criminal procedures and policies stressed leniency for employees and workers of the opium gangs, but there were heavier penalties
for those controlling the networks of growth manufacture and distribution. Americans learned from law professors in Peking in 1973
that capital punishment was reserved for major dealers while intermediate dealers were sent to prison. (57) The New China News Agency
reported on March 29, 1951 that of the 10,000 addicts discovered
in the previous year, 37 had been executed by firing squad. (54)
Difficult cases of addiction were required to go through labor reform similar to the rehabilitation of landowners, business men and
social criminals. Mass meetings were held at which opium, heroin,
and equipment were burned. At one meeting there was a public exhibition of 20 traffickers and addicts who had refused to register
but were exposed and then sent to prison. Americans talking with
former addict in Shanghai in 1974 learned that only 10 major drug

distributors had been executed between 1949 and 1952 in a city of six million which was the center of narcotic addiction and distribution before Liberation. (35)

Opium use continues among the 20 million Chinese living overseas, and is a major health problem in Hong Kong, a British colony on the border of the Peoples Republic of China. This 99% Chinese city has 80,000 to 250,000 opium and heroin addicts in a population of four million (58) despite law enforcement, Western medical and rehabilitation services and acupuncture treatment of addiction. (59) Many young Hong Kong addicts are "mainlining" heroin as is the practice in the United States. (60) The Chinese national minority in many Asian nations including the Philippines, Thailand, Malayasia and Indonesia are the group with most of the opium and narcotic addiction. The World Health Organization reported that in 1963 Taiwan had 40,000 addicts, although there was and continues to be strict police enforcement against addicts. (9) Despite government denials, anonymous sources report the persistance of large numbers of opium addicts in Taiwan in 1972. (61)

The solution in Communist China contrasts vividly to the problem in capitalist Hong Kong which remains a British colony. Still, some attribute both the problem in China and its solution principally to its "culture" and "temperment." (62)

Meng Chien, a representative of the People's Republic of China at the United Nations Commission on Narcotic Drugs in Geneva summarized in 1973, "Narcotic drugs are strictly controlled in our country...no abuse is allowed...Our success in this respect testifies to the strong determination and the clear-cut policy of the Chinese Government and the people and demonstrates the superiority of our socialist system in solving the narcotic problem." (63)

How can this achievement be related to control of drug abuse in the United States? First it remains clear in 1976 that many young people in the United States seek alcohol, narcotics and other drugs as social experiences in both white suburban and black ghetto areas. (2) This need to "turn on" is part of poverty, racism, militarism, a meaningless social environment, a repressive community and a national and family life of frustration and boredom. There is no American equivalent to the change in national purpose which the Chinese underwent with their Liberation of 1949. Clearly the civil rights, peace and cultural revolutions of the sixties did not overcome the problems nor the inertia, hopelessness, powerlessness, and alienation among young people. In fact, American liberal, radical, countercultural and Third World movements have been characteristically victimized by alcohol, narcotic and drug abuse. Only some of these movements have struggled against the addiction of their own members and then with only a moderate degree of success.

The suppression of the opium trade in China by agreement of the government and people in a popular and consistent way contrasts to the United States where there is no such consistent national drug policy. The legal punishment of heroin users in the U.S. contrasts to the commerce in heroin which is protected by an informal but persuasive police - law - crime collaboration which often begins outside the borders of the United States. An example of this is the fact that a significant proportion of the international heroin supply is grown in the Golden Triangle area of the hills of Northern Thailand and Burma where it is protected by a Kuomintang Army left over from prerevolutionary China. During the decade of the U.S. war in Indochina, some of this opium was flown from Laos by Air America, a CIA subsidized airline (64) to Bangkok and Saigon where it was refined into heroin for American soldiers and shipment to the United States. (65) In 1976 the traffic remains from Burma and Thailand to Singapore and Hong Kong to Eastern and Western users including the U.S. (66) This collaboration between the Federal government and heroin import into the United States was first described by poet Allen Ginsberg, (67) then was reported in Ramparts (68) and finally appeared in the daily press (69-75) and the speeches of Attorney General Mitchell. (78) The collaboration between the police narcotics bureau and the narcotic dealers is reported in New York by the Knapp Commission in 1972 (77) but was also known during the Johnson administration (78) and described earlier by former Mafia member Valachi. (79) This is the flourishing American narcotic conspiracy described by McCoy (80) in which government, police, organized crime and the military all have an investment. The prohibitive laws against narcotics keep the price so high as to guarantee tremendous profits, tax-free, to the corporate criminal importer, distributor and seller. (81-83) The lower echelons of the network who are arrested and sometimes imprisoned are nearly always addicts who are considered expendable.

The notion of addict rehabilitation in the United States is still regarded ambivalently. Funds are inadequate. Addicts are rejected by doctors and nurses in most hospitals and health facilities. Because the treatment of addicts is sometimes accompanied by police harrassment or arrest, many fear to come for treatment. Former addicts are social pariahs and can't find employment. There is no public willingness to accept the addict into community life. Anti-addiction campaigns in the United States which have only begun during the last ten years leave most addicts without assistance and focus on two specialized groups: the few who are able to live in a therapeutic community for several years, and a larger number of addicts who accept methadone maintenance treatment. These are very limited systems when contrasted to the Chinese use of total health, community and political rehabilitation for all addicts.

The Chinese solutions to narcotic addiction emphasize the ambivalent and feeble efforts of the United States. The political content of addiction is clear in both societies. Narcotic addiction is a symptom of the unhealthful state of the individual in an unhealthful society. A return to a healthy society with healthy individuals was made in China which used a broad range of political and public health measures to solve the problem of addiction. The inability to do this in our affluent urban society with mass communication, education and technology is striking.

The remaining issues were clarified during my own three week visit to the People's Republic of China in June 1975. Narcotic addiction is virtually unknown in China and so there are no addicts or treatments for addiction. A few former addicts may live in labor camps because of a failure to rehabilitate them. The rehabilitated addicts continue to be useful members of society. This information was reported to me by doctors, law officials, writers, and ordinary people in China. The intensely political nature of the People's Republic as a Marxist dictatorship of the proletariat was something I was not able to fully understand until my visit. I saw how the political and class analysis of national issues worked in the development of a mass line. This was a crucial element in the mobilization of the people for the solution of the narcotic addiction problem.

China's success calls for Americans concerned with health and addiction to study and learn from China. Full diplomatic relations should accelerate an interchange of personnel and scientific knowledge in the near future. It is essential for the United States that the fundamental political basis of addiction begin to receive recognition.

Bibliography

1. Marshall, E., "The Losing Battle Against Heroin," The New Republic, 174:pp. 7-11, Feb. 7, 1976.
2. "NIDA Reports Continued High Drug Abuse by U.S. Population," Psychiatric News, Feb. 6, 1976, American Psychiatric Association, Washington, D.C.
3. Fort, J., The Pleasure Seekers: The Drug Crisis, Youth and Society, pp. 16-22, Bobbs-Merrill, New York, 1969.
4. Epstein, I., From Opium War to Liberation, pp. 4-9, New World Press, Peking, 1956 and a personal communication November 4, 1975.
5. Fairbanks, J., The United States and China, Viking, New York, 1922.

6. Dennett, T., Americans in Eastern Asia, p. 167, Macmillan, New York, 1922.
7. Franke, W., A Century of Chinese Revolution 1851-1949, pp. 33-35, Basil Blackwell, Oxford, 1970.
8. Kawakami, K., "Millions of Orientals Under the Yoke of Opium," New York Times Current History, 21: 583, 1924.
9. Fort, J., Giver of Delight or Liberator of Sin: Drug Use and Education in Asia, Bulletin on Narcotics, 17: 1-11, 1965.
10. Bermann, G. "Mental Health in China." Psychiatry in the Communist World, Ed. Kiev, A., Science House, New York, 1968.
11. Hsu, F., Americans and Chinese, p. 62, Doubleday, New York, 1972.

12. Cerny, J., "Chinese Psychiatry," International Journal of Psychiatry, 1: 229-247, 1965.

13. Fitzgerald, C., "The Early Republic: Miu Kuo Period," p.30, in Republican China Nationalism War and the Rise of Communism, 1911-1949, Ed., Schurmann, F. & Schell, O., Random House, New York, 1967.

14. Adams, L., "China: The Historical Settings of Asia's Profitable Plague," In, McCoy, A., The Politics of Heroin in Southeast Asia, Harper and Row, New York, 1972.

15. Alley, R., "Opium and Imperialism - and the Cleanup of Sandan" China and Us, 3: 9, 12, 1973, U.S. China Peoples Friendship Association, New York.

16. Smedley, A., The Great Road, Monthly Review Press, New York, 1956.

17. Snow, E., Red Star Over China, Random House, New York, 1938.

18. Beldon, J., China Shakes the World, p. 107, Monthly Review Press, New York, 194.

19. Kolman, I., personal communication April 7, 1973, from a medical doctor who was in china 1944-1946.

20. Stanley, M., "Two Experiences of an American Public Health Nurse in China a Quarter of Century Apart." American Journal of Public Health, 63: 111-116, 1973 and a personal communication April 16, 1971.

21. Chou, E., GAC Order on the Banning of Opium and Narcotics, "New China News Agency in Current Background, No. 188, June 30, 1952, American Consulate General, Hong Kong.

22. Canton Registers Opium Addict Peddlars, Canton Nan Fang Jih Pao, Jan. 24, 1951, In Survey of China Mainland Press, No. 55 Jan 24, 1951, American Consulate General, Hong Kong.

23. "The Situation Relating to Opium and Narcotics Suppression in Canton Nan Fang Jih Pao, June 3, 1952, Current Background, No. 188, June 30, 1952, American Consulate General, Hong Kong.

24. Shao-wen, C. "Develop with Fanfare, the Anti-opium and Anti-narcotics Movement", Hanchow Ch'and Ching Jih Pao, June 4, 1952 in Current Background, No. 188, June 30, 1952, American Consulate General, Hong Kong.

25. Survey of China Mainland Press, No. 542, March 31, 1953, American Consulate General, Hong Kong.

26. Horn, J., Away with All Pests, Monthly Review Press, New York, 1969.

27. Horn, J., Talk at the National Meeting of the Medical Committee for Human Rights, Philadelphia, April, 1970.

28. Williams, R., Personal Communication, March 13, 1971.

29. Snow, E., Red China Today, Vintage Books, New York, 1970.

30. Topping, S., "Rural China: Change and Continuity," p. 154, in Report from Red China, Durdin, T., Reston, J., and Topping, S., Quadrangle, New York, 1971.

31. Dimond, E., "Medical Education and Care in People's Republic of China," Journal of American Medical Association, 218: 1552-1557, 1971.

32. Sidel, V., Personal Communication, Dec. 14, 1971.
33. Seldon, M., Personal Communication, Dec. 4, 1972.
34. "A Vast Nation's Quest," Health Rights News, Dec. 1972.
35. "How China Got Rid of Drug Addiction," China and Us, 3: 1, 10, 1974, U.S. China Peoples Friendship Association, New York.
36. The Illicit Narcotic Trade of the Chinese Communists, Asian People's Anti-Communist League, Republic of China, 1957.
37. Deverall, R., Mao Tse-Tung: Stop This Dirty Opium Business, p. 7, Toyoh Printing Co., Tokyo, 1954.
38. Letter from the U.S. Secretary of the Treasury to Senator Proxmire, May 11, 1967, Joint Economic Committee, 90th Congress p. 248, U.S. Government Printing Office, Washington, D.C., 1967.
39. Warner, J., Bureau of Narcotics and Dangerous Drugs, Strategic Intelligence Office, Personal Communication, April 20, 1971.
40. Teltsch, K., "Traffic in Opium Denied by Peking," New York Times, January 14, 1973.
41. "Preposterous Slander - Hsinhua Refutes TASS China Opium Trade Lie," Peking Review, 16: 16-17, 1973.
42. "Red China Exports 10,000 Tons of Narcotics in 1970," China Post, Taiwan, Jan. 21, 1971.
43. Chamberlain, J., "China's Role in Drugs," Detroit Free Press, Feb. 4, 1972.
44. Schmitz, J., "Our New Red Friends Called Pushers," Newsday, Oct. 17, 1972.
45. Li, V., Personal Communication, April 20, 1971.
46. Worth, R., Personal Communication, April 7, 1971.
47. Lau, M., Personal Communication, July 14, 1972.
48. Worth, R., "Health in Rural China: From Village to Commune," American Journal of Hygiene, 77: 228-239, 1963.
49. Service, J. Personal Communication, April 18, 1971.
50. Personal Communication from a physician, Dec. 1, 1971.
51. Myrdal, J., Report from a Chinese Village, New American Library, New York, 1965.
52. Hinton, W., Fanshen, Random House, 1966.
53. Vogel, E., Canton Under Communism, Harper, New York, 1969.
54. "Opium Suppression Day in Canton," Current Background, June 21, 1951, American Consulate General, Hong Kong.
55. Great Achievements in Opium Suppression During the Past Year, New China News Agency, March 29, 1951, in Survey of China Mainland Press, No. 89, March 29, 1951, American Consulate General, Hong Kong.
56. "New Life for Canton's Opium Addicts," Canton Nan Fang Jih Pao, June 3, 1951 in Current Background, No. 86, June 21, 1951, American Consulate General, Hong Kong.
57. Rubenstein, A., "How China Got Rid of Opium," Monthly Review, pp. 58-63, Oct. 1973.
58. Stewart, I., "Hong Kong Chief for Drugs is Due," New York Times, June 26, 1972.
59. Wen, H. and Cheung, S. "Treatment of Drug Addiction by Acupuncture and Electrical Stimulation," American Journal of Acupuncture, 1: 71-75, 1973.

60. Pop-Hennessy, J., <u>Half-Crown Colony</u>, p. 36, Little Brown, Boston, 1969.
61. Personal Communication from a resident of Taiwan, May 10, 1972.
62. Margulies, M., "China Has No Drug Problem - Why?" <u>Parade</u>, Oct. 15, 1972.
63. "China's Stand on Narcotic Drugs," Peking Review, 16: 18-19, 1973.
64. Scott, P., "Air America: Flying the U.S. into Laos," pp. 301-321, in <u>Laos: War and Revolution</u>, Ed., Adams, N. and McCoy, A., Harper and Row, New York, 1970.
65. Feingold, D., "Opium and Politics in Laos," pp. 322-339, in <u>Laos: War and Revolution</u>, Ed., Adams, N. and McCoy, A., Harper and Row, New York, 1970.
66. Woolacott, M., "The Thai Key to the Drug Traffic," <u>San Francisco Sunday Examiner and Chronicle</u>, Feb. 29, 1976.
67. Ginsberg, A., "The CIA and Air Opium," <u>NOLA Express</u>, Dec. 11-24, 1970.
68. Browning, F. and Garrett, B., "The New Opium War," <u>Ramparts</u>, 9: 32-39, 1971.
69. Hoyt, C., "Allies Push GI Drugs, Official Says," <u>Detroit News</u>, June 11, 1971.
70. Ronk, D. "Heroin Rerouted through Laos," <u>Detroit News</u>, June 11, 1971.
71. Childs, M., "GI Drug Scandal a Threat to Thieu," <u>Detroit Free Press</u>, July 19, 1971.
72. "Guards Wink at Opium Flow," <u>The Detroit Free Press</u>, July 26, 1971.
73. Kamm, H., "Asians Doubt the U.S. Can Halt Heroin Flow," <u>New York Times</u>, August, 1971.
74. Hersh, S., "Asian Drug Flow Greater than Realized," <u>New York Times</u>, July 28, 1972.
75. Spielman, H., "The Southeast Asia Connection," <u>New York Times</u>, May 17, 1972.
76. "Mitchel Aim: Oust Drug-Linked Agents," <u>Detroit News</u>, July 8, 1971.
77. Walinsky, A., "The Knapp Connection," <u>Village Voice</u>, March 1, 1973.
78. Lessard, S., "Busting Our Mental Blocks on Drugs and Crime," <u>The Washington Monthly</u>, 3: 6-18, 1971.
79. Maas, P., <u>The Valachi Papers</u>, Bantam Books, New York, 1968.
80. McCoy, A., <u>The Politics of Heroin in Southeast Asia</u>, Harper and Row, New York.
81. "Who Benefits from the American Drug Culture?" <u>Health/PAC Bulletin,</u> Health Policy Advisory Center, New York, June, 1970.
82. "The Opium Trail Heroin and Imperialism," Committee of Concerned Asian Scholars, <u>New England Free Press</u>, Boston, 1971.
83. Lowinger, P., Council of Health Organizations Statement on Drug Use and Abuse, <u>World Journal of Psychosynthesis</u>, 3: 37-38, 1971.

ADDICTION IN GREAT BRITAIN: A CLOSER LOOK

Ernest Drucker

Department of Social Medicine
Monteforiore Hospital and Medical Center
Bronx, New York

The British enjoy an excellent reputation in the area of drug abuse treatment. It is commonly held that their approach has been successful in that:
1. The number of addicts is small and stable.
2. There is an absence of anti-social behavior associated with addiction
3. There is no significant black market of illicit drugs.

If one takes these factors literally they suggest that the British have no drug problem -- at least not in the sense that we know it in the United States. More commonly, however, it is as-sumed that the British have successfully treated "the problem" of heroin addiction and that this success may be attributed largely to an approach based on the medically-supervised prescription of heroin in Drug Treatment Centers.

Professor Lindesmith pointed out in his remarks that if we are to learn from the experiences of others, it is crucial that we carefully evaluate those experiences and their applicability to our own situation. Thus two questions may be asked about the British experience: 1) How comparable was the British drug problem to our own? and 2) How successful was their intervention?

The Population of Addicts

In 1975 there were fewer than 3000 known addicts in Great Britain. Given a total population of 50 million (about 25% that of the U.S.) this means that the rate of addiction in Great Britain is no more than 5% of even the most conservative U.S. estimates. (There are probably 5-10 times more drug workers in the U.S. than there are addicts in Great Britain.) Thus the total number and the prevalence are indeed small. Changes in the incidence over time, however, are critical to interpreting the significance of this statistic. In 1960 there were only 437 known addicts in all of Great Britain, whose total population is more or less constant.

1375

Rapid growth took place in the late 1960's -- the number quadru-
pling in the 5 year period 1964-69. This is referred to as the
heroin "epidemic" or, by the more modest "the minidemic." It is
generally attributed to excessive prescribing on the part of a few
misguided or venal London physicians.

The original addict population of the 1950's (which had been
stable in number for almost 20 years) had a distinct composition.
They were, for the most part, middle-class and middle-aged; a majority were women; and, most importantly, an overwhelming majority
(70-75%) were "therapeutic" addicts, i.e., they became addicted in
the course of medical treatment. About 20% of this group were
themselves health professionals: doctors, dentists, nurses and
pharmacists. Altogether, less than 10% of the entire addict population of Great Britain were classified as "other-than-therapeutic"
heroin addicts.

By 1972 this picture had changed dramatically both in terms of
quantity and quality. The mean age had dropped into the 20's, the
cohort was predominantly male (70-80%), the socio-economic status
was lower than average, and, most significantly, fewer than 10% of
the new cases were "therapeutic" addicts -- i.e., over 90% were
addicted in the course of self-administered use (i.e., abuse). In
the twelve year period 1960-1972 the British "addict" had turned
into a "junkie."

As the population changed so did the milieu in which drug addiction (the "scene") and drug treatment (the "program") took
place. In general, British society is more well-balanced and orderly than our own, but recently the drug scene has begun to differentiate itself from this pattern. Drug-related crimes have risen
steadily and a majority of these relate to the sale and/or possession of illicit narcotics (i.e., heroin, methadone, cocaine). Keeping in mind the small number of British addicts this is a rather
high ratio of drug-related crimes to the population "at risk", primarily the 3000 addicts.* For the last few years this ratio has
been about 1:1 -- i.e., on the average, each British addict is arrested each year. The former medical officer of Brixton Prison in
London reports that in the years 1968-1970 about 750 addicts were
incarcerated, i.e., 75% of the entire adult addict population of
Great Britain. Events reminiscent of the American drug scene have
become more common -- e.g., violence, extortion, a street drug
scene, even reports of corruption in the London narcotics squad.
The relation of violent crimes to drug abuse is not easily
identified in the British statistics.** Thus, while the total im-

---

*Confirming the impression that for the British addict some crim-
 nal involvement is the norm, rather than the exception.
**"Drug-related crimes" were not, at least until very recently, a
  category which the British payed any particular attention to
  since, until very recently, they rarely happened.

pact on the society of criminal activity associated with addiction
may be quantitatively less than the U.S. (i.e., it has less "so-
cial-nuisance" value), there is no indication that the individual
British addict has any better relationship with the law than does
his American counterpart.

Increasingly British addicts find themselves in an adversary
relationship not only with the law but also with the community and
with each other. Most surprising, however, is the fact that today
many British addicts also find themselves pitted against the very
programs that were designed to "cure" them.

The Treatment Scene

In the last 10 years the nature of the British addiction
treatment system has changed considerably. From a group of independent general practitioners treating individual patients there
has evolved a program, i.e., the clinics. The addict has been
placed under the care of the consulting psychiatrist -- often a
specialist in drug abuse. The consulting psychiatrist in turn has
been placed in a clinic and that clinic has been placed in a hospital -- often a teaching hospital. By his removal from the care
of a GP, the British addict has also been removed from the coverage
provided by the assumptions and values of the doctor-patient relationship. This represents a dramatic shift in status and implies
new rules of behavior for him and his condition -- new explanations
and expectations of his illness and a new concept of him as a person. Whereas formerly he had been a patient who was addicted to
drugs (a concept which allowed him to retain his membership in the
society of other patients with other conditions) he is now seen
through a related but very different prism -- that of the "disease
model" of addiction.* In the U.S. the "disease" model replaced the
"criminal" model and this provided a somewhat more humane albeit
more pernicious perspective. In Great Britain, however, the "disease" model replaced the addicted individual himself and (as be-
fits the status of a displaced person) his entitlement to treatment
as a "patient" under the National Health Service -- i.e., through
the physician of his choice.

The British physician and medical educator Marinker has noted
that with increased specialization in medicine the concept of the
doctor-patient relationship has been supplanted by one in which
the "patient" is an inconvenience; where once the disease was a
phenomenon of the patient, now the patient is a phenomenon of the

---

*See Drucker and Sidel for a critique of the disease model of ad-
 diction from a social policy perspective; or consider the appropriateness of the "disease" model of addiction in light of the
 fact that addicts pursue their disease with more industry than
 most of us devote to maintaining our health.

disease. In Great Britain today (as in most American programs) treatment is available only for the "disease", not for the "patient."

History will show that the career of the addict as patient (as opposed to the earlier addict as criminal or the current addict as disease) was short-lived -- perhaps 50 years in Great Britain.* In his rapid transit through that phase in which he was viewed as a "patient" and not as a "disease" the British addict did not distinguish himself. He progressed no better and acheived a cure no more often than those afflicted with other chronic, recurrent conditions. However, and this is the main point, he did no worse. If the general practitioners of that era (who were a diverse lot) occasionally misdiagnosed and mistreated some addicts in ways that led them further into their already well-established state, he did so no more often with these patients than he did with his others. To the degree that a GP was successfully able to cope with the chronic conditions and complex diagnostic demands of his general practice, so would he fare with the addict/patient. The earlier and more genuine stability of the addict population in Great Britain (1910-1960) strongly suggest that someone was doing something right, at least for 50 years.

But what of the new system? I have already indicated that the population of addicts has changed substantially over a 12-year period. Certainly some changes in the approach to addiction would be appropriate. Indeed there are those programs in Great Britain which commit themselves to the innovative and person-oriented treatment of addicts. But such programs are not in the majority. The more common case is the clinic associated with a teaching hospital and staffed by registrars in psychiatry (residents) under the supervision of a consultant -- usually a psychiatrist specializing in the "addiction field" or, recently, "the addictive diseases." These clinics have been described elsewhere and they seem to attract endless attention from American drug experts who visit England.

What gets considerably less scrutiny are the data they produce. The following discussion is based solely on that data.

Three principal trends can be discerned from the statistics of the British clinic system:

1. A shift from heroin to methadone for the maintenance of addicts

---

*The comparable figure for the U.S. is about 15 years counting current (but increasingly rare) patient-care models and the brief American flirtation with morphine maintenance in the 1920's (soon cut short by the Harrison Act and the persecution of those physicians who attempted to treat addicts as patients.)

2. A shift from injectable to oral administration of drugs.
3. A shift from high doses to low doses.

These trends reflect a policy which its adherents believe will move most British addicts towards a "cure" -- i.e., total abstinence. If this is interpreted to mean abstinence from drugs provided by clinics, the policy is a clear success. Of the 1960 group of addicts, 75% were on heroin, morphine or cocaine -- generally receiving large doses. By 1972, following a five-fold increase in the number of addicts, about 65% were on methadone -- the majority of these on methadone alone. Only between 10-15% are on heroin alone and most of these are the surviving members of the old 1960's group. New patients get little or no heroin and, usually, only small oral doses of methadone. Today the average dose of methadone in the British system is under 35 mg/day. (In the Dole-Nyswander model this is considered a marginal maintenance dose).

Many young addicts, hooked on street drugs, don't even bother going to the clinics anymore knowing that it won't meet their needs. The existence of such addicts is, however, not officially recognized despite the assertion that 95-97% of British addicts are "known" to the Home Office. The validity and reliability of the British registry is based on arrests and medical examiners' reports. It was pointed out that the British criminal data are not attuned to analyzing drug-related crimes (other than possession itself). Likewise, in keeping with the statistically "rare" nature of addiction in Britain many medical examiners are inexperienced in the detection of physical signs of addiction (pre or post-mortem). Thus, there is reason to suspect that the oft-cited reliability of the Home Office body count of "known addicts" was more a function of the obliging character and stable life-style of the older group of addicts than of especially good surveillance.*

The clinics themselves and the Department of Health and Social Security keep detailed statistics on drugs prescribed, dosages and patient outcomes. If these are examined from a perspective based on treatment of the "disease" of addiction they indicate some slow progress. That "progress" is based largely on the reduction of doses and termination (or discouragement) of patients, i.e., it represents the implementation of clinic policy. In effect the same clinic system which in 10 years enrolled several thousand

---

*In all liklihood there was a rush to the newly-opened clinics based on high expectations which only later proved to be unfounded. But it was therefore possible quite early in the program to identify and "tag" almost all addicts. As these addicts drop out of the programs they are removed from the "active patient" list but (given the cumulative nature of the statistics) remain "known."

addicts and placed them on maintenance has declared that condition a disease and has discovered a cure -- namely the discontinuation of its own drugs and the termination of its own patients.*

Since the clinics and the disease are progressing well we may inquire after the patients. Here we see a somewhat different picture:

1) British addicts (including clinic patients) abuse illicit drugs regularly and 90-95% "supplement" their ever-shrinking clinic doses with street drugs -- often amphetamines and barbiturates (each more destructive than the opiates they replace).

2) British addicts (including clinic patients) are subject to a high rate of medical illnesses associated with addiction. Despite prescriptions for sterile needles and syringes most British addicts share needles regularly and often shoot-up in public toilets using bowl water for the cooker. One study showed that 40% had hepatitis (probably a low estimate) and 46% had severe abcesses (often associated with shooting crushed barbiturate tablets).

3) British addicts (including clinic patients) rarely are "cured". Despite the tug of war between the addict and the clinic doctor, only about 10% successfully de-toxify and stay drug-free. The remainder continue sporadically on (to them) unsatisfactory doses of the wrong drug and "supplement" with street drugs.

4) British addicts (including clinic patients) suffer a fearful death rate -- double or triple that of U.S. addicts both in programs and on the street. One study in Great Britain found a mortality rate of 6% -- 28 times that of a non-addict control group.

From even this brief over-view it should be apparent that the contemporary British addict is no better off than his American counterpart. In fact, the evidence suggests he does a bit worse. While the British can claim some success for the control of addiction as a "disease" there is little to envy in their results with the patients themselves. Caught between the old addicts and the new junkies the British have opted for a model which may in the short-run limit the spread of disease but offers little hope for its victims.

_____

*This scenario bears a striking resemblance to the changes taking place in the methadone treatment programs in the U.S. which, in the face of arbitrarily-set and often punitive regulations, are driving patients back to the street in droves (e.g., in N.Y.C. there are about twice as many former methadone patients as active ones).

If we can learn anything from the British experience (it seems they haven't learned very well from ours) it is that the "model" matters. Medical models which do not benefit patients are dangerous -- both to the patients and to the community at large. While the British approach (i.e., their application of the prevalent "disease" model) may make some claim to effectiveness in restricting the spread of addiction* it can take little pride in how it deals with individual patients, and it is this failure which ultimately casts doubt upon the value of both the model and the British drug program itself.

---

*This claim cannot be properly evaluated since no other method has ever been tried on a systematic basis with the current British addict, there is therefore no way to differentiate the possible effects of the program from the effects of time itself and other social variations -- i.e., the British addiction scene changed once and it could change again.

Bibliography

1. Heroin Addiction in Britain by Horace Freeland Judson, Vintage Books, 1974.

2. Heroin and Behavior by G.V. Stimson, Halstead (Wiley), 1973.

3. Narcotics Addiction and Control in Great Britain by Edgar May in Dealing With Drug Abuse, Praeger, 1972.

4. Licit and Illicit Drugs by Edward Brecher, Little, Brown, 1972.

A HOLISTIC PERSPECTIVE IN VIEWING
DRUG TAKING BEHAVIOR (abridged)

Edward C. Farley, M.S.W.

Philadelphia Psychiatric Center
Philadelphia, Pennsylvania

An integrated conceptual model of drug taking behavior is presented which was developed from a selected review of the substance
abuse literature and the author's personal experiences. There are
ten conceptual cells that will be filled with selected Initiating
and Sustaining Influences that move people to use psychoactive substances from three analytical perspectives: The Individual, The
Primary Group and The Cultural.

For any behavioral event there are multiple determinants that
vary from person to person. Yet, drug taking behavior is even more
complex and dynamic than ordinary behavior as an examination of the
model's structure suggests. This model artificially isolates aspects of human behavior and social phenomena into separate analytical cells. Thus, any separate cell interpretations are meaningless
without relating it to its contextual whole.

Individual Perspective.

Cell 1: *Psychological Initiating Influences*. Literature re-
viewers have reported two principle psychological patterns that influence the genesis of drug use. The first pattern is basically
healthy curiosity and experimental zeal to experience new sensations. In fact, according to developmental and personality theories an openness to new experiences and a desire to test arbitrarily
set boundaries are elements of a creative and sound personality
structure.

Thus, a motivational impetus for initiating use of psychoactive substances may well spring from a psychological need, but
that need does not have to be a pathological one. On the other
hand, this is not to deny that there are individuals who initially
choose psychoactive substances as adaptive behavior to situations
that they feel that they cannot handle alone. This second psychological initiating pattern is seen as a form of a coping mechanism

where individuals seek drugs either to avoid or block what is considered by them to be problematic situations or negative psychic states.

Cell 2: *Psychological Sustaining Influences*. There are two divergent paths psychological feedback may take in promoting continued drug use. The first path may be characterized as positive reinforcement where the drug taking behavior is continued because it is working. That is to say, the ingested substance is more or less doing the job it is taken to do. The second psychological sustaining path may be characterized as negative reinforcement or entrapment. Here subjective fears of withdrawal illnesses in the curtailment of use or substance craving for repeated applications supercede the earlier positive reinforcement influences.

Cell 3: *Physiological Initiating Influences*. We are here proposing that the brain physiology of adolescents and young adults are at a developmentally critical "readiness" stage for non-materialistic stimulation which arouses behavior to seek out environmental stimulations that can alter consciousness. This hypothesis is based on the work of Piaget, Humanistic Psychology and Learning Theory concepts. Also, this age group does more drug experimentation than any other supports this contention.

Cell 4: *Physiological Sustaining Influences*. There are various levels of cellular and neurological accomodations to a substance's presence and thus different degrees of dependencies.

The human organism adapts gradually thus experimental dabbling will usually not produce a physiological dependence. However, when potent substances are habitually repeated, be it for Social, Recretional or Medicative reasons, there is evidence that various physiological adaptations take place. For instance, increased activity of drug metabolizing enzymes has been reported. Physiological adaptation may also occur in shifting the distribution pattern of these metabolizing enzymes so that a more efficient breakdown process can occur.

These adaptive activities can be viewed as analogous to software programming changes needed for the computer to process material more efficiently. Dependent on the substance used these modifications may lead to a biochemical immunization or tolerance where greater amounts of the substance are needed to produce the same level of effect. The user experiences varying degrees of psychological dependence due to the reinforced belief in the benefits of repeated usage.

In the final stage of dependency we see structural "hardware" (to continue the computer analogy) modifications taking place to accommodate the almost ever present drug presence. These modifications may be in the form of increased production of metabolizing enzymes or changes in the sensitivity of nerve cells. Or they may simply increase production of transmitter receptors for the specialized processing of the specific substance. These structural changes bring with them the dependency syndrome discussed earlier.

Primary Group Perspective.

Cell 5: *Family Group Initiating Influences*. The family is the most important socialization instrument a growing child has. There are numerous studies that show similar drug patterns between parents and their children. But even beyond role modeling of drug behavior is the more important learnings of parental styles of handling life's stress, dissappointments and even joys.

Cell 6: *Family Group Sustaining Influences*. When a child is suspected of drug use, parents usually react quite emotionally and without a proper knowledge or understanding. Often many youth then feel misunderstood, guilty for not measuring up to parental expectations, or just depressed. These feelings further alienate them from their families and may propel many a youthful drug dabbler into self-medicative use and abuse of mood altering substances.

Cell 7: *Peer Group Initiating Influences*. In our society the 14 to 25 age range has a great amount of stress due to the transitional nature of the roles they assume. Most are leaving the idealistic and somewhat sheltered world of the child role but are not yet ready, in society's eyes, for the responsibilities and demands of adulthood. They are bombarded by what is often conflicting role demands from their parents, teachers and friends. On top of this there are new internal sensations (sexual and psychic) that they must learn to cope with and understand. The peer group becomes cemented together by its shared developmental struggles and thus becomes an important social influence on individual behavior. Peer group influence has never been greater than at this age range. Due to the many role stresses, many youthful egos are in disequilibrium and the need for individual acceptance is very high. In many youth groups, drug use is an accepted norm and thus substantial group pressure is exerted on vulnerable individual members to conform.

Cell 8: *Peer Group Sustaining Influences*. Many studies report that acceptance and status is regulated by substance related activities in many peer groups. For instance, a group member who locates a new supply of grass receives social "strokes" from the group. Thus status and continued acceptance are interwoven into group sharing of drugs, turning on new friends and developing distribution schemes.

Cultural Perspective.

Cell 9 and Cell 10: *Societal Values and Norms That Initiate and Sustain Drug Taking Behavior*. The author has selected five

1384

major themes that are cultural in nature that move people to use
and abuse psychoactive substances. The first is the concept of
sociological ambivalence that Merton has developed. By this he
means there is ambivalence built into the structure of social
status and roles that produce stresses and strains. We can see
this by observing the contradictions in our present complex society.
Due to the rapidly changing values one is insecure in many social
situations and can easily become alienated from the society in
which we live. The second cultural factor is our society's
materialistic nature. Science is the religion of our age, but
science ignores any psychic development beyond rational reasoning.
For countless milenniums this area of exploration has been the
realm of various religions. They have nurtured spiritual psychic
growth and provided many altered consciousness states (awe, mystic
rapture, internal bliss, beatific vision, cosmic love, etc.).
Further, they have comforted the anxious and consoled the sorrowful
during troubled times. Many contemporary youth, especially those
involved with drugs, have not benefited from these time-honored
religious services and spiritual experiences. The third cultural
factor is the enormous amount of psychoactive substances that are
available in this country. The impact of the abundant varieties
of pills manufactured by the pharmaceutical companies which flood
the legal market and are often diverted into illicit distribution
channels cannot be overlooked. The fourth cultural factor is the
increased medicalization of the human condition that is taking
place in contemporary America. We are continually and aggressively exposed to licit drug propaganda that promotes its product's
use as an instant and painless solution to most human conditions,
real and imaginary.

One survey of general practitioner's offices and clinics
found that approximately 60% of the patients were there because
they were lonely, depressed, anxious, dissatisfied or unhappy with
life. The authors concluded that most of their troubles and unhappiness came from their inability to measure up to the prevalent
social prescriptions concerning what one ought to get out of life.

The last cultural factor that must be taken up is the negative
effects of legal prohibitions on illicit substances and the subsequent criminalization of their use. These laws should be re-
examined in light of their effect on the total drug using population. Their actual deterrence value and the criminalization effect they have on offenders also should be reconsidered.

Discussion.

It is hoped that this construct will aid in the understanding
of what is often bewildering and conflicting research information
concerning drug use in America and will sensitize decision makers
and researchers to the various factors that influence drug taking

behavior, thus leading to more effective and wider defined social intervention programs. For local practitioners working with prevention, the model may have utility as an educational tool for youth and parents groups as well as an aid in planning programs for schools and church groups.

Finally, there are the many clinicians working in America's ever growing drug rehabilitation industry. Here the model may be used for diagnostic, referral or therapeutic purposes with individual clients. For example, a client and clinician would be asked to rate the various influences effect on their past, present and future drug taking behavior. In addition to provoking client introspective and insights it may well plot the best treatment modality for that particular individual and generate important prognosis data. Referrals could then be guided by these assessments and predictions of successful outcomes eventually developed from careful monitoring the treatments progress.

The above are some suggested field applications of the conceptual model. Its real utility will be in provoking a rethinking of the broader interlocking dimensions of drug taking behavior.

References upon request.

PSYCHOLOGICAL REACTIONS TO THE VIETNAM WITHDRAWAL

Clarita E. Herrera, M.D., and Martin S. Kesselman, M.D.

Psychiatry Service, NY VA Hospital and
Department of Psychiatry
New York University Medical School

Shortly after the Vietnam withdrawal several of us associated with VA Drug Abuse programs discovered we had been sharing a similar impression; that during the period of time that the withdrawal was being implemented and in the succeeding few weeks there had been an unusual increase in the number of serious behavioral outbursts at the New York VA., M.M.T.P. for example dirty urines increased from 10% to 30% during the month of March 1975, the rise being mostly related to abuse of barbiturates and amphetamines. It is our impression that similar observations were made elsewhere but further study was confined to our own institution. It seemed interesting to us to evaluate the validity of these impressions, and the light they might shed on some of the factors contributing to the initiation and maintenance of drug abuse in our population. For many addicted veterans, the experience of war and the need to withstand the emotions that followed in its wake forms a prominent part of the way they explain their addiction to themselves. Psychiatric sequelae of the war experience have been described by Stenger [1] and Lifton [2] among others. However, the relations of these symptoms to premilitary personality disorders remain probematic. Post-discharge drug abuse is a persistent or recurring problem in only a relatively small fraction of veterans compared to the number of drug users in Vietnam [4]. If veterans in our program were in fact attempting to work through the affects aroused by their wartime experience, their reaction to the United States withdrawal might reasonably be expected to shed some light on the extent to which they remained preoccupied with these events.

Methodology

These considerations led to formulation of a crisis research project. Members of the drug treatment staff met together with the two co-authors to formulate an appropriate questionnaire. The questionnaire (Fig. 1) was designed by members of the Mental Health and Behavioral Sciences Council. Personal interviews were conducted over a two (2) week period by the staff of the program, a multidisciplinary team consisting of a nurse, psychologist, drug reha-

habilitation counselor, social worker and physician. The questionnaire was administered in a semi-structured format and answers
were recorded during the interview of immediately afterward bearing
in mind the respondent's feelings and thought, not the rater as the
focus of the interview. Interview time varied from 15 to 45
minutes. Table 1 summarized the statistics for the demographic
variables measured.

Results

All veterans approached agreed to participate in the study.
By contrast, several of the Drug Unit staff felt too emotionally
involved themselves to question patients about what they saw as
heavily charged issues. Contrary to these apprehensions, several
of the participant veterans expressed appreciation of the chance
to formulate their views more clearly and to express their feelings.

Overall no increase over the expected incidence of behavioral
reports or "dirty" urines occurred during this period of study.
However the veterans' responses demonstrated some qualitative
features which would appear to warrant comment:

1. The Vietnam veterans differed from both the older veterans
and those who did not serve in Vietnam. While the latter two
groups tended to see the U.S. withdrawal as a failure of national
policy, for the Vietnam veterans, almost to a man, this aspect was
unimportant. They focused instead on the failure of a relationship
between U.S. support and the Vietnamese people.

2. Not unexpectedly, the Vietnam veteran expressed a more
emotional response in which anger and depression were dominant
feelings: anger at having been "let down" by the Vietnamese people
and regret over time lost and the futility of the entire undertaking.

3. The theme of being "let down" was reflected in several
respects. The Vietnamese had let down the U.S., the V.A. had let
down the veterans, the country as a whole had let down the returning
veterans. There was a substantial feeling of resentment toward the
Vietnamese refugees.

4. In line with this pervasive sense of betrayal, there was
a commonly expressed concern for the women and children left behind
in Vietnam and among the refugees. This appeared to reflect identification with the victimized rather than guilt.

5. None of the veterans felt that the withdrawal had a
significantly changed or re-oriented their views of the role their
personal participation in the war played in their lives.

6. They did however perceive the influx of Vietnamese refugees as threatening their own future opportunities in the areas
of employment, housing, and benefits.

Discussion

The results failed to substantiate an enduring increase in behavioral disturbance related to veterans' reaction to the U.S. Vietnam withdrawal. While this casts considerable doubt on the basis for the initially observed increase in contaminated urines, the fact that the study could not be carried out sooner than a month after the observation which provoked it makes a conclusive interpretation of our results impossible. It is possible that there was an initial response but that it was dampened by the veterans fatalism on one hand and by the strong support provided by their participation in the drug program. Unfortunately, similar evidence is not available from street addicts. One cannot fail to read the protocols, particularly those of the Vietnam veterans, without a strong sense of sadness. These men appear to be expressing a profound sense of helplessness and fatalism toward both the past and future; their sense of personal betrayal and their sensitivity to the plight of the weak and helpless on all sides is quite affecting. They appear to stand apart from any of the major parties to the Vietnam action. Little overt guilt was expressed, rather a sense of shame was implied in many of the answers. For many of the respondents, this was reflected in a mild surprise that the U.S. withdrawal had been "so long in coming" or had occasioned so much interest on the part of the staff. The feeling that we should have stayed or have responded with more aggressive actions such, as bombing the North more vigorously was scarcely considered. One is reminded of Bowlly's[5] scheme of separation, protest and withdrawal. For many of these veterans, withdrawal, passivity and a helpless resignation appear to be at least a current phase of their response to the war.

TABLE 1

Interview Schedule

We are conducting a survey of the attitudes of our veterans toward
the recent events occurring in South Vietnam. Your participation
in this survey is completely voluntary. You are free to refuse
to answer any or all of the questions. We do feel that the information you can give us will assist the hospital staff in understanding the experiences of our veterans as they may be affected
by these type of political events. Any answers you give will be
held in strict confidence; and, of course, no information about
this survey will be included in your files.

   May I go ahead?

1. What is your impression of the events that have taken
  place in South Viet Nam during the past month?

2. How do you feel about these vents?

  Can you characterize your attitude as very strong,
  moderate, mild or indifferent? Favorable or unfavorable?

3. When you first heard of the news about the surrender of
  the South Viet Namese forces, what was your reaction?

  a. Intensity of reaction: intense, moderate, mild
    or indifferent.

  b. Has the news affected you in any other ways?
    Have you noticed any of the following reactions in
    yourself: depression or sadness, anger or bitterness,
    relief or a sense of gladness.

4. Did you serve in Viet Nam?

  Have your attitudes toward your military service in Viet
  Nam been changed or affected in any way by these recents
  events. If so, how?

5. Is there anything else you wish to add?

TABLE II

DEMOGRAPHIC CHARACTERISTICS OF VETERANS SURVEYED

TOTAL NO.   30

SEX: Male - 29   Female - 1

AGE: 25 - 45 years   Mean - 29 years

RACE: Black - 42%   White - 31%   SSSS - 27%

MILITARY DUTY: Vietnam - 82%   Korean - 6%   WW II - 12%

TREATMENT MODALITY:	DETOXIFICATION	MMTP	PADAT
			10%
	38%	52%	
DURATION OF TREATMENT	7 days	22 months	8 weeks
FULL OR PART TIME EMPLOYMENT	22%	47%	33%
EDUCATION OR SKILL DEVELOPMENT PROGRAM	-	28%	33%

Bibliography

1. Stenger, C. Newsletter for Res. in Ment. Health and Behav. Sci. 16:1-4, 1974.

2. Lifton, R.J. Home from the War. Simon and Schuster, 1973.

3. Borus, J.F. Arch. Gen. Psych. 30:554-557, 1974.

4. Robins, L. The Vietnam Drug User Returns; Special Action Office Monograph. U.S. Govt. Printing Office, Wash. D.C. 1973.

5. Bowlly, J. Attachment and Loss. Vol. 1, Basic Book, New York, 1969.

THE STUDY OF AN URBAN POLYDRUG LINKAGE SYSTEM

Mark Bencivengo
Jean C. Sifter
Barry I. Grossman
Richard Cohen

The Coordinating Office for Drug and Alcohol
Abuse Programs, Philadelphia, Pennsylvania

I.   INTRODUCTION

Within the past several years, a new item of terminology has
been added to the drug abuse lexicon. "Polydrug" and the "polydrug
abuser" have recently come to be a focus of concern. The National
Commission on Marijuana and Drug Abuse referred to "America's hidden drug problem"; a reference to the polydrug abuser. Reporting
systems such as DAWN and CODAP indicated substantial numbers who
were using chemical substances other than an opiate in such a way
as to appear in official records. Incidence and prevalence studies
undertaken in several states and on a national level uncovered,
often through the method of self report, significant numbers who
used drugs with a frequency and duration and in quantities sufficient to cause alarm. Further evidence documenting the polydrug
phenomenon came from school administrators, especially in those
schools where primary prevention activities were in place and project staff had attained rapport with groups of students.

The federal response to this accumulating evidence was to fund
a number of projects aimed at drug abusers whose primary drug of
abuse was not heroin or alcohol. Initially the effort was directed
at collecting information and investigating hypotheses. Attempts
were made to establish typologies of polydrug abusers (Wesson et
al, 1975), to describe their characteristics (Kirby and Berry,
1975), and to suggest effective modes of treatment (Hirsch and Imhof, 1975; Marcus, 1975). The literature on the polydrug abuser,
while not yet as extensive as that referring to the abuser of
heroin or alcohol, is growing. What it does point out, is that
due attention should be given to those individuals whose drug of
choice is not heroin, but another chemical substance.

II. A FIRST RESPONSE

The Philadelphia response to drug abuse among adolescents and polydrug abuse in particular has resulted in the establishment of several programs and approaches. In 1972 an LEAA funded court program, Juvenile Drug Identification and Referral Service (JDIRS) was implemented. The purpose of JDIRS was twofold. First, as a research project it was to document the types and extent of drug use among arrested juveniles being held in detention or appearing for hearings. Secondly, the JDIRS was to perform social service screening for these court involved young people and refer those individuals who were in need on to appropriate treatment at drug programs, mental health centers, special schools, etc. The first part was a success, but the second part was not. The main reason for the lack of success in the second part was that there was no organization behind the attempts to forge linkages with treatment programs.

Prior to the closing of JDIRS and on the basis of accumulating evidence, the Coordinating Office for Drug and Alcohol Abuse Programs (CODAAP) initiated, with funds from the Governor's Council on Drug and Alcohol Abuse, a program targeted for the youthful drug abuser. This program was to offer inpatient detoxification services for barbiturate dependent persons. During the client's stay, the program would attempt to motivate the individual to accept extended outpatient treatment. The main problem which led to closing this program was its failure to adequately develop relationships with referal sources. The agency did send letters to schools and the courts and also to community leaders. However, this first attempt to communication was never adequately followed up. By mid 1974, then, two programs which targeted the adolescent drug abuser had been terminated. They had in common the failure to establish the linkages necessary to assure an orderly movement of clients through the system.

III. A SECOND RESPONSE

Approximately two years after the ADAPT and JDIRS experiences, an adolescent polydrug program was conceived that aimed to avoid repeating the mistakes that helped cause the downfall of the prior programs; namely, the lack of an adequate client referral mechanism. Some of the same staff who were involved in both the ADAPT and JDIRS efforts now joined forces to plan and implement the Multi-Agency Adolescent Polydrug Program (MAAPP). It was hoped that this program would finally be able to establish an effective referral linkage system thereby narrowing the treatment gaps for the adolescent polydrug user.

A. The Plan

The plan was to utilize five service providing agencies and one linkage agency whose sole responsibility would be the coordination of services and the actual formation of the linkage system. CODAAP, the agency applying for the grant would have the responsibility for the administrative coordinating, monitoring and evaluation of the linkage and treatment programs.

The target population was chosen: adolescent polydrug users. Young people, ages 12-18 were to be the group served. Five treatment agencies were chosen to provide services for the adolescent and his or her total needs, including but not limited to substance abuse. All agencies were to provide outpatient service at minimum but inpatient and medical services were to be available to all.

B. The Linkage Agency

The linkage agency's functions were:
1) To identify those youth in the schools, criminal justice system and community who are abusing polydrugs;
2) To refer adolescents to the appropriate treatment facilities;
3) To function as a liaison between the School District, the Criminal Justice System, various community agencies, mainly the Crisis Intervention Network, and the five component treatment facilities of the MAAPP.

C. The Five Treatment Agencies

Perhaps one of the greatest problems and a problem that is yet to be completely overcome is the linkage agency's lack of ability to gain the full trust and acceptance of the five treatment agencies. The concept of "liaison" or "linkage" is a difficult one to understand for agencies accustomed to working rather independently of one another. Philadelphia is a city of neighborhoods, and many treatment agencies either have origins in the community or take on the ethnic pride and identity of the community in which they are located. The linkage agency realized this and developed the policy of using geographical areas of residence as the primary basis for deciding upon agency placement for each client. After delivering most referrals to the treatment agencies doorsteps, regularly visiting and calling agency staff, and paving the way for staff access to the schools, a level of cooperation has been reached.

D. Funding Agency Coordination

CODAAP, functioning in its monitoring and coordinating capacity, has held bi-monthly meetings with the counselors from all six agencies. These meetings have progressed from getting-to-know-you stage on to staff training seminars in which inter-agency competition and suspicions surfaced. Finally, after seven months the 25 counselors of six different agencies have united to the point where they are beginning to share information, work with one another and are now proposing the creation of the "MAAPP Forum" in which the six agency Directors will be asked to attend.

IV. RESULTS

After much diligent effort on the part of the linkage agency, the five treatment agencies, and the funding agency, adequate slot utilization was reached by program month eight. The client admission and discharge forms of the Uniform Data Collection System (UDCS) designed by the Pennsylvania Governor's Council on Drug and Alcohol Abuse were chosen as the primary data collection instruments. The first 217 admissions to the MAAPP were scrutinized and compared to 2,612 new admissions to 53 CODAAP administered drug programs in the city of Philadelphia for the month of January 1976.

The primary drugs of abuse for the UDCS general population new admissions are quite different from those used by the MAAPP admissions. Whereas heroin is the primary drug for the general population, MAAPP clients tend to use marijuana as their primary drug. Polydrug clients are also inclined to use more amphetamines, barbiturates, sedatives, hallucinogens and inhalants than the average general admission. The only drug the two groups use somewhat comparably is alcohol. Results also indicated that the polydrug clients tend to use more drugs than the general drug program admission. While 10% of the general admissions use three or more drugs, 40% of the polydrug clients stated that they use three or more drugs.

Demographically, more of the polydrug (MAAPP) admissions are male (63%) as opposed to female (37%). Almost half (47%) are black, 38% are white and 15% are Puerto Rican. The major referral sources for the MAAPP are the schools. Many clients have also been enrolled as referrals from Philadelphia youth detention facilities and from Probation Officers at the Family Court. The age range is 8-26 with the average age being 16 years old. Most MAAPP clients are enrolled in school (85.5%). Almost one-third (29%) of them have been arrested at one time or another.

V. CONCLUSION

The first nine months of this project have been most instructive and prompted several recommendations. Since few of the adolescents currently in treatment exhibit physical deterioration or legal pressure to enter treatment, they are less likely than heroin abusers to seek treatment of their own accord. Therefore, a case finding mechanism strongly integrated into the project is essential. The agency or agencies participating in the case finding function must be prepared to do the groundwork necessary to establish relationships with referral sources which will provide access to clients. Another asset is a knowledge of the city in which the program is being established and appreciation of its community structure. Philadelphia, for example, is a mosaic of neighborhoods. In some communities boundaries are clearly recognized. Gang activity is a chronic problem and the turf concept is strongly held and respected. This has resulted in hazzardous travel for adolescents who venture out of their neighborhoods. Referral agencies must be sensitive to this phenomenon. Communication among program components is also important. This particular program has profited from the time spent bringing everyone together. Throughout this whole effort, the role of the linkage agency cannot be overestimated. It was the attempt at a liaison function which set this project apart from less successful past efforts.

In the future we expect this function will continue to be important. The existing network will continue to be improved. The end result, we expect, will be a progressive yet comprehensive polydrug system which will be accessible to clients from all areas of the city and from all social levels and which will have the ability to respond to the full range of treatment demands encountered. It is projected that any system growth will continue to focus on the important effects of linkages. Certainly this has been a key aspect of the successful treatment of adolescent substance abusers in Philadelphia. It has been difficult yet important lesson.

REFERENCES

1. Drug Use in America: Problems in Perspective. Second Report of the National Commission on Marijuana and Drug Abuse. Washington D.C.; U.S. Government Printing Office, 1973.
2. D.R. Wesson, D.E. Smith and S.E. Lerner, J. Psychedelic Drugs, 7 April-June: 121-134 (1975).
3. M.W. Kirby and G.J. Berry, J. Psychedelic Drugs, 7 April-June: 161-167 (1975).
4. R. Hirsch and J.E. Imhof, J. Psychedelic Drugs, 7 April-June: 181-185 (1975)
5. J.B. Marcus, J. Psychedelic Drugs, 7 April-June: 169-179 (1975).

BELIEVABILITY OF THE MEDIA AS SOURCES OF INFORMATION ON DRUGS

Richard Dembo, Michael Miran, Dean V. Babst and James Schmeidler

Bureau of Social Science Research
New York State Office of Drug Abuse Services
2 World Trade Center
New York, New York 10047

Two related themes dominate the research literature concerning media credibility. There is, first, the growing tradition of work focusing on the relationship of demographic and attitudinal factors to certain information and content formats[1,2,3,4]. A second line of work compares the various media in order to assess their believability when they are pitted against one another[5,6,7,8,9].

While offering insight into the variables that are associated with people's receptivity to the influence of the media, research in both areas has been limited methodologically. Both the relationship and credibility comparison studies have often neglected to include the content of the media in their analysis. In the absence of explicit control for content, the findings of media credibility research gloss over some of the important interactions accounting for individuals' incorporation of their media experiences. In addition, few inquiries have sought to compare the credibility of the media with other relevant information sources.

Information on drugs would appear to be a useful area in which to examine the perceived believability of diverse sources--including the mass media. However, the research that has been completed has, generally, reflected a lack of awareness of mass communication theory. Some important recent work [10,11,12] has grouped the various media into one category, in spite of the fact that drug educators have placed differential stress on the various media. Pamphlets, in particular, have been heavily distributed in recent years.

The present study sought to avoid the methodological problems encountered in previous media credibility research by: (1) examining the believability of various sources of information on drugs, including the several mass media, among junior and senior high school students and (2) studying the differential credence imputed to clusters of the media probed (television, radio, newspaper/magazines and pamphlets) by youths claiming varying substance use behavior.

METHOD

Following approval of the school board of a metropolitan New York City suburban community, a questionnaire was administered to junior and senior high school students (N=682) in the Spring 1974. In addition to gathering demographic and drug use data, the instrument probed, among other things, the perceived believability of a wide range of sources of information on drugs.

Few refusals to participate in the study were encountered. With the exception of the twelfth grade, where 23% of the youngsters (15 of 65) declined to cooperate, all grades from 7 to 12 had completion rates at or near 100%. Due to their involvement in a community volunteer program that was not related to drug use, a number of 12th grade students were not available at the time the survey was conducted.

The high response rate was facilitated by efforts to ensure confidentiality. Students were requested not to put their names on the forms. Sealing labels were provided to secure their answers from scrutiny by persons who were not part of the research team.

Demographic analysis confirmed the near equal representation of boys and girls in the study, and indicated their intact home situations, with 86% of the youths claiming to live with both their parents. Socio-economically, the sample was upper-middle class, with 48% of the pupils' fathers and 39% of their mothers having graduated from college or attended professional or graduate school.

There was little stated use of depressants, L.S.D. or similar substances, narcotics, solvents or stimulants. On the other hand, a majority of the youngsters (66%) indicated they had used alcohol, and 29% marijuana, during the six months prior to the survey. In addition, 21% noted they used a substance (except tobacco) and alcohol so both affected them at the same time and ten percent said they took a substance (except tobacco and alcohol) when another was still having its effects.

RESULTS

In order to learn how the students regard various sources of drug information, they were asked to rate the eighteen sources listed in Table I as "mostly believable" or "mostly not believable." Overall, the mass media were judged to be less believable sources of information on drugs than interpersonal sources. The results indicate that a majority of the young people surveyed felt members of their immediate family, close friends, doctor, staff members of a drug program and a former drug user were most credible. Among the media, students judged television and radio to be least believable with respect to drug information. Interestingly, pamphlets, a specialized medium, appear to be more believable than mental health counselors and the non-media sources listed below this item in Table I.

It is reasonable to assume that media exposure is accounted
for in the data. There is no reason to doubt that the youths have
been exposed to television, radio and newspapers/magazines; and
school authorities have advised that pamphlets on drugs were distributed to students in the two schools that were researched.

Because not all students answered the believability questions,
an analysis was undertaken to learn if pupils with particular demographic, social status and/or substance use characteristics were
significantly more likely to not respond to these items. Study of
the data found only grade in school to be significantly, positively
associated to frequency of no response. Significantly, however,
small no answer differences were obtained among students with varying drug use behaviors, the major independent variables used in
the analysis. These results provided a statistical rationale for
further study of the data. A further analysis of responses to the
believability questions determined that the students replied to the
questions in a serious manner.

Clustering Of The Drug Information Sources

A varimax factor analysis, using the principal factor method,
was undertaken on the interrelationships of the eighteen items to
learn how they clustered together. Six varimax factors emerged.
Two factors are highly loaded on mass media sources; one refers to
friends; a fourth emphasizes medical/treatment personnel; another
is strongly weighted on representatives of various social institutions; and the sixth centers on family sources. (A table depic-
ting these results is available upon request from the senior
author.)

Table II shows the two mass media factors that emerged from
the factor analysis of the believability items. Note for the
first factor the high loadings of television, radio and newspapers/
magazines. Each of these media load on the factor at .63 or
greater. None of the other drug information sources exceeded the
.30 level. The second factor primarily relates to pamphlets,
which has a loading of .60. It has relatively little relationship
to all the other items; none of these load at greater than .31 (a
more detailed table of these factor loadings is available from the
senior author).

Relationship Between Media Source Believability And Substance Use

Examination of the believability of the media as sources of
information on drugs by youngsters with varying substance use behavior was accomplished by developing a drug involvement scale
consisting of the following elements: (1) ever used alcohol;
(2) ever used marijuana; (3) ever used a substance (except tobacco) and alcohol so both affected one at the same time (Poly1);
(4) ever took a substance (except tobacco and alcohol) when
another was still having its effects (Poly2).

Analysis found these items to form a Guttman scale, having a
coefficient of reproducibility of .968. A subject who answered
"yes" to any item was highly likely to answer "yes" to all lower
numbered items; a subject who answered "no" to any item was highly

likely to answer "no" to all higher numbered items. Although constructed on an ever used basis, the youths' scale scores were highly related to their use of alcohol and marijuana more than once a week during the six months prior to administration of the survey. In order to include as many cases as possible into the analysis, believability factor scores were computed for all 682 subjects, with the mean score being given to a non-response to any particular item. The relationships between substance use and the two media credibility factors clearly show that the more students are involved with substances, the less believable they find the media to be as sources of information on drugs (r=.117,P<.01 for Factor 1-television, radio, newspapers/magazines-; r=.123, P<.01 for Factor 2-pamphlets). (A table reporting these results is available from the senior author.)

There were mutual interrelationships among several demographic factors, drug use and the pamphlet believability factor scores (especially school grade). Accordingly, it was necessary to control for the influence of these demographic characteristics in the association between substance use and this medium's credibility. When this was done, the relationships still remained statistically significant.

TABLE I

BELIEVABILITY OF SOURCES OF DRUG INFORMATION (N=682)
(In Percent)

Source	Mostly Believable	Mostly Not Believable	Not Sure	No Answer*
Media				
Pamphlets	49.3	27.3	1.2	22.2
Newspapers/Magazines	35.6	38.1	2.8	23.5
Radio	30.9	43.4	2.2	23.5
Television	28.9	46.7	1.6	22.8
Non-Media				
Doctor	65.0	12.6	0.3	22.1
Former Drug User	63.1	13.8	1.3	21.8
Close Friend	60.0	18.8	1.0	20.2
Staff Member of Program	59.5	13.5	1.3	25.7
Someone in Immediate Family	52.7	28.4	0.6	18.3
Nurse	51.3	21.8	1.8	25.1
Mental Health Counselor	46.7	24.5	1.5	27.3
Teacher/School Staff	44.6	30.5	2.1	22.8
Police Officer	39.0	34.8	0.9	25.3
Social Worker	38.9	33.3	1.3	26.5
Other Relative	35.8	39.4	0.9	23.9
Lawyer	30.2	40.1	1.8	27.9
Clergyman	30.1	37.8	2.8	29.3
Neighbor	22.7	49.8	1.3	26.2

* 12% of the subjects did not answer any of the 18 believability questions.

TABLE II

LOADING OF THE MEDIA SOURCES OF DRUG INFORMATION ITEMS
ON THE TWO VARIMAX FACTORS
(Decimal points omitted)

Source	Factor 1 Television, Radio Newspapers/Magazines	Factor 2 Pamphlets
1. Television	87	00
2. Radio	79	09
3. Newspapers/Magazines	63	31
4. Pamphlets	30	60

REFERENCES

1. B. Westley and W. Severin, Some correlates of media credibility. Journalism Quart. 41: 325-35 (1964).
2. K. Mielke, Education level as a correlate of attitudes toward television. J. of Broadcasting 9: 313-21 (1965).
3. B. Greenberg, Media use and believability: Some multiple correlates. Journalism Quart. 43: 665-70, 732 (1966).
4. Roper Research Associates, Emerging Profiles of Television and Other Mass Media Public Attitudes 1959-1964. Television Information Office, New York, 1967.
5. J. Markham and J. Ranck, Use of the mass media by Penn State students. Journalism Quart. 36: 346-8 (1959).
6. R. Carter and B. Greenberg, Newspaper or television: Which do you believe? Journalism Quart. 42: 29-34 (1965).
7. R. Bishop, M. Boersma and J. Williams, Teenagers and mass media: Credibility canyon. Journalism Quart. 46: 597-99(1969).
8. W.G. Cushing and J.B. Lemert, Has television alerted students' news media preferences? Journalism Quart. 50: 138-51 (1973).
9. L. A. Baxter and J. R. Bittner, High school and college student perceptions of media credibility. Journalism Quart. 51: 517-20 (1974).
10. D. Fejer, R. G. Smart, P. C. Whitehead and L. LaForest, Sources of information about drugs among high school students. Public Opinion Quart. 35: 235-41 (1971).
11. R. G. Smart and D. Fejer, Credibility of sources of drug information for high school students. J. of Drug Issues 2:8-18(1972).
12. G. J. Hanneman, Communicating drug-abuse information among college students. Public Opinion Quart. 37: 171-91 (1973).

THE THOUGHT DISORDER OF THE CANNABIS SYNDROME

Alfred V. Miliman

Maryland Drug Abuse Research and Treatment
Foundation, Inc.
222 E. Redwood Street, Baltimore, Maryland

Data for this study was first obtained in 1965 at a private
psychiatric hospital. Thereafter, subjects were found at 2 high
schools, 2 universities, 2 community colleges, 2 prisons, drug programs, street demonstrations, other hospitals and even at social
events or other meetings where solid information could be obtained.
The person, patient, student or prisoner had no idea of our research purposes in exploring these topics. Over 750 pot smokers
were involved in these longitudinal studies, ranging up to 9 years
per subject, with several hundred "straights" used as controls
when possible. Much of this data was obtained during individual
and group counseling-therapy sessions, once or twice weekly, except with controls. Actual time spent per person exceeded 500
hours in some cases.
Symptoms and patterns began to emerge very early in this study.
One startling fact was the absence in the official record (hospital chart, agency file, etc.) of marijuana use. In 88 of 135
charts for adolescent (ages 13-21 inclusive) psychiatric patients
(1965-1971) there was either no reference to, nor significance
attached to the cannabis or other drug use, yet all 135 were pot
smokers. 7 of the 88 charts specifically stated no drug abuse.
Using the word "syndrome" to mean group of symptoms or pattern of
behavior, what is the Cannabis Syndrome? Does this happen when
you get "high"? No. Getting "stoned" hasn't changed for several
thousand years. The eater (now smoker) of the drug experiences
pleasure; increased excitement combined with a heightening of all
senses; a distortion-usually a magnification-of the dimensions
of space and time; and a keener sense of hearing combined with a
greater susceptibility to increase in pre-existing feelings.
Pleasure, which follows the initial experimentation due to curiosity, is the key to just about all drug abuse, up to the point
of dependence or addiction, or a syndrome, after which there may
be a need as well as a desire.
M-DART considers the condition which follows regular pot
smoking a non-organic brain syndrome combined with a thought dis-

order. It can develop in two weeks or two years. Its growth is gradual, and the victim is rarely aware of the connection with his changing attitudes, feeling and thinking. There are many symptoms, with varying degrees of pre-disposition existing for each, but anyone is vulnerable to some extent. Factors such as age, maturity, talent or skill, dosage, mental and environmental status play a part in prognosis and results. Adjustment to and "enjoyment" of the drug more than once weekly is most significant. If it occurs, the syndrome will soon follow, though in some the effects will seem relatively mild.

As the valid scientific research of the past decade was being published, M-DART found striking similarity with the findings of Drs. Kolansky and Moore, Powelson, Jones, Davis and Nahas in their studies, and even more significant parallels to the laboratory work of Drs. Heath, Stenchover, Kolodny, Morishima, Leuchtenberger, Paton and Zimmerman. We have no doubt that marked changes take place deep in the brain and central nervous system caused by marihuana, or its principal ingredient, THC. We believe it to be soluble in fat, in human tissue. We believe it can cause chromosome breakage. We believe it does interfere in the cell regeneration process, and finally, our historical studies cause us to believe in its carcinogenicity. We consider much of the recent published lab research indicating the above to be brilliant, and explanatory in part of certain findings of our clinical and field work.

Probably 20 to 30 million of our people have been adversely affected by their pot use, and among these are members of every profession, class, age, religion, race and occupation. The following is what to look for to uncover the heavy marijuana user; lesser users will have fewer symptoms:

(1) Diminished drive, lessened ambition, decreased motivation, apathy. The waste of human potential here is tragic. Watch the PH.D. pumping gas, or the biologist turning to the study of ESP.

(2) Shortened attention and concentration span, distractibility, inability to do complex thinking, a peculiar fragmentation in the flow of thought. To see the lessened ability to learn, the failure to apply objective reason and logic, is heartrending. At the college level, our engineers and scientists might soon be in short supply. Our college and other testing scores should be declining, beginning about 1965.

(3) Poor judgement, general loss of effectiveness, impaired communication skills, progressive loss of insight, inability to prepare realistically for the future.

(4) Introversion, an undue pre-occupation with oneself, mystical thinking, a deep interest in eastern religion, astrology, witch-craft, ESP. Interestingly, in African and Asian cultures centuries ago, Cannabis was mother's helper, for an infant or child nibbling a certain type of cookie would be happy and occupied internally, happy all day long, wouldn't need any attention. The harm to the brain at this early age probably was irreversible, and the subsequent ability to learn tremendously impaired.

1403

(5) Magical thinking, which is not magic as we know it, but simply means that the thought connotes the deed or act, opinion becomes fact.

(6) Regression, a slow automatic psychiatric reaction causing a return to juvenile, infantile or primitive emotion-oriented simplistic thinking and reasoning, and involving a very high degree of susceptibility to ego-protective beliefs.

(7) Rationalization, projection, and retrospective falsification, all unconscious and gradual automatic psychiatric processes which change or distort the present or past in one's mind to fill current emotional needs. The pot smoker can easily change reality 180 degrees, as the Battle of Wounded Knee becomes the Massacre at Wounded Knee. The mind of the revisionist historian is fascinating to study.

(8) Flat affect: inappropriate or disassociated thought versus mood; a speech blockage, where talk must be very slow and measured unless it is memorized rhetoric; feelings of inadequacy and helplessness, futility, pessimism, despondency and depression. "Pollution will one day kill us all."

(10) Unusual, weird and bizarre behavior, resulting from a combination of 4, 5, 6, 7 and 8 above. Could we have a Fonda, Hearst, Ellsberg, Rubin, Hoffman, Cleaver, Newton, Seale, Davis, or even Shirley MacLaine otherwise: Or the SLA? Or fraggers in Viet Nam? Or MACOS? M-DART believes not.

During the years 1967-1972, many individuals were encountered who had ultra-strong, valid anti-war, anti-system, counter-culture attitudes. 384 believed with a passion that the U.S. is a very rotten, very sick society; 380 of them were pot smokers. 80 believed our system should be destroyed; 79 of them were into marihuana. 65 believed President Johnson (or Nixon) was a war criminal; 64 had been pot users. 21 hoped for the death of the president; all were "heads". 10 stated, with conviction, that they would kill the president personally if it could be done safely; all were into "grass". No violent revolutionary was encountered who was straight, including 37 SDS members and 42 rock throwers at demonstrations.

During 1975-76, of 41 persons who believed there is a health crisis in the U.S., 32 were marihuana users. Conversely, of 60 who believed the U.S. has the best health service in the world, only 13 had been pot smokers.

A form of psychiatric regression involving simplistic, emotional, cause-oriented, ego-protective thinking was found. A sincerity or passion was present not based on fact, reason, logic or objective study, but on an apparent need to externalize problems, with contradictory or conflicting data ignored or blocked out of conscious, intellectual awareness. Included in these folks who did not think they were right - they knew it - were social workers, sociologists, counselors, psychologists, lawyers, probation officers, teachers, reporters, editors, and many other disciplines. Over 98% of this entire passionate anti-war, anti-system, counter-culture group was under 35 (1967-1972), with prior cannabis use preceding their strong attitudes and viewpoints in nearly 100% of cases.

Symptoms lessened or disappeared in a great many cases following cessation of marijuana use - at times most difficult to effect and concurrent educative, supportive, directive reality counselling therapy. Heavy users became very paranoid, yet even in some social users there was a type of psychosis, or denial of reality.

The following conclusions and theories developed as our study progressed:

(1) Cannabis is a particularly dangerous drug because of the usually subtle and gradual adverse changes in attitude, ability and thinking caused by its regular use.

(2) Many treatment, academic and other professionals are themselves changed by personal pot smoking.

(3) These changes are not realized by the user and, in fact, many users are positive the drug helps them.

(4) An organic brain syndrome may develop from heavy regular use. We believe the cerebral atrophy found by Dr. Campbell in 1972 depicts this condition.

(5) Marijuana use can cause emotional, thinking or related mental disorders.

(6) In every society the past several thousand years, where cannabis or other mild or regular hallucinogenic use was "legal" or widespread, in 2 or 3 generations following introduction, the culture, no matter how advanced, seemed to deteriorate, or if primitive, remained so.

(7) One or more generations of regular pot use by the family may result in possible genetic or organic brain changes, and this condition can be studied in the laboratory. There probably are many Asian, Arab and African communities where cannabis has been used for 50 to 100 generations. Air encephalographic equipment may be available to test infants now.

(8) Marijuana seems to lessen the activity of the left hemisphere of the brain and to enforce the operation of the right.

(9) M-DART believes more people have the Cannabis Syndrome in the U.S. today than abuse all other drugs, including alcohol, combined.

(10) A modern free society such as ours may not survive a legalized reality distorting drug without extreme polarization between producers-achievers-realists versus romantics-talkers-dreamers.

(11) We found the greatest single obstacle to successful treatment of opiate addiction to be chronic marijuana use.

(12) A new category of crime develops from hallucinogenic drug use, with those affected acting passionately and irrationally in the cause of peace, conservation, liberation, mankind, ecology, etc. Would you believe 20,000 bombings by "dissenters", 1967-1972?

(13) Much of the "research" on marijuana is done by biased users of the drug and by shallow questionnaires, interviews, or cursory lab tests.

(14)   To a large extent the polarization and alienation now present in the home, family, church, school, business, college, factory, military, government and country is caused by the Cannabis Syndrome.

(15)   Certain professions teach that "drugs are not the problem, they are merely symptomatic of some other deep, underlying disorder". So long as we continue to believe outmoded theory such as this, our efforts to educate, prevent and treat may be impeded. M-DART findings indicate the drugs, including alcohol, cause the problems in 80% to 90% of cases, though of course degree of susceptibility to subsequent disorder will vary. We found no prior existing psychopathology in over 90% of cases, prior meaning before marijuana use.

In a free society, we must respect opposing viewpoints. The test of "love" is not applying it to those with whom we agree, but to those with whom we differ. I doubt that most pot smokers can pass this test, for their beliefs must be self or ego-protective. It is wrong to condemn something or someone "out there" in the environment without realizing one has the duty to learn that other person's viewpoint and the reasons therefore. The recent refusal by Hopkins and Cornell Universities audiences to permit ex-Premier Ky to make a scheduled address was atrocious, and typical of the impassioned pothead. It has become fashionable today to attack respectable and responsible individuals, officials and institutions without any real knowledge of the facts of each issue or situation because one's ego is fed by criticizing the truly important or adopting great sounding causes.

We have a great need in this country for an informed, open minded, objective and clear-headed citizenry. We must consider and respect each other's views, in a rational manner, before disagreement. If we close our minds to this great need of a free society, the nature of our lives could be drastically changed for the worse. Those who succumb to the use of chemicals for pleasure in life may be leading us to regression and stagnation on a national scale. How can anyone rightfully say that man is not destined to live, work and love in his natural state? The greatest "high" comes from those we love and what we achieve, not from a weed or pill. It is not too late for a return to reality, though for many it may be. These are great times, of hope and aspiration and challenge, for all mankind. If we get the truth about marijuana to the people, the right decisions can and will be made by them.

Pulication of the hundreds of longitudinal case studies hinges upon M-DART's ability to get funding. It will be a near Herculean task, with some individual charts and files from one to two inches thick. We are confident that this will somehow be accomplished, and meanwhile the study continues. For bibliography, references and detailed data, send request to: M-DART, 222 East Redwood Street, Baltimore, Maryland 21202

THE FALLACY OF DRUG REHABILITATION

Edwina D. Frank, Ed. D.
Albert L. Juniel, Jr., A.A.N.
Vernon J. Shorty, Director, DBS

Desire Narcotic Rehabilitation Center

I.   Introduction

    A. Psychological and Social Barriers

II. Impact of Poverty and Social Deprivation

    A. Community Introduction to Drugs

III. Political Barriers

IV. Summary

V.   References

In the preceeding presentation, our analysis resulted in the conclusion that it is not enough to work with the program participant in his individual or group coping efforts. As a part of our theme, Barriers to Rehabilitation, we suggest that any efforts that would focus on rehabilitation, should also take into consideration the alteration of socio-cultural and environmental forces that permit the continuation of circumstances in which addiction develops and thrives. Thus, it is in this context that we coin the term, "fallacy of rehabilitation." For the most part, drug rehabilitation programs are operationalized to focus on assisting the individual to overcome his maladaptive behavior, yet at the same time, we concur that there are political, psychological and social forces that not only serve as barriers to the modification of drug abuse but possibly serve to perpetuate the continual development of drug abuse and abusers. Thus, one aspect of the "fallacy" is in the limitation of rehabilitation efforts to the person in the problem ignoring the environmental influence and the necessity for inclusion of external force alteration as a part of the total process. This is analogous to repairing the damage on one side of a two-way street.

It has long been theorized by persons involved with the treatment aspects of drug addiction that rehabilitation programs supplied with adequate economic resources would have a significant impact on the community. The thrust of this paper is to examine the political, psychological and social barriers to the altering of drug abuse behavior.

Psychological and Social Barriers

We discussed the multi-faceted problems in the community setting in which there are built-in reward systems which perpetuate drug abuse behavior. Certainly, there are alternative approaches. The therapeutic community has had a considerable degree of success. The most successful ones focus on removal from the negative environment more or less reconditioning for a new life style. Even under these circumstances there remain social barriers which inhibit individuals from being able to get to a given point.

The idea of entry or re-entry into the mainstream at the present time is unrealistic; primarily because the straight world is not ready for the "Ex." There would simply not be enough slots if everyone was well and functioning. Among those who are not incorporated into the mainstream are minorities, the aged, the ex-physical or mentally ill, or as one of my colleagues indicates the "ex-anything," even the ex-husband. Persons exhibiting a history of anything other than educated, health, straight and from the right side of the tracks, are automatically alienated from the mainstream. Thus those having a history of drug taking or incarceration have to wait in line a long time to cut through priorities of acceptance into the mainstream.

In a generation when machines have taken over so many human tasks, the effect of economic and social breakdown is felt most by the individuals who have been counted, grouped, classified, programmed for and labeled poor, deprived, and or minorities.

The economic effects are felt in the following areas:
>Inadequate schooling
>Deficient health services
>Crime and juvenile delinquency
>Indecent housing conditions
>Discrimination
>High unemployment
>Family breakdown

The Impact of Poverty and Social Deprivation

Poverty and health reinforce each other. Being poor means more than simply being without money. It means living under conditions that undermine both physical and mental health; people must struggle with malnutrition, with inadequate housing, heating, clothing, sanitary facilities, with substandard working conditions, with rats, roaches, flies, and other symptoms of unsatisfactory living conditions which breed illness or make it worse. Poverty, with all the associated deprivation, is not a necessary state in any society.

Another aspect of social deprivation encompasses cultural isolation. Language differences, as well as, basic values and temperament that are an integral part of a personality, can be affected when the person is placed outside his milieu. Communication impairment is another facet to social deprivation.

Community Introduction to Drugs

The mass availability of drugs in a ghetto community is directly associated with the degree of area infestation. This observation is consistent with the economic theory of supply and demand being a dominant business enterprise factor. The prevalence of drugs in an area then has the power of influencing behavior, drug using patterns, social practice and ultimately life styles. For example, experimentation with drugs out of curiosity or peer group influence can be attributed to easy access to drugs. One might be ever so curious and yet never experiment as a result of not having access to illegal drugs.

The implications for the need of alleviating the affects of poverty on health cuts across many aspects of society. We are at a period of time where many newly impoverished groups are evolving. These include the aged, and newly unemployed. It remains that with the U.S., the majority of populations of minority groups (although not new) remain impoverished. Spanish surnamed, Indian and Blacks are still piled up in urban ghettoes or reservations. One strategy for change introduced by Kenneth Clark in 1964 remains relevant to today's poverties. Although unused, Clark suggested that, "if ghettoes are to be transformed, then forces superior to those which resist change must be mobilized to counteract them. The problem of change in the ghetto is essentially, therefore, a problem of power confrontation and conflict between the power required for change and power resistant to change." The chances for any major transformation in the ghetto are slim until the anguish of the ghetto is in someway shared, not only by its victims but by those who now consider themselves privileged and immune to the ghettoes flagrant pathologies.

Political Barriers

C. Wright Mills, the late sociologist, concluded that there is a power elite composed of the "political directorate," "the corporate rich," and "the ascendant military"....the middle levels consist of "civil servants and elected representatives," "a set of stalemating forces"....and beneath them lie the "practically powerless public." Our collective observations suggest that Mr. Mills' conclusion is an accurate description of why the political recognition, understanding and response to the addiction problem will retain its patchwork direction and never pursue or assume a curative course. The enormous quantity of capital required to purchase drugs, the diverse strategies involved in the transportation of drugs and elaborate system of distribution -- from top to bottom --

indicate the level of involvement of respectable entities and couriers control, influence and limit our approach to sever the prevalence of foreign drugs in this country. On the other hand, lack of strict control of prescribed drugs, (i.e., the potential for a client to have similar drugs prescribed by several physicians for a single medical problem without physician's knowledge), and the wholesale unaccountable distribution of samples to the medical complex play a contributing role to the availability of street drugs for abuse. We are suggesting that the elimination of drugs in our communities would have a tremendous impact on the economy of this country. This means that there is little profit, incentive or public reward for the controlling powers to establish inhibiting processes to stop illegal drug-trafficking, with the realization that to do so would increase the magnitude of our current fiscal concerns. A country that can determine the exact ingredients to land man-rated missiles, data gathering and transmission satellites in precise stellar areas, eliminate skyjacking and perform feats of similar complexity could reduce, if not totally eliminate, the illegal drugs in our communities.

For several years there have been attempts made to design and pass through the legislative process, bills that would insure the provision of decent health care to all citizens regardless of age, ethnic origin or social status. To date, much of this legislature which is essential to the improvement of the quality of life for many remains stalled in various stages of work. It was recently announced that much of the health-care legislation has been out prioritized for congressional consideration for this year and will probably have to wait until next year (an election year) for consideration.

Summary

In 1969, the community residents where this program is located wrote a letter to the president of the United States, asking for assistance in improving the impoverished conditions. In 1975, we find that very little has changed.

Individual rehabilitation efforts, will not rectify the grim social conditions that make it inevitable that the peoples problems repeat themselves over and over again. Social change programs must be implemented to complement programs aimed at individual change. The fallacy lies in the one-sidedness of present efforts.

REFERENCES

Clark, K.   Dark Ghetto, Delimmas of Social Power, Harper
                 Torchbooks, Harper & Row Publishers, New York
                 and Evanston, 1967.

Mills, C.W.   The Power Elite, New York, Oxford University
                 Press, 1966.

PRIMARY PROPOXYPHENE DEPENDENCE

George Czertko, M.D.
John F. Keegan, M.A.
Kenneth G. Schooff, M.D.
Robert R. Freedman, Ph.D.

Department of Substance Abuse
Lafayette Clinic
Detroit, Michigan

Experience on the polydrug unit at Harper Hospital in Detroit, Michigan, during the years 1973 to 1974 substantiated the significant abuse potential of propoxyphene, oxycodone (dihydrohydroxy-codeinone), and other synthetic and semi-synthetic analgesics. These substances are capable of producing physiological as well as psychological dependency. This fact has been well established by other investigators and our experience with two such groups will be presented (1, 2, 3, 4, 5, 6).

One group was composed of nine patients whose primary drug of dependence was propoxyphene. While in the hospital they reported withdrawal symptoms classically seen in the opiate abstinence syndrome, i.e., insomnia, rhinnorhea, lacrimation, anxiety, tremulousness, diaphoresis, craving, myalgia, arthralgia, diarrhea, nausea, abdominal cramping and vomitting. In addition, three had a history of convulsions in the past, although they were not diagnosed as having a convulsive disorder.

All of these patients were introduced to propoxyphene through physician prescription. They all received propoxyphene for a variety of somatic complaints: backaches, headaches, stomach pains, and other vague symptoms and pains. Many had histories of multiple surgical procedures, as well as the other described symptoms. Their ages ranged from 20 to 50 years. Both sexes were equally represented. The length of dependence varied from one to twelve years. Dosage level varied from six to thirty capsules (390 mg. to 2150) of propoxyphene mixtures per day. Six of the nine complained of the described withdrawal symptoms. All expressed craving for the drug.

The propoxyphene dependent group can be separated into three categories on the basis of the length of their hospitalization. The first category consisted of three patients who stayed the entire thirty day period on the polydrug unit. This group was detoxified with propoxyphene napsylate or with propoxyphene hydrochloride. The second group consisted of two patients. One stayed eleven days and one stayed fourteen days. These patients left the hospital immediately after detoxification was completed. The third group consisted of four patients who left the hospital within two days of admission. This group received no propoxyphene and detoxification with propoxyphene was not part of their treatment plan.

Oxycodone, another frequently prescribed semi-synthetic analgesic was found to be the primary drug of dependence with another group of our polydrug patients. This group consisted of seven patients who were similar to the propoxyphene patients in terms of pre-addiction history and exposure to the drug through physician prescription. Physiological addiction is an accepted liability associated with oxycodone use and this population exhibited all the classic symptoms and signs of opiate withdrawal.

In this group the age range was from 24 to 40 years and the sex distribution was five female and two male. The dosage varied from four to sixteen tablets (20 mg. to 80 mg.) of oxycodone per day. Once again they were all introduced to the drug by legitimate prescription. All had a history of multiple drug abuse.

The oxycodone dependent group can be separated into two sub-groups. One group of four patients who stayed for the entire thirty-day period in the hospital was detoxified using methadone. Methadone was prescribed in decreasing dosages not exceeding 15 mgs. over a seven to three day period depending on the severity of their symptoms. The second group consisted of three patients who remained for seven days or less. They were detoxified with oxycodone in decreasing dosages of one tablet per day. They left immediately after detoxification was completed. Both the propoxyphene and the oxycodone groups were compared on the basis of the MMPI, SCL-90 and a neuropsychiatric impairment rating derived from a modified Halstead-Reitan battery. Mean scores on all of the MMPI scales were equivalent. Any differences were found to be statistically insignificant although we realize that with samples of this size the statistics are not very useful.

The oxycodone group showed slightly higher distress levels as measured by the SCL-90 but in no case were the differences between groups significantly different. Both groups also demonstrated equivalent and minimal neuropsychological impairment. The psychological testing indicated that both groups appear neurotic with characteristically high levels of hysteria, depression, hypochondriasis and psychopathy. These findings are also congruent with our clinical impressions and observations of these patients.

Upon initial medical evaluation the oxycodone dependent group was seen as suffering from physiologically based withdrawal symptoms. The similarly reported withdrawal symptoms of the propoxyphene dependent group were, however, interpreted as being of a more psychological as opposed to physiological origin. In retrospect it now appears that the reported withdrawal symptoms in the propoxyphene dependent group were physiologically as well as psychologically determined. There are several reasons for this reappraisal. Individuals using larger doses also reported more withdrawal symptoms both qualitatively and quantitatively. It is standard medical practice to use the narcotic antagonist, Naloxone, as part of the treatment of acute propoxyphene overdosage (7, 8, 9).

Clinical experience indicates that propoxyphene salts may be used to successfully maintain and detoxify opiate dependent individuals (10). Finally, Daftery (11) precipitated withdrawal symptoms identical to those complained of by our patients by the administration of naloxone to propoxyphene dependent individuals.

We now believe that our treatment of propoxyphene dependent patients would have been more successful had we recognized the physiological component of their withdrawal as we did with our oxycodone patients. Comparison between these two groups indicates that the oxycodone dependent patients who were detoxified remained in the hospital longer. In conclusion, while propoxyphene may be useful as an adjunct and/or alternative to methadone (maintenance or detoxification) it must be recognized that it also has addictive liabilities heretofore minimized or unrecognized.

REFERENCES

1. B. Maletzky. Addiction to Propoxyphene (Darvon): A Second Look. International Journal of the Addictions, 9, (1974).

2. J.C. Claghorn and J.C. Schoolar. Propoxyphene Hydrochloride, a Drug of Abuse. JAMA, 196: 12 (1966).

3. A. Elson and E.F. Domino. Dextropropoxyphene Addiction: Observations of a Case. JAMA, 183, 1963, p. 482 - 485.

4. H.F. Fraser and H. Isbell. Pharmacology and Addiction Liability of dl and d-Propoxyphene. Bull. Narcotics, 12, 1960 (Jan. - March), p. 9 - 14.

5. R.C. Wolfe and M. Recdenberg, et. al. Propoxyphene (Darvon[R]) Addiction and Withdrawal Syndrome. Annals of Int. Med., 10: 773 (1969).

6. F.J. Kane and J.T. Norton. Addiction to Propoxyphene. JAMA, 211: 300 (1969).

7. F.H. Lovejoy and A.A. Mitchell. The Management of Propoxyphene Poisoning. Journal of Pediatrics, Vol. 85, July, 1974.

8. L.S. Goodman and A. Gilman eds. The Pharmacological Basis of Therapeutics, 5th edition, New York, Macmillan Publishing Co., Inc., 1975.

9. H.F. Conn, ed. Current Therapy 1975, Philadelphia, W.B. Saunders Co., 1975.

10. F.S. Tennant and B.A. Russell. Propoxyphene Napsylate Treatment of Heroin and Methadone Dependence: One Year's Experience. Journal of Psychedelic Drugs, 6: 2 (1974).

11. A.V. Daftery. Naloxone Challenge In Propoxyphene Dependence. New Eng. J. of Med., 291: 18 (1974).

USE OF MARIHUANA, HASHISH, AND PSYCHEDELICS AMONG WORKERS*

Khalil A. Khavari & Mae J. Humes

Midwest Institute on Drug Use
University of Wisconsin-Milwaukee
Milwaukee, Wisconsin 53201

Misuse of drugs has come to be regarded as one of the most serious problems of our time. It has been variously termed, "a national emergency," "a major national problem," and "an epidemic." A particularly disturbing aspect of the problem are increases in the non-medical use of drugs by members of all strata of society. Within the past few years widespread abuse of a broad range of drugs, in addition to alcohol, has been reported among adolescents, young children, college students, the elderly, military personnel, and members of the nation's work force (1-3). Thus, the problem of drugs and their abuse no longer can be viewed as limited to the rebellious young, the deviant members of society, or to members of any specific racial, ethnic or socio-economic group.

No one seems to know for certain the extent of the problem in business and industry. Traditionally, alcohol has been regarded as the drug most abused by workers, as well as the general popu-lation, and over the years there has been a gradual acceptance of alcoholism as an industrial health problem requiring treatment and rehabilitation. By comparison, use and abuse of other drugs have not received much attention until quite recently.

One indication that a problem exists is the increasing mention of drug use by workers in the popular press and in trade journals. An article published early in 1970, in Time (January 29, 1970) entitled "The Rising Problem of Drugs on the Job" described the problem in dramatic terms:

> First spawned in the ghetto, drug addiction quickly
> spread to the middle class suburbs, colleges and high
> schools. Now, in corporations across the country,
> the cloying whiff of marijuana in the stairwell and
> the hastily dumped syringe in the washroom attest to
> the rapid growth of on-the-job drug users (p. 70).

---

*Supported by NIDA Research Grant DA1080 to K.A. Khavari

Accounts of on-the-job incidents were given:

In a General Motors plant in Los Angeles, undercover
police recently smashed a ring selling drugs at
lunchtime from a camper in the parking lot. . . In
Detroit, an assembly-line worker at the Dodge plant
notes: 'Guys are always stoned. Either they are
high from pills to keep them awake or they're zonked
on a joint they had on a break'. . . To support
their habits, drug dependent workers often become
pushers and ensnare co-workers into narcotic
addiction (p. 70).

Similar reports of drug use in business and industry have
appeared in the press (New York Times, March 22, 1970: The Wall
Street Journal, May 4, 1970; Business Week, August 15, 1970;
Washington Post, April 10, 1972; Chicago Tribune, January 6, 1972
and August 23, 1973).

Surveys conducted by business organizations document a growing concern by management with the problem. The American Management Association asked a large number of firms the question, "Do
you have a drug problem in your company?" Whereas only 7% said
"yes" in 1967, the number had increased to 45% by 1970 (Nation's
Business, November 1972). A market research firm in Chicago
found that one-third of Chicago-area companies surveyed had discovered drug use of drugs was associated with increased absenteeism,
thefts, and personnel turnover (Occupational Health Nursing, 1972,
16-19).

At the "Symposium on Drug Abuse in Industry," held in 1970,
W.P. Gullander, President of the National Association of Manufacturers stated:

No longer can businessmen view the problem of drug
abuse as one, confined to schools and street corners,
or within a single economic level. It is beginning to
infect industrial employees with potentially serious
results to our national economy. . . The long-term
prognosis is alarming, too, in light of the growing
trend toward drug abuse by the school-age population --
the future work force of this nation (4, p. 4).

There is a paucity of scholarly literature to help answer
questions about the magnitude of the problem and its underlying
dynamics. Chambers' work (5,6) represents the only reported major
effort to provide the needed data. In general, the results of
this survey bear out the concern that has been expressed from
other sources. A significant number of individuals within the
population sampled reported use of drugs on the job. Of special
interest was the finding of relationships between the type of

drug used, the user's occupational category and tendencies to use the drug on the job.

Thus, the widely held view that drug abuse is confined to specific marginal populations cannot be supported. Another commonly held notion pertains to group-drug stereotyping. Some examples: heroin is the drug of the ghetto, the minorities, and the poor; sedatives and depressants are used more heavily by blacks than other racial groups; hallucinogens are used most widely by college students and other "intellectuals." The data presented here show significant use of various hallucinogens by members of the work force.

METHOD AND PROCEDURES

The participants in this study were 309 male and female, adult workers from two industrial plants in the midwest. The age range was 18-40 years with a mean of 25.8 years. The ethnic composition of the group was: white = 241; black = 49, and others = 19.

The participants were volunteers recruited to participate in the research by union and labor leaders. The study contained a variety of tests where data were obtained on: personality variables: assessment of past and current drug use: motivation for use of drugs; attitudes toward drug use; self-image; alienation, demographic characteristics; occupational factors, and; work stress and work demands.

Thus, the study was directed at in-depth examination of the above parameters in a volunteer sample of industrial workers. The only pre-selection that was imposed pertained to age, i.e., to participate in the study. This procedure precludes generalizability of the data to the industrial population, since the sampling did not utilize probability sampling or stratified quota sampling. Nonetheless, subject selection procedure used in this study allowed participation by drug users and non-users alike.

The data presented here are based on a self-administered drug use questionnaire. This questionnaire was part of a larger battery of tests, as explained above.

RESULTS AND DISCUSSION

The results are presented in Table I. Marihuana has been tried by 71%, hashish by 47%, LSD by 24%, and Other Psychedelics (DET, DMT, Peyote, Mescaline, STP, Psilocybin, etc.) by 23% of this population.

Of the 71% who reported having tried marihuana 73% considered themselves as "current users" of this substance. Usage frequency was reported by the respondents where 3% indicated usage of marihuana "several times a day," another 6% reported "daily" usage, and 24% reported usage "several times a week" (see Table I).

Of the 47% who reported having tried hashish, 66% considered themselves as "current users" of this drug. However, most respondents reported relatively infrequent use of hashish, as compared to the frequency of usage for marihuana.

"Current usage" for LSD and Other Psychedelics are reported as "less often than monthly" for a substantial percentage of the respondents. Usage for "about once a month" was reported by only 4% for LSD and 6% for Other Psychedelics.

Thus, the results of this study show that marihuana, hashish, LSD, and Other Psychedelics are used by an appreciable number of workers. Their reported usages appear to be similar to other populations such as college students (7).

TABLE I

Percentages for those reporting who have tried and those who consider themselves current users, and their frequency of current use for marihuana, hashish, LSD, and Other Psychedelics (N=309).

Drug	Tried	*Current Use (%)					
		1	2	3	4	5	6
Marihuana	71	18	10	12	24	6	3
Hashish	47	44	15	6	1	–	–
LSD	24	36	4	–	–	–	–
Other Psychedelics	23	36	6	–	–	–	–

*(1 = less often than monthly; 2 = about once a month; 3 = about once a week; 4 = several times a week; 5 = daily; 6 = several times a day.)

REFERENCES

1. R.H. Blum, Students and Drugs, Jossey-Bass, San Francisco, Vol. II, 1970.

2. S.W. Sadava, Psychol. Rep., 33, 75 (1973).

3. C.D. Chambers and R.D. Heckman, Employee Drug Use, Cahners Books, Boston, Mass., 1972.

4. W.W. Stewart (ed.), Drug Abuse in Industry, Halos and Associates, Miami, Fla., 1970.

5. C.D. Chambers, Differential Drug Use Within the New York Labor Force, publication of New York State Narcotic Addiction Control Commission, Albany, N.Y., 1971.

6. C.D. Chambers, An Assessment of Drug Use in the General Population: Special Report No. 1, Drug Use in New York State, publication of New York State Narcotic Addiction Control Commission, Albany, N.Y., 1971.

7. Drug Use in America: Problem in Perspective, U.S. Government Printing Office, Washington, D.C. No. 5266-00003, 1973.

REFERENCES

1. [illegible text]

2. [illegible text]

3. [illegible text]

4. [illegible text]

5. [illegible text]

6. [illegible text]

Cattes, Daniel, 405
Center, Lawrence J., 597, 814
Cetrangol, Michael, 819
Chatterjie, Nithianonda, 1246, 1304
Chavez, Cleofe J., 715
Chorens, Jose A., 76
Chung, Tommy, 611
Clouet, Doris H., 1140
Cohen, Aaron, 948
Cohen, Allan Y., 139
Cohen, Arie, 931, 943
Cohen, Claudia, 745,
Cohen, Melvin, 431, 804
Cohen, Murray J., 190, 364, 403, 533, 948
Cohen, Richard, 1065, 1392
Cohn, Major L., 1233, 1239
Cohn, Marthe, 1233, 1239
Cole, Jonathan O., 1167
Collins, Mary Beth, 1025
Coloni, Randall S., 426
Comstock, Betsy S., 980
Cone, Edward J. 1228
Connaughton, James F., 691, 697
Cox, Michael D., 980
Crawford, Gail A., 64
Crawford, J., 1269
Czertko, George, 1411

D'Amico, Dina A., 280, 764
Dammann, Grace M., 955
Darvish, Harriet S., 619
Davidson, Virginia, 412, 659
Davis, John L., 862
Dawson, Joy, 96
Dayton, Harry E., 1246, 1304
Deaux, Edward, 968
De Leon, George, 227
Demaree, Robert G., 185
Dempsey, George, 76
Demto, Richard, 1397
Denson-Gerber, Judianne, 750
Desiderio, Dawn, 1299
Des Jarlais, Don C., 459
Deutsch, Lionel G., 499
Dickstein, Risa G., 545
DiGregorio, G. John, 1221
Doft, Ellen B., 390
Dogoloff, Lee I., 30

Double, William G., 829
Doyle, Kathleen M., 296, 793, 1050
Drew, Joseph S., 1330
Drucker, Ernest, 1375
Dubin, Gerald H., 287
DuPont, Robert L., 11, 59, 133
DuRocher, Rosemary, 175
Dustman, Robert E., 1179
Dvorchik, Barry H., 1216

Ehn, Shirley E., 644
Eichberg, Robert H., 1097
Ellner, Melvyn, 291
Emlet, Harry E., Jr., 862
Engelsing, Thomas M., 213
Escamilla-Mondanaro, Josette, 722
Evans, Robert J., III, 494

Farley, Edward C., 1382
Farwell, Bruce, 166
Feldman, Harvey W., 589
Ferris, Wayne H., 447
Field, F. H., 1206
Finkelstein, Helene, 526
Finnegan, Loretta P., 691, 697, 702, 726, 745
Flanzer, Jerry P., 514, 581
Fogelman, Eva, 436
Forrest, Catherine K., 309
Foster, Helen Lardner, 759
Foster, Kay, 90
Frank, Blanche, 96
Frank, Edwina D., 586, 1407
Freedman, Lawrence Zelic, 922
Freedman, Robert R., 1411
Freeman, Judith, 381
Freudenberger, Herbert J., 1075, 1080
Fried, Anne, 907
Friesen, George, 589

Gaetano, Ronald J., 161
Galanter, Marc, 222, 907, 912, 1129
Galonsky, Allan J., 240
Gasta, Carla, 1014
Gearing, Frances Rowe, 280, 764
Gerstein, Dean R., 386

Gillis, Roderic, 1330
Gilmore, John, 572
Goodman, Carolyn, 740
Goodman, Nellie, 745
Gottheil, Edward, 166
Greene, Bradford T., 250, 447
Gregory, Judi, 175
Gropper, Bernard A., 232
Grossman, Barry I., 1392
Gubar, George, 872
Gunn, Frank W. 809
Gutjahr, C. L., 1206

Haines, Michael P., 1070
Halikas, James A., 619
Hanbury, Ray, 364, 533
Hanlon, Thomas E., 1289
Hannigan, Patricia, 934
Harding, Wayne M., 1351
Harford, Robert J., 265, 426,
    442, 485, 926
Harris, Marcel, 1274
Hayes, Gwendolyn A., 469
Heit, Daniel, 340
Held, Joy A., 275
Henderson, Gary L., 1211
Hendrix, Henderson, 1085, 1124
Herrera, Clarita E., 1387
Hertzman, Marc, 841
Hesse, Catherine B., 270
Hesse, Rayburn F., 25
Hightower, Vastine, 76
Hoffman, Lee, 526
Hogan, Izola, 926
Hope, Katia, 1010
Horn, Rita, 819
Hou, Ping-wen, 735
Hough, Gordon, 1274
Howe, A. Sidney, 1330
Hughes, Jacqueline, 296
Humes, Mae J., 1415

Inturrisi, Charles E., 1246,
    1304, 1310, 1339

Jackson, G. Graham, 1036
Jackson, Judy S., 881
Jacobs, Phillip E., 390
Jacoby, John Eric, 731, 980

Janke, Peter, 350, 480
Joe, George W., 185
Johnson, Richard P., 648
Judd, Lewis L., 386
Julius, Demetrios A., 1285
Juniel, Albert L., Jr., 586, 1407

Kahn, Robert B., 417, 602
Kaiko, Robert F., 1310, 1339
Kalin, Gail, 1294
Kaplan, S. L., 702, 726
Karras, Athan, 390, 431, 499,
    804, 989
Kauffman, Thomas C., 1085, 1124
Kaufman, Edward, 344, 964, 997
Kaufmann, Pauline, 997
Keegan, John F., 1411
Keil, Thomas J., 452
Kern, Joseph C., 245, 847, 877
Kerr, David H., 330
Kesselman, Martin S., 1387
Kestenbaum, Richard S., 1265,
    1274
Khavari, Khalil A., 1415
King, Olga E., 1094
Kissin, Benjamin, 193
Kleber, Herbert D., 485
Kleinberg, Joel, 265
Kleinhans, Bruce, 265, 426
Klett, C. James, 1327
Koenigsberg, Lee, 829
Koger, James, 390
Kolb, Lawrence C., 37
Kreek, M. J., 1206
Kron, R. E., 702, 726
Kuldau, John M., 213

Labinger, Frances, 735
LaBrosse, Claude R., 881
Langrod, John, 120, 653, 1030
Lau, Christopher, 1118, 1185
LePla, S., 1118
Leukefeld, Carl G., 260
Lewis, David C., 548, 889, 1167,
    1280
Lieberman, Daniel, 166
Lieberman, Louis, 771
Lin, Paul M., 922
Lindesmith, Alfred R., 47
Ling, Walter, 1327